America's Top-Rated Cities

In-Depth Statistics & Comparative Rankings
of the Best Big Cities in America

2025
Thirty-second Edition

America's Top-Rated Cities

In-Depth Statistics & Comparative Rankings
of the Best Big Cities in America

Volume 3: Central Region

Grey House Publishing

Cover images: Minneapolis, Minneapolis

PUBLISHER: Leslie Mackenzie
EDITORIAL DIRECTOR: Stuart Paterson
SENIOR EDITOR: David Garoogian

RESEARCHER & WRITER: Jael Bridgemahon; Laura Mars
MARKETING DIRECTOR: Jessica Moody

Grey House Publishing, Inc.
4919 Route 22
Amenia, NY 12501
518.789.8700 • Fax 845.373.6390
www.greyhouse.com
books@greyhouse.com

While every effort has been made to ensure the reliability of the information presented in this publication, Grey House Publishing neither guarantees the accuracy of the data contained herein nor assumes any responsibility for errors, omissions or discrepancies. Grey House accepts no payment for listing; inclusion in the publication of any organization, agency, institution, publication, service or individual does not imply endorsement of the editors or publisher.

Errors brought to the attention of the publisher and verified to the satisfaction of the publisher will be corrected in future editions.

Except by express prior written permission of the Copyright Proprietor no part of this work may be copied by any means of publication or communication now known or developed hereafter including, but not limited to, use in any directory or compilation or other print publication, in any information storage and retrieval system, in any other electronic device, or in any visual or audio-visual device or product.

This publication is an original and creative work, copyrighted by Grey House Publishing, Inc. and is fully protected by all applicable copyright laws, as well as by laws covering misappropriation, trade secrets and unfair competition.

Grey House has added value to the underlying factual material through one or more of the following efforts: unique and original selection; expression; arrangement; coordination; and classification.

Grey House Publishing, Inc. will defend its rights in this publication.

Copyright © 2025 Grey House Publishing, Inc.
All rights reserved

Thirty-second Edition
Printed in the U.S.A.

Publisher's Cataloging-in-Publication Data
(Prepared by The Donohue Group, Inc.)

America's top-rated cities. Vol. 3, Central region : in-depth statistics & comparative rankings of the best big cities in america. — 1992-

v. : ill. ; cm.
Annual, 1995-
Irregular, 1992-1993
ISSN: 1082-7102

1. Cities and towns—Ratings—Central States—Statistics—Periodicals. 2. Cities and towns—Central States—Statistics—Periodicals. 3. Social indicators—Central States—Periodicals. 4. Quality of life—Central States—Statistics—Periodicals. 5. Central States—Social conditions—Statistics—Periodicals. I. Title: America's top rated cities. II. Title: Central region

HT123.5.S6 A44
307.76/0973/05 95644648

4-Volume Set	ISBN: 979-8-89179-096-4
Volume 1	ISBN: 979-8-89179-098-8
Volume 2	ISBN: 979-8-89179-099-5
Volume 3	**ISBN: 979-8-89179-100-8**
Volume 4	ISBN: 979-8-89179-101-5

Ann Arbor, Michigan

Background	1
Rankings	2
Business Environment	3
Demographics	3
Economy	5
Income	5
Employment	6
City Finances	8
Taxes	8
Transportation	9
Businesses	10
Living Environment	11
Cost of Living	11
Housing	11
Health	12
Education	15
Employers	16
Public Safety	16
Politics	17
Sports	17
Climate	17
Hazardous Waste	17
Air Quality	18

Cedar Rapids, Iowa

Background	21
Rankings	22
Business Environment	23
Demographics	23
Economy	25
Income	25
Employment	26
City Finances	28
Taxes	28
Transportation	29
Businesses	30
Living Environment	31
Cost of Living	31
Housing	31
Health	32
Education	34
Employers	35
Public Safety	36
Politics	36
Sports	36
Climate	36
Hazardous Waste	37
Air Quality	37

Chicago, Illinois

Background	39
Rankings	40
Business Environment	44
Demographics	44
Economy	46
Income	46
Employment	47
City Finances	49
Taxes	49
Transportation	50
Businesses	52
Living Environment	53
Cost of Living	53
Housing	53
Health	54
Education	57
Employers	59
Public Safety	60
Politics	60
Sports	60
Climate	61
Hazardous Waste	61
Air Quality	61

Columbia, Missouri

Background	63
Rankings	64
Business Environment	65
Demographics	65
Economy	67
Income	67
Employment	68
City Finances	70
Taxes	70
Transportation	71
Businesses	72
Living Environment	73
Cost of Living	73
Housing	73
Health	74
Education	76
Employers	77
Public Safety	78
Politics	78
Sports	78
Climate	78
Hazardous Waste	79
Air Quality	79

Davenport, Iowa

Background	81
Rankings	82
Business Environment	83
Demographics	83
Economy	85
Income	85
Employment	86
City Finances	88
Taxes	88
Transportation	89
Businesses	90
Living Environment	91
Cost of Living	91
Housing	92
Health	93
Education	95
Employers	96
Public Safety	96
Politics	96
Sports	96
Climate	97
Hazardous Waste	97
Air Quality	97

Des Moines, Iowa

Background	99
Rankings	100
Business Environment	102
Demographics	102
Economy	104
Income	104
Employment	105
City Finances	107
Taxes	107
Transportation	108
Businesses	109
Living Environment	110
Cost of Living	110
Housing	110
Health	111
Education	113
Employers	114
Public Safety	115
Politics	115
Sports	115
Climate	116
Hazardous Waste	116
Air Quality	116

Detroit, Michigan

Background	119
Rankings	120
Business Environment	123
Demographics	123
Economy	125
Income	125
Employment	126
City Finances	128
Taxes	128
Transportation	129
Businesses	130
Living Environment	131
Cost of Living	131
Housing	131
Health	132
Education	135
Employers	136
Public Safety	137
Politics	137
Sports	137
Climate	138
Hazardous Waste	138
Air Quality	138

Fargo, North Dakota

Background	141
Rankings	142
Business Environment	144
Demographics	144
Economy	146
Income	146
Employment	147
City Finances	149
Taxes	149
Transportation	150
Businesses	151
Living Environment	152
Cost of Living	152
Housing	152
Health	153
Education	155
Employers	156
Public Safety	157
Politics	157
Sports	157
Climate	157
Hazardous Waste	158
Air Quality	158

Fort Wayne, Indiana

Background................................. 161
Rankings.................................. 162
Business Environment..................... 164
   Demographics............................ 164
   Economy................................ 166
   Income 166
   Employment............................. 167
   City Finances.......................... 169
   Taxes 169
   Transportation......................... 170
   Businesses 171
Living Environment....................... 172
   Cost of Living......................... 172
   Housing 172
   Health................................. 173
   Education 175
   Employers.............................. 176
   Public Safety.......................... 176
   Politics 177
   Sports 177
   Climate 177
   Hazardous Waste 178
   Air Quality 178

Green Bay, Wisconsin

Background................................. 181
Rankings.................................. 182
Business Environment..................... 183
   Demographics........................... 183
   Economy................................ 185
   Income 185
   Employment............................. 186
   City Finances.......................... 188
   Taxes 188
   Transportation......................... 189
   Businesses 190
Living Environment....................... 191
   Cost of Living......................... 191
   Housing 191
   Health................................. 192
   Education 194
   Employers.............................. 195
   Public Safety.......................... 196
   Politics 196
   Sports 196
   Climate 196
   Hazardous Waste 197
   Air Quality 197

Indianapolis, Indiana

Background................................. 199
Rankings.................................. 200
Business Environment..................... 202
   Demographics........................... 202
   Economy................................ 204
   Income 204
   Employment............................. 205
   City Finances.......................... 207
   Taxes 207
   Transportation......................... 208
   Businesses 209
Living Environment....................... 210
   Cost of Living......................... 210
   Housing 210
   Health................................. 211
   Education 214
   Employers.............................. 215
   Public Safety.......................... 216
   Politics 216
   Sports 216
   Climate 217
   Hazardous Waste 217
   Air Quality 217

Kansas City, Missouri

Background................................. 219
Rankings.................................. 220
Business Environment..................... 222
   Demographics........................... 222
   Economy................................ 224
   Income 224
   Employment............................. 225
   City Finances.......................... 227
   Taxes 227
   Transportation......................... 228
   Businesses 229
Living Environment....................... 230
   Cost of Living......................... 230
   Housing 230
   Health................................. 231
   Education 234
   Employers.............................. 235
   Public Safety.......................... 235
   Politics 236
   Sports 236
   Climate 236
   Hazardous Waste 237
   Air Quality 237

Lincoln, Nebraska

- **Background** 239
- **Rankings** 240
- **Business Environment** 242
  - Demographics 242
  - Economy 244
  - Income 244
  - Employment 245
  - City Finances 247
  - Taxes 247
  - Transportation 248
  - Businesses 249
- **Living Environment** 250
  - Cost of Living 250
  - Housing 250
  - Health 251
  - Education 253
  - Employers 255
  - Public Safety 255
  - Politics 255
  - Sports 256
  - Climate 256
  - Hazardous Waste 256
  - Air Quality 256

Little Rock, Arkansas

- **Background** 259
- **Rankings** 260
- **Business Environment** 262
  - Demographics 262
  - Economy 264
  - Income 264
  - Employment 265
  - City Finances 267
  - Taxes 267
  - Transportation 268
  - Businesses 269
- **Living Environment** 270
  - Cost of Living 270
  - Housing 270
  - Health 271
  - Education 273
  - Employers 275
  - Public Safety 275
  - Politics 275
  - Sports 276
  - Climate 276
  - Hazardous Waste 276
  - Air Quality 276

Madison, Wisconsin

- **Background** 279
- **Rankings** 280
- **Business Environment** 283
  - Demographics 283
  - Economy 285
  - Income 285
  - Employment 286
  - City Finances 288
  - Taxes 288
  - Transportation 289
  - Businesses 290
- **Living Environment** 291
  - Cost of Living 291
  - Housing 291
  - Health 292
  - Education 295
  - Employers 296
  - Public Safety 296
  - Politics 297
  - Sports 297
  - Climate 297
  - Hazardous Waste 298
  - Air Quality 298

Milwaukee, Wisconsin

- **Background** 301
- **Rankings** 302
- **Business Environment** 304
  - Demographics 304
  - Economy 306
  - Income 306
  - Employment 307
  - City Finances 309
  - Taxes 309
  - Transportation 310
  - Businesses 311
- **Living Environment** 312
  - Cost of Living 312
  - Housing 312
  - Health 313
  - Education 316
  - Employers 317
  - Public Safety 317
  - Politics 318
  - Sports 318
  - Climate 318
  - Hazardous Waste 319
  - Air Quality 319

Minneapolis, Minnesota

Background 321
Rankings 322
Business Environment 325
   Demographics 325
   Economy 327
   Income 327
   Employment 328
   City Finances 330
   Taxes 330
   Transportation 331
   Businesses 332
Living Environment 333
   Cost of Living 333
   Housing 333
   Health 334
   Education 337
   Employers 339
   Public Safety 339
   Politics 340
   Sports 340
   Climate 340
   Hazardous Waste 340
   Air Quality 341

Oklahoma City, Oklahoma

Background 343
Rankings 344
Business Environment 346
   Demographics 346
   Economy 348
   Income 348
   Employment 349
   City Finances 351
   Taxes 351
   Transportation 352
   Businesses 353
Living Environment 354
   Cost of Living 354
   Housing 354
   Health 355
   Education 358
   Employers 359
   Public Safety 359
   Politics 360
   Sports 360
   Climate 360
   Hazardous Waste 361
   Air Quality 361

Omaha, Nebraska

Background 363
Rankings 364
Business Environment 366
   Demographics 366
   Economy 368
   Income 368
   Employment 369
   City Finances 371
   Taxes 371
   Transportation 372
   Businesses 373
Living Environment 374
   Cost of Living 374
   Housing 374
   Health 375
   Education 378
   Employers 379
   Public Safety 380
   Politics 380
   Sports 380
   Climate 381
   Hazardous Waste 381
   Air Quality 381

Rochester, Minnesota

Background 383
Rankings 384
Business Environment 385
   Demographics 385
   Economy 387
   Income 387
   Employment 388
   City Finances 390
   Taxes 390
   Transportation 391
   Businesses 392
Living Environment 393
   Cost of Living 393
   Housing 393
   Health 394
   Education 397
   Employers 398
   Public Safety 398
   Politics 399
   Sports 399
   Climate 399
   Hazardous Waste 399
   Air Quality 399

Table of Contents

Saint Louis, Missouri

Background 401
Rankings 402
Business Environment 405
    Demographics 405
    Economy 407
    Income 407
    Employment 408
    City Finances 410
    Taxes 410
    Transportation 411
    Businesses 412
Living Environment 414
    Cost of Living 414
    Housing 414
    Health 415
    Education 418
    Employers 420
    Public Safety 420
    Politics 421
    Sports 421
    Climate 421
    Hazardous Waste 422
    Air Quality 422

Saint Paul, Minnesota

Background 425
Rankings 426
Business Environment 428
    Demographics 428
    Economy 430
    Income 430
    Employment 431
    City Finances 433
    Taxes 433
    Transportation 434
    Businesses 435
Living Environment 436
    Cost of Living 436
    Housing 436
    Health 437
    Education 440
    Employers 442
    Public Safety 442
    Politics 442
    Sports 443
    Climate 443
    Hazardous Waste 443
    Air Quality 443

Sioux Falls, South Dakota

Background 445
Rankings 446
Business Environment 447
    Demographics 447
    Economy 449
    Income 449
    Employment 450
    City Finances 452
    Taxes 452
    Transportation 453
    Businesses 454
Living Environment 455
    Cost of Living 455
    Housing 455
    Health 456
    Education 458
    Employers 459
    Public Safety 459
    Politics 460
    Sports 460
    Climate 460
    Hazardous Waste 461
    Air Quality 461

Tulsa, Oklahoma

Background 463
Rankings 464
Business Environment 466
    Demographics 466
    Economy 468
    Income 468
    Employment 469
    City Finances 471
    Taxes 471
    Transportation 472
    Businesses 473
Living Environment 474
    Cost of Living 474
    Housing 474
    Health 475
    Education 477
    Employers 478
    Public Safety 479
    Politics 479
    Sports 479
    Climate 479
    Hazardous Waste 480
    Air Quality 480

Wichita, Kansas

Background 483
Rankings 484
Business Environment 486
   Demographics 486
   Economy 488
   Income 488
   Employment 489
   City Finances 491
   Taxes 491
   Transportation 492
   Businesses 493
Living Environment 494
   Cost of Living 494
   Housing 494
   Health 495
   Education 497
   Employers 498
   Public Safety 498
   Politics 499
   Sports 499
   Climate 499
   Hazardous Waste 500
   Air Quality 500

Appendixes

Appendix A: Comparative Statistics A-3
Appendix B: Metropolitan Area Definitions A-171
Appendix C: Government Type & Primary County . . A-175
Appendix D: Chambers of Commerce A-177
Appendix E: State Departments of Labor A-183

Introduction

This thirty-second edition of *America's Top-Rated Cities* is a concise, statistical, 4-volume work identifying America's top-rated cities with estimated populations of 100,000 or more. It profiles 97 cities that have received high marks for business and living based on our unique weighting system.

Each volume covers a different region of the country—Southern, Western, Central, Eastern—and includes a detailed Table of Contents, City Chapters, Appendices, and Maps. Each city chapter incorporates information from hundreds of resources to create the following major sections:

- **Background**—lively narrative of significant, up-to-date news for both businesses and residents. These combine historical facts with current developments, "known-for" annual events, and climate data.
- **Rankings**—fun-to-read, bulleted survey results from over 100 books, magazines, and online articles, ranging from general (Great Places to Live), to specific (Friendliest Cities), and everything in between.
- **Statistical Tables**—88 tables and detailed topics that offer an unparalleled view of each city's Business and Living Environments. They are carefully organized with data that is easy to read and understand.
- **Appendices**—five in all, appear at the end of each volume. These range from listings of Metropolitan Statistical Areas to Comparative Statistics for all 97 cities.

This new edition of *America's Top-Rated Cities* includes cities that not only surveyed well, but ranked highest using the following criteria: population growth, crime, household income, poverty, housing affordability, educational attainment, and unemployment. Part of the criteria, in most cases, is that it be the "primary" city in a given metropolitan area. For example, if the metro area is Raleigh-Cary, North Carolina, we would consider Raleigh, not Cary. This allows for a more equitable core city comparison. In general, the core city of a metro area is defined as having substantial influence on neighboring cities. A final consideration is location—we strive to include as many states in the country as possible.

You'll find that we have included several American cities despite having lower rankings in some categories. New York, Los Angeles, and Miami remain world-class cities despite challenges faced by many large urban centers. We also decided to include all major cities with historic or cultural significance. For example, Detroit, Michigan, the birthplace of the American automotive industry.

New to this edition are:
Volume 1: Midland, TX
Volume 2: Salem, OR
Volume 3: Green Bay, WI; St. Paul, MN

Praise for previous editions:

> "... [ATRC] has...proven its worth to a wide audience...from businesspeople and corporations planning to launch, relocate, or expand their operations to market researchers, real estate professionals, urban planners, job-seekers, students...interested in...reliable, attractively presented statistical information about larger U.S. cities."
> —ARBA

> "... For individuals or businesses looking to relocate, this resource conveniently reports rankings from more than 300 sources for the top 100 U.S. cities. Recommended..."
> —Choice

> "... While patrons are becoming increasingly comfortable locating statistical data online, there is still something to be said for the ease associated with such a compendium of otherwise scattered data. A well-organized and appropriate update..."
> —Library Journal

BACKGROUND
Each city begins with an informative Background that combines history with current events. These narratives often reflect changes that have occurred during the past year, and touch on the city's environment, politics, employment, cultural offerings, and climate, and include interesting trivia. For example: Tampa, Florida was known as the Cigar Capital of the World in the early 1900s; Wilmington, North Carolina was the site of one of the first rebellions in the United States'

revolt against British rule; and the first mail-order business, Montgomery Ward, was established in Chicago in 1872. Current events include: the most devastating fires recorded in the city of Los Angeles destroyed entire neighborhoods, including Pacific Palisades in January 2025; MARTA (Metropolitan Atlanta Rapid Transit Authority) unveiled its first state-of-the-art CQ400 railcar in early 2025; and Jaialdi, a large Basque festival held once every five years, is being held in Boise City in July 2025.

RANKINGS
This section has rankings from over 100 articles and reports. For easy reference, these Rankings are categorized into 16 topics including Business/Finance, Dating/Romance, and Health/Fitness.

The Rankings are presented in an easy-to-read, bulleted format and include results from both annual surveys and one-shot studies. **Fastest Job Growth** . . . **Best Drivers** . . . **Most Well-Read** . . . **Most Wired** . . . **Healthiest for Women** . . . **Best for Minority Entrepreneurs** . . . **Safest** . . . **Best to Retire** . . . **Most Polite** . . . **Best for Moviemakers** . . . **Most Frugal** . . . **Best for Bikes** . . . **Most Cultured** . . . **Least Stressful** . . . **Best for Families** . . . **Most Romantic** . . . **Most Charitable** . . . **Best for Telecommuters** . . . **Best for Singles** . . . **Nerdiest** . . . **Fittest** . . . **Best for Dogs** . . . **Most Tattooed** . . . **Best for Veterans** . . . **Best for Wheelchair Users**, and more.

Sources for these Rankings include both well-known magazines and other organizations, including *The Advocate*, *Condé Nast Traveler*, *Forbes*, *Kiplinger*, and *National Geographic*, as well as American Lung Association, Asthma & Allergy Foundation of America, National Civic League, People for the Ethical Treatment of Animals, and *Site Selection*.

Rankings cover a variety of geographic areas; see Appendix B for full geographic definitions.

STATISTICAL TABLES
Each city chapter includes 88 tables and detailed topics—45 in Business and 43 in Living. Over 90% of statistical data has been updated. This edition also includes new data on the economy from the U.S. Bureau of Economic Analysis and mortality rates from accidental poisonings and exposure to noxious substances.

Business Environment includes hard facts and figures on 8 major categories, including Demographics, Income, Economy, Employment, and Taxes. *Living Environment* includes 11 major categories, such as Cost of Living, Housing, Health, Education, Safety, and Climate.

To compile the Statistical Tables, editors have again turned to a wide range of sources, some well known, such as the Bureau of Labor Statistics, Centers for Disease Control and Prevention, Federal Bureau of Investigation, U.S. Census Bureau, and U.S. Environmental Protection Agency, plus others like The Council for Community and Economic Research, Federal Housing Finance Agency, and Texas A&M Transportation Institute.

APPENDIXES: Data for all cities appear in all volumes.
- **Appendix A**—*Comparative Statistics*
- **Appendix B**—*Metropolitan Area Definitions*
- **Appendix C**—*Government Type and County*
- **Appendix D**—*Chambers of Commerce and Economic Development Organizations*
- **Appendix E**—*State Departments of Labor and Employment*

Material provided by public and private agencies and organizations was supplemented by original research, numerous library sources and Internet sites. *America's Top-Rated Cities* is designed for a wide range of readers: private individuals considering relocating a residence or business; professionals considering expanding their businesses or changing careers; corporations considering relocating, opening up additional offices or creating new divisions; government agencies; general and market researchers; real estate consultants; human resource personnel; urban planners; investors; and urban government students.

Customers who purchase the four-volume set receive free online access to *America's Top-Rated Cities* allowing them to download city reports and sort and rank these cities by 50-plus data points.

AMERICA'S TOP-RATED CITIES

Legend:
- CBSA: Core Based Statistical Area
- STATE
- Top Rated City
- South Region – VOLUME 1
- West Region – VOLUME 2
- Central Region – VOLUME 3
- East Region – VOLUME 4

© Larry Mandelin 2025

Ann Arbor, Michigan

Background

Ann Arbor is located on the Huron River, 36 miles west of Detroit. It was founded in 1824 by John Allen and Elisha W. Rumsey, two East Coast entrepreneurs who named the settlement for their wives—both Ann—and for the community's location within natural groves. In 1851, Ann Arbor was chartered as a city.

After the arrival of the Michigan Central Railroad in 1839, the settlement developed as an agricultural center, and it continues to be such for the rich agricultural area surrounding it.

Before the arrival of settlers, the Ojibwa tribe roamed the area, which they called Washtenaw—the land beyond—which now serves as the county for which Ann Arbor is the seat.

The city manufactures machinery, tools, steel ball bearings, scientific instruments, doors and blinds, cameras, and coil springs. Lasers, computers, hospital and laboratory equipment, automotive parts, and high-tech/software products are also vibrant industries. The University of Michigan Medical Centers and St. Joseph Mercy Hospital employ over 12,000, and the region is also strong in book printing and manufacturing.

Ann Arbor's population is about one-third college or university students. The University of Michigan, the town's largest employer, played a prominent role in Ann Arbor's development as a major Midwest center for aeronautical, space, nuclear, chemical, and metallurgical research. The university's Museum of Natural History is known for an outstanding collection of dinosaur and mastodon skeletons and fossils, detailed dioramas of prehistoric life and Native American cultures, exhibits on Michigan wildlife, anthropology, and geology, and its planetarium. Also located at the university is a 250-acre botanical garden with a conservatory featuring tropical, temperate, and arid houses, over six miles of nature trails, and a variety of outdoor display gardens. The University of Michigan Museum of Art (UMMA), with more than 18,000 works of art from all over the world, and the university's Detroit Observatory, a historic scientific laboratory built in 1854, make this a truly unique, world-class institution. UMMA expanded in 2009, more than doubling its space.

The university is also home to the Gerald R. Ford School of Policy, named in honor of the former President, who graduated from the university in 1935. The 85,000 square-foot Joan and Sanford Weill Hall, designed by the noted firm of Robert A. M. Stern Architects, opened in 2006. The University of Michigan is also the site of the Ford Presidential Library.

Other cultural attractions in the city include: the African American Cultural and Historical Museum; the Ann Arbor Art Center, including two contemporary art galleries and art classes for all ages; the Ann Arbor Hands-On Museum, offering interactive exhibits in physics, mathematics, biology, physiology, botany and geology; and Gallery Von Glahn, specializing in serigraphs, lithographs, and original bronze and porcelain art. The Detroit Institute of Arts displays Diego Rivera's spectacular "Detroit Industry" frescoes. In addition, Ann Arbor offers dozens of artists' guilds, museums, top-rated art fairs, music and film festivals, and its share of fine restaurants with cuisine ranging from Italian to Ethiopian.

In nearby Dearborn are the Henry Ford Estate and Museum and the Automotive Hall of Fame. Historic Ypsilanti hosts the annual Orphan Car Show, which pays homage to elegant vehicles of a bygone era such as the Kaiser, Triumph, and Packard.

With its high-tech industries and great university, Ann Arbor is an exceptionally livable city and full of cultural events, including an annual arts fair, and jazz, film, and summer festivals. The city boasts 161 city parks, 12 golf courses, and more than 40 hiking trails.

Located in the humid continental climate zone, Ann Arbor's summers are hot, winters are cold, and there is an above-average occurrence of snow and rain. Proximity to the Great Lakes causes extreme temperatures, but also results in high humidity and cloud cover two-thirds of the year.

Rankings

General Rankings

- In their annual survey, Livability.com looked at data for more than 2,000 mid-sized U.S. cities to assign a "Livability Score" for each. The top 100 scoring cities make up Livability's "Top 100 Best Places to Live in the U.S." in 2025. Ann Arbor was placed among the top 100 of the customizable list. Criteria: housing and economy; cost of living; environment; education; health care options; transportation; safety; and community amenities. *Livability.com, "Top 100 Best Places to Live in the U.S. in 2025" April 15, 2025*

Business/Finance Rankings

- The Ann Arbor metro area appeared on the Milken Institute "2025 Best Performing Cities" list. Rank: #149 out of 200 large metro areas (based on performance category). Criteria: job growth; wage growth; high-tech growth and impact; community resilience; housing affordability; household broadband access. *Milken Institute, "Best-Performing Cities 2025," January 14, 2025*

Education Rankings

- Personal finance website *WalletHub* analyzed the 150 largest U.S. metropolitan statistical areas to determine where the most educated Americans are putting their degrees to work. Criteria: education levels; percentage of workers with degrees; education quality and attainment gap; public school quality rankings; quality and enrollment of each metro area's universities. Ann Arbor was ranked #1 (#1 = most educated city). *WalletHub.com, "Most & Least Educated Cities in America, 2025" July 2, 2024*

Environmental Rankings

- *Niche* compiled a list of the nation's snowiest cities, based on the National Oceanic and Atmospheric Administration's 30-year average snowfall data. Among cities with a population of at least 50,000, Ann Arbor ranked #19. *Niche.com, Top 25 Snowiest Cities in America, December 10, 2018*

Health/Fitness Rankings

- The Sharecare Community Well-Being Index evaluates 10 individual and social health factors in order to measure what matters to Americans in the communities in which they live. The Ann Arbor metro area ranked #8 in the top 10 across all 10 domains. Criteria: access to healthcare, food, and community resources; housing and transportation; economic security; feeling of purpose; and physical, financial, social, and community well-being. *Sharecare.com, "Community Well-Being Index: 2020 Metro Area & County Rankings Report," August 30, 2021*

Real Estate Rankings

- Ann Arbor was ranked #111 out of 176 metro areas in terms of cost of housing in 2024 by the National Association of Home Builders (#1 = most affordable). Criteria: the portion of an average family's income necessary to pay the mortgage on a median-priced home. *National Association of Home Builders®, NAHB-Wells Fargo Cost of Housing Index, 4th Quarter 2024*

Miscellaneous Rankings

- Despite a wide range of popular international destinations, plugged-in travel influencers and experts continue to rediscover their local regions. Ann Arbor appeared on a *Forbes Advisor* list of places in the U.S. designed to showcase a large variety of destinations. Whether it be discovery of hidden gems, delicious food, or outdoor exploring and daytrips, these places are a must-see. *Forbes.com, "Top 18 Places To Travel In the U.S. In 2024," February 7, 2024*

Business Environment

DEMOGRAPHICS

Population Growth

Area	1990 Census	2000 Census	2010 Census	2020 Census	2023 Estimate[2]	Population Growth 1990-2023 (%)
City	111,018	114,024	113,934	123,851	121,179	9.2
MSA[1]	282,937	322,895	344,791	372,258	368,394	30.2
U.S.	248,709,873	281,421,906	308,745,538	331,449,281	332,387,540	33.6

Note: (1) Figures cover the Ann Arbor, MI Metropolitan Statistical Area; (2) 2019-2023 5-year ACS population estimate
Source: U.S. Census Bureau, 1990 Census, 2000 Census, 2010 Census, 2020 Census, 2019-2023 American Community Survey 5-Year Estimates

Race

Area	White Alone[2] (%)	Black Alone[2] (%)	Asian Alone[2] (%)	AIAN[3] Alone[2] (%)	NHOPI[4] Alone[2] (%)	Other Race Alone[2] (%)	Two or More Races (%)
City	68.8	7.2	15.2	0.3	0.0	1.2	7.3
MSA[1]	69.9	11.6	8.9	0.3	0.0	1.6	7.7
U.S.	63.4	12.4	5.8	0.9	0.2	6.6	10.7

Note: (1) Figures cover the Ann Arbor, MI Metropolitan Statistical Area; (2) Alone is defined as not being in combination with one or more other races; (3) American Indian and Alaska Native; (4) Native Hawaiian and Other Pacific Islander
Source: U.S. Census Bureau, 2019-2023 American Community Survey 5-Year Estimates

Hispanic or Latino Origin

Area	Total (%)	Mexican (%)	Puerto Rican (%)	Cuban (%)	Other (%)
City	5.4	2.3	0.7	0.2	2.3
MSA[1]	5.6	2.8	0.6	0.2	2.1
U.S.	19.0	11.3	1.8	0.7	5.2

Note: Persons of Hispanic or Latino origin can be of any race; (1) Figures cover the Ann Arbor, MI Metropolitan Statistical Area
Source: U.S. Census Bureau, 2019-2023 American Community Survey 5-Year Estimates

Age

Area	Under Age 5	Age 5–19	Age 20–34	Age 35–44	Age 45–54	Age 55–64	Age 65–74	Age 75–84	Age 85+	Median Age
City	3.8	18.7	38.6	10.1	8.2	7.9	7.3	4.0	1.4	27.7
MSA[1]	4.6	19.1	26.4	11.9	11.3	11.3	9.2	4.5	1.5	34.8
U.S.	5.7	19.1	20.2	13.1	12.3	12.8	10.0	4.9	1.9	38.7

Note: (1) Figures cover the Ann Arbor, MI Metropolitan Statistical Area
Source: U.S. Census Bureau, 2019-2023 American Community Survey 5-Year Estimates

Disability by Age

Area	All Ages	Under 18 Years Old	18 to 64 Years Old	65 Years and Over
City	8.1	4.7	6.1	23.8
MSA[1]	10.3	4.1	8.3	26.9
U.S.	13.0	4.7	10.7	32.9

Note: Figures show percent of the civilian noninstitutionalized population that reported having a disability. Disability status is determined from six types of difficulty: vision, hearing, cognitive, ambulatory, self-care, and independent living. For children under 5 years old, hearing and vision difficulty are used to determine disability status. For children between the ages of 5 and 14, disability status is determined from hearing, vision, cognitive, ambulatory, and self-care difficulties. For people aged 15 years and older, they are considered to have a disability if they have difficulty with any one of the six difficulty types; Note: (1) Figures cover the Ann Arbor, MI Metropolitan Statistical Area
Source: U.S. Census Bureau, 2019-2023 American Community Survey 5-Year Estimates

Ancestry

Area	German	Irish	English	American	Italian	Polish	French[2]	European	Scottish
City	16.5	10.7	9.7	2.1	4.5	6.2	2.2	2.7	2.3
MSA[1]	17.8	10.2	11.1	5.1	4.5	6.2	2.5	2.3	2.8
U.S.	12.6	9.4	9.1	5.5	4.9	2.6	2.0	1.6	1.6

Note: Figures are the percentage of the total population reporting a particular ancestry. The nine most commonly reported ancestries in the U.S. are shown. Figures include multiple ancestries (e.g. if a person reported being Irish and Italian, they were included in both columns); (1) Figures cover the Ann Arbor, MI Metropolitan Statistical Area; (2) Excludes Basque
Source: U.S. Census Bureau, 2019-2023 American Community Survey 5-Year Estimates

Foreign-born Population

Area	Percent of Population Born in								
	Any Foreign Country	Asia	Mexico	Europe	Caribbean	Central America[2]	South America	Africa	Canada
City	18.7	11.8	0.5	2.9	0.1	0.3	0.6	1.6	0.7
MSA[1]	12.8	7.3	0.7	2.2	0.1	0.5	0.4	0.9	0.5
U.S.	13.9	4.3	3.3	1.4	1.4	1.2	1.2	0.8	0.2

Note: (1) Figures cover the Ann Arbor, MI Metropolitan Statistical Area; (2) Excludes Mexico.
Source: U.S. Census Bureau, 2019-2023 American Community Survey 5-Year Estimates

Household Size

Area	Persons in Household (%)							Average Household Size
	One	Two	Three	Four	Five	Six	Seven or More	
City	34.0	35.9	14.5	9.9	3.2	1.8	0.7	2.19
MSA[1]	30.6	36.1	14.9	11.5	4.2	1.9	0.9	2.34
U.S.	28.5	33.8	15.4	12.7	5.9	2.3	1.4	2.54

Note: (1) Figures cover the Ann Arbor, MI Metropolitan Statistical Area
Source: U.S. Census Bureau, 2019-2023 American Community Survey 5-Year Estimates

Household Relationships

Area	Householder	Opposite-sex Spouse	Same-sex Spouse	Opposite-sex Unmarried Partner	Same-sex Unmarried Partner	Child[2]	Grandchild	Other Relatives	Non-relatives
City	40.3	13.3	0.3	2.4	0.2	17.1	0.5	1.6	11.5
MSA[1]	39.7	17.0	0.3	2.4	0.2	24.3	1.3	2.5	5.8
U.S.	38.3	17.5	0.2	2.5	0.2	28.3	2.4	4.8	3.4

Note: Figures are percent of the total population; (1) Figures cover the Ann Arbor, MI Metropolitan Statistical Area; (2) Includes biological, adopted, and stepchildren of the householder
Source: U.S. Census Bureau, 2020 Census

Gender

Area	Males	Females	Males per 100 Females
City	60,397	60,782	99.4
MSA[1]	183,761	184,633	99.5
U.S.	164,545,087	167,842,453	98.0

Note: (1) Figures cover the Ann Arbor, MI Metropolitan Statistical Area
Source: U.S. Census Bureau, 2019-2023 American Community Survey 5-Year Estimates

Marital Status

Area	Never Married	Now Married[2]	Separated	Widowed	Divorced
City	55.4	35.4	0.6	2.3	6.3
MSA[1]	42.3	44.6	0.9	3.8	8.4
U.S.	34.1	47.9	1.7	5.6	10.7

Note: Figures are percentages and cover the population 15 years of age and older; (1) Figures cover the Ann Arbor, MI Metropolitan Statistical Area; (2) Excludes separated
Source: U.S. Census Bureau, 2019-2023 American Community Survey 5-Year Estimates

Religious Groups by Family

Area	Catholic	Baptist	Methodist	LDS[2]	Pentecostal	Lutheran	Islam	Adventist	Other
MSA[1]	9.7	2.0	2.4	0.8	1.5	2.3	2.2	0.9	10.0
U.S.	18.7	7.3	3.0	2.0	1.8	1.7	1.3	1.3	11.6

Note: Figures are the number of adherents as a percentage of the total population and cover the eight largest religious groups in the U.S; (1) Figures cover the Ann Arbor, MI Metropolitan Statistical Area; (2) Church of Jesus Christ of Latter-day Saints
Sources: 2020 U.S. Religion Census, Association of Statisticians of American Religious Bodies; The Association of Religion Data Archives (ARDA)

Religious Groups by Tradition

Area	Catholic	Evangelical Protestant	Mainline Protestant	Black Protestant	Islam	Judaism	Hinduism	Orthodox	Buddhism
MSA[1]	9.7	8.1	5.6	2.5	2.2	0.8	0.5	0.4	0.3
U.S.	18.7	16.5	5.2	2.3	1.3	0.6	0.4	0.4	0.3

Note: Figures are the number of adherents as a percentage of the total population; (1) Figures cover the Ann Arbor, MI Metropolitan Statistical Area
Sources: 2020 U.S. Religion Census, Association of Statisticians of American Religious Bodies; The Association of Religion Data Archives (ARDA)

ECONOMY

Real Gross Domestic Product (GDP)

Area	2017	2018	2019	2020	2021	2022	2023	Rank[3]
MSA[1]	24.0	24.6	25.6	25.0	26.3	27.0	27.8	114
U.S.[2]	17,619.1	18,160.7	18,642.5	18,238.9	19,387.6	19,896.6	20,436.3	—

Note: Figures are in billions of chained 2017 dollars; (1) Figures cover the Ann Arbor, MI Metropolitan Statistical Area; (2) Figures cover real GDP within metropolitan areas; (3) Rank is based on 2023 data and ranges from 1 to 384
Source: U.S. Bureau of Economic Analysis

Economic Growth

Area	2014	2015	2016	2017	2018	2019	2020	2021	2022	2023
MSA[1]	1.7	3.7	2.2	3.3	2.5	4.0	-2.5	5.2	2.6	2.9
U.S.[2]	2.6	3.2	2.0	2.7	3.1	2.7	-2.2	6.3	2.6	2.7

Note: Figures are real gross domestic product growth rates and represent percent change from preceding period; (1) Figures cover the Ann Arbor, MI Metropolitan Statistical Area; (2) Figures are the average growth rates within metropolitan areas
Source: U.S. Bureau of Economic Analysis

Metropolitan Area Exports

Area	2018	2019	2020	2021	2022	2023	Rank[2]
MSA[1]	1,538.7	1,432.7	1,183.1	1,230.7	1,334.2	1,196.2	156
U.S.	1,664,056.1	1,645,173.7	1,431,406.6	1,753,941.4	2,062,937.4	2,019,160.5	—

Note: Figures are in millions of dollars; (1) Figures cover the Ann Arbor, MI Metropolitan Statistical Area; (2) Rank is based on 2023 data and ranges from 1 to 386
Source: U.S. Department of Commerce, International Trade Administration, Office of Trade and Economic Analysis, Industry and Analysis, Exports by Metropolitan Area, data extracted April 2, 2025

Building Permits

Area	Single-Family			Multi-Family			Total		
	2023	2024	Pct. Chg.	2023	2024	Pct. Chg.	2023	2024	Pct. Chg.
City	161	28	-82.6	61	266	336.1	222	294	32.4
MSA[1]	485	557	14.8	1,112	636	-42.8	1,597	1,193	-25.3
U.S.	920,000	981,900	6.7	591,100	496,100	-16.1	1,511,100	1,478,000	-2.2

Note: (1) Figures cover the Ann Arbor, MI Metropolitan Statistical Area; Figures represent new, privately-owned housing units authorized (unadjusted data)
Source: U.S. Census Bureau, Building Permits Survey (BPS), 2023, 2024

Bankruptcy Filings

Area	Business Filings			Nonbusiness Filings		
	2023	2024	% Chg.	2023	2024	% Chg.
Washtenaw County	7	8	14.3	396	404	2.0
U.S.	18,926	23,107	22.1	434,064	494,201	13.9

Note: Business filings include Chapter 7, Chapter 9, Chapter 11, Chapter 12, Chapter 13, Chapter 15, and Section 304; Nonbusiness filings include Chapter 7, Chapter 11, and Chapter 13
Source: Administrative Office of the U.S. Courts, Business and Nonbusiness Bankruptcy, County Cases Commenced by Chapter of the Bankruptcy Code, During the 12-Month Period Ending December 31, 2023 and Business and Nonbusiness Bankruptcy, County Cases Commenced by Chapter of the Bankruptcy Code, During the 12-Month Period Ending December 31, 2024

Housing Vacancy Rates

Area	Gross Vacancy Rate[3] (%)			Year-Round Vacancy Rate[4] (%)			Rental Vacancy Rate[5] (%)			Homeowner Vacancy Rate[6] (%)		
	2022	2023	2024	2022	2023	2024	2022	2023	2024	2022	2023	2024
MSA[1]	n/a	n/a	n/a	n/a	n/a	n/a	n/a	n/a	n/a	n/a	n/a	n/a
U.S.[2]	9.1	9.0	9.1	7.5	7.5	7.6	5.7	6.5	6.8	0.8	0.8	1.0

Note: (1) Figures cover the Ann Arbor, MI Metropolitan Statistical Area; (2) Figures cover the 75 largest Metropolitan Statistical Areas; (3) The percentage of the total housing inventory that is vacant; (4) The percentage of the housing inventory (excluding seasonal units) that is year-round vacant; (5) The percentage of rental inventory that is vacant for rent; (6) The percentage of homeowner inventory that is vacant for sale; n/a not available
Source: U.S. Census Bureau, Housing Vacancies and Homeownership Annual Statistics: 2022, 2023, 2024

INCOME

Income

Area	Per Capita ($)	Median Household ($)	Average Household ($)
City	54,604	81,089	121,561
MSA[1]	51,746	87,156	122,847
U.S.	43,289	78,538	110,491

Note: (1) Figures cover the Ann Arbor, MI Metropolitan Statistical Area
Source: U.S. Census Bureau, 2019-2023 American Community Survey 5-Year Estimates

Household Income Distribution

Area	Percent of Households Earning							
	Under $15,000	$15,000 -$24,999	$25,000 -$34,999	$35,000 -$49,999	$50,000 -$74,999	$75,000 -$99,999	$100,000 -$149,999	$150,000 and up
City	12.8	5.7	5.8	8.8	14.4	10.6	15.2	26.8
MSA[1]	8.8	5.3	5.8	9.3	14.9	11.8	17.5	26.6
U.S.	8.5	6.6	6.8	10.4	15.7	12.7	17.4	21.9

Note: (1) Figures cover the Ann Arbor, MI Metropolitan Statistical Area
Source: U.S. Census Bureau, 2019-2023 American Community Survey 5-Year Estimates

Poverty Rate

Area	All Ages	Under 18 Years Old	18 to 64 Years Old	65 Years and Over
City	23.0	13.5	27.9	6.0
MSA[1]	13.8	12.5	16.2	5.9
U.S.	12.4	16.3	11.6	10.4

Note: Figures are percentage of people whose income during the past 12 months was below the poverty level; (1) Figures cover the Ann Arbor, MI Metropolitan Statistical Area
Source: U.S. Census Bureau, 2019-2023 American Community Survey 5-Year Estimates

EMPLOYMENT

Labor Force and Employment

Area	Civilian Labor Force			Workers Employed		
	Dec. 2023	Dec. 2024	% Chg.	Dec. 2023	Dec. 2024	% Chg.
City	66,518	68,304	2.7	64,986	66,059	1.7
MSA[1]	201,644	207,512	2.9	195,986	199,223	1.7
U.S.	166,661,000	167,746,000	0.7	160,754,000	161,294,000	0.3

Note: Data is not seasonally adjusted and covers workers 16 years of age and older; (1) Figures cover the Ann Arbor, MI Metropolitan Statistical Area
Source: Bureau of Labor Statistics, Local Area Unemployment Statistics

Unemployment Rate

Area	2024											
	Jan.	Feb.	Mar.	Apr.	May	Jun.	Jul.	Aug.	Sep.	Oct.	Nov.	Dec.
City	2.5	2.7	2.8	2.6	3.2	3.8	4.2	3.7	3.2	3.1	3.2	3.3
MSA[1]	3.1	3.3	3.4	3.2	3.9	4.6	5.1	4.5	3.9	3.8	3.8	4.0
U.S.	4.1	4.2	3.9	3.5	3.7	4.3	4.5	4.4	3.9	3.9	4.0	3.8

Note: Data is not seasonally adjusted and covers workers 16 years of age and older; (1) Figures cover the Ann Arbor, MI Metropolitan Statistical Area
Source: Bureau of Labor Statistics, Local Area Unemployment Statistics

Average Wages

Occupation	$/Hr.	Occupation	$/Hr.
Accountants and Auditors	41.19	Maintenance and Repair Workers	24.12
Automotive Mechanics	27.70	Marketing Managers	70.18
Bookkeepers	24.68	Network and Computer Systems Admin.	46.70
Carpenters	30.96	Nurses, Licensed Practical	33.06
Cashiers	15.32	Nurses, Registered	46.65
Computer Programmers	39.67	Nursing Assistants	19.82
Computer Systems Analysts	53.91	Office Clerks, General	21.46
Computer User Support Specialists	27.63	Physical Therapists	47.54
Construction Laborers	24.45	Physicians	117.60
Cooks, Restaurant	18.17	Plumbers, Pipefitters and Steamfitters	35.47
Customer Service Representatives	20.90	Police and Sheriff's Patrol Officers	37.47
Dentists	n/a	Postal Service Mail Carriers	28.15
Electricians	37.90	Real Estate Sales Agents	31.11
Engineers, Electrical	52.52	Retail Salespersons	18.46
Fast Food and Counter Workers	15.01	Sales Representatives, Technical/Scientific	105.25
Financial Managers	78.28	Secretaries, Exc. Legal/Medical/Executive	24.23
First-Line Supervisors of Office Workers	33.10	Security Guards	21.89
General and Operations Managers	66.91	Surgeons	n/a
Hairdressers/Cosmetologists	21.16	Teacher Assistants, Exc. Postsecondary[1]	16.34
Home Health and Personal Care Aides	17.05	Teachers, Secondary School, Exc. Sp. Ed.[1]	35.96
Janitors and Cleaners	18.60	Telemarketers	n/a
Landscaping/Groundskeeping Workers	19.91	Truck Drivers, Heavy/Tractor-Trailer	28.12
Lawyers	80.54	Truck Drivers, Light/Delivery Services	23.79
Maids and Housekeeping Cleaners	17.03	Waiters and Waitresses	20.05

Note: Wage data covers the Ann Arbor, MI Metropolitan Statistical Area; (1) Hourly wages were calculated from annual wage data based on a 40 hour work week
Source: Bureau of Labor Statistics, Metro Area Occupational Employment & Wage Estimates, May 2024

Employment by Industry

Sector	MSA[1] Number of Employees	MSA[1] Percent of Total	U.S. Percent of Total
Construction, Mining, and Logging	5,100	2.2	5.5
Financial Activities	6,800	2.9	5.8
Government	87,300	37.3	14.9
Information	5,800	2.5	1.9
Leisure and Hospitality	16,600	7.1	10.4
Manufacturing	12,000	5.1	8.0
Other Services	6,600	2.8	3.7
Private Education and Health Services	35,100	15.0	16.9
Professional and Business Services	29,100	12.4	14.2
Retail Trade	17,100	7.3	10.0
Transportation, Warehousing, and Utilities	5,200	2.2	4.8
Wholesale Trade	7,200	3.1	3.9

Note: Figures are non-farm employment as of December 2024. Figures are not seasonally adjusted and include workers 16 years of age and older; (1) Figures cover the Ann Arbor, MI Metropolitan Statistical Area
Source: Bureau of Labor Statistics, Current Employment Statistics, Employment, Hours, and Earnings

Employment by Occupation

Occupation Classification	City (%)	MSA[1] (%)	U.S. (%)
Management, Business, Science, and Arts	67.2	57.4	42.0
Natural Resources, Construction, and Maintenance	2.3	4.2	8.6
Production, Transportation, and Material Moving	5.1	8.7	13.0
Sales and Office	13.5	15.4	19.9
Service	11.9	14.2	16.5

Note: Figures cover employed civilians 16 years of age and older; (1) Figures cover the Ann Arbor, MI Metropolitan Statistical Area
Source: U.S. Census Bureau, 2019-2023 American Community Survey 5-Year Estimates

Occupations with Greatest Projected Employment Growth: 2022 – 2032

Occupation[1]	2022 Employment	2032 Projected Employment	Numeric Employment Change	Percent Employment Change
Home Health and Personal Care Aides	85,480	100,320	14,840	17.4
Software Developers	42,680	51,380	8,700	20.4
Cooks, Restaurant	38,550	44,610	6,060	15.7
Medical and Health Services Managers	14,350	18,190	3,840	26.8
Light Truck or Delivery Services Drivers	34,630	37,810	3,180	9.2
Medical Assistants	24,670	27,830	3,160	12.8
Nurse Practitioners	7,370	10,410	3,040	41.2
Industrial Machinery Mechanics	20,680	23,650	2,970	14.4
Financial Managers	20,620	23,540	2,920	14.2
Registered Nurses	104,150	106,910	2,760	2.7

Note: Projections cover Michigan; (1) Sorted by numeric employment change
Source: www.projectionscentral.org, State Occupational Projections, 2022–2032 Long-Term Projections

Fastest-Growing Occupations: 2022 – 2032

Occupation[1]	2022 Employment	2032 Projected Employment	Numeric Employment Change	Percent Employment Change
Nurse Practitioners	7,370	10,410	3,040	41.2
Data Scientists	4,020	5,420	1,400	34.8
Statisticians	690	900	210	30.4
Occupational Therapy Assistants	1,410	1,790	380	27.0
Medical and Health Services Managers	14,350	18,190	3,840	26.8
Physician Assistants	5,550	7,000	1,450	26.1
Information Security Analysts (SOC 2018)	2,810	3,530	720	25.6
Epidemiologists	240	300	60	25.0
Solar Photovoltaic Installers	200	250	50	25.0
Actuaries	420	520	100	23.8

Note: Projections cover Michigan; (1) Sorted by percent employment change and excludes occupations with numeric employment change less than 50
Source: www.projectionscentral.org, State Occupational Projections, 2022–2032 Long-Term Projections

CITY FINANCES

City Government Finances

Component	2022 ($000)	2022 ($ per capita)
Total Revenues	328,530	2,754
Total Expenditures	279,643	2,344
Debt Outstanding	265,164	2,223

Source: U.S. Census Bureau, State & Local Government Finances 2022

City Government Revenue by Source

Source	2022 ($000)	2022 ($ per capita)	2022 (%)
General Revenue			
From Federal Government	40,568	340	12.3
From State Government	35,469	297	10.8
From Local Governments	7,679	64	2.3
Taxes			
Property	125,434	1,052	38.2
Sales and Gross Receipts	0	0	0.0
Personal Income	0	0	0.0
Corporate Income	0	0	0.0
Motor Vehicle License	0	0	0.0
Other Taxes	9,315	78	2.8
Current Charges	61,874	519	18.8
Liquor Store	0	0	0.0
Utility	30,553	256	9.3

Source: U.S. Census Bureau, State & Local Government Finances 2022

City Government Expenditures by Function

Function	2022 ($000)	2022 ($ per capita)	2022 (%)
General Direct Expenditures			
Air Transportation	860	7	0.3
Corrections	0	0	0.0
Education	0	0	0.0
Employment Security Administration	0	0	0.0
Financial Administration	4,392	36	1.6
Fire Protection	17,886	150	6.4
General Public Buildings	0	0	0.0
Governmental Administration, Other	3,760	31	1.3
Health	0	0	0.0
Highways	34,929	292	12.5
Hospitals	0	0	0.0
Housing and Community Development	26,843	225	9.6
Interest on General Debt	6,263	52	2.2
Judicial and Legal	7,688	64	2.7
Libraries	0	0	0.0
Parking	0	0	0.0
Parks and Recreation	18,960	159	6.8
Police Protection	32,450	272	11.6
Public Welfare	0	0	0.0
Sewerage	13,506	113	4.8
Solid Waste Management	16,159	135	5.8
Veterans' Services	0	0	0.0
Liquor Store	0	0	0.0
Utility	27,781	232	9.9

Source: U.S. Census Bureau, State & Local Government Finances 2022

TAXES

State Corporate Income Tax Rates

State	Tax Rate (%)	Income Brackets ($)	Num. of Brackets	Financial Institution Tax Rate (%)[a]	Federal Income Tax Ded.
Michigan	6.0	Flat rate	1	(a)	No

Note: Tax rates for tax year 2024; (a) Rates listed are the corporate income tax rate applied to financial institutions or excise taxes based on income. Some states have other taxes based upon the value of deposits or shares.
Source: Federation of Tax Administrators, State Corporate Income Tax Rates, January 1, 2025

State Individual Income Tax Rates

State	Tax Rate (%)	Income Brackets ($)	Personal Exemptions ($)			Standard Ded. ($)	
			Single	Married	Depend.	Single	Married
Michigan	4.25	Flat rate	56000	11,200	5,000	(m1)	(m1)

Note: Tax rates for tax year 2024; Local- and county-level taxes are not included; Federal income tax is not deductible on state income tax returns
Source: Federation of Tax Administrators, State Individual Income Tax Rates, January 1, 2025

Various State Sales and Excise Tax Rates

State	State Sales Tax (%)	Gasoline[1] ($/gal.)	Cigarette[2] ($/pack)	Spirits[3] ($/gal.)	Wine[4] ($/gal.)	Beer[5] ($/gal.)	Recreational Marijuana (%)
Michigan	6	0.48	2.00	14.61	0.51	0.20	(k)

Note: All tax rates as of January 1, 2025; (1) The American Petroleum Institute has developed a methodology for determining the average tax rate on a gallon of fuel. Rates may include any of the following: excise taxes, environmental fees, storage tank fees, other fees or taxes, general sales tax, and local taxes; (2) The federal excise tax of $1.0066 per pack and local taxes are not included; (3) Rates are those applicable to off-premise sales of 40% alcohol by volume (a.b.v.) distilled spirits in 750ml containers. Local excise taxes are excluded; (4) Rates are those applicable to off-premise sales of 11% a.b.v. non-carbonated wine in 750ml containers; (5) Rates are those applicable to off-premise sales of 4.7% a.b.v. beer in 12 ounce containers; (k) 10% excise tax (retail gross receipts)
Source: Tax Foundation, 2025 Facts & Figures: How Does Your State Compare?

State Tax Competitiveness Index

State	Overall Rank	Corporate Tax Rank	Individual Income Tax Rank	Sales Tax Rank	Property Tax Rank	Unemployment Insurance Tax Rank
Michigan	14	9	14	12	28	26

Note: The Tax Foundation's State Tax Competitiveness Index enables policymakers, taxpayers, and business leaders to gauge how their states' tax systems compare. A rank of 1 is best, 50 is worst. Rankings do not average to the total. States without a tax rank equally as 1. DC's scores and rankings do not affect other states. The report shows tax systems as of July 1, 2024 (the beginning of Fiscal Year 2025).
Source: Tax Foundation, State Tax Competitiveness Index 2025

TRANSPORTATION

Means of Transportation to Work

Area	Car/Truck/Van		Public Transportation			Bicycle	Walked	Other Means	Worked at Home
	Drove Alone	Car-pooled	Bus	Subway	Railroad				
City	45.6	5.0	7.3	0.1	0.0	2.4	13.1	0.5	26.2
MSA[1]	61.9	6.3	3.7	0.0	0.0	1.0	5.8	0.8	20.3
U.S.	70.2	8.5	1.7	1.3	0.4	0.4	2.4	1.6	13.5

Note: Figures are percentages and cover workers 16 years of age and older; (1) Figures cover the Ann Arbor, MI Metropolitan Statistical Area
Source: U.S. Census Bureau, 2019-2023 American Community Survey 5-Year Estimates

Travel Time to Work

Area	Less Than 10 Minutes	10 to 19 Minutes	20 to 29 Minutes	30 to 44 Minutes	45 to 59 Minutes	60 to 89 Minutes	90 Minutes or More
City	12.9	45.8	18.9	13.6	5.8	2.3	0.7
MSA[1]	11.2	33.3	25.2	18.5	7.2	3.5	1.2
U.S.	12.6	28.6	21.2	20.8	8.1	6.0	2.8

Note: Note: Figures are percentages and include workers 16 years old and over; (1) Figures cover the Ann Arbor, MI Metropolitan Statistical Area
Source: U.S. Census Bureau, 2019-2023 American Community Survey 5-Year Estimates

Key Congestion Measures

Measure	2000	2010	2015	2020	2022
Annual Hours of Delay, Total (000)	n/a	n/a	6,900	3,239	5,603
Annual Hours of Delay, Per Auto Commuter	n/a	n/a	22	10	18
Annual Congestion Cost, Per Auto Commuter ($)	n/a	n/a	515	255	422

Note: n/a not available
Source: Texas A&M Transportation Institute, 2023 Urban Mobility Report

Freeway Travel Time Index

Measure	1985	1990	1995	2000	2005	2010	2015	2020	2022
Urban Area Index[1]	n/a	n/a	n/a	n/a	n/a	n/a	1.11	1.07	1.09
Urban Area Rank[1,2]	n/a	n/a	n/a	n/a	n/a	n/a	n/a	n/a	n/a

Note: Freeway Travel Time Index—the ratio of travel time in the peak period to the travel time at free-flow conditions. For example, a value of 1.30 indicates a 20-minute free-flow trip takes 26 minutes in the peak (20 minutes x 1.30 = 26 minutes); (1) Covers the Ann Arbor MI urban area; (2) Rank is based on 101 larger urban areas (#1 = highest travel time index); n/a not available
Source: Texas A&M Transportation Institute, 2023 Urban Mobility Report

Public Transportation

Agency Name / Mode of Transportation	Vehicles Operated in Maximum Service[1]	Annual Unlinked Passenger Trips[2] (in thous.)	Annual Passenger Miles[3] (in thous.)
Ann Arbor Transportation Authority (AATA)			
Bus (directly operated)	75	4,350.5	14,417.1
Commuter Bus (purchased transportation)	3	56.8	2,498.2
Demand Response (purchased transportation)	35	113.2	658.1
Vanpool (purchased transportation)	114	160.1	6,046.9

Note: (1) Number of revenue vehicles operated by the given mode and type of service to meet the annual maximum service requirement. This is the revenue vehicle count during the peak season of the year; on the week and day that maximum service is provided. Vehicles operated in maximum service (VOMS) exclude atypical days and one-time special events; (2) Number of passengers who boarded public transportation vehicles. Passengers are counted each time they board a vehicle no matter how many vehicles they use to travel from their origin to their destination. (3) Sum of the distances ridden by all passengers during the entire fiscal year.
Source: Federal Transit Administration, National Transit Database, 2023

Air Transportation

Airport Name and Code / Type of Service	Passenger Airlines[1]	Passenger Enplanements	Freight Carriers[2]	Freight (lbs)
Detroit Metro Wayne County (25 miles) (DTW)				
Domestic service (U.S. carriers only)	30	14,425,694	15	102,703,905
International service (U.S. carriers only)	8	1,270,466	3	30,600,556

Note: (1) Includes all U.S.-based major, minor and commuter airlines that carried at least one passenger during the year; (2) Includes all U.S.-based airlines and freight carriers that transported at least one pound of freight during the year.
Source: Bureau of Transportation Statistics, The Intermodal Transportation Database, Air Carriers: T-100 Domestic Market (U.S. carriers only), 2024; Bureau of Transportation Statistics, The Intermodal Transportation Database, Air Carriers: T-100 International Market (U.S. carriers only), 2024

BUSINESSES

Major Business Headquarters

Company Name	Industry	Rankings Fortune[1]	Rankings Forbes[2]
No companies listed	-	-	-

Note: (1) Companies that produce a 10-K are ranked 1 to 500 based on 2023 revenue; (2) All private companies with at least $2 billion in annual revenue through the end of their most current fiscal year are ranked 1 to 275; companies listed are headquartered in the city; dashes indicate no ranking
Source: Fortune, "Fortune 500," 2024; Forbes, "America's Largest Private Companies," 2024

Fastest-Growing Businesses

According to Deloitte, Ann Arbor is home to one of North America's 500 fastest-growing high-technology companies: **Censys** (#323). Companies are ranked by percentage growth in revenue over a four-year period. Criteria for inclusion: company must be headquartered within North America; must own proprietary intellectual property or technology that is sold to customers in products that contributes to a significant portion of the company's operating revenue; must have been in business for a minumum of four years with 2020 operating revenues of at least $50,000 USD/CD and 2023 operating revenues of at least $5 million USD/CD. *Deloitte, 2024 Technology Fast 500™*

Living Environment

COST OF LIVING

Cost of Living Index

Composite Index	Groceries	Housing	Utilities	Transportation	Health Care	Misc. Goods/Services
n/a	n/a	n/a	n/a	n/a	n/a	n/a

Note: The Cost of Living Index measures regional differences in the cost of consumer goods and services, excluding taxes and non-consumer expenditures, for professional and managerial households in the top income quintile. It is based on more than 50,000 prices covering almost 60 different items for which prices are collected three times a year by chambers of commerce, economic development organizations or university applied economic centers in each participating urban area. The numbers shown should be read as a percentage above or below the national average of 100. For example, a value of 115.4 in the groceries column indicates that grocery prices are 15.4% higher than the national average. Small differences in the index numbers should not be interpreted as significant; n/a not available.
Source: The Council for Community and Economic Research, Cost of Living Index, 2024

Grocery Prices

Area[1]	T-Bone Steak ($/pound)	Frying Chicken ($/pound)	Whole Milk ($/half gal.)	Eggs ($/dozen)	Orange Juice ($/64 oz.)	Coffee ($/11.5 oz.)
City[2]	n/a	n/a	n/a	n/a	n/a	n/a
Avg.	15.42	1.55	4.69	3.25	4.41	5.46
Min.	14.50	1.16	4.43	2.75	4.00	4.85
Max.	17.56	2.89	5.49	4.78	5.54	7.89

*Note: (1) Values for the local area are compared with the average, minimum and maximum values for all 276 areas in the Cost of Living Index; (2) Figures cover the Ann Arbor MI urban area; n/a not available; **T-Bone Steak** (price per pound); **Frying Chicken** (price per pound, whole fryer); **Whole Milk** (half gallon carton); **Eggs** (price per dozen, Grade A, large); **Orange Juice** (64 oz. Tropicana or Florida Natural); **Coffee** (11.5 oz. can, vacuum-packed, Maxwell House, Hills Bros, or Folgers).*
Source: The Council for Community and Economic Research, Cost of Living Index, 2024

Housing and Utility Costs

Area[1]	New Home Price ($)	Apartment Rent ($/month)	All Electric ($/month)	Part Electric ($/month)	Other Energy ($/month)	Telephone ($/month)
City[2]	n/a	n/a	n/a	n/a	n/a	n/a
Avg.	515,975	1,550	210.99	123.07	82.07	194.99
Min.	265,375	692	104.33	53.68	36.26	179.42
Max.	2,775,821	5,719	529.02	397.28	361.63	223.33

*Note: (1) Values for the local area are compared with the average, minimum and maximum values for all 276 areas in the Cost of Living Index; (2) Figures cover the Ann Arbor MI urban area; n/a not available; **New Home Price** (2,400 sf living area, 8,000 sf lot, in urban area with full utilities); **Apartment Rent** (950 sf 2 bedroom/1.5 or 2 bath, unfurnished, excluding all utilities except water); **All Electric** (average monthly cost for an all-electric home); **Part Electric** (average monthly cost for a part-electric home); **Other Energy** (average monthly cost for natural gas, fuel oil, coal, wood, and any other forms of energy except electricity); **Telephone** (price includes the base monthly rate plus taxes and fees for three lines of mobile phone service).*
Source: The Council for Community and Economic Research, Cost of Living Index, 2024

Health Care, Transportation, and Other Costs

Area[1]	Doctor ($/visit)	Dentist ($/visit)	Optometrist ($/visit)	Gasoline ($/gallon)	Beauty Salon ($/visit)	Men's Shirt ($)
City[2]	n/a	n/a	n/a	n/a	n/a	n/a
Avg.	143.77	117.51	129.23	3.32	48.57	38.14
Min.	36.74	58.67	67.33	2.80	24.00	13.41
Max.	270.44	216.82	307.33	5.28	94.00	63.89

*Note: (1) Values for the local area are compared with the average, minimum and maximum values for all 276 areas in the Cost of Living Index; (2) Figures cover the Ann Arbor MI urban area; n/a not available; **Doctor** (general practitioners routine exam of an established patient); **Dentist** (adult teeth cleaning and periodic oral examination); **Optometrist** (full vision eye exam for established adult patient); **Gasoline** (one gallon regular unleaded, national brand, including all taxes, cash price at self-service pump if available); **Beauty Salon** (woman's shampoo, trim, and blow-dry); **Men's Shirt** (cotton/polyester dress shirt, pinpoint weave, long sleeves).*
Source: The Council for Community and Economic Research, Cost of Living Index, 2024

HOUSING

Homeownership Rate

Area	2017 (%)	2018 (%)	2019 (%)	2020 (%)	2021 (%)	2022 (%)	2023 (%)	2024 (%)
MSA[1]	n/a	n/a	n/a	n/a	n/a	n/a	n/a	n/a
U.S.	63.9	64.4	64.6	66.6	65.5	65.8	65.9	65.6

Note: (1) Figures cover the Ann Arbor, MI Metropolitan Statistical Area; n/a not available
Source: U.S. Census Bureau, Housing Vacancies and Homeownership Annual Statistics: 2017-2024

House Price Index (HPI)

Area	National Ranking[2]	Quarterly Change (%)	One-Year Change (%)	Five-Year Change (%)	Since 1991Q1 (%)
MSA[1]	111	0.79	5.63	45.12	265.98
U.S.[3]	–	1.43	4.51	57.13	327.82

Note: The HPI is a weighted repeat sales index. It measures average price changes in repeat sales or refinancings on the same properties. This information is obtained by reviewing repeat mortgage transactions on single-family properties whose mortgages have been purchased or securitized by Fannie Mae or Freddie Mac since January 1975; (1) Figures cover the Ann Arbor, MI Metropolitan Statistical Area; (2) Rankings are based on annual percentage change for all metro areas containing at least 15,000 transactions over the last 10 years and ranges from 1 to 241; (3) figures based on a weighted average of Census Division estimates using a seasonally adjusted, purchase-only index; all figures are for the period ending December 31, 2024
Source: Federal Housing Finance Agency, Change in FHFA Metropolitan Area House Price Indexes, All Transactions Index, 2024Q4

Home Value

Area	Under $100,000	$100,000 -$199,999	$200,000 -$299,999	$300,000 -$399,999	$400,000 -$499,999	$500,000 -$999,999	$1,000,000 or more	Median ($)
City	1.8	5.6	14.3	20.1	23.3	29.4	5.4	435,100
MSA[1]	7.1	11.0	21.8	19.2	16.2	21.4	3.4	353,000
U.S.	12.1	17.8	19.5	14.4	10.5	19.1	6.5	303,400

Note: Figures are percentages except for median and cover owner-occupied housing units; (1) Figures cover the Ann Arbor, MI Metropolitan Statistical Area
Source: U.S. Census Bureau, 2019-2023 American Community Survey 5-Year Estimates

Year Housing Structure Built

Area	2020 or Later	2010 -2019	2000 -2009	1990 -1999	1980 -1989	1970 -1979	1960 -1969	1950 -1959	1940 -1949	Before 1940	Median Year
City	1.3	6.5	6.8	11.2	9.9	16.0	17.9	10.6	4.8	15.2	1971
MSA[1]	1.2	6.4	13.0	16.0	10.5	15.4	12.3	9.1	4.3	11.8	1978
U.S.	1.2	8.9	13.6	12.8	13.0	14.4	10.0	9.7	4.5	11.9	1980

Note: Figures are percentages except for Median Year; Note: (1) Figures cover the Ann Arbor, MI Metropolitan Statistical Area
Source: U.S. Census Bureau, 2019-2023 American Community Survey 5-Year Estimates

Gross Monthly Rent

Area	Under $500	$500 -$999	$1,000 -$1,499	$1,500 -$1,999	$2,000 -$2,499	$2,500 -$2,999	$3,000 and up	Median ($)
City	3.0	11.6	32.6	26.6	14.6	4.9	6.7	1,552
MSA[1]	4.3	14.9	39.0	23.1	10.3	3.5	4.7	1,400
U.S.	6.5	22.3	29.5	20.2	10.8	4.8	5.9	1,348

Note: Figures are percentages except for median; Gross rent is the contract rent plus the estimated average monthly cost of utilities (electricity, gas, and water and sewer) and fuels (oil, coal, kerosene, wood, etc.) if these are paid by the renter (or paid for the renter by someone else); (1) Figures cover the Ann Arbor, MI Metropolitan Statistical Area
Source: U.S. Census Bureau, 2019-2023 American Community Survey 5-Year Estimates

HEALTH

Health Risk Factors

Category	MSA[1] (%)	U.S. (%)
Adults aged 18–64 who have any kind of health care coverage	n/a	90.8
Adults who reported being in good or better health	n/a	81.8
Adults who have been told they have high blood cholesterol	n/a	36.9
Adults who have been told they have high blood pressure	n/a	34.0
Adults who are current smokers	n/a	12.1
Adults who currently use e-cigarettes	n/a	7.7
Adults who currently use chewing tobacco, snuff, or snus	n/a	3.2
Adults who are heavy drinkers[2]	n/a	6.1
Adults who are binge drinkers[3]	n/a	15.2
Adults who are overweight (BMI 25.0 - 29.9)	n/a	34.4
Adults who are obese (BMI 30.0 - 99.8)	n/a	34.3
Adults who participated in any physical activities in the past month	n/a	75.8

Note: All figures are crude prevalence; (1) Figures for the Ann Arbor, MI Metropolitan Statistical Area were not available.
(2) Heavy drinkers are classified as adult men having more than 14 drinks per week and adult women having more than 7 drinks per week; (3) Binge drinkers are classified as males having five or more drinks on one occasion or females having four or more drinks on one occasion
Source: Centers for Disease Control and Prevention, Behavioral Risk Factor Surveillance System, SMART: Selected Metropolitan Area Risk Trends, 2023

Acute and Chronic Health Conditions

Category	MSA[1] (%)	U.S. (%)
Adults who have ever been told they had a heart attack	n/a	4.2
Adults who have ever been told they have angina or coronary heart disease	n/a	4.0
Adults who have ever been told they had a stroke	n/a	3.3
Adults who have ever been told they have asthma	n/a	15.7
Adults who have ever been told they have arthritis	n/a	26.3
Adults who have ever been told they have diabetes[2]	n/a	11.5
Adults who have ever been told they had skin cancer	n/a	5.6
Adults who have ever been told they had any other types of cancer	n/a	8.4
Adults who have ever been told they have COPD	n/a	6.4
Adults who have ever been told they have kidney disease	n/a	3.7
Adults who have ever been told they have a form of depression	n/a	22.0

Note: All figures are crude prevalence; (1) Figures for the Ann Arbor, MI Metropolitan Statistical Area were not available.
(2) Figures do not include pregnancy-related, borderline, or pre-diabetes
Source: Centers for Disease Control and Prevention, Behavioral Risk Factor Surveillance System, SMART: Selected Metropolitan Area Risk Trends, 2023

Health Screening and Vaccination Rates

Category	MSA[1] (%)	U.S. (%)
Adults who have ever been tested for HIV	n/a	37.5
Adults who have had their blood cholesterol checked within the last five years	n/a	87.0
Adults aged 65+ who have had flu shot within the past year	n/a	63.4
Adults aged 65+ who have ever had a pneumonia vaccination	n/a	71.9

Note: All figures are crude prevalence; (1) Figures for the Ann Arbor, MI Metropolitan Statistical Area were not available.
Source: Centers for Disease Control and Prevention, Behavioral Risk Factor Surveillance System, SMART: Selected Metropolitan Area Risk Trends, 2023

Disability Status

Category	MSA[1] (%)	U.S. (%)
Adults who reported being deaf	n/a	7.4
Are you blind or have serious difficulty seeing, even when wearing glasses?	n/a	4.9
Do you have difficulty doing errands alone?	n/a	7.8
Do you have difficulty dressing or bathing?	n/a	3.6
Do you have serious difficulty concentrating/remembering/making decisions?	n/a	13.7
Do you have serious difficulty walking or climbing stairs?	n/a	13.2

Note: All figures are crude prevalence; (1) Figures for the Ann Arbor, MI Metropolitan Statistical Area were not available.
Source: Centers for Disease Control and Prevention, Behavioral Risk Factor Surveillance System, SMART: Selected Metropolitan Area Risk Trends, 2023

Mortality Rates for the Top 10 Causes of Death in the U.S.

ICD-10[a] Sub-Chapter	ICD-10[a] Code	Crude Mortality Rate[2] per 100,000 population	
		County[3]	U.S.
Malignant neoplasms	C00-C97	147.6	182.7
Ischaemic heart diseases	I20-I25	89.3	109.6
Provisional assignment of new diseases of uncertain etiology[1]	U00-U49	27.6	65.3
Other forms of heart disease	I30-I51	38.6	65.1
Other degenerative diseases of the nervous system	G30-G31	47.3	52.4
Other external causes of accidental injury	W00-X59	42.4	52.3
Cerebrovascular diseases	I60-I69	41.7	49.1
Chronic lower respiratory diseases	J40-J47	28.0	43.5
Hypertensive diseases	I10-I15	42.4	38.9
Organic, including symptomatic, mental disorders	F01-F09	22.3	33.9

Note: (a) ICD-10 = International Classification of Diseases 10th Revision; (1) Includes COVID-19, adverse effects to COVID-19 vaccines, SARS, and vaping-related disorders; (2) Crude mortality rates are a three-year average covering 2021-2023; (3) Figures cover Washtenaw County.
Source: Centers for Disease Control and Prevention, National Center for Health Statistics. National Vital Statistics System, Mortality 2018-2023 on CDC WONDER Online Database

Mortality Rates for Selected Causes of Death

Cause of Death	ICD-10[a] Code	Crude Mortality Rate[1] per 100,000 population	
		County[2]	U.S.
Accidental poisoning and exposure to noxious substances	X40-X49	21.3	30.5
Alzheimer disease	G30	40.6	35.4
Assault	X85-Y09	3.8	7.3
COVID-19	U07.1	27.6	65.3
Diabetes mellitus	E10-E14	10.9	30.0
Diseases of the liver	K70-K76	10.4	20.8
Human immunodeficiency virus (HIV) disease	B20-B24	Suppressed	1.5
Influenza and pneumonia	J09-J18	7.3	13.4
Intentional self-harm	X60-X84	12.0	14.7
Malnutrition	E40-E46	3.5	6.0
Obesity and other hyperalimentation	E65-E68	Unreliable	3.1
Renal failure	N17-N19	6.4	16.4
Transport accidents	V01-V99	6.9	14.4

Note: (a) ICD-10 = International Classification of Diseases 10th Revision; (1) Crude mortality rates are a three-year average covering 2021-2023; (2) Figures cover Washtenaw County; Data are suppressed when the data meet the criteria for confidentiality constraints; Crude mortality rates are flagged as unreliable when the rate would be calculated with a numerator of 20 or less.
Source: Centers for Disease Control and Prevention, National Center for Health Statistics. National Vital Statistics System, Mortality 2018-2023 on CDC WONDER Online Database

Health Insurance Coverage

Area	With Health Insurance	With Private Health Insurance	With Public Health Insurance	Without Health Insurance	Population Under Age 19 Without Health Insurance
City	97.2	86.7	20.9	2.8	2.1
MSA[1]	96.7	81.5	28.7	3.3	2.0
U.S.	91.4	67.3	36.3	8.6	5.4

Note: Figures are percentages that cover the civilian noninstitutionalized population; (1) Figures cover the Ann Arbor, MI Metropolitan Statistical Area
Source: U.S. Census Bureau, 2019-2023 American Community Survey 5-Year Estimates

Number of Medical Professionals

Area	MDs[3]	DOs[3,4]	Dentists	Podiatrists	Chiropractors	Optometrists
County[1] (number)	5,206	193	763	33	97	71
County[1] (rate[2])	1,420.9	52.7	208.7	9.0	26.5	19.4
U.S. (rate[2])	302.5	29.2	74.6	6.4	29.5	18.0

Note: Data as of 2023 unless noted; (1) Data covers Washtenaw County; (2) Number of medical professionals per 100,000 population; (3) Data as of 2022 and includes all active, non-federal physicians; (4) Doctor of Osteopathic Medicine
Source: U.S. Department of Health and Human Services, Health Resources and Services Administration, Bureau of Health Professions, Area Resource File (ARF) 2023-2024

Best Hospitals

According to *U.S. News,* the Ann Arbor, MI metro area is home to seven of the best hospitals in the U.S.: **University of Michigan Health Frankel Cardiovascular Center** (12 adult specialties and 11 pediatric specialties); **University of Michigan Health Kellogg Eye Center** (12 adult specialties and 11 pediatric specialties); **University of Michigan Health Rogel Cancer Center** (12 adult specialties and 11 pediatric specialties); **University of Michigan Health Von Voigtlander Women's Hospital** (12 adult specialties and 11 pediatric specialties); **University of Michigan Health-Ann Arbor** (12 adult specialties and 11 pediatric specialties); **University of Michigan Health-Inpatient Rehabilitation at Chelsea Hospital** (12 adult specialties and 11 pediatric specialties); **University of Michigan Hospitals and Health Centers** (12 adult specialties and 11 pediatric specialties). The hospitals listed were nationally ranked in at least one of 15 adult or 11 pediatric specialties. The number of specialties shown cover the parent hospital. Only 160 U.S. hospitals performed well enough to be nationally ranked in one or more specialties. Twenty hospitals in the U.S. made the Honor Roll. The Best Hospitals Honor Roll takes both the national rankings and the procedure and condition ratings into account. Hospitals received points if they were nationally ranked in one of the 15 adult specialties—the higher they ranked, the more points they got—and how many ratings of "high performing" they earned in the 20 procedures and conditions. *U.S. News Online, "America's Best Hospitals 2024-25"*

According to *U.S. News,* the Ann Arbor, MI metro area is home to two of the best children's hospitals in the U.S.: **University of Michigan Health C.S. Mott Children's Hospital** (11 pediatric specialties); **University of Michigan Health C.S. Mott Children's Hospital** (11 pediatric specialties). The hospitals listed were highly ranked in at least one of 11 pediatric specialties. One hundred five children's hospitals in the U.S. were nationally ranked in at least one specialty. Hospitals received points for being ranked in a specialty, and the 10 hospitals with the most points across the 11 specialties make up the Honor Roll. *U.S. News Online, "America's Best Children's Hospitals 2024-25"*

EDUCATION

Public School District Statistics

District Name	Schls	Pupils	Pupil/ Teacher Ratio	Minority Pupils[1] (%)	Total Rev. per Pupil ($)	Total Exp. per Pupil ($)
Ann Arbor Public Schools	32	16,978	13.9	49.7	21,751	22,548

Note: Table includes school districts with 2,000 or more students; (1) Percentage of students that are not non-Hispanic white.
Source: U.S. Department of Education, National Center for Education Statistics, Common Core of Data, Local Education Agency (School District) Universe Survey: School Year 2023-2024; U.S. Department of Education, National Center for Education Statistics, Common Core of Data, School District Finance Survey (F-33): School Year 2021–22

Best High Schools

According to *U.S. News,* Ann Arbor is home to one of the top 500 high schools in the U.S.: **Skyline High School** (#452). Nearly 25,000 public, magnet and charter schools were ranked based on their performance on state assessments and how well they prepare students for college. *U.S. News & World Report, "Best High Schools 2024"*

Highest Level of Education

Area	Less than H.S.	H.S. Diploma	Some College, No Deg.	Associate Degree	Bachelor's Degree	Master's Degree	Prof. School Degree	Doctorate Degree
City	2.4	7.0	8.9	4.0	30.5	26.4	8.7	12.1
MSA[1]	4.2	14.2	16.8	6.7	27.1	19.4	5.1	6.5
U.S.	10.6	26.2	19.4	8.8	21.3	9.8	2.3	1.6

Note: Figures cover persons age 25 and over; (1) Figures cover the Ann Arbor, MI Metropolitan Statistical Area
Source: U.S. Census Bureau, 2019-2023 American Community Survey 5-Year Estimates

Educational Attainment by Race

Area	High School Graduate or Higher (%)					Bachelor's Degree or Higher (%)				
	Total	White	Black	Asian	Hisp.[2]	Total	White	Black	Asian	Hisp.[2]
City	97.6	98.6	92.7	97.2	92.8	77.7	79.7	44.8	85.2	75.5
MSA[1]	95.8	97.1	90.9	95.6	85.8	58.1	60.0	31.5	82.0	47.3
U.S.	89.4	92.9	88.1	88.0	72.5	35.0	37.7	24.7	57.0	19.9

Note: Figures shown cover persons 25 years old and over; (1) Figures cover the Ann Arbor, MI Metropolitan Statistical Area; (2) People of Hispanic origin can be of any race
Source: U.S. Census Bureau, 2019-2023 American Community Survey 5-Year Estimates

School Enrollment by Grade and Control

Area	Preschool (%)		Kindergarten (%)		Grades 1 - 4 (%)		Grades 5 - 8 (%)		Grades 9 - 12 (%)	
	Public	Private	Public	Private	Public	Private	Public	Private	Public	Private
City	44.3	55.7	86.7	13.3	89.6	10.4	87.0	13.0	91.2	8.8
MSA[1]	53.0	47.0	89.6	10.4	85.0	15.0	84.6	15.4	91.8	8.2
U.S.	58.7	41.3	85.2	14.8	87.2	12.8	87.9	12.1	89.0	11.0

Note: Figures shown cover persons 3 years old and over; (1) Figures cover the Ann Arbor, MI Metropolitan Statistical Area
Source: U.S. Census Bureau, 2019-2023 American Community Survey 5-Year Estimates

Higher Education

Four-Year Colleges			Two-Year Colleges			Medical Schools[1]	Law Schools[2]	Voc/ Tech[3]
Public	Private Non-profit	Private For-profit	Public	Private Non-profit	Private For-profit			
2	1	0	1	0	0	1	1	1

Note: Figures cover institutions located within the Ann Arbor, MI Metropolitan Statistical Area and include main campuses only; (1) includes schools accredited by the Liaison Committee on Medical Education and the American Osteopathic Association's Commission on Osteopathic College Accreditation; (2) includes ABA-accredited schools, schools with provisional ABA accreditation, and state accredited schools; (3) includes all schools with programs that are less than 2 years.
Source: National Center for Education Statistics, Integrated Postsecondary Education System (IPEDS), 2023-24; Wikipedia, List of Medical Schools in the United States, accessed May 2, 2025; Wikipedia, List of Law Schools in the United States, accessed May 2, 2025

According to *U.S. News & World Report,* the Ann Arbor, MI metro area is home to one of the top 200 national universities in the U.S.: **University of Michigan—Ann Arbor** (#21 tie). The indicators used to capture academic quality fall into a number of categories: assessment by administrators at peer institutions; retention of students; faculty resources; student selectivity; financial resources; alumni giving; high school counselor ratings of colleges; and graduation rate. *U.S. News & World Report, "America's Best Colleges 2025"*

According to *U.S. News & World Report*, the Ann Arbor, MI metro area is home to one of the top 100 law schools in the U.S.: **University of Michigan—Ann Arbor 1** (#8 tie). The rankings are based on a weighted average of 12 measures of quality: peer assessment score; assessment score by lawyers/judges; median LSAT scores; median undergrad GPA; acceptance rate; employment rates for graduates; placement success; bar passage rate; faculty resources; expenditures per student; student/faculty ratio; and library resources. *U.S. News & World Report, "America's Best Graduate Schools, Law, 2025"*

According to *U.S. News & World Report*, the Ann Arbor, MI metro area is home to one of the top 75 business schools in the U.S.: **University of Michigan—Ann Arbor (Ross)** (#13 tie). The rankings are based on a weighted average of the following nine measures: quality assessment; peer assessment; recruiter assessment; placement success; mean starting salary and bonus; student selectivity; mean GMAT and GRE scores; mean undergraduate GPA; and acceptance rate. *U.S. News & World Report, "America's Best Graduate Schools, Business, 2025"*

EMPLOYERS

Major Employers

Company Name	Industry
Ann Arbor Public Schools	Education
Citizens Insurance Company of America	Finance & insurance
City of Ann Arbor	Municipal government
Domino's Pizza	Food services
Eastern Michigan University	Education
Faurecia Interior Systems	Automotive component mfg.
Ford Motor Company	Automotive component mfg.
General Motors Milford Proving Grounds	OEM research
Grupo Antolin	Automotive component mfg.
Integrated Health Associates (IHA)	Medical centers
JAC Products	Auto component mfg.
ProQuest	Data & information
Terumo Carviocascular Systems	Medical device manufacturer
Thai Summit America	Automotive component mfg.
Thomson Reuters	Software/IT
Toyota Technical Center	Automotive research & development
Trinity Health	Medical centers
Truven Health Analytics	Data & information
University of Michigan	Education
University of Michigan Medical Center	Medical centers

Note: Companies shown are located within the Ann Arbor, MI Metropolitan Statistical Area.
Source: Chambers of Commerce; State Departments of Labor; Wikipedia

PUBLIC SAFETY

Crime Rate

Area	Total Crime Rate	Violent Crime Rate				Property Crime Rate		
		Murder	Rape	Robbery	Aggrav. Assault	Burglary	Larceny-Theft	Motor Vehicle Theft
City	2,058.1	3.4	37.3	39.0	232.1	171.1	1,438.1	137.2
U.S.	2,290.9	5.7	38.0	66.5	264.1	250.7	1,347.2	318.7

Note: Figures are crimes per 100,000 population.
Source: FBI, Table 8, Offenses Known to Law Enforcement, by State by City, 2023

Hate Crimes

Area	Number of Quarters Reported	Number of Incidents per Bias Motivation					
		Race/Ethnicity/Ancestry	Religion	Sexual Orientation	Disability	Gender	Gender Identity
City	4	1	1	1	0	0	0
U.S.	4	5,900	2,699	2,077	187	92	492

Source: Federal Bureau of Investigation, Hate Crime Statistics 2023

Identity Theft Consumer Reports

Area	Reports	Reports per 100,000 Population	Rank[2]
MSA[1]	771	209	144
U.S.	1,135,291	339	-

Note: (1) Figures cover the Ann Arbor, MI Metropolitan Statistical Area; (2) Rank ranges from 1 to 401 where 1 indicates greatest number of identity theft reports per 100,000 population
Source: Federal Trade Commission, Consumer Sentinel Network Data Book 2024

Fraud and Other Consumer Reports

Area	Reports	Reports per 100,000 Population	Rank[2]
MSA[1]	4,321	1,173	136
U.S.	5,360,641	1,601	-

Note: (1) Figures cover the Ann Arbor, MI Metropolitan Statistical Area; (2) Rank ranges from 1 to 401 where 1 indicates greatest number of fraud and other consumer reports per 100,000 population
Source: Federal Trade Commission, Consumer Sentinel Network Data Book 2024

POLITICS

2024 Presidential Election Results

Area	Trump (Rep.)	Harris (Dem.)	Stein (Green)	Kennedy (Ind.)	Oliver (Lib.)	Other
Washtenaw County	26.5	70.7	1.3	0.4	0.4	0.7
U.S.	49.7	48.2	0.6	0.5	0.4	0.6

Note: Results are percentages and may not add to 100% due to rounding
Source: Dave Leip's Atlas of U.S. Presidential Elections

SPORTS

Professional Sports Teams

Team Name	League	Year Established

No teams are located in the metro area
Source: Wikipedia, Major Professional Sports Teams of the United States and Canada, May 1, 2025

CLIMATE

Average and Extreme Temperatures

Temperature	Jan	Feb	Mar	Apr	May	Jun	Jul	Aug	Sep	Oct	Nov	Dec	Yr.
Extreme High (°F)	62	65	81	89	93	104	102	100	98	91	77	68	104
Average High (°F)	30	33	44	58	70	79	83	81	74	61	48	35	58
Average Temp. (°F)	23	26	36	48	59	68	72	71	64	52	40	29	49
Average Low (°F)	16	18	27	37	47	56	61	60	53	41	32	21	39
Extreme Low (°F)	-21	-15	-4	10	25	36	41	38	29	17	9	-10	-21

Note: Figures cover the years 1958-1990
Source: National Climatic Data Center, International Station Meteorological Climate Summary, 9/96

Average Precipitation/Snowfall/Humidity

Precip./Humidity	Jan	Feb	Mar	Apr	May	Jun	Jul	Aug	Sep	Oct	Nov	Dec	Yr.
Avg. Precip. (in.)	1.8	1.8	2.5	3.0	2.9	3.6	3.1	3.4	2.8	2.2	2.6	2.7	32.4
Avg. Snowfall (in.)	10	9	7	2	Tr	0	0	0	0	Tr	3	11	41
Avg. Rel. Hum. 7am (%)	80	79	79	78	78	79	82	86	87	84	82	81	81
Avg. Rel. Hum. 4pm (%)	67	63	59	53	51	52	52	54	55	55	64	70	58

Note: Figures cover the years 1958-1990; Tr = Trace amounts (<0.05 in. of rain; <0.5 in. of snow)
Source: National Climatic Data Center, International Station Meteorological Climate Summary, 9/96

Weather Conditions

Temperature			Daytime Sky			Precipitation		
5°F & below	32°F & below	90°F & above	Clear	Partly cloudy	Cloudy	0.01 inch or more precip.	0.1 inch or more snow/ice	Thunderstorms
15	136	12	74	134	157	135	38	32

Note: Figures are average number of days per year and cover the years 1958-1990
Source: National Climatic Data Center, International Station Meteorological Climate Summary, 9/96

HAZARDOUS WASTE

Superfund Sites

The Ann Arbor, MI metro area is home to one site on the EPA's Superfund National Priorities List (NPL) or Superfund Alternative Approach (SAA) list: **Gelman Sciences Inc** (Proposed NPL). The Superfund alternative approach uses the same investigation and cleanup process and standards that are used for sites listed on the National Priorities List. The SAA is an alternative to listing a site on the NPL; it is not an alternative to Superfund or the Superfund process. There are a total of 1,445 Superfund sites with a status of proposed or final on both lists in the United States. *U.S. Environmental Protection Agency, National Priorities List, May 1, 2025; U.S. Environmental Protection Agency, Superfund Alternative Approach Sites, May 1, 2025*

AIR QUALITY

Air Quality Trends: Ozone

	1990	1995	2000	2005	2010	2015	2020	2021	2022	2023
MSA[1]	0.025	0.034	0.035	0.023	0.034	0.064	0.067	0.063	0.066	0.072
U.S.	0.087	0.089	0.081	0.080	0.072	0.068	0.066	0.067	0.067	0.070

Note: (1) Data covers the Ann Arbor, MI Metropolitan Statistical Area. The values shown are the composite ozone concentration averages among trend sites based on the highest fourth daily maximum 8-hour concentration in parts per million. These trends are based on sites having an adequate record of monitoring data during the trend period. Data from exceptional events are included.
Source: U.S. Environmental Protection Agency, Air Quality Monitoring Information, "Air Quality Trends by City, 1990-2023"

Air Quality Index

Area	Percent of Days when Air Quality was...[2]					AQI Statistics[2]	
	Good	Moderate	Unhealthy for Sensitive Groups	Unhealthy	Very Unhealthy	Maximum	Median
MSA[1]	46.0	50.4	2.5	0.5	0.5	218	52

Note: (1) Data covers the Ann Arbor, MI Metropolitan Statistical Area; (2) Based on 365 days with AQI data in 2023. Air Quality Index (AQI) is an index for reporting daily air quality. EPA calculates the AQI for five major air pollutants regulated by the Clean Air Act: ground-level ozone, particle pollution (aka particulate matter), carbon monoxide, sulfur dioxide, and nitrogen dioxide. The AQI runs from 0 to 500. The higher the AQI value, the greater the level of air pollution and the greater the health concern. There are six AQI categories: "Good" AQI is between 0 and 50. Air quality is considered satisfactory; "Moderate" AQI is between 51 and 100. Air quality is acceptable; "Unhealthy for Sensitive Groups" When AQI values are between 101 and 150, members of sensitive groups may experience health effects; "Unhealthy" When AQI values are between 151 and 200 everyone may begin to experience health effects; "Very Unhealthy" AQI values between 201 and 300 trigger a health alert; "Hazardous" AQI values over 300 trigger warnings of emergency conditions (not shown).
Source: U.S. Environmental Protection Agency, Air Quality Index Report, 2023

Air Quality Index Pollutants

Area	Percent of Days when AQI Pollutant was...[2]					
	Carbon Monoxide	Nitrogen Dioxide	Ozone	Sulfur Dioxide	Particulate Matter 2.5	Particulate Matter 10
MSA[1]	0.0	0.0	33.2	(3)	66.8	0.0

Note: (1) Data covers the Ann Arbor, MI Metropolitan Statistical Area; (2) Based on 365 days with AQI data in 2023. The Air Quality Index (AQI) is an index for reporting daily air quality. EPA calculates the AQI for five major air pollutants regulated by the Clean Air Act: ground-level ozone, particle pollution (also known as particulate matter), carbon monoxide, sulfur dioxide, and nitrogen dioxide. The AQI runs from 0 to 500. The higher the AQI value, the greater the level of air pollution and the greater the health concern; (3) Sulfur dioxide is no longer included in this table because SO_2 concentrations tend to be very localized and not necessarily representative of broad geographical areas like counties and CBSAs.
Source: U.S. Environmental Protection Agency, Air Quality Index Report, 2023

Maximum Air Pollutant Concentrations: Particulate Matter, Ozone, CO and Lead

	Particulate Matter 10 (ug/m^3)	Particulate Matter 2.5 Wtd AM (ug/m^3)	Particulate Matter 2.5 24-Hr (ug/m^3)	Ozone (ppm)	Carbon Monoxide (ppm)	Lead (ug/m^3)
MSA[1] Level	n/a	10.6	33	0.073	n/a	n/a
NAAQS[2]	150	15	35	0.075	9	0.15
Met NAAQS[2]	n/a	Yes	Yes	Yes	n/a	n/a

Note: (1) Data covers the Ann Arbor, MI Metropolitan Statistical Area; Data from exceptional events are included; (2) National Ambient Air Quality Standards; ppm = parts per million; ug/m^3 = micrograms per cubic meter; n/a not available.
Concentrations: Particulate Matter 10 (coarse particulate)—highest second maximum 24-hour concentration; Particulate Matter 2.5 Wtd AM (fine particulate)—highest weighted annual mean concentration; Particulate Matter 2.5 24-Hour (fine particulate)—highest 98th percentile 24-hour concentration; Ozone—highest fourth daily maximum 8-hour concentration; Carbon Monoxide—highest second maximum non-overlapping 8-hour concentration; Lead—maximum running 3-month average
Source: U.S. Environmental Protection Agency, Air Quality Monitoring Information, "Air Quality Statistics by City, 2023"

Maximum Air Pollutant Concentrations: Nitrogen Dioxide and Sulfur Dioxide

	Nitrogen Dioxide AM (ppb)	Nitrogen Dioxide 1-Hr (ppb)	Sulfur Dioxide AM (ppb)	Sulfur Dioxide 1-Hr (ppb)	Sulfur Dioxide 24-Hr (ppb)
MSA[1] Level	n/a	n/a	n/a	n/a	n/a
NAAQS[2]	53	100	30	75	140
Met NAAQS[2]	n/a	n/a	n/a	n/a	n/a

Note: (1) Data covers the Ann Arbor, MI Metropolitan Statistical Area; Data from exceptional events are included; (2) National Ambient Air Quality Standards; ppm = parts per million; ug/m³ = micrograms per cubic meter; n/a not available.
Concentrations: Nitrogen Dioxide AM—highest arithmetic mean concentration; Nitrogen Dioxide 1-Hr—highest 98th percentile 1-hour daily maximum concentration; Sulfur Dioxide AM—highest annual mean concentration; Sulfur Dioxide 1-Hr—highest 99th percentile 1-hour daily maximum concentration; Sulfur Dioxide 24-Hr—highest second maximum 24-hour concentration
Source: U.S. Environmental Protection Agency, Air Quality Monitoring Information, "Air Quality Statistics by City, 2023"

Cedar Rapids, Iowa

Background

Cedar Rapids sits on the Cedar River and is the principal city in eastern Iowa, 100 miles northeast of Des Moines. It is one of the Midwest's most diversified and modern cities.

Prior to European expansion, the site was intermittently home to nomadic bands of Fox, Meskwaki, and Winnebago Indians. Its first western settler was Osgood Shephard, a hunter, trapper, and horse trader who lived in a cabin on the river at the current corner of First Avenue and First Street SE. A stainless-steel sculpture, The Tree of Five Seasons, commemorates Shephard's first settlement, and is a common point of reference for the city's citizens.

Cedar Rapids, first called Rapids City, was incorporated as a town in 1849 and as a city in 1856. By 1858 the city boasted a population of 1,400. The city itself and its immediate environs is steeped in rich ethnic traditions and a pride in the preservation of local performing and visual arts.

Cedar Rapids was the original home of the North Star Oatmeal Mill, which eventually became Quaker Oats, long a giant in the cereal industry. The Cedar Rapids-based company still operates, under one roof, the largest cereal mill in the world.

The city has extensively diversified, however, from its original agricultural focus. Many industries, both locally and internationally owned, provide stability and dynamism to the local economy, which is increasingly tied into a larger global framework. Today, Cedar Rapids today depends on an economy based in food processing, construction machinery, pharmaceuticals, financial services, and biotechnology. It is one of the largest exporters per capita in the United States, with the nearby Eastern Iowa Airport designated as a foreign trade zone. The city is also a major telecommunications hub.

Cedar Rapids is home to Coe College, founded in 1851, and Mount Mercy College, founded in 1928. It maintains one of 93 schools established by The National Capital Language Resource Center (NCLRC) in Washington DC that teach Arabic. Cultural attractions include the Cedar Rapids Museum of Art, the Cedar Rapids Symphony Orchestra, the Science Station, which boasts the first IMAX Theater in Iowa, the History Center, and the National Czech and Slovak Museum and Library. Other area attractions include Duffy's Collectible Cars, Brucemore Mansion, the Iowa Children's Museum, the Indian Creek Nature Center, and the Czech Village. Government buildings are located on Municipal Island in the main channel of the Cedar River. Seventy-five parks and seven public golf courses are in and around the city.

Nearby points of historical interest include the Herbert Hoover Birthplace and Library, and the Amana Colonies, founded in the 1850s as a utopian society by members of a German religious sect. Visitors to the Amana villages view the operations of working farms, wool mills, and bakeries. Cedar Rapids is also the home to a large number of American Muslims, and the city boasts the oldest exclusively Muslim cemetery in the United States and the historic Mother Mosque of America.

Grant Wood—the famous painter of *American Gothic* and other icons of the Great Plains—was a resident of the city and taught there for many years. The Cedar Rapids Museum houses 7,200 works of art, including the world's largest collections of works by Wood, Marvin D. Cone, and Mauricio Lasansky. The Museum also operates the Grant Wood Studio and Visitor Center.

In June 2008, the Cedar River flooded its banks, leaving 1,300 city blocks under water and causing much of the city to be evacuated. Rebuilding efforts included hundreds of homes, a restored City Hall, Paramount Theater, fire stations, library, ground transportation center and a new $37 million office tower on the river's east bank.

In September 2016, when Hurricane Paine threatened to flood Cedar Rapids again, residents and National Guard troops filled more than 250,000 sandbags, preventing major flooding of the city. In 2020 an intense derecho (windstorm) caused major damage to the city.

There are four distinct seasons in Cedar Rapids. Winters are cold and dry, with winds out of the northwest. Some summer days bring rain from the Gulf of Mexico, and hot dry air from the southwest can cause unusually high temperatures. Fall and spring are usually mild, tempered by air from the Pacific. Precipitation throughout the year is moderate.

Rankings

General Rankings

- In their annual survey, Livability.com looked at data for more than 2,000 mid-sized U.S. cities to assign a "Livability Score"for each. The top 100 scoring cities make up Livability's "Top 100 Best Places to Live in the U.S." in 2025. Cedar Rapids was placed among the top 100 of the customizable list. Criteria: housing and economy; cost of living; environment; education; health care options; transportation; safety; and community amenities. *Livability.com, "Top 100 Best Places to Live in the U.S. in 2025" April 15, 2025*

Business/Finance Rankings

- The Cedar Rapids metro area appeared on the Milken Institute "2025 Best Performing Cities" list. Rank: #161 out of 200 large metro areas (based on performance category). Criteria: job growth; wage growth; high-tech growth and impact; community resilience; housing affordability; household broadband access. *Milken Institute, "Best-Performing Cities 2025," January 14, 2025*

Health/Fitness Rankings

- The Cedar Rapids metro area was identified as one of the worst cities for bed bugs in America by pest control company Orkin. The area ranked #39 out of 50 based on the number of bed bug treatments Orkin performed from December 2022 to November 2023. *Orkin, "Chicago Joins Paris In Global Bed Bug Spotlight Ranking As The Worst City On Orkin's U.S. Bed Bug Cities List," January 22, 2024*

Real Estate Rankings

- *WalletHub* compared the most populated U.S. cities to determine which had the best markets for real estate agents. Cedar Rapids ranked #150 where demand was high and pay was the best. Criteria: sales per agent; annual median wage for real-estate agents; monthly average starting salary for real estate agents; real estate job density and competition; unemployment rate; home turnover rate; housing-market health index; and other relevant metrics. *WalletHub.com, "2021 Best Places to Be a Real Estate Agent," May 12, 2021*

- Cedar Rapids was ranked #8 out of 176 metro areas in terms of cost of housing in 2024 by the National Association of Home Builders (#1 = most affordable). Criteria: the portion of an average family's income necessary to pay the mortgage on a median-priced home. *National Association of Home Builders®, NAHB-Wells Fargo Cost of Housing Index, 4th Quarter 2024*

Women/Minorities Rankings

- Personal finance website *WalletHub* compared more than 180 U.S. cities across two key dimensions, "Hispanic Business-Friendliness" and "Hispanic Purchasing Power," to arrive at the most favorable conditions for Hispanic entrepreneurs. Cedar Rapids was ranked #140 out of 182. Criteria includes: share of Hispanic-Owned Businesses; average growth of Hispanic Business revenues; Small Business-Friendliness score; affordability; and number of Hispanics with at least a bachelor's degree. *WalletHub.com, "Best Cities for Hispanic Entrepreneurs," September 4, 2024*

Miscellaneous Rankings

- *WalletHub* compared 148 of the most populated U.S. cities to determine their operating efficiency. A "Quality of Services" score was constructed for each city and then measured against the total budget per capita to reveal which were managed the best. Cedar Rapids ranked #35. Criteria: financial stability; economy; education; safety; health; infrastructure and pollution. *WalletHub.com, "2025's Best- & Worst-Run Cities in America," June 18, 2024*

Business Environment

DEMOGRAPHICS

Population Growth

Area	1990 Census	2000 Census	2010 Census	2020 Census	2023 Estimate[2]	Population Growth 1990-2023 (%)
City	110,829	120,758	126,326	137,710	136,859	23.5
MSA[1]	210,640	237,230	257,940	276,520	275,960	31.0
U.S.	248,709,873	281,421,906	308,745,538	331,449,281	332,387,540	33.6

Note: (1) Figures cover the Cedar Rapids, IA Metropolitan Statistical Area; (2) 2019-2023 5-year ACS population estimate
Source: U.S. Census Bureau, 1990 Census, 2000 Census, 2010 Census, 2020 Census, 2019-2023 American Community Survey 5-Year Estimates

Race

Area	White Alone[2] (%)	Black Alone[2] (%)	Asian Alone[2] (%)	AIAN[3] Alone[2] (%)	NHOPI[4] Alone[2] (%)	Other Race Alone[2] (%)	Two or More Races (%)
City	79.7	8.5	2.6	0.2	0.0	1.4	7.6
MSA[1]	86.2	5.0	2.0	0.3	0.0	1.1	5.5
U.S.	63.4	12.4	5.8	0.9	0.2	6.6	10.7

Note: (1) Figures cover the Cedar Rapids, IA Metropolitan Statistical Area; (2) Alone is defined as not being in combination with one or more other races; (3) American Indian and Alaska Native; (4) Native Hawaiian and Other Pacific Islander
Source: U.S. Census Bureau, 2019-2023 American Community Survey 5-Year Estimates

Hispanic or Latino Origin

Area	Total (%)	Mexican (%)	Puerto Rican (%)	Cuban (%)	Other (%)
City	5.1	3.5	0.4	0.1	1.2
MSA[1]	3.7	2.6	0.2	0.0	0.8
U.S.	19.0	11.3	1.8	0.7	5.2

Note: Persons of Hispanic or Latino origin can be of any race; (1) Figures cover the Cedar Rapids, IA Metropolitan Statistical Area
Source: U.S. Census Bureau, 2019-2023 American Community Survey 5-Year Estimates

Age

Area	Under Age 5	Age 5–19	Age 20–34	Age 35–44	Age 45–54	Age 55–64	Age 65–74	Age 75–84	Age 85+	Median Age
City	5.7	18.7	22.7	13.5	11.4	11.8	9.3	4.7	2.3	36.9
MSA[1]	5.8	19.3	19.1	13.2	12.1	13.1	10.1	5.1	2.2	39.3
U.S.	5.7	19.1	20.2	13.1	12.3	12.8	10.0	4.9	1.9	38.7

Note: (1) Figures cover the Cedar Rapids, IA Metropolitan Statistical Area
Source: U.S. Census Bureau, 2019-2023 American Community Survey 5-Year Estimates

Disability by Age

Area	All Ages	Under 18 Years Old	18 to 64 Years Old	65 Years and Over
City	11.6	4.9	10.0	27.3
MSA[1]	11.5	5.0	9.5	27.3
U.S.	13.0	4.7	10.7	32.9

Note: Figures show percent of the civilian noninstitutionalized population that reported having a disability. Disability status is determined from six types of difficulty: vision, hearing, cognitive, ambulatory, self-care, and independent living. For children under 5 years old, hearing and vision difficulty are used to determine disability status. For children between the ages of 5 and 14, disability status is determined from hearing, vision, cognitive, ambulatory, and self-care difficulties. For people aged 15 years and older, they are considered to have a disability if they have difficulty with any one of the six difficulty types; Note: (1) Figures cover the Cedar Rapids, IA Metropolitan Statistical Area
Source: U.S. Census Bureau, 2019-2023 American Community Survey 5-Year Estimates

Ancestry

Area	German	Irish	English	American	Italian	Polish	French[2]	European	Scottish
City	26.8	13.3	10.4	3.3	1.7	1.4	1.8	1.5	1.6
MSA[1]	31.4	14.1	10.6	4.0	1.6	1.2	1.8	1.7	1.8
U.S.	12.6	9.4	9.1	5.5	4.9	2.6	2.0	1.6	1.6

Note: Figures are the percentage of the total population reporting a particular ancestry. The nine most commonly reported ancestries in the U.S. are shown. Figures include multiple ancestries (e.g. if a person reported being Irish and Italian, they were included in both columns); (1) Figures cover the Cedar Rapids, IA Metropolitan Statistical Area; (2) Excludes Basque
Source: U.S. Census Bureau, 2019-2023 American Community Survey 5-Year Estimates

Foreign-born Population

Area	Percent of Population Born in								
	Any Foreign Country	Asia	Mexico	Europe	Caribbean	Central America[2]	South America	Africa	Canada
City	7.1	2.6	0.7	0.5	0.1	0.3	0.2	2.5	0.1
MSA[1]	4.5	1.8	0.5	0.4	0.1	0.2	0.1	1.3	0.1
U.S.	13.9	4.3	3.3	1.4	1.4	1.2	1.2	0.8	0.2

Note: (1) Figures cover the Cedar Rapids, IA Metropolitan Statistical Area; (2) Excludes Mexico.
Source: U.S. Census Bureau, 2019-2023 American Community Survey 5-Year Estimates

Household Size

Area	Persons in Household (%)							Average Household Size
	One	Two	Three	Four	Five	Six	Seven or More	
City	34.4	35.4	13.5	9.4	5.0	1.1	1.3	2.27
MSA[1]	29.8	37.2	13.8	11.3	5.4	1.4	1.1	2.38
U.S.	28.5	33.8	15.4	12.7	5.9	2.3	1.4	2.54

Note: (1) Figures cover the Cedar Rapids, IA Metropolitan Statistical Area
Source: U.S. Census Bureau, 2019-2023 American Community Survey 5-Year Estimates

Household Relationships

Area	Householder	Opposite-sex Spouse	Same-sex Spouse	Opposite-sex Unmarried Partner	Same-sex Unmarried Partner	Child[2]	Grand-child	Other Relatives	Non-relatives
City	42.2	16.7	0.2	3.5	0.2	26.8	1.3	2.9	3.4
MSA[1]	40.9	19.3	0.1	3.0	0.1	27.9	1.2	2.3	2.5
U.S.	38.3	17.5	0.2	2.5	0.2	28.3	2.4	4.8	3.4

Note: Figures are percent of the total population; (1) Figures cover the Cedar Rapids, IA Metropolitan Statistical Area; (2) Includes biological, adopted, and stepchildren of the householder
Source: U.S. Census Bureau, 2020 Census

Gender

Area	Males	Females	Males per 100 Females
City	67,551	69,308	97.5
MSA[1]	137,287	138,673	99.0
U.S.	164,545,087	167,842,453	98.0

Note: (1) Figures cover the Cedar Rapids, IA Metropolitan Statistical Area
Source: U.S. Census Bureau, 2019-2023 American Community Survey 5-Year Estimates

Marital Status

Area	Never Married	Now Married[2]	Separated	Widowed	Divorced
City	36.8	44.3	1.5	5.0	12.3
MSA[1]	30.9	51.1	1.3	5.2	11.5
U.S.	34.1	47.9	1.7	5.6	10.7

Note: Figures are percentages and cover the population 15 years of age and older; (1) Figures cover the Cedar Rapids, IA Metropolitan Statistical Area; (2) Excludes separated
Source: U.S. Census Bureau, 2019-2023 American Community Survey 5-Year Estimates

Religious Groups by Family

Area	Catholic	Baptist	Methodist	LDS[2]	Pentecostal	Lutheran	Islam	Adventist	Other
MSA[1]	16.8	1.0	5.3	1.0	1.3	8.1	1.3	0.6	9.6
U.S.	18.7	7.3	3.0	2.0	1.8	1.7	1.3	1.3	11.6

Note: Figures are the number of adherents as a percentage of the total population and cover the eight largest religious groups in the U.S; (1) Figures cover the Cedar Rapids, IA Metropolitan Statistical Area; (2) Church of Jesus Christ of Latter-day Saints
Sources: 2020 U.S. Religion Census, Association of Statisticians of American Religious Bodies; The Association of Religion Data Archives (ARDA)

Religious Groups by Tradition

Area	Catholic	Evangelical Protestant	Mainline Protestant	Black Protestant	Islam	Judaism	Hinduism	Orthodox	Buddhism
MSA[1]	16.8	11.9	12.2	0.4	1.3	0.1	0.7	0.1	<0.1
U.S.	18.7	16.5	5.2	2.3	1.3	0.6	0.4	0.4	0.3

Note: Figures are the number of adherents as a percentage of the total population; (1) Figures cover the Cedar Rapids, IA Metropolitan Statistical Area
Sources: 2020 U.S. Religion Census, Association of Statisticians of American Religious Bodies; The Association of Religion Data Archives (ARDA)

ECONOMY

Real Gross Domestic Product (GDP)

Area	2017	2018	2019	2020	2021	2022	2023	Rank[3]
MSA[1]	18.3	18.7	18.3	18.0	19.2	19.0	18.8	155
U.S.[2]	17,619.1	18,160.7	18,642.5	18,238.9	19,387.6	19,896.6	20,436.3	—

Note: Figures are in billions of chained 2017 dollars; (1) Figures cover the Cedar Rapids, IA Metropolitan Statistical Area; (2) Figures cover real GDP within metropolitan areas; (3) Rank is based on 2023 data and ranges from 1 to 384
Source: U.S. Bureau of Economic Analysis

Economic Growth

Area	2014	2015	2016	2017	2018	2019	2020	2021	2022	2023
MSA[1]	4.4	4.0	3.1	0.1	1.8	-1.9	-1.8	6.7	-1.0	-0.9
U.S.[2]	2.6	3.2	2.0	2.7	3.1	2.7	-2.2	6.3	2.6	2.7

Note: Figures are real gross domestic product growth rates and represent percent change from preceding period; (1) Figures cover the Cedar Rapids, IA Metropolitan Statistical Area; (2) Figures are the average growth rates within metropolitan areas
Source: U.S. Bureau of Economic Analysis

Metropolitan Area Exports

Area	2018	2019	2020	2021	2022	2023	Rank[2]
MSA[1]	1,025.0	1,028.4	832.0	980.0	1,018.7	1,175.4	159
U.S.	1,664,056.1	1,645,173.7	1,431,406.6	1,753,941.4	2,062,937.4	2,019,160.5	—

Note: Figures are in millions of dollars; (1) Figures cover the Cedar Rapids, IA Metropolitan Statistical Area; (2) Rank is based on 2023 data and ranges from 1 to 386
Source: U.S. Department of Commerce, International Trade Administration, Office of Trade and Economic Analysis, Industry and Analysis, Exports by Metropolitan Area, data extracted April 2, 2025

Building Permits

Area	Single-Family 2023	Single-Family 2024	Pct. Chg.	Multi-Family 2023	Multi-Family 2024	Pct. Chg.	Total 2023	Total 2024	Pct. Chg.
City	145	143	-1.4	229	465	103.1	374	608	62.6
MSA[1]	467	494	5.8	301	593	97.0	768	1,087	41.5
U.S.	920,000	981,900	6.7	591,100	496,100	-16.1	1,511,100	1,478,000	-2.2

Note: (1) Figures cover the Cedar Rapids, IA Metropolitan Statistical Area; Figures represent new, privately-owned housing units authorized (unadjusted data)
Source: U.S. Census Bureau, Building Permits Survey (BPS), 2023, 2024

Bankruptcy Filings

Area	Business Filings 2023	Business Filings 2024	% Chg.	Nonbusiness Filings 2023	Nonbusiness Filings 2024	% Chg.
Linn County	9	7	-22.2	224	278	24.1
U.S.	18,926	23,107	22.1	434,064	494,201	13.9

Note: Business filings include Chapter 7, Chapter 9, Chapter 11, Chapter 12, Chapter 13, Chapter 15, and Section 304; Nonbusiness filings include Chapter 7, Chapter 11, and Chapter 13
Source: Administrative Office of the U.S. Courts, Business and Nonbusiness Bankruptcy, County Cases Commenced by Chapter of the Bankruptcy Code, During the 12-Month Period Ending December 31, 2023 and Business and Nonbusiness Bankruptcy, County Cases Commenced by Chapter of the Bankruptcy Code, During the 12-Month Period Ending December 31, 2024

Housing Vacancy Rates

Area	Gross Vacancy Rate[3] (%) 2022	2023	2024	Year-Round Vacancy Rate[4] (%) 2022	2023	2024	Rental Vacancy Rate[5] (%) 2022	2023	2024	Homeowner Vacancy Rate[6] (%) 2022	2023	2024
MSA[1]	n/a	n/a	n/a	n/a	n/a	n/a	n/a	n/a	n/a	n/a	n/a	n/a
U.S.[2]	9.1	9.0	9.1	7.5	7.5	7.6	5.7	6.5	6.8	0.8	0.8	1.0

Note: (1) Figures cover the Cedar Rapids, IA Metropolitan Statistical Area; (2) Figures cover the 75 largest Metropolitan Statistical Areas; (3) The percentage of the total housing inventory that is vacant; (4) The percentage of the housing inventory (excluding seasonal units) that is year-round vacant; (5) The percentage of rental inventory that is vacant for rent; (6) The percentage of homeowner inventory that is vacant for sale; n/a not available
Source: U.S. Census Bureau, Housing Vacancies and Homeownership Annual Statistics: 2022, 2023, 2024

INCOME

Income

Area	Per Capita ($)	Median Household ($)	Average Household ($)
City	39,824	67,859	91,040
MSA[1]	41,820	77,084	100,451
U.S.	43,289	78,538	110,491

Note: (1) Figures cover the Cedar Rapids, IA Metropolitan Statistical Area
Source: U.S. Census Bureau, 2019-2023 American Community Survey 5-Year Estimates

Household Income Distribution

Area	Percent of Households Earning							
	Under $15,000	$15,000 -$24,999	$25,000 -$34,999	$35,000 -$49,999	$50,000 -$74,999	$75,000 -$99,999	$100,000 -$149,999	$150,000 and up
City	7.3	6.6	8.9	14.1	18.3	14.2	16.0	14.8
MSA[1]	6.1	6.2	7.2	12.0	17.3	14.5	18.2	18.5
U.S.	8.5	6.6	6.8	10.4	15.7	12.7	17.4	21.9

Note: (1) Figures cover the Cedar Rapids, IA Metropolitan Statistical Area
Source: U.S. Census Bureau, 2019-2023 American Community Survey 5-Year Estimates

Poverty Rate

Area	All Ages	Under 18 Years Old	18 to 64 Years Old	65 Years and Over
City	11.8	14.3	11.9	7.8
MSA[1]	9.7	11.5	9.7	7.5
U.S.	12.4	16.3	11.6	10.4

Note: Figures are percentage of people whose income during the past 12 months was below the poverty level; (1) Figures cover the Cedar Rapids, IA Metropolitan Statistical Area
Source: U.S. Census Bureau, 2019-2023 American Community Survey 5-Year Estimates

EMPLOYMENT

Labor Force and Employment

Area	Civilian Labor Force			Workers Employed		
	Dec. 2023	Dec. 2024	% Chg.	Dec. 2023	Dec. 2024	% Chg.
City	70,086	70,636	0.8	67,783	68,276	0.7
MSA[1]	141,248	142,473	0.9	136,873	137,885	0.7
U.S.	166,661,000	167,746,000	0.7	160,754,000	161,294,000	0.3

Note: Data is not seasonally adjusted and covers workers 16 years of age and older; (1) Figures cover the Cedar Rapids, IA Metropolitan Statistical Area
Source: Bureau of Labor Statistics, Local Area Unemployment Statistics

Unemployment Rate

Area	2024											
	Jan.	Feb.	Mar.	Apr.	May	Jun.	Jul.	Aug.	Sep.	Oct.	Nov.	Dec.
City	3.9	4.3	3.2	2.7	3.6	4.5	4.2	4.0	3.3	3.5	3.6	3.3
MSA[1]	3.9	4.0	3.2	2.5	3.2	3.8	3.8	3.7	3.0	3.3	3.4	3.2
U.S.	4.1	4.2	3.9	3.5	3.7	4.3	4.5	4.4	3.9	3.9	4.0	3.8

Note: Data is not seasonally adjusted and covers workers 16 years of age and older; (1) Figures cover the Cedar Rapids, IA Metropolitan Statistical Area
Source: Bureau of Labor Statistics, Local Area Unemployment Statistics

Average Wages

Occupation	$/Hr.	Occupation	$/Hr.
Accountants and Auditors	39.80	Maintenance and Repair Workers	26.12
Automotive Mechanics	26.02	Marketing Managers	66.98
Bookkeepers	24.03	Network and Computer Systems Admin.	41.23
Carpenters	27.03	Nurses, Licensed Practical	29.02
Cashiers	14.47	Nurses, Registered	37.78
Computer Programmers	39.50	Nursing Assistants	19.56
Computer Systems Analysts	44.19	Office Clerks, General	21.03
Computer User Support Specialists	28.20	Physical Therapists	42.76
Construction Laborers	23.76	Physicians	148.31
Cooks, Restaurant	16.74	Plumbers, Pipefitters and Steamfitters	33.30
Customer Service Representatives	21.95	Police and Sheriff's Patrol Officers	35.70
Dentists	76.51	Postal Service Mail Carriers	28.91
Electricians	26.89	Real Estate Sales Agents	21.00
Engineers, Electrical	53.76	Retail Salespersons	16.36
Fast Food and Counter Workers	13.79	Sales Representatives, Technical/Scientific	49.65
Financial Managers	67.28	Secretaries, Exc. Legal/Medical/Executive	21.59
First-Line Supervisors of Office Workers	31.58	Security Guards	19.04
General and Operations Managers	49.70	Surgeons	n/a
Hairdressers/Cosmetologists	22.37	Teacher Assistants, Exc. Postsecondary[1]	14.24
Home Health and Personal Care Aides	17.35	Teachers, Secondary School, Exc. Sp. Ed.[1]	28.68
Janitors and Cleaners	17.85	Telemarketers	15.78
Landscaping/Groundskeeping Workers	18.72	Truck Drivers, Heavy/Tractor-Trailer	29.58
Lawyers	61.80	Truck Drivers, Light/Delivery Services	24.80
Maids and Housekeeping Cleaners	15.71	Waiters and Waitresses	14.45

Note: Wage data covers the Cedar Rapids, IA Metropolitan Statistical Area; (1) Hourly wages were calculated from annual wage data based on a 40 hour work week
Source: Bureau of Labor Statistics, Metro Area Occupational Employment & Wage Estimates, May 2024

Employment by Industry

Sector	MSA[1] Number of Employees	MSA[1] Percent of Total	U.S. Percent of Total
Construction, Mining, and Logging	8,800	6.3	5.5
Financial Activities	9,200	6.6	5.8
Government	16,700	11.9	14.9
Information	2,800	2.0	1.9
Leisure and Hospitality	11,800	8.4	10.4
Manufacturing	19,900	14.2	8.0
Other Services	5,000	3.6	3.7
Private Education and Health Services	22,800	16.3	16.9
Professional and Business Services	15,600	11.1	14.2
Retail Trade	14,500	10.4	10.0
Transportation, Warehousing, and Utilities	7,100	5.1	4.8
Wholesale Trade	5,800	4.1	3.9

Note: Figures are non-farm employment as of December 2024. Figures are not seasonally adjusted and include workers 16 years of age and older; (1) Figures cover the Cedar Rapids, IA Metropolitan Statistical Area
Source: Bureau of Labor Statistics, Current Employment Statistics, Employment, Hours, and Earnings

Employment by Occupation

Occupation Classification	City (%)	MSA[1] (%)	U.S. (%)
Management, Business, Science, and Arts	38.8	40.2	42.0
Natural Resources, Construction, and Maintenance	8.2	8.8	8.6
Production, Transportation, and Material Moving	17.3	16.1	13.0
Sales and Office	20.7	20.8	19.9
Service	15.1	14.0	16.5

Note: Figures cover employed civilians 16 years of age and older; (1) Figures cover the Cedar Rapids, IA Metropolitan Statistical Area
Source: U.S. Census Bureau, 2019-2023 American Community Survey 5-Year Estimates

Occupations with Greatest Projected Employment Growth: 2022 – 2032

Occupation[1]	2022 Employment	2032 Projected Employment	Numeric Employment Change	Percent Employment Change
Home Health and Personal Care Aides	25,390	32,770	7,380	29.1
Heavy and Tractor-Trailer Truck Drivers	46,210	52,250	6,040	13.1
Registered Nurses	35,700	39,270	3,570	10.0
Stockers and Order Fillers	24,100	27,230	3,130	13.0
Laborers and Freight, Stock, and Material Movers, Hand	33,560	36,540	2,980	8.9
Cooks, Restaurant	13,190	15,840	2,650	20.1
Nursing Assistants (SOC 2018)	22,400	24,690	2,290	10.2
Construction Laborers	14,560	16,720	2,160	14.8
Medical and Health Services Managers	6,200	8,350	2,150	34.7
Financial Managers	8,990	10,870	1,880	20.9

Note: Projections cover Iowa; (1) Sorted by numeric employment change
Source: www.projectionscentral.org, State Occupational Projections, 2022–2032 Long-Term Projections

Fastest-Growing Occupations: 2022 – 2032

Occupation[1]	2022 Employment	2032 Projected Employment	Numeric Employment Change	Percent Employment Change
Wind Turbine Service Technicians	600	920	320	53.3
Nurse Practitioners	2,400	3,670	1,270	52.9
Data Scientists	2,010	2,760	750	37.3
Physical Therapist Assistants	1,260	1,720	460	36.5
Statisticians	400	540	140	35.0
Medical and Health Services Managers	6,200	8,350	2,150	34.7
Occupational Therapy Assistants	470	630	160	34.0
Information Security Analysts (SOC 2018)	1,250	1,670	420	33.6
Substance Abuse, Behavioral Disorder, and Mental Health Counselors	3,190	4,180	990	31.0
Physician Assistants	1,210	1,580	370	30.6

Note: Projections cover Iowa; (1) Sorted by percent employment change and excludes occupations with numeric employment change less than 50
Source: www.projectionscentral.org, State Occupational Projections, 2022–2032 Long-Term Projections

CITY FINANCES

City Government Finances

Component	2022 ($000)	2022 ($ per capita)
Total Revenues	475,654	3,549
Total Expenditures	495,736	3,699
Debt Outstanding	511,962	3,820

Source: U.S. Census Bureau, State & Local Government Finances 2022

City Government Revenue by Source

Source	2022 ($000)	2022 ($ per capita)	2022 (%)
General Revenue			
From Federal Government	66,164	494	13.9
From State Government	48,377	361	10.2
From Local Governments	1,171	9	0.2
Taxes			
Property	128,594	959	27.0
Sales and Gross Receipts	51,051	381	10.7
Personal Income	0	0	0.0
Corporate Income	0	0	0.0
Motor Vehicle License	0	0	0.0
Other Taxes	4,812	36	1.0
Current Charges	119,538	892	25.1
Liquor Store	0	0	0.0
Utility	42,570	318	8.9

Source: U.S. Census Bureau, State & Local Government Finances 2022

City Government Expenditures by Function

Function	2022 ($000)	2022 ($ per capita)	2022 (%)
General Direct Expenditures			
Air Transportation	34,101	254	6.9
Corrections	0	0	0.0
Education	0	0	0.0
Employment Security Administration	0	0	0.0
Financial Administration	6,284	46	1.3
Fire Protection	23,467	175	4.7
General Public Buildings	1,334	10	0.3
Governmental Administration, Other	3,591	26	0.7
Health	1,381	10	0.3
Highways	23,874	178	4.8
Hospitals	0	0	0.0
Housing and Community Development	7,340	54	1.5
Interest on General Debt	11,718	87	2.4
Judicial and Legal	957	7	0.2
Libraries	7,206	53	1.5
Parking	174	1	0.0
Parks and Recreation	14,143	105	2.9
Police Protection	51,879	387	10.5
Public Welfare	0	0	0.0
Sewerage	43,443	324	8.8
Solid Waste Management	23,370	174	4.7
Veterans' Services	0	0	0.0
Liquor Store	0	0	0.0
Utility	54,353	405	11.0

Source: U.S. Census Bureau, State & Local Government Finances 2022

TAXES

State Corporate Income Tax Rates

State	Tax Rate (%)	Income Brackets ($)	Num. of Brackets	Financial Institution Tax Rate (%)[a]	Federal Income Tax Ded.
Iowa	Undetermined	100,000 - 250,001	3	4.7	Yes (h)

Note: Tax rates for tax year 2024; (a) Rates listed are the corporate income tax rate applied to financial institutions or excise taxes based on income. Some states have other taxes based upon the value of deposits or shares; (h) 50% of the federal income tax is deductible.
Source: Federation of Tax Administrators, State Corporate Income Tax Rates, January 1, 2025

State Individual Income Tax Rates

State	Tax Rate (%)	Income Brackets ($)	Personal Exemptions ($)			Standard Ded. ($)	
			Single	Married	Depend.	Single	Married
Iowa (a)	4.4 - 5.7 (bb)	6,210 - 62,100	40	80	40 (c)	–	–

Note: Tax rates for tax year 2024; Local- and county-level taxes are not included; Federal income tax is deductible on state income tax returns; (a) 16 states have statutory provision for automatically adjusting to the rate of inflation the dollar values of the income tax brackets, standard deductions, and/or personal exemptions. Oregon does not index the income brackets for $125,000 and over See: INFL and SPEC above; (c) The personal exemption takes the form of a tax credit instead of a deduction; (bb) Louisiana lawmakers repealed the state's throwout rule, ending the taxation of so-called "nowhere income." Iowa is phasing-in a flat rate by 2027, while Nebraska (LB 754 signed into law) and South Carolina is phasing-in a reduced top rate by 2027.
Source: Federation of Tax Administrators, State Individual Income Tax Rates, January 1, 2025

Various State Sales and Excise Tax Rates

State	State Sales Tax (%)	Gasoline[1] ($/gal.)	Cigarette[2] ($/pack)	Spirits[3] ($/gal.)	Wine[4] ($/gal.)	Beer[5] ($/gal.)	Recreational Marijuana (%)
Iowa	6	0.30	1.36	15.14	1.75	0.19	Not legal

Note: All tax rates as of January 1, 2025; (1) The American Petroleum Institute has developed a methodology for determining the average tax rate on a gallon of fuel. Rates may include any of the following: excise taxes, environmental fees, storage tank fees, other fees or taxes, general sales tax, and local taxes; (2) The federal excise tax of $1.0066 per pack and local taxes are not included; (3) Rates are those applicable to off-premise sales of 40% alcohol by volume (a.b.v.) distilled spirits in 750ml containers. Local excise taxes are excluded; (4) Rates are those applicable to off-premise sales of 11% a.b.v. non-carbonated wine in 750ml containers; (5) Rates are those applicable to off-premise sales of 4.7% a.b.v. beer in 12 ounce containers.
Source: Tax Foundation, 2025 Facts & Figures: How Does Your State Compare?

State Tax Competitiveness Index

State	Overall Rank	Corporate Tax Rank	Individual Income Tax Rank	Sales Tax Rank	Property Tax Rank	Unemployment Insurance Tax Rank
Iowa	20	23	19	11	32	33

Note: The Tax Foundation's State Tax Competitiveness Index enables policymakers, taxpayers, and business leaders to gauge how their states' tax systems compare. A rank of 1 is best, 50 is worst. Rankings do not average to the total. States without a tax rank equally as 1. DC's scores and rankings do not affect other states. The report shows tax systems as of July 1, 2024 (the beginning of Fiscal Year 2025).
Source: Tax Foundation, State Tax Competitiveness Index 2025

TRANSPORTATION

Means of Transportation to Work

Area	Car/Truck/Van		Public Transportation			Bicycle	Walked	Other Means	Worked at Home
	Drove Alone	Car-pooled	Bus	Subway	Railroad				
City	77.0	6.5	0.6	0.0	0.0	0.3	2.2	0.8	12.6
MSA[1]	76.8	6.5	0.5	0.0	0.0	0.2	1.9	0.8	13.3
U.S.	70.2	8.5	1.7	1.3	0.4	0.4	2.4	1.6	13.5

Note: Figures are percentages and cover workers 16 years of age and older; (1) Figures cover the Cedar Rapids, IA Metropolitan Statistical Area
Source: U.S. Census Bureau, 2019-2023 American Community Survey 5-Year Estimates

Travel Time to Work

Area	Less Than 10 Minutes	10 to 19 Minutes	20 to 29 Minutes	30 to 44 Minutes	45 to 59 Minutes	60 to 89 Minutes	90 Minutes or More
City	19.8	47.9	17.9	8.7	1.8	2.5	1.4
MSA[1]	19.1	39.1	20.6	13.0	4.3	2.6	1.3
U.S.	12.6	28.6	21.2	20.8	8.1	6.0	2.8

Note: Note: Figures are percentages and include workers 16 years old and over; (1) Figures cover the Cedar Rapids, IA Metropolitan Statistical Area
Source: U.S. Census Bureau, 2019-2023 American Community Survey 5-Year Estimates

Key Congestion Measures

Measure	2000	2010	2015	2020	2022
Annual Hours of Delay, Total (000)	n/a	n/a	2,974	2,287	2,462
Annual Hours of Delay, Per Auto Commuter	n/a	n/a	15	11	13
Annual Congestion Cost, Per Auto Commuter ($)	n/a	n/a	343	290	292

Note: n/a not available
Source: Texas A&M Transportation Institute, 2023 Urban Mobility Report

Freeway Travel Time Index

Measure	1985	1990	1995	2000	2005	2010	2015	2020	2022
Urban Area Index[1]	n/a	n/a	n/a	n/a	n/a	n/a	1.07	1.07	1.06
Urban Area Rank[1,2]	n/a	n/a	n/a	n/a	n/a	n/a	n/a	n/a	n/a

Note: Freeway Travel Time Index—the ratio of travel time in the peak period to the travel time at free-flow conditions. For example, a value of 1.30 indicates a 20-minute free-flow trip takes 26 minutes in the peak (20 minutes x 1.30 = 26 minutes); (1) Covers the Cedar Rapids IA urban area; (2) Rank is based on 101 larger urban areas (#1 = highest travel time index); n/a not available
Source: Texas A&M Transportation Institute, 2023 Urban Mobility Report

Public Transportation

Agency Name / Mode of Transportation	Vehicles Operated in Maximum Service[1]	Annual Unlinked Passenger Trips[2] (in thous.)	Annual Passenger Miles[3] (in thous.)
Five Seasons Transportation and Parking (FSTP)			
Bus (directly operated)	23	982.3	4,624.3
Demand Response (purchased transportation)	5	14.8	100.3

Note: (1) Number of revenue vehicles operated by the given mode and type of service to meet the annual maximum service requirement. This is the revenue vehicle count during the peak season of the year; on the week and day that maximum service is provided. Vehicles operated in maximum service (VOMS) exclude atypical days and one-time special events; (2) Number of passengers who boarded public transportation vehicles. Passengers are counted each time they board a vehicle no matter how many vehicles they use to travel from their origin to their destination. (3) Sum of the distances ridden by all passengers during the entire fiscal year.
Source: Federal Transit Administration, National Transit Database, 2023

Air Transportation

Airport Name and Code / Type of Service	Passenger Airlines[1]	Passenger Enplanements	Freight Carriers[2]	Freight (lbs)
The Eastern Iowa (CID)				
Domestic service (U.S. carriers only)	23	759,829	9	38,675,634
International service (U.S. carriers only)	1	132	0	0

Note: (1) Includes all U.S.-based major, minor and commuter airlines that carried at least one passenger during the year; (2) Includes all U.S.-based airlines and freight carriers that transported at least one pound of freight during the year.
Source: Bureau of Transportation Statistics, The Intermodal Transportation Database, Air Carriers: T-100 Domestic Market (U.S. carriers only), 2024; Bureau of Transportation Statistics, The Intermodal Transportation Database, Air Carriers: T-100 International Market (U.S. carriers only), 2024

BUSINESSES

Major Business Headquarters

Company Name	Industry	Rankings	
		Fortune[1]	Forbes[2]
No companies listed	-	-	-

Note: (1) Companies that produce a 10-K are ranked 1 to 500 based on 2023 revenue; (2) All private companies with at least $2 billion in annual revenue through the end of their most current fiscal year are ranked 1 to 275; companies listed are headquartered in the city; dashes indicate no ranking
Source: Fortune, "Fortune 500," 2024; Forbes, "America's Largest Private Companies," 2024

Living Environment

COST OF LIVING

Cost of Living Index

Composite Index	Groceries	Housing	Utilities	Transportation	Health Care	Misc. Goods/Services
n/a	n/a	n/a	n/a	n/a	n/a	n/a

Note: The Cost of Living Index measures regional differences in the cost of consumer goods and services, excluding taxes and non-consumer expenditures, for professional and managerial households in the top income quintile. It is based on more than 50,000 prices covering almost 60 different items for which prices are collected three times a year by chambers of commerce, economic development organizations or university applied economic centers in each participating urban area. The numbers shown should be read as a percentage above or below the national average of 100. For example, a value of 115.4 in the groceries column indicates that grocery prices are 15.4% higher than the national average. Small differences in the index numbers should not be interpreted as significant; n/a not available.
Source: The Council for Community and Economic Research, Cost of Living Index, 2024

Grocery Prices

Area[1]	T-Bone Steak ($/pound)	Frying Chicken ($/pound)	Whole Milk ($/half gal.)	Eggs ($/dozen)	Orange Juice ($/64 oz.)	Coffee ($/11.5 oz.)
City[2]	n/a	n/a	n/a	n/a	n/a	n/a
Avg.	15.42	1.55	4.69	3.25	4.41	5.46
Min.	14.50	1.16	4.43	2.75	4.00	4.85
Max.	17.56	2.89	5.49	4.78	5.54	7.89

Note: (1) Values for the local area are compared with the average, minimum and maximum values for all 276 areas in the Cost of Living Index; (2) Figures cover the Cedar Rapids IA urban area; n/a not available; **T-Bone Steak** (price per pound); **Frying Chicken** (price per pound, whole fryer); **Whole Milk** (half gallon carton); **Eggs** (price per dozen, Grade A, large); **Orange Juice** (64 oz. Tropicana or Florida Natural); **Coffee** (11.5 oz. can, vacuum-packed, Maxwell House, Hills Bros, or Folgers).
Source: The Council for Community and Economic Research, Cost of Living Index, 2024

Housing and Utility Costs

Area[1]	New Home Price ($)	Apartment Rent ($/month)	All Electric ($/month)	Part Electric ($/month)	Other Energy ($/month)	Telephone ($/month)
City[2]	n/a	n/a	n/a	n/a	n/a	n/a
Avg.	515,975	1,550	210.99	123.07	82.07	194.99
Min.	265,375	692	104.33	53.68	36.26	179.42
Max.	2,775,821	5,719	529.02	397.28	361.63	223.33

Note: (1) Values for the local area are compared with the average, minimum and maximum values for all 276 areas in the Cost of Living Index; (2) Figures cover the Cedar Rapids IA urban area; n/a not available; **New Home Price** (2,400 sf living area, 8,000 sf lot, in urban area with full utilities); **Apartment Rent** (950 sf 2 bedroom/1.5 or 2 bath, unfurnished, excluding all utilities except water); **All Electric** (average monthly cost for an all-electric home); **Part Electric** (average monthly cost for a part-electric home); **Other Energy** (average monthly cost for natural gas, fuel oil, coal, wood, and any other forms of energy except electricity); **Telephone** (price includes the base monthly rate plus taxes and fees for three lines of mobile phone service).
Source: The Council for Community and Economic Research, Cost of Living Index, 2024

Health Care, Transportation, and Other Costs

Area[1]	Doctor ($/visit)	Dentist ($/visit)	Optometrist ($/visit)	Gasoline ($/gallon)	Beauty Salon ($/visit)	Men's Shirt ($)
City[2]	n/a	n/a	n/a	n/a	n/a	n/a
Avg.	143.77	117.51	129.23	3.32	48.57	38.14
Min.	36.74	58.67	67.33	2.80	24.00	13.41
Max.	270.44	216.82	307.33	5.28	94.00	63.89

Note: (1) Values for the local area are compared with the average, minimum and maximum values for all 276 areas in the Cost of Living Index; (2) Figures cover the Cedar Rapids IA urban area; n/a not available; **Doctor** (general practitioners routine exam of an established patient); **Dentist** (adult teeth cleaning and periodic oral examination); **Optometrist** (full vision eye exam for established adult patient); **Gasoline** (one gallon regular unleaded, national brand, including all taxes, cash price at self-service pump if available); **Beauty Salon** (woman's shampoo, trim, and blow-dry); **Men's Shirt** (cotton/polyester dress shirt, pinpoint weave, long sleeves).
Source: The Council for Community and Economic Research, Cost of Living Index, 2024

HOUSING

Homeownership Rate

Area	2017 (%)	2018 (%)	2019 (%)	2020 (%)	2021 (%)	2022 (%)	2023 (%)	2024 (%)
MSA[1]	n/a	n/a	n/a	n/a	n/a	n/a	n/a	n/a
U.S.	63.9	64.4	64.6	66.6	65.5	65.8	65.9	65.6

Note: (1) Figures cover the Cedar Rapids, IA Metropolitan Statistical Area; n/a not available
Source: U.S. Census Bureau, Housing Vacancies and Homeownership Annual Statistics: 2017-2024

House Price Index (HPI)

Area	National Ranking[2]	Quarterly Change (%)	One-Year Change (%)	Five-Year Change (%)	Since 1991Q1 (%)
MSA[1]	204	-0.20	3.04	39.04	206.71
U.S.[3]	—		1.43	4.51	57.13	327.82

Note: The HPI is a weighted repeat sales index. It measures average price changes in repeat sales or refinancings on the same properties. This information is obtained by reviewing repeat mortgage transactions on single-family properties whose mortgages have been purchased or securitized by Fannie Mae or Freddie Mac since January 1975; (1) Figures cover the Cedar Rapids, IA Metropolitan Statistical Area; (2) Rankings are based on annual percentage change for all metro areas containing at least 15,000 transactions over the last 10 years and ranges from 1 to 241; (3) figures based on a weighted average of Census Division estimates using a seasonally adjusted, purchase-only index; all figures are for the period ending December 31, 2024
Source: Federal Housing Finance Agency, Change in FHFA Metropolitan Area House Price Indexes, All Transactions Index, 2024Q4

Home Value

Area	Under $100,000	$100,000 -$199,999	$200,000 -$299,999	$300,000 -$399,999	$400,000 -$499,999	$500,000 -$999,999	$1,000,000 or more	Median ($)
City	12.5	47.4	24.5	8.5	3.9	2.7	0.5	177,100
MSA[1]	11.7	37.7	25.8	12.6	6.1	5.0	1.0	202,100
U.S.	12.1	17.8	19.5	14.4	10.5	19.1	6.5	303,400

Note: Figures are percentages except for median and cover owner-occupied housing units; (1) Figures cover the Cedar Rapids, IA Metropolitan Statistical Area
Source: U.S. Census Bureau, 2019-2023 American Community Survey 5-Year Estimates

Year Housing Structure Built

Area	2020 or Later	2010 -2019	2000 -2009	1990 -1999	1980 -1989	1970 -1979	1960 -1969	1950 -1959	1940 -1949	Before 1940	Median Year
City	0.8	9.6	11.3	10.9	7.5	14.7	13.9	12.4	4.3	14.7	1973
MSA[1]	0.9	10.2	13.2	12.8	7.4	13.6	11.6	10.2	3.6	16.6	1976
U.S.	1.2	8.9	13.6	12.8	13.0	14.4	10.0	9.7	4.5	11.9	1980

Note: Figures are percentages except for Median Year; Note: (1) Figures cover the Cedar Rapids, IA Metropolitan Statistical Area
Source: U.S. Census Bureau, 2019-2023 American Community Survey 5-Year Estimates

Gross Monthly Rent

Area	Under $500	$500 -$999	$1,000 -$1,499	$1,500 -$1,999	$2,000 -$2,499	$2,500 -$2,999	$3,000 and up	Median ($)
City	7.5	49.3	31.3	8.7	0.9	0.3	2.0	925
MSA[1]	7.8	50.9	29.5	8.0	1.3	0.3	2.2	899
U.S.	6.5	22.3	29.5	20.2	10.8	4.8	5.9	1,348

Note: Figures are percentages except for median; Gross rent is the contract rent plus the estimated average monthly cost of utilities (electricity, gas, and water and sewer) and fuels (oil, coal, kerosene, wood, etc.) if these are paid by the renter (or paid for the renter by someone else); (1) Figures cover the Cedar Rapids, IA Metropolitan Statistical Area
Source: U.S. Census Bureau, 2019-2023 American Community Survey 5-Year Estimates

HEALTH

Health Risk Factors

Category	MSA[1] (%)	U.S. (%)
Adults aged 18–64 who have any kind of health care coverage	93.9	90.8
Adults who reported being in good or better health	83.3	81.8
Adults who have been told they have high blood cholesterol	35.1	36.9
Adults who have been told they have high blood pressure	29.3	34.0
Adults who are current smokers	12.0	12.1
Adults who currently use e-cigarettes	7.1	7.7
Adults who currently use chewing tobacco, snuff, or snus	3.7	3.2
Adults who are heavy drinkers[2]	8.2	6.1
Adults who are binge drinkers[3]	21.8	15.2
Adults who are overweight (BMI 25.0 - 29.9)	37.0	34.4
Adults who are obese (BMI 30.0 - 99.8)	35.0	34.3
Adults who participated in any physical activities in the past month	79.4	75.8

Note: All figures are crude prevalence; (1) Figures cover the Cedar Rapids, IA Metropolitan Statistical Area; (2) Heavy drinkers are classified as adult men having more than 14 drinks per week and adult women having more than 7 drinks per week; (3) Binge drinkers are classified as males having five or more drinks on one occasion or females having four or more drinks on one occasion
Source: Centers for Disease Control and Prevention, Behavioral Risk Factor Surveillance System, SMART: Selected Metropolitan Area Risk Trends, 2023

Acute and Chronic Health Conditions

Category	MSA[1] (%)	U.S. (%)
Adults who have ever been told they had a heart attack	5.2	4.2
Adults who have ever been told they have angina or coronary heart disease	4.2	4.0
Adults who have ever been told they had a stroke	2.6	3.3
Adults who have ever been told they have asthma	14.9	15.7
Adults who have ever been told they have arthritis	26.1	26.3
Adults who have ever been told they have diabetes[2]	10.4	11.5
Adults who have ever been told they had skin cancer	4.8	5.6
Adults who have ever been told they had any other types of cancer	8.5	8.4
Adults who have ever been told they have COPD	6.1	6.4
Adults who have ever been told they have kidney disease	5.7	3.7
Adults who have ever been told they have a form of depression	23.9	22.0

Note: All figures are crude prevalence; (1) Figures cover the Cedar Rapids, IA Metropolitan Statistical Area; (2) Figures do not include pregnancy-related, borderline, or pre-diabetes
Source: Centers for Disease Control and Prevention, Behavioral Risk Factor Surveillance System, SMART: Selected Metropolitan Area Risk Trends, 2023

Health Screening and Vaccination Rates

Category	MSA[1] (%)	U.S. (%)
Adults who have ever been tested for HIV	28.7	37.5
Adults who have had their blood cholesterol checked within the last five years	85.1	87.0
Adults aged 65+ who have had flu shot within the past year	63.5	63.4
Adults aged 65+ who have ever had a pneumonia vaccination	68.1	71.9

Note: All figures are crude prevalence; (1) Figures cover the Cedar Rapids, IA Metropolitan Statistical Area.
Source: Centers for Disease Control and Prevention, Behavioral Risk Factor Surveillance System, SMART: Selected Metropolitan Area Risk Trends, 2023

Disability Status

Category	MSA[1] (%)	U.S. (%)
Adults who reported being deaf	7.9	7.4
Are you blind or have serious difficulty seeing, even when wearing glasses?	3.1	4.9
Do you have difficulty doing errands alone?	8.2	7.8
Do you have difficulty dressing or bathing?	n/a	3.6
Do you have serious difficulty concentrating/remembering/making decisions?	13.6	13.7
Do you have serious difficulty walking or climbing stairs?	10.5	13.2

Note: All figures are crude prevalence; (1) Figures cover the Cedar Rapids, IA Metropolitan Statistical Area.
Source: Centers for Disease Control and Prevention, Behavioral Risk Factor Surveillance System, SMART: Selected Metropolitan Area Risk Trends, 2023

Mortality Rates for the Top 10 Causes of Death in the U.S.

ICD-10[a] Sub-Chapter	ICD-10[a] Code	Crude Mortality Rate[2] per 100,000 population County[3]	U.S.
Malignant neoplasms	C00-C97	178.2	182.7
Ischaemic heart diseases	I20-I25	114.7	109.6
Provisional assignment of new diseases of uncertain etiology[1]	U00-U49	47.2	65.3
Other forms of heart disease	I30-I51	53.1	65.1
Other degenerative diseases of the nervous system	G30-G31	64.1	52.4
Other external causes of accidental injury	W00-X59	49.1	52.3
Cerebrovascular diseases	I60-I69	41.1	49.1
Chronic lower respiratory diseases	J40-J47	46.6	43.5
Hypertensive diseases	I10-I15	36.4	38.9
Organic, including symptomatic, mental disorders	F01-F09	29.7	33.9

Note: (a) ICD-10 = International Classification of Diseases 10th Revision; (1) Includes COVID-19, adverse effects to COVID-19 vaccines, SARS, and vaping-related disorders; (2) Crude mortality rates are a three-year average covering 2021-2023; (3) Figures cover Linn County.
Source: Centers for Disease Control and Prevention, National Center for Health Statistics. National Vital Statistics System, Mortality 2018-2023 on CDC WONDER Online Database

Mortality Rates for Selected Causes of Death

Cause of Death	ICD-10[a] Code	Crude Mortality Rate[1] per 100,000 population	
		County[2]	U.S.
Accidental poisoning and exposure to noxious substances	X40-X49	14.4	30.5
Alzheimer disease	G30	28.4	35.4
Assault	X85-Y09	5.8	7.3
COVID-19	U07.1	47.2	65.3
Diabetes mellitus	E10-E14	26.2	30.0
Diseases of the liver	K70-K76	20.5	20.8
Human immunodeficiency virus (HIV) disease	B20-B24	Suppressed	1.5
Influenza and pneumonia	J09-J18	12.5	13.4
Intentional self-harm	X60-X84	15.7	14.7
Malnutrition	E40-E46	13.7	6.0
Obesity and other hyperalimentation	E65-E68	Suppressed	3.1
Renal failure	N17-N19	15.0	16.4
Transport accidents	V01-V99	9.5	14.4

Note: (a) ICD-10 = International Classification of Diseases 10th Revision; (1) Crude mortality rates are a three-year average covering 2021-2023; (2) Figures cover Linn County; Data are suppressed when the data meet the criteria for confidentiality constraints; Crude mortality rates are flagged as unreliable when the rate would be calculated with a numerator of 20 or less.
Source: Centers for Disease Control and Prevention, National Center for Health Statistics. National Vital Statistics System, Mortality 2018-2023 on CDC WONDER Online Database

Health Insurance Coverage

Area	With Health Insurance	With Private Health Insurance	With Public Health Insurance	Without Health Insurance	Population Under Age 19 Without Health Insurance
City	95.5	71.1	36.8	4.5	1.6
MSA[1]	96.3	74.8	35.1	3.7	1.4
U.S.	91.4	67.3	36.3	8.6	5.4

Note: Figures are percentages that cover the civilian noninstitutionalized population; (1) Figures cover the Cedar Rapids, IA Metropolitan Statistical Area
Source: U.S. Census Bureau, 2019-2023 American Community Survey 5-Year Estimates

Number of Medical Professionals

Area	MDs[3]	DOs[3,4]	Dentists	Podiatrists	Chiropractors	Optometrists
County[1] (number)	415	58	178	20	143	41
County[1] (rate[2])	181.2	25.3	77.7	8.7	62.5	17.9
U.S. (rate[2])	302.5	29.2	74.6	6.4	29.5	18.0

Note: Data as of 2023 unless noted; (1) Data covers Linn County; (2) Number of medical professionals per 100,000 population; (3) Data as of 2022 and includes all active, non-federal physicians; (4) Doctor of Osteopathic Medicine
Source: U.S. Department of Health and Human Services, Health Resources and Services Administration, Bureau of Health Professions, Area Resource File (ARF) 2023-2024

EDUCATION

Public School District Statistics

District Name	Schls	Pupils	Pupil/Teacher Ratio	Minority Pupils[1] (%)	Total Rev. per Pupil ($)	Total Exp. per Pupil ($)
Cedar Rapids CSD	34	15,589	15.0	45.1	18,341	17,848
College Comm School District	10	5,749	15.4	30.3	17,200	22,009

Note: Table includes school districts with 2,000 or more students; (1) Percentage of students that are not non-Hispanic white.
Source: U.S. Department of Education, National Center for Education Statistics, Common Core of Data, Local Education Agency (School District) Universe Survey: School Year 2023-2024; U.S. Department of Education, National Center for Education Statistics, Common Core of Data, School District Finance Survey (F-33): School Year 2021–22

Highest Level of Education

Area	Less than H.S.	H.S. Diploma	Some College, No Deg.	Associate Degree	Bachelor's Degree	Master's Degree	Prof. School Degree	Doctorate Degree
City	5.9	25.9	22.4	12.9	22.2	7.8	2.1	0.8
MSA[1]	4.8	27.8	20.7	13.9	22.2	8.0	1.7	0.9
U.S.	10.6	26.2	19.4	8.8	21.3	9.8	2.3	1.6

Note: Figures cover persons age 25 and over; (1) Figures cover the Cedar Rapids, IA Metropolitan Statistical Area
Source: U.S. Census Bureau, 2019-2023 American Community Survey 5-Year Estimates

Educational Attainment by Race

Area	High School Graduate or Higher (%)					Bachelor's Degree or Higher (%)				
	Total	White	Black	Asian	Hisp.[2]	Total	White	Black	Asian	Hisp.[2]
City	94.1	95.5	81.1	88.4	90.0	32.9	33.6	15.5	55.7	25.0
MSA[1]	95.2	96.1	83.2	90.9	85.2	32.8	33.3	16.5	53.6	24.3
U.S.	89.4	92.9	88.1	88.0	72.5	35.0	37.7	24.7	57.0	19.9

Note: Figures shown cover persons 25 years old and over; (1) Figures cover the Cedar Rapids, IA Metropolitan Statistical Area; (2) People of Hispanic origin can be of any race
Source: U.S. Census Bureau, 2019-2023 American Community Survey 5-Year Estimates

School Enrollment by Grade and Control

Area	Preschool (%)		Kindergarten (%)		Grades 1 - 4 (%)		Grades 5 - 8 (%)		Grades 9 - 12 (%)	
	Public	Private	Public	Private	Public	Private	Public	Private	Public	Private
City	73.1	26.9	85.9	14.1	88.2	11.8	87.2	12.8	86.4	13.6
MSA[1]	74.7	25.3	87.6	12.4	88.4	11.6	88.3	11.7	89.7	10.3
U.S.	58.7	41.3	85.2	14.8	87.2	12.8	87.9	12.1	89.0	11.0

Note: Figures shown cover persons 3 years old and over; (1) Figures cover the Cedar Rapids, IA Metropolitan Statistical Area
Source: U.S. Census Bureau, 2019-2023 American Community Survey 5-Year Estimates

Higher Education

Four-Year Colleges			Two-Year Colleges			Medical Schools[1]	Law Schools[2]	Voc/Tech[3]
Public	Private Non-profit	Private For-profit	Public	Private Non-profit	Private For-profit			
0	3	0	1	1	0	0	0	2

Note: Figures cover institutions located within the Cedar Rapids, IA Metropolitan Statistical Area and include main campuses only; (1) includes schools accredited by the Liaison Committee on Medical Education and the American Osteopathic Association's Commission on Osteopathic College Accreditation; (2) includes ABA-accredited schools, schools with provisional ABA accreditation, and state accredited schools; (3) includes all schools with programs that are less than 2 years.
Source: National Center for Education Statistics, Integrated Postsecondary Education System (IPEDS), 2023-24; Wikipedia, List of Medical Schools in the United States, accessed May 2, 2025; Wikipedia, List of Law Schools in the United States, accessed May 2, 2025

EMPLOYERS

Major Employers

Company Name	Industry
AEGON USA	Insurance
Alliant Energy	Energy
Amana Refrigeration Products	Appliances
Cedar Rapids Community School District	Education
City of Cedar Rapids	Municipal government
Gazette Communications	Publishing
General Mills	Food products
Hy-Vee Food Stores	Grocery stores
Kirkwood Community College	Education
Linn County Offices	Government
Linn-Mar Community Schools	Education
Maytag Appliances	Appliances
MCI	Communications
McLeodUSA Incorporated	Communications
Mercy Medical Center	Healthcare
Nash Finch Company	Retail
Rockwell Collins	Aerospace/defense
St. Luke's Hospital	Education
Wal-Mart Stores	Retail
Yellowbook USA	Publisher

Note: Companies shown are located within the Cedar Rapids, IA Metropolitan Statistical Area.
Source: Chambers of Commerce; State Departments of Labor; Wikipedia

Best Companies to Work For

RSM US, headquartered in Cedar Rapids, is among the "Best Places to Work in IT." To qualify, companies had to have a minimum of 100 total employees and five IT employees. The best places to work were selected based on DEI (diversity, equity, and inclusion) practices; IT turnover, promotions, and growth; IT retention and engagement programs; remote/hybrid working; benefits and perks (such as elder care and child care, flextime, and reimbursement for college tuition); and training and career development opportunities. *Computerworld, "Best Places to Work in IT," 2025*

PUBLIC SAFETY

Crime Rate

Area	Total Crime Rate	Violent Crime Rate				Property Crime Rate		
		Murder	Rape	Robbery	Aggrav. Assault	Burglary	Larceny-Theft	Motor Vehicle Theft
City	3,184.6	5.9	8.1	30.2	255.6	345.4	2,281.7	257.8
U.S.	2,290.9	5.7	38.0	66.5	264.1	250.7	1,347.2	318.7

Note: Figures are crimes per 100,000 population.
Source: FBI, Table 8, Offenses Known to Law Enforcement, by State by City, 2023

Hate Crimes

Area	Number of Quarters Reported	Number of Incidents per Bias Motivation					
		Race/Ethnicity/Ancestry	Religion	Sexual Orientation	Disability	Gender	Gender Identity
City	4	0	0	0	0	0	0
U.S.	4	5,900	2,699	2,077	187	92	492

Source: Federal Bureau of Investigation, Hate Crime Statistics 2023

Identity Theft Consumer Reports

Area	Reports	Reports per 100,000 Population	Rank[2]
MSA[1]	388	141	297
U.S.	1,135,291	339	-

Note: (1) Figures cover the Cedar Rapids, IA Metropolitan Statistical Area; (2) Rank ranges from 1 to 401 where 1 indicates greatest number of identity theft reports per 100,000 population
Source: Federal Trade Commission, Consumer Sentinel Network Data Book 2024

Fraud and Other Consumer Reports

Area	Reports	Reports per 100,000 Population	Rank[2]
MSA[1]	2,209	800	320
U.S.	5,360,641	1,601	-

Note: (1) Figures cover the Cedar Rapids, IA Metropolitan Statistical Area; (2) Rank ranges from 1 to 401 where 1 indicates greatest number of fraud and other consumer reports per 100,000 population
Source: Federal Trade Commission, Consumer Sentinel Network Data Book 2024

POLITICS

2024 Presidential Election Results

Area	Trump (Rep.)	Harris (Dem.)	Stein (Green)	Kennedy (Ind.)	Oliver (Lib.)	Other
Linn County	44.1	54.0	0.0	0.8	0.5	0.6
U.S.	49.7	48.2	0.6	0.5	0.4	0.6

Note: Results are percentages and may not add to 100% due to rounding
Source: Dave Leip's Atlas of U.S. Presidential Elections

SPORTS

Professional Sports Teams

Team Name	League	Year Established

No teams are located in the metro area
Source: Wikipedia, Major Professional Sports Teams of the United States and Canada, May 1, 2025

CLIMATE

Average and Extreme Temperatures

Temperature	Jan	Feb	Mar	Apr	May	Jun	Jul	Aug	Sep	Oct	Nov	Dec	Yr.
Extreme High (°F)	58	66	87	100	94	103	105	105	97	95	76	65	105
Average High (°F)	24	30	43	59	71	81	84	82	73	62	45	29	57
Average Temp. (°F)	15	21	34	48	60	69	73	71	62	50	36	21	47
Average Low (°F)	6	11	24	36	48	58	62	59	50	39	26	12	36
Extreme Low (°F)	-33	-29	-34	-4	25	38	42	38	22	11	-17	-27	-34

Note: Figures cover the years 1960-1995
Source: National Climatic Data Center, International Station Meteorological Climate Summary, 9/96

Average Precipitation/Snowfall/Humidity

Precip./Humidity	Jan	Feb	Mar	Apr	May	Jun	Jul	Aug	Sep	Oct	Nov	Dec	Yr.
Avg. Precip. (in.)	0.8	1.0	2.3	3.6	4.1	4.5	4.8	4.0	3.5	2.5	1.9	1.3	34.4
Avg. Snowfall (in.)	7	7	6	2	Tr	0	0	0	0	Tr	4	8	33
Avg. Rel. Hum. 6am (%)	77	80	82	81	81	83	87	90	89	84	83	82	83
Avg. Rel. Hum. 3pm (%)	68	66	62	52	51	51	55	55	55	52	62	70	58

Note: Figures cover the years 1960-1995; Tr = Trace amounts (<0.05 in. of rain; <0.5 in. of snow)
Source: National Climatic Data Center, International Station Meteorological Climate Summary, 9/96

Weather Conditions

Temperature			Daytime Sky			Precipitation		
5°F & below	32°F & below	90°F & above	Clear	Partly cloudy	Cloudy	0.01 inch or more precip.	0.1 inch or more snow/ice	Thunder-storms
38	156	16	89	132	144	109	28	42

Note: Figures are average number of days per year and cover the years 1960-1995
Source: National Climatic Data Center, International Station Meteorological Climate Summary, 9/96

HAZARDOUS WASTE

Superfund Sites

The Cedar Rapids, IA metro area has no sites on the EPA's Superfund Final National Priorities List (NPL) or Superfund Alternative Approach (SAA) list. The Superfund alternative approach uses the same investigation and cleanup process and standards that are used for sites listed on the National Priorities List. The SAA is an alternative to listing a site on the NPL; it is not an alternative to Superfund or the Superfund process. There are a total of 1,445 Superfund sites with a status of proposed or final on both lists in the United States. *U.S. Environmental Protection Agency, National Priorities List, May 1, 2025; U.S. Environmental Protection Agency, Superfund Alternative Approach Sites, May 1, 2025*

AIR QUALITY

Air Quality Trends: Ozone

	1990	1995	2000	2005	2010	2015	2020	2021	2022	2023
MSA[1]	n/a	n/a	n/a	n/a	n/a	n/a	n/a	n/a	n/a	n/a
U.S.	0.087	0.089	0.081	0.080	0.072	0.068	0.066	0.067	0.067	0.070

Note: (1) Data covers the Cedar Rapids, IA Metropolitan Statistical Area; n/a not available. The values shown are the composite ozone concentration averages among trend sites based on the highest fourth daily maximum 8-hour concentration in parts per million. These trends are based on sites having an adequate record of monitoring data during the trend period. Data from exceptional events are included.
Source: U.S. Environmental Protection Agency, Air Quality Monitoring Information, "Air Quality Trends by City, 1990-2023"

Air Quality Index

Area	Percent of Days when Air Quality was...[2]					AQI Statistics[2]	
	Good	Moderate	Unhealthy for Sensitive Groups	Unhealthy	Very Unhealthy	Maximum	Median
MSA[1]	35.6	59.5	3.8	0.8	0.3	207	54

Note: (1) Data covers the Cedar Rapids, IA Metropolitan Statistical Area; (2) Based on 365 days with AQI data in 2023. Air Quality Index (AQI) is an index for reporting daily air quality. EPA calculates the AQI for five major air pollutants regulated by the Clean Air Act: ground-level ozone, particle pollution (aka particulate matter), carbon monoxide, sulfur dioxide, and nitrogen dioxide. The AQI runs from 0 to 500. The higher the AQI value, the greater the level of air pollution and the greater the health concern. There are six AQI categories: "Good" AQI is between 0 and 50. Air quality is considered satisfactory; "Moderate" AQI is between 51 and 100. Air quality is acceptable; "Unhealthy for Sensitive Groups" When AQI values are between 101 and 150, members of sensitive groups may experience health effects; "Unhealthy" When AQI values are between 151 and 200 everyone may begin to experience health effects; "Very Unhealthy" AQI values between 201 and 300 trigger a health alert; "Hazardous" AQI values over 300 trigger warnings of emergency conditions (not shown).
Source: U.S. Environmental Protection Agency, Air Quality Index Report, 2023

Air Quality Index Pollutants

Area	Percent of Days when AQI Pollutant was...[2]					
	Carbon Monoxide	Nitrogen Dioxide	Ozone	Sulfur Dioxide	Particulate Matter 2.5	Particulate Matter 10
MSA[1]	0.0	0.0	23.6	(3)	76.4	0.0

Note: (1) Data covers the Cedar Rapids, IA Metropolitan Statistical Area; (2) Based on 365 days with AQI data in 2023. The Air Quality Index (AQI) is an index for reporting daily air quality. EPA calculates the AQI for five major air pollutants regulated by the Clean Air Act: ground-level ozone, particle pollution (also known as particulate matter), carbon monoxide, sulfur dioxide, and nitrogen dioxide. The AQI runs from 0 to 500. The higher the AQI value, the greater the level of air pollution and the greater the health concern; (3) Sulfur dioxide is no longer included in this table because SO_2 concentrations tend to be very localized and not necessarily representative of broad geographical areas like counties and CBSAs.
Source: U.S. Environmental Protection Agency, Air Quality Index Report, 2023

Maximum Air Pollutant Concentrations: Particulate Matter, Ozone, CO and Lead

	Particulate Matter 10 (ug/m^3)	Particulate Matter 2.5 Wtd AM (ug/m^3)	Particulate Matter 2.5 24-Hr (ug/m^3)	Ozone (ppm)	Carbon Monoxide (ppm)	Lead (ug/m^3)
MSA[1] Level	68	9.9	25	0.08	n/a	n/a
NAAQS[2]	150	15	35	0.075	9	0.15
Met NAAQS[2]	Yes	Yes	Yes	No	n/a	n/a

Note: (1) Data covers the Cedar Rapids, IA Metropolitan Statistical Area; Data from exceptional events are included; (2) National Ambient Air Quality Standards; ppm = parts per million; ug/m^3 = micrograms per cubic meter; n/a not available.
Concentrations: Particulate Matter 10 (coarse particulate)—highest second maximum 24-hour concentration; Particulate Matter 2.5 Wtd AM (fine particulate)—highest weighted annual mean concentration; Particulate Matter 2.5 24-Hour (fine particulate)—highest 98th percentile 24-hour concentration; Ozone—highest fourth daily maximum 8-hour concentration; Carbon Monoxide—highest second maximum non-overlapping 8-hour concentration; Lead—maximum running 3-month average
Source: U.S. Environmental Protection Agency, Air Quality Monitoring Information, "Air Quality Statistics by City, 2023"

Maximum Air Pollutant Concentrations: Nitrogen Dioxide and Sulfur Dioxide

	Nitrogen Dioxide AM (ppb)	Nitrogen Dioxide 1-Hr (ppb)	Sulfur Dioxide AM (ppb)	Sulfur Dioxide 1-Hr (ppb)	Sulfur Dioxide 24-Hr (ppb)
MSA[1] Level	n/a	n/a	n/a	10	n/a
NAAQS[2]	53	100	30	75	140
Met NAAQS[2]	n/a	n/a	n/a	Yes	n/a

Note: (1) Data covers the Cedar Rapids, IA Metropolitan Statistical Area; Data from exceptional events are included; (2) National Ambient Air Quality Standards; ppm = parts per million; ug/m^3 = micrograms per cubic meter; n/a not available.
Concentrations: Nitrogen Dioxide AM—highest arithmetic mean concentration; Nitrogen Dioxide 1-Hr—highest 98th percentile 1-hour daily maximum concentration; Sulfur Dioxide AM—highest annual mean concentration; Sulfur Dioxide 1-Hr—highest 99th percentile 1-hour daily maximum concentration; Sulfur Dioxide 24-Hr—highest second maximum 24-hour concentration
Source: U.S. Environmental Protection Agency, Air Quality Monitoring Information, "Air Quality Statistics by City, 2023"

Chicago, Illinois

Background

Chicago has many nicknames, including City of Big Shoulders, Windy City, Toddling Town, Second City, and Chi-Town. Whatever one calls Chicago, it has always exemplified a great American city, from a bustling downtown with towering skyscrapers to a quaint collection of tightly packed urban neighborhoods stretching into the suburban landscape, then into the fields of the Illinois prairie. It is the third most populous city in the United States.

Innovation has been part of Chicago's history from the very start. Cyrus McCormick invented his McCormick Reaper in 1831 and put Chicago on the map, revolutionizing harvesting across the world. The first mail-order business, Montgomery Ward, was established in Chicago in 1872. The world's first skyscraper was built in Chicago in 1885 for the Home Insurance Company. In 1907, University of Chicago's Albert Michelson, received the first American Nobel Prize for science. In 1931, Enrico Fermi split the atom underneath the University of Chicago football field. In 1983, Motorola set up the first modern portable cellular phone system in Chicago. The city also boasts 101 Nobel Prize Winners.

Chicago is an international hub for finance, culture, commerce, industry, education, technology, telecommunications, and transportation. It has the largest and most diverse derivatives market in the world, generating 20% of all volume in commodities and financial futures alone. O'Hare International Airport is routinely ranked among the world's top six busiest airports by passenger traffic, and the region is also the nation's railroad hub. Chicago's economy is diverse, with no single industry employing more than 14% of the workforce.

Chicago was the home of former President Barack Obama and his family; the Barack Obama Presidential Center opened in 2020 at the University of Chicago.

When the Willis (formerly Sears) Tower was completed in 1973, it was the tallest building in North America. Today, Chicago is home to the tenth and twenty-second tallest buildings in the world, and the work of homegrown architects Frank Lloyd Wright, Louis Sullivan, and Helmut Jahn. In addition, Mies van der Rohe immigrated here and became one of the most influential architects of the post-World War II era. In 2019, the city elected the first African American women and openly LBGTQ+ mayor.

Present-day Chicago is "greener" than ever with more than 500 parks over 8,000 acres. Lincoln Park covers 1,200 acres. The city is the nation's largest municipal marina with over 6,000 boat slips. Bicycling, walking trails, beaches and golf are all abundant and top notch. The Oceanarium is the world's largest indoor marine mammal pavilion.

Chicago boasts the Art Institute of Chicago, the Adler Planetarium, the Chicago Architecture Foundation, and the Hellenic Museum and Cultural Center. Classical musical offerings include the Chicago Symphony Orchestra, its Chamber Music Series, the Chicago Opera Theater, and the Lyric Opera of Chicago. The city is famous for its eclectic nightlife. You can hear music at dozens of clubs, and comedy at Second City, where such comics as John Belushi, John Candy, Chris Farley, and Stephen Colbert had their start.

Chicago professional sports have long been in the national spotlight. Chicago is home to two major league baseball teams, the Chicago Cubs who play at Wrigley Field in the city's North Side and the Chicago White Sox who play in the city's South Side at U.S. Cellular Field and who won the 2016 World Series, ending a 108-year record World Series drought. The Chicago Bears, the city's NFL team, won thirteen NFL championships, and Chicago's professional basketball team, the Chicago Bulls, is one of the world's most recognized teams. In 2021, Chicago Sky, the city's Women's National Basketball Association team, became WNBA champions.

The Chicago Marathon, one of five world marathon events, has been held every October since 1977. Chicago is also the starting point for the Chicago Yacht Club Race to Mackinac—the longest annual freshwater sailboat race in the world.

Outstanding educational institutions in Chicago include the University of Chicago (1891), Northwestern University (1851), DePaul University, Loyola University, and the School of the Art Institute of Chicago.

Located along the southwest shore of Lake Michigan, the city has a hot-summer humid continental climate and experiences four distinct seasons. Summers are hot and humid, with frequent heat waves. Winters are relatively cold and snowy. Blizzards occasionally occur. Spring and autumn are mild, short seasons, typically with low humidity.

Rankings

General Rankings

- To help military veterans find the best places in which to settle down, *WalletHub* compared the 100 largest U.S. cities across 19 key indicators of livability, affordability and veteran-friendliness. They range from the share of military skill-related jobs to veteran income growth to the availability of VA health facilities. Chicago ranked #93. *Wallethub.com, "Best & Worst Places for Veterans to Live (2025)," November 7, 2024*

- *Insider* listed 23 places in the U.S. that travel industry trends reveal would be popular destinations in 2023. This year the list trends towards cultural and historical happenings, sports events, wellness experiences and invigorating outdoor escapes. According to the website insider.com Chicago is a place to visit in 2023. *Insider, "23 of the Best Places You Should Travel to in the U.S. in 2023," December 17, 2022*

- The human resources consulting firm Mercer ranked 241 major cities worldwide in terms of overall quality of life. Chicago ranked #66. Criteria: political and personal safety, social, and economic factors; medical and health considerations; schools and education; public services and transportation; recreation; connectivity; housing and infrastructure; and climate. *Mercer, "Mercer 2024 Quality of Living Survey," December 2024*

- Chicago appeared on *Travel + Leisure's* list of "The 15 Best Cities in the United States." The city was ranked #9. Criteria: walkability; sights/landmarks; culture; food; friendliness; shopping; and overall value. *Travel + Leisure, "The World's Best Awards 2024" July 9, 2024*

- For its 37th annual "Readers' Choice Awards" survey, *Condé Nast Traveler* ranked its readers' favorite cities in the U.S. Whether it be a longed-for visit or the next big new thing, these are the places travelers loved best. The list was broken into large cities and cities under 250,000. Chicago ranked #1 in the big city category. *Condé Nast Traveler, Readers' Choice Awards 2024, "Best Big Cities in the U.S." October 1, 2024*

Business/Finance Rankings

- According to *Business Insider*, the Chicago metro area is a prime place to run a startup or move an existing business to. The area ranked #14. More than 300 metro areas were analyzed for factors that were of top concern to new business owners. Data was based on the 2019 U.S. Census Bureau American Community Survey, statistics from the CDC, and University of Chicago analysis. Criteria: business formations; percentage of vaccinated population; percentage of households with internet subscriptions; median household income; and share of work that can be done from home. *BusinessInsider.com, "The 20 Best Cities for Starting a Business in 2022 Include Denver, Raleigh, and Olympia," June 7, 2022*

- Payscale.com ranked the 32 largest metro areas in terms of wage growth. The Chicago metro area ranked #14. Criteria: quarterly changes in private industry employee and education professional wage growth from the previous year. *PayScale, "Wage Trends by Metro Area-4th Quarter," February 4, 2025*

- Chicago was cited as one of America's top metros for total corporate facility investment projects in 2024. The area ranked #2 in the Tier 1 (large) metro area category (population over 1 million). *Site Selection, "Top Metros of 2024," March 2025*

- The Chicago metro area appeared on the Milken Institute "2025 Best Performing Cities" list. Rank: #169 out of 200 large metro areas (based on performance category). Criteria: job growth; wage growth; high-tech growth and impact; community resilience; housing affordability; household broadband access. *Milken Institute, "Best-Performing Cities 2025," January 14, 2025*

- Mercer Human Resources Consulting ranked 226 cities worldwide in terms of cost-of-living. Chicago ranked #20 (the lower the ranking, the higher the cost-of-living). The survey measured the comparative cost of over 200 items (such as housing, food, clothing, domestic supplies, transportation, and recreation/entertainment) in each location. *Mercer, "2024 Cost of Living City Ranking," June 17, 2024*

Culture/Performing Arts Rankings

- Chicago was selected as one of the 25 best cities for moviemakers in North America. Great film cities are places where filmmaking dreams can come true, that offer more creative space, lower costs, and great outdoor locations. NYC & LA were intentionally excluded. Criteria: film industry presence and culture; tax incentives; affordability; and proximity of festivals and schools. The city was ranked #4. *MovieMaker Magazine, "Best Places to Live and Work as a Moviemaker, 2025," January 29, 2025*

Education Rankings

- Personal finance website *WalletHub* analyzed the 150 largest U.S. metropolitan statistical areas to determine where the most educated Americans are putting their degrees to work. Criteria: education levels; percentage of workers with degrees; education quality and attainment gap; public school quality rankings; quality and enrollment of each metro area's universities. Chicago was ranked #29 (#1 = most educated city). *WalletHub.com, "Most & Least Educated Cities in America, 2025" July 2, 2024*

Environmental Rankings

- The U.S. Environmental Protection Agency (EPA) released its list of U.S. metropolitan areas with the most ENERGY STAR certified buildings in 2023. The Chicago metro area was ranked #11 out of 25. *U.S. Environmental Protection Agency, "2024 Energy Star Top Cities," May 22, 2024*
- Chicago was highlighted as one of the 25 most ozone-polluted metro areas in the U.S. during 2021 through 2023. The area ranked #15. *American Lung Association, "State of the Air 2025," April 23, 2025*
- Chicago was highlighted as one of the 25 metro areas most polluted by year-round particle pollution (Annual PM 2.5) in the U.S. during 2021 through 2023. The area ranked #13. *American Lung Association, "State of the Air 2025," April 23, 2025*

Food/Drink Rankings

- WalletHub compared the 100 largest U.S. cities across 17 key indicators of vegan- and vegetarian-friendliness. Chicago was ranked #15. Cities were selected based on metrics such as the cost of groceries for vegetarians, the share of restaurants serving meatless options and the number of salad shops per capita. *WalletHub.com, "Best Cities for Vegans & Vegetarians (2025)," September 24, 2024*

Health/Fitness Rankings

- For each of the 100 largest cities in the United States, the American Fitness Index®, compiled in partnership between the American College of Sports Medicine and the Elevance Health Foundation, evaluated community infrastructure and more than 30 health behaviors including preventive health, levels of chronic disease conditions, food insecurity, pedestrian safety, air quality, and community/environment resources that support physical activity. Chicago ranked #18 for "community fitness." *americanfitnessindex.org, "2024 ACSM American Fitness Index Summary Report," July 23, 2024*
- Chicago was identified as one of the 10 most walkable cities in the U.S. by Walk Score. The city ranked #6. Walk Score measures walkability by analyzing hundreds of walking routes to nearby amenities, and also measures pedestrian friendliness by analyzing population density and road metrics such as block length and intersection density. *WalkScore.com, April 13, 2021*
- The Chicago metro area was identified as one of the worst cities for bed bugs in America by pest control company Orkin. The area ranked #1 out of 50 based on the number of bed bug treatments Orkin performed from December 2022 to November 2023. *Orkin, "Chicago Joins Paris In Global Bed Bug Spotlight Ranking As The Worst City On Orkin's U.S. Bed Bug Cities List," January 22, 2024*
- Chicago was identified as a "2025 Allergy Capital." The area ranked #80 out of the nation's 100 largest metropolitan areas. Three groups of factors were used to identify the most challenging cities for people with allergies: annual tree, grass, and weed pollen scores; over the counter allergy medicine use; number of board-certified allergy specialists. *Asthma and Allergy Foundation of America, "2025 Allergy Capitals: The Most Challenging Places to Live with Allergies," March 18, 2025*
- Chicago was identified as a "2024 Asthma Capital." The area ranked #53 out of the nation's 100 largest metropolitan areas. Criteria: estimated asthma prevalence; asthma-related mortality; and ER visits due to asthma. Risk factors analyzed but not factored in the rankings: annual air quality including pollution and ozone levels; public smoking laws; indoor air quality; access to asthma specialists; rescue and controller medication use; uninsured rate; pollen allergy; poverty rate. *Asthma and Allergy Foundation of America, "Asthma Capitals 2024: The Most Challenging Places to Live With Asthma," September 10, 2024*

Pet Rankings

- Chicago was selected by *Sniffspot.com* as one of the most dog-friendly cities in the U.S., ranking #43 out of 50. Criteria: dog parks; hiking; sniffspots; public parks; dog-friendly businesses; housing; dog waste cleanliness; leash laws; dog services; and overall cost. *Sniffspot.com, "The Top 50 Most Dog-Friendly Cities in the U.S.," September 30, 2024*

Real Estate Rankings

- *WalletHub* compared the most populated U.S. cities to determine which had the best markets for real estate agents. Chicago ranked #134 where demand was high and pay was the best. Criteria: sales per agent; annual median wage for real-estate agents; monthly average starting salary for real estate agents; real estate job density and competition; unemployment rate; home turnover rate; housing-market health index; and other relevant metrics. *WalletHub.com, "2021 Best Places to Be a Real Estate Agent," May 12, 2021*

- Chicago was ranked #15 in the top 20 out of the 100 largest metro areas in terms of house price appreciation in 2024 (#1 = highest rate). *Federal Housing Finance Agency, "House Price Index, 4th Quarter 2024," February 25, 2025*

- Chicago was ranked #89 out of 176 metro areas in terms of cost of housing in 2024 by the National Association of Home Builders (#1 = most affordable). Criteria: the portion of an average family's income necessary to pay the mortgage on a median-priced home. *National Association of Home Builders®, NAHB-Wells Fargo Cost of Housing Index, 4th Quarter 2024*

- The nation's largest metro areas were analyzed in terms of the percentage of households entering some stage of foreclosure in 2024. The Chicago metro area ranked #2 out of 5 (#1 = highest foreclosure rate). *ATTOM Data Solutions, "2024 Year-End U.S. Foreclosure Market Report™," January 15, 2025*

Safety Rankings

- Allstate ranked the 100 most populous cities in America in terms of driver safety. Chicago ranked #75. Criteria based on anonymized driving behavior data from Allstate's mobile app powered by Arity: high speed driving (over 80 mph), phone handling, and hard braking. The report helps increase the importance of safety and awareness behind the wheel. *Allstate, "16th Allstate America's Best Drivers Report®" July 11, 2024*

- The National Insurance Crime Bureau ranked the largest metro areas in the U.S. in terms of per capita rates of vehicle theft. The Chicago metro area ranked #3 out of the top 10 (#1 = highest rate). Criteria: number of vehicle theft offenses per 100,000 inhabitants in 2023. *National Insurance Crime Bureau, "Vehicle Thefts Surge Nationwide in 2023," April 9, 2024*

Transportation Rankings

- Chicago was identified as one of the most congested metro areas in the U.S. The area ranked #10 out of 10. Criteria: yearly delay per auto commuter in hours. *Texas A&M Transportation Institute, "2023 Urban Mobility Report," June 2024*

- According to the INRIX "2024 Global Traffic Scorecard," Chicago was identified as one of the most congested metro areas in the U.S. The area ranked #2 out of 10 in the country and among the top 25 most congested in the world. Criteria: average annual time spent in traffic and average cost of congestion per motorist. *Inrix.com, "Employees & Consumers Returned to Downtowns, Traffic Delays & Costs Grew," January 6, 2025*

Women/Minorities Rankings

- *Travel + Leisure* listed the best cities in and around the U.S. for a memorable and fun girls' trip, even on a budget. Whether it is for a special occasion, to make new memories or just to get away, Chicago is sure to have something for all the ladies in your tribe. *Travel + Leisure, "25 Affordable Girls Weekend Getaways That Won't Break the Bank," January 30, 2025*

- Chicago was listed as one of the most LGBTQ-friendly cities in America by *The Advocate*, as compiled by the real estate data site *Clever*. The city ranked #9 out of 15. Criteria, among many: Pride events; gay bars; LGBTQ-affirming healthcare options; state and local laws; number of PFLAG chapters; LGBTQ+ population. *The Advocate, "These Are the 15 Most LGBTQ-Friendly Cities in the U.S." November 1, 2023*

- Personal finance website *WalletHub* compared more than 180 U.S. cities across two key dimensions, "Hispanic Business-Friendliness" and "Hispanic Purchasing Power," to arrive at the most favorable conditions for Hispanic entrepreneurs. Chicago was ranked #76 out of 182. Criteria includes: share of Hispanic-Owned Businesses; average growth of Hispanic Business revenues; Small Business-Friendliness score; affordability; and number of Hispanics with at least a bachelor's degree. *WalletHub.com, "Best Cities for Hispanic Entrepreneurs," September 4, 2024*

Miscellaneous Rankings

- In its roundup of St. Patrick's Day parades, *Gayot* listed the best festivals and parades of all things Irish. The festivities in Chicago as among the best in North America. *Gayot.com, "Best St. Patrick's Day Parades," March 2025*

- In *Condé Nast Traveler* magazine's 2024 Readers' Choice Survey, Chicago made the top ten list of friendliest American cities. Chicago ranked #10. *Condé Nast Traveler, "The Friendliest Cities in the U.S., According to Our Readers"* October 28, 2024

- *WalletHub* compared 148 of the most populated U.S. cities to determine their operating efficiency. A "Quality of Services" score was constructed for each city and then measured against the total budget per capita to reveal which were managed the best. Chicago ranked #137. Criteria: financial stability; economy; education; safety; health; infrastructure and pollution. *WalletHub.com, "2025's Best- & Worst-Run Cities in America," June 18, 2024*

Business Environment

DEMOGRAPHICS

Population Growth

Area	1990 Census	2000 Census	2010 Census	2020 Census	2023 Estimate[2]	Population Growth 1990-2023 (%)
City	2,783,726	2,896,016	2,695,598	2,746,388	2,707,648	-2.7
MSA[1]	8,182,076	9,098,316	9,461,105	9,618,502	9,359,555	14.4
U.S.	248,709,873	281,421,906	308,745,538	331,449,281	332,387,540	33.6

Note: (1) Figures cover the Chicago-Naperville-Elgin, IL-IN Metropolitan Statistical Area; (2) 2019-2023 5-year ACS population estimate
Source: U.S. Census Bureau, 1990 Census, 2000 Census, 2010 Census, 2020 Census, 2019-2023 American Community Survey 5-Year Estimates

Race

Area	White Alone[2] (%)	Black Alone[2] (%)	Asian Alone[2] (%)	AIAN[3] Alone[2] (%)	NHOPI[4] Alone[2] (%)	Other Race Alone[2] (%)	Two or More Races (%)
City	39.0	28.4	7.1	0.9	0.1	12.4	12.0
MSA[1]	55.7	16.2	7.1	0.6	0.0	9.5	10.8
U.S.	63.4	12.4	5.8	0.9	0.2	6.6	10.7

Note: (1) Figures cover the Chicago-Naperville-Elgin, IL-IN Metropolitan Statistical Area; (2) Alone is defined as not being in combination with one or more other races; (3) American Indian and Alaska Native; (4) Native Hawaiian and Other Pacific Islander
Source: U.S. Census Bureau, 2019-2023 American Community Survey 5-Year Estimates

Hispanic or Latino Origin

Area	Total (%)	Mexican (%)	Puerto Rican (%)	Cuban (%)	Other (%)
City	29.6	21.6	3.5	0.4	4.2
MSA[1]	23.8	18.3	2.3	0.3	2.9
U.S.	19.0	11.3	1.8	0.7	5.2

Note: Persons of Hispanic or Latino origin can be of any race; (1) Figures cover the Chicago-Naperville-Elgin, IL-IN Metropolitan Statistical Area
Source: U.S. Census Bureau, 2019-2023 American Community Survey 5-Year Estimates

Age

Area	Percent of Population									Median Age
	Under Age 5	Age 5–19	Age 20–34	Age 35–44	Age 45–54	Age 55–64	Age 65–74	Age 75–84	Age 85+	
City	5.6	16.6	26.7	14.6	11.8	11.2	8.1	3.9	1.7	35.7
MSA[1]	5.6	19.2	20.4	13.6	12.8	12.7	9.3	4.4	1.8	38.4
U.S.	5.7	19.1	20.2	13.1	12.3	12.8	10.0	4.9	1.9	38.7

Note: (1) Figures cover the Chicago-Naperville-Elgin, IL-IN Metropolitan Statistical Area
Source: U.S. Census Bureau, 2019-2023 American Community Survey 5-Year Estimates

Disability by Age

Area	All Ages	Under 18 Years Old	18 to 64 Years Old	65 Years and Over
City	11.9	3.8	9.6	35.4
MSA[1]	10.7	3.6	8.4	30.2
U.S.	13.0	4.7	10.7	32.9

Note: Figures show percent of the civilian noninstitutionalized population that reported having a disability. Disability status is determined from six types of difficulty: vision, hearing, cognitive, ambulatory, self-care, and independent living. For children under 5 years old, hearing and vision difficulty are used to determine disability status. For children between the ages of 5 and 14, disability status is determined from hearing, vision, cognitive, ambulatory, and self-care difficulties. For people aged 15 years and older, they are considered to have a disability if they have difficulty with any one of the six difficulty types; Note: (1) Figures cover the Chicago-Naperville-Elgin, IL-IN Metropolitan Statistical Area
Source: U.S. Census Bureau, 2019-2023 American Community Survey 5-Year Estimates

Ancestry

Area	German	Irish	English	American	Italian	Polish	French[2]	European	Scottish
City	7.4	7.2	3.2	2.0	3.8	5.0	0.9	0.9	0.7
MSA[1]	12.9	10.2	4.8	2.5	6.1	8.0	1.2	1.2	0.9
U.S.	12.6	9.4	9.1	5.5	4.9	2.6	2.0	1.6	1.6

Note: Figures are the percentage of the total population reporting a particular ancestry. The nine most commonly reported ancestries in the U.S. are shown. Figures include multiple ancestries (e.g. if a person reported being Irish and Italian, they were included in both columns); (1) Figures cover the Chicago-Naperville-Elgin, IL-IN Metropolitan Statistical Area; (2) Excludes Basque
Source: U.S. Census Bureau, 2019-2023 American Community Survey 5-Year Estimates

Foreign-born Population

Area	Percent of Population Born in								
	Any Foreign Country	Asia	Mexico	Europe	Caribbean	Central America[2]	South America	Africa	Canada
City	20.7	5.2	8.2	3.3	0.4	0.9	1.4	1.1	0.2
MSA[1]	18.3	5.4	6.5	3.7	0.3	0.6	0.8	0.7	0.2
U.S.	13.9	4.3	3.3	1.4	1.4	1.2	1.2	0.8	0.2

Note: (1) Figures cover the Chicago-Naperville-Elgin, IL-IN Metropolitan Statistical Area; (2) Excludes Mexico.
Source: U.S. Census Bureau, 2019-2023 American Community Survey 5-Year Estimates

Household Size

Area	Persons in Household (%)							Average Household Size
	One	Two	Three	Four	Five	Six	Seven or More	
City	39.2	29.4	13.1	9.9	4.8	2.1	1.5	2.32
MSA[1]	29.9	31.0	15.4	13.5	6.4	2.3	1.5	2.55
U.S.	28.5	33.8	15.4	12.7	5.9	2.3	1.4	2.54

Note: (1) Figures cover the Chicago-Naperville-Elgin, IL-IN Metropolitan Statistical Area
Source: U.S. Census Bureau, 2019-2023 American Community Survey 5-Year Estimates

Household Relationships

Area	Householder	Opposite-sex Spouse	Same-sex Spouse	Opposite-sex Unmarried Partner	Same-sex Unmarried Partner	Child[2]	Grandchild	Other Relatives	Non-relatives
City	41.6	12.2	0.3	3.0	0.3	26.6	3.0	6.4	4.8
MSA[1]	38.2	17.1	0.2	2.3	0.1	30.3	2.4	5.1	2.8
U.S.	38.3	17.5	0.2	2.5	0.2	28.3	2.4	4.8	3.4

Note: Figures are percent of the total population; (1) Figures cover the Chicago-Naperville-Elgin, IL-IN Metropolitan Statistical Area; (2) Includes biological, adopted, and stepchildren of the householder
Source: U.S. Census Bureau, 2020 Census

Gender

Area	Males	Females	Males per 100 Females
City	1,314,256	1,393,392	94.3
MSA[1]	4,607,366	4,752,189	97.0
U.S.	164,545,087	167,842,453	98.0

Note: (1) Figures cover the Chicago-Naperville-Elgin, IL-IN Metropolitan Statistical Area
Source: U.S. Census Bureau, 2019-2023 American Community Survey 5-Year Estimates

Marital Status

Area	Never Married	Now Married[2]	Separated	Widowed	Divorced
City	49.1	35.6	2.2	5.0	8.1
MSA[1]	37.6	46.7	1.6	5.3	8.8
U.S.	34.1	47.9	1.7	5.6	10.7

Note: Figures are percentages and cover the population 15 years of age and older; (1) Figures cover the Chicago-Naperville-Elgin, IL-IN Metropolitan Statistical Area; (2) Excludes separated
Source: U.S. Census Bureau, 2019-2023 American Community Survey 5-Year Estimates

Religious Groups by Family

Area	Catholic	Baptist	Methodist	LDS[2]	Pentecostal	Lutheran	Islam	Adventist	Other
MSA[1]	28.6	3.4	1.4	0.3	1.5	2.1	4.7	1.1	9.2
U.S.	18.7	7.3	3.0	2.0	1.8	1.7	1.3	1.3	11.6

Note: Figures are the number of adherents as a percentage of the total population and cover the eight largest religious groups in the U.S; (1) Figures cover the Chicago-Naperville-Elgin, IL-IN Metropolitan Statistical Area; (2) Church of Jesus Christ of Latter-day Saints
Sources: 2020 U.S. Religion Census, Association of Statisticians of American Religious Bodies; The Association of Religion Data Archives (ARDA)

Religious Groups by Tradition

Area	Catholic	Evangelical Protestant	Mainline Protestant	Black Protestant	Islam	Judaism	Hinduism	Orthodox	Buddhism
MSA[1]	28.6	8.2	3.7	3.6	4.7	0.7	0.4	0.7	0.4
U.S.	18.7	16.5	5.2	2.3	1.3	0.6	0.4	0.4	0.3

Note: Figures are the number of adherents as a percentage of the total population; (1) Figures cover the Chicago-Naperville-Elgin, IL-IN Metropolitan Statistical Area
Sources: 2020 U.S. Religion Census, Association of Statisticians of American Religious Bodies; The Association of Religion Data Archives (ARDA)

ECONOMY

Real Gross Domestic Product (GDP)

Area	2017	2018	2019	2020	2021	2022	2023	Rank[3]
MSA[1]	674.6	691.2	697.5	659.6	698.0	715.6	725.7	3
U.S.[2]	17,619.1	18,160.7	18,642.5	18,238.9	19,387.6	19,896.6	20,436.3	—

Note: Figures are in billions of chained 2017 dollars; (1) Figures cover the Chicago-Naperville-Elgin, IL-IN Metropolitan Statistical Area; (2) Figures cover real GDP within metropolitan areas; (3) Rank is based on 2023 data and ranges from 1 to 384
Source: U.S. Bureau of Economic Analysis

Economic Growth

Area	2014	2015	2016	2017	2018	2019	2020	2021	2022	2023
MSA[1]	2.3	2.4	0.8	1.4	2.5	0.9	-5.4	5.8	2.5	1.4
U.S.[2]	2.6	3.2	2.0	2.7	3.1	2.7	-2.2	6.3	2.6	2.7

Note: Figures are real gross domestic product growth rates and represent percent change from preceding period; (1) Figures cover the Chicago-Naperville-Elgin, IL-IN Metropolitan Statistical Area; (2) Figures are the average growth rates within metropolitan areas
Source: U.S. Bureau of Economic Analysis

Metropolitan Area Exports

Area	2018	2019	2020	2021	2022	2023	Rank[2]
MSA[1]	47,287.8	42,438.8	41,279.4	54,498.1	63,374.6	56,656.6	5
U.S.	1,664,056.1	1,645,173.7	1,431,406.6	1,753,941.4	2,062,937.4	2,019,160.5	—

Note: Figures are in millions of dollars; (1) Figures cover the Chicago-Naperville-Elgin, IL-IN Metropolitan Statistical Area; (2) Rank is based on 2023 data and ranges from 1 to 386
Source: U.S. Department of Commerce, International Trade Administration, Office of Trade and Economic Analysis, Industry and Analysis, Exports by Metropolitan Area, data extracted April 2, 2025

Building Permits

Area	Single-Family			Multi-Family			Total		
	2023	2024	Pct. Chg.	2023	2024	Pct. Chg.	2023	2024	Pct. Chg.
City	290	325	12.1	3,326	4,046	21.6	3,616	4,371	20.9
MSA[1]	8,452	9,509	12.5	6,576	8,555	30.1	15,028	18,064	20.2
U.S.	920,000	981,900	6.7	591,100	496,100	-16.1	1,511,100	1,478,000	-2.2

Note: (1) Figures cover the Chicago-Naperville-Elgin, IL-IN Metropolitan Statistical Area; Figures represent new, privately-owned housing units authorized (unadjusted data)
Source: U.S. Census Bureau, Building Permits Survey (BPS), 2023, 2024

Bankruptcy Filings

Area	Business Filings			Nonbusiness Filings		
	2023	2024	% Chg.	2023	2024	% Chg.
Cook County	361	479	32.7	12,419	13,840	11.4
U.S.	18,926	23,107	22.1	434,064	494,201	13.9

Note: Business filings include Chapter 7, Chapter 9, Chapter 11, Chapter 12, Chapter 13, Chapter 15, and Section 304; Nonbusiness filings include Chapter 7, Chapter 11, and Chapter 13
Source: Administrative Office of the U.S. Courts, Business and Nonbusiness Bankruptcy, County Cases Commenced by Chapter of the Bankruptcy Code, During the 12-Month Period Ending December 31, 2023 and Business and Nonbusiness Bankruptcy, County Cases Commenced by Chapter of the Bankruptcy Code, During the 12-Month Period Ending December 31, 2024

Housing Vacancy Rates

Area	Gross Vacancy Rate[3] (%)			Year-Round Vacancy Rate[4] (%)			Rental Vacancy Rate[5] (%)			Homeowner Vacancy Rate[6] (%)		
	2022	2023	2024	2022	2023	2024	2022	2023	2024	2022	2023	2024
MSA[1]	7.3	6.0	5.8	7.1	5.8	5.6	6.1	5.6	5.1	1.1	0.5	0.6
U.S.[2]	9.1	9.0	9.1	7.5	7.5	7.6	5.7	6.5	6.8	0.8	0.8	1.0

Note: (1) Figures cover the Chicago-Naperville-Elgin, IL-IN Metropolitan Statistical Area; (2) Figures cover the 75 largest Metropolitan Statistical Areas; (3) The percentage of the total housing inventory that is vacant; (4) The percentage of the housing inventory (excluding seasonal units) that is year-round vacant; (5) The percentage of rental inventory that is vacant for rent; (6) The percentage of homeowner inventory that is vacant for sale
Source: U.S. Census Bureau, Housing Vacancies and Homeownership Annual Statistics: 2022, 2023, 2024

INCOME

Income

Area	Per Capita ($)	Median Household ($)	Average Household ($)
City	48,148	75,134	112,443
MSA[1]	48,107	88,850	122,980
U.S.	43,289	78,538	110,491

Note: (1) Figures cover the Chicago-Naperville-Elgin, IL-IN Metropolitan Statistical Area
Source: U.S. Census Bureau, 2019-2023 American Community Survey 5-Year Estimates

Household Income Distribution

Area	Percent of Households Earning							
	Under $15,000	$15,000 -$24,999	$25,000 -$34,999	$35,000 -$49,999	$50,000 -$74,999	$75,000 -$99,999	$100,000 -$149,999	$150,000 and up
City	12.1	7.2	6.9	9.8	14.0	11.7	16.0	22.4
MSA[1]	8.1	5.6	5.9	9.0	14.2	12.5	18.4	26.4
U.S.	8.5	6.6	6.8	10.4	15.7	12.7	17.4	21.9

Note: (1) Figures cover the Chicago-Naperville-Elgin, IL-IN Metropolitan Statistical Area
Source: U.S. Census Bureau, 2019-2023 American Community Survey 5-Year Estimates

Poverty Rate

Area	All Ages	Under 18 Years Old	18 to 64 Years Old	65 Years and Over
City	16.8	24.0	14.6	17.1
MSA[1]	11.1	14.8	10.0	10.2
U.S.	12.4	16.3	11.6	10.4

Note: Figures are percentage of people whose income during the past 12 months was below the poverty level; (1) Figures cover the Chicago-Naperville-Elgin, IL-IN Metropolitan Statistical Area
Source: U.S. Census Bureau, 2019-2023 American Community Survey 5-Year Estimates

EMPLOYMENT

Labor Force and Employment

Area	Civilian Labor Force			Workers Employed		
	Dec. 2023	Dec. 2024	% Chg.	Dec. 2023	Dec. 2024	% Chg.
City	1,391,216	1,432,019	2.9	1,330,946	1,363,159	2.4
MD[1]	3,780,647	3,890,015	2.9	3,630,697	3,719,159	2.4
U.S.	166,661,000	167,746,000	0.7	160,754,000	161,294,000	0.3

Note: Data is not seasonally adjusted and covers workers 16 years of age and older; (1) Figures cover the Chicago-Naperville-Schaumburg, IL Metropolitan Division
Source: Bureau of Labor Statistics, Local Area Unemployment Statistics

Unemployment Rate

Area	2024											
	Jan.	Feb.	Mar.	Apr.	May	Jun.	Jul.	Aug.	Sep.	Oct.	Nov.	Dec.
City	5.0	5.5	5.1	5.1	5.6	6.9	6.7	6.4	5.8	5.8	5.4	4.8
MD[1]	4.7	5.2	4.8	4.6	5.1	6.2	6.0	5.7	5.1	5.1	4.8	4.4
U.S.	4.1	4.2	3.9	3.5	3.7	4.3	4.5	4.4	3.9	3.9	4.0	3.8

Note: Data is not seasonally adjusted and covers workers 16 years of age and older; (1) Figures cover the Chicago-Naperville-Schaumburg, IL Metropolitan Division
Source: Bureau of Labor Statistics, Local Area Unemployment Statistics

Average Wages

Occupation	$/Hr.	Occupation	$/Hr.
Accountants and Auditors	44.28	Maintenance and Repair Workers	27.90
Automotive Mechanics	28.71	Marketing Managers	78.03
Bookkeepers	25.75	Network and Computer Systems Admin.	49.76
Carpenters	38.11	Nurses, Licensed Practical	34.69
Cashiers	16.33	Nurses, Registered	45.47
Computer Programmers	46.08	Nursing Assistants	21.85
Computer Systems Analysts	48.09	Office Clerks, General	23.22
Computer User Support Specialists	30.31	Physical Therapists	52.46
Construction Laborers	34.99	Physicians	109.22
Cooks, Restaurant	18.66	Plumbers, Pipefitters and Steamfitters	44.43
Customer Service Representatives	23.30	Police and Sheriff's Patrol Officers	47.28
Dentists	89.54	Postal Service Mail Carriers	29.11
Electricians	44.39	Real Estate Sales Agents	29.28
Engineers, Electrical	57.06	Retail Salespersons	18.67
Fast Food and Counter Workers	16.05	Sales Representatives, Technical/Scientific	58.57
Financial Managers	88.31	Secretaries, Exc. Legal/Medical/Executive	25.84
First-Line Supervisors of Office Workers	35.22	Security Guards	21.16
General and Operations Managers	68.58	Surgeons	161.04
Hairdressers/Cosmetologists	20.23	Teacher Assistants, Exc. Postsecondary[1]	18.41
Home Health and Personal Care Aides	17.79	Teachers, Secondary School, Exc. Sp. Ed.[1]	42.55
Janitors and Cleaners	19.25	Telemarketers	17.05
Landscaping/Groundskeeping Workers	21.26	Truck Drivers, Heavy/Tractor-Trailer	31.25
Lawyers	89.56	Truck Drivers, Light/Delivery Services	25.40
Maids and Housekeeping Cleaners	19.33	Waiters and Waitresses	16.76

Note: Wage data covers the Chicago-Naperville-Elgin, IL-IN Metropolitan Statistical Area; (1) Hourly wages were calculated from annual wage data based on a 40 hour work week
Source: Bureau of Labor Statistics, Metro Area Occupational Employment & Wage Estimates, May 2024

Employment by Industry

Sector	MD[1] Number of Employees	MD[1] Percent of Total	U.S. Percent of Total
Construction	128,300	3.4	5.1
Financial Activities	277,100	7.2	5.8
Government	427,900	11.2	14.9
Information	70,000	1.8	1.9
Leisure and Hospitality	373,600	9.8	10.4
Manufacturing	279,900	7.3	8.0
Mining and Logging	1,300	<0.1	0.4
Other Services	157,200	4.1	3.7
Private Education and Health Services	652,200	17.0	16.9
Professional and Business Services	688,500	18.0	14.2
Retail Trade	332,600	8.7	10.0
Transportation, Warehousing, and Utilities	250,300	6.5	4.8
Wholesale Trade	188,600	4.9	3.9

Note: Figures are non-farm employment as of December 2024. Figures are not seasonally adjusted and include workers 16 years of age and older; (1) Figures cover the Chicago-Naperville-Schaumburg, IL Metropolitan Division
Source: Bureau of Labor Statistics, Current Employment Statistics, Employment, Hours, and Earnings

Employment by Occupation

Occupation Classification	City (%)	MSA[1] (%)	U.S. (%)
Management, Business, Science, and Arts	48.1	44.2	42.0
Natural Resources, Construction, and Maintenance	4.8	6.6	8.6
Production, Transportation, and Material Moving	12.1	14.0	13.0
Sales and Office	17.9	19.8	19.9
Service	17.2	15.4	16.5

Note: Figures cover employed civilians 16 years of age and older; (1) Figures cover the Chicago-Naperville-Elgin, IL-IN Metropolitan Statistical Area
Source: U.S. Census Bureau, 2019-2023 American Community Survey 5-Year Estimates

Occupations with Greatest Projected Employment Growth: 2022 – 2032

Occupation[1]	2022 Employment	2032 Projected Employment	Numeric Employment Change	Percent Employment Change
Home Health and Personal Care Aides	108,190	124,190	16,000	14.8
Software Developers	58,810	70,390	11,580	19.7
Cooks, Restaurant	52,430	63,780	11,350	21.6
General and Operations Managers	192,820	201,600	8,780	4.6
Laborers and Freight, Stock, and Material Movers, Hand	203,480	211,740	8,260	4.1
Stockers and Order Fillers	97,920	104,400	6,480	6.6
Financial Managers	46,470	52,870	6,400	13.8
Light Truck or Delivery Services Drivers	53,210	58,020	4,810	9.0
Registered Nurses	138,050	142,310	4,260	3.1
Medical and Health Services Managers	16,940	21,120	4,180	24.7

Note: Projections cover Illinois; (1) Sorted by numeric employment change
Source: www.projectionscentral.org, State Occupational Projections, 2022–2032 Long-Term Projections

Fastest-Growing Occupations: 2022 – 2032

Occupation[1]	2022 Employment	2032 Projected Employment	Numeric Employment Change	Percent Employment Change
Gaming Dealers	1,040	2,620	1,580	151.9
First-Line Supervisors of Gambling Services Workers	310	720	410	132.3
Gaming Managers	70	150	80	114.3
Gaming Service Workers, All Other	170	350	180	105.9
Gaming Cage Workers	180	370	190	105.6
Solar Photovoltaic Installers	260	510	250	96.2
Gaming Change Persons and Booth Cashiers	320	600	280	87.5
Nurse Practitioners	8,970	12,660	3,690	41.1
Data Scientists	6,410	8,310	1,900	29.6
Statisticians	620	800	180	29.0

Note: Projections cover Illinois; (1) Sorted by percent employment change and excludes occupations with numeric employment change less than 50
Source: www.projectionscentral.org, State Occupational Projections, 2022–2032 Long-Term Projections

CITY FINANCES

City Government Finances

Component	2022 ($000)	2022 ($ per capita)
Total Revenues	12,391,075	4,628
Total Expenditures	9,790,554	3,656
Debt Outstanding	23,158,939	8,649

Source: U.S. Census Bureau, State & Local Government Finances 2022

City Government Revenue by Source

Source	2022 ($000)	2022 ($ per capita)	2022 (%)
General Revenue			
From Federal Government	1,843,629	689	14.9
From State Government	1,728,449	646	13.9
From Local Governments	75,766	28	0.6
Taxes			
Property	1,570,534	587	12.7
Sales and Gross Receipts	2,233,587	834	18.0
Personal Income	0	0	0.0
Corporate Income	0	0	0.0
Motor Vehicle License	30,954	12	0.2
Other Taxes	413,132	154	3.3
Current Charges	1,962,192	733	15.8
Liquor Store	0	0	0.0
Utility	764,059	285	6.2

Source: U.S. Census Bureau, State & Local Government Finances 2022

City Government Expenditures by Function

Function	2022 ($000)	2022 ($ per capita)	2022 (%)
General Direct Expenditures			
Air Transportation	1,596,145	596	16.3
Corrections	0	0	0.0
Education	0	0	0.0
Employment Security Administration	0	0	0.0
Financial Administration	150,765	56	1.5
Fire Protection	670,955	250	6.9
General Public Buildings	229,693	85	2.3
Governmental Administration, Other	58,009	21	0.6
Health	225,441	84	2.3
Highways	626,455	234	6.4
Hospitals	0	0	0.0
Housing and Community Development	374,070	139	3.8
Interest on General Debt	1,014,633	378	10.4
Judicial and Legal	31,151	11	0.3
Libraries	103,558	38	1.1
Parking	7,382	2	0.1
Parks and Recreation	29,949	11	0.3
Police Protection	1,653,933	617	16.9
Public Welfare	392,007	146	4.0
Sewerage	292,201	109	3.0
Solid Waste Management	172,112	64	1.8
Veterans' Services	0	0	0.0
Liquor Store	0	0	0.0
Utility	419,628	156	4.3

Source: U.S. Census Bureau, State & Local Government Finances 2022

TAXES

State Corporate Income Tax Rates

State	Tax Rate (%)	Income Brackets ($)	Num. of Brackets	Financial Institution Tax Rate (%)[a]	Federal Income Tax Ded.
Illinois	9.5 (g)	Flat rate	1	9.5 (g)	No

Note: Tax rates for tax year 2024; (a) Rates listed are the corporate income tax rate applied to financial institutions or excise taxes based on income. Some states have other taxes based upon the value of deposits or shares; (g) The Illinois rate of 9.5% is the sum of a corporate income tax rate of 7.0% plus a replacement tax of 2.5%.
Source: Federation of Tax Administrators, State Corporate Income Tax Rates, January 1, 2025

State Individual Income Tax Rates

State	Tax Rate (%)	Income Brackets ($)	Personal Exemptions ($)			Standard Ded. ($)	
			Single	Married	Depend.	Single	Married
Illinois (a)	4.95	Flat rate	2,775	5,550	2,775	—	—

Note: Tax rates for tax year 2024; Local- and county-level taxes are not included; Federal income tax is not deductible on state income tax returns; (a) 16 states have statutory provision for automatically adjusting to the rate of inflation the dollar values of the income tax brackets, standard deductions, and/or personal exemptions. Oregon does not index the income brackets for $125,000 and over See: INFL and SPEC above.
Source: Federation of Tax Administrators, State Individual Income Tax Rates, January 1, 2025

Various State Sales and Excise Tax Rates

State	State Sales Tax (%)	Gasoline[1] ($/gal.)	Cigarette[2] ($/pack)	Spirits[3] ($/gal.)	Wine[4] ($/gal.)	Beer[5] ($/gal.)	Recreational Marijuana (%)
Illinois	6.25	0.66	2.98	8.55	1.39	0.23	(g)

Note: All tax rates as of January 1, 2025; (1) The American Petroleum Institute has developed a methodology for determining the average tax rate on a gallon of fuel. Rates may include any of the following: excise taxes, environmental fees, storage tank fees, other fees or taxes, general sales tax, and local taxes; (2) The federal excise tax of $1.0066 per pack and local taxes are not included; (3) Rates are those applicable to off-premise sales of 40% alcohol by volume (a.b.v.) distilled spirits in 750ml containers. Local excise taxes are excluded; (4) Rates are those applicable to off-premise sales of 11% a.b.v. non-carbonated wine in 750ml containers; (5) Rates are those applicable to off-premise sales of 4.7% a.b.v. beer in 12 ounce containers; (g) 7% excise tax of value at wholesale level; 10% tax on cannabis flower or products with less than or equal to 35% THC; 20% tax on products infused with cannabis, such as edible products; 25% tax on any product with a THC concentration higher than 35%
Source: Tax Foundation, 2025 Facts & Figures: How Does Your State Compare?

State Tax Competitiveness Index

State	Overall Rank	Corporate Tax Rank	Individual Income Tax Rank	Sales Tax Rank	Property Tax Rank	Unemployment Insurance Tax Rank
Illinois	37	42	13	38	41	43

Note: The Tax Foundation's State Tax Competitiveness Index enables policymakers, taxpayers, and business leaders to gauge how their states' tax systems compare. A rank of 1 is best, 50 is worst. Rankings do not average to the total. States without a tax rank equally as 1. DC's scores and rankings do not affect other states. The report shows tax systems as of July 1, 2024 (the beginning of Fiscal Year 2025).
Source: Tax Foundation, State Tax Competitiveness Index 2025

TRANSPORTATION

Means of Transportation to Work

Area	Car/Truck/Van		Public Transportation			Bicycle	Walked	Other Means	Worked at Home
	Drove Alone	Car-pooled	Bus	Subway	Railroad				
City	46.0	7.4	9.5	8.5	1.2	1.4	5.7	2.1	18.3
MSA[1]	63.6	7.8	3.3	2.9	2.0	0.6	2.8	1.6	15.6
U.S.	70.2	8.5	1.7	1.3	0.4	0.4	2.4	1.6	13.5

Note: Figures are percentages and cover workers 16 years of age and older; (1) Figures cover the Chicago-Naperville-Elgin, IL-IN Metropolitan Statistical Area
Source: U.S. Census Bureau, 2019-2023 American Community Survey 5-Year Estimates

Travel Time to Work

Area	Less Than 10 Minutes	10 to 19 Minutes	20 to 29 Minutes	30 to 44 Minutes	45 to 59 Minutes	60 to 89 Minutes	90 Minutes or More
City	5.2	17.2	19.2	29.8	14.6	10.9	3.0
MSA[1]	8.9	22.3	19.5	25.3	11.9	9.3	2.9
U.S.	12.6	28.6	21.2	20.8	8.1	6.0	2.8

Note: Note: Figures are percentages and include workers 16 years old and over; (1) Figures cover the Chicago-Naperville-Elgin, IL-IN Metropolitan Statistical Area
Source: U.S. Census Bureau, 2019-2023 American Community Survey 5-Year Estimates

Key Congestion Measures

Measure	2000	2010	2015	2020	2022
Annual Hours of Delay, Total (000)	221,112	280,745	315,669	172,876	306,001
Annual Hours of Delay, Per Auto Commuter	52	59	70	39	72
Annual Congestion Cost, Per Auto Commuter ($)	1,551	1,566	1,627	953	1,675

Note: Figures cover the Chicago IL-IN urban area
Source: Texas A&M Transportation Institute, 2023 Urban Mobility Report

Freeway Travel Time Index

Measure	1985	1990	1995	2000	2005	2010	2015	2020	2022
Urban Area Index[1]	1.16	1.19	1.23	1.25	1.27	1.26	1.29	1.10	1.30
Urban Area Rank[1,2]	10	12	8	16	18	19	18	29	11

Note: Freeway Travel Time Index—the ratio of travel time in the peak period to the travel time at free-flow conditions. For example, a value of 1.30 indicates a 20-minute free-flow trip takes 26 minutes in the peak (20 minutes x 1.30 = 26 minutes); (1) Covers the Chicago IL-IN urban area; (2) Rank is based on 101 larger urban areas (#1 = highest travel time index)
Source: Texas A&M Transportation Institute, 2023 Urban Mobility Report

Public Transportation

Agency Name / Mode of Transportation	Vehicles Operated in Maximum Service[1]	Annual Unlinked Passenger Trips[2] (in thous.)	Annual Passenger Miles[3] (in thous.)
Chicago Transit Authority (CTA)			
Bus (directly operated)	1,307	161,699.4	403,793.2
Heavy Rail (directly operated)	838	117,447.1	686,884.5
Northeast Illinois Regional Commuter Railroad (Metra)			
Commuter Rail (directly operated)	447	13,742.4	296,062.3
Commuter Rail (purchased transportation)	465	18,245.7	410,043.3

Note: (1) Number of revenue vehicles operated by the given mode and type of service to meet the annual maximum service requirement. This is the revenue vehicle count during the peak season of the year; on the week and day that maximum service is provided. Vehicles operated in maximum service (VOMS) exclude atypical days and one-time special events; (2) Number of passengers who boarded public transportation vehicles. Passengers are counted each time they board a vehicle no matter how many vehicles they use to travel from their origin to their destination. (3) Sum of the distances ridden by all passengers during the entire fiscal year.
Source: Federal Transit Administration, National Transit Database, 2023

Air Transportation

Airport Name and Code / Type of Service	Passenger Airlines[1]	Passenger Enplanements	Freight Carriers[2]	Freight (lbs)
O'Hare International (ORD)				
Domestic service (U.S. carriers only)	36	31,613,389	20	381,088,910
International service (U.S. carriers only)	14	3,346,832	8	164,447,740
Midway International (MDW)				
Domestic service (U.S. carriers only)	22	10,016,976	2	17,026,306
International service (U.S. carriers only)	5	117,256	1	51

Note: (1) Includes all U.S.-based major, minor and commuter airlines that carried at least one passenger during the year; (2) Includes all U.S.-based airlines and freight carriers that transported at least one pound of freight during the year.
Source: Bureau of Transportation Statistics, The Intermodal Transportation Database, Air Carriers: T-100 Domestic Market (U.S. carriers only), 2024; Bureau of Transportation Statistics, The Intermodal Transportation Database, Air Carriers: T-100 International Market (U.S. carriers only), 2024

Chicago, Illinois

BUSINESSES

Major Business Headquarters

Company Name	Industry	Fortune[1]	Forbes[2]
Amsted Industries	Capital goods	-	144
Archer Daniels Midland	Food production	43	-
Berlin Packaging	Materials	-	206
Clune Construction	Construction	-	259
Conagra Brands	Food consumer products	336	-
Echo Global Logistics	Transportation	-	168
Exelon	Utilities: gas and electric	187	-
GE HealthCare Technologies	Medical products and equipment	206	-
Heico Cos	Capital goods	-	210
Jones Lang LaSalle	Real estate	193	-
Kellanova	Food consumer products	272	-
Kirkland & Ellis	Services	-	86
Kraft Heinz	Food consumer products	156	-
LKQ	Wholesalers: diversified	305	-
McDonald's	Food services	162	-
Molson Coors Beverage	Beverages	352	-
Mondelez International	Food consumer products	115	-
Motorola Solutions	Network and other communications equipment	395	-
Newly Weds Foods	Food, drink & tobacco	-	226
Northern Trust	Commercial banks	342	-
Old Republic International	Insurance: property and casualty (stock)	491	-
R.R. Donnelley & Sons	Business services & supplies	-	148
Sidley Austin	Services	-	204
United Airlines Holdings	Airlines	83	-
Walsh Group	Construction	-	92

Note: (1) Companies that produce a 10-K are ranked 1 to 500 based on 2023 revenue; (2) All private companies with at least $2 billion in annual revenue through the end of their most current fiscal year are ranked 1 to 275; companies listed are headquartered in the city; dashes indicate no ranking
Source: Fortune, "Fortune 500," 2024; Forbes, "America's Largest Private Companies," 2024

Fastest-Growing Businesses

According to *Inc.*, Chicago is home to 10 of America's 500 fastest-growing private companies: **Kin Insurance** (#37); **ProxyPics** (#59); **Slumber Stay** (#69); **Sanguine Strategic Advisors** (#94); **iLoan** (#199); **Songfinch** (#238); **Atwix** (#273); **1440** (#309); **Aberdeen Advisors** (#335); **FARE Holdings** (#471). Criteria: must be an independent, privately-held, for-profit, U.S. corporation, proprietorship or partnership as of December 31, 2023; revenues must be at least $100,000 in 2020 and $2 million in 2023; must have four-year operating/sales history. *Inc., "America's 500 Fastest-Growing Private Companies," 2024*

According to *Initiative for a Competitive Inner City (ICIC)*, Chicago is home to 12 of America's 100 fastest-growing "inner city" companies: **A & L Environmental** (#4); **Adelante Construction Group** (#7); **Vitalizing Business Solutions** (#12); **Rudd Resources** (#22); **Supply Logistics & Procurement Services** (#32); **Nova Enterprises** (#46); **Jones Software Corporation** (#52); **Laystrom Manufacturing** (#59); **HUSarchitecture** (#63); **LaSalle Network** (#75); **Sandstorm** (#76); **Bush Infotech Group dba Kristine Fallon Associates dba KFA** (#100). To be eligible for the IC100, companies have to be independently operated, privately held, for-profit businesses with revenues of at least $50,000 in 2019 and $500,000 in 2023, and headquartered in an under-resourced community. Recognizing that concentrated poverty exists within metropolitan areas outside of big cities (and that poverty overall is suburbanizing), ICIC defines under-resourced communities as large low-income, high-poverty areas located in the urban and suburban parts of all but the smallest metropolitan areas. Companies were ranked overall by revenue growth over the five-year period between 2019 and 2023. *Initiative for a Competitive Inner City (ICIC), "Inner City 100 Companies," 2024*

According to Deloitte, Chicago is home to six of North America's 500 fastest-growing high-technology companies: **Zero Hash** (#4); **Fingerprint** (#40); **Vivid Seats** (#71); **Xeris Biopharma Holdings** (#169); **LogicGate** (#387); **RLDatix** (#476). Companies are ranked by percentage growth in revenue over a four-year period. Criteria for inclusion: company must be headquartered within North America; must own proprietary intellectual property or technology that is sold to customers in products that contributes to a significant portion of the company's operating revenue; must have been in business for a minumum of four years with 2020 operating revenues of at least $50,000 USD/CD and 2023 operating revenues of at least $5 million USD/CD. *Deloitte, 2024 Technology Fast 500™*

Living Environment

COST OF LIVING

Cost of Living Index

Composite Index	Groceries	Housing	Utilities	Transportation	Health Care	Misc. Goods/Services
115.1	103.9	140.1	96.7	107.3	107.9	107.0

Note: The Cost of Living Index measures regional differences in the cost of consumer goods and services, excluding taxes and non-consumer expenditures, for professional and managerial households in the top income quintile. It is based on more than 50,000 prices covering almost 60 different items for which prices are collected three times a year by chambers of commerce, economic development organizations or university applied economic centers in each participating urban area. The numbers shown should be read as a percentage above or below the national average of 100. For example, a value of 115.4 in the groceries column indicates that grocery prices are 15.4% higher than the national average. Small differences in the index numbers should not be interpreted as significant; Figures cover the Chicago IL urban area.
Source: The Council for Community and Economic Research, Cost of Living Index, 2024

Grocery Prices

Area[1]	T-Bone Steak ($/pound)	Frying Chicken ($/pound)	Whole Milk ($/half gal.)	Eggs ($/dozen)	Orange Juice ($/64 oz.)	Coffee ($/11.5 oz.)
City[2]	15.52	1.45	4.88	3.50	4.50	5.80
Avg.	15.42	1.55	4.69	3.25	4.41	5.46
Min.	14.50	1.16	4.43	2.75	4.00	4.85
Max.	17.56	2.89	5.49	4.78	5.54	7.89

Note: (1) Values for the local area are compared with the average, minimum and maximum values for all 276 areas in the Cost of Living Index; (2) Figures cover the Chicago IL urban area; **T-Bone Steak** (price per pound); **Frying Chicken** (price per pound, whole fryer); **Whole Milk** (half gallon carton); **Eggs** (price per dozen, Grade A, large); **Orange Juice** (64 oz. Tropicana or Florida Natural); **Coffee** (11.5 oz. can, vacuum-packed, Maxwell House, Hills Bros, or Folgers).
Source: The Council for Community and Economic Research, Cost of Living Index, 2024

Housing and Utility Costs

Area[1]	New Home Price ($)	Apartment Rent ($/month)	All Electric ($/month)	Part Electric ($/month)	Other Energy ($/month)	Telephone ($/month)
City[2]	566,384	3,240	-	113.94	70.31	212.43
Avg.	515,975	1,550	210.99	123.07	82.07	194.99
Min.	265,375	692	104.33	53.68	36.26	179.42
Max.	2,775,821	5,719	529.02	397.28	361.63	223.33

Note: (1) Values for the local area are compared with the average, minimum and maximum values for all 276 areas in the Cost of Living Index; (2) Figures cover the Chicago IL urban area; **New Home Price** (2,400 sf living area, 8,000 sf lot, in urban area with full utilities); **Apartment Rent** (950 sf 2 bedroom/1.5 or 2 bath, unfurnished, excluding all utilities except water); **All Electric** (average monthly cost for an all-electric home); **Part Electric** (average monthly cost for a part-electric home); **Other Energy** (average monthly cost for natural gas, fuel oil, coal, wood, and any other forms of energy except electricity); **Telephone** (price includes the base monthly rate plus taxes and fees for three lines of mobile phone service).
Source: The Council for Community and Economic Research, Cost of Living Index, 2024

Health Care, Transportation, and Other Costs

Area[1]	Doctor ($/visit)	Dentist ($/visit)	Optometrist ($/visit)	Gasoline ($/gallon)	Beauty Salon ($/visit)	Men's Shirt ($)
City[2]	179.67	126.00	113.83	3.55	62.23	34.52
Avg.	143.77	117.51	129.23	3.32	48.57	38.14
Min.	36.74	58.67	67.33	2.80	24.00	13.41
Max.	270.44	216.82	307.33	5.28	94.00	63.89

Note: (1) Values for the local area are compared with the average, minimum and maximum values for all 276 areas in the Cost of Living Index; (2) Figures cover the Chicago IL urban area; **Doctor** (general practitioners routine exam of an established patient); **Dentist** (adult teeth cleaning and periodic oral examination); **Optometrist** (full vision eye exam for established adult patient); **Gasoline** (one gallon regular unleaded, national brand, including all taxes, cash price at self-service pump if available); **Beauty Salon** (woman's shampoo, trim, and blow-dry); **Men's Shirt** (cotton/polyester dress shirt, pinpoint weave, long sleeves).
Source: The Council for Community and Economic Research, Cost of Living Index, 2024

HOUSING

Homeownership Rate

Area	2017 (%)	2018 (%)	2019 (%)	2020 (%)	2021 (%)	2022 (%)	2023 (%)	2024 (%)
MSA[1]	64.1	64.6	63.4	66.0	67.5	66.8	67.3	68.0
U.S.	63.9	64.4	64.6	66.6	65.5	65.8	65.9	65.6

Note: (1) Figures cover the Chicago-Naperville-Elgin, IL-IN Metropolitan Statistical Area
Source: U.S. Census Bureau, Housing Vacancies and Homeownership Annual Statistics: 2017-2024

House Price Index (HPI)

Area	National Ranking[2]	Quarterly Change (%)	One-Year Change (%)	Five-Year Change (%)	Since 1991Q1 (%)
MD[1]	70	0.05	6.77	43.67	208.59
U.S.[3]	—	1.43	4.51	57.13	327.82

Note: The HPI is a weighted repeat sales index. It measures average price changes in repeat sales or refinancings on the same properties. This information is obtained by reviewing repeat mortgage transactions on single-family properties whose mortgages have been purchased or securitized by Fannie Mae or Freddie Mac since January 1975; (1) Figures cover the Chicago-Naperville-Arlington Heights, IL Metropolitan Division; (2) Rankings are based on annual percentage change for all metro areas containing at least 15,000 transactions over the last 10 years and ranges from 1 to 241; (3) figures based on a weighted average of Census Division estimates using a seasonally adjusted, purchase-only index; all figures are for the period ending December 31, 2024
Source: Federal Housing Finance Agency, Change in FHFA Metropolitan Area House Price Indexes, All Transactions Index, 2024Q4

Home Value

Area	Under $100,000	$100,000 -$199,999	$200,000 -$299,999	$300,000 -$399,999	$400,000 -$499,999	$500,000 -$999,999	$1,000,000 or more	Median ($)
City	6.6	16.0	24.7	17.7	11.1	18.1	5.8	315,200
MSA[1]	6.2	16.9	26.5	19.9	12.0	15.0	3.5	301,900
U.S.	12.1	17.8	19.5	14.4	10.5	19.1	6.5	303,400

Note: Figures are percentages except for median and cover owner-occupied housing units; (1) Figures cover the Chicago-Naperville-Elgin, IL-IN Metropolitan Statistical Area
Source: U.S. Census Bureau, 2019-2023 American Community Survey 5-Year Estimates

Year Housing Structure Built

Area	2020 or Later	2010 -2019	2000 -2009	1990 -1999	1980 -1989	1970 -1979	1960 -1969	1950 -1959	1940 -1949	Before 1940	Median Year
City	0.4	5.1	8.2	4.9	5.0	7.9	9.7	11.6	8.2	39.1	1952
MSA[1]	0.5	4.6	11.5	10.7	9.2	13.9	11.6	12.4	5.5	20.1	1970
U.S.	1.2	8.9	13.6	12.8	13.0	14.4	10.0	9.7	4.5	11.9	1980

Note: Figures are percentages except for Median Year; Note: (1) Figures cover the Chicago-Naperville-Elgin, IL-IN Metropolitan Statistical Area
Source: U.S. Census Bureau, 2019-2023 American Community Survey 5-Year Estimates

Gross Monthly Rent

Area	Under $500	$500 -$999	$1,000 -$1,499	$1,500 -$1,999	$2,000 -$2,499	$2,500 -$2,999	$3,000 and up	Median ($)
City	7.2	17.6	32.2	20.1	11.6	5.4	5.9	1,380
MSA[1]	5.8	16.7	35.4	21.8	11.0	4.6	4.6	1,378
U.S.	6.5	22.3	29.5	20.2	10.8	4.8	5.9	1,348

Note: Figures are percentages except for median; Gross rent is the contract rent plus the estimated average monthly cost of utilities (electricity, gas, and water and sewer) and fuels (oil, coal, kerosene, wood, etc.) if these are paid by the renter (or paid for the renter by someone else); (1) Figures cover the Chicago-Naperville-Elgin, IL-IN Metropolitan Statistical Area
Source: U.S. Census Bureau, 2019-2023 American Community Survey 5-Year Estimates

HEALTH

Health Risk Factors

Category	MSA[1] (%)	U.S. (%)
Adults aged 18–64 who have any kind of health care coverage	89.8	90.8
Adults who reported being in good or better health	82.5	81.8
Adults who have been told they have high blood cholesterol	35.4	36.9
Adults who have been told they have high blood pressure	31.4	34.0
Adults who are current smokers	9.5	12.1
Adults who currently use e-cigarettes	5.1	7.7
Adults who currently use chewing tobacco, snuff, or snus	2.3	3.2
Adults who are heavy drinkers[2]	4.8	6.1
Adults who are binge drinkers[3]	17.6	15.2
Adults who are overweight (BMI 25.0 - 29.9)	36.0	34.4
Adults who are obese (BMI 30.0 - 99.8)	33.6	34.3
Adults who participated in any physical activities in the past month	78.9	75.8

Note: All figures are crude prevalence; (1) Figures cover the Chicago-Naperville-Elgin, IL-IN-WI Metropolitan Statistical Area; (2) Heavy drinkers are classified as adult men having more than 14 drinks per week and adult women having more than 7 drinks per week; (3) Binge drinkers are classified as males having five or more drinks on one occasion or females having four or more drinks on one occasion
Source: Centers for Disease Control and Prevention, Behaviorial Risk Factor Surveillance System, SMART: Selected Metropolitan Area Risk Trends, 2023

Acute and Chronic Health Conditions

Category	MSA[1] (%)	U.S. (%)
Adults who have ever been told they had a heart attack	2.7	4.2
Adults who have ever been told they have angina or coronary heart disease	2.7	4.0
Adults who have ever been told they had a stroke	2.5	3.3
Adults who have ever been told they have asthma	14.3	15.7
Adults who have ever been told they have arthritis	22.0	26.3
Adults who have ever been told they have diabetes[2]	11.0	11.5
Adults who have ever been told they had skin cancer	3.8	5.6
Adults who have ever been told they had any other types of cancer	7.0	8.4
Adults who have ever been told they have COPD	5.2	6.4
Adults who have ever been told they have kidney disease	3.2	3.7
Adults who have ever been told they have a form of depression	17.0	22.0

Note: All figures are crude prevalence; (1) Figures cover the Chicago-Naperville-Elgin, IL-IN-WI Metropolitan Statistical Area; (2) Figures do not include pregnancy-related, borderline, or pre-diabetes
Source: Centers for Disease Control and Prevention, Behavioral Risk Factor Surveillance System, SMART: Selected Metropolitan Area Risk Trends, 2023

Health Screening and Vaccination Rates

Category	MSA[1] (%)	U.S. (%)
Adults who have ever been tested for HIV	36.3	37.5
Adults who have had their blood cholesterol checked within the last five years	89.7	87.0
Adults aged 65+ who have had flu shot within the past year	70.1	63.4
Adults aged 65+ who have ever had a pneumonia vaccination	71.1	71.9

Note: All figures are crude prevalence; (1) Figures cover the Chicago-Naperville-Elgin, IL-IN-WI Metropolitan Statistical Area.
Source: Centers for Disease Control and Prevention, Behavioral Risk Factor Surveillance System, SMART: Selected Metropolitan Area Risk Trends, 2023

Disability Status

Category	MSA[1] (%)	U.S. (%)
Adults who reported being deaf	4.6	7.4
Are you blind or have serious difficulty seeing, even when wearing glasses?	4.2	4.9
Do you have difficulty doing errands alone?	6.4	7.8
Do you have difficulty dressing or bathing?	2.9	3.6
Do you have serious difficulty concentrating/remembering/making decisions?	10.9	13.7
Do you have serious difficulty walking or climbing stairs?	11.8	13.2

Note: All figures are crude prevalence; (1) Figures cover the Chicago-Naperville-Elgin, IL-IN-WI Metropolitan Statistical Area.
Source: Centers for Disease Control and Prevention, Behavioral Risk Factor Surveillance System, SMART: Selected Metropolitan Area Risk Trends, 2023

Mortality Rates for the Top 10 Causes of Death in the U.S.

ICD-10[a] Sub-Chapter	ICD-10[a] Code	Crude Mortality Rate[2] per 100,000 population	
		County[3]	U.S.
Malignant neoplasms	C00-C97	166.2	182.7
Ischaemic heart diseases	I20-I25	84.9	109.6
Provisional assignment of new diseases of uncertain etiology[1]	U00-U49	49.1	65.3
Other forms of heart disease	I30-I51	80.0	65.1
Other degenerative diseases of the nervous system	G30-G31	41.4	52.4
Other external causes of accidental injury	W00-X59	53.6	52.3
Cerebrovascular diseases	I60-I69	51.3	49.1
Chronic lower respiratory diseases	J40-J47	26.5	43.5
Hypertensive diseases	I10-I15	36.7	38.9
Organic, including symptomatic, mental disorders	F01-F09	29.7	33.9

Note: (a) ICD-10 = International Classification of Diseases 10th Revision; (1) Includes COVID-19, adverse effects to COVID-19 vaccines, SARS, and vaping-related disorders; (2) Crude mortality rates are a three-year average covering 2021-2023; (3) Figures cover Cook County.
Source: Centers for Disease Control and Prevention, National Center for Health Statistics. National Vital Statistics System, Mortality 2018-2023 on CDC WONDER Online Database

Mortality Rates for Selected Causes of Death

Cause of Death	ICD-10[a] Code	Crude Mortality Rate[1] per 100,000 population	
		County[2]	U.S.
Accidental poisoning and exposure to noxious substances	X40-X49	38.9	30.5
Alzheimer disease	G30	26.2	35.4
Assault	X85-Y09	17.9	7.3
COVID-19	U07.1	49.1	65.3
Diabetes mellitus	E10-E14	24.6	30.0
Diseases of the liver	K70-K76	15.1	20.8
Human immunodeficiency virus (HIV) disease	B20-B24	1.4	1.5
Influenza and pneumonia	J09-J18	14.3	13.4
Intentional self-harm	X60-X84	9.8	14.7
Malnutrition	E40-E46	4.4	6.0
Obesity and other hyperalimentation	E65-E68	2.3	3.1
Renal failure	N17-N19	20.0	16.4
Transport accidents	V01-V99	10.1	14.4

Note: (a) ICD-10 = International Classification of Diseases 10th Revision; (1) Crude mortality rates are a three-year average covering 2021-2023; (2) Figures cover Cook County; Data are suppressed when the data meet the criteria for confidentiality constraints; Crude mortality rates are flagged as unreliable when the rate would be calculated with a numerator of 20 or less.
Source: Centers for Disease Control and Prevention, National Center for Health Statistics. National Vital Statistics System, Mortality 2018-2023 on CDC WONDER Online Database

Health Insurance Coverage

Area	With Health Insurance	With Private Health Insurance	With Public Health Insurance	Without Health Insurance	Population Under Age 19 Without Health Insurance
City	90.2	61.6	35.8	9.8	4.0
MSA[1]	92.4	69.8	32.5	7.6	3.5
U.S.	91.4	67.3	36.3	8.6	5.4

Note: Figures are percentages that cover the civilian noninstitutionalized population; (1) Figures cover the Chicago-Naperville-Elgin, IL-IN Metropolitan Statistical Area
Source: U.S. Census Bureau, 2019-2023 American Community Survey 5-Year Estimates

Number of Medical Professionals

Area	MDs[3]	DOs[3,4]	Dentists	Podiatrists	Chiropractors	Optometrists
County[1] (number)	24,160	1,751	5,111	656	1,530	1,143
County[1] (rate[2])	472.9	34.3	100.5	12.9	30.1	22.5
U.S. (rate[2])	302.5	29.2	74.6	6.4	29.5	18.0

Note: Data as of 2023 unless noted; (1) Data covers Cook County; (2) Number of medical professionals per 100,000 population; (3) Data as of 2022 and includes all active, non-federal physicians; (4) Doctor of Osteopathic Medicine
Source: U.S. Department of Health and Human Services, Health Resources and Services Administration, Bureau of Health Professions, Area Resource File (ARF) 2023-2024

Best Hospitals

According to *U.S. News,* the Chicago-Naperville-Elgin, IL-IN metro area is home to 11 of the best hospitals in the U.S.: **Advocate Christ Medical Center** (4 adult specialties and 1 pediatric specialty); **Advocate Good Shepherd Hospital** (1 adult specialty); **Advocate Lutheran General Hospital** (1 adult specialty); **Endeavor Health NorthShore Hospitals** (4 adult specialties); **Midwest Orthopaedics at Rush University Medical Center** (11 adult specialties); **Northwestern Medicine Lake Forest Hospital** (3 adult specialties); **Northwestern Medicine Marianjoy Rehabilitation Hospital** (1 adult specialty); **Northwestern Medicine-Northwestern Memorial Hospital** (Honor Roll/11 adult specialties); **Rush University Medical Center** (Honor Roll/11 adult specialties); **Shirley Ryan AbilityLab** (1 adult specialty); **University of Chicago Medical Center** (10 adult specialties and 4 pediatric specialties). The hospitals listed were nationally ranked in at least one of 15 adult or 11 pediatric specialties. The number of specialties shown cover the parent hospital. Only 160 U.S. hospitals performed well enough to be nationally ranked in one or more specialties. Twenty hospitals in the U.S. made the Honor Roll. The Best Hospitals Honor Roll takes both the national rankings and the procedure and condition ratings into account. Hospitals received points if they were nationally ranked in one of the 15 adult specialties—the higher they ranked, the more points they got—and how many ratings of "high performing" they earned in the 20 procedures and conditions. *U.S. News Online,* "America's Best Hospitals 2024-25"

According to *U.S. News,* the Chicago-Naperville-Elgin, IL-IN metro area is home to five of the best children's hospitals in the U.S.: **Advocate Children's Hospital** (1 pediatric specialty); **Advocate Children's Heart Institute** (1 pediatric specialty); **Ann & Robert H. Lurie Children's Hospital of Chicago** (11 pediatric specialties); **Ann and Robert H. Lurie Children's Hospital-Prentice Women's Hospital** (11 pediatric specialties); **University of Chicago Comer Children's Hospital** (4 pediatric specialties). The hospitals listed were highly ranked in at least one of 11 pediatric special-

Chicago, Illinois 57

ties. One hundred five children's hospitals in the U.S. were nationally ranked in at least one specialty. Hospitals received points for being ranked in a specialty, and the 10 hospitals with the most points across the 11 specialties make up the Honor Roll. *U.S. News Online, "America's Best Children's Hospitals 2024-25"*

EDUCATION

Public School District Statistics

District Name	Schls	Pupils	Pupil/Teacher Ratio	Minority Pupils[1] (%)	Total Rev. per Pupil ($)	Total Exp. per Pupil ($)
City of Chicago SD 299	643	322,809	13.9	88.9	25,577	25,599

Note: Table includes school districts with 2,000 or more students; (1) Percentage of students that are not non-Hispanic white.
Source: U.S. Department of Education, National Center for Education Statistics, Common Core of Data, Local Education Agency (School District) Universe Survey: School Year 2023-2024; U.S. Department of Education, National Center for Education Statistics, Common Core of Data, School District Finance Survey (F-33): School Year 2021–22

Best High Schools

According to *U.S. News,* Chicago is home to seven of the top 500 high schools in the U.S.: **Payton College Preparatory High School** (#5); **Northside College Preparatory High School** (#35); **Young Magnet High School** (#52); **Jones College Prep High School** (#53); **Lane Technical High School** (#60); **Brooks College Prep Academy High School** (#305); **Hancock College Preparatory High School** (#327). Nearly 25,000 public, magnet and charter schools were ranked based on their performance on state assessments and how well they prepare students for college. *U.S. News & World Report, "Best High Schools 2024"*

Highest Level of Education

Area	Less than H.S.	H.S. Diploma	Some College, No Deg.	Associate Degree	Bachelor's Degree	Master's Degree	Prof. School Degree	Doctorate Degree
City	13.2	21.3	16.4	5.8	24.9	12.8	3.6	2.0
MSA[1]	10.3	23.2	18.4	7.3	24.4	12.1	2.8	1.6
U.S.	10.6	26.2	19.4	8.8	21.3	9.8	2.3	1.6

Note: Figures cover persons age 25 and over; (1) Figures cover the Chicago-Naperville-Elgin, IL-IN Metropolitan Statistical Area
Source: U.S. Census Bureau, 2019-2023 American Community Survey 5-Year Estimates

Educational Attainment by Race

Area	High School Graduate or Higher (%)					Bachelor's Degree or Higher (%)				
	Total	White	Black	Asian	Hisp.[2]	Total	White	Black	Asian	Hisp.[2]
City	86.8	93.4	87.4	88.3	71.9	43.3	61.9	25.2	65.0	20.4
MSA[1]	89.7	94.4	89.4	91.3	71.8	40.9	47.4	25.8	67.0	18.6
U.S.	89.4	92.9	88.1	88.0	72.5	35.0	37.7	24.7	57.0	19.9

Note: Figures shown cover persons 25 years old and over; (1) Figures cover the Chicago-Naperville-Elgin, IL-IN Metropolitan Statistical Area; (2) People of Hispanic origin can be of any race
Source: U.S. Census Bureau, 2019-2023 American Community Survey 5-Year Estimates

School Enrollment by Grade and Control

Area	Preschool (%)		Kindergarten (%)		Grades 1 - 4 (%)		Grades 5 - 8 (%)		Grades 9 - 12 (%)	
	Public	Private	Public	Private	Public	Private	Public	Private	Public	Private
City	56.4	43.6	81.6	18.4	82.8	17.2	83.6	16.4	85.2	14.8
MSA[1]	56.8	43.2	84.8	15.2	87.6	12.4	88.1	11.9	90.0	10.0
U.S.	58.7	41.3	85.2	14.8	87.2	12.8	87.9	12.1	89.0	11.0

Note: Figures shown cover persons 3 years old and over; (1) Figures cover the Chicago-Naperville-Elgin, IL-IN Metropolitan Statistical Area
Source: U.S. Census Bureau, 2019-2023 American Community Survey 5-Year Estimates

Higher Education

Four-Year Colleges			Two-Year Colleges			Medical Schools[1]	Law Schools[2]	Voc/Tech[3]
Public	Private Non-profit	Private For-profit	Public	Private Non-profit	Private For-profit			
7	56	7	21	2	9	7	7	64

Note: Figures cover institutions located within the Chicago-Naperville-Elgin, IL-IN Metropolitan Statistical Area and include main campuses only; (1) includes schools accredited by the Liaison Committee on Medical Education and the American Osteopathic Association's Commission on Osteopathic College Accreditation; (2) includes ABA-accredited schools, schools with provisional ABA accreditation, and state accredited schools; (3) includes all schools with programs that are less than 2 years.
Source: National Center for Education Statistics, Integrated Postsecondary Education System (IPEDS), 2023-24; Wikipedia, List of Medical Schools in the United States, accessed May 2, 2025; Wikipedia, List of Law Schools in the United States, accessed May 2, 2025

According to *U.S. News & World Report,* the Chicago-Naperville-Elgin, IL-IN metro area is home to six of the top 200 national universities in the U.S.: **Northwestern University** (#6 tie); **University of Chicago** (#11 tie); **University of Illinois—Chicago** (#80 tie); **Illinois Institute of Technology** (#105 tie); **Loyola University Chicago** (#132 tie); **DePaul University** (#165 tie). The indicators used to capture academic quality fall into a number of categories: assessment by administrators at peer institutions; retention of students; faculty resources; student selectivity; financial resources; alumni giving; high school counselor ratings of colleges; and graduation rate. *U.S. News & World Report,* "America's Best Colleges 2025"

According to *U.S. News & World Report,* the Chicago-Naperville-Elgin, IL-IN metro area is home to two of the top 100 liberal arts colleges in the U.S.: **Wheaton College (IL)** (#53 tie); **Lake Forest College** (#77 tie). The indicators used to capture academic quality fall into a number of categories: assessment by administrators at peer institutions; retention of students; faculty resources; student selectivity; financial resources; alumni giving; high school counselor ratings of colleges; and graduation rate. *U.S. News & World Report,* "America's Best Colleges 2025"

According to *U.S. News & World Report,* the Chicago-Naperville-Elgin, IL-IN metro area is home to three of the top 100 law schools in the U.S.: **University of Chicago** (#3); **Northwestern University (Pritzker) 1** (#10 tie); **Loyola University Chicago** (#79 tie). The rankings are based on a weighted average of 12 measures of quality: peer assessment score; assessment score by lawyers/judges; median LSAT scores; median undergrad GPA; acceptance rate; employment rates for graduates; placement success; bar passage rate; faculty resources; expenditures per student; student/faculty ratio; and library resources. *U.S. News & World Report,* "America's Best Graduate Schools, Law, 2025"

According to *U.S. News & World Report,* the Chicago-Naperville-Elgin, IL-IN metro area is home to two of the top medical schools for research in the U.S.: **Rush University** (Tier 2); **University of Illinois** (Tier 2). *U.S. News* placed medical and osteopathic schools into tiers based on their research productivity, faculty and admissions data. Each school's tier was derived from its overall score, calculated by summing the weighted normalized values generated across several factors of academic quality, outlined below. There are four tiers, with tier 1 medical schools as the highest-performing and tier 4 as the lowest-performing. Only tier 1 and 2 schools are shown. Because of the tier presentation, *U.S. News* calculated overall scores based on their percentile performance among all rated schools instead of dividing against the rescaled score of the No. 1-performing schools. Tier 1 included schools with overall scores of 85 to 99. The cutoffs for tiers 2 through 4 were schools scoring 50 to 84, 15 to 49 and 1 to 14, respectively. The rankings are based on a weighted average of the following measures of quality: total research activity; average research activity per faculty member; total NIH research grants at the medical school and its affiliated hospitals; average NIH research grants per faculty; median MCAT total score; median undergraduate GPA; acceptance rate; and faculty resources. *U.S. News & World Report,* "America's Best Graduate Schools, Medical, 2025"

According to *U.S. News & World Report,* the Chicago-Naperville-Elgin, IL-IN metro area is home to one of the top medical schools for primary care in the U.S.: **University of Illinois** (Tier 2). *U.S. News* placed medical and osteopathic schools into tiers based on their research productivity, faculty and admissions data. Each school's tier was derived from its overall score, calculated by summing the weighted normalized values generated across several factors of academic quality, outlined below. There are four tiers, with tier 1 medical schools as the highest-performing and tier 4 as the lowest-performing. Only tier 1 and 2 schools are shown. Because of the tier presentation, *U.S. News* calculated overall scores based on their percentile performance among all rated schools instead of dividing against the rescaled score of the No. 1-performing schools. Tier 1 included schools with overall scores of 85 to 99. The cutoffs for tiers 2 through 4 were schools scoring 50 to 84, 15 to 49 and 1 to 14, respectively. The rankings are based on a weighted average of the following measures of quality: graduates practicing in primary care specialties; graduates entering primary care residencies; median MCAT total score; median undergraduate GPA; acceptance rate; and faculty resources. *U.S. News & World Report,* "America's Best Graduate Schools, Medical, 2025"

According to *U.S. News & World Report,* the Chicago-Naperville-Elgin, IL-IN metro area is home to two of the top 75 business schools in the U.S.: **Northwestern University (Kellogg)** (#2 tie); **University of Chicago (Booth)** (#4). The rankings are based on a weighted average of the following nine measures: quality assessment; peer assessment; recruiter assessment; placement success; mean starting salary and bonus; student selectivity; mean GMAT and GRE scores; mean undergraduate GPA; and acceptance rate. *U.S. News & World Report,* "America's Best Graduate Schools, Business, 2025"

EMPLOYERS

Major Employers

Company Name	Industry
Abbott Laboratories	Pharmaceutical preparations
Accenture	Management consulting, technology services
Allstate	Fire, marine, & casualty insurance
Aon	Management consulting
Archdiocese of Chicago	Ecclesiastical jurisdiction
AT&T Illinois	Telecommunications
Boeing	Aerospace
Chicago Public Schools	Education
Chicago Transit Authority	Public transportation
City of Chicago	Municipal government
Cook County, Illinois	Government
Illinois Institute of Technology	Higher education
Jewel-Osco	Grocery
JPMorgan Chase	Financial services
Northwestern University	Higher education
United Airlines	Airline
United Parcel Service	Package delivery services
University of Chicago Medical Center	General medical & surgical hospitals
University of Illinois at Chicago	Higher education
Walgreens	Pharmacies

Note: Companies shown are located within the Chicago-Naperville-Elgin, IL-IN Metropolitan Statistical Area. Source: Chambers of Commerce; State Departments of Labor; Wikipedia

Best Companies to Work For

BDO USA; Hyatt Hotels Corporation; RSM US, headquartered in Chicago, are among "The 100 Best Companies to Work For." To pick the best companies, *Fortune* partnered with the Great Place to Work Institute. Using their proprietary Trust Index™ survey, the core of what creates great a workplace is measured—key behaviors that drive trust in management, connection with colleagues, and loyalty to the company. To be eligible for the *Fortune* 100 Best Companies to Work For list, employers must have 1,000 or more employees in the U.S. and cannot be a government agency. *Fortune, "The 100 Best Companies to Work For," 2025*

BDO USA; RSM US, headquartered in Chicago, are among "Fortune's Best Workplaces for Parents." To pick the best companies, *Fortune* partnered with the Great Place to Work Institute. To be considered for the list, companies must be Great Place To Work-Certified and have at least 50 responses from parents in the US. The survey enables employees to share confidential quantitative and qualitative feedback about their organization's culture by responding to 60 statements on a 5-point scale and answering two open-ended questions. Collectively, these statements describe a great employee experience, defined by high levels of trust, respect, credibility, fairness, pride, and camaraderie. In addition, companies provide organizational data like size, location, industry, demographics, roles, and levels; and provide information about parental leave, adoption, flexible schedule, childcare and dependent health care benefits. *Fortune, "Best Workplaces for Parents," 2024*

Basis Technologies; BDO USA; Hyatt Hotels Corporation; McDermott Will and Emery, headquartered in Chicago, are among "Fortune's Best Workplaces for Women." To pick the best companies, *Fortune* partnered with the Great Place to Work Institute. To be considered for the list, companies must be Great Place To Work-Certified. Companies must also employ at least 50 women, at least 20% of their non-executive managers must be female, and at least one executive must be female. To determine the Best Workplaces for Women, Great Place To Work measured the differences in women's survey responses to those of their peers and assesses the impact of demographics and roles on the quality and consistency of women's experiences. Great Place To Work also analyzed the gender balance of each workplace, how it compared to each company's industry, and patterns in representation as women rise from front-line positions to the board of directors. *Fortune, "Best Workplaces for Women," 2024*

Cambell Street Senior Living; MPAC Healthcare; Q-Centrix, headquartered in Chicago, are among "Best Workplaces in Health Care." To determine the Best Workplaces in Health Care list, Great Place To Work analyzed the survey responses of over 185,000 employees from Great Place To Work-Certified companies in the health care industry. Survey data analysis and company-provided datapoints are then factored into a combined score to compare and rank the companies that create the most consistently positive experience for all employees in this industry. *Fortune, "Best Workplaces in Health Care," 2024*

Revantage, headquartered in Chicago, is among "Best Workplaces in Real Estate." To determine the Best Workplaces in Real Estate list, Great Place To Work analyzed the survey responses of over 29,000 employees from Great Place To Work-Certified companies in the real estate industry. Survey data analysis and company-provided datapoints are then factored into a combined score to compare and rank the companies that create the most consistently positive experience for all employees in this industry. *Fortune, "Best Workplaces in Real Estate," 2024*

ADM; CME Group; Enova; Health Care Service Corporation; Motorola Solutions; Nitel, headquartered in Chicago, are among the "Best Places to Work in IT." To qualify, companies had to have a minimum of 100 total employees and five IT employees. The best places to work were selected based on DEI (diversity, equity, and inclusion) practices; IT turnover, promotions, and growth; IT retention and engagement programs; remote/hybrid working; benefits and perks (such as elder care and child care, flextime, and reimbursement for college tuition); and training and career development opportunities. *Computerworld, "Best Places to Work in IT," 2025*

PUBLIC SAFETY

Crime Rate

Area	Total Crime Rate	Violent Crime Rate				Property Crime Rate		
		Murder	Rape	Robbery	Aggrav. Assault	Burglary	Larceny-Theft	Motor Vehicle Theft
City	4,038.7	19.0	47.3	412.3	128.1	280.1	2,145.0	1,006.8
U.S.	2,290.9	5.7	38.0	66.5	264.1	250.7	1,347.2	318.7

Note: Figures are crimes per 100,000 population.
Source: FBI, Table 8, Offenses Known to Law Enforcement, by State by City, 2023

Hate Crimes

Area	Number of Quarters Reported	Number of Incidents per Bias Motivation					
		Race/Ethnicity/Ancestry	Religion	Sexual Orientation	Disability	Gender	Gender Identity
City[1]	4	99	41	44	1	0	7
U.S.	4	5,900	2,699	2,077	187	92	492

Note: (1) Figures include at least one incident reported with more than one bias motivation.
Source: Federal Bureau of Investigation, Hate Crime Statistics 2023

Identity Theft Consumer Reports

Area	Reports	Reports per 100,000 Population	Rank[2]
MSA[1]	37,486	401	22
U.S.	1,135,291	339	-

Note: (1) Figures cover the Chicago-Naperville-Elgin, IL-IN Metropolitan Statistical Area; (2) Rank ranges from 1 to 401 where 1 indicates greatest number of identity theft reports per 100,000 population
Source: Federal Trade Commission, Consumer Sentinel Network Data Book 2024

Fraud and Other Consumer Reports

Area	Reports	Reports per 100,000 Population	Rank[2]
MSA[1]	158,000	1,688	35
U.S.	5,360,641	1,601	-

Note: (1) Figures cover the Chicago-Naperville-Elgin, IL-IN Metropolitan Statistical Area; (2) Rank ranges from 1 to 401 where 1 indicates greatest number of fraud and other consumer reports per 100,000 population
Source: Federal Trade Commission, Consumer Sentinel Network Data Book 2024

POLITICS

2024 Presidential Election Results

Area	Trump (Rep.)	Harris (Dem.)	Stein (Green)	Kennedy (Ind.)	Oliver (Lib.)	Other
Cook County	28.1	69.6	0.9	1.2	0.1	0.2
U.S.	49.7	48.2	0.6	0.5	0.4	0.6

Note: Results are percentages and may not add to 100% due to rounding
Source: Dave Leip's Atlas of U.S. Presidential Elections

SPORTS

Professional Sports Teams

Team Name	League	Year Established
Chicago Bears	National Football League (NFL)	1921
Chicago Blackhawks	National Hockey League (NHL)	1926
Chicago Bulls	National Basketball Association (NBA)	1966
Chicago Cubs	Major League Baseball (MLB)	1874
Chicago Fire	Major League Soccer (MLS)	1997
Chicago White Sox	Major League Baseball (MLB)	1900

Note: Includes teams located in the Chicago-Naperville-Elgin, IL-IN Metropolitan Statistical Area.
Source: Wikipedia, Major Professional Sports Teams of the United States and Canada, May 1, 2025

CLIMATE

Average and Extreme Temperatures

Temperature	Jan	Feb	Mar	Apr	May	Jun	Jul	Aug	Sep	Oct	Nov	Dec	Yr.
Extreme High (°F)	65	71	88	91	93	104	102	100	99	91	78	71	104
Average High (°F)	29	33	45	59	70	79	84	82	75	63	48	34	59
Average Temp. (°F)	21	26	37	49	59	69	73	72	65	53	40	27	49
Average Low (°F)	13	17	28	39	48	57	63	62	54	42	32	19	40
Extreme Low (°F)	-27	-17	-8	7	24	36	40	41	28	17	1	-25	-27

Note: Figures cover the years 1958-1990
Source: National Climatic Data Center, International Station Meteorological Climate Summary, 9/96

Average Precipitation/Snowfall/Humidity

Precip./Humidity	Jan	Feb	Mar	Apr	May	Jun	Jul	Aug	Sep	Oct	Nov	Dec	Yr.
Avg. Precip. (in.)	1.6	1.4	2.7	3.6	3.3	3.7	3.7	4.1	3.7	2.4	2.8	2.3	35.4
Avg. Snowfall (in.)	11	8	7	2	Tr	0	0	0	0	1	2	9	39
Avg. Rel. Hum. 6am (%)	76	77	79	77	77	78	82	85	85	82	80	80	80
Avg. Rel. Hum. 3pm (%)	65	63	59	53	51	52	54	55	55	53	61	68	57

Note: Figures cover the years 1958-1990; Tr = Trace amounts (<0.05 in. of rain; <0.5 in. of snow)
Source: National Climatic Data Center, International Station Meteorological Climate Summary, 9/96

Weather Conditions

Temperature			Daytime Sky			Precipitation		
5°F & below	32°F & below	90°F & above	Clear	Partly cloudy	Cloudy	0.01 inch or more precip.	0.1 inch or more snow/ice	Thunder-storms
21	132	17	84	135	146	125	31	38

Note: Figures are average number of days per year and cover the years 1958-1990
Source: National Climatic Data Center, International Station Meteorological Climate Summary, 9/96

HAZARDOUS WASTE

Superfund Sites

The Chicago-Naperville-Schaumburg, IL metro division is home to 20 sites on the EPA's Superfund National Priorities List (NPL) or Superfund Alternative Approach (SAA) list: **Acme Steel Coke Plant** (Final NPL); **Amoco Chemicals (Joliet Landfill)** (Final NPL); **Ellsworth Industrial Park** (SAA); **Estech General Chemical Company** (Final NPL); **Joliet Army Ammunition Plant (Load-Assembly-Packing Area)** (Final NPL); **Joliet Army Ammunition Plant (Manufacturing Area)** (Final NPL); **Kerr-Mcgee (Kress Creek/West Branch Of Dupage River)** (Final NPL); **Kerr-Mcgee (Residential Areas)** (Final NPL); **Lake Calumet Cluster** (Final NPL); **Lenz Oil Service, Inc.** (Final NPL); **Peoples Gas Crawford Station Former Mgp** (SAA); **Peoples Gas Light & Coke - 22nd St** (SAA); **Peoples Gas Light & Coke - Division St** (SAA); **Peoples Gas Light & Coke North Station** (SAA); **Peoples Gas Light & Coke Willow St Station** (SAA); **Peoples Gas North Shore Avenue Station Former Mgp** (SAA); **Peoples Gas South Station Former Mgp** (SAA); **Peoples Gas Throop Street Former Mgp** (SAA); **Schroud Property** (Final NPL); **Woodstock Municipal Landfill** (Final NPL). The Superfund alternative approach uses the same investigation and cleanup process and standards that are used for sites listed on the National Priorities List. The SAA is an alternative to listing a site on the NPL; it is not an alternative to Superfund or the Superfund process. There are a total of 1,445 Superfund sites with a status of proposed or final on both lists in the United States. *U.S. Environmental Protection Agency, National Priorities List, May 1, 2025; U.S. Environmental Protection Agency, Superfund Alternative Approach Sites, May 1, 2025*

AIR QUALITY

Air Quality Trends: Ozone

	1990	1995	2000	2005	2010	2015	2020	2021	2022	2023
MSA[1]	0.074	0.094	0.073	0.084	0.070	0.066	0.076	0.071	0.070	0.081
U.S.	0.087	0.089	0.081	0.080	0.072	0.068	0.066	0.067	0.067	0.070

Note: (1) Data covers the Chicago-Naperville-Elgin, IL-IN Metropolitan Statistical Area. The values shown are the composite ozone concentration averages among trend sites based on the highest fourth daily maximum 8-hour concentration in parts per million. These trends are based on sites having an adequate record of monitoring data during the trend period. Data from exceptional events are included.
Source: U.S. Environmental Protection Agency, Air Quality Monitoring Information, "Air Quality Trends by City, 1990-2023"

Air Quality Index

Area	Percent of Days when Air Quality was...[2]					AQI Statistics[2]	
	Good	Moderate	Unhealthy for Sensitive Groups	Unhealthy	Very Unhealthy	Maximum	Median
MSA[1]	20.8	67.4	9.0	2.2	0.5	246	60

Note: (1) Data covers the Chicago-Naperville-Elgin, IL-IN Metropolitan Statistical Area; (2) Based on 365 days with AQI data in 2023. Air Quality Index (AQI) is an index for reporting daily air quality. EPA calculates the AQI for five major air pollutants regulated by the Clean Air Act: ground-level ozone, particle pollution (aka particulate matter), carbon monoxide, sulfur dioxide, and nitrogen dioxide. The AQI runs from 0 to 500. The higher the AQI value, the greater the level of air pollution and the greater the health concern. There are six AQI categories: "Good" AQI is between 0 and 50. Air quality is considered satisfactory; "Moderate" AQI is between 51 and 100. Air quality is acceptable; "Unhealthy for Sensitive Groups" When AQI values are between 101 and 150, members of sensitive groups may experience health effects; "Unhealthy" When AQI values are between 151 and 200 everyone may begin to experience health effects; "Very Unhealthy" AQI values between 201 and 300 trigger a health alert; "Hazardous" AQI values over 300 trigger warnings of emergency conditions (not shown).
Source: U.S. Environmental Protection Agency, Air Quality Index Report, 2023

Air Quality Index Pollutants

Area	Percent of Days when AQI Pollutant was...[2]					
	Carbon Monoxide	Nitrogen Dioxide	Ozone	Sulfur Dioxide	Particulate Matter 2.5	Particulate Matter 10
MSA[1]	0.0	1.6	27.1	(3)	67.7	3.6

Note: (1) Data covers the Chicago-Naperville-Elgin, IL-IN Metropolitan Statistical Area; (2) Based on 365 days with AQI data in 2023. The Air Quality Index (AQI) is an index for reporting daily air quality. EPA calculates the AQI for five major air pollutants regulated by the Clean Air Act: ground-level ozone, particle pollution (also known as particulate matter), carbon monoxide, sulfur dioxide, and nitrogen dioxide. The AQI runs from 0 to 500. The higher the AQI value, the greater the level of air pollution and the greater the health concern; (3) Sulfur dioxide is no longer included in this table because SO_2 concentrations tend to be very localized and not necessarily representative of broad geographical areas like counties and CBSAs.
Source: U.S. Environmental Protection Agency, Air Quality Index Report, 2023

Maximum Air Pollutant Concentrations: Particulate Matter, Ozone, CO and Lead

	Particulate Matter 10 (ug/m^3)	Particulate Matter 2.5 Wtd AM (ug/m^3)	Particulate Matter 2.5 24-Hr (ug/m^3)	Ozone (ppm)	Carbon Monoxide (ppm)	Lead (ug/m^3)
MSA[1] Level	137	11.2	31	0.086	1	0.1
NAAQS[2]	150	15	35	0.075	9	0.15
Met NAAQS[2]	Yes	Yes	Yes	No	Yes	Yes

Note: (1) Data covers the Chicago-Naperville-Elgin, IL-IN Metropolitan Statistical Area; Data from exceptional events are included; (2) National Ambient Air Quality Standards; ppm = parts per million; ug/m^3 = micrograms per cubic meter; n/a not available.
Concentrations: Particulate Matter 10 (coarse particulate)—highest second maximum 24-hour concentration; Particulate Matter 2.5 Wtd AM (fine particulate)—highest weighted annual mean concentration; Particulate Matter 2.5 24-Hour (fine particulate)—highest 98th percentile 24-hour concentration; Ozone—highest fourth daily maximum 8-hour concentration; Carbon Monoxide—highest second maximum non-overlapping 8-hour concentration; Lead—maximum running 3-month average
Source: U.S. Environmental Protection Agency, Air Quality Monitoring Information, "Air Quality Statistics by City, 2023"

Maximum Air Pollutant Concentrations: Nitrogen Dioxide and Sulfur Dioxide

	Nitrogen Dioxide AM (ppb)	Nitrogen Dioxide 1-Hr (ppb)	Sulfur Dioxide AM (ppb)	Sulfur Dioxide 1-Hr (ppb)	Sulfur Dioxide 24-Hr (ppb)
MSA[1] Level	17	54	n/a	79	n/a
NAAQS[2]	53	100	30	75	140
Met NAAQS[2]	Yes	Yes	n/a	No	n/a

Note: (1) Data covers the Chicago-Naperville-Elgin, IL-IN Metropolitan Statistical Area; Data from exceptional events are included; (2) National Ambient Air Quality Standards; ppm = parts per million; ug/m^3 = micrograms per cubic meter; n/a not available.
Concentrations: Nitrogen Dioxide AM—highest arithmetic mean concentration; Nitrogen Dioxide 1-Hr—highest 98th percentile 1-hour daily maximum concentration; Sulfur Dioxide AM—highest annual mean concentration; Sulfur Dioxide 1-Hr—highest 99th percentile 1-hour daily maximum concentration; Sulfur Dioxide 24-Hr—highest second maximum 24-hour concentration
Source: U.S. Environmental Protection Agency, Air Quality Monitoring Information, "Air Quality Statistics by City, 2023"

Columbia, Missouri

Background

Columbia is located in Boone County, in northern mid-Missouri. It's a college town teeming with bright young minds and technological breakthroughs. The founding of its colleges and university dovetails with the growth and founding of the city itself. A settlement called Smithton grew from the Smithton Land Company's 2,000-acre land purchase on the other side of Flat Branch, not far from where Lewis and Clark traveled during their 1803 explorations. In 1821 the settlement moved across the river and Columbia was established. Daniel Boone and sons ran a salt lick about forty miles away.

Six counties competed for the right to host Missouri's university when it was founded in 1838, the first public university west of the Mississippi River. Boone County won the honor by raising more than $118,000 in land, cash, and buildings. It was forced to repeat its largess decades later, when the academic hall burned down and talk turned to moving the university. The city responded by raising $50,000 to build Jesse Hall, now a local landmark.

Two other institutions of higher learning contribute to Columbia's focus on education. Stephens College, a private women's college, was founded in 1833, and Columbia College was founded as the Christian Female College in 1851, now with 30,000 students. This school was the first women's college west of the Mississippi chartered by a state legislature; it became co-ed in 1970.

Although these three institutions help to define the historic downtown area, it is the state's massive flagship University of Missouri—with a rare combination of law school, medical school, and veterinary school all on the same campus—that is Boone County's largest employer. As a major research institution "Mizzou," as it is known, conducts nearly $400 million in research and houses a nuclear research reactor on campus. It is the nation's largest supplier of radioisotopes for diagnosing and treating cancer and hosts interdisciplinary research in a range of scientific enterprises, including biofuels, energy logistics, energy policy, wind, biomass, and solar. The licensing of products invented by MU products by various companies is a huge market.

The MU Life Science Business Incubator encourages and supports business based on these technologies. The Indian pharma company Shasun collaborated to create a cancer treatment, Shasun-NBI. Also in the city is Discovery Ridge, with other research centers under development.

The campus also houses a well-regarded journalism school and IRE, Investigative Reporters and Editors, Inc. The Missouri School of Journalism was founded in 1908 by Walter Williams and was the first college or university to offer a journalism degree. The school operates KOMU-TV8, the local NBC affiliate; KBIA, the local NPR radio station; and the Columbia Missourian, a daily newspaper, offering journalism students real-life experience in broadcast and print news. The 1,250-acre campus is also home to a botanic garden and several cultural opportunities enjoyed by the community at large, including the Missouri Theatre Center for the Arts, Jesse Auditorium, and the university's Museum of Art and Architecture. The State Historical Society of Missouri also operates a research center at the university.

The county's other large employers include University Hospital and Clinics, Columbia Public Schools, Boone Hospital Center, the City of Columbia, and the U.S. Dept. of Veterans Affairs.

The city operates a regional airport, a short line railroad, and utilities for both water and electricity. Its Office of Cultural Affairs distributes art guides and a cultural newsletter, funds local arts organizations, and supports local arts opportunities. Columbia's "percent for art" program allows one percent of the cost of new city construction or renovation to be used for site-specific public art. The town is also full of galleries and various arts organizations.

Columbia has a humid continental climate marked by sharp seasonal contrasts in temperature. Precipitation tends to be greatest and most frequent in the latter half of spring, when severe weather is also most common. Snow averages about 16 inches per season, mostly from December to March.

Rankings

General Rankings

- In their annual survey, Livability.com looked at data for more than 2,000 mid-sized U.S. cities to assign a "Livability Score" for each. The top 100 scoring cities make up Livability's "Top 100 Best Places to Live in the U.S." in 2025. Columbia was placed among the top 100 of the customizable list. Criteria: housing and economy; cost of living; environment; education; health care options; transportation; safety; and community amenities. *Livability.com, "Top 100 Best Places to Live in the U.S. in 2025" April 15, 2025*

Business/Finance Rankings

- The Columbia metro area appeared on the Milken Institute "2025 Best Performing Cities" list. Rank: #75 out of 203 small metro areas (based on performance category). Criteria: job growth; wage growth; high-tech growth and impact; community resilience; housing affordability; household broadband access. *Milken Institute, "Best-Performing Cities 2025," January 14, 2025*

Real Estate Rankings

- Columbia was ranked #62 out of 176 metro areas in terms of cost of housing in 2024 by the National Association of Home Builders (#1 = most affordable). Criteria: the portion of an average family's income necessary to pay the mortgage on a median-priced home. *National Association of Home Builders®, NAHB-Wells Fargo Cost of Housing Index, 4th Quarter 2024*

Seniors/Retirement Rankings

- Columbia made the 2024 *Forbes* list of "25 Best Places to Retire." Criteria, focused on overall affordability as well as quality of life indicators, include: housing/living costs compared to the national average and taxes; air quality; crime rates; median home prices; risk associated with climate-change/natural hazards; availability of medical care; bikeability; walkability; healthy living. *Forbes.com, "The Best Places to Retire in 2024: Las Cruces and Other Unexpected Hot Spots," May 10, 2024*

Miscellaneous Rankings

- Columbia was selected as a 2024 Digital Cities Survey winner. The city ranked #2 in the mid-sized city (125,000 to 249,999 population) category. The survey examined and assessed how city governments are utilizing new technology and modernized applications to provide residents an array of contactless services and conveniences. Survey questions focused on ten initiatives: cybersecurity; citizen experience; disaster recovery; business intelligence; IT personnel retention; data governance; business automation; AI/machine learning; application modernization; and IT collaboration. *Center for Digital Government, "2024 Digital Cities Survey," November 5, 2024*

Business Environment

DEMOGRAPHICS

Population Growth

Area	1990 Census	2000 Census	2010 Census	2020 Census	2023 Estimate[2]	Population Growth 1990-2023 (%)
City	71,069	84,531	108,500	126,254	127,200	79.0
MSA[1]	122,010	145,666	172,786	210,864	212,850	74.5
U.S.	248,709,873	281,421,906	308,745,538	331,449,281	332,387,540	33.6

Note: (1) Figures cover the Columbia, MO Metropolitan Statistical Area; (2) 2019-2023 5-year ACS population estimate
Source: U.S. Census Bureau, 1990 Census, 2000 Census, 2010 Census, 2020 Census, 2019-2023 American Community Survey 5-Year Estimates

Race

Area	White Alone[2] (%)	Black Alone[2] (%)	Asian Alone[2] (%)	AIAN[3] Alone[2] (%)	NHOPI[4] Alone[2] (%)	Other Race Alone[2] (%)	Two or More Races (%)
City	74.3	12.1	6.1	0.1	0.1	1.2	6.1
MSA[1]	79.2	9.0	4.1	0.2	0.1	1.3	6.1
U.S.	63.4	12.4	5.8	0.9	0.2	6.6	10.7

Note: (1) Figures cover the Columbia, MO Metropolitan Statistical Area; (2) Alone is defined as not being in combination with one or more other races; (3) American Indian and Alaska Native; (4) Native Hawaiian and Other Pacific Islander
Source: U.S. Census Bureau, 2019-2023 American Community Survey 5-Year Estimates

Hispanic or Latino Origin

Area	Total (%)	Mexican (%)	Puerto Rican (%)	Cuban (%)	Other (%)
City	4.3	2.5	0.2	0.2	1.3
MSA[1]	4.1	2.7	0.2	0.1	1.0
U.S.	19.0	11.3	1.8	0.7	5.2

Note: Persons of Hispanic or Latino origin can be of any race; (1) Figures cover the Columbia, MO Metropolitan Statistical Area
Source: U.S. Census Bureau, 2019-2023 American Community Survey 5-Year Estimates

Age

Area	Under Age 5	Age 5–19	Age 20–34	Age 35–44	Age 45–54	Age 55–64	Age 65–74	Age 75–84	Age 85+	Median Age
City	5.4	20.7	32.4	12.5	8.9	8.8	6.4	3.3	1.6	29.2
MSA[1]	5.5	20.2	26.9	12.3	10.3	10.9	8.5	3.9	1.5	33.1
U.S.	5.7	19.1	20.2	13.1	12.3	12.8	10.0	4.9	1.9	38.7

Note: (1) Figures cover the Columbia, MO Metropolitan Statistical Area
Source: U.S. Census Bureau, 2019-2023 American Community Survey 5-Year Estimates

Disability by Age

Area	All Ages	Under 18 Years Old	18 to 64 Years Old	65 Years and Over
City	11.9	5.4	10.5	32.2
MSA[1]	13.0	5.3	11.5	31.9
U.S.	13.0	4.7	10.7	32.9

Note: Figures show percent of the civilian noninstitutionalized population that reported having a disability. Disability status is determined from six types of difficulty: vision, hearing, cognitive, ambulatory, self-care, and independent living. For children under 5 years old, hearing and vision difficulty are used to determine disability status. For children between the ages of 5 and 14, disability status is determined from hearing, vision, cognitive, ambulatory, and self-care difficulties. For people aged 15 years and older, they are considered to have a disability if they have difficulty with any one of the six difficulty types; Note: (1) Figures cover the Columbia, MO Metropolitan Statistical Area
Source: U.S. Census Bureau, 2019-2023 American Community Survey 5-Year Estimates

Ancestry

Area	German	Irish	English	American	Italian	Polish	French[2]	European	Scottish
City	24.0	12.1	13.5	5.1	3.4	1.6	1.9	2.2	2.3
MSA[1]	24.4	11.8	13.9	6.4	2.8	1.4	1.9	2.2	2.1
U.S.	12.6	9.4	9.1	5.5	4.9	2.6	2.0	1.6	1.6

Note: Figures are the percentage of the total population reporting a particular ancestry. The nine most commonly reported ancestries in the U.S. are shown. Figures include multiple ancestries (e.g. if a person reported being Irish and Italian, they were included in both columns); (1) Figures cover the Columbia, MO Metropolitan Statistical Area; (2) Excludes Basque
Source: U.S. Census Bureau, 2019-2023 American Community Survey 5-Year Estimates

Foreign-born Population

Area	Percent of Population Born in								
	Any Foreign Country	Asia	Mexico	Europe	Caribbean	Central America[2]	South America	Africa	Canada
City	8.1	4.9	0.6	0.4	0.3	0.2	0.5	1.1	0.0
MSA[1]	5.8	3.4	0.6	0.4	0.2	0.1	0.3	0.7	0.0
U.S.	13.9	4.3	3.3	1.4	1.4	1.2	1.2	0.8	0.2

Note: (1) Figures cover the Columbia, MO Metropolitan Statistical Area; (2) Excludes Mexico.
Source: U.S. Census Bureau, 2019-2023 American Community Survey 5-Year Estimates

Household Size

Area	Persons in Household (%)							Average Household Size
	One	Two	Three	Four	Five	Six	Seven or More	
City	34.5	33.8	13.4	12.2	4.6	1.0	0.5	2.29
MSA[1]	31.1	36.1	13.7	12.2	5.0	1.2	0.8	2.37
U.S.	28.5	33.8	15.4	12.7	5.9	2.3	1.4	2.54

Note: (1) Figures cover the Columbia, MO Metropolitan Statistical Area
Source: U.S. Census Bureau, 2019-2023 American Community Survey 5-Year Estimates

Household Relationships

Area	Householder	Opposite-sex Spouse	Same-sex Spouse	Opposite-sex Unmarried Partner	Same-sex Unmarried Partner	Child[2]	Grand-child	Other Relatives	Non-relatives
City	40.5	14.1	0.2	2.8	0.2	22.4	1.0	2.5	7.8
MSA[1]	39.8	16.5	0.2	2.8	0.2	24.9	1.4	2.5	5.7
U.S.	38.3	17.5	0.2	2.5	0.2	28.3	2.4	4.8	3.4

Note: Figures are percent of the total population; (1) Figures cover the Columbia, MO Metropolitan Statistical Area; (2) Includes biological, adopted, and stepchildren of the householder
Source: U.S. Census Bureau, 2020 Census

Gender

Area	Males	Females	Males per 100 Females
City	61,139	66,061	92.5
MSA[1]	103,590	109,260	94.8
U.S.	164,545,087	167,842,453	98.0

Note: (1) Figures cover the Columbia, MO Metropolitan Statistical Area
Source: U.S. Census Bureau, 2019-2023 American Community Survey 5-Year Estimates

Marital Status

Area	Never Married	Now Married[2]	Separated	Widowed	Divorced
City	49.8	37.9	1.0	3.4	8.0
MSA[1]	41.1	44.4	1.1	4.3	9.2
U.S.	34.1	47.9	1.7	5.6	10.7

Note: Figures are percentages and cover the population 15 years of age and older; (1) Figures cover the Columbia, MO Metropolitan Statistical Area; (2) Excludes separated
Source: U.S. Census Bureau, 2019-2023 American Community Survey 5-Year Estimates

Religious Groups by Family

Area	Catholic	Baptist	Methodist	LDS[2]	Pentecostal	Lutheran	Islam	Adventist	Other
MSA[1]	7.1	9.0	3.5	1.7	1.1	1.6	1.4	1.2	12.4
U.S.	18.7	7.3	3.0	2.0	1.8	1.7	1.3	1.3	11.6

Note: Figures are the number of adherents as a percentage of the total population and cover the eight largest religious groups in the U.S; (1) Figures cover the Columbia, MO Metropolitan Statistical Area; (2) Church of Jesus Christ of Latter-day Saints
Sources: 2020 U.S. Religion Census, Association of Statisticians of American Religious Bodies; The Association of Religion Data Archives (ARDA)

Religious Groups by Tradition

Area	Catholic	Evangelical Protestant	Mainline Protestant	Black Protestant	Islam	Judaism	Hinduism	Orthodox	Buddhism
MSA[1]	7.1	19.4	6.3	1.9	1.4	0.2	0.1	0.1	<0.1
U.S.	18.7	16.5	5.2	2.3	1.3	0.6	0.4	0.4	0.3

Note: Figures are the number of adherents as a percentage of the total population; (1) Figures cover the Columbia, MO Metropolitan Statistical Area
Sources: 2020 U.S. Religion Census, Association of Statisticians of American Religious Bodies; The Association of Religion Data Archives (ARDA)

ECONOMY

Real Gross Domestic Product (GDP)

Area	2017	2018	2019	2020	2021	2022	2023	Rank[3]
MSA[1]	10.0	10.0	10.4	10.1	10.6	10.7	11.0	213
U.S.[2]	17,619.1	18,160.7	18,642.5	18,238.9	19,387.6	19,896.6	20,436.3	—

Note: Figures are in billions of chained 2017 dollars; (1) Figures cover the Columbia, MO Metropolitan Statistical Area; (2) Figures cover real GDP within metropolitan areas; (3) Rank is based on 2023 data and ranges from 1 to 384
Source: U.S. Bureau of Economic Analysis

Economic Growth

Area	2014	2015	2016	2017	2018	2019	2020	2021	2022	2023
MSA[1]	0.4	2.1	0.4	2.4	0.6	4.0	-2.9	5.1	0.5	2.8
U.S.[2]	2.6	3.2	2.0	2.7	3.1	2.7	-2.2	6.3	2.6	2.7

Note: Figures are real gross domestic product growth rates and represent percent change from preceding period; (1) Figures cover the Columbia, MO Metropolitan Statistical Area; (2) Figures are the average growth rates within metropolitan areas
Source: U.S. Bureau of Economic Analysis

Metropolitan Area Exports

Area	2018	2019	2020	2021	2022	2023	Rank[2]
MSA[1]	238.6	291.4	256.2	335.4	368.7	474.1	230
U.S.	1,664,056.1	1,645,173.7	1,431,406.6	1,753,941.4	2,062,937.4	2,019,160.5	—

Note: Figures are in millions of dollars; (1) Figures cover the Columbia, MO Metropolitan Statistical Area; (2) Rank is based on 2023 data and ranges from 1 to 386
Source: U.S. Department of Commerce, International Trade Administration, Office of Trade and Economic Analysis, Industry and Analysis, Exports by Metropolitan Area, data extracted April 2, 2025

Building Permits

Area	Single-Family			Multi-Family			Total		
	2023	2024	Pct. Chg.	2023	2024	Pct. Chg.	2023	2024	Pct. Chg.
City	314	461	46.8	56	549	880.4	370	1,010	173.0
MSA[1]	609	763	25.3	72	568	688.9	681	1,331	95.4
U.S.	920,000	981,900	6.7	591,100	496,100	-16.1	1,511,100	1,478,000	-2.2

Note: (1) Figures cover the Columbia, MO Metropolitan Statistical Area; Figures represent new, privately-owned housing units authorized (unadjusted data)
Source: U.S. Census Bureau, Building Permits Survey (BPS), 2023, 2024

Bankruptcy Filings

Area	Business Filings			Nonbusiness Filings		
	2023	2024	% Chg.	2023	2024	% Chg.
Boone County	3	5	66.7	191	201	5.2
U.S.	18,926	23,107	22.1	434,064	494,201	13.9

Note: Business filings include Chapter 7, Chapter 9, Chapter 11, Chapter 12, Chapter 13, Chapter 15, and Section 304; Nonbusiness filings include Chapter 7, Chapter 11, and Chapter 13
Source: Administrative Office of the U.S. Courts, Business and Nonbusiness Bankruptcy, County Cases Commenced by Chapter of the Bankruptcy Code, During the 12-Month Period Ending December 31, 2023 and Business and Nonbusiness Bankruptcy, County Cases Commenced by Chapter of the Bankruptcy Code, During the 12-Month Period Ending December 31, 2024

Housing Vacancy Rates

Area	Gross Vacancy Rate[3] (%)			Year-Round Vacancy Rate[4] (%)			Rental Vacancy Rate[5] (%)			Homeowner Vacancy Rate[6] (%)		
	2022	2023	2024	2022	2023	2024	2022	2023	2024	2022	2023	2024
MSA[1]	n/a	n/a	n/a	n/a	n/a	n/a	n/a	n/a	n/a	n/a	n/a	n/a
U.S.[2]	9.1	9.0	9.1	7.5	7.5	7.6	5.7	6.5	6.8	0.8	0.8	1.0

Note: (1) Figures cover the Columbia, MO Metropolitan Statistical Area; (2) Figures cover the 75 largest Metropolitan Statistical Areas; (3) The percentage of the total housing inventory that is vacant; (4) The percentage of the housing inventory (excluding seasonal units) that is year-round vacant; (5) The percentage of rental inventory that is vacant for rent; (6) The percentage of homeowner inventory that is vacant for sale; n/a not available
Source: U.S. Census Bureau, Housing Vacancies and Homeownership Annual Statistics: 2022, 2023, 2024

INCOME

Income

Area	Per Capita ($)	Median Household ($)	Average Household ($)
City	37,359	64,488	91,425
MSA[1]	37,799	69,463	93,435
U.S.	43,289	78,538	110,491

Note: (1) Figures cover the Columbia, MO Metropolitan Statistical Area
Source: U.S. Census Bureau, 2019-2023 American Community Survey 5-Year Estimates

Household Income Distribution

Area	Percent of Households Earning							
	Under $15,000	$15,000 -$24,999	$25,000 -$34,999	$35,000 -$49,999	$50,000 -$74,999	$75,000 -$99,999	$100,000 -$149,999	$150,000 and up
City	12.4	8.3	8.5	10.8	17.1	11.8	14.3	17.0
MSA[1]	10.3	7.4	7.6	11.1	17.3	13.3	16.6	16.2
U.S.	8.5	6.6	6.8	10.4	15.7	12.7	17.4	21.9

Note: (1) Figures cover the Columbia, MO Metropolitan Statistical Area
Source: U.S. Census Bureau, 2019-2023 American Community Survey 5-Year Estimates

Poverty Rate

Area	All Ages	Under 18 Years Old	18 to 64 Years Old	65 Years and Over
City	20.0	13.4	23.5	10.7
MSA[1]	16.5	14.6	18.8	9.0
U.S.	12.4	16.3	11.6	10.4

Note: Figures are percentage of people whose income during the past 12 months was below the poverty level; (1) Figures cover the Columbia, MO Metropolitan Statistical Area
Source: U.S. Census Bureau, 2019-2023 American Community Survey 5-Year Estimates

EMPLOYMENT

Labor Force and Employment

Area	Civilian Labor Force			Workers Employed		
	Dec. 2023	Dec. 2024	% Chg.	Dec. 2023	Dec. 2024	% Chg.
City	69,206	70,699	2.2	67,566	68,998	2.1
MSA[1]	113,118	115,648	2.2	110,484	112,817	2.1
U.S.	166,661,000	167,746,000	0.7	160,754,000	161,294,000	0.3

Note: Data is not seasonally adjusted and covers workers 16 years of age and older; (1) Figures cover the Columbia, MO Metropolitan Statistical Area
Source: Bureau of Labor Statistics, Local Area Unemployment Statistics

Unemployment Rate

Area	2024											
	Jan.	Feb.	Mar.	Apr.	May	Jun.	Jul.	Aug.	Sep.	Oct.	Nov.	Dec.
City	3.1	2.9	3.2	2.7	3.3	3.6	3.8	3.4	2.4	2.7	2.8	2.4
MSA[1]	3.2	3.0	3.2	2.7	3.2	3.5	3.7	3.3	2.4	2.7	2.7	2.4
U.S.	4.1	4.2	3.9	3.5	3.7	4.3	4.5	4.4	3.9	3.9	4.0	3.8

Note: Data is not seasonally adjusted and covers workers 16 years of age and older; (1) Figures cover the Columbia, MO Metropolitan Statistical Area
Source: Bureau of Labor Statistics, Local Area Unemployment Statistics

Average Wages

Occupation	$/Hr.	Occupation	$/Hr.
Accountants and Auditors	35.97	Maintenance and Repair Workers	22.42
Automotive Mechanics	23.99	Marketing Managers	59.28
Bookkeepers	23.55	Network and Computer Systems Admin.	43.70
Carpenters	26.93	Nurses, Licensed Practical	28.34
Cashiers	14.42	Nurses, Registered	39.72
Computer Programmers	n/a	Nursing Assistants	18.73
Computer Systems Analysts	44.38	Office Clerks, General	20.78
Computer User Support Specialists	27.69	Physical Therapists	43.86
Construction Laborers	28.79	Physicians	149.57
Cooks, Restaurant	16.00	Plumbers, Pipefitters and Steamfitters	30.64
Customer Service Representatives	20.94	Police and Sheriff's Patrol Officers	28.96
Dentists	105.42	Postal Service Mail Carriers	28.47
Electricians	30.08	Real Estate Sales Agents	24.50
Engineers, Electrical	n/a	Retail Salespersons	16.22
Fast Food and Counter Workers	14.25	Sales Representatives, Technical/Scientific	46.86
Financial Managers	67.68	Secretaries, Exc. Legal/Medical/Executive	20.78
First-Line Supervisors of Office Workers	31.10	Security Guards	18.70
General and Operations Managers	46.12	Surgeons	n/a
Hairdressers/Cosmetologists	20.40	Teacher Assistants, Exc. Postsecondary[1]	15.25
Home Health and Personal Care Aides	17.18	Teachers, Secondary School, Exc. Sp. Ed.[1]	26.79
Janitors and Cleaners	16.98	Telemarketers	n/a
Landscaping/Groundskeeping Workers	17.79	Truck Drivers, Heavy/Tractor-Trailer	26.84
Lawyers	71.41	Truck Drivers, Light/Delivery Services	22.33
Maids and Housekeeping Cleaners	15.77	Waiters and Waitresses	15.03

Note: Wage data covers the Columbia, MO Metropolitan Statistical Area; (1) Hourly wages were calculated from annual wage data based on a 40 hour work week
Source: Bureau of Labor Statistics, Metro Area Occupational Employment & Wage Estimates, May 2024

Employment by Industry

Sector	MSA[1] Number of Employees	MSA[1] Percent of Total	U.S. Percent of Total
Construction	4,200	3.5	5.1
Financial Activities	9,200	7.6	5.8
Government	37,900	31.5	14.9
Information	1,300	1.1	1.9
Leisure and Hospitality	12,700	10.6	10.4
Manufacturing	5,600	4.7	8.0
Mining and Logging	100	0.1	0.4
Other Services	3,400	2.8	3.7
Private Education and Health Services	16,700	13.9	16.9
Professional and Business Services	10,900	9.1	14.2
Retail Trade	12,200	10.1	10.0
Transportation, Warehousing, and Utilities	3,100	2.6	4.8
Wholesale Trade	3,000	2.5	3.9

Note: Figures are non-farm employment as of December 2024. Figures are not seasonally adjusted and include workers 16 years of age and older; (1) Figures cover the Columbia, MO Metropolitan Statistical Area
Source: Bureau of Labor Statistics, Current Employment Statistics, Employment, Hours, and Earnings

Employment by Occupation

Occupation Classification	City (%)	MSA[1] (%)	U.S. (%)
Management, Business, Science, and Arts	51.5	48.1	42.0
Natural Resources, Construction, and Maintenance	4.4	7.3	8.6
Production, Transportation, and Material Moving	8.1	9.8	13.0
Sales and Office	17.8	18.3	19.9
Service	18.3	16.6	16.5

Note: Figures cover employed civilians 16 years of age and older; (1) Figures cover the Columbia, MO Metropolitan Statistical Area
Source: U.S. Census Bureau, 2019-2023 American Community Survey 5-Year Estimates

Occupations with Greatest Projected Employment Growth: 2022 – 2032

Occupation[1]	2022 Employment	2032 Projected Employment	Numeric Employment Change	Percent Employment Change
Home Health and Personal Care Aides	79,380	91,510	12,130	15.3
Registered Nurses	76,960	84,580	7,620	9.9
Cooks, Restaurant	31,980	39,310	7,330	22.9
General and Operations Managers	97,060	102,780	5,720	5.9
Software Developers	19,530	24,690	5,160	26.4
Stockers and Order Fillers	57,940	62,820	4,880	8.4
Laborers and Freight, Stock, and Material Movers, Hand	43,160	46,620	3,460	8.0
Nurse Practitioners	7,520	10,670	3,150	41.9
Medical and Health Services Managers	9,950	13,050	3,100	31.2
Maintenance and Repair Workers, General	32,440	34,810	2,370	7.3

Note: Projections cover Missouri; (1) Sorted by numeric employment change
Source: www.projectionscentral.org, State Occupational Projections, 2022–2032 Long-Term Projections

Fastest-Growing Occupations: 2022 – 2032

Occupation[1]	2022 Employment	2032 Projected Employment	Numeric Employment Change	Percent Employment Change
Nurse Practitioners	7,520	10,670	3,150	41.9
Data Scientists	4,320	5,950	1,630	37.7
Information Security Analysts (SOC 2018)	3,470	4,640	1,170	33.7
Computer and Information Research Scientists (SOC 2018)	540	710	170	31.5
Medical and Health Services Managers	9,950	13,050	3,100	31.2
Physical Therapist Assistants	2,520	3,240	720	28.6
Occupational Therapy Assistants	1,160	1,490	330	28.4
Veterinary Technologists and Technicians	2,080	2,640	560	26.9
Speech-Language Pathologists	4,030	5,100	1,070	26.6
Software Developers	19,530	24,690	5,160	26.4

Note: Projections cover Missouri; (1) Sorted by percent employment change and excludes occupations with numeric employment change less than 50
Source: www.projectionscentral.org, State Occupational Projections, 2022–2032 Long-Term Projections

Columbia, Missouri

CITY FINANCES

City Government Finances

Component	2022 ($000)	2022 ($ per capita)
Total Revenues	386,580	3,098
Total Expenditures	359,507	2,881
Debt Outstanding	297,448	2,384

Source: U.S. Census Bureau, State & Local Government Finances 2022

City Government Revenue by Source

Source	2022 ($000)	2022 ($ per capita)	2022 (%)
General Revenue			
From Federal Government	25,810	207	6.7
From State Government	6,786	54	1.8
From Local Governments	26,649	214	6.9
Taxes			
Property	9,147	73	2.4
Sales and Gross Receipts	61,682	494	16.0
Personal Income	0	0	0.0
Corporate Income	0	0	0.0
Motor Vehicle License	1,714	14	0.4
Other Taxes	2,352	19	0.6
Current Charges	68,464	549	17.7
Liquor Store	0	0	0.0
Utility	164,663	1,320	42.6

Source: U.S. Census Bureau, State & Local Government Finances 2022

City Government Expenditures by Function

Function	2022 ($000)	2022 ($ per capita)	2022 (%)
General Direct Expenditures			
Air Transportation	19,447	155	5.4
Corrections	0	0	0.0
Education	0	0	0.0
Employment Security Administration	0	0	0.0
Financial Administration	4,007	32	1.1
Fire Protection	14,857	119	4.1
General Public Buildings	143	1	0.0
Governmental Administration, Other	6,763	54	1.9
Health	8,458	67	2.4
Highways	23,657	189	6.6
Hospitals	0	0	0.0
Housing and Community Development	2,246	18	0.6
Interest on General Debt	3,176	25	0.9
Judicial and Legal	2,353	18	0.7
Libraries	0	0	0.0
Parking	2,972	23	0.8
Parks and Recreation	15,265	122	4.2
Police Protection	20,690	165	5.8
Public Welfare	1,054	8	0.3
Sewerage	15,684	125	4.4
Solid Waste Management	22,516	180	6.3
Veterans' Services	0	0	0.0
Liquor Store	0	0	0.0
Utility	155,526	1,246	43.3

Source: U.S. Census Bureau, State & Local Government Finances 2022

TAXES

State Corporate Income Tax Rates

State	Tax Rate (%)	Income Brackets ($)	Num. of Brackets	Financial Institution Tax Rate (%)[a]	Federal Income Tax Ded.
Missouri	4.0	Flat rate	1	4.48	Yes (h)

Note: Tax rates for tax year 2024; (a) Rates listed are the corporate income tax rate applied to financial institutions or excise taxes based on income. Some states have other taxes based upon the value of deposits or shares; (h) 50% of the federal income tax is deductible.
Source: Federation of Tax Administrators, State Corporate Income Tax Rates, January 1, 2025

State Individual Income Tax Rates

State	Tax Rate (%)	Income Brackets ($)	Personal Exemptions ($)			Standard Ded. ($)	
			Single	Married	Depend.	Single	Married
Missouri (a)	0.0 - 4.8	1,207 - 8,449	(d)	(d)	(d)	14,600	29,200 (d)

Note: Tax rates for tax year 2024; Local- and county-level taxes are not included; The deduction for federal SALT deductions is limited to $5,000 for individuals and $10,000 for joint returns in Missouri and Montana, and to $7,800 for all filers in Oregon; (a) 16 states have statutory provision for automatically adjusting to the rate of inflation the dollar values of the income tax brackets, standard deductions, and/or personal exemptions. Oregon does not index the income brackets for $125,000 and over See: INFL and SPEC above; (d) These states use the personal exemption/standard deduction amounts provided in the federal Internal Revenue Code. Montana personal exemption subject to repeal under Section 15-30-2114.
Source: Federation of Tax Administrators, State Individual Income Tax Rates, January 1, 2025

Various State Sales and Excise Tax Rates

State	State Sales Tax (%)	Gasoline[1] ($/gal.)	Cigarette[2] ($/pack)	Spirits[3] ($/gal.)	Wine[4] ($/gal.)	Beer[5] ($/gal.)	Recreational Marijuana (%)
Missouri	4.225	0.27	0.17	2.00	0.42	0.06	(m)

Note: All tax rates as of January 1, 2025; (1) The American Petroleum Institute has developed a methodology for determining the average tax rate on a gallon of fuel. Rates may include any of the following: excise taxes, environmental fees, storage tank fees, other fees or taxes, general sales tax, and local taxes; (2) The federal excise tax of $1.0066 per pack and local taxes are not included; (3) Rates are those applicable to off-premise sales of 40% alcohol by volume (a.b.v.) distilled spirits in 750ml containers. Local excise taxes are excluded; (4) Rates are those applicable to off-premise sales of 11% a.b.v. non-carbonated wine in 750ml containers; (5) Rates are those applicable to off-premise sales of 4.7% a.b.v. beer in 12 ounce containers; (m) 6% excise tax (retail price)
Source: Tax Foundation, 2025 Facts & Figures: How Does Your State Compare?

State Tax Competitiveness Index

State	Overall Rank	Corporate Tax Rank	Individual Income Tax Rank	Sales Tax Rank	Property Tax Rank	Unemployment Insurance Tax Rank
Missouri	13	4	20	24	11	5

Note: The Tax Foundation's State Tax Competitiveness Index enables policymakers, taxpayers, and business leaders to gauge how their states' tax systems compare. A rank of 1 is best, 50 is worst. Rankings do not average to the total. States without a tax rank equally as 1. DC's scores and rankings do not affect other states. The report shows tax systems as of July 1, 2024 (the beginning of Fiscal Year 2025).
Source: Tax Foundation, State Tax Competitiveness Index 2025

TRANSPORTATION

Means of Transportation to Work

Area	Car/Truck/Van		Public Transportation			Bicycle	Walked	Other Means	Worked at Home
	Drove Alone	Car-pooled	Bus	Subway	Railroad				
City	74.1	7.6	1.1	0.0	0.0	1.0	5.6	0.9	9.6
MSA[1]	76.0	8.8	0.7	0.0	0.0	0.7	3.8	1.0	8.9
U.S.	70.2	8.5	1.7	1.3	0.4	0.4	2.4	1.6	13.5

Note: Figures are percentages and cover workers 16 years of age and older; (1) Figures cover the Columbia, MO Metropolitan Statistical Area
Source: U.S. Census Bureau, 2019-2023 American Community Survey 5-Year Estimates

Travel Time to Work

Area	Less Than 10 Minutes	10 to 19 Minutes	20 to 29 Minutes	30 to 44 Minutes	45 to 59 Minutes	60 to 89 Minutes	90 Minutes or More
City	19.5	54.4	14.3	7.2	2.1	1.2	1.3
MSA[1]	17.1	44.0	20.2	11.8	3.4	1.7	1.8
U.S.	12.6	28.6	21.2	20.8	8.1	6.0	2.8

Note: Note: Figures are percentages and include workers 16 years old and over; (1) Figures cover the Columbia, MO Metropolitan Statistical Area
Source: U.S. Census Bureau, 2019-2023 American Community Survey 5-Year Estimates

Key Congestion Measures

Measure	2000	2010	2015	2020	2022
Annual Hours of Delay, Total (000)	n/a	n/a	2,665	2,006	3,429
Annual Hours of Delay, Per Auto Commuter	n/a	n/a	19	14	25
Annual Congestion Cost, Per Auto Commuter ($)	n/a	n/a	447	375	623

Note: n/a not available
Source: Texas A&M Transportation Institute, 2023 Urban Mobility Report

Freeway Travel Time Index

Measure	1985	1990	1995	2000	2005	2010	2015	2020	2022
Urban Area Index[1]	n/a	n/a	n/a	n/a	n/a	n/a	1.10	1.07	1.13
Urban Area Rank[1,2]	n/a	n/a	n/a	n/a	n/a	n/a	n/a	n/a	n/a

Note: Freeway Travel Time Index—the ratio of travel time in the peak period to the travel time at free-flow conditions. For example, a value of 1.30 indicates a 20-minute free-flow trip takes 26 minutes in the peak (20 minutes x 1.30 = 26 minutes); (1) Covers the Columbia MO urban area; (2) Rank is based on 101 larger urban areas (#1 = highest travel time index); n/a not available
Source: Texas A&M Transportation Institute, 2023 Urban Mobility Report

Public Transportation

Agency Name / Mode of Transportation	Vehicles Operated in Maximum Service[1]	Annual Unlinked Passenger Trips[2] (in thous.)	Annual Passenger Miles[3] (in thous.)
Columbia Transit (CT)			
Bus (directly operated)	12	854.4	2,136.0
Demand Response (directly operated)	15	56.7	310.3

Note: (1) Number of revenue vehicles operated by the given mode and type of service to meet the annual maximum service requirement. This is the revenue vehicle count during the peak season of the year; on the week and day that maximum service is provided. Vehicles operated in maximum service (VOMS) exclude atypical days and one-time special events; (2) Number of passengers who boarded public transportation vehicles. Passengers are counted each time they board a vehicle no matter how many vehicles they use to travel from their origin to their destination. (3) Sum of the distances ridden by all passengers during the entire fiscal year.
Source: Federal Transit Administration, National Transit Database, 2023

Air Transportation

Airport Name and Code / Type of Service	Passenger Airlines[1]	Passenger Enplanements	Freight Carriers[2]	Freight (lbs)
Columbia Regional (COU)				
Domestic service (U.S. carriers only)	15	103,069	2	4,991
International service (U.S. carriers only)	0	0	0	0

Note: (1) Includes all U.S.-based major, minor and commuter airlines that carried at least one passenger during the year; (2) Includes all U.S.-based airlines and freight carriers that transported at least one pound of freight during the year.
Source: Bureau of Transportation Statistics, The Intermodal Transportation Database, Air Carriers: T-100 Domestic Market (U.S. carriers only), 2024; Bureau of Transportation Statistics, The Intermodal Transportation Database, Air Carriers: T-100 International Market (U.S. carriers only), 2024

BUSINESSES

Major Business Headquarters

Company Name	Industry	Rankings Fortune[1]	Forbes[2]
No companies listed	-	-	-

Note: (1) Companies that produce a 10-K are ranked 1 to 500 based on 2023 revenue; (2) All private companies with at least $2 billion in annual revenue through the end of their most current fiscal year are ranked 1 to 275; companies listed are headquartered in the city; dashes indicate no ranking
Source: Fortune, "Fortune 500," 2024; Forbes, "America's Largest Private Companies," 2024

Living Environment

COST OF LIVING

Cost of Living Index

Composite Index	Groceries	Housing	Utilities	Trans-portation	Health Care	Misc. Goods/Services
90.0	96.2	79.7	96.8	84.8	98.8	94.3

Note: The Cost of Living Index measures regional differences in the cost of consumer goods and services, excluding taxes and non-consumer expenditures, for professional and managerial households in the top income quintile. It is based on more than 50,000 prices covering almost 60 different items for which prices are collected three times a year by chambers of commerce, economic development organizations or university applied economic centers in each participating urban area. The numbers shown should be read as a percentage above or below the national average of 100. For example, a value of 115.4 in the groceries column indicates that grocery prices are 15.4% higher than the national average. Small differences in the index numbers should not be interpreted as significant; Figures cover the Columbia MO urban area.
Source: The Council for Community and Economic Research, Cost of Living Index, 2024

Grocery Prices

Area[1]	T-Bone Steak ($/pound)	Frying Chicken ($/pound)	Whole Milk ($/half gal.)	Eggs ($/dozen)	Orange Juice ($/64 oz.)	Coffee ($/11.5 oz.)
City[2]	15.51	1.47	4.69	3.41	4.45	5.17
Avg.	15.42	1.55	4.69	3.25	4.41	5.46
Min.	14.50	1.16	4.43	2.75	4.00	4.85
Max.	17.56	2.89	5.49	4.78	5.54	7.89

*Note: (1) Values for the local area are compared with the average, minimum and maximum values for all 276 areas in the Cost of Living Index; (2) Figures cover the Columbia MO urban area; **T-Bone Steak** (price per pound); **Frying Chicken** (price per pound, whole fryer); **Whole Milk** (half gallon carton); **Eggs** (price per dozen, Grade A, large); **Orange Juice** (64 oz. Tropicana or Florida Natural); **Coffee** (11.5 oz. can, vacuum-packed, Maxwell House, Hills Bros, or Folgers).*
Source: The Council for Community and Economic Research, Cost of Living Index, 2024

Housing and Utility Costs

Area[1]	New Home Price ($)	Apartment Rent ($/month)	All Electric ($/month)	Part Electric ($/month)	Other Energy ($/month)	Telephone ($/month)
City[2]	451,668	1,041	-	114.12	78.36	199.61
Avg.	515,975	1,550	210.99	123.07	82.07	194.99
Min.	265,375	692	104.33	53.68	36.26	179.42
Max.	2,775,821	5,719	529.02	397.28	361.63	223.33

*Note: (1) Values for the local area are compared with the average, minimum and maximum values for all 276 areas in the Cost of Living Index; (2) Figures cover the Columbia MO urban area; **New Home Price** (2,400 sf living area, 8,000 sf lot, in urban area with full utilities); **Apartment Rent** (950 sf 2 bedroom/1.5 or 2 bath, unfurnished, excluding all utilities except water); **All Electric** (average monthly cost for an all-electric home); **Part Electric** (average monthly cost for a part-electric home); **Other Energy** (average monthly cost for natural gas, fuel oil, coal, wood, and any other forms of energy except electricity); **Telephone** (price includes the base monthly rate plus taxes and fees for three lines of mobile phone service).*
Source: The Council for Community and Economic Research, Cost of Living Index, 2024

Health Care, Transportation, and Other Costs

Area[1]	Doctor ($/visit)	Dentist ($/visit)	Optometrist ($/visit)	Gasoline ($/gallon)	Beauty Salon ($/visit)	Men's Shirt ($)
City[2]	182.67	95.67	138.50	3.10	45.42	37.14
Avg.	143.77	117.51	129.23	3.32	48.57	38.14
Min.	36.74	58.67	67.33	2.80	24.00	13.41
Max.	270.44	216.82	307.33	5.28	94.00	63.89

*Note: (1) Values for the local area are compared with the average, minimum and maximum values for all 276 areas in the Cost of Living Index; (2) Figures cover the Columbia MO urban area; **Doctor** (general practitioners routine exam of an established patient); **Dentist** (adult teeth cleaning and periodic oral examination); **Optometrist** (full vision eye exam for established adult patient); **Gasoline** (one gallon regular unleaded, national brand, including all taxes, cash price at self-service pump if available); **Beauty Salon** (woman's shampoo, trim, and blow-dry); **Men's Shirt** (cotton/polyester dress shirt, pinpoint weave, long sleeves).*
Source: The Council for Community and Economic Research, Cost of Living Index, 2024

HOUSING

Homeownership Rate

Area	2017 (%)	2018 (%)	2019 (%)	2020 (%)	2021 (%)	2022 (%)	2023 (%)	2024 (%)
MSA[1]	n/a	n/a	n/a	n/a	n/a	n/a	n/a	n/a
U.S.	63.9	64.4	64.6	66.6	65.5	65.8	65.9	65.6

Note: (1) Figures cover the Columbia, MO Metropolitan Statistical Area; n/a not available
Source: U.S. Census Bureau, Housing Vacancies and Homeownership Annual Statistics: 2017-2024

House Price Index (HPI)

Area	National Ranking[2]	Quarterly Change (%)	One-Year Change (%)	Five-Year Change (%)	Since 1991Q1 (%)
MSA[1]	24	0.09	8.46	58.84	279.40
U.S.[3]	–	1.43	4.51	57.13	327.82

Note: The HPI is a weighted repeat sales index. It measures average price changes in repeat sales or refinancings on the same properties. This information is obtained by reviewing repeat mortgage transactions on single-family properties whose mortgages have been purchased or securitized by Fannie Mae or Freddie Mac since January 1975; (1) Figures cover the Columbia, MO Metropolitan Statistical Area; (2) Rankings are based on annual percentage change for all metro areas containing at least 15,000 transactions over the last 10 years and ranges from 1 to 241; (3) figures based on a weighted average of Census Division estimates using a seasonally adjusted, purchase-only index; all figures are for the period ending December 31, 2024
Source: Federal Housing Finance Agency, Change in FHFA Metropolitan Area House Price Indexes, All Transactions Index, 2024Q4

Home Value

Area	Under $100,000	$100,000 -$199,999	$200,000 -$299,999	$300,000 -$399,999	$400,000 -$499,999	$500,000 -$999,999	$1,000,000 or more	Median ($)
City	6.6	23.2	30.2	18.4	10.8	10.1	0.8	268,300
MSA[1]	11.1	26.8	26.5	15.4	9.6	9.0	1.6	242,500
U.S.	12.1	17.8	19.5	14.4	10.5	19.1	6.5	303,400

Note: Figures are percentages except for median and cover owner-occupied housing units; (1) Figures cover the Columbia, MO Metropolitan Statistical Area
Source: U.S. Census Bureau, 2019-2023 American Community Survey 5-Year Estimates

Year Housing Structure Built

Area	2020 or Later	2010 -2019	2000 -2009	1990 -1999	1980 -1989	1970 -1979	1960 -1969	1950 -1959	1940 -1949	Before 1940	Median Year
City	0.8	17.5	20.3	17.0	12.3	9.9	10.3	4.5	2.4	5.0	1993
MSA[1]	1.0	14.0	17.9	16.8	13.2	13.1	9.7	4.6	2.4	7.3	1990
U.S.	1.2	8.9	13.6	12.8	13.0	14.4	10.0	9.7	4.5	11.9	1980

Note: Figures are percentages except for Median Year; Note: (1) Figures cover the Columbia, MO Metropolitan Statistical Area
Source: U.S. Census Bureau, 2019-2023 American Community Survey 5-Year Estimates

Gross Monthly Rent

Area	Under $500	$500 -$999	$1,000 -$1,499	$1,500 -$1,999	$2,000 -$2,499	$2,500 -$2,999	$3,000 and up	Median ($)
City	4.0	39.3	38.9	9.8	5.8	1.4	0.8	1,067
MSA[1]	4.7	41.2	38.4	9.2	4.6	1.1	0.8	1,041
U.S.	6.5	22.3	29.5	20.2	10.8	4.8	5.9	1,348

Note: Figures are percentages except for median; Gross rent is the contract rent plus the estimated average monthly cost of utilities (electricity, gas, and water and sewer) and fuels (oil, coal, kerosene, wood, etc.) if these are paid by the renter (or paid for the renter by someone else); (1) Figures cover the Columbia, MO Metropolitan Statistical Area
Source: U.S. Census Bureau, 2019-2023 American Community Survey 5-Year Estimates

HEALTH

Health Risk Factors

Category	MSA[1] (%)	U.S. (%)
Adults aged 18–64 who have any kind of health care coverage	n/a	90.8
Adults who reported being in good or better health	n/a	81.8
Adults who have been told they have high blood cholesterol	n/a	36.9
Adults who have been told they have high blood pressure	n/a	34.0
Adults who are current smokers	n/a	12.1
Adults who currently use e-cigarettes	n/a	7.7
Adults who currently use chewing tobacco, snuff, or snus	n/a	3.2
Adults who are heavy drinkers[2]	n/a	6.1
Adults who are binge drinkers[3]	n/a	15.2
Adults who are overweight (BMI 25.0 - 29.9)	n/a	34.4
Adults who are obese (BMI 30.0 - 99.8)	n/a	34.3
Adults who participated in any physical activities in the past month	n/a	75.8

Note: All figures are crude prevalence; (1) Figures for the Columbia, MO Metropolitan Statistical Area were not available.
(2) Heavy drinkers are classified as adult men having more than 14 drinks per week and adult women having more than 7 drinks per week; (3) Binge drinkers are classified as males having five or more drinks on one occasion or females having four or more drinks on one occasion
Source: Centers for Disease Control and Prevention, Behaviorial Risk Factor Surveillance System, SMART: Selected Metropolitan Area Risk Trends, 2023

Acute and Chronic Health Conditions

Category	MSA[1] (%)	U.S. (%)
Adults who have ever been told they had a heart attack	n/a	4.2
Adults who have ever been told they have angina or coronary heart disease	n/a	4.0
Adults who have ever been told they had a stroke	n/a	3.3
Adults who have ever been told they have asthma	n/a	15.7
Adults who have ever been told they have arthritis	n/a	26.3
Adults who have ever been told they have diabetes[2]	n/a	11.5
Adults who have ever been told they had skin cancer	n/a	5.6
Adults who have ever been told they had any other types of cancer	n/a	8.4
Adults who have ever been told they have COPD	n/a	6.4
Adults who have ever been told they have kidney disease	n/a	3.7
Adults who have ever been told they have a form of depression	n/a	22.0

Note: All figures are crude prevalence; (1) Figures for the Columbia, MO Metropolitan Statistical Area were not available.
(2) Figures do not include pregnancy-related, borderline, or pre-diabetes
Source: Centers for Disease Control and Prevention, Behavioral Risk Factor Surveillance System, SMART: Selected Metropolitan Area Risk Trends, 2023

Health Screening and Vaccination Rates

Category	MSA[1] (%)	U.S. (%)
Adults who have ever been tested for HIV	n/a	37.5
Adults who have had their blood cholesterol checked within the last five years	n/a	87.0
Adults aged 65+ who have had flu shot within the past year	n/a	63.4
Adults aged 65+ who have ever had a pneumonia vaccination	n/a	71.9

Note: All figures are crude prevalence; (1) Figures for the Columbia, MO Metropolitan Statistical Area were not available.
Source: Centers for Disease Control and Prevention, Behavioral Risk Factor Surveillance System, SMART: Selected Metropolitan Area Risk Trends, 2023

Disability Status

Category	MSA[1] (%)	U.S. (%)
Adults who reported being deaf	n/a	7.4
Are you blind or have serious difficulty seeing, even when wearing glasses?	n/a	4.9
Do you have difficulty doing errands alone?	n/a	7.8
Do you have difficulty dressing or bathing?	n/a	3.6
Do you have serious difficulty concentrating/remembering/making decisions?	n/a	13.7
Do you have serious difficulty walking or climbing stairs?	n/a	13.2

Note: All figures are crude prevalence; (1) Figures for the Columbia, MO Metropolitan Statistical Area were not available.
Source: Centers for Disease Control and Prevention, Behavioral Risk Factor Surveillance System, SMART: Selected Metropolitan Area Risk Trends, 2023

Mortality Rates for the Top 10 Causes of Death in the U.S.

ICD-10[a] Sub-Chapter	ICD-10[a] Code	Crude Mortality Rate[2] per 100,000 population	
		County[3]	U.S.
Malignant neoplasms	C00-C97	143.3	182.7
Ischaemic heart diseases	I20-I25	61.6	109.6
Provisional assignment of new diseases of uncertain etiology[1]	U00-U49	28.6	65.3
Other forms of heart disease	I30-I51	55.4	65.1
Other degenerative diseases of the nervous system	G30-G31	39.8	52.4
Other external causes of accidental injury	W00-X59	41.0	52.3
Cerebrovascular diseases	I60-I69	31.8	49.1
Chronic lower respiratory diseases	J40-J47	36.1	43.5
Hypertensive diseases	I10-I15	25.2	38.9
Organic, including symptomatic, mental disorders	F01-F09	26.3	33.9

Note: (a) ICD-10 = International Classification of Diseases 10th Revision; (1) Includes COVID-19, adverse effects to COVID-19 vaccines, SARS, and vaping-related disorders; (2) Crude mortality rates are a three-year average covering 2021-2023; (3) Figures cover Boone County.
Source: Centers for Disease Control and Prevention, National Center for Health Statistics. National Vital Statistics System, Mortality 2018-2023 on CDC WONDER Online Database

Mortality Rates for Selected Causes of Death

Cause of Death	ICD-10[a] Code	Crude Mortality Rate[1] per 100,000 population	
		County[2]	U.S.
Accidental poisoning and exposure to noxious substances	X40-X49	26.5	30.5
Alzheimer disease	G30	24.0	35.4
Assault	X85-Y09	6.4	7.3
COVID-19	U07.1	28.6	65.3
Diabetes mellitus	E10-E14	19.0	30.0
Diseases of the liver	K70-K76	16.0	20.8
Human immunodeficiency virus (HIV) disease	B20-B24	Suppressed	1.5
Influenza and pneumonia	J09-J18	9.4	13.4
Intentional self-harm	X60-X84	15.6	14.7
Malnutrition	E40-E46	5.2	6.0
Obesity and other hyperalimentation	E65-E68	Unreliable	3.1
Renal failure	N17-N19	11.9	16.4
Transport accidents	V01-V99	10.3	14.4

Note: (a) ICD-10 = International Classification of Diseases 10th Revision; (1) Crude mortality rates are a three-year average covering 2021-2023; (2) Figures cover Boone County; Data are suppressed when the data meet the criteria for confidentiality constraints; Crude mortality rates are flagged as unreliable when the rate would be calculated with a numerator of 20 or less.
Source: Centers for Disease Control and Prevention, National Center for Health Statistics. National Vital Statistics System, Mortality 2018-2023 on CDC WONDER Online Database

Health Insurance Coverage

Area	With Health Insurance	With Private Health Insurance	With Public Health Insurance	Without Health Insurance	Population Under Age 19 Without Health Insurance
City	93.6	79.1	23.3	6.4	4.7
MSA[1]	93.4	77.7	26.6	6.6	4.4
U.S.	91.4	67.3	36.3	8.6	5.4

Note: Figures are percentages that cover the civilian noninstitutionalized population; (1) Figures cover the Columbia, MO Metropolitan Statistical Area
Source: U.S. Census Bureau, 2019-2023 American Community Survey 5-Year Estimates

Number of Medical Professionals

Area	MDs[3]	DOs[3,4]	Dentists	Podiatrists	Chiropractors	Optometrists
County[1] (number)	1,622	180	149	11	78	53
County[1] (rate[2])	864.2	95.9	78.6	5.8	41.2	28.0
U.S. (rate[2])	302.5	29.2	74.6	6.4	29.5	18.0

Note: Data as of 2023 unless noted; (1) Data covers Boone County; (2) Number of medical professionals per 100,000 population; (3) Data as of 2022 and includes all active, non-federal physicians; (4) Doctor of Osteopathic Medicine
Source: U.S. Department of Health and Human Services, Health Resources and Services Administration, Bureau of Health Professions, Area Resource File (ARF) 2023-2024

EDUCATION

Public School District Statistics

District Name	Schls	Pupils	Pupil/ Teacher Ratio	Minority Pupils[1] (%)	Total Rev. per Pupil ($)	Total Exp. per Pupil ($)
Columbia 93	36	18,769	13.1	46.2	16,523	15,957

Note: Table includes school districts with 2,000 or more students; (1) Percentage of students that are not non-Hispanic white.
Source: U.S. Department of Education, National Center for Education Statistics, Common Core of Data, Local Education Agency (School District) Universe Survey: School Year 2023-2024; U.S. Department of Education, National Center for Education Statistics, Common Core of Data, School District Finance Survey (F-33): School Year 2021–22

Highest Level of Education

Area	Less than H.S.	H.S. Diploma	Some College, No Deg.	Associate Degree	Bachelor's Degree	Master's Degree	Prof. School Degree	Doctorate Degree
City	4.7	16.9	15.7	6.2	30.1	15.7	4.8	5.9
MSA[1]	6.0	22.6	16.6	7.3	26.7	13.0	3.5	4.2
U.S.	10.6	26.2	19.4	8.8	21.3	9.8	2.3	1.6

Note: Figures cover persons age 25 and over; (1) Figures cover the Columbia, MO Metropolitan Statistical Area
Source: U.S. Census Bureau, 2019-2023 American Community Survey 5-Year Estimates

Columbia, Missouri

Educational Attainment by Race

Area	High School Graduate or Higher (%)					Bachelor's Degree or Higher (%)				
	Total	White	Black	Asian	Hisp.[2]	Total	White	Black	Asian	Hisp.[2]
City	95.3	96.4	92.0	94.2	86.7	56.5	59.4	33.9	72.5	48.5
MSA[1]	94.0	94.6	91.5	92.8	87.6	47.5	48.9	28.5	71.0	38.4
U.S.	89.4	92.9	88.1	88.0	72.5	35.0	37.7	24.7	57.0	19.9

Note: Figures shown cover persons 25 years old and over; (1) Figures cover the Columbia, MO Metropolitan Statistical Area; (2) People of Hispanic origin can be of any race
Source: U.S. Census Bureau, 2019-2023 American Community Survey 5-Year Estimates

School Enrollment by Grade and Control

Area	Preschool (%)		Kindergarten (%)		Grades 1 - 4 (%)		Grades 5 - 8 (%)		Grades 9 - 12 (%)	
	Public	Private	Public	Private	Public	Private	Public	Private	Public	Private
City	49.7	50.3	85.6	14.4	87.0	13.0	89.5	10.5	91.0	9.0
MSA[1]	55.0	45.0	87.6	12.4	84.6	15.4	90.4	9.6	90.7	9.3
U.S.	58.7	41.3	85.2	14.8	87.2	12.8	87.9	12.1	89.0	11.0

Note: Figures shown cover persons 3 years old and over; (1) Figures cover the Columbia, MO Metropolitan Statistical Area
Source: U.S. Census Bureau, 2019-2023 American Community Survey 5-Year Estimates

Higher Education

Four-Year Colleges			Two-Year Colleges			Medical Schools[1]	Law Schools[2]	Voc/ Tech[3]
Public	Private Non-profit	Private For-profit	Public	Private Non-profit	Private For-profit			
1	4	0	0	0	0	1	1	1

Note: Figures cover institutions located within the Columbia, MO Metropolitan Statistical Area and include main campuses only; (1) includes schools accredited by the Liaison Committee on Medical Education and the American Osteopathic Association's Commission on Osteopathic College Accreditation; (2) includes ABA-accredited schools, schools with provisional ABA accreditation, and state accredited schools; (3) includes all schools with programs that are less than 2 years.
Source: National Center for Education Statistics, Integrated Postsecondary Education System (IPEDS), 2023-24; Wikipedia, List of Medical Schools in the United States, accessed May 2, 2025; Wikipedia, List of Law Schools in the United States, accessed May 2, 2025

According to *U.S. News & World Report,* the Columbia, MO metro area is home to one of the top 200 national universities in the U.S.: **University of Missouri** (#109 tie). The indicators used to capture academic quality fall into a number of categories: assessment by administrators at peer institutions; retention of students; faculty resources; student selectivity; financial resources; alumni giving; high school counselor ratings of colleges; and graduation rate. *U.S. News & World Report, "America's Best Colleges 2025".*

According to *U.S. News & World Report,* the Columbia, MO metro area is home to one of the top 100 law schools in the U.S.: **University of Missouri** (#57 tie). The rankings are based on a weighted average of 12 measures of quality: peer assessment score; assessment score by lawyers/judges; median LSAT scores; median undergrad GPA; acceptance rate; employment rates for graduates; placement success; bar passage rate; faculty resources; expenditures per student; student/faculty ratio; and library resources. *U.S. News & World Report, "America's Best Graduate Schools, Law, 2025"*

EMPLOYERS

Major Employers

Company Name	Industry
BJC Health System	Hospital management
City of Columbia	Courts
Columbia College	Colleges & universities
Columbia Public Schools	Education
Kraft Foods Global	Frankfurters, from purchased meat
MBS Textbook Exchange	Books, periodicals, & newspapers
MCI Worldcom Communications	Telephone communication, except radio
Regional Medical Pharmacy	Home health care services
Schneider Electric USA	Switchgear & switchboard apparatus
Shelter Insurance Companies	Fire, marine, & casualty insurance
State Farm Mutual Automobile Insurance	Insurance agents & brokers
University of Missouri Hospital	General medical & surgical hospitals
University of Missouri System	Colleges & universities
University Physicians Hospital	Gynecologist
Veterans Health Administration	Administration of veterans' affairs

Note: Companies shown are located within the Columbia, MO Metropolitan Statistical Area.
Source: Chambers of Commerce; State Departments of Labor; Wikipedia

Best Companies to Work For

Veterans United Home Loans, headquartered in Columbia, is among "The 100 Best Companies to Work For." To pick the best companies, *Fortune* partnered with the Great Place to Work Institute.

Using their proprietary Trust Index™ survey, the core of what creates great a workplace is measured—key behaviors that drive trust in management, connection with colleagues, and loyalty to the company. To be eligible for the *Fortune* 100 Best Companies to Work For list, employers must have 1,000 or more employees in the U.S. and cannot be a government agency. *Fortune, "The 100 Best Companies to Work For," 2025*

PUBLIC SAFETY

Crime Rate

Area	Total Crime Rate	Violent Crime Rate				Property Crime Rate		
		Murder	Rape	Robbery	Aggrav. Assault	Burglary	Larceny -Theft	Motor Vehicle Theft
City	2,897.3	7.7	59.4	33.2	285.5	307.1	1,859.5	344.9
U.S.	2,290.9	5.7	38.0	66.5	264.1	250.7	1,347.2	318.7

Note: Figures are crimes per 100,000 population.
Source: FBI, Table 8, Offenses Known to Law Enforcement, by State by City, 2023

Hate Crimes

Area	Number of Quarters Reported	Number of Incidents per Bias Motivation					
		Race/Ethnicity/ Ancestry	Religion	Sexual Orientation	Disability	Gender	Gender Identity
City	4	1	0	0	0	0	0
U.S.	4	5,900	2,699	2,077	187	92	492

Source: Federal Bureau of Investigation, Hate Crime Statistics 2023

Identity Theft Consumer Reports

Area	Reports	Reports per 100,000 Population	Rank[2]
MSA[1]	295	139	301
U.S.	1,135,291	339	-

Note: (1) Figures cover the Columbia, MO Metropolitan Statistical Area; (2) Rank ranges from 1 to 401 where 1 indicates greatest number of identity theft reports per 100,000 population
Source: Federal Trade Commission, Consumer Sentinel Network Data Book 2024

Fraud and Other Consumer Reports

Area	Reports	Reports per 100,000 Population	Rank[2]
MSA[1]	1,921	903	262
U.S.	5,360,641	1,601	-

Note: (1) Figures cover the Columbia, MO Metropolitan Statistical Area; (2) Rank ranges from 1 to 401 where 1 indicates greatest number of fraud and other consumer reports per 100,000 population
Source: Federal Trade Commission, Consumer Sentinel Network Data Book 2024

POLITICS

2024 Presidential Election Results

Area	Trump (Rep.)	Harris (Dem.)	Stein (Green)	Kennedy (Ind.)	Oliver (Lib.)	Other
Boone County	43.9	53.6	0.9	0.0	1.1	0.4
U.S.	49.7	48.2	0.6	0.5	0.4	0.6

Note: Results are percentages and may not add to 100% due to rounding
Source: Dave Leip's Atlas of U.S. Presidential Elections

SPORTS

Professional Sports Teams

Team Name	League	Year Established

No teams are located in the metro area
Source: Wikipedia, Major Professional Sports Teams of the United States and Canada, May 1, 2025

CLIMATE

Average and Extreme Temperatures

Temperature	Jan	Feb	Mar	Apr	May	Jun	Jul	Aug	Sep	Oct	Nov	Dec	Yr.
Extreme High (°F)	74	76	85	90	90	103	111	110	101	93	83	76	111
Average High (°F)	36	42	54	66	74	83	89	87	79	67	53	41	64
Average Temp. (°F)	28	33	44	55	64	73	78	76	68	56	44	33	54
Average Low (°F)	19	23	34	44	53	62	67	65	57	45	34	24	44
Extreme Low (°F)	-19	-15	-5	19	29	40	48	42	32	22	0	-20	-20

Note: Figures cover the years 1969-1995
Source: National Climatic Data Center, International Station Meteorological Climate Summary, 9/96

Average Precipitation/Snowfall/Humidity

Precip./Humidity	Jan	Feb	Mar	Apr	May	Jun	Jul	Aug	Sep	Oct	Nov	Dec	Yr.
Avg. Precip. (in.)	1.6	2.0	3.2	4.3	5.1	3.9	3.9	3.8	3.7	3.1	3.5	2.6	40.6
Avg. Snowfall (in.)	7	7	4	1	0	0	0	0	0	Tr	2	5	25
Avg. Rel. Hum. 6am (%)	80	80	79	79	85	86	87	89	88	84	82	81	83
Avg. Rel. Hum. 3pm (%)	62	59	53	52	57	56	53	52	54	53	59	64	56

Note: Figures cover the years 1969-1995; Tr = Trace amounts (<0.05 in. of rain; <0.5 in. of snow)
Source: National Climatic Data Center, International Station Meteorological Climate Summary, 9/96

Weather Conditions

Temperature			Daytime Sky			Precipitation		
10°F & below	32°F & below	90°F & above	Clear	Partly cloudy	Cloudy	0.01 inch or more precip.	0.1 inch or more snow/ice	Thunder-storms
17	108	36	99	127	139	110	17	52

Note: Figures are average number of days per year and cover the years 1969-1995
Source: National Climatic Data Center, International Station Meteorological Climate Summary, 9/96

HAZARDOUS WASTE

Superfund Sites

The Columbia, MO metro area has no sites on the EPA's Superfund Final National Priorities List (NPL) or Superfund Alternative Approach (SAA) list. The Superfund alternative approach uses the same investigation and cleanup process and standards that are used for sites listed on the National Priorities List. The SAA is an alternative to listing a site on the NPL; it is not an alternative to Superfund or the Superfund process. There are a total of 1,445 Superfund sites with a status of proposed or final on both lists in the United States. *U.S. Environmental Protection Agency, National Priorities List, May 1, 2025; U.S. Environmental Protection Agency, Superfund Alternative Approach Sites, May 1, 2025*

AIR QUALITY

Air Quality Trends: Ozone

	1990	1995	2000	2005	2010	2015	2020	2021	2022	2023
MSA[1]	n/a	n/a	n/a	n/a	n/a	n/a	n/a	n/a	n/a	n/a
U.S.	0.087	0.089	0.081	0.080	0.072	0.068	0.066	0.067	0.067	0.070

Note: (1) Data covers the Columbia, MO Metropolitan Statistical Area; n/a not available. The values shown are the composite ozone concentration averages among trend sites based on the highest fourth daily maximum 8-hour concentration in parts per million. These trends are based on sites having an adequate record of monitoring data during the trend period. Data from exceptional events are included.
Source: U.S. Environmental Protection Agency, Air Quality Monitoring Information, "Air Quality Trends by City, 1990-2023"

Air Quality Index

Area	Percent of Days when Air Quality was...[2]					AQI Statistics[2]	
	Good	Moderate	Unhealthy for Sensitive Groups	Unhealthy	Very Unhealthy	Maximum	Median
MSA[1]	79.9	18.0	2.0	0.0	0.0	143	42

Note: (1) Data covers the Columbia, MO Metropolitan Statistical Area; (2) Based on 244 days with AQI data in 2023. Air Quality Index (AQI) is an index for reporting daily air quality. EPA calculates the AQI for five major air pollutants regulated by the Clean Air Act: ground-level ozone, particle pollution (aka particulate matter), carbon monoxide, sulfur dioxide, and nitrogen dioxide. The AQI runs from 0 to 500. The higher the AQI value, the greater the level of air pollution and the greater the health concern. There are six AQI categories: "Good" AQI is between 0 and 50. Air quality is considered satisfactory; "Moderate" AQI is between 51 and 100. Air quality is acceptable; "Unhealthy for Sensitive Groups" When AQI values are between 101 and 150, members of sensitive groups may experience health effects; "Unhealthy" When AQI values are between 151 and 200 everyone may begin to experience health effects; "Very Unhealthy" AQI values between 201 and 300 trigger a health alert; "Hazardous" AQI values over 300 trigger warnings of emergency conditions (not shown).
Source: U.S. Environmental Protection Agency, Air Quality Index Report, 2023

Air Quality Index Pollutants

Area	Percent of Days when AQI Pollutant was...[2]					
	Carbon Monoxide	Nitrogen Dioxide	Ozone	Sulfur Dioxide	Particulate Matter 2.5	Particulate Matter 10
MSA[1]	0.0	0.0	100.0	(3)	0.0	0.0

Note: (1) Data covers the Columbia, MO Metropolitan Statistical Area; (2) Based on 244 days with AQI data in 2023. The Air Quality Index (AQI) is an index for reporting daily air quality. EPA calculates the AQI for five major air pollutants regulated by the Clean Air Act: ground-level ozone, particle pollution (also known as particulate matter), carbon monoxide, sulfur dioxide, and nitrogen dioxide. The AQI runs from 0 to 500. The higher the AQI value, the greater the level of air pollution and the greater the health concern; (3) Sulfur dioxide is no longer included in this table because SO_2 concentrations tend to be very localized and not necessarily representative of broad geographical areas like counties and CBSAs.
Source: U.S. Environmental Protection Agency, Air Quality Index Report, 2023

Maximum Air Pollutant Concentrations: Particulate Matter, Ozone, CO and Lead

	Particulate Matter 10 (ug/m^3)	Particulate Matter 2.5 Wtd AM (ug/m^3)	Particulate Matter 2.5 24-Hr (ug/m^3)	Ozone (ppm)	Carbon Monoxide (ppm)	Lead (ug/m^3)
MSA[1] Level	n/a	n/a	n/a	0.072	n/a	n/a
NAAQS[2]	150	15	35	0.075	9	0.15
Met NAAQS[2]	n/a	n/a	n/a	Yes	n/a	n/a

Note: (1) Data covers the Columbia, MO Metropolitan Statistical Area; Data from exceptional events are included; (2) National Ambient Air Quality Standards; ppm = parts per million; ug/m^3 = micrograms per cubic meter; n/a not available.
Concentrations: Particulate Matter 10 (coarse particulate)—highest second maximum 24-hour concentration; Particulate Matter 2.5 Wtd AM (fine particulate)—highest weighted annual mean concentration; Particulate Matter 2.5 24-Hour (fine particulate)—highest 98th percentile 24-hour concentration; Ozone—highest fourth daily maximum 8-hour concentration; Carbon Monoxide—highest second maximum non-overlapping 8-hour concentration; Lead—maximum running 3-month average
Source: U.S. Environmental Protection Agency, Air Quality Monitoring Information, "Air Quality Statistics by City, 2023"

Maximum Air Pollutant Concentrations: Nitrogen Dioxide and Sulfur Dioxide

	Nitrogen Dioxide AM (ppb)	Nitrogen Dioxide 1-Hr (ppb)	Sulfur Dioxide AM (ppb)	Sulfur Dioxide 1-Hr (ppb)	Sulfur Dioxide 24-Hr (ppb)
MSA[1] Level	n/a	n/a	n/a	n/a	n/a
NAAQS[2]	53	100	30	75	140
Met NAAQS[2]	n/a	n/a	n/a	n/a	n/a

Note: (1) Data covers the Columbia, MO Metropolitan Statistical Area; Data from exceptional events are included; (2) National Ambient Air Quality Standards; ppm = parts per million; ug/m^3 = micrograms per cubic meter; n/a not available.
Concentrations: Nitrogen Dioxide AM—highest arithmetic mean concentration; Nitrogen Dioxide 1-Hr—highest 98th percentile 1-hour daily maximum concentration; Sulfur Dioxide AM—highest annual mean concentration; Sulfur Dioxide 1-Hr—highest 99th percentile 1-hour daily maximum concentration; Sulfur Dioxide 24-Hr—highest second maximum 24-hour concentration
Source: U.S. Environmental Protection Agency, Air Quality Monitoring Information, "Air Quality Statistics by City, 2023"

Davenport, Iowa

Background

Davenport was incorporated in 1836 on the site of the bloody "Black Hawk War" between the Native American Sac tribe and eastern settlers who were intent on westward expansion. In 1828, John Quincy Adams had declared that all land east of the Mississippi would be sold to settlers. When Chief Black Hawk and his warriors refused to leave their land, the Black Hawk War ensued, resulting in a treaty now known as the Black Hawk Purchase. Credit Island, which had originally been a fur trading post, hosted the treaty signing between the Sac chief and Colonel George Davenport, from whom Davenport derives its name.

In 1856, a new bridge was constructed between Davenport and Rock Island, Illinois—the first railroad bridge to span the Mississippi. Months later, the riverboat *Effie Afton*, struck and damaged the bridge. The ensuing court case, *Hurd v. Rock Island Railroad Company*, remained the most notable case in the law career of Abraham Lincoln.

The decade preceding the Civil War saw a major influx of German immigrants to Davenport, increasing the population fivefold; it is estimated that about 50 percent of today's Davenport citizenry are of German descent. Many of these immigrants were fleeing political persecution and were instrumental in the creation of the Republican Party. The culture and work ethic of these immigrants remains a key factor in the Davenport ethos of hard work and industry. The washing machine was invented in Davenport and Davenport earned the moniker of "Washing Machine Capital of the World" for the number of washing machine manufacturers in the city at the turn of the 20th century.

In 1861, Davenport's next door neighbor, Rock Island, opened a munitions arsenal to help the Union war efforts. It is now home to the largest, government-owned weapons manufacturing facility in the United States, and a designated national historic landmark. Today, Davenport supports a diverse base of manufacturing industries that include everything from farm and military machinery to publishing products and food processing. Its central, mid-continent location makes Davenport an important, inland U.S. Customs Port of Entry for freight distribution. It is also designated a Foreign Trade Zone.

The largest employers in the area include John Deere & Co., and Genesis Health System. Davenport is also headquarters to Von Maur department stores, and publisher Lee Enterprises.

Davenport is home to four institutes of higher learning, including the Catholic liberal arts St. Ambrose University, the city's oldest college. The Palmer College of Chiropractic, the first college of its kind, was established by the inventor of chiropractic practice and Davenport resident Daniel David Palmer. Within commuting distance of Davenport are Augustana College (Rock Island), the University of Iowa (Iowa City), and Knox College (Galesburg).

Iowa's first municipal art museum, the Figge Museum, is home to the *Grant Wood Archive*. The collection features Wood's wire-rimmed glasses, his easel and painting tools, and the iconic cameo broach in both the portrait of his mother, *Woman with Plants*, 1929, and his most famous painting, *American Gothic*, 1930.

Davenport has a humid continental climate. Summers are very warm to hot with high humidity. Winters have cold temperatures and often high winds, with snow likely from November through February. Average snowfall in Davenport is about 31 inches per year. Substantial weather changes frequently occur at three- to four-day intervals. Although several minor tornadoes have occurred, no devastating tornado has ever touched down in Davenport. Flooding, however, is often a problem in Davenport, and floods have occurred most recently in 1990, 2008, 2029, and 2023.

Rankings

General Rankings

- In their annual survey, Livability.com looked at data for more than 2,000 mid-sized U.S. cities to assign a "Livability Score"for each. The top 100 scoring cities make up Livability's "Top 100 Best Places to Live in the U.S." in 2025. Davenport was placed among the top 100 of the customizable list. Criteria: housing and economy; cost of living; environment; education; health care options; transportation; safety; and community amenities. *Livability.com, "Top 100 Best Places to Live in the U.S. in 2025" April 15, 2025*

Business/Finance Rankings

- The Davenport metro area appeared on the Milken Institute "2025 Best Performing Cities" list. Rank: #181 out of 200 large metro areas (based on performance category). Criteria: job growth; wage growth; high-tech growth and impact; community resilience; housing affordability; household broadband access. *Milken Institute, "Best-Performing Cities 2025," January 14, 2025*

Education Rankings

- Personal finance website *WalletHub* analyzed the 150 largest U.S. metropolitan statistical areas to determine where the most educated Americans are putting their degrees to work. Criteria: education levels; percentage of workers with degrees; education quality and attainment gap; public school quality rankings; quality and enrollment of each metro area's universities. Davenport was ranked #110 (#1 = most educated city). *WalletHub.com, "Most & Least Educated Cities in America, 2025" July 2, 2024*

Health/Fitness Rankings

- The Davenport metro area was identified as one of the worst cities for bed bugs in America by pest control company Orkin. The area ranked #29 out of 50 based on the number of bed bug treatments Orkin performed from December 2022 to November 2023. *Orkin, "Chicago Joins Paris In Global Bed Bug Spotlight Ranking As The Worst City On Orkin's U.S. Bed Bug Cities List," January 22, 2024*

Real Estate Rankings

- The Davenport metro area was identified as one of the 20 most affordable housing markets in the U.S. in 2024. The area ranked #6 out of 226 markets. Criteria: qualification for a mortgage loan with a 10 percent down payment on a typical home. *National Association of Realtors®, Qualifying Income Based on Sales Price of Existing Single-Family Homes for Metropolitan Areas, February 6, 2025*

- Davenport was ranked #6 out of 176 metro areas in terms of cost of housing in 2024 by the National Association of Home Builders (#1 = most affordable). Criteria: the portion of an average family's income necessary to pay the mortgage on a median-priced home. *National Association of Home Builders®, NAHB-Wells Fargo Cost of Housing Index, 4th Quarter 2024*

Business Environment

DEMOGRAPHICS

Population Growth

Area	1990 Census	2000 Census	2010 Census	2020 Census	2023 Estimate[2]	Population Growth 1990-2023 (%)
City	95,705	98,359	99,685	101,724	101,083	5.6
MSA[1]	368,151	376,019	379,690	384,324	381,864	3.7
U.S.	248,709,873	281,421,906	308,745,538	331,449,281	332,387,540	33.6

Note: (1) Figures cover the Davenport-Moline-Rock Island, IA-IL Metropolitan Statistical Area; (2) 2019-2023 5-year ACS population estimate
Source: U.S. Census Bureau, 1990 Census, 2000 Census, 2010 Census, 2020 Census, 2019-2023 American Community Survey 5-Year Estimates

Race

Area	White Alone[2] (%)	Black Alone[2] (%)	Asian Alone[2] (%)	AIAN[3] Alone[2] (%)	NHOPI[4] Alone[2] (%)	Other Race Alone[2] (%)	Two or More Races (%)
City	75.9	11.2	2.0	0.3	0.1	2.1	8.5
MSA[1]	79.4	7.7	2.4	0.2	0.1	2.8	7.5
U.S.	63.4	12.4	5.8	0.9	0.2	6.6	10.7

Note: (1) Figures cover the Davenport-Moline-Rock Island, IA-IL Metropolitan Statistical Area; (2) Alone is defined as not being in combination with one or more other races; (3) American Indian and Alaska Native; (4) Native Hawaiian and Other Pacific Islander
Source: U.S. Census Bureau, 2019-2023 American Community Survey 5-Year Estimates

Hispanic or Latino Origin

Area	Total (%)	Mexican (%)	Puerto Rican (%)	Cuban (%)	Other (%)
City	9.1	8.0	0.4	0.1	0.6
MSA[1]	9.5	8.3	0.4	0.1	0.8
U.S.	19.0	11.3	1.8	0.7	5.2

Note: Persons of Hispanic or Latino origin can be of any race; (1) Figures cover the Davenport-Moline-Rock Island, IA-IL Metropolitan Statistical Area
Source: U.S. Census Bureau, 2019-2023 American Community Survey 5-Year Estimates

Age

Area	Percent of Population									Median Age
	Under Age 5	Age 5–19	Age 20–34	Age 35–44	Age 45–54	Age 55–64	Age 65–74	Age 75–84	Age 85+	
City	6.1	17.9	22.1	13.4	11.1	12.9	9.8	4.6	2.2	37.8
MSA[1]	5.7	19.6	17.9	12.9	11.8	13.2	11.1	5.6	2.3	40.2
U.S.	5.7	19.1	20.2	13.1	12.3	12.8	10.0	4.9	1.9	38.7

Note: (1) Figures cover the Davenport-Moline-Rock Island, IA-IL Metropolitan Statistical Area
Source: U.S. Census Bureau, 2019-2023 American Community Survey 5-Year Estimates

Disability by Age

Area	All Ages	Under 18 Years Old	18 to 64 Years Old	65 Years and Over
City	13.9	5.5	11.8	33.3
MSA[1]	13.5	5.7	10.9	30.9
U.S.	13.0	4.7	10.7	32.9

Note: Figures show percent of the civilian noninstitutionalized population that reported having a disability. Disability status is determined from six types of difficulty: vision, hearing, cognitive, ambulatory, self-care, and independent living. For children under 5 years old, hearing and vision difficulty are used to determine disability status. For children between the ages of 5 and 14, disability status is determined from hearing, vision, cognitive, ambulatory, and self-care difficulties. For people aged 15 years and older, they are considered to have a disability if they have difficulty with any one of the six difficulty types; Note: (1) Figures cover the Davenport-Moline-Rock Island, IA-IL Metropolitan Statistical Area
Source: U.S. Census Bureau, 2019-2023 American Community Survey 5-Year Estimates

Ancestry

Area	German	Irish	English	American	Italian	Polish	French[2]	European	Scottish
City	28.1	14.7	8.7	3.0	2.6	1.9	1.3	1.1	1.8
MSA[1]	25.2	13.0	9.4	3.8	2.5	1.9	1.5	1.5	1.5
U.S.	12.6	9.4	9.1	5.5	4.9	2.6	2.0	1.6	1.6

Note: Figures are the percentage of the total population reporting a particular ancestry. The nine most commonly reported ancestries in the U.S. are shown. Figures include multiple ancestries (e.g. if a person reported being Irish and Italian, they were included in both columns); (1) Figures cover the Davenport-Moline-Rock Island, IA-IL Metropolitan Statistical Area; (2) Excludes Basque
Source: U.S. Census Bureau, 2019-2023 American Community Survey 5-Year Estimates

Foreign-born Population

Area	Percent of Population Born in								
	Any Foreign Country	Asia	Mexico	Europe	Caribbean	Central America[2]	South America	Africa	Canada
City	4.6	1.5	1.5	0.5	0.0	0.1	0.0	0.6	0.2
MSA[1]	5.4	1.8	1.7	0.4	0.1	0.1	0.1	1.1	0.1
U.S.	13.9	4.3	3.3	1.4	1.4	1.2	1.2	0.8	0.2

Note: (1) Figures cover the Davenport-Moline-Rock Island, IA-IL Metropolitan Statistical Area; (2) Excludes Mexico.
Source: U.S. Census Bureau, 2019-2023 American Community Survey 5-Year Estimates

Household Size

Area	Persons in Household (%)							Average Household Size
	One	Two	Three	Four	Five	Six	Seven or More	
City	34.9	35.3	13.1	9.5	5.1	1.4	0.7	2.25
MSA[1]	31.5	35.8	13.6	11.3	5.3	1.8	0.8	2.32
U.S.	28.5	33.8	15.4	12.7	5.9	2.3	1.4	2.54

Note: (1) Figures cover the Davenport-Moline-Rock Island, IA-IL Metropolitan Statistical Area
Source: U.S. Census Bureau, 2019-2023 American Community Survey 5-Year Estimates

Household Relationships

Area	Householder	Opposite-sex Spouse	Same-sex Spouse	Opposite-sex Unmarried Partner	Same-sex Unmarried Partner	Child[2]	Grandchild	Other Relatives	Non-relatives
City	41.9	15.9	0.2	3.7	0.2	27.0	2.0	3.0	3.2
MSA[1]	41.4	18.8	0.2	2.9	0.1	27.9	1.8	2.5	2.2
U.S.	38.3	17.5	0.2	2.5	0.2	28.3	2.4	4.8	3.4

Note: Figures are percent of the total population; (1) Figures cover the Davenport-Moline-Rock Island, IA-IL Metropolitan Statistical Area; (2) Includes biological, adopted, and stepchildren of the householder
Source: U.S. Census Bureau, 2020 Census

Gender

Area	Males	Females	Males per 100 Females
City	50,102	50,981	98.3
MSA[1]	189,025	192,839	98.0
U.S.	164,545,087	167,842,453	98.0

Note: (1) Figures cover the Davenport-Moline-Rock Island, IA-IL Metropolitan Statistical Area
Source: U.S. Census Bureau, 2019-2023 American Community Survey 5-Year Estimates

Marital Status

Area	Never Married	Now Married[2]	Separated	Widowed	Divorced
City	37.3	44.0	1.0	5.6	12.0
MSA[1]	31.1	50.1	1.2	6.2	11.5
U.S.	34.1	47.9	1.7	5.6	10.7

Note: Figures are percentages and cover the population 15 years of age and older; (1) Figures cover the Davenport-Moline-Rock Island, IA-IL Metropolitan Statistical Area; (2) Excludes separated
Source: U.S. Census Bureau, 2019-2023 American Community Survey 5-Year Estimates

Religious Groups by Family

Area	Catholic	Baptist	Methodist	LDS[2]	Pentecostal	Lutheran	Islam	Adventist	Other
MSA[1]	13.2	3.2	3.6	0.8	1.5	6.6	0.7	0.8	6.7
U.S.	18.7	7.3	3.0	2.0	1.8	1.7	1.3	1.3	11.6

Note: Figures are the number of adherents as a percentage of the total population and cover the eight largest religious groups in the U.S.; (1) Figures cover the Davenport-Moline-Rock Island, IA-IL Metropolitan Statistical Area; (2) Church of Jesus Christ of Latter-day Saints
Sources: 2020 U.S. Religion Census, Association of Statisticians of American Religious Bodies; The Association of Religion Data Archives (ARDA)

Religious Groups by Tradition

Area	Catholic	Evangelical Protestant	Mainline Protestant	Black Protestant	Islam	Judaism	Hinduism	Orthodox	Buddhism
MSA[1]	13.2	8.5	10.6	1.9	0.7	0.1	0.2	0.1	n/a
U.S.	18.7	16.5	5.2	2.3	1.3	0.6	0.4	0.4	0.3

Note: Figures are the number of adherents as a percentage of the total population; (1) Figures cover the Davenport-Moline-Rock Island, IA-IL Metropolitan Statistical Area
Sources: 2020 U.S. Religion Census, Association of Statisticians of American Religious Bodies; The Association of Religion Data Archives (ARDA)

ECONOMY

Real Gross Domestic Product (GDP)

Area	2017	2018	2019	2020	2021	2022	2023	Rank[3]
MSA[1]	21.6	21.4	21.6	21.0	21.6	22.0	22.4	136
U.S.[2]	17,619.1	18,160.7	18,642.5	18,238.9	19,387.6	19,896.6	20,436.3	—

Note: Figures are in billions of chained 2017 dollars; (1) Figures cover the Davenport-Moline-Rock Island, IA-IL Metropolitan Statistical Area; (2) Figures cover real GDP within metropolitan areas; (3) Rank is based on 2023 data and ranges from 1 to 384
Source: U.S. Bureau of Economic Analysis

Economic Growth

Area	2014	2015	2016	2017	2018	2019	2020	2021	2022	2023
MSA[1]	0.4	-1.4	-0.7	1.0	-0.7	0.8	-2.4	2.8	1.6	2.1
U.S.[2]	2.6	3.2	2.0	2.7	3.1	2.7	-2.2	6.3	2.6	2.7

Note: Figures are real gross domestic product growth rates and represent percent change from preceding period; (1) Figures cover the Davenport-Moline-Rock Island, IA-IL Metropolitan Statistical Area; (2) Figures are the average growth rates within metropolitan areas
Source: U.S. Bureau of Economic Analysis

Metropolitan Area Exports

Area	2018	2019	2020	2021	2022	2023	Rank[2]
MSA[1]	6,761.9	6,066.3	5,097.5	6,341.0	8,173.6	6,050.0	57
U.S.	1,664,056.1	1,645,173.7	1,431,406.6	1,753,941.4	2,062,937.4	2,019,160.5	—

Note: Figures are in millions of dollars; (1) Figures cover the Davenport-Moline-Rock Island, IA-IL Metropolitan Statistical Area; (2) Rank is based on 2023 data and ranges from 1 to 386
Source: U.S. Department of Commerce, International Trade Administration, Office of Trade and Economic Analysis, Industry and Analysis, Exports by Metropolitan Area, data extracted April 2, 2025

Building Permits

Area	Single-Family			Multi-Family			Total		
	2023	2024	Pct. Chg.	2023	2024	Pct. Chg.	2023	2024	Pct. Chg.
City	94	149	58.5	121	162	33.9	215	311	44.7
MSA[1]	366	401	9.6	248	564	127.4	614	965	57.2
U.S.	920,000	981,900	6.7	591,100	496,100	-16.1	1,511,100	1,478,000	-2.2

Note: (1) Figures cover the Davenport-Moline-Rock Island, IA-IL Metropolitan Statistical Area; Figures represent new, privately-owned housing units authorized (unadjusted data)
Source: U.S. Census Bureau, Building Permits Survey (BPS), 2023, 2024

Bankruptcy Filings

Area	Business Filings			Nonbusiness Filings		
	2023	2024	% Chg.	2023	2024	% Chg.
Scott County	9	4	-55.6	157	158	0.6
U.S.	18,926	23,107	22.1	434,064	494,201	13.9

Note: Business filings include Chapter 7, Chapter 9, Chapter 11, Chapter 12, Chapter 13, Chapter 15, and Section 304; Nonbusiness filings include Chapter 7, Chapter 11, and Chapter 13
Source: Administrative Office of the U.S. Courts, Business and Nonbusiness Bankruptcy, County Cases Commenced by Chapter of the Bankruptcy Code, During the 12-Month Period Ending December 31, 2023 and Business and Nonbusiness Bankruptcy, County Cases Commenced by Chapter of the Bankruptcy Code, During the 12-Month Period Ending December 31, 2024

Housing Vacancy Rates

Area	Gross Vacancy Rate[3] (%)			Year-Round Vacancy Rate[4] (%)			Rental Vacancy Rate[5] (%)			Homeowner Vacancy Rate[6] (%)		
	2022	2023	2024	2022	2023	2024	2022	2023	2024	2022	2023	2024
MSA[1]	n/a	n/a	n/a	n/a	n/a	n/a	n/a	n/a	n/a	n/a	n/a	n/a
U.S.[2]	9.1	9.0	9.1	7.5	7.5	7.6	5.7	6.5	6.8	0.8	0.8	1.0

Note: (1) Figures cover the Davenport-Moline-Rock Island, IA-IL Metropolitan Statistical Area; (2) Figures cover the 75 largest Metropolitan Statistical Areas; (3) The percentage of the total housing inventory that is vacant; (4) The percentage of the housing inventory (excluding seasonal units) that is year-round vacant; (5) The percentage of rental inventory that is vacant for rent; (6) The percentage of homeowner inventory that is vacant for sale; n/a not available
Source: U.S. Census Bureau, Housing Vacancies and Homeownership Annual Statistics: 2022, 2023, 2024

INCOME

Income

Area	Per Capita ($)	Median Household ($)	Average Household ($)
City	36,583	64,497	83,699
MSA[1]	39,357	71,925	93,006
U.S.	43,289	78,538	110,491

Note: (1) Figures cover the Davenport-Moline-Rock Island, IA-IL Metropolitan Statistical Area
Source: U.S. Census Bureau, 2019-2023 American Community Survey 5-Year Estimates

Household Income Distribution

Area	Percent of Households Earning							
	Under $15,000	$15,000 -$24,999	$25,000 -$34,999	$35,000 -$49,999	$50,000 -$74,999	$75,000 -$99,999	$100,000 -$149,999	$150,000 and up
City	10.8	7.0	8.8	11.5	19.0	13.5	17.4	12.0
MSA[1]	9.0	6.9	7.5	11.5	17.0	13.6	18.6	16.0
U.S.	8.5	6.6	6.8	10.4	15.7	12.7	17.4	21.9

Note: (1) Figures cover the Davenport-Moline-Rock Island, IA-IL Metropolitan Statistical Area
Source: U.S. Census Bureau, 2019-2023 American Community Survey 5-Year Estimates

Poverty Rate

Area	All Ages	Under 18 Years Old	18 to 64 Years Old	65 Years and Over
City	15.6	20.7	15.0	11.3
MSA[1]	12.4	16.9	12.0	8.3
U.S.	12.4	16.3	11.6	10.4

Note: Figures are percentage of people whose income during the past 12 months was below the poverty level; (1) Figures cover the Davenport-Moline-Rock Island, IA-IL Metropolitan Statistical Area
Source: U.S. Census Bureau, 2019-2023 American Community Survey 5-Year Estimates

EMPLOYMENT

Labor Force and Employment

Area	Civilian Labor Force			Workers Employed		
	Dec. 2023	Dec. 2024	% Chg.	Dec. 2023	Dec. 2024	% Chg.
City	49,490	49,873	0.8	47,766	47,656	-0.2
MSA[1]	184,725	184,714	0.0	177,254	176,542	-0.4
U.S.	166,661,000	167,746,000	0.7	160,754,000	161,294,000	0.3

Note: Data is not seasonally adjusted and covers workers 16 years of age and older; (1) Figures cover the Davenport-Moline-Rock Island, IA-IL Metropolitan Statistical Area
Source: Bureau of Labor Statistics, Local Area Unemployment Statistics

Unemployment Rate

Area	2024											
	Jan.	Feb.	Mar.	Apr.	May	Jun.	Jul.	Aug.	Sep.	Oct.	Nov.	Dec.
City	4.2	3.6	3.5	3.0	3.8	4.5	4.8	4.9	5.1	4.9	4.9	4.4
MSA[1]	5.2	4.8	4.5	4.0	4.2	4.7	4.8	4.9	5.2	5.0	4.8	4.4
U.S.	4.1	4.2	3.9	3.5	3.7	4.3	4.5	4.4	3.9	3.9	4.0	3.8

Note: Data is not seasonally adjusted and covers workers 16 years of age and older; (1) Figures cover the Davenport-Moline-Rock Island, IA-IL Metropolitan Statistical Area
Source: Bureau of Labor Statistics, Local Area Unemployment Statistics

Average Wages

Occupation	$/Hr.	Occupation	$/Hr.
Accountants and Auditors	39.77	Maintenance and Repair Workers	25.55
Automotive Mechanics	25.81	Marketing Managers	69.88
Bookkeepers	23.07	Network and Computer Systems Admin.	40.45
Carpenters	28.79	Nurses, Licensed Practical	28.99
Cashiers	14.78	Nurses, Registered	36.47
Computer Programmers	38.43	Nursing Assistants	18.90
Computer Systems Analysts	42.15	Office Clerks, General	20.19
Computer User Support Specialists	27.46	Physical Therapists	45.91
Construction Laborers	27.61	Physicians	133.88
Cooks, Restaurant	16.58	Plumbers, Pipefitters and Steamfitters	34.59
Customer Service Representatives	20.62	Police and Sheriff's Patrol Officers	34.22
Dentists	95.43	Postal Service Mail Carriers	28.67
Electricians	34.34	Real Estate Sales Agents	31.72
Engineers, Electrical	54.36	Retail Salespersons	16.82
Fast Food and Counter Workers	14.11	Sales Representatives, Technical/Scientific	46.92
Financial Managers	69.21	Secretaries, Exc. Legal/Medical/Executive	21.95
First-Line Supervisors of Office Workers	30.67	Security Guards	19.78
General and Operations Managers	52.32	Surgeons	n/a
Hairdressers/Cosmetologists	21.43	Teacher Assistants, Exc. Postsecondary[1]	15.98
Home Health and Personal Care Aides	16.37	Teachers, Secondary School, Exc. Sp. Ed.[1]	32.25
Janitors and Cleaners	17.91	Telemarketers	15.38
Landscaping/Groundskeeping Workers	18.79	Truck Drivers, Heavy/Tractor-Trailer	26.97
Lawyers	67.21	Truck Drivers, Light/Delivery Services	22.49
Maids and Housekeeping Cleaners	15.51	Waiters and Waitresses	14.76

Note: Wage data covers the Davenport-Moline-Rock Island, IA-IL Metropolitan Statistical Area; (1) Hourly wages were calculated from annual wage data based on a 40 hour work week
Source: Bureau of Labor Statistics, Metro Area Occupational Employment & Wage Estimates, May 2024

Employment by Industry

Sector	MSA[1] Number of Employees	MSA[1] Percent of Total	U.S. Percent of Total
Construction, Mining, and Logging	10,400	5.7	5.5
Financial Activities	7,400	4.1	5.8
Government	26,200	14.4	14.9
Information	1,400	0.8	1.9
Leisure and Hospitality	17,700	9.7	10.4
Manufacturing	23,300	12.8	8.0
Other Services	6,800	3.7	3.7
Private Education and Health Services	27,200	15.0	16.9
Professional and Business Services	20,500	11.3	14.2
Retail Trade	21,300	11.7	10.0
Transportation, Warehousing, and Utilities	7,600	4.2	4.8
Wholesale Trade	11,800	6.5	3.9

Note: Figures are non-farm employment as of December 2024. Figures are not seasonally adjusted and include workers 16 years of age and older; (1) Figures cover the Davenport-Moline-Rock Island, IA-IL Metropolitan Statistical Area
Source: Bureau of Labor Statistics, Current Employment Statistics, Employment, Hours, and Earnings

Employment by Occupation

Occupation Classification	City (%)	MSA[1] (%)	U.S. (%)
Management, Business, Science, and Arts	37.5	38.1	42.0
Natural Resources, Construction, and Maintenance	8.5	8.9	8.6
Production, Transportation, and Material Moving	17.6	17.3	13.0
Sales and Office	19.2	19.6	19.9
Service	17.3	16.2	16.5

Note: Figures cover employed civilians 16 years of age and older; (1) Figures cover the Davenport-Moline-Rock Island, IA-IL Metropolitan Statistical Area
Source: U.S. Census Bureau, 2019-2023 American Community Survey 5-Year Estimates

Occupations with Greatest Projected Employment Growth: 2022 – 2032

Occupation[1]	2022 Employment	2032 Projected Employment	Numeric Employment Change	Percent Employment Change
Home Health and Personal Care Aides	25,390	32,770	7,380	29.1
Heavy and Tractor-Trailer Truck Drivers	46,210	52,250	6,040	13.1
Registered Nurses	35,700	39,270	3,570	10.0
Stockers and Order Fillers	24,100	27,230	3,130	13.0
Laborers and Freight, Stock, and Material Movers, Hand	33,560	36,540	2,980	8.9
Cooks, Restaurant	13,190	15,840	2,650	20.1
Nursing Assistants (SOC 2018)	22,400	24,690	2,290	10.2
Construction Laborers	14,560	16,720	2,160	14.8
Medical and Health Services Managers	6,200	8,350	2,150	34.7
Financial Managers	8,990	10,870	1,880	20.9

Note: Projections cover Iowa; (1) Sorted by numeric employment change
Source: www.projectionscentral.org, State Occupational Projections, 2022–2032 Long-Term Projections

Fastest-Growing Occupations: 2022 – 2032

Occupation[1]	2022 Employment	2032 Projected Employment	Numeric Employment Change	Percent Employment Change
Wind Turbine Service Technicians	600	920	320	53.3
Nurse Practitioners	2,400	3,670	1,270	52.9
Data Scientists	2,010	2,760	750	37.3
Physical Therapist Assistants	1,260	1,720	460	36.5
Statisticians	400	540	140	35.0
Medical and Health Services Managers	6,200	8,350	2,150	34.7
Occupational Therapy Assistants	470	630	160	34.0
Information Security Analysts (SOC 2018)	1,250	1,670	420	33.6
Substance Abuse, Behavioral Disorder, and Mental Health Counselors	3,190	4,180	990	31.0
Physician Assistants	1,210	1,580	370	30.6

Note: Projections cover Iowa; (1) Sorted by percent employment change and excludes occupations with numeric employment change less than 50
Source: www.projectionscentral.org, State Occupational Projections, 2022–2032 Long-Term Projections

CITY FINANCES

City Government Finances

Component	2022 ($000)	2022 ($ per capita)
Total Revenues	228,226	2,242
Total Expenditures	160,204	1,574
Debt Outstanding	234,790	2,306

Source: U.S. Census Bureau, State & Local Government Finances 2022

City Government Revenue by Source

Source	2022 ($000)	2022 ($ per capita)	2022 (%)
General Revenue			
From Federal Government	15,231	150	6.7
From State Government	21,418	210	9.4
From Local Governments	609	6	0.3
Taxes			
Property	85,403	839	37.4
Sales and Gross Receipts	32,261	317	14.1
Personal Income	0	0	0.0
Corporate Income	0	0	0.0
Motor Vehicle License	0	0	0.0
Other Taxes	3,463	34	1.5
Current Charges	49,065	482	21.5
Liquor Store	0	0	0.0
Utility	379	4	0.2

Source: U.S. Census Bureau, State & Local Government Finances 2022

City Government Expenditures by Function

Function	2022 ($000)	2022 ($ per capita)	2022 (%)
General Direct Expenditures			
Air Transportation	316	3	0.2
Corrections	0	0	0.0
Education	0	0	0.0
Employment Security Administration	0	0	0.0
Financial Administration	2,366	23	1.5
Fire Protection	21,036	206	13.1
General Public Buildings	1,773	17	1.1
Governmental Administration, Other	2,762	27	1.7
Health	0	0	0.0
Highways	17,951	176	11.2
Hospitals	0	0	0.0
Housing and Community Development	9,576	94	6.0
Interest on General Debt	7,481	73	4.7
Judicial and Legal	0	0	0.0
Libraries	5,864	57	3.7
Parking	954	9	0.6
Parks and Recreation	8,176	80	5.1
Police Protection	29,253	287	18.3
Public Welfare	0	0	0.0
Sewerage	16,646	163	10.4
Solid Waste Management	5,516	54	3.4
Veterans' Services	0	0	0.0
Liquor Store	0	0	0.0
Utility	6,741	66	4.2

Source: U.S. Census Bureau, State & Local Government Finances 2022

TAXES

State Corporate Income Tax Rates

State	Tax Rate (%)	Income Brackets ($)	Num. of Brackets	Financial Institution Tax Rate (%)[a]	Federal Income Tax Ded.
Iowa	Undetermined	100,000 - 250,001	3	4.7	Yes (h)

Note: Tax rates for tax year 2024; (a) Rates listed are the corporate income tax rate applied to financial institutions or excise taxes based on income. Some states have other taxes based upon the value of deposits or shares; (h) 50% of the federal income tax is deductible.
Source: Federation of Tax Administrators, State Corporate Income Tax Rates, January 1, 2025

State Individual Income Tax Rates

State	Tax Rate (%)	Income Brackets ($)	Personal Exemptions ($)			Standard Ded. ($)	
			Single	Married	Depend.	Single	Married
Iowa (a)	4.4 - 5.7 (bb)	6,210 - 62,100	40	80	40 (c)	—	—

Note: Tax rates for tax year 2024; Local- and county-level taxes are not included; Federal income tax is deductible on state income tax returns; (a) 16 states have statutory provision for automatically adjusting to the rate of inflation the dollar values of the income tax brackets, standard deductions, and/or personal exemptions. Oregon does not index the income brackets for $125,000 and over See: INFL and SPEC above; (c) The personal exemption takes the form of a tax credit instead of a deduction; (bb) Louisiana lawmakers repealed the state's throwout rule, ending the taxation of so-called "nowhere income." Iowa is phasing-in a flat rate by 2027, while Nebraska (LB 754 signed into law) and South Carolina is phasing-in a reduced top rate by 2027.
Source: Federation of Tax Administrators, State Individual Income Tax Rates, January 1, 2025

Various State Sales and Excise Tax Rates

State	State Sales Tax (%)	Gasoline[1] ($/gal.)	Cigarette[2] ($/pack)	Spirits[3] ($/gal.)	Wine[4] ($/gal.)	Beer[5] ($/gal.)	Recreational Marijuana (%)
Iowa	6	0.30	1.36	15.14	1.75	0.19	Not legal

Note: All tax rates as of January 1, 2025; (1) The American Petroleum Institute has developed a methodology for determining the average tax rate on a gallon of fuel. Rates may include any of the following: excise taxes, environmental fees, storage tank fees, other fees or taxes, general sales tax, and local taxes; (2) The federal excise tax of $1.0066 per pack and local taxes are not included; (3) Rates are those applicable to off-premise sales of 40% alcohol by volume (a.b.v.) distilled spirits in 750ml containers. Local excise taxes are excluded; (4) Rates are those applicable to off-premise sales of 11% a.b.v. non-carbonated wine in 750ml containers; (5) Rates are those applicable to off-premise sales of 4.7% a.b.v. beer in 12 ounce containers.
Source: Tax Foundation, 2025 Facts & Figures: How Does Your State Compare?

State Tax Competitiveness Index

State	Overall Rank	Corporate Tax Rank	Individual Income Tax Rank	Sales Tax Rank	Property Tax Rank	Unemployment Insurance Tax Rank
Iowa	20	23	19	11	32	33

Note: The Tax Foundation's State Tax Competitiveness Index enables policymakers, taxpayers, and business leaders to gauge how their states' tax systems compare. A rank of 1 is best, 50 is worst. Rankings do not average to the total. States without a tax rank equally as 1. DC's scores and rankings do not affect other states. The report shows tax systems as of July 1, 2024 (the beginning of Fiscal Year 2025).
Source: Tax Foundation, State Tax Competitiveness Index 2025

TRANSPORTATION

Means of Transportation to Work

Area	Car/Truck/Van		Public Transportation			Bicycle	Walked	Other Means	Worked at Home
	Drove Alone	Car-pooled	Bus	Subway	Railroad				
City	78.8	7.3	0.8	0.0	0.1	0.2	2.7	1.1	8.9
MSA[1]	80.1	7.2	0.8	0.0	0.0	0.1	2.4	0.9	8.4
U.S.	70.2	8.5	1.7	1.3	0.4	0.4	2.4	1.6	13.5

Note: Figures are percentages and cover workers 16 years of age and older; (1) Figures cover the Davenport-Moline-Rock Island, IA-IL Metropolitan Statistical Area
Source: U.S. Census Bureau, 2019-2023 American Community Survey 5-Year Estimates

Travel Time to Work

Area	Less Than 10 Minutes	10 to 19 Minutes	20 to 29 Minutes	30 to 44 Minutes	45 to 59 Minutes	60 to 89 Minutes	90 Minutes or More
City	15.3	45.9	24.3	8.4	2.9	2.0	1.1
MSA[1]	18.0	35.9	26.0	12.4	3.7	2.6	1.4
U.S.	12.6	28.6	21.2	20.8	8.1	6.0	2.8

Note: Note: Figures are percentages and include workers 16 years old and over; (1) Figures cover the Davenport-Moline-Rock Island, IA-IL Metropolitan Statistical Area
Source: U.S. Census Bureau, 2019-2023 American Community Survey 5-Year Estimates

Key Congestion Measures

Measure	2000	2010	2015	2020	2022
Annual Hours of Delay, Total (000)	n/a	n/a	4,084	2,579	4,185
Annual Hours of Delay, Per Auto Commuter	n/a	n/a	14	9	15
Annual Congestion Cost, Per Auto Commuter ($)	n/a	n/a	320	216	346

Note: n/a not available
Source: Texas A&M Transportation Institute, 2023 Urban Mobility Report

Freeway Travel Time Index

Measure	1985	1990	1995	2000	2005	2010	2015	2020	2022
Urban Area Index[1]	n/a	n/a	n/a	n/a	n/a	n/a	1.05	1.04	1.06
Urban Area Rank[1,2]	n/a	n/a	n/a	n/a	n/a	n/a	n/a	n/a	n/a

Note: Freeway Travel Time Index—the ratio of travel time in the peak period to the travel time at free-flow conditions. For example, a value of 1.30 indicates a 20-minute free-flow trip takes 26 minutes in the peak (20 minutes x 1.30 = 26 minutes); (1) Covers the Davenport IA-IL urban area; (2) Rank is based on 101 larger urban areas (#1 = highest travel time index); n/a not available
Source: Texas A&M Transportation Institute, 2023 Urban Mobility Report

Public Transportation

Agency Name / Mode of Transportation	Vehicles Operated in Maximum Service[1]	Annual Unlinked Passenger Trips[2] (in thous.)	Annual Passenger Miles[3] (in thous.)
Davenport Public Transit			
Bus (directly operated)	14	391.9	n/a

Note: (1) Number of revenue vehicles operated by the given mode and type of service to meet the annual maximum service requirement. This is the revenue vehicle count during the peak season of the year; on the week and day that maximum service is provided. Vehicles operated in maximum service (VOMS) exclude atypical days and one-time special events; (2) Number of passengers who boarded public transportation vehicles. Passengers are counted each time they board a vehicle no matter how many vehicles they use to travel from their origin to their destination. (3) Sum of the distances ridden by all passengers during the entire fiscal year.
Source: Federal Transit Administration, National Transit Database, 2023

Air Transportation

Airport Name and Code / Type of Service	Passenger Airlines[1]	Passenger Enplanements	Freight Carriers[2]	Freight (lbs)
Quad City International Airport (MLI)				
Domestic service (U.S. carriers only)	11	326,491	2	115
International service (U.S. carriers only)	0	0	0	0

Note: (1) Includes all U.S.-based major, minor and commuter airlines that carried at least one passenger during the year; (2) Includes all U.S.-based airlines and freight carriers that transported at least one pound of freight during the year.
Source: Bureau of Transportation Statistics, The Intermodal Transportation Database, Air Carriers: T-100 Domestic Market (U.S. carriers only), 2024; Bureau of Transportation Statistics, The Intermodal Transportation Database, Air Carriers: T-100 International Market (U.S. carriers only), 2024

BUSINESSES

Major Business Headquarters

Company Name	Industry	Rankings Fortune[1]	Rankings Forbes[2]
No companies listed	-	-	-

Note: (1) Companies that produce a 10-K are ranked 1 to 500 based on 2023 revenue; (2) All private companies with at least $2 billion in annual revenue through the end of their most current fiscal year are ranked 1 to 275; companies listed are headquartered in the city; dashes indicate no ranking
Source: Fortune, "Fortune 500," 2024; Forbes, "America's Largest Private Companies," 2024

Living Environment

COST OF LIVING

Cost of Living Index

Composite Index	Groceries	Housing	Utilities	Transportation	Health Care	Misc. Goods/Services
90.1	97.4	76.8	83.2	105.1	97.3	94.6

Note: The Cost of Living Index measures regional differences in the cost of consumer goods and services, excluding taxes and non-consumer expenditures, for professional and managerial households in the top income quintile. It is based on more than 50,000 prices covering almost 60 different items for which prices are collected three times a year by chambers of commerce, economic development organizations or university applied economic centers in each participating urban area. The numbers shown should be read as a percentage above or below the national average of 100. For example, a value of 115.4 in the groceries column indicates that grocery prices are 15.4% higher than the national average. Small differences in the index numbers should not be interpreted as significant; Figures cover the Davenport-Moline-Rock Is IA-IL urban area.
Source: The Council for Community and Economic Research, Cost of Living Index, 2024

Grocery Prices

Area[1]	T-Bone Steak ($/pound)	Frying Chicken ($/pound)	Whole Milk ($/half gal.)	Eggs ($/dozen)	Orange Juice ($/64 oz.)	Coffee ($/11.5 oz.)
City[2]	15.52	1.43	4.92	3.35	4.44	5.02
Avg.	15.42	1.55	4.69	3.25	4.41	5.46
Min.	14.50	1.16	4.43	2.75	4.00	4.85
Max.	17.56	2.89	5.49	4.78	5.54	7.89

*Note: (1) Values for the local area are compared with the average, minimum and maximum values for all 276 areas in the Cost of Living Index; (2) Figures cover the Davenport-Moline-Rock Is IA-IL urban area; **T-Bone Steak** (price per pound); **Frying Chicken** (price per pound, whole fryer); **Whole Milk** (half gallon carton); **Eggs** (price per dozen, Grade A, large); **Orange Juice** (64 oz. Tropicana or Florida Natural); **Coffee** (11.5 oz. can, vacuum-packed, Maxwell House, Hills Bros, or Folgers).*
Source: The Council for Community and Economic Research, Cost of Living Index, 2024

Housing and Utility Costs

Area[1]	New Home Price ($)	Apartment Rent ($/month)	All Electric ($/month)	Part Electric ($/month)	Other Energy ($/month)	Telephone ($/month)
City[2]	387,652	1,218	-	85.51	62.12	200.43
Avg.	515,975	1,550	210.99	123.07	82.07	194.99
Min.	265,375	692	104.33	53.68	36.26	179.42
Max.	2,775,821	5,719	529.02	397.28	361.63	223.33

*Note: (1) Values for the local area are compared with the average, minimum and maximum values for all 276 areas in the Cost of Living Index; (2) Figures cover the Davenport-Moline-Rock Is IA-IL urban area; **New Home Price** (2,400 sf living area, 8,000 sf lot, in urban area with full utilities); **Apartment Rent** (950 sf 2 bedroom/1.5 or 2 bath, unfurnished, excluding all utilities except water); **All Electric** (average monthly cost for an all-electric home); **Part Electric** (average monthly cost for a part-electric home); **Other Energy** (average monthly cost for natural gas, fuel oil, coal, wood, and any other forms of energy except electricity); **Telephone** (price includes the base monthly rate plus taxes and fees for three lines of mobile phone service).*
Source: The Council for Community and Economic Research, Cost of Living Index, 2024

Health Care, Transportation, and Other Costs

Area[1]	Doctor ($/visit)	Dentist ($/visit)	Optometrist ($/visit)	Gasoline ($/gallon)	Beauty Salon ($/visit)	Men's Shirt ($)
City[2]	167.17	105.92	108.62	3.41	39.87	34.38
Avg.	143.77	117.51	129.23	3.32	48.57	38.14
Min.	36.74	58.67	67.33	2.80	24.00	13.41
Max.	270.44	216.82	307.33	5.28	94.00	63.89

*Note: (1) Values for the local area are compared with the average, minimum and maximum values for all 276 areas in the Cost of Living Index; (2) Figures cover the Davenport-Moline-Rock Is IA-IL urban area; **Doctor** (general practitioners routine exam of an established patient); **Dentist** (adult teeth cleaning and periodic oral examination); **Optometrist** (full vision eye exam for established adult patient); **Gasoline** (one gallon regular unleaded, national brand, including all taxes, cash price at self-service pump if available); **Beauty Salon** (woman's shampoo, trim, and blow-dry); **Men's Shirt** (cotton/polyester dress shirt, pinpoint weave, long sleeves).*
Source: The Council for Community and Economic Research, Cost of Living Index, 2024

HOUSING

Homeownership Rate

Area	2017 (%)	2018 (%)	2019 (%)	2020 (%)	2021 (%)	2022 (%)	2023 (%)	2024 (%)
MSA[1]	n/a	n/a	n/a	n/a	n/a	n/a	n/a	n/a
U.S.	63.9	64.4	64.6	66.6	65.5	65.8	65.9	65.6

Note: (1) Figures cover the Davenport-Moline-Rock Island, IA-IL Metropolitan Statistical Area; n/a not available
Source: U.S. Census Bureau, Housing Vacancies and Homeownership Annual Statistics: 2017-2024

House Price Index (HPI)

Area	National Ranking[2]	Quarterly Change (%)	One-Year Change (%)	Five-Year Change (%)	Since 1991Q1 (%)
MSA[1]	143	-0.86	4.87	39.11	236.99
U.S.[3]	—	1.43	4.51	57.13	327.82

Note: The HPI is a weighted repeat sales index. It measures average price changes in repeat sales or refinancings on the same properties. This information is obtained by reviewing repeat mortgage transactions on single-family properties whose mortgages have been purchased or securitized by Fannie Mae or Freddie Mac since January 1975; (1) Figures cover the Davenport-Moline-Rock Island, IA-IL Metropolitan Statistical Area; (2) Rankings are based on annual percentage change for all metro areas containing at least 15,000 transactions over the last 10 years and ranges from 1 to 241; (3) figures based on a weighted average of Census Division estimates using a seasonally adjusted, purchase-only index; all figures are for the period ending December 31, 2024
Source: Federal Housing Finance Agency, Change in FHFA Metropolitan Area House Price Indexes, All Transactions Index, 2024Q4

Home Value

Area	Under $100,000	$100,000 -$199,999	$200,000 -$299,999	$300,000 -$399,999	$400,000 -$499,999	$500,000 -$999,999	$1,000,000 or more	Median ($)
City	18.4	45.7	19.6	9.4	3.8	2.8	0.3	162,900
MSA[1]	20.4	38.7	21.3	9.7	5.0	4.2	0.7	170,000
U.S.	12.1	17.8	19.5	14.4	10.5	19.1	6.5	303,400

Note: Figures are percentages except for median and cover owner-occupied housing units; (1) Figures cover the Davenport-Moline-Rock Island, IA-IL Metropolitan Statistical Area
Source: U.S. Census Bureau, 2019-2023 American Community Survey 5-Year Estimates

Year Housing Structure Built

Area	2020 or Later	2010 -2019	2000 -2009	1990 -1999	1980 -1989	1970 -1979	1960 -1969	1950 -1959	1940 -1949	Before 1940	Median Year
City	0.6	4.8	9.1	8.4	6.9	15.3	12.8	11.8	6.0	24.2	1966
MSA[1]	0.6	5.3	8.4	7.9	7.0	16.0	13.7	12.1	6.9	22.1	1966
U.S.	1.2	8.9	13.6	12.8	13.0	14.4	10.0	9.7	4.5	11.9	1980

Note: Figures are percentages except for Median Year; Note: (1) Figures cover the Davenport-Moline-Rock Island, IA-IL Metropolitan Statistical Area
Source: U.S. Census Bureau, 2019-2023 American Community Survey 5-Year Estimates

Gross Monthly Rent

Area	Under $500	$500 -$999	$1,000 -$1,499	$1,500 -$1,999	$2,000 -$2,499	$2,500 -$2,999	$3,000 and up	Median ($)
City	7.1	52.5	29.5	6.8	1.6	0.1	2.4	930
MSA[1]	11.1	50.2	27.2	7.3	1.5	0.8	1.9	899
U.S.	6.5	22.3	29.5	20.2	10.8	4.8	5.9	1,348

Note: Figures are percentages except for median; Gross rent is the contract rent plus the estimated average monthly cost of utilities (electricity, gas, and water and sewer) and fuels (oil, coal, kerosene, wood, etc.) if these are paid by the renter (or paid for the renter by someone else); (1) Figures cover the Davenport-Moline-Rock Island, IA-IL Metropolitan Statistical Area
Source: U.S. Census Bureau, 2019-2023 American Community Survey 5-Year Estimates

HEALTH

Health Risk Factors

Category	MSA[1] (%)	U.S. (%)
Adults aged 18–64 who have any kind of health care coverage	n/a	90.8
Adults who reported being in good or better health	n/a	81.8
Adults who have been told they have high blood cholesterol	n/a	36.9
Adults who have been told they have high blood pressure	n/a	34.0
Adults who are current smokers	n/a	12.1
Adults who currently use e-cigarettes	n/a	7.7
Adults who currently use chewing tobacco, snuff, or snus	n/a	3.2
Adults who are heavy drinkers[2]	n/a	6.1
Adults who are binge drinkers[3]	n/a	15.2
Adults who are overweight (BMI 25.0 - 29.9)	n/a	34.4
Adults who are obese (BMI 30.0 - 99.8)	n/a	34.3
Adults who participated in any physical activities in the past month	n/a	75.8

Note: All figures are crude prevalence; (1) Figures for the Davenport-Moline-Rock Island, IA-IL Metropolitan Statistical Area were not available.
(2) Heavy drinkers are classified as adult men having more than 14 drinks per week and adult women having more than 7 drinks per week; (3) Binge drinkers are classified as males having five or more drinks on one occasion or females having four or more drinks on one occasion
Source: Centers for Disease Control and Prevention, Behavioral Risk Factor Surveillance System, SMART: Selected Metropolitan Area Risk Trends, 2023

Acute and Chronic Health Conditions

Category	MSA[1] (%)	U.S. (%)
Adults who have ever been told they had a heart attack	n/a	4.2
Adults who have ever been told they have angina or coronary heart disease	n/a	4.0
Adults who have ever been told they had a stroke	n/a	3.3
Adults who have ever been told they have asthma	n/a	15.7
Adults who have ever been told they have arthritis	n/a	26.3
Adults who have ever been told they have diabetes[2]	n/a	11.5
Adults who have ever been told they had skin cancer	n/a	5.6
Adults who have ever been told they had any other types of cancer	n/a	8.4
Adults who have ever been told they have COPD	n/a	6.4
Adults who have ever been told they have kidney disease	n/a	3.7
Adults who have ever been told they have a form of depression	n/a	22.0

Note: All figures are crude prevalence; (1) Figures for the Davenport-Moline-Rock Island, IA-IL Metropolitan Statistical Area were not available.
(2) Figures do not include pregnancy-related, borderline, or pre-diabetes
Source: Centers for Disease Control and Prevention, Behavioral Risk Factor Surveillance System, SMART: Selected Metropolitan Area Risk Trends, 2023

Health Screening and Vaccination Rates

Category	MSA[1] (%)	U.S. (%)
Adults who have ever been tested for HIV	n/a	37.5
Adults who have had their blood cholesterol checked within the last five years	n/a	87.0
Adults aged 65+ who have had flu shot within the past year	n/a	63.4
Adults aged 65+ who have ever had a pneumonia vaccination	n/a	71.9

Note: All figures are crude prevalence; (1) Figures for the Davenport-Moline-Rock Island, IA-IL Metropolitan Statistical Area were not available.
Source: Centers for Disease Control and Prevention, Behavioral Risk Factor Surveillance System, SMART: Selected Metropolitan Area Risk Trends, 2023

Disability Status

Category	MSA[1] (%)	U.S. (%)
Adults who reported being deaf	n/a	7.4
Are you blind or have serious difficulty seeing, even when wearing glasses?	n/a	4.9
Do you have difficulty doing errands alone?	n/a	7.8
Do you have difficulty dressing or bathing?	n/a	3.6
Do you have serious difficulty concentrating/remembering/making decisions?	n/a	13.7
Do you have serious difficulty walking or climbing stairs?	n/a	13.2

Note: All figures are crude prevalence; (1) Figures for the Davenport-Moline-Rock Island, IA-IL Metropolitan Statistical Area were not available.
Source: Centers for Disease Control and Prevention, Behavioral Risk Factor Surveillance System, SMART: Selected Metropolitan Area Risk Trends, 2023

Mortality Rates for the Top 10 Causes of Death in the U.S.

ICD-10[a] Sub-Chapter	ICD-10[a] Code	Crude Mortality Rate[2] per 100,000 population	
		County[3]	U.S.
Malignant neoplasms	C00-C97	190.3	182.7
Ischaemic heart diseases	I20-I25	132.5	109.6
Provisional assignment of new diseases of uncertain etiology[1]	U00-U49	47.3	65.3
Other forms of heart disease	I30-I51	66.6	65.1
Other degenerative diseases of the nervous system	G30-G31	38.9	52.4
Other external causes of accidental injury	W00-X59	51.5	52.3
Cerebrovascular diseases	I60-I69	51.1	49.1
Chronic lower respiratory diseases	J40-J47	57.4	43.5
Hypertensive diseases	I10-I15	55.1	38.9
Organic, including symptomatic, mental disorders	F01-F09	40.0	33.9

Note: (a) ICD-10 = International Classification of Diseases 10th Revision; (1) Includes COVID-19, adverse effects to COVID-19 vaccines, SARS, and vaping-related disorders; (2) Crude mortality rates are a three-year average covering 2021-2023; (3) Figures cover Scott County.
Source: Centers for Disease Control and Prevention, National Center for Health Statistics. National Vital Statistics System, Mortality 2018-2023 on CDC WONDER Online Database

Mortality Rates for Selected Causes of Death

Cause of Death	ICD-10[a] Code	Crude Mortality Rate[1] per 100,000 population	
		County[2]	U.S.
Accidental poisoning and exposure to noxious substances	X40-X49	18.2	30.5
Alzheimer disease	G30	29.5	35.4
Assault	X85-Y09	5.7	7.3
COVID-19	U07.1	47.3	65.3
Diabetes mellitus	E10-E14	18.0	30.0
Diseases of the liver	K70-K76	20.5	20.8
Human immunodeficiency virus (HIV) disease	B20-B24	Suppressed	1.5
Influenza and pneumonia	J09-J18	14.0	13.4
Intentional self-harm	X60-X84	15.9	14.7
Malnutrition	E40-E46	6.1	6.0
Obesity and other hyperalimentation	E65-E68	4.6	3.1
Renal failure	N17-N19	12.3	16.4
Transport accidents	V01-V99	9.4	14.4

Note: (a) ICD-10 = International Classification of Diseases 10th Revision; (1) Crude mortality rates are a three-year average covering 2021-2023; (2) Figures cover Scott County; Data are suppressed when the data meet the criteria for confidentiality constraints; Crude mortality rates are flagged as unreliable when the rate would be calculated with a numerator of 20 or less.
Source: Centers for Disease Control and Prevention, National Center for Health Statistics. National Vital Statistics System, Mortality 2018-2023 on CDC WONDER Online Database

Health Insurance Coverage

Area	With Health Insurance	With Private Health Insurance	With Public Health Insurance	Without Health Insurance	Population Under Age 19 Without Health Insurance
City	92.8	65.0	41.1	7.2	4.7
MSA[1]	94.5	71.3	38.0	5.5	3.7
U.S.	91.4	67.3	36.3	8.6	5.4

Note: Figures are percentages that cover the civilian noninstitutionalized population; (1) Figures cover the Davenport-Moline-Rock Island, IA-IL Metropolitan Statistical Area
Source: U.S. Census Bureau, 2019-2023 American Community Survey 5-Year Estimates

Number of Medical Professionals

Area	MDs[3]	DOs[3,4]	Dentists	Podiatrists	Chiropractors	Optometrists
County[1] (number)	446	98	149	9	332	29
County[1] (rate[2])	256.4	56.3	85.5	5.2	190.5	16.6
U.S. (rate[2])	302.5	29.2	74.6	6.4	29.5	18.0

Note: Data as of 2023 unless noted; (1) Data covers Scott County; (2) Number of medical professionals per 100,000 population; (3) Data as of 2022 and includes all active, non-federal physicians; (4) Doctor of Osteopathic Medicine
Source: U.S. Department of Health and Human Services, Health Resources and Services Administration, Bureau of Health Professions, Area Resource File (ARF) 2023-2024

EDUCATION

Public School District Statistics

District Name	Schls	Pupils	Pupil/ Teacher Ratio	Minority Pupils[1] (%)	Total Rev. per Pupil ($)	Total Exp. per Pupil ($)
Davenport Comm School District	27	13,523	13.9	50.4	17,057	14,427

Note: Table includes school districts with 2,000 or more students; (1) Percentage of students that are not non-Hispanic white.
Source: U.S. Department of Education, National Center for Education Statistics, Common Core of Data, Local Education Agency (School District) Universe Survey: School Year 2023-2024; U.S. Department of Education, National Center for Education Statistics, Common Core of Data, School District Finance Survey (F-33): School Year 2021–22

Highest Level of Education

Area	Less than H.S.	H.S. Diploma	Some College, No Deg.	Associate Degree	Bachelor's Degree	Master's Degree	Prof. School Degree	Doctorate Degree
City	7.4	28.8	22.1	11.7	18.9	8.2	1.8	1.1
MSA[1]	7.6	29.3	22.7	11.1	18.6	8.2	1.5	1.1
U.S.	10.6	26.2	19.4	8.8	21.3	9.8	2.3	1.6

Note: Figures cover persons age 25 and over; (1) Figures cover the Davenport-Moline-Rock Island, IA-IL Metropolitan Statistical Area
Source: U.S. Census Bureau, 2019-2023 American Community Survey 5-Year Estimates

Educational Attainment by Race

Area	High School Graduate or Higher (%)					Bachelor's Degree or Higher (%)				
	Total	White	Black	Asian	Hisp.[2]	Total	White	Black	Asian	Hisp.[2]
City	92.6	94.7	87.4	84.3	78.3	30.0	31.7	16.8	59.3	15.0
MSA[1]	92.4	94.5	83.5	82.5	77.4	29.4	30.4	14.2	61.6	16.8
U.S.	89.4	92.9	88.1	88.0	72.5	35.0	37.7	24.7	57.0	19.9

Note: Figures shown cover persons 25 years old and over; (1) Figures cover the Davenport-Moline-Rock Island, IA-IL Metropolitan Statistical Area; (2) People of Hispanic origin can be of any race
Source: U.S. Census Bureau, 2019-2023 American Community Survey 5-Year Estimates

School Enrollment by Grade and Control

Area	Preschool (%)		Kindergarten (%)		Grades 1 - 4 (%)		Grades 5 - 8 (%)		Grades 9 - 12 (%)	
	Public	Private	Public	Private	Public	Private	Public	Private	Public	Private
City	52.6	47.4	86.2	13.8	79.3	20.7	86.4	13.6	92.5	7.5
MSA[1]	65.1	34.9	87.2	12.8	87.0	13.0	91.2	8.8	92.2	7.8
U.S.	58.7	41.3	85.2	14.8	87.2	12.8	87.9	12.1	89.0	11.0

Note: Figures shown cover persons 3 years old and over; (1) Figures cover the Davenport-Moline-Rock Island, IA-IL Metropolitan Statistical Area
Source: U.S. Census Bureau, 2019-2023 American Community Survey 5-Year Estimates

Higher Education

Four-Year Colleges			Two-Year Colleges			Medical Schools[1]	Law Schools[2]	Voc/ Tech[3]
Public	Private Non-profit	Private For-profit	Public	Private Non-profit	Private For-profit			
0	4	1	2	0	2	0	0	1

Note: Figures cover institutions located within the Davenport-Moline-Rock Island, IA-IL Metropolitan Statistical Area and include main campuses only; (1) includes schools accredited by the Liaison Committee on Medical Education and the American Osteopathic Association's Commission on Osteopathic College Accreditation; (2) includes ABA-accredited schools, schools with provisional ABA accreditation, and state accredited schools; (3) includes all schools with programs that are less than 2 years.
Source: National Center for Education Statistics, Integrated Postsecondary Education System (IPEDS), 2023-24; Wikipedia, List of Medical Schools in the United States, accessed May 2, 2025; Wikipedia, List of Law Schools in the United States, accessed May 2, 2025

According to *U.S. News & World Report,* the Davenport-Moline-Rock Island, IA-IL metro area is home to one of the top 100 liberal arts colleges in the U.S.: **Augustana College** (#100 tie). The indicators used to capture academic quality fall into a number of categories: assessment by administrators at peer institutions; retention of students; faculty resources; student selectivity; financial resources; alumni giving; high school counselor ratings of colleges; and graduation rate. *U.S. News & World Report,* "America's Best Colleges 2025"

EMPLOYERS

Major Employers

Company Name	Industry
Alcoa	Manufacturer
Deere and Company	Manufacturer
Genesis Health System	Healthcare
HNI Corporation/The Hon Company/Allsteel	Manufacturer
Hy-Vee Food Stores	Grocery stores
Kraft Foods/Oscar Mayer	Food processing
Rock Island Arsenal	U.S. military
Trinity Regional Health System	Healthcare
Tyson Fresh Meats	Food processing
XPAC	Service, parts, packaging

Note: Companies shown are located within the Davenport-Moline-Rock Island, IA-IL Metropolitan Statistical Area.
Source: Chambers of Commerce; State Departments of Labor; Wikipedia

PUBLIC SAFETY

Crime Rate

Area	Total Crime Rate	Violent Crime Rate				Property Crime Rate		
		Murder	Rape	Robbery	Aggrav. Assault	Burglary	Larceny-Theft	Motor Vehicle Theft
City	4,501.0	9.0	102.1	91.1	488.4	688.6	2,601.3	520.5
U.S.	2,290.9	5.7	38.0	66.5	264.1	250.7	1,347.2	318.7

Note: Figures are crimes per 100,000 population.
Source: FBI, Table 8, Offenses Known to Law Enforcement, by State by City, 2023

Hate Crimes

Area	Number of Quarters Reported	Number of Incidents per Bias Motivation					
		Race/Ethnicity/Ancestry	Religion	Sexual Orientation	Disability	Gender	Gender Identity
City	4	0	0	0	0	0	0
U.S.	4	5,900	2,699	2,077	187	92	492

Source: Federal Bureau of Investigation, Hate Crime Statistics 2023

Identity Theft Consumer Reports

Area	Reports	Reports per 100,000 Population	Rank[2]
MSA[1]	620	162	235
U.S.	1,135,291	339	-

Note: (1) Figures cover the Davenport-Moline-Rock Island, IA-IL Metropolitan Statistical Area; (2) Rank ranges from 1 to 401 where 1 indicates greatest number of identity theft reports per 100,000 population
Source: Federal Trade Commission, Consumer Sentinel Network Data Book 2024

Fraud and Other Consumer Reports

Area	Reports	Reports per 100,000 Population	Rank[2]
MSA[1]	3,376	884	279
U.S.	5,360,641	1,601	-

Note: (1) Figures cover the Davenport-Moline-Rock Island, IA-IL Metropolitan Statistical Area; (2) Rank ranges from 1 to 401 where 1 indicates greatest number of fraud and other consumer reports per 100,000 population
Source: Federal Trade Commission, Consumer Sentinel Network Data Book 2024

POLITICS

2024 Presidential Election Results

Area	Trump (Rep.)	Harris (Dem.)	Stein (Green)	Kennedy (Ind.)	Oliver (Lib.)	Other
Scott County	51.0	47.1	0.0	0.8	0.5	0.6
U.S.	49.7	48.2	0.6	0.5	0.4	0.6

Note: Results are percentages and may not add to 100% due to rounding
Source: Dave Leip's Atlas of U.S. Presidential Elections

SPORTS

Professional Sports Teams

Team Name	League	Year Established

No teams are located in the metro area
Source: Wikipedia, Major Professional Sports Teams of the United States and Canada, May 1, 2025

CLIMATE

Average and Extreme Temperatures

Temperature	Jan	Feb	Mar	Apr	May	Jun	Jul	Aug	Sep	Oct	Nov	Dec	Yr.
Extreme High (°F)	65	70	91	93	98	103	105	108	99	95	76	69	108
Average High (°F)	29	34	45	61	72	82	86	84	76	65	48	33	60
Average Temp. (°F)	20	25	36	51	62	72	76	74	65	54	39	25	50
Average Low (°F)	11	16	27	40	51	61	66	64	54	43	29	17	40
Extreme Low (°F)	-24	-20	-22	9	28	42	47	40	28	14	-3	-22	-24

Note: Figures cover the years 1945-1990
Source: National Climatic Data Center, International Station Meteorological Climate Summary, 9/96

Average Precipitation/Snowfall/Humidity

Precip./Humidity	Jan	Feb	Mar	Apr	May	Jun	Jul	Aug	Sep	Oct	Nov	Dec	Yr.
Avg. Precip. (in.)	1.1	1.1	2.3	3.1	3.8	4.4	3.5	3.9	3.1	2.4	1.7	1.2	31.8
Avg. Snowfall (in.)	8	7	7	2	Tr	0	0	0	Tr	Tr	3	7	33
Avg. Rel. Hum. 6am (%)	77	79	79	78	78	81	83	86	85	80	79	80	80
Avg. Rel. Hum. 3pm (%)	65	63	57	50	51	52	52	54	52	50	58	66	56

Note: Figures cover the years 1945-1990; Tr = Trace amounts (<0.05 in. of rain; <0.5 in. of snow)
Source: National Climatic Data Center, International Station Meteorological Climate Summary, 9/96

Weather Conditions

Temperature			Daytime Sky			Precipitation		
5°F & below	32°F & below	90°F & above	Clear	Partly cloudy	Cloudy	0.01 inch or more precip.	0.1 inch or more snow/ice	Thunder-storms
25	137	26	99	128	138	106	25	46

Note: Figures are average number of days per year and cover the years 1945-1990
Source: National Climatic Data Center, International Station Meteorological Climate Summary, 9/96

HAZARDOUS WASTE

Superfund Sites

The Davenport-Moline-Rock Island, IA-IL metro area has no sites on the EPA's Superfund Final National Priorities List (NPL) or Superfund Alternative Approach (SAA) list. The Superfund alternative approach uses the same investigation and cleanup process and standards that are used for sites listed on the National Priorities List. The SAA is an alternative to listing a site on the NPL; it is not an alternative to Superfund or the Superfund process. There are a total of 1,445 Superfund sites with a status of proposed or final on both lists in the United States. *U.S. Environmental Protection Agency, National Priorities List, May 1, 2025; U.S. Environmental Protection Agency, Superfund Alternative Approach Sites, May 1, 2025*

AIR QUALITY

Air Quality Trends: Ozone

	1990	1995	2000	2005	2010	2015	2020	2021	2022	2023
MSA[1]	0.065	0.072	0.064	0.065	0.057	0.060	0.063	0.066	0.061	0.079
U.S.	0.087	0.089	0.081	0.080	0.072	0.068	0.066	0.067	0.067	0.070

Note: (1) Data covers the Davenport-Moline-Rock Island, IA-IL Metropolitan Statistical Area. The values shown are the composite ozone concentration averages among trend sites based on the highest fourth daily maximum 8-hour concentration in parts per million. These trends are based on sites having an adequate record of monitoring data during the trend period. Data from exceptional events are included.
Source: U.S. Environmental Protection Agency, Air Quality Monitoring Information, "Air Quality Trends by City, 1990-2023"

Air Quality Index

Area	Percent of Days when Air Quality was...[2]					AQI Statistics[2]	
	Good	Moderate	Unhealthy for Sensitive Groups	Unhealthy	Very Unhealthy	Maximum	Median
MSA[1]	37.3	56.4	5.2	0.8	0.3	232	54

Note: (1) Data covers the Davenport-Moline-Rock Island, IA-IL Metropolitan Statistical Area; (2) Based on 365 days with AQI data in 2023. Air Quality Index (AQI) is an index for reporting daily air quality. EPA calculates the AQI for five major air pollutants regulated by the Clean Air Act: ground-level ozone, particle pollution (aka particulate matter), carbon monoxide, sulfur dioxide, and nitrogen dioxide. The AQI runs from 0 to 500. The higher the AQI value, the greater the level of air pollution and the greater the health concern. There are six AQI categories: "Good" AQI is between 0 and 50. Air quality is considered satisfactory; "Moderate" AQI is between 51 and 100. Air quality is acceptable; "Unhealthy for Sensitive Groups" When AQI values are between 101 and 150, members of sensitive groups may experience health effects; "Unhealthy" When AQI values are between 151 and 200 everyone may begin to experience health effects; "Very Unhealthy" AQI values between 201 and 300 trigger a health alert; "Hazardous" AQI values over 300 trigger warnings of emergency conditions (not shown).
Source: U.S. Environmental Protection Agency, Air Quality Index Report, 2023

Air Quality Index Pollutants

Area	Percent of Days when AQI Pollutant was...[2]					
	Carbon Monoxide	Nitrogen Dioxide	Ozone	Sulfur Dioxide	Particulate Matter 2.5	Particulate Matter 10
MSA[1]	0.0	0.0	30.4	(3)	62.2	7.4

Note: (1) Data covers the Davenport-Moline-Rock Island, IA-IL Metropolitan Statistical Area; (2) Based on 365 days with AQI data in 2023. The Air Quality Index (AQI) is an index for reporting daily air quality. EPA calculates the AQI for five major air pollutants regulated by the Clean Air Act: ground-level ozone, particle pollution (also known as particulate matter), carbon monoxide, sulfur dioxide, and nitrogen dioxide. The AQI runs from 0 to 500. The higher the AQI value, the greater the level of air pollution and the greater the health concern; (3) Sulfur dioxide is no longer included in this table because SO_2 concentrations tend to be very localized and not necessarily representative of broad geographical areas like counties and CBSAs.
Source: U.S. Environmental Protection Agency, Air Quality Index Report, 2023

Maximum Air Pollutant Concentrations: Particulate Matter, Ozone, CO and Lead

	Particulate Matter 10 (ug/m^3)	Particulate Matter 2.5 Wtd AM (ug/m^3)	Particulate Matter 2.5 24-Hr (ug/m^3)	Ozone (ppm)	Carbon Monoxide (ppm)	Lead (ug/m^3)
MSA[1] Level	109	10.4	28	0.08	1	n/a
NAAQS[2]	150	15	35	0.075	9	0.15
Met NAAQS[2]	Yes	Yes	Yes	No	Yes	n/a

Note: (1) Data covers the Davenport-Moline-Rock Island, IA-IL Metropolitan Statistical Area; Data from exceptional events are included; (2) National Ambient Air Quality Standards; ppm = parts per million; ug/m^3 = micrograms per cubic meter; n/a not available.
Concentrations: Particulate Matter 10 (coarse particulate)—highest second maximum 24-hour concentration; Particulate Matter 2.5 Wtd AM (fine particulate)—highest weighted annual mean concentration; Particulate Matter 2.5 24-Hour (fine particulate)—highest 98th percentile 24-hour concentration; Ozone—highest fourth daily maximum 8-hour concentration; Carbon Monoxide—highest second maximum non-overlapping 8-hour concentration; Lead—maximum running 3-month average
Source: U.S. Environmental Protection Agency, Air Quality Monitoring Information, "Air Quality Statistics by City, 2023"

Maximum Air Pollutant Concentrations: Nitrogen Dioxide and Sulfur Dioxide

	Nitrogen Dioxide AM (ppb)	Nitrogen Dioxide 1-Hr (ppb)	Sulfur Dioxide AM (ppb)	Sulfur Dioxide 1-Hr (ppb)	Sulfur Dioxide 24-Hr (ppb)
MSA[1] Level	n/a	n/a	n/a	4	n/a
NAAQS[2]	53	100	30	75	140
Met NAAQS[2]	n/a	n/a	n/a	Yes	n/a

Note: (1) Data covers the Davenport-Moline-Rock Island, IA-IL Metropolitan Statistical Area; Data from exceptional events are included; (2) National Ambient Air Quality Standards; ppm = parts per million; ug/m^3 = micrograms per cubic meter; n/a not available.
Concentrations: Nitrogen Dioxide AM—highest arithmetic mean concentration; Nitrogen Dioxide 1-Hr—highest 98th percentile 1-hour daily maximum concentration; Sulfur Dioxide AM—highest annual mean concentration; Sulfur Dioxide 1-Hr—highest 99th percentile 1-hour daily maximum concentration; Sulfur Dioxide 24-Hr—highest second maximum 24-hour concentration
Source: U.S. Environmental Protection Agency, Air Quality Monitoring Information, "Air Quality Statistics by City, 2023"

Des Moines, Iowa

Background

In 1843, Fort Des Moines was founded at the confluence of the Des Moines and Raccoon rivers. Though the fort was initially established to protect local Native American populations, within two years the area was opened to white settlers. By 1857, the state capital was moved from Iowa City to Des Moines. Today, this capital city is also Iowa's largest.

The city is often on best-of lists extolling its reasonable cost of living, quality of life, or job opportunities. It has taken an active role in acquiring properties in its downtown for redevelopment, and takes a progressive approach to planning, having joined with other counties and regional partners to plan for transportation and other future needs. The Capital Corridor encourages the development of creative high-value growth and development for industry, including animal science.

Des Moines's significant industries include the financial services industry, and Greater Des Moines has a high concentration of employment in financial services. Logistics, bioscience, and data centers are also significant economic sectors in the city.

Greater Des Moines is home to the first statewide fiber optics network in the country. The city proper boasts world-class architecture including the Des Moines Art Center, designed in 1944 by Eliel Saarinen, a Finnish architect and then-president of the renowned Cranbrook Academy of Art in Detroit. In 1968, I.M. Pei, architect of the Pyramid du Louvre and the East Wing of the National Gallery of Art in Washington, D.C., designed a gallery addition to the main Art Center structure. In 1985, Richard Meier, who designed the Museum of Modern Art in Florence, Italy, designed an addition to the Art Center's north wing and went on to design the famed Getty Center in Los Angeles. The city's Home Federal Savings and Loan Building was designed by Mies van der Rohe, of the famous German Bauhaus School of Design, and a sculpture, The Crusoe Umbrella, designed by pop artist Claes Oldenberg, stands in the middle of Nollen Plaza, a wooded park and popular gathering place.

The Greater Des Moines Botanical Center includes Iowa's first "living wall." Des Moines Civic Center offers ballet, symphony, and other performances. The Science Center of Iowa features hands-on science and technology exhibits, an IMAX theater, and a planetarium with an interactive program and laser light show.

Every four years, Des Moines becomes the center of national attention as correspondents from all over the U.S. and abroad arrive to cover the Iowa political caucuses, which has become a financial boon for the state.

Located in the heart of North America, Des Moines has a continental climate, resulting in a seasonal contrast in both temperature and precipitation. Exceptionally high summer rains have caused the nearby Des Moines River and Raccoon River to breach the city's levees in 1993 and again in 2008. The winter is a season of cold, dry air, interrupted by occasional storms of short duration. The autumn is characteristically sunny with diminishing precipitation.

Rankings

Business/Finance Rankings

- For its annual survey of the "Cheapest U.S. Cities to Live In," Kiplinger applied Cost of Living Index statistics developed by the Council for Community and Economic Research to U.S. Census Bureau population and median household income data for 265 urban areas. Only areas with at least 50,000 residents were considered. In the resulting ranking, Des Moines ranked #14. *Kiplinger.com, "The 25 Cheapest Places to Live: U.S. Cities Edition," January 19, 2025*

- The Des Moines metro area appeared on the Milken Institute "2025 Best Performing Cities" list. Rank: #96 out of 200 large metro areas (based on performance category). Criteria: job growth; wage growth; high-tech growth and impact; community resilience; housing affordability; household broadband access. *Milken Institute, "Best-Performing Cities 2025," January 14, 2025*

Education Rankings

- Personal finance website *WalletHub* analyzed the 150 largest U.S. metropolitan statistical areas to determine where the most educated Americans are putting their degrees to work. Criteria: education levels; percentage of workers with degrees; education quality and attainment gap; public school quality rankings; quality and enrollment of each metro area's universities. Des Moines was ranked #54 (#1 = most educated city). *WalletHub.com, "Most & Least Educated Cities in America, 2025" July 2, 2024*

Environmental Rankings

- The U.S. Environmental Protection Agency (EPA) released its list of mid-size U.S. metropolitan areas with the most ENERGY STAR certified buildings in 2023. The Des Moines metro area was ranked #7 out of 10. *U.S. Environmental Protection Agency, "2024 Energy Star Top Cities," May 22, 2024*

Health/Fitness Rankings

- Des Moines was identified as a "2025 Allergy Capital." The area ranked #32 out of the nation's 100 largest metropolitan areas. Three groups of factors were used to identify the most challenging cities for people with allergies: annual tree, grass, and weed pollen scores; over the counter allergy medicine use; number of board-certified allergy specialists. *Asthma and Allergy Foundation of America, "2025 Allergy Capitals: The Most Challenging Places to Live with Allergies," March 18, 2025*

- Des Moines was identified as a "2024 Asthma Capital." The area ranked #100 out of the nation's 100 largest metropolitan areas. Criteria: estimated asthma prevalence; asthma-related mortality; and ER visits due to asthma. Risk factors analyzed but not factored in the rankings: annual air quality including pollution and ozone levels; public smoking laws; indoor air quality; access to asthma specialists; rescue and controller medication use; uninsured rate; pollen allergy; poverty rate. *Asthma and Allergy Foundation of America, "Asthma Capitals 2024: The Most Challenging Places to Live With Asthma," September 10, 2024*

Real Estate Rankings

- *WalletHub* compared the most populated U.S. cities to determine which had the best markets for real estate agents. Des Moines ranked #61 where demand was high and pay was the best. Criteria: sales per agent; annual median wage for real-estate agents; monthly average starting salary for real estate agents; real estate job density and competition; unemployment rate; home turnover rate; housing-market health index; and other relevant metrics. *WalletHub.com, "2021 Best Places to Be a Real Estate Agent," May 12, 2021*

- Des Moines was ranked #32 out of 176 metro areas in terms of cost of housing in 2024 by the National Association of Home Builders (#1 = most affordable). Criteria: the portion of an average family's income necessary to pay the mortgage on a median-priced home. *National Association of Home Builders®, NAHB-Wells Fargo Cost of Housing Index, 4th Quarter 2024*

Safety Rankings

- Allstate ranked the 100 most populous cities in America in terms of driver safety. Des Moines ranked #18. Criteria based on anonymized driving behavior data from Allstate's mobile app powered by Arity: high speed driving (over 80 mph), phone handling, and hard braking. The report helps increase the importance of safety and awareness behind the wheel. *Allstate, "16th Allstate America's Best Drivers Report®" July 11, 2024*

Women/Minorities Rankings

- Personal finance website *WalletHub* compared more than 180 U.S. cities across two key dimensions, "Hispanic Business-Friendliness" and "Hispanic Purchasing Power," to arrive at the most favorable conditions for Hispanic entrepreneurs. Des Moines was ranked #70 out of 182. Criteria includes: share of Hispanic-Owned Businesses; average growth of Hispanic Business revenues; Small Business-Friendliness score; affordability; and number of Hispanics with at least a bachelor's degree. *WalletHub.com, "Best Cities for Hispanic Entrepreneurs," September 4, 2024*

Miscellaneous Rankings

- *WalletHub* compared 148 of the most populated U.S. cities to determine their operating efficiency. A "Quality of Services" score was constructed for each city and then measured against the total budget per capita to reveal which were managed the best. Des Moines ranked #80. Criteria: financial stability; economy; education; safety; health; infrastructure and pollution. *WalletHub.com, "2025's Best- & Worst-Run Cities in America," June 18, 2024*

Business Environment

DEMOGRAPHICS

Population Growth

Area	1990 Census	2000 Census	2010 Census	2020 Census	2023 Estimate[2]	Population Growth 1990-2023 (%)
City	193,569	198,682	203,433	214,133	212,464	9.8
MSA[1]	416,346	481,394	569,633	709,466	720,331	73.0
U.S.	248,709,873	281,421,906	308,745,538	331,449,281	332,387,540	33.6

Note: (1) Figures cover the Des Moines-West Des Moines, IA Metropolitan Statistical Area; (2) 2019-2023 5-year ACS population estimate
Source: U.S. Census Bureau, 1990 Census, 2000 Census, 2010 Census, 2020 Census, 2019-2023 American Community Survey 5-Year Estimates

Race

Area	White Alone[2] (%)	Black Alone[2] (%)	Asian Alone[2] (%)	AIAN[3] Alone[2] (%)	NHOPI[4] Alone[2] (%)	Other Race Alone[2] (%)	Two or More Races (%)
City	66.9	12.0	6.2	0.5	0.0	5.2	9.1
MSA[1]	81.5	5.7	4.2	0.3	0.0	2.5	5.8
U.S.	63.4	12.4	5.8	0.9	0.2	6.6	10.7

Note: (1) Figures cover the Des Moines-West Des Moines, IA Metropolitan Statistical Area; (2) Alone is defined as not being in combination with one or more other races; (3) American Indian and Alaska Native; (4) Native Hawaiian and Other Pacific Islander
Source: U.S. Census Bureau, 2019-2023 American Community Survey 5-Year Estimates

Hispanic or Latino Origin

Area	Total (%)	Mexican (%)	Puerto Rican (%)	Cuban (%)	Other (%)
City	16.0	11.4	0.6	0.3	3.8
MSA[1]	8.4	5.7	0.4	0.1	2.2
U.S.	19.0	11.3	1.8	0.7	5.2

Note: Persons of Hispanic or Latino origin can be of any race; (1) Figures cover the Des Moines-West Des Moines, IA Metropolitan Statistical Area
Source: U.S. Census Bureau, 2019-2023 American Community Survey 5-Year Estimates

Age

Area	Under Age 5	Age 5–19	Age 20–34	Age 35–44	Age 45–54	Age 55–64	Age 65–74	Age 75–84	Age 85+	Median Age
City	6.8	19.2	24.7	13.0	11.8	11.9	7.7	3.3	1.5	34.6
MSA[1]	6.5	20.7	20.4	14.4	12.1	11.7	8.6	4.0	1.7	36.7
U.S.	5.7	19.1	20.2	13.1	12.3	12.8	10.0	4.9	1.9	38.7

Note: (1) Figures cover the Des Moines-West Des Moines, IA Metropolitan Statistical Area
Source: U.S. Census Bureau, 2019-2023 American Community Survey 5-Year Estimates

Disability by Age

Area	All Ages	Under 18 Years Old	18 to 64 Years Old	65 Years and Over
City	14.3	5.8	13.4	35.2
MSA[1]	10.8	3.8	9.3	29.8
U.S.	13.0	4.7	10.7	32.9

Note: Figures show percent of the civilian noninstitutionalized population that reported having a disability. Disability status is determined from six types of difficulty: vision, hearing, cognitive, ambulatory, self-care, and independent living. For children under 5 years old, hearing and vision difficulty are used to determine disability status. For children between the ages of 5 and 14, disability status is determined from hearing, vision, cognitive, ambulatory, and self-care difficulties. For people aged 15 years and older, they are considered to have a disability if they have difficulty with any one of the six difficulty types; Note: (1) Figures cover the Des Moines-West Des Moines, IA Metropolitan Statistical Area
Source: U.S. Census Bureau, 2019-2023 American Community Survey 5-Year Estimates

Ancestry

Area	German	Irish	English	American	Italian	Polish	French[2]	European	Scottish
City	19.1	12.4	9.2	3.1	3.5	1.0	1.4	1.5	1.3
MSA[1]	25.8	13.5	11.3	3.8	3.1	1.2	1.6	2.3	1.7
U.S.	12.6	9.4	9.1	5.5	4.9	2.6	2.0	1.6	1.6

Note: Figures are the percentage of the total population reporting a particular ancestry. The nine most commonly reported ancestries in the U.S. are shown. Figures include multiple ancestries (e.g. if a person reported being Irish and Italian, they were included in both columns); (1) Figures cover the Des Moines-West Des Moines, IA Metropolitan Statistical Area; (2) Excludes Basque
Source: U.S. Census Bureau, 2019-2023 American Community Survey 5-Year Estimates

Foreign-born Population

Area	Percent of Population Born in								
	Any Foreign Country	Asia	Mexico	Europe	Caribbean	Central America[2]	South America	Africa	Canada
City	14.0	4.4	3.6	0.8	0.2	1.6	0.1	3.2	0.1
MSA[1]	8.6	3.1	1.6	1.0	0.1	0.8	0.3	1.6	0.1
U.S.	13.9	4.3	3.3	1.4	1.4	1.2	1.2	0.8	0.2

Note: (1) Figures cover the Des Moines-West Des Moines, IA Metropolitan Statistical Area; (2) Excludes Mexico.
Source: U.S. Census Bureau, 2019-2023 American Community Survey 5-Year Estimates

Household Size

Area	Persons in Household (%)							Average Household Size
	One	Two	Three	Four	Five	Six	Seven or More	
City	37.1	30.7	13.2	10.3	4.8	2.1	1.8	2.30
MSA[1]	29.6	33.9	14.0	12.8	6.4	2.1	1.1	2.44
U.S.	28.5	33.8	15.4	12.7	5.9	2.3	1.4	2.54

Note: (1) Figures cover the Des Moines-West Des Moines, IA Metropolitan Statistical Area
Source: U.S. Census Bureau, 2019-2023 American Community Survey 5-Year Estimates

Household Relationships

Area	House-holder	Opposite-sex Spouse	Same-sex Spouse	Opposite-sex Unmarried Partner	Same-sex Unmarried Partner	Child[2]	Grand-child	Other Relatives	Non-relatives
City	41.1	14.2	0.3	3.5	0.2	27.9	2.0	4.4	3.9
MSA[1]	39.6	19.2	0.2	2.7	0.1	29.6	1.3	2.8	2.6
U.S.	38.3	17.5	0.2	2.5	0.2	28.3	2.4	4.8	3.4

Note: Figures are percent of the total population; (1) Figures cover the Des Moines-West Des Moines, IA Metropolitan Statistical Area; (2) Includes biological, adopted, and stepchildren of the householder
Source: U.S. Census Bureau, 2020 Census

Gender

Area	Males	Females	Males per 100 Females
City	105,131	107,333	97.9
MSA[1]	359,219	361,112	99.5
U.S.	164,545,087	167,842,453	98.0

Note: (1) Figures cover the Des Moines-West Des Moines, IA Metropolitan Statistical Area
Source: U.S. Census Bureau, 2019-2023 American Community Survey 5-Year Estimates

Marital Status

Area	Never Married	Now Married[2]	Separated	Widowed	Divorced
City	40.8	38.8	2.3	5.7	12.5
MSA[1]	31.7	51.3	1.3	5.0	10.7
U.S.	34.1	47.9	1.7	5.6	10.7

Note: Figures are percentages and cover the population 15 years of age and older; (1) Figures cover the Des Moines-West Des Moines, IA Metropolitan Statistical Area; (2) Excludes separated
Source: U.S. Census Bureau, 2019-2023 American Community Survey 5-Year Estimates

Religious Groups by Family

Area	Catholic	Baptist	Methodist	LDS[2]	Pentecostal	Lutheran	Islam	Adventist	Other
MSA[1]	12.1	1.8	4.0	0.9	2.5	6.6	1.6	0.8	8.7
U.S.	18.7	7.3	3.0	2.0	1.8	1.7	1.3	1.3	11.6

Note: Figures are the number of adherents as a percentage of the total population and cover the eight largest religious groups in the U.S; (1) Figures cover the Des Moines-West Des Moines, IA Metropolitan Statistical Area; (2) Church of Jesus Christ of Latter-day Saints
Sources: 2020 U.S. Religion Census, Association of Statisticians of American Religious Bodies; The Association of Religion Data Archives (ARDA)

Religious Groups by Tradition

Area	Catholic	Evangelical Protestant	Mainline Protestant	Black Protestant	Islam	Judaism	Hinduism	Orthodox	Buddhism
MSA[1]	12.1	10.3	12.2	1.0	1.6	<0.1	0.2	0.1	0.1
U.S.	18.7	16.5	5.2	2.3	1.3	0.6	0.4	0.4	0.3

Note: Figures are the number of adherents as a percentage of the total population; (1) Figures cover the Des Moines-West Des Moines, IA Metropolitan Statistical Area
Sources: 2020 U.S. Religion Census, Association of Statisticians of American Religious Bodies; The Association of Religion Data Archives (ARDA)

ECONOMY

Real Gross Domestic Product (GDP)

Area	2017	2018	2019	2020	2021	2022	2023	Rank[3]
MSA[1]	51.8	51.9	54.2	55.6	60.7	59.8	60.4	57
U.S.[2]	17,619.1	18,160.7	18,642.5	18,238.9	19,387.6	19,896.6	20,436.3	—

Note: Figures are in billions of chained 2017 dollars; (1) Figures cover the Des Moines-West Des Moines, IA Metropolitan Statistical Area; (2) Figures cover real GDP within metropolitan areas; (3) Rank is based on 2023 data and ranges from 1 to 384
Source: U.S. Bureau of Economic Analysis

Economic Growth

Area	2014	2015	2016	2017	2018	2019	2020	2021	2022	2023
MSA[1]	12.6	8.5	3.8	-1.3	0.2	4.3	2.6	9.3	-1.5	1.0
U.S.[2]	2.6	3.2	2.0	2.7	3.1	2.7	-2.2	6.3	2.6	2.7

Note: Figures are real gross domestic product growth rates and represent percent change from preceding period; (1) Figures cover the Des Moines-West Des Moines, IA Metropolitan Statistical Area; (2) Figures are the average growth rates within metropolitan areas
Source: U.S. Bureau of Economic Analysis

Metropolitan Area Exports

Area	2018	2019	2020	2021	2022	2023	Rank[2]
MSA[1]	1,293.7	1,437.8	1,414.0	1,706.6	1,706.8	2,175.7	110
U.S.	1,664,056.1	1,645,173.7	1,431,406.6	1,753,941.4	2,062,937.4	2,019,160.5	—

Note: Figures are in millions of dollars; (1) Figures cover the Des Moines-West Des Moines, IA Metropolitan Statistical Area; (2) Rank is based on 2023 data and ranges from 1 to 386
Source: U.S. Department of Commerce, International Trade Administration, Office of Trade and Economic Analysis, Industry and Analysis, Exports by Metropolitan Area, data extracted April 2, 2025

Building Permits

Area	Single-Family			Multi-Family			Total		
	2023	2024	Pct. Chg.	2023	2024	Pct. Chg.	2023	2024	Pct. Chg.
City	248	218	-12.1	321	400	24.6	569	618	8.6
MSA[1]	3,689	3,717	0.8	1,311	1,347	2.7	5,000	5,064	1.3
U.S.	920,000	981,900	6.7	591,100	496,100	-16.1	1,511,100	1,478,000	-2.2

Note: (1) Figures cover the Des Moines-West Des Moines, IA Metropolitan Statistical Area; Figures represent new, privately-owned housing units authorized (unadjusted data)
Source: U.S. Census Bureau, Building Permits Survey (BPS), 2023, 2024

Bankruptcy Filings

Area	Business Filings			Nonbusiness Filings		
	2023	2024	% Chg.	2023	2024	% Chg.
Polk County	15	13	-13.3	566	594	4.9
U.S.	18,926	23,107	22.1	434,064	494,201	13.9

Note: Business filings include Chapter 7, Chapter 9, Chapter 11, Chapter 12, Chapter 13, Chapter 15, and Section 304; Nonbusiness filings include Chapter 7, Chapter 11, and Chapter 13
Source: Administrative Office of the U.S. Courts, Business and Nonbusiness Bankruptcy, County Cases Commenced by Chapter of the Bankruptcy Code, During the 12-Month Period Ending December 31, 2023 and Business and Nonbusiness Bankruptcy, County Cases Commenced by Chapter of the Bankruptcy Code, During the 12-Month Period Ending December 31, 2024

Housing Vacancy Rates

Area	Gross Vacancy Rate[3] (%)			Year-Round Vacancy Rate[4] (%)			Rental Vacancy Rate[5] (%)			Homeowner Vacancy Rate[6] (%)		
	2022	2023	2024	2022	2023	2024	2022	2023	2024	2022	2023	2024
MSA[1]	n/a	n/a	n/a	n/a	n/a	n/a	n/a	n/a	n/a	n/a	n/a	n/a
U.S.[2]	9.1	9.0	9.1	7.5	7.5	7.6	5.7	6.5	6.8	0.8	0.8	1.0

Note: (1) Figures cover the Des Moines-West Des Moines, IA Metropolitan Statistical Area; (2) Figures cover the 75 largest Metropolitan Statistical Areas; (3) The percentage of the total housing inventory that is vacant; (4) The percentage of the housing inventory (excluding seasonal units) that is year-round vacant; (5) The percentage of rental inventory that is vacant for rent; (6) The percentage of homeowner inventory that is vacant for sale; n/a not available
Source: U.S. Census Bureau, Housing Vacancies and Homeownership Annual Statistics: 2022, 2023, 2024

INCOME

Income

Area	Per Capita ($)	Median Household ($)	Average Household ($)
City	36,459	63,966	83,728
MSA[1]	44,796	84,209	109,864
U.S.	43,289	78,538	110,491

Note: (1) Figures cover the Des Moines-West Des Moines, IA Metropolitan Statistical Area
Source: U.S. Census Bureau, 2019-2023 American Community Survey 5-Year Estimates

Household Income Distribution

Area	Percent of Households Earning							
	Under $15,000	$15,000 -$24,999	$25,000 -$34,999	$35,000 -$49,999	$50,000 -$74,999	$75,000 -$99,999	$100,000 -$149,999	$150,000 and up
City	8.8	7.7	7.2	14.3	19.3	15.4	15.2	12.1
MSA[1]	5.6	5.4	6.1	11.0	16.5	14.0	19.1	22.4
U.S.	8.5	6.6	6.8	10.4	15.7	12.7	17.4	21.9

Note: (1) Figures cover the Des Moines-West Des Moines, IA Metropolitan Statistical Area
Source: U.S. Census Bureau, 2019-2023 American Community Survey 5-Year Estimates

Poverty Rate

Area	All Ages	Under 18 Years Old	18 to 64 Years Old	65 Years and Over
City	14.9	22.1	13.1	10.8
MSA[1]	8.9	11.0	8.5	7.1
U.S.	12.4	16.3	11.6	10.4

Note: Figures are percentage of people whose income during the past 12 months was below the poverty level; (1) Figures cover the Des Moines-West Des Moines, IA Metropolitan Statistical Area
Source: U.S. Census Bureau, 2019-2023 American Community Survey 5-Year Estimates

EMPLOYMENT

Labor Force and Employment

Area	Civilian Labor Force			Workers Employed		
	Dec. 2023	Dec. 2024	% Chg.	Dec. 2023	Dec. 2024	% Chg.
City	113,506	113,721	0.2	109,944	109,495	-0.4
MSA[1]	394,185	394,876	0.2	384,347	382,847	-0.4
U.S.	166,661,000	167,746,000	0.7	160,754,000	161,294,000	0.3

Note: Data is not seasonally adjusted and covers workers 16 years of age and older; (1) Figures cover the Des Moines-West Des Moines, IA Metropolitan Statistical Area
Source: Bureau of Labor Statistics, Local Area Unemployment Statistics

Unemployment Rate

Area	2024											
	Jan.	Feb.	Mar.	Apr.	May	Jun.	Jul.	Aug.	Sep.	Oct.	Nov.	Dec.
City	4.3	3.8	3.5	2.6	3.1	3.6	4.1	4.4	3.5	3.7	3.9	3.7
MSA[1]	3.3	2.9	2.7	2.1	2.6	3.1	3.5	3.6	3.0	3.1	3.2	3.0
U.S.	4.1	4.2	3.9	3.5	3.7	4.3	4.5	4.4	3.9	3.9	4.0	3.8

Note: Data is not seasonally adjusted and covers workers 16 years of age and older; (1) Figures cover the Des Moines-West Des Moines, IA Metropolitan Statistical Area
Source: Bureau of Labor Statistics, Local Area Unemployment Statistics

Average Wages

Occupation	$/Hr.	Occupation	$/Hr.
Accountants and Auditors	40.26	Maintenance and Repair Workers	25.62
Automotive Mechanics	26.59	Marketing Managers	70.53
Bookkeepers	24.64	Network and Computer Systems Admin.	44.92
Carpenters	28.46	Nurses, Licensed Practical	30.46
Cashiers	14.74	Nurses, Registered	38.30
Computer Programmers	45.02	Nursing Assistants	20.34
Computer Systems Analysts	47.37	Office Clerks, General	21.64
Computer User Support Specialists	29.14	Physical Therapists	46.36
Construction Laborers	24.89	Physicians	117.95
Cooks, Restaurant	17.75	Plumbers, Pipefitters and Steamfitters	32.51
Customer Service Representatives	24.02	Police and Sheriff's Patrol Officers	39.83
Dentists	93.83	Postal Service Mail Carriers	30.06
Electricians	32.28	Real Estate Sales Agents	20.22
Engineers, Electrical	69.53	Retail Salespersons	17.08
Fast Food and Counter Workers	14.21	Sales Representatives, Technical/Scientific	60.11
Financial Managers	77.18	Secretaries, Exc. Legal/Medical/Executive	22.86
First-Line Supervisors of Office Workers	33.94	Security Guards	19.84
General and Operations Managers	54.24	Surgeons	207.59
Hairdressers/Cosmetologists	22.00	Teacher Assistants, Exc. Postsecondary[1]	15.17
Home Health and Personal Care Aides	17.30	Teachers, Secondary School, Exc. Sp. Ed.[1]	29.25
Janitors and Cleaners	17.35	Telemarketers	15.86
Landscaping/Groundskeeping Workers	19.53	Truck Drivers, Heavy/Tractor-Trailer	29.34
Lawyers	64.42	Truck Drivers, Light/Delivery Services	22.55
Maids and Housekeeping Cleaners	15.83	Waiters and Waitresses	15.00

Note: Wage data covers the Des Moines-West Des Moines, IA Metropolitan Statistical Area; (1) Hourly wages were calculated from annual wage data based on a 40 hour work week
Source: Bureau of Labor Statistics, Metro Area Occupational Employment & Wage Estimates, May 2024

Employment by Industry

Sector	MSA[1]		U.S.
	Number of Employees	Percent of Total	Percent of Total
Construction, Mining, and Logging	24,400	5.9	5.5
Financial Activities	56,000	13.6	5.8
Government	52,700	12.8	14.9
Information	6,100	1.5	1.9
Leisure and Hospitality	36,200	8.8	10.4
Manufacturing	22,400	5.4	8.0
Other Services	13,600	3.3	3.7
Private Education and Health Services	62,600	15.2	16.9
Professional and Business Services	55,300	13.4	14.2
Retail Trade	43,600	10.6	10.0
Transportation, Warehousing, and Utilities	19,700	4.8	4.8
Wholesale Trade	20,000	4.8	3.9

Note: Figures are non-farm employment as of December 2024. Figures are not seasonally adjusted and include workers 16 years of age and older; (1) Figures cover the Des Moines-West Des Moines, IA Metropolitan Statistical Area
Source: Bureau of Labor Statistics, Current Employment Statistics, Employment, Hours, and Earnings

Employment by Occupation

Occupation Classification	City (%)	MSA[1] (%)	U.S. (%)
Management, Business, Science, and Arts	36.9	45.4	42.0
Natural Resources, Construction, and Maintenance	9.1	8.2	8.6
Production, Transportation, and Material Moving	16.1	12.4	13.0
Sales and Office	20.5	20.1	19.9
Service	17.4	13.8	16.5

Note: Figures cover employed civilians 16 years of age and older; (1) Figures cover the Des Moines-West Des Moines, IA Metropolitan Statistical Area
Source: U.S. Census Bureau, 2019-2023 American Community Survey 5-Year Estimates

Occupations with Greatest Projected Employment Growth: 2022 – 2032

Occupation[1]	2022 Employment	2032 Projected Employment	Numeric Employment Change	Percent Employment Change
Home Health and Personal Care Aides	25,390	32,770	7,380	29.1
Heavy and Tractor-Trailer Truck Drivers	46,210	52,250	6,040	13.1
Registered Nurses	35,700	39,270	3,570	10.0
Stockers and Order Fillers	24,100	27,230	3,130	13.0
Laborers and Freight, Stock, and Material Movers, Hand	33,560	36,540	2,980	8.9
Cooks, Restaurant	13,190	15,840	2,650	20.1
Nursing Assistants (SOC 2018)	22,400	24,690	2,290	10.2
Construction Laborers	14,560	16,720	2,160	14.8
Medical and Health Services Managers	6,200	8,350	2,150	34.7
Financial Managers	8,990	10,870	1,880	20.9

Note: Projections cover Iowa; (1) Sorted by numeric employment change
Source: www.projectionscentral.org, State Occupational Projections, 2022–2032 Long-Term Projections

Fastest-Growing Occupations: 2022 – 2032

Occupation[1]	2022 Employment	2032 Projected Employment	Numeric Employment Change	Percent Employment Change
Wind Turbine Service Technicians	600	920	320	53.3
Nurse Practitioners	2,400	3,670	1,270	52.9
Data Scientists	2,010	2,760	750	37.3
Physical Therapist Assistants	1,260	1,720	460	36.5
Statisticians	400	540	140	35.0
Medical and Health Services Managers	6,200	8,350	2,150	34.7
Occupational Therapy Assistants	470	630	160	34.0
Information Security Analysts (SOC 2018)	1,250	1,670	420	33.6
Substance Abuse, Behavioral Disorder, and Mental Health Counselors	3,190	4,180	990	31.0
Physician Assistants	1,210	1,580	370	30.6

Note: Projections cover Iowa; (1) Sorted by percent employment change and excludes occupations with numeric employment change less than 50
Source: www.projectionscentral.org, State Occupational Projections, 2022–2032 Long-Term Projections

CITY FINANCES

City Government Finances

Component	2022 ($000)	2022 ($ per capita)
Total Revenues	678,089	3,194
Total Expenditures	646,497	3,045
Debt Outstanding	693,674	3,267

Source: U.S. Census Bureau, State & Local Government Finances 2022

City Government Revenue by Source

Source	2022 ($000)	2022 ($ per capita)	2022 (%)
General Revenue			
From Federal Government	46,180	218	6.8
From State Government	42,716	201	6.3
From Local Governments	8,859	42	1.3
Taxes			
Property	179,725	847	26.5
Sales and Gross Receipts	102,393	482	15.1
Personal Income	0	0	0.0
Corporate Income	0	0	0.0
Motor Vehicle License	0	0	0.0
Other Taxes	4,279	20	0.6
Current Charges	174,060	820	25.7
Liquor Store	0	0	0.0
Utility	90,643	427	13.4

Source: U.S. Census Bureau, State & Local Government Finances 2022

City Government Expenditures by Function

Function	2022 ($000)	2022 ($ per capita)	2022 (%)
General Direct Expenditures			
Air Transportation	44,925	211	6.9
Corrections	0	0	0.0
Education	0	0	0.0
Employment Security Administration	0	0	0.0
Financial Administration	6,412	30	1.0
Fire Protection	47,174	222	7.3
General Public Buildings	6,442	30	1.0
Governmental Administration, Other	13,881	65	2.1
Health	1,268	6	0.2
Highways	127,640	601	19.7
Hospitals	0	0	0.0
Housing and Community Development	27,820	131	4.3
Interest on General Debt	25,414	119	3.9
Judicial and Legal	1,950	9	0.3
Libraries	10,305	48	1.6
Parking	7,518	35	1.2
Parks and Recreation	14,336	67	2.2
Police Protection	76,152	358	11.8
Public Welfare	10,193	48	1.6
Sewerage	92,869	437	14.4
Solid Waste Management	14,330	67	2.2
Veterans' Services	0	0	0.0
Liquor Store	0	0	0.0
Utility	63,328	298	9.8

Source: U.S. Census Bureau, State & Local Government Finances 2022

TAXES

State Corporate Income Tax Rates

State	Tax Rate (%)	Income Brackets ($)	Num. of Brackets	Financial Institution Tax Rate (%)[a]	Federal Income Tax Ded.
Iowa	Undetermined	100,000 - 250,001	3	4.7	Yes (h)

Note: Tax rates for tax year 2024; (a) Rates listed are the corporate income tax rate applied to financial institutions or excise taxes based on income. Some states have other taxes based upon the value of deposits or shares; (h) 50% of the federal income tax is deductible.
Source: Federation of Tax Administrators, State Corporate Income Tax Rates, January 1, 2025

State Individual Income Tax Rates

State	Tax Rate (%)	Income Brackets ($)	Personal Exemptions ($)			Standard Ded. ($)	
			Single	Married	Depend.	Single	Married
Iowa (a)	4.4 - 5.7 (bb)	6,210 - 62,100	40	80	40 (c)	—	—

Note: Tax rates for tax year 2024; Local- and county-level taxes are not included; Federal income tax is deductible on state income tax returns; (a) 16 states have statutory provision for automatically adjusting to the rate of inflation the dollar values of the income tax brackets, standard deductions, and/or personal exemptions. Oregon does not index the income brackets for $125,000 and over See: INFL and SPEC above; (c) The personal exemption takes the form of a tax credit instead of a deduction; (bb) Louisiana lawmakers repealed the state's throwout rule, ending the taxation of so-called "nowhere income." Iowa is phasing-in a flat rate by 2027, while Nebraska (LB 754 signed into law) and South Carolina is phasing-in a reduced top rate by 2027.
Source: Federation of Tax Administrators, State Individual Income Tax Rates, January 1, 2025

Various State Sales and Excise Tax Rates

State	State Sales Tax (%)	Gasoline[1] ($/gal.)	Cigarette[2] ($/pack)	Spirits[3] ($/gal.)	Wine[4] ($/gal.)	Beer[5] ($/gal.)	Recreational Marijuana (%)
Iowa	6	0.30	1.36	15.14	1.75	0.19	Not legal

Note: All tax rates as of January 1, 2025; (1) The American Petroleum Institute has developed a methodology for determining the average tax rate on a gallon of fuel. Rates may include any of the following: excise taxes, environmental fees, storage tank fees, other fees or taxes, general sales tax, and local taxes; (2) The federal excise tax of $1.0066 per pack and local taxes are not included; (3) Rates are those applicable to off-premise sales of 40% alcohol by volume (a.b.v.) distilled spirits in 750ml containers. Local excise taxes are excluded; (4) Rates are those applicable to off-premise sales of 11% a.b.v. non-carbonated wine in 750ml containers; (5) Rates are those applicable to off-premise sales of 4.7% a.b.v. beer in 12 ounce containers.
Source: Tax Foundation, 2025 Facts & Figures: How Does Your State Compare?

State Tax Competitiveness Index

State	Overall Rank	Corporate Tax Rank	Individual Income Tax Rank	Sales Tax Rank	Property Tax Rank	Unemployment Insurance Tax Rank
Iowa	20	23	19	11	32	33

Note: The Tax Foundation's State Tax Competitiveness Index enables policymakers, taxpayers, and business leaders to gauge how their states' tax systems compare. A rank of 1 is best, 50 is worst. Rankings do not average to the total. States without a tax rank equally as 1. DC's scores and rankings do not affect other states. The report shows tax systems as of July 1, 2024 (the beginning of Fiscal Year 2025).
Source: Tax Foundation, State Tax Competitiveness Index 2025

TRANSPORTATION

Means of Transportation to Work

Area	Car/Truck/Van Drove Alone	Car/Truck/Van Carpooled	Public Transportation Bus	Public Transportation Subway	Public Transportation Railroad	Bicycle	Walked	Other Means	Worked at Home
City	72.3	11.2	1.1	0.0	0.0	0.4	2.2	1.3	11.4
MSA[1]	74.3	7.9	0.4	0.0	0.0	0.2	1.6	1.2	14.3
U.S.	70.2	8.5	1.3	1.3	0.4	0.4	2.4	1.6	13.5

Note: Figures are percentages and cover workers 16 years of age and older; (1) Figures cover the Des Moines-West Des Moines, IA Metropolitan Statistical Area
Source: U.S. Census Bureau, 2019-2023 American Community Survey 5-Year Estimates

Travel Time to Work

Area	Less Than 10 Minutes	10 to 19 Minutes	20 to 29 Minutes	30 to 44 Minutes	45 to 59 Minutes	60 to 89 Minutes	90 Minutes or More
City	14.1	43.0	25.7	11.9	2.0	1.9	1.5
MSA[1]	15.2	35.6	26.7	15.6	3.8	1.7	1.3
U.S.	12.6	28.6	21.2	20.8	8.1	6.0	2.8

Note: Note: Figures are percentages and include workers 16 years old and over; (1) Figures cover the Des Moines-West Des Moines, IA Metropolitan Statistical Area
Source: U.S. Census Bureau, 2019-2023 American Community Survey 5-Year Estimates

Key Congestion Measures

Measure	2000	2010	2015	2020	2022
Annual Hours of Delay, Total (000)	n/a	n/a	8,528	3,468	6,591
Annual Hours of Delay, Per Auto Commuter	n/a	n/a	17	7	13
Annual Congestion Cost, Per Auto Commuter ($)	n/a	n/a	397	171	318

Note: n/a not available
Source: Texas A&M Transportation Institute, 2023 Urban Mobility Report

Freeway Travel Time Index

Measure	1985	1990	1995	2000	2005	2010	2015	2020	2022
Urban Area Index[1]	n/a	n/a	n/a	n/a	n/a	n/a	1.07	1.04	1.06
Urban Area Rank[1,2]	n/a	n/a	n/a	n/a	n/a	n/a	n/a	n/a	n/a

Note: Freeway Travel Time Index—the ratio of travel time in the peak period to the travel time at free-flow conditions. For example, a value of 1.30 indicates a 20-minute free-flow trip takes 26 minutes in the peak (20 minutes x 1.30 = 26 minutes); (1) Covers the Des Moines IA urban area; (2) Rank is based on 101 larger urban areas (#1 = highest travel time index); n/a not available
Source: Texas A&M Transportation Institute, 2023 Urban Mobility Report

Public Transportation

Agency Name / Mode of Transportation	Vehicles Operated in Maximum Service[1]	Annual Unlinked Passenger Trips[2] (in thous.)	Annual Passenger Miles[3] (in thous.)
Des Moines Metropolitan Transit Authority (MTA)			
Bus (directly operated)	86	3,041.5	12,673.9
Demand Response (directly operated)	27	103.4	792.7
Demand Response - Taxi	2	8.0	58.5
Vanpool (directly operated)	35	69.3	3,155.9

Note: (1) Number of revenue vehicles operated by the given mode and type of service to meet the annual maximum service requirement. This is the revenue vehicle count during the peak season of the year; on the week and day that maximum service is provided. Vehicles operated in maximum service (VOMS) exclude atypical days and one-time special events; (2) Number of passengers who boarded public transportation vehicles. Passengers are counted each time they board a vehicle no matter how many vehicles they use to travel from their origin to their destination. (3) Sum of the distances ridden by all passengers during the entire fiscal year.
Source: Federal Transit Administration, National Transit Database, 2023

Air Transportation

Airport Name and Code / Type of Service	Passenger Airlines[1]	Passenger Enplanements	Freight Carriers[2]	Freight (lbs)
Des Moines International (DSM)				
Domestic service (U.S. carriers only)	26	1,554,180	10	25,004,926
International service (U.S. carriers only)	1	529	0	0

Note: (1) Includes all U.S.-based major, minor and commuter airlines that carried at least one passenger during the year; (2) Includes all U.S.-based airlines and freight carriers that transported at least one pound of freight during the year.
Source: Bureau of Transportation Statistics, The Intermodal Transportation Database, Air Carriers: T-100 Domestic Market (U.S. carriers only), 2024; Bureau of Transportation Statistics, The Intermodal Transportation Database, Air Carriers: T-100 International Market (U.S. carriers only), 2024

BUSINESSES

Major Business Headquarters

Company Name	Industry	Rankings	
		Fortune[1]	Forbes[2]
Principal Financial	Insurance: life, health (stock)	310	-

Note: (1) Companies that produce a 10-K are ranked 1 to 500 based on 2023 revenue; (2) All private companies with at least $2 billion in annual revenue through the end of their most current fiscal year are ranked 1 to 275; companies listed are headquartered in the city; dashes indicate no ranking
Source: Fortune, "Fortune 500," 2024; Forbes, "America's Largest Private Companies," 2024

Living Environment

COST OF LIVING

Cost of Living Index

Composite Index	Groceries	Housing	Utilities	Transportation	Health Care	Misc. Goods/Services
85.8	99.6	66.1	80.8	93.2	87.2	94.9

Note: The Cost of Living Index measures regional differences in the cost of consumer goods and services, excluding taxes and non-consumer expenditures, for professional and managerial households in the top income quintile. It is based on more than 50,000 prices covering almost 60 different items for which prices are collected three times a year by chambers of commerce, economic development organizations or university applied economic centers in each participating urban area. The numbers shown should be read as a percentage above or below the national average of 100. For example, a value of 115.4 in the groceries column indicates that grocery prices are 15.4% higher than the national average. Small differences in the index numbers should not be interpreted as significant; Figures cover the Des Moines IA urban area.
Source: The Council for Community and Economic Research, Cost of Living Index, 2024

Grocery Prices

Area[1]	T-Bone Steak ($/pound)	Frying Chicken ($/pound)	Whole Milk ($/half gal.)	Eggs ($/dozen)	Orange Juice ($/64 oz.)	Coffee ($/11.5 oz.)
City[2]	15.52	1.44	4.76	3.47	4.47	4.94
Avg.	15.42	1.55	4.69	3.25	4.41	5.46
Min.	14.50	1.16	4.43	2.75	4.00	4.85
Max.	17.56	2.89	5.49	4.78	5.54	7.89

Note: (1) Values for the local area are compared with the average, minimum and maximum values for all 276 areas in the Cost of Living Index; (2) Figures cover the Des Moines IA urban area; **T-Bone Steak** (price per pound); **Frying Chicken** (price per pound, whole fryer); **Whole Milk** (half gallon carton); **Eggs** (price per dozen, Grade A, large); **Orange Juice** (64 oz. Tropicana or Florida Natural); **Coffee** (11.5 oz. can, vacuum-packed, Maxwell House, Hills Bros, or Folgers).
Source: The Council for Community and Economic Research, Cost of Living Index, 2024

Housing and Utility Costs

Area[1]	New Home Price ($)	Apartment Rent ($/month)	All Electric ($/month)	Part Electric ($/month)	Other Energy ($/month)	Telephone ($/month)
City[2]	359,756	846	-	84.52	63.10	188.12
Avg.	515,975	1,550	210.99	123.07	82.07	194.99
Min.	265,375	692	104.33	53.68	36.26	179.42
Max.	2,775,821	5,719	529.02	397.28	361.63	223.33

Note: (1) Values for the local area are compared with the average, minimum and maximum values for all 276 areas in the Cost of Living Index; (2) Figures cover the Des Moines IA urban area; **New Home Price** (2,400 sf living area, 8,000 sf lot, in urban area with full utilities); **Apartment Rent** (950 sf 2 bedroom/1.5 or 2 bath, unfurnished, excluding all utilities except water); **All Electric** (average monthly cost for an all-electric home); **Part Electric** (average monthly cost for a part-electric home); **Other Energy** (average monthly cost for natural gas, fuel oil, coal, wood, and any other forms of energy except electricity); **Telephone** (price includes the base monthly rate plus taxes and fees for three lines of mobile phone service).
Source: The Council for Community and Economic Research, Cost of Living Index, 2024

Health Care, Transportation, and Other Costs

Area[1]	Doctor ($/visit)	Dentist ($/visit)	Optometrist ($/visit)	Gasoline ($/gallon)	Beauty Salon ($/visit)	Men's Shirt ($)
City[2]	119.38	101.96	128.70	3.15	42.46	37.61
Avg.	143.77	117.51	129.23	3.32	48.57	38.14
Min.	36.74	58.67	67.33	2.80	24.00	13.41
Max.	270.44	216.82	307.33	5.28	94.00	63.89

Note: (1) Values for the local area are compared with the average, minimum and maximum values for all 276 areas in the Cost of Living Index; (2) Figures cover the Des Moines IA urban area; **Doctor** (general practitioners routine exam of an established patient); **Dentist** (adult teeth cleaning and periodic oral examination); **Optometrist** (full vision eye exam for established adult patient); **Gasoline** (one gallon regular unleaded, national brand, including all taxes, cash price at self-service pump if available); **Beauty Salon** (woman's shampoo, trim, and blow-dry); **Men's Shirt** (cotton/polyester dress shirt, pinpoint weave, long sleeves).
Source: The Council for Community and Economic Research, Cost of Living Index, 2024

HOUSING

Homeownership Rate

Area	2017 (%)	2018 (%)	2019 (%)	2020 (%)	2021 (%)	2022 (%)	2023 (%)	2024 (%)
MSA[1]	n/a	n/a	n/a	n/a	n/a	n/a	n/a	n/a
U.S.	63.9	64.4	64.6	66.6	65.5	65.8	65.9	65.6

Note: (1) Figures cover the Des Moines-West Des Moines, IA Metropolitan Statistical Area; n/a not available
Source: U.S. Census Bureau, Housing Vacancies and Homeownership Annual Statistics: 2017-2024

House Price Index (HPI)

Area	National Ranking[2]	Quarterly Change (%)	One-Year Change (%)	Five-Year Change (%)	Since 1991Q1 (%)
MSA[1]	174	-0.70	4.10	43.67	253.81
U.S.[3]	–	1.43	4.51	57.13	327.82

Note: The HPI is a weighted repeat sales index. It measures average price changes in repeat sales or refinancings on the same properties. This information is obtained by reviewing repeat mortgage transactions on single-family properties whose mortgages have been purchased or securitized by Fannie Mae or Freddie Mac since January 1975; (1) Figures cover the Des Moines-West Des Moines, IA Metropolitan Statistical Area; (2) Rankings are based on annual percentage change for all metro areas containing at least 15,000 transactions over the last 10 years and ranges from 1 to 241; (3) figures based on a weighted average of Census Division estimates using a seasonally adjusted, purchase-only index; all figures are for the period ending December 31, 2024
Source: Federal Housing Finance Agency, Change in FHFA Metropolitan Area House Price Indexes, All Transactions Index, 2024Q4

Home Value

Area	Under $100,000	$100,000 -$199,999	$200,000 -$299,999	$300,000 -$399,999	$400,000 -$499,999	$500,000 -$999,999	$1,000,000 or more	Median ($)
City	13.7	44.2	27.4	8.7	2.6	2.7	0.7	183,700
MSA[1]	8.7	25.7	28.2	18.3	9.0	9.0	1.1	252,400
U.S.	12.1	17.8	19.5	14.4	10.5	19.1	6.5	303,400

Note: Figures are percentages except for median and cover owner-occupied housing units; (1) Figures cover the Des Moines-West Des Moines, IA Metropolitan Statistical Area
Source: U.S. Census Bureau, 2019-2023 American Community Survey 5-Year Estimates

Year Housing Structure Built

Area	2020 or Later	2010 -2019	2000 -2009	1990 -1999	1980 -1989	1970 -1979	1960 -1969	1950 -1959	1940 -1949	Before 1940	Median Year
City	0.6	6.9	7.3	6.8	6.4	12.8	9.5	14.6	7.3	27.8	1960
MSA[1]	2.2	15.6	15.3	12.1	7.8	12.5	7.5	8.3	3.5	15.3	1984
U.S.	1.2	8.9	13.6	12.8	14.4	10.0	9.7	4.5	11.9	1980

Note: Figures are percentages except for Median Year; Note: (1) Figures cover the Des Moines-West Des Moines, IA Metropolitan Statistical Area
Source: U.S. Census Bureau, 2019-2023 American Community Survey 5-Year Estimates

Gross Monthly Rent

Area	Under $500	$500 -$999	$1,000 -$1,499	$1,500 -$1,999	$2,000 -$2,499	$2,500 -$2,999	$3,000 and up	Median ($)
City	5.4	39.0	40.2	12.9	2.0	0.2	0.3	1,054
MSA[1]	4.6	33.5	42.0	15.1	3.4	0.5	0.9	1,113
U.S.	6.5	22.3	29.5	20.2	10.8	4.8	5.9	1,348

Note: Figures are percentages except for median; Gross rent is the contract rent plus the estimated average monthly cost of utilities (electricity, gas, and water and sewer) and fuels (oil, coal, kerosene, wood, etc.) if these are paid by the renter (or paid for the renter by someone else); (1) Figures cover the Des Moines-West Des Moines, IA Metropolitan Statistical Area
Source: U.S. Census Bureau, 2019-2023 American Community Survey 5-Year Estimates

HEALTH

Health Risk Factors

Category	MSA[1] (%)	U.S. (%)
Adults aged 18–64 who have any kind of health care coverage	92.7	90.8
Adults who reported being in good or better health	82.4	81.8
Adults who have been told they have high blood cholesterol	37.2	36.9
Adults who have been told they have high blood pressure	33.3	34.0
Adults who are current smokers	12.8	12.1
Adults who currently use e-cigarettes	9.1	7.7
Adults who currently use chewing tobacco, snuff, or snus	4.5	3.2
Adults who are heavy drinkers[2]	7.1	6.1
Adults who are binge drinkers[3]	20.0	15.2
Adults who are overweight (BMI 25.0 - 29.9)	35.2	34.4
Adults who are obese (BMI 30.0 - 99.8)	37.1	34.3
Adults who participated in any physical activities in the past month	77.1	75.8

Note: All figures are crude prevalence; (1) Figures cover the Des Moines-West Des Moines, IA Metropolitan Statistical Area; (2) Heavy drinkers are classified as adult men having more than 14 drinks per week and adult women having more than 7 drinks per week; (3) Binge drinkers are classified as males having five or more drinks on one occasion or females having four or more drinks on one occasion
Source: Centers for Disease Control and Prevention, Behavioral Risk Factor Surveillance System, SMART: Selected Metropolitan Area Risk Trends, 2023

Acute and Chronic Health Conditions

Category	MSA[1] (%)	U.S. (%)
Adults who have ever been told they had a heart attack	3.8	4.2
Adults who have ever been told they have angina or coronary heart disease	3.6	4.0
Adults who have ever been told they had a stroke	2.4	3.3
Adults who have ever been told they have asthma	13.3	15.7
Adults who have ever been told they have arthritis	27.1	26.3
Adults who have ever been told they have diabetes[2]	10.7	11.5
Adults who have ever been told they had skin cancer	5.7	5.6
Adults who have ever been told they had any other types of cancer	7.0	8.4
Adults who have ever been told they have COPD	5.2	6.4
Adults who have ever been told they have kidney disease	3.8	3.7
Adults who have ever been told they have a form of depression	20.2	22.0

Note: All figures are crude prevalence; (1) Figures cover the Des Moines-West Des Moines, IA Metropolitan Statistical Area; (2) Figures do not include pregnancy-related, borderline, or pre-diabetes
Source: Centers for Disease Control and Prevention, Behavioral Risk Factor Surveillance System, SMART: Selected Metropolitan Area Risk Trends, 2023

Health Screening and Vaccination Rates

Category	MSA[1] (%)	U.S. (%)
Adults who have ever been tested for HIV	30.5	37.5
Adults who have had their blood cholesterol checked within the last five years	84.0	87.0
Adults aged 65+ who have had flu shot within the past year	70.0	63.4
Adults aged 65+ who have ever had a pneumonia vaccination	72.5	71.9

Note: All figures are crude prevalence; (1) Figures cover the Des Moines-West Des Moines, IA Metropolitan Statistical Area.
Source: Centers for Disease Control and Prevention, Behavioral Risk Factor Surveillance System, SMART: Selected Metropolitan Area Risk Trends, 2023

Disability Status

Category	MSA[1] (%)	U.S. (%)
Adults who reported being deaf	6.1	7.4
Are you blind or have serious difficulty seeing, even when wearing glasses?	4.3	4.9
Do you have difficulty doing errands alone?	7.5	7.8
Do you have difficulty dressing or bathing?	3.3	3.6
Do you have serious difficulty concentrating/remembering/making decisions?	13.5	13.7
Do you have serious difficulty walking or climbing stairs?	11.5	13.2

Note: All figures are crude prevalence; (1) Figures cover the Des Moines-West Des Moines, IA Metropolitan Statistical Area.
Source: Centers for Disease Control and Prevention, Behavioral Risk Factor Surveillance System, SMART: Selected Metropolitan Area Risk Trends, 2023

Mortality Rates for the Top 10 Causes of Death in the U.S.

ICD-10[a] Sub-Chapter	ICD-10[a] Code	Crude Mortality Rate[2] per 100,000 population	
		County[3]	U.S.
Malignant neoplasms	C00-C97	166.2	182.7
Ischaemic heart diseases	I20-I25	102.4	109.6
Provisional assignment of new diseases of uncertain etiology[1]	U00-U49	44.4	65.3
Other forms of heart disease	I30-I51	60.5	65.1
Other degenerative diseases of the nervous system	G30-G31	47.1	52.4
Other external causes of accidental injury	W00-X59	50.6	52.3
Cerebrovascular diseases	I60-I69	34.1	49.1
Chronic lower respiratory diseases	J40-J47	38.9	43.5
Hypertensive diseases	I10-I15	20.0	38.9
Organic, including symptomatic, mental disorders	F01-F09	33.3	33.9

Note: (a) ICD-10 = International Classification of Diseases 10th Revision; (1) Includes COVID-19, adverse effects to COVID-19 vaccines, SARS, and vaping-related disorders; (2) Crude mortality rates are a three-year average covering 2021-2023; (3) Figures cover Polk County.
Source: Centers for Disease Control and Prevention, National Center for Health Statistics. National Vital Statistics System, Mortality 2018-2023 on CDC WONDER Online Database

Mortality Rates for Selected Causes of Death

Cause of Death	ICD-10[a] Code	Crude Mortality Rate[1] per 100,000 population County[2]	U.S.
Accidental poisoning and exposure to noxious substances	X40-X49	24.6	30.5
Alzheimer disease	G30	38.0	35.4
Assault	X85-Y09	3.1	7.3
COVID-19	U07.1	44.4	65.3
Diabetes mellitus	E10-E14	22.8	30.0
Diseases of the liver	K70-K76	17.1	20.8
Human immunodeficiency virus (HIV) disease	B20-B24	Unreliable	1.5
Influenza and pneumonia	J09-J18	8.4	13.4
Intentional self-harm	X60-X84	16.7	14.7
Malnutrition	E40-E46	9.6	6.0
Obesity and other hyperalimentation	E65-E68	3.1	3.1
Renal failure	N17-N19	10.6	16.4
Transport accidents	V01-V99	10.0	14.4

Note: (a) ICD-10 = International Classification of Diseases 10th Revision; (1) Crude mortality rates are a three-year average covering 2021-2023; (2) Figures cover Polk County; Data are suppressed when the data meet the criteria for confidentiality constraints; Crude mortality rates are flagged as unreliable when the rate would be calculated with a numerator of 20 or less.
Source: Centers for Disease Control and Prevention, National Center for Health Statistics. National Vital Statistics System, Mortality 2018-2023 on CDC WONDER Online Database

Health Insurance Coverage

Area	With Health Insurance	With Private Health Insurance	With Public Health Insurance	Without Health Insurance	Population Under Age 19 Without Health Insurance
City	93.3	62.0	42.7	6.7	2.2
MSA[1]	95.5	75.1	32.5	4.5	2.3
U.S.	91.4	67.3	36.3	8.6	5.4

Note: Figures are percentages that cover the civilian noninstitutionalized population; (1) Figures cover the Des Moines-West Des Moines, IA Metropolitan Statistical Area
Source: U.S. Census Bureau, 2019-2023 American Community Survey 5-Year Estimates

Number of Medical Professionals

Area	MDs[3]	DOs[3,4]	Dentists	Podiatrists	Chiropractors	Optometrists
County[1] (number)	1,108	596	408	62	322	107
County[1] (rate[2])	221.1	118.9	80.8	12.3	63.7	21.2
U.S. (rate[2])	302.5	29.2	74.6	6.4	29.5	18.0

Note: Data as of 2023 unless noted; (1) Data covers Polk County; (2) Number of medical professionals per 100,000 population; (3) Data as of 2022 and includes all active, non-federal physicians; (4) Doctor of Osteopathic Medicine
Source: U.S. Department of Health and Human Services, Health Resources and Services Administration, Bureau of Health Professions, Area Resource File (ARF) 2023-2024

EDUCATION

Public School District Statistics

District Name	Schls	Pupils	Pupil/ Teacher Ratio	Minority Pupils[1] (%)	Total Rev. per Pupil ($)	Total Exp. per Pupil ($)
Des Moines Independent CSD	59	30,277	14.6	67.9	17,634	16,255

Note: Table includes school districts with 2,000 or more students; (1) Percentage of students that are not non-Hispanic white.
Source: U.S. Department of Education, National Center for Education Statistics, Common Core of Data, Local Education Agency (School District) Universe Survey: School Year 2023-2024; U.S. Department of Education, National Center for Education Statistics, Common Core of Data, School District Finance Survey (F-33): School Year 2021–22

Highest Level of Education

Area	Less than H.S.	H.S. Diploma	Some College, No Deg.	Associate Degree	Bachelor's Degree	Master's Degree	Prof. School Degree	Doctorate Degree
City	12.7	29.1	20.0	9.1	19.9	6.3	1.8	0.9
MSA[1]	6.5	25.0	19.0	10.4	26.4	9.0	2.1	1.5
U.S.	10.6	26.2	19.4	8.8	21.3	9.8	2.3	1.6

Note: Figures cover persons age 25 and over; (1) Figures cover the Des Moines-West Des Moines, IA Metropolitan Statistical Area
Source: U.S. Census Bureau, 2019-2023 American Community Survey 5-Year Estimates

Educational Attainment by Race

Area	High School Graduate or Higher (%)					Bachelor's Degree or Higher (%)				
	Total	White	Black	Asian	Hisp.[2]	Total	White	Black	Asian	Hisp.[2]
City	87.3	93.7	79.3	61.3	60.1	29.0	33.5	15.8	23.0	10.8
MSA[1]	93.5	96.3	82.0	73.9	69.3	39.1	40.8	20.1	44.7	17.4
U.S.	89.4	92.9	88.1	88.0	72.5	35.0	37.7	24.7	57.0	19.9

Note: Figures shown cover persons 25 years old and over; (1) Figures cover the Des Moines-West Des Moines, IA Metropolitan Statistical Area; (2) People of Hispanic origin can be of any race
Source: U.S. Census Bureau, 2019-2023 American Community Survey 5-Year Estimates

School Enrollment by Grade and Control

Area	Preschool (%)		Kindergarten (%)		Grades 1 - 4 (%)		Grades 5 - 8 (%)		Grades 9 - 12 (%)	
	Public	Private	Public	Private	Public	Private	Public	Private	Public	Private
City	76.4	23.6	88.0	12.0	90.8	9.2	91.8	8.2	93.8	6.2
MSA[1]	68.1	31.9	87.6	12.4	91.2	8.8	89.9	10.1	91.5	8.5
U.S.	58.7	41.3	85.2	14.8	87.2	12.8	87.9	12.1	89.0	11.0

Note: Figures shown cover persons 3 years old and over; (1) Figures cover the Des Moines-West Des Moines, IA Metropolitan Statistical Area
Source: U.S. Census Bureau, 2019-2023 American Community Survey 5-Year Estimates

Higher Education

Four-Year Colleges			Two-Year Colleges			Medical Schools[1]	Law Schools[2]	Voc/Tech[3]
Public	Private Non-profit	Private For-profit	Public	Private Non-profit	Private For-profit			
0	6	0	1	1	3	1	1	1

Note: Figures cover institutions located within the Des Moines-West Des Moines, IA Metropolitan Statistical Area and include main campuses only; (1) includes schools accredited by the Liaison Committee on Medical Education and the American Osteopathic Association's Commission on Osteopathic College Accreditation; (2) includes ABA-accredited schools, schools with provisional ABA accreditation, and state accredited schools; (3) includes all schools with programs that are less than 2 years.
Source: National Center for Education Statistics, Integrated Postsecondary Education System (IPEDS), 2023-24; Wikipedia, List of Medical Schools in the United States, accessed May 2, 2025; Wikipedia, List of Law Schools in the United States, accessed May 2, 2025

According to *U.S. News & World Report*, the Des Moines-West Des Moines, IA metro area is home to one of the top 200 national universities in the U.S.: **Drake University** (#179 tie). The indicators used to capture academic quality fall into a number of categories: assessment by administrators at peer institutions; retention of students; faculty resources; student selectivity; financial resources; alumni giving; high school counselor ratings of colleges; and graduation rate. *U.S. News & World Report, "America's Best Colleges 2025"*

According to *U.S. News & World Report*, the Des Moines-West Des Moines, IA metro area is home to one of the top 100 law schools in the U.S.: **Drake University** (#84 tie). The rankings are based on a weighted average of 12 measures of quality: peer assessment score; assessment score by lawyers/judges; median LSAT scores; median undergrad GPA; acceptance rate; employment rates for graduates; placement success; bar passage rate; faculty resources; expenditures per student; student/faculty ratio; and library resources. *U.S. News & World Report, "America's Best Graduate Schools, Law, 2025"*

EMPLOYERS

Major Employers

Company Name	Industry
Bridgestone Americas Tire Operations	Global distribution center for tires
DuPont Pioneer	Crop inputs for worldwide agribusiness
Emerson Process Management Fisher Div	Control valves & systems, divisional headquarters
Grinnell Mutual Reinsurance Company	Reinsurance
Hy-Vee Food Stores	Retail grocery & drugstore chain
JBS USA	Pork processing & packaging
John Deere companies	Agricultural machinery, consumer financial services
Lennox Manufacturing	Heating & air conditioners
Mercer	Insurance
Mercy Medical Center	Healthcare
Meredith Corporation	Magazine, book publishing, tv, integrated marketing
Nationwide	Insurance
Principal Financial Group	Financial services
United Parcel Service	Package delivery services
UnityPoint Health	Healthcare
Vermeer Manufacturing Company	Manufacturing
Wellmark	Health insurance
Wells Fargo	Financial services & home mortgage

Note: Companies shown are located within the Des Moines-West Des Moines, IA Metropolitan Statistical Area.
Source: Chambers of Commerce; State Departments of Labor; Wikipedia

Best Companies to Work For

BH Management Services, headquartered in Des Moines, is among "Fortune's Best Workplaces for Women." To pick the best companies, *Fortune* partnered with the Great Place to Work Institute. To be considered for the list, companies must be Great Place To Work-Certified. Companies must also employ at least 50 women, at least 20% of their non-executive managers must be female, and at least one executive must be female. To determine the Best Workplaces for Women, Great Place To Work measured the differences in women's survey responses to those of their peers and assesses the impact of demographics and roles on the quality and consistency of women's experiences. Great Place To Work also analyzed the gender balance of each workplace, how it compared to each company's industry, and patterns in representation as women rise from front-line positions to the board of directors. *Fortune, "Best Workplaces for Women," 2024*

BH Management Services, headquartered in Des Moines, is among "Best Workplaces in Real Estate." To determine the Best Workplaces in Real Estate list, Great Place To Work analyzed the survey responses of over 29,000 employees from Great Place To Work-Certified companies in the real estate industry. Survey data analysis and company-provided datapoints are then factored into a combined score to compare and rank the companies that create the most consistently positive experience for all employees in this industry. *Fortune, "Best Workplaces in Real Estate," 2024*

PUBLIC SAFETY

Crime Rate

Area	Total Crime Rate	Violent Crime Rate				Property Crime Rate		
		Murder	Rape	Robbery	Aggrav. Assault	Burglary	Larceny-Theft	Motor Vehicle Theft
City	4,056.1	4.3	69.2	90.6	542.8	451.2	2,271.3	626.7
U.S.	2,290.9	5.7	38.0	66.5	264.1	250.7	1,347.2	318.7

Note: Figures are crimes per 100,000 population.
Source: FBI, Table 8, Offenses Known to Law Enforcement, by State by City, 2023

Hate Crimes

Area	Number of Quarters Reported	Number of Incidents per Bias Motivation					
		Race/Ethnicity/Ancestry	Religion	Sexual Orientation	Disability	Gender	Gender Identity
City	4	6	2	3	0	0	0
U.S.	4	5,900	2,699	2,077	187	92	492

Source: Federal Bureau of Investigation, Hate Crime Statistics 2023

Identity Theft Consumer Reports

Area	Reports	Reports per 100,000 Population	Rank[2]
MSA[1]	1,147	159	241
U.S.	1,135,291	339	-

Note: (1) Figures cover the Des Moines-West Des Moines, IA Metropolitan Statistical Area; (2) Rank ranges from 1 to 401 where 1 indicates greatest number of identity theft reports per 100,000 population
Source: Federal Trade Commission, Consumer Sentinel Network Data Book 2024

Fraud and Other Consumer Reports

Area	Reports	Reports per 100,000 Population	Rank[2]
MSA[1]	6,021	836	306
U.S.	5,360,641	1,601	-

Note: (1) Figures cover the Des Moines-West Des Moines, IA Metropolitan Statistical Area; (2) Rank ranges from 1 to 401 where 1 indicates greatest number of fraud and other consumer reports per 100,000 population
Source: Federal Trade Commission, Consumer Sentinel Network Data Book 2024

POLITICS

2024 Presidential Election Results

Area	Trump (Rep.)	Harris (Dem.)	Stein (Green)	Kennedy (Ind.)	Oliver (Lib.)	Other
Polk County	43.7	54.5	0.0	0.6	0.5	0.7
U.S.	49.7	48.2	0.6	0.5	0.4	0.6

Note: Results are percentages and may not add to 100% due to rounding
Source: Dave Leip's Atlas of U.S. Presidential Elections

SPORTS

Professional Sports Teams

Team Name	League	Year Established

No teams are located in the metro area
Source: Wikipedia, Major Professional Sports Teams of the United States and Canada, May 1, 2025

Des Moines, Iowa

CLIMATE

Average and Extreme Temperatures

Temperature	Jan	Feb	Mar	Apr	May	Jun	Jul	Aug	Sep	Oct	Nov	Dec	Yr.
Extreme High (°F)	65	70	91	93	98	103	105	108	99	95	76	69	108
Average High (°F)	29	34	45	61	72	82	86	84	76	65	48	33	60
Average Temp. (°F)	20	25	36	51	62	72	76	74	65	54	39	25	50
Average Low (°F)	11	16	27	40	51	61	66	64	54	43	29	17	40
Extreme Low (°F)	-24	-20	-22	9	28	42	47	40	28	14	-3	-22	-24

Note: Figures cover the years 1945-1990
Source: National Climatic Data Center, International Station Meteorological Climate Summary, 9/96

Average Precipitation/Snowfall/Humidity

Precip./Humidity	Jan	Feb	Mar	Apr	May	Jun	Jul	Aug	Sep	Oct	Nov	Dec	Yr.
Avg. Precip. (in.)	1.1	1.1	2.3	3.1	3.8	4.4	3.5	3.9	3.1	2.4	1.7	1.2	31.8
Avg. Snowfall (in.)	8	7	7	2	Tr	0	0	0	Tr	Tr	3	7	33
Avg. Rel. Hum. 6am (%)	77	79	79	78	78	81	83	86	85	80	79	80	80
Avg. Rel. Hum. 3pm (%)	65	63	57	50	51	52	52	54	52	50	58	66	56

Note: Figures cover the years 1945-1990; Tr = Trace amounts (<0.05 in. of rain; <0.5 in. of snow)
Source: National Climatic Data Center, International Station Meteorological Climate Summary, 9/96

Weather Conditions

Temperature			Daytime Sky			Precipitation		
5°F & below	32°F & below	90°F & above	Clear	Partly cloudy	Cloudy	0.01 inch or more precip.	0.1 inch or more snow/ice	Thunder-storms
25	137	26	99	128	138	106	25	46

Note: Figures are average number of days per year and cover the years 1945-1990
Source: National Climatic Data Center, International Station Meteorological Climate Summary, 9/96

HAZARDOUS WASTE

Superfund Sites

The Des Moines-West Des Moines, IA metro area is home to four sites on the EPA's Superfund National Priorities List (NPL) or Superfund Alternative Approach (SAA) list: **Des Moines TCE** (Final NPL); **Lot 46 Valley Gardens TCE** (Final NPL); **Midwest Manufacturing/North Farm** (Final NPL); **Railroad Avenue Groundwater Contamination** (Final NPL). The Superfund alternative approach uses the same investigation and cleanup process and standards that are used for sites listed on the National Priorities List. The SAA is an alternative to listing a site on the NPL; it is not an alternative to Superfund or the Superfund process. There are a total of 1,445 Superfund sites with a status of proposed or final on both lists in the United States. *U.S. Environmental Protection Agency, National Priorities List, May 1, 2025; U.S. Environmental Protection Agency, Superfund Alternative Approach Sites, May 1, 2025*

AIR QUALITY

Air Quality Trends: Ozone

	1990	1995	2000	2005	2010	2015	2020	2021	2022	2023
MSA[1]	n/a	n/a	n/a	n/a	n/a	n/a	n/a	n/a	n/a	n/a
U.S.	0.087	0.089	0.081	0.080	0.072	0.068	0.066	0.067	0.067	0.070

Note: (1) Data covers the Des Moines-West Des Moines, IA Metropolitan Statistical Area; n/a not available. The values shown are the composite ozone concentration averages among trend sites based on the highest fourth daily maximum 8-hour concentration in parts per million. These trends are based on sites having an adequate record of monitoring data during the trend period. Data from exceptional events are included.
Source: U.S. Environmental Protection Agency, Air Quality Monitoring Information, "Air Quality Trends by City, 1990-2023"

Air Quality Index

Area	Percent of Days when Air Quality was...[2]					AQI Statistics[2]	
	Good	Moderate	Unhealthy for Sensitive Groups	Unhealthy	Very Unhealthy	Maximum	Median
MSA[1]	46.0	49.9	3.3	0.8	0.0	166	52

Note: (1) Data covers the Des Moines-West Des Moines, IA Metropolitan Statistical Area; (2) Based on 365 days with AQI data in 2023. Air Quality Index (AQI) is an index for reporting daily air quality. EPA calculates the AQI for five major air pollutants regulated by the Clean Air Act: ground-level ozone, particle pollution (aka particulate matter), carbon monoxide, sulfur dioxide, and nitrogen dioxide. The AQI runs from 0 to 500. The higher the AQI value, the greater the level of air pollution and the greater the health concern. There are six AQI categories: "Good" AQI is between 0 and 50. Air quality is considered satisfactory; "Moderate" AQI is between 51 and 100. Air quality is acceptable; "Unhealthy for Sensitive Groups" When AQI values are between 101 and 150, members of sensitive groups may experience health effects; "Unhealthy" When AQI values are between 151 and 200 everyone may begin to experience health effects; "Very Unhealthy" AQI values between 201 and 300 trigger a health alert; "Hazardous" AQI values over 300 trigger warnings of emergency conditions (not shown).
Source: U.S. Environmental Protection Agency, Air Quality Index Report, 2023

Air Quality Index Pollutants

Area	Percent of Days when AQI Pollutant was...[2]					
	Carbon Monoxide	Nitrogen Dioxide	Ozone	Sulfur Dioxide	Particulate Matter 2.5	Particulate Matter 10
MSA[1]	0.0	0.8	22.2	(3)	77.0	0.0

Note: (1) Data covers the Des Moines-West Des Moines, IA Metropolitan Statistical Area; (2) Based on 365 days with AQI data in 2023. The Air Quality Index (AQI) is an index for reporting daily air quality. EPA calculates the AQI for five major air pollutants regulated by the Clean Air Act: ground-level ozone, particle pollution (also known as particulate matter), carbon monoxide, sulfur dioxide, and nitrogen dioxide. The AQI runs from 0 to 500. The higher the AQI value, the greater the level of air pollution and the greater the health concern; (3) Sulfur dioxide is no longer included in this table because SO_2 concentrations tend to be very localized and not necessarily representative of broad geographical areas like counties and CBSAs.
Source: U.S. Environmental Protection Agency, Air Quality Index Report, 2023

Maximum Air Pollutant Concentrations: Particulate Matter, Ozone, CO and Lead

	Particulate Matter 10 (ug/m^3)	Particulate Matter 2.5 Wtd AM (ug/m^3)	Particulate Matter 2.5 24-Hr (ug/m^3)	Ozone (ppm)	Carbon Monoxide (ppm)	Lead (ug/m^3)
MSA[1] Level	56	10.2	31	0.077	n/a	n/a
NAAQS[2]	150	15	35	0.075	9	0.15
Met NAAQS[2]	Yes	Yes	Yes	No	n/a	n/a

Note: (1) Data covers the Des Moines-West Des Moines, IA Metropolitan Statistical Area; Data from exceptional events are included; (2) National Ambient Air Quality Standards; ppm = parts per million; ug/m^3 = micrograms per cubic meter; n/a not available.
Concentrations: Particulate Matter 10 (coarse particulate)—highest second maximum 24-hour concentration; Particulate Matter 2.5 Wtd AM (fine particulate)—highest weighted annual mean concentration; Particulate Matter 2.5 24-Hour (fine particulate)—highest 98th percentile 24-hour concentration; Ozone—highest fourth daily maximum 8-hour concentration; Carbon Monoxide—highest second maximum non-overlapping 8-hour concentration; Lead—maximum running 3-month average
Source: U.S. Environmental Protection Agency, Air Quality Monitoring Information, "Air Quality Statistics by City, 2023"

Maximum Air Pollutant Concentrations: Nitrogen Dioxide and Sulfur Dioxide

	Nitrogen Dioxide AM (ppb)	Nitrogen Dioxide 1-Hr (ppb)	Sulfur Dioxide AM (ppb)	Sulfur Dioxide 1-Hr (ppb)	Sulfur Dioxide 24-Hr (ppb)
MSA[1] Level	n/a	n/a	n/a	n/a	n/a
NAAQS[2]	53	100	30	75	140
Met NAAQS[2]	n/a	n/a	n/a	n/a	n/a

Note: (1) Data covers the Des Moines-West Des Moines, IA Metropolitan Statistical Area; Data from exceptional events are included; (2) National Ambient Air Quality Standards; ppm = parts per million; ug/m^3 = micrograms per cubic meter; n/a not available.
Concentrations: Nitrogen Dioxide AM—highest arithmetic mean concentration; Nitrogen Dioxide 1-Hr—highest 98th percentile 1-hour daily maximum concentration; Sulfur Dioxide AM—highest annual mean concentration; Sulfur Dioxide 1-Hr—highest 99th percentile 1-hour daily maximum concentration; Sulfur Dioxide 24-Hr—highest second maximum 24-hour concentration
Source: U.S. Environmental Protection Agency, Air Quality Monitoring Information, "Air Quality Statistics by City, 2023"

Detroit, Michigan

Background

Detroit is named after the Detroit River, connecting Lake Huron with Lake Erie. The name is French for 'strait' and refers to the city being situated on a narrow passage of water linking Lake Erie and Lake St. Clair. It is the most populous city in Michigan and the largest U.S. city on the US-Canada border, known for music, art, architecture and automobiles.

During the late 19th and early 20th century, it became an important industrial hub at the center of the Great Lakes region. As its population continued to rise due to the expansion of the automotive industry, the Detroit River became the busiest commercial hub in the world.

In the mid-20th century, Detroit began to decline, due to industrial restructuring, loss of auto industry jobs, and rapid suburbanization; in 2013, it became the largest U.S. city to file for bankruptcy. City leaders and residents rallied, however, and Detroit found itself recovering by the end of 2014. Among many post-bankruptcy efforts to improve city services, the largest fix was the city's street lighting. Forty percent didn't work, resulting in public safety issues and abandonment of housing. Outdated lights were replaced with 65,000 LED lights and in 2016, Detroit became the largest U.S. city with all LED street lighting.

Renovation and revitalization continue. The landmark Michigan Central Station, now owned by the Ford Motor Company, reopened in June 2024 after 30 years of decay. Revitalization of Detroit's waterfront has been ongoing, including a new multifaceted public space with playgrounds, sports venues, and concert space all in concert with the local ecosystem. Future plans include a new movie theater, and a luxury mega hotel, Hotel Water Square.

Detroit's diverse culture, especially its music culture, has had international influence. The city gave rise to Motown and techno, and played a significant role in the development of jazz, hip-hop, rock, and punk.

Today, the city anchors the second-largest regional economy in the Midwest, still known as the center of the U.S. automotive industry. The "Big Three" auto manufacturers—General Motors, Ford, and Stellantis (formerly Fiat Chrysler)—are all headquartered in Metro Detroit.

Detroit accounts for Michigan's national ranking in life sciences, information technology, and advanced manufacturing, and its technology sector is fifth in the U.S. for total employment. Tourism is important to Detroit's economy, comprising nine percent of the area's two million jobs. About 16.5 million people visit the area annually spending an estimated $9.2 billion.

Detroit Metropolitan Airport (DTW) is one of America's largest and most recently modernized facilities. In addition to six major runways, Boeing 747 maintenance facilities, and an attached Westin Hotel, it's a hub for Delta Air Lines. Detroit and its Canadian neighbor city Windsor is the second-busiest international crossing in North America.

It is one of twelve American cities to have teams from the four major North American sports and since 2017, and the only U.S. city to have its MLB, NFL, NBA, and NHL teams play within its downtown district. The three active major sports venues within the city are Comerica Park (home of the Detroit Tigers), Ford Field (home of the Detroit Lions), and Little Caesars Arena (home of the Detroit Red Wings and Detroit Pistons). Detroit is known for its avid hockey fans, who have given the city the moniker "Hockeytown."

In addition to sports, top attractions in the region are The Henry Ford museum complex, Detroit Institute of Arts, Motown Museum, Ford Piquette Avenue original Model T factory, Detroit Riverfront, Guardian Building art deco landmark, Belle Isle state park comprising 987 acres, conservatory aquarium, Detroit historical museum, Fox Theatre and Greektown. Annual festivals include Movement Electronic and Indie Arts & Crafts Fest.

Detroit's climate is continental, with very cold winters and warm to hot summers, during which there are quite frequent thunderstorms. Although the winter is cold and the summer is rainy, the city sees lots of sunshine.

Rankings

General Rankings

- To help military veterans find the best places in which to settle down, *WalletHub* compared the 100 largest U.S. cities across 19 key indicators of livability, affordability and veteran-friendliness. They range from the share of military skill-related jobs to veteran income growth to the availability of VA health facilities. Detroit ranked #99. *Wallethub.com, "Best & Worst Places for Veterans to Live (2025)," November 7, 2024*

- Detroit was selected as one of the best places to live in the United States by *Money* magazine. The city placed among the top 50. This year's list focused on cities built around community spirit, thoughtful policy and civic engagement. Instead of relying on a predetermined dataset, the cities and towns were grouped according to their strengths and chosen due their affordability, good schools and strong job markets. *Money, "The 50 Best Places to Live in the U.S., 2024" April 8, 2024*

- The human resources consulting firm Mercer ranked 241 major cities worldwide in terms of overall quality of life. Detroit ranked #75. Criteria: political and personal safety, social, and economic factors; medical and health considerations; schools and education; public services and transportation; recreation; connectivity; housing and infrastructure; and climate. *Mercer, "Mercer 2024 Quality of Living Survey," December 2024*

Business/Finance Rankings

- WalletHub's latest report ranked 182 cities by the average credit score of its residents. Detroit was ranked #182 among the ten cities with the lowest average credit score, based on WalletHub's 2024 fourth quarter data. *WalletHub.com, "2025's Cities With the Highest & Lowest Credit Scores," March 6, 2025*

- Payscale.com ranked the 32 largest metro areas in terms of wage growth. The Detroit metro area ranked #14. Criteria: quarterly changes in private industry employee and education professional wage growth from the previous year. *PayScale, "Wage Trends by Metro Area-4th Quarter," February 4, 2025*

- The Detroit metro area appeared on the Milken Institute "2025 Best Performing Cities" list. Rank: #197 out of 200 large metro areas (based on performance category). Criteria: job growth; wage growth; high-tech growth and impact; community resilience; housing affordability; household broadband access. *Milken Institute, "Best-Performing Cities 2025," January 14, 2025*

- Mercer Human Resources Consulting ranked 226 cities worldwide in terms of cost-of-living. Detroit ranked #81 (the lower the ranking, the higher the cost-of-living). The survey measured the comparative cost of over 200 items (such as housing, food, clothing, domestic supplies, transportation, and recreation/entertainment) in each location. *Mercer, "2024 Cost of Living City Ranking," June 17, 2024*

Dating/Romance Rankings

- *Apartment List* conducted its Annual Renter Satisfaction Survey and asked renters "how satisfied are you with opportunities for dating in your current city." The cities were ranked from highest to lowest based on their satisfaction scores. Detroit ranked #6 out of 10 cities. *Apartment List, "Best Cities for Dating 2022 with Local Dating Insights from Bumble," February 7, 2022*

Education Rankings

- Personal finance website *WalletHub* analyzed the 150 largest U.S. metropolitan statistical areas to determine where the most educated Americans are putting their degrees to work. Criteria: education levels; percentage of workers with degrees; education quality and attainment gap; public school quality rankings; quality and enrollment of each metro area's universities. Detroit was ranked #80 (#1 = most educated city). *WalletHub.com, "Most & Least Educated Cities in America, 2025" July 2, 2024*

Environmental Rankings

- The U.S. Environmental Protection Agency (EPA) released its list of U.S. metropolitan areas with the most ENERGY STAR certified buildings in 2023. The Detroit metro area was ranked #24 out of 25. *U.S. Environmental Protection Agency, "2024 Energy Star Top Cities," May 22, 2024*

- Detroit was highlighted as one of the 25 metro areas most polluted by year-round particle pollution (Annual PM 2.5) in the U.S. during 2021 through 2023. The area ranked #6. *American Lung Association, "State of the Air 2025," April 23, 2025*

- Detroit was highlighted as one of the 25 metro areas most polluted by short-term particle pollution (24-hour PM 2.5) in the U.S. during 2021 through 2023. The area ranked #22. *American Lung Association, "State of the Air 2025," April 23, 2025*

Health/Fitness Rankings

- For each of the 100 largest cities in the United States, the American Fitness Index®, compiled in partnership between the American College of Sports Medicine and the Elevance Health Foundation, evaluated community infrastructure and more than 30 health behaviors including preventive health, levels of chronic disease conditions, food insecurity, pedestrian safety, air quality, and community/environment resources that support physical activity. Detroit ranked #79 for "community fitness." *americanfitnessindex.org, "2024 ACSM American Fitness Index Summary Report," July 23, 2024*

- The Detroit metro area was identified as one of the worst cities for bed bugs in America by pest control company Orkin. The area ranked #6 out of 50 based on the number of bed bug treatments Orkin performed from December 2022 to November 2023. *Orkin, "Chicago Joins Paris In Global Bed Bug Spotlight Ranking As The Worst City On Orkin's U.S. Bed Bug Cities List," January 22, 2024*

- Detroit was identified as a "2025 Allergy Capital." The area ranked #86 out of the nation's 100 largest metropolitan areas. Three groups of factors were used to identify the most challenging cities for people with allergies: annual tree, grass, and weed pollen scores; over the counter allergy medicine use; number of board-certified allergy specialists. *Asthma and Allergy Foundation of America, "2025 Allergy Capitals: The Most Challenging Places to Live with Allergies," March 18, 2025*

- Detroit was identified as a "2024 Asthma Capital." The area ranked #3 out of the nation's 100 largest metropolitan areas. Criteria: estimated asthma prevalence; asthma-related mortality; and ER visits due to asthma. Risk factors analyzed but not factored in the rankings: annual air quality including pollution and ozone levels; public smoking laws; indoor air quality; access to asthma specialists; rescue and controller medication use; uninsured rate; pollen allergy; poverty rate. *Asthma and Allergy Foundation of America, "Asthma Capitals 2024: The Most Challenging Places to Live With Asthma," September 10, 2024*

Real Estate Rankings

- *WalletHub* compared the most populated U.S. cities to determine which had the best markets for real estate agents. Detroit ranked #172 where demand was high and pay was the best. Criteria: sales per agent; annual median wage for real-estate agents; monthly average starting salary for real estate agents; real estate job density and competition; unemployment rate; home turnover rate; housing-market health index; and other relevant metrics. *WalletHub.com, "2021 Best Places to Be a Real Estate Agent," May 12, 2021*

- The Detroit metro area was identified as one of the 20 best housing markets in the U.S. in 2024. The area ranked #15 out of 226 markets. Criteria: year-over-year change of median sales price of existing single-family homes between the 4th quarter of 2023 and the 4th quarter of 2024. *National Association of Realtors®, Median Sales Price of Existing Single-Family Homes for Metropolitan Areas, 4th Quarter 2024*

- Detroit was ranked #32 out of 176 metro areas in terms of cost of housing in 2024 by the National Association of Home Builders (#1 = most affordable). Criteria: the portion of an average family's income necessary to pay the mortgage on a median-priced home. *National Association of Home Builders®, NAHB-Wells Fargo Cost of Housing Index, 4th Quarter 2024*

Safety Rankings

- To identify the most dangerous cities in America, *24/7 Wall St.* focused on violent crime categories—murder, non-negligent manslaughter, rape, robbery, and aggravated assault—as reported for every 100,000 residents using data from the FBI's 2020 annual Uniform Crime Report. For cities with populations over 25,000, Detroit was ranked #3. *247wallst.com, "America's Most Dangerous Cities" November 12, 2021*

- Statistics drawn from the FBI's Uniform Crime Report were used to rank the cities where violent crime rose the most year over year from 2019 to 2020. Only cities with 25,000 or more residents were included. *24/7 Wall St.* found that Detroit placed #23 of those with a notable surge in incidents of violent crime. *247wallst.com, "American Cities Where Crime Is Soaring," March 4, 2022*

- Allstate ranked the 100 most populous cities in America in terms of driver safety. Detroit ranked #85. Criteria based on anonymized driving behavior data from Allstate's mobile app powered by Arity: high speed driving (over 80 mph), phone handling, and hard braking. The report helps increase the importance of safety and awareness behind the wheel. *Allstate, "16th Allstate America's Best Drivers Report®" July 11, 2024*

- Detroit was identified as one of the most dangerous cities in America by NeighborhoodScout. The city ranked #6 out of 100 (#1 = most dangerous). Criteria: number of violent crimes per 1,000 residents. The editors evaluated cities with 25,000 or more residents. *NeighborhoodScout.com, "2023 Top 100 Most Dangerous Cities in the U.S.," January 12, 2023*

Women/Minorities Rankings

- Personal finance website *WalletHub* compared more than 180 U.S. cities across two key dimensions, "Hispanic Business-Friendliness" and "Hispanic Purchasing Power," to arrive at the most favorable conditions for Hispanic entrepreneurs. Detroit was ranked #179 out of 182. Criteria includes: share of Hispanic-Owned Businesses; average growth of Hispanic Business revenues; Small Business-Friendliness score; affordability; and number of Hispanics with at least a bachelor's degree. *WalletHub.com, "Best Cities for Hispanic Entrepreneurs," September 4, 2024*

Miscellaneous Rankings

- *WalletHub* compared 148 of the most populated U.S. cities to determine their operating efficiency. A "Quality of Services" score was constructed for each city and then measured against the total budget per capita to reveal which were managed the best. Detroit ranked #140. Criteria: financial stability; economy; education; safety; health; infrastructure and pollution. *WalletHub.com, "2025's Best- & Worst-Run Cities in America," June 18, 2024*

Business Environment

DEMOGRAPHICS

Population Growth

Area	1990 Census	2000 Census	2010 Census	2020 Census	2023 Estimate[2]	Population Growth 1990-2023 (%)
City	1,027,974	951,270	713,777	639,111	636,644	-38.1
MSA[1]	4,248,699	4,452,557	4,296,250	4,392,041	4,367,620	2.8
U.S.	248,709,873	281,421,906	308,745,538	331,449,281	332,387,540	33.6

Note: (1) Figures cover the Detroit-Warren-Dearborn, MI Metropolitan Statistical Area; (2) 2019-2023 5-year ACS population estimate
Source: U.S. Census Bureau, 1990 Census, 2000 Census, 2010 Census, 2020 Census, 2019-2023 American Community Survey 5-Year Estimates

Race

Area	White Alone[2] (%)	Black Alone[2] (%)	Asian Alone[2] (%)	AIAN[3] Alone[2] (%)	NHOPI[4] Alone[2] (%)	Other Race Alone[2] (%)	Two or More Races (%)
City	11.7	76.8	1.6	0.4	0.0	4.6	4.8
MSA[1]	65.6	21.5	4.8	0.2	0.0	1.9	5.9
U.S.	63.4	12.4	5.8	0.9	0.2	6.6	10.7

Note: (1) Figures cover the Detroit-Warren-Dearborn, MI Metropolitan Statistical Area; (2) Alone is defined as not being in combination with one or more other races; (3) American Indian and Alaska Native; (4) Native Hawaiian and Other Pacific Islander
Source: U.S. Census Bureau, 2019-2023 American Community Survey 5-Year Estimates

Hispanic or Latino Origin

Area	Total (%)	Mexican (%)	Puerto Rican (%)	Cuban (%)	Other (%)
City	8.0	5.5	0.9	0.2	1.3
MSA[1]	5.1	3.4	0.6	0.1	1.0
U.S.	19.0	11.3	1.8	0.7	5.2

Note: Persons of Hispanic or Latino origin can be of any race; (1) Figures cover the Detroit-Warren-Dearborn, MI Metropolitan Statistical Area
Source: U.S. Census Bureau, 2019-2023 American Community Survey 5-Year Estimates

Age

Area	Percent of Population									Median Age
	Under Age 5	Age 5–19	Age 20–34	Age 35–44	Age 45–54	Age 55–64	Age 65–74	Age 75–84	Age 85+	
City	6.8	20.8	22.2	11.8	11.8	11.8	9.0	4.1	1.7	35.1
MSA[1]	5.6	18.4	19.6	12.2	12.9	14.0	10.5	4.8	2.0	40.2
U.S.	5.7	19.1	20.2	13.1	12.3	12.8	10.0	4.9	1.9	38.7

Note: (1) Figures cover the Detroit-Warren-Dearborn, MI Metropolitan Statistical Area
Source: U.S. Census Bureau, 2019-2023 American Community Survey 5-Year Estimates

Disability by Age

Area	All Ages	Under 18 Years Old	18 to 64 Years Old	65 Years and Over
City	19.6	6.0	19.7	42.6
MSA[1]	14.0	4.6	11.9	33.5
U.S.	13.0	4.7	10.7	32.9

Note: Figures show percent of the civilian noninstitutionalized population that reported having a disability. Disability status is determined from six types of difficulty: vision, hearing, cognitive, ambulatory, self-care, and independent living. For children under 5 years old, hearing and vision difficulty are used to determine disability status. For children between the ages of 5 and 14, disability status is determined from hearing, vision, cognitive, ambulatory, and self-care difficulties. For people aged 15 years and older, they are considered to have a disability if they have difficulty with any one of the six difficulty types; Note: (1) Figures cover the Detroit-Warren-Dearborn, MI Metropolitan Statistical Area
Source: U.S. Census Bureau, 2019-2023 American Community Survey 5-Year Estimates

Ancestry

Area	German	Irish	English	American	Italian	Polish	French[2]	European	Scottish
City	1.8	1.6	1.1	4.4	0.8	1.1	0.5	0.2	0.3
MSA[1]	14.3	9.1	7.9	4.0	5.8	8.9	2.8	1.5	2.0
U.S.	12.6	9.4	9.1	5.5	4.9	2.6	2.0	1.6	1.6

Note: Figures are the percentage of the total population reporting a particular ancestry. The nine most commonly reported ancestries in the U.S. are shown. Figures include multiple ancestries (e.g. if a person reported being Irish and Italian, they were included in both columns); (1) Figures cover the Detroit-Warren-Dearborn, MI Metropolitan Statistical Area; (2) Excludes Basque
Source: U.S. Census Bureau, 2019-2023 American Community Survey 5-Year Estimates

Foreign-born Population

Area	Percent of Population Born in								
	Any Foreign Country	Asia	Mexico	Europe	Caribbean	Central America[2]	South America	Africa	Canada
City	6.0	2.4	1.7	0.2	0.3	0.5	0.1	0.5	0.2
MSA[1]	10.3	6.0	0.8	1.9	0.2	0.2	0.2	0.4	0.5
U.S.	13.9	4.3	3.3	1.4	1.4	1.2	1.2	0.8	0.2

Note: (1) Figures cover the Detroit-Warren-Dearborn, MI Metropolitan Statistical Area; (2) Excludes Mexico.
Source: U.S. Census Bureau, 2019-2023 American Community Survey 5-Year Estimates

Household Size

Area	Persons in Household (%)							Average Household Size
	One	Two	Three	Four	Five	Six	Seven or More	
City	42.5	25.3	13.8	8.9	4.8	2.7	1.9	2.47
MSA[1]	31.9	32.8	15.0	11.9	5.3	1.9	1.2	2.46
U.S.	28.5	33.8	15.4	12.7	5.9	2.3	1.4	2.54

Note: (1) Figures cover the Detroit-Warren-Dearborn, MI Metropolitan Statistical Area
Source: U.S. Census Bureau, 2019-2023 American Community Survey 5-Year Estimates

Household Relationships

Area	Householder	Opposite-sex Spouse	Same-sex Spouse	Opposite-sex Unmarried Partner	Same-sex Unmarried Partner	Child[2]	Grandchild	Other Relatives	Non-relatives
City	39.8	7.3	0.1	2.9	0.2	32.0	4.8	7.3	3.9
MSA[1]	40.1	17.2	0.1	2.5	0.1	30.1	2.3	4.2	2.4
U.S.	38.3	17.5	0.2	2.5	0.2	28.3	2.4	4.8	3.4

Note: Figures are percent of the total population; (1) Figures cover the Detroit-Warren-Dearborn, MI Metropolitan Statistical Area; (2) Includes biological, adopted, and stepchildren of the householder
Source: U.S. Census Bureau, 2020 Census

Gender

Area	Males	Females	Males per 100 Females
City	302,503	334,141	90.5
MSA[1]	2,140,962	2,226,658	96.2
U.S.	164,545,087	167,842,453	98.0

Note: (1) Figures cover the Detroit-Warren-Dearborn, MI Metropolitan Statistical Area
Source: U.S. Census Bureau, 2019-2023 American Community Survey 5-Year Estimates

Marital Status

Area	Never Married	Now Married[2]	Separated	Widowed	Divorced
City	57.0	22.0	2.9	6.3	11.9
MSA[1]	35.9	45.7	1.2	6.0	11.2
U.S.	34.1	47.9	1.7	5.6	10.7

Note: Figures are percentages and cover the population 15 years of age and older; (1) Figures cover the Detroit-Warren-Dearborn, MI Metropolitan Statistical Area; (2) Excludes separated
Source: U.S. Census Bureau, 2019-2023 American Community Survey 5-Year Estimates

Religious Groups by Family

Area	Catholic	Baptist	Methodist	LDS[2]	Pentecostal	Lutheran	Islam	Adventist	Other
MSA[1]	18.6	4.8	1.7	0.3	2.1	2.2	4.5	1.0	8.5
U.S.	18.7	7.3	3.0	2.0	1.8	1.7	1.3	1.3	11.6

Note: Figures are the number of adherents as a percentage of the total population and cover the eight largest religious groups in the U.S; (1) Figures cover the Detroit-Warren-Dearborn, MI Metropolitan Statistical Area; (2) Church of Jesus Christ of Latter-day Saints
Sources: 2020 U.S. Religion Census, Association of Statisticians of American Religious Bodies; The Association of Religion Data Archives (ARDA)

Religious Groups by Tradition

Area	Catholic	Evangelical Protestant	Mainline Protestant	Black Protestant	Islam	Judaism	Hinduism	Orthodox	Buddhism
MSA[1]	18.6	9.1	3.3	5.1	4.5	0.8	0.3	0.8	0.2
U.S.	18.7	16.5	5.2	2.3	1.3	0.6	0.4	0.4	0.3

Note: Figures are the number of adherents as a percentage of the total population; (1) Figures cover the Detroit-Warren-Dearborn, MI Metropolitan Statistical Area
Sources: 2020 U.S. Religion Census, Association of Statisticians of American Religious Bodies; The Association of Religion Data Archives (ARDA)

ECONOMY

Real Gross Domestic Product (GDP)

Area	2017	2018	2019	2020	2021	2022	2023	Rank[3]
MSA[1]	256.2	261.5	262.7	249.7	263.7	271.7	276.5	16
U.S.[2]	17,619.1	18,160.7	18,642.5	18,238.9	19,387.6	19,896.6	20,436.3	—

Note: Figures are in billions of chained 2017 dollars; (1) Figures cover the Detroit-Warren-Dearborn, MI Metropolitan Statistical Area; (2) Figures cover real GDP within metropolitan areas; (3) Rank is based on 2023 data and ranges from 1 to 384
Source: U.S. Bureau of Economic Analysis

Economic Growth

Area	2014	2015	2016	2017	2018	2019	2020	2021	2022	2023
MSA[1]	1.4	1.7	1.9	0.9	2.1	0.4	-4.9	5.6	3.0	1.8
U.S.[2]	2.6	3.2	2.0	2.7	3.1	2.7	-2.2	6.3	2.6	2.7

Note: Figures are real gross domestic product growth rates and represent percent change from preceding period; (1) Figures cover the Detroit-Warren-Dearborn, MI Metropolitan Statistical Area; (2) Figures are the average growth rates within metropolitan areas
Source: U.S. Bureau of Economic Analysis

Metropolitan Area Exports

Area	2018	2019	2020	2021	2022	2023	Rank[2]
MSA[1]	44,131.4	41,070.4	30,715.1	35,433.2	40,395.3	45,591.4	7
U.S.	1,664,056.1	1,645,173.7	1,431,406.6	1,753,941.4	2,062,937.4	2,019,160.5	—

Note: Figures are in millions of dollars; (1) Figures cover the Detroit-Warren-Dearborn, MI Metropolitan Statistical Area; (2) Rank is based on 2023 data and ranges from 1 to 386
Source: U.S. Department of Commerce, International Trade Administration, Office of Trade and Economic Analysis, Industry and Analysis, Exports by Metropolitan Area, data extracted April 2, 2025

Building Permits

Area	Single-Family			Multi-Family			Total		
	2023	2024	Pct. Chg.	2023	2024	Pct. Chg.	2023	2024	Pct. Chg.
City	397	483	21.7	828	1,436	73.4	1,225	1,919	56.7
MSA[1]	4,541	4,878	7.4	2,193	2,826	28.9	6,734	7,704	14.4
U.S.	920,000	981,900	6.7	591,100	496,100	-16.1	1,511,100	1,478,000	-2.2

Note: (1) Figures cover the Detroit-Warren-Dearborn, MI Metropolitan Statistical Area; Figures represent new, privately-owned housing units authorized (unadjusted data)
Source: U.S. Census Bureau, Building Permits Survey (BPS), 2023, 2024

Bankruptcy Filings

Area	Business Filings			Nonbusiness Filings		
	2023	2024	% Chg.	2023	2024	% Chg.
Wayne County	43	58	34.9	6,087	6,501	6.8
U.S.	18,926	23,107	22.1	434,064	494,201	13.9

Note: Business filings include Chapter 7, Chapter 9, Chapter 11, Chapter 12, Chapter 13, Chapter 15, and Section 304; Nonbusiness filings include Chapter 7, Chapter 11, and Chapter 13
Source: Administrative Office of the U.S. Courts, Business and Nonbusiness Bankruptcy, County Cases Commenced by Chapter of the Bankruptcy Code, During the 12-Month Period Ending December 31, 2023 and Business and Nonbusiness Bankruptcy, County Cases Commenced by Chapter of the Bankruptcy Code, During the 12-Month Period Ending December 31, 2024

Housing Vacancy Rates

Area	Gross Vacancy Rate[3] (%)			Year-Round Vacancy Rate[4] (%)			Rental Vacancy Rate[5] (%)			Homeowner Vacancy Rate[6] (%)		
	2022	2023	2024	2022	2023	2024	2022	2023	2024	2022	2023	2024
MSA[1]	7.1	9.0	9.4	6.6	8.7	9.3	4.5	9.3	8.7	0.9	1.0	1.1
U.S.[2]	9.1	9.0	9.1	7.5	7.5	7.6	5.7	6.5	6.8	0.8	0.8	1.0

Note: (1) Figures cover the Detroit-Warren-Dearborn, MI Metropolitan Statistical Area; (2) Figures cover the 75 largest Metropolitan Statistical Areas; (3) The percentage of the total housing inventory that is vacant; (4) The percentage of the housing inventory (excluding seasonal units) that is year-round vacant; (5) The percentage of rental inventory that is vacant for rent; (6) The percentage of homeowner inventory that is vacant for sale
Source: U.S. Census Bureau, Housing Vacancies and Homeownership Annual Statistics: 2022, 2023, 2024

INCOME

Income

Area	Per Capita ($)	Median Household ($)	Average Household ($)
City	24,029	39,575	56,528
MSA[1]	42,145	75,123	102,705
U.S.	43,289	78,538	110,491

Note: (1) Figures cover the Detroit-Warren-Dearborn, MI Metropolitan Statistical Area
Source: U.S. Census Bureau, 2019-2023 American Community Survey 5-Year Estimates

Household Income Distribution

Area	Percent of Households Earning							
	Under $15,000	$15,000 -$24,999	$25,000 -$34,999	$35,000 -$49,999	$50,000 -$74,999	$75,000 -$99,999	$100,000 -$149,999	$150,000 and up
City	22.8	12.2	10.2	15.2	15.1	9.5	9.2	5.8
MSA[1]	9.3	6.7	7.0	11.1	15.7	12.8	17.0	20.2
U.S.	8.5	6.6	6.8	10.4	15.7	12.7	17.4	21.9

Note: (1) Figures cover the Detroit-Warren-Dearborn, MI Metropolitan Statistical Area
Source: U.S. Census Bureau, 2019-2023 American Community Survey 5-Year Estimates

Poverty Rate

Area	All Ages	Under 18 Years Old	18 to 64 Years Old	65 Years and Over
City	31.5	44.2	28.8	20.9
MSA[1]	13.2	19.1	12.0	10.2
U.S.	12.4	16.3	11.6	10.4

Note: Figures are percentage of people whose income during the past 12 months was below the poverty level; (1) Figures cover the Detroit-Warren-Dearborn, MI Metropolitan Statistical Area
Source: U.S. Census Bureau, 2019-2023 American Community Survey 5-Year Estimates

EMPLOYMENT

Labor Force and Employment

Area	Civilian Labor Force			Workers Employed		
	Dec. 2023	Dec. 2024	% Chg.	Dec. 2023	Dec. 2024	% Chg.
City	252,407	254,935	1.0	235,064	230,371	-2.0
MD[1]	816,930	814,679	-0.3	784,713	769,048	-2.0
U.S.	166,661,000	167,746,000	0.7	160,754,000	161,294,000	0.3

Note: Data is not seasonally adjusted and covers workers 16 years of age and older; (1) Figures cover the Detroit-Dearborn-Livonia, MI Metropolitan Division
Source: Bureau of Labor Statistics, Local Area Unemployment Statistics

Unemployment Rate

Area	2024											
	Jan.	Feb.	Mar.	Apr.	May	Jun.	Jul.	Aug.	Sep.	Oct.	Nov.	Dec.
City	8.3	8.3	8.1	7.4	8.6	10.0	12.7	9.7	9.6	10.8	10.6	9.6
MD[1]	4.8	4.8	4.7	4.3	5.0	5.8	7.5	5.6	5.6	6.3	6.2	5.6
U.S.	4.1	4.2	3.9	3.5	3.7	4.3	4.5	4.4	3.9	3.9	4.0	3.8

Note: Data is not seasonally adjusted and covers workers 16 years of age and older; (1) Figures cover the Detroit-Dearborn-Livonia, MI Metropolitan Division
Source: Bureau of Labor Statistics, Local Area Unemployment Statistics

Average Wages

Occupation	$/Hr.	Occupation	$/Hr.
Accountants and Auditors	43.77	Maintenance and Repair Workers	24.30
Automotive Mechanics	27.01	Marketing Managers	72.83
Bookkeepers	25.39	Network and Computer Systems Admin.	48.72
Carpenters	31.70	Nurses, Licensed Practical	32.31
Cashiers	14.88	Nurses, Registered	44.56
Computer Programmers	39.07	Nursing Assistants	19.58
Computer Systems Analysts	50.95	Office Clerks, General	22.38
Computer User Support Specialists	29.25	Physical Therapists	47.96
Construction Laborers	26.26	Physicians	79.84
Cooks, Restaurant	18.06	Plumbers, Pipefitters and Steamfitters	36.88
Customer Service Representatives	22.70	Police and Sheriff's Patrol Officers	36.19
Dentists	93.92	Postal Service Mail Carriers	28.48
Electricians	36.41	Real Estate Sales Agents	32.41
Engineers, Electrical	53.76	Retail Salespersons	19.31
Fast Food and Counter Workers	14.34	Sales Representatives, Technical/Scientific	68.16
Financial Managers	77.60	Secretaries, Exc. Legal/Medical/Executive	23.38
First-Line Supervisors of Office Workers	33.92	Security Guards	19.17
General and Operations Managers	65.30	Surgeons	n/a
Hairdressers/Cosmetologists	21.26	Teacher Assistants, Exc. Postsecondary[1]	15.96
Home Health and Personal Care Aides	15.95	Teachers, Secondary School, Exc. Sp. Ed.[1]	34.65
Janitors and Cleaners	17.41	Telemarketers	16.11
Landscaping/Groundskeeping Workers	19.93	Truck Drivers, Heavy/Tractor-Trailer	27.01
Lawyers	69.97	Truck Drivers, Light/Delivery Services	21.91
Maids and Housekeeping Cleaners	16.33	Waiters and Waitresses	19.88

Note: Wage data covers the Detroit-Warren-Dearborn, MI Metropolitan Statistical Area; (1) Hourly wages were calculated from annual wage data based on a 40 hour work week
Source: Bureau of Labor Statistics, Metro Area Occupational Employment & Wage Estimates, May 2024

Employment by Industry

Sector	MD[1] Number of Employees	MD[1] Percent of Total	U.S. Percent of Total
Construction, Mining, and Logging	83,900	4.0	5.5
Financial Activities	128,900	6.2	5.8
Government	198,700	9.6	14.9
Information	29,700	1.4	1.9
Leisure and Hospitality	188,000	9.1	10.4
Manufacturing	250,600	12.1	8.0
Other Services	78,000	3.8	3.7
Private Education and Health Services	335,600	16.2	16.9
Professional and Business Services	382,000	18.4	14.2
Retail Trade	204,600	9.9	10.0
Transportation, Warehousing, and Utilities	107,400	5.2	4.8
Wholesale Trade	85,800	4.1	3.9

Note: Figures are non-farm employment as of December 2024. Figures are not seasonally adjusted and include workers 16 years of age and older; (1) Figures cover the Detroit-Dearborn-Livonia, MI Metropolitan Division
Source: Bureau of Labor Statistics, Current Employment Statistics, Employment, Hours, and Earnings

Employment by Occupation

Occupation Classification	City (%)	MSA[1] (%)	U.S. (%)
Management, Business, Science, and Arts	27.7	42.5	42.0
Natural Resources, Construction, and Maintenance	6.1	6.8	8.6
Production, Transportation, and Material Moving	23.7	15.2	13.0
Sales and Office	19.4	19.9	19.9
Service	23.1	15.6	16.5

Note: Figures cover employed civilians 16 years of age and older; (1) Figures cover the Detroit-Warren-Dearborn, MI Metropolitan Statistical Area
Source: U.S. Census Bureau, 2019-2023 American Community Survey 5-Year Estimates

Occupations with Greatest Projected Employment Growth: 2022 – 2032

Occupation[1]	2022 Employment	2032 Projected Employment	Numeric Employment Change	Percent Employment Change
Home Health and Personal Care Aides	85,480	100,320	14,840	17.4
Software Developers	42,680	51,380	8,700	20.4
Cooks, Restaurant	38,550	44,610	6,060	15.7
Medical and Health Services Managers	14,350	18,190	3,840	26.8
Light Truck or Delivery Services Drivers	34,630	37,810	3,180	9.2
Medical Assistants	24,670	27,830	3,160	12.8
Nurse Practitioners	7,370	10,410	3,040	41.2
Industrial Machinery Mechanics	20,680	23,650	2,970	14.4
Financial Managers	20,620	23,540	2,920	14.2
Registered Nurses	104,150	106,910	2,760	2.7

Note: Projections cover Michigan; (1) Sorted by numeric employment change
Source: www.projectionscentral.org, State Occupational Projections, 2022–2032 Long-Term Projections

Fastest-Growing Occupations: 2022 – 2032

Occupation[1]	2022 Employment	2032 Projected Employment	Numeric Employment Change	Percent Employment Change
Nurse Practitioners	7,370	10,410	3,040	41.2
Data Scientists	4,020	5,420	1,400	34.8
Statisticians	690	900	210	30.4
Occupational Therapy Assistants	1,410	1,790	380	27.0
Medical and Health Services Managers	14,350	18,190	3,840	26.8
Physician Assistants	5,550	7,000	1,450	26.1
Information Security Analysts (SOC 2018)	2,810	3,530	720	25.6
Epidemiologists	240	300	60	25.0
Solar Photovoltaic Installers	200	250	50	25.0
Actuaries	420	520	100	23.8

Note: Projections cover Michigan; (1) Sorted by percent employment change and excludes occupations with numeric employment change less than 50
Source: www.projectionscentral.org, State Occupational Projections, 2022–2032 Long-Term Projections

CITY FINANCES

City Government Finances

Component	2022 ($000)	2022 ($ per capita)
Total Revenues	2,735,698	4,112
Total Expenditures	2,461,430	3,699
Debt Outstanding	2,831,834	4,256

Source: U.S. Census Bureau, State & Local Government Finances 2022

City Government Revenue by Source

Source	2022 ($000)	2022 ($ per capita)	2022 (%)
General Revenue			
From Federal Government	489,615	736	17.9
From State Government	363,383	546	13.3
From Local Governments	35,833	54	1.3
Taxes			
Property	338,294	508	12.4
Sales and Gross Receipts	302,543	455	11.1
Personal Income	380,558	572	13.9
Corporate Income	0	0	0.0
Motor Vehicle License	0	0	0.0
Other Taxes	39,668	60	1.5
Current Charges	555,853	835	20.3
Liquor Store	0	0	0.0
Utility	124,598	187	4.6

Source: U.S. Census Bureau, State & Local Government Finances 2022

City Government Expenditures by Function

Function	2022 ($000)	2022 ($ per capita)	2022 (%)
General Direct Expenditures			
Air Transportation	3,400	5	0.1
Corrections	0	0	0.0
Education	0	0	0.0
Employment Security Administration	0	0	0.0
Financial Administration	49,639	74	2.0
Fire Protection	137,094	206	5.6
General Public Buildings	0	0	0.0
Governmental Administration, Other	28,908	43	1.2
Health	86,997	130	3.5
Highways	95,157	143	3.9
Hospitals	0	0	0.0
Housing and Community Development	157,780	237	6.4
Interest on General Debt	116,720	175	4.7
Judicial and Legal	42,219	63	1.7
Libraries	27,714	41	1.1
Parking	1,277	1	0.1
Parks and Recreation	57,786	86	2.3
Police Protection	332,420	499	13.5
Public Welfare	0	0	0.0
Sewerage	310,488	466	12.6
Solid Waste Management	78,048	117	3.2
Veterans' Services	0	0	0.0
Liquor Store	0	0	0.0
Utility	350,436	526	14.2

Source: U.S. Census Bureau, State & Local Government Finances 2022

TAXES

State Corporate Income Tax Rates

State	Tax Rate (%)	Income Brackets ($)	Num. of Brackets	Financial Institution Tax Rate (%)[a]	Federal Income Tax Ded.
Michigan	6.0	Flat rate	1	(a)	No

Note: Tax rates for tax year 2024; (a) Rates listed are the corporate income tax rate applied to financial institutions or excise taxes based on income. Some states have other taxes based upon the value of deposits or shares.
Source: Federation of Tax Administrators, State Corporate Income Tax Rates, January 1, 2025

State Individual Income Tax Rates

State	Tax Rate (%)	Income Brackets ($)	Personal Exemptions ($) Single	Personal Exemptions ($) Married	Personal Exemptions ($) Depend.	Standard Ded. ($) Single	Standard Ded. ($) Married
Michigan	4.25	Flat rate	56000	11,200	5,000	(m1)	(m1)

Note: Tax rates for tax year 2024; Local- and county-level taxes are not included; Federal income tax is not deductible on state income tax returns
Source: Federation of Tax Administrators, State Individual Income Tax Rates, January 1, 2025

Various State Sales and Excise Tax Rates

State	State Sales Tax (%)	Gasoline[1] ($/gal.)	Cigarette[2] ($/pack)	Spirits[3] ($/gal.)	Wine[4] ($/gal.)	Beer[5] ($/gal.)	Recreational Marijuana (%)
Michigan	6	0.48	2.00	14.61	0.51	0.20	(k)

Note: All tax rates as of January 1, 2025; (1) The American Petroleum Institute has developed a methodology for determining the average tax rate on a gallon of fuel. Rates may include any of the following: excise taxes, environmental fees, storage tank fees, other fees or taxes, general sales tax, and local taxes; (2) The federal excise tax of $1.0066 per pack and local taxes are not included; (3) Rates are those applicable to off-premise sales of 40% alcohol by volume (a.b.v.) distilled spirits in 750ml containers. Local excise taxes are excluded; (4) Rates are those applicable to off-premise sales of 11% a.b.v. non-carbonated wine in 750ml containers; (5) Rates are those applicable to off-premise sales of 4.7% a.b.v. beer in 12 ounce containers; (k) 10% excise tax (retail gross receipts)
Source: Tax Foundation, 2025 Facts & Figures: How Does Your State Compare?

State Tax Competitiveness Index

State	Overall Rank	Corporate Tax Rank	Individual Income Tax Rank	Sales Tax Rank	Property Tax Rank	Unemployment Insurance Tax Rank
Michigan	14	9	14	12	28	26

Note: The Tax Foundation's State Tax Competitiveness Index enables policymakers, taxpayers, and business leaders to gauge how their states' tax systems compare. A rank of 1 is best, 50 is worst. Rankings do not average to the total. States without a tax rank equally as 1. DC's scores and rankings do not affect other states. The report shows tax systems as of July 1, 2024 (the beginning of Fiscal Year 2025).
Source: Tax Foundation, State Tax Competitiveness Index 2025

TRANSPORTATION

Means of Transportation to Work

Area	Car/Truck/Van Drove Alone	Car/Truck/Van Car-pooled	Public Transportation Bus	Public Transportation Subway	Public Transportation Railroad	Bicycle	Walked	Other Means	Worked at Home
City	66.3	11.0	5.9	0.0	0.0	0.5	3.1	3.1	10.1
MSA[1]	74.8	7.6	1.0	0.0	0.0	0.2	1.3	1.2	13.8
U.S.	70.2	8.5	1.7	1.3	0.4	0.4	2.4	1.6	13.5

Note: Figures are percentages and cover workers 16 years of age and older; (1) Figures cover the Detroit-Warren-Dearborn, MI Metropolitan Statistical Area
Source: U.S. Census Bureau, 2019-2023 American Community Survey 5-Year Estimates

Travel Time to Work

Area	Less Than 10 Minutes	10 to 19 Minutes	20 to 29 Minutes	30 to 44 Minutes	45 to 59 Minutes	60 to 89 Minutes	90 Minutes or More
City	8.1	30.2	27.0	22.3	6.0	4.0	2.3
MSA[1]	10.0	27.0	23.7	24.2	8.5	4.8	1.7
U.S.	12.6	28.6	21.2	20.8	8.1	6.0	2.8

Note: Note: Figures are percentages and include workers 16 years old and over; (1) Figures cover the Detroit-Warren-Dearborn, MI Metropolitan Statistical Area
Source: U.S. Census Bureau, 2019-2023 American Community Survey 5-Year Estimates

Key Congestion Measures

Measure	2000	2010	2015	2020	2022
Annual Hours of Delay, Total (000)	138,866	138,614	160,898	92,996	151,205
Annual Hours of Delay, Per Auto Commuter	52	51	60	35	61
Annual Congestion Cost, Per Auto Commuter ($)	1,524	1,209	1,297	794	1,277

Note: Figures cover the Detroit MI urban area
Source: Texas A&M Transportation Institute, 2023 Urban Mobility Report

Freeway Travel Time Index

Measure	1985	1990	1995	2000	2005	2010	2015	2020	2022
Urban Area Index[1]	1.17	1.20	1.23	1.24	1.25	1.23	1.24	1.12	1.20
Urban Area Rank[1,2]	9	9	8	18	25	28	26	10	36

Note: Freeway Travel Time Index—the ratio of travel time in the peak period to the travel time at free-flow conditions. For example, a value of 1.30 indicates a 20-minute free-flow trip takes 26 minutes in the peak (20 minutes x 1.30 = 26 minutes); (1) Covers the Detroit MI urban area; (2) Rank is based on 101 larger urban areas (#1 = highest travel time index)
Source: Texas A&M Transportation Institute, 2023 Urban Mobility Report

Public Transportation

Agency Name / Mode of Transportation	Vehicles Operated in Maximum Service[1]	Annual Unlinked Passenger Trips[2] (in thous.)	Annual Passenger Miles[3] (in thous.)
City of Detroit dba Detroit Dept of Transportation			
Bus (directly operated)	152	10,229.5	52,320.6
Demand Response (purchased transportation)	75	241.8	2,424.3
Detroit Transportation Corp.			
Monorail and Automated Guideway (directly operated)	4	608.3	839.4
M-1 Rail dba QLINE Detroit			
Streetcar Rail (directly operated)	4	938.6	1,525.9
Suburban Mobility Authority for Regional Transportation			
Bus (directly operated)	142	4,489.6	43,282.9
Demand Response (directly operated)	95	238.9	1,945.2
Demand Response (purchased transportation)	20	99.0	442.2

Note: (1) Number of revenue vehicles operated by the given mode and type of service to meet the annual maximum service requirement. This is the revenue vehicle count during the peak season of the year; on the week and day that maximum service is provided. Vehicles operated in maximum service (VOMS) exclude atypical days and one-time special events; (2) Number of passengers who boarded public transportation vehicles. Passengers are counted each time they board a vehicle no matter how many vehicles they use to travel from their origin to their destination. (3) Sum of the distances ridden by all passengers during the entire fiscal year.
Source: Federal Transit Administration, National Transit Database, 2023

Air Transportation

Airport Name and Code / Type of Service	Passenger Airlines[1]	Passenger Enplanements	Freight Carriers[2]	Freight (lbs)
Detroit Metro Wayne County (DTW)				
Domestic service (U.S. carriers only)	30	14,425,694	15	102,703,905
International service (U.S. carriers only)	8	1,270,466	3	30,600,556

Note: (1) Includes all U.S.-based major, minor and commuter airlines that carried at least one passenger during the year; (2) Includes all U.S.-based airlines and freight carriers that transported at least one pound of freight during the year.
Source: Bureau of Transportation Statistics, The Intermodal Transportation Database, Air Carriers: T-100 Domestic Market (U.S. carriers only), 2024; Bureau of Transportation Statistics, The Intermodal Transportation Database, Air Carriers: T-100 International Market (U.S. carriers only), 2024

BUSINESSES

Major Business Headquarters

Company Name	Industry	Fortune[1]	Forbes[2]
Ally Financial	Diversified financials	257	-
DTE Energy	Utilities: gas and electric	318	-
General Motors	Motor vehicles & parts	19	-
Ilitch Holdings	Hotels, restaurants & leisure	-	125
Walbridge	Construction	-	105

Note: (1) Companies that produce a 10-K are ranked 1 to 500 based on 2023 revenue; (2) All private companies with at least $2 billion in annual revenue through the end of their most current fiscal year are ranked 1 to 275; companies listed are headquartered in the city; dashes indicate no ranking
Source: Fortune, "Fortune 500," 2024; Forbes, "America's Largest Private Companies," 2024

Fastest-Growing Businesses

According to *Initiative for a Competitive Inner City (ICIC)*, Detroit is home to two of America's 100 fastest-growing "inner city" companies: **DMC Group dba DMC Construction** (#43); **PTI Quality Containment Solutions** (#68). To be eligible for the IC100, companies have to be independently operated, privately held, for-profit businesses with revenues of at least $50,000 in 2019 and $500,000 in 2023, and headquartered in an under-resourced community. Recognizing that concentrated poverty exists within metropolitan areas outside of big cities (and that poverty overall is suburbanizing), ICIC defines under-resourced communities as large low-income, high-poverty areas located in the urban and suburban parts of all but the smallest metropolitan areas. Companies were ranked overall by revenue growth over the five-year period between 2019 and 2023. *Initiative for a Competitive Inner City (ICIC), "Inner City 100 Companies," 2024*

Living Environment

COST OF LIVING

Cost of Living Index

Composite Index	Groceries	Housing	Utilities	Trans-portation	Health Care	Misc. Goods/Services
103.3	101.0	106.0	100.6	103.7	107.0	102.0

Note: The Cost of Living Index measures regional differences in the cost of consumer goods and services, excluding taxes and non-consumer expenditures, for professional and managerial households in the top income quintile. It is based on more than 50,000 prices covering almost 60 different items for which prices are collected three times a year by chambers of commerce, economic development organizations or university applied economic centers in each participating urban area. The numbers shown should be read as a percentage above or below the national average of 100. For example, a value of 115.4 in the groceries column indicates that grocery prices are 15.4% higher than the national average. Small differences in the index numbers should not be interpreted as significant; Figures cover the Detroit MI urban area.
Source: The Council for Community and Economic Research, Cost of Living Index, 2024

Grocery Prices

Area[1]	T-Bone Steak ($/pound)	Frying Chicken ($/pound)	Whole Milk ($/half gal.)	Eggs ($/dozen)	Orange Juice ($/64 oz.)	Coffee ($/11.5 oz.)
City[2]	15.53	1.73	4.80	3.37	4.41	5.64
Avg.	15.42	1.55	4.69	3.25	4.41	5.46
Min.	14.50	1.16	4.43	2.75	4.00	4.85
Max.	17.56	2.89	5.49	4.78	5.54	7.89

Note: (1) Values for the local area are compared with the average, minimum and maximum values for all 276 areas in the Cost of Living Index; (2) Figures cover the Detroit MI urban area; **T-Bone Steak** (price per pound); **Frying Chicken** (price per pound, whole fryer); **Whole Milk** (half gallon carton); **Eggs** (price per dozen, Grade A, large); **Orange Juice** (64 oz. Tropicana or Florida Natural); **Coffee** (11.5 oz. can, vacuum-packed, Maxwell House, Hills Bros, or Folgers).
Source: The Council for Community and Economic Research, Cost of Living Index, 2024

Housing and Utility Costs

Area[1]	New Home Price ($)	Apartment Rent ($/month)	All Electric ($/month)	Part Electric ($/month)	Other Energy ($/month)	Telephone ($/month)
City[2]	568,077	1,560	-	134.21	78.36	187.38
Avg.	515,975	1,550	210.99	123.07	82.07	194.99
Min.	265,375	692	104.33	53.68	36.26	179.42
Max.	2,775,821	5,719	529.02	397.28	361.63	223.33

Note: (1) Values for the local area are compared with the average, minimum and maximum values for all 276 areas in the Cost of Living Index; (2) Figures cover the Detroit MI urban area; **New Home Price** (2,400 sf living area, 8,000 sf lot, in urban area with full utilities); **Apartment Rent** (950 sf 2 bedroom/1.5 or 2 bath, unfurnished, excluding all utilities except water); **All Electric** (average monthly cost for an all-electric home); **Part Electric** (average monthly cost for a part-electric home); **Other Energy** (average monthly cost for natural gas, fuel oil, coal, wood, and any other forms of energy except electricity); **Telephone** (price includes the base monthly rate plus taxes and fees for three lines of mobile phone service).
Source: The Council for Community and Economic Research, Cost of Living Index, 2024

Health Care, Transportation, and Other Costs

Area[1]	Doctor ($/visit)	Dentist ($/visit)	Optometrist ($/visit)	Gasoline ($/gallon)	Beauty Salon ($/visit)	Men's Shirt ($)
City[2]	183.09	126.33	95.64	3.42	60.83	52.14
Avg.	143.77	117.51	129.23	3.32	48.57	38.14
Min.	36.74	58.67	67.33	2.80	24.00	13.41
Max.	270.44	216.82	307.33	5.28	94.00	63.89

Note: (1) Values for the local area are compared with the average, minimum and maximum values for all 276 areas in the Cost of Living Index; (2) Figures cover the Detroit MI urban area; **Doctor** (general practitioners routine exam of an established patient); **Dentist** (adult teeth cleaning and periodic oral examination); **Optometrist** (full vision eye exam for established adult patient); **Gasoline** (one gallon regular unleaded, national brand, including all taxes, cash price at self-service pump if available); **Beauty Salon** (woman's shampoo, trim, and blow-dry); **Men's Shirt** (cotton/polyester dress shirt, pinpoint weave, long sleeves).
Source: The Council for Community and Economic Research, Cost of Living Index, 2024

HOUSING

Homeownership Rate

Area	2017 (%)	2018 (%)	2019 (%)	2020 (%)	2021 (%)	2022 (%)	2023 (%)	2024 (%)
MSA[1]	70.2	70.9	70.2	71.8	71.6	71.9	73.5	72.0
U.S.	63.9	64.4	64.6	66.6	65.5	65.8	65.9	65.6

Note: (1) Figures cover the Detroit-Warren-Dearborn, MI Metropolitan Statistical Area
Source: U.S. Census Bureau, Housing Vacancies and Homeownership Annual Statistics: 2017-2024

House Price Index (HPI)

Area	National Ranking[2]	Quarterly Change (%)	One-Year Change (%)	Five-Year Change (%)	Since 1991Q1 (%)
MD[1]	40	0.25	7.71	52.17	227.11
U.S.[3]	–	1.43	4.51	57.13	327.82

Note: The HPI is a weighted repeat sales index. It measures average price changes in repeat sales or refinancings on the same properties. This information is obtained by reviewing repeat mortgage transactions on single-family properties whose mortgages have been purchased or securitized by Fannie Mae or Freddie Mac since January 1975; (1) Figures cover the Detroit-Dearborn-Livonia, MI Metropolitan Division; (2) Rankings are based on annual percentage change for all metro areas containing at least 15,000 transactions over the last 10 years and ranges from 1 to 241; (3) figures based on a weighted average of Census Division estimates using a seasonally adjusted, purchase-only index; all figures are for the period ending December 31, 2024
Source: Federal Housing Finance Agency, Change in FHFA Metropolitan Area House Price Indexes, All Transactions Index, 2024Q4

Home Value

Area	Under $100,000	$100,000 -$199,999	$200,000 -$299,999	$300,000 -$399,999	$400,000 -$499,999	$500,000 -$999,999	$1,000,000 or more	Median ($)
City	63.8	21.8	7.7	3.4	1.3	1.6	0.4	76,800
MSA[1]	16.3	23.8	24.2	15.1	9.2	9.8	1.5	237,100
U.S.	12.1	17.8	19.5	14.4	10.5	19.1	6.5	303,400

Note: Figures are percentages except for median and cover owner-occupied housing units; (1) Figures cover the Detroit-Warren-Dearborn, MI Metropolitan Statistical Area
Source: U.S. Census Bureau, 2019-2023 American Community Survey 5-Year Estimates

Year Housing Structure Built

Area	2020 or Later	2010 -2019	2000 -2009	1990 -1999	1980 -1989	1970 -1979	1960 -1969	1950 -1959	1940 -1949	Before 1940	Median Year
City	0.1	1.5	2.7	2.3	3.2	4.9	7.8	21.8	20.4	35.2	1947
MSA[1]	0.5	4.0	8.7	11.1	9.0	14.5	12.4	18.3	8.8	12.8	1968
U.S.	1.2	8.9	13.6	12.8	13.0	14.4	10.0	9.7	4.5	11.9	1980

Note: Figures are percentages except for Median Year; Note: (1) Figures cover the Detroit-Warren-Dearborn, MI Metropolitan Statistical Area
Source: U.S. Census Bureau, 2019-2023 American Community Survey 5-Year Estimates

Gross Monthly Rent

Area	Under $500	$500 -$999	$1,000 -$1,499	$1,500 -$1,999	$2,000 -$2,499	$2,500 -$2,999	$3,000 and up	Median ($)
City	11.7	35.1	39.5	10.0	2.5	0.8	0.4	1,034
MSA[1]	7.5	26.8	41.4	16.4	4.7	1.3	1.8	1,162
U.S.	6.5	22.3	29.5	20.2	10.8	4.8	5.9	1,348

Note: Figures are percentages except for median; Gross rent is the contract rent plus the estimated average monthly cost of utilities (electricity, gas, and water and sewer) and fuels (oil, coal, kerosene, wood, etc.) if these are paid by the renter (or paid for the renter by someone else); (1) Figures cover the Detroit-Warren-Dearborn, MI Metropolitan Statistical Area
Source: U.S. Census Bureau, 2019-2023 American Community Survey 5-Year Estimates

HEALTH

Health Risk Factors

Category	MSA[1] (%)	U.S. (%)
Adults aged 18–64 who have any kind of health care coverage	n/a	90.8
Adults who reported being in good or better health	n/a	81.8
Adults who have been told they have high blood cholesterol	n/a	36.9
Adults who have been told they have high blood pressure	n/a	34.0
Adults who are current smokers	n/a	12.1
Adults who currently use e-cigarettes	n/a	7.7
Adults who currently use chewing tobacco, snuff, or snus	n/a	3.2
Adults who are heavy drinkers[2]	n/a	6.1
Adults who are binge drinkers[3]	n/a	15.2
Adults who are overweight (BMI 25.0 - 29.9)	n/a	34.4
Adults who are obese (BMI 30.0 - 99.8)	n/a	34.3
Adults who participated in any physical activities in the past month	n/a	75.8

Note: All figures are crude prevalence; (1) Figures for the Detroit-Warren-Dearborn, MI Metropolitan Statistical Area were not available.
(2) Heavy drinkers are classified as adult men having more than 14 drinks per week and adult women having more than 7 drinks per week; (3) Binge drinkers are classified as males having five or more drinks on one occasion or females having four or more drinks on one occasion
Source: Centers for Disease Control and Prevention, Behaviorial Risk Factor Surveillance System, SMART: Selected Metropolitan Area Risk Trends, 2023

Acute and Chronic Health Conditions

Category	MSA[1] (%)	U.S. (%)
Adults who have ever been told they had a heart attack	n/a	4.2
Adults who have ever been told they have angina or coronary heart disease	n/a	4.0
Adults who have ever been told they had a stroke	n/a	3.3
Adults who have ever been told they have asthma	n/a	15.7
Adults who have ever been told they have arthritis	n/a	26.3
Adults who have ever been told they have diabetes[2]	n/a	11.5
Adults who have ever been told they had skin cancer	n/a	5.6
Adults who have ever been told they had any other types of cancer	n/a	8.4
Adults who have ever been told they have COPD	n/a	6.4
Adults who have ever been told they have kidney disease	n/a	3.7
Adults who have ever been told they have a form of depression	n/a	22.0

Note: All figures are crude prevalence; (1) Figures for the Detroit-Warren-Dearborn, MI Metropolitan Statistical Area were not available.
(2) Figures do not include pregnancy-related, borderline, or pre-diabetes
Source: Centers for Disease Control and Prevention, Behavioral Risk Factor Surveillance System, SMART: Selected Metropolitan Area Risk Trends, 2023

Health Screening and Vaccination Rates

Category	MSA[1] (%)	U.S. (%)
Adults who have ever been tested for HIV	n/a	37.5
Adults who have had their blood cholesterol checked within the last five years	n/a	87.0
Adults aged 65+ who have had flu shot within the past year	n/a	63.4
Adults aged 65+ who have ever had a pneumonia vaccination	n/a	71.9

Note: All figures are crude prevalence; (1) Figures for the Detroit-Warren-Dearborn, MI Metropolitan Statistical Area were not available.
Source: Centers for Disease Control and Prevention, Behavioral Risk Factor Surveillance System, SMART: Selected Metropolitan Area Risk Trends, 2023

Disability Status

Category	MSA[1] (%)	U.S. (%)
Adults who reported being deaf	n/a	7.4
Are you blind or have serious difficulty seeing, even when wearing glasses?	n/a	4.9
Do you have difficulty doing errands alone?	n/a	7.8
Do you have difficulty dressing or bathing?	n/a	3.6
Do you have serious difficulty concentrating/remembering/making decisions?	n/a	13.7
Do you have serious difficulty walking or climbing stairs?	n/a	13.2

Note: All figures are crude prevalence; (1) Figures for the Detroit-Warren-Dearborn, MI Metropolitan Statistical Area were not available.
Source: Centers for Disease Control and Prevention, Behavioral Risk Factor Surveillance System, SMART: Selected Metropolitan Area Risk Trends, 2023

Mortality Rates for the Top 10 Causes of Death in the U.S.

ICD-10[a] Sub-Chapter	ICD-10[a] Code	Crude Mortality Rate[2] per 100,000 population	
		County[3]	U.S.
Malignant neoplasms	C00-C97	198.1	182.7
Ischaemic heart diseases	I20-I25	161.3	109.6
Provisional assignment of new diseases of uncertain etiology[1]	U00-U49	74.8	65.3
Other forms of heart disease	I30-I51	71.0	65.1
Other degenerative diseases of the nervous system	G30-G31	33.7	52.4
Other external causes of accidental injury	W00-X59	66.7	52.3
Cerebrovascular diseases	I60-I69	58.1	49.1
Chronic lower respiratory diseases	J40-J47	41.1	43.5
Hypertensive diseases	I10-I15	66.5	38.9
Organic, including symptomatic, mental disorders	F01-F09	27.4	33.9

Note: (a) ICD-10 = International Classification of Diseases 10th Revision; (1) Includes COVID-19, adverse effects to COVID-19 vaccines, SARS, and vaping-related disorders; (2) Crude mortality rates are a three-year average covering 2021-2023; (3) Figures cover Wayne County.
Source: Centers for Disease Control and Prevention, National Center for Health Statistics. National Vital Statistics System, Mortality 2018-2023 on CDC WONDER Online Database

Mortality Rates for Selected Causes of Death

Cause of Death	ICD-10[a] Code	Crude Mortality Rate[1] per 100,000 population	
		County[2]	U.S.
Accidental poisoning and exposure to noxious substances	X40-X49	50.5	30.5
Alzheimer disease	G30	26.6	35.4
Assault	X85-Y09	19.8	7.3
COVID-19	U07.1	74.8	65.3
Diabetes mellitus	E10-E14	33.4	30.0
Diseases of the liver	K70-K76	19.6	20.8
Human immunodeficiency virus (HIV) disease	B20-B24	2.5	1.5
Influenza and pneumonia	J09-J18	19.3	13.4
Intentional self-harm	X60-X84	13.1	14.7
Malnutrition	E40-E46	12.5	6.0
Obesity and other hyperalimentation	E65-E68	3.0	3.1
Renal failure	N17-N19	23.1	16.4
Transport accidents	V01-V99	14.5	14.4

Note: (a) ICD-10 = International Classification of Diseases 10th Revision; (1) Crude mortality rates are a three-year average covering 2021-2023; (2) Figures cover Wayne County; Data are suppressed when the data meet the criteria for confidentiality constraints; Crude mortality rates are flagged as unreliable when the rate would be calculated with a numerator of 20 or less.
Source: Centers for Disease Control and Prevention, National Center for Health Statistics. National Vital Statistics System, Mortality 2018-2023 on CDC WONDER Online Database

Health Insurance Coverage

Area	With Health Insurance	With Private Health Insurance	With Public Health Insurance	Without Health Insurance	Population Under Age 19 Without Health Insurance
City	92.5	41.8	62.6	7.5	2.7
MSA[1]	95.1	70.0	40.0	4.9	2.6
U.S.	91.4	67.3	36.3	8.6	5.4

Note: Figures are percentages that cover the civilian noninstitutionalized population; (1) Figures cover the Detroit-Warren-Dearborn, MI Metropolitan Statistical Area
Source: U.S. Census Bureau, 2019-2023 American Community Survey 5-Year Estimates

Number of Medical Professionals

Area	MDs[3]	DOs[3,4]	Dentists	Podiatrists	Chiropractors	Optometrists
County[1] (number)	6,120	1,071	1,402	171	334	217
County[1] (rate[2])	348.3	61.0	80.1	9.8	19.1	12.4
U.S. (rate[2])	302.5	29.2	74.6	6.4	29.5	18.0

Note: Data as of 2023 unless noted; (1) Data covers Wayne County; (2) Number of medical professionals per 100,000 population; (3) Data as of 2022 and includes all active, non-federal physicians; (4) Doctor of Osteopathic Medicine
Source: U.S. Department of Health and Human Services, Health Resources and Services Administration, Bureau of Health Professions, Area Resource File (ARF) 2023-2024

Best Hospitals

According to *U.S. News*, the Detroit-Warren-Dearborn, MI metro area is home to three of the best hospitals in the U.S.: **Corewell Health Beaumont Grosse Pointe Hospital** (1 adult specialty); **Corewell Health William Beaumont University Hospital** (9 adult specialties); **Henry Ford Hospital** (1 adult specialty). The hospitals listed were nationally ranked in at least one of 15 adult or 11 pediatric specialties. The number of specialties shown cover the parent hospital. Only 160 U.S. hospitals performed well enough to be nationally ranked in one or more specialties. Twenty hospitals in the U.S. made the Honor Roll. The Best Hospitals Honor Roll takes both the national rankings and the procedure and condition ratings into account. Hospitals received points if they were nationally ranked in one of the 15 adult specialties—the higher they ranked, the more points they got—and how many ratings of "high performing" they earned in the 20 procedures and conditions. *U.S. News Online, "America's Best Hospitals 2024-25"*

According to *U.S. News*, the Detroit-Warren-Dearborn, MI metro area is home to one of the best children's hospitals in the U.S.: **Children's Hospital of Michigan** (1 pediatric specialty). The hospital listed was highly ranked in at least one of 11 pediatric specialties. One hundred five children's hospitals in the U.S. were nationally ranked in at least one specialty. Hospitals received points for being ranked in a specialty, and the 10 hospitals with the most points across the 11 specialties make up the Honor Roll. *U.S. News Online, "America's Best Children's Hospitals 2024-25"*

EDUCATION

Public School District Statistics

District Name	Schls	Pupils	Pupil/Teacher Ratio	Minority Pupils[1] (%)	Total Rev. per Pupil ($)	Total Exp. per Pupil ($)
Cesar Chavez Academy	4	2,226	16.9	96.5	13,778	12,304
Detroit Public Schools Community Dist.	106	48,271	16.2	97.6	27,346	22,228

Note: Table includes school districts with 2,000 or more students; (1) Percentage of students that are not non-Hispanic white.
Source: U.S. Department of Education, National Center for Education Statistics, Common Core of Data, Local Education Agency (School District) Universe Survey: School Year 2023-2024; U.S. Department of Education, National Center for Education Statistics, Common Core of Data, School District Finance Survey (F-33): School Year 2021–22

Highest Level of Education

Area	Less than H.S.	H.S. Diploma	Some College, No Deg.	Associate Degree	Bachelor's Degree	Master's Degree	Prof. School Degree	Doctorate Degree
City	16.6	33.2	25.4	7.2	10.5	5.4	1.0	0.7
MSA[1]	8.8	26.0	22.0	9.2	20.4	10.3	2.2	1.1
U.S.	10.6	26.2	19.4	8.8	21.3	9.8	2.3	1.6

Note: Figures cover persons age 25 and over; (1) Figures cover the Detroit-Warren-Dearborn, MI Metropolitan Statistical Area
Source: U.S. Census Bureau, 2019-2023 American Community Survey 5-Year Estimates

Educational Attainment by Race

Area	High School Graduate or Higher (%)					Bachelor's Degree or Higher (%)				
	Total	White	Black	Asian	Hisp.[2]	Total	White	Black	Asian	Hisp.[2]
City	83.4	84.3	85.3	75.5	56.8	17.6	37.4	14.1	43.5	11.6
MSA[1]	91.2	92.9	88.4	89.5	76.9	34.1	36.5	19.4	66.4	26.5
U.S.	89.4	92.9	88.1	88.0	72.5	35.0	37.7	24.7	57.0	19.9

Note: Figures shown cover persons 25 years old and over; (1) Figures cover the Detroit-Warren-Dearborn, MI Metropolitan Statistical Area; (2) People of Hispanic origin can be of any race
Source: U.S. Census Bureau, 2019-2023 American Community Survey 5-Year Estimates

School Enrollment by Grade and Control

Area	Preschool (%)		Kindergarten (%)		Grades 1 - 4 (%)		Grades 5 - 8 (%)		Grades 9 - 12 (%)	
	Public	Private	Public	Private	Public	Private	Public	Private	Public	Private
City	81.6	18.4	91.8	8.2	93.4	6.6	92.1	7.9	92.4	7.6
MSA[1]	62.5	37.5	86.9	13.1	88.7	11.3	89.8	10.2	89.9	10.1
U.S.	58.7	41.3	85.2	14.8	87.2	12.8	87.9	12.1	89.0	11.0

Note: Figures shown cover persons 3 years old and over; (1) Figures cover the Detroit-Warren-Dearborn, MI Metropolitan Statistical Area
Source: U.S. Census Bureau, 2019-2023 American Community Survey 5-Year Estimates

Higher Education

Four-Year Colleges			Two-Year Colleges			Medical Schools[1]	Law Schools[2]	Voc/Tech[3]
Public	Private Non-profit	Private For-profit	Public	Private Non-profit	Private For-profit			
5	12	2	4	2	6	1	2	30

Note: Figures cover institutions located within the Detroit-Warren-Dearborn, MI Metropolitan Statistical Area and include main campuses only; (1) includes schools accredited by the Liaison Committee on Medical Education and the American Osteopathic Association's Commission on Osteopathic College Accreditation; (2) includes ABA-accredited schools, schools with provisional ABA accreditation, and state accredited schools; (3) includes all schools with programs that are less than 2 years.
Source: National Center for Education Statistics, Integrated Postsecondary Education System (IPEDS), 2023-24; Wikipedia, List of Medical Schools in the United States, accessed May 2, 2025; Wikipedia, List of Law Schools in the United States, accessed May 2, 2025

According to *U.S. News & World Report*, the Detroit-Warren-Dearborn, MI metro area is home to two of the top 200 national universities in the U.S.: **Wayne State University** (#179 tie); **University of Detroit Mercy** (#189 tie). The indicators used to capture academic quality fall into a number of categories: assessment by administrators at peer institutions; retention of students; faculty resources; student selectivity; financial resources; alumni giving; high school counselor ratings of colleges; and graduation rate. *U.S. News & World Report, "America's Best Colleges 2025"*

According to *U.S. News & World Report*, the Detroit-Warren-Dearborn, MI metro area is home to one of the top 100 law schools in the U.S.: **Wayne State University** (#71 tie). The rankings are based on a weighted average of 12 measures of quality: peer assessment score; assessment score by lawyers/judges; median LSAT scores; median undergrad GPA; acceptance rate; employment rates for graduates; placement success; bar passage rate; faculty resources; expenditures per student; student/faculty ratio; and library resources. *U.S. News & World Report, "America's Best Graduate Schools, Law, 2025"*

According to *U.S. News & World Report*, the Detroit-Warren-Dearborn, MI metro area is home to one of the top medical schools for research in the U.S.: **Wayne State University** (Tier 2). *U.S. News* placed medical and osteopathic schools into tiers based on their research productivity, faculty and admissions data. Each school's tier was derived from its overall score, calculated by summing the weighted normalized values generated across several factors of academic quality, outlined below. There are four tiers, with tier 1 medical schools as the highest-performing and tier 4 as the lowest-performing. Only tier 1 and 2 schools are shown. Because of the tier presentation, *U.S. News* calculated overall scores based on their percentile performance among all rated schools instead of dividing against the rescaled score of the No. 1-performing schools. Tier 1 included schools with overall scores of 85 to 99. The cutoffs for tiers 2 through 4 were schools scoring 50 to 84, 15 to 49 and 1 to 14, respectively. The rankings are based on a weighted average of the following measures of quality: total research activity; average research activity per faculty member; total NIH research grants at the medical school and its affiliated hospitals; average NIH research grants per faculty; median MCAT total score; median undergraduate GPA; acceptance rate; and faculty resources. *U.S. News & World Report, "America's Best Graduate Schools, Medical, 2025"*

EMPLOYERS

Major Employers

Company Name	Industry
Blue Cross Blue Shield of Michigan	Insurance
City of Detroit	Local government
Detroit Medical Center	Healthcare
Detroit Public Schools Community District	Education
DTE Energy	Energy
Fiat Chrysler	Automobile manufacture and assembly
Ford Motor Company	Automobile manufacture and assembly
General Motors	Automobile manufacture and assembly
Henry Ford Health System	Healthcare
Ilitch Holdings Inc.	Food, sports, entertainment brands
Rocket Companies Inc.	Financial services
State of Michigan	State government
U.S. Government	Federal government
U.S. Postal Service	Postal service
University of Michigan	Higher education

Note: Companies shown are located within the Detroit-Warren-Dearborn, MI Metropolitan Statistical Area.
Source: Chambers of Commerce; State Departments of Labor; Wikipedia

Best Companies to Work For

Ally Financial; Rocket Companies, headquartered in Detroit, are among "The 100 Best Companies to Work For." To pick the best companies, *Fortune* partnered with the Great Place to Work Institute. Using their proprietary Trust Index™ survey, the core of what creates great a workplace is measured—key behaviors that drive trust in management, connection with colleagues, and loyalty to the company. To be eligible for the *Fortune* 100 Best Companies to Work For list, employers must have 1,000 or more employees in the U.S. and cannot be a government agency. *Fortune, "The 100 Best Companies to Work For," 2025*

Rocket Companies, headquartered in Detroit, is among "Fortune's Best Workplaces for Parents." To pick the best companies, *Fortune* partnered with the Great Place to Work Institute. To be considered for the list, companies must be Great Place To Work-Certified and have at least 50 responses from parents in the US. The survey enables employees to share confidential quantitative and qualitative feedback about their organization's culture by responding to 60 statements on a 5-point scale and answering two open-ended questions. Collectively, these statements describe a great employee experience, defined by high levels of trust, respect, credibility, fairness, pride, and camaraderie. In addition, companies provide organizational data like size, location, industry, demographics, roles, and levels; and provide information about parental leave, adoption, flexible schedule, childcare and dependent health care benefits. *Fortune, "Best Workplaces for Parents," 2024*

Rocket Companies, headquartered in Detroit, is among "Fortune's Best Workplaces for Women." To pick the best companies, *Fortune* partnered with the Great Place to Work Institute. To be considered for the list, companies must be Great Place To Work-Certified. Companies must also employ at least 50 women, at least 20% of their non-executive managers must be female, and at least one executive must be female. To determine the Best Workplaces for Women, Great Place To Work measured the differences in women's survey responses to those of their peers and assesses the impact of demographics and roles on the quality and consistency of women's experiences. Great Place To Work also analyzed the gender balance of each workplace, how it compared to each company's industry, and patterns in representation as women rise from front-line positions to the board of directors. *Fortune, "Best Workplaces for Women," 2024*

Rocket Companies, headquartered in Detroit, is among "Best Workplaces in Real Estate." To determine the Best Workplaces in Real Estate list, Great Place To Work analyzed the survey responses of over 29,000 employees from Great Place To Work-Certified companies in the real estate industry. Survey data analysis and company-provided datapoints are then factored into a combined score to compare and rank the companies that create the most consistently positive experience for all employees in this industry. *Fortune, "Best Workplaces in Real Estate," 2024*

PUBLIC SAFETY

Crime Rate

Area	Total Crime Rate	Violent Crime Rate				Property Crime Rate		
		Murder	Rape	Robbery	Aggrav. Assault	Burglary	Larceny-Theft	Motor Vehicle Theft
City	6,785.7	40.6	109.3	225.5	1,676.7	756.9	2,485.8	1,490.8
U.S.	2,290.9	5.7	38.0	66.5	264.1	250.7	1,347.2	318.7

Note: Figures are crimes per 100,000 population.
Source: FBI, Table 8, Offenses Known to Law Enforcement, by State by City, 2023

Hate Crimes

Area	Number of Quarters Reported	Number of Incidents per Bias Motivation					
		Race/Ethnicity/Ancestry	Religion	Sexual Orientation	Disability	Gender	Gender Identity
City[1]	4	28	2	9	0	0	0
U.S.	4	5,900	2,699	2,077	187	92	492

Note: (1) Figures include at least one incident reported with more than one bias motivation.
Source: Federal Bureau of Investigation, Hate Crime Statistics 2023

Identity Theft Consumer Reports

Area	Reports	Reports per 100,000 Population	Rank[2]
MSA[1]	15,687	359	34
U.S.	1,135,291	339	-

Note: (1) Figures cover the Detroit-Warren-Dearborn, MI Metropolitan Statistical Area; (2) Rank ranges from 1 to 401 where 1 indicates greatest number of identity theft reports per 100,000 population
Source: Federal Trade Commission, Consumer Sentinel Network Data Book 2024

Fraud and Other Consumer Reports

Area	Reports	Reports per 100,000 Population	Rank[2]
MSA[1]	66,361	1,519	52
U.S.	5,360,641	1,601	-

Note: (1) Figures cover the Detroit-Warren-Dearborn, MI Metropolitan Statistical Area; (2) Rank ranges from 1 to 401 where 1 indicates greatest number of fraud and other consumer reports per 100,000 population
Source: Federal Trade Commission, Consumer Sentinel Network Data Book 2024

POLITICS

2024 Presidential Election Results

Area	Trump (Rep.)	Harris (Dem.)	Stein (Green)	Kennedy (Ind.)	Oliver (Lib.)	Other
Wayne County	33.6	62.5	2.4	0.4	0.3	0.8
U.S.	49.7	48.2	0.6	0.5	0.4	0.6

Note: Results are percentages and may not add to 100% due to rounding
Source: Dave Leip's Atlas of U.S. Presidential Elections

SPORTS

Professional Sports Teams

Team Name	League	Year Established
Detroit Lions	National Football League (NFL)	1934
Detroit Pistons	National Basketball Association (NBA)	1957
Detroit Red Wings	National Hockey League (NHL)	1926
Detroit Tigers	Major League Baseball (MLB)	1901

Note: Includes teams located in the Detroit-Warren-Dearborn, MI Metropolitan Statistical Area.
Source: Wikipedia, Major Professional Sports Teams of the United States and Canada, May 1, 2025

CLIMATE

Average and Extreme Temperatures

Temperature	Jan	Feb	Mar	Apr	May	Jun	Jul	Aug	Sep	Oct	Nov	Dec	Yr.
Extreme High (°F)	62	65	81	89	93	104	102	100	98	91	77	68	104
Average High (°F)	30	33	44	58	70	79	83	81	74	61	48	35	58
Average Temp. (°F)	23	26	36	48	59	68	72	71	64	52	40	29	49
Average Low (°F)	16	18	27	37	47	56	61	60	53	41	32	21	39
Extreme Low (°F)	-21	-15	-4	10	25	36	41	38	29	17	9	-10	-21

Note: Figures cover the years 1958-1990
Source: National Climatic Data Center, International Station Meteorological Climate Summary, 9/96

Average Precipitation/Snowfall/Humidity

Precip./Humidity	Jan	Feb	Mar	Apr	May	Jun	Jul	Aug	Sep	Oct	Nov	Dec	Yr.
Avg. Precip. (in.)	1.8	1.8	2.5	3.0	2.9	3.6	3.1	3.4	2.8	2.2	2.6	2.7	32.4
Avg. Snowfall (in.)	10	9	7	2	Tr	0	0	0	0	Tr	3	11	41
Avg. Rel. Hum. 7am (%)	80	79	79	78	78	79	82	86	87	84	82	81	81
Avg. Rel. Hum. 4pm (%)	67	63	59	53	51	52	52	54	55	55	64	70	58

Note: Figures cover the years 1958-1990; Tr = Trace amounts (<0.05 in. of rain; <0.5 in. of snow)
Source: National Climatic Data Center, International Station Meteorological Climate Summary, 9/96

Weather Conditions

Temperature			Daytime Sky			Precipitation		
5°F & below	32°F & below	90°F & above	Clear	Partly cloudy	Cloudy	0.01 inch or more precip.	0.1 inch or more snow/ice	Thunder-storms
15	136	12	74	134	157	135	38	32

Note: Figures are average number of days per year and cover the years 1958-1990
Source: National Climatic Data Center, International Station Meteorological Climate Summary, 9/96

HAZARDOUS WASTE

Superfund Sites

The Detroit-Dearborn-Livonia, MI metro division is home to two sites on the EPA's Superfund National Priorities List (NPL) or Superfund Alternative Approach (SAA) list: **Dsc McLouth Steel Gibraltar Plant** (Final NPL); **McLouth Steel Corp** (Final NPL). The Superfund alternative approach uses the same investigation and cleanup process and standards that are used for sites listed on the National Priorities List. The SAA is an alternative to listing a site on the NPL; it is not an alternative to Superfund or the Superfund process. There are a total of 1,445 Superfund sites with a status of proposed or final on both lists in the United States. *U.S. Environmental Protection Agency, National Priorities List, May 1, 2025; U.S. Environmental Protection Agency, Superfund Alternative Approach Sites, May 1, 2025*

AIR QUALITY

Air Quality Trends: Ozone

	1990	1995	2000	2005	2010	2015	2020	2021	2022	2023
MSA[1]	0.083	0.088	0.076	0.083	0.074	0.068	0.072	0.069	0.068	0.074
U.S.	0.087	0.089	0.081	0.080	0.072	0.068	0.066	0.067	0.067	0.070

Note: (1) Data covers the Detroit-Warren-Dearborn, MI Metropolitan Statistical Area. The values shown are the composite ozone concentration averages among trend sites based on the highest fourth daily maximum 8-hour concentration in parts per million. These trends are based on sites having an adequate record of monitoring data during the trend period. Data from exceptional events are included.
Source: U.S. Environmental Protection Agency, Air Quality Monitoring Information, "Air Quality Trends by City, 1990-2023"

Air Quality Index

Area	Percent of Days when Air Quality was...[2]					AQI Statistics[2]	
	Good	Moderate	Unhealthy for Sensitive Groups	Unhealthy	Very Unhealthy	Maximum	Median
MSA[1]	18.6	74.0	6.3	0.8	0.3	226	61

Note: (1) Data covers the Detroit-Warren-Dearborn, MI Metropolitan Statistical Area; (2) Based on 365 days with AQI data in 2023. Air Quality Index (AQI) is an index for reporting daily air quality. EPA calculates the AQI for five major air pollutants regulated by the Clean Air Act: ground-level ozone, particle pollution (aka particulate matter), carbon monoxide, sulfur dioxide, and nitrogen dioxide. The AQI runs from 0 to 500. The higher the AQI value, the greater the level of air pollution and the greater the health concern. There are six AQI categories: "Good" AQI is between 0 and 50. Air quality is considered satisfactory; "Moderate" AQI is between 51 and 100. Air quality is acceptable; "Unhealthy for Sensitive Groups" When AQI values are between 101 and 150, members of sensitive groups may experience health effects; "Unhealthy" When AQI values are between 151 and 200 everyone may begin to experience health effects; "Very Unhealthy" AQI values between 201 and 300 trigger a health alert; "Hazardous" AQI values over 300 trigger warnings of emergency conditions (not shown).
Source: U.S. Environmental Protection Agency, Air Quality Index Report, 2023

Air Quality Index Pollutants

Area	Percent of Days when AQI Pollutant was...[2]					
	Carbon Monoxide	Nitrogen Dioxide	Ozone	Sulfur Dioxide	Particulate Matter 2.5	Particulate Matter 10
MSA[1]	0.0	0.5	11.5	(3)	87.9	0.0

Note: (1) Data covers the Detroit-Warren-Dearborn, MI Metropolitan Statistical Area; (2) Based on 365 days with AQI data in 2023. The Air Quality Index (AQI) is an index for reporting daily air quality. EPA calculates the AQI for five major air pollutants regulated by the Clean Air Act: ground-level ozone, particle pollution (also known as particulate matter), carbon monoxide, sulfur dioxide, and nitrogen dioxide. The AQI runs from 0 to 500. The higher the AQI value, the greater the level of air pollution and the greater the health concern; (3) Sulfur dioxide is no longer included in this table because SO_2 concentrations tend to be very localized and not necessarily representative of broad geographical areas like counties and CBSAs.
Source: U.S. Environmental Protection Agency, Air Quality Index Report, 2023

Maximum Air Pollutant Concentrations: Particulate Matter, Ozone, CO and Lead

	Particulate Matter 10 (ug/m^3)	Particulate Matter 2.5 Wtd AM (ug/m^3)	Particulate Matter 2.5 24-Hr (ug/m^3)	Ozone (ppm)	Carbon Monoxide (ppm)	Lead (ug/m^3)
MSA[1] Level	161	14.7	46	0.079	2	0.03
NAAQS[2]	150	15	35	0.075	9	0.15
Met NAAQS[2]	No	Yes	No	No	Yes	Yes

Note: (1) Data covers the Detroit-Warren-Dearborn, MI Metropolitan Statistical Area; Data from exceptional events are included; (2) National Ambient Air Quality Standards; ppm = parts per million; ug/m^3 = micrograms per cubic meter; n/a not available.
Concentrations: Particulate Matter 10 (coarse particulate)—highest second maximum 24-hour concentration; Particulate Matter 2.5 Wtd AM (fine particulate)—highest weighted annual mean concentration; Particulate Matter 2.5 24-Hour (fine particulate)—highest 98th percentile 24-hour concentration; Ozone—highest fourth daily maximum 8-hour concentration; Carbon Monoxide—highest second maximum non-overlapping 8-hour concentration; Lead—maximum running 3-month average
Source: U.S. Environmental Protection Agency, Air Quality Monitoring Information, "Air Quality Statistics by City, 2023"

Maximum Air Pollutant Concentrations: Nitrogen Dioxide and Sulfur Dioxide

	Nitrogen Dioxide AM (ppb)	Nitrogen Dioxide 1-Hr (ppb)	Sulfur Dioxide AM (ppb)	Sulfur Dioxide 1-Hr (ppb)	Sulfur Dioxide 24-Hr (ppb)
MSA[1] Level	14	50	n/a	55	n/a
NAAQS[2]	53	100	30	75	140
Met NAAQS[2]	Yes	Yes	n/a	Yes	n/a

Note: (1) Data covers the Detroit-Warren-Dearborn, MI Metropolitan Statistical Area; Data from exceptional events are included; (2) National Ambient Air Quality Standards; ppm = parts per million; ug/m^3 = micrograms per cubic meter; n/a not available.
Concentrations: Nitrogen Dioxide AM—highest arithmetic mean concentration; Nitrogen Dioxide 1-Hr—highest 98th percentile 1-hour daily maximum concentration; Sulfur Dioxide AM—highest annual mean concentration; Sulfur Dioxide 1-Hr—highest 99th percentile 1-hour daily maximum concentration; Sulfur Dioxide 24-Hr—highest second maximum 24-hour concentration
Source: U.S. Environmental Protection Agency, Air Quality Monitoring Information, "Air Quality Statistics by City, 2023"

Fargo, North Dakota

Background

Fargo sits on the western bank of the Red River in the Red River Valley in the southeastern part of the state. The city is in Cass County and about 300 miles northwest of Minneapolis.

Originally a stopping point for steamboats on the Red River in the later part of the 19th century, Fargo was founded in 1871 and named Centralia, but renamed Fargo in honor of the Northern Pacific Railway Director Wells Fargo. It began to flourish after the arrival of the railroad and became known as the Gateway to the West. During the 1880s, Fargo was also known for its lenient divorce laws.

A major fire in 1893 destroyed hundreds of homes and businesses but the city was quickly rebuilt with new brick buildings, new streets, and a water system. The North Dakota State Agricultural College was founded in 1890 as the state's land-grant university and was accredited by the North Central Association in 1915. The school eventually became North Dakota State University in the 1960s.

Fargo grew rapidly after World War II as the connection of two interstates, I-29 and I-94, revolutionized travel in the region and allowed for further expansion in the southern and western parts of the city. In 1972, the West Acres Shopping Center was constructed near the intersection of the two interstates and served as a catalyst for retail growth in the area.

Fargo is the crossroads and economic center of eastern North Dakota and western Minnesota. Though the economy of the region was historically dependent on agriculture, other sectors have become increasingly prevalent in recent years, including food processing, manufacturing, technology, retail trade, higher education, and healthcare. The University is the city's largest public sector employer.

A significant landmark in Fargo is the main campus of North Dakota State University, which has a full-time enrollment of nearly 12,000. The city also features many public parks including Percy Godwin Park, Lindenwood Park, Mickelson Field, Island Park, Roosevelt Playground, and Oak Grove Park.

As the city continues to energize the downtown area, the Renaissance Zone and Storefront Rehab programs encourage new business, renovate deteriorating buildings, and increase the availability of housing in the downtown area. The renovated Fargo Public Library's main downtown branch is popular with the city's residents.

Fargo, an Academy Award-winning 1996 film named after the city, shows the city briefly at the film's opening scene set in a bar. *Fargo*, the TV series based on the film, debuted on FX in 2014. The city was featured in its seventh episode of season 1, "Who Shaves the Barber?" and more prominently in season 2. The series was filmed in Calgary, Alberta, Canada.

Because of its location in the Great Plains and its distance from both mountains and oceans, Fargo has an extreme humid continental climate, featuring long, bitterly cold winters, the coldest in the contiguous United States. Summers are warm to hot and humid. Snowfall averages about 51 inches per season. Spring and autumn are short and highly variable seasons. Summers have frequent thunderstorms. Annual precipitation of about 24 inches is concentrated in the warmer months.

Rankings

General Rankings

- In their annual survey, Livability.com looked at data for more than 2,000 mid-sized U.S. cities to assign a "Livability Score"for each. The top 100 scoring cities make up Livability's "Top 100 Best Places to Live in the U.S." in 2025. Fargo was placed among the top 100 of the customizable list. Criteria: housing and economy; cost of living; environment; education; health care options; transportation; safety; and community amenities. *Livability.com, "Top 100 Best Places to Live in the U.S. in 2025" April 15, 2025*

Business/Finance Rankings

- The Fargo metro area appeared on the Milken Institute "2025 Best Performing Cities" list. Rank: #36 out of 203 small metro areas (based on performance category). Criteria: job growth; wage growth; high-tech growth and impact; community resilience; housing affordability; household broadband access. *Milken Institute, "Best-Performing Cities 2025," January 14, 2025*

Environmental Rankings

- *Niche* compiled a list of the nation's snowiest cities, based on the National Oceanic and Atmospheric Administration's 30-year average snowfall data. Among cities with a population of at least 50,000, Fargo ranked #18. *Niche.com, Top 25 Snowiest Cities in America, December 10, 2018*

- Fargo was highlighted as one of the 25 metro areas most polluted by short-term particle pollution (24-hour PM 2.5) in the U.S. during 2021 through 2023. The area ranked #18. *American Lung Association, "State of the Air 2025," April 23, 2025*

Real Estate Rankings

- *WalletHub* compared the most populated U.S. cities to determine which had the best markets for real estate agents. Fargo ranked #35 where demand was high and pay was the best. Criteria: sales per agent; annual median wage for real-estate agents; monthly average starting salary for real estate agents; real estate job density and competition; unemployment rate; home turnover rate; housing-market health index; and other relevant metrics. *WalletHub.com, "2021 Best Places to Be a Real Estate Agent," May 12, 2021*

- Fargo was ranked #40 out of 176 metro areas in terms of cost of housing in 2024 by the National Association of Home Builders (#1 = most affordable). Criteria: the portion of an average family's income necessary to pay the mortgage on a median-priced home. *National Association of Home Builders®, NAHB-Wells Fargo Cost of Housing Index, 4th Quarter 2024*

Seniors/Retirement Rankings

- Fargo made the 2024 *Forbes* list of "25 Best Places to Retire." Criteria, focused on overall affordability as well as quality of life indicators, include: housing/living costs compared to the national average and taxes; air quality; crime rates; median home prices; risk associated with climate-change/natural hazards; availability of medical care; bikeability; walkability; healthy living. *Forbes.com, "The Best Places to Retire in 2024: Las Cruces and Other Unexpected Hot Spots," May 10, 2024*

Sports/Recreation Rankings

- Fargo was chosen as a bicycle friendly community by the League of American Bicyclists. A "Bicycle Friendly Community" welcomes cyclists by providing safe and supportive accommodation for cycling and encouraging people to bike for transportation and recreation. There are four award levels: Platinum; Gold; Silver; and Bronze. The community achieved an award level of Bronze. *League of American Bicyclists, "2024 Awards-New & Renewing Bicycle Friendly Communities List," January 28, 2025*

Women/Minorities Rankings

- Personal finance website *WalletHub* compared more than 180 U.S. cities across two key dimensions, "Hispanic Business-Friendliness" and "Hispanic Purchasing Power," to arrive at the most favorable conditions for Hispanic entrepreneurs. Fargo was ranked #119 out of 182. Criteria includes: share of Hispanic-Owned Businesses; average growth of Hispanic Business revenues; Small Business-Friendliness score; affordability; and number of Hispanics with at least a bachelor's degree. *WalletHub.com, "Best Cities for Hispanic Entrepreneurs," September 4, 2024*

Miscellaneous Rankings

- *WalletHub* compared 148 of the most populated U.S. cities to determine their operating efficiency. A "Quality of Services" score was constructed for each city and then measured against the total budget per capita to reveal which were managed the best. Fargo ranked #59. Criteria: financial stability; economy; education; safety; health; infrastructure and pollution. *WalletHub.com, "2025's Best- & Worst-Run Cities in America," June 18, 2024*

Business Environment

DEMOGRAPHICS

Population Growth

Area	1990 Census	2000 Census	2010 Census	2020 Census	2023 Estimate[2]	Population Growth 1990-2023 (%)
City	74,372	90,599	105,549	125,990	129,064	73.5
MSA[1]	153,296	174,367	208,777	249,843	254,914	66.3
U.S.	248,709,873	281,421,906	308,745,538	331,449,281	332,387,540	33.6

Note: (1) Figures cover the Fargo, ND-MN Metropolitan Statistical Area; (2) 2019-2023 5-year ACS population estimate
Source: U.S. Census Bureau, 1990 Census, 2000 Census, 2010 Census, 2020 Census, 2019-2023 American Community Survey 5-Year Estimates

Race

Area	White Alone[2] (%)	Black Alone[2] (%)	Asian Alone[2] (%)	AIAN[3] Alone[2] (%)	NHOPI[4] Alone[2] (%)	Other Race Alone[2] (%)	Two or More Races (%)
City	80.8	8.3	3.9	1.0	0.0	1.1	5.0
MSA[1]	84.2	6.1	2.7	0.9	0.1	0.9	5.1
U.S.	63.4	12.4	5.8	0.9	0.2	6.6	10.7

Note: (1) Figures cover the Fargo, ND-MN Metropolitan Statistical Area; (2) Alone is defined as not being in combination with one or more other races; (3) American Indian and Alaska Native; (4) Native Hawaiian and Other Pacific Islander
Source: U.S. Census Bureau, 2019-2023 American Community Survey 5-Year Estimates

Hispanic or Latino Origin

Area	Total (%)	Mexican (%)	Puerto Rican (%)	Cuban (%)	Other (%)
City	3.7	2.2	0.6	0.0	0.8
MSA[1]	3.8	2.5	0.4	0.0	0.8
U.S.	19.0	11.3	1.8	0.7	5.2

Note: Persons of Hispanic or Latino origin can be of any race; (1) Figures cover the Fargo, ND-MN Metropolitan Statistical Area
Source: U.S. Census Bureau, 2019-2023 American Community Survey 5-Year Estimates

Age

Area	Percent of Population									Median Age
	Under Age 5	Age 5–19	Age 20–34	Age 35–44	Age 45–54	Age 55–64	Age 65–74	Age 75–84	Age 85+	
City	6.0	18.4	30.1	12.8	9.0	10.1	7.9	3.9	1.8	32.2
MSA[1]	6.5	20.6	26.1	13.8	10.0	9.9	7.7	3.6	1.7	33.0
U.S.	5.7	19.1	20.2	13.1	12.3	12.8	10.0	4.9	1.9	38.7

Note: (1) Figures cover the Fargo, ND-MN Metropolitan Statistical Area
Source: U.S. Census Bureau, 2019-2023 American Community Survey 5-Year Estimates

Disability by Age

Area	All Ages	Under 18 Years Old	18 to 64 Years Old	65 Years and Over
City	11.4	5.4	9.0	32.6
MSA[1]	11.0	4.1	9.3	32.1
U.S.	13.0	4.7	10.7	32.9

Note: Figures show percent of the civilian noninstitutionalized population that reported having a disability. Disability status is determined from six types of difficulty: vision, hearing, cognitive, ambulatory, self-care, and independent living. For children under 5 years old, hearing and vision difficulty are used to determine disability status. For children between the ages of 5 and 14, disability status is determined from hearing, vision, cognitive, ambulatory, and self-care difficulties. For people aged 15 years and older, they are considered to have a disability if they have difficulty with any one of the six difficulty types; Note: (1) Figures cover the Fargo, ND-MN Metropolitan Statistical Area
Source: U.S. Census Bureau, 2019-2023 American Community Survey 5-Year Estimates

Ancestry

Area	German	Irish	English	American	Italian	Polish	French[2]	European	Scottish
City	32.9	8.1	5.2	2.9	1.3	2.2	3.4	0.8	1.4
MSA[1]	33.8	7.6	5.1	2.5	1.4	2.2	3.2	0.9	1.3
U.S.	12.6	9.4	9.1	5.5	4.9	2.6	2.0	1.6	1.6

Note: Figures are the percentage of the total population reporting a particular ancestry. The nine most commonly reported ancestries in the U.S. are shown. Figures include multiple ancestries (e.g. if a person reported being Irish and Italian, they were included in both columns); (1) Figures cover the Fargo, ND-MN Metropolitan Statistical Area; (2) Excludes Basque
Source: U.S. Census Bureau, 2019-2023 American Community Survey 5-Year Estimates

Foreign-born Population

Area	Percent of Population Born in								
	Any Foreign Country	Asia	Mexico	Europe	Caribbean	Central America[2]	South America	Africa	Canada
City	9.7	3.2	0.1	0.6	0.1	0.0	0.1	4.9	0.4
MSA[1]	6.9	2.4	0.2	0.5	0.1	0.0	0.1	3.2	0.3
U.S.	13.9	4.3	3.3	1.4	1.4	1.2	1.2	0.8	0.2

Note: (1) Figures cover the Fargo, ND-MN Metropolitan Statistical Area; (2) Excludes Mexico.
Source: U.S. Census Bureau, 2019-2023 American Community Survey 5-Year Estimates

Household Size

Area	Persons in Household (%)							Average Household Size
	One	Two	Three	Four	Five	Six	Seven or More	
City	41.1	33.0	11.6	9.3	3.4	1.1	0.5	2.10
MSA[1]	35.2	33.4	13.1	11.0	5.0	1.5	0.8	2.28
U.S.	28.5	33.8	15.4	12.7	5.9	2.3	1.4	2.54

Note: (1) Figures cover the Fargo, ND-MN Metropolitan Statistical Area
Source: U.S. Census Bureau, 2019-2023 American Community Survey 5-Year Estimates

Household Relationships

Area	House-holder	Opposite-sex Spouse	Same-sex Spouse	Opposite-sex Unmarried Partner	Same-sex Unmarried Partner	Child[2]	Grand-child	Other Relatives	Non-relatives
City	44.5	15.5	0.1	3.6	0.2	23.5	0.7	2.5	5.0
MSA[1]	41.5	17.7	0.1	3.2	0.1	27.0	0.7	2.2	3.9
U.S.	38.3	17.5	0.2	2.5	0.2	28.3	2.4	4.8	3.4

Note: Figures are percent of the total population; (1) Figures cover the Fargo, ND-MN Metropolitan Statistical Area; (2) Includes biological, adopted, and stepchildren of the householder
Source: U.S. Census Bureau, 2020 Census

Gender

Area	Males	Females	Males per 100 Females
City	65,129	63,935	101.9
MSA[1]	128,561	126,353	101.7
U.S.	164,545,087	167,842,453	98.0

Note: (1) Figures cover the Fargo, ND-MN Metropolitan Statistical Area
Source: U.S. Census Bureau, 2019-2023 American Community Survey 5-Year Estimates

Marital Status

Area	Never Married	Now Married[2]	Separated	Widowed	Divorced
City	44.3	41.2	1.0	3.8	9.6
MSA[1]	38.8	47.3	0.9	3.9	9.1
U.S.	34.1	47.9	1.7	5.6	10.7

Note: Figures are percentages and cover the population 15 years of age and older; (1) Figures cover the Fargo, ND-MN Metropolitan Statistical Area; (2) Excludes separated
Source: U.S. Census Bureau, 2019-2023 American Community Survey 5-Year Estimates

Religious Groups by Family

Area	Catholic	Baptist	Methodist	LDS[2]	Pentecostal	Lutheran	Islam	Adventist	Other
MSA[1]	14.2	0.2	1.0	0.6	1.3	24.0	<0.1	0.6	8.1
U.S.	18.7	7.3	3.0	2.0	1.8	1.7	1.3	1.3	11.6

Note: Figures are the number of adherents as a percentage of the total population and cover the eight largest religious groups in the U.S; (1) Figures cover the Fargo, ND-MN Metropolitan Statistical Area; (2) Church of Jesus Christ of Latter-day Saints
Sources: 2020 U.S. Religion Census, Association of Statisticians of American Religious Bodies; The Association of Religion Data Archives (ARDA)

Religious Groups by Tradition

Area	Catholic	Evangelical Protestant	Mainline Protestant	Black Protestant	Islam	Judaism	Hinduism	Orthodox	Buddhism
MSA[1]	14.2	11.1	23.4	n/a	<0.1	<0.1	n/a	0.1	n/a
U.S.	18.7	16.5	5.2	2.3	1.3	0.6	0.4	0.4	0.3

Note: Figures are the number of adherents as a percentage of the total population; (1) Figures cover the Fargo, ND-MN Metropolitan Statistical Area
Sources: 2020 U.S. Religion Census, Association of Statisticians of American Religious Bodies; The Association of Religion Data Archives (ARDA)

Fargo, North Dakota

ECONOMY

Real Gross Domestic Product (GDP)

Area	2017	2018	2019	2020	2021	2022	2023	Rank[3]
MSA[1]	15.0	15.1	15.4	14.9	15.7	15.8	16.3	167
U.S.[2]	17,619.1	18,160.7	18,642.5	18,238.9	19,387.6	19,896.6	20,436.3	—

Note: Figures are in billions of chained 2017 dollars; (1) Figures cover the Fargo, ND-MN Metropolitan Statistical Area; (2) Figures cover real GDP within metropolitan areas; (3) Rank is based on 2023 data and ranges from 1 to 384
Source: U.S. Bureau of Economic Analysis

Economic Growth

Area	2014	2015	2016	2017	2018	2019	2020	2021	2022	2023
MSA[1]	7.0	3.5	-0.3	3.3	0.7	2.5	-3.4	5.3	0.4	3.6
U.S.[2]	2.6	3.2	2.0	2.7	3.1	2.7	-2.2	6.3	2.6	2.7

Note: Figures are real gross domestic product growth rates and represent percent change from preceding period; (1) Figures cover the Fargo, ND-MN Metropolitan Statistical Area; (2) Figures are the average growth rates within metropolitan areas
Source: U.S. Bureau of Economic Analysis

Metropolitan Area Exports

Area	2018	2019	2020	2021	2022	2023	Rank[2]
MSA[1]	553.5	515.0	438.3	539.4	518.7	880.1	185
U.S.	1,664,056.1	1,645,173.7	1,431,406.6	1,753,941.4	2,062,937.4	2,019,160.5	—

Note: Figures are in millions of dollars; (1) Figures cover the Fargo, ND-MN Metropolitan Statistical Area; (2) Rank is based on 2023 data and ranges from 1 to 386
Source: U.S. Department of Commerce, International Trade Administration, Office of Trade and Economic Analysis, Industry and Analysis, Exports by Metropolitan Area, data extracted April 2, 2025

Building Permits

Area	Single-Family			Multi-Family			Total		
	2023	2024	Pct. Chg.	2023	2024	Pct. Chg.	2023	2024	Pct. Chg.
City	292	241	-17.5	980	410	-58.2	1,272	651	-48.8
MSA[1]	885	832	-6.0	1,204	660	-45.2	2,089	1,492	-28.6
U.S.	920,000	981,900	6.7	591,100	496,100	-16.1	1,511,100	1,478,000	-2.2

Note: (1) Figures cover the Fargo, ND-MN Metropolitan Statistical Area; Figures represent new, privately-owned housing units authorized (unadjusted data)
Source: U.S. Census Bureau, Building Permits Survey (BPS), 2023, 2024

Bankruptcy Filings

Area	Business Filings			Nonbusiness Filings		
	2023	2024	% Chg.	2023	2024	% Chg.
Cass County	5	14	180.0	129	132	2.3
U.S.	18,926	23,107	22.1	434,064	494,201	13.9

Note: Business filings include Chapter 7, Chapter 9, Chapter 11, Chapter 12, Chapter 13, Chapter 15, and Section 304; Nonbusiness filings include Chapter 7, Chapter 11, and Chapter 13
Source: Administrative Office of the U.S. Courts, Business and Nonbusiness Bankruptcy, County Cases Commenced by Chapter of the Bankruptcy Code, During the 12-Month Period Ending December 31, 2023 and Business and Nonbusiness Bankruptcy, County Cases Commenced by Chapter of the Bankruptcy Code, During the 12-Month Period Ending December 31, 2024

Housing Vacancy Rates

Area	Gross Vacancy Rate[3] (%)			Year-Round Vacancy Rate[4] (%)			Rental Vacancy Rate[5] (%)			Homeowner Vacancy Rate[6] (%)		
	2022	2023	2024	2022	2023	2024	2022	2023	2024	2022	2023	2024
MSA[1]	n/a	n/a	n/a	n/a	n/a	n/a	n/a	n/a	n/a	n/a	n/a	n/a
U.S.[2]	9.1	9.0	9.1	7.5	7.5	7.6	5.7	6.5	6.8	0.8	0.8	1.0

Note: (1) Figures cover the Fargo, ND-MN Metropolitan Statistical Area; (2) Figures cover the 75 largest Metropolitan Statistical Areas; (3) The percentage of the total housing inventory that is vacant; (4) The percentage of the housing inventory (excluding seasonal units) that is year-round vacant; (5) The percentage of rental inventory that is vacant for rent; (6) The percentage of homeowner inventory that is vacant for sale; n/a not available
Source: U.S. Census Bureau, Housing Vacancies and Homeownership Annual Statistics: 2022, 2023, 2024

INCOME

Income

Area	Per Capita ($)	Median Household ($)	Average Household ($)
City	42,212	66,029	91,129
MSA[1]	43,099	75,523	100,645
U.S.	43,289	78,538	110,491

Note: (1) Figures cover the Fargo, ND-MN Metropolitan Statistical Area
Source: U.S. Census Bureau, 2019-2023 American Community Survey 5-Year Estimates

Household Income Distribution

Area	Percent of Households Earning							
	Under $15,000	$15,000 -$24,999	$25,000 -$34,999	$35,000 -$49,999	$50,000 -$74,999	$75,000 -$99,999	$100,000 -$149,999	$150,000 and up
City	8.5	7.3	9.2	12.9	18.1	13.8	15.2	15.0
MSA[1]	7.8	6.5	7.5	11.4	16.5	13.8	18.0	18.5
U.S.	8.5	6.6	6.8	10.4	15.7	12.7	17.4	21.9

Note: (1) Figures cover the Fargo, ND-MN Metropolitan Statistical Area
Source: U.S. Census Bureau, 2019-2023 American Community Survey 5-Year Estimates

Poverty Rate

Area	All Ages	Under 18 Years Old	18 to 64 Years Old	65 Years and Over
City	12.8	14.6	13.7	6.0
MSA[1]	11.4	11.8	12.2	6.7
U.S.	12.4	16.3	11.6	10.4

Note: Figures are percentage of people whose income during the past 12 months was below the poverty level; (1) Figures cover the Fargo, ND-MN Metropolitan Statistical Area
Source: U.S. Census Bureau, 2019-2023 American Community Survey 5-Year Estimates

EMPLOYMENT

Labor Force and Employment

Area	Civilian Labor Force			Workers Employed		
	Dec. 2023	Dec. 2024	% Chg.	Dec. 2023	Dec. 2024	% Chg.
City	75,385	76,672	1.7	73,971	74,762	1.1
MSA[1]	149,293	152,175	1.9	146,516	148,732	1.5
U.S.	166,661,000	167,746,000	0.7	160,754,000	161,294,000	0.3

Note: Data is not seasonally adjusted and covers workers 16 years of age and older; (1) Figures cover the Fargo, ND-MN Metropolitan Statistical Area
Source: Bureau of Labor Statistics, Local Area Unemployment Statistics

Unemployment Rate

Area	2024											
	Jan.	Feb.	Mar.	Apr.	May	Jun.	Jul.	Aug.	Sep.	Oct.	Nov.	Dec.
City	2.5	2.6	2.7	2.3	2.0	2.5	2.2	2.3	1.9	1.9	2.2	2.5
MSA[1]	2.5	2.7	2.7	2.2	2.0	2.6	2.3	2.3	1.8	1.8	2.0	2.3
U.S.	4.1	4.2	3.9	3.5	3.7	4.3	4.5	4.4	3.9	3.9	4.0	3.8

Note: Data is not seasonally adjusted and covers workers 16 years of age and older; (1) Figures cover the Fargo, ND-MN Metropolitan Statistical Area
Source: Bureau of Labor Statistics, Local Area Unemployment Statistics

Average Wages

Occupation	$/Hr.	Occupation	$/Hr.
Accountants and Auditors	36.22	Maintenance and Repair Workers	25.20
Automotive Mechanics	26.79	Marketing Managers	66.41
Bookkeepers	24.09	Network and Computer Systems Admin.	40.53
Carpenters	29.49	Nurses, Licensed Practical	28.38
Cashiers	15.21	Nurses, Registered	39.76
Computer Programmers	43.27	Nursing Assistants	19.70
Computer Systems Analysts	50.62	Office Clerks, General	24.78
Computer User Support Specialists	30.52	Physical Therapists	43.52
Construction Laborers	25.14	Physicians	165.27
Cooks, Restaurant	17.42	Plumbers, Pipefitters and Steamfitters	31.67
Customer Service Representatives	21.49	Police and Sheriff's Patrol Officers	36.83
Dentists	100.00	Postal Service Mail Carriers	30.03
Electricians	33.30	Real Estate Sales Agents	34.07
Engineers, Electrical	50.36	Retail Salespersons	18.57
Fast Food and Counter Workers	14.66	Sales Representatives, Technical/Scientific	54.80
Financial Managers	75.72	Secretaries, Exc. Legal/Medical/Executive	21.50
First-Line Supervisors of Office Workers	33.25	Security Guards	20.01
General and Operations Managers	56.75	Surgeons	n/a
Hairdressers/Cosmetologists	20.05	Teacher Assistants, Exc. Postsecondary[1]	18.13
Home Health and Personal Care Aides	18.76	Teachers, Secondary School, Exc. Sp. Ed.[1]	29.54
Janitors and Cleaners	18.02	Telemarketers	n/a
Landscaping/Groundskeeping Workers	20.93	Truck Drivers, Heavy/Tractor-Trailer	27.21
Lawyers	60.13	Truck Drivers, Light/Delivery Services	24.35
Maids and Housekeeping Cleaners	16.65	Waiters and Waitresses	16.96

Note: Wage data covers the Fargo, ND-MN Metropolitan Statistical Area; (1) Hourly wages were calculated from annual wage data based on a 40 hour work week
Source: Bureau of Labor Statistics, Metro Area Occupational Employment & Wage Estimates, May 2024

Employment by Industry

Sector	MSA[1] Number of Employees	MSA[1] Percent of Total	U.S. Percent of Total
Construction, Mining, and Logging	9,200	6.0	5.5
Financial Activities	10,900	7.1	5.8
Government	21,500	14.0	14.9
Information	2,300	1.5	1.9
Leisure and Hospitality	14,800	9.6	10.4
Manufacturing	12,300	8.0	8.0
Other Services	5,100	3.3	3.7
Private Education and Health Services	30,200	19.6	16.9
Professional and Business Services	14,600	9.5	14.2
Retail Trade	15,800	10.3	10.0
Transportation, Warehousing, and Utilities	8,000	5.2	4.8
Wholesale Trade	9,100	5.9	3.9

Note: Figures are non-farm employment as of December 2024. Figures are not seasonally adjusted and include workers 16 years of age and older; (1) Figures cover the Fargo, ND-MN Metropolitan Statistical Area
Source: Bureau of Labor Statistics, Current Employment Statistics, Employment, Hours, and Earnings

Employment by Occupation

Occupation Classification	City (%)	MSA[1] (%)	U.S. (%)
Management, Business, Science, and Arts	42.6	44.2	42.0
Natural Resources, Construction, and Maintenance	7.2	8.0	8.6
Production, Transportation, and Material Moving	12.0	11.5	13.0
Sales and Office	20.3	19.7	19.9
Service	17.9	16.6	16.5

Note: Figures cover employed civilians 16 years of age and older; (1) Figures cover the Fargo, ND-MN Metropolitan Statistical Area
Source: U.S. Census Bureau, 2019-2023 American Community Survey 5-Year Estimates

Occupations with Greatest Projected Employment Growth: 2022 – 2032

Occupation[1]	2022 Employment	2032 Projected Employment	Numeric Employment Change	Percent Employment Change
Home Health and Personal Care Aides	7,310	9,010	1,700	23.3
Heavy and Tractor-Trailer Truck Drivers	11,450	13,040	1,590	13.9
Registered Nurses	11,500	12,700	1,200	10.4
General and Operations Managers	10,430	11,510	1,080	10.4
Cooks, Restaurant	3,820	4,770	950	24.9
Laborers and Freight, Stock, and Material Movers, Hand	9,180	10,050	870	9.5
Nursing Assistants (SOC 2018)	7,450	8,080	630	8.5
Retail Salespersons	11,730	12,360	630	5.4
Janitors and Cleaners, Except Maids and Housekeeping Cleaners	7,840	8,460	620	7.9
Construction Laborers	4,090	4,690	600	14.7

Note: Projections cover North Dakota; (1) Sorted by numeric employment change
Source: www.projectionscentral.org, State Occupational Projections, 2022–2032 Long-Term Projections

Fastest-Growing Occupations: 2022 – 2032

Occupation[1]	2022 Employment	2032 Projected Employment	Numeric Employment Change	Percent Employment Change
Nurse Practitioners	580	860	280	48.3
Wind Turbine Service Technicians	240	330	90	37.5
Information Security Analysts (SOC 2018)	250	330	80	32.0
Physician Assistants	320	420	100	31.3
Medical and Health Services Managers	630	820	190	30.2
Software Developers	2,030	2,560	530	26.1
Veterinary Assistants and Laboratory Animal Caretakers	230	290	60	26.1
Veterinary Technologists and Technicians	280	350	70	25.0
Cooks, Restaurant	3,820	4,770	950	24.9
Personal Financial Advisors	590	730	140	23.7

Note: Projections cover North Dakota; (1) Sorted by percent employment change and excludes occupations with numeric employment change less than 50
Source: www.projectionscentral.org, State Occupational Projections, 2022–2032 Long-Term Projections

CITY FINANCES

City Government Finances

Component	2022 ($000)	2022 ($ per capita)
Total Revenues	437,608	3,495
Total Expenditures	410,223	3,276
Debt Outstanding	913,432	7,295

Source: U.S. Census Bureau, State & Local Government Finances 2022

City Government Revenue by Source

Source	2022 ($000)	2022 ($ per capita)	2022 (%)
General Revenue			
From Federal Government	27,520	220	6.3
From State Government	111,574	891	25.5
From Local Governments	134	1	0.0
Taxes			
Property	35,492	283	8.1
Sales and Gross Receipts	71,539	571	16.3
Personal Income	0	0	0.0
Corporate Income	0	0	0.0
Motor Vehicle License	0	0	0.0
Other Taxes	7,742	62	1.8
Current Charges	74,768	597	17.1
Liquor Store	0	0	0.0
Utility	28,540	228	6.5

Source: U.S. Census Bureau, State & Local Government Finances 2022

City Government Expenditures by Function

Function	2022 ($000)	2022 ($ per capita)	2022 (%)
General Direct Expenditures			
Air Transportation	19,272	153	4.7
Corrections	0	0	0.0
Education	0	0	0.0
Employment Security Administration	0	0	0.0
Financial Administration	2,801	22	0.7
Fire Protection	16,565	132	4.0
General Public Buildings	2,231	17	0.5
Governmental Administration, Other	4,392	35	1.1
Health	18,349	146	4.5
Highways	59,432	474	14.5
Hospitals	0	0	0.0
Housing and Community Development	2,583	20	0.6
Interest on General Debt	33,608	268	8.2
Judicial and Legal	2,312	18	0.6
Libraries	5,059	40	1.2
Parking	1,710	13	0.4
Parks and Recreation	12,258	97	3.0
Police Protection	23,835	190	5.8
Public Welfare	571	4	0.1
Sewerage	47,614	380	11.6
Solid Waste Management	13,282	106	3.2
Veterans' Services	0	0	0.0
Liquor Store	0	0	0.0
Utility	37,927	302	9.2

Source: U.S. Census Bureau, State & Local Government Finances 2022

TAXES

State Corporate Income Tax Rates

State	Tax Rate (%)	Income Brackets ($)	Num. of Brackets	Financial Institution Tax Rate (%)[a]	Federal Income Tax Ded.
North Dakota	1.41 - 4.31 (q)	25,000 - 50,001	3	1.41 - 4.31 (q)	No

Note: Tax rates for tax year 2024; (a) Rates listed are the corporate income tax rate applied to financial institutions or excise taxes based on income. Some states have other taxes based upon the value of deposits or shares; (q) North Dakota imposes a 3.5% surtax for filers electing to use the water's edge method to apportion income.
Source: Federation of Tax Administrators, State Corporate Income Tax Rates, January 1, 2025

State Individual Income Tax Rates

State	Tax Rate (%)	Income Brackets ($)	Personal Exemptions ($)			Standard Ded. ($)	
			Single	Married	Depend.	Single	Married
North Dakota (a)	0.0 - 2.5	41,775 - 458,350 (t)	(d)	(d)	(d)	14,600	29,200 (d)

Note: Tax rates for tax year 2024; Local- and county-level taxes are not included; Federal income tax is not deductible on state income tax returns; (a) 16 states have statutory provision for automatically adjusting to the rate of inflation the dollar values of the income tax brackets, standard deductions, and/or personal exemptions. Oregon does not index the income brackets for $125,000 and over See: INFL and SPEC above; (d) These states use the personal exemption/standard deduction amounts provided in the federal Internal Revenue Code. Montana personal exemption subject to repeal under Section 15-30-2114; (t) The income brackets reported for North Dakota are for single individuals. For married couples filing jointly, the same tax rates apply to income brackets ranging from $74,757 to $458,350. The number of brackets was reduced to three from five in 2024.
Source: Federation of Tax Administrators, State Individual Income Tax Rates, January 1, 2025

Various State Sales and Excise Tax Rates

State	State Sales Tax (%)	Gasoline[1] ($/gal.)	Cigarette[2] ($/pack)	Spirits[3] ($/gal.)	Wine[4] ($/gal.)	Beer[5] ($/gal.)	Recreational Marijuana (%)
North Dakota	5	0.23	0.44	4.93	1.17	0.43	Not legal

Note: All tax rates as of January 1, 2025; (1) The American Petroleum Institute has developed a methodology for determining the average tax rate on a gallon of fuel. Rates may include any of the following: excise taxes, environmental fees, storage tank fees, other fees or taxes, general sales tax, and local taxes; (2) The federal excise tax of $1.0066 per pack and local taxes are not included; (3) Rates are those applicable to off-premise sales of 40% alcohol by volume (a.b.v.) distilled spirits in 750ml containers. Local excise taxes are excluded; (4) Rates are those applicable to off-premise sales of 11% a.b.v. non-carbonated wine in 750ml containers; (5) Rates are those applicable to off-premise sales of 4.7% a.b.v. beer in 12 ounce containers.
Source: Tax Foundation, 2025 Facts & Figures: How Does Your State Compare?

State Tax Competitiveness Index

State	Overall Rank	Corporate Tax Rank	Individual Income Tax Rank	Sales Tax Rank	Property Tax Rank	Unemployment Insurance Tax Rank
North Dakota	9	7	17	15	4	12

Note: The Tax Foundation's State Tax Competitiveness Index enables policymakers, taxpayers, and business leaders to gauge how their states' tax systems compare. A rank of 1 is best, 50 is worst. Rankings do not average to the total. States without a tax rank equally as 1. DC's scores and rankings do not affect other states. The report shows tax systems as of July 1, 2024 (the beginning of Fiscal Year 2025).
Source: Tax Foundation, State Tax Competitiveness Index 2025

TRANSPORTATION

Means of Transportation to Work

Area	Car/Truck/Van		Public Transportation			Bicycle	Walked	Other Means	Worked at Home
	Drove Alone	Car-pooled	Bus	Subway	Railroad				
City	78.7	6.6	0.7	0.0	0.1	0.3	3.5	2.0	8.1
MSA[1]	78.5	6.8	0.7	0.0	0.0	0.3	2.8	1.6	9.3
U.S.	70.2	8.5	1.7	1.3	0.4	0.4	2.4	1.6	13.5

Note: Figures are percentages and cover workers 16 years of age and older; (1) Figures cover the Fargo, ND-MN Metropolitan Statistical Area
Source: U.S. Census Bureau, 2019-2023 American Community Survey 5-Year Estimates

Travel Time to Work

Area	Less Than 10 Minutes	10 to 19 Minutes	20 to 29 Minutes	30 to 44 Minutes	45 to 59 Minutes	60 to 89 Minutes	90 Minutes or More
City	20.1	56.1	15.1	4.6	1.5	1.7	0.9
MSA[1]	17.7	51.4	18.0	7.1	2.4	1.9	1.5
U.S.	12.6	28.6	21.2	20.8	8.1	6.0	2.8

Note: Note: Figures are percentages and include workers 16 years old and over; (1) Figures cover the Fargo, ND-MN Metropolitan Statistical Area
Source: U.S. Census Bureau, 2019-2023 American Community Survey 5-Year Estimates

Key Congestion Measures

Measure	2000	2010	2015	2020	2022
Annual Hours of Delay, Total (000)	n/a	n/a	2,648	1,506	2,225
Annual Hours of Delay, Per Auto Commuter	n/a	n/a	15	8	12
Annual Congestion Cost, Per Auto Commuter ($)	n/a	n/a	334	186	260

Note: n/a not available
Source: Texas A&M Transportation Institute, 2023 Urban Mobility Report

Freeway Travel Time Index

Measure	1985	1990	1995	2000	2005	2010	2015	2020	2022
Urban Area Index[1]	n/a	n/a	n/a	n/a	n/a	n/a	1.15	1.04	1.07
Urban Area Rank[1,2]	n/a	n/a	n/a	n/a	n/a	n/a	n/a	n/a	n/a

Note: Freeway Travel Time Index—the ratio of travel time in the peak period to the travel time at free-flow conditions. For example, a value of 1.30 indicates a 20-minute free-flow trip takes 26 minutes in the peak (20 minutes x 1.30 = 26 minutes); (1) Covers the Fargo ND-MN urban area; (2) Rank is based on 101 larger urban areas (#1 = highest travel time index); n/a not available
Source: Texas A&M Transportation Institute, 2023 Urban Mobility Report

Public Transportation

Agency Name / Mode of Transportation	Vehicles Operated in Maximum Service[1]	Annual Unlinked Passenger Trips[2] (in thous.)	Annual Passenger Miles[3] (in thous.)
Fargo Metropolitan Area Transit (MAT)			
Bus (purchased transportation)	24	859.7	2,836.9
Demand Response (purchased transportation)	13	57.5	325.0

Note: (1) Number of revenue vehicles operated by the given mode and type of service to meet the annual maximum service requirement. This is the revenue vehicle count during the peak season of the year; on the week and day that maximum service is provided. Vehicles operated in maximum service (VOMS) exclude atypical days and one-time special events; (2) Number of passengers who boarded public transportation vehicles. Passengers are counted each time they board a vehicle no matter how many vehicles they use to travel from their origin to their destination. (3) Sum of the distances ridden by all passengers during the entire fiscal year.
Source: Federal Transit Administration, National Transit Database, 2023

Air Transportation

Airport Name and Code / Type of Service	Passenger Airlines[1]	Passenger Enplanements	Freight Carriers[2]	Freight (lbs)
Hector International (FAR)				
Domestic service (U.S. carriers only)	13	552,342	6	32,650,130
International service (U.S. carriers only)	2	180	2	1,401,736

Note: (1) Includes all U.S.-based major, minor and commuter airlines that carried at least one passenger during the year; (2) Includes all U.S.-based airlines and freight carriers that transported at least one pound of freight during the year.
Source: Bureau of Transportation Statistics, The Intermodal Transportation Database, Air Carriers: T-100 Domestic Market (U.S. carriers only), 2024; Bureau of Transportation Statistics, The Intermodal Transportation Database, Air Carriers: T-100 International Market (U.S. carriers only), 2024

BUSINESSES

Major Business Headquarters

Company Name	Industry	Rankings Fortune[1]	Forbes[2]
No companies listed	-	-	-

Note: (1) Companies that produce a 10-K are ranked 1 to 500 based on 2023 revenue; (2) All private companies with at least $2 billion in annual revenue through the end of their most current fiscal year are ranked 1 to 275; companies listed are headquartered in the city; dashes indicate no ranking
Source: Fortune, "Fortune 500," 2024; Forbes, "America's Largest Private Companies," 2024

Living Environment

COST OF LIVING

Cost of Living Index

Composite Index	Groceries	Housing	Utilities	Transportation	Health Care	Misc. Goods/Services
97.3	97.9	85.1	80.1	98.8	118.1	108.0

Note: The Cost of Living Index measures regional differences in the cost of consumer goods and services, excluding taxes and non-consumer expenditures, for professional and managerial households in the top income quintile. It is based on more than 50,000 prices covering almost 60 different items for which prices are collected three times a year by chambers of commerce, economic development organizations or university applied economic centers in each participating urban area. The numbers shown should be read as a percentage above or below the national average of 100. For example, a value of 115.4 in the groceries column indicates that grocery prices are 15.4% higher than the national average. Small differences in the index numbers should not be interpreted as significant; Figures cover the Fargo-Moorhead ND-MN urban area.
Source: The Council for Community and Economic Research, Cost of Living Index, 2024

Grocery Prices

Area[1]	T-Bone Steak ($/pound)	Frying Chicken ($/pound)	Whole Milk ($/half gal.)	Eggs ($/dozen)	Orange Juice ($/64 oz.)	Coffee ($/11.5 oz.)
City[2]	15.51	1.46	4.85	3.12	4.28	5.46
Avg.	15.42	1.55	4.69	3.25	4.41	5.46
Min.	14.50	1.16	4.43	2.75	4.00	4.85
Max.	17.56	2.89	5.49	4.78	5.54	7.89

Note: (1) Values for the local area are compared with the average, minimum and maximum values for all 276 areas in the Cost of Living Index; (2) Figures cover the Fargo-Moorhead ND-MN urban area; **T-Bone Steak** (price per pound); **Frying Chicken** (price per pound, whole fryer); **Whole Milk** (half gallon carton); **Eggs** (price per dozen, Grade A, large); **Orange Juice** (64 oz. Tropicana or Florida Natural); **Coffee** (11.5 oz. can, vacuum-packed, Maxwell House, Hills Bros, or Folgers).
Source: The Council for Community and Economic Research, Cost of Living Index, 2024

Housing and Utility Costs

Area[1]	New Home Price ($)	Apartment Rent ($/month)	All Electric ($/month)	Part Electric ($/month)	Other Energy ($/month)	Telephone ($/month)
City[2]	390,066	1,596	-	81.39	58.17	197.46
Avg.	515,975	1,550	210.99	123.07	82.07	194.99
Min.	265,375	692	104.33	53.68	36.26	179.42
Max.	2,775,821	5,719	529.02	397.28	361.63	223.33

Note: (1) Values for the local area are compared with the average, minimum and maximum values for all 276 areas in the Cost of Living Index; (2) Figures cover the Fargo-Moorhead ND-MN urban area; **New Home Price** (2,400 sf living area, 8,000 sf lot, in urban area with full utilities); **Apartment Rent** (950 sf 2 bedroom/1.5 or 2 bath, unfurnished, excluding all utilities except water); **All Electric** (average monthly cost for an all-electric home); **Part Electric** (average monthly cost for a part-electric home); **Other Energy** (average monthly cost for natural gas, fuel oil, coal, wood, and any other forms of energy except electricity); **Telephone** (price includes the base monthly rate plus taxes and fees for three lines of mobile phone service).
Source: The Council for Community and Economic Research, Cost of Living Index, 2024

Health Care, Transportation, and Other Costs

Area[1]	Doctor ($/visit)	Dentist ($/visit)	Optometrist ($/visit)	Gasoline ($/gallon)	Beauty Salon ($/visit)	Men's Shirt ($)
City[2]	230.71	124.67	113.44	3.12	40.47	44.83
Avg.	143.77	117.51	129.23	3.32	48.57	38.14
Min.	36.74	58.67	67.33	2.80	24.00	13.41
Max.	270.44	216.82	307.33	5.28	94.00	63.89

Note: (1) Values for the local area are compared with the average, minimum and maximum values for all 276 areas in the Cost of Living Index; (2) Figures cover the Fargo-Moorhead ND-MN urban area; **Doctor** (general practitioners routine exam of an established patient); **Dentist** (adult teeth cleaning and periodic oral examination); **Optometrist** (full vision eye exam for established adult patient); **Gasoline** (one gallon regular unleaded, national brand, including all taxes, cash price at self-service pump if available); **Beauty Salon** (woman's shampoo, trim, and blow-dry); **Men's Shirt** (cotton/polyester dress shirt, pinpoint weave, long sleeves).
Source: The Council for Community and Economic Research, Cost of Living Index, 2024

HOUSING

Homeownership Rate

Area	2017 (%)	2018 (%)	2019 (%)	2020 (%)	2021 (%)	2022 (%)	2023 (%)	2024 (%)
MSA[1]	n/a	n/a	n/a	n/a	n/a	n/a	n/a	n/a
U.S.	63.9	64.4	64.6	66.6	65.5	65.8	65.9	65.6

Note: (1) Figures cover the Fargo, ND-MN Metropolitan Statistical Area; n/a not available
Source: U.S. Census Bureau, Housing Vacancies and Homeownership Annual Statistics: 2017-2024

House Price Index (HPI)

Area	National Ranking[2]	Quarterly Change (%)	One-Year Change (%)	Five-Year Change (%)	Since 1991Q1 (%)
MSA[1]	214	-1.86	2.52	33.66	292.25
U.S.[3]	–	1.43	4.51	57.13	327.82

Note: The HPI is a weighted repeat sales index. It measures average price changes in repeat sales or refinancings on the same properties. This information is obtained by reviewing repeat mortgage transactions on single-family properties whose mortgages have been purchased or securitized by Fannie Mae or Freddie Mac since January 1975; (1) Figures cover the Fargo, ND-MN Metropolitan Statistical Area; (2) Rankings are based on annual percentage change for all metro areas containing at least 15,000 transactions over the last 10 years and ranges from 1 to 241; (3) figures based on a weighted average of Census Division estimates using a seasonally adjusted, purchase-only index; all figures are for the period ending December 31, 2024
Source: Federal Housing Finance Agency, Change in FHFA Metropolitan Area House Price Indexes, All Transactions Index, 2024Q4

Home Value

Area	Under $100,000	$100,000 -$199,999	$200,000 -$299,999	$300,000 -$399,999	$400,000 -$499,999	$500,000 -$999,999	$1,000,000 or more	Median ($)
City	6.0	16.7	36.1	22.1	9.0	8.7	1.4	269,800
MSA[1]	6.0	16.9	33.8	21.7	10.4	9.8	1.5	276,600
U.S.	12.1	17.8	19.5	14.4	10.5	19.1	6.5	303,400

Note: Figures are percentages except for median and cover owner-occupied housing units; (1) Figures cover the Fargo, ND-MN Metropolitan Statistical Area
Source: U.S. Census Bureau, 2019-2023 American Community Survey 5-Year Estimates

Year Housing Structure Built

Area	2020 or Later	2010 -2019	2000 -2009	1990 -1999	1980 -1989	1970 -1979	1960 -1969	1950 -1959	1940 -1949	Before 1940	Median Year
City	1.3	20.3	14.9	14.5	11.5	13.7	5.8	7.7	2.5	7.9	1991
MSA[1]	1.9	19.2	17.1	13.2	9.8	14.3	6.5	7.4	2.2	8.2	1991
U.S.	1.2	8.9	13.6	12.8	13.0	14.4	10.0	9.7	4.5	11.9	1980

Note: Figures are percentages except for Median Year; Note: (1) Figures cover the Fargo, ND-MN Metropolitan Statistical Area
Source: U.S. Census Bureau, 2019-2023 American Community Survey 5-Year Estimates

Gross Monthly Rent

Area	Under $500	$500 -$999	$1,000 -$1,499	$1,500 -$1,999	$2,000 -$2,499	$2,500 -$2,999	$3,000 and up	Median ($)
City	4.3	56.5	27.7	8.1	1.6	0.7	1.1	916
MSA[1]	4.7	52.7	29.3	9.2	2.5	0.8	0.9	940
U.S.	6.5	22.3	29.5	20.2	10.8	4.8	5.9	1,348

Note: Figures are percentages except for median; Gross rent is the contract rent plus the estimated average monthly cost of utilities (electricity, gas, and water and sewer) and fuels (oil, coal, kerosene, wood, etc.) if these are paid by the renter (or paid for the renter by someone else); (1) Figures cover the Fargo, ND-MN Metropolitan Statistical Area
Source: U.S. Census Bureau, 2019-2023 American Community Survey 5-Year Estimates

HEALTH

Health Risk Factors

Category	MSA[1] (%)	U.S. (%)
Adults aged 18–64 who have any kind of health care coverage	96.0	90.8
Adults who reported being in good or better health	86.3	81.8
Adults who have been told they have high blood cholesterol	34.3	36.9
Adults who have been told they have high blood pressure	28.2	34.0
Adults who are current smokers	12.1	12.1
Adults who currently use e-cigarettes	10.7	7.7
Adults who currently use chewing tobacco, snuff, or snus	3.5	3.2
Adults who are heavy drinkers[2]	6.4	6.1
Adults who are binge drinkers[3]	21.2	15.2
Adults who are overweight (BMI 25.0 - 29.9)	35.4	34.4
Adults who are obese (BMI 30.0 - 99.8)	34.3	34.3
Adults who participated in any physical activities in the past month	81.6	75.8

Note: All figures are crude prevalence; (1) Figures cover the Fargo, ND-MN Metropolitan Statistical Area; (2) Heavy drinkers are classified as adult men having more than 14 drinks per week and adult women having more than 7 drinks per week; (3) Binge drinkers are classified as males having five or more drinks on one occasion or females having four or more drinks on one occasion
Source: Centers for Disease Control and Prevention, Behavioral Risk Factor Surveillance System, SMART: Selected Metropolitan Area Risk Trends, 2023

Acute and Chronic Health Conditions

Category	MSA[1] (%)	U.S. (%)
Adults who have ever been told they had a heart attack	3.6	4.2
Adults who have ever been told they have angina or coronary heart disease	3.3	4.0
Adults who have ever been told they had a stroke	2.0	3.3
Adults who have ever been told they have asthma	13.5	15.7
Adults who have ever been told they have arthritis	22.2	26.3
Adults who have ever been told they have diabetes[2]	8.4	11.5
Adults who have ever been told they had skin cancer	4.2	5.6
Adults who have ever been told they had any other types of cancer	6.6	8.4
Adults who have ever been told they have COPD	4.2	6.4
Adults who have ever been told they have kidney disease	3.5	3.7
Adults who have ever been told they have a form of depression	25.9	22.0

Note: All figures are crude prevalence; (1) Figures cover the Fargo, ND-MN Metropolitan Statistical Area; (2) Figures do not include pregnancy-related, borderline, or pre-diabetes
Source: Centers for Disease Control and Prevention, Behavioral Risk Factor Surveillance System, SMART: Selected Metropolitan Area Risk Trends, 2023

Health Screening and Vaccination Rates

Category	MSA[1] (%)	U.S. (%)
Adults who have ever been tested for HIV	33.8	37.5
Adults who have had their blood cholesterol checked within the last five years	81.9	87.0
Adults aged 65+ who have had flu shot within the past year	68.1	63.4
Adults aged 65+ who have ever had a pneumonia vaccination	74.5	71.9

Note: All figures are crude prevalence; (1) Figures cover the Fargo, ND-MN Metropolitan Statistical Area.
Source: Centers for Disease Control and Prevention, Behavioral Risk Factor Surveillance System, SMART: Selected Metropolitan Area Risk Trends, 2023

Disability Status

Category	MSA[1] (%)	U.S. (%)
Adults who reported being deaf	6.1	7.4
Are you blind or have serious difficulty seeing, even when wearing glasses?	2.8	4.9
Do you have difficulty doing errands alone?	8.0	7.8
Do you have difficulty dressing or bathing?	2.4	3.6
Do you have serious difficulty concentrating/remembering/making decisions?	12.1	13.7
Do you have serious difficulty walking or climbing stairs?	7.8	13.2

Note: All figures are crude prevalence; (1) Figures cover the Fargo, ND-MN Metropolitan Statistical Area.
Source: Centers for Disease Control and Prevention, Behavioral Risk Factor Surveillance System, SMART: Selected Metropolitan Area Risk Trends, 2023

Mortality Rates for the Top 10 Causes of Death in the U.S.

ICD-10[a] Sub-Chapter	ICD-10[a] Code	Crude Mortality Rate[2] per 100,000 population	
		County[3]	U.S.
Malignant neoplasms	C00-C97	129.6	182.7
Ischaemic heart diseases	I20-I25	55.9	109.6
Provisional assignment of new diseases of uncertain etiology[1]	U00-U49	31.6	65.3
Other forms of heart disease	I30-I51	47.3	65.1
Other degenerative diseases of the nervous system	G30-G31	39.4	52.4
Other external causes of accidental injury	W00-X59	41.2	52.3
Cerebrovascular diseases	I60-I69	30.4	49.1
Chronic lower respiratory diseases	J40-J47	26.1	43.5
Hypertensive diseases	I10-I15	19.6	38.9
Organic, including symptomatic, mental disorders	F01-F09	27.4	33.9

Note: (a) ICD-10 = International Classification of Diseases 10th Revision; (1) Includes COVID-19, adverse effects to COVID-19 vaccines, SARS, and vaping-related disorders; (2) Crude mortality rates are a three-year average covering 2021-2023; (3) Figures cover Cass County.
Source: Centers for Disease Control and Prevention, National Center for Health Statistics. National Vital Statistics System, Mortality 2018-2023 on CDC WONDER Online Database

Mortality Rates for Selected Causes of Death

Cause of Death	ICD-10[a] Code	Crude Mortality Rate[1] per 100,000 population	
		County[2]	U.S.
Accidental poisoning and exposure to noxious substances	X40-X49	15.6	30.5
Alzheimer disease	G30	28.3	35.4
Assault	X85-Y09	Unreliable	7.3
COVID-19	U07.1	31.6	65.3
Diabetes mellitus	E10-E14	15.5	30.0
Diseases of the liver	K70-K76	16.3	20.8
Human immunodeficiency virus (HIV) disease	B20-B24	Suppressed	1.5
Influenza and pneumonia	J09-J18	9.4	13.4
Intentional self-harm	X60-X84	15.6	14.7
Malnutrition	E40-E46	5.2	6.0
Obesity and other hyperalimentation	E65-E68	9.6	3.1
Renal failure	N17-N19	7.6	16.4
Transport accidents	V01-V99	6.6	14.4

Note: (a) ICD-10 = International Classification of Diseases 10th Revision; (1) Crude mortality rates are a three-year average covering 2021-2023; (2) Figures cover Cass County; Data are suppressed when the data meet the criteria for confidentiality constraints; Crude mortality rates are flagged as unreliable when the rate would be calculated with a numerator of 20 or less.
Source: Centers for Disease Control and Prevention, National Center for Health Statistics. National Vital Statistics System, Mortality 2018-2023 on CDC WONDER Online Database

Health Insurance Coverage

Area	With Health Insurance	With Private Health Insurance	With Public Health Insurance	Without Health Insurance	Population Under Age 19 Without Health Insurance
City	93.9	79.5	26.0	6.1	4.5
MSA[1]	94.8	80.6	25.8	5.2	4.2
U.S.	91.4	67.3	36.3	8.6	5.4

Note: Figures are percentages that cover the civilian noninstitutionalized population; (1) Figures cover the Fargo, ND-MN Metropolitan Statistical Area
Source: U.S. Census Bureau, 2019-2023 American Community Survey 5-Year Estimates

Number of Medical Professionals

Area	MDs[3]	DOs[3,4]	Dentists	Podiatrists	Chiropractors	Optometrists
County[1] (number)	774	51	154	10	149	66
County[1] (rate[2])	401.6	26.5	78.4	5.1	75.9	33.6
U.S. (rate[2])	302.5	29.2	74.6	6.4	29.5	18.0

Note: Data as of 2023 unless noted; (1) Data covers Cass County; (2) Number of medical professionals per 100,000 population; (3) Data as of 2022 and includes all active, non-federal physicians; (4) Doctor of Osteopathic Medicine
Source: U.S. Department of Health and Human Services, Health Resources and Services Administration, Bureau of Health Professions, Area Resource File (ARF) 2023-2024

EDUCATION

Public School District Statistics

District Name	Schls	Pupils	Pupil/ Teacher Ratio	Minority Pupils[1] (%)	Total Rev. per Pupil ($)	Total Exp. per Pupil ($)
Fargo 1	26	11,484	12.0	34.6	18,923	18,379

Note: Table includes school districts with 2,000 or more students; (1) Percentage of students that are not non-Hispanic white.
Source: U.S. Department of Education, National Center for Education Statistics, Common Core of Data, Local Education Agency (School District) Universe Survey: School Year 2023-2024; U.S. Department of Education, National Center for Education Statistics, Common Core of Data, School District Finance Survey (F-33): School Year 2021–22

Highest Level of Education

Area	Less than H.S.	H.S. Diploma	Some College, No Deg.	Associate Degree	Bachelor's Degree	Master's Degree	Prof. School Degree	Doctorate Degree
City	4.7	18.7	20.7	12.7	29.0	9.9	2.0	2.3
MSA[1]	4.4	19.1	20.8	13.5	28.4	9.7	1.9	2.3
U.S.	10.6	26.2	19.4	8.8	21.3	9.8	2.3	1.6

Note: Figures cover persons age 25 and over; (1) Figures cover the Fargo, ND-MN Metropolitan Statistical Area
Source: U.S. Census Bureau, 2019-2023 American Community Survey 5-Year Estimates

Educational Attainment by Race

Area	High School Graduate or Higher (%)					Bachelor's Degree or Higher (%)				
	Total	White	Black	Asian	Hisp.[2]	Total	White	Black	Asian	Hisp.[2]
City	95.3	96.6	82.3	87.0	95.2	43.2	44.3	20.1	69.9	31.7
MSA[1]	95.6	96.6	84.7	88.7	89.2	42.2	43.0	24.6	67.9	30.1
U.S.	89.4	92.9	88.1	88.0	72.5	35.0	37.7	24.7	57.0	19.9

Note: Figures shown cover persons 25 years old and over; (1) Figures cover the Fargo, ND-MN Metropolitan Statistical Area; (2) People of Hispanic origin can be of any race
Source: U.S. Census Bureau, 2019-2023 American Community Survey 5-Year Estimates

School Enrollment by Grade and Control

Area	Preschool (%)		Kindergarten (%)		Grades 1 - 4 (%)		Grades 5 - 8 (%)		Grades 9 - 12 (%)	
	Public	Private	Public	Private	Public	Private	Public	Private	Public	Private
City	46.4	53.6	89.8	10.2	91.9	8.1	92.1	7.9	94.3	5.7
MSA[1]	65.0	35.0	90.0	10.0	89.1	10.9	90.7	9.3	91.7	8.3
U.S.	58.7	41.3	85.2	14.8	87.2	12.8	87.9	12.1	89.0	11.0

Note: Figures shown cover persons 3 years old and over; (1) Figures cover the Fargo, ND-MN Metropolitan Statistical Area
Source: U.S. Census Bureau, 2019-2023 American Community Survey 5-Year Estimates

Higher Education

Four-Year Colleges			Two-Year Colleges			Medical Schools[1]	Law Schools[2]	Voc/ Tech[3]
Public	Private Non-profit	Private For-profit	Public	Private Non-profit	Private For-profit			
2	1	1	0	0	1	0	0	2

Note: Figures cover institutions located within the Fargo, ND-MN Metropolitan Statistical Area and include main campuses only; (1) includes schools accredited by the Liaison Committee on Medical Education and the American Osteopathic Association's Commission on Osteopathic College Accreditation; (2) includes ABA-accredited schools, schools with provisional ABA accreditation, and state accredited schools; (3) includes all schools with programs that are less than 2 years.
Source: National Center for Education Statistics, Integrated Postsecondary Education System (IPEDS), 2023-24; Wikipedia, List of Medical Schools in the United States, accessed May 2, 2025; Wikipedia, List of Law Schools in the United States, accessed May 2, 2025

EMPLOYERS

Major Employers

Company Name	Industry
BlueCross BlueShield of North Dakota	Insurance
City of Fargo	Municipal government
CNH Industrial America	Agriculture equipment
Concordia College	Education
Essentia Health	General medical & surgical hospitals
Fargo Public School District	Education
John Deere Electronic Solutions	Manufacturers
Microsoft	Computer software
Minnesota State University Moorhead	Education
Moorhead Area Public Schools	Education
Noridian Heathcare Solutions	Insurance
North Dakota State University	Education
Sanford Fargo Medical Center	Healthcare services
U.S. Bank	Financial services
Veterans Affairs	General medical & surgical hospitals
West Fargo Public School	Education

Note: Companies shown are located within the Fargo, ND-MN Metropolitan Statistical Area.
Source: Chambers of Commerce; State Departments of Labor; Wikipedia

Best Companies to Work For

Noridian Healthcare Solutions, headquartered in Fargo, is among the "Best Places to Work in IT." To qualify, companies had to have a minimum of 100 total employees and five IT employees. The best places to work were selected based on DEI (diversity, equity, and inclusion) practices; IT turnover, promotions, and growth; IT retention and engagement programs; remote/hybrid working; benefits and perks (such as elder care and child care, flextime, and reimbursement for college tuition); and training and career development opportunities. *Computerworld, "Best Places to Work in IT," 2025*

Fargo, North Dakota

PUBLIC SAFETY

Crime Rate

Area	Total Crime Rate	Violent Crime Rate				Property Crime Rate		
		Murder	Rape	Robbery	Aggrav. Assault	Burglary	Larceny-Theft	Motor Vehicle Theft
City	4,394.2	1.5	71.5	75.2	367.2	768.6	2,690.1	420.1
U.S.	2,290.9	5.7	38.0	66.5	264.1	250.7	1,347.2	318.7

Note: Figures are crimes per 100,000 population.
Source: FBI, Table 8, Offenses Known to Law Enforcement, by State by City, 2023

Hate Crimes

Area	Number of Quarters Reported	Number of Incidents per Bias Motivation					
		Race/Ethnicity/Ancestry	Religion	Sexual Orientation	Disability	Gender	Gender Identity
City	4	0	0	0	0	0	0
U.S.	4	5,900	2,699	2,077	187	92	492

Source: Federal Bureau of Investigation, Hate Crime Statistics 2023

Identity Theft Consumer Reports

Area	Reports	Reports per 100,000 Population	Rank[2]
MSA[1]	378	148	275
U.S.	1,135,291	339	-

Note: (1) Figures cover the Fargo, ND-MN Metropolitan Statistical Area; (2) Rank ranges from 1 to 401 where 1 indicates greatest number of identity theft reports per 100,000 population
Source: Federal Trade Commission, Consumer Sentinel Network Data Book 2024

Fraud and Other Consumer Reports

Area	Reports	Reports per 100,000 Population	Rank[2]
MSA[1]	2,183	856	294
U.S.	5,360,641	1,601	-

Note: (1) Figures cover the Fargo, ND-MN Metropolitan Statistical Area; (2) Rank ranges from 1 to 401 where 1 indicates greatest number of fraud and other consumer reports per 100,000 population
Source: Federal Trade Commission, Consumer Sentinel Network Data Book 2024

POLITICS

2024 Presidential Election Results

Area	Trump (Rep.)	Harris (Dem.)	Stein (Green)	Kennedy (Ind.)	Oliver (Lib.)	Other
Cass County	52.7	44.4	0.0	0.0	1.8	1.1
U.S.	49.7	48.2	0.6	0.5	0.4	0.6

Note: Results are percentages and may not add to 100% due to rounding
Source: Dave Leip's Atlas of U.S. Presidential Elections

SPORTS

Professional Sports Teams

Team Name	League	Year Established

No teams are located in the metro area
Source: Wikipedia, Major Professional Sports Teams of the United States and Canada, May 1, 2025

CLIMATE

Average and Extreme Temperatures

Temperature	Jan	Feb	Mar	Apr	May	Jun	Jul	Aug	Sep	Oct	Nov	Dec	Yr.
Extreme High (°F)	52	66	78	100	98	100	106	106	102	93	74	57	106
Average High (°F)	15	21	34	54	69	77	83	81	70	57	36	21	52
Average Temp. (°F)	6	12	26	43	56	66	71	69	58	46	28	13	41
Average Low (°F)	-3	3	17	32	44	54	59	57	46	35	19	4	31
Extreme Low (°F)	-36	-34	-34	-7	20	30	36	33	19	5	-24	-32	-36

Note: Figures cover the years 1948-1995
Source: National Climatic Data Center, International Station Meteorological Climate Summary, 9/96

Average Precipitation/Snowfall/Humidity

Precip./Humidity	Jan	Feb	Mar	Apr	May	Jun	Jul	Aug	Sep	Oct	Nov	Dec	Yr.
Avg. Precip. (in.)	0.6	0.5	1.0	1.7	2.3	3.1	3.2	2.4	1.8	1.5	0.8	0.6	19.6
Avg. Snowfall (in.)	9	6	7	3	Tr	0	0	0	Tr	1	6	7	40
Avg. Rel. Hum. 6am (%)	75	77	82	79	77	82	86	86	85	80	81	78	81
Avg. Rel. Hum. 3pm (%)	70	71	67	51	45	50	50	47	49	51	65	73	57

Note: Figures cover the years 1948-1995; Tr = Trace amounts (<0.05 in. of rain; <0.5 in. of snow)
Source: National Climatic Data Center, International Station Meteorological Climate Summary, 9/96

Weather Conditions

Temperature			Daytime Sky			Precipitation		
5°F & below	32°F & below	90°F & above	Clear	Partly cloudy	Cloudy	0.01 inch or more precip.	0.1 inch or more snow/ice	Thunderstorms
65	180	15	81	145	139	100	38	31

Note: Figures are average number of days per year and cover the years 1948-1995
Source: National Climatic Data Center, International Station Meteorological Climate Summary, 9/96

HAZARDOUS WASTE

Superfund Sites

The Fargo, ND-MN metro area has no sites on the EPA's Superfund Final National Priorities List (NPL) or Superfund Alternative Approach (SAA) list. The Superfund alternative approach uses the same investigation and cleanup process and standards that are used for sites listed on the National Priorities List. The SAA is an alternative to listing a site on the NPL; it is not an alternative to Superfund or the Superfund process. There are a total of 1,445 Superfund sites with a status of proposed or final on both lists in the United States. *U.S. Environmental Protection Agency, National Priorities List, May 1, 2025; U.S. Environmental Protection Agency, Superfund Alternative Approach Sites, May 1, 2025*

AIR QUALITY

Air Quality Trends: Ozone

	1990	1995	2000	2005	2010	2015	2020	2021	2022	2023
MSA[1]	n/a	n/a	n/a	n/a	n/a	n/a	n/a	n/a	n/a	n/a
U.S.	0.087	0.089	0.081	0.080	0.072	0.068	0.066	0.067	0.067	0.070

Note: (1) Data covers the Fargo, ND-MN Metropolitan Statistical Area; n/a not available. The values shown are the composite ozone concentration averages among trend sites based on the highest fourth daily maximum 8-hour concentration in parts per million. These trends are based on sites having an adequate record of monitoring data during the trend period. Data from exceptional events are included.
Source: U.S. Environmental Protection Agency, Air Quality Monitoring Information, "Air Quality Trends by City, 1990-2023"

Air Quality Index

Area	Percent of Days when Air Quality was...[2]					AQI Statistics[2]	
	Good	Moderate	Unhealthy for Sensitive Groups	Unhealthy	Very Unhealthy	Maximum	Median
MSA[1]	50.3	46.4	2.8	0.6	0.0	175	50

Note: (1) Data covers the Fargo, ND-MN Metropolitan Statistical Area; (2) Based on 358 days with AQI data in 2023. Air Quality Index (AQI) is an index for reporting daily air quality. EPA calculates the AQI for five major air pollutants regulated by the Clean Air Act: ground-level ozone, particle pollution (aka particulate matter), carbon monoxide, sulfur dioxide, and nitrogen dioxide. The AQI runs from 0 to 500. The higher the AQI value, the greater the level of air pollution and the greater the health concern. There are six AQI categories: "Good" AQI is between 0 and 50. Air quality is considered satisfactory; "Moderate" AQI is between 51 and 100. Air quality is acceptable; "Unhealthy for Sensitive Groups" When AQI values are between 101 and 150, members of sensitive groups may experience health effects; "Unhealthy" When AQI values are between 151 and 200 everyone may begin to experience health effects; "Very Unhealthy" AQI values between 201 and 300 trigger a health alert; "Hazardous" AQI values over 300 trigger warnings of emergency conditions (not shown).
Source: U.S. Environmental Protection Agency, Air Quality Index Report, 2023

Air Quality Index Pollutants

Area	Percent of Days when AQI Pollutant was...[2]					
	Carbon Monoxide	Nitrogen Dioxide	Ozone	Sulfur Dioxide	Particulate Matter 2.5	Particulate Matter 10
MSA[1]	0.0	0.3	31.3	(3)	68.4	0.0

Note: (1) Data covers the Fargo, ND-MN Metropolitan Statistical Area; (2) Based on 358 days with AQI data in 2023. The Air Quality Index (AQI) is an index for reporting daily air quality. EPA calculates the AQI for five major air pollutants regulated by the Clean Air Act: ground-level ozone, particle pollution (also known as particulate matter), carbon monoxide, sulfur dioxide, and nitrogen dioxide. The AQI runs from 0 to 500. The higher the AQI value, the greater the level of air pollution and the greater the health concern; (3) Sulfur dioxide is no longer included in this table because SO_2 concentrations tend to be very localized and not necessarily representative of broad geographical areas like counties and CBSAs.
Source: U.S. Environmental Protection Agency, Air Quality Index Report, 2023

Maximum Air Pollutant Concentrations: Particulate Matter, Ozone, CO and Lead

	Particulate Matter 10 (ug/m³)	Particulate Matter 2.5 Wtd AM (ug/m³)	Particulate Matter 2.5 24-Hr (ug/m³)	Ozone (ppm)	Carbon Monoxide (ppm)	Lead (ug/m³)
MSA¹ Level	n/a	11.5	39	0.07	n/a	n/a
NAAQS²	150	15	35	0.075	9	0.15
Met NAAQS²	n/a	Yes	No	Yes	n/a	n/a

Note: (1) Data covers the Fargo, ND-MN Metropolitan Statistical Area; Data from exceptional events are included; (2) National Ambient Air Quality Standards; ppm = parts per million; ug/m³ = micrograms per cubic meter; n/a not available.
Concentrations: Particulate Matter 10 (coarse particulate)—highest second maximum 24-hour concentration; Particulate Matter 2.5 Wtd AM (fine particulate)—highest weighted annual mean concentration; Particulate Matter 2.5 24-Hour (fine particulate)—highest 98th percentile 24-hour concentration; Ozone—highest fourth daily maximum 8-hour concentration; Carbon Monoxide—highest second maximum non-overlapping 8-hour concentration; Lead—maximum running 3-month average
Source: U.S. Environmental Protection Agency, Air Quality Monitoring Information, "Air Quality Statistics by City, 2023"

Maximum Air Pollutant Concentrations: Nitrogen Dioxide and Sulfur Dioxide

	Nitrogen Dioxide AM (ppb)	Nitrogen Dioxide 1-Hr (ppb)	Sulfur Dioxide AM (ppb)	Sulfur Dioxide 1-Hr (ppb)	Sulfur Dioxide 24-Hr (ppb)
MSA¹ Level	4	n/a	n/a	3	n/a
NAAQS²	53	100	30	75	140
Met NAAQS²	Yes	n/a	n/a	Yes	n/a

Note: (1) Data covers the Fargo, ND-MN Metropolitan Statistical Area; Data from exceptional events are included; (2) National Ambient Air Quality Standards; ppm = parts per million; ug/m³ = micrograms per cubic meter; n/a not available.
Concentrations: Nitrogen Dioxide AM—highest arithmetic mean concentration; Nitrogen Dioxide 1-Hr—highest 98th percentile 1-hour daily maximum concentration; Sulfur Dioxide AM—highest annual mean concentration; Sulfur Dioxide 1-Hr—highest 99th percentile 1-hour daily maximum concentration; Sulfur Dioxide 24-Hr—highest second maximum 24-hour concentration
Source: U.S. Environmental Protection Agency, Air Quality Monitoring Information, "Air Quality Statistics by City, 2023"

Fort Wayne, Indiana

Background

Fort Wayne lies 100 miles northeast of Indianapolis, at the confluence of the St. Mary and St. Joseph rivers, which form the Maumee River. The waters, spanned by 21 bridges, divide the city into three parts.

Once the stronghold of the Miami Native American tribe, the area was prominent in frontier history. The Miami ruled the lower peninsula region, fighting against the Iroquois who were armed by the English colonists. Later, the Miami tribe established itself in the Wabash Valley and built a village at the Lakeside district in Fort Wayne. They continued to side with the British during the American Revolution, after which President Washington ordered armies into the center of the Miami Territory to stop the Miami war parties, which was encouraged by the British to attack the new nation. After Chief Little Turtle, one of the most feared and respected tribal leaders, defeated the army of General Arthur St. Clair, Washington sought the help of General "Mad" Anthony Wayne, who succeeded in defeating the rebellious tribes. Wayne marched on Miamitown and built the first American fort there. When the fort was turned over to Colonel John Hamtramck on October 21, 1794, the colonel immediately changed the name to Fort Wayne.

Fort Wayne's industrial growth began with the building of the Wabash and Erie Canal in the 1830s and was further stimulated in the 1850s when the railroad reached the region.

Nearly equidistant from Chicago, Cincinnati, and Detroit, the city is a regional transportation and communications center. Although rich in dairy, livestock, and vegetable farming, it is primarily a diversified industrial center, with several strong clusters of industry including advanced manufacturing, defense engineering, automotive-related development and production (home to the world's first full-size hybrid pickup truck), life science, higher education, aerospace/avionics-related, logistics and finance. Fort Wayne also enjoys additional prosperity due to its proximity to Warsaw, Indiana, termed the Orthopedic Capitol of the World due to its many orthopedic-implant manufacturers.

Institutions of higher education in the city include Indiana's Institute of Technology, Indiana University-Purdue University at Fort Wayne, and University of St. Francis. The city is also home to the Northeast Indiana Innovation Center, designed to attract high-tech businesses and provide community outreach to local entrepreneurs and schools. Ongoing projects include the Core Incubation System, which specializes in biomedical, information systems, and advanced manufacturing plans, and the Digital Kids Initiative, which promotes early mastery of digital skills. The city has developed a blueprint for preservation and restoration of various downtown districts, including the Landing District, the Old Canal District, and the Barr Street District, which features an "International Marketplace," a diverse group of businesses representing a variety of ethnicities and cultural centers serving them.

Fort Wayne is sometimes referred to as the "City of Churches," an unofficial moniker dating to the late-19th century when the city was the regional hub of Catholic, Lutheran, and Episcopal faiths. Today, there are over 350 churches in the city.

Parkview Field is home to the TinCaps, baseball's minor league team affiliated with the San Diego Padres. Not far from Parkview Field are condominiums, shops and a centrally located Courtyard Marriott hotel. Fort Wayne's Grand Wayne Convention Center encompasses 225,000 square feet.

Fort Wayne's varied cultural and educational attractions combined with a low cost of living continue to earn Fort Wayne many "best of" awards. Arts events are held at the Allen County War Memorial Coliseum, Foellinger Outdoor Theater, and IPFW Performing Arts Center. Additional attractions include the Foellinger-Freimann Botanical Conservatory with a Tropical House and cascading waterfall; Sonoran Desert House; Woody the talking tree and exhibit; Fort Wayne Museum of Art; the nationally acclaimed Fort Wayne Children's Zoo; and Lincoln Museum with its award-winning exhibit honoring the life and legacy of our 16th president.

The land surrounding the city is generally level to the south and east, rolling to the west and southwest, and quite hilly to the north and northwest. The climate is influenced by the Great Lakes, with rain constant throughout the warmer months. Damaging hailstorms occur approximately twice a year, and severe flooding is possible. While snow generally covers the ground for about a month during the winter, heavy snowstorms are infrequent. Except for considerable cloudiness during the winter, Fort Wayne enjoys a good Midwestern average for sunshine.

Rankings

General Rankings

- To help military veterans find the best places in which to settle down, *WalletHub* compared the 100 largest U.S. cities across 19 key indicators of livability, affordability and veteran-friendliness. They range from the share of military skill-related jobs to veteran income growth to the availability of VA health facilities. Fort Wayne ranked #89. *Wallethub.com, "Best & Worst Places for Veterans to Live (2025)," November 7, 2024*

- *US News & World Report* conducted a survey of more than 3,500 people and analyzed the 150 largest metropolitan areas to determine what matters most when selecting the next place to live. Fort Wayne ranked #20 out of the top 25 as having the best combination of desirable factors. Criteria: cost of living; quality of life and education; climate; job market; desirability; and other factors. *realestate.usnews.com, "Best Places to Live in the U.S. in 2024-2025," May 21, 2024*

- *Insider* listed 23 places in the U.S. that travel industry trends reveal would be popular destinations in 2023. This year the list trends towards cultural and historical happenings, sports events, wellness experiences and invigorating outdoor escapes. According to the website insider.com Fort Wayne is a place to visit in 2023. *Insider, "23 of the Best Places You Should Travel to in the U.S. in 2023," December 17, 2022*

Business/Finance Rankings

- The Fort Wayne metro area appeared on the Milken Institute "2025 Best Performing Cities" list. Rank: #147 out of 200 large metro areas (based on performance category). Criteria: job growth; wage growth; high-tech growth and impact; community resilience; housing affordability; household broadband access. *Milken Institute, "Best-Performing Cities 2025," January 14, 2025*

Education Rankings

- Personal finance website *WalletHub* analyzed the 150 largest U.S. metropolitan statistical areas to determine where the most educated Americans are putting their degrees to work. Criteria: education levels; percentage of workers with degrees; education quality and attainment gap; public school quality rankings; quality and enrollment of each metro area's universities. Fort Wayne was ranked #112 (#1 = most educated city). *WalletHub.com, "Most & Least Educated Cities in America, 2025" July 2, 2024*

Health/Fitness Rankings

- For each of the 100 largest cities in the United States, the American Fitness Index®, compiled in partnership between the American College of Sports Medicine and the Elevance Health Foundation, evaluated community infrastructure and more than 30 health behaviors including preventive health, levels of chronic disease conditions, food insecurity, pedestrian safety, air quality, and community/environment resources that support physical activity. Fort Wayne ranked #83 for "community fitness." *americanfitnessindex.org, "2024 ACSM American Fitness Index Summary Report," July 23, 2024*

- The Fort Wayne metro area was identified as one of the worst cities for bed bugs in America by pest control company Orkin. The area ranked #40 out of 50 based on the number of bed bug treatments Orkin performed from December 2022 to November 2023. *Orkin, "Chicago Joins Paris In Global Bed Bug Spotlight Ranking As The Worst City On Orkin's U.S. Bed Bug Cities List," January 22, 2024*

Real Estate Rankings

- *WalletHub* compared the most populated U.S. cities to determine which had the best markets for real estate agents. Fort Wayne ranked #86 where demand was high and pay was the best. Criteria: sales per agent; annual median wage for real-estate agents; monthly average starting salary for real estate agents; real estate job density and competition; unemployment rate; home turnover rate; housing-market health index; and other relevant metrics. *WalletHub.com, "2021 Best Places to Be a Real Estate Agent," May 12, 2021*

- Fort Wayne was ranked #28 out of 176 metro areas in terms of cost of housing in 2024 by the National Association of Home Builders (#1 = most affordable). Criteria: the portion of an average family's income necessary to pay the mortgage on a median-priced home. *National Association of Home Builders®, NAHB-Wells Fargo Cost of Housing Index, 4th Quarter 2024*

Women/Minorities Rankings

- Personal finance website *WalletHub* compared more than 180 U.S. cities across two key dimensions, "Hispanic Business-Friendliness" and "Hispanic Purchasing Power," to arrive at the most favorable conditions for Hispanic entrepreneurs. Fort Wayne was ranked #151 out of 182. Criteria includes: share of Hispanic-Owned Businesses; average growth of Hispanic Business revenues; Small Business-Friendliness score; affordability; and number of Hispanics with at least a bachelor's degree. *WalletHub.com, "Best Cities for Hispanic Entrepreneurs," September 4, 2024*

Miscellaneous Rankings

- *WalletHub* compared 148 of the most populated U.S. cities to determine their operating efficiency. A "Quality of Services" score was constructed for each city and then measured against the total budget per capita to reveal which were managed the best. Fort Wayne ranked #8. Criteria: financial stability; economy; education; safety; health; infrastructure and pollution. *WalletHub.com, "2025's Best- & Worst-Run Cities in America," June 18, 2024*

Business Environment

DEMOGRAPHICS

Population Growth

Area	1990 Census	2000 Census	2010 Census	2020 Census	2023 Estimate[2]	Population Growth 1990-2023 (%)
City	205,671	205,727	253,691	263,886	266,235	29.4
MSA[1]	354,435	390,156	416,257	419,601	451,440	27.4
U.S.	248,709,873	281,421,906	308,745,538	331,449,281	332,387,540	33.6

Note: (1) Figures cover the Fort Wayne, IN Metropolitan Statistical Area; (2) 2019-2023 5-year ACS population estimate
Source: U.S. Census Bureau, 1990 Census, 2000 Census, 2010 Census, 2020 Census, 2019-2023 American Community Survey 5-Year Estimates

Race

Area	White Alone[2] (%)	Black Alone[2] (%)	Asian Alone[2] (%)	AIAN[3] Alone[2] (%)	NHOPI[4] Alone[2] (%)	Other Race Alone[2] (%)	Two or More Races (%)
City	66.4	14.6	5.8	0.4	0.0	4.3	8.4
MSA[1]	75.6	9.5	4.3	0.3	0.0	3.2	7.1
U.S.	63.4	12.4	5.8	0.9	0.2	6.6	10.7

Note: (1) Figures cover the Fort Wayne, IN Metropolitan Statistical Area; (2) Alone is defined as not being in combination with one or more other races; (3) American Indian and Alaska Native; (4) Native Hawaiian and Other Pacific Islander
Source: U.S. Census Bureau, 2019-2023 American Community Survey 5-Year Estimates

Hispanic or Latino Origin

Area	Total (%)	Mexican (%)	Puerto Rican (%)	Cuban (%)	Other (%)
City	10.5	7.7	0.7	0.1	2.2
MSA[1]	8.0	5.7	0.6	0.1	1.7
U.S.	19.0	11.3	1.8	0.7	5.2

Note: Persons of Hispanic or Latino origin can be of any race; (1) Figures cover the Fort Wayne, IN Metropolitan Statistical Area
Source: U.S. Census Bureau, 2019-2023 American Community Survey 5-Year Estimates

Age

Area	Percent of Population									Median Age
	Under Age 5	Age 5–19	Age 20–34	Age 35–44	Age 45–54	Age 55–64	Age 65–74	Age 75–84	Age 85+	
City	7.0	20.0	22.9	12.5	11.4	11.3	8.8	4.1	2.0	35.0
MSA[1]	6.7	21.0	20.2	12.6	11.7	12.1	9.5	4.3	1.9	36.8
U.S.	5.7	19.1	20.2	13.1	12.3	12.8	10.0	4.9	1.9	38.7

Note: (1) Figures cover the Fort Wayne, IN Metropolitan Statistical Area
Source: U.S. Census Bureau, 2019-2023 American Community Survey 5-Year Estimates

Disability by Age

Area	All Ages	Under 18 Years Old	18 to 64 Years Old	65 Years and Over
City	13.6	5.3	12.5	32.5
MSA[1]	12.4	4.7	11.1	30.4
U.S.	13.0	4.7	10.7	32.9

Note: Figures show percent of the civilian noninstitutionalized population that reported having a disability. Disability status is determined from six types of difficulty: vision, hearing, cognitive, ambulatory, self-care, and independent living. For children under 5 years old, hearing and vision difficulty are used to determine disability status. For children between the ages of 5 and 14, disability status is determined from hearing, vision, cognitive, ambulatory, and self-care difficulties. For people aged 15 years and older, they are considered to have a disability if they have difficulty with any one of the six difficulty types; Note: (1) Figures cover the Fort Wayne, IN Metropolitan Statistical Area
Source: U.S. Census Bureau, 2019-2023 American Community Survey 5-Year Estimates

Ancestry

Area	German	Irish	English	American	Italian	Polish	French[2]	European	Scottish
City	22.5	9.0	9.2	5.0	2.1	1.9	2.4	2.3	1.9
MSA[1]	26.1	9.0	9.8	5.8	2.2	2.0	2.8	2.6	1.8
U.S.	12.6	9.4	9.1	5.5	4.9	2.6	2.0	1.6	1.6

Note: Figures are the percentage of the total population reporting a particular ancestry. The nine most commonly reported ancestries in the U.S. are shown. Figures include multiple ancestries (e.g. if a person reported being Irish and Italian, they were included in both columns); (1) Figures cover the Fort Wayne, IN Metropolitan Statistical Area; (2) Excludes Basque
Source: U.S. Census Bureau, 2019-2023 American Community Survey 5-Year Estimates

Foreign-born Population

Area	Percent of Population Born in								
	Any Foreign Country	Asia	Mexico	Europe	Caribbean	Central America[2]	South America	Africa	Canada
City	9.0	4.4	2.1	0.5	0.2	1.0	0.2	0.5	0.2
MSA[1]	6.9	3.3	1.4	0.5	0.1	0.7	0.2	0.4	0.2
U.S.	13.9	4.3	3.3	1.4	1.4	1.2	1.2	0.8	0.2

Note: (1) Figures cover the Fort Wayne, IN Metropolitan Statistical Area; (2) Excludes Mexico.
Source: U.S. Census Bureau, 2019-2023 American Community Survey 5-Year Estimates

Household Size

Area	Persons in Household (%)							Average Household Size
	One	Two	Three	Four	Five	Six	Seven or More	
City	33.5	33.1	13.3	10.7	5.4	2.5	1.4	2.39
MSA[1]	29.7	34.7	13.4	11.7	6.1	2.7	1.6	2.48
U.S.	28.5	33.8	15.4	12.7	5.9	2.3	1.4	2.54

Note: (1) Figures cover the Fort Wayne, IN Metropolitan Statistical Area
Source: U.S. Census Bureau, 2019-2023 American Community Survey 5-Year Estimates

Household Relationships

Area	Householder	Opposite-sex Spouse	Same-sex Spouse	Opposite-sex Unmarried Partner	Same-sex Unmarried Partner	Child[2]	Grandchild	Other Relatives	Non-relatives
City	40.7	15.6	0.2	3.1	0.2	29.7	2.0	3.4	3.0
MSA[1]	39.5	18.0	0.2	2.7	0.1	30.5	1.9	2.9	2.5
U.S.	38.3	17.5	0.2	2.5	0.2	28.3	2.4	4.8	3.4

Note: Figures are percent of the total population; (1) Figures cover the Fort Wayne, IN Metropolitan Statistical Area; (2) Includes biological, adopted, and stepchildren of the householder
Source: U.S. Census Bureau, 2020 Census

Gender

Area	Males	Females	Males per 100 Females
City	129,959	136,276	95.4
MSA[1]	222,504	228,936	97.2
U.S.	164,545,087	167,842,453	98.0

Note: (1) Figures cover the Fort Wayne, IN Metropolitan Statistical Area
Source: U.S. Census Bureau, 2019-2023 American Community Survey 5-Year Estimates

Marital Status

Area	Never Married	Now Married[2]	Separated	Widowed	Divorced
City	37.2	42.9	1.5	5.9	12.5
MSA[1]	31.8	49.9	1.3	5.5	11.5
U.S.	34.1	47.9	1.7	5.6	10.7

Note: Figures are percentages and cover the population 15 years of age and older; (1) Figures cover the Fort Wayne, IN Metropolitan Statistical Area; (2) Excludes separated
Source: U.S. Census Bureau, 2019-2023 American Community Survey 5-Year Estimates

Religious Groups by Family

Area	Catholic	Baptist	Methodist	LDS[2]	Pentecostal	Lutheran	Islam	Adventist	Other
MSA[1]	13.1	8.1	3.9	0.4	1.1	7.1	1.0	0.9	17.6
U.S.	18.7	7.3	3.0	2.0	1.8	1.7	1.3	1.3	11.6

Note: Figures are the number of adherents as a percentage of the total population and cover the eight largest religious groups in the U.S; (1) Figures cover the Fort Wayne, IN Metropolitan Statistical Area; (2) Church of Jesus Christ of Latter-day Saints
Sources: 2020 U.S. Religion Census, Association of Statisticians of American Religious Bodies; The Association of Religion Data Archives (ARDA)

Religious Groups by Tradition

Area	Catholic	Evangelical Protestant	Mainline Protestant	Black Protestant	Islam	Judaism	Hinduism	Orthodox	Buddhism
MSA[1]	13.1	24.7	6.1	6.5	1.0	0.1	0.1	0.2	0.4
U.S.	18.7	16.5	5.2	2.3	1.3	0.6	0.4	0.4	0.3

Note: Figures are the number of adherents as a percentage of the total population; (1) Figures cover the Fort Wayne, IN Metropolitan Statistical Area
Sources: 2020 U.S. Religion Census, Association of Statisticians of American Religious Bodies; The Association of Religion Data Archives (ARDA)

ECONOMY

Real Gross Domestic Product (GDP)

Area	2017	2018	2019	2020	2021	2022	2023	Rank[3]
MSA[1]	22.4	23.3	23.5	21.8	23.4	24.3	24.7	120
U.S.[2]	17,619.1	18,160.7	18,642.5	18,238.9	19,387.6	19,896.6	20,436.3	—

Note: Figures are in billions of chained 2017 dollars; (1) Figures cover the Fort Wayne, IN Metropolitan Statistical Area; (2) Figures cover real GDP within metropolitan areas; (3) Rank is based on 2023 data and ranges from 1 to 384
Source: U.S. Bureau of Economic Analysis

Economic Growth

Area	2014	2015	2016	2017	2018	2019	2020	2021	2022	2023
MSA[1]	7.7	4.3	3.2	3.8	3.8	0.7	-7.1	7.2	4.2	1.4
U.S.[2]	2.6	3.2	2.0	2.7	3.1	2.7	-2.2	6.3	2.6	2.7

Note: Figures are real gross domestic product growth rates and represent percent change from preceding period; (1) Figures cover the Fort Wayne, IN Metropolitan Statistical Area; (2) Figures are the average growth rates within metropolitan areas
Source: U.S. Bureau of Economic Analysis

Metropolitan Area Exports

Area	2018	2019	2020	2021	2022	2023	Rank[2]
MSA[1]	1,593.3	1,438.5	1,144.6	1,592.7	1,787.5	2,032.1	115
U.S.	1,664,056.1	1,645,173.7	1,431,406.6	1,753,941.4	2,062,937.4	2,019,160.5	—

Note: Figures are in millions of dollars; (1) Figures cover the Fort Wayne, IN Metropolitan Statistical Area; (2) Rank is based on 2023 data and ranges from 1 to 386
Source: U.S. Department of Commerce, International Trade Administration, Office of Trade and Economic Analysis, Industry and Analysis, Exports by Metropolitan Area, data extracted April 2, 2025

Building Permits

Area	Single-Family			Multi-Family			Total		
	2023	2024	Pct. Chg.	2023	2024	Pct. Chg.	2023	2024	Pct. Chg.
City	n/a	n/a	n/a	n/a	n/a	n/a	n/a	n/a	n/a
MSA[1]	1,680	1,409	-16.1	756	625	-17.3	2,436	2,034	-16.5
U.S.	920,000	981,900	6.7	591,100	496,100	-16.1	1,511,100	1,478,000	-2.2

Note: (1) Figures cover the Fort Wayne, IN Metropolitan Statistical Area; Figures represent new, privately-owned housing units authorized (unadjusted data)
Source: U.S. Census Bureau, Building Permits Survey (BPS), 2023, 2024

Bankruptcy Filings

Area	Business Filings			Nonbusiness Filings		
	2023	2024	% Chg.	2023	2024	% Chg.
Allen County	17	17	0.0	924	959	3.8
U.S.	18,926	23,107	22.1	434,064	494,201	13.9

Note: Business filings include Chapter 7, Chapter 9, Chapter 11, Chapter 12, Chapter 13, Chapter 15, and Section 304; Nonbusiness filings include Chapter 7, Chapter 11, and Chapter 13
Source: Administrative Office of the U.S. Courts, Business and Nonbusiness Bankruptcy, County Cases Commenced by Chapter of the Bankruptcy Code, During the 12-Month Period Ending December 31, 2023 and Business and Nonbusiness Bankruptcy, County Cases Commenced by Chapter of the Bankruptcy Code, During the 12-Month Period Ending December 31, 2024

Housing Vacancy Rates

Area	Gross Vacancy Rate[3] (%)			Year-Round Vacancy Rate[4] (%)			Rental Vacancy Rate[5] (%)			Homeowner Vacancy Rate[6] (%)		
	2022	2023	2024	2022	2023	2024	2022	2023	2024	2022	2023	2024
MSA[1]	n/a	n/a	n/a	n/a	n/a	n/a	n/a	n/a	n/a	n/a	n/a	n/a
U.S.[2]	9.1	9.0	9.1	7.5	7.5	7.6	5.7	6.5	6.8	0.8	0.8	1.0

Note: (1) Figures cover the Fort Wayne, IN Metropolitan Statistical Area; (2) Figures cover the 75 largest Metropolitan Statistical Areas; (3) The percentage of the total housing inventory that is vacant; (4) The percentage of the housing inventory (excluding seasonal units) that is year-round vacant; (5) The percentage of rental inventory that is vacant for rent; (6) The percentage of homeowner inventory that is vacant for sale; n/a not available
Source: U.S. Census Bureau, Housing Vacancies and Homeownership Annual Statistics: 2022, 2023, 2024

INCOME

Income

Area	Per Capita ($)	Median Household ($)	Average Household ($)
City	32,884	60,293	78,764
MSA[1]	36,444	69,378	90,705
U.S.	43,289	78,538	110,491

Note: (1) Figures cover the Fort Wayne, IN Metropolitan Statistical Area
Source: U.S. Census Bureau, 2019-2023 American Community Survey 5-Year Estimates

Household Income Distribution

Area	Percent of Households Earning							
	Under $15,000	$15,000 -$24,999	$25,000 -$34,999	$35,000 -$49,999	$50,000 -$74,999	$75,000 -$99,999	$100,000 -$149,999	$150,000 and up
City	9.3	7.9	9.6	14.5	19.5	14.1	15.2	9.9
MSA[1]	7.2	6.9	7.9	12.8	18.9	15.0	17.0	14.1
U.S.	8.5	6.6	6.8	10.4	15.7	12.7	17.4	21.9

Note: (1) Figures cover the Fort Wayne, IN Metropolitan Statistical Area
Source: U.S. Census Bureau, 2019-2023 American Community Survey 5-Year Estimates

Poverty Rate

Area	All Ages	Under 18 Years Old	18 to 64 Years Old	65 Years and Over
City	15.6	22.5	14.3	9.1
MSA[1]	11.8	16.1	11.1	7.3
U.S.	12.4	16.3	11.6	10.4

Note: Figures are percentage of people whose income during the past 12 months was below the poverty level;
(1) Figures cover the Fort Wayne, IN Metropolitan Statistical Area
Source: U.S. Census Bureau, 2019-2023 American Community Survey 5-Year Estimates

EMPLOYMENT

Labor Force and Employment

Area	Civilian Labor Force			Workers Employed		
	Dec. 2023	Dec. 2024	% Chg.	Dec. 2023	Dec. 2024	% Chg.
City	130,643	133,106	1.9	126,751	127,554	0.6
MSA[1]	220,472	224,223	1.7	214,223	215,591	0.6
U.S.	166,661,000	167,746,000	0.7	160,754,000	161,294,000	0.3

Note: Data is not seasonally adjusted and covers workers 16 years of age and older; (1) Figures cover the Fort Wayne, IN Metropolitan Statistical Area
Source: Bureau of Labor Statistics, Local Area Unemployment Statistics

Unemployment Rate

Area	2024											
	Jan.	Feb.	Mar.	Apr.	May	Jun.	Jul.	Aug.	Sep.	Oct.	Nov.	Dec.
City	3.9	4.3	4.1	3.4	3.9	4.4	6.0	4.4	4.0	4.1	4.4	4.2
MSA[1]	3.8	4.1	3.9	3.2	3.7	4.2	5.8	4.1	3.7	3.8	4.1	3.8
U.S.	4.1	4.2	3.9	3.5	3.7	4.3	4.5	4.4	3.9	3.9	4.0	3.8

Note: Data is not seasonally adjusted and covers workers 16 years of age and older; (1) Figures cover the Fort Wayne, IN Metropolitan Statistical Area
Source: Bureau of Labor Statistics, Local Area Unemployment Statistics

Average Wages

Occupation	$/Hr.	Occupation	$/Hr.
Accountants and Auditors	38.36	Maintenance and Repair Workers	25.25
Automotive Mechanics	24.39	Marketing Managers	n/a
Bookkeepers	22.76	Network and Computer Systems Admin.	39.62
Carpenters	27.40	Nurses, Licensed Practical	29.69
Cashiers	13.68	Nurses, Registered	39.85
Computer Programmers	39.45	Nursing Assistants	18.10
Computer Systems Analysts	44.73	Office Clerks, General	21.10
Computer User Support Specialists	26.58	Physical Therapists	46.11
Construction Laborers	23.81	Physicians	144.14
Cooks, Restaurant	15.90	Plumbers, Pipefitters and Steamfitters	35.26
Customer Service Representatives	21.57	Police and Sheriff's Patrol Officers	36.57
Dentists	98.97	Postal Service Mail Carriers	28.41
Electricians	31.08	Real Estate Sales Agents	37.39
Engineers, Electrical	49.63	Retail Salespersons	16.08
Fast Food and Counter Workers	13.24	Sales Representatives, Technical/Scientific	52.60
Financial Managers	65.40	Secretaries, Exc. Legal/Medical/Executive	20.58
First-Line Supervisors of Office Workers	33.46	Security Guards	20.23
General and Operations Managers	64.53	Surgeons	n/a
Hairdressers/Cosmetologists	16.40	Teacher Assistants, Exc. Postsecondary[1]	15.68
Home Health and Personal Care Aides	15.55	Teachers, Secondary School, Exc. Sp. Ed.[1]	30.99
Janitors and Cleaners	16.97	Telemarketers	n/a
Landscaping/Groundskeeping Workers	17.85	Truck Drivers, Heavy/Tractor-Trailer	28.99
Lawyers	65.81	Truck Drivers, Light/Delivery Services	21.73
Maids and Housekeeping Cleaners	14.93	Waiters and Waitresses	14.84

Note: Wage data covers the Fort Wayne, IN Metropolitan Statistical Area; (1) Hourly wages were calculated from annual wage data based on a 40 hour work week
Source: Bureau of Labor Statistics, Metro Area Occupational Employment & Wage Estimates, May 2024

Employment by Industry

Sector	MSA[1] Number of Employees	MSA[1] Percent of Total	U.S. Percent of Total
Construction, Mining, and Logging	13,200	5.5	5.5
Financial Activities	12,300	5.1	5.8
Government	23,100	9.6	14.9
Information	1,800	0.8	1.9
Leisure and Hospitality	21,100	8.8	10.4
Manufacturing	37,900	15.8	8.0
Other Services	13,400	5.6	3.7
Private Education and Health Services	45,900	19.2	16.9
Professional and Business Services	22,900	9.6	14.2
Retail Trade	25,000	10.4	10.0
Transportation, Warehousing, and Utilities	11,900	5.0	4.8
Wholesale Trade	11,000	4.6	3.9

Note: Figures are non-farm employment as of December 2024. Figures are not seasonally adjusted and include workers 16 years of age and older; (1) Figures cover the Fort Wayne, IN Metropolitan Statistical Area
Source: Bureau of Labor Statistics, Current Employment Statistics, Employment, Hours, and Earnings

Employment by Occupation

Occupation Classification	City (%)	MSA[1] (%)	U.S. (%)
Management, Business, Science, and Arts	35.6	37.8	42.0
Natural Resources, Construction, and Maintenance	6.4	7.5	8.6
Production, Transportation, and Material Moving	21.3	20.1	13.0
Sales and Office	20.2	19.6	19.9
Service	16.5	15.0	16.5

Note: Figures cover employed civilians 16 years of age and older; (1) Figures cover the Fort Wayne, IN Metropolitan Statistical Area
Source: U.S. Census Bureau, 2019-2023 American Community Survey 5-Year Estimates

Occupations with Greatest Projected Employment Growth: 2022 – 2032

Occupation[1]	2022 Employment	2032 Projected Employment	Numeric Employment Change	Percent Employment Change
Home Health and Personal Care Aides	44,830	54,650	9,820	21.9
Laborers and Freight, Stock, and Material Movers, Hand	105,700	112,240	6,540	6.2
Cooks, Restaurant	27,930	34,350	6,420	23.0
Software Developers	12,170	16,000	3,830	31.5
Registered Nurses	67,390	71,020	3,630	5.4
Fast Food and Counter Workers	91,680	94,980	3,300	3.6
Medical and Health Services Managers	10,690	13,820	3,130	29.3
Stockers and Order Fillers	58,190	61,320	3,130	5.4
Nurse Practitioners	6,550	9,550	3,000	45.8
Medical Assistants	20,210	23,170	2,960	14.6

Note: Projections cover Indiana; (1) Sorted by numeric employment change
Source: www.projectionscentral.org, State Occupational Projections, 2022–2032 Long-Term Projections

Fastest-Growing Occupations: 2022 – 2032

Occupation[1]	2022 Employment	2032 Projected Employment	Numeric Employment Change	Percent Employment Change
Nurse Practitioners	6,550	9,550	3,000	45.8
Information Security Analysts (SOC 2018)	1,150	1,570	420	36.5
Data Scientists	2,200	2,980	780	35.5
Statisticians	270	360	90	33.3
Software Developers	12,170	16,000	3,830	31.5
Medical and Health Services Managers	10,690	13,820	3,130	29.3
Occupational Therapy Assistants	1,000	1,280	280	28.0
Physician Assistants	1,640	2,100	460	28.0
Veterinary Assistants and Laboratory Animal Caretakers	2,680	3,410	730	27.2
Veterinary Technologists and Technicians	2,880	3,660	780	27.1

Note: Projections cover Indiana; (1) Sorted by percent employment change and excludes occupations with numeric employment change less than 50
Source: www.projectionscentral.org, State Occupational Projections, 2022–2032 Long-Term Projections

CITY FINANCES

City Government Finances

Component	2022 ($000)	2022 ($ per capita)
Total Revenues	460,147	1,689
Total Expenditures	323,307	1,187
Debt Outstanding	582,036	2,137

Source: U.S. Census Bureau, State & Local Government Finances 2022

City Government Revenue by Source

Source	2022 ($000)	2022 ($ per capita)	2022 (%)
General Revenue			
From Federal Government	26,601	98	5.8
From State Government	24,360	89	5.3
From Local Governments	18,511	68	4.0
Taxes			
Property	157,927	580	34.3
Sales and Gross Receipts	0	0	0.0
Personal Income	80,427	295	17.5
Corporate Income	0	0	0.0
Motor Vehicle License	11,006	40	2.4
Other Taxes	996	4	0.2
Current Charges	24,988	92	5.4
Liquor Store	0	0	0.0
Utility	63,544	233	13.8

Source: U.S. Census Bureau, State & Local Government Finances 2022

City Government Expenditures by Function

Function	2022 ($000)	2022 ($ per capita)	2022 (%)
General Direct Expenditures			
Air Transportation	0	0	0.0
Corrections	0	0	0.0
Education	0	0	0.0
Employment Security Administration	0	0	0.0
Financial Administration	10,470	38	3.2
Fire Protection	49,661	182	15.4
General Public Buildings	1,510	5	0.5
Governmental Administration, Other	3,938	14	1.2
Health	5,274	19	1.6
Highways	64,360	236	19.9
Hospitals	0	0	0.0
Housing and Community Development	17,861	65	5.5
Interest on General Debt	22,921	84	7.1
Judicial and Legal	708	2	0.2
Libraries	0	0	0.0
Parking	2,803	10	0.9
Parks and Recreation	24,264	89	7.5
Police Protection	73,560	270	22.8
Public Welfare	0	0	0.0
Sewerage	12,917	47	4.0
Solid Waste Management	11,537	42	3.6
Veterans' Services	0	0	0.0
Liquor Store	0	0	0.0
Utility	19,995	73	6.2

Source: U.S. Census Bureau, State & Local Government Finances 2022

TAXES

State Corporate Income Tax Rates

State	Tax Rate (%)	Income Brackets ($)	Num. of Brackets	Financial Institution Tax Rate (%)[a]	Federal Income Tax Ded.
Indiana	4.9	Flat rate	1	4.9	No

Note: Tax rates for tax year 2024; (a) Rates listed are the corporate income tax rate applied to financial institutions or excise taxes based on income. Some states have other taxes based upon the value of deposits or shares.
Source: Federation of Tax Administrators, State Corporate Income Tax Rates, January 1, 2025

State Individual Income Tax Rates

State	Tax Rate (%)	Income Brackets ($)	Personal Exemptions ($)			Standard Ded. ($)	
			Single	Married	Depend.	Single	Married
Indiana	3.05	Flat rate	1,000	2,000	2,500 (i)	–	–

Note: Tax rates for tax year 2024; Local- and county-level taxes are not included; Federal income tax is not deductible on state income tax returns; (i) GA moves to a flat tax rate regime, eliminates the personal exemption and increases the standard deduction amounts for single, HOH and married jointly filers.
Source: Federation of Tax Administrators, State Individual Income Tax Rates, January 1, 2025

Various State Sales and Excise Tax Rates

State	State Sales Tax (%)	Gasoline[1] ($/gal.)	Cigarette[2] ($/pack)	Spirits[3] ($/gal.)	Wine[4] ($/gal.)	Beer[5] ($/gal.)	Recreational Marijuana (%)
Indiana	7	0.53	1.00	2.68	0.47	0.12	Not legal

Note: All tax rates as of January 1, 2025; (1) The American Petroleum Institute has developed a methodology for determining the average tax rate on a gallon of fuel. Rates may include any of the following: excise taxes, environmental fees, storage tank fees, other fees or taxes, general sales tax, and local taxes; (2) The federal excise tax of $1.0066 per pack and local taxes are not included; (3) Rates are those applicable to off-premise sales of 40% alcohol by volume (a.b.v.) distilled spirits in 750ml containers. Local excise taxes are excluded; (4) Rates are those applicable to off-premise sales of 11% a.b.v. non-carbonated wine in 750ml containers; (5) Rates are those applicable to off-premise sales of 4.7% a.b.v. beer in 12 ounce containers.
Source: Tax Foundation, 2025 Facts & Figures: How Does Your State Compare?

State Tax Competitiveness Index

State	Overall Rank	Corporate Tax Rank	Individual Income Tax Rank	Sales Tax Rank	Property Tax Rank	Unemployment Insurance Tax Rank
Indiana	10	8	16	17	5	13

Note: The Tax Foundation's State Tax Competitiveness Index enables policymakers, taxpayers, and business leaders to gauge how their states' tax systems compare. A rank of 1 is best, 50 is worst. Rankings do not average to the total. States without a tax rank equally as 1. DC's scores and rankings do not affect other states. The report shows tax systems as of July 1, 2024 (the beginning of Fiscal Year 2025).
Source: Tax Foundation, State Tax Competitiveness Index 2025

TRANSPORTATION

Means of Transportation to Work

Area	Car/Truck/Van Drove Alone	Car/Truck/Van Carpooled	Public Transportation Bus	Public Transportation Subway	Public Transportation Railroad	Bicycle	Walked	Other Means	Worked at Home
City	78.1	9.9	1.1	0.0	0.0	0.3	1.5	0.8	8.2
MSA[1]	79.9	9.1	0.7	0.0	0.0	0.3	1.2	0.7	8.1
U.S.	70.2	8.5	1.7	1.3	0.4	0.4	2.4	1.6	13.5

Note: Figures are percentages and cover workers 16 years of age and older; (1) Figures cover the Fort Wayne, IN Metropolitan Statistical Area
Source: U.S. Census Bureau, 2019-2023 American Community Survey 5-Year Estimates

Travel Time to Work

Area	Less Than 10 Minutes	10 to 19 Minutes	20 to 29 Minutes	30 to 44 Minutes	45 to 59 Minutes	60 to 89 Minutes	90 Minutes or More
City	13.1	38.1	27.8	13.7	2.9	2.2	2.2
MSA[1]	13.8	34.9	28.2	15.9	3.4	1.9	2.0
U.S.	12.6	28.6	21.2	20.8	8.1	6.0	2.8

Note: Note: Figures are percentages and include workers 16 years old and over; (1) Figures cover the Fort Wayne, IN Metropolitan Statistical Area
Source: U.S. Census Bureau, 2019-2023 American Community Survey 5-Year Estimates

Key Congestion Measures

Measure	2000	2010	2015	2020	2022
Annual Hours of Delay, Total (000)	n/a	n/a	5,835	2,768	4,664
Annual Hours of Delay, Per Auto Commuter	n/a	n/a	18	8	14
Annual Congestion Cost, Per Auto Commuter ($)	n/a	n/a	417	208	345

Note: n/a not available
Source: Texas A&M Transportation Institute, 2023 Urban Mobility Report

Freeway Travel Time Index

Measure	1985	1990	1995	2000	2005	2010	2015	2020	2022
Urban Area Index[1]	n/a	n/a	n/a	n/a	n/a	n/a	1.09	1.04	1.08
Urban Area Rank[1,2]	n/a	n/a	n/a	n/a	n/a	n/a	n/a	n/a	n/a

Note: Freeway Travel Time Index—the ratio of travel time in the peak period to the travel time at free-flow conditions. For example, a value of 1.30 indicates a 20-minute free-flow trip takes 26 minutes in the peak (20 minutes x 1.30 = 26 minutes); (1) Covers the Fort Wayne IN urban area; (2) Rank is based on 101 larger urban areas (#1 = highest travel time index); n/a not available
Source: Texas A&M Transportation Institute, 2023 Urban Mobility Report

Public Transportation

Agency Name / Mode of Transportation	Vehicles Operated in Maximum Service[1]	Annual Unlinked Passenger Trips[2] (in thous.)	Annual Passenger Miles[3] (in thous.)
Fort Wayne Public Transportation Corp. (Citilink)			
Bus (directly operated)	25	1,500.0	6,229.4
Demand Response (directly operated)	15	62.0	435.4

Note: (1) Number of revenue vehicles operated by the given mode and type of service to meet the annual maximum service requirement. This is the revenue vehicle count during the peak season of the year; on the week and day that maximum service is provided. Vehicles operated in maximum service (VOMS) exclude atypical days and one-time special events; (2) Number of passengers who boarded public transportation vehicles. Passengers are counted each time they board a vehicle no matter how many vehicles they use to travel from their origin to their destination. (3) Sum of the distances ridden by all passengers during the entire fiscal year.
Source: Federal Transit Administration, National Transit Database, 2023

Air Transportation

Airport Name and Code / Type of Service	Passenger Airlines[1]	Passenger Enplanements	Freight Carriers[2]	Freight (lbs)
Fort Wayne International (FWA)				
Domestic service (U.S. carriers only)	11	424,439	9	17,596,074
International service (U.S. carriers only)	0	0	1	29,220

Note: (1) Includes all U.S.-based major, minor and commuter airlines that carried at least one passenger during the year; (2) Includes all U.S.-based airlines and freight carriers that transported at least one pound of freight during the year.
Source: Bureau of Transportation Statistics, The Intermodal Transportation Database, Air Carriers: T-100 Domestic Market (U.S. carriers only), 2024; Bureau of Transportation Statistics, The Intermodal Transportation Database, Air Carriers: T-100 International Market (U.S. carriers only), 2024

BUSINESSES

Major Business Headquarters

Company Name	Industry	Rankings	
		Fortune[1]	Forbes[2]
Steel Dynamics	Metals	221	-

Note: (1) Companies that produce a 10-K are ranked 1 to 500 based on 2023 revenue; (2) All private companies with at least $2 billion in annual revenue through the end of their most current fiscal year are ranked 1 to 275; companies listed are headquartered in the city; dashes indicate no ranking
Source: Fortune, "Fortune 500," 2024; Forbes, "America's Largest Private Companies," 2024

Living Environment

COST OF LIVING

Cost of Living Index

Composite Index	Groceries	Housing	Utilities	Transportation	Health Care	Misc. Goods/Services
90.3	99.0	77.5	91.0	100.4	97.4	93.1

Note: The Cost of Living Index measures regional differences in the cost of consumer goods and services, excluding taxes and non-consumer expenditures, for professional and managerial households in the top income quintile. It is based on more than 50,000 prices covering almost 60 different items for which prices are collected three times a year by chambers of commerce, economic development organizations or university applied economic centers in each participating urban area. The numbers shown should be read as a percentage above or below the national average of 100. For example, a value of 115.4 in the groceries column indicates that grocery prices are 15.4% higher than the national average. Small differences in the index numbers should not be interpreted as significant; Figures cover the Fort Wayne-Allen County IN urban area.
Source: The Council for Community and Economic Research, Cost of Living Index, 2024

Grocery Prices

Area[1]	T-Bone Steak ($/pound)	Frying Chicken ($/pound)	Whole Milk ($/half gal.)	Eggs ($/dozen)	Orange Juice ($/64 oz.)	Coffee ($/11.5 oz.)
City[2]	15.51	1.66	4.69	3.49	4.36	5.41
Avg.	15.42	1.55	4.69	3.25	4.41	5.46
Min.	14.50	1.16	4.43	2.75	4.00	4.85
Max.	17.56	2.89	5.49	4.78	5.54	7.89

Note: (1) Values for the local area are compared with the average, minimum and maximum values for all 276 areas in the Cost of Living Index; (2) Figures cover the Fort Wayne-Allen County IN urban area; **T-Bone Steak** (price per pound); **Frying Chicken** (price per pound, whole fryer); **Whole Milk** (half gallon carton); **Eggs** (price per dozen, Grade A, large); **Orange Juice** (64 oz. Tropicana or Florida Natural); **Coffee** (11.5 oz. can, vacuum-packed, Maxwell House, Hills Bros, or Folgers).
Source: The Council for Community and Economic Research, Cost of Living Index, 2024

Housing and Utility Costs

Area[1]	New Home Price ($)	Apartment Rent ($/month)	All Electric ($/month)	Part Electric ($/month)	Other Energy ($/month)	Telephone ($/month)
City[2]	364,871	1,370	-	109.31	68.72	192.42
Avg.	515,975	1,550	210.99	123.07	82.07	194.99
Min.	265,375	692	104.33	53.68	36.26	179.42
Max.	2,775,821	5,719	529.02	397.28	361.63	223.33

Note: (1) Values for the local area are compared with the average, minimum and maximum values for all 276 areas in the Cost of Living Index; (2) Figures cover the Fort Wayne-Allen County IN urban area; **New Home Price** (2,400 sf living area, 8,000 sf lot, in urban area with full utilities); **Apartment Rent** (950 sf 2 bedroom/1.5 or 2 bath, unfurnished, excluding all utilities except water); **All Electric** (average monthly cost for an all-electric home); **Part Electric** (average monthly cost for a part-electric home); **Other Energy** (average monthly cost for natural gas, fuel oil, coal, wood, and any other forms of energy except electricity); **Telephone** (price includes the base monthly rate plus taxes and fees for three lines of mobile phone service).
Source: The Council for Community and Economic Research, Cost of Living Index, 2024

Health Care, Transportation, and Other Costs

Area[1]	Doctor ($/visit)	Dentist ($/visit)	Optometrist ($/visit)	Gasoline ($/gallon)	Beauty Salon ($/visit)	Men's Shirt ($)
City[2]	137.75	106.33	122.67	3.32	33.28	39.34
Avg.	143.77	117.51	129.23	3.32	48.57	38.14
Min.	36.74	58.67	67.33	2.80	24.00	13.41
Max.	270.44	216.82	307.33	5.28	94.00	63.89

Note: (1) Values for the local area are compared with the average, minimum and maximum values for all 276 areas in the Cost of Living Index; (2) Figures cover the Fort Wayne-Allen County IN urban area; **Doctor** (general practitioners routine exam of an established patient); **Dentist** (adult teeth cleaning and periodic oral examination); **Optometrist** (full vision eye exam for established adult patient); **Gasoline** (one gallon regular unleaded, national brand, including all taxes, cash price at self-service pump if available); **Beauty Salon** (woman's shampoo, trim, and blow-dry); **Men's Shirt** (cotton/polyester dress shirt, pinpoint weave, long sleeves).
Source: The Council for Community and Economic Research, Cost of Living Index, 2024

HOUSING

Homeownership Rate

Area	2017 (%)	2018 (%)	2019 (%)	2020 (%)	2021 (%)	2022 (%)	2023 (%)	2024 (%)
MSA[1]	n/a	n/a	n/a	n/a	n/a	n/a	n/a	n/a
U.S.	63.9	64.4	64.6	66.6	65.5	65.8	65.9	65.6

Note: (1) Figures cover the Fort Wayne, IN Metropolitan Statistical Area; n/a not available
Source: U.S. Census Bureau, Housing Vacancies and Homeownership Annual Statistics: 2017-2024

Fort Wayne, Indiana

House Price Index (HPI)

Area	National Ranking[2]	Quarterly Change (%)	One-Year Change (%)	Five-Year Change (%)	Since 1991Q1 (%)
MSA[1]	32	1.26	7.98	72.59	239.64
U.S.[3]	–	1.43	4.51	57.13	327.82

Note: The HPI is a weighted repeat sales index. It measures average price changes in repeat sales or refinancings on the same properties. This information is obtained by reviewing repeat mortgage transactions on single-family properties whose mortgages have been purchased or securitized by Fannie Mae or Freddie Mac since January 1975; (1) Figures cover the Fort Wayne, IN Metropolitan Statistical Area; (2) Rankings are based on annual percentage change for all metro areas containing at least 15,000 transactions over the last 10 years and ranges from 1 to 241; (3) figures based on a weighted average of Census Division estimates using a seasonally adjusted, purchase-only index; all figures are for the period ending December 31, 2024
Source: Federal Housing Finance Agency, Change in FHFA Metropolitan Area House Price Indexes, All Transactions Index, 2024Q4

Home Value

Area	Under $100,000	$100,000 -$199,999	$200,000 -$299,999	$300,000 -$399,999	$400,000 -$499,999	$500,000 -$999,999	$1,000,000 or more	Median ($)
City	19.8	42.0	25.3	7.7	2.8	2.0	0.3	169,700
MSA[1]	16.3	35.8	25.6	11.4	5.1	5.0	0.7	194,000
U.S.	12.1	17.8	19.5	14.4	10.5	19.1	6.5	303,400

Note: Figures are percentages except for median and cover owner-occupied housing units; (1) Figures cover the Fort Wayne, IN Metropolitan Statistical Area
Source: U.S. Census Bureau, 2019-2023 American Community Survey 5-Year Estimates

Year Housing Structure Built

Area	2020 or Later	2010 -2019	2000 -2009	1990 -1999	1980 -1989	1970 -1979	1960 -1969	1950 -1959	1940 -1949	Before 1940	Median Year
City	0.5	3.4	7.4	12.9	11.3	16.9	15.5	12.0	5.7	14.4	1971
MSA[1]	1.0	7.6	11.5	13.5	10.2	14.7	12.3	9.9	4.7	14.5	1976
U.S.	1.2	8.9	13.6	12.8	13.0	14.4	10.0	9.7	4.5	11.9	1980

Note: Figures are percentages except for Median Year; Note: (1) Figures cover the Fort Wayne, IN Metropolitan Statistical Area
Source: U.S. Census Bureau, 2019-2023 American Community Survey 5-Year Estimates

Gross Monthly Rent

Area	Under $500	$500 -$999	$1,000 -$1,499	$1,500 -$1,999	$2,000 -$2,499	$2,500 -$2,999	$3,000 and up	Median ($)
City	6.7	48.7	37.3	5.3	1.4	0.4	0.3	959
MSA[1]	6.6	48.2	36.5	6.1	1.7	0.5	0.4	963
U.S.	6.5	22.3	29.5	20.2	10.8	4.8	5.9	1,348

Note: Figures are percentages except for median; Gross rent is the contract rent plus the estimated average monthly cost of utilities (electricity, gas, and water and sewer) and fuels (oil, coal, kerosene, wood, etc.) if these are paid by the renter (or paid for the renter by someone else); (1) Figures cover the Fort Wayne, IN Metropolitan Statistical Area
Source: U.S. Census Bureau, 2019-2023 American Community Survey 5-Year Estimates

HEALTH

Health Risk Factors

Category	MSA[1] (%)	U.S. (%)
Adults aged 18–64 who have any kind of health care coverage	90.0	90.8
Adults who reported being in good or better health	82.8	81.8
Adults who have been told they have high blood cholesterol	34.8	36.9
Adults who have been told they have high blood pressure	38.1	34.0
Adults who are current smokers	9.5	12.1
Adults who currently use e-cigarettes	7.2	7.7
Adults who currently use chewing tobacco, snuff, or snus	3.1	3.2
Adults who are heavy drinkers[2]	4.1	6.1
Adults who are binge drinkers[3]	15.6	15.2
Adults who are overweight (BMI 25.0 - 29.9)	31.4	34.4
Adults who are obese (BMI 30.0 - 99.8)	41.1	34.3
Adults who participated in any physical activities in the past month	79.4	75.8

Note: All figures are crude prevalence; (1) Figures cover the Fort Wayne, IN Metropolitan Statistical Area; (2) Heavy drinkers are classified as adult men having more than 14 drinks per week and adult women having more than 7 drinks per week; (3) Binge drinkers are classified as males having five or more drinks on one occasion or females having four or more drinks on one occasion
Source: Centers for Disease Control and Prevention, Behavioral Risk Factor Surveillance System, SMART: Selected Metropolitan Area Risk Trends, 2023

Acute and Chronic Health Conditions

Category	MSA[1] (%)	U.S. (%)
Adults who have ever been told they had a heart attack	4.1	4.2
Adults who have ever been told they have angina or coronary heart disease	4.4	4.0
Adults who have ever been told they had a stroke	3.4	3.3
Adults who have ever been told they have asthma	15.0	15.7
Adults who have ever been told they have arthritis	25.3	26.3
Adults who have ever been told they have diabetes[2]	13.5	11.5
Adults who have ever been told they had skin cancer	4.8	5.6
Adults who have ever been told they had any other types of cancer	6.6	8.4
Adults who have ever been told they have COPD	6.2	6.4
Adults who have ever been told they have kidney disease	3.7	3.7
Adults who have ever been told they have a form of depression	27.2	22.0

Note: All figures are crude prevalence; (1) Figures cover the Fort Wayne, IN Metropolitan Statistical Area; (2) Figures do not include pregnancy-related, borderline, or pre-diabetes
Source: Centers for Disease Control and Prevention, Behaviorial Risk Factor Surveillance System, SMART: Selected Metropolitan Area Risk Trends, 2023

Health Screening and Vaccination Rates

Category	MSA[1] (%)	U.S. (%)
Adults who have ever been tested for HIV	32.1	37.5
Adults who have had their blood cholesterol checked within the last five years	85.4	87.0
Adults aged 65+ who have had flu shot within the past year	60.4	63.4
Adults aged 65+ who have ever had a pneumonia vaccination	72.7	71.9

Note: All figures are crude prevalence; (1) Figures cover the Fort Wayne, IN Metropolitan Statistical Area.
Source: Centers for Disease Control and Prevention, Behaviorial Risk Factor Surveillance System, SMART: Selected Metropolitan Area Risk Trends, 2023

Disability Status

Category	MSA[1] (%)	U.S. (%)
Adults who reported being deaf	6.5	7.4
Are you blind or have serious difficulty seeing, even when wearing glasses?	4.7	4.9
Do you have difficulty doing errands alone?	8.3	7.8
Do you have difficulty dressing or bathing?	3.4	3.6
Do you have serious difficulty concentrating/remembering/making decisions?	14.3	13.7
Do you have serious difficulty walking or climbing stairs?	10.4	13.2

Note: All figures are crude prevalence; (1) Figures cover the Fort Wayne, IN Metropolitan Statistical Area.
Source: Centers for Disease Control and Prevention, Behaviorial Risk Factor Surveillance System, SMART: Selected Metropolitan Area Risk Trends, 2023

Mortality Rates for the Top 10 Causes of Death in the U.S.

ICD-10[a] Sub-Chapter	ICD-10[a] Code	Crude Mortality Rate[2] per 100,000 population	
		County[3]	U.S.
Malignant neoplasms	C00-C97	187.2	182.7
Ischaemic heart diseases	I20-I25	91.8	109.6
Provisional assignment of new diseases of uncertain etiology[1]	U00-U49	53.6	65.3
Other forms of heart disease	I30-I51	56.1	65.1
Other degenerative diseases of the nervous system	G30-G31	37.9	52.4
Other external causes of accidental injury	W00-X59	53.9	52.3
Cerebrovascular diseases	I60-I69	50.7	49.1
Chronic lower respiratory diseases	J40-J47	51.0	43.5
Hypertensive diseases	I10-I15	47.7	38.9
Organic, including symptomatic, mental disorders	F01-F09	41.7	33.9

Note: (a) ICD-10 = International Classification of Diseases 10th Revision; (1) Includes COVID-19, adverse effects to COVID-19 vaccines, SARS, and vaping-related disorders; (2) Crude mortality rates are a three-year average covering 2021-2023; (3) Figures cover Allen County.
Source: Centers for Disease Control and Prevention, National Center for Health Statistics. National Vital Statistics System, Mortality 2018-2023 on CDC WONDER Online Database

Mortality Rates for Selected Causes of Death

Cause of Death	ICD-10[a] Code	Crude Mortality Rate[1] per 100,000 population	
		County[2]	U.S.
Accidental poisoning and exposure to noxious substances	X40-X49	31.4	30.5
Alzheimer disease	G30	30.0	35.4
Assault	X85-Y09	8.4	7.3
COVID-19	U07.1	53.6	65.3
Diabetes mellitus	E10-E14	45.0	30.0
Diseases of the liver	K70-K76	19.0	20.8
Human immunodeficiency virus (HIV) disease	B20-B24	Unreliable	1.5
Influenza and pneumonia	J09-J18	7.8	13.4
Intentional self-harm	X60-X84	17.3	14.7
Malnutrition	E40-E46	4.3	6.0
Obesity and other hyperalimentation	E65-E68	2.3	3.1
Renal failure	N17-N19	14.9	16.4
Transport accidents	V01-V99	11.6	14.4

Note: (a) ICD-10 = International Classification of Diseases 10th Revision; (1) Crude mortality rates are a three-year average covering 2021-2023; (2) Figures cover Allen County; Data are suppressed when the data meet the criteria for confidentiality constraints; Crude mortality rates are flagged as unreliable when the rate would be calculated with a numerator of 20 or less.
Source: Centers for Disease Control and Prevention, National Center for Health Statistics. National Vital Statistics System, Mortality 2018-2023 on CDC WONDER Online Database

Health Insurance Coverage

Area	With Health Insurance	With Private Health Insurance	With Public Health Insurance	Without Health Insurance	Population Under Age 19 Without Health Insurance
City	90.6	62.9	38.1	9.4	6.7
MSA[1]	92.0	68.5	34.5	8.0	6.3
U.S.	91.4	67.3	36.3	8.6	5.4

Note: Figures are percentages that cover the civilian noninstitutionalized population; (1) Figures cover the Fort Wayne, IN Metropolitan Statistical Area
Source: U.S. Census Bureau, 2019-2023 American Community Survey 5-Year Estimates

Number of Medical Professionals

Area	MDs[3]	DOs[3,4]	Dentists	Podiatrists	Chiropractors	Optometrists
County[1] (number)	1,065	131	287	22	94	105
County[1] (rate[2])	272.1	33.5	72.7	5.6	23.8	26.6
U.S. (rate[2])	302.5	29.2	74.6	6.4	29.5	18.0

Note: Data as of 2023 unless noted; (1) Data covers Allen County; (2) Number of medical professionals per 100,000 population; (3) Data as of 2022 and includes all active, non-federal physicians; (4) Doctor of Osteopathic Medicine
Source: U.S. Department of Health and Human Services, Health Resources and Services Administration, Bureau of Health Professions, Area Resource File (ARF) 2023-2024

EDUCATION

Public School District Statistics

District Name	Schls	Pupils	Pupil/ Teacher Ratio	Minority Pupils[1] (%)	Total Rev. per Pupil ($)	Total Exp. per Pupil ($)
Fort Wayne Community Schools	50	28,506	13.3	64.4	16,150	15,804
M S D Southwest Allen Co. Schls	10	7,555	15.1	26.2	13,202	12,427
Northwest Allen County Schools	12	8,383	16.9	22.1	13,193	13,212

Note: Table includes school districts with 2,000 or more students; (1) Percentage of students that are not non-Hispanic white.
Source: U.S. Department of Education, National Center for Education Statistics, Common Core of Data, Local Education Agency (School District) Universe Survey: School Year 2023-2024; U.S. Department of Education, National Center for Education Statistics, Common Core of Data, School District Finance Survey (F-33): School Year 2021–22

Highest Level of Education

Area	Less than H.S.	H.S. Diploma	Some College, No Deg.	Associate Degree	Bachelor's Degree	Master's Degree	Prof. School Degree	Doctorate Degree
City	11.1	28.7	21.8	9.9	19.4	7.2	1.1	0.9
MSA[1]	9.3	29.7	20.7	10.6	20.0	7.3	1.5	0.9
U.S.	10.6	26.2	19.4	8.8	21.3	9.8	2.3	1.6

Note: Figures cover persons age 25 and over; (1) Figures cover the Fort Wayne, IN Metropolitan Statistical Area
Source: U.S. Census Bureau, 2019-2023 American Community Survey 5-Year Estimates

Educational Attainment by Race

Area	High School Graduate or Higher (%)					Bachelor's Degree or Higher (%)				
	Total	White	Black	Asian	Hisp.[2]	Total	White	Black	Asian	Hisp.[2]
City	88.9	94.1	87.7	49.2	65.7	28.5	33.1	13.9	19.7	15.4
MSA[1]	90.7	93.8	88.5	59.3	68.5	29.7	32.0	15.8	29.2	16.9
U.S.	89.4	92.9	88.1	88.0	72.5	35.0	37.7	24.7	57.0	19.9

Note: Figures shown cover persons 25 years old and over; (1) Figures cover the Fort Wayne, IN Metropolitan Statistical Area; (2) People of Hispanic origin can be of any race
Source: U.S. Census Bureau, 2019-2023 American Community Survey 5-Year Estimates

School Enrollment by Grade and Control

Area	Preschool (%)		Kindergarten (%)		Grades 1 - 4 (%)		Grades 5 - 8 (%)		Grades 9 - 12 (%)	
	Public	Private	Public	Private	Public	Private	Public	Private	Public	Private
City	45.6	54.4	70.8	29.2	78.5	21.5	82.0	18.0	79.2	20.8
MSA[1]	44.1	55.9	73.2	26.8	75.7	24.3	76.8	23.2	81.3	18.7
U.S.	58.7	41.3	85.2	14.8	87.2	12.8	87.9	12.1	89.0	11.0

Note: Figures shown cover persons 3 years old and over; (1) Figures cover the Fort Wayne, IN Metropolitan Statistical Area
Source: U.S. Census Bureau, 2019-2023 American Community Survey 5-Year Estimates

Higher Education

Four-Year Colleges			Two-Year Colleges			Medical Schools[1]	Law Schools[2]	Voc/ Tech[3]
Public	Private Non-profit	Private For-profit	Public	Private Non-profit	Private For-profit			
1	4	0	0	0	2	0	0	2

Note: Figures cover institutions located within the Fort Wayne, IN Metropolitan Statistical Area and include main campuses only; (1) includes schools accredited by the Liaison Committee on Medical Education and the American Osteopathic Association's Commission on Osteopathic College Accreditation; (2) includes ABA-accredited schools, schools with provisional ABA accreditation, and state accredited schools; (3) includes all schools with programs that are less than 2 years.
Source: National Center for Education Statistics, Integrated Postsecondary Education System (IPEDS), 2023-24; Wikipedia, List of Medical Schools in the United States, accessed May 2, 2025; Wikipedia, List of Law Schools in the United States, accessed May 2, 2025

EMPLOYERS

Major Employers

Company Name	Industry
Allen County Government	Government
BAE Systems Platform Solutions	Aircraft electronics
Benchmark Human Services	Services for people with disabilities
BFGoodrich	Rubber tire manufacturing
City of Fort Wayne	Municipal government
Dana Corp.	Motor vehicle parts manufacturing
Edy's Grand Ice Cream	Ice cream & other frozen treats
Fort Wayne Community Schools	Elementary & secondary schools
Fort Wayne Metals Research Products Corp.	Wire for medical devices
Frontier Communications Corp.	Wired telecommunications carriers
General Motors	Motor vehicle manufacturing
Harris Corporation	Wireless networking systems & satellite imaging systems
IPFW	University
Ivy Tech Community College- Northeast	Community college
Lincoln Financial Group	Insurance carriers
Lutheran Health Network	General medical & surgical hospitals
Norfolk Southern Corp2	Rail transportation
Northwest Allen County Schools	Elementary & secondary schools
Parker Hannifin Corporation	Metal product manufacturing for a/c systems
Parkview Health Systems	General medical & surgical hospitals

Note: Companies shown are located within the Fort Wayne, IN Metropolitan Statistical Area.
Source: Chambers of Commerce; State Departments of Labor; Wikipedia

PUBLIC SAFETY

Crime Rate

Area	Total Crime Rate	Violent Crime Rate				Property Crime Rate		
		Murder	Rape	Robbery	Aggrav. Assault	Burglary	Larceny -Theft	Motor Vehicle Theft
City	2,623.8	9.6	43.7	64.9	153.1	251.0	1,800.3	301.0
U.S.	2,290.9	5.7	38.0	66.5	264.1	250.7	1,347.2	318.7

Note: Figures are crimes per 100,000 population.
Source: FBI, Table 8, Offenses Known to Law Enforcement, by State by City, 2023

Hate Crimes

Area	Number of Quarters Reported	Number of Incidents per Bias Motivation					
		Race/Ethnicity/Ancestry	Religion	Sexual Orientation	Disability	Gender	Gender Identity
City	4	6	2	4	0	1	0
U.S.	4	5,900	2,699	2,077	187	92	492

Source: Federal Bureau of Investigation, Hate Crime Statistics 2023

Identity Theft Consumer Reports

Area	Reports	Reports per 100,000 Population	Rank[2]
MSA[1]	732	162	236
U.S.	1,135,291	339	-

Note: (1) Figures cover the Fort Wayne, IN Metropolitan Statistical Area; (2) Rank ranges from 1 to 401 where 1 indicates greatest number of identity theft reports per 100,000 population
Source: Federal Trade Commission, Consumer Sentinel Network Data Book 2024

Fraud and Other Consumer Reports

Area	Reports	Reports per 100,000 Population	Rank[2]
MSA[1]	4,431	982	223
U.S.	5,360,641	1,601	-

Note: (1) Figures cover the Fort Wayne, IN Metropolitan Statistical Area; (2) Rank ranges from 1 to 401 where 1 indicates greatest number of fraud and other consumer reports per 100,000 population
Source: Federal Trade Commission, Consumer Sentinel Network Data Book 2024

POLITICS

2024 Presidential Election Results

Area	Trump (Rep.)	Harris (Dem.)	Stein (Green)	Kennedy (Ind.)	Oliver (Lib.)	Other
Allen County	55.2	42.7	0.0	0.9	0.8	0.4
U.S.	49.7	48.2	0.6	0.5	0.4	0.6

Note: Results are percentages and may not add to 100% due to rounding
Source: Dave Leip's Atlas of U.S. Presidential Elections

SPORTS

Professional Sports Teams

Team Name	League	Year Established

No teams are located in the metro area
Source: Wikipedia, Major Professional Sports Teams of the United States and Canada, May 1, 2025

CLIMATE

Average and Extreme Temperatures

Temperature	Jan	Feb	Mar	Apr	May	Jun	Jul	Aug	Sep	Oct	Nov	Dec	Yr.
Extreme High (°F)	69	69	82	88	94	106	103	101	100	90	79	71	106
Average High (°F)	31	35	46	60	71	81	84	82	76	64	49	36	60
Average Temp. (°F)	24	27	37	49	60	70	74	72	65	53	41	29	50
Average Low (°F)	16	19	28	39	49	59	63	61	53	42	32	22	40
Extreme Low (°F)	-22	-18	-10	7	27	38	44	38	29	19	-1	-18	-22

Note: Figures cover the years 1948-1990
Source: National Climatic Data Center, International Station Meteorological Climate Summary, 9/96

Average Precipitation/Snowfall/Humidity

Precip./Humidity	Jan	Feb	Mar	Apr	May	Jun	Jul	Aug	Sep	Oct	Nov	Dec	Yr.
Avg. Precip. (in.)	2.3	2.1	2.9	3.4	3.6	3.8	3.6	3.4	2.6	2.7	2.8	2.7	35.9
Avg. Snowfall (in.)	8	8	5	2	Tr	0	0	0	0	Tr	3	7	33
Avg. Rel. Hum. 7am (%)	81	81	80	77	76	78	81	86	86	84	83	83	81
Avg. Rel. Hum. 4pm (%)	71	68	62	54	52	52	53	55	53	55	67	74	59

Note: Figures cover the years 1948-1990; Tr = Trace amounts (<0.05 in. of rain; <0.5 in. of snow)
Source: National Climatic Data Center, International Station Meteorological Climate Summary, 9/96

Weather Conditions

Temperature			Daytime Sky			Precipitation		
5°F & below	32°F & below	90°F & above	Clear	Partly cloudy	Cloudy	0.01 inch or more precip.	0.1 inch or more snow/ice	Thunder-storms
16	131	16	75	140	150	131	31	39

Note: Figures are average number of days per year and cover the years 1948-1990
Source: National Climatic Data Center, International Station Meteorological Climate Summary, 9/96

HAZARDOUS WASTE

Superfund Sites

The Fort Wayne, IN metro area is home to two sites on the EPA's Superfund National Priorities List (NPL) or Superfund Alternative Approach (SAA) list: **Fort Wayne Reduction Dump** (Final NPL); **Wayne Waste Oil** (Final NPL). The Superfund alternative approach uses the same investigation and cleanup process and standards that are used for sites listed on the National Priorities List. The SAA is an alternative to listing a site on the NPL; it is not an alternative to Superfund or the Superfund process. There are a total of 1,445 Superfund sites with a status of proposed or final on both lists in the United States. *U.S. Environmental Protection Agency, National Priorities List, May 1, 2025; U.S. Environmental Protection Agency, Superfund Alternative Approach Sites, May 1, 2025*

AIR QUALITY

Air Quality Trends: Ozone

	1990	1995	2000	2005	2010	2015	2020	2021	2022	2023
MSA[1]	0.086	0.094	0.086	0.081	0.067	0.061	0.064	0.062	0.064	0.067
U.S.	0.087	0.089	0.081	0.080	0.072	0.068	0.066	0.067	0.067	0.070

Note: (1) Data covers the Fort Wayne, IN Metropolitan Statistical Area. The values shown are the composite ozone concentration averages among trend sites based on the highest fourth daily maximum 8-hour concentration in parts per million. These trends are based on sites having an adequate record of monitoring data during the trend period. Data from exceptional events are included.
Source: U.S. Environmental Protection Agency, Air Quality Monitoring Information, "Air Quality Trends by City, 1990-2023"

Air Quality Index

Area	Percent of Days when Air Quality was...[2]					AQI Statistics[2]	
	Good	Moderate	Unhealthy for Sensitive Groups	Unhealthy	Very Unhealthy	Maximum	Median
MSA[1]	45.2	52.1	1.9	0.5	0.3	223	52

Note: (1) Data covers the Fort Wayne, IN Metropolitan Statistical Area; (2) Based on 365 days with AQI data in 2023. Air Quality Index (AQI) is an index for reporting daily air quality. EPA calculates the AQI for five major air pollutants regulated by the Clean Air Act: ground-level ozone, particle pollution (aka particulate matter), carbon monoxide, sulfur dioxide, and nitrogen dioxide. The AQI runs from 0 to 500. The higher the AQI value, the greater the level of air pollution and the greater the health concern. There are six AQI categories: "Good" AQI is between 0 and 50. Air quality is considered satisfactory; "Moderate" AQI is between 51 and 100. Air quality is acceptable; "Unhealthy for Sensitive Groups" When AQI values are between 101 and 150, members of sensitive groups may experience health effects; "Unhealthy" When AQI values are between 151 and 200 everyone may begin to experience health effects; "Very Unhealthy" AQI values between 201 and 300 trigger a health alert; "Hazardous" AQI values over 300 trigger warnings of emergency conditions (not shown).
Source: U.S. Environmental Protection Agency, Air Quality Index Report, 2023

Air Quality Index Pollutants

Area	Percent of Days when AQI Pollutant was...[2]					
	Carbon Monoxide	Nitrogen Dioxide	Ozone	Sulfur Dioxide	Particulate Matter 2.5	Particulate Matter 10
MSA[1]	0.0	0.0	38.9	(3)	61.1	0.0

Note: (1) Data covers the Fort Wayne, IN Metropolitan Statistical Area; (2) Based on 365 days with AQI data in 2023. The Air Quality Index (AQI) is an index for reporting daily air quality. EPA calculates the AQI for five major air pollutants regulated by the Clean Air Act: ground-level ozone, particle pollution (also known as particulate matter), carbon monoxide, sulfur dioxide, and nitrogen dioxide. The AQI runs from 0 to 500. The higher the AQI value, the greater the level of air pollution and the greater the health concern; (3) Sulfur dioxide is no longer included in this table because SO_2 concentrations tend to be very localized and not necessarily representative of broad geographical areas like counties and CBSAs.
Source: U.S. Environmental Protection Agency, Air Quality Index Report, 2023

Maximum Air Pollutant Concentrations: Particulate Matter, Ozone, CO and Lead

	Particulate Matter 10 (ug/m^3)	Particulate Matter 2.5 Wtd AM (ug/m^3)	Particulate Matter 2.5 24-Hr (ug/m^3)	Ozone (ppm)	Carbon Monoxide (ppm)	Lead (ug/m^3)
MSA[1] Level	n/a	10	33	0.075	n/a	n/a
NAAQS[2]	150	15	35	0.075	9	0.15
Met NAAQS[2]	n/a	Yes	Yes	Yes	n/a	n/a

Note: (1) Data covers the Fort Wayne, IN Metropolitan Statistical Area; Data from exceptional events are included; (2) National Ambient Air Quality Standards; ppm = parts per million; ug/m^3 = micrograms per cubic meter; n/a not available.
Concentrations: Particulate Matter 10 (coarse particulate)—highest second maximum 24-hour concentration; Particulate Matter 2.5 Wtd AM (fine particulate)—highest weighted annual mean concentration; Particulate Matter 2.5 24-Hour (fine particulate)—highest 98th percentile 24-hour concentration; Ozone—highest fourth daily maximum 8-hour concentration; Carbon Monoxide—highest second maximum non-overlapping 8-hour concentration; Lead—maximum running 3-month average
Source: U.S. Environmental Protection Agency, Air Quality Monitoring Information, "Air Quality Statistics by City, 2023"

Maximum Air Pollutant Concentrations: Nitrogen Dioxide and Sulfur Dioxide

	Nitrogen Dioxide AM (ppb)	Nitrogen Dioxide 1-Hr (ppb)	Sulfur Dioxide AM (ppb)	Sulfur Dioxide 1-Hr (ppb)	Sulfur Dioxide 24-Hr (ppb)
MSA[1] Level	n/a	n/a	n/a	n/a	n/a
NAAQS[2]	53	100	30	75	140
Met NAAQS[2]	n/a	n/a	n/a	n/a	n/a

Note: (1) Data covers the Fort Wayne, IN Metropolitan Statistical Area; Data from exceptional events are included; (2) National Ambient Air Quality Standards; ppm = parts per million; ug/m^3 = micrograms per cubic meter; n/a not available.
Concentrations: Nitrogen Dioxide AM—highest arithmetic mean concentration; Nitrogen Dioxide 1-Hr—highest 98th percentile 1-hour daily maximum concentration; Sulfur Dioxide AM—highest annual mean concentration; Sulfur Dioxide 1-Hr—highest 99th percentile 1-hour daily maximum concentration; Sulfur Dioxide 24-Hr—highest second maximum 24-hour concentration
Source: U.S. Environmental Protection Agency, Air Quality Monitoring Information, "Air Quality Statistics by City, 2023"

Green Bay, Wisconsin

Background

The city of Green Bay takes its name from an inlet at the mouth of the Fox River, off Lake Michigan. Laid out on both sides of the river, Green Bay is the oldest city in Wisconsin, the seat of Brown County, and the third most populous in the state. Among the many things the city is known for, stands outs are the Port of Green Bay, with 14 docks on the Fox River that connect to both domestic and international ports, and the nation's oldest professional football team, the Green Bay Packers, who play in Lambeau Field, the longest continuously occupied stadium in the NFL.

Prior to European settlement, the area was home to Winnebago and other horticultural tribes. French explorer Jean Nicolet, who was seeking a route to the Pacific to Asia, was the first recorded European visitor. He landed his canoe in 1634 about 10 miles south of the present city, finding a community of friendly Winnebago and Oneida people.

Mostly French explorers and traders established a trading post at the mouth of the river, founding Fort St. Francis in 1720. In 1745, the first permanent settlement was Le Baye in the present city. The Tank House, built by the voyageur Joseph Roy in 1766, is thought to be the oldest house in the state. Green Bay is also home to the oldest Roman Catholic bishopric in the area. Although the French influence was paramount, many of the fur traders who came into the area were associated with the American fur baron John Jacob Astor, who constructed warehouses and other buildings.

Settlers regarded themselves as French citizens until the fort was occupied by the British in 1763. From 1763 until the War of 1812, they were under British control. When the Americans garrisoned Fort Howard, the city was brought firmly under rule of the new republic. The first newspaper in the state, the *Green Bay Intelligencer*, was established in 1833. In 1854, the city of Green Bay was chartered and, in 1893, the adjoining Fort Howard was incorporated into it. In the late nineteenth century, Green Bay was a major port for the thriving lumber trade.

Today, Green Bay is the flagship city and economic hub of northeastern Wisconsin. Forest products, particularly paper, are still a mainstay of the local economy, giving the city the nickname the "Toilet Paper Capital of the World." Northern Paper Company, Fort Howard Paper Company, and Hoberg Paper Company were among Green Bay's first paper manufacturers, and Northern offered the first splinter-free toilet paper in the early 1930s. Packing companies were part of the city's early economy, including Acme Packing Company and Indian Packing Company, the namesake of the Green Bay Packers. Top employers today include Bellin Health, Schneider National, Humana, Aurora BayCare Medical Center, and Oneida Nation of Wisconsin.

The city's downtown combines office space and residences along the Fox River and boasts a popular walking/biking trail along the river's east side. The CityDeck riverfront boardwalk is about a quarter mile long. The recently renovated Broadway corridor and the KI Convention Center add to the city's economy.

Popular cultural attractions include the Children's Museum of Green Bay, the National Railroad Museum, the Meyer Theatre, The Tarlton Theatre, the Green Bay Film Festival, and the Civic Symphony of Green Bay.

Natural attractions include the Bay Beach Wildlife Sanctuary, Green Bay Botanical Garden and 70 parks and trails.

In 2020, Green Bay Metro partnered with Via Transportation to launch GBM Paratransit, a service for riders with disabilities. Due to the success of that program, the partners launched GBM On Demand, the first micro-transit service in the state of Wisconsin.

Higher education in Green Bay includes Bellin College of Nursing, College of Menominee Nation, Northeast Wisconsin Technical College, and Green Bay campuses for Concordia University, Lakeland College, Medical College of Wisconsin, and University of Wisconsin.

Green Bay has four distinct seasons, with warm summers, and snowy, windy winters. Summer temperatures average at 81 degrees and winter temperatures average 12 degrees. Rainy season is April to October.

Rankings

General Rankings

- *US News & World Report* conducted a survey of more than 3,500 people and analyzed the 150 largest metropolitan areas to determine what matters most when selecting the next place to live. Green Bay ranked #12 out of the top 25 as having the best combination of desirable factors. Criteria: cost of living; quality of life and education; climate; job market; desirability; and other factors. *realestate.usnews.com, "Best Places to Live in the U.S. in 2024-2025," May 21, 2024*

- In their annual survey, Livability.com looked at data for more than 2,000 mid-sized U.S. cities to assign a "Livability Score"for each. The top 100 scoring cities make up Livability's "Top 100 Best Places to Live in the U.S." in 2025. Green Bay was placed among the top 100 of the customizable list. Criteria: housing and economy; cost of living; environment; education; health care options; transportation; safety; and community amenities. *Livability.com, "Top 100 Best Places to Live in the U.S. in 2025" April 15, 2025*

Business/Finance Rankings

- The Green Bay metro area appeared on the Milken Institute "2025 Best Performing Cities" list. Rank: #170 out of 200 large metro areas (based on performance category). Criteria: job growth; wage growth; high-tech growth and impact; community resilience; housing affordability; household broadband access. *Milken Institute, "Best-Performing Cities 2025," January 14, 2025*

Real Estate Rankings

- Green Bay was ranked #72 out of 176 metro areas in terms of cost of housing in 2024 by the National Association of Home Builders (#1 = most affordable). Criteria: the portion of an average family's income necessary to pay the mortgage on a median-priced home. *National Association of Home Builders®, NAHB-Wells Fargo Cost of Housing Index, 4th Quarter 2024*

Business Environment

DEMOGRAPHICS

Population Growth

Area	1990 Census	2000 Census	2010 Census	2020 Census	2023 Estimate[2]	Population Growth 1990-2023 (%)
City	96,466	102,313	104,057	107,395	106,585	10.5
MSA[1]	243,698	282,599	306,241	328,268	329,375	35.2
U.S.	248,709,873	281,421,906	308,745,538	331,449,281	332,387,540	33.6

Note: (1) Figures cover the Green Bay, WI Metropolitan Statistical Area; (2) 2019-2023 5-year ACS population estimate
Source: U.S. Census Bureau, 1990 Census, 2000 Census, 2010 Census, 2020 Census, 2019-2023 American Community Survey 5-Year Estimates

Race

Area	White Alone[2] (%)	Black Alone[2] (%)	Asian Alone[2] (%)	AIAN[3] Alone[2] (%)	NHOPI[4] Alone[2] (%)	Other Race Alone[2] (%)	Two or More Races (%)
City	69.9	3.8	4.1	3.3	0.0	7.1	11.8
MSA[1]	82.9	2.2	2.7	1.7	0.0	3.3	7.1
U.S.	63.4	12.4	5.8	0.9	0.2	6.6	10.7

Note: (1) Figures cover the Green Bay, WI Metropolitan Statistical Area; (2) Alone is defined as not being in combination with one or more other races; (3) American Indian and Alaska Native; (4) Native Hawaiian and Other Pacific Islander
Source: U.S. Census Bureau, 2019-2023 American Community Survey 5-Year Estimates

Hispanic or Latino Origin

Area	Total (%)	Mexican (%)	Puerto Rican (%)	Cuban (%)	Other (%)
City	18.1	13.8	2.3	0.1	1.9
MSA[1]	8.7	6.2	1.0	0.1	1.3
U.S.	19.0	11.3	1.8	0.7	5.2

Note: Persons of Hispanic or Latino origin can be of any race; (1) Figures cover the Green Bay, WI Metropolitan Statistical Area
Source: U.S. Census Bureau, 2019-2023 American Community Survey 5-Year Estimates

Age

Area	Percent of Population									Median Age
	Under Age 5	Age 5–19	Age 20–34	Age 35–44	Age 45–54	Age 55–64	Age 65–74	Age 75–84	Age 85+	
City	6.5	20.5	21.8	13.5	11.6	12.2	8.3	3.7	1.7	35.7
MSA[1]	5.7	19.6	18.8	12.9	12.1	13.9	10.4	4.8	1.7	39.2
U.S.	5.7	19.1	20.2	13.1	12.3	12.8	10.0	4.9	1.9	38.7

Note: (1) Figures cover the Green Bay, WI Metropolitan Statistical Area
Source: U.S. Census Bureau, 2019-2023 American Community Survey 5-Year Estimates

Disability by Age

Area	All Ages	Under 18 Years Old	18 to 64 Years Old	65 Years and Over
City	15.0	7.1	13.9	34.3
MSA[1]	12.0	4.4	10.6	27.3
U.S.	13.0	4.7	10.7	32.9

Note: Figures show percent of the civilian noninstitutionalized population that reported having a disability. Disability status is determined from six types of difficulty: vision, hearing, cognitive, ambulatory, self-care, and independent living. For children under 5 years old, hearing and vision difficulty are used to determine disability status. For children between the ages of 5 and 14, disability status is determined from hearing, vision, cognitive, ambulatory, and self-care difficulties. For people aged 15 years and older, they are considered to have a disability if they have difficulty with any one of the six difficulty types; Note: (1) Figures cover the Green Bay, WI Metropolitan Statistical Area
Source: U.S. Census Bureau, 2019-2023 American Community Survey 5-Year Estimates

Ancestry

Area	German	Irish	English	American	Italian	Polish	French[2]	European	Scottish
City	26.6	8.2	4.6	3.6	2.0	7.2	3.0	1.6	1.0
MSA[1]	33.7	9.3	4.9	4.0	2.2	9.4	3.5	1.6	0.7
U.S.	12.6	9.4	9.1	5.5	4.9	2.6	2.0	1.6	1.6

Note: Figures are the percentage of the total population reporting a particular ancestry. The nine most commonly reported ancestries in the U.S. are shown. Figures include multiple ancestries (e.g. if a person reported being Irish and Italian, they were included in both columns); (1) Figures cover the Green Bay, WI Metropolitan Statistical Area; (2) Excludes Basque
Source: U.S. Census Bureau, 2019-2023 American Community Survey 5-Year Estimates

Foreign-born Population

Area	Percent of Population Born in								
	Any Foreign Country	Asia	Mexico	Europe	Caribbean	Central America[2]	South America	Africa	Canada
City	8.8	2.1	4.5	0.4	0.2	0.5	0.3	0.6	0.2
MSA[1]	4.8	1.5	1.9	0.5	0.1	0.3	0.2	0.2	0.1
U.S.	13.9	4.3	3.3	1.4	1.4	1.2	1.2	0.8	0.2

Note: (1) Figures cover the Green Bay, WI Metropolitan Statistical Area; (2) Excludes Mexico.
Source: U.S. Census Bureau, 2019-2023 American Community Survey 5-Year Estimates

Household Size

Area	Persons in Household (%)							Average Household Size
	One	Two	Three	Four	Five	Six	Seven or More	
City	35.7	32.4	12.0	11.7	4.8	2.0	1.3	2.35
MSA[1]	29.3	37.6	13.1	12.1	5.2	1.8	0.8	2.38
U.S.	28.5	33.8	15.4	12.7	5.9	2.3	1.4	2.54

Note: (1) Figures cover the Green Bay, WI Metropolitan Statistical Area
Source: U.S. Census Bureau, 2019-2023 American Community Survey 5-Year Estimates

Household Relationships

Area	Householder	Opposite-sex Spouse	Same-sex Spouse	Opposite-sex Unmarried Partner	Same-sex Unmarried Partner	Child[2]	Grandchild	Other Relatives	Non-relatives
City	40.7	15.2	0.2	4.0	0.2	28.6	1.6	3.4	3.0
MSA[1]	40.5	19.8	0.1	3.3	0.1	28.1	1.2	2.2	2.2
U.S.	38.3	17.5	0.2	2.5	0.2	28.3	2.4	4.8	3.4

Note: Figures are percent of the total population; (1) Figures cover the Green Bay, WI Metropolitan Statistical Area; (2) Includes biological, adopted, and stepchildren of the householder
Source: U.S. Census Bureau, 2020 Census

Gender

Area	Males	Females	Males per 100 Females
City	52,829	53,756	98.3
MSA[1]	165,274	164,101	100.7
U.S.	164,545,087	167,842,453	98.0

Note: (1) Figures cover the Green Bay, WI Metropolitan Statistical Area
Source: U.S. Census Bureau, 2019-2023 American Community Survey 5-Year Estimates

Marital Status

Area	Never Married	Now Married[2]	Separated	Widowed	Divorced
City	39.4	41.0	1.1	4.9	13.5
MSA[1]	31.8	51.2	0.6	5.2	11.1
U.S.	34.1	47.9	1.7	5.6	10.7

Note: Figures are percentages and cover the population 15 years of age and older; (1) Figures cover the Green Bay, WI Metropolitan Statistical Area; (2) Excludes separated
Source: U.S. Census Bureau, 2019-2023 American Community Survey 5-Year Estimates

Religious Groups by Family

Area	Catholic	Baptist	Methodist	LDS[2]	Pentecostal	Lutheran	Islam	Adventist	Other
MSA[1]	31.8	0.3	1.4	0.5	1.1	10.8	0.4	0.9	7.0
U.S.	18.7	7.3	3.0	2.0	1.8	1.7	1.3	1.3	11.6

Note: Figures are the number of adherents as a percentage of the total population and cover the eight largest religious groups in the U.S; (1) Figures cover the Green Bay, WI Metropolitan Statistical Area; (2) Church of Jesus Christ of Latter-day Saints
Sources: 2020 U.S. Religion Census, Association of Statisticians of American Religious Bodies; The Association of Religion Data Archives (ARDA)

Religious Groups by Tradition

Area	Catholic	Evangelical Protestant	Mainline Protestant	Black Protestant	Islam	Judaism	Hinduism	Orthodox	Buddhism
MSA[1]	31.8	14.6	6.2	<0.1	0.4	n/a	n/a	<0.1	<0.1
U.S.	18.7	16.5	5.2	2.3	1.3	0.6	0.4	0.4	0.3

Note: Figures are the number of adherents as a percentage of the total population; (1) Figures cover the Green Bay, WI Metropolitan Statistical Area
Sources: 2020 U.S. Religion Census, Association of Statisticians of American Religious Bodies; The Association of Religion Data Archives (ARDA)

Green Bay, Wisconsin

ECONOMY

Real Gross Domestic Product (GDP)

Area	2017	2018	2019	2020	2021	2022	2023	Rank[3]
MSA[1]	20.0	20.6	20.7	20.1	20.5	20.8	21.1	144
U.S.[2]	17,619.1	18,160.7	18,642.5	18,238.9	19,387.6	19,896.6	20,436.3	—

Note: Figures are in billions of chained 2017 dollars; (1) Figures cover the Green Bay, WI Metropolitan Statistical Area; (2) Figures cover real GDP within metropolitan areas; (3) Rank is based on 2023 data and ranges from 1 to 384
Source: U.S. Bureau of Economic Analysis

Economic Growth

Area	2014	2015	2016	2017	2018	2019	2020	2021	2022	2023
MSA[1]	6.3	2.8	1.0	-0.2	3.2	0.4	-2.8	1.9	1.4	1.3
U.S.[2]	2.6	3.2	2.0	2.7	3.1	2.7	-2.2	6.3	2.6	2.7

Note: Figures are real gross domestic product growth rates and represent percent change from preceding period; (1) Figures cover the Green Bay, WI Metropolitan Statistical Area; (2) Figures are the average growth rates within metropolitan areas
Source: U.S. Bureau of Economic Analysis

Metropolitan Area Exports

Area	2018	2019	2020	2021	2022	2023	Rank[2]
MSA[1]	1,044.3	928.2	736.4	765.6	855.1	835.1	190
U.S.	1,664,056.1	1,645,173.7	1,431,406.6	1,753,941.4	2,062,937.4	2,019,160.5	—

Note: Figures are in millions of dollars; (1) Figures cover the Green Bay, WI Metropolitan Statistical Area; (2) Rank is based on 2023 data and ranges from 1 to 386
Source: U.S. Department of Commerce, International Trade Administration, Office of Trade and Economic Analysis, Industry and Analysis, Exports by Metropolitan Area, data extracted April 2, 2025

Building Permits

Area	Single-Family 2023	Single-Family 2024	Single-Family Pct. Chg.	Multi-Family 2023	Multi-Family 2024	Multi-Family Pct. Chg.	Total 2023	Total 2024	Total Pct. Chg.
City	37	42	13.5	0	434	—	37	476	1,186.5
MSA[1]	578	717	24.0	415	1,108	167.0	993	1,825	83.8
U.S.	920,000	981,900	6.7	591,100	496,100	-16.1	1,511,100	1,478,000	-2.2

Note: (1) Figures cover the Green Bay, WI Metropolitan Statistical Area; Figures represent new, privately-owned housing units authorized (unadjusted data)
Source: U.S. Census Bureau, Building Permits Survey (BPS), 2023, 2024

Bankruptcy Filings

Area	Business Filings 2023	Business Filings 2024	% Chg.	Nonbusiness Filings 2023	Nonbusiness Filings 2024	% Chg.
Brown County	5	10	100.0	320	408	27.5
U.S.	18,926	23,107	22.1	434,064	494,201	13.9

Note: Business filings include Chapter 7, Chapter 9, Chapter 11, Chapter 12, Chapter 13, Chapter 15, and Section 304; Nonbusiness filings include Chapter 7, Chapter 11, and Chapter 13
Source: Administrative Office of the U.S. Courts, Business and Nonbusiness Bankruptcy, County Cases Commenced by Chapter of the Bankruptcy Code, During the 12-Month Period Ending December 31, 2023 and Business and Nonbusiness Bankruptcy, County Cases Commenced by Chapter of the Bankruptcy Code, During the 12-Month Period Ending December 31, 2024

Housing Vacancy Rates

Area	Gross Vacancy Rate[3] (%) 2022	2023	2024	Year-Round Vacancy Rate[4] (%) 2022	2023	2024	Rental Vacancy Rate[5] (%) 2022	2023	2024	Homeowner Vacancy Rate[6] (%) 2022	2023	2024
MSA[1]	n/a	n/a	n/a	n/a	n/a	n/a	n/a	n/a	n/a	n/a	n/a	n/a
U.S.[2]	9.1	9.0	9.1	7.5	7.5	7.6	5.7	6.5	6.8	0.8	0.8	1.0

Note: (1) Figures cover the Green Bay, WI Metropolitan Statistical Area; (2) Figures cover the 75 largest Metropolitan Statistical Areas; (3) The percentage of the total housing inventory that is vacant; (4) The percentage of the housing inventory (excluding seasonal units) that is year-round vacant; (5) The percentage of rental inventory that is vacant for rent; (6) The percentage of homeowner inventory that is vacant for sale; n/a not available
Source: U.S. Census Bureau, Housing Vacancies and Homeownership Annual Statistics: 2022, 2023, 2024

INCOME

Income

Area	Per Capita ($)	Median Household ($)	Average Household ($)
City	34,514	62,546	81,363
MSA[1]	40,606	77,459	98,052
U.S.	43,289	78,538	110,491

Note: (1) Figures cover the Green Bay, WI Metropolitan Statistical Area
Source: U.S. Census Bureau, 2019-2023 American Community Survey 5-Year Estimates

Household Income Distribution

Area	Percent of Households Earning							
	Under $15,000	$15,000 -$24,999	$25,000 -$34,999	$35,000 -$49,999	$50,000 -$74,999	$75,000 -$99,999	$100,000 -$149,999	$150,000 and up
City	9.5	8.6	7.4	13.6	19.7	14.6	16.2	10.4
MSA[1]	6.7	5.6	7.0	11.1	17.9	14.8	20.8	16.1
U.S.	8.5	6.6	6.8	10.4	15.7	12.7	17.4	21.9

Note: (1) Figures cover the Green Bay, WI Metropolitan Statistical Area
Source: U.S. Census Bureau, 2019-2023 American Community Survey 5-Year Estimates

Poverty Rate

Area	All Ages	Under 18 Years Old	18 to 64 Years Old	65 Years and Over
City	16.5	23.4	15.0	11.0
MSA[1]	9.5	11.6	9.3	7.5
U.S.	12.4	16.3	11.6	10.4

Note: Figures are percentage of people whose income during the past 12 months was below the poverty level; (1) Figures cover the Green Bay, WI Metropolitan Statistical Area
Source: U.S. Census Bureau, 2019-2023 American Community Survey 5-Year Estimates

EMPLOYMENT

Labor Force and Employment

Area	Civilian Labor Force			Workers Employed		
	Dec. 2023	Dec. 2024	% Chg.	Dec. 2023	Dec. 2024	% Chg.
City	53,842	54,171	0.6	52,558	52,661	0.2
MSA[1]	174,722	175,808	0.6	170,734	171,226	0.3
U.S.	166,661,000	167,746,000	0.7	160,754,000	161,294,000	0.3

Note: Data is not seasonally adjusted and covers workers 16 years of age and older; (1) Figures cover the Green Bay, WI Metropolitan Statistical Area
Source: Bureau of Labor Statistics, Local Area Unemployment Statistics

Unemployment Rate

Area	2024											
	Jan.	Feb.	Mar.	Apr.	May	Jun.	Jul.	Aug.	Sep.	Oct.	Nov.	Dec.
City	2.7	3.2	3.3	2.8	2.8	3.3	3.1	2.8	2.5	2.5	2.6	2.8
MSA[1]	2.6	3.1	3.1	2.6	2.6	3.0	2.9	2.6	2.3	2.3	2.4	2.6
U.S.	4.1	4.2	3.9	3.5	3.7	4.3	4.5	4.4	3.9	3.9	4.0	3.8

Note: Data is not seasonally adjusted and covers workers 16 years of age and older; (1) Figures cover the Green Bay, WI Metropolitan Statistical Area
Source: Bureau of Labor Statistics, Local Area Unemployment Statistics

Average Wages

Occupation	$/Hr.	Occupation	$/Hr.
Accountants and Auditors	40.76	Maintenance and Repair Workers	25.64
Automotive Mechanics	27.11	Marketing Managers	75.74
Bookkeepers	23.58	Network and Computer Systems Admin.	41.79
Carpenters	30.80	Nurses, Licensed Practical	28.26
Cashiers	14.24	Nurses, Registered	41.77
Computer Programmers	45.19	Nursing Assistants	19.98
Computer Systems Analysts	48.58	Office Clerks, General	21.47
Computer User Support Specialists	28.66	Physical Therapists	47.00
Construction Laborers	26.49	Physicians	196.56
Cooks, Restaurant	17.71	Plumbers, Pipefitters and Steamfitters	39.90
Customer Service Representatives	22.50	Police and Sheriff's Patrol Officers	39.06
Dentists	81.11	Postal Service Mail Carriers	29.14
Electricians	33.62	Real Estate Sales Agents	28.56
Engineers, Electrical	47.47	Retail Salespersons	17.47
Fast Food and Counter Workers	13.45	Sales Representatives, Technical/Scientific	31.64
Financial Managers	72.06	Secretaries, Exc. Legal/Medical/Executive	22.49
First-Line Supervisors of Office Workers	32.86	Security Guards	20.67
General and Operations Managers	64.79	Surgeons	n/a
Hairdressers/Cosmetologists	18.07	Teacher Assistants, Exc. Postsecondary[1]	17.43
Home Health and Personal Care Aides	15.70	Teachers, Secondary School, Exc. Sp. Ed.[1]	29.58
Janitors and Cleaners	16.94	Telemarketers	n/a
Landscaping/Groundskeeping Workers	19.50	Truck Drivers, Heavy/Tractor-Trailer	27.16
Lawyers	69.46	Truck Drivers, Light/Delivery Services	22.51
Maids and Housekeeping Cleaners	16.12	Waiters and Waitresses	14.93

Note: Wage data covers the Green Bay, WI Metropolitan Statistical Area; (1) Hourly wages were calculated from annual wage data based on a 40 hour work week
Source: Bureau of Labor Statistics, Metro Area Occupational Employment & Wage Estimates, May 2024

Employment by Industry

Sector	MSA[1] Number of Employees	MSA[1] Percent of Total	U.S. Percent of Total
Construction, Mining, and Logging	8,700	4.8	5.5
Financial Activities	8,600	4.7	5.8
Government	21,600	11.8	14.9
Information	1,700	0.9	1.9
Leisure and Hospitality	17,900	9.8	10.4
Manufacturing	33,100	18.1	8.0
Other Services	8,000	4.4	3.7
Private Education and Health Services	28,800	15.8	16.9
Professional and Business Services	19,100	10.5	14.2
Retail Trade	17,300	9.5	10.0
Transportation, Warehousing, and Utilities	8,700	4.8	4.8
Wholesale Trade	9,000	4.9	3.9

Note: Figures are non-farm employment as of December 2024. Figures are not seasonally adjusted and include workers 16 years of age and older; (1) Figures cover the Green Bay, WI Metropolitan Statistical Area
Source: Bureau of Labor Statistics, Current Employment Statistics, Employment, Hours, and Earnings

Employment by Occupation

Occupation Classification	City (%)	MSA[1] (%)	U.S. (%)
Management, Business, Science, and Arts	32.5	37.2	42.0
Natural Resources, Construction, and Maintenance	8.0	9.3	8.6
Production, Transportation, and Material Moving	22.5	19.0	13.0
Sales and Office	19.8	19.4	19.9
Service	17.3	15.1	16.5

Note: Figures cover employed civilians 16 years of age and older; (1) Figures cover the Green Bay, WI Metropolitan Statistical Area
Source: U.S. Census Bureau, 2019-2023 American Community Survey 5-Year Estimates

Occupations with Greatest Projected Employment Growth: 2022 – 2032

Occupation[1]	2022 Employment	2032 Projected Employment	Numeric Employment Change	Percent Employment Change
Home Health and Personal Care Aides	80,600	94,000	13,400	16.6
Cooks, Restaurant	24,790	32,190	7,400	29.9
Laborers and Freight, Stock, and Material Movers, Hand	68,280	75,240	6,960	10.2
Stockers and Order Fillers	51,890	58,550	6,660	12.8
Software Developers	19,270	25,280	6,010	31.2
Fast Food and Counter Workers	56,080	60,930	4,850	8.6
Industrial Machinery Mechanics	16,970	21,220	4,250	25.0
Construction Laborers	23,620	27,590	3,970	16.8
Heavy and Tractor-Trailer Truck Drivers	52,250	56,180	3,930	7.5
Registered Nurses	62,260	65,570	3,310	5.3

Note: Projections cover Wisconsin; (1) Sorted by numeric employment change
Source: www.projectionscentral.org, State Occupational Projections, 2022–2032 Long-Term Projections

Fastest-Growing Occupations: 2022 – 2032

Occupation[1]	2022 Employment	2032 Projected Employment	Numeric Employment Change	Percent Employment Change
Nurse Practitioners	4,950	7,480	2,530	51.1
Data Scientists	2,860	4,090	1,230	43.0
Travel Agents	920	1,270	350	38.0
Animal Trainers	1,180	1,610	430	36.4
Statisticians	360	490	130	36.1
Information Security Analysts (SOC 2018)	2,410	3,220	810	33.6
Aircraft Service Attendants	150	200	50	33.3
Physician Assistants	2,980	3,950	970	32.6
Actuaries	990	1,310	320	32.3
Chemical Engineers	350	460	110	31.4

Note: Projections cover Wisconsin; (1) Sorted by percent employment change and excludes occupations with numeric employment change less than 50
Source: www.projectionscentral.org, State Occupational Projections, 2022–2032 Long-Term Projections

CITY FINANCES

City Government Finances

Component	2022 ($000)	2022 ($ per capita)
Total Revenues	209,653	2,019
Total Expenditures	208,294	2,006
Debt Outstanding	302,087	2,909

Source: U.S. Census Bureau, State & Local Government Finances 2022

City Government Revenue by Source

Source	2022 ($000)	2022 ($ per capita)	2022 (%)
General Revenue			
From Federal Government	5,157	50	2.5
From State Government	34,401	331	16.4
From Local Governments	10,815	104	5.2
Taxes			
Property	66,992	645	32.0
Sales and Gross Receipts	405	4	0.2
Personal Income	0	0	0.0
Corporate Income	0	0	0.0
Motor Vehicle License	0	0	0.0
Other Taxes	2,551	25	1.2
Current Charges	49,030	472	23.4
Liquor Store	0	0	0.0
Utility	25,474	245	12.2

Source: U.S. Census Bureau, State & Local Government Finances 2022

City Government Expenditures by Function

Function	2022 ($000)	2022 ($ per capita)	2022 (%)
General Direct Expenditures			
Air Transportation	0	0	0.0
Corrections	0	0	0.0
Education	0	0	0.0
Employment Security Administration	0	0	0.0
Financial Administration	2,794	26	1.3
Fire Protection	28,378	273	13.6
General Public Buildings	689	6	0.3
Governmental Administration, Other	3,254	31	1.6
Health	488	4	0.2
Highways	20,962	201	10.1
Hospitals	0	0	0.0
Housing and Community Development	413	4	0.2
Interest on General Debt	8,346	80	4.0
Judicial and Legal	1,135	10	0.5
Libraries	0	0	0.0
Parking	2,866	27	1.4
Parks and Recreation	11,086	106	5.3
Police Protection	28,713	276	13.8
Public Welfare	0	0	0.0
Sewerage	36,455	351	17.5
Solid Waste Management	6,270	60	3.0
Veterans' Services	0	0	0.0
Liquor Store	0	0	0.0
Utility	43,777	421	21.0

Source: U.S. Census Bureau, State & Local Government Finances 2022

TAXES

State Corporate Income Tax Rates

State	Tax Rate (%)	Income Brackets ($)	Num. of Brackets	Financial Institution Tax Rate (%)[a]	Federal Income Tax Ded.
Wisconsin	7.9	Flat rate	1	7.9	No

Note: Tax rates for tax year 2024; (a) Rates listed are the corporate income tax rate applied to financial institutions or excise taxes based on income. Some states have other taxes based upon the value of deposits or shares.
Source: Federation of Tax Administrators, State Corporate Income Tax Rates, January 1, 2025

State Individual Income Tax Rates

State	Tax Rate (%)	Income Brackets ($)	Personal Exemptions ($)			Standard Ded. ($)	
			Single	Married	Depend.	Single	Married
Wisconsin (a)	3.5 - 7.65	13,810 - 304,170 (y)	700	1,400	700	14,600	29,200 (z)

Note: Tax rates for tax year 2024; Local- and county-level taxes are not included; Federal income tax is not deductible on state income tax returns; (a) 16 states have statutory provision for automatically adjusting to the rate of inflation the dollar values of the income tax brackets, standard deductions, and/or personal exemptions. Oregon does not index the income brackets for $125,000 and over See: INFL and SPEC above; (y) The Wisconsin income brackets reported are for single individuals. For married taxpayers filing jointly, the same tax rates apply income brackets ranging from $18,420, to $405,550 in 2023; (z) Alabama standard deduction is phased out for incomes over $25,500 after 2017 (MFJ, HOH and Single); $12,750 for MFS. Rhode Island exemptions & standard deductions phased out for incomes over $274,650; Wisconsin standard deduciton phases out for income over $124,500.
Source: Federation of Tax Administrators, State Individual Income Tax Rates, January 1, 2025

Various State Sales and Excise Tax Rates

State	State Sales Tax (%)	Gasoline[1] ($/gal.)	Cigarette[2] ($/pack)	Spirits[3] ($/gal.)	Wine[4] ($/gal.)	Beer[5] ($/gal.)	Recreational Marijuana (%)
Wisconsin	5	0.33	2.52	3.25	0.25	0.06	Not legal

Note: All tax rates as of January 1, 2025; (1) The American Petroleum Institute has developed a methodology for determining the average tax rate on a gallon of fuel. Rates may include any of the following: excise taxes, environmental fees, storage tank fees, other fees or taxes, general sales tax, and local taxes; (2) The federal excise tax of $1.0066 per pack and local taxes are not included; (3) Rates are those applicable to off-premise sales of 40% alcohol by volume (a.b.v.) distilled spirits in 750ml containers. Local excise taxes are excluded; (4) Rates are those applicable to off-premise sales of 11% a.b.v. non-carbonated wine in 750ml containers; (5) Rates are those applicable to off-premise sales of 4.7% a.b.v. beer in 12 ounce containers.
Source: Tax Foundation, 2025 Facts & Figures: How Does Your State Compare?

State Tax Competitiveness Index

State	Overall Rank	Corporate Tax Rank	Individual Income Tax Rank	Sales Tax Rank	Property Tax Rank	Unemployment Insurance Tax Rank
Wisconsin	19	30	35	6	8	32

Note: The Tax Foundation's State Tax Competitiveness Index enables policymakers, taxpayers, and business leaders to gauge how their states' tax systems compare. A rank of 1 is best, 50 is worst. Rankings do not average to the total. States without a tax rank equally as 1. DC's scores and rankings do not affect other states. The report shows tax systems as of July 1, 2024 (the beginning of Fiscal Year 2025).
Source: Tax Foundation, State Tax Competitiveness Index 2025

TRANSPORTATION

Means of Transportation to Work

Area	Car/Truck/Van		Public Transportation			Bicycle	Walked	Other Means	Worked at Home
	Drove Alone	Car-pooled	Bus	Subway	Railroad				
City	75.9	10.7	1.0	0.0	0.0	0.4	2.3	1.1	8.5
MSA[1]	78.7	7.8	0.4	0.0	0.0	0.2	1.7	0.9	10.4
U.S.	70.2	8.5	1.7	1.3	0.4	0.4	2.4	1.6	13.5

Note: Figures are percentages and cover workers 16 years of age and older; (1) Figures cover the Green Bay, WI Metropolitan Statistical Area
Source: U.S. Census Bureau, 2019-2023 American Community Survey 5-Year Estimates

Travel Time to Work

Area	Less Than 10 Minutes	10 to 19 Minutes	20 to 29 Minutes	30 to 44 Minutes	45 to 59 Minutes	60 to 89 Minutes	90 Minutes or More
City	18.1	47.5	18.0	9.1	3.9	1.9	1.5
MSA[1]	16.8	39.6	22.4	13.1	4.3	2.1	1.7
U.S.	12.6	28.6	21.2	20.8	8.1	6.0	2.8

Note: Note: Figures are percentages and include workers 16 years old and over; (1) Figures cover the Green Bay, WI Metropolitan Statistical Area
Source: U.S. Census Bureau, 2019-2023 American Community Survey 5-Year Estimates

Key Congestion Measures

Measure	2000	2010	2015	2020	2022
Annual Hours of Delay, Total (000)	n/a	n/a	3,394	1,805	3,960
Annual Hours of Delay, Per Auto Commuter	n/a	n/a	15	8	18
Annual Congestion Cost, Per Auto Commuter ($)	n/a	n/a	356	203	420

Note: n/a not available
Source: Texas A&M Transportation Institute, 2023 Urban Mobility Report

Freeway Travel Time Index

Measure	1985	1990	1995	2000	2005	2010	2015	2020	2022
Urban Area Index[1]	n/a	n/a	n/a	n/a	n/a	n/a	1.05	1.03	1.06
Urban Area Rank[1,2]	n/a	n/a	n/a	n/a	n/a	n/a	n/a	n/a	n/a

Note: Freeway Travel Time Index—the ratio of travel time in the peak period to the travel time at free-flow conditions. For example, a value of 1.30 indicates a 20-minute free-flow trip takes 26 minutes in the peak (20 minutes x 1.30 = 26 minutes); (1) Covers the Green Bay WI urban area; (2) Rank is based on 101 larger urban areas (#1 = highest travel time index); n/a not available
Source: Texas A&M Transportation Institute, 2023 Urban Mobility Report

Public Transportation

Agency Name / Mode of Transportation	Vehicles Operated in Maximum Service[1]	Annual Unlinked Passenger Trips[2] (in thous.)	Annual Passenger Miles[3] (in thous.)
Green Bay Metro			
Bus (directly operated)	15	758.4	2,315.8
Demand Response (purchased transportation)	12	77.7	368.3

Note: (1) Number of revenue vehicles operated by the given mode and type of service to meet the annual maximum service requirement. This is the revenue vehicle count during the peak season of the year; on the week and day that maximum service is provided. Vehicles operated in maximum service (VOMS) exclude atypical days and one-time special events; (2) Number of passengers who boarded public transportation vehicles. Passengers are counted each time they board a vehicle no matter how many vehicles they use to travel from their origin to their destination. (3) Sum of the distances ridden by all passengers during the entire fiscal year.
Source: Federal Transit Administration, National Transit Database, 2023

Air Transportation

Airport Name and Code / Type of Service	Passenger Airlines[1]	Passenger Enplanements	Freight Carriers[2]	Freight (lbs)
Green Bay-Austin Straubel International Airport (GRB)				
Domestic service (U.S. carriers only)	16	337,321	5	219,751
International service (U.S. carriers only)	3	190	0	0

Note: (1) Includes all U.S.-based major, minor and commuter airlines that carried at least one passenger during the year; (2) Includes all U.S.-based airlines and freight carriers that transported at least one pound of freight during the year.
Source: Bureau of Transportation Statistics, The Intermodal Transportation Database, Air Carriers: T-100 Domestic Market (U.S. carriers only), 2024; Bureau of Transportation Statistics, The Intermodal Transportation Database, Air Carriers: T-100 International Market (U.S. carriers only), 2024

BUSINESSES

Major Business Headquarters

Company Name	Industry	Rankings Fortune[1]	Rankings Forbes[2]
Schreiber Foods	Food, drink & tobacco	-	91

Note: (1) Companies that produce a 10-K are ranked 1 to 500 based on 2023 revenue; (2) All private companies with at least $2 billion in annual revenue through the end of their most current fiscal year are ranked 1 to 275; companies listed are headquartered in the city; dashes indicate no ranking
Source: Fortune, "Fortune 500," 2024; Forbes, "America's Largest Private Companies," 2024

Fastest-Growing Businesses

According to *Initiative for a Competitive Inner City (ICIC)*, Green Bay is home to one of America's 100 fastest-growing "inner city" companies: **American Tent** (#38). To be eligible for the IC100, companies have to be independently operated, privately held, for-profit businesses with revenues of at least $50,000 in 2019 and $500,000 in 2023, and headquartered in an under-resourced community. Recognizing that concentrated poverty exists within metropolitan areas outside of big cities (and that poverty overall is suburbanizing), ICIC defines under-resourced communities as large low-income, high-poverty areas located in the urban and suburban parts of all but the smallest metropolitan areas. Companies were ranked overall by revenue growth over the five-year period between 2019 and 2023.
Initiative for a Competitive Inner City (ICIC), "Inner City 100 Companies," 2024

Living Environment

COST OF LIVING

Cost of Living Index

Composite Index	Groceries	Housing	Utilities	Trans-portation	Health Care	Misc. Goods/Services
90.5	97.9	80.9	82.0	102.8	95.1	93.4

Note: The Cost of Living Index measures regional differences in the cost of consumer goods and services, excluding taxes and non-consumer expenditures, for professional and managerial households in the top income quintile. It is based on more than 50,000 prices covering almost 60 different items for which prices are collected three times a year by chambers of commerce, economic development organizations or university applied economic centers in each participating urban area. The numbers shown should be read as a percentage above or below the national average of 100. For example, a value of 115.4 in the groceries column indicates that grocery prices are 15.4% higher than the national average. Small differences in the index numbers should not be interpreted as significant; Figures cover the Green Bay WI urban area.
Source: The Council for Community and Economic Research, Cost of Living Index, 2024

Grocery Prices

Area[1]	T-Bone Steak ($/pound)	Frying Chicken ($/pound)	Whole Milk ($/half gal.)	Eggs ($/dozen)	Orange Juice ($/64 oz.)	Coffee ($/11.5 oz.)
City[2]	15.51	1.42	4.70	3.25	4.43	5.29
Avg.	15.42	1.55	4.69	3.25	4.41	5.46
Min.	14.50	1.16	4.43	2.75	4.00	4.85
Max.	17.56	2.89	5.49	4.78	5.54	7.89

Note: (1) Values for the local area are compared with the average, minimum and maximum values for all 276 areas in the Cost of Living Index; (2) Figures cover the Green Bay WI urban area; **T-Bone Steak** (price per pound); **Frying Chicken** (price per pound, whole fryer); **Whole Milk** (half gallon carton); **Eggs** (price per dozen, Grade A, large); **Orange Juice** (64 oz. Tropicana or Florida Natural); **Coffee** (11.5 oz. can, vacuum-packed, Maxwell House, Hills Bros, or Folgers).
Source: The Council for Community and Economic Research, Cost of Living Index, 2024

Housing and Utility Costs

Area[1]	New Home Price ($)	Apartment Rent ($/month)	All Electric ($/month)	Part Electric ($/month)	Other Energy ($/month)	Telephone ($/month)
City[2]	447,400	1,055	-	90.06	61.14	188.34
Avg.	515,975	1,550	210.99	123.07	82.07	194.99
Min.	265,375	692	104.33	53.68	36.26	179.42
Max.	2,775,821	5,719	529.02	397.28	361.63	223.33

Note: (1) Values for the local area are compared with the average, minimum and maximum values for all 276 areas in the Cost of Living Index; (2) Figures cover the Green Bay WI urban area; **New Home Price** (2,400 sf living area, 8,000 sf lot, in urban area with full utilities); **Apartment Rent** (950 sf 2 bedroom/1.5 or 2 bath, unfurnished, excluding all utilities except water); **All Electric** (average monthly cost for an all-electric home); **Part Electric** (average monthly cost for a part-electric home); **Other Energy** (average monthly cost for natural gas, fuel oil, coal, wood, and any other forms of energy except electricity); **Telephone** (price includes the base monthly rate plus taxes and fees for three lines of mobile phone service).
Source: The Council for Community and Economic Research, Cost of Living Index, 2024

Health Care, Transportation, and Other Costs

Area[1]	Doctor ($/visit)	Dentist ($/visit)	Optometrist ($/visit)	Gasoline ($/gallon)	Beauty Salon ($/visit)	Men's Shirt ($)
City[2]	167.58	112.11	84.28	3.14	30.42	26.22
Avg.	143.77	117.51	129.23	3.32	48.57	38.14
Min.	36.74	58.67	67.33	2.80	24.00	13.41
Max.	270.44	216.82	307.33	5.28	94.00	63.89

Note: (1) Values for the local area are compared with the average, minimum and maximum values for all 276 areas in the Cost of Living Index; (2) Figures cover the Green Bay WI urban area; **Doctor** (general practitioners routine exam of an established patient); **Dentist** (adult teeth cleaning and periodic oral examination); **Optometrist** (full vision eye exam for established adult patient); **Gasoline** (one gallon regular unleaded, national brand, including all taxes, cash price at self-service pump if available); **Beauty Salon** (woman's shampoo, trim, and blow-dry); **Men's Shirt** (cotton/polyester dress shirt, pinpoint weave, long sleeves).
Source: The Council for Community and Economic Research, Cost of Living Index, 2024

HOUSING

Homeownership Rate

Area	2017 (%)	2018 (%)	2019 (%)	2020 (%)	2021 (%)	2022 (%)	2023 (%)	2024 (%)
MSA[1]	n/a	n/a	n/a	n/a	n/a	n/a	n/a	n/a
U.S.	63.9	64.4	64.6	66.6	65.5	65.8	65.9	65.6

Note: (1) Figures cover the Green Bay, WI Metropolitan Statistical Area; n/a not available
Source: U.S. Census Bureau, Housing Vacancies and Homeownership Annual Statistics: 2017-2024

House Price Index (HPI)

Area	National Ranking[2]	Quarterly Change (%)	One-Year Change (%)	Five-Year Change (%)	Since 1991Q1 (%)
MSA[1]	103	-1.16	5.89	63.68	299.15
U.S.[3]	–	1.43	4.51	57.13	327.82

Note: The HPI is a weighted repeat sales index. It measures average price changes in repeat sales or refinancings on the same properties. This information is obtained by reviewing repeat mortgage transactions on single-family properties whose mortgages have been purchased or securitized by Fannie Mae or Freddie Mac since January 1975; (1) Figures cover the Green Bay, WI Metropolitan Statistical Area; (2) Rankings are based on annual percentage change for all metro areas containing at least 15,000 transactions over the last 10 years and ranges from 1 to 241; (3) figures based on a weighted average of Census Division estimates using a seasonally adjusted, purchase-only index; all figures are for the period ending December 31, 2024
Source: Federal Housing Finance Agency, Change in FHFA Metropolitan Area House Price Indexes, All Transactions Index, 2024Q4

Home Value

Area	Under $100,000	$100,000 -$199,999	$200,000 -$299,999	$300,000 -$399,999	$400,000 -$499,999	$500,000 -$999,999	$1,000,000 or more	Median ($)
City	8.5	46.2	29.0	8.4	4.0	3.6	0.3	191,500
MSA[1]	7.8	29.2	31.1	15.7	8.0	7.3	0.9	238,700
U.S.	12.1	17.8	19.5	14.4	10.5	19.1	6.5	303,400

Note: Figures are percentages except for median and cover owner-occupied housing units; (1) Figures cover the Green Bay, WI Metropolitan Statistical Area
Source: U.S. Census Bureau, 2019-2023 American Community Survey 5-Year Estimates

Year Housing Structure Built

Area	2020 or Later	2010 -2019	2000 -2009	1990 -1999	1980 -1989	1970 -1979	1960 -1969	1950 -1959	1940 -1949	Before 1940	Median Year
City	0.4	3.2	7.3	9.8	12.5	17.9	12.6	16.1	5.9	14.4	1971
MSA[1]	1.0	8.5	13.4	15.1	11.6	15.5	9.9	9.3	4.0	11.7	1980
U.S.	1.2	8.9	13.6	12.8	13.0	14.4	10.0	9.7	4.5	11.9	1980

Note: Figures are percentages except for Median Year; Note: (1) Figures cover the Green Bay, WI Metropolitan Statistical Area
Source: U.S. Census Bureau, 2019-2023 American Community Survey 5-Year Estimates

Gross Monthly Rent

Area	Under $500	$500 -$999	$1,000 -$1,499	$1,500 -$1,999	$2,000 -$2,499	$2,500 -$2,999	$3,000 and up	Median ($)
City	6.7	55.0	31.7	5.1	0.7	0.1	0.6	904
MSA[1]	4.8	50.7	35.3	6.6	1.4	0.4	0.8	959
U.S.	6.5	22.3	29.5	20.2	10.8	4.8	5.9	1,348

Note: Figures are percentages except for median; Gross rent is the contract rent plus the estimated average monthly cost of utilities (electricity, gas, and water and sewer) and fuels (oil, coal, kerosene, wood, etc.) if these are paid by the renter (or paid for the renter by someone else); (1) Figures cover the Green Bay, WI Metropolitan Statistical Area
Source: U.S. Census Bureau, 2019-2023 American Community Survey 5-Year Estimates

HEALTH

Health Risk Factors

Category	MSA[1] (%)	U.S. (%)
Adults aged 18–64 who have any kind of health care coverage	94.2	90.8
Adults who reported being in good or better health	82.4	81.8
Adults who have been told they have high blood cholesterol	35.5	36.9
Adults who have been told they have high blood pressure	32.3	34.0
Adults who are current smokers	11.2	12.1
Adults who currently use e-cigarettes	6.8	7.7
Adults who currently use chewing tobacco, snuff, or snus	1.4	3.2
Adults who are heavy drinkers[2]	7.5	6.1
Adults who are binge drinkers[3]	13.3	15.2
Adults who are overweight (BMI 25.0 - 29.9)	28.0	34.4
Adults who are obese (BMI 30.0 - 99.8)	44.2	34.3
Adults who participated in any physical activities in the past month	72.8	75.8

Note: All figures are crude prevalence; (1) Figures cover the Green Bay, WI Metropolitan Statistical Area; (2) Heavy drinkers are classified as adult men having more than 14 drinks per week and adult women having more than 7 drinks per week; (3) Binge drinkers are classified as males having five or more drinks on one occasion or females having four or more drinks on one occasion
Source: Centers for Disease Control and Prevention, Behaviorial Risk Factor Surveillance System, SMART: Selected Metropolitan Area Risk Trends, 2023

Acute and Chronic Health Conditions

Category	MSA[1] (%)	U.S. (%)
Adults who have ever been told they had a heart attack	4.6	4.2
Adults who have ever been told they have angina or coronary heart disease	3.6	4.0
Adults who have ever been told they had a stroke	4.5	3.3
Adults who have ever been told they have asthma	15.8	15.7
Adults who have ever been told they have arthritis	24.2	26.3
Adults who have ever been told they have diabetes[2]	9.7	11.5
Adults who have ever been told they had skin cancer	5.5	5.6
Adults who have ever been told they had any other types of cancer	9.9	8.4
Adults who have ever been told they have COPD	5.3	6.4
Adults who have ever been told they have kidney disease	4.1	3.7
Adults who have ever been told they have a form of depression	24.4	22.0

Note: All figures are crude prevalence; (1) Figures cover the Green Bay, WI Metropolitan Statistical Area; (2) Figures do not include pregnancy-related, borderline, or pre-diabetes
Source: Centers for Disease Control and Prevention, Behavioral Risk Factor Surveillance System, SMART: Selected Metropolitan Area Risk Trends, 2023

Health Screening and Vaccination Rates

Category	MSA[1] (%)	U.S. (%)
Adults who have ever been tested for HIV	29.8	37.5
Adults who have had their blood cholesterol checked within the last five years	86.3	87.0
Adults aged 65+ who have had flu shot within the past year	71.1	63.4
Adults aged 65+ who have ever had a pneumonia vaccination	70.9	71.9

Note: All figures are crude prevalence; (1) Figures cover the Green Bay, WI Metropolitan Statistical Area.
Source: Centers for Disease Control and Prevention, Behavioral Risk Factor Surveillance System, SMART: Selected Metropolitan Area Risk Trends, 2023

Disability Status

Category	MSA[1] (%)	U.S. (%)
Adults who reported being deaf	5.9	7.4
Are you blind or have serious difficulty seeing, even when wearing glasses?	4.7	4.9
Do you have difficulty doing errands alone?	10.7	7.8
Do you have difficulty dressing or bathing?	5.1	3.6
Do you have serious difficulty concentrating/remembering/making decisions?	15.2	13.7
Do you have serious difficulty walking or climbing stairs?	12.9	13.2

Note: All figures are crude prevalence; (1) Figures cover the Green Bay, WI Metropolitan Statistical Area.
Source: Centers for Disease Control and Prevention, Behavioral Risk Factor Surveillance System, SMART: Selected Metropolitan Area Risk Trends, 2023

Mortality Rates for the Top 10 Causes of Death in the U.S.

ICD-10[a] Sub-Chapter	ICD-10[a] Code	Crude Mortality Rate[2] per 100,000 population	
		County[3]	U.S.
Malignant neoplasms	C00-C97	168.4	182.7
Ischaemic heart diseases	I20-I25	117.0	109.6
Provisional assignment of new diseases of uncertain etiology[1]	U00-U49	41.9	65.3
Other forms of heart disease	I30-I51	55.6	65.1
Other degenerative diseases of the nervous system	G30-G31	48.1	52.4
Other external causes of accidental injury	W00-X59	61.8	52.3
Cerebrovascular diseases	I60-I69	34.4	49.1
Chronic lower respiratory diseases	J40-J47	28.5	43.5
Hypertensive diseases	I10-I15	40.2	38.9
Organic, including symptomatic, mental disorders	F01-F09	36.2	33.9

Note: (a) ICD-10 = International Classification of Diseases 10th Revision; (1) Includes COVID-19, adverse effects to COVID-19 vaccines, SARS, and vaping-related disorders; (2) Crude mortality rates are a three-year average covering 2021-2023; (3) Figures cover Brown County.
Source: Centers for Disease Control and Prevention, National Center for Health Statistics. National Vital Statistics System, Mortality 2018-2023 on CDC WONDER Online Database

Mortality Rates for Selected Causes of Death

Cause of Death	ICD-10[a] Code	Crude Mortality Rate[1] per 100,000 population	
		County[2]	U.S.
Accidental poisoning and exposure to noxious substances	X40-X49	21.8	30.5
Alzheimer disease	G30	38.5	35.4
Assault	X85-Y09	Unreliable	7.3
COVID-19	U07.1	41.9	65.3
Diabetes mellitus	E10-E14	15.2	30.0
Diseases of the liver	K70-K76	14.2	20.8
Human immunodeficiency virus (HIV) disease	B20-B24	Suppressed	1.5
Influenza and pneumonia	J09-J18	7.3	13.4
Intentional self-harm	X60-X84	16.0	14.7
Malnutrition	E40-E46	5.7	6.0
Obesity and other hyperalimentation	E65-E68	Unreliable	3.1
Renal failure	N17-N19	13.9	16.4
Transport accidents	V01-V99	7.9	14.4

Note: (a) ICD-10 = International Classification of Diseases 10th Revision; (1) Crude mortality rates are a three-year average covering 2021-2023; (2) Figures cover Brown County; Data are suppressed when the data meet the criteria for confidentiality constraints; Crude mortality rates are flagged as unreliable when the rate would be calculated with a numerator of 20 or less.
Source: Centers for Disease Control and Prevention, National Center for Health Statistics. National Vital Statistics System, Mortality 2018-2023 on CDC WONDER Online Database

Health Insurance Coverage

Area	With Health Insurance	With Private Health Insurance	With Public Health Insurance	Without Health Insurance	Population Under Age 19 Without Health Insurance
City	91.6	59.8	40.9	8.4	4.9
MSA[1]	94.8	72.2	34.1	5.2	3.4
U.S.	91.4	67.3	36.3	8.6	5.4

Note: Figures are percentages that cover the civilian noninstitutionalized population; (1) Figures cover the Green Bay, WI Metropolitan Statistical Area
Source: U.S. Census Bureau, 2019-2023 American Community Survey 5-Year Estimates

Number of Medical Professionals

Area	MDs[3]	DOs[3,4]	Dentists	Podiatrists	Chiropractors	Optometrists
County[1] (number)	717	69	219	9	137	54
County[1] (rate[2])	265.5	25.6	80.7	3.3	50.5	19.9
U.S. (rate[2])	302.5	29.2	74.6	6.4	29.5	18.0

Note: Data as of 2023 unless noted; (1) Data covers Brown County; (2) Number of medical professionals per 100,000 population; (3) Data as of 2022 and includes all active, non-federal physicians; (4) Doctor of Osteopathic Medicine
Source: U.S. Department of Health and Human Services, Health Resources and Services Administration, Bureau of Health Professions, Area Resource File (ARF) 2023-2024

EDUCATION

Public School District Statistics

District Name	Schls	Pupils	Pupil/Teacher Ratio	Minority Pupils[1] (%)	Total Rev. per Pupil ($)	Total Exp. per Pupil ($)
Ashwaubenon School District	5	3,197	15.0	26.7	14,544	15,390
Green Bay Area PSD	44	18,579	12.9	62.6	19,631	18,203

Note: Table includes school districts with 2,000 or more students; (1) Percentage of students that are not non-Hispanic white.
Source: U.S. Department of Education, National Center for Education Statistics, Common Core of Data, Local Education Agency (School District) Universe Survey: School Year 2023-2024; U.S. Department of Education, National Center for Education Statistics, Common Core of Data, School District Finance Survey (F-33): School Year 2021–22

Highest Level of Education

Area	Less than H.S.	H.S. Diploma	Some College, No Deg.	Associate Degree	Bachelor's Degree	Master's Degree	Prof. School Degree	Doctorate Degree
City	11.0	31.4	20.4	11.7	18.4	5.3	1.2	0.7
MSA[1]	6.7	31.3	19.1	13.0	21.0	6.8	1.3	0.8
U.S.	10.6	26.2	19.4	8.8	21.3	9.8	2.3	1.6

Note: Figures cover persons age 25 and over; (1) Figures cover the Green Bay, WI Metropolitan Statistical Area
Source: U.S. Census Bureau, 2019-2023 American Community Survey 5-Year Estimates

Educational Attainment by Race

Area	High School Graduate or Higher (%)					Bachelor's Degree or Higher (%)				
	Total	White	Black	Asian	Hisp.[2]	Total	White	Black	Asian	Hisp.[2]
City	89.0	92.6	69.5	84.3	65.8	25.5	27.8	16.2	32.8	11.5
MSA[1]	93.3	95.2	74.2	85.9	69.6	29.9	30.8	18.3	44.5	15.5
U.S.	89.4	92.9	88.1	88.0	72.5	35.0	37.7	24.7	57.0	19.9

Note: Figures shown cover persons 25 years old and over; (1) Figures cover the Green Bay, WI Metropolitan Statistical Area; (2) People of Hispanic origin can be of any race
Source: U.S. Census Bureau, 2019-2023 American Community Survey 5-Year Estimates

School Enrollment by Grade and Control

Area	Preschool (%)		Kindergarten (%)		Grades 1 - 4 (%)		Grades 5 - 8 (%)		Grades 9 - 12 (%)	
	Public	Private	Public	Private	Public	Private	Public	Private	Public	Private
City	71.0	29.0	86.2	13.8	87.3	12.7	89.8	10.2	90.4	9.6
MSA[1]	68.0	32.0	84.2	15.8	86.1	13.9	87.0	13.0	90.5	9.5
U.S.	58.7	41.3	85.2	14.8	87.2	12.8	87.9	12.1	89.0	11.0

Note: Figures shown cover persons 3 years old and over; (1) Figures cover the Green Bay, WI Metropolitan Statistical Area
Source: U.S. Census Bureau, 2019-2023 American Community Survey 5-Year Estimates

Higher Education

Four-Year Colleges			Two-Year Colleges			Medical Schools[1]	Law Schools[2]	Voc/Tech[3]
Public	Private Non-profit	Private For-profit	Public	Private Non-profit	Private For-profit			
1	2	1	1	0	0	0	0	2

Note: Figures cover institutions located within the Green Bay, WI Metropolitan Statistical Area and include main campuses only; (1) includes schools accredited by the Liaison Committee on Medical Education and the American Osteopathic Association's Commission on Osteopathic College Accreditation; (2) includes ABA-accredited schools, schools with provisional ABA accreditation, and state accredited schools; (3) includes all schools with programs that are less than 2 years.
Source: National Center for Education Statistics, Integrated Postsecondary Education System (IPEDS), 2023-24; Wikipedia, List of Medical Schools in the United States, accessed May 2, 2025; Wikipedia, List of Law Schools in the United States, accessed May 2, 2025

According to *U.S. News & World Report*, the Green Bay, WI metro area is home to one of the top 100 liberal arts colleges in the U.S.: **St. Norbert College** (#90 tie). The indicators used to capture academic quality fall into a number of categories: assessment by administrators at peer institutions; retention of students; faculty resources; student selectivity; financial resources; alumni giving; high school counselor ratings of colleges; and graduation rate. *U.S. News & World Report*, "America's Best Colleges 2025"

EMPLOYERS

Major Employers

Company Name	Industry
American Foods Group	Food manufacturing
APAC Customer Services	Business management
Associated Bank	Financial services
Aurora Health Care	Healthcare
Bellin Health	Healthcare
Georgia-Pacific	Paper manufacturing
Green Bay Packaging	Paper manufacturing
Green Bay Packers	NFL franchise
H.J. Martin and Son	Interior design
JBS	Food manufacturing
Nicolet National Bank	Financial services
Procter & Gamble Paper Products	Paper manufacturing
Schreiber Foods	Food manufacturing
Schwabe North America	Health products
St. Mary's Hospital Medical Center	Healthcare
St. Vincent Hospital	Healthcare
Wal-Mart Stores	Retail
Wisconsin Public Service	Utilities

Note: Companies shown are located within the Green Bay, WI Metropolitan Statistical Area.
Source: Chambers of Commerce; State Departments of Labor; Wikipedia

PUBLIC SAFETY

Crime Rate

Area	Total Crime Rate	Violent Crime Rate				Property Crime Rate		
		Murder	Rape	Robbery	Aggrav. Assault	Burglary	Larceny-Theft	Motor Vehicle Theft
City	1,915.3	5.7	66.3	31.3	283.4	215.1	1,029.2	284.3
U.S.	2,290.9	5.7	38.0	66.5	264.1	250.7	1,347.2	318.7

Note: Figures are crimes per 100,000 population.
Source: FBI, Table 8, Offenses Known to Law Enforcement, by State by City, 2023

Hate Crimes

Area	Number of Quarters Reported	Number of Incidents per Bias Motivation					
		Race/Ethnicity/Ancestry	Religion	Sexual Orientation	Disability	Gender	Gender Identity
City	4	2	1	1	0	0	0
U.S.	4	5,900	2,699	2,077	187	92	492

Source: Federal Bureau of Investigation, Hate Crime Statistics 2023

Identity Theft Consumer Reports

Area	Reports	Reports per 100,000 Population	Rank[2]
MSA[1]	350	106	375
U.S.	1,135,291	339	-

Note: (1) Figures cover the Green Bay, WI Metropolitan Statistical Area; (2) Rank ranges from 1 to 401 where 1 indicates greatest number of identity theft reports per 100,000 population
Source: Federal Trade Commission, Consumer Sentinel Network Data Book 2024

Fraud and Other Consumer Reports

Area	Reports	Reports per 100,000 Population	Rank[2]
MSA[1]	2,496	758	344
U.S.	5,360,641	1,601	-

Note: (1) Figures cover the Green Bay, WI Metropolitan Statistical Area; (2) Rank ranges from 1 to 401 where 1 indicates greatest number of fraud and other consumer reports per 100,000 population
Source: Federal Trade Commission, Consumer Sentinel Network Data Book 2024

POLITICS

2024 Presidential Election Results

Area	Trump (Rep.)	Harris (Dem.)	Stein (Green)	Kennedy (Ind.)	Oliver (Lib.)	Other
Brown County	53.0	45.5	0.2	0.5	0.3	0.5
U.S.	49.7	48.2	0.6	0.5	0.4	0.6

Note: Results are percentages and may not add to 100% due to rounding
Source: Dave Leip's Atlas of U.S. Presidential Elections

SPORTS

Professional Sports Teams

Team Name	League	Year Established
Green Bay Packers	National Football League (NFL)	1921

Note: Includes teams located in the Green Bay, WI Metropolitan Statistical Area.
Source: Wikipedia, Major Professional Sports Teams of the United States and Canada, May 1, 2025

CLIMATE

Average and Extreme Temperatures

Temperature	Jan	Feb	Mar	Apr	May	Jun	Jul	Aug	Sep	Oct	Nov	Dec	Yr.
Extreme High (°F)	50	55	77	89	91	98	99	99	95	88	72	62	99
Average High (°F)	23	27	38	54	67	76	81	78	70	58	42	28	54
Average Temp. (°F)	15	19	29	44	55	65	70	68	59	48	34	21	44
Average Low (°F)	6	10	21	34	44	53	58	56	48	38	26	13	34
Extreme Low (°F)	-31	-26	-29	7	21	32	40	38	24	15	-9	-27	-31

Note: Figures cover the years 1949-1990
Source: National Climatic Data Center, International Station Meteorological Climate Summary, 9/96

Green Bay, Wisconsin

Average Precipitation/Snowfall/Humidity

Precip./Humidity	Jan	Feb	Mar	Apr	May	Jun	Jul	Aug	Sep	Oct	Nov	Dec	Yr.
Avg. Precip. (in.)	1.1	1.1	1.9	2.6	2.9	3.2	3.3	3.3	3.2	2.2	2.0	1.4	28.3
Avg. Snowfall (in.)	11	8	9	2	Tr	0	0	0	Tr	Tr	5	11	46
Avg. Rel. Hum. 6am (%)	77	79	81	79	79	82	86	90	89	85	82	80	83
Avg. Rel. Hum. 3pm (%)	68	65	63	54	52	55	55	58	59	59	67	71	60

Note: Figures cover the years 1949-1990; Tr = Trace amounts (<0.05 in. of rain; <0.5 in. of snow)
Source: National Climatic Data Center, International Station Meteorological Climate Summary, 9/96

Weather Conditions

Temperature			Daytime Sky			Precipitation		
5°F & below	32°F & below	90°F & above	Clear	Partly cloudy	Cloudy	0.01 inch or more precip.	0.1 inch or more snow/ice	Thunder-storms
39	163	7	86	125	154	120	40	33

Note: Figures are average number of days per year and cover the years 1949-1990
Source: National Climatic Data Center, International Station Meteorological Climate Summary, 9/96

HAZARDOUS WASTE

Superfund Sites

The Green Bay, WI metro area is home to four sites on the EPA's Superfund National Priorities List (NPL) or Superfund Alternative Approach (SAA) list: **Algoma Municipal Landfill** (Final NPL); **Better Brite Plating Co. Chrome and Zinc Shops** (Final NPL); **Fox River Nrda/Pcb Releases** (Proposed NPL); **Wpsc Green Bay Mgp** (SAA). The Superfund alternative approach uses the same investigation and cleanup process and standards that are used for sites listed on the National Priorities List. The SAA is an alternative to listing a site on the NPL; it is not an alternative to Superfund or the Superfund process. There are a total of 1,445 Superfund sites with a status of proposed or final on both lists in the United States. *U.S. Environmental Protection Agency, National Priorities List, May 1, 2025; U.S. Environmental Protection Agency, Superfund Alternative Approach Sites, May 1, 2025*

AIR QUALITY

Air Quality Trends: Ozone

	1990	1995	2000	2005	2010	2015	2020	2021	2022	2023
MSA[1]	n/a	n/a	n/a	n/a	n/a	n/a	n/a	n/a	n/a	n/a
U.S.	0.087	0.089	0.081	0.080	0.072	0.068	0.066	0.067	0.067	0.070

Note: (1) Data covers the Green Bay, WI Metropolitan Statistical Area; n/a not available. The values shown are the composite ozone concentration averages among trend sites based on the highest fourth daily maximum 8-hour concentration in parts per million. These trends are based on sites having an adequate record of monitoring data during the trend period. Data from exceptional events are included.
Source: U.S. Environmental Protection Agency, Air Quality Monitoring Information, "Air Quality Trends by City, 1990-2023"

Air Quality Index

Area	Percent of Days when Air Quality was...[2]					AQI Statistics[2]	
	Good	Moderate	Unhealthy for Sensitive Groups	Unhealthy	Very Unhealthy	Maximum	Median
MSA[1]	57.0	38.1	3.3	1.6	0.0	182	46

Note: (1) Data covers the Green Bay, WI Metropolitan Statistical Area; (2) Based on 365 days with AQI data in 2023. Air Quality Index (AQI) is an index for reporting daily air quality. EPA calculates the AQI for five major air pollutants regulated by the Clean Air Act: ground-level ozone, particle pollution (aka particulate matter), carbon monoxide, sulfur dioxide, and nitrogen dioxide. The AQI runs from 0 to 500. The higher the AQI value, the greater the level of air pollution and the greater the health concern. There are six AQI categories: "Good" AQI is between 0 and 50. Air quality is considered satisfactory; "Moderate" AQI is between 51 and 100. Air quality is acceptable; "Unhealthy for Sensitive Groups" When AQI values are between 101 and 150, members of sensitive groups may experience health effects; "Unhealthy" When AQI values are between 151 and 200 everyone may begin to experience health effects; "Very Unhealthy" AQI values between 201 and 300 trigger a health alert; "Hazardous" AQI values over 300 trigger warnings of emergency conditions (not shown).
Source: U.S. Environmental Protection Agency, Air Quality Index Report, 2023

Air Quality Index Pollutants

Area	Percent of Days when AQI Pollutant was...[2]					
	Carbon Monoxide	Nitrogen Dioxide	Ozone	Sulfur Dioxide	Particulate Matter 2.5	Particulate Matter 10
MSA[1]	0.0	0.0	35.9	(3)	64.1	0.0

Note: (1) Data covers the Green Bay, WI Metropolitan Statistical Area; (2) Based on 365 days with AQI data in 2023. The Air Quality Index (AQI) is an index for reporting daily air quality. EPA calculates the AQI for five major air pollutants regulated by the Clean Air Act: ground-level ozone, particle pollution (also known as particulate matter), carbon monoxide, sulfur dioxide, and nitrogen dioxide. The AQI runs from 0 to 500. The higher the AQI value, the greater the level of air pollution and the greater the health concern; (3) Sulfur dioxide is no longer included in this table because SO_2 concentrations tend to be very localized and not necessarily representative of broad geographical areas like counties and CBSAs.
Source: U.S. Environmental Protection Agency, Air Quality Index Report, 2023

Maximum Air Pollutant Concentrations: Particulate Matter, Ozone, CO and Lead

	Particulate Matter 10 (ug/m^3)	Particulate Matter 2.5 Wtd AM (ug/m^3)	Particulate Matter 2.5 24-Hr (ug/m^3)	Ozone (ppm)	Carbon Monoxide (ppm)	Lead (ug/m^3)
MSA[1] Level	n/a	9.5	38	0.075	n/a	n/a
NAAQS[2]	150	15	35	0.075	9	0.15
Met NAAQS[2]	n/a	Yes	No	Yes	n/a	n/a

Note: (1) Data covers the Green Bay, WI Metropolitan Statistical Area; Data from exceptional events are included; (2) National Ambient Air Quality Standards; ppm = parts per million; ug/m^3 = micrograms per cubic meter; n/a not available.
Concentrations: Particulate Matter 10 (coarse particulate)—highest second maximum 24-hour concentration; Particulate Matter 2.5 Wtd AM (fine particulate)—highest weighted annual mean concentration; Particulate Matter 2.5 24-Hour (fine particulate)—highest 98th percentile 24-hour concentration; Ozone—highest fourth daily maximum 8-hour concentration; Carbon Monoxide—highest second maximum non-overlapping 8-hour concentration; Lead—maximum running 3-month average
Source: U.S. Environmental Protection Agency, Air Quality Monitoring Information, "Air Quality Statistics by City, 2023"

Maximum Air Pollutant Concentrations: Nitrogen Dioxide and Sulfur Dioxide

	Nitrogen Dioxide AM (ppb)	Nitrogen Dioxide 1-Hr (ppb)	Sulfur Dioxide AM (ppb)	Sulfur Dioxide 1-Hr (ppb)	Sulfur Dioxide 24-Hr (ppb)
MSA[1] Level	n/a	n/a	n/a	n/a	n/a
NAAQS[2]	53	100	30	75	140
Met NAAQS[2]	n/a	n/a	n/a	n/a	n/a

Note: (1) Data covers the Green Bay, WI Metropolitan Statistical Area; Data from exceptional events are included; (2) National Ambient Air Quality Standards; ppm = parts per million; ug/m^3 = micrograms per cubic meter; n/a not available.
Concentrations: Nitrogen Dioxide AM—highest arithmetic mean concentration; Nitrogen Dioxide 1-Hr—highest 98th percentile 1-hour daily maximum concentration; Sulfur Dioxide AM—highest annual mean concentration; Sulfur Dioxide 1-Hr—highest 99th percentile 1-hour daily maximum concentration; Sulfur Dioxide 24-Hr—highest second maximum 24-hour concentration
Source: U.S. Environmental Protection Agency, Air Quality Monitoring Information, "Air Quality Statistics by City, 2023"

Indianapolis, Indiana

Background

Indianapolis is known as the "Crossroads of America" in the northeast region of Indiana along the White River. It sits within the northern manufacturing belt and the midwestern corn belt, and its economy reflects both influences. Indianapolis' industrial sector includes transportation, airplane and truck parts, paper and rubber products, and computer software. It is also a leading grain market, as well as the largest meat-processing center outside of Chicago.

Despite pollution and other problems of urban decay in the late twentieth century, Indianapolis has made significant strides, completing dozens of major downtown projects, including Dolphin Adventure at the Indianapolis Zoo, Eiteljorg Museum of American Indians and Western Art expansion, Eli Lilly and Company Insulin Finishing Building, the Indianapolis Museum of Art expansion, and Circle Centre, a retail and entertainment complex that draws one million visitors a month.

The city is bisected by more interstate highways than any other city in the nation, making it accessible from many locations and within a day's drive of half the country's population. As a result, it's a popular choice for conventions and offers excellent facilities at the Indiana Convention Center and Lucas Oil Stadium. The Indianapolis Artsgarden, offering more than 300 free performances and exhibits each year, is linked to the Convention Center by a skywalk, and is a world-class venue for the arts.

The city is home to one of the finest children's museums in the United States, and its 85 parks offer many outdoor activities.

Indianapolis has been called the rising food star of the Midwest, with top-notch restaurants in the Fletcher Place neighborhood and a number of city chefs and restaurateurs as recent semifinalists in the James Beard Foundation Awards. Microbreweries are a staple in the city, with more than 150 craft breweries. The city also hosts many popular farmers markets.

Known as the "Racing Capital of the World," Indianapolis hosts the world's three biggest single-day sporting events at the world-famous Indianapolis Motor Speedway: Indy 500; Brickyard 400; and SAP United States Grand Prix. The National Collegiate Athletic Association is also in Indianapolis, as is the NCAA Hall of Champions. Housing divisions of both Indiana and Purdue Universities make for a lively learning center.

Gainbridge Fieldhouse is an indoor arena located in downtown Indianapolis. It opened in November 1999 to replace Market Square Arena. The arena is the home of the Indiana Pacers of the National Basketball Association and the Indiana Fever of the Women's National Basketball Association.

The Indianapolis Art Museum is one of the largest general museums in the United States. Collections include works of Gaugin, Seurat, and Turner. The museum has integrated its galleries with other properties on its campus, including the Virginia B. Fairbanks Art & Nature Park and the Oldfields-Lilly House.

Indianapolis was initially planned by Alexander Ralston, the American engineer who assisted French architect Pierre L'Enfant in planning Washington, D.C. Like the nation's capital, Indianapolis is laid out on a mile-square grid and is easily navigable. Its centerpiece is Monument Circle, home of the 284-foot Soldiers and Sailors Monument, with a 32-story panoramic view of the Indianapolis skyline.

Indianapolis has a temperate climate, with very warm summers and no dry season. Very cold winter weather sometime occurs with continental polar air from northern latitudes. In the summer, tropical air from the Gulf of Mexico brings warm temperatures and moderate humidity.

Rankings

General Rankings

- To help military veterans find the best places in which to settle down, *WalletHub* compared the 100 largest U.S. cities across 19 key indicators of livability, affordability and veteran-friendliness. They range from the share of military skill-related jobs to veteran income growth to the availability of VA health facilities. Indianapolis ranked #96. *Wallethub.com, "Best & Worst Places for Veterans to Live (2025)," November 7, 2024*

- *Insider* listed 23 places in the U.S. that travel industry trends reveal would be popular destinations in 2023. This year the list trends towards cultural and historical happenings, sports events, wellness experiences and invigorating outdoor escapes. According to the website insider.com Indianapolis is a place to visit in 2023. *Insider, "23 of the Best Places You Should Travel to in the U.S. in 2023," December 17, 2022*

Business/Finance Rankings

- The Indianapolis metro area appeared on the Milken Institute "2025 Best Performing Cities" list. Rank: #39 out of 200 large metro areas (based on performance category). Criteria: job growth; wage growth; high-tech growth and impact; community resilience; housing affordability; household broadband access. *Milken Institute, "Best-Performing Cities 2025," January 14, 2025*

Education Rankings

- Personal finance website *WalletHub* analyzed the 150 largest U.S. metropolitan statistical areas to determine where the most educated Americans are putting their degrees to work. Criteria: education levels; percentage of workers with degrees; education quality and attainment gap; public school quality rankings; quality and enrollment of each metro area's universities. Indianapolis was ranked #73 (#1 = most educated city). *WalletHub.com, "Most & Least Educated Cities in America, 2025" July 2, 2024*

Environmental Rankings

- Indianapolis was highlighted as one of the 25 metro areas most polluted by year-round particle pollution (Annual PM 2.5) in the U.S. during 2021 through 2023. The area ranked #11. *American Lung Association, "State of the Air 2025," April 23, 2025*

- Indianapolis was highlighted as one of the 25 metro areas most polluted by short-term particle pollution (24-hour PM 2.5) in the U.S. during 2021 through 2023. The area ranked #21. *American Lung Association, "State of the Air 2025," April 23, 2025*

Health/Fitness Rankings

- For each of the 100 largest cities in the United States, the American Fitness Index®, compiled in partnership between the American College of Sports Medicine and the Elevance Health Foundation, evaluated community infrastructure and more than 30 health behaviors including preventive health, levels of chronic disease conditions, food insecurity, pedestrian safety, air quality, and community/environment resources that support physical activity. Indianapolis ranked #94 for "community fitness." *americanfitnessindex.org, "2024 ACSM American Fitness Index Summary Report," July 23, 2024*

- The Indianapolis metro area was identified as one of the worst cities for bed bugs in America by pest control company Orkin. The area ranked #8 out of 50 based on the number of bed bug treatments Orkin performed from December 2022 to November 2023. *Orkin, "Chicago Joins Paris In Global Bed Bug Spotlight Ranking As The Worst City On Orkin's U.S. Bed Bug Cities List," January 22, 2024*

- Indianapolis was identified as a "2025 Allergy Capital." The area ranked #74 out of the nation's 100 largest metropolitan areas. Three groups of factors were used to identify the most challenging cities for people with allergies: annual tree, grass, and weed pollen scores; over the counter allergy medicine use; number of board-certified allergy specialists. *Asthma and Allergy Foundation of America, "2025 Allergy Capitals: The Most Challenging Places to Live with Allergies," March 18, 2025*

- Indianapolis was identified as a "2024 Asthma Capital." The area ranked #61 out of the nation's 100 largest metropolitan areas. Criteria: estimated asthma prevalence; asthma-related mortality; and ER visits due to asthma. Risk factors analyzed but not factored in the rankings: annual air quality including pollution and ozone levels; public smoking laws; indoor air quality; access to asthma specialists; rescue and controller medication use; uninsured rate; pollen allergy; poverty rate. *Asthma and Allergy Foundation of America, "Asthma Capitals 2024: The Most Challenging Places to Live With Asthma," September 10, 2024*

Real Estate Rankings

- *WalletHub* compared the most populated U.S. cities to determine which had the best markets for real estate agents. Indianapolis ranked #94 where demand was high and pay was the best. Criteria: sales per agent; annual median wage for real-estate agents; monthly average starting salary for real estate agents; real estate job density and competition; unemployment rate; home turnover rate; housing-market health index; and other relevant metrics. *WalletHub.com, "2021 Best Places to Be a Real Estate Agent," May 12, 2021*

- The Indianapolis metro area was identified as one of the top 16 housing markets to invest in for 2025 by *Forbes*. Criteria: stable local economies with good population growth and increase in jobs providing good support for home prices and rents. *Forbes.com, "Best Local Markets For Real Estate Investing In 2025," November 6, 2024*

- The Indianapolis metro area was identified as one of the 10 worst condo markets in the U.S. in 2024. The area ranked #57 out of 63 markets. Criteria: year-over-year change of median sales price of existing apartment condo-coop homes between the 4th quarter of 2023 and the 4th quarter of 2024. *National Association of Realtors®, Median Sales Price of Existing Apartment Condo-Coops Homes for Metropolitan Areas, 4th Quarter 2024*

- Indianapolis was ranked #52 out of 176 metro areas in terms of cost of housing in 2024 by the National Association of Home Builders (#1 = most affordable). Criteria: the portion of an average family's income necessary to pay the mortgage on a median-priced home. *National Association of Home Builders®, NAHB-Wells Fargo Cost of Housing Index, 4th Quarter 2024*

Safety Rankings

- Allstate ranked the 100 most populous cities in America in terms of driver safety. Indianapolis ranked #23. Criteria based on anonymized driving behavior data from Allstate's mobile app powered by Arity: high speed driving (over 80 mph), phone handling, and hard braking. The report helps increase the importance of safety and awareness behind the wheel. *Allstate, "16th Allstate America's Best Drivers Report®" July 11, 2024*

Women/Minorities Rankings

- Personal finance website *WalletHub* compared more than 180 U.S. cities across two key dimensions, "Hispanic Business-Friendliness" and "Hispanic Purchasing Power," to arrive at the most favorable conditions for Hispanic entrepreneurs. Indianapolis was ranked #111 out of 182. Criteria includes: share of Hispanic-Owned Businesses; average growth of Hispanic Business revenues; Small Business-Friendliness score; affordability; and number of Hispanics with at least a bachelor's degree. *WalletHub.com, "Best Cities for Hispanic Entrepreneurs," September 4, 2024*

Miscellaneous Rankings

- *WalletHub* compared 148 of the most populated U.S. cities to determine their operating efficiency. A "Quality of Services" score was constructed for each city and then measured against the total budget per capita to reveal which were managed the best. Indianapolis ranked #93. Criteria: financial stability; economy; education; safety; health; infrastructure and pollution. *WalletHub.com, "2025's Best- & Worst-Run Cities in America," June 18, 2024*

Business Environment

DEMOGRAPHICS

Population Growth

Area	1990 Census	2000 Census	2010 Census	2020 Census	2023 Estimate[2]	Population Growth 1990-2023 (%)
City	730,993	781,870	820,445	887,642	882,043	20.7
MSA[1]	1,294,217	1,525,104	1,756,241	2,111,040	2,106,327	62.7
U.S.	248,709,873	281,421,906	308,745,538	331,449,281	332,387,540	33.6

Note: (1) Figures cover the Indianapolis-Carmel-Greenwood, IN Metropolitan Statistical Area; (2) 2019-2023 5-year ACS population estimate
Source: U.S. Census Bureau, 1990 Census, 2000 Census, 2010 Census, 2020 Census, 2019-2023 American Community Survey 5-Year Estimates

Race

Area	White Alone[2] (%)	Black Alone[2] (%)	Asian Alone[2] (%)	AIAN[3] Alone[2] (%)	NHOPI[4] Alone[2] (%)	Other Race Alone[2] (%)	Two or More Races (%)
City	53.6	28.1	4.1	0.5	0.0	5.7	8.0
MSA[1]	70.8	15.1	3.8	0.3	0.0	3.4	6.5
U.S.	63.4	12.4	5.8	0.9	0.2	6.6	10.7

Note: (1) Figures cover the Indianapolis-Carmel-Greenwood, IN Metropolitan Statistical Area; (2) Alone is defined as not being in combination with one or more other races; (3) American Indian and Alaska Native; (4) Native Hawaiian and Other Pacific Islander
Source: U.S. Census Bureau, 2019-2023 American Community Survey 5-Year Estimates

Hispanic or Latino Origin

Area	Total (%)	Mexican (%)	Puerto Rican (%)	Cuban (%)	Other (%)
City	13.3	8.7	0.8	0.3	3.5
MSA[1]	8.6	5.4	0.6	0.2	2.4
U.S.	19.0	11.3	1.8	0.7	5.2

Note: Persons of Hispanic or Latino origin can be of any race; (1) Figures cover the Indianapolis-Carmel-Greenwood, IN Metropolitan Statistical Area
Source: U.S. Census Bureau, 2019-2023 American Community Survey 5-Year Estimates

Age

Area	Percent of Population									Median Age
	Under Age 5	Age 5–19	Age 20–34	Age 35–44	Age 45–54	Age 55–64	Age 65–74	Age 75–84	Age 85+	
City	7.0	20.5	23.8	13.2	11.2	11.4	8.1	3.3	1.5	34.1
MSA[1]	6.3	20.6	20.5	13.7	12.4	12.2	8.8	3.9	1.6	36.7
U.S.	5.7	19.1	20.2	13.1	12.3	12.8	10.0	4.9	1.9	38.7

Note: (1) Figures cover the Indianapolis-Carmel-Greenwood, IN Metropolitan Statistical Area
Source: U.S. Census Bureau, 2019-2023 American Community Survey 5-Year Estimates

Disability by Age

Area	All Ages	Under 18 Years Old	18 to 64 Years Old	65 Years and Over
City	13.5	5.1	12.6	34.6
MSA[1]	12.4	5.0	10.9	32.1
U.S.	13.0	4.7	10.7	32.9

Note: Figures show percent of the civilian noninstitutionalized population that reported having a disability. Disability status is determined from six types of difficulty: vision, hearing, cognitive, ambulatory, self-care, and independent living. For children under 5 years old, hearing and vision difficulty are used to determine disability status. For children between the ages of 5 and 14, disability status is determined from hearing, vision, cognitive, ambulatory, and self-care difficulties. For people aged 15 years and older, they are considered to have a disability if they have difficulty with any one of the six difficulty types; Note: (1) Figures cover the Indianapolis-Carmel-Greenwood, IN Metropolitan Statistical Area
Source: U.S. Census Bureau, 2019-2023 American Community Survey 5-Year Estimates

Ancestry

Area	German	Irish	English	American	Italian	Polish	French[2]	European	Scottish
City	12.8	7.9	8.0	4.5	2.0	1.4	1.4	1.4	1.5
MSA[1]	16.6	9.4	10.9	7.3	2.5	1.7	1.5	1.7	1.8
U.S.	12.6	9.4	9.1	5.5	4.9	2.6	2.0	1.6	1.6

Note: Figures are the percentage of the total population reporting a particular ancestry. The nine most commonly reported ancestries in the U.S. are shown. Figures include multiple ancestries (e.g. if a person reported being Irish and Italian, they were included in both columns); (1) Figures cover the Indianapolis-Carmel-Greenwood, IN Metropolitan Statistical Area; (2) Excludes Basque
Source: U.S. Census Bureau, 2019-2023 American Community Survey 5-Year Estimates

Foreign-born Population

Area	Percent of Population Born in								
	Any Foreign Country	Asia	Mexico	Europe	Caribbean	Central America[2]	South America	Africa	Canada
City	11.6	3.1	3.2	0.5	0.7	1.3	0.6	2.2	0.1
MSA[1]	8.4	2.8	1.8	0.6	0.4	0.7	0.5	1.5	0.1
U.S.	13.9	4.3	3.3	1.4	1.4	1.2	1.2	0.8	0.2

Note: (1) Figures cover the Indianapolis-Carmel-Greenwood, IN Metropolitan Statistical Area; (2) Excludes Mexico.
Source: U.S. Census Bureau, 2019-2023 American Community Survey 5-Year Estimates

Household Size

Area	Persons in Household (%)							Average Household Size
	One	Two	Three	Four	Five	Six	Seven or More	
City	36.6	31.9	13.1	9.8	5.4	1.9	1.3	2.41
MSA[1]	29.6	33.8	14.7	12.7	6.1	1.9	1.1	2.50
U.S.	28.5	33.8	15.4	12.7	5.9	2.3	1.4	2.54

Note: (1) Figures cover the Indianapolis-Carmel-Greenwood, IN Metropolitan Statistical Area
Source: U.S. Census Bureau, 2019-2023 American Community Survey 5-Year Estimates

Household Relationships

Area	Householder	Opposite-sex Spouse	Same-sex Spouse	Opposite-sex Unmarried Partner	Same-sex Unmarried Partner	Child[2]	Grandchild	Other Relatives	Non-relatives
City	40.7	14.0	0.3	3.4	0.3	28.6	2.5	4.5	3.9
MSA[1]	39.2	17.9	0.2	2.8	0.2	29.6	2.1	3.5	2.8
U.S.	38.3	17.5	0.2	2.5	0.2	28.3	2.4	4.8	3.4

Note: Figures are percent of the total population; (1) Figures cover the Indianapolis-Carmel-Greenwood, IN Metropolitan Statistical Area; (2) Includes biological, adopted, and stepchildren of the householder
Source: U.S. Census Bureau, 2020 Census

Gender

Area	Males	Females	Males per 100 Females
City	428,660	453,383	94.5
MSA[1]	1,034,791	1,071,536	96.6
U.S.	164,545,087	167,842,453	98.0

Note: (1) Figures cover the Indianapolis-Carmel-Greenwood, IN Metropolitan Statistical Area
Source: U.S. Census Bureau, 2019-2023 American Community Survey 5-Year Estimates

Marital Status

Area	Never Married	Now Married[2]	Separated	Widowed	Divorced
City	41.1	40.4	1.7	4.8	12.0
MSA[1]	32.7	49.7	1.2	4.9	11.5
U.S.	34.1	47.9	1.7	5.6	10.7

Note: Figures are percentages and cover the population 15 years of age and older; (1) Figures cover the Indianapolis-Carmel-Greenwood, IN Metropolitan Statistical Area; (2) Excludes separated
Source: U.S. Census Bureau, 2019-2023 American Community Survey 5-Year Estimates

Religious Groups by Family

Area	Catholic	Baptist	Methodist	LDS[2]	Pentecostal	Lutheran	Islam	Adventist	Other
MSA[1]	11.5	6.2	3.3	0.7	1.3	1.1	1.1	1.0	17.4
U.S.	18.7	7.3	3.0	2.0	1.8	1.7	1.3	1.3	11.6

Note: Figures are the number of adherents as a percentage of the total population and cover the eight largest religious groups in the U.S; (1) Figures cover the Indianapolis-Carmel-Greenwood, IN Metropolitan Statistical Area; (2) Church of Jesus Christ of Latter-day Saints
Sources: 2020 U.S. Religion Census, Association of Statisticians of American Religious Bodies; The Association of Religion Data Archives (ARDA)

Religious Groups by Tradition

Area	Catholic	Evangelical Protestant	Mainline Protestant	Black Protestant	Islam	Judaism	Hinduism	Orthodox	Buddhism
MSA[1]	11.5	16.8	7.6	4.2	1.1	0.4	0.2	0.3	0.1
U.S.	18.7	16.5	5.2	2.3	1.3	0.6	0.4	0.4	0.3

Note: Figures are the number of adherents as a percentage of the total population; (1) Figures cover the Indianapolis-Carmel-Greenwood, IN Metropolitan Statistical Area
Sources: 2020 U.S. Religion Census, Association of Statisticians of American Religious Bodies; The Association of Religion Data Archives (ARDA)

ECONOMY

Real Gross Domestic Product (GDP)

Area	2017	2018	2019	2020	2021	2022	2023	Rank[3]
MSA[1]	135.9	140.7	143.8	142.8	152.5	158.8	161.8	28
U.S.[2]	17,619.1	18,160.7	18,642.5	18,238.9	19,387.6	19,896.6	20,436.3	—

Note: Figures are in billions of chained 2017 dollars; (1) Figures cover the Indianapolis-Carmel-Greenwood, IN Metropolitan Statistical Area; (2) Figures cover real GDP within metropolitan areas; (3) Rank is based on 2023 data and ranges from 1 to 384
Source: U.S. Bureau of Economic Analysis

Economic Growth

Area	2014	2015	2016	2017	2018	2019	2020	2021	2022	2023
MSA[1]	2.1	-2.5	2.4	2.4	3.6	2.2	-0.7	6.8	4.1	1.9
U.S.[2]	2.6	3.2	2.0	2.7	3.1	2.7	-2.2	6.3	2.6	2.7

Note: Figures are real gross domestic product growth rates and represent percent change from preceding period; (1) Figures cover the Indianapolis-Carmel-Greenwood, IN Metropolitan Statistical Area; (2) Figures are the average growth rates within metropolitan areas
Source: U.S. Bureau of Economic Analysis

Metropolitan Area Exports

Area	2018	2019	2020	2021	2022	2023	Rank[2]
MSA[1]	11,069.9	11,148.7	11,100.4	12,740.4	14,671.5	23,080.6	20
U.S.	1,664,056.1	1,645,173.7	1,431,406.6	1,753,941.4	2,062,937.4	2,019,160.5	—

Note: Figures are in millions of dollars; (1) Figures cover the Indianapolis-Carmel-Greenwood, IN Metropolitan Statistical Area; (2) Rank is based on 2023 data and ranges from 1 to 386
Source: U.S. Department of Commerce, International Trade Administration, Office of Trade and Economic Analysis, Industry and Analysis, Exports by Metropolitan Area, data extracted April 2, 2025

Building Permits

Area	Single-Family 2023	Single-Family 2024	Single-Family Pct. Chg.	Multi-Family 2023	Multi-Family 2024	Multi-Family Pct. Chg.	Total 2023	Total 2024	Total Pct. Chg.
City	896	1,170	30.6	1,517	653	-57.0	2,413	1,823	-24.5
MSA[1]	7,252	9,168	26.4	5,302	2,620	-50.6	12,554	11,788	-6.1
U.S.	920,000	981,900	6.7	591,100	496,100	-16.1	1,511,100	1,478,000	-2.2

Note: (1) Figures cover the Indianapolis-Carmel-Greenwood, IN Metropolitan Statistical Area; Figures represent new, privately-owned housing units authorized (unadjusted data)
Source: U.S. Census Bureau, Building Permits Survey (BPS), 2023, 2024

Bankruptcy Filings

Area	Business Filings 2023	Business Filings 2024	Business % Chg.	Nonbusiness Filings 2023	Nonbusiness Filings 2024	Nonbusiness % Chg.
Marion County	45	43	-4.4	2,601	3,166	21.7
U.S.	18,926	23,107	22.1	434,064	494,201	13.9

Note: Business filings include Chapter 7, Chapter 9, Chapter 11, Chapter 12, Chapter 13, Chapter 15, and Section 304; Nonbusiness filings include Chapter 7, Chapter 11, and Chapter 13
Source: Administrative Office of the U.S. Courts, Business and Nonbusiness Bankruptcy, County Cases Commenced by Chapter of the Bankruptcy Code, During the 12-Month Period Ending December 31, 2023 and Business and Nonbusiness Bankruptcy, County Cases Commenced by Chapter of the Bankruptcy Code, During the 12-Month Period Ending December 31, 2024

Housing Vacancy Rates

Area	Gross Vacancy Rate[3] (%) 2022	2023	2024	Year-Round Vacancy Rate[4] (%) 2022	2023	2024	Rental Vacancy Rate[5] (%) 2022	2023	2024	Homeowner Vacancy Rate[6] (%) 2022	2023	2024
MSA[1]	7.7	6.2	6.7	7.2	5.6	5.8	11.0	8.8	9.2	1.0	0.8	0.8
U.S.[2]	9.1	9.0	9.1	7.5	7.5	7.6	5.7	6.5	6.8	0.8	0.8	1.0

Note: (1) Figures cover the Indianapolis-Carmel-Greenwood, IN Metropolitan Statistical Area; (2) Figures cover the 75 largest Metropolitan Statistical Areas; (3) The percentage of the total housing inventory that is vacant; (4) The percentage of the housing inventory (excluding seasonal units) that is year-round vacant; (5) The percentage of rental inventory that is vacant for rent; (6) The percentage of homeowner inventory that is vacant for sale
Source: U.S. Census Bureau, Housing Vacancies and Homeownership Annual Statistics: 2022, 2023, 2024

INCOME

Income

Area	Per Capita ($)	Median Household ($)	Average Household ($)
City	36,194	62,995	86,913
MSA[1]	42,522	77,065	106,219
U.S.	43,289	78,538	110,491

Note: (1) Figures cover the Indianapolis-Carmel-Greenwood, IN Metropolitan Statistical Area
Source: U.S. Census Bureau, 2019-2023 American Community Survey 5-Year Estimates

Household Income Distribution

Area	Percent of Households Earning							
	Under $15,000	$15,000 -$24,999	$25,000 -$34,999	$35,000 -$49,999	$50,000 -$74,999	$75,000 -$99,999	$100,000 -$149,999	$150,000 and up
City	10.7	7.5	8.2	13.5	18.7	12.5	15.0	13.8
MSA[1]	7.7	6.0	6.6	11.2	17.3	13.2	17.5	20.5
U.S.	8.5	6.6	6.8	10.4	15.7	12.7	17.4	21.9

Note: (1) Figures cover the Indianapolis-Carmel-Greenwood, IN Metropolitan Statistical Area
Source: U.S. Census Bureau, 2019-2023 American Community Survey 5-Year Estimates

Poverty Rate

Area	All Ages	Under 18 Years Old	18 to 64 Years Old	65 Years and Over
City	15.7	21.2	14.3	11.5
MSA[1]	10.5	13.6	9.8	8.3
U.S.	12.4	16.3	11.6	10.4

Note: Figures are percentage of people whose income during the past 12 months was below the poverty level; (1) Figures cover the Indianapolis-Carmel-Greenwood, IN Metropolitan Statistical Area
Source: U.S. Census Bureau, 2019-2023 American Community Survey 5-Year Estimates

EMPLOYMENT

Labor Force and Employment

Area	Civilian Labor Force			Workers Employed		
	Dec. 2023	Dec. 2024	% Chg.	Dec. 2023	Dec. 2024	% Chg.
City	468,727	483,276	3.1	453,754	464,036	2.3
MSA[1]	1,114,296	1,147,341	3.0	1,082,623	1,106,085	2.2
U.S.	166,661,000	167,746,000	0.7	160,754,000	161,294,000	0.3

Note: Data is not seasonally adjusted and covers workers 16 years of age and older; (1) Figures cover the Indianapolis-Carmel-Greenwood, IN Metropolitan Statistical Area
Source: Bureau of Labor Statistics, Local Area Unemployment Statistics

Unemployment Rate

Area	2024											
	Jan.	Feb.	Mar.	Apr.	May	Jun.	Jul.	Aug.	Sep.	Oct.	Nov.	Dec.
City	3.9	4.3	4.2	3.6	4.0	4.4	4.7	4.5	4.1	4.0	4.2	4.0
MSA[1]	3.6	3.9	3.9	3.2	3.6	4.0	4.3	4.0	3.6	3.6	3.9	3.6
U.S.	4.1	4.2	3.9	3.5	3.7	4.3	4.5	4.4	3.9	3.9	4.0	3.8

Note: Data is not seasonally adjusted and covers workers 16 years of age and older; (1) Figures cover the Indianapolis-Carmel-Greenwood, IN Metropolitan Statistical Area
Source: Bureau of Labor Statistics, Local Area Unemployment Statistics

Average Wages

Occupation	$/Hr.	Occupation	$/Hr.
Accountants and Auditors	41.42	Maintenance and Repair Workers	25.58
Automotive Mechanics	25.35	Marketing Managers	64.61
Bookkeepers	23.97	Network and Computer Systems Admin.	43.51
Carpenters	30.07	Nurses, Licensed Practical	30.93
Cashiers	13.91	Nurses, Registered	42.93
Computer Programmers	47.00	Nursing Assistants	18.85
Computer Systems Analysts	50.67	Office Clerks, General	22.26
Computer User Support Specialists	29.12	Physical Therapists	47.40
Construction Laborers	25.60	Physicians	154.93
Cooks, Restaurant	16.96	Plumbers, Pipefitters and Steamfitters	33.46
Customer Service Representatives	22.07	Police and Sheriff's Patrol Officers	38.34
Dentists	89.99	Postal Service Mail Carriers	29.29
Electricians	32.56	Real Estate Sales Agents	36.12
Engineers, Electrical	53.74	Retail Salespersons	16.89
Fast Food and Counter Workers	14.01	Sales Representatives, Technical/Scientific	55.71
Financial Managers	75.66	Secretaries, Exc. Legal/Medical/Executive	21.53
First-Line Supervisors of Office Workers	36.11	Security Guards	21.17
General and Operations Managers	72.23	Surgeons	222.23
Hairdressers/Cosmetologists	17.77	Teacher Assistants, Exc. Postsecondary[1]	16.14
Home Health and Personal Care Aides	15.78	Teachers, Secondary School, Exc. Sp. Ed.[1]	32.97
Janitors and Cleaners	16.98	Telemarketers	18.55
Landscaping/Groundskeeping Workers	18.81	Truck Drivers, Heavy/Tractor-Trailer	30.71
Lawyers	82.32	Truck Drivers, Light/Delivery Services	24.66
Maids and Housekeeping Cleaners	15.57	Waiters and Waitresses	15.51

Note: Wage data covers the Indianapolis-Carmel-Greenwood, IN Metropolitan Statistical Area; (1) Hourly wages were calculated from annual wage data based on a 40 hour work week
Source: Bureau of Labor Statistics, Metro Area Occupational Employment & Wage Estimates, May 2024

Employment by Industry

Sector	MSA[1] Number of Employees	MSA[1] Percent of Total	U.S. Percent of Total
Construction	64,900	5.5	5.1
Financial Activities	74,300	6.3	5.8
Government	149,100	12.6	14.9
Information	11,500	1.0	1.9
Leisure and Hospitality	108,200	9.1	10.4
Manufacturing	96,000	8.1	8.0
Mining and Logging	700	0.1	0.4
Other Services	48,800	4.1	3.7
Private Education and Health Services	187,900	15.8	16.9
Professional and Business Services	186,000	15.7	14.2
Retail Trade	104,400	8.8	10.0
Transportation, Warehousing, and Utilities	98,200	8.3	4.8
Wholesale Trade	56,000	4.7	3.9

Note: Figures are non-farm employment as of December 2024. Figures are not seasonally adjusted and include workers 16 years of age and older; (1) Figures cover the Indianapolis-Carmel-Greenwood, IN Metropolitan Statistical Area
Source: Bureau of Labor Statistics, Current Employment Statistics, Employment, Hours, and Earnings

Employment by Occupation

Occupation Classification	City (%)	MSA[1] (%)	U.S. (%)
Management, Business, Science, and Arts	40.0	43.7	42.0
Natural Resources, Construction, and Maintenance	7.2	7.3	8.6
Production, Transportation, and Material Moving	17.3	14.8	13.0
Sales and Office	20.3	20.2	19.9
Service	15.2	14.0	16.5

Note: Figures cover employed civilians 16 years of age and older; (1) Figures cover the Indianapolis-Carmel-Greenwood, IN Metropolitan Statistical Area
Source: U.S. Census Bureau, 2019-2023 American Community Survey 5-Year Estimates

Occupations with Greatest Projected Employment Growth: 2022 – 2032

Occupation[1]	2022 Employment	2032 Projected Employment	Numeric Employment Change	Percent Employment Change
Home Health and Personal Care Aides	44,830	54,650	9,820	21.9
Laborers and Freight, Stock, and Material Movers, Hand	105,700	112,240	6,540	6.2
Cooks, Restaurant	27,930	34,350	6,420	23.0
Software Developers	12,170	16,000	3,830	31.5
Registered Nurses	67,390	71,020	3,630	5.4
Fast Food and Counter Workers	91,680	94,980	3,300	3.6
Medical and Health Services Managers	10,690	13,820	3,130	29.3
Stockers and Order Fillers	58,190	61,320	3,130	5.4
Nurse Practitioners	6,550	9,550	3,000	45.8
Medical Assistants	20,210	23,170	2,960	14.6

Note: Projections cover Indiana; (1) Sorted by numeric employment change
Source: www.projectionscentral.org, State Occupational Projections, 2022–2032 Long-Term Projections

Fastest-Growing Occupations: 2022 – 2032

Occupation[1]	2022 Employment	2032 Projected Employment	Numeric Employment Change	Percent Employment Change
Nurse Practitioners	6,550	9,550	3,000	45.8
Information Security Analysts (SOC 2018)	1,150	1,570	420	36.5
Data Scientists	2,200	2,980	780	35.5
Statisticians	270	360	90	33.3
Software Developers	12,170	16,000	3,830	31.5
Medical and Health Services Managers	10,690	13,820	3,130	29.3
Occupational Therapy Assistants	1,000	1,280	280	28.0
Physician Assistants	1,640	2,100	460	28.0
Veterinary Assistants and Laboratory Animal Caretakers	2,680	3,410	730	27.2
Veterinary Technologists and Technicians	2,880	3,660	780	27.1

Note: Projections cover Indiana; (1) Sorted by percent employment change and excludes occupations with numeric employment change less than 50
Source: www.projectionscentral.org, State Occupational Projections, 2022–2032 Long-Term Projections

CITY FINANCES

City Government Finances

Component	2022 ($000)	2022 ($ per capita)
Total Revenues	4,621,024	5,264
Total Expenditures	4,449,276	5,068
Debt Outstanding	5,948,748	6,776

Source: U.S. Census Bureau, State & Local Government Finances 2022

City Government Revenue by Source

Source	2022 ($000)	2022 ($ per capita)	2022 (%)
General Revenue			
From Federal Government	119,890	137	2.6
From State Government	590,993	673	12.8
From Local Governments	27,415	31	0.6
Taxes			
Property	540,157	615	11.7
Sales and Gross Receipts	43,219	49	0.9
Personal Income	566,802	646	12.3
Corporate Income	0	0	0.0
Motor Vehicle License	1,935	2	0.0
Other Taxes	48,540	55	1.1
Current Charges	1,912,206	2,178	41.4
Liquor Store	0	0	0.0
Utility	578,069	658	12.5

Source: U.S. Census Bureau, State & Local Government Finances 2022

City Government Expenditures by Function

Function	2022 ($000)	2022 ($ per capita)	2022 (%)
General Direct Expenditures			
Air Transportation	139,697	159	3.1
Corrections	146,400	166	3.3
Education	0	0	0.0
Employment Security Administration	0	0	0.0
Financial Administration	34,000	38	0.8
Fire Protection	156,067	177	3.5
General Public Buildings	0	0	0.0
Governmental Administration, Other	20,300	23	0.5
Health	225,654	257	5.1
Highways	169,297	192	3.8
Hospitals	1,499,993	1,708	33.7
Housing and Community Development	152,380	173	3.4
Interest on General Debt	177,283	201	4.0
Judicial and Legal	118,979	135	2.7
Libraries	0	0	0.0
Parking	4,475	5	0.1
Parks and Recreation	75,890	86	1.7
Police Protection	240,723	274	5.4
Public Welfare	0	0	0.0
Sewerage	352,815	401	7.9
Solid Waste Management	50,553	57	1.1
Veterans' Services	0	0	0.0
Liquor Store	0	0	0.0
Utility	753,271	858	16.9

Source: U.S. Census Bureau, State & Local Government Finances 2022

TAXES

State Corporate Income Tax Rates

State	Tax Rate (%)	Income Brackets ($)	Num. of Brackets	Financial Institution Tax Rate (%)[a]	Federal Income Tax Ded.
Indiana	4.9	Flat rate	1	4.9	No

Note: Tax rates for tax year 2024; (a) Rates listed are the corporate income tax rate applied to financial institutions or excise taxes based on income. Some states have other taxes based upon the value of deposits or shares.
Source: Federation of Tax Administrators, State Corporate Income Tax Rates, January 1, 2025

State Individual Income Tax Rates

State	Tax Rate (%)	Income Brackets ($)	Personal Exemptions ($)			Standard Ded. ($)	
			Single	Married	Depend.	Single	Married
Indiana	3.05	Flat rate	1,000	2,000	2,500 (i)	–	–

Note: Tax rates for tax year 2024; Local- and county-level taxes are not included; Federal income tax is not deductible on state income tax returns; (i) GA moves to a flat tax rate regime, eliminates the personal exemption and increases the standard deduction amounts for single, HOH and married jointly filers.
Source: Federation of Tax Administrators, State Individual Income Tax Rates, January 1, 2025

Various State Sales and Excise Tax Rates

State	State Sales Tax (%)	Gasoline[1] ($/gal.)	Cigarette[2] ($/pack)	Spirits[3] ($/gal.)	Wine[4] ($/gal.)	Beer[5] ($/gal.)	Recreational Marijuana (%)
Indiana	7	0.53	1.00	2.68	0.47	0.12	Not legal

Note: All tax rates as of January 1, 2025; (1) The American Petroleum Institute has developed a methodology for determining the average tax rate on a gallon of fuel. Rates may include any of the following: excise taxes, environmental fees, storage tank fees, other fees or taxes, general sales tax, and local taxes; (2) The federal excise tax of $1.0066 per pack and local taxes are not included; (3) Rates are those applicable to off-premise sales of 40% alcohol by volume (a.b.v.) distilled spirits in 750ml containers. Local excise taxes are excluded; (4) Rates are those applicable to off-premise sales of 11% a.b.v. non-carbonated wine in 750ml containers; (5) Rates are those applicable to off-premise sales of 4.7% a.b.v. beer in 12 ounce containers.
Source: Tax Foundation, 2025 Facts & Figures: How Does Your State Compare?

State Tax Competitiveness Index

State	Overall Rank	Corporate Tax Rank	Individual Income Tax Rank	Sales Tax Rank	Property Tax Rank	Unemployment Insurance Tax Rank
Indiana	10	8	16	17	5	13

Note: The Tax Foundation's State Tax Competitiveness Index enables policymakers, taxpayers, and business leaders to gauge how their states' tax systems compare. A rank of 1 is best, 50 is worst. Rankings do not average to the total. States without a tax rank equally as 1. DC's scores and rankings do not affect other states. The report shows tax systems as of July 1, 2024 (the beginning of Fiscal Year 2025).
Source: Tax Foundation, State Tax Competitiveness Index 2025

TRANSPORTATION

Means of Transportation to Work

Area	Car/Truck/Van		Public Transportation			Bicycle	Walked	Other Means	Worked at Home
	Drove Alone	Carpooled	Bus	Subway	Railroad				
City	73.7	9.6	1.4	0.0	0.0	0.4	1.8	0.9	12.3
MSA[1]	74.5	8.4	0.6	0.0	0.0	0.3	1.3	0.9	14.0
U.S.	70.2	8.5	1.7	1.3	0.4	0.4	2.4	1.6	13.5

Note: Figures are percentages and cover workers 16 years of age and older; (1) Figures cover the Indianapolis-Carmel-Greenwood, IN Metropolitan Statistical Area
Source: U.S. Census Bureau, 2019-2023 American Community Survey 5-Year Estimates

Travel Time to Work

Area	Less Than 10 Minutes	10 to 19 Minutes	20 to 29 Minutes	30 to 44 Minutes	45 to 59 Minutes	60 to 89 Minutes	90 Minutes or More
City	9.8	29.6	28.6	23.1	4.5	2.5	2.0
MSA[1]	11.3	27.6	24.2	24.6	7.2	3.3	1.9
U.S.	12.6	28.6	21.2	20.8	8.1	6.0	2.8

Note: Note: Figures are percentages and include workers 16 years old and over; (1) Figures cover the Indianapolis-Carmel-Greenwood, IN Metropolitan Statistical Area
Source: U.S. Census Bureau, 2019-2023 American Community Survey 5-Year Estimates

Key Congestion Measures

Measure	2000	2010	2015	2020	2022
Annual Hours of Delay, Total (000)	21,747	35,485	41,413	23,362	45,367
Annual Hours of Delay, Per Auto Commuter	39	42	46	26	51
Annual Congestion Cost, Per Auto Commuter ($)	663	859	926	544	1,067

Note: Figures cover the Indianapolis IN urban area
Source: Texas A&M Transportation Institute, 2023 Urban Mobility Report

Freeway Travel Time Index

Measure	1985	1990	1995	2000	2005	2010	2015	2020	2022
Urban Area Index[1]	1.09	1.11	1.14	1.17	1.17	1.17	1.18	1.06	1.17
Urban Area Rank[1,2]	36	42	41	36	49	41	41	75	44

Note: Freeway Travel Time Index—the ratio of travel time in the peak period to the travel time at free-flow conditions. For example, a value of 1.30 indicates a 20-minute free-flow trip takes 26 minutes in the peak (20 minutes x 1.30 = 26 minutes); (1) Covers the Indianapolis IN urban area; (2) Rank is based on 101 larger urban areas (#1 = highest travel time index)
Source: Texas A&M Transportation Institute, 2023 Urban Mobility Report

Public Transportation

Agency Name / Mode of Transportation	Vehicles Operated in Maximum Service[1]	Annual Unlinked Passenger Trips[2] (in thous.)	Annual Passenger Miles[3] (in thous.)
Indianapolis and Marion County Public Transportation (IndyGo)			
Bus (directly operated)	105	5,619.5	30,184.8
Bus (purchased transportation)	1	13.9	48.5
Bus Rapid Transit (directly operated)	12	1,097.0	3,211.7
Demand Response (purchased transportation)	44	131.7	1,430.9
Demand Response - Transportation Network Company	32	26.9	329.1

Note: (1) Number of revenue vehicles operated by the given mode and type of service to meet the annual maximum service requirement. This is the revenue vehicle count during the peak season of the year; on the week and day that maximum service is provided. Vehicles operated in maximum service (VOMS) exclude atypical days and one-time special events; (2) Number of passengers who boarded public transportation vehicles. Passengers are counted each time they board a vehicle no matter how many vehicles they use to travel from their origin to their destination. (3) Sum of the distances ridden by all passengers during the entire fiscal year.
Source: Federal Transit Administration, National Transit Database, 2023

Air Transportation

Airport Name and Code / Type of Service	Passenger Airlines[1]	Passenger Enplanements	Freight Carriers[2]	Freight (lbs)
Indianapolis International (IND)				
Domestic service (U.S. carriers only)	33	5,146,280	16	841,534,701
International service (U.S. carriers only)	7	15,945	3	70,911,731

Note: (1) Includes all U.S.-based major, minor and commuter airlines that carried at least one passenger during the year; (2) Includes all U.S.-based airlines and freight carriers that transported at least one pound of freight during the year.
Source: Bureau of Transportation Statistics, The Intermodal Transportation Database, Air Carriers: T-100 Domestic Market (U.S. carriers only), 2024; Bureau of Transportation Statistics, The Intermodal Transportation Database, Air Carriers: T-100 International Market (U.S. carriers only), 2024

BUSINESSES

Major Business Headquarters

Company Name	Industry	Rankings	
		Fortune[1]	Forbes[2]
Corteva	Food production	238	-
Elevance Health	Health care: insurance and managed care	20	-
Eli Lilly	Pharmaceuticals	127	-

Note: (1) Companies that produce a 10-K are ranked 1 to 500 based on 2023 revenue; (2) All private companies with at least $2 billion in annual revenue through the end of their most current fiscal year are ranked 1 to 275; companies listed are headquartered in the city; dashes indicate no ranking
Source: Fortune, "Fortune 500," 2024; Forbes, "America's Largest Private Companies," 2024

Fastest-Growing Businesses

According to *Inc.*, Indianapolis is home to one of America's 500 fastest-growing private companies: **Stepping Stones Behavioral Solutions** (#468). Criteria: must be an independent, privately-held, for-profit, U.S. corporation, proprietorship or partnership as of December 31, 2023; revenues must be at least $100,000 in 2020 and $2 million in 2023; must have four-year operating/sales history. *Inc.*, "America's 500 Fastest-Growing Private Companies," 2024

Living Environment

COST OF LIVING

Cost of Living Index

Composite Index	Groceries	Housing	Utilities	Transportation	Health Care	Misc. Goods/Services
88.8	98.0	76.9	88.4	98.0	86.9	92.5

Note: The Cost of Living Index measures regional differences in the cost of consumer goods and services, excluding taxes and non-consumer expenditures, for professional and managerial households in the top income quintile. It is based on more than 50,000 prices covering almost 60 different items for which prices are collected three times a year by chambers of commerce, economic development organizations or university applied economic centers in each participating urban area. The numbers shown should be read as a percentage above or below the national average of 100. For example, a value of 115.4 in the groceries column indicates that grocery prices are 15.4% higher than the national average. Small differences in the index numbers should not be interpreted as significant; Figures cover the Indianapolis IN urban area.
Source: The Council for Community and Economic Research, Cost of Living Index, 2024

Grocery Prices

Area[1]	T-Bone Steak ($/pound)	Frying Chicken ($/pound)	Whole Milk ($/half gal.)	Eggs ($/dozen)	Orange Juice ($/64 oz.)	Coffee ($/11.5 oz.)
City[2]	15.51	1.63	4.67	3.40	4.33	5.39
Avg.	15.42	1.55	4.69	3.25	4.41	5.46
Min.	14.50	1.16	4.43	2.75	4.00	4.85
Max.	17.56	2.89	5.49	4.78	5.54	7.89

Note: (1) Values for the local area are compared with the average, minimum and maximum values for all 276 areas in the Cost of Living Index; (2) Figures cover the Indianapolis IN urban area; **T-Bone Steak** (price per pound); **Frying Chicken** (price per pound, whole fryer); **Whole Milk** (half gallon carton); **Eggs** (price per dozen, Grade A, large); **Orange Juice** (64 oz. Tropicana or Florida Natural); **Coffee** (11.5 oz. can, vacuum-packed, Maxwell House, Hills Bros, or Folgers).
Source: The Council for Community and Economic Research, Cost of Living Index, 2024

Housing and Utility Costs

Area[1]	New Home Price ($)	Apartment Rent ($/month)	All Electric ($/month)	Part Electric ($/month)	Other Energy ($/month)	Telephone ($/month)
City[2]	360,369	1,336	-	99.46	70.12	192.42
Avg.	515,975	1,550	210.99	123.07	82.07	194.99
Min.	265,375	692	104.33	53.68	36.26	179.42
Max.	2,775,821	5,719	529.02	397.28	361.63	223.33

Note: (1) Values for the local area are compared with the average, minimum and maximum values for all 276 areas in the Cost of Living Index; (2) Figures cover the Indianapolis IN urban area; **New Home Price** (2,400 sf living area, 8,000 sf lot, in urban area with full utilities); **Apartment Rent** (950 sf 2 bedroom/1.5 or 2 bath, unfurnished, excluding all utilities except water); **All Electric** (average monthly cost for an all-electric home); **Part Electric** (average monthly cost for a part-electric home); **Other Energy** (average monthly cost for natural gas, fuel oil, coal, wood, and any other forms of energy except electricity); **Telephone** (price includes the base monthly rate plus taxes and fees for three lines of mobile phone service).
Source: The Council for Community and Economic Research, Cost of Living Index, 2024

Health Care, Transportation, and Other Costs

Area[1]	Doctor ($/visit)	Dentist ($/visit)	Optometrist ($/visit)	Gasoline ($/gallon)	Beauty Salon ($/visit)	Men's Shirt ($)
City[2]	112.66	105.53	77.80	3.35	39.07	43.61
Avg.	143.77	117.51	129.23	3.32	48.57	38.14
Min.	36.74	58.67	67.33	2.80	24.00	13.41
Max.	270.44	216.82	307.33	5.28	94.00	63.89

Note: (1) Values for the local area are compared with the average, minimum and maximum values for all 276 areas in the Cost of Living Index; (2) Figures cover the Indianapolis IN urban area; **Doctor** (general practitioners routine exam of an established patient); **Dentist** (adult teeth cleaning and periodic oral examination); **Optometrist** (full vision eye exam for established adult patient); **Gasoline** (one gallon regular unleaded, national brand, including all taxes, cash price at self-service pump if available); **Beauty Salon** (woman's shampoo, trim, and blow-dry); **Men's Shirt** (cotton/polyester dress shirt, pinpoint weave, long sleeves).
Source: The Council for Community and Economic Research, Cost of Living Index, 2024

HOUSING

Homeownership Rate

Area	2017 (%)	2018 (%)	2019 (%)	2020 (%)	2021 (%)	2022 (%)	2023 (%)	2024 (%)
MSA[1]	63.9	64.3	66.2	70.0	70.1	68.8	70.2	69.6
U.S.	63.9	64.4	64.6	66.6	65.5	65.8	65.9	65.6

Note: (1) Figures cover the Indianapolis-Carmel-Greenwood, IN Metropolitan Statistical Area
Source: U.S. Census Bureau, Housing Vacancies and Homeownership Annual Statistics: 2017-2024

House Price Index (HPI)

Area	National Ranking[2]	Quarterly Change (%)	One-Year Change (%)	Five-Year Change (%)	Since 1991Q1 (%)
MSA[1]	136	1.08	4.99	59.79	247.41
U.S.[3]	–	1.43	4.51	57.13	327.82

Note: The HPI is a weighted repeat sales index. It measures average price changes in repeat sales or refinancings on the same properties. This information is obtained by reviewing repeat mortgage transactions on single-family properties whose mortgages have been purchased or securitized by Fannie Mae or Freddie Mac since January 1975; (1) Figures cover the Indianapolis-Carmel-Anderson, IN Metropolitan Statistical Area; (2) Rankings are based on annual percentage change for all metro areas containing at least 15,000 transactions over the last 10 years and ranges from 1 to 241; (3) figures based on a weighted average of Census Division estimates using a seasonally adjusted, purchase-only index; all figures are for the period ending December 31, 2024
Source: Federal Housing Finance Agency, Change in FHFA Metropolitan Area House Price Indexes, All Transactions Index, 2024Q4

Home Value

Area	Under $100,000	$100,000 -$199,999	$200,000 -$299,999	$300,000 -$399,999	$400,000 -$499,999	$500,000 -$999,999	$1,000,000 or more	Median ($)
City	14.2	33.3	28.5	11.6	5.2	6.1	1.1	207,000
MSA[1]	10.9	25.6	27.2	15.9	8.9	9.9	1.7	244,000
U.S.	12.1	17.8	19.5	14.4	10.5	19.1	6.5	303,400

Note: Figures are percentages except for median and cover owner-occupied housing units; (1) Figures cover the Indianapolis-Carmel-Greenwood, IN Metropolitan Statistical Area
Source: U.S. Census Bureau, 2019-2023 American Community Survey 5-Year Estimates

Year Housing Structure Built

Area	2020 or Later	2010 -2019	2000 -2009	1990 -1999	1980 -1989	1970 -1979	1960 -1969	1950 -1959	1940 -1949	Before 1940	Median Year
City	0.6	6.5	9.9	12.0	11.2	12.1	13.4	12.1	6.0	16.1	1972
MSA[1]	1.4	10.4	14.9	15.5	9.9	11.7	10.3	9.4	4.3	12.2	1982
U.S.	1.2	8.9	13.6	12.8	13.0	14.4	10.0	9.7	4.5	11.9	1980

Note: Figures are percentages except for Median Year; Note: (1) Figures cover the Indianapolis-Carmel-Greenwood, IN Metropolitan Statistical Area
Source: U.S. Census Bureau, 2019-2023 American Community Survey 5-Year Estimates

Gross Monthly Rent

Area	Under $500	$500 -$999	$1,000 -$1,499	$1,500 -$1,999	$2,000 -$2,499	$2,500 -$2,999	$3,000 and up	Median ($)
City	4.8	32.8	43.9	13.7	3.2	1.0	0.6	1,112
MSA[1]	4.8	30.7	41.9	15.6	4.7	1.4	0.9	1,142
U.S.	6.5	22.3	29.5	20.2	10.8	4.8	5.9	1,348

Note: Figures are percentages except for median; Gross rent is the contract rent plus the estimated average monthly cost of utilities (electricity, gas, and water and sewer) and fuels (oil, coal, kerosene, wood, etc.) if these are paid by the renter (or paid for the renter by someone else); (1) Figures cover the Indianapolis-Carmel-Greenwood, IN Metropolitan Statistical Area
Source: U.S. Census Bureau, 2019-2023 American Community Survey 5-Year Estimates

HEALTH

Health Risk Factors

Category	MSA[1] (%)	U.S. (%)
Adults aged 18–64 who have any kind of health care coverage	90.3	90.8
Adults who reported being in good or better health	81.4	81.8
Adults who have been told they have high blood cholesterol	37.6	36.9
Adults who have been told they have high blood pressure	36.2	34.0
Adults who are current smokers	13.4	12.1
Adults who currently use e-cigarettes	8.5	7.7
Adults who currently use chewing tobacco, snuff, or snus	2.4	3.2
Adults who are heavy drinkers[2]	5.1	6.1
Adults who are binge drinkers[3]	15.4	15.2
Adults who are overweight (BMI 25.0 - 29.9)	35.1	34.4
Adults who are obese (BMI 30.0 - 99.8)	34.9	34.3
Adults who participated in any physical activities in the past month	78.8	75.8

Note: All figures are crude prevalence; (1) Figures cover the Indianapolis-Carmel-Anderson, IN Metropolitan Statistical Area; (2) Heavy drinkers are classified as adult men having more than 14 drinks per week and adult women having more than 7 drinks per week; (3) Binge drinkers are classified as males having five or more drinks on one occasion or females having four or more drinks on one occasion
Source: Centers for Disease Control and Prevention, Behavioral Risk Factor Surveillance System, SMART: Selected Metropolitan Area Risk Trends, 2023

Acute and Chronic Health Conditions

Category	MSA[1] (%)	U.S. (%)
Adults who have ever been told they had a heart attack	4.7	4.2
Adults who have ever been told they have angina or coronary heart disease	4.0	4.0
Adults who have ever been told they had a stroke	3.8	3.3
Adults who have ever been told they have asthma	16.8	15.7
Adults who have ever been told they have arthritis	27.4	26.3
Adults who have ever been told they have diabetes[2]	12.7	11.5
Adults who have ever been told they had skin cancer	5.1	5.6
Adults who have ever been told they had any other types of cancer	8.4	8.4
Adults who have ever been told they have COPD	7.5	6.4
Adults who have ever been told they have kidney disease	4.6	3.7
Adults who have ever been told they have a form of depression	24.0	22.0

Note: All figures are crude prevalence; (1) Figures cover the Indianapolis-Carmel-Anderson, IN Metropolitan Statistical Area; (2) Figures do not include pregnancy-related, borderline, or pre-diabetes
Source: Centers for Disease Control and Prevention, Behavioral Risk Factor Surveillance System, SMART: Selected Metropolitan Area Risk Trends, 2023

Health Screening and Vaccination Rates

Category	MSA[1] (%)	U.S. (%)
Adults who have ever been tested for HIV	36.7	37.5
Adults who have had their blood cholesterol checked within the last five years	89.0	87.0
Adults aged 65+ who have had flu shot within the past year	66.3	63.4
Adults aged 65+ who have ever had a pneumonia vaccination	74.4	71.9

Note: All figures are crude prevalence; (1) Figures cover the Indianapolis-Carmel-Anderson, IN Metropolitan Statistical Area.
Source: Centers for Disease Control and Prevention, Behavioral Risk Factor Surveillance System, SMART: Selected Metropolitan Area Risk Trends, 2023

Disability Status

Category	MSA[1] (%)	U.S. (%)
Adults who reported being deaf	5.8	7.4
Are you blind or have serious difficulty seeing, even when wearing glasses?	4.6	4.9
Do you have difficulty doing errands alone?	6.5	7.8
Do you have difficulty dressing or bathing?	2.6	3.6
Do you have serious difficulty concentrating/remembering/making decisions?	13.3	13.7
Do you have serious difficulty walking or climbing stairs?	12.5	13.2

Note: All figures are crude prevalence; (1) Figures cover the Indianapolis-Carmel-Anderson, IN Metropolitan Statistical Area.
Source: Centers for Disease Control and Prevention, Behavioral Risk Factor Surveillance System, SMART: Selected Metropolitan Area Risk Trends, 2023

Mortality Rates for the Top 10 Causes of Death in the U.S.

ICD-10[a] Sub-Chapter	ICD-10[a] Code	Crude Mortality Rate[2] per 100,000 population	
		County[3]	U.S.
Malignant neoplasms	C00-C97	177.0	182.7
Ischaemic heart diseases	I20-I25	86.5	109.6
Provisional assignment of new diseases of uncertain etiology[1]	U00-U49	56.1	65.3
Other forms of heart disease	I30-I51	57.3	65.1
Other degenerative diseases of the nervous system	G30-G31	41.1	52.4
Other external causes of accidental injury	W00-X59	87.7	52.3
Cerebrovascular diseases	I60-I69	40.2	49.1
Chronic lower respiratory diseases	J40-J47	51.9	43.5
Hypertensive diseases	I10-I15	36.0	38.9
Organic, including symptomatic, mental disorders	F01-F09	31.6	33.9

Note: (a) ICD-10 = International Classification of Diseases 10th Revision; (1) Includes COVID-19, adverse effects to COVID-19 vaccines, SARS, and vaping-related disorders; (2) Crude mortality rates are a three-year average covering 2021-2023; (3) Figures cover Marion County.
Source: Centers for Disease Control and Prevention, National Center for Health Statistics. National Vital Statistics System, Mortality 2018-2023 on CDC WONDER Online Database

Mortality Rates for Selected Causes of Death

Cause of Death	ICD-10[a] Code	Crude Mortality Rate[1] per 100,000 population	
		County[2]	U.S.
Accidental poisoning and exposure to noxious substances	X40-X49	68.4	30.5
Alzheimer disease	G30	23.2	35.4
Assault	X85-Y09	22.9	7.3
COVID-19	U07.1	56.1	65.3
Diabetes mellitus	E10-E14	30.0	30.0
Diseases of the liver	K70-K76	19.6	20.8
Human immunodeficiency virus (HIV) disease	B20-B24	1.8	1.5
Influenza and pneumonia	J09-J18	7.5	13.4
Intentional self-harm	X60-X84	14.7	14.7
Malnutrition	E40-E46	7.4	6.0
Obesity and other hyperalimentation	E65-E68	3.3	3.1
Renal failure	N17-N19	20.6	16.4
Transport accidents	V01-V99	17.6	14.4

Note: (a) ICD-10 = International Classification of Diseases 10th Revision; (1) Crude mortality rates are a three-year average covering 2021-2023; (2) Figures cover Marion County; Data are suppressed when the data meet the criteria for confidentiality constraints; Crude mortality rates are flagged as unreliable when the rate would be calculated with a numerator of 20 or less.
Source: Centers for Disease Control and Prevention, National Center for Health Statistics. National Vital Statistics System, Mortality 2018-2023 on CDC WONDER Online Database

Health Insurance Coverage

Area	With Health Insurance	With Private Health Insurance	With Public Health Insurance	Without Health Insurance	Population Under Age 19 Without Health Insurance
City	91.0	62.3	38.6	9.0	5.7
MSA[1]	93.0	70.9	32.9	7.0	4.6
U.S.	91.4	67.3	36.3	8.6	5.4

Note: Figures are percentages that cover the civilian noninstitutionalized population; (1) Figures cover the Indianapolis-Carmel-Greenwood, IN Metropolitan Statistical Area
Source: U.S. Census Bureau, 2019-2023 American Community Survey 5-Year Estimates

Number of Medical Professionals

Area	MDs[3]	DOs[3,4]	Dentists	Podiatrists	Chiropractors	Optometrists
County[1] (number)	4,605	306	924	67	169	214
County[1] (rate[2])	475.0	31.6	95.4	6.9	17.5	22.1
U.S. (rate[2])	302.5	29.2	74.6	6.4	29.5	18.0

Note: Data as of 2023 unless noted; (1) Data covers Marion County; (2) Number of medical professionals per 100,000 population; (3) Data as of 2022 and includes all active, non-federal physicians; (4) Doctor of Osteopathic Medicine
Source: U.S. Department of Health and Human Services, Health Resources and Services Administration, Bureau of Health Professions, Area Resource File (ARF) 2023-2024

Best Hospitals

According to *U.S. News,* the Indianapolis-Carmel-Greenwood, IN metro area is home to one of the best hospitals in the U.S.: **Rehabilitation Hospital of Indiana** (1 adult specialty). The hospital listed was nationally ranked in at least one of 15 adult or 11 pediatric specialties. The number of specialties shown cover the parent hospital. Only 160 U.S. hospitals performed well enough to be nationally ranked in one or more specialties. Twenty hospitals in the U.S. made the Honor Roll. The Best Hospitals Honor Roll takes both the national rankings and the procedure and condition ratings into account. Hospitals received points if they were nationally ranked in one of the 15 adult specialties—the higher they ranked, the more points they got—and how many ratings of "high performing" they earned in the 20 procedures and conditions. *U.S. News Online, "America's Best Hospitals 2024-25"*

According to *U.S. News,* the Indianapolis-Carmel-Greenwood, IN metro area is home to one of the best children's hospitals in the U.S.: **Riley Hospital for Children at IU Health** (11 pediatric specialties). The hospital listed was highly ranked in at least one of 11 pediatric specialties. One hundred five children's hospitals in the U.S. were nationally ranked in at least one specialty. Hospitals received points for being ranked in a specialty, and the 10 hospitals with the most points across the 11 specialties make up the Honor Roll. *U.S. News Online, "America's Best Children's Hospitals 2024-25"*

EDUCATION

Public School District Statistics

District Name	Schls	Pupils	Pupil/Teacher Ratio	Minority Pupils[1] (%)	Total Rev. per Pupil ($)	Total Exp. per Pupil ($)
Franklin Township Com Sch Corp	11	11,240	18.5	44.0	13,814	12,954
Indiana Connections Academy	1	5,475	32.2	26.3	7,529	8,562
Indianapolis Public Schools	48	21,863	14.0	81.0	26,465	26,790
M S D Decatur Township	10	6,655	15.6	52.2	16,041	14,768
M S D Lawrence Township	17	16,502	18.8	83.4	15,995	14,366
M S D Pike Township	13	10,617	16.0	93.6	15,770	14,885
M S D Warren Township	16	11,440	15.6	85.9	16,329	18,845
M S D Washington Township	14	10,735	15.3	71.8	19,644	19,331
M S D Wayne Township	18	15,799	16.3	78.3	17,301	18,276
Perry Township Schools	21	16,044	16.3	65.7	15,840	13,927

Note: Table includes school districts with 2,000 or more students; (1) Percentage of students that are not non-Hispanic white.
Source: U.S. Department of Education, National Center for Education Statistics, Common Core of Data, Local Education Agency (School District) Universe Survey: School Year 2023-2024; U.S. Department of Education, National Center for Education Statistics, Common Core of Data, School District Finance Survey (F-33): School Year 2021–22

Best High Schools

According to U.S. News, Indianapolis is home to one of the top 500 high schools in the U.S.: **Herron High School** (#316). Nearly 25,000 public, magnet and charter schools were ranked based on their performance on state assessments and how well they prepare students for college. U.S. News & World Report, "Best High Schools 2024"

Highest Level of Education

Area	Less than H.S.	H.S. Diploma	Some College, No Deg.	Associate Degree	Bachelor's Degree	Master's Degree	Prof. School Degree	Doctorate Degree
City	12.5	26.8	18.9	7.7	21.7	8.8	2.3	1.4
MSA[1]	8.9	26.7	18.4	8.1	24.1	9.9	2.4	1.5
U.S.	10.6	26.2	19.4	8.8	21.3	9.8	2.3	1.6

Note: Figures cover persons age 25 and over; (1) Figures cover the Indianapolis-Carmel-Greenwood, IN Metropolitan Statistical Area
Source: U.S. Census Bureau, 2019-2023 American Community Survey 5-Year Estimates

Educational Attainment by Race

Area	High School Graduate or Higher (%)					Bachelor's Degree or Higher (%)				
	Total	White	Black	Asian	Hisp.[2]	Total	White	Black	Asian	Hisp.[2]
City	87.5	91.3	87.9	70.4	64.5	34.2	41.0	22.1	41.0	18.6
MSA[1]	91.1	93.5	88.2	81.4	70.5	37.8	40.4	24.9	54.4	24.0
U.S.	89.4	92.9	88.1	88.0	72.5	35.0	37.7	24.7	57.0	19.9

Note: Figures shown cover persons 25 years old and over; (1) Figures cover the Indianapolis-Carmel-Greenwood, IN Metropolitan Statistical Area; (2) People of Hispanic origin can be of any race
Source: U.S. Census Bureau, 2019-2023 American Community Survey 5-Year Estimates

School Enrollment by Grade and Control

Area	Preschool (%)		Kindergarten (%)		Grades 1 - 4 (%)		Grades 5 - 8 (%)		Grades 9 - 12 (%)	
	Public	Private	Public	Private	Public	Private	Public	Private	Public	Private
City	61.1	38.9	85.4	14.6	82.9	17.1	83.7	16.3	85.2	14.8
MSA[1]	53.8	46.2	84.3	15.7	85.1	14.9	85.7	14.3	87.4	12.6
U.S.	58.7	41.3	85.2	14.8	87.2	12.8	87.9	12.1	89.0	11.0

Note: Figures shown cover persons 3 years old and over; (1) Figures cover the Indianapolis-Carmel-Greenwood, IN Metropolitan Statistical Area
Source: U.S. Census Bureau, 2019-2023 American Community Survey 5-Year Estimates

Higher Education

Four-Year Colleges			Two-Year Colleges			Medical Schools[1]	Law Schools[2]	Voc/Tech[3]
Public	Private Non-profit	Private For-profit	Public	Private Non-profit	Private For-profit			
1	9	2	1	0	5	2	1	8

Note: Figures cover institutions located within the Indianapolis-Carmel-Greenwood, IN Metropolitan Statistical Area and include main campuses only; (1) includes schools accredited by the Liaison Committee on Medical Education and the American Osteopathic Association's Commission on Osteopathic College Accreditation; (2) includes ABA-accredited schools, schools with provisional ABA accreditation, and state accredited schools; (3) includes all schools with programs that are less than 2 years.
Source: National Center for Education Statistics, Integrated Postsecondary Education System (IPEDS), 2023-24; Wikipedia, List of Medical Schools in the United States, accessed May 2, 2025; Wikipedia, List of Law Schools in the United States, accessed May 2, 2025

According to *U.S. News & World Report*, the Indianapolis-Carmel-Greenwood, IN metro area is home to one of the top 200 national universities in the U.S.: **Indiana University Indianapolis** (#196 tie). The indicators used to capture academic quality fall into a number of categories: assessment by administrators at peer institutions; retention of students; faculty resources; student selectivity; financial resources; alumni giving; high school counselor ratings of colleges; and graduation rate. *U.S. News & World Report, "America's Best Colleges 2025"*

According to *U.S. News & World Report*, the Indianapolis-Carmel-Greenwood, IN metro area is home to one of the top medical schools for research in the U.S.: **Indiana University** (Tier 2). *U.S. News* placed medical and osteopathic schools into tiers based on their research productivity, faculty and admissions data. Each school's tier was derived from its overall score, calculated by summing the weighted normalized values generated across several factors of academic quality, outlined below. There are four tiers, with tier 1 medical schools as the highest-performing and tier 4 as the lowest-performing. Only tier 1 and 2 schools are shown. Because of the tier presentation, *U.S. News* calculated overall scores based on their percentile performance among all rated schools instead of dividing against the rescaled score of the No. 1-performing schools. Tier 1 included schools with overall scores of 85 to 99. The cutoffs for tiers 2 through 4 were schools scoring 50 to 84, 15 to 49 and 1 to 14, respectively. The rankings are based on a weighted average of the following measures of quality: total research activity; average research activity per faculty member; total NIH research grants at the medical school and its affiliated hospitals; average NIH research grants per faculty; median MCAT total score; median undergraduate GPA; acceptance rate; and faculty resources. *U.S. News & World Report, "America's Best Graduate Schools, Medical, 2025"*

EMPLOYERS

Major Employers

Company Name	Industry
Amazon.com	Online retail
Anthem	Healthcare
City of Indianapolis	Local government
Community Health Network	Healthcare
Cummins	Manufacturing
Eli Lilly	Pharmaceutical
Indiana Department of Transportation	Public transportation
Indiana State Police	Police
Indiana University	Higher education
Indiana University Health	Healthcare network
Indianapolis Public Schools	School districts
Roche Diagnositcs Corp.	Biotech industry
Salesforce	Customer realations management
State of Indiana	Government
United States Postal Service	U.S. postal service

Note: Companies shown are located within the Indianapolis-Carmel-Greenwood, IN Metropolitan Statistical Area.
Source: Chambers of Commerce; State Departments of Labor; Wikipedia

Best Companies to Work For

Elevance Health, headquartered in Indianapolis, is among "The 100 Best Companies to Work For." To pick the best companies, *Fortune* partnered with the Great Place to Work Institute. Using their proprietary Trust Index™ survey, the core of what creates great a workplace is measured—key behaviors that drive trust in management, connection with colleagues, and loyalty to the company. To be eligible for the *Fortune* 100 Best Companies to Work For list, employers must have 1,000 or more employees in the U.S. and cannot be a government agency. *Fortune, "The 100 Best Companies to Work For," 2025*

Elevance Health, headquartered in Indianapolis, is among "Fortune's Best Workplaces for Women." To pick the best companies, *Fortune* partnered with the Great Place to Work Institute. To be considered for the list, companies must be Great Place To Work-Certified. Companies must also employ at least 50 women, at least 20% of their non-executive managers must be female, and at least one executive must be female. To determine the Best Workplaces for Women, Great Place To Work measured the differences in women's survey responses to those of their peers and assesses the impact of demographics and roles on the quality and consistency of women's experiences. Great Place To Work also analyzed the gender balance of each workplace, how it compared to each company's industry, and patterns in representation as women rise from front-line positions to the board of directors. *Fortune, "Best Workplaces for Women," 2024*

Elevance Health, headquartered in Indianapolis, is among "Best Workplaces in Health Care." To determine the Best Workplaces in Health Care list, Great Place To Work analyzed the survey responses of over 185,000 employees from Great Place To Work-Certified companies in the health care industry. Survey data analysis and company-provided datapoints are then factored into a combined score to compare and rank the companies that create the most consistently positive experience for all employees in this industry. *Fortune, "Best Workplaces in Health Care," 2024*

PUBLIC SAFETY

Crime Rate

Area	Total Crime Rate	Violent Crime Rate				Property Crime Rate		
		Murder	Rape	Robbery	Aggrav. Assault	Burglary	Larceny-Theft	Motor Vehicle Theft
City	4,653.4	18.9	55.9	174.2	782.0	615.8	2,229.9	776.8
U.S.	2,290.9	5.7	38.0	66.5	264.1	250.7	1,347.2	318.7

Note: Figures are crimes per 100,000 population.
Source: FBI, Table 8, Offenses Known to Law Enforcement, by State by City, 2023

Hate Crimes

Area	Number of Quarters Reported	Number of Incidents per Bias Motivation					
		Race/Ethnicity/Ancestry	Religion	Sexual Orientation	Disability	Gender	Gender Identity
City	4	17	2	7	0	0	0
U.S.	4	5,900	2,699	2,077	187	92	492

Source: Federal Bureau of Investigation, Hate Crime Statistics 2023

Identity Theft Consumer Reports

Area	Reports	Reports per 100,000 Population	Rank[2]
MSA[1]	6,570	312	61
U.S.	1,135,291	339	-

Note: (1) Figures cover the Indianapolis-Carmel-Greenwood, IN Metropolitan Statistical Area; (2) Rank ranges from 1 to 401 where 1 indicates greatest number of identity theft reports per 100,000 population
Source: Federal Trade Commission, Consumer Sentinel Network Data Book 2024

Fraud and Other Consumer Reports

Area	Reports	Reports per 100,000 Population	Rank[2]
MSA[1]	31,318	1,487	61
U.S.	5,360,641	1,601	-

Note: (1) Figures cover the Indianapolis-Carmel-Greenwood, IN Metropolitan Statistical Area; (2) Rank ranges from 1 to 401 where 1 indicates greatest number of fraud and other consumer reports per 100,000 population
Source: Federal Trade Commission, Consumer Sentinel Network Data Book 2024

POLITICS

2024 Presidential Election Results

Area	Trump (Rep.)	Harris (Dem.)	Stein (Green)	Kennedy (Ind.)	Oliver (Lib.)	Other
Marion County	35.1	62.6	0.0	0.9	0.8	0.7
U.S.	49.7	48.2	0.6	0.5	0.4	0.6

Note: Results are percentages and may not add to 100% due to rounding
Source: Dave Leip's Atlas of U.S. Presidential Elections

SPORTS

Professional Sports Teams

Team Name	League	Year Established
Indiana Pacers	National Basketball Association (NBA)	1967
Indianapolis Colts	National Football League (NFL)	1984

Note: Includes teams located in the Indianapolis-Carmel-Greenwood, IN Metropolitan Statistical Area.
Source: Wikipedia, Major Professional Sports Teams of the United States and Canada, May 1, 2025

CLIMATE

Average and Extreme Temperatures

Temperature	Jan	Feb	Mar	Apr	May	Jun	Jul	Aug	Sep	Oct	Nov	Dec	Yr.
Extreme High (°F)	71	72	85	89	93	102	104	102	100	90	81	74	104
Average High (°F)	35	39	50	63	73	82	85	84	78	66	51	39	62
Average Temp. (°F)	27	31	41	52	63	72	76	73	67	55	43	31	53
Average Low (°F)	18	22	31	41	52	61	65	63	55	44	33	23	42
Extreme Low (°F)	-22	-21	-7	18	28	39	48	41	34	20	-2	-23	-23

Note: Figures cover the years 1948-1990
Source: National Climatic Data Center, International Station Meteorological Climate Summary, 9/96

Average Precipitation/Snowfall/Humidity

Precip./Humidity	Jan	Feb	Mar	Apr	May	Jun	Jul	Aug	Sep	Oct	Nov	Dec	Yr.
Avg. Precip. (in.)	2.8	2.5	3.6	3.6	4.0	3.9	4.3	3.4	2.9	2.6	3.3	3.3	40.2
Avg. Snowfall (in.)	7	6	4	1	Tr	0	0	0	0	Tr	2	5	25
Avg. Rel. Hum. 7am (%)	81	81	79	77	79	80	84	87	87	85	83	83	82
Avg. Rel. Hum. 4pm (%)	68	64	59	53	53	53	56	56	53	53	63	70	59

Note: Figures cover the years 1948-1990; Tr = Trace amounts (<0.05 in. of rain; <0.5 in. of snow)
Source: National Climatic Data Center, International Station Meteorological Climate Summary, 9/96

Weather Conditions

Temperature			Daytime Sky			Precipitation		
10°F & below	32°F & below	90°F & above	Clear	Partly cloudy	Cloudy	0.01 inch or more precip.	0.1 inch or more snow/ice	Thunder-storms
19	119	19	83	128	154	127	24	43

Note: Figures are average number of days per year and cover the years 1948-1990
Source: National Climatic Data Center, International Station Meteorological Climate Summary, 9/96

HAZARDOUS WASTE

Superfund Sites

The Indianapolis-Carmel-Greenwood, IN metro area is home to six sites on the EPA's Superfund National Priorities List (NPL) or Superfund Alternative Approach (SAA) list: **Broadway Street Corridor Groundwater Contamination** (Final NPL); **Envirochem Corp.** (Final NPL); **Keystone Corridor Ground Water Contamination** (Final NPL); **Northside Sanitary Landfill, Inc** (Final NPL); **Pike and Mulberry Streets PCE Plume** (Final NPL); **Reilly Tar & Chemical Corp. (Indianapolis Plant)** (Final NPL). The Superfund alternative approach uses the same investigation and cleanup process and standards that are used for sites listed on the National Priorities List. The SAA is an alternative to listing a site on the NPL; it is not an alternative to Superfund or the Superfund process. There are a total of 1,445 Superfund sites with a status of proposed or final on both lists in the United States. *U.S. Environmental Protection Agency, National Priorities List, May 1, 2025; U.S. Environmental Protection Agency, Superfund Alternative Approach Sites, May 1, 2025*

AIR QUALITY

Air Quality Trends: Ozone

	1990	1995	2000	2005	2010	2015	2020	2021	2022	2023
MSA[1]	0.085	0.095	0.081	0.081	0.070	0.065	0.065	0.067	0.070	0.073
U.S.	0.087	0.089	0.081	0.080	0.072	0.068	0.066	0.067	0.067	0.070

Note: (1) Data covers the Indianapolis-Carmel-Greenwood, IN Metropolitan Statistical Area. The values shown are the composite ozone concentration averages among trend sites based on the highest fourth daily maximum 8-hour concentration in parts per million. These trends are based on sites having an adequate record of monitoring data during the trend period. Data from exceptional events are included.
Source: U.S. Environmental Protection Agency, Air Quality Monitoring Information, "Air Quality Trends by City, 1990-2023"

Air Quality Index

Area	Percent of Days when Air Quality was...[2]					AQI Statistics[2]	
	Good	Moderate	Unhealthy for Sensitive Groups	Unhealthy	Very Unhealthy	Maximum	Median
MSA[1]	21.9	71.5	5.5	0.5	0.5	259	60

Note: (1) Data covers the Indianapolis-Carmel-Greenwood, IN Metropolitan Statistical Area; (2) Based on 365 days with AQI data in 2023. Air Quality Index (AQI) is an index for reporting daily air quality. EPA calculates the AQI for five major air pollutants regulated by the Clean Air Act: ground-level ozone, particle pollution (aka particulate matter), carbon monoxide, sulfur dioxide, and nitrogen dioxide. The AQI runs from 0 to 500. The higher the AQI value, the greater the level of air pollution and the greater the health concern. There are six AQI categories: "Good" AQI is between 0 and 50. Air quality is considered satisfactory; "Moderate" AQI is between 51 and 100. Air quality is acceptable; "Unhealthy for Sensitive Groups" When AQI values are between 101 and 150, members of sensitive groups may experience health effects; "Unhealthy" When AQI values are between 151 and 200 everyone may begin to experience health effects; "Very Unhealthy" AQI values between 201 and 300 trigger a health alert; "Hazardous" AQI values over 300 trigger warnings of emergency conditions (not shown).
Source: U.S. Environmental Protection Agency, Air Quality Index Report, 2023

Air Quality Index Pollutants

Area	Percent of Days when AQI Pollutant was...[2]					
	Carbon Monoxide	Nitrogen Dioxide	Ozone	Sulfur Dioxide	Particulate Matter 2.5	Particulate Matter 10
MSA[1]	0.0	0.0	19.2	(3)	80.8	0.0

Note: (1) Data covers the Indianapolis-Carmel-Greenwood, IN Metropolitan Statistical Area; (2) Based on 365 days with AQI data in 2023. The Air Quality Index (AQI) is an index for reporting daily air quality. EPA calculates the AQI for five major air pollutants regulated by the Clean Air Act: ground-level ozone, particle pollution (also known as particulate matter), carbon monoxide, sulfur dioxide, and nitrogen dioxide. The AQI runs from 0 to 500. The higher the AQI value, the greater the level of air pollution and the greater the health concern; (3) Sulfur dioxide is no longer included in this table because SO_2 concentrations tend to be very localized and not necessarily representative of broad geographical areas like counties and CBSAs.
Source: U.S. Environmental Protection Agency, Air Quality Index Report, 2023

Maximum Air Pollutant Concentrations: Particulate Matter, Ozone, CO and Lead

	Particulate Matter 10 (ug/m^3)	Particulate Matter 2.5 Wtd AM (ug/m^3)	Particulate Matter 2.5 24-Hr (ug/m^3)	Ozone (ppm)	Carbon Monoxide (ppm)	Lead (ug/m^3)
MSA[1] Level	147	13.7	44	0.077	2	n/a
NAAQS[2]	150	15	35	0.075	9	0.15
Met NAAQS[2]	Yes	Yes	No	No	Yes	n/a

Note: (1) Data covers the Indianapolis-Carmel-Greenwood, IN Metropolitan Statistical Area; Data from exceptional events are included; (2) National Ambient Air Quality Standards; ppm = parts per million; ug/m^3 = micrograms per cubic meter; n/a not available.
Concentrations: Particulate Matter 10 (coarse particulate)—highest second maximum 24-hour concentration; Particulate Matter 2.5 Wtd AM (fine particulate)—highest weighted annual mean concentration; Particulate Matter 2.5 24-Hour (fine particulate)—highest 98th percentile 24-hour concentration; Ozone—highest fourth daily maximum 8-hour concentration; Carbon Monoxide—highest second maximum non-overlapping 8-hour concentration; Lead—maximum running 3-month average
Source: U.S. Environmental Protection Agency, Air Quality Monitoring Information, "Air Quality Statistics by City, 2023"

Maximum Air Pollutant Concentrations: Nitrogen Dioxide and Sulfur Dioxide

	Nitrogen Dioxide AM (ppb)	Nitrogen Dioxide 1-Hr (ppb)	Sulfur Dioxide AM (ppb)	Sulfur Dioxide 1-Hr (ppb)	Sulfur Dioxide 24-Hr (ppb)
MSA[1] Level	13	44	n/a	3	n/a
NAAQS[2]	53	100	30	75	140
Met NAAQS[2]	Yes	Yes	n/a	Yes	n/a

Note: (1) Data covers the Indianapolis-Carmel-Greenwood, IN Metropolitan Statistical Area; Data from exceptional events are included; (2) National Ambient Air Quality Standards; ppm = parts per million; ug/m^3 = micrograms per cubic meter; n/a not available.
Concentrations: Nitrogen Dioxide AM—highest arithmetic mean concentration; Nitrogen Dioxide 1-Hr—highest 98th percentile 1-hour daily maximum concentration; Sulfur Dioxide AM—highest annual mean concentration; Sulfur Dioxide 1-Hr—highest 99th percentile 1-hour daily maximum concentration; Sulfur Dioxide 24-Hr—highest second maximum 24-hour concentration
Source: U.S. Environmental Protection Agency, Air Quality Monitoring Information, "Air Quality Statistics by City, 2023"

Kansas City, Missouri

Background

Kansas City, on the western boundary of the state, and its sister city of the same name on the other side of the Kansas/Missouri border in Kansas, make up the greater Kansas City metropolitan area.

The territory of the Kansa (or Kaw) tribe received intermittent visits from white settlers during the eighteenth and nineteenth centuries. In 1724, a fort was built in the vicinity, and in 1804, Meriwether Lewis and William Clark explored the area on behalf of President Jefferson for the Louisiana Purchase. In 1821, the site was a trading post established by Francois Chouteau, who established the American Fur Company.

A combination of gold prospectors passing through on their way to California, via steamboat, rail, and coach, and the migration of would-be settlers to California and the Southwest stimulated economic activity in Kansas City during the 1800s. Three major trails—Santa Fe, California, and Oregon—all originated in Jackson County.

It was in this solid Midwestern city that the jazz clubs on 18th Street and Vine gave birth to the careers of Charlie Parker and Count Basie. Today a new generation of artists upholds Kansas City's reputation for great jazz, performing in dozens of clubs featuring live jazz nightly.

Kansas City is also home to more than 100 barbecue restaurants in the metropolitan area and each fall hosts what it claims is the world's biggest barbecue contest.

As one might expect from the heartland of America, Kansas City's major industries are hard wheat and cattle. The city continues to transform its skyline with modern skyscrapers among the more traditional nineteenth-century buildings. The city boasts over 100 parks and playgrounds, suburban areas with an above-average living standard, European statues that line wide stretching boulevards, and a foreign trade zone where foreign countries can store their goods free of import duties. It offers something for everyone, from cultural and sporting events to casinos and gaming, from hot barbecue to even hotter jazz.

In 2019, the USDA opened two federal research labs in the Kansas City area. The Stowers Institute for Medical Research, adjacent to the University of Missouri-Kansas City main campus, and National Bio and Agro-Defense Facility (NBAF) in Manhattan Kansas, two hours from Kansas City.

The Kansas City International Airport is a modern and growing transportation hub. A new airport terminal opened in 2023, the largest infrastructure project in the city's history. The historic Union Station's restored grand hall, with its 95-foot ceilings, shares space with the Science City Museum, theaters, restaurants, and shops.

The city maintains its own symphony, lyric opera, and ballet. It boasts dozens of museums and art galleries, many with free admission. The Kansas City Zoo offers over 200 acres of exhibits, including the Orangutan Primadome and a penguin exhibit. Visitors to the Harley-Davidson plant can see how a "Hog" is built; other attractions include the Children's Peace Pavilion, the Kansas City Renaissance Festival, and Fiesta Hispana, a yearly celebration of Hispanic heritage.

The NFL's Kansas City Chiefs won Super Bowl LIV in 2020 and again in 2023 and 2024. Also in 2020, the Sprint Center was renamed T-Mobile Center, poised to host future NBA and NHL franchises.

The National Weather Service office at Kansas City is very near the geographical center of the United States. The gently rolling terrain with no topographic impediments allows a free sweep of air from all directions, often creating conflict between warm, moist air from the Gulf of Mexico and cold polar air from the north. The summer season is characterized by warm days, mild nights, and moderate humidity. Winters are not severely cold, and sizeable snowfalls are rare.

Rankings

General Rankings

- To help military veterans find the best places in which to settle down, *WalletHub* compared the 100 largest U.S. cities across 19 key indicators of livability, affordability and veteran-friendliness. They range from the share of military skill-related jobs to veteran income growth to the availability of VA health facilities. Kansas City ranked #52. *Wallethub.com, "Best & Worst Places for Veterans to Live (2025)," November 7, 2024*

- *Insider* listed 23 places in the U.S. that travel industry trends reveal would be popular destinations in 2023. This year the list trends towards cultural and historical happenings, sports events, wellness experiences and invigorating outdoor escapes. According to the website insider.com Kansas City is a place to visit in 2023. *Insider, "23 of the Best Places You Should Travel to in the U.S. in 2023," December 17, 2022*

Business/Finance Rankings

- Payscale.com ranked the 32 largest metro areas in terms of wage growth. The Kansas City metro area ranked #1. Criteria: quarterly changes in private industry employee and education professional wage growth from the previous year. *PayScale, "Wage Trends by Metro Area-4th Quarter," February 4, 2025*

- Kansas City was cited as one of America's top metros for total corporate facility investment projects in 2024. The area ranked #7 in the Tier 1 (large) metro area category (population over 1 million). *Site Selection, "Top Metros of 2024," March 2025*

- The Kansas City metro area appeared on the Milken Institute "2025 Best Performing Cities" list. Rank: #92 out of 200 large metro areas (based on performance category). Criteria: job growth; wage growth; high-tech growth and impact; community resilience; housing affordability; household broadband access. *Milken Institute, "Best-Performing Cities 2025," January 14, 2025*

Culture/Performing Arts Rankings

- Kansas City was selected as one of the 25 best cities for moviemakers in North America. Great film cities are places where filmmaking dreams can come true, that offer more creative space, lower costs, and great outdoor locations. NYC & LA were intentionally excluded. Criteria: film industry presence and culture; tax incentives; affordability; and proximity of festivals and schools. The city was ranked #23. *MovieMaker Magazine, "Best Places to Live and Work as a Moviemaker, 2025," January 29, 2025*

Education Rankings

- Personal finance website *WalletHub* analyzed the 150 largest U.S. metropolitan statistical areas to determine where the most educated Americans are putting their degrees to work. Criteria: education levels; percentage of workers with degrees; education quality and attainment gap; public school quality rankings; quality and enrollment of each metro area's universities. Kansas City was ranked #39 (#1 = most educated city). *WalletHub.com, "Most & Least Educated Cities in America, 2025" July 2, 2024*

Health/Fitness Rankings

- For each of the 100 largest cities in the United States, the American Fitness Index®, compiled in partnership between the American College of Sports Medicine and the Elevance Health Foundation, evaluated community infrastructure and more than 30 health behaviors including preventive health, levels of chronic disease conditions, food insecurity, pedestrian safety, air quality, and community/environment resources that support physical activity. Kansas City ranked #82 for "community fitness." *americanfitnessindex.org, "2024 ACSM American Fitness Index Summary Report," July 23, 2024*

- Kansas City was identified as a "2025 Allergy Capital." The area ranked #54 out of the nation's 100 largest metropolitan areas. Three groups of factors were used to identify the most challenging cities for people with allergies: annual tree, grass, and weed pollen scores; over the counter allergy medicine use; number of board-certified allergy specialists. *Asthma and Allergy Foundation of America, "2025 Allergy Capitals: The Most Challenging Places to Live with Allergies," March 18, 2025*

- Kansas City was identified as a "2024 Asthma Capital." The area ranked #65 out of the nation's 100 largest metropolitan areas. Criteria: estimated asthma prevalence; asthma-related mortality; and ER visits due to asthma. Risk factors analyzed but not factored in the rankings: annual air quality including pollution and ozone levels; public smoking laws; indoor air quality; access to asthma specialists; rescue and controller medication use; uninsured rate; pollen allergy; poverty rate. *Asthma and Allergy Foundation of America, "Asthma Capitals 2024: The Most Challenging Places to Live With Asthma," September 10, 2024*

Pet Rankings

- Kansas City was selected by *Sniffspot.com* as one of the most dog-friendly cities in the U.S., ranking #31 out of 50. Criteria: dog parks; hiking; sniffspots; public parks; dog-friendly businesses; housing; dog waste cleanliness; leash laws; dog services; and overall cost. *Sniffspot.com, "The Top 50 Most Dog-Friendly Cities in the U.S.," September 30, 2024*

Real Estate Rankings

- *WalletHub* compared the most populated U.S. cities to determine which had the best markets for real estate agents. Kansas City ranked #26 where demand was high and pay was the best. Criteria: sales per agent; annual median wage for real-estate agents; monthly average starting salary for real estate agents; real estate job density and competition; unemployment rate; home turnover rate; housing-market health index; and other relevant metrics. *WalletHub.com, "2021 Best Places to Be a Real Estate Agent," May 12, 2021*

- Kansas City was ranked #76 out of 176 metro areas in terms of cost of housing in 2024 by the National Association of Home Builders (#1 = most affordable). Criteria: the portion of an average family's income necessary to pay the mortgage on a median-priced home. *National Association of Home Builders®, NAHB-Wells Fargo Cost of Housing Index, 4th Quarter 2024*

Safety Rankings

- To identify the most dangerous cities in America, *24/7 Wall St.* focused on violent crime categories—murder, non-negligent manslaughter, rape, robbery, and aggravated assault—as reported for every 100,000 residents using data from the FBI's 2020 annual Uniform Crime Report. For cities with populations over 25,000, Kansas City was ranked #15. *247wallst.com, "America's Most Dangerous Cities" November 12, 2021*

- Allstate ranked the 100 most populous cities in America in terms of driver safety. Kansas City ranked #19. Criteria based on anonymized driving behavior data from Allstate's mobile app powered by Arity: high speed driving (over 80 mph), phone handling, and hard braking. The report helps increase the importance of safety and awareness behind the wheel. *Allstate, "16th Allstate America's Best Drivers Report®" July 11, 2024*

- Kansas City was identified as one of the most dangerous cities in America by NeighborhoodScout. The city ranked #25 out of 100 (#1 = most dangerous). Criteria: number of violent crimes per 1,000 residents. The editors evaluated cities with 25,000 or more residents. *NeighborhoodScout.com, "2023 Top 100 Most Dangerous Cities in the U.S.," January 12, 2023*

Women/Minorities Rankings

- Personal finance website *WalletHub* compared more than 180 U.S. cities across two key dimensions, "Hispanic Business-Friendliness" and "Hispanic Purchasing Power," to arrive at the most favorable conditions for Hispanic entrepreneurs. Kansas City was ranked #85 out of 182. Criteria includes: share of Hispanic-Owned Businesses; average growth of Hispanic Business revenues; Small Business-Friendliness score; affordability; and number of Hispanics with at least a bachelor's degree. *WalletHub.com, "Best Cities for Hispanic Entrepreneurs," September 4, 2024*

Miscellaneous Rankings

- *MoveHub* ranked 446 hipster cities across 20 countries, using its new and improved alternative Hipster Index and Kansas City came out as #38 among the top 50. Criteria: population over 150,000; number of vintage boutiques; density of tattoo parlors; vegan places to eat; coffee shops; and density of vinyl record stores. *MoveHub.com, "The Hipster Index: Brighton Pips Portland to Global Top Spot," July 28, 2021*

- *WalletHub* compared 148 of the most populated U.S. cities to determine their operating efficiency. A "Quality of Services" score was constructed for each city and then measured against the total budget per capita to reveal which were managed the best. Kansas City ranked #115. Criteria: financial stability; economy; education; safety; health; infrastructure and pollution. *WalletHub.com, "2025's Best- & Worst-Run Cities in America," June 18, 2024*

Business Environment

DEMOGRAPHICS

Population Growth

Area	1990 Census	2000 Census	2010 Census	2020 Census	2023 Estimate[2]	Population Growth 1990-2023 (%)
City	434,967	441,545	459,787	508,090	508,233	16.8
MSA[1]	1,636,528	1,836,038	2,035,334	2,192,035	2,202,006	34.6
U.S.	248,709,873	281,421,906	308,745,538	331,449,281	332,387,540	33.6

Note: (1) Figures cover the Kansas City, MO-KS Metropolitan Statistical Area; (2) 2019-2023 5-year ACS population estimate
Source: U.S. Census Bureau, 1990 Census, 2000 Census, 2010 Census, 2020 Census, 2019-2023 American Community Survey 5-Year Estimates

Race

Area	White Alone[2] (%)	Black Alone[2] (%)	Asian Alone[2] (%)	AIAN[3] Alone[2] (%)	NHOPI[4] Alone[2] (%)	Other Race Alone[2] (%)	Two or More Races (%)
City	57.8	25.8	2.7	0.4	0.3	4.5	8.6
MSA[1]	73.0	11.9	2.9	0.4	0.2	3.7	7.8
U.S.	63.4	12.4	5.8	0.9	0.2	6.6	10.7

Note: (1) Figures cover the Kansas City, MO-KS Metropolitan Statistical Area; (2) Alone is defined as not being in combination with one or more other races; (3) American Indian and Alaska Native; (4) Native Hawaiian and Other Pacific Islander
Source: U.S. Census Bureau, 2019-2023 American Community Survey 5-Year Estimates

Hispanic or Latino Origin

Area	Total (%)	Mexican (%)	Puerto Rican (%)	Cuban (%)	Other (%)
City	12.3	8.3	0.6	0.4	3.0
MSA[1]	10.6	7.5	0.5	0.3	2.3
U.S.	19.0	11.3	1.8	0.7	5.2

Note: Persons of Hispanic or Latino origin can be of any race; (1) Figures cover the Kansas City, MO-KS Metropolitan Statistical Area
Source: U.S. Census Bureau, 2019-2023 American Community Survey 5-Year Estimates

Age

Area	Under Age 5	Age 5–19	Age 20–34	Age 35–44	Age 45–54	Age 55–64	Age 65–74	Age 75–84	Age 85+	Median Age
City	6.2	18.7	24.1	13.7	11.4	11.8	8.8	3.6	1.7	35.7
MSA[1]	6.1	20.1	19.9	13.7	12.2	12.6	9.4	4.4	1.8	37.8
U.S.	5.7	19.1	20.2	13.1	12.3	12.8	10.0	4.9	1.9	38.7

Note: (1) Figures cover the Kansas City, MO-KS Metropolitan Statistical Area
Source: U.S. Census Bureau, 2019-2023 American Community Survey 5-Year Estimates

Disability by Age

Area	All Ages	Under 18 Years Old	18 to 64 Years Old	65 Years and Over
City	12.8	3.7	11.6	33.3
MSA[1]	12.0	4.4	10.3	31.1
U.S.	13.0	4.7	10.7	32.9

Note: Figures show percent of the civilian noninstitutionalized population that reported having a disability. Disability status is determined from six types of difficulty: vision, hearing, cognitive, ambulatory, self-care, and independent living. For children under 5 years old, hearing and vision difficulty are used to determine disability status. For children between the ages of 5 and 14, disability status is determined from hearing, vision, cognitive, ambulatory, and self-care difficulties. For people aged 15 years and older, they are considered to have a disability if they have difficulty with any one of the six difficulty types; Note: (1) Figures cover the Kansas City, MO-KS Metropolitan Statistical Area
Source: U.S. Census Bureau, 2019-2023 American Community Survey 5-Year Estimates

Ancestry

Area	German	Irish	English	American	Italian	Polish	French[2]	European	Scottish
City	15.2	10.0	9.5	4.1	3.7	1.6	1.5	2.3	1.4
MSA[1]	19.5	11.8	12.5	4.6	3.0	1.5	1.9	3.4	1.8
U.S.	12.6	9.4	9.1	5.5	4.9	2.6	2.0	1.6	1.6

Note: Figures are the percentage of the total population reporting a particular ancestry. The nine most commonly reported ancestries in the U.S. are shown. Figures include multiple ancestries (e.g. if a person reported being Irish and Italian, they were included in both columns); (1) Figures cover the Kansas City, MO-KS Metropolitan Statistical Area; (2) Excludes Basque
Source: U.S. Census Bureau, 2019-2023 American Community Survey 5-Year Estimates

Foreign-born Population

Area	Percent of Population Born in								
	Any Foreign Country	Asia	Mexico	Europe	Caribbean	Central America[2]	South America	Africa	Canada
City	8.5	2.2	2.2	0.6	0.5	0.9	0.4	1.5	0.1
MSA[1]	7.2	2.2	2.0	0.6	0.3	0.8	0.3	0.8	0.1
U.S.	13.9	4.3	3.3	1.4	1.4	1.2	1.2	0.8	0.2

Note: (1) Figures cover the Kansas City, MO-KS Metropolitan Statistical Area; (2) Excludes Mexico.
Source: U.S. Census Bureau, 2019-2023 American Community Survey 5-Year Estimates

Household Size

Area	Persons in Household (%)							Average Household Size
	One	Two	Three	Four	Five	Six	Seven or More	
City	37.7	31.3	12.3	10.8	4.7	2.1	1.0	2.28
MSA[1]	29.8	34.3	14.1	12.6	5.8	2.3	1.2	2.46
U.S.	28.5	33.8	15.4	12.7	5.9	2.3	1.4	2.54

Note: (1) Figures cover the Kansas City, MO-KS Metropolitan Statistical Area
Source: U.S. Census Bureau, 2019-2023 American Community Survey 5-Year Estimates

Household Relationships

Area	Householder	Opposite-sex Spouse	Same-sex Spouse	Opposite-sex Unmarried Partner	Same-sex Unmarried Partner	Child[2]	Grandchild	Other Relatives	Non-relatives
City	42.6	14.5	0.3	3.3	0.3	27.2	2.3	4.0	3.8
MSA[1]	39.6	18.4	0.2	2.6	0.2	29.4	2.0	3.3	2.7
U.S.	38.3	17.5	0.2	2.5	0.2	28.3	2.4	4.8	3.4

Note: Figures are percent of the total population; (1) Figures cover the Kansas City, MO-KS Metropolitan Statistical Area; (2) Includes biological, adopted, and stepchildren of the householder
Source: U.S. Census Bureau, 2020 Census

Gender

Area	Males	Females	Males per 100 Females
City	245,780	262,453	93.6
MSA[1]	1,087,932	1,114,074	97.7
U.S.	164,545,087	167,842,453	98.0

Note: (1) Figures cover the Kansas City, MO-KS Metropolitan Statistical Area
Source: U.S. Census Bureau, 2019-2023 American Community Survey 5-Year Estimates

Marital Status

Area	Never Married	Now Married[2]	Separated	Widowed	Divorced
City	39.5	40.6	1.9	4.8	13.2
MSA[1]	31.3	50.3	1.5	5.1	11.8
U.S.	34.1	47.9	1.7	5.6	10.7

Note: Figures are percentages and cover the population 15 years of age and older; (1) Figures cover the Kansas City, MO-KS Metropolitan Statistical Area; (2) Excludes separated
Source: U.S. Census Bureau, 2019-2023 American Community Survey 5-Year Estimates

Religious Groups by Family

Area	Catholic	Baptist	Methodist	LDS[2]	Pentecostal	Lutheran	Islam	Adventist	Other
MSA[1]	11.3	9.1	5.0	1.6	2.7	1.7	1.0	1.0	12.1
U.S.	18.7	7.3	3.0	2.0	1.8	1.7	1.3	1.3	11.6

Note: Figures are the number of adherents as a percentage of the total population and cover the eight largest religious groups in the U.S; (1) Figures cover the Kansas City, MO-KS Metropolitan Statistical Area; (2) Church of Jesus Christ of Latter-day Saints
Sources: 2020 U.S. Religion Census, Association of Statisticians of American Religious Bodies; The Association of Religion Data Archives (ARDA)

Religious Groups by Tradition

Area	Catholic	Evangelical Protestant	Mainline Protestant	Black Protestant	Islam	Judaism	Hinduism	Orthodox	Buddhism
MSA[1]	11.3	19.1	7.1	3.6	1.0	0.3	0.4	0.1	0.2
U.S.	18.7	16.5	5.2	2.3	1.3	0.6	0.4	0.4	0.3

Note: Figures are the number of adherents as a percentage of the total population; (1) Figures cover the Kansas City, MO-KS Metropolitan Statistical Area
Sources: 2020 U.S. Religion Census, Association of Statisticians of American Religious Bodies; The Association of Religion Data Archives (ARDA)

Kansas City, Missouri

ECONOMY

Real Gross Domestic Product (GDP)

Area	2017	2018	2019	2020	2021	2022	2023	Rank[3]
MSA[1]	133.8	136.4	139.5	136.8	141.7	148.9	152.8	32
U.S.[2]	17,619.1	18,160.7	18,642.5	18,238.9	19,387.6	19,896.6	20,436.3	—

Note: Figures are in billions of chained 2017 dollars; (1) Figures cover the Kansas City, MO-KS Metropolitan Statistical Area; (2) Figures cover real GDP within metropolitan areas; (3) Rank is based on 2023 data and ranges from 1 to 384
Source: U.S. Bureau of Economic Analysis

Economic Growth

Area	2014	2015	2016	2017	2018	2019	2020	2021	2022	2023
MSA[1]	2.7	3.8	0.5	3.3	2.0	2.3	-1.9	3.6	5.0	2.7
U.S.[2]	2.6	3.2	2.0	2.7	3.1	2.7	-2.2	6.3	2.6	2.7

Note: Figures are real gross domestic product growth rates and represent percent change from preceding period; (1) Figures cover the Kansas City, MO-KS Metropolitan Statistical Area; (2) Figures are the average growth rates within metropolitan areas
Source: U.S. Bureau of Economic Analysis

Metropolitan Area Exports

Area	2018	2019	2020	2021	2022	2023	Rank[2]
MSA[1]	7,316.9	7,652.6	7,862.7	9,177.6	9,623.5	10,627.2	40
U.S.	1,664,056.1	1,645,173.7	1,431,406.6	1,753,941.4	2,062,937.4	2,019,160.5	—

Note: Figures are in millions of dollars; (1) Figures cover the Kansas City, MO-KS Metropolitan Statistical Area; (2) Rank is based on 2023 data and ranges from 1 to 386
Source: U.S. Department of Commerce, International Trade Administration, Office of Trade and Economic Analysis, Industry and Analysis, Exports by Metropolitan Area, data extracted April 2, 2025

Building Permits

Area	Single-Family 2023	Single-Family 2024	Single-Family Pct. Chg.	Multi-Family 2023	Multi-Family 2024	Multi-Family Pct. Chg.	Total 2023	Total 2024	Total Pct. Chg.
City	776	429	-44.7	458	2,449	434.7	1,234	2,878	133.2
MSA[1]	4,299	4,875	13.4	3,215	4,273	32.9	7,514	9,148	21.7
U.S.	920,000	981,900	6.7	591,100	496,100	-16.1	1,511,100	1,478,000	-2.2

Note: (1) Figures cover the Kansas City, MO-KS Metropolitan Statistical Area; Figures represent new, privately-owned housing units authorized (unadjusted data)
Source: U.S. Census Bureau, Building Permits Survey (BPS), 2023, 2024

Bankruptcy Filings

Area	Business Filings 2023	Business Filings 2024	% Chg.	Nonbusiness Filings 2023	Nonbusiness Filings 2024	% Chg.
Jackson County	22	27	22.7	1,186	1,166	-1.7
U.S.	18,926	23,107	22.1	434,064	494,201	13.9

Note: Business filings include Chapter 7, Chapter 9, Chapter 11, Chapter 12, Chapter 13, Chapter 15, and Section 304; Nonbusiness filings include Chapter 7, Chapter 11, and Chapter 13
Source: Administrative Office of the U.S. Courts, Business and Nonbusiness Bankruptcy, County Cases Commenced by Chapter of the Bankruptcy Code, During the 12-Month Period Ending December 31, 2023 and Business and Nonbusiness Bankruptcy, County Cases Commenced by Chapter of the Bankruptcy Code, During the 12-Month Period Ending December 31, 2024

Housing Vacancy Rates

Area	Gross Vacancy Rate[3] (%) 2022	2023	2024	Year-Round Vacancy Rate[4] (%) 2022	2023	2024	Rental Vacancy Rate[5] (%) 2022	2023	2024	Homeowner Vacancy Rate[6] (%) 2022	2023	2024
MSA[1]	7.1	7.0	6.9	7.1	6.6	6.3	7.8	7.6	8.9	0.6	1.2	0.9
U.S.[2]	9.1	9.0	9.1	7.5	7.5	7.6	5.7	6.5	6.8	0.8	0.8	1.0

Note: (1) Figures cover the Kansas City, MO-KS Metropolitan Statistical Area; (2) Figures cover the 75 largest Metropolitan Statistical Areas; (3) The percentage of the total housing inventory that is vacant; (4) The percentage of the housing inventory (excluding seasonal units) that is year-round vacant; (5) The percentage of rental inventory that is vacant for rent; (6) The percentage of homeowner inventory that is vacant for sale
Source: U.S. Census Bureau, Housing Vacancies and Homeownership Annual Statistics: 2022, 2023, 2024

INCOME

Income

Area	Per Capita ($)	Median Household ($)	Average Household ($)
City	40,112	67,449	91,703
MSA[1]	44,205	81,927	108,186
U.S.	43,289	78,538	110,491

Note: (1) Figures cover the Kansas City, MO-KS Metropolitan Statistical Area
Source: U.S. Census Bureau, 2019-2023 American Community Survey 5-Year Estimates

Household Income Distribution

Area	Percent of Households Earning							
	Under $15,000	$15,000 -$24,999	$25,000 -$34,999	$35,000 -$49,999	$50,000 -$74,999	$75,000 -$99,999	$100,000 -$149,999	$150,000 and up
City	10.3	7.2	7.5	12.5	17.2	12.6	16.9	15.7
MSA[1]	6.9	5.7	6.4	10.4	16.6	13.3	19.1	21.3
U.S.	8.5	6.6	6.8	10.4	15.7	12.7	17.4	21.9

Note: (1) Figures cover the Kansas City, MO-KS Metropolitan Statistical Area
Source: U.S. Census Bureau, 2019-2023 American Community Survey 5-Year Estimates

Poverty Rate

Area	All Ages	Under 18 Years Old	18 to 64 Years Old	65 Years and Over
City	14.6	20.5	12.9	12.4
MSA[1]	10.0	13.2	9.2	8.5
U.S.	12.4	16.3	11.6	10.4

Note: Figures are percentage of people whose income during the past 12 months was below the poverty level; (1) Figures cover the Kansas City, MO-KS Metropolitan Statistical Area
Source: U.S. Census Bureau, 2019-2023 American Community Survey 5-Year Estimates

EMPLOYMENT

Labor Force and Employment

Area	Civilian Labor Force			Workers Employed		
	Dec. 2023	Dec. 2024	% Chg.	Dec. 2023	Dec. 2024	% Chg.
City	261,274	264,629	1.3	252,452	255,316	1.1
MSA[1]	1,160,004	1,182,211	1.9	1,127,092	1,144,249	1.5
U.S.	166,661,000	167,746,000	0.7	160,754,000	161,294,000	0.3

Note: Data is not seasonally adjusted and covers workers 16 years of age and older; (1) Figures cover the Kansas City, MO-KS Metropolitan Statistical Area
Source: Bureau of Labor Statistics, Local Area Unemployment Statistics

Unemployment Rate

Area	2024											
	Jan.	Feb.	Mar.	Apr.	May	Jun.	Jul.	Aug.	Sep.	Oct.	Nov.	Dec.
City	3.9	4.1	4.1	3.5	4.0	4.1	4.6	4.2	3.3	3.6	3.6	3.5
MSA[1]	3.5	3.8	3.8	3.2	3.6	3.8	4.2	3.9	3.2	3.5	3.3	3.2
U.S.	4.1	4.2	3.9	3.5	3.7	4.3	4.5	4.4	3.9	3.9	4.0	3.8

Note: Data is not seasonally adjusted and covers workers 16 years of age and older; (1) Figures cover the Kansas City, MO-KS Metropolitan Statistical Area
Source: Bureau of Labor Statistics, Local Area Unemployment Statistics

Average Wages

Occupation	$/Hr.	Occupation	$/Hr.
Accountants and Auditors	41.41	Maintenance and Repair Workers	25.52
Automotive Mechanics	26.51	Marketing Managers	69.71
Bookkeepers	24.38	Network and Computer Systems Admin.	44.91
Carpenters	31.38	Nurses, Licensed Practical	30.67
Cashiers	15.02	Nurses, Registered	41.12
Computer Programmers	46.73	Nursing Assistants	20.02
Computer Systems Analysts	48.94	Office Clerks, General	22.34
Computer User Support Specialists	28.37	Physical Therapists	46.79
Construction Laborers	26.74	Physicians	76.04
Cooks, Restaurant	18.07	Plumbers, Pipefitters and Steamfitters	36.37
Customer Service Representatives	21.64	Police and Sheriff's Patrol Officers	33.12
Dentists	89.46	Postal Service Mail Carriers	29.08
Electricians	35.72	Real Estate Sales Agents	40.62
Engineers, Electrical	51.97	Retail Salespersons	17.76
Fast Food and Counter Workers	14.34	Sales Representatives, Technical/Scientific	57.49
Financial Managers	76.99	Secretaries, Exc. Legal/Medical/Executive	21.49
First-Line Supervisors of Office Workers	34.02	Security Guards	22.78
General and Operations Managers	53.13	Surgeons	n/a
Hairdressers/Cosmetologists	20.28	Teacher Assistants, Exc. Postsecondary[1]	15.24
Home Health and Personal Care Aides	15.65	Teachers, Secondary School, Exc. Sp. Ed.[1]	29.47
Janitors and Cleaners	17.70	Telemarketers	18.48
Landscaping/Groundskeeping Workers	20.15	Truck Drivers, Heavy/Tractor-Trailer	28.62
Lawyers	84.26	Truck Drivers, Light/Delivery Services	23.71
Maids and Housekeeping Cleaners	16.32	Waiters and Waitresses	17.04

Note: Wage data covers the Kansas City, MO-KS Metropolitan Statistical Area; (1) Hourly wages were calculated from annual wage data based on a 40 hour work week
Source: Bureau of Labor Statistics, Metro Area Occupational Employment & Wage Estimates, May 2024

Employment by Industry

Sector	MSA[1] Number of Employees	MSA[1] Percent of Total	U.S. Percent of Total
Construction	60,000	5.2	5.1
Financial Activities	79,900	6.9	5.8
Government	155,500	13.4	14.9
Information	16,900	1.5	1.9
Leisure and Hospitality	111,400	9.6	10.4
Manufacturing	91,000	7.9	8.0
Mining and Logging	900	0.1	0.4
Other Services	42,600	3.7	3.7
Private Education and Health Services	177,700	15.3	16.9
Professional and Business Services	185,800	16.0	14.2
Retail Trade	115,200	9.9	10.0
Transportation, Warehousing, and Utilities	69,300	6.0	4.8
Wholesale Trade	52,900	4.6	3.9

Note: Figures are non-farm employment as of December 2024. Figures are not seasonally adjusted and include workers 16 years of age and older; (1) Figures cover the Kansas City, MO-KS Metropolitan Statistical Area
Source: Bureau of Labor Statistics, Current Employment Statistics, Employment, Hours, and Earnings

Employment by Occupation

Occupation Classification	City (%)	MSA[1] (%)	U.S. (%)
Management, Business, Science, and Arts	43.9	44.5	42.0
Natural Resources, Construction, and Maintenance	6.4	7.5	8.6
Production, Transportation, and Material Moving	13.4	13.2	13.0
Sales and Office	20.4	20.4	19.9
Service	15.9	14.4	16.5

Note: Figures cover employed civilians 16 years of age and older; (1) Figures cover the Kansas City, MO-KS Metropolitan Statistical Area
Source: U.S. Census Bureau, 2019-2023 American Community Survey 5-Year Estimates

Occupations with Greatest Projected Employment Growth: 2022 – 2032

Occupation[1]	2022 Employment	2032 Projected Employment	Numeric Employment Change	Percent Employment Change
Home Health and Personal Care Aides	79,380	91,510	12,130	15.3
Registered Nurses	76,960	84,580	7,620	9.9
Cooks, Restaurant	31,980	39,310	7,330	22.9
General and Operations Managers	97,060	102,780	5,720	5.9
Software Developers	19,530	24,690	5,160	26.4
Stockers and Order Fillers	57,940	62,820	4,880	8.4
Laborers and Freight, Stock, and Material Movers, Hand	43,160	46,620	3,460	8.0
Nurse Practitioners	7,520	10,670	3,150	41.9
Medical and Health Services Managers	9,950	13,050	3,100	31.2
Maintenance and Repair Workers, General	32,440	34,810	2,370	7.3

Note: Projections cover Missouri; (1) Sorted by numeric employment change
Source: www.projectionscentral.org, State Occupational Projections, 2022–2032 Long-Term Projections

Fastest-Growing Occupations: 2022 – 2032

Occupation[1]	2022 Employment	2032 Projected Employment	Numeric Employment Change	Percent Employment Change
Nurse Practitioners	7,520	10,670	3,150	41.9
Data Scientists	4,320	5,950	1,630	37.7
Information Security Analysts (SOC 2018)	3,470	4,640	1,170	33.7
Computer and Information Research Scientists (SOC 2018)	540	710	170	31.5
Medical and Health Services Managers	9,950	13,050	3,100	31.2
Physical Therapist Assistants	2,520	3,240	720	28.6
Occupational Therapy Assistants	1,160	1,490	330	28.4
Veterinary Technologists and Technicians	2,080	2,640	560	26.9
Speech-Language Pathologists	4,030	5,100	1,070	26.6
Software Developers	19,530	24,690	5,160	26.4

Note: Projections cover Missouri; (1) Sorted by percent employment change and excludes occupations with numeric employment change less than 50
Source: www.projectionscentral.org, State Occupational Projections, 2022–2032 Long-Term Projections

CITY FINANCES

City Government Finances

Component	2022 ($000)	2022 ($ per capita)
Total Revenues	2,497,952	5,024
Total Expenditures	2,459,223	4,947
Debt Outstanding	4,549,455	9,151

Source: U.S. Census Bureau, State & Local Government Finances 2022

City Government Revenue by Source

Source	2022 ($000)	2022 ($ per capita)	2022 (%)
General Revenue			
From Federal Government	163,384	329	6.5
From State Government	6,422	13	0.3
From Local Governments	313,155	630	12.5
Taxes			
Property	186,933	376	7.5
Sales and Gross Receipts	423,174	851	16.9
Personal Income	293,677	591	11.8
Corporate Income	64,653	130	2.6
Motor Vehicle License	5,746	12	0.2
Other Taxes	9,569	19	0.4
Current Charges	520,976	1,048	20.9
Liquor Store	0	0	0.0
Utility	183,383	369	7.3

Source: U.S. Census Bureau, State & Local Government Finances 2022

City Government Expenditures by Function

Function	2022 ($000)	2022 ($ per capita)	2022 (%)
General Direct Expenditures			
Air Transportation	504,274	1,014	20.5
Corrections	0	0	0.0
Education	0	0	0.0
Employment Security Administration	0	0	0.0
Financial Administration	17,118	34	0.7
Fire Protection	218,832	440	8.9
General Public Buildings	0	0	0.0
Governmental Administration, Other	55,840	112	2.3
Health	66,730	134	2.7
Highways	170,809	343	6.9
Hospitals	0	0	0.0
Housing and Community Development	120,690	242	4.9
Interest on General Debt	156,983	315	6.4
Judicial and Legal	17,248	34	0.7
Libraries	0	0	0.0
Parking	4,622	9	0.2
Parks and Recreation	76,159	153	3.1
Police Protection	232,817	468	9.5
Public Welfare	5,460	11	0.2
Sewerage	195,877	394	8.0
Solid Waste Management	0	0	0.0
Veterans' Services	0	0	0.0
Liquor Store	0	0	0.0
Utility	124,335	250	5.1

Source: U.S. Census Bureau, State & Local Government Finances 2022

TAXES

State Corporate Income Tax Rates

State	Tax Rate (%)	Income Brackets ($)	Num. of Brackets	Financial Institution Tax Rate (%)[a]	Federal Income Tax Ded.
Missouri	4.0	Flat rate	1	4.48	Yes (h)

Note: Tax rates for tax year 2024; (a) Rates listed are the corporate income tax rate applied to financial institutions or excise taxes based on income. Some states have other taxes based upon the value of deposits or shares; (h) 50% of the federal income tax is deductible.
Source: Federation of Tax Administrators, State Corporate Income Tax Rates, January 1, 2025

State Individual Income Tax Rates

State	Tax Rate (%)	Income Brackets ($)	Personal Exemptions ($)			Standard Ded. ($)	
			Single	Married	Depend.	Single	Married
Missouri (a)	0.0 - 4.8	1,207 - 8,449	(d)	(d)	(d)	14,600	29,200 (d)

Note: Tax rates for tax year 2024; Local- and county-level taxes are not included; The deduction for federal SALT deductions is limited to $5,000 for individuals and $10,000 for joint returns in Missouri and Montana, and to $7,800 for all filers in Oregon; (a) 16 states have statutory provision for automatically adjusting to the rate of inflation the dollar values of the income tax brackets, standard deductions, and/or personal exemptions. Oregon does not index the income brackets for $125,000 and over See: INFL and SPEC above; (d) These states use the personal exemption/standard deduction amounts provided in the federal Internal Revenue Code. Montana personal exemption subject to repeal under Section 15-30-2114.
Source: Federation of Tax Administrators, State Individual Income Tax Rates, January 1, 2025

Various State Sales and Excise Tax Rates

State	State Sales Tax (%)	Gasoline[1] ($/gal.)	Cigarette[2] ($/pack)	Spirits[3] ($/gal.)	Wine[4] ($/gal.)	Beer[5] ($/gal.)	Recreational Marijuana (%)
Missouri	4.225	0.27	0.17	2.00	0.42	0.06	(m)

Note: All tax rates as of January 1, 2025; (1) The American Petroleum Institute has developed a methodology for determining the average tax rate on a gallon of fuel. Rates may include any of the following: excise taxes, environmental fees, storage tank fees, other fees or taxes, general sales tax, and local taxes; (2) The federal excise tax of $1.0066 per pack and local taxes are not included; (3) Rates are those applicable to off-premise sales of 40% alcohol by volume (a.b.v.) distilled spirits in 750ml containers. Local excise taxes are excluded; (4) Rates are those applicable to off-premise sales of 11% a.b.v. non-carbonated wine in 750ml containers; (5) Rates are those applicable to off-premise sales of 4.7% a.b.v. beer in 12 ounce containers; (m) 6% excise tax (retail price)
Source: Tax Foundation, 2025 Facts & Figures: How Does Your State Compare?

State Tax Competitiveness Index

State	Overall Rank	Corporate Tax Rank	Individual Income Tax Rank	Sales Tax Rank	Property Tax Rank	Unemployment Insurance Tax Rank
Missouri	13	4	20	24	11	5

Note: The Tax Foundation's State Tax Competitiveness Index enables policymakers, taxpayers, and business leaders to gauge how their states' tax systems compare. A rank of 1 is best, 50 is worst. Rankings do not average to the total. States without a tax rank equally as 1. DC's scores and rankings do not affect other states. The report shows tax systems as of July 1, 2024 (the beginning of Fiscal Year 2025).
Source: Tax Foundation, State Tax Competitiveness Index 2025

TRANSPORTATION

Means of Transportation to Work

Area	Car/Truck/Van		Public Transportation			Bicycle	Walked	Other Means	Worked at Home
	Drove Alone	Car-pooled	Bus	Subway	Railroad				
City	72.7	7.4	1.9	0.0	0.0	0.2	1.5	1.5	14.8
MSA[1]	75.0	6.9	0.6	0.0	0.0	0.1	1.1	1.1	15.2
U.S.	70.2	8.5	1.7	1.3	0.4	0.4	2.4	1.6	13.5

Note: Figures are percentages and cover workers 16 years of age and older; (1) Figures cover the Kansas City, MO-KS Metropolitan Statistical Area
Source: U.S. Census Bureau, 2019-2023 American Community Survey 5-Year Estimates

Travel Time to Work

Area	Less Than 10 Minutes	10 to 19 Minutes	20 to 29 Minutes	30 to 44 Minutes	45 to 59 Minutes	60 to 89 Minutes	90 Minutes or More
City	11.7	35.0	28.3	18.3	3.5	1.8	1.4
MSA[1]	12.4	30.9	26.3	20.9	5.7	2.4	1.4
U.S.	12.6	28.6	21.2	20.8	8.1	6.0	2.8

Note: Note: Figures are percentages and include workers 16 years old and over; (1) Figures cover the Kansas City, MO-KS Metropolitan Statistical Area
Source: U.S. Census Bureau, 2019-2023 American Community Survey 5-Year Estimates

Key Congestion Measures

Measure	2000	2010	2015	2020	2022
Annual Hours of Delay, Total (000)	29,273	40,503	47,011	35,061	52,696
Annual Hours of Delay, Per Auto Commuter	34	40	45	34	54
Annual Congestion Cost, Per Auto Commuter ($)	816	897	963	776	1,156

Note: Figures cover the Kansas City MO-KS urban area
Source: Texas A&M Transportation Institute, 2023 Urban Mobility Report

Freeway Travel Time Index

Measure	1985	1990	1995	2000	2005	2010	2015	2020	2022
Urban Area Index[1]	1.06	1.10	1.11	1.13	1.14	1.14	1.15	1.10	1.15
Urban Area Rank[1,2]	53	47	66	72	73	71	67	29	54

Note: Freeway Travel Time Index—the ratio of travel time in the peak period to the travel time at free-flow conditions. For example, a value of 1.30 indicates a 20-minute free-flow trip takes 26 minutes in the peak (20 minutes x 1.30 = 26 minutes); (1) Covers the Kansas City MO-KS urban area; (2) Rank is based on 101 larger urban areas (#1 = highest travel time index)
Source: Texas A&M Transportation Institute, 2023 Urban Mobility Report

Public Transportation

Agency Name / Mode of Transportation	Vehicles Operated in Maximum Service[1]	Annual Unlinked Passenger Trips[2] (in thous.)	Annual Passenger Miles[3] (in thous.)
Kansas City Area Transportation Authority (KCATA)			
Bus (directly operated)	120	10,841.7	36,800.3
Bus Rapid Transit (directly operated)	28	943.7	2,834.9
Demand Response (directly operated)	9	65.7	227.9
Demand Response (purchased transportation)	31	80.7	591.5
Demand Response - Taxi	93	291.7	2,797.8
Vanpool (purchased transportation)	28	52.4	1,823.2

Note: (1) Number of revenue vehicles operated by the given mode and type of service to meet the annual maximum service requirement. This is the revenue vehicle count during the peak season of the year; on the week and day that maximum service is provided. Vehicles operated in maximum service (VOMS) exclude atypical days and one-time special events; (2) Number of passengers who boarded public transportation vehicles. Passengers are counted each time they board a vehicle no matter how many vehicles they use to travel from their origin to their destination. (3) Sum of the distances ridden by all passengers during the entire fiscal year.
Source: Federal Transit Administration, National Transit Database, 2023

Air Transportation

Airport Name and Code / Type of Service	Passenger Airlines[1]	Passenger Enplanements	Freight Carriers[2]	Freight (lbs)
Kansas City International (MCI)				
Domestic service (U.S. carriers only)	26	5,828,768	19	126,624,806
International service (U.S. carriers only)	5	77,552	1	12,857

Note: (1) Includes all U.S.-based major, minor and commuter airlines that carried at least one passenger during the year; (2) Includes all U.S.-based airlines and freight carriers that transported at least one pound of freight during the year.
Source: Bureau of Transportation Statistics, The Intermodal Transportation Database, Air Carriers: T-100 Domestic Market (U.S. carriers only), 2024; Bureau of Transportation Statistics, The Intermodal Transportation Database, Air Carriers: T-100 International Market (U.S. carriers only), 2024

BUSINESSES

Major Business Headquarters

Company Name	Industry	Rankings Fortune[1]	Rankings Forbes[2]
Burns & McDonnell	Construction	-	81
Hallmark	Media	-	178
JE Dunn Construction Group	Construction	-	97

Note: (1) Companies that produce a 10-K are ranked 1 to 500 based on 2023 revenue; (2) All private companies with at least $2 billion in annual revenue through the end of their most current fiscal year are ranked 1 to 275; companies listed are headquartered in the city; dashes indicate no ranking
Source: Fortune, "Fortune 500," 2024; Forbes, "America's Largest Private Companies," 2024

Living Environment

COST OF LIVING

Cost of Living Index

Composite Index	Groceries	Housing	Utilities	Transportation	Health Care	Misc. Goods/Services
91.1	97.3	87.5	105.6	89.3	83.8	89.1

Note: The Cost of Living Index measures regional differences in the cost of consumer goods and services, excluding taxes and non-consumer expenditures, for professional and managerial households in the top income quintile. It is based on more than 50,000 prices covering almost 60 different items for which prices are collected three times a year by chambers of commerce, economic development organizations or university applied economic centers in each participating urban area. The numbers shown should be read as a percentage above or below the national average of 100. For example, a value of 115.4 in the groceries column indicates that grocery prices are 15.4% higher than the national average. Small differences in the index numbers should not be interpreted as significant; Figures cover the Kansas City MO-KS urban area.
Source: The Council for Community and Economic Research, Cost of Living Index, 2024

Grocery Prices

Area[1]	T-Bone Steak ($/pound)	Frying Chicken ($/pound)	Whole Milk ($/half gal.)	Eggs ($/dozen)	Orange Juice ($/64 oz.)	Coffee ($/11.5 oz.)
City[2]	15.52	1.45	4.70	3.17	4.38	5.06
Avg.	15.42	1.55	4.69	3.25	4.41	5.46
Min.	14.50	1.16	4.43	2.75	4.00	4.85
Max.	17.56	2.89	5.49	4.78	5.54	7.89

Note: (1) Values for the local area are compared with the average, minimum and maximum values for all 276 areas in the Cost of Living Index; (2) Figures cover the Kansas City MO-KS urban area; **T-Bone Steak** (price per pound); **Frying Chicken** (price per pound, whole fryer); **Whole Milk** (half gallon carton); **Eggs** (price per dozen, Grade A, large); **Orange Juice** (64 oz. Tropicana or Florida Natural); **Coffee** (11.5 oz. can, vacuum-packed, Maxwell House, Hills Bros, or Folgers).
Source: The Council for Community and Economic Research, Cost of Living Index, 2024

Housing and Utility Costs

Area[1]	New Home Price ($)	Apartment Rent ($/month)	All Electric ($/month)	Part Electric ($/month)	Other Energy ($/month)	Telephone ($/month)
City[2]	429,449	1,506	-	103.82	115.85	202.40
Avg.	515,975	1,550	210.99	123.07	82.07	194.99
Min.	265,375	692	104.33	53.68	36.26	179.42
Max.	2,775,821	5,719	529.02	397.28	361.63	223.33

Note: (1) Values for the local area are compared with the average, minimum and maximum values for all 276 areas in the Cost of Living Index; (2) Figures cover the Kansas City MO-KS urban area; **New Home Price** (2,400 sf living area, 8,000 sf lot, in urban area with full utilities); **Apartment Rent** (950 sf 2 bedroom/1.5 or 2 bath, unfurnished, excluding all utilities except water); **All Electric** (average monthly cost for an all-electric home); **Part Electric** (average monthly cost for a part-electric home); **Other Energy** (average monthly cost for natural gas, fuel oil, coal, wood, and any other forms of energy except electricity); **Telephone** (price includes the base monthly rate plus taxes and fees for three lines of mobile phone service).
Source: The Council for Community and Economic Research, Cost of Living Index, 2024

Health Care, Transportation, and Other Costs

Area[1]	Doctor ($/visit)	Dentist ($/visit)	Optometrist ($/visit)	Gasoline ($/gallon)	Beauty Salon ($/visit)	Men's Shirt ($)
City[2]	95.79	108.20	95.10	3.06	34.80	29.79
Avg.	143.77	117.51	129.23	3.32	48.57	38.14
Min.	36.74	58.67	67.33	2.80	24.00	13.41
Max.	270.44	216.82	307.33	5.28	94.00	63.89

Note: (1) Values for the local area are compared with the average, minimum and maximum values for all 276 areas in the Cost of Living Index; (2) Figures cover the Kansas City MO-KS urban area; **Doctor** (general practitioners routine exam of an established patient); **Dentist** (adult teeth cleaning and periodic oral examination); **Optometrist** (full vision eye exam for established adult patient); **Gasoline** (one gallon regular unleaded, national brand, including all taxes, cash price at self-service pump if available); **Beauty Salon** (woman's shampoo, trim, and blow-dry); **Men's Shirt** (cotton/polyester dress shirt, pinpoint weave, long sleeves).
Source: The Council for Community and Economic Research, Cost of Living Index, 2024

HOUSING

Homeownership Rate

Area	2017 (%)	2018 (%)	2019 (%)	2020 (%)	2021 (%)	2022 (%)	2023 (%)	2024 (%)
MSA[1]	62.4	64.3	65.0	66.7	63.8	63.8	64.1	65.3
U.S.	63.9	64.4	64.6	66.6	65.5	65.8	65.9	65.6

Note: (1) Figures cover the Kansas City, MO-KS Metropolitan Statistical Area
Source: U.S. Census Bureau, Housing Vacancies and Homeownership Annual Statistics: 2017-2024

House Price Index (HPI)

Area	National Ranking[2]	Quarterly Change (%)	One-Year Change (%)	Five-Year Change (%)	Since 1991Q1 (%)
MSA[1]	149	-0.76	4.78	56.68	300.63
U.S.[3]	–	1.43	4.51	57.13	327.82

Note: The HPI is a weighted repeat sales index. It measures average price changes in repeat sales or refinancings on the same properties. This information is obtained by reviewing repeat mortgage transactions on single-family properties whose mortgages have been purchased or securitized by Fannie Mae or Freddie Mac since January 1975; (1) Figures cover the Kansas City, MO-KS Metropolitan Statistical Area; (2) Rankings are based on annual percentage change for all metro areas containing at least 15,000 transactions over the last 10 years and ranges from 1 to 241; (3) figures based on a weighted average of Census Division estimates using a seasonally adjusted, purchase-only index; all figures are for the period ending December 31, 2024
Source: Federal Housing Finance Agency, Change in FHFA Metropolitan Area House Price Indexes, All Transactions Index, 2024Q4

Home Value

Area	Under $100,000	$100,000 -$199,999	$200,000 -$299,999	$300,000 -$399,999	$400,000 -$499,999	$500,000 -$999,999	$1,000,000 or more	Median ($)
City	16.8	25.8	25.2	14.7	8.5	7.8	1.2	227,000
MSA[1]	10.8	22.1	25.5	17.5	10.4	11.8	1.8	265,400
U.S.	12.1	17.8	19.5	14.4	10.5	19.1	6.5	303,400

Note: Figures are percentages except for median and cover owner-occupied housing units; (1) Figures cover the Kansas City, MO-KS Metropolitan Statistical Area
Source: U.S. Census Bureau, 2019-2023 American Community Survey 5-Year Estimates

Year Housing Structure Built

Area	2020 or Later	2010 -2019	2000 -2009	1990 -1999	1980 -1989	1970 -1979	1960 -1969	1950 -1959	1940 -1949	Before 1940	Median Year
City	1.0	8.2	10.1	8.5	8.6	11.4	12.0	13.2	5.5	21.6	1968
MSA[1]	1.2	8.8	13.5	13.3	12.0	14.1	11.2	10.6	4.0	11.4	1979
U.S.	1.2	8.9	13.6	12.8	13.0	14.4	10.0	9.7	4.5	11.9	1980

Note: Figures are percentages except for Median Year; Note: (1) Figures cover the Kansas City, MO-KS Metropolitan Statistical Area
Source: U.S. Census Bureau, 2019-2023 American Community Survey 5-Year Estimates

Gross Monthly Rent

Area	Under $500	$500 -$999	$1,000 -$1,499	$1,500 -$1,999	$2,000 -$2,499	$2,500 -$2,999	$3,000 and up	Median ($)
City	6.7	25.9	41.6	18.6	4.6	1.5	1.2	1,186
MSA[1]	5.4	25.3	41.7	18.9	5.6	1.4	1.6	1,201
U.S.	6.5	22.3	29.5	20.2	10.8	4.8	5.9	1,348

Note: Figures are percentages except for median; Gross rent is the contract rent plus the estimated average monthly cost of utilities (electricity, gas, and water and sewer) and fuels (oil, coal, kerosene, wood, etc.) if these are paid by the renter (or paid for the renter by someone else); (1) Figures cover the Kansas City, MO-KS Metropolitan Statistical Area
Source: U.S. Census Bureau, 2019-2023 American Community Survey 5-Year Estimates

HEALTH

Health Risk Factors

Category	MSA[1] (%)	U.S. (%)
Adults aged 18–64 who have any kind of health care coverage	90.7	90.8
Adults who reported being in good or better health	83.6	81.8
Adults who have been told they have high blood cholesterol	40.8	36.9
Adults who have been told they have high blood pressure	34.6	34.0
Adults who are current smokers	13.9	12.1
Adults who currently use e-cigarettes	7.5	7.7
Adults who currently use chewing tobacco, snuff, or snus	3.4	3.2
Adults who are heavy drinkers[2]	6.1	6.1
Adults who are binge drinkers[3]	16.0	15.2
Adults who are overweight (BMI 25.0 - 29.9)	34.4	34.4
Adults who are obese (BMI 30.0 - 99.8)	35.1	34.3
Adults who participated in any physical activities in the past month	75.0	75.8

Note: All figures are crude prevalence; (1) Figures cover the Kansas City, MO-KS Metropolitan Statistical Area; (2) Heavy drinkers are classified as adult men having more than 14 drinks per week and adult women having more than 7 drinks per week; (3) Binge drinkers are classified as males having five or more drinks on one occasion or females having four or more drinks on one occasion
Source: Centers for Disease Control and Prevention, Behavioral Risk Factor Surveillance System, SMART: Selected Metropolitan Area Risk Trends, 2023

Acute and Chronic Health Conditions

Category	MSA[1] (%)	U.S. (%)
Adults who have ever been told they had a heart attack	3.7	4.2
Adults who have ever been told they have angina or coronary heart disease	3.6	4.0
Adults who have ever been told they had a stroke	3.2	3.3
Adults who have ever been told they have asthma	15.0	15.7
Adults who have ever been told they have arthritis	25.2	26.3
Adults who have ever been told they have diabetes[2]	10.9	11.5
Adults who have ever been told they had skin cancer	5.7	5.6
Adults who have ever been told they had any other types of cancer	8.3	8.4
Adults who have ever been told they have COPD	5.8	6.4
Adults who have ever been told they have kidney disease	3.3	3.7
Adults who have ever been told they have a form of depression	21.7	22.0

Note: All figures are crude prevalence; (1) Figures cover the Kansas City, MO-KS Metropolitan Statistical Area; (2) Figures do not include pregnancy-related, borderline, or pre-diabetes
Source: Centers for Disease Control and Prevention, Behavioral Risk Factor Surveillance System, SMART: Selected Metropolitan Area Risk Trends, 2023

Health Screening and Vaccination Rates

Category	MSA[1] (%)	U.S. (%)
Adults who have ever been tested for HIV	36.0	37.5
Adults who have had their blood cholesterol checked within the last five years	87.4	87.0
Adults aged 65+ who have had flu shot within the past year	68.1	63.4
Adults aged 65+ who have ever had a pneumonia vaccination	76.5	71.9

Note: All figures are crude prevalence; (1) Figures cover the Kansas City, MO-KS Metropolitan Statistical Area.
Source: Centers for Disease Control and Prevention, Behavioral Risk Factor Surveillance System, SMART: Selected Metropolitan Area Risk Trends, 2023

Disability Status

Category	MSA[1] (%)	U.S. (%)
Adults who reported being deaf	7.0	7.4
Are you blind or have serious difficulty seeing, even when wearing glasses?	4.4	4.9
Do you have difficulty doing errands alone?	8.2	7.8
Do you have difficulty dressing or bathing?	3.9	3.6
Do you have serious difficulty concentrating/remembering/making decisions?	14.3	13.7
Do you have serious difficulty walking or climbing stairs?	12.8	13.2

Note: All figures are crude prevalence; (1) Figures cover the Kansas City, MO-KS Metropolitan Statistical Area.
Source: Centers for Disease Control and Prevention, Behavioral Risk Factor Surveillance System, SMART: Selected Metropolitan Area Risk Trends, 2023

Mortality Rates for the Top 10 Causes of Death in the U.S.

ICD-10[a] Sub-Chapter	ICD-10[a] Code	Crude Mortality Rate[2] per 100,000 population	
		County[3]	U.S.
Malignant neoplasms	C00-C97	185.6	182.7
Ischaemic heart diseases	I20-I25	106.9	109.6
Provisional assignment of new diseases of uncertain etiology[1]	U00-U49	67.7	65.3
Other forms of heart disease	I30-I51	63.0	65.1
Other degenerative diseases of the nervous system	G30-G31	47.4	52.4
Other external causes of accidental injury	W00-X59	64.8	52.3
Cerebrovascular diseases	I60-I69	45.3	49.1
Chronic lower respiratory diseases	J40-J47	45.6	43.5
Hypertensive diseases	I10-I15	35.7	38.9
Organic, including symptomatic, mental disorders	F01-F09	42.1	33.9

Note: (a) ICD-10 = International Classification of Diseases 10th Revision; (1) Includes COVID-19, adverse effects to COVID-19 vaccines, SARS, and vaping-related disorders; (2) Crude mortality rates are a three-year average covering 2021-2023; (3) Figures cover Jackson County.
Source: Centers for Disease Control and Prevention, National Center for Health Statistics. National Vital Statistics System, Mortality 2018-2023 on CDC WONDER Online Database

Mortality Rates for Selected Causes of Death

Cause of Death	ICD-10[a] Code	Crude Mortality Rate[1] per 100,000 population County[2]	U.S.
Accidental poisoning and exposure to noxious substances	X40-X49	38.6	30.5
Alzheimer disease	G30	18.4	35.4
Assault	X85-Y09	26.0	7.3
COVID-19	U07.1	67.7	65.3
Diabetes mellitus	E10-E14	28.3	30.0
Diseases of the liver	K70-K76	21.0	20.8
Human immunodeficiency virus (HIV) disease	B20-B24	2.1	1.5
Influenza and pneumonia	J09-J18	12.2	13.4
Intentional self-harm	X60-X84	21.5	14.7
Malnutrition	E40-E46	12.7	6.0
Obesity and other hyperalimentation	E65-E68	1.9	3.1
Renal failure	N17-N19	23.4	16.4
Transport accidents	V01-V99	16.7	14.4

Note: (a) ICD-10 = International Classification of Diseases 10th Revision; (1) Crude mortality rates are a three-year average covering 2021-2023; (2) Figures cover Jackson County; Data are suppressed when the data meet the criteria for confidentiality constraints; Crude mortality rates are flagged as unreliable when the rate would be calculated with a numerator of 20 or less.
Source: Centers for Disease Control and Prevention, National Center for Health Statistics. National Vital Statistics System, Mortality 2018-2023 on CDC WONDER Online Database

Health Insurance Coverage

Area	With Health Insurance	With Private Health Insurance	With Public Health Insurance	Without Health Insurance	Population Under Age 19 Without Health Insurance
City	88.7	68.3	29.8	11.3	7.4
MSA[1]	91.1	74.1	27.9	8.9	5.6
U.S.	91.4	67.3	36.3	8.6	5.4

Note: Figures are percentages that cover the civilian noninstitutionalized population; (1) Figures cover the Kansas City, MO-KS Metropolitan Statistical Area
Source: U.S. Census Bureau, 2019-2023 American Community Survey 5-Year Estimates

Number of Medical Professionals

Area	MDs[3]	DOs[3,4]	Dentists	Podiatrists	Chiropractors	Optometrists
County[1] (number)	2,462	789	679	51	354	145
County[1] (rate[2])	343.6	110.1	94.5	7.1	49.3	20.2
U.S. (rate[2])	302.5	29.2	74.6	6.4	29.5	18.0

Note: Data as of 2023 unless noted; (1) Data covers Jackson County; (2) Number of medical professionals per 100,000 population; (3) Data as of 2022 and includes all active, non-federal physicians; (4) Doctor of Osteopathic Medicine
Source: U.S. Department of Health and Human Services, Health Resources and Services Administration, Bureau of Health Professions, Area Resource File (ARF) 2023-2024

Best Hospitals

According to *U.S. News,* the Kansas City, MO-KS metro area is home to one of the best hospitals in the U.S.: **University of Kansas Hospital** (6 adult specialties). The hospital listed was nationally ranked in at least one of 15 adult or 11 pediatric specialties. The number of specialties shown cover the parent hospital. Only 160 U.S. hospitals performed well enough to be nationally ranked in one or more specialties. Twenty hospitals in the U.S. made the Honor Roll. The Best Hospitals Honor Roll takes both the national rankings and the procedure and condition ratings into account. Hospitals received points if they were nationally ranked in one of the 15 adult specialties—the higher they ranked, the more points they got—and how many ratings of "high performing" they earned in the 20 procedures and conditions. *U.S. News Online, "America's Best Hospitals 2024-25"*

According to *U.S. News,* the Kansas City, MO-KS metro area is home to one of the best children's hospitals in the U.S.: **Children's Mercy Kansas City Hospital** (11 pediatric specialties). The hospital listed was highly ranked in at least one of 11 pediatric specialties. One hundred five children's hospitals in the U.S. were nationally ranked in at least one specialty. Hospitals received points for being ranked in a specialty, and the 10 hospitals with the most points across the 11 specialties make up the Honor Roll. *U.S. News Online, "America's Best Children's Hospitals 2024-25"*

EDUCATION

Public School District Statistics

District Name	Schls	Pupils	Pupil/ Teacher Ratio	Minority Pupils[1] (%)	Total Rev. per Pupil ($)	Total Exp. per Pupil ($)
Center 58	8	2,454	11.8	82.7	21,518	20,469
Hickman Mills C-1	13	4,981	12.7	90.3	18,700	18,564
Kansas City 33	33	14,694	12.5	89.5	21,825	19,566
North Kansas City 74	34	21,015	13.8	49.3	16,985	19,814
Park Hill	20	11,915	13.4	36.8	16,916	15,923

Note: Table includes school districts with 2,000 or more students; (1) Percentage of students that are not non-Hispanic white.
Source: U.S. Department of Education, National Center for Education Statistics, Common Core of Data, Local Education Agency (School District) Universe Survey: School Year 2023-2024; U.S. Department of Education, National Center for Education Statistics, Common Core of Data, School District Finance Survey (F-33): School Year 2021–22

Best High Schools

According to *U.S. News*, Kansas City is home to one of the top 500 high schools in the U.S.: **Lincoln College Prep.** (#457). Nearly 25,000 public, magnet and charter schools were ranked based on their performance on state assessments and how well they prepare students for college. *U.S. News & World Report, "Best High Schools 2024"*

Highest Level of Education

Area	Less than H.S.	H.S. Diploma	Some College, No Deg.	Associate Degree	Bachelor's Degree	Master's Degree	Prof. School Degree	Doctorate Degree
City	8.2	25.0	21.6	7.4	23.8	10.1	2.7	1.2
MSA[1]	6.9	24.9	21.1	7.9	24.4	11.0	2.5	1.3
U.S.	10.6	26.2	19.4	8.8	21.3	9.8	2.3	1.6

Note: Figures cover persons age 25 and over; (1) Figures cover the Kansas City, MO-KS Metropolitan Statistical Area
Source: U.S. Census Bureau, 2019-2023 American Community Survey 5-Year Estimates

Educational Attainment by Race

Area	High School Graduate or Higher (%)					Bachelor's Degree or Higher (%)				
	Total	White	Black	Asian	Hisp.[2]	Total	White	Black	Asian	Hisp.[2]
City	91.8	94.9	89.8	89.9	73.9	37.8	47.4	17.5	49.5	20.7
MSA[1]	93.1	95.0	90.9	89.1	75.0	39.2	42.6	21.9	56.7	20.9
U.S.	89.4	92.9	88.1	88.0	72.5	35.0	37.7	24.7	57.0	19.9

Note: Figures shown cover persons 25 years old and over; (1) Figures cover the Kansas City, MO-KS Metropolitan Statistical Area; (2) People of Hispanic origin can be of any race
Source: U.S. Census Bureau, 2019-2023 American Community Survey 5-Year Estimates

School Enrollment by Grade and Control

Area	Preschool (%)		Kindergarten (%)		Grades 1 - 4 (%)		Grades 5 - 8 (%)		Grades 9 - 12 (%)	
	Public	Private	Public	Private	Public	Private	Public	Private	Public	Private
City	61.2	38.8	86.8	13.2	85.4	14.6	87.0	13.0	83.4	16.6
MSA[1]	60.8	39.2	86.2	13.8	87.9	12.1	88.5	11.5	88.5	11.5
U.S.	58.7	41.3	85.2	14.8	87.2	12.8	87.9	12.1	89.0	11.0

Note: Figures shown cover persons 3 years old and over; (1) Figures cover the Kansas City, MO-KS Metropolitan Statistical Area
Source: U.S. Census Bureau, 2019-2023 American Community Survey 5-Year Estimates

Higher Education

Four-Year Colleges			Two-Year Colleges			Medical Schools[1]	Law Schools[2]	Voc/ Tech[3]
Public	Private Non-profit	Private For-profit	Public	Private Non-profit	Private For-profit			
1	18	2	3	0	3	3	1	11

Note: Figures cover institutions located within the Kansas City, MO-KS Metropolitan Statistical Area and include main campuses only; (1) includes schools accredited by the Liaison Committee on Medical Education and the American Osteopathic Association's Commission on Osteopathic College Accreditation; (2) includes ABA-accredited schools, schools with provisional ABA accreditation, and state accredited schools; (3) includes all schools with programs that are less than 2 years.
Source: National Center for Education Statistics, Integrated Postsecondary Education System (IPEDS), 2023-24; Wikipedia, List of Medical Schools in the United States, accessed May 2, 2025; Wikipedia, List of Law Schools in the United States, accessed May 2, 2025

According to *U.S. News & World Report,* the Kansas City, MO-KS metro area is home to one of the top 100 law schools in the U.S.: **University of Missouri—Kansas City** (#99 tie). The rankings are based on a weighted average of 12 measures of quality: peer assessment score; assessment score by lawyers/judges; median LSAT scores; median undergrad GPA; acceptance rate; employment rates for graduates; placement success; bar passage rate; faculty resources; expenditures per student; student/faculty ratio; and library resources. *U.S. News & World Report, "America's Best Graduate Schools, Law, 2025"*

According to *U.S. News & World Report*, the Kansas City, MO-KS metro area is home to one of the top medical schools for research in the U.S.: **University of Kansas Medical Center** (Tier 2). *U.S. News* placed medical and osteopathic schools into tiers based on their research productivity, faculty and admissions data. Each school's tier was derived from its overall score, calculated by summing the weighted normalized values generated across several factors of academic quality, outlined below. There are four tiers, with tier 1 medical schools as the highest-performing and tier 4 as the lowest-performing. Only tier 1 and 2 schools are shown. Because of the tier presentation, *U.S. News* calculated overall scores based on their percentile performance among all rated schools instead of dividing against the rescaled score of the No. 1-performing schools. Tier 1 included schools with overall scores of 85 to 99. The cutoffs for tiers 2 through 4 were schools scoring 50 to 84, 15 to 49 and 1 to 14, respectively. The rankings are based on a weighted average of the following measures of quality: total research activity; average research activity per faculty member; total NIH research grants at the medical school and its affiliated hospitals; average NIH research grants per faculty; median MCAT total score; median undergraduate GPA; acceptance rate; and faculty resources. *U.S. News & World Report, "America's Best Graduate Schools, Medical, 2025"*

According to *U.S. News & World Report*, the Kansas City, MO-KS metro area is home to one of the top medical schools for primary care in the U.S.: **University of Kansas Medical Center** (Tier 1). *U.S. News* placed medical and osteopathic schools into tiers based on their research productivity, faculty and admissions data. Each school's tier was derived from its overall score, calculated by summing the weighted normalized values generated across several factors of academic quality, outlined below. There are four tiers, with tier 1 medical schools as the highest-performing and tier 4 as the lowest-performing. Only tier 1 and 2 schools are shown. Because of the tier presentation, *U.S. News* calculated overall scores based on their percentile performance among all rated schools instead of dividing against the rescaled score of the No. 1-performing schools. Tier 1 included schools with overall scores of 85 to 99. The cutoffs for tiers 2 through 4 were schools scoring 50 to 84, 15 to 49 and 1 to 14, respectively. The rankings are based on a weighted average of the following measures of quality: graduates practicing in primary care specialties; graduates entering primary care residencies; median MCAT total score; median undergraduate GPA; acceptance rate; and faculty resources. *U.S. News & World Report, "America's Best Graduate Schools, Medical, 2025"*

EMPLOYERS

Major Employers

Company Name	Industry
B&V Baker Guam JV	Engineering services
Black and Veatch Corp	Engineering services
DST Systems	Data processing
Embarq Corporation	Telephone communications
Ford Motor Company	Automobile assembly
Hallmark Cards	Greeting cards
HCA Midwest Division	Hospital management
Honeywell International	Search & navigation equipment
Internal Revenue Service	Taxation department, government
North Kansas City Hospital	General medical & surgical hospitals
Park University	Colleges & universities
Performance Contracting	Drywall
St. Lukes Hospital of Kansas	General medical & surgical hospitals
United Auto Workers	Labor union
University of Kansas	Medical centers
University of Missouri System	General medical & surgical hospitals

Note: Companies shown are located within the Kansas City, MO-KS Metropolitan Statistical Area.
Source: Chambers of Commerce; State Departments of Labor; Wikipedia

PUBLIC SAFETY

Crime Rate

Area	Total Crime Rate	Violent Crime Rate				Property Crime Rate		
		Murder	Rape	Robbery	Aggrav. Assault	Burglary	Larceny-Theft	Motor Vehicle Theft
City	6,436.1	35.5	78.5	241.2	1,122.5	549.6	2,633.3	1,775.6
U.S.	2,290.9	5.7	38.0	66.5	264.1	250.7	1,347.2	318.7

Note: Figures are crimes per 100,000 population.
Source: FBI, Table 8, Offenses Known to Law Enforcement, by State by City, 2023

Hate Crimes

Area	Number of Quarters Reported	Number of Incidents per Bias Motivation					
		Race/Ethnicity/Ancestry	Religion	Sexual Orientation	Disability	Gender	Gender Identity
City[1]	4	28	5	7	0	1	4
U.S.	4	5,900	2,699	2,077	187	92	492

Note: (1) Figures include at least one incident reported with more than one bias motivation.
Source: Federal Bureau of Investigation, Hate Crime Statistics 2023

Identity Theft Consumer Reports

Area	Reports	Reports per 100,000 Population	Rank[2]
MSA[1]	4,247	193	175
U.S.	1,135,291	339	-

Note: (1) Figures cover the Kansas City, MO-KS Metropolitan Statistical Area; (2) Rank ranges from 1 to 401 where 1 indicates greatest number of identity theft reports per 100,000 population
Source: Federal Trade Commission, Consumer Sentinel Network Data Book 2024

Fraud and Other Consumer Reports

Area	Reports	Reports per 100,000 Population	Rank[2]
MSA[1]	24,559	1,115	158
U.S.	5,360,641	1,601	-

Note: (1) Figures cover the Kansas City, MO-KS Metropolitan Statistical Area; (2) Rank ranges from 1 to 401 where 1 indicates greatest number of fraud and other consumer reports per 100,000 population
Source: Federal Trade Commission, Consumer Sentinel Network Data Book 2024

POLITICS

2024 Presidential Election Results

Area	Trump (Rep.)	Harris (Dem.)	Stein (Green)	Kennedy (Ind.)	Oliver (Lib.)	Other
Jackson County	39.3	58.5	0.8	0.0	0.8	0.6
U.S.	49.7	48.2	0.6	0.5	0.4	0.6

Note: Results are percentages and may not add to 100% due to rounding
Source: Dave Leip's Atlas of U.S. Presidential Elections

SPORTS

Professional Sports Teams

Team Name	League	Year Established
Kansas City Chiefs	National Football League (NFL)	1963
Kansas City Royals	Major League Baseball (MLB)	1969
Sporting Kansas City	Major League Soccer (MLS)	1996

Note: Includes teams located in the Kansas City, MO-KS Metropolitan Statistical Area.
Source: Wikipedia, Major Professional Sports Teams of the United States and Canada, May 1, 2025

CLIMATE

Average and Extreme Temperatures

Temperature	Jan	Feb	Mar	Apr	May	Jun	Jul	Aug	Sep	Oct	Nov	Dec	Yr.
Extreme High (°F)	69	76	86	93	92	105	107	109	102	92	82	70	109
Average High (°F)	35	40	54	65	74	84	90	87	79	66	52	39	64
Average Temp. (°F)	26	31	44	55	64	74	79	77	68	56	43	30	54
Average Low (°F)	17	22	34	44	54	63	69	66	58	45	34	21	44
Extreme Low (°F)	-17	-19	-10	12	30	42	54	43	33	21	1	-23	-23

Note: Figures cover the years 1972-1990
Source: National Climatic Data Center, International Station Meteorological Climate Summary, 9/96

Average Precipitation/Snowfall/Humidity

Precip./Humidity	Jan	Feb	Mar	Apr	May	Jun	Jul	Aug	Sep	Oct	Nov	Dec	Yr.
Avg. Precip. (in.)	1.1	1.2	2.8	3.0	5.5	4.1	3.8	4.1	4.9	3.6	2.1	1.6	38.1
Avg. Snowfall (in.)	6	5	3	1	0	0	0	0	0	Tr	1	5	21
Avg. Rel. Hum. 6am (%)	76	77	78	77	82	84	84	86	86	80	79	78	80
Avg. Rel. Hum. 3pm (%)	58	59	54	50	54	54	51	53	53	51	57	60	54

Note: Figures cover the years 1972-1990; Tr = Trace amounts (<0.05 in. of rain; <0.5 in. of snow)
Source: National Climatic Data Center, International Station Meteorological Climate Summary, 9/96

Weather Conditions

Temperature			Daytime Sky			Precipitation		
10°F & below	32°F & below	90°F & above	Clear	Partly cloudy	Cloudy	0.01 inch or more precip.	0.1 inch or more snow/ice	Thunder-storms
22	110	39	112	134	119	103	17	51

Note: Figures are average number of days per year and cover the years 1972-1990
Source: National Climatic Data Center, International Station Meteorological Climate Summary, 9/96

HAZARDOUS WASTE

Superfund Sites

The Kansas City, MO-KS metro area is home to six sites on the EPA's Superfund National Priorities List (NPL) or Superfund Alternative Approach (SAA) list: **Armour Road** (Final NPL); **Chemical Commodities, Inc.** (Final NPL); **Conservation Chemical Co.** (Final NPL); **Doepke Disposal (Holliday)** (Final NPL); **Lake City Army Ammunition Plant (Northwest Lagoon)** (Final NPL); **Lee Chemical** (Final NPL). The Superfund alternative approach uses the same investigation and cleanup process and standards that are used for sites listed on the National Priorities List. The SAA is an alternative to listing a site on the NPL; it is not an alternative to Superfund or the Superfund process. There are a total of 1,445 Superfund sites with a status of proposed or final on both lists in the United States. *U.S. Environmental Protection Agency, National Priorities List, May 1, 2025; U.S. Environmental Protection Agency, Superfund Alternative Approach Sites, May 1, 2025*

AIR QUALITY

Air Quality Trends: Ozone

	1990	1995	2000	2005	2010	2015	2020	2021	2022	2023
MSA[1]	0.075	0.095	0.087	0.082	0.067	0.063	0.064	0.067	0.066	0.074
U.S.	0.087	0.089	0.081	0.080	0.072	0.068	0.066	0.067	0.067	0.070

Note: (1) Data covers the Kansas City, MO-KS Metropolitan Statistical Area. The values shown are the composite ozone concentration averages among trend sites based on the highest fourth daily maximum 8-hour concentration in parts per million. These trends are based on sites having an adequate record of monitoring data during the trend period. Data from exceptional events are included.
Source: U.S. Environmental Protection Agency, Air Quality Monitoring Information, "Air Quality Trends by City, 1990-2023"

Air Quality Index

Area	Percent of Days when Air Quality was...[2]					AQI Statistics[2]	
	Good	Moderate	Unhealthy for Sensitive Groups	Unhealthy	Very Unhealthy	Maximum	Median
MSA[1]	34.0	58.1	6.8	1.1	0.0	166	55

Note: (1) Data covers the Kansas City, MO-KS Metropolitan Statistical Area; (2) Based on 365 days with AQI data in 2023. Air Quality Index (AQI) is an index for reporting daily air quality. EPA calculates the AQI for five major air pollutants regulated by the Clean Air Act: ground-level ozone, particle pollution (aka particulate matter), carbon monoxide, sulfur dioxide, and nitrogen dioxide. The AQI runs from 0 to 500. The higher the AQI value, the greater the level of air pollution and the greater the health concern. There are six AQI categories: "Good" AQI is between 0 and 50. Air quality is considered satisfactory; "Moderate" AQI is between 51 and 100. Air quality is acceptable; "Unhealthy for Sensitive Groups" When AQI values are between 101 and 150, members of sensitive groups may experience health effects; "Unhealthy" When AQI values are between 151 and 200 everyone may begin to experience health effects; "Very Unhealthy" AQI values between 201 and 300 trigger a health alert; "Hazardous" AQI values over 300 trigger warnings of emergency conditions (not shown).
Source: U.S. Environmental Protection Agency, Air Quality Index Report, 2023

Air Quality Index Pollutants

Area	Percent of Days when AQI Pollutant was...[2]					
	Carbon Monoxide	Nitrogen Dioxide	Ozone	Sulfur Dioxide	Particulate Matter 2.5	Particulate Matter 10
MSA[1]	0.0	1.4	39.5	(3)	55.6	3.6

Note: (1) Data covers the Kansas City, MO-KS Metropolitan Statistical Area; (2) Based on 365 days with AQI data in 2023. The Air Quality Index (AQI) is an index for reporting daily air quality. EPA calculates the AQI for five major air pollutants regulated by the Clean Air Act: ground-level ozone, particle pollution (also known as particulate matter), carbon monoxide, sulfur dioxide, and nitrogen dioxide. The AQI runs from 0 to 500. The higher the AQI value, the greater the level of air pollution and the greater the health concern; (3) Sulfur dioxide is no longer included in this table because SO_2 concentrations tend to be very localized and not necessarily representative of broad geographical areas like counties and CBSAs.
Source: U.S. Environmental Protection Agency, Air Quality Index Report, 2023

Maximum Air Pollutant Concentrations: Particulate Matter, Ozone, CO and Lead

	Particulate Matter 10 (ug/m^3)	Particulate Matter 2.5 Wtd AM (ug/m^3)	Particulate Matter 2.5 24-Hr (ug/m^3)	Ozone (ppm)	Carbon Monoxide (ppm)	Lead (ug/m^3)
MSA[1] Level	256	9.6	27	0.077	1	n/a
NAAQS[2]	150	15	35	0.075	9	0.15
Met NAAQS[2]	No	Yes	Yes	No	Yes	n/a

Note: (1) Data covers the Kansas City, MO-KS Metropolitan Statistical Area; Data from exceptional events are included; (2) National Ambient Air Quality Standards; ppm = parts per million; ug/m^3 = micrograms per cubic meter; n/a not available.
Concentrations: Particulate Matter 10 (coarse particulate)—highest second maximum 24-hour concentration; Particulate Matter 2.5 Wtd AM (fine particulate)—highest weighted annual mean concentration; Particulate Matter 2.5 24-Hour (fine particulate)—highest 98th percentile 24-hour concentration; Ozone—highest fourth daily maximum 8-hour concentration; Carbon Monoxide—highest second maximum non-overlapping 8-hour concentration; Lead—maximum running 3-month average
Source: U.S. Environmental Protection Agency, Air Quality Monitoring Information, "Air Quality Statistics by City, 2023"

Maximum Air Pollutant Concentrations: Nitrogen Dioxide and Sulfur Dioxide

	Nitrogen Dioxide AM (ppb)	Nitrogen Dioxide 1-Hr (ppb)	Sulfur Dioxide AM (ppb)	Sulfur Dioxide 1-Hr (ppb)	Sulfur Dioxide 24-Hr (ppb)
MSA[1] Level	11	45	n/a	6	n/a
NAAQS[2]	53	100	30	75	140
Met NAAQS[2]	Yes	Yes	n/a	Yes	n/a

Note: (1) Data covers the Kansas City, MO-KS Metropolitan Statistical Area; Data from exceptional events are included; (2) National Ambient Air Quality Standards; ppm = parts per million; ug/m^3 = micrograms per cubic meter; n/a not available.
Concentrations: Nitrogen Dioxide AM—highest arithmetic mean concentration; Nitrogen Dioxide 1-Hr—highest 98th percentile 1-hour daily maximum concentration; Sulfur Dioxide AM—highest annual mean concentration; Sulfur Dioxide 1-Hr—highest 99th percentile 1-hour daily maximum concentration; Sulfur Dioxide 24-Hr—highest second maximum 24-hour concentration
Source: U.S. Environmental Protection Agency, Air Quality Monitoring Information, "Air Quality Statistics by City, 2023"

Lincoln, Nebraska

Background

Lincoln, the capital of Nebraska and the seat of Lancaster County is in the southeastern part of the state. It is a thriving and multifaceted city with a fascinating history and a dynamic and expanding contemporary economy and cultural life. Lincoln today is the second-largest city in Nebraska.

The site first attracted the attention of settlers in 1856 when commercial explorers found saline deposits on the banks of the Salt Creek, known today as Capitol Beach Lake. Salt was the first major commercial activity in the city, with two large salt "boilers," Cox and Peckham, supplying this vital resource to farmers and townspeople in a wide stretch of the Plains region. Captain W.T. Donovan came to the area as a salt company representative, settling there permanently in 1867. He named the town Lancaster, after his home in Pennsylvania, which also became the county name.

Omaha was the capital of Nebraska until statehood and a drive began to move the capital south of the Platte River. The new Capitol City was sited at Lancaster. State Senator J.H.N. Patrick proposed changing the name to Lincoln because he thought it would discourage Democratic support, and Lincoln it became.

In the 1880s—a dynamic period of Lincoln's early economic growth—William Jennings Bryan came to town as a lawyer and budding politician and two years later was elected to the U.S. Congress. Another Lincoln luminary from this period was General John J. Pershing, who was an instructor in military science at the recently established University of Nebraska.

Lincoln was designated a "refugee-friendly" city by the U.S. Department of State in the 1970s and is home to over 30,000 immigrants and refugees from about 150 different countries. In 2021 the city's school district served about 2,400 immigrant or refugee families. Lincoln's bilingual liaisons help families who speak 130 languages.

The city's downtown is a modern entertainment, commercial, and office center, with the historic Haymarket District on its west edge. The state capitol building, designed by Bertram Grosvenor Goodhue in 1919, offers a modernist central white stone column, visible from surrounding prairie hilltops for miles, that still defines the Lincoln skyline. In addition to recent downtown restoration and improved flood control, a major renovation to downtown's historic Atrium was completed in 2022, now a spectacular office space for new and existing businesses.

Lincoln is also a city of 166 parks, including a children's zoo and wilderness park, with more than half of them designated as neighborhood and mini parks.

The University of Nebraska is city's largest institution of higher learning, and its football team attracts crowds of 90,000 to Memorial Stadium. The University of Nebraska is a major hub of cultural activity in the city and is the site of the State Museum of Natural History. Nebraska Wesleyan University and Union College are also located in Lincoln.

The city offers rich cultural resources that draw on its increasingly cosmopolitan character, as well as on the rural traditions of the state. The Lied Center for Performing Arts, on the University of Nebraska's downtown campus, features a full range of musical and dramatic performances, and the city hosts the Nebraska State Fair in early September.

The State of Nebraska is the city's largest employer, followed by the public schools and the University of Nebraska-Lincoln. Health care is a major industry in the city, that's also home to Kawasaki, Burlington Northern Railroad and Duncan Aviation. The joint County-City Building houses the mayor's office, the city council, Lancaster County commissioner's office; county, district, and juvenile courts, and the judicial center is connected to the County-City Building by elevated walkways.

The climate in Lincoln is characterized by the robust and dramatic range of the Great Plains area. Most precipitation falls April through September, and thunderstorms are predominant in the summer months. Lincoln lies in a valley that affords considerable protection against tornadoes, although more than 25 Federal Signal warning sirens throughout the city are still tested every Wednesday morning, except in the winter months.

Rankings

General Rankings

- To help military veterans find the best places in which to settle down, *WalletHub* compared the 100 largest U.S. cities across 19 key indicators of livability, affordability and veteran-friendliness. They range from the share of military skill-related jobs to veteran income growth to the availability of VA health facilities. Lincoln ranked #47. *Wallethub.com, "Best & Worst Places for Veterans to Live (2025)," November 7, 2024*

- *US News & World Report* conducted a survey of more than 3,500 people and analyzed the 150 largest metropolitan areas to determine what matters most when selecting the next place to live. Lincoln ranked #24 out of the top 25 as having the best combination of desirable factors. Criteria: cost of living; quality of life and education; climate; job market; desirability; and other factors. *realestate.usnews.com, "Best Places to Live in the U.S. in 2024-2025," May 21, 2024*

- In their annual survey, Livability.com looked at data for more than 2,000 mid-sized U.S. cities to assign a "Livability Score" for each. The top 100 scoring cities make up Livability's "Top 100 Best Places to Live in the U.S." in 2025. Lincoln was placed among the top 100 of the customizable list. Criteria: housing and economy; cost of living; environment; education; health care options; transportation; safety; and community amenities. *Livability.com, "Top 100 Best Places to Live in the U.S. in 2025" April 15, 2025*

Business/Finance Rankings

- The Lincoln metro area appeared on the Milken Institute "2025 Best Performing Cities" list. Rank: #66 out of 200 large metro areas (based on performance category). Criteria: job growth; wage growth; high-tech growth and impact; community resilience; housing affordability; household broadband access. *Milken Institute, "Best-Performing Cities 2025," January 14, 2025*

Children/Family Rankings

- Lincoln was selected as one of the best cities for newlyweds by *Rent.com*. The city ranked #8 of 15. Criteria: cost of living; availability of affordable rental inventory; annual household income; entertainment, culture and restaurant options; percentage of married couples; concentration of millennials; and safety. *Rent.com, "The 15 Best Cities for Newlyweds," September 2, 2021*

Environmental Rankings

- The U.S. Conference of Mayors and Walmart Stores sponsor the Mayors' Climate Protection Awards Program which recognize mayors for outstanding and innovative practices that address the climate crisis: increase energy efficiency in their cities, reduce carbon emissions and expand renewable energy. Lincoln received an Honorable Mention in the large city category. *U.S. Conference of Mayors, "2024 Mayors' Climate Protection Awards," June 20, 2024*

Health/Fitness Rankings

- For each of the 100 largest cities in the United States, the American Fitness Index®, compiled in partnership between the American College of Sports Medicine and the Elevance Health Foundation, evaluated community infrastructure and more than 30 health behaviors including preventive health, levels of chronic disease conditions, food insecurity, pedestrian safety, air quality, and community/environment resources that support physical activity. Lincoln ranked #23 for "community fitness." *americanfitnessindex.org, "2024 ACSM American Fitness Index Summary Report," July 23, 2024*

Real Estate Rankings

- *WalletHub* compared the most populated U.S. cities to determine which had the best markets for real estate agents. Lincoln ranked #32 where demand was high and pay was the best. Criteria: sales per agent; annual median wage for real-estate agents; monthly average starting salary for real estate agents; real estate job density and competition; unemployment rate; home turnover rate; housing-market health index; and other relevant metrics. *WalletHub.com, "2021 Best Places to Be a Real Estate Agent," May 12, 2021*

- Lincoln was ranked #62 out of 176 metro areas in terms of cost of housing in 2024 by the National Association of Home Builders (#1 = most affordable). Criteria: the portion of an average family's income necessary to pay the mortgage on a median-priced home. *National Association of Home Builders®, NAHB-Wells Fargo Cost of Housing Index, 4th Quarter 2024*

Seniors/Retirement Rankings

- Lincoln made the 2024 *Forbes* list of "25 Best Places to Retire." Criteria, focused on overall affordability as well as quality of life indicators, include: housing/living costs compared to the national average and taxes; air quality; crime rates; median home prices; risk associated with climate-change/natural hazards; availability of medical care; bikeability; walkability; healthy living. *Forbes.com, "The Best Places to Retire in 2024: Las Cruces and Other Unexpected Hot Spots," May 10, 2024*

Women/Minorities Rankings

- Personal finance website *WalletHub* compared more than 180 U.S. cities across two key dimensions, "Hispanic Business-Friendliness" and "Hispanic Purchasing Power," to arrive at the most favorable conditions for Hispanic entrepreneurs. Lincoln was ranked #108 out of 182. Criteria includes: share of Hispanic-Owned Businesses; average growth of Hispanic Business revenues; Small Business-Friendliness score; affordability; and number of Hispanics with at least a bachelor's degree. *WalletHub.com, "Best Cities for Hispanic Entrepreneurs," September 4, 2024*

Miscellaneous Rankings

- *WalletHub* compared 148 of the most populated U.S. cities to determine their operating efficiency. A "Quality of Services" score was constructed for each city and then measured against the total budget per capita to reveal which were managed the best. Lincoln ranked #24. Criteria: financial stability; economy; education; safety; health; infrastructure and pollution. *WalletHub.com, "2025's Best- & Worst-Run Cities in America," June 18, 2024*

Business Environment

DEMOGRAPHICS

Population Growth

Area	1990 Census	2000 Census	2010 Census	2020 Census	2023 Estimate[2]	Population Growth 1990-2023 (%)
City	193,629	225,581	258,379	291,082	291,932	50.8
MSA[1]	229,091	266,787	302,157	340,217	341,309	49.0
U.S.	248,709,873	281,421,906	308,745,538	331,449,281	332,387,540	33.6

Note: (1) Figures cover the Lincoln, NE Metropolitan Statistical Area; (2) 2019-2023 5-year ACS population estimate
Source: U.S. Census Bureau, 1990 Census, 2000 Census, 2010 Census, 2020 Census, 2019-2023 American Community Survey 5-Year Estimates

Race

Area	White Alone[2] (%)	Black Alone[2] (%)	Asian Alone[2] (%)	AIAN[3] Alone[2] (%)	NHOPI[4] Alone[2] (%)	Other Race Alone[2] (%)	Two or More Races (%)
City	80.9	4.2	4.5	0.7	0.1	2.3	7.4
MSA[1]	83.0	3.6	3.9	0.7	0.1	2.0	6.8
U.S.	63.4	12.4	5.8	0.9	0.2	6.6	10.7

Note: (1) Figures cover the Lincoln, NE Metropolitan Statistical Area; (2) Alone is defined as not being in combination with one or more other races; (3) American Indian and Alaska Native; (4) Native Hawaiian and Other Pacific Islander
Source: U.S. Census Bureau, 2019-2023 American Community Survey 5-Year Estimates

Hispanic or Latino Origin

Area	Total (%)	Mexican (%)	Puerto Rican (%)	Cuban (%)	Other (%)
City	8.8	5.7	0.4	0.2	2.5
MSA[1]	8.0	5.2	0.4	0.2	2.2
U.S.	19.0	11.3	1.8	0.7	5.2

Note: Persons of Hispanic or Latino origin can be of any race; (1) Figures cover the Lincoln, NE Metropolitan Statistical Area
Source: U.S. Census Bureau, 2019-2023 American Community Survey 5-Year Estimates

Age

Area	Percent of Population									Median Age
	Under Age 5	Age 5–19	Age 20–34	Age 35–44	Age 45–54	Age 55–64	Age 65–74	Age 75–84	Age 85+	
City	5.9	20.0	26.1	12.8	10.4	10.4	8.8	4.0	1.7	33.4
MSA[1]	5.9	20.6	24.1	12.8	10.7	10.9	9.3	4.0	1.7	34.4
U.S.	5.7	19.1	20.2	13.1	12.3	12.8	10.0	4.9	1.9	38.7

Note: (1) Figures cover the Lincoln, NE Metropolitan Statistical Area
Source: U.S. Census Bureau, 2019-2023 American Community Survey 5-Year Estimates

Disability by Age

Area	All Ages	Under 18 Years Old	18 to 64 Years Old	65 Years and Over
City	12.0	4.8	10.6	29.5
MSA[1]	11.8	4.5	10.2	29.6
U.S.	13.0	4.7	10.7	32.9

Note: Figures show percent of the civilian noninstitutionalized population that reported having a disability. Disability status is determined from six types of difficulty: vision, hearing, cognitive, ambulatory, self-care, and independent living. For children under 5 years old, hearing and vision difficulty are used to determine disability status. For children between the ages of 5 and 14, disability status is determined from hearing, vision, cognitive, ambulatory, and self-care difficulties. For people aged 15 years and older, they are considered to have a disability if they have difficulty with any one of the six difficulty types; Note: (1) Figures cover the Lincoln, NE Metropolitan Statistical Area
Source: U.S. Census Bureau, 2019-2023 American Community Survey 5-Year Estimates

Ancestry

Area	German	Irish	English	American	Italian	Polish	French[2]	European	Scottish
City	30.2	11.0	9.3	3.4	1.9	2.2	1.7	1.8	1.4
MSA[1]	32.0	10.9	9.3	3.6	1.8	2.1	1.6	1.7	1.3
U.S.	12.6	9.4	9.1	5.5	4.9	2.6	2.0	1.6	1.6

Note: Figures are the percentage of the total population reporting a particular ancestry. The nine most commonly reported ancestries in the U.S. are shown. Figures include multiple ancestries (e.g. if a person reported being Irish and Italian, they were included in both columns); (1) Figures cover the Lincoln, NE Metropolitan Statistical Area; (2) Excludes Basque
Source: U.S. Census Bureau, 2019-2023 American Community Survey 5-Year Estimates

Foreign-born Population

Area	Percent of Population Born in								
	Any Foreign Country	Asia	Mexico	Europe	Caribbean	Central America[2]	South America	Africa	Canada
City	9.2	4.9	1.3	0.9	0.4	0.6	0.3	0.8	0.1
MSA[1]	8.1	4.3	1.1	0.8	0.3	0.5	0.3	0.7	0.1
U.S.	13.9	4.3	3.3	1.4	1.4	1.2	1.2	0.8	0.2

Note: (1) Figures cover the Lincoln, NE Metropolitan Statistical Area; (2) Excludes Mexico.
Source: U.S. Census Bureau, 2019-2023 American Community Survey 5-Year Estimates

Household Size

Area	Persons in Household (%)							Average Household Size
	One	Two	Three	Four	Five	Six	Seven or More	
City	32.7	34.1	13.7	11.0	4.9	2.5	1.0	2.31
MSA[1]	30.8	35.3	13.6	11.4	5.2	2.5	1.1	2.35
U.S.	28.5	33.8	15.4	12.7	5.9	2.3	1.4	2.54

Note: (1) Figures cover the Lincoln, NE Metropolitan Statistical Area
Source: U.S. Census Bureau, 2019-2023 American Community Survey 5-Year Estimates

Household Relationships

Area	House-holder	Opposite-sex Spouse	Same-sex Spouse	Opposite-sex Unmarried Partner	Same-sex Unmarried Partner	Child[2]	Grand-child	Other Relatives	Non-relatives
City	40.1	16.9	0.2	2.8	0.1	26.6	1.1	2.7	4.6
MSA[1]	39.5	17.9	0.2	2.6	0.1	27.2	1.1	2.6	4.1
U.S.	38.3	17.5	0.2	2.5	0.2	28.3	2.4	4.8	3.4

Note: Figures are percent of the total population; (1) Figures cover the Lincoln, NE Metropolitan Statistical Area; (2) Includes biological, adopted, and stepchildren of the householder
Source: U.S. Census Bureau, 2020 Census

Gender

Area	Males	Females	Males per 100 Females
City	146,855	145,077	101.2
MSA[1]	172,052	169,257	101.7
U.S.	164,545,087	167,842,453	98.0

Note: (1) Figures cover the Lincoln, NE Metropolitan Statistical Area
Source: U.S. Census Bureau, 2019-2023 American Community Survey 5-Year Estimates

Marital Status

Area	Never Married	Now Married[2]	Separated	Widowed	Divorced
City	39.6	45.4	0.8	4.2	10.0
MSA[1]	37.2	48.2	0.8	4.2	9.6
U.S.	34.1	47.9	1.7	5.6	10.7

Note: Figures are percentages and cover the population 15 years of age and older; (1) Figures cover the Lincoln, NE Metropolitan Statistical Area; (2) Excludes separated
Source: U.S. Census Bureau, 2019-2023 American Community Survey 5-Year Estimates

Religious Groups by Family

Area	Catholic	Baptist	Methodist	LDS[2]	Pentecostal	Lutheran	Islam	Adventist	Other
MSA[1]	13.2	1.0	5.7	1.2	3.1	9.1	0.1	1.8	10.0
U.S.	18.7	7.3	3.0	2.0	1.8	1.7	1.3	1.3	11.6

Note: Figures are the number of adherents as a percentage of the total population and cover the eight largest religious groups in the U.S; (1) Figures cover the Lincoln, NE Metropolitan Statistical Area; (2) Church of Jesus Christ of Latter-day Saints
Sources: 2020 U.S. Religion Census, Association of Statisticians of American Religious Bodies; The Association of Religion Data Archives (ARDA)

Religious Groups by Tradition

Area	Catholic	Evangelical Protestant	Mainline Protestant	Black Protestant	Islam	Judaism	Hinduism	Orthodox	Buddhism
MSA[1]	13.2	16.6	12.9	0.3	0.1	0.1	0.1	0.1	0.1
U.S.	18.7	16.5	5.2	2.3	1.3	0.6	0.4	0.4	0.3

Note: Figures are the number of adherents as a percentage of the total population; (1) Figures cover the Lincoln, NE Metropolitan Statistical Area
Sources: 2020 U.S. Religion Census, Association of Statisticians of American Religious Bodies; The Association of Religion Data Archives (ARDA)

ECONOMY

Real Gross Domestic Product (GDP)

Area	2017	2018	2019	2020	2021	2022	2023	Rank[3]
MSA[1]	19.6	19.9	20.3	20.2	21.1	22.1	22.8	130
U.S.[2]	17,619.1	18,160.7	18,642.5	18,238.9	19,387.6	19,896.6	20,436.3	—

Note: Figures are in billions of chained 2017 dollars; (1) Figures cover the Lincoln, NE Metropolitan Statistical Area; (2) Figures cover real GDP within metropolitan areas; (3) Rank is based on 2023 data and ranges from 1 to 384
Source: U.S. Bureau of Economic Analysis

Economic Growth

Area	2014	2015	2016	2017	2018	2019	2020	2021	2022	2023
MSA[1]	4.9	3.5	1.7	5.3	2.0	1.9	-0.7	4.5	4.6	3.3
U.S.[2]	2.6	3.2	2.0	2.7	3.1	2.7	-2.2	6.3	2.6	2.7

Note: Figures are real gross domestic product growth rates and represent percent change from preceding period; (1) Figures cover the Lincoln, NE Metropolitan Statistical Area; (2) Figures are the average growth rates within metropolitan areas
Source: U.S. Bureau of Economic Analysis

Metropolitan Area Exports

Area	2018	2019	2020	2021	2022	2023	Rank[2]
MSA[1]	885.6	807.0	726.3	872.6	1,161.3	1,082.2	165
U.S.	1,664,056.1	1,645,173.7	1,431,406.6	1,753,941.4	2,062,937.4	2,019,160.5	—

Note: Figures are in millions of dollars; (1) Figures cover the Lincoln, NE Metropolitan Statistical Area; (2) Rank is based on 2023 data and ranges from 1 to 386
Source: U.S. Department of Commerce, International Trade Administration, Office of Trade and Economic Analysis, Industry and Analysis, Exports by Metropolitan Area, data extracted April 2, 2025

Building Permits

Area	Single-Family			Multi-Family			Total		
	2023	2024	Pct. Chg.	2023	2024	Pct. Chg.	2023	2024	Pct. Chg.
City	699	937	34.0	1,282	793	-38.1	1,981	1,730	-12.7
MSA[1]	849	1,077	26.9	1,288	959	-25.5	2,137	2,036	-4.7
U.S.	920,000	981,900	6.7	591,100	496,100	-16.1	1,511,100	1,478,000	-2.2

Note: (1) Figures cover the Lincoln, NE Metropolitan Statistical Area; Figures represent new, privately-owned housing units authorized (unadjusted data)
Source: U.S. Census Bureau, Building Permits Survey (BPS), 2023, 2024

Bankruptcy Filings

Area	Business Filings			Nonbusiness Filings		
	2023	2024	% Chg.	2023	2024	% Chg.
Lancaster County	11	15	36.4	367	405	10.4
U.S.	18,926	23,107	22.1	434,064	494,201	13.9

Note: Business filings include Chapter 7, Chapter 9, Chapter 11, Chapter 12, Chapter 13, Chapter 15, and Section 304; Nonbusiness filings include Chapter 7, Chapter 11, and Chapter 13
Source: Administrative Office of the U.S. Courts, Business and Nonbusiness Bankruptcy, County Cases Commenced by Chapter of the Bankruptcy Code, During the 12-Month Period Ending December 31, 2023 and Business and Nonbusiness Bankruptcy, County Cases Commenced by Chapter of the Bankruptcy Code, During the 12-Month Period Ending December 31, 2024

Housing Vacancy Rates

Area	Gross Vacancy Rate[3] (%)			Year-Round Vacancy Rate[4] (%)			Rental Vacancy Rate[5] (%)			Homeowner Vacancy Rate[6] (%)		
	2022	2023	2024	2022	2023	2024	2022	2023	2024	2022	2023	2024
MSA[1]	n/a	n/a	n/a	n/a	n/a	n/a	n/a	n/a	n/a	n/a	n/a	n/a
U.S.[2]	9.1	9.0	9.1	7.5	7.5	7.6	5.7	6.5	6.8	0.8	0.8	1.0

Note: (1) Figures cover the Lincoln, NE Metropolitan Statistical Area; (2) Figures cover the 75 largest Metropolitan Statistical Areas; (3) The percentage of the total housing inventory that is vacant; (4) The percentage of the housing inventory (excluding seasonal units) that is year-round vacant; (5) The percentage of rental inventory that is vacant for rent; (6) The percentage of homeowner inventory that is vacant for sale; n/a not available
Source: U.S. Census Bureau, Housing Vacancies and Homeownership Annual Statistics: 2022, 2023, 2024

INCOME

Income

Area	Per Capita ($)	Median Household ($)	Average Household ($)
City	39,187	69,991	94,181
MSA[1]	40,527	73,095	99,081
U.S.	43,289	78,538	110,491

Note: (1) Figures cover the Lincoln, NE Metropolitan Statistical Area
Source: U.S. Census Bureau, 2019-2023 American Community Survey 5-Year Estimates

Household Income Distribution

Area	Percent of Households Earning							
	Under $15,000	$15,000 -$24,999	$25,000 -$34,999	$35,000 -$49,999	$50,000 -$74,999	$75,000 -$99,999	$100,000 -$149,999	$150,000 and up
City	8.1	6.4	8.2	12.5	18.3	14.0	17.1	15.6
MSA[1]	7.4	6.1	7.7	12.0	17.9	13.8	18.0	17.1
U.S.	8.5	6.6	6.8	10.4	15.7	12.7	17.4	21.9

Note: (1) Figures cover the Lincoln, NE Metropolitan Statistical Area
Source: U.S. Census Bureau, 2019-2023 American Community Survey 5-Year Estimates

Poverty Rate

Area	All Ages	Under 18 Years Old	18 to 64 Years Old	65 Years and Over
City	12.6	13.0	13.6	8.0
MSA[1]	11.4	11.3	12.5	7.6
U.S.	12.4	16.3	11.6	10.4

Note: Figures are percentage of people whose income during the past 12 months was below the poverty level;
(1) Figures cover the Lincoln, NE Metropolitan Statistical Area
Source: U.S. Census Bureau, 2019-2023 American Community Survey 5-Year Estimates

EMPLOYMENT

Labor Force and Employment

Area	Civilian Labor Force			Workers Employed		
	Dec. 2023	Dec. 2024	% Chg.	Dec. 2023	Dec. 2024	% Chg.
City	164,857	168,647	2.3	161,204	164,571	2.1
MSA[1]	191,591	195,942	2.3	187,422	191,304	2.1
U.S.	166,661,000	167,746,000	0.7	160,754,000	161,294,000	0.3

Note: Data is not seasonally adjusted and covers workers 16 years of age and older; (1) Figures cover the Lincoln, NE Metropolitan Statistical Area
Source: Bureau of Labor Statistics, Local Area Unemployment Statistics

Unemployment Rate

Area	2024											
	Jan.	Feb.	Mar.	Apr.	May	Jun.	Jul.	Aug.	Sep.	Oct.	Nov.	Dec.
City	2.5	2.7	2.5	2.2	2.5	3.0	2.7	2.8	2.4	2.6	2.6	2.4
MSA[1]	2.4	2.6	2.4	2.2	2.5	3.0	2.6	2.7	2.4	2.6	2.5	2.4
U.S.	4.1	4.2	3.9	3.5	3.7	4.3	4.5	4.4	3.9	3.9	4.0	3.8

Note: Data is not seasonally adjusted and covers workers 16 years of age and older; (1) Figures cover the Lincoln, NE Metropolitan Statistical Area
Source: Bureau of Labor Statistics, Local Area Unemployment Statistics

Average Wages

Occupation	$/Hr.	Occupation	$/Hr.
Accountants and Auditors	34.67	Maintenance and Repair Workers	24.63
Automotive Mechanics	25.66	Marketing Managers	54.33
Bookkeepers	22.74	Network and Computer Systems Admin.	42.93
Carpenters	25.07	Nurses, Licensed Practical	28.51
Cashiers	14.50	Nurses, Registered	39.04
Computer Programmers	43.25	Nursing Assistants	19.33
Computer Systems Analysts	40.47	Office Clerks, General	18.58
Computer User Support Specialists	28.07	Physical Therapists	44.86
Construction Laborers	21.86	Physicians	136.23
Cooks, Restaurant	17.81	Plumbers, Pipefitters and Steamfitters	30.39
Customer Service Representatives	19.65	Police and Sheriff's Patrol Officers	40.64
Dentists	85.28	Postal Service Mail Carriers	30.57
Electricians	29.82	Real Estate Sales Agents	27.17
Engineers, Electrical	47.88	Retail Salespersons	16.38
Fast Food and Counter Workers	14.42	Sales Representatives, Technical/Scientific	40.00
Financial Managers	68.94	Secretaries, Exc. Legal/Medical/Executive	22.03
First-Line Supervisors of Office Workers	30.73	Security Guards	20.05
General and Operations Managers	50.12	Surgeons	n/a
Hairdressers/Cosmetologists	17.48	Teacher Assistants, Exc. Postsecondary[1]	13.52
Home Health and Personal Care Aides	16.47	Teachers, Secondary School, Exc. Sp. Ed.[1]	29.94
Janitors and Cleaners	16.83	Telemarketers	14.12
Landscaping/Groundskeeping Workers	18.75	Truck Drivers, Heavy/Tractor-Trailer	38.54
Lawyers	54.48	Truck Drivers, Light/Delivery Services	22.72
Maids and Housekeeping Cleaners	15.57	Waiters and Waitresses	19.50

Note: Wage data covers the Lincoln, NE Metropolitan Statistical Area; (1) Hourly wages were calculated from annual wage data based on a 40 hour work week
Source: Bureau of Labor Statistics, Metro Area Occupational Employment & Wage Estimates, May 2024

Employment by Industry

Sector	MSA[1] Number of Employees	MSA[1] Percent of Total	U.S. Percent of Total
Construction, Mining, and Logging	10,800	5.4	5.5
Financial Activities	10,700	5.4	5.8
Government	43,500	21.8	14.9
Information	3,900	2.0	1.9
Leisure and Hospitality	19,400	9.7	10.4
Manufacturing	14,700	7.4	8.0
Other Services	8,500	4.3	3.7
Private Education and Health Services	33,900	17.0	16.9
Professional and Business Services	20,500	10.3	14.2
Retail Trade	18,600	9.3	10.0
Transportation, Warehousing, and Utilities	10,500	5.3	4.8
Wholesale Trade	4,300	2.2	3.9

Note: Figures are non-farm employment as of December 2024. Figures are not seasonally adjusted and include workers 16 years of age and older; (1) Figures cover the Lincoln, NE Metropolitan Statistical Area
Source: Bureau of Labor Statistics, Current Employment Statistics, Employment, Hours, and Earnings

Employment by Occupation

Occupation Classification	City (%)	MSA[1] (%)	U.S. (%)
Management, Business, Science, and Arts	42.4	42.9	42.0
Natural Resources, Construction, and Maintenance	7.3	7.9	8.6
Production, Transportation, and Material Moving	12.2	12.2	13.0
Sales and Office	21.0	20.6	19.9
Service	17.1	16.4	16.5

Note: Figures cover employed civilians 16 years of age and older; (1) Figures cover the Lincoln, NE Metropolitan Statistical Area
Source: U.S. Census Bureau, 2019-2023 American Community Survey 5-Year Estimates

Occupations with Greatest Projected Employment Growth: 2022 – 2032

Occupation[1]	2022 Employment	2032 Projected Employment	Numeric Employment Change	Percent Employment Change
Home Health and Personal Care Aides	10,120	12,360	2,240	22.1
Stockers and Order Fillers	14,130	16,070	1,940	13.7
Software Developers	7,780	9,680	1,900	24.4
Fast Food and Counter Workers	26,230	28,120	1,890	7.2
Heavy and Tractor-Trailer Truck Drivers	27,030	28,840	1,810	6.7
Registered Nurses	22,900	24,670	1,770	7.7
General and Operations Managers	22,330	23,990	1,660	7.4
Laborers and Freight, Stock, and Material Movers, Hand	18,030	19,440	1,410	7.8
Nursing Assistants (SOC 2018)	16,290	17,540	1,250	7.7
Cooks, Restaurant	4,450	5,680	1,230	27.6

Note: Projections cover Nebraska; (1) Sorted by numeric employment change
Source: www.projectionscentral.org, State Occupational Projections, 2022–2032 Long-Term Projections

Fastest-Growing Occupations: 2022 – 2032

Occupation[1]	2022 Employment	2032 Projected Employment	Numeric Employment Change	Percent Employment Change
Gaming Dealers	30	100	70	233.3
Wind Turbine Service Technicians	320	530	210	65.6
Nurse Practitioners	1,790	2,430	640	35.8
Occupational Therapy Assistants	250	330	80	32.0
Data Scientists	1,400	1,830	430	30.7
Physical Therapist Assistants	1,120	1,450	330	29.5
Information Security Analysts (SOC 2018)	670	860	190	28.4
Cooks, Restaurant	4,450	5,680	1,230	27.6
Lodging Managers	480	600	120	25.0
Software Developers	7,780	9,680	1,900	24.4

Note: Projections cover Nebraska; (1) Sorted by percent employment change and excludes occupations with numeric employment change less than 50
Source: www.projectionscentral.org, State Occupational Projections, 2022–2032 Long-Term Projections

CITY FINANCES

City Government Finances

Component	2022 ($000)	2022 ($ per capita)
Total Revenues	483,375	1,664
Total Expenditures	525,088	1,808
Debt Outstanding	68,285	235

Source: U.S. Census Bureau, State & Local Government Finances 2022

City Government Revenue by Source

Source	2022 ($000)	2022 ($ per capita)	2022 (%)
General Revenue			
From Federal Government	43,286	149	9.0
From State Government	29,222	101	6.0
From Local Governments	2,472	9	0.5
Taxes			
Property	84,973	293	17.6
Sales and Gross Receipts	77,660	267	16.1
Personal Income	0	0	0.0
Corporate Income	0	0	0.0
Motor Vehicle License	6,978	24	1.4
Other Taxes	53,597	184	11.1
Current Charges	88,250	304	18.3
Liquor Store	0	0	0.0
Utility	45,253	156	9.4

Source: U.S. Census Bureau, State & Local Government Finances 2022

City Government Expenditures by Function

Function	2022 ($000)	2022 ($ per capita)	2022 (%)
General Direct Expenditures			
Air Transportation	0	0	0.0
Corrections	0	0	0.0
Education	0	0	0.0
Employment Security Administration	0	0	0.0
Financial Administration	4,549	15	0.9
Fire Protection	34,419	118	6.6
General Public Buildings	3,983	13	0.8
Governmental Administration, Other	6,316	21	1.2
Health	9,188	31	1.7
Highways	104,133	358	19.8
Hospitals	0	0	0.0
Housing and Community Development	9,060	31	1.7
Interest on General Debt	4,960	17	0.9
Judicial and Legal	0	0	0.0
Libraries	15,264	52	2.9
Parking	5,511	19	1.0
Parks and Recreation	45,793	157	8.7
Police Protection	53,835	185	10.3
Public Welfare	13,221	45	2.5
Sewerage	33,118	114	6.3
Solid Waste Management	16,020	55	3.1
Veterans' Services	0	0	0.0
Liquor Store	0	0	0.0
Utility	128,478	442	24.5

Source: U.S. Census Bureau, State & Local Government Finances 2022

TAXES

State Corporate Income Tax Rates

State	Tax Rate (%)	Income Brackets ($)	Num. of Brackets	Financial Institution Tax Rate (%)[a]	Federal Income Tax Ded.
Nebraska	3.99 - 5.2	100,000	2	(a)	No

Note: Tax rates for tax year 2024; (a) Rates listed are the corporate income tax rate applied to financial institutions or excise taxes based on income. Some states have other taxes based upon the value of deposits or shares.
Source: Federation of Tax Administrators, State Corporate Income Tax Rates, January 1, 2025

State Individual Income Tax Rates

State	Tax Rate (%)	Income Brackets ($)	Personal Exemptions ($)			Standard Ded. ($)	
			Single	Married	Depend.	Single	Married
Nebraska (a)	2.46 - 5.84 (bb)	2,399 - 29,000 (b)	157	314	157 (c)	7,900	15,800

Note: Tax rates for tax year 2024; Local- and county-level taxes are not included; Federal income tax is not deductible on state income tax returns; (a) 16 states have statutory provision for automatically adjusting to the rate of inflation the dollar values of the income tax brackets, standard deductions, and/or personal exemptions. Oregon does not index the income brackets for $125,000 and over See: INFL and SPEC above; (b) For joint returns, taxes are twice the tax on half the couple's income. California brackets violate this formula at the two highest tax brackets in 2024; (c) The personal exemption takes the form of a tax credit instead of a deduction; (bb) Louisiana lawmakers repealed the state's throwout rule, ending the taxation of so-called "nowhere income." Iowa is phasing-in a flat rate by 2027, while Nebraska (LB 754 signed into law) and South Carolina is phasing-in a reduced top rate by 2027.
Source: Federation of Tax Administrators, State Individual Income Tax Rates, January 1, 2025

Various State Sales and Excise Tax Rates

State	State Sales Tax (%)	Gasoline[1] ($/gal.)	Cigarette[2] ($/pack)	Spirits[3] ($/gal.)	Wine[4] ($/gal.)	Beer[5] ($/gal.)	Recreational Marijuana (%)
Nebraska	5.5	0.31	0.64	3.75	0.95	0.31	Not legal

Note: All tax rates as of January 1, 2025; (1) The American Petroleum Institute has developed a methodology for determining the average tax rate on a gallon of fuel. Rates may include any of the following: excise taxes, environmental fees, storage tank fees, other fees or taxes, general sales tax, and local taxes; (2) The federal excise tax of $1.0066 per pack and local taxes are not included; (3) Rates are those applicable to off-premise sales of 40% alcohol by volume (a.b.v.) distilled spirits in 750ml containers. Local excise taxes are excluded; (4) Rates are those applicable to off-premise sales of 11% a.b.v. non-carbonated wine in 750ml containers; (5) Rates are those applicable to off-premise sales of 4.7% a.b.v. beer in 12 ounce containers.
Source: Tax Foundation, 2025 Facts & Figures: How Does Your State Compare?

State Tax Competitiveness Index

State	Overall Rank	Corporate Tax Rank	Individual Income Tax Rank	Sales Tax Rank	Property Tax Rank	Unemployment Insurance Tax Rank
Nebraska	24	20	26	13	45	3

Note: The Tax Foundation's State Tax Competitiveness Index enables policymakers, taxpayers, and business leaders to gauge how their states' tax systems compare. A rank of 1 is best, 50 is worst. Rankings do not average to the total. States without a tax rank equally as 1. DC's scores and rankings do not affect other states. The report shows tax systems as of July 1, 2024 (the beginning of Fiscal Year 2025).
Source: Tax Foundation, State Tax Competitiveness Index 2025

TRANSPORTATION

Means of Transportation to Work

Area	Car/Truck/Van		Public Transportation			Bicycle	Walked	Other Means	Worked at Home
	Drove Alone	Car-pooled	Bus	Subway	Railroad				
City	75.7	8.6	0.9	0.0	0.0	0.9	3.2	0.8	10.0
MSA[1]	76.3	8.5	0.8	0.0	0.0	0.8	3.0	0.7	9.9
U.S.	70.2	8.5	1.7	1.3	0.4	0.4	2.4	1.6	13.5

Note: Figures are percentages and cover workers 16 years of age and older; (1) Figures cover the Lincoln, NE Metropolitan Statistical Area
Source: U.S. Census Bureau, 2019-2023 American Community Survey 5-Year Estimates

Travel Time to Work

Area	Less Than 10 Minutes	10 to 19 Minutes	20 to 29 Minutes	30 to 44 Minutes	45 to 59 Minutes	60 to 89 Minutes	90 Minutes or More
City	16.8	46.0	22.5	8.9	2.9	2.1	1.0
MSA[1]	17.0	42.8	23.2	10.6	3.2	2.3	1.0
U.S.	12.6	28.6	21.2	20.8	8.1	6.0	2.8

Note: Note: Figures are percentages and include workers 16 years old and over; (1) Figures cover the Lincoln, NE Metropolitan Statistical Area
Source: U.S. Census Bureau, 2019-2023 American Community Survey 5-Year Estimates

Key Congestion Measures

Measure	2000	2010	2015	2020	2022
Annual Hours of Delay, Total (000)	n/a	n/a	4,612	2,054	5,197
Annual Hours of Delay, Per Auto Commuter	n/a	n/a	16	7	17
Annual Congestion Cost, Per Auto Commuter ($)	n/a	n/a	369	171	408

Note: n/a not available
Source: Texas A&M Transportation Institute, 2023 Urban Mobility Report

Freeway Travel Time Index

Measure	1985	1990	1995	2000	2005	2010	2015	2020	2022
Urban Area Index[1]	n/a	n/a	n/a	n/a	n/a	n/a	1.09	1.03	1.09
Urban Area Rank[1,2]	n/a	n/a	n/a	n/a	n/a	n/a	n/a	n/a	n/a

Note: Freeway Travel Time Index—the ratio of travel time in the peak period to the travel time at free-flow conditions. For example, a value of 1.30 indicates a 20-minute free-flow trip takes 26 minutes in the peak (20 minutes x 1.30 = 26 minutes); (1) Covers the Lincoln NE urban area; (2) Rank is based on 101 larger urban areas (#1 = highest travel time index); n/a not available
Source: Texas A&M Transportation Institute, 2023 Urban Mobility Report

Public Transportation

Agency Name / Mode of Transportation	Vehicles Operated in Maximum Service[1]	Annual Unlinked Passenger Trips[2] (in thous.)	Annual Passenger Miles[3] (in thous.)
StarTran			
Bus (directly operated)	54	2,020.2	5,728.3
Demand Response (directly operated)	19	91.9	561.1

Note: (1) Number of revenue vehicles operated by the given mode and type of service to meet the annual maximum service requirement. This is the revenue vehicle count during the peak season of the year; on the week and day that maximum service is provided. Vehicles operated in maximum service (VOMS) exclude atypical days and one-time special events; (2) Number of passengers who boarded public transportation vehicles. Passengers are counted each time they board a vehicle no matter how many vehicles they use to travel from their origin to their destination. (3) Sum of the distances ridden by all passengers during the entire fiscal year.
Source: Federal Transit Administration, National Transit Database, 2023

Air Transportation

Airport Name and Code / Type of Service	Passenger Airlines[1]	Passenger Enplanements	Freight Carriers[2]	Freight (lbs)
Lincoln Municipal (LNK)				
Domestic service (U.S. carriers only)	18	129,832	2	28,926
International service (U.S. carriers only)	0	0	0	0

Note: (1) Includes all U.S.-based major, minor and commuter airlines that carried at least one passenger during the year; (2) Includes all U.S.-based airlines and freight carriers that transported at least one pound of freight during the year.
Source: Bureau of Transportation Statistics, The Intermodal Transportation Database, Air Carriers: T-100 Domestic Market (U.S. carriers only), 2024; Bureau of Transportation Statistics, The Intermodal Transportation Database, Air Carriers: T-100 International Market (U.S. carriers only), 2024

BUSINESSES

Major Business Headquarters

Company Name	Industry	Rankings	
		Fortune[1]	Forbes[2]
No companies listed	-	-	-

Note: (1) Companies that produce a 10-K are ranked 1 to 500 based on 2023 revenue; (2) All private companies with at least $2 billion in annual revenue through the end of their most current fiscal year are ranked 1 to 275; companies listed are headquartered in the city; dashes indicate no ranking
Source: Fortune, "Fortune 500," 2024; Forbes, "America's Largest Private Companies," 2024

Living Environment

COST OF LIVING

Cost of Living Index

Composite Index	Groceries	Housing	Utilities	Transportation	Health Care	Misc. Goods/Services
94.3	99.3	77.6	92.2	99.5	105.4	103.5

Note: The Cost of Living Index measures regional differences in the cost of consumer goods and services, excluding taxes and non-consumer expenditures, for professional and managerial households in the top income quintile. It is based on more than 50,000 prices covering almost 60 different items for which prices are collected three times a year by chambers of commerce, economic development organizations or university applied economic centers in each participating urban area. The numbers shown should be read as a percentage above or below the national average of 100. For example, a value of 115.4 in the groceries column indicates that grocery prices are 15.4% higher than the national average. Small differences in the index numbers should not be interpreted as significant; Figures cover the Lincoln NE urban area.
Source: The Council for Community and Economic Research, Cost of Living Index, 2024

Grocery Prices

Area[1]	T-Bone Steak ($/pound)	Frying Chicken ($/pound)	Whole Milk ($/half gal.)	Eggs ($/dozen)	Orange Juice ($/64 oz.)	Coffee ($/11.5 oz.)
City[2]	15.51	1.44	4.68	3.13	4.43	5.17
Avg.	15.42	1.55	4.69	3.25	4.41	5.46
Min.	14.50	1.16	4.43	2.75	4.00	4.85
Max.	17.56	2.89	5.49	4.78	5.54	7.89

Note: (1) Values for the local area are compared with the average, minimum and maximum values for all 276 areas in the Cost of Living Index; (2) Figures cover the Lincoln NE urban area; **T-Bone Steak** (price per pound); **Frying Chicken** (price per pound, whole fryer); **Whole Milk** (half gallon carton); **Eggs** (price per dozen, Grade A, large); **Orange Juice** (64 oz. Tropicana or Florida Natural); **Coffee** (11.5 oz. can, vacuum-packed, Maxwell House, Hills Bros, or Folgers).
Source: The Council for Community and Economic Research, Cost of Living Index, 2024

Housing and Utility Costs

Area[1]	New Home Price ($)	Apartment Rent ($/month)	All Electric ($/month)	Part Electric ($/month)	Other Energy ($/month)	Telephone ($/month)
City[2]	390,814	1,216	-	90.57	84.28	204.27
Avg.	515,975	1,550	210.99	123.07	82.07	194.99
Min.	265,375	692	104.33	53.68	36.26	179.42
Max.	2,775,821	5,719	529.02	397.28	361.63	223.33

Note: (1) Values for the local area are compared with the average, minimum and maximum values for all 276 areas in the Cost of Living Index; (2) Figures cover the Lincoln NE urban area; **New Home Price** (2,400 sf living area, 8,000 sf lot, in urban area with full utilities); **Apartment Rent** (950 sf 2 bedroom/1.5 or 2 bath, unfurnished, excluding all utilities except water); **All Electric** (average monthly cost for an all-electric home); **Part Electric** (average monthly cost for a part-electric home); **Other Energy** (average monthly cost for natural gas, fuel oil, coal, wood, and any other forms of energy except electricity); **Telephone** (price includes the base monthly rate plus taxes and fees for three lines of mobile phone service).
Source: The Council for Community and Economic Research, Cost of Living Index, 2024

Health Care, Transportation, and Other Costs

Area[1]	Doctor ($/visit)	Dentist ($/visit)	Optometrist ($/visit)	Gasoline ($/gallon)	Beauty Salon ($/visit)	Men's Shirt ($)
City[2]	183.29	113.07	119.17	3.25	42.20	52.31
Avg.	143.77	117.51	129.23	3.32	48.57	38.14
Min.	36.74	58.67	67.33	2.80	24.00	13.41
Max.	270.44	216.82	307.33	5.28	94.00	63.89

Note: (1) Values for the local area are compared with the average, minimum and maximum values for all 276 areas in the Cost of Living Index; (2) Figures cover the Lincoln NE urban area; **Doctor** (general practitioners routine exam of an established patient); **Dentist** (adult teeth cleaning and periodic oral examination); **Optometrist** (full vision eye exam for established adult patient); **Gasoline** (one gallon regular unleaded, national brand, including all taxes, cash price at self-service pump if available); **Beauty Salon** (woman's shampoo, trim, and blow-dry); **Men's Shirt** (cotton/polyester dress shirt, pinpoint weave, long sleeves).
Source: The Council for Community and Economic Research, Cost of Living Index, 2024

HOUSING

Homeownership Rate

Area	2017 (%)	2018 (%)	2019 (%)	2020 (%)	2021 (%)	2022 (%)	2023 (%)	2024 (%)
MSA[1]	n/a	n/a	n/a	n/a	n/a	n/a	n/a	n/a
U.S.	63.9	64.4	64.6	66.6	65.5	65.8	65.9	65.6

Note: (1) Figures cover the Lincoln, NE Metropolitan Statistical Area; n/a not available
Source: U.S. Census Bureau, Housing Vacancies and Homeownership Annual Statistics: 2017-2024

House Price Index (HPI)

Area	National Ranking[2]	Quarterly Change (%)	One-Year Change (%)	Five-Year Change (%)	Since 1991Q1 (%)
MSA[1]	60	0.91	6.97	52.28	300.89
U.S.[3]	—	1.43	4.51	57.13	327.82

Note: The HPI is a weighted repeat sales index. It measures average price changes in repeat sales or refinancings on the same properties. This information is obtained by reviewing repeat mortgage transactions on single-family properties whose mortgages have been purchased or securitized by Fannie Mae or Freddie Mac since January 1975; (1) Figures cover the Lincoln, NE Metropolitan Statistical Area; (2) Rankings are based on annual percentage change for all metro areas containing at least 15,000 transactions over the last 10 years and ranges from 1 to 241; (3) figures based on a weighted average of Census Division estimates using a seasonally adjusted, purchase-only index; all figures are for the period ending December 31, 2024
Source: Federal Housing Finance Agency, Change in FHFA Metropolitan Area House Price Indexes, All Transactions Index, 2024Q4

Home Value

Area	Under $100,000	$100,000 -$199,999	$200,000 -$299,999	$300,000 -$399,999	$400,000 -$499,999	$500,000 -$999,999	$1,000,000 or more	Median ($)
City	5.9	26.1	34.7	18.1	7.5	6.6	1.1	248,200
MSA[1]	5.8	24.3	32.7	18.0	8.9	8.9	1.3	257,500
U.S.	12.1	17.8	19.5	14.4	10.5	19.1	6.5	303,400

Note: Figures are percentages except for median and cover owner-occupied housing units; (1) Figures cover the Lincoln, NE Metropolitan Statistical Area
Source: U.S. Census Bureau, 2019-2023 American Community Survey 5-Year Estimates

Year Housing Structure Built

Area	2020 or Later	2010 -2019	2000 -2009	1990 -1999	1980 -1989	1970 -1979	1960 -1969	1950 -1959	1940 -1949	Before 1940	Median Year
City	1.0	11.9	14.2	13.6	10.1	14.5	8.7	10.3	3.2	12.4	1981
MSA[1]	1.1	11.9	14.3	13.5	9.6	14.7	8.9	9.5	3.2	13.1	1981
U.S.	1.2	8.9	13.6	12.8	13.0	14.4	10.0	9.7	4.5	11.9	1980

Note: Figures are percentages except for Median Year; Note: (1) Figures cover the Lincoln, NE Metropolitan Statistical Area
Source: U.S. Census Bureau, 2019-2023 American Community Survey 5-Year Estimates

Gross Monthly Rent

Area	Under $500	$500 -$999	$1,000 -$1,499	$1,500 -$1,999	$2,000 -$2,499	$2,500 -$2,999	$3,000 and up	Median ($)
City	4.7	41.3	37.3	12.0	3.0	0.5	1.4	1,045
MSA[1]	4.8	41.4	37.2	11.8	2.9	0.5	1.4	1,043
U.S.	6.5	22.3	29.5	20.2	10.8	4.8	5.9	1,348

Note: Figures are percentages except for median; Gross rent is the contract rent plus the estimated average monthly cost of utilities (electricity, gas, and water and sewer) and fuels (oil, coal, kerosene, wood, etc.) if these are paid by the renter (or paid for the renter by someone else); (1) Figures cover the Lincoln, NE Metropolitan Statistical Area
Source: U.S. Census Bureau, 2019-2023 American Community Survey 5-Year Estimates

HEALTH

Health Risk Factors

Category	MSA[1] (%)	U.S. (%)
Adults aged 18–64 who have any kind of health care coverage	90.4	90.8
Adults who reported being in good or better health	85.1	81.8
Adults who have been told they have high blood cholesterol	31.9	36.9
Adults who have been told they have high blood pressure	30.6	34.0
Adults who are current smokers	10.2	12.1
Adults who currently use e-cigarettes	10.0	7.7
Adults who currently use chewing tobacco, snuff, or snus	3.8	3.2
Adults who are heavy drinkers[2]	6.3	6.1
Adults who are binge drinkers[3]	20.0	15.2
Adults who are overweight (BMI 25.0 - 29.9)	33.1	34.4
Adults who are obese (BMI 30.0 - 99.8)	33.6	34.3
Adults who participated in any physical activities in the past month	81.1	75.8

Note: All figures are crude prevalence; (1) Figures cover the Lincoln, NE Metropolitan Statistical Area; (2) Heavy drinkers are classified as adult men having more than 14 drinks per week and adult women having more than 7 drinks per week; (3) Binge drinkers are classified as males having five or more drinks on one occasion or females having four or more drinks on one occasion
Source: Centers for Disease Control and Prevention, Behaviorial Risk Factor Surveillance System, SMART: Selected Metropolitan Area Risk Trends, 2023

Acute and Chronic Health Conditions

Category	MSA[1] (%)	U.S. (%)
Adults who have ever been told they had a heart attack	3.7	4.2
Adults who have ever been told they have angina or coronary heart disease	3.6	4.0
Adults who have ever been told they had a stroke	2.3	3.3
Adults who have ever been told they have asthma	12.6	15.7
Adults who have ever been told they have arthritis	23.0	26.3
Adults who have ever been told they have diabetes[2]	9.7	11.5
Adults who have ever been told they had skin cancer	5.9	5.6
Adults who have ever been told they had any other types of cancer	8.4	8.4
Adults who have ever been told they have COPD	5.4	6.4
Adults who have ever been told they have kidney disease	3.8	3.7
Adults who have ever been told they have a form of depression	20.2	22.0

Note: All figures are crude prevalence; (1) Figures cover the Lincoln, NE Metropolitan Statistical Area; (2) Figures do not include pregnancy-related, borderline, or pre-diabetes
Source: Centers for Disease Control and Prevention, Behaviorial Risk Factor Surveillance System, SMART: Selected Metropolitan Area Risk Trends, 2023

Health Screening and Vaccination Rates

Category	MSA[1] (%)	U.S. (%)
Adults who have ever been tested for HIV	26.1	37.5
Adults who have had their blood cholesterol checked within the last five years	85.2	87.0
Adults aged 65+ who have had flu shot within the past year	67.7	63.4
Adults aged 65+ who have ever had a pneumonia vaccination	77.7	71.9

Note: All figures are crude prevalence; (1) Figures cover the Lincoln, NE Metropolitan Statistical Area.
Source: Centers for Disease Control and Prevention, Behaviorial Risk Factor Surveillance System, SMART: Selected Metropolitan Area Risk Trends, 2023

Disability Status

Category	MSA[1] (%)	U.S. (%)
Adults who reported being deaf	6.8	7.4
Are you blind or have serious difficulty seeing, even when wearing glasses?	2.2	4.9
Do you have difficulty doing errands alone?	7.8	7.8
Do you have difficulty dressing or bathing?	2.6	3.6
Do you have serious difficulty concentrating/remembering/making decisions?	11.1	13.7
Do you have serious difficulty walking or climbing stairs?	10.8	13.2

Note: All figures are crude prevalence; (1) Figures cover the Lincoln, NE Metropolitan Statistical Area.
Source: Centers for Disease Control and Prevention, Behaviorial Risk Factor Surveillance System, SMART: Selected Metropolitan Area Risk Trends, 2023

Mortality Rates for the Top 10 Causes of Death in the U.S.

ICD-10[a] Sub-Chapter	ICD-10[a] Code	Crude Mortality Rate[2] per 100,000 population	
		County[3]	U.S.
Malignant neoplasms	C00-C97	159.8	182.7
Ischaemic heart diseases	I20-I25	67.5	109.6
Provisional assignment of new diseases of uncertain etiology[1]	U00-U49	31.7	65.3
Other forms of heart disease	I30-I51	58.0	65.1
Other degenerative diseases of the nervous system	G30-G31	65.9	52.4
Other external causes of accidental injury	W00-X59	25.1	52.3
Cerebrovascular diseases	I60-I69	40.9	49.1
Chronic lower respiratory diseases	J40-J47	40.5	43.5
Hypertensive diseases	I10-I15	46.0	38.9
Organic, including symptomatic, mental disorders	F01-F09	21.1	33.9

Note: (a) ICD-10 = International Classification of Diseases 10th Revision; (1) Includes COVID-19, adverse effects to COVID-19 vaccines, SARS, and vaping-related disorders; (2) Crude mortality rates are a three-year average covering 2021-2023; (3) Figures cover Lancaster County.
Source: Centers for Disease Control and Prevention, National Center for Health Statistics. National Vital Statistics System, Mortality 2018-2023 on CDC WONDER Online Database

Mortality Rates for Selected Causes of Death

Cause of Death	ICD-10[a] Code	Crude Mortality Rate[1] per 100,000 population	
		County[2]	U.S.
Accidental poisoning and exposure to noxious substances	X40-X49	11.0	30.5
Alzheimer disease	G30	30.3	35.4
Assault	X85-Y09	3.1	7.3
COVID-19	U07.1	31.7	65.3
Diabetes mellitus	E10-E14	21.3	30.0
Diseases of the liver	K70-K76	16.2	20.8
Human immunodeficiency virus (HIV) disease	B20-B24	Suppressed	1.5
Influenza and pneumonia	J09-J18	9.0	13.4
Intentional self-harm	X60-X84	14.3	14.7
Malnutrition	E40-E46	10.0	6.0
Obesity and other hyperalimentation	E65-E68	2.5	3.1
Renal failure	N17-N19	9.1	16.4
Transport accidents	V01-V99	9.1	14.4

Note: (a) ICD-10 = International Classification of Diseases 10th Revision; (1) Crude mortality rates are a three-year average covering 2021-2023; (2) Figures cover Lancaster County; Data are suppressed when the data meet the criteria for confidentiality constraints; Crude mortality rates are flagged as unreliable when the rate would be calculated with a numerator of 20 or less.
Source: Centers for Disease Control and Prevention, National Center for Health Statistics. National Vital Statistics System, Mortality 2018-2023 on CDC WONDER Online Database

Health Insurance Coverage

Area	With Health Insurance	With Private Health Insurance	With Public Health Insurance	Without Health Insurance	Population Under Age 19 Without Health Insurance
City	93.3	76.3	28.6	6.7	3.9
MSA[1]	93.7	77.6	28.1	6.3	3.8
U.S.	91.4	67.3	36.3	8.6	5.4

Note: Figures are percentages that cover the civilian noninstitutionalized population; (1) Figures cover the Lincoln, NE Metropolitan Statistical Area
Source: U.S. Census Bureau, 2019-2023 American Community Survey 5-Year Estimates

Number of Medical Professionals

Area	MDs[3]	DOs[3,4]	Dentists	Podiatrists	Chiropractors	Optometrists
County[1] (number)	701	55	356	18	163	67
County[1] (rate[2])	215.9	16.9	109.0	5.5	49.9	20.5
U.S. (rate[2])	302.5	29.2	74.6	6.4	29.5	18.0

Note: Data as of 2023 unless noted; (1) Data covers Lancaster County; (2) Number of medical professionals per 100,000 population; (3) Data as of 2022 and includes all active, non-federal physicians; (4) Doctor of Osteopathic Medicine
Source: U.S. Department of Health and Human Services, Health Resources and Services Administration, Bureau of Health Professions, Area Resource File (ARF) 2023-2024

EDUCATION

Public School District Statistics

District Name	Schls	Pupils	Pupil/ Teacher Ratio	Minority Pupils[1] (%)	Total Rev. per Pupil ($)	Total Exp. per Pupil ($)
Lincoln Public Schools	78	41,654	13.6	38.5	14,706	14,943

Note: Table includes school districts with 2,000 or more students; (1) Percentage of students that are not non-Hispanic white.
Source: U.S. Department of Education, National Center for Education Statistics, Common Core of Data, Local Education Agency (School District) Universe Survey: School Year 2023-2024; U.S. Department of Education, National Center for Education Statistics, Common Core of Data, School District Finance Survey (F-33): School Year 2021–22

Highest Level of Education

Area	Less than H.S.	H.S. Diploma	Some College, No Deg.	Associate Degree	Bachelor's Degree	Master's Degree	Prof. School Degree	Doctorate Degree
City	7.0	20.4	20.3	11.4	26.4	9.8	2.3	2.5
MSA[1]	6.4	20.9	20.1	11.9	26.2	9.8	2.1	2.4
U.S.	10.6	26.2	19.4	8.8	21.3	9.8	2.3	1.6

Note: Figures cover persons age 25 and over; (1) Figures cover the Lincoln, NE Metropolitan Statistical Area
Source: U.S. Census Bureau, 2019-2023 American Community Survey 5-Year Estimates

Educational Attainment by Race

Area	High School Graduate or Higher (%)					Bachelor's Degree or Higher (%)				
	Total	White	Black	Asian	Hisp.[2]	Total	White	Black	Asian	Hisp.[2]
City	93.0	95.2	86.6	81.2	70.7	41.0	42.7	25.0	43.3	21.1
MSA[1]	93.6	95.4	86.4	81.1	71.1	40.6	42.0	24.8	43.2	20.9
U.S.	89.4	92.9	88.1	88.0	72.5	35.0	37.7	24.7	57.0	19.9

Note: Figures shown cover persons 25 years old and over; (1) Figures cover the Lincoln, NE Metropolitan Statistical Area; (2) People of Hispanic origin can be of any race
Source: U.S. Census Bureau, 2019-2023 American Community Survey 5-Year Estimates

School Enrollment by Grade and Control

Area	Preschool (%)		Kindergarten (%)		Grades 1 - 4 (%)		Grades 5 - 8 (%)		Grades 9 - 12 (%)	
	Public	Private	Public	Private	Public	Private	Public	Private	Public	Private
City	53.4	46.6	79.0	21.0	82.6	17.4	84.2	15.8	90.3	9.7
MSA[1]	54.3	45.7	79.6	20.4	81.9	18.1	84.4	15.6	90.5	9.5
U.S.	58.7	41.3	85.2	14.8	87.2	12.8	87.9	12.1	89.0	11.0

Note: Figures shown cover persons 3 years old and over; (1) Figures cover the Lincoln, NE Metropolitan Statistical Area
Source: U.S. Census Bureau, 2019-2023 American Community Survey 5-Year Estimates

Higher Education

Four-Year Colleges			Two-Year Colleges			Medical Schools[1]	Law Schools[2]	Voc/Tech[3]
Public	Private Non-profit	Private For-profit	Public	Private Non-profit	Private For-profit			
1	4	0	1	0	5	0	1	0

Note: Figures cover institutions located within the Lincoln, NE Metropolitan Statistical Area and include main campuses only; (1) includes schools accredited by the Liaison Committee on Medical Education and the American Osteopathic Association's Commission on Osteopathic College Accreditation; (2) includes ABA-accredited schools, schools with provisional ABA accreditation, and state accredited schools; (3) includes all schools with programs that are less than 2 years.
Source: National Center for Education Statistics, Integrated Postsecondary Education System (IPEDS), 2023-24; Wikipedia, List of Medical Schools in the United States, accessed May 2, 2025; Wikipedia, List of Law Schools in the United States, accessed May 2, 2025

According to *U.S. News & World Report,* the Lincoln, NE metro area is home to one of the top 200 national universities in the U.S.: **University of Nebraska — Lincoln** (#152 tie). The indicators used to capture academic quality fall into a number of categories: assessment by administrators at peer institutions; retention of students; faculty resources; student selectivity; financial resources; alumni giving; high school counselor ratings of colleges; and graduation rate. *U.S. News & World Report, "America's Best Colleges 2025"*

According to *U.S. News & World Report,* the Lincoln, NE metro area is home to one of the top 100 law schools in the U.S.: **University of Nebraska—Lincoln** (#71 tie). The rankings are based on a weighted average of 12 measures of quality: peer assessment score; assessment score by lawyers/judges; median LSAT scores; median undergrad GPA; acceptance rate; employment rates for graduates; placement success; bar passage rate; faculty resources; expenditures per student; student/faculty ratio; and library resources. *U.S. News & World Report, "America's Best Graduate Schools, Law, 2025"*

EMPLOYERS

Major Employers

Company Name	Industry
Bank of the West	Financial services
Cargill Meat Solutions	Food processing
CHI Health Bergan Mercy	Healthcare
CHI Health Saint Elizabeth	Healthcare
Con Agra Foods Inc	Food manufacturing
Creighton University	Education
First Data	Commerce
Health & Human Svc Dept	Government
JBS USA	Food processing
Methodist Hospital	Healthcare
Mutual of Omaha Insurance Co	Insurance
Nebraska Medical Center	Healthcare
Nebraska Medicine	Healthcare
Offutt AFB	U.S. military
PayPal	Payment services
Smithfield Farmland	Agriculture
Tyson Fresh Meats	Food processing
Union Pacific Railroad Co	Railroad
University of NE Medical Ctr	Healthcare
University of Nebraska	Education

Note: Companies shown are located within the Lincoln, NE Metropolitan Statistical Area.
Source: Chambers of Commerce; State Departments of Labor; Wikipedia

PUBLIC SAFETY

Crime Rate

Area	Total Crime Rate	Violent Crime Rate				Property Crime Rate		
		Murder	Rape	Robbery	Aggrav. Assault	Burglary	Larceny-Theft	Motor Vehicle Theft
City	3,052.3	2.4	90.4	52.9	220.4	252.4	2,106.4	327.5
U.S.	2,290.9	5.7	38.0	66.5	264.1	250.7	1,347.2	318.7

Note: Figures are crimes per 100,000 population.
Source: FBI, Table 8, Offenses Known to Law Enforcement, by State by City, 2023

Hate Crimes

Area	Number of Quarters Reported	Number of Incidents per Bias Motivation					
		Race/Ethnicity/Ancestry	Religion	Sexual Orientation	Disability	Gender	Gender Identity
City[1]	4	5	1	2	0	0	1
U.S.	4	5,900	2,699	2,077	187	92	492

Note: (1) Figures include at least one incident reported with more than one bias motivation.
Source: Federal Bureau of Investigation, Hate Crime Statistics 2023

Identity Theft Consumer Reports

Area	Reports	Reports per 100,000 Population	Rank[2]
MSA[1]	423	124	324
U.S.	1,135,291	339	-

Note: (1) Figures cover the Lincoln, NE Metropolitan Statistical Area; (2) Rank ranges from 1 to 401 where 1 indicates greatest number of identity theft reports per 100,000 population
Source: Federal Trade Commission, Consumer Sentinel Network Data Book 2024

Fraud and Other Consumer Reports

Area	Reports	Reports per 100,000 Population	Rank[2]
MSA[1]	2,743	804	319
U.S.	5,360,641	1,601	-

Note: (1) Figures cover the Lincoln, NE Metropolitan Statistical Area; (2) Rank ranges from 1 to 401 where 1 indicates greatest number of fraud and other consumer reports per 100,000 population
Source: Federal Trade Commission, Consumer Sentinel Network Data Book 2024

POLITICS

2024 Presidential Election Results

Area	Trump (Rep.)	Harris (Dem.)	Stein (Green)	Kennedy (Ind.)	Oliver (Lib.)	Other
Lancaster County	46.8	51.0	0.4	0.0	0.8	1.1
U.S.	49.7	48.2	0.6	0.5	0.4	0.6

Note: Results are percentages and may not add to 100% due to rounding
Source: Dave Leip's Atlas of U.S. Presidential Elections

SPORTS

Professional Sports Teams

Team Name	League	Year Established
No teams are located in the metro area		

Source: Wikipedia, Major Professional Sports Teams of the United States and Canada, May 1, 2025

CLIMATE

Average and Extreme Temperatures

Temperature	Jan	Feb	Mar	Apr	May	Jun	Jul	Aug	Sep	Oct	Nov	Dec	Yr.
Extreme High (°F)	73	77	89	97	99	107	108	107	101	93	82	69	108
Average High (°F)	33	38	50	64	74	85	89	86	78	66	49	36	62
Average Temp. (°F)	22	28	39	52	62	73	78	75	66	53	38	26	51
Average Low (°F)	11	16	27	39	50	60	66	64	53	40	27	16	39
Extreme Low (°F)	-33	-24	-19	3	24	39	45	39	26	11	-5	-27	-33

Note: Figures cover the years 1948-1995
Source: National Climatic Data Center, International Station Meteorological Climate Summary, 9/96

Average Precipitation/Snowfall/Humidity

Precip./Humidity	Jan	Feb	Mar	Apr	May	Jun	Jul	Aug	Sep	Oct	Nov	Dec	Yr.
Avg. Precip. (in.)	0.8	0.8	2.4	2.9	4.1	3.7	3.7	3.4	3.1	1.9	1.4	0.9	29.1
Avg. Snowfall (in.)	6	5	6	1	Tr	0	0	0	Tr	Tr	3	6	27
Avg. Rel. Hum. 6am (%)	78	81	81	80	83	83	83	86	84	80	80	80	82
Avg. Rel. Hum. 3pm (%)	61	60	55	47	51	49	48	51	49	46	54	60	53

Note: Figures cover the years 1948-1995; Tr = Trace amounts (<0.05 in. of rain; <0.5 in. of snow)
Source: National Climatic Data Center, International Station Meteorological Climate Summary, 9/96

Weather Conditions

Temperature			Daytime Sky			Precipitation		
5°F & below	32°F & below	90°F & above	Clear	Partly cloudy	Cloudy	0.01 inch or more precip.	0.1 inch or more snow/ice	Thunder-storms
25	145	40	108	135	122	94	19	46

Note: Figures are average number of days per year and cover the years 1948-1995
Source: National Climatic Data Center, International Station Meteorological Climate Summary, 9/96

HAZARDOUS WASTE

Superfund Sites

The Lincoln, NE metro area has no sites on the EPA's Superfund Final National Priorities List (NPL) or Superfund Alternative Approach (SAA) list. The Superfund alternative approach uses the same investigation and cleanup process and standards that are used for sites listed on the National Priorities List. The SAA is an alternative to listing a site on the NPL; it is not an alternative to Superfund or the Superfund process. There are a total of 1,445 Superfund sites with a status of proposed or final on both lists in the United States. *U.S. Environmental Protection Agency, National Priorities List, May 1, 2025; U.S. Environmental Protection Agency, Superfund Alternative Approach Sites, May 1, 2025*

AIR QUALITY

Air Quality Trends: Ozone

	1990	1995	2000	2005	2010	2015	2020	2021	2022	2023
MSA[1]	0.057	0.060	0.057	0.056	0.050	0.061	0.054	0.059	0.055	0.068
U.S.	0.087	0.089	0.081	0.080	0.072	0.068	0.066	0.067	0.067	0.070

Note: (1) Data covers the Lincoln, NE Metropolitan Statistical Area. The values shown are the composite ozone concentration averages among trend sites based on the highest fourth daily maximum 8-hour concentration in parts per million. These trends are based on sites having an adequate record of monitoring data during the trend period. Data from exceptional events are included.
Source: U.S. Environmental Protection Agency, Air Quality Monitoring Information, "Air Quality Trends by City, 1990-2023"

Air Quality Index

Area	Percent of Days when Air Quality was...[2]					AQI Statistics[2]	
	Good	Moderate	Unhealthy for Sensitive Groups	Unhealthy	Very Unhealthy	Maximum	Median
MSA[1]	69.6	29.3	0.7	0.4	0.0	160	42

Note: (1) Data covers the Lincoln, NE Metropolitan Statistical Area; (2) Based on 283 days with AQI data in 2023. Air Quality Index (AQI) is an index for reporting daily air quality. EPA calculates the AQI for five major air pollutants regulated by the Clean Air Act: ground-level ozone, particle pollution (aka particulate matter), carbon monoxide, sulfur dioxide, and nitrogen dioxide. The AQI runs from 0 to 500. The higher the AQI value, the greater the level of air pollution and the greater the health concern. There are six AQI categories: "Good" AQI is between 0 and 50. Air quality is considered satisfactory; "Moderate" AQI is between 51 and 100. Air quality is acceptable; "Unhealthy for Sensitive Groups" When AQI values are between 101 and 150, members of sensitive groups may experience health effects; "Unhealthy" When AQI values are between 151 and 200 everyone may begin to experience health effects; "Very Unhealthy" AQI values between 201 and 300 trigger a health alert; "Hazardous" AQI values over 300 trigger warnings of emergency conditions (not shown).
Source: U.S. Environmental Protection Agency, Air Quality Index Report, 2023

Air Quality Index Pollutants

Area	Percent of Days when AQI Pollutant was...[2]					
	Carbon Monoxide	Nitrogen Dioxide	Ozone	Sulfur Dioxide	Particulate Matter 2.5	Particulate Matter 10
MSA[1]	0.0	0.0	74.9	(3)	25.1	0.0

Note: (1) Data covers the Lincoln, NE Metropolitan Statistical Area; (2) Based on 283 days with AQI data in 2023. The Air Quality Index (AQI) is an index for reporting daily air quality. EPA calculates the AQI for five major air pollutants regulated by the Clean Air Act: ground-level ozone, particle pollution (also known as particulate matter), carbon monoxide, sulfur dioxide, and nitrogen dioxide. The AQI runs from 0 to 500. The higher the AQI value, the greater the level of air pollution and the greater the health concern; (3) Sulfur dioxide is no longer included in this table because SO_2 concentrations tend to be very localized and not necessarily representative of broad geographical areas like counties and CBSAs.
Source: U.S. Environmental Protection Agency, Air Quality Index Report, 2023

Maximum Air Pollutant Concentrations: Particulate Matter, Ozone, CO and Lead

	Particulate Matter 10 (ug/m^3)	Particulate Matter 2.5 Wtd AM (ug/m^3)	Particulate Matter 2.5 24-Hr (ug/m^3)	Ozone (ppm)	Carbon Monoxide (ppm)	Lead (ug/m^3)
MSA[1] Level	n/a	n/a	n/a	0.068	n/a	n/a
NAAQS[2]	150	15	35	0.075	9	0.15
Met NAAQS[2]	n/a	n/a	n/a	Yes	n/a	n/a

Note: (1) Data covers the Lincoln, NE Metropolitan Statistical Area; Data from exceptional events are included; (2) National Ambient Air Quality Standards; ppm = parts per million; ug/m^3 = micrograms per cubic meter; n/a not available.
Concentrations: Particulate Matter 10 (coarse particulate)—highest second maximum 24-hour concentration; Particulate Matter 2.5 Wtd AM (fine particulate)—highest weighted annual mean concentration; Particulate Matter 2.5 24-Hour (fine particulate)—highest 98th percentile 24-hour concentration; Ozone—highest fourth daily maximum 8-hour concentration; Carbon Monoxide—highest second maximum non-overlapping 8-hour concentration; Lead—maximum running 3-month average
Source: U.S. Environmental Protection Agency, Air Quality Monitoring Information, "Air Quality Statistics by City, 2023"

Maximum Air Pollutant Concentrations: Nitrogen Dioxide and Sulfur Dioxide

	Nitrogen Dioxide AM (ppb)	Nitrogen Dioxide 1-Hr (ppb)	Sulfur Dioxide AM (ppb)	Sulfur Dioxide 1-Hr (ppb)	Sulfur Dioxide 24-Hr (ppb)
MSA[1] Level	n/a	n/a	n/a	n/a	n/a
NAAQS[2]	53	100	30	75	140
Met NAAQS[2]	n/a	n/a	n/a	n/a	n/a

Note: (1) Data covers the Lincoln, NE Metropolitan Statistical Area; Data from exceptional events are included; (2) National Ambient Air Quality Standards; ppm = parts per million; ug/m^3 = micrograms per cubic meter; n/a not available.
Concentrations: Nitrogen Dioxide AM—highest arithmetic mean concentration; Nitrogen Dioxide 1-Hr—highest 98th percentile 1-hour daily maximum concentration; Sulfur Dioxide AM—highest annual mean concentration; Sulfur Dioxide 1-Hr—highest 99th percentile 1-hour daily maximum concentration; Sulfur Dioxide 24-Hr—highest second maximum 24-hour concentration
Source: U.S. Environmental Protection Agency, Air Quality Monitoring Information, "Air Quality Statistics by City, 2023"

Little Rock, Arkansas

Background

Little Rock is the capital of Arkansas and the most populous city in the state. It is located along the banks of the Arkansas River and marks the point where the flat Mississippi Delta ends and the foothills of the Quachita Mountains begin. The city is best known for its place in the history of the United States Civil Rights Movement and for its connection to former President William Jefferson Clinton, who served as the Governor of Arkansas before being elected our forty-second President.

The area that is now Little Rock was originally inhabited by Native American tribes including the Quapaw, Choctaw, and Cherokee, but the first Europeans in the area were Spanish, who passed through in the mid-sixteenth century. The city got its name from a rock formation on the southern side of the Arkansas River that was a landmark for river crossings. When French explorer Jean-Baptiste Benard de la Harpe arrived in the area in 1722, he called the area *Le petite roche*, or "the little rock," and the nickname stuck. La Harpe built a trading post on the site, but it would be more than 100 years before the city officially incorporated in 1831. When Arkansas became the 25th American state in 1836, Little Rock was chosen as its capital.

Initially the city grew quickly, but many projects, including the railroad between Little Rock and Memphis, were put on hold during the Civil War. Post-war reconstruction brought a wealth of new development and by the turn of the century, its transformation from a small, sleepy frontier town to a thriving, modern city was complete. After the Great Depression ended in the early 1930s, residents began to move out to the suburbs and new roads were built to accommodate the city's changing layout.

In 1957 the city was thrown into the national spotlight with Little Rock Nine—nine African American students who enrolled in the all-white Central High School, claiming it was their right, based on the U.S. Supreme Court's ruling on *Brown v. Board of Education*. Governor Orval Faubus sent the National Guard to prevent the students from entering the school, but they were eventually admitted under the protection of the U.S. Army sent by President Eisenhower.

Little Rock was brought to national prominence again in 1992 when Governor Bill Clinton started his presidential election campaign, and again when he gave his election-night acceptance speech from the steps of the Old State House in downtown Little Rock. Clinton has since solidified his link to the city through the William J. Clinton Presidential Center and Park.

Today, the city has a diverse economy built upon manufacturing, education, healthcare, and commercial trade. Many major corporations have headquarters in the city. The Little Rock Port is part of a comprehensive industrial business zone on the Arkansas River. In 2016, Little Rock joined "What Works Cities," a national initiative to help American cities enhance their use of data, improve services, and engage residents. In 2021, the city received the organization's silver certification, based on data governance, open data and results-driven contracting.

The Pulaski County Pedestrian and Bicycle Bridge, at 3,463 feet, is the world's longest bridge for pedestrians and bicyclists only. Prominent charitable organization Heifer International has its world headquarters in Little Rock. The area's Dickey-Stephens Park, a 7,000-seat baseball park, is home to minor league team Arkansas Travelers.

Attractions in Little Rock include the MacArthur Museum of Arkansas Military History, the Arkansas Museum of Discovery, and the Old State House Museum. In addition, the William J. Clinton Presidential Center and Park houses the Clinton Presidential Library and the headquarters of the Clinton Foundation. A section of downtown's Main Street, called Creative Corridor, combines the arts, entertainment, business, and culture, and is home to the Arkansas Repertory Theatre, Arkansas Symphony Orchestra, and Ballet Arkansas. Other cultural attractions in Little Rock include the Arkansas Arts Center, the Robinson Center Music Hall, and Wildwood Center for the Performing Arts. The city's major institutions of higher learning are the University of Arkansas at Little Rock and the University of Arkansas for Medical Sciences.

Little Rock has a humid subtropical climate, typical of the southern United States. Summers are generally hot, while winters are cooler; high humidity persists all year round. Rainfall can be heavy at times during the spring and fall but the city rarely receives any snow. A deadly tornado touched down 10 miles west of the city in 2014, when powerful storms killed 16 people in three states. In April of 2017, a deadly flood devastated the city.

Rankings

General Rankings

- In their annual survey, Livability.com looked at data for more than 2,000 mid-sized U.S. cities to assign a "Livability Score" for each. The top 100 scoring cities make up Livability's "Top 100 Best Places to Live in the U.S." in 2025. Little Rock was placed among the top 100 of the customizable list. Criteria: housing and economy; cost of living; environment; education; health care options; transportation; safety; and community amenities. *Livability.com, "Top 100 Best Places to Live in the U.S. in 2025" April 15, 2025*

Business/Finance Rankings

- The Little Rock metro area appeared on the Milken Institute "2025 Best Performing Cities" list. Rank: #77 out of 200 large metro areas (based on performance category). Criteria: job growth; wage growth; high-tech growth and impact; community resilience; housing affordability; household broadband access. *Milken Institute, "Best-Performing Cities 2025," January 14, 2025*

Education Rankings

- Personal finance website *WalletHub* analyzed the 150 largest U.S. metropolitan statistical areas to determine where the most educated Americans are putting their degrees to work. Criteria: education levels; percentage of workers with degrees; education quality and attainment gap; public school quality rankings; quality and enrollment of each metro area's universities. Little Rock was ranked #75 (#1 = most educated city). *WalletHub.com, "Most & Least Educated Cities in America, 2025" July 2, 2024*

Environmental Rankings

- Little Rock was highlighted as one of the top 22 cleanest metro areas for short-term particle pollution (24-hour PM 2.5) in the U.S. during 2021 through 2023. Monitors in these cities reported no days with unhealthful PM 2.5 levels. *American Lung Association, "State of the Air 2025," April 23, 2025*

Health/Fitness Rankings

- Little Rock was identified as a "2025 Allergy Capital." The area ranked #6 out of the nation's 100 largest metropolitan areas. Three groups of factors were used to identify the most challenging cities for people with allergies: annual tree, grass, and weed pollen scores; over the counter allergy medicine use; number of board-certified allergy specialists. *Asthma and Allergy Foundation of America, "2025 Allergy Capitals: The Most Challenging Places to Live with Allergies," March 18, 2025*

- Little Rock was identified as a "2024 Asthma Capital." The area ranked #94 out of the nation's 100 largest metropolitan areas. Criteria: estimated asthma prevalence; asthma-related mortality; and ER visits due to asthma. Risk factors analyzed but not factored in the rankings: annual air quality including pollution and ozone levels; public smoking laws; indoor air quality; access to asthma specialists; rescue and controller medication use; uninsured rate; pollen allergy; poverty rate. *Asthma and Allergy Foundation of America, "Asthma Capitals 2024: The Most Challenging Places to Live With Asthma," September 10, 2024*

Real Estate Rankings

- *WalletHub* compared the most populated U.S. cities to determine which had the best markets for real estate agents. Little Rock ranked #119 where demand was high and pay was the best. Criteria: sales per agent; annual median wage for real-estate agents; monthly average starting salary for real estate agents; real estate job density and competition; unemployment rate; home turnover rate; housing-market health index; and other relevant metrics. *WalletHub.com, "2021 Best Places to Be a Real Estate Agent," May 12, 2021*

- The Little Rock metro area was identified as one of the top 16 housing markets to invest in for 2025 by *Forbes*. Criteria: stable local economies with good population growth and increase in jobs providing good support for home prices and rents. *Forbes.com, "Best Local Markets For Real Estate Investing In 2025," November 6, 2024*

- Little Rock was ranked #16 out of 176 metro areas in terms of cost of housing in 2024 by the National Association of Home Builders (#1 = most affordable). Criteria: the portion of an average family's income necessary to pay the mortgage on a median-priced home. *National Association of Home Builders®, NAHB-Wells Fargo Cost of Housing Index, 4th Quarter 2024*

Safety Rankings

- To identify the most dangerous cities in America, *24/7 Wall St.* focused on violent crime categories—murder, non-negligent manslaughter, rape, robbery, and aggravated assault—as reported for every 100,000 residents using data from the FBI's 2020 annual Uniform Crime Report. For cities with populations over 25,000, Little Rock was ranked #6. *247wallst.com, "America's Most Dangerous Cities" November 12, 2021*

- Statistics drawn from the FBI's Uniform Crime Report were used to rank the cities where violent crime rose the most year over year from 2019 to 2020. Only cities with 25,000 or more residents were included. *24/7 Wall St.* found that Little Rock placed #7 of those with a notable surge in incidents of violent crime. *247wallst.com, "American Cities Where Crime Is Soaring," March 4, 2022*

- Allstate ranked the 100 most populous cities in America in terms of driver safety. Little Rock ranked #47. Criteria based on anonymized driving behavior data from Allstate's mobile app powered by Arity: high speed driving (over 80 mph), phone handling, and hard braking. The report helps increase the importance of safety and awareness behind the wheel. *Allstate, "16th Allstate America's Best Drivers Report®" July 11, 2024*

- Little Rock was identified as one of the most dangerous cities in America by NeighborhoodScout. The city ranked #9 out of 100 (#1 = most dangerous). Criteria: number of violent crimes per 1,000 residents. The editors evaluated cities with 25,000 or more residents. *NeighborhoodScout.com, "2023 Top 100 Most Dangerous Cities in the U.S.," January 12, 2023*

Women/Minorities Rankings

- Personal finance website *WalletHub* compared more than 180 U.S. cities across two key dimensions, "Hispanic Business-Friendliness" and "Hispanic Purchasing Power," to arrive at the most favorable conditions for Hispanic entrepreneurs. Little Rock was ranked #115 out of 182. Criteria includes: share of Hispanic-Owned Businesses; average growth of Hispanic Business revenues; Small Business-Friendliness score; affordability; and number of Hispanics with at least a bachelor's degree. *WalletHub.com, "Best Cities for Hispanic Entrepreneurs," September 4, 2024*

Miscellaneous Rankings

- *WalletHub* compared 148 of the most populated U.S. cities to determine their operating efficiency. A "Quality of Services" score was constructed for each city and then measured against the total budget per capita to reveal which were managed the best. Little Rock ranked #52. Criteria: financial stability; economy; education; safety; health; infrastructure and pollution. *WalletHub.com, "2025's Best- & Worst-Run Cities in America," June 18, 2024*

Business Environment

DEMOGRAPHICS

Population Growth

Area	1990 Census	2000 Census	2010 Census	2020 Census	2023 Estimate[2]	Population Growth 1990-2023 (%)
City	177,519	183,133	193,524	202,591	202,739	14.2
MSA[1]	535,034	610,518	699,757	748,031	753,605	40.9
U.S.	248,709,873	281,421,906	308,745,538	331,449,281	332,387,540	33.6

Note: (1) Figures cover the Little Rock-North Little Rock-Conway, AR Metropolitan Statistical Area; (2) 2019-2023 5-year ACS population estimate
Source: U.S. Census Bureau, 1990 Census, 2000 Census, 2010 Census, 2020 Census, 2019-2023 American Community Survey 5-Year Estimates

Race

Area	White Alone[2] (%)	Black Alone[2] (%)	Asian Alone[2] (%)	AIAN[3] Alone[2] (%)	NHOPI[4] Alone[2] (%)	Other Race Alone[2] (%)	Two or More Races (%)
City	46.3	39.4	3.0	0.3	0.1	4.2	6.6
MSA[1]	65.9	23.5	1.6	0.3	0.0	2.8	5.8
U.S.	63.4	12.4	5.8	0.9	0.2	6.6	10.7

Note: (1) Figures cover the Little Rock-North Little Rock-Conway, AR Metropolitan Statistical Area; (2) Alone is defined as not being in combination with one or more other races; (3) American Indian and Alaska Native; (4) Native Hawaiian and Other Pacific Islander
Source: U.S. Census Bureau, 2019-2023 American Community Survey 5-Year Estimates

Hispanic or Latino Origin

Area	Total (%)	Mexican (%)	Puerto Rican (%)	Cuban (%)	Other (%)
City	10.4	6.8	0.2	0.1	3.3
MSA[1]	7.1	4.6	0.3	0.1	2.1
U.S.	19.0	11.3	1.8	0.7	5.2

Note: Persons of Hispanic or Latino origin can be of any race; (1) Figures cover the Little Rock-North Little Rock-Conway, AR Metropolitan Statistical Area
Source: U.S. Census Bureau, 2019-2023 American Community Survey 5-Year Estimates

Age

Area	Percent of Population									Median Age
	Under Age 5	Age 5–19	Age 20–34	Age 35–44	Age 45–54	Age 55–64	Age 65–74	Age 75–84	Age 85+	
City	6.7	19.9	21.8	13.4	12.1	11.0	9.2	4.0	2.0	36.4
MSA[1]	6.1	19.8	20.8	13.3	11.9	12.2	9.7	4.6	1.7	37.4
U.S.	5.7	19.1	20.2	13.1	12.3	12.8	10.0	4.9	1.9	38.7

Note: (1) Figures cover the Little Rock-North Little Rock-Conway, AR Metropolitan Statistical Area
Source: U.S. Census Bureau, 2019-2023 American Community Survey 5-Year Estimates

Disability by Age

Area	All Ages	Under 18 Years Old	18 to 64 Years Old	65 Years and Over
City	13.9	6.8	12.0	33.8
MSA[1]	15.5	5.7	13.6	37.4
U.S.	13.0	4.7	10.7	32.9

Note: Figures show percent of the civilian noninstitutionalized population that reported having a disability. Disability status is determined from six types of difficulty: vision, hearing, cognitive, ambulatory, self-care, and independent living. For children under 5 years old, hearing and vision difficulty are used to determine disability status. For children between the ages of 5 and 14, disability status is determined from hearing, vision, cognitive, ambulatory, and self-care difficulties. For people aged 15 years and older, they are considered to have a disability if they have difficulty with any one of the six difficulty types; Note: (1) Figures cover the Little Rock-North Little Rock-Conway, AR Metropolitan Statistical Area
Source: U.S. Census Bureau, 2019-2023 American Community Survey 5-Year Estimates

Ancestry

Area	German	Irish	English	American	Italian	Polish	French[2]	European	Scottish
City	7.5	6.5	10.4	4.6	1.2	0.7	1.3	1.7	1.7
MSA[1]	8.5	8.4	11.7	6.6	1.4	0.8	1.4	1.6	1.8
U.S.	12.6	9.4	9.1	5.5	4.9	2.6	2.0	1.6	1.6

Note: Figures are the percentage of the total population reporting a particular ancestry. The nine most commonly reported ancestries in the U.S. are shown. Figures include multiple ancestries (e.g. if a person reported being Irish and Italian, they were included in both columns); (1) Figures cover the Little Rock-North Little Rock-Conway, AR Metropolitan Statistical Area; (2) Excludes Basque
Source: U.S. Census Bureau, 2019-2023 American Community Survey 5-Year Estimates

Foreign-born Population

Area	Percent of Population Born in								
	Any Foreign Country	Asia	Mexico	Europe	Caribbean	Central America[2]	South America	Africa	Canada
City	7.9	2.7	2.1	0.6	0.1	1.6	0.3	0.4	0.1
MSA[1]	4.6	1.3	1.4	0.4	0.1	0.9	0.2	0.2	0.1
U.S.	13.9	4.3	3.3	1.4	1.4	1.2	1.2	0.8	0.2

Note: (1) Figures cover the Little Rock-North Little Rock-Conway, AR Metropolitan Statistical Area; (2) Excludes Mexico.
Source: U.S. Census Bureau, 2019-2023 American Community Survey 5-Year Estimates

Household Size

Area	Persons in Household (%)							Average Household Size
	One	Two	Three	Four	Five	Six	Seven or More	
City	39.4	31.1	13.5	9.1	4.3	1.4	1.1	2.28
MSA[1]	31.7	34.1	15.2	11.0	5.3	1.7	1.0	2.41
U.S.	28.5	33.8	15.4	12.7	5.9	2.3	1.4	2.54

Note: (1) Figures cover the Little Rock-North Little Rock-Conway, AR Metropolitan Statistical Area
Source: U.S. Census Bureau, 2019-2023 American Community Survey 5-Year Estimates

Household Relationships

Area	Householder	Opposite-sex Spouse	Same-sex Spouse	Opposite-sex Unmarried Partner	Same-sex Unmarried Partner	Child[2]	Grandchild	Other Relatives	Non-relatives
City	43.5	14.5	0.3	2.4	0.3	27.1	2.3	3.9	3.1
MSA[1]	40.8	17.7	0.2	2.3	0.2	27.9	2.6	3.6	2.7
U.S.	38.3	17.5	0.2	2.5	0.2	28.3	2.4	4.8	3.4

Note: Figures are percent of the total population; (1) Figures cover the Little Rock-North Little Rock-Conway, AR Metropolitan Statistical Area; (2) Includes biological, adopted, and stepchildren of the householder
Source: U.S. Census Bureau, 2020 Census

Gender

Area	Males	Females	Males per 100 Females
City	95,597	107,142	89.2
MSA[1]	365,071	388,534	94.0
U.S.	164,545,087	167,842,453	98.0

Note: (1) Figures cover the Little Rock-North Little Rock-Conway, AR Metropolitan Statistical Area
Source: U.S. Census Bureau, 2019-2023 American Community Survey 5-Year Estimates

Marital Status

Area	Never Married	Now Married[2]	Separated	Widowed	Divorced
City	38.6	41.0	1.5	5.5	13.4
MSA[1]	31.5	48.0	1.7	5.9	12.9
U.S.	34.1	47.9	1.7	5.6	10.7

Note: Figures are percentages and cover the population 15 years of age and older; (1) Figures cover the Little Rock-North Little Rock-Conway, AR Metropolitan Statistical Area; (2) Excludes separated
Source: U.S. Census Bureau, 2019-2023 American Community Survey 5-Year Estimates

Religious Groups by Family

Area	Catholic	Baptist	Methodist	LDS[2]	Pentecostal	Lutheran	Islam	Adventist	Other
MSA[1]	4.9	23.5	6.2	0.8	3.7	0.4	0.4	1.0	13.6
U.S.	18.7	7.3	3.0	2.0	1.8	1.7	1.3	1.3	11.6

Note: Figures are the number of adherents as a percentage of the total population and cover the eight largest religious groups in the U.S; (1) Figures cover the Little Rock-North Little Rock-Conway, AR Metropolitan Statistical Area; (2) Church of Jesus Christ of Latter-day Saints
Sources: 2020 U.S. Religion Census, Association of Statisticians of American Religious Bodies; The Association of Religion Data Archives (ARDA)

Religious Groups by Tradition

Area	Catholic	Evangelical Protestant	Mainline Protestant	Black Protestant	Islam	Judaism	Hinduism	Orthodox	Buddhism
MSA[1]	4.9	32.1	6.6	8.5	0.4	0.1	<0.1	0.1	0.1
U.S.	18.7	16.5	5.2	2.3	1.3	0.6	0.4	0.4	0.3

Note: Figures are the number of adherents as a percentage of the total population; (1) Figures cover the Little Rock-North Little Rock-Conway, AR Metropolitan Statistical Area
Sources: 2020 U.S. Religion Census, Association of Statisticians of American Religious Bodies; The Association of Religion Data Archives (ARDA)

ECONOMY

Real Gross Domestic Product (GDP)

Area	2017	2018	2019	2020	2021	2022	2023	Rank[3]
MSA[1]	36.5	37.1	37.4	37.7	39.4	39.9	41.3	82
U.S.[2]	17,619.1	18,160.7	18,642.5	18,238.9	19,387.6	19,896.6	20,436.3	—

Note: Figures are in billions of chained 2017 dollars; (1) Figures cover the Little Rock-North Little Rock-Conway, AR Metropolitan Statistical Area; (2) Figures cover real GDP within metropolitan areas; (3) Rank is based on 2023 data and ranges from 1 to 384
Source: U.S. Bureau of Economic Analysis

Economic Growth

Area	2014	2015	2016	2017	2018	2019	2020	2021	2022	2023
MSA[1]	1.1	1.4	1.1	-0.8	1.5	0.8	0.8	4.6	1.1	3.5
U.S.[2]	2.6	3.2	2.0	2.7	3.1	2.7	-2.2	6.3	2.6	2.7

Note: Figures are real gross domestic product growth rates and represent percent change from preceding period; (1) Figures cover the Little Rock-North Little Rock-Conway, AR Metropolitan Statistical Area; (2) Figures are the average growth rates within metropolitan areas
Source: U.S. Bureau of Economic Analysis

Metropolitan Area Exports

Area	2018	2019	2020	2021	2022	2023	Rank[2]
MSA[1]	1,607.4	1,642.5	n/a	1,370.6	1,373.7	1,464.0	134
U.S.	1,664,056.1	1,645,173.7	1,431,406.6	1,753,941.4	2,062,937.4	2,019,160.5	—

Note: Figures are in millions of dollars; (1) Figures cover the Little Rock-North Little Rock-Conway, AR Metropolitan Statistical Area; (2) Rank is based on 2023 data and ranges from 1 to 386
Source: U.S. Department of Commerce, International Trade Administration, Office of Trade and Economic Analysis, Industry and Analysis, Exports by Metropolitan Area, data extracted April 2, 2025

Building Permits

Area	Single-Family 2023	Single-Family 2024	Single-Family Pct. Chg.	Multi-Family 2023	Multi-Family 2024	Multi-Family Pct. Chg.	Total 2023	Total 2024	Total Pct. Chg.
City	703	468	-33.4	230	18	-92.2	933	486	-47.9
MSA[1]	1,932	2,055	6.4	732	551	-24.7	2,664	2,606	-2.2
U.S.	920,000	981,900	6.7	591,100	496,100	-16.1	1,511,100	1,478,000	-2.2

Note: (1) Figures cover the Little Rock-North Little Rock-Conway, AR Metropolitan Statistical Area; Figures represent new, privately-owned housing units authorized (unadjusted data)
Source: U.S. Census Bureau, Building Permits Survey (BPS), 2023, 2024

Bankruptcy Filings

Area	Business Filings 2023	Business Filings 2024	% Chg.	Nonbusiness Filings 2023	Nonbusiness Filings 2024	% Chg.
Pulaski County	17	29	70.6	1,436	1,390	-3.2
U.S.	18,926	23,107	22.1	434,064	494,201	13.9

Note: Business filings include Chapter 7, Chapter 9, Chapter 11, Chapter 12, Chapter 13, Chapter 15, and Section 304; Nonbusiness filings include Chapter 7, Chapter 11, and Chapter 13
Source: Administrative Office of the U.S. Courts, Business and Nonbusiness Bankruptcy, County Cases Commenced by Chapter of the Bankruptcy Code, During the 12-Month Period Ending December 31, 2023 and Business and Nonbusiness Bankruptcy, County Cases Commenced by Chapter of the Bankruptcy Code, During the 12-Month Period Ending December 31, 2024

Housing Vacancy Rates

Area	Gross Vacancy Rate[3] (%) 2022	2023	2024	Year-Round Vacancy Rate[4] (%) 2022	2023	2024	Rental Vacancy Rate[5] (%) 2022	2023	2024	Homeowner Vacancy Rate[6] (%) 2022	2023	2024
MSA[1]	9.4	10.1	10.7	9.2	9.8	9.9	11.4	10.8	11.7	0.7	0.9	0.6
U.S.[2]	9.1	9.0	9.1	7.5	7.5	7.6	5.7	6.5	6.8	0.8	0.8	1.0

Note: (1) Figures cover the Little Rock-North Little Rock-Conway, AR Metropolitan Statistical Area; (2) Figures cover the 75 largest Metropolitan Statistical Areas; (3) The percentage of the total housing inventory that is vacant; (4) The percentage of the housing inventory (excluding seasonal units) that is year-round vacant; (5) The percentage of rental inventory that is vacant for rent; (6) The percentage of homeowner inventory that is vacant for sale
Source: U.S. Census Bureau, Housing Vacancies and Homeownership Annual Statistics: 2022, 2023, 2024

INCOME

Income

Area	Per Capita ($)	Median Household ($)	Average Household ($)
City	43,242	60,583	98,728
MSA[1]	37,678	65,309	90,691
U.S.	43,289	78,538	110,491

Note: (1) Figures cover the Little Rock-North Little Rock-Conway, AR Metropolitan Statistical Area
Source: U.S. Census Bureau, 2019-2023 American Community Survey 5-Year Estimates

Household Income Distribution

Area	Percent of Households Earning							
	Under $15,000	$15,000 -$24,999	$25,000 -$34,999	$35,000 -$49,999	$50,000 -$74,999	$75,000 -$99,999	$100,000 -$149,999	$150,000 and up
City	10.7	8.2	9.9	13.9	15.6	11.3	13.1	17.2
MSA[1]	9.9	7.9	8.8	12.9	17.0	12.7	16.1	14.8
U.S.	8.5	6.6	6.8	10.4	15.7	12.7	17.4	21.9

Note: (1) Figures cover the Little Rock-North Little Rock-Conway, AR Metropolitan Statistical Area
Source: U.S. Census Bureau, 2019-2023 American Community Survey 5-Year Estimates

Poverty Rate

Area	All Ages	Under 18 Years Old	18 to 64 Years Old	65 Years and Over
City	16.4	25.1	15.1	7.8
MSA[1]	14.2	19.7	13.5	8.7
U.S.	12.4	16.3	11.6	10.4

Note: Figures are percentage of people whose income during the past 12 months was below the poverty level; (1) Figures cover the Little Rock-North Little Rock-Conway, AR Metropolitan Statistical Area
Source: U.S. Census Bureau, 2019-2023 American Community Survey 5-Year Estimates

EMPLOYMENT

Labor Force and Employment

Area	Civilian Labor Force			Workers Employed		
	Dec. 2023	Dec. 2024	% Chg.	Dec. 2023	Dec. 2024	% Chg.
City	100,778	102,786	2.0	97,463	99,326	1.9
MSA[1]	371,026	378,813	2.1	359,838	366,941	2.0
U.S.	166,661,000	167,746,000	0.7	160,754,000	161,294,000	0.3

Note: Data is not seasonally adjusted and covers workers 16 years of age and older; (1) Figures cover the Little Rock-North Little Rock-Conway, AR Metropolitan Statistical Area
Source: Bureau of Labor Statistics, Local Area Unemployment Statistics

Unemployment Rate

Area	2024											
	Jan.	Feb.	Mar.	Apr.	May	Jun.	Jul.	Aug.	Sep.	Oct.	Nov.	Dec.
City	3.8	3.8	3.6	3.3	3.4	3.8	4.0	3.6	3.3	3.3	3.4	3.4
MSA[1]	3.5	3.5	3.2	2.9	3.1	3.5	3.7	3.3	3.0	2.9	3.0	3.1
U.S.	4.1	4.2	3.9	3.5	3.7	4.3	4.5	4.4	3.9	3.9	4.0	3.8

Note: Data is not seasonally adjusted and covers workers 16 years of age and older; (1) Figures cover the Little Rock-North Little Rock-Conway, AR Metropolitan Statistical Area
Source: Bureau of Labor Statistics, Local Area Unemployment Statistics

Average Wages

Occupation	$/Hr.	Occupation	$/Hr.
Accountants and Auditors	36.16	Maintenance and Repair Workers	22.43
Automotive Mechanics	23.85	Marketing Managers	55.96
Bookkeepers	22.54	Network and Computer Systems Admin.	40.49
Carpenters	23.06	Nurses, Licensed Practical	26.10
Cashiers	13.71	Nurses, Registered	39.00
Computer Programmers	45.30	Nursing Assistants	16.82
Computer Systems Analysts	29.95	Office Clerks, General	19.51
Computer User Support Specialists	26.42	Physical Therapists	45.58
Construction Laborers	18.42	Physicians	113.68
Cooks, Restaurant	15.24	Plumbers, Pipefitters and Steamfitters	25.08
Customer Service Representatives	19.85	Police and Sheriff's Patrol Officers	28.58
Dentists	92.76	Postal Service Mail Carriers	29.24
Electricians	24.62	Real Estate Sales Agents	n/a
Engineers, Electrical	51.32	Retail Salespersons	15.97
Fast Food and Counter Workers	13.24	Sales Representatives, Technical/Scientific	38.95
Financial Managers	60.66	Secretaries, Exc. Legal/Medical/Executive	19.79
First-Line Supervisors of Office Workers	28.31	Security Guards	18.85
General and Operations Managers	42.89	Surgeons	n/a
Hairdressers/Cosmetologists	14.46	Teacher Assistants, Exc. Postsecondary[1]	15.65
Home Health and Personal Care Aides	13.31	Teachers, Secondary School, Exc. Sp. Ed.[1]	27.84
Janitors and Cleaners	15.15	Telemarketers	n/a
Landscaping/Groundskeeping Workers	16.67	Truck Drivers, Heavy/Tractor-Trailer	28.31
Lawyers	65.50	Truck Drivers, Light/Delivery Services	21.58
Maids and Housekeeping Cleaners	13.80	Waiters and Waitresses	14.13

Note: Wage data covers the Little Rock-North Little Rock-Conway, AR Metropolitan Statistical Area; (1) Hourly wages were calculated from annual wage data based on a 40 hour work week
Source: Bureau of Labor Statistics, Metro Area Occupational Employment & Wage Estimates, May 2024

Employment by Industry

Sector	MSA[1] Number of Employees	MSA[1] Percent of Total	U.S. Percent of Total
Construction, Mining, and Logging	21,700	5.4	5.5
Financial Activities	28,300	7.1	5.8
Government	71,500	17.8	14.9
Information	5,100	1.3	1.9
Leisure and Hospitality	34,200	8.5	10.4
Manufacturing	21,500	5.4	8.0
Other Services	19,100	4.8	3.7
Private Education and Health Services	68,000	16.9	16.9
Professional and Business Services	49,800	12.4	14.2
Retail Trade	40,000	10.0	10.0
Transportation, Warehousing, and Utilities	23,900	6.0	4.8
Wholesale Trade	18,300	4.6	3.9

Note: Figures are non-farm employment as of December 2024. Figures are not seasonally adjusted and include workers 16 years of age and older; (1) Figures cover the Little Rock-North Little Rock-Conway, AR Metropolitan Statistical Area
Source: Bureau of Labor Statistics, Current Employment Statistics, Employment, Hours, and Earnings

Employment by Occupation

Occupation Classification	City (%)	MSA[1] (%)	U.S. (%)
Management, Business, Science, and Arts	48.7	41.8	42.0
Natural Resources, Construction, and Maintenance	5.4	8.8	8.6
Production, Transportation, and Material Moving	9.6	12.3	13.0
Sales and Office	21.2	21.9	19.9
Service	15.2	15.1	16.5

Note: Figures cover employed civilians 16 years of age and older; (1) Figures cover the Little Rock-North Little Rock-Conway, AR Metropolitan Statistical Area
Source: U.S. Census Bureau, 2019-2023 American Community Survey 5-Year Estimates

Occupations with Greatest Projected Employment Growth: 2022 – 2032

Occupation[1]	2022 Employment	2032 Projected Employment	Numeric Employment Change	Percent Employment Change
Home Health and Personal Care Aides	20,310	24,670	4,360	21.5
Stockers and Order Fillers	28,690	32,370	3,680	12.8
General and Operations Managers	34,520	38,140	3,620	10.5
Cooks, Restaurant	12,540	15,530	2,990	23.8
Registered Nurses	28,750	30,920	2,170	7.5
Medical and Health Services Managers	6,680	8,760	2,080	31.1
Fast Food and Counter Workers	37,020	38,930	1,910	5.2
Laborers and Freight, Stock, and Material Movers, Hand	29,070	30,950	1,880	6.5
Nurse Practitioners	3,000	4,840	1,840	61.3
Retail Salespersons	32,180	33,950	1,770	5.5

Note: Projections cover Arkansas; (1) Sorted by numeric employment change
Source: www.projectionscentral.org, State Occupational Projections, 2022–2032 Long-Term Projections

Fastest-Growing Occupations: 2022 – 2032

Occupation[1]	2022 Employment	2032 Projected Employment	Numeric Employment Change	Percent Employment Change
Nurse Practitioners	3,000	4,840	1,840	61.3
Occupational Therapy Assistants	500	670	170	34.0
Physician Assistants	870	1,160	290	33.3
Information Security Analysts (SOC 2018)	950	1,260	310	32.6
Software Developers	5,360	7,080	1,720	32.1
Labor Relations Specialists	380	500	120	31.6
Medical and Health Services Managers	6,680	8,760	2,080	31.1
Operations Research Analysts	230	300	70	30.4
Recreational Vehicle Service Technicians	200	260	60	30.0
Physical Therapist Assistants	1,400	1,790	390	27.9

Note: Projections cover Arkansas; (1) Sorted by percent employment change and excludes occupations with numeric employment change less than 50
Source: www.projectionscentral.org, State Occupational Projections, 2022–2032 Long-Term Projections

CITY FINANCES

City Government Finances

Component	2022 ($000)	2022 ($ per capita)
Total Revenues	601,220	3,039
Total Expenditures	582,827	2,946
Debt Outstanding	488,230	2,467

Source: U.S. Census Bureau, State & Local Government Finances 2022

City Government Revenue by Source

Source	2022 ($000)	2022 ($ per capita)	2022 (%)
General Revenue			
From Federal Government	37,359	189	6.2
From State Government	57,060	288	9.5
From Local Governments	57,692	292	9.6
Taxes			
Property	63,838	323	10.6
Sales and Gross Receipts	146,098	738	24.3
Personal Income	0	0	0.0
Corporate Income	0	0	0.0
Motor Vehicle License	0	0	0.0
Other Taxes	9,679	49	1.6
Current Charges	184,930	935	30.8
Liquor Store	0	0	0.0
Utility	0	0	0.0

Source: U.S. Census Bureau, State & Local Government Finances 2022

City Government Expenditures by Function

Function	2022 ($000)	2022 ($ per capita)	2022 (%)
General Direct Expenditures			
Air Transportation	37,615	190	6.5
Corrections	0	0	0.0
Education	0	0	0.0
Employment Security Administration	0	0	0.0
Financial Administration	10,007	50	1.7
Fire Protection	57,316	289	9.8
General Public Buildings	1,048	5	0.2
Governmental Administration, Other	6,388	32	1.1
Health	36,822	186	6.3
Highways	33,034	167	5.7
Hospitals	0	0	0.0
Housing and Community Development	8,922	45	1.5
Interest on General Debt	19,576	98	3.4
Judicial and Legal	4,555	23	0.8
Libraries	120	< 1	< 0.1
Parking	1,129	5	0.2
Parks and Recreation	102,640	518	17.6
Police Protection	80,293	405	13.8
Public Welfare	0	0	0.0
Sewerage	62,241	314	10.7
Solid Waste Management	19,212	97	3.3
Veterans' Services	0	0	0.0
Liquor Store	0	0	0.0
Utility	0	0	0.0

Source: U.S. Census Bureau, State & Local Government Finances 2022

TAXES

State Corporate Income Tax Rates

State	Tax Rate (%)	Income Brackets ($)	Num. of Brackets	Financial Institution Tax Rate (%)[a]	Federal Income Tax Ded.
Arkansas	1.0 - 4.8	3,000 - 26,000	5	1.0 - 4.8	No

Note: Tax rates for tax year 2024; (a) Rates listed are the corporate income tax rate applied to financial institutions or excise taxes based on income. Some states have other taxes based upon the value of deposits or shares.
Source: Federation of Tax Administrators, State Corporate Income Tax Rates, January 1, 2025

State Individual Income Tax Rates

State	Tax Rate (%)	Income Brackets ($)	Personal Exemptions ($)			Standard Ded. ($)	
			Single	Married	Depend.	Single	Married
Arkansas (a)	2.0 - 4.7 (f)	5,300 - 24,300	29	58	29 (c)	2,340	4,680

Note: Tax rates for tax year 2024; Local- and county-level taxes are not included; Federal income tax is not deductible on state income tax returns; (a) 16 states have statutory provision for automatically adjusting to the rate of inflation the dollar values of the income tax brackets, standard deductions, and/or personal exemptions. Oregon does not index the income brackets for $125,000 and over See: INFL and SPEC above; (c) The personal exemption takes the form of a tax credit instead of a deduction; (f) During a September special session the legislature approved tax cuts that will benefit Arkansans in two ways. An income tax reduction will lower the top rate from 4.7 to 4.4 percent for individuals. The tax relief measure includes a one-time credit of $150 for all taxpayers whose incomes was below $89,600 in 2023. Arkansas has separate brackets for taxpayers with income under $84,500 in 2023.
Source: Federation of Tax Administrators, State Individual Income Tax Rates, January 1, 2025

Various State Sales and Excise Tax Rates

State	State Sales Tax (%)	Gasoline[1] ($/gal.)	Cigarette[2] ($/pack)	Spirits[3] ($/gal.)	Wine[4] ($/gal.)	Beer[5] ($/gal.)	Recreational Marijuana (%)
Arkansas	6.5	0.25	1.15	9.47	1.58	0.38	Not legal

Note: All tax rates as of January 1, 2025; (1) The American Petroleum Institute has developed a methodology for determining the average tax rate on a gallon of fuel. Rates may include any of the following: excise taxes, environmental fees, storage tank fees, other fees or taxes, general sales tax, and local taxes; (2) The federal excise tax of $1.0066 per pack and local taxes are not included; (3) Rates are those applicable to off-premise sales of 40% alcohol by volume (a.b.v.) distilled spirits in 750ml containers. Local excise taxes are excluded; (4) Rates are those applicable to off-premise sales of 11% a.b.v. non-carbonated wine in 750ml containers; (5) Rates are those applicable to off-premise sales of 4.7% a.b.v. beer in 12 ounce containers.
Source: Tax Foundation, 2025 Facts & Figures: How Does Your State Compare?

State Tax Competitiveness Index

State	Overall Rank	Corporate Tax Rank	Individual Income Tax Rank	Sales Tax Rank	Property Tax Rank	Unemployment Insurance Tax Rank
Arkansas	36	15	39	44	19	11

Note: The Tax Foundation's State Tax Competitiveness Index enables policymakers, taxpayers, and business leaders to gauge how their states' tax systems compare. A rank of 1 is best, 50 is worst. Rankings do not average to the total. States without a tax rank equally as 1. DC's scores and rankings do not affect other states. The report shows tax systems as of July 1, 2024 (the beginning of Fiscal Year 2025).
Source: Tax Foundation, State Tax Competitiveness Index 2025

TRANSPORTATION

Means of Transportation to Work

Area	Car/Truck/Van		Public Transportation			Bicycle	Walked	Other Means	Worked at Home
	Drove Alone	Car-pooled	Bus	Subway	Railroad				
City	76.5	8.9	1.0	0.0	0.0	0.2	1.8	0.9	10.8
MSA[1]	79.2	8.8	0.5	0.0	0.0	0.1	1.2	1.0	9.1
U.S.	70.2	8.5	1.7	1.3	0.4	0.4	2.4	1.6	13.5

Note: Figures are percentages and cover workers 16 years of age and older; (1) Figures cover the Little Rock-North Little Rock-Conway, AR Metropolitan Statistical Area
Source: U.S. Census Bureau, 2019-2023 American Community Survey 5-Year Estimates

Travel Time to Work

Area	Less Than 10 Minutes	10 to 19 Minutes	20 to 29 Minutes	30 to 44 Minutes	45 to 59 Minutes	60 to 89 Minutes	90 Minutes or More
City	15.3	46.6	22.6	10.7	2.2	1.7	0.9
MSA[1]	13.2	32.4	22.2	21.1	6.6	3.1	1.5
U.S.	12.6	28.6	21.2	20.8	8.1	6.0	2.8

Note: Note: Figures are percentages and include workers 16 years old and over; (1) Figures cover the Little Rock-North Little Rock-Conway, AR Metropolitan Statistical Area
Source: U.S. Census Bureau, 2019-2023 American Community Survey 5-Year Estimates

Key Congestion Measures

Measure	2000	2010	2015	2020	2022
Annual Hours of Delay, Total (000)	7,628	16,142	17,871	14,655	21,802
Annual Hours of Delay, Per Auto Commuter	27	35	40	33	51
Annual Congestion Cost, Per Auto Commuter ($)	489	824	840	743	1,014

Note: Figures cover the Little Rock AR urban area
Source: Texas A&M Transportation Institute, 2023 Urban Mobility Report

Freeway Travel Time Index

Measure	1985	1990	1995	2000	2005	2010	2015	2020	2022
Urban Area Index[1]	1.03	1.04	1.06	1.10	1.12	1.14	1.13	1.10	1.15
Urban Area Rank[1,2]	89	94	93	85	86	71	83	29	54

Note: Freeway Travel Time Index—the ratio of travel time in the peak period to the travel time at free-flow conditions. For example, a value of 1.30 indicates a 20-minute free-flow trip takes 26 minutes in the peak (20 minutes x 1.30 = 26 minutes); (1) Covers the Little Rock AR urban area; (2) Rank is based on 101 larger urban areas (#1 = highest travel time index)
Source: Texas A&M Transportation Institute, 2023 Urban Mobility Report

Public Transportation

Agency Name / Mode of Transportation	Vehicles Operated in Maximum Service[1]	Annual Unlinked Passenger Trips[2] (in thous.)	Annual Passenger Miles[3] (in thous.)
Central Arkansas Transit Authority (CATA)			
Bus (directly operated)	34	1,732.7	5,450.2
Demand Response (directly operated)	30	193.3	985.0
Demand Response (purchased transportation)	9	27.9	203.1
Streetcar Rail (directly operated)	2	65.0	120.4
Vanpool (purchased transportation)	11	18.2	724.5

Note: (1) Number of revenue vehicles operated by the given mode and type of service to meet the annual maximum service requirement. This is the revenue vehicle count during the peak season of the year; on the week and day that maximum service is provided. Vehicles operated in maximum service (VOMS) exclude atypical days and one-time special events; (2) Number of passengers who boarded public transportation vehicles. Passengers are counted each time they board a vehicle no matter how many vehicles they use to travel from their origin to their destination. (3) Sum of the distances ridden by all passengers during the entire fiscal year.
Source: Federal Transit Administration, National Transit Database, 2023

Air Transportation

Airport Name and Code / Type of Service	Passenger Airlines[1]	Passenger Enplanements	Freight Carriers[2]	Freight (lbs)
Little Rock National Airport (LIT)				
Domestic service (U.S. carriers only)	18	1,145,632	11	10,878,097
International service (U.S. carriers only)	0	0	0	0

Note: (1) Includes all U.S.-based major, minor and commuter airlines that carried at least one passenger during the year; (2) Includes all U.S.-based airlines and freight carriers that transported at least one pound of freight during the year.
Source: Bureau of Transportation Statistics, The Intermodal Transportation Database, Air Carriers: T-100 Domestic Market (U.S. carriers only), 2024; Bureau of Transportation Statistics, The Intermodal Transportation Database, Air Carriers: T-100 International Market (U.S. carriers only), 2024

BUSINESSES

Major Business Headquarters

Company Name	Industry	Rankings	
		Fortune[1]	Forbes[2]
No companies listed	-	-	-

Note: (1) Companies that produce a 10-K are ranked 1 to 500 based on 2023 revenue; (2) All private companies with at least $2 billion in annual revenue through the end of their most current fiscal year are ranked 1 to 275; companies listed are headquartered in the city; dashes indicate no ranking
Source: Fortune, "Fortune 500," 2024; Forbes, "America's Largest Private Companies," 2024

Little Rock, Arkansas

Living Environment

COST OF LIVING

Cost of Living Index

Composite Index	Groceries	Housing	Utilities	Transportation	Health Care	Misc. Goods/Services
93.4	97.3	77.6	84.2	94.5	84.6	107.8

Note: The Cost of Living Index measures regional differences in the cost of consumer goods and services, excluding taxes and non-consumer expenditures, for professional and managerial households in the top income quintile. It is based on more than 50,000 prices covering almost 60 different items for which prices are collected three times a year by chambers of commerce, economic development organizations or university applied economic centers in each participating urban area. The numbers shown should be read as a percentage above or below the national average of 100. For example, a value of 115.4 in the groceries column indicates that grocery prices are 15.4% higher than the national average. Small differences in the index numbers should not be interpreted as significant; Figures cover the Little Rock-North Little Rock AR urban area.
Source: The Council for Community and Economic Research, Cost of Living Index, 2024

Grocery Prices

Area[1]	T-Bone Steak ($/pound)	Frying Chicken ($/pound)	Whole Milk ($/half gal.)	Eggs ($/dozen)	Orange Juice ($/64 oz.)	Coffee ($/11.5 oz.)
City[2]	14.86	1.43	4.62	3.40	4.31	5.24
Avg.	15.42	1.55	4.69	3.25	4.41	5.46
Min.	14.50	1.16	4.43	2.75	4.00	4.85
Max.	17.56	2.89	5.49	4.78	5.54	7.89

Note: (1) Values for the local area are compared with the average, minimum and maximum values for all 276 areas in the Cost of Living Index; (2) Figures cover the Little Rock-North Little Rock AR urban area; **T-Bone Steak** (price per pound); **Frying Chicken** (price per pound, whole fryer); **Whole Milk** (half gallon carton); **Eggs** (price per dozen, Grade A, large); **Orange Juice** (64 oz. Tropicana or Florida Natural); **Coffee** (11.5 oz. can, vacuum-packed, Maxwell House, Hills Bros, or Folgers).
Source: The Council for Community and Economic Research, Cost of Living Index, 2024

Housing and Utility Costs

Area[1]	New Home Price ($)	Apartment Rent ($/month)	All Electric ($/month)	Part Electric ($/month)	Other Energy ($/month)	Telephone ($/month)
City[2]	407,536	1,155	-	76.85	69.20	208.40
Avg.	515,975	1,550	210.99	123.07	82.07	194.99
Min.	265,375	692	104.33	53.68	36.26	179.42
Max.	2,775,821	5,719	529.02	397.28	361.63	223.33

Note: (1) Values for the local area are compared with the average, minimum and maximum values for all 276 areas in the Cost of Living Index; (2) Figures cover the Little Rock-North Little Rock AR urban area; **New Home Price** (2,400 sf living area, 8,000 sf lot, in urban area with full utilities); **Apartment Rent** (950 sf 2 bedroom/1.5 or 2 bath, unfurnished, excluding all utilities except water); **All Electric** (average monthly cost for an all-electric home); **Part Electric** (average monthly cost for a part-electric home); **Other Energy** (average monthly cost for natural gas, fuel oil, coal, wood, and any other forms of energy except electricity); **Telephone** (price includes the base monthly rate plus taxes and fees for three lines of mobile phone service).
Source: The Council for Community and Economic Research, Cost of Living Index, 2024

Health Care, Transportation, and Other Costs

Area[1]	Doctor ($/visit)	Dentist ($/visit)	Optometrist ($/visit)	Gasoline ($/gallon)	Beauty Salon ($/visit)	Men's Shirt ($)
City[2]	133.00	83.67	105.53	2.95	52.55	47.99
Avg.	143.77	117.51	129.23	3.32	48.57	38.14
Min.	36.74	58.67	67.33	2.80	24.00	13.41
Max.	270.44	216.82	307.33	5.28	94.00	63.89

Note: (1) Values for the local area are compared with the average, minimum and maximum values for all 276 areas in the Cost of Living Index; (2) Figures cover the Little Rock-North Little Rock AR urban area; **Doctor** (general practitioners routine exam of an established patient); **Dentist** (adult teeth cleaning and periodic oral examination); **Optometrist** (full vision eye exam for established adult patient); **Gasoline** (one gallon regular unleaded, national brand, including all taxes, cash price at self-service pump if available); **Beauty Salon** (woman's shampoo, trim, and blow-dry); **Men's Shirt** (cotton/polyester dress shirt, pinpoint weave, long sleeves).
Source: The Council for Community and Economic Research, Cost of Living Index, 2024

HOUSING

Homeownership Rate

Area	2017 (%)	2018 (%)	2019 (%)	2020 (%)	2021 (%)	2022 (%)	2023 (%)	2024 (%)
MSA[1]	61.0	62.2	65.0	67.7	64.6	64.4	62.6	61.7
U.S.	63.9	64.4	64.6	66.6	65.5	65.8	65.9	65.6

Note: (1) Figures cover the Little Rock-North Little Rock-Conway, AR Metropolitan Statistical Area
Source: U.S. Census Bureau, Housing Vacancies and Homeownership Annual Statistics: 2017-2024

House Price Index (HPI)

Area	National Ranking[2]	Quarterly Change (%)	One-Year Change (%)	Five-Year Change (%)	Since 1991Q1 (%)
MSA[1]	197	-1.14	3.23	47.11	222.55
U.S.[3]	—	1.43	4.51	57.13	327.82

Note: The HPI is a weighted repeat sales index. It measures average price changes in repeat sales or refinancings on the same properties. This information is obtained by reviewing repeat mortgage transactions on single-family properties whose mortgages have been purchased or securitized by Fannie Mae or Freddie Mac since January 1975; (1) Figures cover the Little Rock-North Little Rock-Conway, AR Metropolitan Statistical Area; (2) Rankings are based on annual percentage change for all metro areas containing at least 15,000 transactions over the last 10 years and ranges from 1 to 241; (3) figures based on a weighted average of Census Division estimates using a seasonally adjusted, purchase-only index; all figures are for the period ending December 31, 2024
Source: Federal Housing Finance Agency, Change in FHFA Metropolitan Area House Price Indexes, All Transactions Index, 2024Q4

Home Value

Area	Under $100,000	$100,000 -$199,999	$200,000 -$299,999	$300,000 -$399,999	$400,000 -$499,999	$500,000 -$999,999	$1,000,000 or more	Median ($)
City	15.5	28.7	22.6	12.2	8.1	10.2	2.6	221,200
MSA[1]	17.5	32.8	24.9	11.9	5.4	6.1	1.5	199,300
U.S.	12.1	17.8	19.5	14.4	10.5	19.1	6.5	303,400

Note: Figures are percentages except for median and cover owner-occupied housing units; (1) Figures cover the Little Rock-North Little Rock-Conway, AR Metropolitan Statistical Area
Source: U.S. Census Bureau, 2019-2023 American Community Survey 5-Year Estimates

Year Housing Structure Built

Area	2020 or Later	2010 -2019	2000 -2009	1990 -1999	1980 -1989	1970 -1979	1960 -1969	1950 -1959	1940 -1949	Before 1940	Median Year
City	0.4	9.7	11.7	11.8	13.1	17.9	14.7	8.5	4.9	7.2	1978
MSA[1]	1.3	13.5	17.7	15.3	13.9	15.3	9.9	6.3	3.2	3.7	1988
U.S.	1.2	8.9	13.6	12.8	13.0	14.4	10.0	9.7	4.5	11.9	1980

Note: Figures are percentages except for Median Year; Note: (1) Figures cover the Little Rock-North Little Rock-Conway, AR Metropolitan Statistical Area
Source: U.S. Census Bureau, 2019-2023 American Community Survey 5-Year Estimates

Gross Monthly Rent

Area	Under $500	$500 -$999	$1,000 -$1,499	$1,500 -$1,999	$2,000 -$2,499	$2,500 -$2,999	$3,000 and up	Median ($)
City	5.2	38.1	39.8	12.0	2.8	0.8	1.2	1,067
MSA[1]	6.2	43.2	37.0	10.4	1.7	0.6	0.9	1,007
U.S.	6.5	22.3	29.5	20.2	10.8	4.8	5.9	1,348

Note: Figures are percentages except for median; Gross rent is the contract rent plus the estimated average monthly cost of utilities (electricity, gas, and water and sewer) and fuels (oil, coal, kerosene, wood, etc.) if these are paid by the renter (or paid for the renter by someone else); (1) Figures cover the Little Rock-North Little Rock-Conway, AR Metropolitan Statistical Area
Source: U.S. Census Bureau, 2019-2023 American Community Survey 5-Year Estimates

HEALTH

Health Risk Factors

Category	MSA[1] (%)	U.S. (%)
Adults aged 18–64 who have any kind of health care coverage	87.4	90.8
Adults who reported being in good or better health	78.8	81.8
Adults who have been told they have high blood cholesterol	40.3	36.9
Adults who have been told they have high blood pressure	42.1	34.0
Adults who are current smokers	15.1	12.1
Adults who currently use e-cigarettes	9.0	7.7
Adults who currently use chewing tobacco, snuff, or snus	2.9	3.2
Adults who are heavy drinkers[2]	6.4	6.1
Adults who are binge drinkers[3]	16.0	15.2
Adults who are overweight (BMI 25.0 - 29.9)	33.2	34.4
Adults who are obese (BMI 30.0 - 99.8)	36.6	34.3
Adults who participated in any physical activities in the past month	72.8	75.8

Note: All figures are crude prevalence; (1) Figures cover the Little Rock-North Little Rock-Conway, AR Metropolitan Statistical Area; (2) Heavy drinkers are classified as adult men having more than 14 drinks per week and adult women having more than 7 drinks per week; (3) Binge drinkers are classified as males having five or more drinks on one occasion or females having four or more drinks on one occasion
Source: Centers for Disease Control and Prevention, Behavioral Risk Factor Surveillance System, SMART: Selected Metropolitan Area Risk Trends, 2023

Acute and Chronic Health Conditions

Category	MSA[1] (%)	U.S. (%)
Adults who have ever been told they had a heart attack	3.8	4.2
Adults who have ever been told they have angina or coronary heart disease	5.1	4.0
Adults who have ever been told they had a stroke	4.8	3.3
Adults who have ever been told they have asthma	13.4	15.7
Adults who have ever been told they have arthritis	27.0	26.3
Adults who have ever been told they have diabetes[2]	12.6	11.5
Adults who have ever been told they had skin cancer	6.0	5.6
Adults who have ever been told they had any other types of cancer	8.8	8.4
Adults who have ever been told they have COPD	7.4	6.4
Adults who have ever been told they have kidney disease	4.1	3.7
Adults who have ever been told they have a form of depression	23.7	22.0

Note: All figures are crude prevalence; (1) Figures cover the Little Rock-North Little Rock-Conway, AR Metropolitan Statistical Area; (2) Figures do not include pregnancy-related, borderline, or pre-diabetes
Source: Centers for Disease Control and Prevention, Behavioral Risk Factor Surveillance System, SMART: Selected Metropolitan Area Risk Trends, 2023

Health Screening and Vaccination Rates

Category	MSA[1] (%)	U.S. (%)
Adults who have ever been tested for HIV	39.5	37.5
Adults who have had their blood cholesterol checked within the last five years	86.1	87.0
Adults aged 65+ who have had flu shot within the past year	72.0	63.4
Adults aged 65+ who have ever had a pneumonia vaccination	76.8	71.9

Note: All figures are crude prevalence; (1) Figures cover the Little Rock-North Little Rock-Conway, AR Metropolitan Statistical Area.
Source: Centers for Disease Control and Prevention, Behavioral Risk Factor Surveillance System, SMART: Selected Metropolitan Area Risk Trends, 2023

Disability Status

Category	MSA[1] (%)	U.S. (%)
Adults who reported being deaf	7.9	7.4
Are you blind or have serious difficulty seeing, even when wearing glasses?	7.5	4.9
Do you have difficulty doing errands alone?	10.5	7.8
Do you have difficulty dressing or bathing?	6.1	3.6
Do you have serious difficulty concentrating/remembering/making decisions?	19.0	13.7
Do you have serious difficulty walking or climbing stairs?	17.4	13.2

Note: All figures are crude prevalence; (1) Figures cover the Little Rock-North Little Rock-Conway, AR Metropolitan Statistical Area.
Source: Centers for Disease Control and Prevention, Behavioral Risk Factor Surveillance System, SMART: Selected Metropolitan Area Risk Trends, 2023

Mortality Rates for the Top 10 Causes of Death in the U.S.

ICD-10[a] Sub-Chapter	ICD-10[a] Code	Crude Mortality Rate[2] per 100,000 population	
		County[3]	U.S.
Malignant neoplasms	C00-C97	192.0	182.7
Ischaemic heart diseases	I20-I25	106.6	109.6
Provisional assignment of new diseases of uncertain etiology[1]	U00-U49	57.5	65.3
Other forms of heart disease	I30-I51	50.9	65.1
Other degenerative diseases of the nervous system	G30-G31	91.1	52.4
Other external causes of accidental injury	W00-X59	50.5	52.3
Cerebrovascular diseases	I60-I69	54.5	49.1
Chronic lower respiratory diseases	J40-J47	45.9	43.5
Hypertensive diseases	I10-I15	73.0	38.9
Organic, including symptomatic, mental disorders	F01-F09	16.0	33.9

Note: (a) ICD-10 = International Classification of Diseases 10th Revision; (1) Includes COVID-19, adverse effects to COVID-19 vaccines, SARS, and vaping-related disorders; (2) Crude mortality rates are a three-year average covering 2021-2023; (3) Figures cover Pulaski County.
Source: Centers for Disease Control and Prevention, National Center for Health Statistics. National Vital Statistics System, Mortality 2018-2023 on CDC WONDER Online Database

Mortality Rates for Selected Causes of Death

Cause of Death	ICD-10[a] Code	Crude Mortality Rate[1] per 100,000 population	
		County[2]	U.S.
Accidental poisoning and exposure to noxious substances	X40-X49	30.5	30.5
Alzheimer disease	G30	60.3	35.4
Assault	X85-Y09	23.2	7.3
COVID-19	U07.1	57.5	65.3
Diabetes mellitus	E10-E14	45.4	30.0
Diseases of the liver	K70-K76	24.7	20.8
Human immunodeficiency virus (HIV) disease	B20-B24	3.1	1.5
Influenza and pneumonia	J09-J18	15.6	13.4
Intentional self-harm	X60-X84	15.5	14.7
Malnutrition	E40-E46	8.4	6.0
Obesity and other hyperalimentation	E65-E68	5.3	3.1
Renal failure	N17-N19	24.0	16.4
Transport accidents	V01-V99	22.9	14.4

Note: (a) ICD-10 = International Classification of Diseases 10th Revision; (1) Crude mortality rates are a three-year average covering 2021-2023; (2) Figures cover Pulaski County; Data are suppressed when the data meet the criteria for confidentiality constraints; Crude mortality rates are flagged as unreliable when the rate would be calculated with a numerator of 20 or less.
Source: Centers for Disease Control and Prevention, National Center for Health Statistics. National Vital Statistics System, Mortality 2018-2023 on CDC WONDER Online Database

Health Insurance Coverage

Area	With Health Insurance	With Private Health Insurance	With Public Health Insurance	Without Health Insurance	Population Under Age 19 Without Health Insurance
City	90.0	62.0	39.1	10.0	7.0
MSA[1]	91.7	65.3	39.2	8.3	5.1
U.S.	91.4	67.3	36.3	8.6	5.4

Note: Figures are percentages that cover the civilian noninstitutionalized population; (1) Figures cover the Little Rock-North Little Rock-Conway, AR Metropolitan Statistical Area
Source: U.S. Census Bureau, 2019-2023 American Community Survey 5-Year Estimates

Number of Medical Professionals

Area	MDs[3]	DOs[3,4]	Dentists	Podiatrists	Chiropractors	Optometrists
County[1] (number)	3,284	121	321	21	96	91
County[1] (rate[2])	822.8	30.3	80.2	5.2	24.0	22.7
U.S. (rate[2])	302.5	29.2	74.6	6.4	29.5	18.0

Note: Data as of 2023 unless noted; (1) Data covers Pulaski County; (2) Number of medical professionals per 100,000 population; (3) Data as of 2022 and includes all active, non-federal physicians; (4) Doctor of Osteopathic Medicine
Source: U.S. Department of Health and Human Services, Health Resources and Services Administration, Bureau of Health Professions, Area Resource File (ARF) 2023-2024

Best Hospitals

According to *U.S. News*, the Little Rock-North Little Rock-Conway, AR metro area is home to one of the best children's hospitals in the U.S.: **Arkansas Children's Hospital** (7 pediatric specialties). The hospital listed was highly ranked in at least one of 11 pediatric specialties. One hundred five children's hospitals in the U.S. were nationally ranked in at least one specialty. Hospitals received points for being ranked in a specialty, and the 10 hospitals with the most points across the 11 specialties make up the Honor Roll. *U.S. News Online, "America's Best Children's Hospitals 2024-25"*

EDUCATION

Public School District Statistics

District Name	Schls	Pupils	Pupil/ Teacher Ratio	Minority Pupils[1] (%)	Total Rev. per Pupil ($)	Total Exp. per Pupil ($)
Arkansas Virtual Academy	3	3,936	14.3	33.6	9,684	9,121
Estem High Charter	5	2,739	13.6	86.7	11,716	11,688
Lisa Academy Charter	11	4,015	14.2	75.1	12,200	11,632
Little Rock School District	40	21,105	14.8	80.9	16,622	15,987
Pulaski Co. Spec. School Dist.	26	12,290	13.1	66.3	16,738	16,702

Note: Table includes school districts with 2,000 or more students; (1) Percentage of students that are not non-Hispanic white.
Source: U.S. Department of Education, National Center for Education Statistics, Common Core of Data, Local Education Agency (School District) Universe Survey: School Year 2023-2024; U.S. Department of Education, National Center for Education Statistics, Common Core of Data, School District Finance Survey (F-33): School Year 2021–22

Highest Level of Education

Area	Less than H.S.	H.S. Diploma	Some College, No Deg.	Associate Degree	Bachelor's Degree	Master's Degree	Prof. School Degree	Doctorate Degree
City	7.7	21.2	20.7	6.5	25.0	11.7	4.7	2.6
MSA[1]	7.9	29.1	21.7	8.4	20.3	8.8	2.4	1.4
U.S.	10.6	26.2	19.4	8.8	21.3	9.8	2.3	1.6

Note: Figures cover persons age 25 and over; (1) Figures cover the Little Rock-North Little Rock-Conway, AR Metropolitan Statistical Area
Source: U.S. Census Bureau, 2019-2023 American Community Survey 5-Year Estimates

Educational Attainment by Race

Area	High School Graduate or Higher (%)					Bachelor's Degree or Higher (%)				
	Total	White	Black	Asian	Hisp.[2]	Total	White	Black	Asian	Hisp.[2]
City	92.3	96.3	91.5	92.7	63.7	44.0	58.0	26.6	73.5	13.5
MSA[1]	92.1	93.9	91.4	89.9	68.2	32.9	35.4	25.8	55.9	17.4
U.S.	89.4	92.9	88.1	88.0	72.5	35.0	37.7	24.7	57.0	19.9

Note: Figures shown cover persons 25 years old and over; (1) Figures cover the Little Rock-North Little Rock-Conway, AR Metropolitan Statistical Area; (2) People of Hispanic origin can be of any race
Source: U.S. Census Bureau, 2019-2023 American Community Survey 5-Year Estimates

School Enrollment by Grade and Control

Area	Preschool (%)		Kindergarten (%)		Grades 1 - 4 (%)		Grades 5 - 8 (%)		Grades 9 - 12 (%)	
	Public	Private	Public	Private	Public	Private	Public	Private	Public	Private
City	66.2	33.8	86.5	13.5	78.2	21.8	76.0	24.0	77.5	22.5
MSA[1]	69.9	30.1	86.8	13.2	86.2	13.8	85.4	14.6	87.1	12.9
U.S.	58.7	41.3	85.2	14.8	87.2	12.8	87.9	12.1	89.0	11.0

Note: Figures shown cover persons 3 years old and over; (1) Figures cover the Little Rock-North Little Rock-Conway, AR Metropolitan Statistical Area
Source: U.S. Census Bureau, 2019-2023 American Community Survey 5-Year Estimates

Higher Education

Four-Year Colleges			Two-Year Colleges			Medical Schools[1]	Law Schools[2]	Voc/ Tech[3]
Public	Private Non-profit	Private For-profit	Public	Private Non-profit	Private For-profit			
4	5	1	1	2	0	1	1	11

Note: Figures cover institutions located within the Little Rock-North Little Rock-Conway, AR Metropolitan Statistical Area and include main campuses only; (1) includes schools accredited by the Liaison Committee on Medical Education and the American Osteopathic Association's Commission on Osteopathic College Accreditation; (2) includes ABA-accredited schools, schools with provisional ABA accreditation, and state accredited schools; (3) includes all schools with programs that are less than 2 years.
Source: National Center for Education Statistics, Integrated Postsecondary Education System (IPEDS), 2023-24; Wikipedia, List of Medical Schools in the United States, accessed May 2, 2025; Wikipedia, List of Law Schools in the United States, accessed May 2, 2025

According to *U.S. News & World Report,* the Little Rock-North Little Rock-Conway, AR metro area is home to one of the top medical schools for research in the U.S.: **University of Arkansas for Medical Sciences** (Tier 2). *U.S. News* placed medical and osteopathic schools into tiers based on their research productivity, faculty and admissions data. Each school's tier was derived from its overall score, calculated by summing the weighted normalized values generated across several factors of academic quality, outlined below. There are four tiers, with tier 1 medical schools as the highest-performing and tier 4 as the lowest-performing. Only tier 1 and 2 schools are shown. Because of the tier presentation, *U.S. News* calculated overall scores based on their percentile performance among all rated schools instead of dividing against the rescaled score of the No. 1-performing schools. Tier 1 included schools with overall scores of 85 to 99. The cutoffs for tiers 2 through 4 were schools scoring 50 to 84, 15 to 49 and 1 to 14, respectively. The rankings are based on a weighted average of the following measures of quality: total research activity; average research activity per faculty member; total NIH research grants at the medical school and its affiliated hospitals; average NIH research grants per faculty; median MCAT total score; median undergraduate GPA; acceptance rate; and faculty resources. *U.S. News & World Report, "America's Best Graduate Schools, Medical, 2025"*

According to *U.S. News & World Report,* the Little Rock-North Little Rock-Conway, AR metro area is home to one of the top medical schools for primary care in the U.S.: **University of Arkansas for Medical Sciences** (Tier 1). *U.S. News* placed medical and osteopathic schools into tiers based on their research productivity, faculty and admissions data. Each school's tier was derived from its overall score, calculated by summing the weighted normalized values generated across several factors of academic quality, outlined below. There are four tiers, with tier 1 medical schools as the highest-performing and tier 4 as the lowest-performing. Only tier 1 and 2 schools are shown. Because of the tier presentation, *U.S. News* calculated overall scores based on their percentile performance among all rated schools instead of dividing against the rescaled score of the No. 1-performing schools. Tier 1 included schools with overall scores of 85 to 99. The cutoffs for tiers 2 through 4 were schools scoring

50 to 84, 15 to 49 and 1 to 14, respectively. The rankings are based on a weighted average of the following measures of quality: graduates practicing in primary care specialties; graduates entering primary care residencies; median MCAT total score; median undergraduate GPA; acceptance rate; and faculty resources. *U.S. News & World Report, "America's Best Graduate Schools, Medical, 2025"*

EMPLOYERS

Major Employers

Company Name	Industry
Arkansas Blue Cross and Blue Shield	Hospitals and medical service plans
Arkansas Childrens Hospital	Specialty hospitals, except psychiatric
Baptist Health Systems	General medical & surgical hospitals
Dassault Falcon Jet Corp	Aviation and or aeronautical engineering
Dept of Highway and Trans Arkansas	Regulation, administration of transportation
Dept of Finance & Admin Arkansas	Finance, taxation, and monetary policy
Fidelity Information Systems	Data processing services
Loreal USA	Toilet preparations
Mountaire Farms	Broiler, fryer and roaster chickens
Pulaski County	General practice, attorney
St. Vincent Health System	Medical services organization
United States Dept of Veteran Affairs	General medical & surgical hospitals
University of Arkansas System	Colleges & universities
Valor Telecommunications	Voice telephone communications
Veterans Health Administration	Administration of veterans' affairs

Note: Companies shown are located within the Little Rock-North Little Rock-Conway, AR Metropolitan Statistical Area.
Source: Chambers of Commerce; State Departments of Labor; Wikipedia

PUBLIC SAFETY

Crime Rate

Area	Total Crime Rate	Violent Crime Rate				Property Crime Rate		
		Murder	Rape	Robbery	Aggrav. Assault	Burglary	Larceny-Theft	Motor Vehicle Theft
City	7,228.6	30.5	122.2	223.2	1,425.2	925.7	4,003.7	498.1
U.S.	2,290.9	5.7	38.0	66.5	264.1	250.7	1,347.2	318.7

Note: Figures are crimes per 100,000 population.
Source: FBI, Table 8, Offenses Known to Law Enforcement, by State by City, 2023

Hate Crimes

Area	Number of Quarters Reported	Number of Incidents per Bias Motivation					
		Race/Ethnicity/Ancestry	Religion	Sexual Orientation	Disability	Gender	Gender Identity
City	4	0	0	0	0	0	0
U.S.	4	5,900	2,699	2,077	187	92	492

Source: Federal Bureau of Investigation, Hate Crime Statistics 2023

Identity Theft Consumer Reports

Area	Reports	Reports per 100,000 Population	Rank[2]
MSA[1]	2,641	350	36
U.S.	1,135,291	339	-

Note: (1) Figures cover the Little Rock-North Little Rock-Conway, AR Metropolitan Statistical Area; (2) Rank ranges from 1 to 401 where 1 indicates greatest number of identity theft reports per 100,000 population
Source: Federal Trade Commission, Consumer Sentinel Network Data Book 2024

Fraud and Other Consumer Reports

Area	Reports	Reports per 100,000 Population	Rank[2]
MSA[1]	10,233	1,358	84
U.S.	5,360,641	1,601	-

Note: (1) Figures cover the Little Rock-North Little Rock-Conway, AR Metropolitan Statistical Area; (2) Rank ranges from 1 to 401 where 1 indicates greatest number of fraud and other consumer reports per 100,000 population
Source: Federal Trade Commission, Consumer Sentinel Network Data Book 2024

POLITICS

2024 Presidential Election Results

Area	Trump (Rep.)	Harris (Dem.)	Stein (Green)	Kennedy (Ind.)	Oliver (Lib.)	Other
Pulaski County	37.7	59.8	0.6	1.1	0.5	0.3
U.S.	49.7	48.2	0.6	0.5	0.4	0.6

Note: Results are percentages and may not add to 100% due to rounding
Source: Dave Leip's Atlas of U.S. Presidential Elections

SPORTS

Professional Sports Teams

Team Name	League	Year Established
No teams are located in the metro area		

Source: Wikipedia, Major Professional Sports Teams of the United States and Canada, May 1, 2025

CLIMATE

Average and Extreme Temperatures

Temperature	Jan	Feb	Mar	Apr	May	Jun	Jul	Aug	Sep	Oct	Nov	Dec	Yr.
Extreme High (°F)	83	85	91	95	98	105	112	108	103	97	86	80	112
Average High (°F)	50	54	63	73	81	89	92	91	85	75	62	53	73
Average Temp. (°F)	40	45	53	63	71	79	82	81	74	63	52	43	62
Average Low (°F)	30	34	42	51	60	68	72	70	63	51	41	34	51
Extreme Low (°F)	-4	-5	17	28	40	46	54	52	38	29	17	-1	-5

Note: Figures cover the years 1948-1990
Source: National Climatic Data Center, International Station Meteorological Climate Summary, 9/96

Average Precipitation/Snowfall/Humidity

Precip./Humidity	Jan	Feb	Mar	Apr	May	Jun	Jul	Aug	Sep	Oct	Nov	Dec	Yr.
Avg. Precip. (in.)	4.1	4.2	4.9	5.2	5.4	3.6	3.5	3.2	3.8	3.5	4.8	4.5	50.7
Avg. Snowfall (in.)	3	2	1	Tr	0	0	0	0	0	0	Tr	1	5
Avg. Rel. Hum. 6am (%)	80	80	78	81	86	86	87	88	87	86	82	80	84
Avg. Rel. Hum. 3pm (%)	57	54	50	50	53	52	54	52	52	48	52	57	53

Note: Figures cover the years 1948-1990; Tr = Trace amounts (<0.05 in. of rain; <0.5 in. of snow)
Source: National Climatic Data Center, International Station Meteorological Climate Summary, 9/96

Weather Conditions

Temperature			Daytime Sky			Precipitation		
10°F & below	32°F & below	90°F & above	Clear	Partly cloudy	Cloudy	0.01 inch or more precip.	0.1 inch or more snow/ice	Thunder-storms
1	57	73	110	142	113	104	4	57

Note: Figures are average number of days per year and cover the years 1948-1990
Source: National Climatic Data Center, International Station Meteorological Climate Summary, 9/96

HAZARDOUS WASTE

Superfund Sites

The Little Rock-North Little Rock-Conway, AR metro area is home to one site on the EPA's Superfund National Priorities List (NPL) or Superfund Alternative Approach (SAA) list: **Vertac, Inc.** (Final NPL). The Superfund alternative approach uses the same investigation and cleanup process and standards that are used for sites listed on the National Priorities List. The SAA is an alternative to listing a site on the NPL; it is not an alternative to Superfund or the Superfund process. There are a total of 1,445 Superfund sites with a status of proposed or final on both lists in the United States. *U.S. Environmental Protection Agency, National Priorities List, May 1, 2025; U.S. Environmental Protection Agency, Superfund Alternative Approach Sites, May 1, 2025*

AIR QUALITY

Air Quality Trends: Ozone

	1990	1995	2000	2005	2010	2015	2020	2021	2022	2023
MSA[1]	0.080	0.086	0.090	0.083	0.072	0.063	0.062	0.066	0.063	0.067
U.S.	0.087	0.089	0.081	0.080	0.072	0.068	0.066	0.067	0.067	0.070

Note: (1) Data covers the Little Rock-North Little Rock-Conway, AR Metropolitan Statistical Area. The values shown are the composite ozone concentration averages among trend sites based on the highest fourth daily maximum 8-hour concentration in parts per million. These trends are based on sites having an adequate record of monitoring data during the trend period. Data from exceptional events are included.
Source: U.S. Environmental Protection Agency, Air Quality Monitoring Information, "Air Quality Trends by City, 1990-2023"

Air Quality Index

Area	Percent of Days when Air Quality was...[2]					AQI Statistics[2]	
	Good	Moderate	Unhealthy for Sensitive Groups	Unhealthy	Very Unhealthy	Maximum	Median
MSA[1]	33.4	65.2	1.1	0.3	0.0	174	55

Note: (1) Data covers the Little Rock-North Little Rock-Conway, AR Metropolitan Statistical Area; (2) Based on 365 days with AQI data in 2023. Air Quality Index (AQI) is an index for reporting daily air quality. EPA calculates the AQI for five major air pollutants regulated by the Clean Air Act: ground-level ozone, particle pollution (aka particulate matter), carbon monoxide, sulfur dioxide, and nitrogen dioxide. The AQI runs from 0 to 500. The higher the AQI value, the greater the level of air pollution and the greater the health concern. There are six AQI categories: "Good" AQI is between 0 and 50. Air quality is considered satisfactory; "Moderate" AQI is between 51 and 100. Air quality is acceptable; "Unhealthy for Sensitive Groups" When AQI values are between 101 and 150, members of sensitive groups may experience health effects; "Unhealthy" When AQI values are between 151 and 200 everyone may begin to experience health effects; "Very Unhealthy" AQI values between 201 and 300 trigger a health alert; "Hazardous" AQI values over 300 trigger warnings of emergency conditions (not shown).
Source: U.S. Environmental Protection Agency, Air Quality Index Report, 2023

Air Quality Index Pollutants

Area	Percent of Days when AQI Pollutant was...[2]					
	Carbon Monoxide	Nitrogen Dioxide	Ozone	Sulfur Dioxide	Particulate Matter 2.5	Particulate Matter 10
MSA[1]	0.0	0.0	16.4	(3)	83.6	0.0

Note: (1) Data covers the Little Rock-North Little Rock-Conway, AR Metropolitan Statistical Area; (2) Based on 365 days with AQI data in 2023. The Air Quality Index (AQI) is an index for reporting daily air quality. EPA calculates the AQI for five major air pollutants regulated by the Clean Air Act: ground-level ozone, particle pollution (also known as particulate matter), carbon monoxide, sulfur dioxide, and nitrogen dioxide. The AQI runs from 0 to 500. The higher the AQI value, the greater the level of air pollution and the greater the health concern; (3) Sulfur dioxide is no longer included in this table because SO_2 concentrations tend to be very localized and not necessarily representative of broad geographical areas like counties and CBSAs.
Source: U.S. Environmental Protection Agency, Air Quality Index Report, 2023

Maximum Air Pollutant Concentrations: Particulate Matter, Ozone, CO and Lead

	Particulate Matter 10 (ug/m³)	Particulate Matter 2.5 Wtd AM (ug/m³)	Particulate Matter 2.5 24-Hr (ug/m³)	Ozone (ppm)	Carbon Monoxide (ppm)	Lead (ug/m³)
MSA[1] Level	39	10.8	23	0.07	1	n/a
NAAQS[2]	150	15	35	0.075	9	0.15
Met NAAQS[2]	Yes	Yes	Yes	Yes	Yes	n/a

Note: (1) Data covers the Little Rock-North Little Rock-Conway, AR Metropolitan Statistical Area; Data from exceptional events are included; (2) National Ambient Air Quality Standards; ppm = parts per million; ug/m³ = micrograms per cubic meter; n/a not available.
Concentrations: Particulate Matter 10 (coarse particulate)—highest second maximum 24-hour concentration; Particulate Matter 2.5 Wtd AM (fine particulate)—highest weighted annual mean concentration; Particulate Matter 2.5 24-Hour (fine particulate)—highest 98th percentile 24-hour concentration; Ozone—highest fourth daily maximum 8-hour concentration; Carbon Monoxide—highest second maximum non-overlapping 8-hour concentration; Lead—maximum running 3-month average
Source: U.S. Environmental Protection Agency, Air Quality Monitoring Information, "Air Quality Statistics by City, 2023"

Maximum Air Pollutant Concentrations: Nitrogen Dioxide and Sulfur Dioxide

	Nitrogen Dioxide AM (ppb)	Nitrogen Dioxide 1-Hr (ppb)	Sulfur Dioxide AM (ppb)	Sulfur Dioxide 1-Hr (ppb)	Sulfur Dioxide 24-Hr (ppb)
MSA[1] Level	3	13	n/a	4	n/a
NAAQS[2]	53	100	30	75	140
Met NAAQS[2]	Yes	Yes	n/a	Yes	n/a

Note: (1) Data covers the Little Rock-North Little Rock-Conway, AR Metropolitan Statistical Area; Data from exceptional events are included; (2) National Ambient Air Quality Standards; ppm = parts per million; ug/m³ = micrograms per cubic meter; n/a not available.
Concentrations: Nitrogen Dioxide AM—highest arithmetic mean concentration; Nitrogen Dioxide 1-Hr—highest 98th percentile 1-hour daily maximum concentration; Sulfur Dioxide AM—highest annual mean concentration; Sulfur Dioxide 1-Hr—highest 99th percentile 1-hour daily maximum concentration; Sulfur Dioxide 24-Hr—highest second maximum 24-hour concentration
Source: U.S. Environmental Protection Agency, Air Quality Monitoring Information, "Air Quality Statistics by City, 2023"

Madison, Wisconsin

Background

Madison was selected as Wisconsin's territorial capital in 1836 before construction of the city began in 1838. Despite repeated attempts to move the capital elsewhere by members of the legislature, it has maintained its status. It was named for President James Madison in 1836 and incorporated into a village in 1856. When Wisconsin attained statehood in 1848, the University of Wisconsin (one of the largest in the country) was established.

Most of the city, including its business center, is situated on an isthmus between Lake Mendota and Lake Minona in the south-central part of the state. Two other lakes, Kengonsa and Waubesa, lie to the south. By ordinance, the city's skyline is dominated by the capitol dome, which weighs 2,500 tons.

Madison serves as the trade center of a rich agricultural and dairy region. Food processing is a major industry. Batteries, dairy equipment, and machine tools are produced there as well.

Wisconsin state government and the University of Wisconsin-Madison remain the two largest Madison employers. Madison continues to evolve from a government-based economy to consumer services and a base for high-tech, particularly in the health, biotech, and advertising sectors. Beginning in the early 1990s, the city experienced a steady economic boom fostered by the development of high-tech companies and UW-Madison working with local businesses and entrepreneurs to transfer the results of academic research into real-world applications, especially bio-tech applications. UW-Madison also offers fully online degrees. Businesses are attracted to Madison's skill base, taking advantage of the area's high level of education.

The city has received numerous awards, beginning in 1948 when it was named Best Place to Live in America by *Life* magazine. Although Madison is a progressive, eclectic city, it also offers the atmosphere of a small town with many picturesque communities, four lakes, and over 300 parks. There are a total of 29,000 acres designated for recreational use, including 46 miles of hiking trails, over 150 miles of bicycle trails, 92 miles of shoreline for swimming and boating, and 20 golf courses. The city claims to be the bike capital of the Midwest, with more bikes than cars and more than 200 miles of scenic biking and hiking trails.

Madison's many restaurants boast a large variety of ethnic food, from Greek and Italian to Japanese, Mexican, and Middle Eastern, as well as many brew pubs.

Cultural life in Madison is centered downtown at the Madison Civic Center and its associated sites. Project Overture renovated and redeveloped a variety of cultural venues, including the Madison Museum of Contemporary Art with innovative design and sculpture-garden rooftop. A 2,250-seat hall houses the Madison Symphony Orchestra, whose old home, the Oscar Meyer Theater, is used by groups such as the CTM Family Theatre and the Wisconsin Chamber group. Keeping the goal of architectural integration in mind, facades of nearby buildings have been refurbished and preserved.

In 2018, Forward Madison FC became the city's first professional soccer team.

Another major attraction in Madison is the Olbrich Botanical Gardens, with 16 acres of outdoor display gardens, including sunken, perennial, rose, rock, herb, and wildflower gardens. Over 340,000 visitors a year enjoy the gardens, which include a lush, tropical conservatory filled with exotic plants, bright flowers, a rushing waterfall, and free-flying birds.

Madison is home to many institutions of higher learning, including the University of Wisconsin-Madison, Edgewood College, Herzing College, Lakeland College, and Madison Media Institute.

The area has the typical continental climate of interior North America with a large annual temperature range and frequent short-period temperature changes. The city lies in the path of the frequent cyclones and anticyclones that move eastward over this area during fall, winter, and spring. Frequent polar air masses and occasional influxes of arctic air affect the area during the winter months. Summers are pleasant, with only occasional periods of extreme heat or high humidity.

Rankings

General Rankings

- To help military veterans find the best places in which to settle down, *WalletHub* compared the 100 largest U.S. cities across 19 key indicators of livability, affordability and veteran-friendliness. They range from the share of military skill-related jobs to veteran income growth to the availability of VA health facilities. Madison ranked #8. *Wallethub.com, "Best & Worst Places for Veterans to Live (2025)," November 7, 2024*

- *US News & World Report* conducted a survey of more than 3,500 people and analyzed the 150 largest metropolitan areas to determine what matters most when selecting the next place to live. Madison ranked #14 out of the top 25 as having the best combination of desirable factors. Criteria: cost of living; quality of life and education; climate; job market; desirability; and other factors. *realestate.usnews.com, "Best Places to Live in the U.S. in 2024-2025," May 21, 2024*

- Madison was selected as one of the happiest places to live in America by *Outside Magazine*. Criteria centered on overall well being; effect of climate change; inclusivity; affordability; outdoor access; and other demographic and population figures. Local experts shared highlights from hands-on experience in each location. *Outside Magazine, "The 15 Happiest Places to Live in the U.S.," September 18, 2023*

- In their annual survey, Livability.com looked at data for more than 2,000 mid-sized U.S. cities to assign a "Livability Score" for each. The top 100 scoring cities make up Livability's "Top 100 Best Places to Live in the U.S." in 2025. Madison was placed among the top 100 of the customizable list. Criteria: housing and economy; cost of living; environment; education; health care options; transportation; safety; and community amenities. *Livability.com, "Top 100 Best Places to Live in the U.S. in 2025" April 15, 2025*

Business/Finance Rankings

- According to *Business Insider*, the Madison metro area is a prime place to run a startup or move an existing business to. The area ranked #13. More than 300 metro areas were analyzed for factors that were of top concern to new business owners. Data was based on the 2019 U.S. Census Bureau American Community Survey, statistics from the CDC, and University of Chicago analysis. Criteria: business formations; percentage of vaccinated population; percentage of households with internet subscriptions; median household income; and share of work that can be done from home. *BusinessInsider.com, "The 20 Best Cities for Starting a Business in 2022 Include Denver, Raleigh, and Olympia," June 7, 2022*

- The Madison metro area appeared on the Milken Institute "2025 Best Performing Cities" list. Rank: #74 out of 200 large metro areas (based on performance category). Criteria: job growth; wage growth; high-tech growth and impact; community resilience; housing affordability; household broadband access. *Milken Institute, "Best-Performing Cities 2025," January 14, 2025*

Education Rankings

- Personal finance website *WalletHub* analyzed the 150 largest U.S. metropolitan statistical areas to determine where the most educated Americans are putting their degrees to work. Criteria: education levels; percentage of workers with degrees; education quality and attainment gap; public school quality rankings; quality and enrollment of each metro area's universities. Madison was ranked #5 (#1 = most educated city). *WalletHub.com, "Most & Least Educated Cities in America, 2025" July 2, 2024*

Environmental Rankings

- The U.S. Conference of Mayors and Walmart Stores sponsor the Mayors' Climate Protection Awards Program which recognize mayors for outstanding and innovative practices that address the climate crisis: increase energy efficiency in their cities, reduce carbon emissions and expand renewable energy. Madison received an Honorable Mention in the large city category. *U.S. Conference of Mayors, "2024 Mayors' Climate Protection Awards," June 20, 2024*

Food/Drink Rankings

- WalletHub compared the 100 largest U.S. cities across 17 key indicators of vegan- and vegetarian-friendliness. Madison was ranked #17. Cities were selected based on metrics such as the cost of groceries for vegetarians, the share of restaurants serving meatless options and the number of salad shops per capita. *WalletHub.com, "Best Cities for Vegans & Vegetarians (2025)," September 24, 2024*

Health/Fitness Rankings

- For each of the 100 largest cities in the United States, the American Fitness Index®, compiled in partnership between the American College of Sports Medicine and the Elevance Health Foundation, evaluated community infrastructure and more than 30 health behaviors including preventive health, levels of chronic disease conditions, food insecurity, pedestrian safety, air quality, and community/environment resources that support physical activity. Madison ranked #5 for "community fitness." *americanfitnessindex.org*, *"2024 ACSM American Fitness Index Summary Report,"* July 23, 2024

- Madison was identified as a "2025 Allergy Capital." The area ranked #93 out of the nation's 100 largest metropolitan areas. Three groups of factors were used to identify the most challenging cities for people with allergies: annual tree, grass, and weed pollen scores; over the counter allergy medicine use; number of board-certified allergy specialists. *Asthma and Allergy Foundation of America, "2025 Allergy Capitals: The Most Challenging Places to Live with Allergies," March 18, 2025*

- Madison was identified as a "2024 Asthma Capital." The area ranked #97 out of the nation's 100 largest metropolitan areas. Criteria: estimated asthma prevalence; asthma-related mortality; and ER visits due to asthma. Risk factors analyzed but not factored in the rankings: annual air quality including pollution and ozone levels; public smoking laws; indoor air quality; access to asthma specialists; rescue and controller medication use; uninsured rate; pollen allergy; poverty rate. *Asthma and Allergy Foundation of America, "Asthma Capitals 2024: The Most Challenging Places to Live With Asthma," September 10, 2024*

Pet Rankings

- Madison was selected by *Sniffspot.com* as one of the most dog-friendly cities in the U.S., ranking #50 out of 50. Criteria: dog parks; hiking; sniffspots; public parks; dog-friendly businesses; housing; dog waste cleanliness; leash laws; dog services; and overall cost. *Sniffspot.com, "The Top 50 Most Dog-Friendly Cities in the U.S.," September 30, 2024*

Real Estate Rankings

- *WalletHub* compared the most populated U.S. cities to determine which had the best markets for real estate agents. Madison ranked #60 where demand was high and pay was the best. Criteria: sales per agent; annual median wage for real-estate agents; monthly average starting salary for real estate agents; real estate job density and competition; unemployment rate; home turnover rate; housing-market health index; and other relevant metrics. *WalletHub.com, "2021 Best Places to Be a Real Estate Agent," May 12, 2021*

- Madison was ranked #96 out of 176 metro areas in terms of cost of housing in 2024 by the National Association of Home Builders (#1 = most affordable). Criteria: the portion of an average family's income necessary to pay the mortgage on a median-priced home. *National Association of Home Builders®, NAHB-Wells Fargo Cost of Housing Index, 4th Quarter 2024*

Safety Rankings

- Allstate ranked the 100 most populous cities in America in terms of driver safety. Madison ranked #48. Criteria based on anonymized driving behavior data from Allstate's mobile app powered by Arity: high speed driving (over 80 mph), phone handling, and hard braking. The report helps increase the importance of safety and awareness behind the wheel. *Allstate, "16th Allstate America's Best Drivers Report®" July 11, 2024*

Women/Minorities Rankings

- Personal finance website *WalletHub* compared more than 180 U.S. cities across two key dimensions, "Hispanic Business-Friendliness" and "Hispanic Purchasing Power," to arrive at the most favorable conditions for Hispanic entrepreneurs. Madison was ranked #89 out of 182. Criteria includes: share of Hispanic-Owned Businesses; average growth of Hispanic Business revenues; Small Business-Friendliness score; affordability; and number of Hispanics with at least a bachelor's degree. *WalletHub.com, "Best Cities for Hispanic Entrepreneurs," September 4, 2024*

Miscellaneous Rankings

- *MoveHub* ranked 446 hipster cities across 20 countries, using its new and improved alternative Hipster Index and Madison came out as #30 among the top 50. Criteria: population over 150,000; number of vintage boutiques; density of tattoo parlors; vegan places to eat; coffee shops; and density of vinyl record stores. *MoveHub.com, "The Hipster Index: Brighton Pips Portland to Global Top Spot," July 28, 2021*

- *WalletHub* compared 148 of the most populated U.S. cities to determine their operating efficiency. A "Quality of Services" score was constructed for each city and then measured against the total budget per capita to reveal which were managed the best. Madison ranked #21. Criteria: financial stability; economy; education; safety; health; infrastructure and pollution. *WalletHub.com, "2025's Best- & Worst-Run Cities in America," June 18, 2024*

Business Environment

DEMOGRAPHICS

Population Growth

Area	1990 Census	2000 Census	2010 Census	2020 Census	2023 Estimate[2]	Population Growth 1990-2023 (%)
City	193,451	208,054	233,209	269,840	275,568	42.4
MSA[1]	432,323	501,774	568,593	680,796	683,967	58.2
U.S.	248,709,873	281,421,906	308,745,538	331,449,281	332,387,540	33.6

Note: (1) Figures cover the Madison, WI Metropolitan Statistical Area; (2) 2019-2023 5-year ACS population estimate
Source: U.S. Census Bureau, 1990 Census, 2000 Census, 2010 Census, 2020 Census, 2019-2023 American Community Survey 5-Year Estimates

Race

Area	White Alone[2] (%)	Black Alone[2] (%)	Asian Alone[2] (%)	AIAN[3] Alone[2] (%)	NHOPI[4] Alone[2] (%)	Other Race Alone[2] (%)	Two or More Races (%)
City	73.0	7.1	8.0	0.4	0.0	2.1	9.4
MSA[1]	81.4	4.5	5.0	0.3	0.1	1.7	7.1
U.S.	63.4	12.4	5.8	0.9	0.2	6.6	10.7

Note: (1) Figures cover the Madison, WI Metropolitan Statistical Area; (2) Alone is defined as not being in combination with one or more other races; (3) American Indian and Alaska Native; (4) Native Hawaiian and Other Pacific Islander
Source: U.S. Census Bureau, 2019-2023 American Community Survey 5-Year Estimates

Hispanic or Latino Origin

Area	Total (%)	Mexican (%)	Puerto Rican (%)	Cuban (%)	Other (%)
City	9.3	5.7	0.7	0.2	2.8
MSA[1]	6.9	4.2	0.6	0.1	1.9
U.S.	19.0	11.3	1.8	0.7	5.2

Note: Persons of Hispanic or Latino origin can be of any race; (1) Figures cover the Madison, WI Metropolitan Statistical Area
Source: U.S. Census Bureau, 2019-2023 American Community Survey 5-Year Estimates

Age

Area	Percent of Population									Median Age
	Under Age 5	Age 5–19	Age 20–34	Age 35–44	Age 45–54	Age 55–64	Age 65–74	Age 75–84	Age 85+	
City	4.8	16.9	33.7	12.8	9.6	9.5	7.7	3.6	1.4	31.8
MSA[1]	5.2	18.3	23.8	13.6	11.6	12.0	9.6	4.2	1.7	36.9
U.S.	5.7	19.1	20.2	13.1	12.3	12.8	10.0	4.9	1.9	38.7

Note: (1) Figures cover the Madison, WI Metropolitan Statistical Area
Source: U.S. Census Bureau, 2019-2023 American Community Survey 5-Year Estimates

Disability by Age

Area	All Ages	Under 18 Years Old	18 to 64 Years Old	65 Years and Over
City	9.1	4.1	7.5	24.6
MSA[1]	9.4	3.8	7.6	24.3
U.S.	13.0	4.7	10.7	32.9

Note: Figures show percent of the civilian noninstitutionalized population that reported having a disability. Disability status is determined from six types of difficulty: vision, hearing, cognitive, ambulatory, self-care, and independent living. For children under 5 years old, hearing and vision difficulty are used to determine disability status. For children between the ages of 5 and 14, disability status is determined from hearing, vision, cognitive, ambulatory, and self-care difficulties. For people aged 15 years and older, they are considered to have a disability if they have difficulty with any one of the six difficulty types; Note: (1) Figures cover the Madison, WI Metropolitan Statistical Area
Source: U.S. Census Bureau, 2019-2023 American Community Survey 5-Year Estimates

Ancestry

Area	German	Irish	English	American	Italian	Polish	French[2]	European	Scottish
City	28.4	12.2	9.2	1.9	4.0	5.5	2.0	2.0	1.9
MSA[1]	34.3	12.8	9.8	2.6	3.5	5.0	2.3	1.9	1.7
U.S.	12.6	9.4	9.1	5.5	4.9	2.6	2.0	1.6	1.6

Note: Figures are the percentage of the total population reporting a particular ancestry. The nine most commonly reported ancestries in the U.S. are shown. Figures include multiple ancestries (e.g. if a person reported being Irish and Italian, they were included in both columns); (1) Figures cover the Madison, WI Metropolitan Statistical Area; (2) Excludes Basque
Source: U.S. Census Bureau, 2019-2023 American Community Survey 5-Year Estimates

Foreign-born Population

Area	Percent of Population Born in								
	Any Foreign Country	Asia	Mexico	Europe	Caribbean	Central America[2]	South America	Africa	Canada
City	11.6	5.5	1.9	1.4	0.2	0.2	1.1	1.0	0.2
MSA[1]	7.6	3.3	1.3	1.0	0.1	0.2	0.8	0.6	0.2
U.S.	13.9	4.3	3.3	1.4	1.4	1.2	1.2	0.8	0.2

Note: (1) Figures cover the Madison, WI Metropolitan Statistical Area; (2) Excludes Mexico.
Source: U.S. Census Bureau, 2019-2023 American Community Survey 5-Year Estimates

Household Size

Area	Persons in Household (%)							Average Household Size
	One	Two	Three	Four	Five	Six	Seven or More	
City	39.0	35.2	12.0	9.1	3.3	0.8	0.7	2.09
MSA[1]	32.9	36.5	13.2	11.1	4.3	1.4	0.7	2.25
U.S.	28.5	33.8	15.4	12.7	5.9	2.3	1.4	2.54

Note: (1) Figures cover the Madison, WI Metropolitan Statistical Area
Source: U.S. Census Bureau, 2019-2023 American Community Survey 5-Year Estimates

Household Relationships

Area	Householder	Opposite-sex Spouse	Same-sex Spouse	Opposite-sex Unmarried Partner	Same-sex Unmarried Partner	Child[2]	Grandchild	Other Relatives	Non-relatives
City	44.8	14.5	0.4	3.8	0.3	19.7	0.7	2.4	8.2
MSA[1]	42.2	18.6	0.3	3.3	0.2	25.0	0.8	2.1	4.5
U.S.	38.3	17.5	0.2	2.5	0.2	28.3	2.4	4.8	3.4

Note: Figures are percent of the total population; (1) Figures cover the Madison, WI Metropolitan Statistical Area; (2) Includes biological, adopted, and stepchildren of the householder
Source: U.S. Census Bureau, 2020 Census

Gender

Area	Males	Females	Males per 100 Females
City	137,655	137,913	99.8
MSA[1]	343,409	340,558	100.8
U.S.	164,545,087	167,842,453	98.0

Note: (1) Figures cover the Madison, WI Metropolitan Statistical Area
Source: U.S. Census Bureau, 2019-2023 American Community Survey 5-Year Estimates

Marital Status

Area	Never Married	Now Married[2]	Separated	Widowed	Divorced
City	50.7	37.5	0.8	3.0	8.0
MSA[1]	37.6	48.1	0.7	4.1	9.5
U.S.	34.1	47.9	1.7	5.6	10.7

Note: Figures are percentages and cover the population 15 years of age and older; (1) Figures cover the Madison, WI Metropolitan Statistical Area; (2) Excludes separated
Source: U.S. Census Bureau, 2019-2023 American Community Survey 5-Year Estimates

Religious Groups by Family

Area	Catholic	Baptist	Methodist	LDS[2]	Pentecostal	Lutheran	Islam	Adventist	Other
MSA[1]	14.4	0.5	2.0	0.7	0.2	9.2	1.2	0.7	8.4
U.S.	18.7	7.3	3.0	2.0	1.8	1.7	1.3	1.3	11.6

Note: Figures are the number of adherents as a percentage of the total population and cover the eight largest religious groups in the U.S; (1) Figures cover the Madison, WI Metropolitan Statistical Area; (2) Church of Jesus Christ of Latter-day Saints
Sources: 2020 U.S. Religion Census, Association of Statisticians of American Religious Bodies; The Association of Religion Data Archives (ARDA)

Religious Groups by Tradition

Area	Catholic	Evangelical Protestant	Mainline Protestant	Black Protestant	Islam	Judaism	Hinduism	Orthodox	Buddhism
MSA[1]	14.4	8.0	10.6	0.2	1.2	0.4	0.1	0.1	0.9
U.S.	18.7	16.5	5.2	2.3	1.3	0.6	0.4	0.4	0.3

Note: Figures are the number of adherents as a percentage of the total population; (1) Figures cover the Madison, WI Metropolitan Statistical Area
Sources: 2020 U.S. Religion Census, Association of Statisticians of American Religious Bodies; The Association of Religion Data Archives (ARDA)

ECONOMY

Real Gross Domestic Product (GDP)

Area	2017	2018	2019	2020	2021	2022	2023	Rank[3]
MSA[1]	47.4	49.3	50.6	49.4	52.3	53.4	55.1	59
U.S.[2]	17,619.1	18,160.7	18,642.5	18,238.9	19,387.6	19,896.6	20,436.3	—

Note: Figures are in billions of chained 2017 dollars; (1) Figures cover the Madison, WI Metropolitan Statistical Area; (2) Figures cover real GDP within metropolitan areas; (3) Rank is based on 2023 data and ranges from 1 to 384
Source: U.S. Bureau of Economic Analysis

Economic Growth

Area	2014	2015	2016	2017	2018	2019	2020	2021	2022	2023
MSA[1]	5.0	3.7	3.3	1.5	3.9	2.7	-2.4	5.9	2.2	3.2
U.S.[2]	2.6	3.2	2.0	2.7	3.1	2.7	-2.2	6.3	2.6	2.7

Note: Figures are real gross domestic product growth rates and represent percent change from preceding period; (1) Figures cover the Madison, WI Metropolitan Statistical Area; (2) Figures are the average growth rates within metropolitan areas
Source: U.S. Bureau of Economic Analysis

Metropolitan Area Exports

Area	2018	2019	2020	2021	2022	2023	Rank[2]
MSA[1]	2,460.2	2,337.6	2,450.5	2,756.3	2,893.8	2,822.9	90
U.S.	1,664,056.1	1,645,173.7	1,431,406.6	1,753,941.4	2,062,937.4	2,019,160.5	—

Note: Figures are in millions of dollars; (1) Figures cover the Madison, WI Metropolitan Statistical Area; (2) Rank is based on 2023 data and ranges from 1 to 386
Source: U.S. Department of Commerce, International Trade Administration, Office of Trade and Economic Analysis, Industry and Analysis, Exports by Metropolitan Area, data extracted April 2, 2025

Building Permits

Area	Single-Family			Multi-Family			Total		
	2023	2024	Pct. Chg.	2023	2024	Pct. Chg.	2023	2024	Pct. Chg.
City	332	250	-24.7	2,288	2,562	12.0	2,620	2,812	7.3
MSA[1]	1,534	1,679	9.5	3,827	4,159	8.7	5,361	5,838	8.9
U.S.	920,000	981,900	6.7	591,100	496,100	-16.1	1,511,100	1,478,000	-2.2

Note: (1) Figures cover the Madison, WI Metropolitan Statistical Area; Figures represent new, privately-owned housing units authorized (unadjusted data)
Source: U.S. Census Bureau, Building Permits Survey (BPS), 2023, 2024

Bankruptcy Filings

Area	Business Filings			Nonbusiness Filings		
	2023	2024	% Chg.	2023	2024	% Chg.
Dane County	25	21	-16.0	437	494	13.0
U.S.	18,926	23,107	22.1	434,064	494,201	13.9

Note: Business filings include Chapter 7, Chapter 9, Chapter 11, Chapter 12, Chapter 13, Chapter 15, and Section 304; Nonbusiness filings include Chapter 7, Chapter 11, and Chapter 13
Source: Administrative Office of the U.S. Courts, Business and Nonbusiness Bankruptcy, County Cases Commenced by Chapter of the Bankruptcy Code, During the 12-Month Period Ending December 31, 2023 and Business and Nonbusiness Bankruptcy, County Cases Commenced by Chapter of the Bankruptcy Code, During the 12-Month Period Ending December 31, 2024

Housing Vacancy Rates

Area	Gross Vacancy Rate[3] (%)			Year-Round Vacancy Rate[4] (%)			Rental Vacancy Rate[5] (%)			Homeowner Vacancy Rate[6] (%)		
	2022	2023	2024	2022	2023	2024	2022	2023	2024	2022	2023	2024
MSA[1]	n/a	n/a	n/a	n/a	n/a	n/a	n/a	n/a	n/a	n/a	n/a	n/a
U.S.[2]	9.1	9.0	9.1	7.5	7.5	7.6	5.7	6.5	6.8	0.8	0.8	1.0

Note: (1) Figures cover the Madison, WI Metropolitan Statistical Area; (2) Figures cover the 75 largest Metropolitan Statistical Areas; (3) The percentage of the total housing inventory that is vacant; (4) The percentage of the housing inventory (excluding seasonal units) that is year-round vacant; (5) The percentage of rental inventory that is vacant for rent; (6) The percentage of homeowner inventory that is vacant for sale; n/a not available
Source: U.S. Census Bureau, Housing Vacancies and Homeownership Annual Statistics: 2022, 2023, 2024

INCOME

Income

Area	Per Capita ($)	Median Household ($)	Average Household ($)
City	48,557	76,983	104,969
MSA[1]	49,799	86,827	113,809
U.S.	43,289	78,538	110,491

Note: (1) Figures cover the Madison, WI Metropolitan Statistical Area
Source: U.S. Census Bureau, 2019-2023 American Community Survey 5-Year Estimates

Household Income Distribution

Area	Percent of Households Earning							
	Under $15,000	$15,000 -$24,999	$25,000 -$34,999	$35,000 -$49,999	$50,000 -$74,999	$75,000 -$99,999	$100,000 -$149,999	$150,000 and up
City	9.4	6.2	7.2	10.3	15.5	12.8	17.6	20.9
MSA[1]	6.5	5.2	6.1	9.4	16.1	13.5	19.4	23.8
U.S.	8.5	6.6	6.8	10.4	15.7	12.7	17.4	21.9

Note: (1) Figures cover the Madison, WI Metropolitan Statistical Area
Source: U.S. Census Bureau, 2019-2023 American Community Survey 5-Year Estimates

Poverty Rate

Area	All Ages	Under 18 Years Old	18 to 64 Years Old	65 Years and Over
City	16.2	13.1	18.7	7.0
MSA[1]	10.0	8.5	11.4	6.1
U.S.	12.4	16.3	11.6	10.4

Note: Figures are percentage of people whose income during the past 12 months was below the poverty level; (1) Figures cover the Madison, WI Metropolitan Statistical Area
Source: U.S. Census Bureau, 2019-2023 American Community Survey 5-Year Estimates

EMPLOYMENT

Labor Force and Employment

Area	Civilian Labor Force			Workers Employed		
	Dec. 2023	Dec. 2024	% Chg.	Dec. 2023	Dec. 2024	% Chg.
City	167,700	168,775	0.6	164,752	165,214	0.3
MSA[1]	410,987	413,894	0.7	403,502	404,881	0.3
U.S.	166,661,000	167,746,000	0.7	160,754,000	161,294,000	0.3

Note: Data is not seasonally adjusted and covers workers 16 years of age and older; (1) Figures cover the Madison, WI Metropolitan Statistical Area
Source: Bureau of Labor Statistics, Local Area Unemployment Statistics

Unemployment Rate

Area	2024											
	Jan.	Feb.	Mar.	Apr.	May	Jun.	Jul.	Aug.	Sep.	Oct.	Nov.	Dec.
City	1.9	2.2	2.4	2.2	2.3	2.8	2.6	2.3	2.2	2.1	2.1	2.1
MSA[1]	2.1	2.5	2.5	2.2	2.3	2.7	2.6	2.3	2.1	2.1	2.2	2.2
U.S.	4.1	4.2	3.9	3.5	3.7	4.3	4.5	4.4	3.9	3.9	4.0	3.8

Note: Data is not seasonally adjusted and covers workers 16 years of age and older; (1) Figures cover the Madison, WI Metropolitan Statistical Area
Source: Bureau of Labor Statistics, Local Area Unemployment Statistics

Average Wages

Occupation	$/Hr.	Occupation	$/Hr.
Accountants and Auditors	41.87	Maintenance and Repair Workers	26.12
Automotive Mechanics	28.99	Marketing Managers	67.95
Bookkeepers	25.40	Network and Computer Systems Admin.	41.94
Carpenters	32.44	Nurses, Licensed Practical	30.71
Cashiers	15.63	Nurses, Registered	46.09
Computer Programmers	42.40	Nursing Assistants	21.62
Computer Systems Analysts	46.04	Office Clerks, General	21.81
Computer User Support Specialists	29.81	Physical Therapists	47.86
Construction Laborers	27.12	Physicians	156.17
Cooks, Restaurant	18.70	Plumbers, Pipefitters and Steamfitters	42.99
Customer Service Representatives	23.53	Police and Sheriff's Patrol Officers	38.38
Dentists	98.38	Postal Service Mail Carriers	29.38
Electricians	36.51	Real Estate Sales Agents	32.13
Engineers, Electrical	51.89	Retail Salespersons	17.90
Fast Food and Counter Workers	14.40	Sales Representatives, Technical/Scientific	43.29
Financial Managers	77.53	Secretaries, Exc. Legal/Medical/Executive	24.50
First-Line Supervisors of Office Workers	36.80	Security Guards	21.74
General and Operations Managers	69.40	Surgeons	n/a
Hairdressers/Cosmetologists	17.58	Teacher Assistants, Exc. Postsecondary[1]	18.13
Home Health and Personal Care Aides	17.03	Teachers, Secondary School, Exc. Sp. Ed.[1]	30.40
Janitors and Cleaners	18.27	Telemarketers	17.61
Landscaping/Groundskeeping Workers	21.04	Truck Drivers, Heavy/Tractor-Trailer	27.62
Lawyers	69.54	Truck Drivers, Light/Delivery Services	23.52
Maids and Housekeeping Cleaners	16.72	Waiters and Waitresses	17.52

Note: Wage data covers the Madison, WI Metropolitan Statistical Area; (1) Hourly wages were calculated from annual wage data based on a 40 hour work week
Source: Bureau of Labor Statistics, Metro Area Occupational Employment & Wage Estimates, May 2024

Employment by Industry

Sector	MSA[1] Number of Employees	MSA[1] Percent of Total	U.S. Percent of Total
Construction, Mining, and Logging	19,800	4.6	5.5
Financial Activities	23,800	5.5	5.8
Government	96,400	22.4	14.9
Information	21,600	5.0	1.9
Leisure and Hospitality	36,100	8.4	10.4
Manufacturing	37,600	8.7	8.0
Other Services	21,300	5.0	3.7
Private Education and Health Services	56,200	13.1	16.9
Professional and Business Services	52,400	12.2	14.2
Retail Trade	39,000	9.1	10.0
Transportation, Warehousing, and Utilities	10,800	2.5	4.8
Wholesale Trade	15,300	3.6	3.9

Note: Figures are non-farm employment as of December 2024. Figures are not seasonally adjusted and include workers 16 years of age and older; (1) Figures cover the Madison, WI Metropolitan Statistical Area
Source: Bureau of Labor Statistics, Current Employment Statistics, Employment, Hours, and Earnings

Employment by Occupation

Occupation Classification	City (%)	MSA[1] (%)	U.S. (%)
Management, Business, Science, and Arts	57.7	52.4	42.0
Natural Resources, Construction, and Maintenance	3.5	6.2	8.6
Production, Transportation, and Material Moving	8.5	10.5	13.0
Sales and Office	15.9	17.4	19.9
Service	14.4	13.4	16.5

Note: Figures cover employed civilians 16 years of age and older; (1) Figures cover the Madison, WI Metropolitan Statistical Area
Source: U.S. Census Bureau, 2019-2023 American Community Survey 5-Year Estimates

Occupations with Greatest Projected Employment Growth: 2022 – 2032

Occupation[1]	2022 Employment	2032 Projected Employment	Numeric Employment Change	Percent Employment Change
Home Health and Personal Care Aides	80,600	94,000	13,400	16.6
Cooks, Restaurant	24,790	32,190	7,400	29.9
Laborers and Freight, Stock, and Material Movers, Hand	68,280	75,240	6,960	10.2
Stockers and Order Fillers	51,890	58,550	6,660	12.8
Software Developers	19,270	25,280	6,010	31.2
Fast Food and Counter Workers	56,080	60,930	4,850	8.6
Industrial Machinery Mechanics	16,970	21,220	4,250	25.0
Construction Laborers	23,620	27,590	3,970	16.8
Heavy and Tractor-Trailer Truck Drivers	52,250	56,180	3,930	7.5
Registered Nurses	62,260	65,570	3,310	5.3

Note: Projections cover Wisconsin; (1) Sorted by numeric employment change
Source: www.projectionscentral.org, State Occupational Projections, 2022–2032 Long-Term Projections

Fastest-Growing Occupations: 2022 – 2032

Occupation[1]	2022 Employment	2032 Projected Employment	Numeric Employment Change	Percent Employment Change
Nurse Practitioners	4,950	7,480	2,530	51.1
Data Scientists	2,860	4,090	1,230	43.0
Travel Agents	920	1,270	350	38.0
Animal Trainers	1,180	1,610	430	36.4
Statisticians	360	490	130	36.1
Information Security Analysts (SOC 2018)	2,410	3,220	810	33.6
Aircraft Service Attendants	150	200	50	33.3
Physician Assistants	2,980	3,950	970	32.6
Actuaries	990	1,310	320	32.3
Chemical Engineers	350	460	110	31.4

Note: Projections cover Wisconsin; (1) Sorted by percent employment change and excludes occupations with numeric employment change less than 50
Source: www.projectionscentral.org, State Occupational Projections, 2022–2032 Long-Term Projections

CITY FINANCES

City Government Finances

Component	2022 ($000)	2022 ($ per capita)
Total Revenues	669,011	2,543
Total Expenditures	654,893	2,489
Debt Outstanding	1,148,122	4,364

Source: U.S. Census Bureau, State & Local Government Finances 2022

City Government Revenue by Source

Source	2022 ($000)	2022 ($ per capita)	2022 (%)
General Revenue			
From Federal Government	64,103	244	9.6
From State Government	84,041	319	12.6
From Local Governments	15,143	58	2.3
Taxes			
Property	281,112	1,068	42.0
Sales and Gross Receipts	12,088	46	1.8
Personal Income	0	0	0.0
Corporate Income	0	0	0.0
Motor Vehicle License	0	0	0.0
Other Taxes	17,516	67	2.6
Current Charges	115,884	440	17.3
Liquor Store	0	0	0.0
Utility	51,663	196	7.7

Source: U.S. Census Bureau, State & Local Government Finances 2022

City Government Expenditures by Function

Function	2022 ($000)	2022 ($ per capita)	2022 (%)
General Direct Expenditures			
Air Transportation	0	0	0.0
Corrections	0	0	0.0
Education	0	0	0.0
Employment Security Administration	0	0	0.0
Financial Administration	6,920	26	1.1
Fire Protection	64,586	245	9.9
General Public Buildings	2,651	10	0.4
Governmental Administration, Other	18,647	70	2.8
Health	7,387	28	1.1
Highways	65,733	249	10.0
Hospitals	0	0	0.0
Housing and Community Development	52,706	200	8.0
Interest on General Debt	46,609	177	7.1
Judicial and Legal	3,136	11	0.5
Libraries	19,653	74	3.0
Parking	13,475	51	2.1
Parks and Recreation	40,935	155	6.3
Police Protection	83,281	316	12.7
Public Welfare	17,965	68	2.7
Sewerage	42,489	161	6.5
Solid Waste Management	14,759	56	2.3
Veterans' Services	0	0	0.0
Liquor Store	0	0	0.0
Utility	93,032	353	14.2

Source: U.S. Census Bureau, State & Local Government Finances 2022

TAXES

State Corporate Income Tax Rates

State	Tax Rate (%)	Income Brackets ($)	Num. of Brackets	Financial Institution Tax Rate (%)[a]	Federal Income Tax Ded.
Wisconsin	7.9	Flat rate	1	7.9	No

Note: Tax rates for tax year 2024; (a) Rates listed are the corporate income tax rate applied to financial institutions or excise taxes based on income. Some states have other taxes based upon the value of deposits or shares.
Source: Federation of Tax Administrators, State Corporate Income Tax Rates, January 1, 2025

State Individual Income Tax Rates

State	Tax Rate (%)	Income Brackets ($)	Personal Exemptions ($)			Standard Ded. ($)	
			Single	Married	Depend.	Single	Married
Wisconsin (a)	3.5 - 7.65	13,810 - 304,170 (y)	700	1,400	700	14,600	29,200 (z)

Note: Tax rates for tax year 2024; Local- and county-level taxes are not included; Federal income tax is not deductible on state income tax returns; (a) 16 states have statutory provision for automatically adjusting to the rate of inflation the dollar values of the income tax brackets, standard deductions, and/or personal exemptions. Oregon does not index the income brackets for $125,000 and over See: INFL and SPEC above; (y) The Wisconsin income brackets reported are for single individuals. For married taxpayers filing jointly, the same tax rates apply income brackets ranging from $18,420, to $405,550 in 2023; (z) Alabama standard deduction is phased out for incomes over $25,500 after 2017 (MFJ, HOH and Single); $12,750 for MFS. Rhode Island exemptions & standard deductions phased out for incomes over $274,650; Wisconsin standard deduciton phases out for income over $124,500.
Source: Federation of Tax Administrators, State Individual Income Tax Rates, January 1, 2025

Various State Sales and Excise Tax Rates

State	State Sales Tax (%)	Gasoline[1] ($/gal.)	Cigarette[2] ($/pack)	Spirits[3] ($/gal.)	Wine[4] ($/gal.)	Beer[5] ($/gal.)	Recreational Marijuana (%)
Wisconsin	5	0.33	2.52	3.25	0.25	0.06	Not legal

Note: All tax rates as of January 1, 2025; (1) The American Petroleum Institute has developed a methodology for determining the average tax rate on a gallon of fuel. Rates may include any of the following: excise taxes, environmental fees, storage tank fees, other fees or taxes, general sales tax, and local taxes; (2) The federal excise tax of $1.0066 per pack and local taxes are not included; (3) Rates are those applicable to off-premise sales of 40% alcohol by volume (a.b.v.) distilled spirits in 750ml containers. Local excise taxes are excluded; (4) Rates are those applicable to off-premise sales of 11% a.b.v. non-carbonated wine in 750ml containers; (5) Rates are those applicable to off-premise sales of 4.7% a.b.v. beer in 12 ounce containers.
Source: Tax Foundation, 2025 Facts & Figures: How Does Your State Compare?

State Tax Competitiveness Index

State	Overall Rank	Corporate Tax Rank	Individual Income Tax Rank	Sales Tax Rank	Property Tax Rank	Unemployment Insurance Tax Rank
Wisconsin	19	30	35	6	8	32

Note: The Tax Foundation's State Tax Competitiveness Index enables policymakers, taxpayers, and business leaders to gauge how their states' tax systems compare. A rank of 1 is best, 50 is worst. Rankings do not average to the total. States without a tax rank equally as 1. DC's scores and rankings do not affect other states. The report shows tax systems as of July 1, 2024 (the beginning of Fiscal Year 2025).
Source: Tax Foundation, State Tax Competitiveness Index 2025

TRANSPORTATION

Means of Transportation to Work

Area	Car/Truck/Van		Public Transportation			Bicycle	Walked	Other Means	Worked at Home
	Drove Alone	Car-pooled	Bus	Subway	Railroad				
City	57.6	5.9	5.6	0.0	0.1	3.1	8.2	1.3	18.2
MSA[1]	67.3	5.9	2.6	0.0	0.0	1.6	4.8	1.1	16.7
U.S.	70.2	8.5	1.7	1.3	0.4	0.4	2.4	1.6	13.5

Note: Figures are percentages and cover workers 16 years of age and older; (1) Figures cover the Madison, WI Metropolitan Statistical Area
Source: U.S. Census Bureau, 2019-2023 American Community Survey 5-Year Estimates

Travel Time to Work

Area	Less Than 10 Minutes	10 to 19 Minutes	20 to 29 Minutes	30 to 44 Minutes	45 to 59 Minutes	60 to 89 Minutes	90 Minutes or More
City	14.4	40.3	25.5	14.3	3.2	1.7	0.6
MSA[1]	15.8	32.4	25.5	17.6	5.0	2.5	1.1
U.S.	12.6	28.6	21.2	20.8	8.1	6.0	2.8

Note: Note: Figures are percentages and include workers 16 years old and over; (1) Figures cover the Madison, WI Metropolitan Statistical Area
Source: U.S. Census Bureau, 2019-2023 American Community Survey 5-Year Estimates

Key Congestion Measures

Measure	2000	2010	2015	2020	2022
Annual Hours of Delay, Total (000)	4,474	8,637	10,435	7,945	12,420
Annual Hours of Delay, Per Auto Commuter	23	33	37	28	45
Annual Congestion Cost, Per Auto Commuter ($)	421	644	717	575	859

Note: Figures cover the Madison WI urban area
Source: Texas A&M Transportation Institute, 2023 Urban Mobility Report

Freeway Travel Time Index

Measure	1985	1990	1995	2000	2005	2010	2015	2020	2022
Urban Area Index[1]	1.08	1.08	1.09	1.11	1.14	1.14	1.15	1.05	1.17
Urban Area Rank[1,2]	40	62	77	79	73	71	67	85	44

Note: Freeway Travel Time Index—the ratio of travel time in the peak period to the travel time at free-flow conditions. For example, a value of 1.30 indicates a 20-minute free-flow trip takes 26 minutes in the peak (20 minutes x 1.30 = 26 minutes); (1) Covers the Madison WI urban area; (2) Rank is based on 101 larger urban areas (#1 = highest travel time index)
Source: Texas A&M Transportation Institute, 2023 Urban Mobility Report

Public Transportation

Agency Name / Mode of Transportation	Vehicles Operated in Maximum Service[1]	Annual Unlinked Passenger Trips[2] (in thous.)	Annual Passenger Miles[3] (in thous.)
Metro Transit System (Metro)			
Bus (directly operated)	150	9,403.9	32,819.6
Demand Response - Taxi	27	110.7	537.5

Note: (1) Number of revenue vehicles operated by the given mode and type of service to meet the annual maximum service requirement. This is the revenue vehicle count during the peak season of the year; on the week and day that maximum service is provided. Vehicles operated in maximum service (VOMS) exclude atypical days and one-time special events; (2) Number of passengers who boarded public transportation vehicles. Passengers are counted each time they board a vehicle no matter how many vehicles they use to travel from their origin to their destination. (3) Sum of the distances ridden by all passengers during the entire fiscal year.
Source: Federal Transit Administration, National Transit Database, 2023

Air Transportation

Airport Name and Code / Type of Service	Passenger Airlines[1]	Passenger Enplanements	Freight Carriers[2]	Freight (lbs)
Dane County Regional-Truax Field (MSN)				
Domestic service (U.S. carriers only)	21	1,154,944	9	13,143,530
International service (U.S. carriers only)	2	89	0	0

Note: (1) Includes all U.S.-based major, minor and commuter airlines that carried at least one passenger during the year; (2) Includes all U.S.-based airlines and freight carriers that transported at least one pound of freight during the year.
Source: Bureau of Transportation Statistics, The Intermodal Transportation Database, Air Carriers: T-100 Domestic Market (U.S. carriers only), 2024; Bureau of Transportation Statistics, The Intermodal Transportation Database, Air Carriers: T-100 International Market (U.S. carriers only), 2024

BUSINESSES

Major Business Headquarters

Company Name	Industry	Rankings Fortune[1]	Forbes[2]
American Family Insurance Group	Insurance: property and casualty (stock)	243	-

Note: (1) Companies that produce a 10-K are ranked 1 to 500 based on 2023 revenue; (2) All private companies with at least $2 billion in annual revenue through the end of their most current fiscal year are ranked 1 to 275; companies listed are headquartered in the city; dashes indicate no ranking
Source: Fortune, "Fortune 500," 2024; Forbes, "America's Largest Private Companies," 2024

Fastest-Growing Businesses

According to *Inc.*, Madison is home to two of America's 500 fastest-growing private companies: **Recovery.com** (#196); **Veda Data Solutions** (#417). Criteria: must be an independent, privately-held, for-profit, U.S. corporation, proprietorship or partnership as of December 31, 2023; revenues must be at least $100,000 in 2020 and $2 million in 2023; must have four-year operating/sales history. *Inc., "America's 500 Fastest-Growing Private Companies," 2024*

Living Environment

COST OF LIVING

Cost of Living Index

Composite Index	Groceries	Housing	Utilities	Transportation	Health Care	Misc. Goods/Services
104.7	98.8	106.4	98.8	98.3	113.2	107.8

Note: The Cost of Living Index measures regional differences in the cost of consumer goods and services, excluding taxes and non-consumer expenditures, for professional and managerial households in the top income quintile. It is based on more than 50,000 prices covering almost 60 different items for which prices are collected three times a year by chambers of commerce, economic development organizations or university applied economic centers in each participating urban area. The numbers shown should be read as a percentage above or below the national average of 100. For example, a value of 115.4 in the groceries column indicates that grocery prices are 15.4% higher than the national average. Small differences in the index numbers should not be interpreted as significant; Figures cover the Madison WI urban area.
Source: The Council for Community and Economic Research, Cost of Living Index, 2024

Grocery Prices

Area[1]	T-Bone Steak ($/pound)	Frying Chicken ($/pound)	Whole Milk ($/half gal.)	Eggs ($/dozen)	Orange Juice ($/64 oz.)	Coffee ($/11.5 oz.)
City[2]	15.51	1.43	4.77	3.34	4.44	5.60
Avg.	15.42	1.55	4.69	3.25	4.41	5.46
Min.	14.50	1.16	4.43	2.75	4.00	4.85
Max.	17.56	2.89	5.49	4.78	5.54	7.89

Note: (1) Values for the local area are compared with the average, minimum and maximum values for all 276 areas in the Cost of Living Index; (2) Figures cover the Madison WI urban area; **T-Bone Steak** (price per pound); **Frying Chicken** (price per pound, whole fryer); **Whole Milk** (half gallon carton); **Eggs** (price per dozen, Grade A, large); **Orange Juice** (64 oz. Tropicana or Florida Natural); **Coffee** (11.5 oz. can, vacuum-packed, Maxwell House, Hills Bros, or Folgers).
Source: The Council for Community and Economic Research, Cost of Living Index, 2024

Housing and Utility Costs

Area[1]	New Home Price ($)	Apartment Rent ($/month)	All Electric ($/month)	Part Electric ($/month)	Other Energy ($/month)	Telephone ($/month)
City[2]	622,141	1,233	-	126.81	79.79	187.45
Avg.	515,975	1,550	210.99	123.07	82.07	194.99
Min.	265,375	692	104.33	53.68	36.26	179.42
Max.	2,775,821	5,719	529.02	397.28	361.63	223.33

Note: (1) Values for the local area are compared with the average, minimum and maximum values for all 276 areas in the Cost of Living Index; (2) Figures cover the Madison WI urban area; **New Home Price** (2,400 sf living area, 8,000 sf lot, in urban area with full utilities); **Apartment Rent** (950 sf 2 bedroom/1.5 or 2 bath, unfurnished, excluding all utilities except water); **All Electric** (average monthly cost for an all-electric home); **Part Electric** (average monthly cost for a part-electric home); **Other Energy** (average monthly cost for natural gas, fuel oil, coal, wood, and any other forms of energy except electricity); **Telephone** (price includes the base monthly rate plus taxes and fees for three lines of mobile phone service).
Source: The Council for Community and Economic Research, Cost of Living Index, 2024

Health Care, Transportation, and Other Costs

Area[1]	Doctor ($/visit)	Dentist ($/visit)	Optometrist ($/visit)	Gasoline ($/gallon)	Beauty Salon ($/visit)	Men's Shirt ($)
City[2]	236.64	124.37	72.86	3.27	76.22	41.80
Avg.	143.77	117.51	129.23	3.32	48.57	38.14
Min.	36.74	58.67	67.33	2.80	24.00	13.41
Max.	270.44	216.82	307.33	5.28	94.00	63.89

Note: (1) Values for the local area are compared with the average, minimum and maximum values for all 276 areas in the Cost of Living Index; (2) Figures cover the Madison WI urban area; **Doctor** (general practitioners routine exam of an established patient); **Dentist** (adult teeth cleaning and periodic oral examination); **Optometrist** (full vision eye exam for established adult patient); **Gasoline** (one gallon regular unleaded, national brand, including all taxes, cash price at self-service pump if available); **Beauty Salon** (woman's shampoo, trim, and blow-dry); **Men's Shirt** (cotton/polyester dress shirt, pinpoint weave, long sleeves).
Source: The Council for Community and Economic Research, Cost of Living Index, 2024

HOUSING

Homeownership Rate

Area	2017 (%)	2018 (%)	2019 (%)	2020 (%)	2021 (%)	2022 (%)	2023 (%)	2024 (%)
MSA[1]	n/a	n/a	n/a	n/a	n/a	n/a	n/a	n/a
U.S.	63.9	64.4	64.6	66.6	65.5	65.8	65.9	65.6

Note: (1) Figures cover the Madison, WI Metropolitan Statistical Area; n/a not available
Source: U.S. Census Bureau, Housing Vacancies and Homeownership Annual Statistics: 2017-2024

House Price Index (HPI)

Area	National Ranking[2]	Quarterly Change (%)	One-Year Change (%)	Five-Year Change (%)	Since 1991Q1 (%)
MSA[1]	118	0.61	5.50	54.87	369.35
U.S.[3]	—	1.43	4.51	57.13	327.82

Note: The HPI is a weighted repeat sales index. It measures average price changes in repeat sales or refinancings on the same properties. This information is obtained by reviewing repeat mortgage transactions on single-family properties whose mortgages have been purchased or securitized by Fannie Mae or Freddie Mac since January 1975; (1) Figures cover the Madison, WI Metropolitan Statistical Area; (2) Rankings are based on annual percentage change for all metro areas containing at least 15,000 transactions over the last 10 years and ranges from 1 to 241; (3) figures based on a weighted average of Census Division estimates using a seasonally adjusted, purchase-only index; all figures are for the period ending December 31, 2024
Source: Federal Housing Finance Agency, Change in FHFA Metropolitan Area House Price Indexes, All Transactions Index, 2024Q4

Home Value

Area	Under $100,000	$100,000 -$199,999	$200,000 -$299,999	$300,000 -$399,999	$400,000 -$499,999	$500,000 -$999,999	$1,000,000 or more	Median ($)
City	2.9	9.1	25.1	27.7	16.5	17.0	1.8	346,900
MSA[1]	3.7	11.6	24.1	23.9	16.0	18.4	2.3	344,600
U.S.	12.1	17.8	19.5	14.4	10.5	19.1	6.5	303,400

Note: Figures are percentages except for median and cover owner-occupied housing units; (1) Figures cover the Madison, WI Metropolitan Statistical Area
Source: U.S. Census Bureau, 2019-2023 American Community Survey 5-Year Estimates

Year Housing Structure Built

Area	2020 or Later	2010 -2019	2000 -2009	1990 -1999	1980 -1989	1970 -1979	1960 -1969	1950 -1959	1940 -1949	Before 1940	Median Year
City	0.9	11.8	14.3	11.8	9.5	12.8	11.9	9.2	4.3	13.4	1979
MSA[1]	1.2	11.5	15.9	14.2	10.4	13.6	9.2	7.5	3.3	13.1	1983
U.S.	1.2	8.9	13.6	12.8	13.0	14.4	10.0	9.7	4.5	11.9	1980

Note: Figures are percentages except for Median Year; Note: (1) Figures cover the Madison, WI Metropolitan Statistical Area
Source: U.S. Census Bureau, 2019-2023 American Community Survey 5-Year Estimates

Gross Monthly Rent

Area	Under $500	$500 -$999	$1,000 -$1,499	$1,500 -$1,999	$2,000 -$2,499	$2,500 -$2,999	$3,000 and up	Median ($)
City	3.6	15.5	41.6	26.0	8.2	2.4	2.7	1,364
MSA[1]	3.9	19.6	41.6	23.8	6.9	1.9	2.2	1,300
U.S.	6.5	22.3	29.5	20.2	10.8	4.8	5.9	1,348

Note: Figures are percentages except for median; Gross rent is the contract rent plus the estimated average monthly cost of utilities (electricity, gas, and water and sewer) and fuels (oil, coal, kerosene, wood, etc.) if these are paid by the renter (or paid for the renter by someone else); (1) Figures cover the Madison, WI Metropolitan Statistical Area
Source: U.S. Census Bureau, 2019-2023 American Community Survey 5-Year Estimates

HEALTH

Health Risk Factors

Category	MSA[1] (%)	U.S. (%)
Adults aged 18–64 who have any kind of health care coverage	93.3	90.8
Adults who reported being in good or better health	87.0	81.8
Adults who have been told they have high blood cholesterol	30.1	36.9
Adults who have been told they have high blood pressure	25.2	34.0
Adults who are current smokers	8.0	12.1
Adults who currently use e-cigarettes	5.5	7.7
Adults who currently use chewing tobacco, snuff, or snus	2.0	3.2
Adults who are heavy drinkers[2]	6.7	6.1
Adults who are binge drinkers[3]	18.9	15.2
Adults who are overweight (BMI 25.0 - 29.9)	32.7	34.4
Adults who are obese (BMI 30.0 - 99.8)	32.3	34.3
Adults who participated in any physical activities in the past month	80.1	75.8

Note: All figures are crude prevalence; (1) Figures cover the Madison, WI Metropolitan Statistical Area; (2) Heavy drinkers are classified as adult men having more than 14 drinks per week and adult women having more than 7 drinks per week; (3) Binge drinkers are classified as males having five or more drinks on one occasion or females having four or more drinks on one occasion
Source: Centers for Disease Control and Prevention, Behavorial Risk Factor Surveillance System, SMART: Selected Metropolitan Area Risk Trends, 2023

Acute and Chronic Health Conditions

Category	MSA[1] (%)	U.S. (%)
Adults who have ever been told they had a heart attack	2.5	4.2
Adults who have ever been told they have angina or coronary heart disease	2.7	4.0
Adults who have ever been told they had a stroke	1.7	3.3
Adults who have ever been told they have asthma	12.1	15.7
Adults who have ever been told they have arthritis	20.1	26.3
Adults who have ever been told they have diabetes[2]	7.4	11.5
Adults who have ever been told they had skin cancer	5.3	5.6
Adults who have ever been told they had any other types of cancer	7.6	8.4
Adults who have ever been told they have COPD	3.8	6.4
Adults who have ever been told they have kidney disease	2.5	3.7
Adults who have ever been told they have a form of depression	24.8	22.0

Note: All figures are crude prevalence; (1) Figures cover the Madison, WI Metropolitan Statistical Area; (2) Figures do not include pregnancy-related, borderline, or pre-diabetes
Source: Centers for Disease Control and Prevention, Behaviorial Risk Factor Surveillance System, SMART: Selected Metropolitan Area Risk Trends, 2023

Health Screening and Vaccination Rates

Category	MSA[1] (%)	U.S. (%)
Adults who have ever been tested for HIV	33.8	37.5
Adults who have had their blood cholesterol checked within the last five years	85.1	87.0
Adults aged 65+ who have had flu shot within the past year	75.1	63.4
Adults aged 65+ who have ever had a pneumonia vaccination	67.2	71.9

Note: All figures are crude prevalence; (1) Figures cover the Madison, WI Metropolitan Statistical Area.
Source: Centers for Disease Control and Prevention, Behaviorial Risk Factor Surveillance System, SMART: Selected Metropolitan Area Risk Trends, 2023

Disability Status

Category	MSA[1] (%)	U.S. (%)
Adults who reported being deaf	6.0	7.4
Are you blind or have serious difficulty seeing, even when wearing glasses?	4.2	4.9
Do you have difficulty doing errands alone?	6.5	7.8
Do you have difficulty dressing or bathing?	3.3	3.6
Do you have serious difficulty concentrating/remembering/making decisions?	10.2	13.7
Do you have serious difficulty walking or climbing stairs?	8.8	13.2

Note: All figures are crude prevalence; (1) Figures cover the Madison, WI Metropolitan Statistical Area.
Source: Centers for Disease Control and Prevention, Behaviorial Risk Factor Surveillance System, SMART: Selected Metropolitan Area Risk Trends, 2023

Mortality Rates for the Top 10 Causes of Death in the U.S.

ICD-10[a] Sub-Chapter	ICD-10[a] Code	Crude Mortality Rate[2] per 100,000 population	
		County[3]	U.S.
Malignant neoplasms	C00-C97	142.5	182.7
Ischaemic heart diseases	I20-I25	72.6	109.6
Provisional assignment of new diseases of uncertain etiology[1]	U00-U49	20.4	65.3
Other forms of heart disease	I30-I51	47.1	65.1
Other degenerative diseases of the nervous system	G30-G31	36.5	52.4
Other external causes of accidental injury	W00-X59	67.4	52.3
Cerebrovascular diseases	I60-I69	28.8	49.1
Chronic lower respiratory diseases	J40-J47	20.0	43.5
Hypertensive diseases	I10-I15	17.0	38.9
Organic, including symptomatic, mental disorders	F01-F09	39.9	33.9

Note: (a) ICD-10 = International Classification of Diseases 10th Revision; (1) Includes COVID-19, adverse effects to COVID-19 vaccines, SARS, and vaping-related disorders; (2) Crude mortality rates are a three-year average covering 2021-2023; (3) Figures cover Dane County.
Source: Centers for Disease Control and Prevention, National Center for Health Statistics. National Vital Statistics System, Mortality 2018-2023 on CDC WONDER Online Database

Mortality Rates for Selected Causes of Death

Cause of Death	ICD-10[a] Code	Crude Mortality Rate[1] per 100,000 population	
		County[2]	U.S.
Accidental poisoning and exposure to noxious substances	X40-X49	25.4	30.5
Alzheimer disease	G30	28.9	35.4
Assault	X85-Y09	2.6	7.3
COVID-19	U07.1	20.4	65.3
Diabetes mellitus	E10-E14	13.4	30.0
Diseases of the liver	K70-K76	12.5	20.8
Human immunodeficiency virus (HIV) disease	B20-B24	Suppressed	1.5
Influenza and pneumonia	J09-J18	5.9	13.4
Intentional self-harm	X60-X84	13.6	14.7
Malnutrition	E40-E46	1.9	6.0
Obesity and other hyperalimentation	E65-E68	1.6	3.1
Renal failure	N17-N19	7.6	16.4
Transport accidents	V01-V99	7.8	14.4

Note: (a) ICD-10 = International Classification of Diseases 10th Revision; (1) Crude mortality rates are a three-year average covering 2021-2023; (2) Figures cover Dane County; Data are suppressed when the data meet the criteria for confidentiality constraints; Crude mortality rates are flagged as unreliable when the rate would be calculated with a numerator of 20 or less.
Source: Centers for Disease Control and Prevention, National Center for Health Statistics. National Vital Statistics System, Mortality 2018-2023 on CDC WONDER Online Database

Health Insurance Coverage

Area	With Health Insurance	With Private Health Insurance	With Public Health Insurance	Without Health Insurance	Population Under Age 19 Without Health Insurance
City	95.7	81.9	24.1	4.3	2.9
MSA[1]	96.3	82.6	26.5	3.7	2.8
U.S.	91.4	67.3	36.3	8.6	5.4

Note: Figures are percentages that cover the civilian noninstitutionalized population; (1) Figures cover the Madison, WI Metropolitan Statistical Area
Source: U.S. Census Bureau, 2019-2023 American Community Survey 5-Year Estimates

Number of Medical Professionals

Area	MDs[3]	DOs[3,4]	Dentists	Podiatrists	Chiropractors	Optometrists
County[1] (number)	3,801	159	445	30	264	126
County[1] (rate[2])	669.0	28.0	77.3	5.2	45.9	21.9
U.S. (rate[2])	302.5	29.2	74.6	6.4	29.5	18.0

Note: Data as of 2023 unless noted; (1) Data covers Dane County; (2) Number of medical professionals per 100,000 population; (3) Data as of 2022 and includes all active, non-federal physicians; (4) Doctor of Osteopathic Medicine
Source: U.S. Department of Health and Human Services, Health Resources and Services Administration, Bureau of Health Professions, Area Resource File (ARF) 2023-2024

Best Hospitals

According to *U.S. News*, the Madison, WI metro area is home to one of the best hospitals in the U.S.: **UW Health University Hospital** (7 adult specialties and 1 pediatric specialty). The hospital listed was nationally ranked in at least one of 15 adult or 11 pediatric specialties. The number of specialties shown cover the parent hospital. Only 160 U.S. hospitals performed well enough to be nationally ranked in one or more specialties. Twenty hospitals in the U.S. made the Honor Roll. The Best Hospitals Honor Roll takes both the national rankings and the procedure and condition ratings into account. Hospitals received points if they were nationally ranked in one of the 15 adult specialties—the higher they ranked, the more points they got—and how many ratings of "high performing" they earned in the 20 procedures and conditions. *U.S. News Online, "America's Best Hospitals 2024-25"*

According to *U.S. News*, the Madison, WI metro area is home to one of the best children's hospitals in the U.S.: **American Family Children's Hospital** (1 pediatric specialty). The hospital listed was highly ranked in at least one of 11 pediatric specialties. One hundred five children's hospitals in the U.S. were nationally ranked in at least one specialty. Hospitals received points for being ranked in a specialty, and the 10 hospitals with the most points across the 11 specialties make up the Honor Roll. *U.S. News Online, "America's Best Children's Hospitals 2024-25"*

EDUCATION

Public School District Statistics

District Name	Schls	Pupils	Pupil/ Teacher Ratio	Minority Pupils[1] (%)	Total Rev. per Pupil ($)	Total Exp. per Pupil ($)
Madison Metropolitan SD	54	25,247	12.3	60.7	21,107	20,303

Note: Table includes school districts with 2,000 or more students; (1) Percentage of students that are not non-Hispanic white.
Source: U.S. Department of Education, National Center for Education Statistics, Common Core of Data, Local Education Agency (School District) Universe Survey: School Year 2023-2024; U.S. Department of Education, National Center for Education Statistics, Common Core of Data, School District Finance Survey (F-33): School Year 2021–22

Highest Level of Education

Area	Less than H.S.	H.S. Diploma	Some College, No Deg.	Associate Degree	Bachelor's Degree	Master's Degree	Prof. School Degree	Doctorate Degree
City	4.3	14.6	14.4	7.5	33.5	16.0	3.7	6.0
MSA[1]	4.1	20.2	16.6	9.7	29.9	12.7	2.9	3.8
U.S.	10.6	26.2	19.4	8.8	21.3	9.8	2.3	1.6

Note: Figures cover persons age 25 and over; (1) Figures cover the Madison, WI Metropolitan Statistical Area
Source: U.S. Census Bureau, 2019-2023 American Community Survey 5-Year Estimates

Educational Attainment by Race

Area	High School Graduate or Higher (%)					Bachelor's Degree or Higher (%)				
	Total	White	Black	Asian	Hisp.[2]	Total	White	Black	Asian	Hisp.[2]
City	95.7	97.7	91.9	92.5	78.5	59.2	62.9	25.6	70.4	37.4
MSA[1]	95.9	97.1	91.4	92.5	78.5	49.3	50.1	25.9	69.7	33.2
U.S.	89.4	92.9	88.1	88.0	72.5	35.0	37.7	24.7	57.0	19.9

Note: Figures shown cover persons 25 years old and over; (1) Figures cover the Madison, WI Metropolitan Statistical Area; (2) People of Hispanic origin can be of any race
Source: U.S. Census Bureau, 2019-2023 American Community Survey 5-Year Estimates

School Enrollment by Grade and Control

Area	Preschool (%)		Kindergarten (%)		Grades 1 - 4 (%)		Grades 5 - 8 (%)		Grades 9 - 12 (%)	
	Public	Private	Public	Private	Public	Private	Public	Private	Public	Private
City	47.1	52.9	87.9	12.1	88.1	11.9	89.4	10.6	89.8	10.2
MSA[1]	64.6	35.4	89.5	10.5	88.4	11.6	90.8	9.2	93.5	6.5
U.S.	58.7	41.3	85.2	14.8	87.2	12.8	87.9	12.1	89.0	11.0

Note: Figures shown cover persons 3 years old and over; (1) Figures cover the Madison, WI Metropolitan Statistical Area
Source: U.S. Census Bureau, 2019-2023 American Community Survey 5-Year Estimates

Higher Education

Four-Year Colleges			Two-Year Colleges			Medical Schools[1]	Law Schools[2]	Voc/ Tech[3]
Public	Private Non-profit	Private For-profit	Public	Private Non-profit	Private For-profit			
2	2	0	0	0	0	1	1	4

Note: Figures cover institutions located within the Madison, WI Metropolitan Statistical Area and include main campuses only; (1) includes schools accredited by the Liaison Committee on Medical Education and the American Osteopathic Association's Commission on Osteopathic College Accreditation; (2) includes ABA-accredited schools, schools with provisional ABA accreditation, and state accredited schools; (3) includes all schools with programs that are less than 2 years.
Source: National Center for Education Statistics, Integrated Postsecondary Education System (IPEDS), 2023-24; Wikipedia, List of Medical Schools in the United States, accessed May 2, 2025; Wikipedia, List of Law Schools in the United States, accessed May 2, 2025

According to *U.S. News & World Report*, the Madison, WI metro area is home to one of the top 200 national universities in the U.S.: **University of Wisconsin—Madison** (#39 tie). The indicators used to capture academic quality fall into a number of categories: assessment by administrators at peer institutions; retention of students; faculty resources; student selectivity; financial resources; alumni giving; high school counselor ratings of colleges; and graduation rate. *U.S. News & World Report*, "America's Best Colleges 2025"

According to *U.S. News & World Report*, the Madison, WI metro area is home to one of the top 100 law schools in the U.S.: **University of Wisconsin—Madison** (#28 tie). The rankings are based on a weighted average of 12 measures of quality: peer assessment score; assessment score by lawyers/judges; median LSAT scores; median undergrad GPA; acceptance rate; employment rates for graduates; placement success; bar passage rate; faculty resources; expenditures per student; student/faculty ratio; and library resources. *U.S. News & World Report*, "America's Best Graduate Schools, Law, 2025"

According to *U.S. News & World Report,* the Madison, WI metro area is home to one of the top medical schools for research in the U.S.: **University of Wisconsin—Madison** (Tier 2). *U.S. News* placed medical and osteopathic schools into tiers based on their research productivity, faculty and admissions data. Each school's tier was derived from its overall score, calculated by summing the weighted normalized values generated across several factors of academic quality, outlined below. There are four tiers, with tier 1 medical schools as the highest-performing and tier 4 as the lowest-performing. Only tier 1 and 2 schools are shown. Because of the tier presentation, *U.S. News* calculated overall scores based on their percentile performance among all rated schools instead of dividing against the rescaled score of the No. 1-performing schools. Tier 1 included schools with overall scores of 85 to 99. The cutoffs for tiers 2 through 4 were schools scoring 50 to 84, 15 to 49 and 1 to 14, respectively. The rankings are based on a weighted average of the following measures of quality: total research activity; average research activity per faculty member; total NIH research grants at the medical school and its affiliated hospitals; average NIH research grants per faculty; median MCAT total score; median undergraduate GPA; acceptance rate; and faculty resources. *U.S. News & World Report, "America's Best Graduate Schools, Medical, 2025"*

According to *U.S. News & World Report,* the Madison, WI metro area is home to one of the top medical schools for primary care in the U.S.: **University of Wisconsin—Madison** (Tier 2). *U.S. News* placed medical and osteopathic schools into tiers based on their research productivity, faculty and admissions data. Each school's tier was derived from its overall score, calculated by summing the weighted normalized values generated across several factors of academic quality, outlined below. There are four tiers, with tier 1 medical schools as the highest-performing and tier 4 as the lowest-performing. Only tier 1 and 2 schools are shown. Because of the tier presentation, *U.S. News* calculated overall scores based on their percentile performance among all rated schools instead of dividing against the rescaled score of the No. 1-performing schools. Tier 1 included schools with overall scores of 85 to 99. The cutoffs for tiers 2 through 4 were schools scoring 50 to 84, 15 to 49 and 1 to 14, respectively. The rankings are based on a weighted average of the following measures of quality: graduates practicing in primary care specialties; graduates entering primary care residencies; median MCAT total score; median undergraduate GPA; acceptance rate; and faculty resources. *U.S. News & World Report, "America's Best Graduate Schools, Medical, 2025"*

According to *U.S. News & World Report,* the Madison, WI metro area is home to one of the top 75 business schools in the U.S.: **University of Wisconsin—Madison** (#40 tie). The rankings are based on a weighted average of the following nine measures: quality assessment; peer assessment; recruiter assessment; placement success; mean starting salary and bonus; student selectivity; mean GMAT and GRE scores; mean undergraduate GPA; and acceptance rate. *U.S. News & World Report, "America's Best Graduate Schools, Business, 2025"*

EMPLOYERS

Major Employers

Company Name	Industry
American Family Mutual Insurance Co.	Fire, marine, & casualty insurance
City of Madison	Local government
Community Living Alliance	Social services for the handicapped
Labcorp Drug Development	Druggists preparations
TruStage Financial Group	Commercial and consumer insurance
University of Wisconsin Hospitals	General medical & surgical hospitals
University of Wisconsin-Madison	Higher education
Veterans Health Administration	General medical & surgical hospitals
WI Dept of Workforce Development	Administration of social & manpower programs
Wisconsin Department of Administration	Administration of general economic programs
Wisconsin Department of Health Services	Administration of public health programs
Wisconsin Department of Natural Resources	Land, mineral, & wildlife conservation
Wisconsin Department of Transportation	Regulation, administration of transportation
Wisconsin Dept of Natural Resources	Land, mineral, & wildlife conservation
Wisconsin Physicians Srvc Ins Corp	Hospital & medical services plans

Note: Companies shown are located within the Madison, WI Metropolitan Statistical Area.
Source: Chambers of Commerce; State Departments of Labor; Wikipedia

PUBLIC SAFETY

Crime Rate

Area	Total Crime Rate	Violent Crime Rate				Property Crime Rate		
		Murder	Rape	Robbery	Aggrav. Assault	Burglary	Larceny-Theft	Motor Vehicle Theft
City	2,636.1	3.6	27.7	44.5	225.4	280.4	1,859.0	195.5
U.S.	2,290.9	5.7	38.0	66.5	264.1	250.7	1,347.2	318.7

Note: Figures are crimes per 100,000 population.
Source: FBI, Table 8, Offenses Known to Law Enforcement, by State by City, 2023

Hate Crimes

Area	Number of Quarters Reported	Number of Incidents per Bias Motivation					
		Race/Ethnicity/ Ancestry	Religion	Sexual Orientation	Disability	Gender	Gender Identity
City	4	5	2	0	0	0	0
U.S.	4	5,900	2,699	2,077	187	92	492

Source: Federal Bureau of Investigation, Hate Crime Statistics 2023

Identity Theft Consumer Reports

Area	Reports	Reports per 100,000 Population	Rank[2]
MSA[1]	1,123	164	231
U.S.	1,135,291	339	-

Note: (1) Figures cover the Madison, WI Metropolitan Statistical Area; (2) Rank ranges from 1 to 401 where 1 indicates greatest number of identity theft reports per 100,000 population
Source: Federal Trade Commission, Consumer Sentinel Network Data Book 2024

Fraud and Other Consumer Reports

Area	Reports	Reports per 100,000 Population	Rank[2]
MSA[1]	6,855	1,002	207
U.S.	5,360,641	1,601	-

Note: (1) Figures cover the Madison, WI Metropolitan Statistical Area; (2) Rank ranges from 1 to 401 where 1 indicates greatest number of fraud and other consumer reports per 100,000 population
Source: Federal Trade Commission, Consumer Sentinel Network Data Book 2024

POLITICS

2024 Presidential Election Results

Area	Trump (Rep.)	Harris (Dem.)	Stein (Green)	Kennedy (Ind.)	Oliver (Lib.)	Other
Dane County	23.4	74.9	0.5	0.4	0.3	0.6
U.S.	49.7	48.2	0.6	0.5	0.4	0.6

Note: Results are percentages and may not add to 100% due to rounding
Source: Dave Leip's Atlas of U.S. Presidential Elections

SPORTS

Professional Sports Teams

Team Name	League	Year Established

No teams are located in the metro area
Source: Wikipedia, Major Professional Sports Teams of the United States and Canada, May 1, 2025

CLIMATE

Average and Extreme Temperatures

Temperature	Jan	Feb	Mar	Apr	May	Jun	Jul	Aug	Sep	Oct	Nov	Dec	Yr.
Extreme High (°F)	56	61	82	94	93	101	104	102	99	90	76	62	104
Average High (°F)	26	30	42	58	70	79	84	81	72	61	44	30	57
Average Temp. (°F)	17	21	32	46	57	67	72	69	61	50	36	23	46
Average Low (°F)	8	12	22	35	45	54	59	57	49	38	27	14	35
Extreme Low (°F)	-37	-28	-29	0	19	31	36	35	25	13	-8	-25	-37

Note: Figures cover the years 1948-1990
Source: National Climatic Data Center, International Station Meteorological Climate Summary, 9/96

Average Precipitation/Snowfall/Humidity

Precip./Humidity	Jan	Feb	Mar	Apr	May	Jun	Jul	Aug	Sep	Oct	Nov	Dec	Yr.
Avg. Precip. (in.)	1.1	1.1	2.1	2.9	3.2	3.8	3.9	3.9	3.0	2.3	2.0	1.7	31.1
Avg. Snowfall (in.)	10	7	9	2	Tr	0	0	0	Tr	Tr	4	11	42
Avg. Rel. Hum. 6am (%)	78	80	81	80	79	81	85	89	90	85	84	82	83
Avg. Rel. Hum. 3pm (%)	66	63	59	50	50	51	53	55	55	54	64	69	57

Note: Figures cover the years 1948-1990; Tr = Trace amounts (<0.05 in. of rain; <0.5 in. of snow)
Source: National Climatic Data Center, International Station Meteorological Climate Summary, 9/96

Weather Conditions

Temperature			Daytime Sky			Precipitation		
5°F & below	32°F & below	90°F & above	Clear	Partly cloudy	Cloudy	0.01 inch or more precip.	0.1 inch or more snow/ice	Thunder-storms
35	161	14	88	119	158	118	38	40

Note: Figures are average number of days per year and cover the years 1948-1990
Source: National Climatic Data Center, International Station Meteorological Climate Summary, 9/96

HAZARDOUS WASTE **Superfund Sites**

The Madison, WI metro area is home to five sites on the EPA's Superfund National Priorities List (NPL) or Superfund Alternative Approach (SAA) list: **City Disposal Corp. Landfill** (Final NPL); **Hagen Farm** (Final NPL); **Madison Metropolitan Sewerage District Lagoons** (Final NPL); **Refuse Hideaway Landfill** (Final NPL); **Stoughton City Landfill** (Final NPL). The Superfund alternative approach uses the same investigation and cleanup process and standards that are used for sites listed on the National Priorities List. The SAA is an alternative to listing a site on the NPL; it is not an alternative to Superfund or the Superfund process. There are a total of 1,445 Superfund sites with a status of proposed or final on both lists in the United States. *U.S. Environmental Protection Agency, National Priorities List, May 1, 2025; U.S. Environmental Protection Agency, Superfund Alternative Approach Sites, May 1, 2025*

AIR QUALITY **Air Quality Trends: Ozone**

	1990	1995	2000	2005	2010	2015	2020	2021	2022	2023
MSA[1]	0.077	0.084	0.072	0.079	0.062	0.064	0.070	0.066	0.062	0.082
U.S.	0.087	0.089	0.081	0.080	0.072	0.068	0.066	0.067	0.067	0.070

Note: (1) Data covers the Madison, WI Metropolitan Statistical Area. The values shown are the composite ozone concentration averages among trend sites based on the highest fourth daily maximum 8-hour concentration in parts per million. These trends are based on sites having an adequate record of monitoring data during the trend period. Data from exceptional events are included.
Source: U.S. Environmental Protection Agency, Air Quality Monitoring Information, "Air Quality Trends by City, 1990-2023"

Air Quality Index

Area	Percent of Days when Air Quality was...[2]					AQI Statistics[2]	
	Good	Moderate	Unhealthy for Sensitive Groups	Unhealthy	Very Unhealthy	Maximum	Median
MSA[1]	49.6	43.6	5.5	0.5	0.8	268	51

Note: (1) Data covers the Madison, WI Metropolitan Statistical Area; (2) Based on 365 days with AQI data in 2023. Air Quality Index (AQI) is an index for reporting daily air quality. EPA calculates the AQI for five major air pollutants regulated by the Clean Air Act: ground-level ozone, particle pollution (aka particulate matter), carbon monoxide, sulfur dioxide, and nitrogen dioxide. The AQI runs from 0 to 500. The higher the AQI value, the greater the level of air pollution and the greater the health concern. There are six AQI categories: "Good" AQI is between 0 and 50. Air quality is considered satisfactory; "Moderate" AQI is between 51 and 100. Air quality is acceptable; "Unhealthy for Sensitive Groups" When AQI values are between 101 and 150, members of sensitive groups may experience health effects; "Unhealthy" When AQI values are between 151 and 200 everyone may begin to experience health effects; "Very Unhealthy" AQI values between 201 and 300 trigger a health alert; "Hazardous" AQI values over 300 trigger warnings of emergency conditions (not shown).
Source: U.S. Environmental Protection Agency, Air Quality Index Report, 2023

Air Quality Index Pollutants

Area	Percent of Days when AQI Pollutant was...[2]					
	Carbon Monoxide	Nitrogen Dioxide	Ozone	Sulfur Dioxide	Particulate Matter 2.5	Particulate Matter 10
MSA[1]	0.0	0.0	31.5	(3)	68.5	0.0

Note: (1) Data covers the Madison, WI Metropolitan Statistical Area; (2) Based on 365 days with AQI data in 2023. The Air Quality Index (AQI) is an index for reporting daily air quality. EPA calculates the AQI for five major air pollutants regulated by the Clean Air Act: ground-level ozone, particle pollution (also known as particulate matter), carbon monoxide, sulfur dioxide, and nitrogen dioxide. The AQI runs from 0 to 500. The higher the AQI value, the greater the level of air pollution and the greater the health concern; (3) Sulfur dioxide is no longer included in this table because SO_2 concentrations tend to be very localized and not necessarily representative of broad geographical areas like counties and CBSAs.
Source: U.S. Environmental Protection Agency, Air Quality Index Report, 2023

Maximum Air Pollutant Concentrations: Particulate Matter, Ozone, CO and Lead

	Particulate Matter 10 (ug/m^3)	Particulate Matter 2.5 Wtd AM (ug/m^3)	Particulate Matter 2.5 24-Hr (ug/m^3)	Ozone (ppm)	Carbon Monoxide (ppm)	Lead (ug/m^3)
MSA[1] Level	208	10.7	39	0.082	n/a	n/a
NAAQS[2]	150	15	35	0.075	9	0.15
Met NAAQS[2]	No	Yes	No	No	n/a	n/a

Note: (1) Data covers the Madison, WI Metropolitan Statistical Area; Data from exceptional events are included; (2) National Ambient Air Quality Standards; ppm = parts per million; ug/m^3 = micrograms per cubic meter; n/a not available.
Concentrations: Particulate Matter 10 (coarse particulate)—highest second maximum 24-hour concentration; Particulate Matter 2.5 Wtd AM (fine particulate)—highest weighted annual mean concentration; Particulate Matter 2.5 24-Hour (fine particulate)—highest 98th percentile 24-hour concentration; Ozone—highest fourth daily maximum 8-hour concentration; Carbon Monoxide—highest second maximum non-overlapping 8-hour concentration; Lead—maximum running 3-month average
Source: U.S. Environmental Protection Agency, Air Quality Monitoring Information, "Air Quality Statistics by City, 2023"

Maximum Air Pollutant Concentrations: Nitrogen Dioxide and Sulfur Dioxide

	Nitrogen Dioxide AM (ppb)	Nitrogen Dioxide 1-Hr (ppb)	Sulfur Dioxide AM (ppb)	Sulfur Dioxide 1-Hr (ppb)	Sulfur Dioxide 24-Hr (ppb)
MSA[1] Level	n/a	n/a	n/a	n/a	n/a
NAAQS[2]	53	100	30	75	140
Met NAAQS[2]	n/a	n/a	n/a	n/a	n/a

Note: (1) Data covers the Madison, WI Metropolitan Statistical Area; Data from exceptional events are included; (2) National Ambient Air Quality Standards; ppm = parts per million; ug/m^3 = micrograms per cubic meter; n/a not available.
Concentrations: Nitrogen Dioxide AM—highest arithmetic mean concentration; Nitrogen Dioxide 1-Hr—highest 98th percentile 1-hour daily maximum concentration; Sulfur Dioxide AM—highest annual mean concentration; Sulfur Dioxide 1-Hr—highest 99th percentile 1-hour daily maximum concentration; Sulfur Dioxide 24-Hr—highest second maximum 24-hour concentration
Source: U.S. Environmental Protection Agency, Air Quality Monitoring Information, "Air Quality Statistics by City, 2023"

Milwaukee, Wisconsin

Background

Milwaukee originally began as a trading post for French fur traders. Its favorable location on the western shore of Lake Michigan and at the confluence of the Milwaukee, Menomonee, and Kinnickinnic rivers made the site a natural meeting place. In 1818, Solomon Laurent Juneau, a son-in-law of a French fur trader, became Milwaukee's first founder and permanent white settler.

During the 1840s, Milwaukee saw a wave of German immigrants hit its shores. Many of these exiles were unsuccessful revolutionaries in the overthrow of the German monarchy. Despite their lack of success back home, however, they had considerable influence in the new country. Politically, they produced three socialist mayors; economically, they founded Pabst and Schlitz breweries in the city; culturally, Germans founded the Goethe House cultural resource center located in the central library of the Milwaukee Public Library system.

Today, Milwaukee is diverse, home to more than a dozen nationalities, including Irish, Mexican, Serbian, Scandinavian, Polish, Italian, German, and Puerto Rican, as well as a large and thriving African American population. While the brewing manufacturers remain major employers in the city that was once the number one producer of beer worldwide, Milwaukee's economy has widely diversified, with six Fortune 500 companies in the city. Prominent industries include healthcare, financial services, education, and manufacturing.

Culture and entertainment thrive in Milwaukee. The Milwaukee Public Museum features exhibits devoted to science, technology, and natural history, and includes the first IMAX(r) theater in Wisconsin. The city is home to the Florentine Opera Company, the Milwaukee Symphony Orchestra, the Milwaukee Ballet, the Milwaukee Repertory Theater, and the Milwaukee Shakespeare Company. The annual lakefront music festival Summerfest is considered the largest music festival in the world with nearly a million people attending yearly. The Milwaukee Art Museum is known worldwide with the breathtaking Quadracci Pavilion designed by Santiago Calatrava. Discovery World, the city's largest science museum, is known for its high-tech, hands-on exhibits.

The city is home to numerous colleges and universities, including Marquette University and the University of Wisconsin-Milwaukee.

Milwaukee is home to two professional sports teams, the Brewers of Major League Baseball and the Bucks of the National Basketball Association. In addition, Milwaukee is considered a home market for the popular Green Bay Packers football team, who play about an hour away. Among college sports, Marquette University's men's basketball team, the Golden Eagles, is a popular draw, playing in the competitive Big East conference.

Milwaukee has a continental climate, and its weather is quite changeable. Temperatures vary widely through the year. In winter, arctic air masses from Canada bring frigid winter temperatures, while in summer high temperatures occur with brisk, hot winds from the southwest. Lake Michigan and the other Great Lakes mitigates these extremes; in late autumn and winter, the coldest air masses from the northwest are often warmed by the lakes before they can reach the city.

Rankings

General Rankings

- To help military veterans find the best places in which to settle down, *WalletHub* compared the 100 largest U.S. cities across 19 key indicators of livability, affordability and veteran-friendliness. They range from the share of military skill-related jobs to veteran income growth to the availability of VA health facilities. Milwaukee ranked #73. *Wallethub.com, "Best & Worst Places for Veterans to Live (2025)," November 7, 2024*

- For its 37th annual "Readers' Choice Awards" survey, *Condé Nast Traveler* ranked its readers' favorite cities in the U.S. Whether it be a longed-for visit or the next big new thing, these are the places travelers loved best. The list was broken into large cities and cities under 250,000. Milwaukee ranked #3 in the big city category. *Condé Nast Traveler, Readers' Choice Awards 2024, "Best Big Cities in the U.S." October 1, 2024*

Business/Finance Rankings

- Payscale.com ranked the 32 largest metro areas in terms of wage growth. The Milwaukee metro area ranked #32. Criteria: quarterly changes in private industry employee and education professional wage growth from the previous year. *PayScale, "Wage Trends by Metro Area-4th Quarter," February 4, 2025*

- The Milwaukee metro area appeared on the Milken Institute "2025 Best Performing Cities" list. Rank: #191 out of 200 large metro areas (based on performance category). Criteria: job growth; wage growth; high-tech growth and impact; community resilience; housing affordability; household broadband access. *Milken Institute, "Best-Performing Cities 2025," January 14, 2025*

Education Rankings

- Personal finance website *WalletHub* analyzed the 150 largest U.S. metropolitan statistical areas to determine where the most educated Americans are putting their degrees to work. Criteria: education levels; percentage of workers with degrees; education quality and attainment gap; public school quality rankings; quality and enrollment of each metro area's universities. Milwaukee was ranked #55 (#1 = most educated city). *WalletHub.com, "Most & Least Educated Cities in America, 2025" July 2, 2024*

Health/Fitness Rankings

- For each of the 100 largest cities in the United States, the American Fitness Index®, compiled in partnership between the American College of Sports Medicine and the Elevance Health Foundation, evaluated community infrastructure and more than 30 health behaviors including preventive health, levels of chronic disease conditions, food insecurity, pedestrian safety, air quality, and community/environment resources that support physical activity. Milwaukee ranked #36 for "community fitness." *americanfitnessindex.org, "2024 ACSM American Fitness Index Summary Report," July 23, 2024*

- The Milwaukee metro area was identified as one of the worst cities for bed bugs in America by pest control company Orkin. The area ranked #25 out of 50 based on the number of bed bug treatments Orkin performed from December 2022 to November 2023. *Orkin, "Chicago Joins Paris In Global Bed Bug Spotlight Ranking As The Worst City On Orkin's U.S. Bed Bug Cities List," January 22, 2024*

- Milwaukee was identified as a "2025 Allergy Capital." The area ranked #87 out of the nation's 100 largest metropolitan areas. Three groups of factors were used to identify the most challenging cities for people with allergies: annual tree, grass, and weed pollen scores; over the counter allergy medicine use; number of board-certified allergy specialists. *Asthma and Allergy Foundation of America, "2025 Allergy Capitals: The Most Challenging Places to Live with Allergies," March 18, 2025*

- Milwaukee was identified as a "2024 Asthma Capital." The area ranked #76 out of the nation's 100 largest metropolitan areas. Criteria: estimated asthma prevalence; asthma-related mortality; and ER visits due to asthma. Risk factors analyzed but not factored in the rankings: annual air quality including pollution and ozone levels; public smoking laws; indoor air quality; access to asthma specialists; rescue and controller medication use; uninsured rate; pollen allergy; poverty rate. *Asthma and Allergy Foundation of America, "Asthma Capitals 2024: The Most Challenging Places to Live With Asthma," September 10, 2024*

Pet Rankings

- Milwaukee was selected by *Sniffspot.com* as one of the most dog-friendly cities in the U.S., ranking #35 out of 50. Criteria: dog parks; hiking; sniffspots; public parks; dog-friendly businesses; housing; dog waste cleanliness; leash laws; dog services; and overall cost. *Sniffspot.com, "The Top 50 Most Dog-Friendly Cities in the U.S.," September 30, 2024*

Real Estate Rankings

- *WalletHub* compared the most populated U.S. cities to determine which had the best markets for real estate agents. Milwaukee ranked #92 where demand was high and pay was the best. Criteria: sales per agent; annual median wage for real-estate agents; monthly average starting salary for real estate agents; real estate job density and competition; unemployment rate; home turnover rate; housing-market health index; and other relevant metrics. *WalletHub.com, "2021 Best Places to Be a Real Estate Agent," May 12, 2021*

- The Milwaukee metro area was identified as one of the nations's 20 hottest housing markets in 2025. Criteria: unique listing views as an indicator of demand and number of days on the market as an indicator of pace. The area ranked #11. *Realtor.com, "January 2025 Top 20 Hottest Housing Markets," February 11, 2025*

- Milwaukee was ranked #111 out of 176 metro areas in terms of cost of housing in 2024 by the National Association of Home Builders (#1 = most affordable). Criteria: the portion of an average family's income necessary to pay the mortgage on a median-priced home. *National Association of Home Builders®, NAHB-Wells Fargo Cost of Housing Index, 4th Quarter 2024*

Safety Rankings

- To identify the most dangerous cities in America, *24/7 Wall St.* focused on violent crime categories—murder, non-negligent manslaughter, rape, robbery, and aggravated assault—as reported for every 100,000 residents using data from the FBI's 2020 annual Uniform Crime Report. For cities with populations over 25,000, Milwaukee was ranked #13. *247wallst.com, "America's Most Dangerous Cities" November 12, 2021*

- Statistics drawn from the FBI's Uniform Crime Report were used to rank the cities where violent crime rose the most year over year from 2019 to 2020. Only cities with 25,000 or more residents were included. *24/7 Wall St.* found that Milwaukee placed #15 of those with a notable surge in incidents of violent crime. *247wallst.com, "American Cities Where Crime Is Soaring," March 4, 2022*

- Allstate ranked the 100 most populous cities in America in terms of driver safety. Milwaukee ranked #27. Criteria based on anonymized driving behavior data from Allstate's mobile app powered by Arity: high speed driving (over 80 mph), phone handling, and hard braking. The report helps increase the importance of safety and awareness behind the wheel. *Allstate, "16th Allstate America's Best Drivers Report®" July 11, 2024*

- Milwaukee was identified as one of the most dangerous cities in America by NeighborhoodScout. The city ranked #13 out of 100 (#1 = most dangerous). Criteria: number of violent crimes per 1,000 residents. The editors evaluated cities with 25,000 or more residents. *NeighborhoodScout.com, "2023 Top 100 Most Dangerous Cities in the U.S.," January 12, 2023*

Women/Minorities Rankings

- Milwaukee was listed as one of the most LGBTQ-friendly cities in America by *The Advocate*, as compiled by the real estate data site *Clever*. The city ranked #15 out of 15. Criteria, among many: Pride events; gay bars; LGBTQ-affirming healthcare options; state and local laws; number of PFLAG chapters; LGBTQ+ population. *The Advocate, "These Are the 15 Most LGBTQ-Friendly Cities in the U.S." November 1, 2023*

- Personal finance website *WalletHub* compared more than 180 U.S. cities across two key dimensions, "Hispanic Business-Friendliness" and "Hispanic Purchasing Power," to arrive at the most favorable conditions for Hispanic entrepreneurs. Milwaukee was ranked #165 out of 182. Criteria includes: share of Hispanic-Owned Businesses; average growth of Hispanic Business revenues; Small Business-Friendliness score; affordability; and number of Hispanics with at least a bachelor's degree. *WalletHub.com, "Best Cities for Hispanic Entrepreneurs," September 4, 2024*

Miscellaneous Rankings

- *WalletHub* compared 148 of the most populated U.S. cities to determine their operating efficiency. A "Quality of Services" score was constructed for each city and then measured against the total budget per capita to reveal which were managed the best. Milwaukee ranked #92. Criteria: financial stability; economy; education; safety; health; infrastructure and pollution. *WalletHub.com, "2025's Best- & Worst-Run Cities in America," June 18, 2024*

Business Environment

DEMOGRAPHICS

Population Growth

Area	1990 Census	2000 Census	2010 Census	2020 Census	2023 Estimate[2]	Population Growth 1990-2023 (%)
City	628,095	596,974	594,833	577,222	569,756	-9.3
MSA[1]	1,432,149	1,500,741	1,555,908	1,574,731	1,566,361	9.4
U.S.	248,709,873	281,421,906	308,745,538	331,449,281	332,387,540	33.6

Note: (1) Figures cover the Milwaukee-Waukesha, WI Metropolitan Statistical Area; (2) 2019-2023 5-year ACS population estimate
Source: U.S. Census Bureau, 1990 Census, 2000 Census, 2010 Census, 2020 Census, 2019-2023 American Community Survey 5-Year Estimates

Race

Area	White Alone[2] (%)	Black Alone[2] (%)	Asian Alone[2] (%)	AIAN[3] Alone[2] (%)	NHOPI[4] Alone[2] (%)	Other Race Alone[2] (%)	Two or More Races (%)
City	36.5	38.6	4.8	0.7	0.0	6.9	12.4
MSA[1]	67.4	16.1	4.0	0.4	0.0	3.8	8.3
U.S.	63.4	12.4	5.8	0.9	0.2	6.6	10.7

Note: (1) Figures cover the Milwaukee-Waukesha, WI Metropolitan Statistical Area; (2) Alone is defined as not being in combination with one or more other races; (3) American Indian and Alaska Native; (4) Native Hawaiian and Other Pacific Islander
Source: U.S. Census Bureau, 2019-2023 American Community Survey 5-Year Estimates

Hispanic or Latino Origin

Area	Total (%)	Mexican (%)	Puerto Rican (%)	Cuban (%)	Other (%)
City	20.7	13.7	4.9	0.1	1.9
MSA[1]	11.8	7.7	2.6	0.1	1.4
U.S.	19.0	11.3	1.8	0.7	5.2

Note: Persons of Hispanic or Latino origin can be of any race; (1) Figures cover the Milwaukee-Waukesha, WI Metropolitan Statistical Area
Source: U.S. Census Bureau, 2019-2023 American Community Survey 5-Year Estimates

Age

Area	Under Age 5	Age 5–19	Age 20–34	Age 35–44	Age 45–54	Age 55–64	Age 65–74	Age 75–84	Age 85+	Median Age
City	6.9	22.2	25.1	13.0	10.6	10.4	7.4	3.0	1.4	32.2
MSA[1]	5.9	19.3	19.8	13.1	11.9	13.2	10.0	4.5	2.1	38.5
U.S.	5.7	19.1	20.2	13.1	12.3	12.8	10.0	4.9	1.9	38.7

Note: (1) Figures cover the Milwaukee-Waukesha, WI Metropolitan Statistical Area
Source: U.S. Census Bureau, 2019-2023 American Community Survey 5-Year Estimates

Disability by Age

Area	All Ages	Under 18 Years Old	18 to 64 Years Old	65 Years and Over
City	13.2	4.8	12.5	35.3
MSA[1]	11.3	4.0	9.4	28.9
U.S.	13.0	4.7	10.7	32.9

Note: Figures show percent of the civilian noninstitutionalized population that reported having a disability. Disability status is determined from six types of difficulty: vision, hearing, cognitive, ambulatory, self-care, and independent living. For children under 5 years old, hearing and vision difficulty are used to determine disability status. For children between the ages of 5 and 14, disability status is determined from hearing, vision, cognitive, ambulatory, and self-care difficulties. For people aged 15 years and older, they are considered to have a disability if they have difficulty with any one of the six difficulty types; Note: (1) Figures cover the Milwaukee-Waukesha, WI Metropolitan Statistical Area
Source: U.S. Census Bureau, 2019-2023 American Community Survey 5-Year Estimates

Ancestry

Area	German	Irish	English	American	Italian	Polish	French[2]	European	Scottish
City	15.1	5.4	2.2	1.4	2.4	5.5	1.2	1.0	0.5
MSA[1]	31.6	9.3	5.0	2.4	4.3	9.8	2.1	1.4	0.9
U.S.	12.6	9.4	9.1	5.5	4.9	2.6	2.0	1.6	1.6

Note: Figures are the percentage of the total population reporting a particular ancestry. The nine most commonly reported ancestries in the U.S. are shown. Figures include multiple ancestries (e.g. if a person reported being Irish and Italian, they were included in both columns); (1) Figures cover the Milwaukee-Waukesha, WI Metropolitan Statistical Area; (2) Excludes Basque
Source: U.S. Census Bureau, 2019-2023 American Community Survey 5-Year Estimates

Foreign-born Population

Area	Percent of Population Born in								
	Any Foreign Country	Asia	Mexico	Europe	Caribbean	Central America[2]	South America	Africa	Canada
City	10.8	2.8	5.1	0.6	0.3	0.4	0.3	1.0	0.1
MSA[1]	7.6	2.7	2.4	1.1	0.2	0.2	0.3	0.6	0.1
U.S.	13.9	4.3	3.3	1.4	1.4	1.2	1.2	0.8	0.2

Note: (1) Figures cover the Milwaukee-Waukesha, WI Metropolitan Statistical Area; (2) Excludes Mexico.
Source: U.S. Census Bureau, 2019-2023 American Community Survey 5-Year Estimates

Household Size

Area	Persons in Household (%)							Average Household Size
	One	Two	Three	Four	Five	Six	Seven or More	
City	38.7	29.0	13.7	9.4	5.6	2.1	1.6	2.40
MSA[1]	33.0	34.4	13.7	11.3	5.1	1.7	0.9	2.37
U.S.	28.5	33.8	15.4	12.7	5.9	2.3	1.4	2.54

Note: (1) Figures cover the Milwaukee-Waukesha, WI Metropolitan Statistical Area
Source: U.S. Census Bureau, 2019-2023 American Community Survey 5-Year Estimates

Household Relationships

Area	House-holder	Opposite-sex Spouse	Same-sex Spouse	Opposite-sex Unmarried Partner	Same-sex Unmarried Partner	Child[2]	Grand-child	Other Relatives	Non-relatives
City	40.8	10.2	0.2	3.6	0.2	30.2	2.7	4.9	4.4
MSA[1]	41.3	17.5	0.2	2.9	0.2	28.7	1.6	3.1	2.7
U.S.	38.3	17.5	0.2	2.5	0.2	28.3	2.4	4.8	3.4

Note: Figures are percent of the total population; (1) Figures cover the Milwaukee-Waukesha, WI Metropolitan Statistical Area; (2) Includes biological, adopted, and stepchildren of the householder
Source: U.S. Census Bureau, 2020 Census

Gender

Area	Males	Females	Males per 100 Females
City	275,637	294,119	93.7
MSA[1]	768,160	798,201	96.2
U.S.	164,545,087	167,842,453	98.0

Note: (1) Figures cover the Milwaukee-Waukesha, WI Metropolitan Statistical Area
Source: U.S. Census Bureau, 2019-2023 American Community Survey 5-Year Estimates

Marital Status

Area	Never Married	Now Married[2]	Separated	Widowed	Divorced
City	54.7	29.2	1.9	4.3	9.9
MSA[1]	37.7	45.9	1.2	5.1	10.1
U.S.	34.1	47.9	1.7	5.6	10.7

Note: Figures are percentages and cover the population 15 years of age and older; (1) Figures cover the Milwaukee-Waukesha, WI Metropolitan Statistical Area; (2) Excludes separated
Source: U.S. Census Bureau, 2019-2023 American Community Survey 5-Year Estimates

Religious Groups by Family

Area	Catholic	Baptist	Methodist	LDS[2]	Pentecostal	Lutheran	Islam	Adventist	Other
MSA[1]	24.5	3.0	1.0	0.4	2.8	9.1	2.8	0.9	10.7
U.S.	18.7	7.3	3.0	2.0	1.8	1.7	1.3	1.3	11.6

Note: Figures are the number of adherents as a percentage of the total population and cover the eight largest religious groups in the U.S; (1) Figures cover the Milwaukee-Waukesha, WI Metropolitan Statistical Area; (2) Church of Jesus Christ of Latter-day Saints
Sources: 2020 U.S. Religion Census, Association of Statisticians of American Religious Bodies; The Association of Religion Data Archives (ARDA)

Religious Groups by Tradition

Area	Catholic	Evangelical Protestant	Mainline Protestant	Black Protestant	Islam	Judaism	Hinduism	Orthodox	Buddhism
MSA[1]	24.5	16.3	5.4	3.3	2.8	0.4	0.4	0.5	0.4
U.S.	18.7	16.5	5.2	2.3	1.3	0.6	0.4	0.4	0.3

Note: Figures are the number of adherents as a percentage of the total population; (1) Figures cover the Milwaukee-Waukesha, WI Metropolitan Statistical Area
Sources: 2020 U.S. Religion Census, Association of Statisticians of American Religious Bodies; The Association of Religion Data Archives (ARDA)

ECONOMY

Real Gross Domestic Product (GDP)

Area	2017	2018	2019	2020	2021	2022	2023	Rank[3]
MSA[1]	99.3	100.8	102.3	98.2	102.4	105.2	106.6	39
U.S.[2]	17,619.1	18,160.7	18,642.5	18,238.9	19,387.6	19,896.6	20,436.3	—

Note: Figures are in billions of chained 2017 dollars; (1) Figures cover the Milwaukee-Waukesha, WI Metropolitan Statistical Area; (2) Figures cover real GDP within metropolitan areas; (3) Rank is based on 2023 data and ranges from 1 to 384
Source: U.S. Bureau of Economic Analysis

Economic Growth

Area	2014	2015	2016	2017	2018	2019	2020	2021	2022	2023
MSA[1]	0.6	1.2	0.5	1.5	1.6	1.5	-4.0	4.3	2.7	1.4
U.S.[2]	2.6	3.2	2.0	2.7	3.1	2.7	-2.2	6.3	2.6	2.7

Note: Figures are real gross domestic product growth rates and represent percent change from preceding period; (1) Figures cover the Milwaukee-Waukesha, WI Metropolitan Statistical Area; (2) Figures are the average growth rates within metropolitan areas
Source: U.S. Bureau of Economic Analysis

Metropolitan Area Exports

Area	2018	2019	2020	2021	2022	2023	Rank[2]
MSA[1]	7,337.6	6,896.3	6,624.0	7,282.8	8,742.5	9,352.5	45
U.S.	1,664,056.1	1,645,173.7	1,431,406.6	1,753,941.4	2,062,937.4	2,019,160.5	—

Note: Figures are in millions of dollars; (1) Figures cover the Milwaukee-Waukesha, WI Metropolitan Statistical Area; (2) Rank is based on 2023 data and ranges from 1 to 386
Source: U.S. Department of Commerce, International Trade Administration, Office of Trade and Economic Analysis, Industry and Analysis, Exports by Metropolitan Area, data extracted April 2, 2025

Building Permits

Area	Single-Family			Multi-Family			Total		
	2023	2024	Pct. Chg.	2023	2024	Pct. Chg.	2023	2024	Pct. Chg.
City	61	72	18.0	36	164	355.6	97	236	143.3
MSA[1]	1,408	1,712	21.6	1,436	2,346	63.4	2,844	4,058	42.7
U.S.	920,000	981,900	6.7	591,100	496,100	-16.1	1,511,100	1,478,000	-2.2

Note: (1) Figures cover the Milwaukee-Waukesha, WI Metropolitan Statistical Area; Figures represent new, privately-owned housing units authorized (unadjusted data)
Source: U.S. Census Bureau, Building Permits Survey (BPS), 2023, 2024

Bankruptcy Filings

Area	Business Filings			Nonbusiness Filings		
	2023	2024	% Chg.	2023	2024	% Chg.
Milwaukee County	24	40	66.7	2,881	3,306	14.8
U.S.	18,926	23,107	22.1	434,064	494,201	13.9

Note: Business filings include Chapter 7, Chapter 9, Chapter 11, Chapter 12, Chapter 13, Chapter 15, and Section 304; Nonbusiness filings include Chapter 7, Chapter 11, and Chapter 13
Source: Administrative Office of the U.S. Courts, Business and Nonbusiness Bankruptcy, County Cases Commenced by Chapter of the Bankruptcy Code, During the 12-Month Period Ending December 31, 2023 and Business and Nonbusiness Bankruptcy, County Cases Commenced by Chapter of the Bankruptcy Code, During the 12-Month Period Ending December 31, 2024

Housing Vacancy Rates

Area	Gross Vacancy Rate[3] (%)			Year-Round Vacancy Rate[4] (%)			Rental Vacancy Rate[5] (%)			Homeowner Vacancy Rate[6] (%)		
	2022	2023	2024	2022	2023	2024	2022	2023	2024	2022	2023	2024
MSA[1]	5.2	6.7	5.6	5.1	6.6	5.1	5.9	4.1	4.8	0.1	0.8	0.4
U.S.[2]	9.1	9.0	9.1	7.5	7.5	7.6	5.7	6.5	6.8	0.8	0.8	1.0

Note: (1) Figures cover the Milwaukee-Waukesha, WI Metropolitan Statistical Area; (2) Figures cover the 75 largest Metropolitan Statistical Areas; (3) The percentage of the total housing inventory that is vacant; (4) The percentage of the housing inventory (excluding seasonal units) that is year-round vacant; (5) The percentage of rental inventory that is vacant for rent; (6) The percentage of homeowner inventory that is vacant for sale
Source: U.S. Census Bureau, Housing Vacancies and Homeownership Annual Statistics: 2022, 2023, 2024

INCOME

Income

Area	Per Capita ($)	Median Household ($)	Average Household ($)
City	29,679	51,888	70,559
MSA[1]	44,476	76,404	104,403
U.S.	43,289	78,538	110,491

Note: (1) Figures cover the Milwaukee-Waukesha, WI Metropolitan Statistical Area
Source: U.S. Census Bureau, 2019-2023 American Community Survey 5-Year Estimates

Household Income Distribution

Area	Percent of Households Earning							
	Under $15,000	$15,000 -$24,999	$25,000 -$34,999	$35,000 -$49,999	$50,000 -$74,999	$75,000 -$99,999	$100,000 -$149,999	$150,000 and up
City	14.5	9.7	10.4	13.8	18.0	12.0	12.7	8.9
MSA[1]	8.5	6.5	7.4	10.4	16.3	13.1	17.8	20.0
U.S.	8.5	6.6	6.8	10.4	15.7	12.7	17.4	21.9

Note: (1) Figures cover the Milwaukee-Waukesha, WI Metropolitan Statistical Area
Source: U.S. Census Bureau, 2019-2023 American Community Survey 5-Year Estimates

Poverty Rate

Area	All Ages	Under 18 Years Old	18 to 64 Years Old	65 Years and Over
City	23.3	32.5	20.7	16.7
MSA[1]	12.4	17.0	11.2	10.3
U.S.	12.4	16.3	11.6	10.4

Note: Figures are percentage of people whose income during the past 12 months was below the poverty level;
(1) Figures cover the Milwaukee-Waukesha, WI Metropolitan Statistical Area
Source: U.S. Census Bureau, 2019-2023 American Community Survey 5-Year Estimates

EMPLOYMENT

Labor Force and Employment

Area	Civilian Labor Force			Workers Employed		
	Dec. 2023	Dec. 2024	% Chg.	Dec. 2023	Dec. 2024	% Chg.
City	273,443	274,723	0.5	264,071	263,797	-0.1
MSA[1]	822,104	825,110	0.4	800,656	800,116	-0.1
U.S.	166,661,000	167,746,000	0.7	160,754,000	161,294,000	0.3

Note: Data is not seasonally adjusted and covers workers 16 years of age and older; (1) Figures cover the Milwaukee-Waukesha, WI Metropolitan Statistical Area
Source: Bureau of Labor Statistics, Local Area Unemployment Statistics

Unemployment Rate

Area	2024											
	Jan.	Feb.	Mar.	Apr.	May	Jun.	Jul.	Aug.	Sep.	Oct.	Nov.	Dec.
City	3.9	4.5	4.6	4.2	4.0	4.9	4.9	4.8	3.8	3.9	4.1	4.0
MSA[1]	3.0	3.5	3.6	3.2	3.1	3.8	3.7	3.4	2.9	2.9	3.1	3.0
U.S.	4.1	4.2	3.9	3.5	3.7	4.3	4.5	4.4	3.9	3.9	4.0	3.8

Note: Data is not seasonally adjusted and covers workers 16 years of age and older; (1) Figures cover the Milwaukee-Waukesha, WI Metropolitan Statistical Area
Source: Bureau of Labor Statistics, Local Area Unemployment Statistics

Average Wages

Occupation	$/Hr.	Occupation	$/Hr.
Accountants and Auditors	43.31	Maintenance and Repair Workers	26.01
Automotive Mechanics	28.74	Marketing Managers	71.02
Bookkeepers	24.38	Network and Computer Systems Admin.	46.35
Carpenters	32.43	Nurses, Licensed Practical	30.73
Cashiers	14.53	Nurses, Registered	43.77
Computer Programmers	43.19	Nursing Assistants	21.00
Computer Systems Analysts	50.52	Office Clerks, General	21.09
Computer User Support Specialists	30.47	Physical Therapists	48.16
Construction Laborers	28.30	Physicians	115.37
Cooks, Restaurant	18.61	Plumbers, Pipefitters and Steamfitters	41.81
Customer Service Representatives	23.48	Police and Sheriff's Patrol Officers	41.03
Dentists	97.31	Postal Service Mail Carriers	28.92
Electricians	35.83	Real Estate Sales Agents	36.71
Engineers, Electrical	50.13	Retail Salespersons	17.62
Fast Food and Counter Workers	13.86	Sales Representatives, Technical/Scientific	43.52
Financial Managers	78.61	Secretaries, Exc. Legal/Medical/Executive	23.21
First-Line Supervisors of Office Workers	35.29	Security Guards	21.24
General and Operations Managers	68.07	Surgeons	n/a
Hairdressers/Cosmetologists	19.57	Teacher Assistants, Exc. Postsecondary[1]	17.98
Home Health and Personal Care Aides	15.84	Teachers, Secondary School, Exc. Sp. Ed.[1]	34.09
Janitors and Cleaners	17.69	Telemarketers	17.30
Landscaping/Groundskeeping Workers	19.82	Truck Drivers, Heavy/Tractor-Trailer	28.14
Lawyers	86.63	Truck Drivers, Light/Delivery Services	22.92
Maids and Housekeeping Cleaners	17.09	Waiters and Waitresses	16.18

Note: Wage data covers the Milwaukee-Waukesha, WI Metropolitan Statistical Area; (1) Hourly wages were calculated from annual wage data based on a 40 hour work week
Source: Bureau of Labor Statistics, Metro Area Occupational Employment & Wage Estimates, May 2024

Employment by Industry

Sector	MSA[1] Number of Employees	MSA[1] Percent of Total	U.S. Percent of Total
Construction	36,700	4.2	5.1
Financial Activities	47,500	5.5	5.8
Government	83,300	9.6	14.9
Information	11,300	1.3	1.9
Leisure and Hospitality	79,600	9.2	10.4
Manufacturing	110,800	12.8	8.0
Mining and Logging	500	0.1	0.4
Other Services	43,700	5.1	3.7
Private Education and Health Services	179,700	20.8	16.9
Professional and Business Services	121,500	14.0	14.2
Retail Trade	77,600	9.0	10.0
Transportation, Warehousing, and Utilities	34,400	4.0	4.8
Wholesale Trade	38,700	4.5	3.9

Note: Figures are non-farm employment as of December 2024. Figures are not seasonally adjusted and include workers 16 years of age and older; (1) Figures cover the Milwaukee-Waukesha, WI Metropolitan Statistical Area
Source: Bureau of Labor Statistics, Current Employment Statistics, Employment, Hours, and Earnings

Employment by Occupation

Occupation Classification	City (%)	MSA[1] (%)	U.S. (%)
Management, Business, Science, and Arts	34.4	43.7	42.0
Natural Resources, Construction, and Maintenance	6.0	6.5	8.6
Production, Transportation, and Material Moving	20.1	15.1	13.0
Sales and Office	17.9	19.5	19.9
Service	21.6	15.3	16.5

Note: Figures cover employed civilians 16 years of age and older; (1) Figures cover the Milwaukee-Waukesha, WI Metropolitan Statistical Area
Source: U.S. Census Bureau, 2019-2023 American Community Survey 5-Year Estimates

Occupations with Greatest Projected Employment Growth: 2022 – 2032

Occupation[1]	2022 Employment	2032 Projected Employment	Numeric Employment Change	Percent Employment Change
Home Health and Personal Care Aides	80,600	94,000	13,400	16.6
Cooks, Restaurant	24,790	32,190	7,400	29.9
Laborers and Freight, Stock, and Material Movers, Hand	68,280	75,240	6,960	10.2
Stockers and Order Fillers	51,890	58,550	6,660	12.8
Software Developers	19,270	25,280	6,010	31.2
Fast Food and Counter Workers	56,080	60,930	4,850	8.6
Industrial Machinery Mechanics	16,970	21,220	4,250	25.0
Construction Laborers	23,620	27,590	3,970	16.8
Heavy and Tractor-Trailer Truck Drivers	52,250	56,180	3,930	7.5
Registered Nurses	62,260	65,570	3,310	5.3

Note: Projections cover Wisconsin; (1) Sorted by numeric employment change
Source: www.projectionscentral.org, State Occupational Projections, 2022–2032 Long-Term Projections

Fastest-Growing Occupations: 2022 – 2032

Occupation[1]	2022 Employment	2032 Projected Employment	Numeric Employment Change	Percent Employment Change
Nurse Practitioners	4,950	7,480	2,530	51.1
Data Scientists	2,860	4,090	1,230	43.0
Travel Agents	920	1,270	350	38.0
Animal Trainers	1,180	1,610	430	36.4
Statisticians	360	490	130	36.1
Information Security Analysts (SOC 2018)	2,410	3,220	810	33.6
Aircraft Service Attendants	150	200	50	33.3
Physician Assistants	2,980	3,950	970	32.6
Actuaries	990	1,310	320	32.3
Chemical Engineers	350	460	110	31.4

Note: Projections cover Wisconsin; (1) Sorted by percent employment change and excludes occupations with numeric employment change less than 50
Source: www.projectionscentral.org, State Occupational Projections, 2022–2032 Long-Term Projections

CITY FINANCES

City Government Finances

Component	2022 ($000)	2022 ($ per capita)
Total Revenues	1,315,708	2,234
Total Expenditures	1,364,847	2,317
Debt Outstanding	1,548,517	2,629

Source: U.S. Census Bureau, State & Local Government Finances 2022

City Government Revenue by Source

Source	2022 ($000)	2022 ($ per capita)	2022 (%)
General Revenue			
From Federal Government	151,777	258	11.5
From State Government	295,927	502	22.5
From Local Governments	86,073	146	6.5
Taxes			
Property	362,175	615	27.5
Sales and Gross Receipts	0	0	0.0
Personal Income	0	0	0.0
Corporate Income	0	0	0.0
Motor Vehicle License	8,928	15	0.7
Other Taxes	17,282	29	1.3
Current Charges	249,255	423	18.9
Liquor Store	0	0	0.0
Utility	82,043	139	6.2

Source: U.S. Census Bureau, State & Local Government Finances 2022

City Government Expenditures by Function

Function	2022 ($000)	2022 ($ per capita)	2022 (%)
General Direct Expenditures			
Air Transportation	0	0	0.0
Corrections	9,600	16	0.7
Education	0	0	0.0
Employment Security Administration	0	0	0.0
Financial Administration	97	< 1	< 0.1
Fire Protection	133,030	225	9.7
General Public Buildings	35,988	61	2.6
Governmental Administration, Other	157,873	268	11.6
Health	48,757	82	3.6
Highways	158,385	268	11.6
Hospitals	0	0	0.0
Housing and Community Development	27,423	46	2.0
Interest on General Debt	59,717	101	4.4
Judicial and Legal	16,620	28	1.2
Libraries	31,304	53	2.3
Parking	24,685	41	1.8
Parks and Recreation	3,772	6	0.3
Police Protection	310,739	527	22.8
Public Welfare	0	0	0.0
Sewerage	68,467	116	5.0
Solid Waste Management	43,894	74	3.2
Veterans' Services	0	0	0.0
Liquor Store	0	0	0.0
Utility	86,591	147	6.3

Source: U.S. Census Bureau, State & Local Government Finances 2022

TAXES

State Corporate Income Tax Rates

State	Tax Rate (%)	Income Brackets ($)	Num. of Brackets	Financial Institution Tax Rate (%)[a]	Federal Income Tax Ded.
Wisconsin	7.9	Flat rate	1	7.9	No

Note: Tax rates for tax year 2024; (a) Rates listed are the corporate income tax rate applied to financial institutions or excise taxes based on income. Some states have other taxes based upon the value of deposits or shares.
Source: Federation of Tax Administrators, State Corporate Income Tax Rates, January 1, 2025

State Individual Income Tax Rates

State	Tax Rate (%)	Income Brackets ($)	Personal Exemptions ($)			Standard Ded. ($)	
			Single	Married	Depend.	Single	Married
Wisconsin (a)	3.5 - 7.65	13,810 - 304,170 (y)	700	1,400	700	14,600	29,200 (z)

Note: Tax rates for tax year 2024; Local- and county-level taxes are not included; Federal income tax is not deductible on state income tax returns; (a) 16 states have statutory provision for automatically adjusting to the rate of inflation the dollar values of the income tax brackets, standard deductions, and/or personal exemptions. Oregon does not index the income brackets for $125,000 and over See: INFL and SPEC above; (y) The Wisconsin income brackets reported are for single individuals. For married taxpayers filing jointly, the same tax rates apply income brackets ranging from $18,420, to $405,550 in 2023; (z) Alabama standard deduction is phased out for incomes over $25,500 after 2017 (MFJ, HOH and Single); $12,750 for MFS. Rhode Island exemptions & standard deductions phased out for incomes over $274,650; Wisconsin standard deduciton phases out for income over $124,500.
Source: Federation of Tax Administrators, State Individual Income Tax Rates, January 1, 2025

Various State Sales and Excise Tax Rates

State	State Sales Tax (%)	Gasoline[1] ($/gal.)	Cigarette[2] ($/pack)	Spirits[3] ($/gal.)	Wine[4] ($/gal.)	Beer[5] ($/gal.)	Recreational Marijuana (%)
Wisconsin	5	0.33	2.52	3.25	0.25	0.06	Not legal

Note: All tax rates as of January 1, 2025; (1) The American Petroleum Institute has developed a methodology for determining the average tax rate on a gallon of fuel. Rates may include any of the following: excise taxes, environmental fees, storage tank fees, other fees or taxes, general sales tax, and local taxes; (2) The federal excise tax of $1.0066 per pack and local taxes are not included; (3) Rates are those applicable to off-premise sales of 40% alcohol by volume (a.b.v.) distilled spirits in 750ml containers. Local excise taxes are excluded; (4) Rates are those applicable to off-premise sales of 11% a.b.v. non-carbonated wine in 750ml containers; (5) Rates are those applicable to off-premise sales of 4.7% a.b.v. beer in 12 ounce containers.
Source: Tax Foundation, 2025 Facts & Figures: How Does Your State Compare?

State Tax Competitiveness Index

State	Overall Rank	Corporate Tax Rank	Individual Income Tax Rank	Sales Tax Rank	Property Tax Rank	Unemployment Insurance Tax Rank
Wisconsin	19	30	35	6	8	32

Note: The Tax Foundation's State Tax Competitiveness Index enables policymakers, taxpayers, and business leaders to gauge how their states' tax systems compare. A rank of 1 is best, 50 is worst. Rankings do not average to the total. States without a tax rank equally as 1. DC's scores and rankings do not affect other states. The report shows tax systems as of July 1, 2024 (the beginning of Fiscal Year 2025).
Source: Tax Foundation, State Tax Competitiveness Index 2025

TRANSPORTATION

Means of Transportation to Work

Area	Car/Truck/Van Drove Alone	Car/Truck/Van Carpooled	Public Transportation Bus	Public Transportation Subway	Public Transportation Railroad	Bicycle	Walked	Other Means	Worked at Home
City	67.8	10.0	5.3	0.0	0.0	0.5	4.0	1.2	11.2
MSA[1]	73.8	7.1	2.1	0.0	0.0	0.3	2.2	0.9	13.5
U.S.	70.2	8.5	1.7	1.3	0.4	0.4	2.4	1.6	13.5

Note: Figures are percentages and cover workers 16 years of age and older; (1) Figures cover the Milwaukee-Waukesha, WI Metropolitan Statistical Area
Source: U.S. Census Bureau, 2019-2023 American Community Survey 5-Year Estimates

Travel Time to Work

Area	Less Than 10 Minutes	10 to 19 Minutes	20 to 29 Minutes	30 to 44 Minutes	45 to 59 Minutes	60 to 89 Minutes	90 Minutes or More
City	10.6	36.2	26.5	18.9	3.4	2.9	1.6
MSA[1]	12.3	32.4	26.0	20.7	4.7	2.5	1.4
U.S.	12.6	28.6	21.2	20.8	8.1	6.0	2.8

Note: Note: Figures are percentages and include workers 16 years old and over; (1) Figures cover the Milwaukee-Waukesha, WI Metropolitan Statistical Area
Source: U.S. Census Bureau, 2019-2023 American Community Survey 5-Year Estimates

Key Congestion Measures

Measure	2000	2010	2015	2020	2022
Annual Hours of Delay, Total (000)	26,505	33,479	37,896	24,340	42,607
Annual Hours of Delay, Per Auto Commuter	33	40	44	29	54
Annual Congestion Cost, Per Auto Commuter ($)	942	945	988	673	1,163

Note: Figures cover the Milwaukee WI urban area
Source: Texas A&M Transportation Institute, 2023 Urban Mobility Report

Freeway Travel Time Index

Measure	1985	1990	1995	2000	2005	2010	2015	2020	2022
Urban Area Index[1]	1.08	1.12	1.14	1.15	1.16	1.16	1.17	1.07	1.16
Urban Area Rank[1,2]	40	35	41	53	57	54	46	57	50

Note: Freeway Travel Time Index—the ratio of travel time in the peak period to the travel time at free-flow conditions. For example, a value of 1.30 indicates a 20-minute free-flow trip takes 26 minutes in the peak (20 minutes x 1.30 = 26 minutes); (1) Covers the Milwaukee WI urban area; (2) Rank is based on 101 larger urban areas (#1 = highest travel time index)
Source: Texas A&M Transportation Institute, 2023 Urban Mobility Report

Public Transportation

Agency Name / Mode of Transportation	Vehicles Operated in Maximum Service[1]	Annual Unlinked Passenger Trips[2] (in thous.)	Annual Passenger Miles[3] (in thous.)
Milwaukee County Transit System (MCTS)			
Bus (purchased transportation)	290	22,384.3	73,141.6
Demand Response (purchased transportation)	80	350.8	2,315.2

Note: (1) Number of revenue vehicles operated by the given mode and type of service to meet the annual maximum service requirement. This is the revenue vehicle count during the peak season of the year; on the week and day that maximum service is provided. Vehicles operated in maximum service (VOMS) exclude atypical days and one-time special events; (2) Number of passengers who boarded public transportation vehicles. Passengers are counted each time they board a vehicle no matter how many vehicles they use to travel from their origin to their destination. (3) Sum of the distances ridden by all passengers during the entire fiscal year.
Source: Federal Transit Administration, National Transit Database, 2023

Air Transportation

Airport Name and Code / Type of Service	Passenger Airlines[1]	Passenger Enplanements	Freight Carriers[2]	Freight (lbs)
General Mitchell International (MKE)				
Domestic service (U.S. carriers only)	26	3,070,094	13	55,217,999
International service (U.S. carriers only)	5	13,060	0	0

Note: (1) Includes all U.S.-based major, minor and commuter airlines that carried at least one passenger during the year; (2) Includes all U.S.-based airlines and freight carriers that transported at least one pound of freight during the year.
Source: Bureau of Transportation Statistics, The Intermodal Transportation Database, Air Carriers: T-100 Domestic Market (U.S. carriers only), 2024; Bureau of Transportation Statistics, The Intermodal Transportation Database, Air Carriers: T-100 International Market (U.S. carriers only), 2024

BUSINESSES

Major Business Headquarters

Company Name	Industry	Rankings	
		Fortune[1]	Forbes[2]
Fiserv	Financial data services	215	-
ManpowerGroup	Temporary help	219	-
Northwestern Mutual	Insurance: life, health (mutual)	110	-
Rockwell Automation	Electronics, electrical equip.	430	-
WEC Energy Group	Utilities: gas and electric	435	-

Note: (1) Companies that produce a 10-K are ranked 1 to 500 based on 2023 revenue; (2) All private companies with at least $2 billion in annual revenue through the end of their most current fiscal year are ranked 1 to 275; companies listed are headquartered in the city; dashes indicate no ranking
Source: Fortune, "Fortune 500," 2024; Forbes, "America's Largest Private Companies," 2024

Living Environment

COST OF LIVING

Cost of Living Index

Composite Index	Groceries	Housing	Utilities	Transportation	Health Care	Misc. Goods/Services
100.5	100.8	104.2	94.0	102.7	105.0	97.7

Note: The Cost of Living Index measures regional differences in the cost of consumer goods and services, excluding taxes and non-consumer expenditures, for professional and managerial households in the top income quintile. It is based on more than 50,000 prices covering almost 60 different items for which prices are collected three times a year by chambers of commerce, economic development organizations or university applied economic centers in each participating urban area. The numbers shown should be read as a percentage above or below the national average of 100. For example, a value of 115.4 in the groceries column indicates that grocery prices are 15.4% higher than the national average. Small differences in the index numbers should not be interpreted as significant; Figures cover the Milwaukee-Waukesha WI urban area.
Source: The Council for Community and Economic Research, Cost of Living Index, 2024

Grocery Prices

Area[1]	T-Bone Steak ($/pound)	Frying Chicken ($/pound)	Whole Milk ($/half gal.)	Eggs ($/dozen)	Orange Juice ($/64 oz.)	Coffee ($/11.5 oz.)
City[2]	15.50	1.43	4.80	3.34	4.45	5.96
Avg.	15.42	1.55	4.69	3.25	4.41	5.46
Min.	14.50	1.16	4.43	2.75	4.00	4.85
Max.	17.56	2.89	5.49	4.78	5.54	7.89

Note: (1) Values for the local area are compared with the average, minimum and maximum values for all 276 areas in the Cost of Living Index; (2) Figures cover the Milwaukee-Waukesha WI urban area; **T-Bone Steak** (price per pound); **Frying Chicken** (price per pound, whole fryer); **Whole Milk** (half gallon carton); **Eggs** (price per dozen, Grade A, large); **Orange Juice** (64 oz. Tropicana or Florida Natural); **Coffee** (11.5 oz. can, vacuum-packed, Maxwell House, Hills Bros, or Folgers).
Source: The Council for Community and Economic Research, Cost of Living Index, 2024

Housing and Utility Costs

Area[1]	New Home Price ($)	Apartment Rent ($/month)	All Electric ($/month)	Part Electric ($/month)	Other Energy ($/month)	Telephone ($/month)
City[2]	541,477	1,627	-	123.28	67.66	187.62
Avg.	515,975	1,550	210.99	123.07	82.07	194.99
Min.	265,375	692	104.33	53.68	36.26	179.42
Max.	2,775,821	5,719	529.02	397.28	361.63	223.33

Note: (1) Values for the local area are compared with the average, minimum and maximum values for all 276 areas in the Cost of Living Index; (2) Figures cover the Milwaukee-Waukesha WI urban area; **New Home Price** (2,400 sf living area, 8,000 sf lot, in urban area with full utilities); **Apartment Rent** (950 sf 2 bedroom/1.5 or 2 bath, unfurnished, excluding all utilities except water); **All Electric** (average monthly cost for an all-electric home); **Part Electric** (average monthly cost for a part-electric home); **Other Energy** (average monthly cost for natural gas, fuel oil, coal, wood, and any other forms of energy except electricity); **Telephone** (price includes the base monthly rate plus taxes and fees for three lines of mobile phone service).
Source: The Council for Community and Economic Research, Cost of Living Index, 2024

Health Care, Transportation, and Other Costs

Area[1]	Doctor ($/visit)	Dentist ($/visit)	Optometrist ($/visit)	Gasoline ($/gallon)	Beauty Salon ($/visit)	Men's Shirt ($)
City[2]	174.22	122.03	86.17	3.30	44.20	32.41
Avg.	143.77	117.51	129.23	3.32	48.57	38.14
Min.	36.74	58.67	67.33	2.80	24.00	13.41
Max.	270.44	216.82	307.33	5.28	94.00	63.89

Note: (1) Values for the local area are compared with the average, minimum and maximum values for all 276 areas in the Cost of Living Index; (2) Figures cover the Milwaukee-Waukesha WI urban area; **Doctor** (general practitioners routine exam of an established patient); **Dentist** (adult teeth cleaning and periodic oral examination); **Optometrist** (full vision eye exam for established adult patient); **Gasoline** (one gallon regular unleaded, national brand, including all taxes, cash price at self-service pump if available); **Beauty Salon** (woman's shampoo, trim, and blow-dry); **Men's Shirt** (cotton/polyester dress shirt, pinpoint weave, long sleeves).
Source: The Council for Community and Economic Research, Cost of Living Index, 2024

HOUSING

Homeownership Rate

Area	2017 (%)	2018 (%)	2019 (%)	2020 (%)	2021 (%)	2022 (%)	2023 (%)	2024 (%)
MSA[1]	63.9	62.3	56.9	58.5	56.8	57.3	60.0	62.7
U.S.	63.9	64.4	64.6	66.6	65.5	65.8	65.9	65.6

Note: (1) Figures cover the Milwaukee-Waukesha, WI Metropolitan Statistical Area
Source: U.S. Census Bureau, Housing Vacancies and Homeownership Annual Statistics: 2017-2024

House Price Index (HPI)

Area	National Ranking[2]	Quarterly Change (%)	One-Year Change (%)	Five-Year Change (%)	Since 1991Q1 (%)
MSA[1]	49	0.11	7.27	55.07	296.31
U.S.[3]	–	1.43	4.51	57.13	327.82

Note: The HPI is a weighted repeat sales index. It measures average price changes in repeat sales or refinancings on the same properties. This information is obtained by reviewing repeat mortgage transactions on single-family properties whose mortgages have been purchased or securitized by Fannie Mae or Freddie Mac since January 1975; (1) Figures cover the Milwaukee-Waukesha-West Allis, WI Metropolitan Statistical Area; (2) Rankings are based on annual percentage change for all metro areas containing at least 15,000 transactions over the last 10 years and ranges from 1 to 241; (3) figures based on a weighted average of Census Division estimates using a seasonally adjusted, purchase-only index; all figures are for the period ending December 31, 2024
Source: Federal Housing Finance Agency, Change in FHFA Metropolitan Area House Price Indexes, All Transactions Index, 2024Q4

Home Value

Area	Under $100,000	$100,000 -$199,999	$200,000 -$299,999	$300,000 -$399,999	$400,000 -$499,999	$500,000 -$999,999	$1,000,000 or more	Median ($)
City	19.7	43.3	25.1	5.9	2.6	2.6	0.8	172,000
MSA[1]	7.4	19.6	27.2	19.0	11.7	13.0	2.1	283,800
U.S.	12.1	17.8	19.5	14.4	10.5	19.1	6.5	303,400

Note: Figures are percentages except for median and cover owner-occupied housing units; (1) Figures cover the Milwaukee-Waukesha, WI Metropolitan Statistical Area
Source: U.S. Census Bureau, 2019-2023 American Community Survey 5-Year Estimates

Year Housing Structure Built

Area	2020 or Later	2010 -2019	2000 -2009	1990 -1999	1980 -1989	1970 -1979	1960 -1969	1950 -1959	1940 -1949	Before 1940	Median Year
City	0.3	3.5	3.7	3.5	3.8	9.2	11.6	18.8	10.9	34.7	1952
MSA[1]	0.7	5.5	8.2	10.4	7.6	13.1	11.6	15.3	7.0	20.7	1966
U.S.	1.2	8.9	13.6	12.8	13.0	14.4	10.0	9.7	4.5	11.9	1980

Note: Figures are percentages except for Median Year; Note: (1) Figures cover the Milwaukee-Waukesha, WI Metropolitan Statistical Area
Source: U.S. Census Bureau, 2019-2023 American Community Survey 5-Year Estimates

Gross Monthly Rent

Area	Under $500	$500 -$999	$1,000 -$1,499	$1,500 -$1,999	$2,000 -$2,499	$2,500 -$2,999	$3,000 and up	Median ($)
City	7.0	39.6	38.2	10.7	2.4	1.0	1.1	1,033
MSA[1]	6.0	33.5	39.6	14.3	3.8	1.5	1.3	1,105
U.S.	6.5	22.3	29.5	20.2	10.8	4.8	5.9	1,348

Note: Figures are percentages except for median; Gross rent is the contract rent plus the estimated average monthly cost of utilities (electricity, gas, and water and sewer) and fuels (oil, coal, kerosene, wood, etc.) if these are paid by the renter (or paid for the renter by someone else); (1) Figures cover the Milwaukee-Waukesha, WI Metropolitan Statistical Area
Source: U.S. Census Bureau, 2019-2023 American Community Survey 5-Year Estimates

HEALTH

Health Risk Factors

Category	MSA[1] (%)	U.S. (%)
Adults aged 18–64 who have any kind of health care coverage	92.6	90.8
Adults who reported being in good or better health	80.5	81.8
Adults who have been told they have high blood cholesterol	35.6	36.9
Adults who have been told they have high blood pressure	35.0	34.0
Adults who are current smokers	10.6	12.1
Adults who currently use e-cigarettes	6.3	7.7
Adults who currently use chewing tobacco, snuff, or snus	2.6	3.2
Adults who are heavy drinkers[2]	7.8	6.1
Adults who are binge drinkers[3]	18.6	15.2
Adults who are overweight (BMI 25.0 - 29.9)	32.9	34.4
Adults who are obese (BMI 30.0 - 99.8)	34.3	34.3
Adults who participated in any physical activities in the past month	75.8	75.8

Note: All figures are crude prevalence; (1) Figures cover the Milwaukee-Waukesha-West Allis, WI Metropolitan Statistical Area; (2) Heavy drinkers are classified as adult men having more than 14 drinks per week and adult women having more than 7 drinks per week; (3) Binge drinkers are classified as males having five or more drinks on one occasion or females having four or more drinks on one occasion
Source: Centers for Disease Control and Prevention, Behavioral Risk Factor Surveillance System, SMART: Selected Metropolitan Area Risk Trends, 2023

Acute and Chronic Health Conditions

Category	MSA[1] (%)	U.S. (%)
Adults who have ever been told they had a heart attack	4.0	4.2
Adults who have ever been told they have angina or coronary heart disease	5.3	4.0
Adults who have ever been told they had a stroke	3.6	3.3
Adults who have ever been told they have asthma	16.5	15.7
Adults who have ever been told they have arthritis	25.3	26.3
Adults who have ever been told they have diabetes[2]	12.1	11.5
Adults who have ever been told they had skin cancer	4.9	5.6
Adults who have ever been told they had any other types of cancer	8.3	8.4
Adults who have ever been told they have COPD	5.6	6.4
Adults who have ever been told they have kidney disease	4.6	3.7
Adults who have ever been told they have a form of depression	22.8	22.0

Note: All figures are crude prevalence; (1) Figures cover the Milwaukee-Waukesha-West Allis, WI Metropolitan Statistical Area; (2) Figures do not include pregnancy-related, borderline, or pre-diabetes
Source: Centers for Disease Control and Prevention, Behavioral Risk Factor Surveillance System, SMART: Selected Metropolitan Area Risk Trends, 2023

Health Screening and Vaccination Rates

Category	MSA[1] (%)	U.S. (%)
Adults who have ever been tested for HIV	37.3	37.5
Adults who have had their blood cholesterol checked within the last five years	89.2	87.0
Adults aged 65+ who have had flu shot within the past year	69.3	63.4
Adults aged 65+ who have ever had a pneumonia vaccination	77.7	71.9

Note: All figures are crude prevalence; (1) Figures cover the Milwaukee-Waukesha-West Allis, WI Metropolitan Statistical Area.
Source: Centers for Disease Control and Prevention, Behavioral Risk Factor Surveillance System, SMART: Selected Metropolitan Area Risk Trends, 2023

Disability Status

Category	MSA[1] (%)	U.S. (%)
Adults who reported being deaf	5.7	7.4
Are you blind or have serious difficulty seeing, even when wearing glasses?	4.6	4.9
Do you have difficulty doing errands alone?	7.8	7.8
Do you have difficulty dressing or bathing?	4.9	3.6
Do you have serious difficulty concentrating/remembering/making decisions?	11.6	13.7
Do you have serious difficulty walking or climbing stairs?	13.7	13.2

Note: All figures are crude prevalence; (1) Figures cover the Milwaukee-Waukesha-West Allis, WI Metropolitan Statistical Area.
Source: Centers for Disease Control and Prevention, Behavioral Risk Factor Surveillance System, SMART: Selected Metropolitan Area Risk Trends, 2023

Mortality Rates for the Top 10 Causes of Death in the U.S.

ICD-10[a] Sub-Chapter	ICD-10[a] Code	Crude Mortality Rate[2] per 100,000 population	
		County[3]	U.S.
Malignant neoplasms	C00-C97	174.5	182.7
Ischaemic heart diseases	I20-I25	116.1	109.6
Provisional assignment of new diseases of uncertain etiology[1]	U00-U49	43.8	65.3
Other forms of heart disease	I30-I51	57.8	65.1
Other degenerative diseases of the nervous system	G30-G31	32.6	52.4
Other external causes of accidental injury	W00-X59	108.1	52.3
Cerebrovascular diseases	I60-I69	44.9	49.1
Chronic lower respiratory diseases	J40-J47	37.6	43.5
Hypertensive diseases	I10-I15	40.8	38.9
Organic, including symptomatic, mental disorders	F01-F09	46.3	33.9

Note: (a) ICD-10 = International Classification of Diseases 10th Revision; (1) Includes COVID-19, adverse effects to COVID-19 vaccines, SARS, and vaping-related disorders; (2) Crude mortality rates are a three-year average covering 2021-2023; (3) Figures cover Milwaukee County.
Source: Centers for Disease Control and Prevention, National Center for Health Statistics. National Vital Statistics System, Mortality 2018-2023 on CDC WONDER Online Database

Mortality Rates for Selected Causes of Death

Cause of Death	ICD-10[a] Code	Crude Mortality Rate[1] per 100,000 population	
		County[2]	U.S.
Accidental poisoning and exposure to noxious substances	X40-X49	67.3	30.5
Alzheimer disease	G30	26.3	35.4
Assault	X85-Y09	22.7	7.3
COVID-19	U07.1	43.8	65.3
Diabetes mellitus	E10-E14	26.4	30.0
Diseases of the liver	K70-K76	18.2	20.8
Human immunodeficiency virus (HIV) disease	B20-B24	1.0	1.5
Influenza and pneumonia	J09-J18	9.3	13.4
Intentional self-harm	X60-X84	14.2	14.7
Malnutrition	E40-E46	8.0	6.0
Obesity and other hyperalimentation	E65-E68	2.7	3.1
Renal failure	N17-N19	14.6	16.4
Transport accidents	V01-V99	12.5	14.4

Note: (a) ICD-10 = International Classification of Diseases 10th Revision; (1) Crude mortality rates are a three-year average covering 2021-2023; (2) Figures cover Milwaukee County; Data are suppressed when the data meet the criteria for confidentiality constraints; Crude mortality rates are flagged as unreliable when the rate would be calculated with a numerator of 20 or less.
Source: Centers for Disease Control and Prevention, National Center for Health Statistics. National Vital Statistics System, Mortality 2018-2023 on CDC WONDER Online Database

Health Insurance Coverage

Area	With Health Insurance	With Private Health Insurance	With Public Health Insurance	Without Health Insurance	Population Under Age 19 Without Health Insurance
City	90.9	52.2	46.7	9.1	3.6
MSA[1]	94.6	70.6	35.5	5.4	2.8
U.S.	91.4	67.3	36.3	8.6	5.4

Note: Figures are percentages that cover the civilian noninstitutionalized population; (1) Figures cover the Milwaukee-Waukesha, WI Metropolitan Statistical Area
Source: U.S. Census Bureau, 2019-2023 American Community Survey 5-Year Estimates

Number of Medical Professionals

Area	MDs[3]	DOs[3,4]	Dentists	Podiatrists	Chiropractors	Optometrists
County[1] (number)	3,965	336	850	65	202	111
County[1] (rate[2])	431.6	36.6	92.8	7.1	22.0	12.1
U.S. (rate[2])	302.5	29.2	74.6	6.4	29.5	18.0

Note: Data as of 2023 unless noted; (1) Data covers Milwaukee County; (2) Number of medical professionals per 100,000 population; (3) Data as of 2022 and includes all active, non-federal physicians; (4) Doctor of Osteopathic Medicine
Source: U.S. Department of Health and Human Services, Health Resources and Services Administration, Bureau of Health Professions, Area Resource File (ARF) 2023-2024

Best Hospitals

According to *U.S. News,* the Milwaukee-Waukesha, WI metro area is home to two of the best hospitals in the U.S.: **Aurora St. Luke's Medical Center** (1 adult specialty); **Froedtert Hospital and the Medical College of Wisconsin** (1 adult specialty). The hospitals listed were nationally ranked in at least one of 15 adult or 11 pediatric specialties. The number of specialties shown cover the parent hospital. Only 160 U.S. hospitals performed well enough to be nationally ranked in one or more specialties. Twenty hospitals in the U.S. made the Honor Roll. The Best Hospitals Honor Roll takes both the national rankings and the procedure and condition ratings into account. Hospitals received points if they were nationally ranked in one of the 15 adult specialties—the higher they ranked, the more points they got—and how many ratings of "high performing" they earned in the 20 procedures and conditions. *U.S. News Online, "America's Best Hospitals 2024-25"*

According to *U.S. News,* the Milwaukee-Waukesha, WI metro area is home to one of the best children's hospitals in the U.S.: **Children's Wisconsin** (8 pediatric specialties). The hospital listed was highly ranked in at least one of 11 pediatric specialties. One hundred five children's hospitals in the U.S. were nationally ranked in at least one specialty. Hospitals received points for being ranked in a specialty, and the 10 hospitals with the most points across the 11 specialties make up the Honor Roll. *U.S. News Online, "America's Best Children's Hospitals 2024-25"*

EDUCATION

Public School District Statistics

District Name	Schls	Pupils	Pupil/ Teacher Ratio	Minority Pupils[1] (%)	Total Rev. per Pupil ($)	Total Exp. per Pupil ($)
Milwaukee School District	156	66,864	17.3	91.1	19,185	19,598

Note: Table includes school districts with 2,000 or more students; (1) Percentage of students that are not non-Hispanic white.
Source: U.S. Department of Education, National Center for Education Statistics, Common Core of Data, Local Education Agency (School District) Universe Survey: School Year 2023-2024; U.S. Department of Education, National Center for Education Statistics, Common Core of Data, School District Finance Survey (F-33): School Year 2021–22

Best High Schools

According to *U.S. News*, Milwaukee is home to one of the top 500 high schools in the U.S.: **Reagan College Preparatory High School** (#458). Nearly 25,000 public, magnet and charter schools were ranked based on their performance on state assessments and how well they prepare students for college. *U.S. News & World Report, "Best High Schools 2024"*

Highest Level of Education

Area	Less than H.S.	H.S. Diploma	Some College, No Deg.	Associate Degree	Bachelor's Degree	Master's Degree	Prof. School Degree	Doctorate Degree
City	14.5	30.8	20.9	7.3	17.2	7.0	1.4	1.0
MSA[1]	7.3	25.6	19.3	9.0	25.2	9.8	2.2	1.5
U.S.	10.6	26.2	19.4	8.8	21.3	9.8	2.3	1.6

Note: Figures cover persons age 25 and over; (1) Figures cover the Milwaukee-Waukesha, WI Metropolitan Statistical Area
Source: U.S. Census Bureau, 2019-2023 American Community Survey 5-Year Estimates

Educational Attainment by Race

Area	High School Graduate or Higher (%)					Bachelor's Degree or Higher (%)				
	Total	White	Black	Asian	Hisp.[2]	Total	White	Black	Asian	Hisp.[2]
City	85.5	92.8	86.0	74.3	64.6	26.6	41.0	13.7	32.7	12.0
MSA[1]	92.7	96.2	86.7	86.3	72.7	38.8	44.4	15.3	53.9	18.1
U.S.	89.4	92.9	88.1	88.0	72.5	35.0	37.7	24.7	57.0	19.9

Note: Figures shown cover persons 25 years old and over; (1) Figures cover the Milwaukee-Waukesha, WI Metropolitan Statistical Area; (2) People of Hispanic origin can be of any race
Source: U.S. Census Bureau, 2019-2023 American Community Survey 5-Year Estimates

School Enrollment by Grade and Control

Area	Preschool (%)		Kindergarten (%)		Grades 1 - 4 (%)		Grades 5 - 8 (%)		Grades 9 - 12 (%)	
	Public	Private	Public	Private	Public	Private	Public	Private	Public	Private
City	77.0	23.0	73.9	26.1	75.5	24.5	73.9	26.1	79.9	20.1
MSA[1]	59.4	40.6	75.9	24.1	78.5	21.5	78.7	21.3	84.9	15.1
U.S.	58.7	41.3	85.2	14.8	87.2	12.8	87.9	12.1	89.0	11.0

Note: Figures shown cover persons 3 years old and over; (1) Figures cover the Milwaukee-Waukesha, WI Metropolitan Statistical Area
Source: U.S. Census Bureau, 2019-2023 American Community Survey 5-Year Estimates

Higher Education

Four-Year Colleges			Two-Year Colleges			Medical Schools[1]	Law Schools[2]	Voc/ Tech[3]
Public	Private Non-profit	Private For-profit	Public	Private Non-profit	Private For-profit			
2	15	0	2	0	2	1	1	3

Note: Figures cover institutions located within the Milwaukee-Waukesha, WI Metropolitan Statistical Area and include main campuses only; (1) includes schools accredited by the Liaison Committee on Medical Education and the American Osteopathic Association's Commission on Osteopathic College Accreditation; (2) includes ABA-accredited schools, schools with provisional ABA accreditation, and state accredited schools; (3) includes all schools with programs that are less than 2 years.
Source: National Center for Education Statistics, Integrated Postsecondary Education System (IPEDS), 2023-24; Wikipedia, List of Medical Schools in the United States, accessed May 2, 2025; Wikipedia, List of Law Schools in the United States, accessed May 2, 2025

According to *U.S. News & World Report*, the Milwaukee-Waukesha, WI metro area is home to one of the top 200 national universities in the U.S.: **Marquette University** (#86 tie). The indicators used to capture academic quality fall into a number of categories: assessment by administrators at peer institutions; retention of students; faculty resources; student selectivity; financial resources; alumni giving; high school counselor ratings of colleges; and graduation rate. *U.S. News & World Report, "America's Best Colleges 2025"*

According to *U.S. News & World Report,* the Milwaukee-Waukesha, WI metro area is home to one of the top 100 law schools in the U.S.: **Marquette University** (#59 tie). The rankings are based on a weighted average of 12 measures of quality: peer assessment score; assessment score by lawyers/judges; median LSAT scores; median undergrad GPA; acceptance rate; employment rates for graduates; placement success; bar passage rate; faculty resources; expenditures per student; student/faculty ratio; and library resources. *U.S. News & World Report,* "America's Best Graduate Schools, Law, 2025"

EMPLOYERS

Major Employers

Company Name	Industry
Advocate Aurora Health	Healthcare
Ascension Wisconsin	Healthcare
BMO Harris Bank	Financial services
Briggs & Stratton Corp.	Manufacturing
Children's Wisconisn	Healthcare
City of Milwaukee	Local government
Froedtert Health	Healthcare
GE Healthcare	Medical technologies and services
Kohl's	Retailer
Medical College of Wisconsin	Private medial school
Milwaukee Tool	Retail
Northwestern Mutual	Financial services
Quad	Marketing solutions
Rockwell Automation	Industrial machinery & equipment
US Bank	Financial services

Note: Companies shown are located within the Milwaukee-Waukesha, WI Metropolitan Statistical Area.
Source: Chambers of Commerce; State Departments of Labor; Wikipedia

Best Companies to Work For

Baird, headquartered in Milwaukee, is among "The 100 Best Companies to Work For." To pick the best companies, *Fortune* partnered with the Great Place to Work Institute. Using their proprietary Trust Index™ survey, the core of what creates great a workplace is measured—key behaviors that drive trust in management, connection with colleagues, and loyalty to the company. To be eligible for the *Fortune* 100 Best Companies to Work For list, employers must have 1,000 or more employees in the U.S. and cannot be a government agency. *Fortune,* "The 100 Best Companies to Work For," 2025

Baird, headquartered in Milwaukee, is among "Fortune's Best Workplaces for Parents." To pick the best companies, *Fortune* partnered with the Great Place to Work Institute. To be considered for the list, companies must be Great Place To Work-Certified and have at least 50 responses from parents in the US. The survey enables employees to share confidential quantitative and qualitative feedback about their organization's culture by responding to 60 statements on a 5-point scale and answering two open-ended questions. Collectively, these statements describe a great employee experience, defined by high levels of trust, respect, credibility, fairness, pride, and camaraderie. In addition, companies provide organizational data like size, location, industry, demographics, roles, and levels; and provide information about parental leave, adoption, flexible schedule, childcare and dependent health care benefits. *Fortune,* "Best Workplaces for Parents," 2024

Baird, headquartered in Milwaukee, is among "Fortune's Best Workplaces for Women." To pick the best companies, *Fortune* partnered with the Great Place to Work Institute. To be considered for the list, companies must be Great Place To Work-Certified. Companies must also employ at least 50 women, at least 20% of their non-executive managers must be female, and at least one executive must be female. To determine the Best Workplaces for Women, Great Place To Work measured the differences in women's survey responses to those of their peers and assesses the impact of demographics and roles on the quality and consistency of women's experiences. Great Place To Work also analyzed the gender balance of each workplace, how it compared to each company's industry, and patterns in representation as women rise from front-line positions to the board of directors. *Fortune,* "Best Workplaces for Women," 2024

PUBLIC SAFETY

Crime Rate

Area	Total Crime Rate	Violent Crime Rate				Property Crime Rate		
		Murder	Rape	Robbery	Aggrav. Assault	Burglary	Larceny -Theft	Motor Vehicle Theft
City	4,136.0	31.0	74.3	284.4	1,048.0	418.1	1,278.7	1,001.6
U.S.	2,290.9	5.7	38.0	66.5	264.1	250.7	1,347.2	318.7

Note: Figures are crimes per 100,000 population.
Source: FBI, Table 8, Offenses Known to Law Enforcement, by State by City, 2023

Hate Crimes

Area	Number of Quarters Reported	Number of Incidents per Bias Motivation					
		Race/Ethnicity/Ancestry	Religion	Sexual Orientation	Disability	Gender	Gender Identity
City[1]	4	2	0	1	0	0	0
U.S.	4	5,900	2,699	2,077	187	92	492

Note: (1) Figures include at least one incident reported with more than one bias motivation.
Source: Federal Bureau of Investigation, Hate Crime Statistics 2023

Identity Theft Consumer Reports

Area	Reports	Reports per 100,000 Population	Rank[2]
MSA[1]	3,882	248	104
U.S.	1,135,291	339	-

Note: (1) Figures cover the Milwaukee-Waukesha, WI Metropolitan Statistical Area; (2) Rank ranges from 1 to 401 where 1 indicates greatest number of identity theft reports per 100,000 population
Source: Federal Trade Commission, Consumer Sentinel Network Data Book 2024

Fraud and Other Consumer Reports

Area	Reports	Reports per 100,000 Population	Rank[2]
MSA[1]	19,316	1,233	117
U.S.	5,360,641	1,601	-

Note: (1) Figures cover the Milwaukee-Waukesha, WI Metropolitan Statistical Area; (2) Rank ranges from 1 to 401 where 1 indicates greatest number of fraud and other consumer reports per 100,000 population
Source: Federal Trade Commission, Consumer Sentinel Network Data Book 2024

POLITICS

2024 Presidential Election Results

Area	Trump (Rep.)	Harris (Dem.)	Stein (Green)	Kennedy (Ind.)	Oliver (Lib.)	Other
Milwaukee County	29.7	68.2	0.7	0.4	0.2	0.7
U.S.	49.7	48.2	0.6	0.5	0.4	0.6

Note: Results are percentages and may not add to 100% due to rounding
Source: Dave Leip's Atlas of U.S. Presidential Elections

SPORTS

Professional Sports Teams

Team Name	League	Year Established
Milwaukee Brewers	Major League Baseball (MLB)	1970
Milwaukee Bucks	National Basketball Association (NBA)	1968

Note: Includes teams located in the Milwaukee-Waukesha, WI Metropolitan Statistical Area.
Source: Wikipedia, Major Professional Sports Teams of the United States and Canada, May 1, 2025

CLIMATE

Average and Extreme Temperatures

Temperature	Jan	Feb	Mar	Apr	May	Jun	Jul	Aug	Sep	Oct	Nov	Dec	Yr.
Extreme High (°F)	60	65	82	91	92	101	101	103	98	89	77	63	103
Average High (°F)	27	31	40	54	65	76	80	79	71	60	45	32	55
Average Temp. (°F)	20	24	33	45	55	66	71	70	62	51	38	25	47
Average Low (°F)	12	16	26	36	45	55	62	61	53	42	30	18	38
Extreme Low (°F)	-26	-19	-10	12	21	36	40	44	28	18	-5	-20	-26

Note: Figures cover the years 1948-1990
Source: National Climatic Data Center, International Station Meteorological Climate Summary, 9/96

Average Precipitation/Snowfall/Humidity

Precip./Humidity	Jan	Feb	Mar	Apr	May	Jun	Jul	Aug	Sep	Oct	Nov	Dec	Yr.
Avg. Precip. (in.)	1.6	1.4	2.6	3.3	2.9	3.4	3.6	3.4	2.9	2.3	2.3	2.2	32.0
Avg. Snowfall (in.)	13	10	9	2	Tr	0	0	0	0	Tr	3	11	49
Avg. Rel. Hum. 6am (%)	76	77	78	78	77	79	82	86	86	82	80	80	80
Avg. Rel. Hum. 3pm (%)	68	66	64	58	58	58	59	62	61	61	66	70	63

Note: Figures cover the years 1948-1990; Tr = Trace amounts (<0.05 in. of rain; <0.5 in. of snow)
Source: National Climatic Data Center, International Station Meteorological Climate Summary, 9/96

Weather Conditions

Temperature			Daytime Sky			Precipitation		
5°F & below	32°F & below	90°F & above	Clear	Partly cloudy	Cloudy	0.01 inch or more precip.	0.1 inch or more snow/ice	Thunder-storms
22	141	10	90	118	157	126	38	35

Note: Figures are average number of days per year and cover the years 1948-1990
Source: National Climatic Data Center, International Station Meteorological Climate Summary, 9/96

HAZARDOUS WASTE

Superfund Sites

The Milwaukee-Waukesha, WI metro area is home to nine sites on the EPA's Superfund National Priorities List (NPL) or Superfund Alternative Approach (SAA) list: **Amcast Industrial Corporation** (Final NPL); **Burnham Canal - Miller Compressing Company** (SAA); **Cedar Creek** (SAA); **Lauer I Sanitary Landfill** (Final NPL); **Master Disposal Service Landfill** (Final NPL); **Moss-American Co., Inc. (Kerr-Mcgee Oil Co.)** (Final NPL); **Muskego Sanitary Landfill** (Final NPL); **Solvay Coke And Gas Company** (SAA); **Waste Management Of Wisconsin, Inc. (Brookfield Sanitary Landfill)** (Final NPL). The Superfund alternative approach uses the same investigation and cleanup process and standards that are used for sites listed on the National Priorities List. The SAA is an alternative to listing a site on the NPL; it is not an alternative to Superfund or the Superfund process. There are a total of 1,445 Superfund sites with a status of proposed or final on both lists in the United States. *U.S. Environmental Protection Agency, National Priorities List, May 1, 2025; U.S. Environmental Protection Agency, Superfund Alternative Approach Sites, May 1, 2025*

AIR QUALITY

Air Quality Trends: Ozone

	1990	1995	2000	2005	2010	2015	2020	2021	2022	2023
MSA[1]	0.095	0.106	0.082	0.092	0.079	0.069	0.074	0.072	0.073	0.077
U.S.	0.087	0.089	0.081	0.080	0.072	0.068	0.066	0.067	0.067	0.070

Note: (1) Data covers the Milwaukee-Waukesha, WI Metropolitan Statistical Area. The values shown are the composite ozone concentration averages among trend sites based on the highest fourth daily maximum 8-hour concentration in parts per million. These trends are based on sites having an adequate record of monitoring data during the trend period. Data from exceptional events are included.
Source: U.S. Environmental Protection Agency, Air Quality Monitoring Information, "Air Quality Trends by City, 1990-2023"

Air Quality Index

Area	Percent of Days when Air Quality was...[2]					AQI Statistics[2]	
	Good	Moderate	Unhealthy for Sensitive Groups	Unhealthy	Very Unhealthy	Maximum	Median
MSA[1]	43.6	48.8	6.6	0.3	0.8	270	53

Note: (1) Data covers the Milwaukee-Waukesha, WI Metropolitan Statistical Area; (2) Based on 365 days with AQI data in 2023. Air Quality Index (AQI) is an index for reporting daily air quality. EPA calculates the AQI for five major air pollutants regulated by the Clean Air Act: ground-level ozone, particle pollution (aka particulate matter), carbon monoxide, sulfur dioxide, and nitrogen dioxide. The AQI runs from 0 to 500. The higher the AQI value, the greater the level of air pollution and the greater the health concern. There are six AQI categories: "Good" AQI is between 0 and 50. Air quality is considered satisfactory; "Moderate" AQI is between 51 and 100. Air quality is acceptable; "Unhealthy for Sensitive Groups" When AQI values are between 101 and 150, members of sensitive groups may experience health effects; "Unhealthy" When AQI values are between 151 and 200 everyone may begin to experience health effects; "Very Unhealthy" AQI values between 201 and 300 trigger a health alert; "Hazardous" AQI values over 300 trigger warnings of emergency conditions (not shown).
Source: U.S. Environmental Protection Agency, Air Quality Index Report, 2023

Air Quality Index Pollutants

Area	Percent of Days when AQI Pollutant was...[2]					
	Carbon Monoxide	Nitrogen Dioxide	Ozone	Sulfur Dioxide	Particulate Matter 2.5	Particulate Matter 10
MSA[1]	0.0	1.4	31.5	(3)	67.1	0.0

Note: (1) Data covers the Milwaukee-Waukesha, WI Metropolitan Statistical Area; (2) Based on 365 days with AQI data in 2023. The Air Quality Index (AQI) is an index for reporting daily air quality. EPA calculates the AQI for five major air pollutants regulated by the Clean Air Act: ground-level ozone, particle pollution (also known as particulate matter), carbon monoxide, sulfur dioxide, and nitrogen dioxide. The AQI runs from 0 to 500. The higher the AQI value, the greater the level of air pollution and the greater the health concern; (3) Sulfur dioxide is no longer included in this table because SO_2 concentrations tend to be very localized and not necessarily representative of broad geographical areas like counties and CBSAs.
Source: U.S. Environmental Protection Agency, Air Quality Index Report, 2023

Maximum Air Pollutant Concentrations: Particulate Matter, Ozone, CO and Lead

	Particulate Matter 10 (ug/m^3)	Particulate Matter 2.5 Wtd AM (ug/m^3)	Particulate Matter 2.5 24-Hr (ug/m^3)	Ozone (ppm)	Carbon Monoxide (ppm)	Lead (ug/m^3)
MSA[1] Level	209	11	39	0.08	1	n/a
NAAQS[2]	150	15	35	0.075	9	0.15
Met NAAQS[2]	No	Yes	No	No	Yes	n/a

Note: (1) Data covers the Milwaukee-Waukesha, WI Metropolitan Statistical Area; Data from exceptional events are included; (2) National Ambient Air Quality Standards; ppm = parts per million; ug/m^3 = micrograms per cubic meter; n/a not available.
Concentrations: Particulate Matter 10 (coarse particulate)—highest second maximum 24-hour concentration; Particulate Matter 2.5 Wtd AM (fine particulate)—highest weighted annual mean concentration; Particulate Matter 2.5 24-Hour (fine particulate)—highest 98th percentile 24-hour concentration; Ozone—highest fourth daily maximum 8-hour concentration; Carbon Monoxide—highest second maximum non-overlapping 8-hour concentration; Lead—maximum running 3-month average
Source: U.S. Environmental Protection Agency, Air Quality Monitoring Information, "Air Quality Statistics by City, 2023"

Maximum Air Pollutant Concentrations: Nitrogen Dioxide and Sulfur Dioxide

	Nitrogen Dioxide AM (ppb)	Nitrogen Dioxide 1-Hr (ppb)	Sulfur Dioxide AM (ppb)	Sulfur Dioxide 1-Hr (ppb)	Sulfur Dioxide 24-Hr (ppb)
MSA[1] Level	11	46	n/a	3	n/a
NAAQS[2]	53	100	30	75	140
Met NAAQS[2]	Yes	Yes	n/a	Yes	n/a

Note: (1) Data covers the Milwaukee-Waukesha, WI Metropolitan Statistical Area; Data from exceptional events are included; (2) National Ambient Air Quality Standards; ppm = parts per million; ug/m^3 = micrograms per cubic meter; n/a not available.
Concentrations: Nitrogen Dioxide AM—highest arithmetic mean concentration; Nitrogen Dioxide 1-Hr—highest 98th percentile 1-hour daily maximum concentration; Sulfur Dioxide AM—highest annual mean concentration; Sulfur Dioxide 1-Hr—highest 99th percentile 1-hour daily maximum concentration; Sulfur Dioxide 24-Hr—highest second maximum 24-hour concentration
Source: U.S. Environmental Protection Agency, Air Quality Monitoring Information, "Air Quality Statistics by City, 2023"

Minneapolis, Minnesota

Background

Minneapolis is a vibrant, cosmopolitan city that boasts sunlit skyscrapers, sparkling lakes, many cultural offerings and abundant recreation. Known for performing and visual arts, education, finance, advertising, and manufacturing, Minneapolis is also a hub of trade, industry, transportation and finance for the Upper Midwest.

In 1680, a French Franciscan priest, Father Louis Hennepin, was the area's first white man to arrive on the scene. In 1819, Fort Snelling was established to protect fur traders from the Sioux and Chippewa tribes. In 1848, two towns, St. Anthony (later named St. Paul), and Minneapolis, grew simultaneously, thus forming the metropolitan area known today as the Twin Cities. A tide of Swedish, German, and Norwegian immigrants came in the late nineteenth century, giving the city a decidedly Scandinavian flavor. Its many lakes gave Minneapolis its name, which comes from the Dakota word "minne," or "of the waters," and the Greek "polis," or city.

Minneapolis's traditional industries are lumber and flour milling. Since the 1950s, electronics, computers, and other science related industries, have played a vital role in the city's economy, as has printing and advertising. Seventeen Fortune 500 companies are based in Minneapolis, including UnitedHealth Group, Target, General Mills, and Ameriprise Financial.

Minneapolis has the fourth-highest percentage of LGBTQ individuals behind San Francisco, Seattle, and Atlanta. In 2013, the city was among 25 U.S. cities to receive the highest possible score from the Human Rights Campaign. In contrast, the city has experienced continued unrest in the wake of the 2020 death of African American George Floyd at the hands of Minneapolis police.

Well-known for its cultural and artistic offerings, Minneapolis occupies more theater seats per capita than any U.S. city outside of New York. The Minneapolis Institute of Arts has more than 100,000 pieces of art with renovated African Art galleries. A Michael Graves-designed wing holds contemporary and modern works. Other area attractions include the Science Museum of Minnesota, the Minneapolis Zoo, and the Charles A. Lindbergh Historic Site.

The Minneapolis metro area has four professional sports teams. The National Football League's (NFL) Minnesota Vikings and Major League Baseball's (MLB) Minnesota Twins have played in the state since 1961. The Minnesota Timberwolves returned National Basketball Association (NBA) basketball to Minneapolis in 1989, and were followed by Minnesota Lynx (WNBA) in 1999. Both basketball teams play in the Target Center. In the 2010s, the Lynx were the most-successful Minnesota professional sports team and a dominant force in the Women's National Basketball Association, winning four WNBA championships from 2011 to 2017. The Minnesota Wild, a National Hockey League (NHL) team, play at the Xcel Energy Center; and the Major League Soccer team Minnesota United FC play at Allianz Field, both of which are located in Saint Paul.

Minneapolis is home to many award-winning restaurants and chefs. Minneapolis-based individuals who have won the food industry James Beard Foundation Award include chef Gavin Kaysen, writer Dara Moskowitz Grumdahl, television personality Andrew Zimmern, and chef Sean Sherman, whose restaurant Owamni received James Beard's 2022 best new restaurant award.

More than five miles of downtown Minneapolis are connected by comfortable, climate-controlled glass "skyways" one flight above ground. The city hosts a Northstar Corridor commuter line between downtown and Big Lake on existing railroad tracks, and a Green Line linking downtown, the University of Minnesota, and downtown St. Paul. Old rail lines and bridges within the city have been converted for bicycles and pedestrians.

Minneapolis experiences a continental climate that is typical of southern parts of the Upper Midwest, with cold, snowy winters and hot, humid summers. The difference between average temperatures in the coldest winter month and the warmest summer month is about 58 degrees. The Minneapolis area experiences a full range of precipitation and related weather events, including snow, sleet, ice, rain, thunderstorms, and fog.

Rankings

General Rankings

- To help military veterans find the best places in which to settle down, *WalletHub* compared the 100 largest U.S. cities across 19 key indicators of livability, affordability and veteran-friendliness. They range from the share of military skill-related jobs to veteran income growth to the availability of VA health facilities. Minneapolis ranked #24. *Wallethub.com, "Best & Worst Places for Veterans to Live (2025)," November 7, 2024*

- Minneapolis was selected as one of the happiest places to live in America by *Outside Magazine*. Criteria centered on overall well being; effect of climate change; inclusivity; affordability; outdoor access; and other demographic and population figures. Local experts shared highlights from hands-on experience in each location. *Outside Magazine, "The 15 Happiest Places to Live in the U.S.," September 18, 2023*

- The human resources consulting firm Mercer ranked 241 major cities worldwide in terms of overall quality of life. Minneapolis ranked #71. Criteria: political and personal safety, social, and economic factors; medical and health considerations; schools and education; public services and transportation; recreation; connectivity; housing and infrastructure; and climate. *Mercer, "Mercer 2024 Quality of Living Survey," December 2024*

- In their annual survey, Livability.com looked at data for more than 2,000 mid-sized U.S. cities to assign a "Livability Score" for each. The top 100 scoring cities make up Livability's "Top 100 Best Places to Live in the U.S." in 2025. Minneapolis was placed among the top 100 of the customizable list. Criteria: housing and economy; cost of living; environment; education; health care options; transportation; safety; and community amenities. *Livability.com, "Top 100 Best Places to Live in the U.S. in 2025" April 15, 2025*

Business/Finance Rankings

- Payscale.com ranked the 32 largest metro areas in terms of wage growth. The Minneapolis metro area ranked #18. Criteria: quarterly changes in private industry employee and education professional wage growth from the previous year. *PayScale, "Wage Trends by Metro Area-4th Quarter," February 4, 2025*

- The Minneapolis metro area appeared on the Milken Institute "2025 Best Performing Cities" list. Rank: #125 out of 200 large metro areas (based on performance category). Criteria: job growth; wage growth; high-tech growth and impact; community resilience; housing affordability; household broadband access. *Milken Institute, "Best-Performing Cities 2025," January 14, 2025*

- Mercer Human Resources Consulting ranked 226 cities worldwide in terms of cost-of-living. Minneapolis ranked #59 (the lower the ranking, the higher the cost-of-living). The survey measured the comparative cost of over 200 items (such as housing, food, clothing, domestic supplies, transportation, and recreation/entertainment) in each location. *Mercer, "2024 Cost of Living City Ranking," June 17, 2024*

Education Rankings

- Personal finance website *WalletHub* analyzed the 150 largest U.S. metropolitan statistical areas to determine where the most educated Americans are putting their degrees to work. Criteria: education levels; percentage of workers with degrees; education quality and attainment gap; public school quality rankings; quality and enrollment of each metro area's universities. Minneapolis was ranked #18 (#1 = most educated city). *WalletHub.com, "Most & Least Educated Cities in America, 2025" July 2, 2024*

Environmental Rankings

- *Niche* compiled a list of the nation's snowiest cities, based on the National Oceanic and Atmospheric Administration's 30-year average snowfall data. Among cities with a population of at least 50,000, Minneapolis ranked #24. *Niche.com, Top 25 Snowiest Cities in America, December 10, 2018*

- Sperling's *BestPlaces* assessed the 50 largest metropolitan areas of the United States for the likelihood of dangerously extreme weather events or earthquakes. In general the Southeast and South-Central regions have the highest risk of weather extremes and earthquakes, while the Pacific Northwest enjoys the lowest risk. Of the least risky metropolitan areas, the Minneapolis metro area was ranked #7. *Bestplaces.net, "Avoid Natural Disasters: BestPlaces Reveals The Top 10 Safest Places to Live," October 25, 2017*

- The U.S. Environmental Protection Agency (EPA) released its list of U.S. metropolitan areas with the most ENERGY STAR certified buildings in 2023. The Minneapolis metro area was ranked #16 out of 25. *U.S. Environmental Protection Agency, "2024 Energy Star Top Cities," May 22, 2024*

Health/Fitness Rankings

- For each of the 100 largest cities in the United States, the American Fitness Index®, compiled in partnership between the American College of Sports Medicine and the Elevance Health Foundation, evaluated community infrastructure and more than 30 health behaviors including preventive health, levels of chronic disease conditions, food insecurity, pedestrian safety, air quality, and community/environment resources that support physical activity. Minneapolis ranked #6 for "community fitness." *americanfitnessindex.org, "2024 ACSM American Fitness Index Summary Report," July 23, 2024*

- The Minneapolis metro area was identified as one of the worst cities for bed bugs in America by pest control company Orkin. The area ranked #47 out of 50 based on the number of bed bug treatments Orkin performed from December 2022 to November 2023. *Orkin, "Chicago Joins Paris In Global Bed Bug Spotlight Ranking As The Worst City On Orkin's U.S. Bed Bug Cities List," January 22, 2024*

- Minneapolis was identified as a "2025 Allergy Capital." The area ranked #90 out of the nation's 100 largest metropolitan areas. Three groups of factors were used to identify the most challenging cities for people with allergies: annual tree, grass, and weed pollen scores; over the counter allergy medicine use; number of board-certified allergy specialists. *Asthma and Allergy Foundation of America, "2025 Allergy Capitals: The Most Challenging Places to Live with Allergies," March 18, 2025*

- Minneapolis was identified as a "2024 Asthma Capital." The area ranked #47 out of the nation's 100 largest metropolitan areas. Criteria: estimated asthma prevalence; asthma-related mortality; and ER visits due to asthma. Risk factors analyzed but not factored in the rankings: annual air quality including pollution and ozone levels; public smoking laws; indoor air quality; access to asthma specialists; rescue and controller medication use; uninsured rate; pollen allergy; poverty rate. *Asthma and Allergy Foundation of America, "Asthma Capitals 2024: The Most Challenging Places to Live With Asthma," September 10, 2024*

Pet Rankings

- Minneapolis was selected by *Sniffspot.com* as one of the most dog-friendly cities in the U.S., ranking #12 out of 50. Criteria: dog parks; hiking; sniffspots; public parks; dog-friendly businesses; housing; dog waste cleanliness; leash laws; dog services; and overall cost. *Sniffspot.com, "The Top 50 Most Dog-Friendly Cities in the U.S.," September 30, 2024*

Real Estate Rankings

- *WalletHub* compared the most populated U.S. cities to determine which had the best markets for real estate agents. Minneapolis ranked #96 where demand was high and pay was the best. Criteria: sales per agent; annual median wage for real-estate agents; monthly average starting salary for real estate agents; real estate job density and competition; unemployment rate; home turnover rate; housing-market health index; and other relevant metrics. *WalletHub.com, "2021 Best Places to Be a Real Estate Agent," May 12, 2021*

- Minneapolis was ranked #62 out of 176 metro areas in terms of cost of housing in 2024 by the National Association of Home Builders (#1 = most affordable). Criteria: the portion of an average family's income necessary to pay the mortgage on a median-priced home. *National Association of Home Builders®, NAHB-Wells Fargo Cost of Housing Index, 4th Quarter 2024*

Safety Rankings

- To identify the most dangerous cities in America, *24/7 Wall St.* focused on violent crime categories—murder, non-negligent manslaughter, rape, robbery, and aggravated assault—as reported for every 100,000 residents using data from the FBI's 2020 annual Uniform Crime Report. For cities with populations over 25,000, Minneapolis was ranked #48. *247wallst.com, "America's Most Dangerous Cities" November 12, 2021*

- Statistics drawn from the FBI's Uniform Crime Report were used to rank the cities where violent crime rose the most year over year from 2019 to 2020. Only cities with 25,000 or more residents were included. *24/7 Wall St.* found that Minneapolis placed #21 of those with a notable surge in incidents of violent crime. *247wallst.com, "American Cities Where Crime Is Soaring," March 4, 2022*

- Allstate ranked the 100 most populous cities in America in terms of driver safety. Minneapolis ranked #2. Criteria based on anonymized driving behavior data from Allstate's mobile app powered by Arity: high speed driving (over 80 mph), phone handling, and hard braking. The report helps increase the importance of safety and awareness behind the wheel. *Allstate, "16th Allstate America's Best Drivers Report®" July 11, 2024*

- Minneapolis was identified as one of the most dangerous cities in America by NeighborhoodScout. The city ranked #36 out of 100 (#1 = most dangerous). Criteria: number of violent crimes per 1,000 residents. The editors evaluated cities with 25,000 or more residents. *NeighborhoodScout.com, "2023 Top 100 Most Dangerous Cities in the U.S.," January 12, 2023*

Women/Minorities Rankings

- Personal finance website *WalletHub* compared more than 180 U.S. cities across two key dimensions, "Hispanic Business-Friendliness" and "Hispanic Purchasing Power," to arrive at the most favorable conditions for Hispanic entrepreneurs. Minneapolis was ranked #163 out of 182. Criteria includes: share of Hispanic-Owned Businesses; average growth of Hispanic Business revenues; Small Business-Friendliness score; affordability; and number of Hispanics with at least a bachelor's degree. *WalletHub.com, "Best Cities for Hispanic Entrepreneurs," September 4, 2024*

Miscellaneous Rankings

- *MoveHub* ranked 446 hipster cities across 20 countries, using its new and improved alternative Hipster Index and Minneapolis came out as #13 among the top 50. Criteria: population over 150,000; number of vintage boutiques; density of tattoo parlors; vegan places to eat; coffee shops; and density of vinyl record stores. *MoveHub.com, "The Hipster Index: Brighton Pips Portland to Global Top Spot," July 28, 2021*

- *WalletHub* compared 148 of the most populated U.S. cities to determine their operating efficiency. A "Quality of Services" score was constructed for each city and then measured against the total budget per capita to reveal which were managed the best. Minneapolis ranked #96. Criteria: financial stability; economy; education; safety; health; infrastructure and pollution. *WalletHub.com, "2025's Best- & Worst-Run Cities in America," June 18, 2024*

Business Environment

DEMOGRAPHICS

Population Growth

Area	1990 Census	2000 Census	2010 Census	2020 Census	2023 Estimate[2]	Population Growth 1990-2023 (%)
City	368,383	382,618	382,578	429,954	426,845	15.9
MSA[1]	2,538,834	2,968,806	3,279,833	3,690,261	3,693,351	45.5
U.S.	248,709,873	281,421,906	308,745,538	331,449,281	332,387,540	33.6

Note: (1) Figures cover the Minneapolis-St. Paul-Bloomington, MN-WI Metropolitan Statistical Area; (2) 2019-2023 5-year ACS population estimate
Source: U.S. Census Bureau, 1990 Census, 2000 Census, 2010 Census, 2020 Census, 2019-2023 American Community Survey 5-Year Estimates

Race

Area	White Alone[2] (%)	Black Alone[2] (%)	Asian Alone[2] (%)	AIAN[3] Alone[2] (%)	NHOPI[4] Alone[2] (%)	Other Race Alone[2] (%)	Two or More Races (%)
City	61.6	18.3	5.2	1.1	0.1	4.9	8.9
MSA[1]	73.8	8.9	6.9	0.5	0.0	3.0	6.8
U.S.	63.4	12.4	5.8	0.9	0.2	6.6	10.7

Note: (1) Figures cover the Minneapolis-St. Paul-Bloomington, MN-WI Metropolitan Statistical Area; (2) Alone is defined as not being in combination with one or more other races; (3) American Indian and Alaska Native; (4) Native Hawaiian and Other Pacific Islander
Source: U.S. Census Bureau, 2019-2023 American Community Survey 5-Year Estimates

Hispanic or Latino Origin

Area	Total (%)	Mexican (%)	Puerto Rican (%)	Cuban (%)	Other (%)
City	10.5	5.9	0.4	0.2	4.0
MSA[1]	6.7	4.1	0.3	0.1	2.1
U.S.	19.0	11.3	1.8	0.7	5.2

Note: Persons of Hispanic or Latino origin can be of any race; (1) Figures cover the Minneapolis-St. Paul-Bloomington, MN-WI Metropolitan Statistical Area
Source: U.S. Census Bureau, 2019-2023 American Community Survey 5-Year Estimates

Age

Area	Percent of Population									Median Age
	Under Age 5	Age 5–19	Age 20–34	Age 35–44	Age 45–54	Age 55–64	Age 65–74	Age 75–84	Age 85+	
City	5.7	17.1	30.9	14.9	10.7	9.9	7.0	2.7	1.1	33.0
MSA[1]	6.1	19.7	20.0	14.1	12.2	12.8	9.1	4.2	1.7	37.8
U.S.	5.7	19.1	20.2	13.1	12.3	12.8	10.0	4.9	1.9	38.7

Note: (1) Figures cover the Minneapolis-St. Paul-Bloomington, MN-WI Metropolitan Statistical Area
Source: U.S. Census Bureau, 2019-2023 American Community Survey 5-Year Estimates

Disability by Age

Area	All Ages	Under 18 Years Old	18 to 64 Years Old	65 Years and Over
City	11.6	4.8	10.7	30.5
MSA[1]	10.4	4.0	8.6	27.9
U.S.	13.0	4.7	10.7	32.9

Note: Figures show percent of the civilian noninstitutionalized population that reported having a disability. Disability status is determined from six types of difficulty: vision, hearing, cognitive, ambulatory, self-care, and independent living. For children under 5 years old, hearing and vision difficulty are used to determine disability status. For children between the ages of 5 and 14, disability status is determined from hearing, vision, cognitive, ambulatory, and self-care difficulties. For people aged 15 years and older, they are considered to have a disability if they have difficulty with any one of the six difficulty types; Note: (1) Figures cover the Minneapolis-St. Paul-Bloomington, MN-WI Metropolitan Statistical Area
Source: U.S. Census Bureau, 2019-2023 American Community Survey 5-Year Estimates

Ancestry

Area	German	Irish	English	American	Italian	Polish	French[2]	European	Scottish
City	21.0	10.7	7.4	1.7	2.6	3.9	2.7	2.0	1.4
MSA[1]	27.4	10.7	6.9	3.1	2.5	4.0	2.9	2.0	1.2
U.S.	12.6	9.4	9.1	5.5	4.9	2.6	2.0	1.6	1.6

Note: Figures are the percentage of the total population reporting a particular ancestry. The nine most commonly reported ancestries in the U.S. are shown. Figures include multiple ancestries (e.g. if a person reported being Irish and Italian, they were included in both columns); (1) Figures cover the Minneapolis-St. Paul-Bloomington, MN-WI Metropolitan Statistical Area; (2) Excludes Basque
Source: U.S. Census Bureau, 2019-2023 American Community Survey 5-Year Estimates

Foreign-born Population

Area	Percent of Population Born in								
	Any Foreign Country	Asia	Mexico	Europe	Caribbean	Central America[2]	South America	Africa	Canada
City	14.1	3.2	1.8	1.0	0.2	0.3	1.5	5.7	0.3
MSA[1]	10.7	4.0	1.2	1.0	0.2	0.4	0.6	3.1	0.2
U.S.	13.9	4.3	3.3	1.4	1.4	1.2	1.2	0.8	0.2

Note: (1) Figures cover the Minneapolis-St. Paul-Bloomington, MN-WI Metropolitan Statistical Area; (2) Excludes Mexico.
Source: U.S. Census Bureau, 2019-2023 American Community Survey 5-Year Estimates

Household Size

Area	Persons in Household (%)							Average Household Size
	One	Two	Three	Four	Five	Six	Seven or More	
City	42.0	30.8	11.5	9.2	3.5	1.5	1.4	2.16
MSA[1]	28.9	34.2	14.3	13.3	5.8	2.1	1.4	2.49
U.S.	28.5	33.8	15.4	12.7	5.9	2.3	1.4	2.54

Note: (1) Figures cover the Minneapolis-St. Paul-Bloomington, MN-WI Metropolitan Statistical Area
Source: U.S. Census Bureau, 2019-2023 American Community Survey 5-Year Estimates

Household Relationships

Area	Householder	Opposite-sex Spouse	Same-sex Spouse	Opposite-sex Unmarried Partner	Same-sex Unmarried Partner	Child[2]	Grand-child	Other Relatives	Non-relatives
City	43.7	12.0	0.6	3.9	0.5	22.1	1.1	3.5	8.0
MSA[1]	38.9	18.7	0.2	2.8	0.2	29.4	1.2	3.3	3.3
U.S.	38.3	17.5	0.2	2.5	0.2	28.3	2.4	4.8	3.4

Note: Figures are percent of the total population; (1) Figures cover the Minneapolis-St. Paul-Bloomington, MN-WI Metropolitan Statistical Area; (2) Includes biological, adopted, and stepchildren of the householder
Source: U.S. Census Bureau, 2020 Census

Gender

Area	Males	Females	Males per 100 Females
City	218,753	208,092	105.1
MSA[1]	1,842,197	1,851,154	99.5
U.S.	164,545,087	167,842,453	98.0

Note: (1) Figures cover the Minneapolis-St. Paul-Bloomington, MN-WI Metropolitan Statistical Area
Source: U.S. Census Bureau, 2019-2023 American Community Survey 5-Year Estimates

Marital Status

Area	Never Married	Now Married[2]	Separated	Widowed	Divorced
City	52.0	33.9	1.2	2.9	9.9
MSA[1]	34.1	50.7	0.9	4.3	10.0
U.S.	34.1	47.9	1.7	5.6	10.7

Note: Figures are percentages and cover the population 15 years of age and older; (1) Figures cover the Minneapolis-St. Paul-Bloomington, MN-WI Metropolitan Statistical Area; (2) Excludes separated
Source: U.S. Census Bureau, 2019-2023 American Community Survey 5-Year Estimates

Religious Groups by Family

Area	Catholic	Baptist	Methodist	LDS[2]	Pentecostal	Lutheran	Islam	Adventist	Other
MSA[1]	19.8	0.8	1.4	0.5	2.5	10.7	2.9	0.7	7.4
U.S.	18.7	7.3	3.0	2.0	1.8	1.7	1.3	1.3	11.6

Note: Figures are the number of adherents as a percentage of the total population and cover the eight largest religious groups in the U.S; (1) Figures cover the Minneapolis-St. Paul-Bloomington, MN-WI Metropolitan Statistical Area; (2) Church of Jesus Christ of Latter-day Saints
Sources: 2020 U.S. Religion Census, Association of Statisticians of American Religious Bodies; The Association of Religion Data Archives (ARDA)

Religious Groups by Tradition

Area	Catholic	Evangelical Protestant	Mainline Protestant	Black Protestant	Islam	Judaism	Hinduism	Orthodox	Buddhism
MSA[1]	19.8	10.6	10.3	0.5	2.9	0.6	0.2	0.3	0.3
U.S.	18.7	16.5	5.2	2.3	1.3	0.6	0.4	0.4	0.3

Note: Figures are the number of adherents as a percentage of the total population; (1) Figures cover the Minneapolis-St. Paul-Bloomington, MN-WI Metropolitan Statistical Area
Sources: 2020 U.S. Religion Census, Association of Statisticians of American Religious Bodies; The Association of Religion Data Archives (ARDA)

ECONOMY

Real Gross Domestic Product (GDP)

Area	2017	2018	2019	2020	2021	2022	2023	Rank[3]
MSA[1]	257.8	265.7	270.1	260.6	275.7	281.3	286.7	15
U.S.[2]	17,619.1	18,160.7	18,642.5	18,238.9	19,387.6	19,896.6	20,436.3	—

Note: Figures are in billions of chained 2017 dollars; (1) Figures cover the Minneapolis-St. Paul-Bloomington, MN-WI Metropolitan Statistical Area; (2) Figures cover real GDP within metropolitan areas; (3) Rank is based on 2023 data and ranges from 1 to 384
Source: U.S. Bureau of Economic Analysis

Economic Growth

Area	2014	2015	2016	2017	2018	2019	2020	2021	2022	2023
MSA[1]	3.8	2.2	1.6	1.9	3.1	1.6	-3.5	5.8	2.0	2.0
U.S.[2]	2.6	3.2	2.0	2.7	3.1	2.7	-2.2	6.3	2.6	2.7

Note: Figures are real gross domestic product growth rates and represent percent change from preceding period; (1) Figures cover the Minneapolis-St. Paul-Bloomington, MN-WI Metropolitan Statistical Area; (2) Figures are the average growth rates within metropolitan areas
Source: U.S. Bureau of Economic Analysis

Metropolitan Area Exports

Area	2018	2019	2020	2021	2022	2023	Rank[2]
MSA[1]	20,016.2	18,633.0	17,109.5	21,098.8	21,964.3	22,209.4	23
U.S.	1,664,056.1	1,645,173.7	1,431,406.6	1,753,941.4	2,062,937.4	2,019,160.5	—

Note: Figures are in millions of dollars; (1) Figures cover the Minneapolis-St. Paul-Bloomington, MN-WI Metropolitan Statistical Area; (2) Rank is based on 2023 data and ranges from 1 to 386
Source: U.S. Department of Commerce, International Trade Administration, Office of Trade and Economic Analysis, Industry and Analysis, Exports by Metropolitan Area, data extracted April 2, 2025

Building Permits

Area	Single-Family			Multi-Family			Total		
	2023	2024	Pct. Chg.	2023	2024	Pct. Chg.	2023	2024	Pct. Chg.
City	70	65	-7.1	1,458	387	-73.5	1,528	452	-70.4
MSA[1]	8,245	9,300	12.8	10,388	4,722	-54.5	18,633	14,022	-24.7
U.S.	920,000	981,900	6.7	591,100	496,100	-16.1	1,511,100	1,478,000	-2.2

Note: (1) Figures cover the Minneapolis-St. Paul-Bloomington, MN-WI Metropolitan Statistical Area; Figures represent new, privately-owned housing units authorized (unadjusted data)
Source: U.S. Census Bureau, Building Permits Survey (BPS), 2023, 2024

Bankruptcy Filings

Area	Business Filings			Nonbusiness Filings		
	2023	2024	% Chg.	2023	2024	% Chg.
Hennepin County	64	77	20.3	1,473	1,952	32.5
U.S.	18,926	23,107	22.1	434,064	494,201	13.9

Note: Business filings include Chapter 7, Chapter 9, Chapter 11, Chapter 12, Chapter 13, Chapter 15, and Section 304; Nonbusiness filings include Chapter 7, Chapter 11, and Chapter 13
Source: Administrative Office of the U.S. Courts, Business and Nonbusiness Bankruptcy, County Cases Commenced by Chapter of the Bankruptcy Code, During the 12-Month Period Ending December 31, 2023 and Business and Nonbusiness Bankruptcy, County Cases Commenced by Chapter of the Bankruptcy Code, During the 12-Month Period Ending December 31, 2024

Housing Vacancy Rates

Area	Gross Vacancy Rate[3] (%)			Year-Round Vacancy Rate[4] (%)			Rental Vacancy Rate[5] (%)			Homeowner Vacancy Rate[6] (%)		
	2022	2023	2024	2022	2023	2024	2022	2023	2024	2022	2023	2024
MSA[1]	4.8	5.5	4.9	4.5	5.3	4.6	6.7	8.1	5.2	0.8	0.5	0.4
U.S.[2]	9.1	9.0	9.1	7.5	7.5	7.6	5.7	6.5	6.8	0.8	0.8	1.0

Note: (1) Figures cover the Minneapolis-St. Paul-Bloomington, MN-WI Metropolitan Statistical Area; (2) Figures cover the 75 largest Metropolitan Statistical Areas; (3) The percentage of the total housing inventory that is vacant; (4) The percentage of the housing inventory (excluding seasonal units) that is year-round vacant; (5) The percentage of rental inventory that is vacant for rent; (6) The percentage of homeowner inventory that is vacant for sale
Source: U.S. Census Bureau, Housing Vacancies and Homeownership Annual Statistics: 2022, 2023, 2024

INCOME

Income

Area	Per Capita ($)	Median Household ($)	Average Household ($)
City	50,605	80,269	112,607
MSA[1]	51,500	98,180	128,647
U.S.	43,289	78,538	110,491

Note: (1) Figures cover the Minneapolis-St. Paul-Bloomington, MN-WI Metropolitan Statistical Area
Source: U.S. Census Bureau, 2019-2023 American Community Survey 5-Year Estimates

Household Income Distribution

Area	Percent of Households Earning							
	Under $15,000	$15,000 -$24,999	$25,000 -$34,999	$35,000 -$49,999	$50,000 -$74,999	$75,000 -$99,999	$100,000 -$149,999	$150,000 and up
City	9.5	6.6	6.2	9.7	15.2	12.3	17.3	23.1
MSA[1]	5.5	4.5	4.9	8.5	14.5	13.0	20.3	28.9
U.S.	8.5	6.6	6.8	10.4	15.7	12.7	17.4	21.9

Note: (1) Figures cover the Minneapolis-St. Paul-Bloomington, MN-WI Metropolitan Statistical Area
Source: U.S. Census Bureau, 2019-2023 American Community Survey 5-Year Estimates

Poverty Rate

Area	All Ages	Under 18 Years Old	18 to 64 Years Old	65 Years and Over
City	16.4	19.8	15.7	14.2
MSA[1]	8.2	9.6	7.7	7.7
U.S.	12.4	16.3	11.6	10.4

Note: Figures are percentage of people whose income during the past 12 months was below the poverty level; (1) Figures cover the Minneapolis-St. Paul-Bloomington, MN-WI Metropolitan Statistical Area
Source: U.S. Census Bureau, 2019-2023 American Community Survey 5-Year Estimates

EMPLOYMENT

Labor Force and Employment

Area	Civilian Labor Force			Workers Employed		
	Dec. 2023	Dec. 2024	% Chg.	Dec. 2023	Dec. 2024	% Chg.
City	244,672	245,657	0.4	238,965	239,886	0.4
MSA[1]	2,005,284	2,015,070	0.5	1,956,084	1,964,999	0.5
U.S.	166,661,000	167,746,000	0.7	160,754,000	161,294,000	0.3

Note: Data is not seasonally adjusted and covers workers 16 years of age and older; (1) Figures cover the Minneapolis-St. Paul-Bloomington, MN-WI Metropolitan Statistical Area
Source: Bureau of Labor Statistics, Local Area Unemployment Statistics

Unemployment Rate

Area	2024											
	Jan.	Feb.	Mar.	Apr.	May	Jun.	Jul.	Aug.	Sep.	Oct.	Nov.	Dec.
City	2.8	3.0	2.8	2.6	2.5	3.3	3.4	3.4	2.9	2.7	2.5	2.3
MSA[1]	3.1	3.3	3.1	2.7	2.6	3.5	3.4	3.4	2.7	2.4	2.4	2.5
U.S.	4.1	4.2	3.9	3.5	3.7	4.3	4.5	4.4	3.9	3.9	4.0	3.8

Note: Data is not seasonally adjusted and covers workers 16 years of age and older; (1) Figures cover the Minneapolis-St. Paul-Bloomington, MN-WI Metropolitan Statistical Area
Source: Bureau of Labor Statistics, Local Area Unemployment Statistics

Average Wages

Occupation	$/Hr.	Occupation	$/Hr.
Accountants and Auditors	45.40	Maintenance and Repair Workers	28.72
Automotive Mechanics	29.52	Marketing Managers	85.36
Bookkeepers	26.89	Network and Computer Systems Admin.	48.14
Carpenters	35.62	Nurses, Licensed Practical	30.75
Cashiers	16.35	Nurses, Registered	49.42
Computer Programmers	50.83	Nursing Assistants	22.60
Computer Systems Analysts	53.62	Office Clerks, General	24.20
Computer User Support Specialists	33.76	Physical Therapists	47.65
Construction Laborers	30.67	Physicians	159.99
Cooks, Restaurant	20.11	Plumbers, Pipefitters and Steamfitters	42.95
Customer Service Representatives	24.54	Police and Sheriff's Patrol Officers	42.99
Dentists	108.57	Postal Service Mail Carriers	29.62
Electricians	41.70	Real Estate Sales Agents	34.01
Engineers, Electrical	54.81	Retail Salespersons	18.56
Fast Food and Counter Workers	16.17	Sales Representatives, Technical/Scientific	50.40
Financial Managers	85.12	Secretaries, Exc. Legal/Medical/Executive	25.28
First-Line Supervisors of Office Workers	37.88	Security Guards	24.99
General and Operations Managers	59.75	Surgeons	180.26
Hairdressers/Cosmetologists	22.01	Teacher Assistants, Exc. Postsecondary[1]	20.05
Home Health and Personal Care Aides	17.88	Teachers, Secondary School, Exc. Sp. Ed.[1]	35.70
Janitors and Cleaners	19.66	Telemarketers	22.16
Landscaping/Groundskeeping Workers	22.32	Truck Drivers, Heavy/Tractor-Trailer	31.39
Lawyers	79.57	Truck Drivers, Light/Delivery Services	25.01
Maids and Housekeeping Cleaners	19.15	Waiters and Waitresses	13.95

Note: Wage data covers the Minneapolis-St. Paul-Bloomington, MN-WI Metropolitan Statistical Area; (1) Hourly wages were calculated from annual wage data based on a 40 hour work week
Source: Bureau of Labor Statistics, Metro Area Occupational Employment & Wage Estimates, May 2024

Employment by Industry

Sector	MSA[1] Number of Employees	MSA[1] Percent of Total	U.S. Percent of Total
Construction, Mining, and Logging	85,600	4.3	5.5
Financial Activities	143,800	7.2	5.8
Government	262,700	13.2	14.9
Information	27,500	1.4	1.9
Leisure and Hospitality	176,800	8.9	10.4
Manufacturing	199,500	10.0	8.0
Other Services	76,900	3.9	3.7
Private Education and Health Services	378,700	19.0	16.9
Professional and Business Services	287,200	14.4	14.2
Retail Trade	183,200	9.2	10.0
Transportation, Warehousing, and Utilities	87,100	4.4	4.8
Wholesale Trade	84,000	4.2	3.9

Note: Figures are non-farm employment as of December 2024. Figures are not seasonally adjusted and include workers 16 years of age and older; (1) Figures cover the Minneapolis-St. Paul-Bloomington, MN-WI Metropolitan Statistical Area
Source: Bureau of Labor Statistics, Current Employment Statistics, Employment, Hours, and Earnings

Employment by Occupation

Occupation Classification	City (%)	MSA[1] (%)	U.S. (%)
Management, Business, Science, and Arts	56.4	48.6	42.0
Natural Resources, Construction, and Maintenance	3.4	6.4	8.6
Production, Transportation, and Material Moving	9.4	12.3	13.0
Sales and Office	16.3	18.8	19.9
Service	14.5	14.0	16.5

Note: Figures cover employed civilians 16 years of age and older; (1) Figures cover the Minneapolis-St. Paul-Bloomington, MN-WI Metropolitan Statistical Area
Source: U.S. Census Bureau, 2019-2023 American Community Survey 5-Year Estimates

Occupations with Greatest Projected Employment Growth: 2022 – 2032

Occupation[1]	2022 Employment	2032 Projected Employment	Numeric Employment Change	Percent Employment Change
Home Health and Personal Care Aides	113,680	129,520	15,840	13.9
Software Developers	38,590	47,920	9,330	24.2
General and Operations Managers	76,000	81,170	5,170	6.8
Laborers and Freight, Stock, and Material Movers, Hand	55,000	58,700	3,700	6.7
Registered Nurses	68,040	71,630	3,590	5.3
Stockers and Order Fillers	42,970	46,440	3,470	8.1
Market Research Analysts and Marketing Specialists	23,920	27,220	3,300	13.8
Cooks, Restaurant	26,770	30,010	3,240	12.1
Industrial Engineers	18,230	21,260	3,030	16.6
Medical and Health Services Managers	10,910	13,760	2,850	26.1

Note: Projections cover Minnesota; (1) Sorted by numeric employment change
Source: www.projectionscentral.org, State Occupational Projections, 2022–2032 Long-Term Projections

Fastest-Growing Occupations: 2022 – 2032

Occupation[1]	2022 Employment	2032 Projected Employment	Numeric Employment Change	Percent Employment Change
Wind Turbine Service Technicians	360	540	180	50.0
Nurse Practitioners	5,570	8,010	2,440	43.8
Epidemiologists	260	370	110	42.3
Data Scientists	2,290	3,070	780	34.1
Statisticians	660	860	200	30.3
Information Security Analysts (SOC 2018)	2,910	3,730	820	28.2
Physician Assistants	3,830	4,900	1,070	27.9
Medical and Health Services Managers	10,910	13,760	2,850	26.1
Actuaries	1,150	1,430	280	24.3
Physical Therapist Assistants	1,320	1,640	320	24.2

Note: Projections cover Minnesota; (1) Sorted by percent employment change and excludes occupations with numeric employment change less than 50
Source: www.projectionscentral.org, State Occupational Projections, 2022–2032 Long-Term Projections

Minneapolis, Minnesota

CITY FINANCES

City Government Finances

Component	2022 ($000)	2022 ($ per capita)
Total Revenues	1,173,002	2,708
Total Expenditures	1,498,215	3,459
Debt Outstanding	879,064	2,030

Source: U.S. Census Bureau, State & Local Government Finances 2022

City Government Revenue by Source

Source	2022 ($000)	2022 ($ per capita)	2022 (%)
General Revenue			
From Federal Government	52,978	122	4.5
From State Government	130,261	301	11.1
From Local Governments	13,304	31	1.1
Taxes			
Property	356,101	822	30.4
Sales and Gross Receipts	69,480	160	5.9
Personal Income	0	0	0.0
Corporate Income	0	0	0.0
Motor Vehicle License	0	0	0.0
Other Taxes	42,021	97	3.6
Current Charges	345,240	797	29.4
Liquor Store	0	0	0.0
Utility	85,424	197	7.3

Source: U.S. Census Bureau, State & Local Government Finances 2022

City Government Expenditures by Function

Function	2022 ($000)	2022 ($ per capita)	2022 (%)
General Direct Expenditures			
Air Transportation	0	0	0.0
Corrections	0	0	0.0
Education	0	0	0.0
Employment Security Administration	0	0	0.0
Financial Administration	23,971	55	1.6
Fire Protection	73,450	169	4.9
General Public Buildings	39,368	90	2.6
Governmental Administration, Other	18,172	42	1.2
Health	18,596	42	1.2
Highways	184,260	425	12.3
Hospitals	0	0	0.0
Housing and Community Development	188,105	434	12.6
Interest on General Debt	18,997	43	1.3
Judicial and Legal	16,491	38	1.1
Libraries	0	0	0.0
Parking	74,921	173	5.0
Parks and Recreation	131,553	303	8.8
Police Protection	169,457	391	11.3
Public Welfare	0	0	0.0
Sewerage	147,982	341	9.9
Solid Waste Management	52,373	120	3.5
Veterans' Services	0	0	0.0
Liquor Store	0	0	0.0
Utility	128,589	296	8.6

Source: U.S. Census Bureau, State & Local Government Finances 2022

TAXES

State Corporate Income Tax Rates

State	Tax Rate (%)	Income Brackets ($)	Num. of Brackets	Financial Institution Tax Rate (%)[a]	Federal Income Tax Ded.
Minnesota	9.8 (l)	Flat rate	1	9.8 (l)	No

Note: Tax rates for tax year 2024; (a) Rates listed are the corporate income tax rate applied to financial institutions or excise taxes based on income. Some states have other taxes based upon the value of deposits or shares; (l) In addition, Minnesota levies a 5.8% tentative minimum tax on Alternative Minimum Taxable Income. Minnesota also imposes a surtax ranging up to $11,570.
Source: Federation of Tax Administrators, State Corporate Income Tax Rates, January 1, 2025

State Individual Income Tax Rates

State	Tax Rate (%)	Income Brackets ($)	Personal Exemptions ($)			Standard Ded. ($)	
			Single	Married	Depend.	Single	Married
Minnesota (a)	5.35 - 9.85	31,690 - 193,240 (n)	(d)	(d)	5,150	14,575	29,150

Note: Tax rates for tax year 2024; Local- and county-level taxes are not included; Federal income tax is not deductible on state income tax returns; (a) 16 states have statutory provision for automatically adjusting to the rate of inflation the dollar values of the income tax brackets, standard deductions, and/or personal exemptions. Oregon does not index the income brackets for $125,000 and over See: INFL and SPEC above; (d) These states use the personal exemption/standard deduction amounts provided in the federal Internal Revenue Code. Montana personal exemption subject to repeal under Section 15-30-2114; (n) The income brackets reported for Minnesota are for single individuals. For married couples filing jointly, the same tax rates apply to income brackets ranging from $46,331 to $321,450.
Source: Federation of Tax Administrators, State Individual Income Tax Rates, January 1, 2025

Various State Sales and Excise Tax Rates

State	State Sales Tax (%)	Gasoline[1] ($/gal.)	Cigarette[2] ($/pack)	Spirits[3] ($/gal.)	Wine[4] ($/gal.)	Beer[5] ($/gal.)	Recreational Marijuana (%)
Minnesota	6.875	0.32	3.83	8.74	1.25	0.47	(l)

Note: All tax rates as of January 1, 2025; (1) The American Petroleum Institute has developed a methodology for determining the average tax rate on a gallon of fuel. Rates may include any of the following: excise taxes, environmental fees, storage tank fees, other fees or taxes, general sales tax, and local taxes; (2) The federal excise tax of $1.0066 per pack and local taxes are not included; (3) Rates are those applicable to off-premise sales of 40% alcohol by volume (a.b.v.) distilled spirits in 750ml containers. Local excise taxes are excluded; (4) Rates are those applicable to off-premise sales of 11% a.b.v. non-carbonated wine in 750ml containers; (5) Rates are those applicable to off-premise sales of 4.7% a.b.v. beer in 12 ounce containers; (l) 10% excise tax (retail gross receipts)
Source: Tax Foundation, 2025 Facts & Figures: How Does Your State Compare?

State Tax Competitiveness Index

State	Overall Rank	Corporate Tax Rank	Individual Income Tax Rank	Sales Tax Rank	Property Tax Rank	Unemployment Insurance Tax Rank
Minnesota	44	43	44	34	26	42

Note: The Tax Foundation's State Tax Competitiveness Index enables policymakers, taxpayers, and business leaders to gauge how their states' tax systems compare. A rank of 1 is best, 50 is worst. Rankings do not average to the total. States without a tax rank equally as 1. DC's scores and rankings do not affect other states. The report shows tax systems as of July 1, 2024 (the beginning of Fiscal Year 2025).
Source: Tax Foundation, State Tax Competitiveness Index 2025

TRANSPORTATION

Means of Transportation to Work

Area	Car/Truck/Van		Public Transportation			Bicycle	Walked	Other Means	Worked at Home
	Drove Alone	Car-pooled	Bus	Subway	Railroad				
City	53.4	5.9	6.3	0.2	0.0	2.3	6.0	2.5	23.3
MSA[1]	67.7	7.1	2.2	0.0	0.0	0.5	2.0	1.4	19.0
U.S.	70.2	8.5	1.7	1.3	0.4	0.4	2.4	1.6	13.5

Note: Figures are percentages and cover workers 16 years of age and older; (1) Figures cover the Minneapolis-St. Paul-Bloomington, MN-WI Metropolitan Statistical Area
Source: U.S. Census Bureau, 2019-2023 American Community Survey 5-Year Estimates

Travel Time to Work

Area	Less Than 10 Minutes	10 to 19 Minutes	20 to 29 Minutes	30 to 44 Minutes	45 to 59 Minutes	60 to 89 Minutes	90 Minutes or More
City	8.3	36.1	28.8	19.2	4.2	2.4	1.0
MSA[1]	11.1	29.6	25.3	22.3	6.9	3.5	1.4
U.S.	12.6	28.6	21.2	20.8	8.1	6.0	2.8

Note: Note: Figures are percentages and include workers 16 years old and over; (1) Figures cover the Minneapolis-St. Paul-Bloomington, MN-WI Metropolitan Statistical Area
Source: U.S. Census Bureau, 2019-2023 American Community Survey 5-Year Estimates

Key Congestion Measures

Measure	2000	2010	2015	2020	2022
Annual Hours of Delay, Total (000)	68,767	84,317	99,730	59,835	103,024
Annual Hours of Delay, Per Auto Commuter	47	47	53	32	59
Annual Congestion Cost, Per Auto Commuter ($)	1,045	1,017	1,112	693	1,208

Note: Figures cover the Minneapolis-St. Paul MN-WI urban area
Source: Texas A&M Transportation Institute, 2023 Urban Mobility Report

Freeway Travel Time Index

Measure	1985	1990	1995	2000	2005	2010	2015	2020	2022
Urban Area Index[1]	1.10	1.14	1.21	1.27	1.28	1.25	1.25	1.11	1.24
Urban Area Rank[1,2]	27	26	16	10	14	21	24	20	22

Note: Freeway Travel Time Index—the ratio of travel time in the peak period to the travel time at free-flow conditions. For example, a value of 1.30 indicates a 20-minute free-flow trip takes 26 minutes in the peak (20 minutes x 1.30 = 26 minutes); (1) Covers the Minneapolis-St. Paul MN-WI urban area; (2) Rank is based on 101 larger urban areas (#1 = highest travel time index)
Source: Texas A&M Transportation Institute, 2023 Urban Mobility Report

Public Transportation

Agency Name / Mode of Transportation	Vehicles Operated in Maximum Service[1]	Annual Unlinked Passenger Trips[2] (in thous.)	Annual Passenger Miles[3] (in thous.)
Metro Transit			
Bus (directly operated)	480	30,124.0	119,831.3
Commuter Rail (purchased transportation)	20	97.3	2,501.4
Light Rail (directly operated)	48	14,755.9	52,841.2

Note: (1) Number of revenue vehicles operated by the given mode and type of service to meet the annual maximum service requirement. This is the revenue vehicle count during the peak season of the year; on the week and day that maximum service is provided. Vehicles operated in maximum service (VOMS) exclude atypical days and one-time special events; (2) Number of passengers who boarded public transportation vehicles. Passengers are counted each time they board a vehicle no matter how many vehicles they use to travel from their origin to their destination. (3) Sum of the distances ridden by all passengers during the entire fiscal year.
Source: Federal Transit Administration, National Transit Database, 2023

Air Transportation

Airport Name and Code / Type of Service	Passenger Airlines[1]	Passenger Enplanements	Freight Carriers[2]	Freight (lbs)
Minneapolis-St. Paul International (MSP)				
Domestic service (U.S. carriers only)	33	16,321,623	18	158,998,803
International service (U.S. carriers only)	7	1,411,075	3	26,482,102

Note: (1) Includes all U.S.-based major, minor and commuter airlines that carried at least one passenger during the year; (2) Includes all U.S.-based airlines and freight carriers that transported at least one pound of freight during the year.
Source: Bureau of Transportation Statistics, The Intermodal Transportation Database, Air Carriers: T-100 Domestic Market (U.S. carriers only), 2024; Bureau of Transportation Statistics, The Intermodal Transportation Database, Air Carriers: T-100 International Market (U.S. carriers only), 2024

BUSINESSES

Major Business Headquarters

Company Name	Industry	Fortune[1]	Forbes[2]
Ameriprise Financial	Diversified financials	254	-
Cargill	Food & drink	-	1
General Mills	Food consumer products	203	-
Mortenson	Construction	-	119
Ryan Companies	Construction	-	194
Target	General merchandisers	37	-
Thrivent Financial for Lutherans	Insurance: life, health (mutual)	405	-
U.S. Bancorp	Commercial banks	107	-
Xcel Energy	Utilities: gas and electric	302	-

Note: (1) Companies that produce a 10-K are ranked 1 to 500 based on 2023 revenue; (2) All private companies with at least $2 billion in annual revenue through the end of their most current fiscal year are ranked 1 to 275; companies listed are headquartered in the city; dashes indicate no ranking
Source: Fortune, "Fortune 500," 2024; Forbes, "America's Largest Private Companies," 2024

Fastest-Growing Businesses

According to Deloitte, Minneapolis is home to one of North America's 500 fastest-growing high-technology companies: **CVRx** (#213). Companies are ranked by percentage growth in revenue over a four-year period. Criteria for inclusion: company must be headquartered within North America; must own proprietary intellectual property or technology that is sold to customers in products that contributes to a significant portion of the company's operating revenue; must have been in business for a minumum of four years with 2020 operating revenues of at least $50,000 USD/CD and 2023 operating revenues of at least $5 million USD/CD. *Deloitte, 2024 Technology Fast 500™*

Living Environment

COST OF LIVING

Cost of Living Index

Composite Index	Groceries	Housing	Utilities	Transportation	Health Care	Misc. Goods/Services
93.6	102.6	82.9	96.6	96.4	96.0	96.5

Note: The Cost of Living Index measures regional differences in the cost of consumer goods and services, excluding taxes and non-consumer expenditures, for professional and managerial households in the top income quintile. It is based on more than 50,000 prices covering almost 60 different items for which prices are collected three times a year by chambers of commerce, economic development organizations or university applied economic centers in each participating urban area. The numbers shown should be read as a percentage above or below the national average of 100. For example, a value of 115.4 in the groceries column indicates that grocery prices are 15.4% higher than the national average. Small differences in the index numbers should not be interpreted as significant; Figures cover the Minneapolis MN urban area.
Source: The Council for Community and Economic Research, Cost of Living Index, 2024

Grocery Prices

Area[1]	T-Bone Steak ($/pound)	Frying Chicken ($/pound)	Whole Milk ($/half gal.)	Eggs ($/dozen)	Orange Juice ($/64 oz.)	Coffee ($/11.5 oz.)
City[2]	15.53	1.44	4.66	3.56	4.49	5.23
Avg.	15.42	1.55	4.69	3.25	4.41	5.46
Min.	14.50	1.16	4.43	2.75	4.00	4.85
Max.	17.56	2.89	5.49	4.78	5.54	7.89

Note: (1) Values for the local area are compared with the average, minimum and maximum values for all 276 areas in the Cost of Living Index; (2) Figures cover the Minneapolis MN urban area; **T-Bone Steak** (price per pound); **Frying Chicken** (price per pound, whole fryer); **Whole Milk** (half gallon carton); **Eggs** (price per dozen, Grade A, large); **Orange Juice** (64 oz. Tropicana or Florida Natural); **Coffee** (11.5 oz. can, vacuum-packed, Maxwell House, Hills Bros, or Folgers).
Source: The Council for Community and Economic Research, Cost of Living Index, 2024

Housing and Utility Costs

Area[1]	New Home Price ($)	Apartment Rent ($/month)	All Electric ($/month)	Part Electric ($/month)	Other Energy ($/month)	Telephone ($/month)
City[2]	405,152	1,419	-	98.70	98.25	191.53
Avg.	515,975	1,550	210.99	123.07	82.07	194.99
Min.	265,375	692	104.33	53.68	36.26	179.42
Max.	2,775,821	5,719	529.02	397.28	361.63	223.33

Note: (1) Values for the local area are compared with the average, minimum and maximum values for all 276 areas in the Cost of Living Index; (2) Figures cover the Minneapolis MN urban area; **New Home Price** (2,400 sf living area, 8,000 sf lot, in urban area with full utilities); **Apartment Rent** (950 sf 2 bedroom/1.5 or 2 bath, unfurnished, excluding all utilities except water); **All Electric** (average monthly cost for an all-electric home); **Part Electric** (average monthly cost for a part-electric home); **Other Energy** (average monthly cost for natural gas, fuel oil, coal, wood, and any other forms of energy except electricity); **Telephone** (price includes the base monthly rate plus taxes and fees for three lines of mobile phone service).
Source: The Council for Community and Economic Research, Cost of Living Index, 2024

Health Care, Transportation, and Other Costs

Area[1]	Doctor ($/visit)	Dentist ($/visit)	Optometrist ($/visit)	Gasoline ($/gallon)	Beauty Salon ($/visit)	Men's Shirt ($)
City[2]	170.09	100.86	120.48	3.16	40.96	41.19
Avg.	143.77	117.51	129.23	3.32	48.57	38.14
Min.	36.74	58.67	67.33	2.80	24.00	13.41
Max.	270.44	216.82	307.33	5.28	94.00	63.89

Note: (1) Values for the local area are compared with the average, minimum and maximum values for all 276 areas in the Cost of Living Index; (2) Figures cover the Minneapolis MN urban area; **Doctor** (general practitioners routine exam of an established patient); **Dentist** (adult teeth cleaning and periodic oral examination); **Optometrist** (full vision eye exam for established adult patient); **Gasoline** (one gallon regular unleaded, national brand, including all taxes, cash price at self-service pump if available); **Beauty Salon** (woman's shampoo, trim, and blow-dry); **Men's Shirt** (cotton/polyester dress shirt, pinpoint weave, long sleeves).
Source: The Council for Community and Economic Research, Cost of Living Index, 2024

HOUSING

Homeownership Rate

Area	2017 (%)	2018 (%)	2019 (%)	2020 (%)	2021 (%)	2022 (%)	2023 (%)	2024 (%)
MSA[1]	70.1	67.8	70.2	73.0	75.0	73.0	72.0	67.8
U.S.	63.9	64.4	64.6	66.6	65.5	65.8	65.9	65.6

Note: (1) Figures cover the Minneapolis-St. Paul-Bloomington, MN-WI Metropolitan Statistical Area
Source: U.S. Census Bureau, Housing Vacancies and Homeownership Annual Statistics: 2017-2024

House Price Index (HPI)

Area	National Ranking[2]	Quarterly Change (%)	One-Year Change (%)	Five-Year Change (%)	Since 1991Q1 (%)
MSA[1]	153	0.20	4.68	37.75	302.55
U.S.[3]	—	1.43	4.51	57.13	327.82

Note: The HPI is a weighted repeat sales index. It measures average price changes in repeat sales or refinancings on the same properties. This information is obtained by reviewing repeat mortgage transactions on single-family properties whose mortgages have been purchased or securitized by Fannie Mae or Freddie Mac since January 1975; (1) Figures cover the Minneapolis-St. Paul-Bloomington, MN-WI Metropolitan Statistical Area; (2) Rankings are based on annual percentage change for all metro areas containing at least 15,000 transactions over the last 10 years and ranges from 1 to 241; (3) figures based on a weighted average of Census Division estimates using a seasonally adjusted, purchase-only index; all figures are for the period ending December 31, 2024
Source: Federal Housing Finance Agency, Change in FHFA Metropolitan Area House Price Indexes, All Transactions Index, 2024Q4

Home Value

Area	Under $100,000	$100,000 -$199,999	$200,000 -$299,999	$300,000 -$399,999	$400,000 -$499,999	$500,000 -$999,999	$1,000,000 or more	Median ($)
City	2.9	10.4	25.0	25.6	14.0	18.1	4.0	345,600
MSA[1]	4.0	7.4	24.9	25.1	16.1	19.6	2.9	354,400
U.S.	12.1	17.8	14.4	10.5	19.1	19.1	6.5	303,400

Note: Figures are percentages except for median and cover owner-occupied housing units; (1) Figures cover the Minneapolis-St. Paul-Bloomington, MN-WI Metropolitan Statistical Area
Source: U.S. Census Bureau, 2019-2023 American Community Survey 5-Year Estimates

Year Housing Structure Built

Area	2020 or Later	2010 -2019	2000 -2009	1990 -1999	1980 -1989	1970 -1979	1960 -1969	1950 -1959	1940 -1949	Before 1940	Median Year
City	1.0	8.8	6.2	4.2	6.8	8.2	6.8	8.2	6.2	43.6	1950
MSA[1]	1.3	8.6	13.3	13.4	13.8	13.9	9.3	9.1	3.6	13.6	1980
U.S.	1.2	8.9	13.6	12.8	13.0	14.4	10.0	9.7	4.5	11.9	1980

Note: Figures are percentages except for Median Year; Note: (1) Figures cover the Minneapolis-St. Paul-Bloomington, MN-WI Metropolitan Statistical Area
Source: U.S. Census Bureau, 2019-2023 American Community Survey 5-Year Estimates

Gross Monthly Rent

Area	Under $500	$500 -$999	$1,000 -$1,499	$1,500 -$1,999	$2,000 -$2,499	$2,500 -$2,999	$3,000 and up	Median ($)
City	8.7	16.4	35.0	22.5	10.8	3.3	3.3	1,329
MSA[1]	6.6	14.0	36.6	25.6	10.8	3.3	3.2	1,396
U.S.	6.5	22.3	29.5	20.2	10.8	4.8	5.9	1,348

Note: Figures are percentages except for median; Gross rent is the contract rent plus the estimated average monthly cost of utilities (electricity, gas, and water and sewer) and fuels (oil, coal, kerosene, wood, etc.) if these are paid by the renter (or paid for the renter by someone else); (1) Figures cover the Minneapolis-St. Paul-Bloomington, MN-WI Metropolitan Statistical Area
Source: U.S. Census Bureau, 2019-2023 American Community Survey 5-Year Estimates

HEALTH

Health Risk Factors

Category	MSA[1] (%)	U.S. (%)
Adults aged 18–64 who have any kind of health care coverage	93.3	90.8
Adults who reported being in good or better health	84.5	81.8
Adults who have been told they have high blood cholesterol	34.0	36.9
Adults who have been told they have high blood pressure	30.6	34.0
Adults who are current smokers	10.5	12.1
Adults who currently use e-cigarettes	6.7	7.7
Adults who currently use chewing tobacco, snuff, or snus	2.6	3.2
Adults who are heavy drinkers[2]	5.5	6.1
Adults who are binge drinkers[3]	16.3	15.2
Adults who are overweight (BMI 25.0 - 29.9)	34.6	34.4
Adults who are obese (BMI 30.0 - 99.8)	31.3	34.3
Adults who participated in any physical activities in the past month	78.5	75.8

Note: All figures are crude prevalence; (1) Figures cover the Minneapolis-St. Paul-Bloomington, MN-WI Metropolitan Statistical Area; (2) Heavy drinkers are classified as adult men having more than 14 drinks per week and adult women having more than 7 drinks per week; (3) Binge drinkers are classified as males having five or more drinks on one occasion or females having four or more drinks on one occasion
Source: Centers for Disease Control and Prevention, Behavioral Risk Factor Surveillance System, SMART: Selected Metropolitan Area Risk Trends, 2023

Acute and Chronic Health Conditions

Category	MSA[1] (%)	U.S. (%)
Adults who have ever been told they had a heart attack	3.4	4.2
Adults who have ever been told they have angina or coronary heart disease	3.4	4.0
Adults who have ever been told they had a stroke	2.9	3.3
Adults who have ever been told they have asthma	13.9	15.7
Adults who have ever been told they have arthritis	20.4	26.3
Adults who have ever been told they have diabetes[2]	10.0	11.5
Adults who have ever been told they had skin cancer	5.1	5.6
Adults who have ever been told they had any other types of cancer	7.9	8.4
Adults who have ever been told they have COPD	3.9	6.4
Adults who have ever been told they have kidney disease	3.3	3.7
Adults who have ever been told they have a form of depression	23.3	22.0

Note: All figures are crude prevalence; (1) Figures cover the Minneapolis-St. Paul-Bloomington, MN-WI Metropolitan Statistical Area; (2) Figures do not include pregnancy-related, borderline, or pre-diabetes
Source: Centers for Disease Control and Prevention, Behaviorial Risk Factor Surveillance System, SMART: Selected Metropolitan Area Risk Trends, 2023

Health Screening and Vaccination Rates

Category	MSA[1] (%)	U.S. (%)
Adults who have ever been tested for HIV	36.3	37.5
Adults who have had their blood cholesterol checked within the last five years	86.7	87.0
Adults aged 65+ who have had flu shot within the past year	69.0	63.4
Adults aged 65+ who have ever had a pneumonia vaccination	72.7	71.9

Note: All figures are crude prevalence; (1) Figures cover the Minneapolis-St. Paul-Bloomington, MN-WI Metropolitan Statistical Area.
Source: Centers for Disease Control and Prevention, Behaviorial Risk Factor Surveillance System, SMART: Selected Metropolitan Area Risk Trends, 2023

Disability Status

Category	MSA[1] (%)	U.S. (%)
Adults who reported being deaf	5.6	7.4
Are you blind or have serious difficulty seeing, even when wearing glasses?	3.7	4.9
Do you have difficulty doing errands alone?	7.2	7.8
Do you have difficulty dressing or bathing?	3.0	3.6
Do you have serious difficulty concentrating/remembering/making decisions?	11.7	13.7
Do you have serious difficulty walking or climbing stairs?	10.4	13.2

Note: All figures are crude prevalence; (1) Figures cover the Minneapolis-St. Paul-Bloomington, MN-WI Metropolitan Statistical Area.
Source: Centers for Disease Control and Prevention, Behaviorial Risk Factor Surveillance System, SMART: Selected Metropolitan Area Risk Trends, 2023

Mortality Rates for the Top 10 Causes of Death in the U.S.

ICD-10[a] Sub-Chapter	ICD-10[a] Code	Crude Mortality Rate[2] per 100,000 population	
		County[3]	U.S.
Malignant neoplasms	C00-C97	151.9	182.7
Ischaemic heart diseases	I20-I25	53.5	109.6
Provisional assignment of new diseases of uncertain etiology[1]	U00-U49	33.5	65.3
Other forms of heart disease	I30-I51	44.8	65.1
Other degenerative diseases of the nervous system	G30-G31	39.4	52.4
Other external causes of accidental injury	W00-X59	68.2	52.3
Cerebrovascular diseases	I60-I69	36.9	49.1
Chronic lower respiratory diseases	J40-J47	26.5	43.5
Hypertensive diseases	I10-I15	30.2	38.9
Organic, including symptomatic, mental disorders	F01-F09	48.2	33.9

Note: (a) ICD-10 = International Classification of Diseases 10th Revision; (1) Includes COVID-19, adverse effects to COVID-19 vaccines, SARS, and vaping-related disorders; (2) Crude mortality rates are a three-year average covering 2021-2023; (3) Figures cover Hennepin County.
Source: Centers for Disease Control and Prevention, National Center for Health Statistics. National Vital Statistics System, Mortality 2018-2023 on CDC WONDER Online Database

Mortality Rates for Selected Causes of Death

Cause of Death	ICD-10[a] Code	Crude Mortality Rate[1] per 100,000 population	
		County[2]	U.S.
Accidental poisoning and exposure to noxious substances	X40-X49	35.6	30.5
Alzheimer disease	G30	32.1	35.4
Assault	X85-Y09	6.8	7.3
COVID-19	U07.1	33.5	65.3
Diabetes mellitus	E10-E14	22.5	30.0
Diseases of the liver	K70-K76	18.5	20.8
Human immunodeficiency virus (HIV) disease	B20-B24	1.1	1.5
Influenza and pneumonia	J09-J18	7.7	13.4
Intentional self-harm	X60-X84	11.6	14.7
Malnutrition	E40-E46	2.6	6.0
Obesity and other hyperalimentation	E65-E68	2.5	3.1
Renal failure	N17-N19	7.9	16.4
Transport accidents	V01-V99	7.4	14.4

Note: (a) ICD-10 = International Classification of Diseases 10th Revision; (1) Crude mortality rates are a three-year average covering 2021-2023; (2) Figures cover Hennepin County; Data are suppressed when the data meet the criteria for confidentiality constraints; Crude mortality rates are flagged as unreliable when the rate would be calculated with a numerator of 20 or less.
Source: Centers for Disease Control and Prevention, National Center for Health Statistics. National Vital Statistics System, Mortality 2018-2023 on CDC WONDER Online Database

Health Insurance Coverage

Area	With Health Insurance	With Private Health Insurance	With Public Health Insurance	Without Health Insurance	Population Under Age 19 Without Health Insurance
City	94.1	69.5	32.8	5.9	2.8
MSA[1]	95.7	77.3	30.9	4.3	2.7
U.S.	91.4	67.3	36.3	8.6	5.4

Note: Figures are percentages that cover the civilian noninstitutionalized population; (1) Figures cover the Minneapolis-St. Paul-Bloomington, MN-WI Metropolitan Statistical Area
Source: U.S. Census Bureau, 2019-2023 American Community Survey 5-Year Estimates

Number of Medical Professionals

Area	MDs[3]	DOs[3,4]	Dentists	Podiatrists	Chiropractors	Optometrists
County[1] (number)	7,191	415	1,341	72	1,009	293
County[1] (rate[2])	570.7	32.9	106.5	5.7	80.2	23.3
U.S. (rate[2])	302.5	29.2	74.6	6.4	29.5	18.0

Note: Data as of 2023 unless noted; (1) Data covers Hennepin County; (2) Number of medical professionals per 100,000 population; (3) Data as of 2022 and includes all active, non-federal physicians; (4) Doctor of Osteopathic Medicine
Source: U.S. Department of Health and Human Services, Health Resources and Services Administration, Bureau of Health Professions, Area Resource File (ARF) 2023-2024

Best Hospitals

According to *U.S. News,* the Minneapolis-St. Paul-Bloomington, MN-WI metro area is home to two of the best hospitals in the U.S.: **Courage Kenny Rehabilitation Institute at Abbott Northwestern Hospital** (1 adult specialty); **M Health Fairview University of Minnesota Medical Center** (3 pediatric specialties). The hospitals listed were nationally ranked in at least one of 15 adult or 11 pediatric specialties. The number of specialties shown cover the parent hospital. Only 160 U.S. hospitals performed well enough to be nationally ranked in one or more specialties. Twenty hospitals in the U.S. made the Honor Roll. The Best Hospitals Honor Roll takes both the national rankings and the procedure and condition ratings into account. Hospitals received points if they were nationally ranked in one of the 15 adult specialties—the higher they ranked, the more points they got—and how many ratings of "high performing" they earned in the 20 procedures and conditions. *U.S. News Online,* "America's Best Hospitals 2024-25"

According to *U.S. News,* the Minneapolis-St. Paul-Bloomington, MN-WI metro area is home to two of the best children's hospitals in the U.S.: **M Health Fairview Masonic Children's Hospital** (3 pediatric specialties); **M Health Fairview Masonic Children's Hospital-Children's Minnesota** (3 pediatric specialties). The hospitals listed were highly ranked in at least one of 11 pediatric specialties. One hundred five children's hospitals in the U.S. were nationally ranked in at least one specialty. Hospitals received points for being ranked in a specialty, and the 10 hospitals with the most points across the 11 specialties make up the Honor Roll. *U.S. News Online,* "America's Best Children's Hospitals 2024-25"

EDUCATION

Public School District Statistics

District Name	Schls	Pupils	Pupil/ Teacher Ratio	Minority Pupils[1] (%)	Total Rev. per Pupil ($)	Total Exp. per Pupil ($)
Minneapolis Public School District	98	29,063	13.2	61.7	25,997	26,112
Minnesota Transitions Charter	9	4,943	23.2	38.9	14,527	13,698

Note: Table includes school districts with 2,000 or more students; (1) Percentage of students that are not non-Hispanic white.
Source: U.S. Department of Education, National Center for Education Statistics, Common Core of Data, Local Education Agency (School District) Universe Survey: School Year 2023-2024; U.S. Department of Education, National Center for Education Statistics, Common Core of Data, School District Finance Survey (F-33): School Year 2021–22

Highest Level of Education

Area	Less than H.S.	H.S. Diploma	Some College, No Deg.	Associate Degree	Bachelor's Degree	Master's Degree	Prof. School Degree	Doctorate Degree
City	8.9	13.8	15.7	7.2	32.7	14.8	4.1	2.9
MSA[1]	5.8	20.2	18.7	10.5	29.1	11.3	2.7	1.9
U.S.	10.6	26.2	19.4	8.8	21.3	9.8	2.3	1.6

Note: Figures cover persons age 25 and over; (1) Figures cover the Minneapolis-St. Paul-Bloomington, MN-WI Metropolitan Statistical Area
Source: U.S. Census Bureau, 2019-2023 American Community Survey 5-Year Estimates

Educational Attainment by Race

Area	High School Graduate or Higher (%)					Bachelor's Degree or Higher (%)				
	Total	White	Black	Asian	Hisp.[2]	Total	White	Black	Asian	Hisp.[2]
City	91.1	97.2	74.9	86.3	71.6	54.5	65.6	19.1	62.7	31.0
MSA[1]	94.2	97.0	84.0	83.5	76.4	44.9	47.7	25.1	47.6	27.2
U.S.	89.4	92.9	88.1	88.0	72.5	35.0	37.7	24.7	57.0	19.9

Note: Figures shown cover persons 25 years old and over; (1) Figures cover the Minneapolis-St. Paul-Bloomington, MN-WI Metropolitan Statistical Area; (2) People of Hispanic origin can be of any race
Source: U.S. Census Bureau, 2019-2023 American Community Survey 5-Year Estimates

School Enrollment by Grade and Control

Area	Preschool (%)		Kindergarten (%)		Grades 1 - 4 (%)		Grades 5 - 8 (%)		Grades 9 - 12 (%)	
	Public	Private	Public	Private	Public	Private	Public	Private	Public	Private
City	53.1	46.9	86.3	13.7	86.2	13.8	87.0	13.0	88.8	11.2
MSA[1]	60.7	39.3	85.8	14.2	88.3	11.7	88.7	11.3	91.5	8.5
U.S.	58.7	41.3	85.2	14.8	87.2	12.8	87.9	12.1	89.0	11.0

Note: Figures shown cover persons 3 years old and over; (1) Figures cover the Minneapolis-St. Paul-Bloomington, MN-WI Metropolitan Statistical Area
Source: U.S. Census Bureau, 2019-2023 American Community Survey 5-Year Estimates

Higher Education

Four-Year Colleges			Two-Year Colleges			Medical Schools[1]	Law Schools[2]	Voc/ Tech[3]
Public	Private Non-profit	Private For-profit	Public	Private Non-profit	Private For-profit			
3	21	4	10	0	0	1	3	8

Note: Figures cover institutions located within the Minneapolis-St. Paul-Bloomington, MN-WI Metropolitan Statistical Area and include main campuses only; (1) includes schools accredited by the Liaison Committee on Medical Education and the American Osteopathic Association's Commission on Osteopathic College Accreditation; (2) includes ABA-accredited schools, schools with provisional ABA accreditation, and state accredited schools; (3) includes all schools with programs that are less than 2 years.
Source: National Center for Education Statistics, Integrated Postsecondary Education System (IPEDS), 2023-24; Wikipedia, List of Medical Schools in the United States, accessed May 2, 2025; Wikipedia, List of Law Schools in the United States, accessed May 2, 2025

According to *U.S. News & World Report*, the Minneapolis-St. Paul-Bloomington, MN-WI metro area is home to two of the top 200 national universities in the U.S.: **University of Minnesota—Twin Cities** (#54 tie); **University of St. Thomas (MN)** (#148 tie). The indicators used to capture academic quality fall into a number of categories: assessment by administrators at peer institutions; retention of students; faculty resources; student selectivity; financial resources; alumni giving; high school counselor ratings of colleges; and graduation rate. *U.S. News & World Report*, "America's Best Colleges 2025"

According to *U.S. News & World Report*, the Minneapolis-St. Paul-Bloomington, MN-WI metro area is home to one of the top 100 liberal arts colleges in the U.S.: **Macalester College** (#26 tie). The indicators used to capture academic quality fall into a number of categories: assessment by administrators at peer institutions; retention of students; faculty resources; student selectivity; financial resources; alumni giving; high school counselor ratings of colleges; and graduation rate. *U.S. News & World Report, "America's Best Colleges 2025"*

According to *U.S. News & World Report,* the Minneapolis-St. Paul-Bloomington, MN-WI metro area is home to two of the top 100 law schools in the U.S.: **University of Minnesota** (#20 tie); **University of St. Thomas** (#94 tie). The rankings are based on a weighted average of 12 measures of quality: peer assessment score; assessment score by lawyers/judges; median LSAT scores; median undergrad GPA; acceptance rate; employment rates for graduates; placement success; bar passage rate; faculty resources; expenditures per student; student/faculty ratio; and library resources. *U.S. News & World Report, "America's Best Graduate Schools, Law, 2025"*

According to *U.S. News & World Report,* the Minneapolis-St. Paul-Bloomington, MN-WI metro area is home to one of the top medical schools for research in the U.S.: **University of Minnesota** (Tier 2). *U.S. News* placed medical and osteopathic schools into tiers based on their research productivity, faculty and admissions data. Each school's tier was derived from its overall score, calculated by summing the weighted normalized values generated across several factors of academic quality, outlined below. There are four tiers, with tier 1 medical schools as the highest-performing and tier 4 as the lowest-performing. Only tier 1 and 2 schools are shown. Because of the tier presentation, *U.S. News* calculated overall scores based on their percentile performance among all rated schools instead of dividing against the rescaled score of the No. 1-performing schools. Tier 1 included schools with overall scores of 85 to 99. The cutoffs for tiers 2 through 4 were schools scoring 50 to 84, 15 to 49 and 1 to 14, respectively. The rankings are based on a weighted average of the following measures of quality: total research activity; average research activity per faculty member; total NIH research grants at the medical school and its affiliated hospitals; average NIH research grants per faculty; median MCAT total score; median undergraduate GPA; acceptance rate; and faculty resources. *U.S. News & World Report, "America's Best Graduate Schools, Medical, 2025"*

According to *U.S. News & World Report,* the Minneapolis-St. Paul-Bloomington, MN-WI metro area is home to one of the top medical schools for primary care in the U.S.: **University of Minnesota** (Tier 1). *U.S. News* placed medical and osteopathic schools into tiers based on their research productivity, faculty and admissions data. Each school's tier was derived from its overall score, calculated by summing the weighted normalized values generated across several factors of academic quality, outlined below. There are four tiers, with tier 1 medical schools as the highest-performing and tier 4 as the lowest-performing. Only tier 1 and 2 schools are shown. Because of the tier presentation, *U.S. News* calculated overall scores based on their percentile performance among all rated schools instead of dividing against the rescaled score of the No. 1-performing schools. Tier 1 included schools with overall scores of 85 to 99. The cutoffs for tiers 2 through 4 were schools scoring 50 to 84, 15 to 49 and 1 to 14, respectively. The rankings are based on a weighted average of the following measures of quality: graduates practicing in primary care specialties; graduates entering primary care residencies; median MCAT total score; median undergraduate GPA; acceptance rate; and faculty resources. *U.S. News & World Report, "America's Best Graduate Schools, Medical, 2025"*

According to *U.S. News & World Report,* the Minneapolis-St. Paul-Bloomington, MN-WI metro area is home to one of the top 75 business schools in the U.S.: **University of Minnesota—Twin Cities (Carlson)** (#35 tie). The rankings are based on a weighted average of the following nine measures: quality assessment; peer assessment; recruiter assessment; placement success; mean starting salary and bonus; student selectivity; mean GMAT and GRE scores; mean undergraduate GPA; and acceptance rate. *U.S. News & World Report, "America's Best Graduate Schools, Business, 2025"*

EMPLOYERS

Major Employers

Company Name	Industry
3M Company	Adhesives, sealants
Ameriprise Financial	Investment advice
Anderson Corporation	Millwork
Aware Integrated	Hospital & medical services plans
Bethesda Healtheast Hospital	General medical & surgical hospitals
Carlson Holdings	Hotels & motels
City of Minneapolis	Municipal government
County of Hennepin	County government
Hennepin County	County government
Honeywell International	Aircraft engines & engine parts
Lawson Software	Application computer software
Medtronic	Electromedical equipment
Minnesota Department of Human Services	Family services agency
Minnesota Department of Transportation	Regulation, administration of transportation
North Memorial Hospital	General medical & surgical hospitals
Regents of the University of Minnesota	Specialty outpatient clinics
Rosemount Apple Valley and Eagan	Personal service agents, brokers, & bureaus
St. Paul Fire & Marine Insurance Company	Fire, marine, & casualty insurance
Thomson Legal Regulatory	Books, publishing & printing
United Parcel Service	Package delivery services

Note: Companies shown are located within the Minneapolis-St. Paul-Bloomington, MN-WI Metropolitan Statistical Area.
Source: Chambers of Commerce; State Departments of Labor; Wikipedia

Best Companies to Work For

Allianz Life; Target Corporation, headquartered in Minneapolis, are among "The 100 Best Companies to Work For." To pick the best companies, *Fortune* partnered with the Great Place to Work Institute. Using their proprietary Trust Index™ survey, the core of what creates great a workplace is measured—key behaviors that drive trust in management, connection with colleagues, and loyalty to the company. To be eligible for the *Fortune* 100 Best Companies to Work For list, employers must have 1,000 or more employees in the U.S. and cannot be a government agency. *Fortune, "The 100 Best Companies to Work For," 2025*

Dayforce, headquartered in Minneapolis, is among the "Best Places to Work in IT." To qualify, companies had to have a minimum of 100 total employees and five IT employees. The best places to work were selected based on DEI (diversity, equity, and inclusion) practices; IT turnover, promotions, and growth; IT retention and engagement programs; remote/hybrid working; benefits and perks (such as elder care and child care, flextime, and reimbursement for college tuition); and training and career development opportunities. *Computerworld, "Best Places to Work in IT," 2025*

PUBLIC SAFETY

Crime Rate

Area	Total Crime Rate	Violent Crime Rate				Property Crime Rate		
		Murder	Rape	Robbery	Aggrav. Assault	Burglary	Larceny-Theft	Motor Vehicle Theft
City	6,384.2	17.0	86.7	339.8	688.1	605.7	2,806.3	1,840.7
U.S.	2,290.9	5.7	38.0	66.5	264.1	250.7	1,347.2	318.7

Note: Figures are crimes per 100,000 population.
Source: FBI, Table 8, Offenses Known to Law Enforcement, by State by City, 2023

Hate Crimes

Area	Number of Quarters Reported	Number of Incidents per Bias Motivation					
		Race/Ethnicity/Ancestry	Religion	Sexual Orientation	Disability	Gender	Gender Identity
City[1]	4	11	10	10	0	0	3
U.S.	4	5,900	2,699	2,077	187	92	492

Note: (1) Figures include at least one incident reported with more than one bias motivation.
Source: Federal Bureau of Investigation, Hate Crime Statistics 2023

Identity Theft Consumer Reports

Area	Reports	Reports per 100,000 Population	Rank[2]
MSA[1]	5,552	150	262
U.S.	1,135,291	339	-

Note: (1) Figures cover the Minneapolis-St. Paul-Bloomington, MN-WI Metropolitan Statistical Area; (2) Rank ranges from 1 to 401 where 1 indicates greatest number of identity theft reports per 100,000 population
Source: Federal Trade Commission, Consumer Sentinel Network Data Book 2024

Fraud and Other Consumer Reports

Area	Reports	Reports per 100,000 Population	Rank[2]
MSA[1]	38,139	1,033	191
U.S.	5,360,641	1,601	-

Note: (1) Figures cover the Minneapolis-St. Paul-Bloomington, MN-WI Metropolitan Statistical Area; (2) Rank ranges from 1 to 401 where 1 indicates greatest number of fraud and other consumer reports per 100,000 population
Source: Federal Trade Commission, Consumer Sentinel Network Data Book 2024

POLITICS

2024 Presidential Election Results

Area	Trump (Rep.)	Harris (Dem.)	Stein (Green)	Kennedy (Ind.)	Oliver (Lib.)	Other
Hennepin County	27.4	69.8	0.8	0.6	0.5	1.0
U.S.	49.7	48.2	0.6	0.5	0.4	0.6

Note: Results are percentages and may not add to 100% due to rounding
Source: Dave Leip's Atlas of U.S. Presidential Elections

SPORTS

Professional Sports Teams

Team Name	League	Year Established
Minnesota Timberwolves	National Basketball Association (NBA)	1989
Minnesota Twins	Major League Baseball (MLB)	1961
Minnesota United FC	Major League Soccer (MLS)	2017
Minnesota Vikings	National Football League (NFL)	1961
Minnesota Wild	National Hockey League (NHL)	2000

Note: Includes teams located in the Minneapolis-St. Paul-Bloomington, MN-WI Metropolitan Statistical Area.
Source: Wikipedia, Major Professional Sports Teams of the United States and Canada, May 1, 2025

CLIMATE

Average and Extreme Temperatures

Temperature	Jan	Feb	Mar	Apr	May	Jun	Jul	Aug	Sep	Oct	Nov	Dec	Yr.
Extreme High (°F)	57	60	83	95	96	102	105	101	98	89	74	63	105
Average High (°F)	21	27	38	56	69	79	84	81	71	59	41	26	54
Average Temp. (°F)	12	18	30	46	59	69	74	71	61	50	33	19	45
Average Low (°F)	3	9	21	36	48	58	63	61	50	39	25	11	35
Extreme Low (°F)	-34	-28	-32	2	18	37	43	39	26	15	-17	-29	-34

Note: Figures cover the years 1948-1990
Source: National Climatic Data Center, International Station Meteorological Climate Summary, 9/96

Average Precipitation/Snowfall/Humidity

Precip./Humidity	Jan	Feb	Mar	Apr	May	Jun	Jul	Aug	Sep	Oct	Nov	Dec	Yr.
Avg. Precip. (in.)	0.8	0.8	1.9	2.2	3.1	4.0	3.8	3.6	2.5	1.9	1.4	1.0	27.1
Avg. Snowfall (in.)	11	9	12	3	Tr	0	0	0	Tr	Tr	7	10	52
Avg. Rel. Hum. 6am (%)	75	76	77	75	75	79	81	84	85	81	80	79	79
Avg. Rel. Hum. 3pm (%)	64	62	58	48	47	50	50	52	53	52	62	68	55

Note: Figures cover the years 1948-1990; Tr = Trace amounts (<0.05 in. of rain; <0.5 in. of snow)
Source: National Climatic Data Center, International Station Meteorological Climate Summary, 9/96

Weather Conditions

Temperature			Daytime Sky			Precipitation		
5°F & below	32°F & below	90°F & above	Clear	Partly cloudy	Cloudy	0.01 inch or more precip.	0.1 inch or more snow/ice	Thunder-storms
45	156	16	93	125	147	113	41	37

Note: Figures are average number of days per year and cover the years 1948-1990
Source: National Climatic Data Center, International Station Meteorological Climate Summary, 9/96

HAZARDOUS WASTE

Superfund Sites

The Minneapolis-St. Paul-Bloomington, MN-WI metro area is home to 17 sites on the EPA's Superfund National Priorities List (NPL) or Superfund Alternative Approach (SAA) list: **Baytown Township Ground Water Plume** (Final NPL); **FMC Corp. (Fridley Plant)** (Final NPL); **Freeway Sanitary Landfill** (Final NPL); **General Mills/Henkel Corp.** (Final NPL); **Highway 100 and County Road 3 Groundwater Plume** (Final NPL); **Joslyn Manufacturing & Supply Co.** (Final NPL); **Koppers Coke** (Final NPL); **Kurt Manufacturing Co.** (Final NPL); **Macgillis & Gibbs Co./Bell Lumber & Pole Co.** (Final NPL); **Naval Industrial Reserve Ordnance Plant** (Final NPL); **New Brighton/Arden Hills/Tcaap (USARMY)** (Final NPL); **Oakdale Dump** (Final NPL); **Reilly Tar & Chemical Corp. (Saint Louis Park Plant)** (Final NPL); **South Andover Site** (Final NPL); **South Minneapolis Residential Soil Contamination** (Final NPL); **Southeast Hennepin Area**

AIR QUALITY

Groundwater and Vapor (Final NPL); **Spring Park Municipal Well Field** (Final NPL). The Superfund alternative approach uses the same investigation and cleanup process and standards that are used for sites listed on the National Priorities List. The SAA is an alternative to listing a site on the NPL; it is not an alternative to Superfund or the Superfund process. There are a total of 1,445 Superfund sites with a status of proposed or final on both lists in the United States. *U.S. Environmental Protection Agency, National Priorities List, May 1, 2025; U.S. Environmental Protection Agency, Superfund Alternative Approach Sites, May 1, 2025*

Air Quality Trends: Ozone

	1990	1995	2000	2005	2010	2015	2020	2021	2022	2023
MSA[1]	0.068	0.084	0.065	0.074	0.066	0.061	0.060	0.067	0.057	0.077
U.S.	0.087	0.089	0.081	0.080	0.072	0.068	0.066	0.067	0.067	0.070

Note: (1) Data covers the Minneapolis-St. Paul-Bloomington, MN-WI Metropolitan Statistical Area. The values shown are the composite ozone concentration averages among trend sites based on the highest fourth daily maximum 8-hour concentration in parts per million. These trends are based on sites having an adequate record of monitoring data during the trend period. Data from exceptional events are included.
Source: U.S. Environmental Protection Agency, Air Quality Monitoring Information, "Air Quality Trends by City, 1990-2023"

Air Quality Index

Area	Percent of Days when Air Quality was...[2]					AQI Statistics[2]	
	Good	Moderate	Unhealthy for Sensitive Groups	Unhealthy	Very Unhealthy	Maximum	Median
MSA[1]	36.7	55.1	6.6	1.6	0.0	190	55

Note: (1) Data covers the Minneapolis-St. Paul-Bloomington, MN-WI Metropolitan Statistical Area; (2) Based on 365 days with AQI data in 2023. Air Quality Index (AQI) is an index for reporting daily air quality. EPA calculates the AQI for five major air pollutants regulated by the Clean Air Act: ground-level ozone, particle pollution (aka particulate matter), carbon monoxide, sulfur dioxide, and nitrogen dioxide. The AQI runs from 0 to 500. The higher the AQI value, the greater the level of air pollution and the greater the health concern. There are six AQI categories: "Good" AQI is between 0 and 50. Air quality is considered satisfactory; "Moderate" AQI is between 51 and 100. Air quality is acceptable; "Unhealthy for Sensitive Groups" When AQI values are between 101 and 150, members of sensitive groups may experience health effects; "Unhealthy" When AQI values are between 151 and 200 everyone may begin to experience health effects; "Very Unhealthy" AQI values between 201 and 300 trigger a health alert; "Hazardous" AQI values over 300 trigger warnings of emergency conditions (not shown).
Source: U.S. Environmental Protection Agency, Air Quality Index Report, 2023

Air Quality Index Pollutants

Area	Percent of Days when AQI Pollutant was...[2]					
	Carbon Monoxide	Nitrogen Dioxide	Ozone	Sulfur Dioxide	Particulate Matter 2.5	Particulate Matter 10
MSA[1]	0.3	0.8	33.4	(3)	61.1	4.4

Note: (1) Data covers the Minneapolis-St. Paul-Bloomington, MN-WI Metropolitan Statistical Area; (2) Based on 365 days with AQI data in 2023. The Air Quality Index (AQI) is an index for reporting daily air quality. EPA calculates the AQI for five major air pollutants regulated by the Clean Air Act: ground-level ozone, particle pollution (also known as particulate matter), carbon monoxide, sulfur dioxide, and nitrogen dioxide. The AQI runs from 0 to 500. The higher the AQI value, the greater the level of air pollution and the greater the health concern; (3) Sulfur dioxide is no longer included in this table because SO_2 concentrations tend to be very localized and not necessarily representative of broad geographical areas like counties and CBSAs.
Source: U.S. Environmental Protection Agency, Air Quality Index Report, 2023

Maximum Air Pollutant Concentrations: Particulate Matter, Ozone, CO and Lead

	Particulate Matter 10 (ug/m³)	Particulate Matter 2.5 Wtd AM (ug/m³)	Particulate Matter 2.5 24-Hr (ug/m³)	Ozone (ppm)	Carbon Monoxide (ppm)	Lead (ug/m³)
MSA[1] Level	118	10.6	41	0.079	4	0.46
NAAQS[2]	150	15	35	0.075	9	0.15
Met NAAQS[2]	Yes	Yes	No	No	Yes	No

Note: (1) Data covers the Minneapolis-St. Paul-Bloomington, MN-WI Metropolitan Statistical Area; Data from exceptional events are included; (2) National Ambient Air Quality Standards; ppm = parts per million; ug/m³ = micrograms per cubic meter; n/a not available.
Concentrations: Particulate Matter 10 (coarse particulate)—highest second maximum 24-hour concentration; Particulate Matter 2.5 Wtd AM (fine particulate)—highest weighted annual mean concentration; Particulate Matter 2.5 24-Hour (fine particulate)—highest 98th percentile 24-hour concentration; Ozone—highest fourth daily maximum 8-hour concentration; Carbon Monoxide—highest second maximum non-overlapping 8-hour concentration; Lead—maximum running 3-month average
Source: U.S. Environmental Protection Agency, Air Quality Monitoring Information, "Air Quality Statistics by City, 2023"

Maximum Air Pollutant Concentrations: Nitrogen Dioxide and Sulfur Dioxide

	Nitrogen Dioxide AM (ppb)	Nitrogen Dioxide 1-Hr (ppb)	Sulfur Dioxide AM (ppb)	Sulfur Dioxide 1-Hr (ppb)	Sulfur Dioxide 24-Hr (ppb)
MSA[1] Level	12	45	n/a	14	n/a
NAAQS[2]	53	100	30	75	140
Met NAAQS[2]	Yes	Yes	n/a	Yes	n/a

Note: (1) Data covers the Minneapolis-St. Paul-Bloomington, MN-WI Metropolitan Statistical Area; Data from exceptional events are included; (2) National Ambient Air Quality Standards; ppm = parts per million; ug/m^3 = micrograms per cubic meter; n/a not available.
Concentrations: Nitrogen Dioxide AM—highest arithmetic mean concentration; Nitrogen Dioxide 1-Hr—highest 98th percentile 1-hour daily maximum concentration; Sulfur Dioxide AM—highest annual mean concentration; Sulfur Dioxide 1-Hr—highest 99th percentile 1-hour daily maximum concentration; Sulfur Dioxide 24-Hr—highest second maximum 24-hour concentration
Source: U.S. Environmental Protection Agency, Air Quality Monitoring Information, "Air Quality Statistics by City, 2023"

Oklahoma City, Oklahoma

Background

The 1992 film *Far and Away*, directed by Ron Howard, shows Tom Cruise charging away on his horse to claim land in the Oklahoma Territory. That dramatic scene depicted a true event from the great Oklahoma land run of 1889. A pistol was fired from the Oklahoma Station house of the Santa Fe Railroad and 10,000 homesteaders raced away to stake land claims in central Oklahoma territory. Overnight, Oklahoma City (aka OKC) had been founded.

The town grew quickly along the tracks of the Santa Fe Railroad. Soon it became a distribution center for the territory's crops and livestock and still today. By 1910 the city had become the state capital, which also furthered growth. In 1928, growth went through the ceiling when oil was discovered within the city limits, forever changing the economic face of Oklahoma City from one of livestock and feed to one of livestock, feed, and oil.

After World War II, Oklahoma City, like many other cities, entered aircraft and related industries. The Tinker Air Force Base and the Federal Aviation Administration's Mike Monroney Aeronautical Center—home to the largest concentration of Dept. of Transportation personnel outside of Washington, D.C.—have made Oklahoma City a leading aviation center. Major economic sectors for the Greater Oklahoma City region—the geographic center of the continent—also include energy, bioscience, and logistics. Major employers in the city include INTEGRIS Health and Hobby Lobby.

The area caters to a Western lifestyle, home to the National Cowboy and Western Heritage Museum, with its famous 18-foot-tall sculpture "End of the Trail" by James Earle Fraser. The Oklahoma History Center, affiliated with the Smithsonian Institute, occupies a 215,000 square foot building on an 18-acre campus. The Red Earth Museum features 1,400 items of Native American art and a research center. To the north of Oklahoma City's Capitol building is the Tribal Flag Plaza, displaying the 39 native tribal flags of Oklahoma. Each September the State Fair is held in Oklahoma City, and each January the International Finals Rodeo is held at the State Fair Park. If swinging a bat is more your style than riding a bronco, there's the National Softball Hall of Fame and Museum.

In the mid-1960s, Oklahoma City hired famed architect I.M. Pei to redesign its downtown area. Taking inspiration from the Tivoli Gardens of Copenhagen, the downtown boasts the Myriad Gardens, a 12-acre recreational park with gardens, and amphitheater. The seven-story Crystal Bridge Tropical Conservatory was completely restored and reopened in 2022.

The city is also home to the Oklahoma City Thunder, a professional basketball team, the only team in the major professional North American sports leagues based in the state of Oklahoma.

A national tragedy occurred in Oklahoma City on April 19, 1995, when a terrorist truck bomb destroyed part of the Alfred P. Murray Federal Building in the downtown area, killing 168 people and injuring more than 500. The Oklahoma City National Memorial commemorates those people whose lives were ended or forever changed on that day.

Oklahoma City's weather is changeable. There are pronounced daily and seasonal temperature changes and considerable variation in seasonal and annual precipitation. Summers are long and usually hot, while winters are comparatively mild and short. The city is in Tornado Alley, which is frequently visited in the springtime by violent thunderstorms producing damaging winds, large hail, and tornadoes.

Rankings

General Rankings

- To help military veterans find the best places in which to settle down, *WalletHub* compared the 100 largest U.S. cities across 19 key indicators of livability, affordability and veteran-friendliness. They range from the share of military skill-related jobs to veteran income growth to the availability of VA health facilities. Oklahoma City ranked #32. *Wallethub.com, "Best & Worst Places for Veterans to Live (2025)," November 7, 2024*

- *US News & World Report* conducted a survey of more than 3,500 people and analyzed the 150 largest metropolitan areas to determine what matters most when selecting the next place to live. Oklahoma City ranked #16 out of the top 25 as having the best combination of desirable factors. Criteria: cost of living; quality of life and education; climate; job market; desirability; and other factors. *realestate.usnews.com, "Best Places to Live in the U.S. in 2024-2025," May 21, 2024*

- Oklahoma City was selected as one of the best places to live in the United States by *Money* magazine. The city placed among the top 50. This year's list focused on cities built around community spirit, thoughtful policy and civic engagement. Instead of relying on a predetermined dataset, the cities and towns were grouped according to their strengths and chosen due their affordability, good schools and strong job markets. *Money, "The 50 Best Places to Live in the U.S., 2024" April 8, 2024*

Business/Finance Rankings

- For its annual survey of the "Cheapest U.S. Cities to Live In," Kiplinger applied Cost of Living Index statistics developed by the Council for Community and Economic Research to U.S. Census Bureau population and median household income data for 265 urban areas. Only areas with at least 50,000 residents were considered. In the resulting ranking, Oklahoma City ranked #3. *Kiplinger.com, "The 25 Cheapest Places to Live: U.S. Cities Edition," January 19, 2025*

- The Oklahoma City metro area appeared on the Milken Institute "2025 Best Performing Cities" list. Rank: #58 out of 200 large metro areas (based on performance category). Criteria: job growth; wage growth; high-tech growth and impact; community resilience; housing affordability; household broadband access. *Milken Institute, "Best-Performing Cities 2025," January 14, 2025*

Culture/Performing Arts Rankings

- Oklahoma City was selected as one of the 25 best cities for moviemakers in North America. Great film cities are places where filmmaking dreams can come true, that offer more creative space, lower costs, and great outdoor locations. NYC & LA were intentionally excluded. Criteria: film industry presence and culture; tax incentives; affordability; and proximity of festivals and schools. The city was ranked #13. *MovieMaker Magazine, "Best Places to Live and Work as a Moviemaker, 2025," January 29, 2025*

Education Rankings

- Personal finance website *WalletHub* analyzed the 150 largest U.S. metropolitan statistical areas to determine where the most educated Americans are putting their degrees to work. Criteria: education levels; percentage of workers with degrees; education quality and attainment gap; public school quality rankings; quality and enrollment of each metro area's universities. Oklahoma City was ranked #86 (#1 = most educated city). *WalletHub.com, "Most & Least Educated Cities in America, 2025" July 2, 2024*

Environmental Rankings

- Sperling's *BestPlaces* assessed the 50 largest metropolitan areas of the United States for the likelihood of dangerously extreme weather events or earthquakes. In general the Southeast and South-Central regions have the highest risk of weather extremes and earthquakes, while the Pacific Northwest enjoys the lowest risk. Of the most risky metropolitan areas, the Oklahoma City metro area was ranked #3. *Bestplaces.net, "Avoid Natural Disasters: BestPlaces Reveals The Top 10 Safest Places to Live," October 25, 2017*

Health/Fitness Rankings

- For each of the 100 largest cities in the United States, the American Fitness Index®, compiled in partnership between the American College of Sports Medicine and the Elevance Health Foundation, evaluated community infrastructure and more than 30 health behaviors including preventive health, levels of chronic disease conditions, food insecurity, pedestrian safety, air quality, and community/environment resources that support physical activity. Oklahoma City ranked #100 for "community fitness." *americanfitnessindex.org, "2024 ACSM American Fitness Index Summary Report," July 23, 2024*

- The Oklahoma City metro area was identified as one of the worst cities for bed bugs in America by pest control company Orkin. The area ranked #48 out of 50 based on the number of bed bug treatments Orkin performed from December 2022 to November 2023. *Orkin, "Chicago Joins Paris In Global Bed Bug Spotlight Ranking As The Worst City On Orkin's U.S. Bed Bug Cities List," January 22, 2024*

- Oklahoma City was identified as a "2025 Allergy Capital." The area ranked #3 out of the nation's 100 largest metropolitan areas. Three groups of factors were used to identify the most challenging cities for people with allergies: annual tree, grass, and weed pollen scores; over the counter allergy medicine use; number of board-certified allergy specialists. *Asthma and Allergy Foundation of America, "2025 Allergy Capitals: The Most Challenging Places to Live with Allergies," March 18, 2025*

- Oklahoma City was identified as a "2024 Asthma Capital." The area ranked #66 out of the nation's 100 largest metropolitan areas. Criteria: estimated asthma prevalence; asthma-related mortality; and ER visits due to asthma. Risk factors analyzed but not factored in the rankings: annual air quality including pollution and ozone levels; public smoking laws; indoor air quality; access to asthma specialists; rescue and controller medication use; uninsured rate; pollen allergy; poverty rate. *Asthma and Allergy Foundation of America, "Asthma Capitals 2024: The Most Challenging Places to Live With Asthma," September 10, 2024*

Real Estate Rankings

- *WalletHub* compared the most populated U.S. cities to determine which had the best markets for real estate agents. Oklahoma City ranked #126 where demand was high and pay was the best. Criteria: sales per agent; annual median wage for real-estate agents; monthly average starting salary for real estate agents; real estate job density and competition; unemployment rate; home turnover rate; housing-market health index; and other relevant metrics. *WalletHub.com, "2021 Best Places to Be a Real Estate Agent," May 12, 2021*

- Oklahoma City was ranked #40 out of 176 metro areas in terms of cost of housing in 2024 by the National Association of Home Builders (#1 = most affordable). Criteria: the portion of an average family's income necessary to pay the mortgage on a median-priced home. *National Association of Home Builders®, NAHB-Wells Fargo Cost of Housing Index, 4th Quarter 2024*

Safety Rankings

- Allstate ranked the 100 most populous cities in America in terms of driver safety. Oklahoma City ranked #44. Criteria based on anonymized driving behavior data from Allstate's mobile app powered by Arity: high speed driving (over 80 mph), phone handling, and hard braking. The report helps increase the importance of safety and awareness behind the wheel. *Allstate, "16th Allstate America's Best Drivers Report®" July 11, 2024*

Women/Minorities Rankings

- Personal finance website *WalletHub* compared more than 180 U.S. cities across two key dimensions, "Hispanic Business-Friendliness" and "Hispanic Purchasing Power," to arrive at the most favorable conditions for Hispanic entrepreneurs. Oklahoma City was ranked #21 out of 182. Criteria includes: share of Hispanic-Owned Businesses; average growth of Hispanic Business revenues; Small Business-Friendliness score; affordability; and number of Hispanics with at least a bachelor's degree. *WalletHub.com, "Best Cities for Hispanic Entrepreneurs," September 4, 2024*

Miscellaneous Rankings

- *WalletHub* compared 148 of the most populated U.S. cities to determine their operating efficiency. A "Quality of Services" score was constructed for each city and then measured against the total budget per capita to reveal which were managed the best. Oklahoma City ranked #5. Criteria: financial stability; economy; education; safety; health; infrastructure and pollution. *WalletHub.com, "2025's Best- & Worst-Run Cities in America," June 18, 2024*

Business Environment

DEMOGRAPHICS

Population Growth

Area	1990 Census	2000 Census	2010 Census	2020 Census	2023 Estimate[2]	Population Growth 1990-2023 (%)
City	445,065	506,132	579,999	681,054	688,693	54.7
MSA[1]	971,042	1,095,421	1,252,987	1,425,695	1,445,122	48.8
U.S.	248,709,873	281,421,906	308,745,538	331,449,281	332,387,540	33.6

Note: (1) Figures cover the Oklahoma City, OK Metropolitan Statistical Area; (2) 2019-2023 5-year ACS population estimate
Source: U.S. Census Bureau, 1990 Census, 2000 Census, 2010 Census, 2020 Census, 2019-2023 American Community Survey 5-Year Estimates

Race

Area	White Alone[2] (%)	Black Alone[2] (%)	Asian Alone[2] (%)	AIAN[3] Alone[2] (%)	NHOPI[4] Alone[2] (%)	Other Race Alone[2] (%)	Two or More Races (%)
City	58.4	13.4	4.5	3.4	0.1	5.8	14.4
MSA[1]	66.5	9.8	3.3	3.6	0.1	3.9	12.8
U.S.	63.4	12.4	5.8	0.9	0.2	6.6	10.7

Note: (1) Figures cover the Oklahoma City, OK Metropolitan Statistical Area; (2) Alone is defined as not being in combination with one or more other races; (3) American Indian and Alaska Native; (4) Native Hawaiian and Other Pacific Islander
Source: U.S. Census Bureau, 2019-2023 American Community Survey 5-Year Estimates

Hispanic or Latino Origin

Area	Total (%)	Mexican (%)	Puerto Rican (%)	Cuban (%)	Other (%)
City	21.7	17.3	0.5	0.1	3.8
MSA[1]	15.3	11.9	0.5	0.1	2.8
U.S.	19.0	11.3	1.8	0.7	5.2

Note: Persons of Hispanic or Latino origin can be of any race; (1) Figures cover the Oklahoma City, OK Metropolitan Statistical Area
Source: U.S. Census Bureau, 2019-2023 American Community Survey 5-Year Estimates

Age

Area	Under Age 5	Age 5–19	Age 20–34	Age 35–44	Age 45–54	Age 55–64	Age 65–74	Age 75–84	Age 85+	Median Age
City	6.8	20.5	22.6	14.2	11.4	11.1	8.3	3.8	1.2	35.0
MSA[1]	6.3	21.0	21.7	13.7	11.4	11.5	8.9	4.2	1.4	35.8
U.S.	5.7	19.1	20.2	13.1	12.3	12.8	10.0	4.9	1.9	38.7

Note: (1) Figures cover the Oklahoma City, OK Metropolitan Statistical Area
Source: U.S. Census Bureau, 2019-2023 American Community Survey 5-Year Estimates

Disability by Age

Area	All Ages	Under 18 Years Old	18 to 64 Years Old	65 Years and Over
City	13.9	5.6	12.5	36.6
MSA[1]	14.7	5.2	13.0	38.3
U.S.	13.0	4.7	10.7	32.9

Note: Figures show percent of the civilian noninstitutionalized population that reported having a disability. Disability status is determined from six types of difficulty: vision, hearing, cognitive, ambulatory, self-care, and independent living. For children under 5 years old, hearing and vision difficulty are used to determine disability status. For children between the ages of 5 and 14, disability status is determined from hearing, vision, cognitive, ambulatory, and self-care difficulties. For people aged 15 years and older, they are considered to have a disability if they have difficulty with any one of the six difficulty types; Note: (1) Figures cover the Oklahoma City, OK Metropolitan Statistical Area
Source: U.S. Census Bureau, 2019-2023 American Community Survey 5-Year Estimates

Ancestry

Area	German	Irish	English	American	Italian	Polish	French[2]	European	Scottish
City	10.1	7.8	9.5	5.3	1.5	0.7	1.2	1.9	1.7
MSA[1]	11.8	9.0	11.2	6.2	1.7	0.8	1.5	2.0	1.9
U.S.	12.6	9.4	9.1	5.5	4.9	2.6	2.0	1.6	1.6

Note: Figures are the percentage of the total population reporting a particular ancestry. The nine most commonly reported ancestries in the U.S. are shown. Figures include multiple ancestries (e.g. if a person reported being Irish and Italian, they were included in both columns); (1) Figures cover the Oklahoma City, OK Metropolitan Statistical Area; (2) Excludes Basque
Source: U.S. Census Bureau, 2019-2023 American Community Survey 5-Year Estimates

Foreign-born Population

Area	Percent of Population Born in								
	Any Foreign Country	Asia	Mexico	Europe	Caribbean	Central America[2]	South America	Africa	Canada
City	12.0	3.1	5.4	0.5	0.2	1.3	0.5	0.7	0.2
MSA[1]	8.2	2.3	3.4	0.5	0.1	0.8	0.4	0.5	0.2
U.S.	13.9	4.3	3.3	1.4	1.4	1.2	1.2	0.8	0.2

Note: (1) Figures cover the Oklahoma City, OK Metropolitan Statistical Area; (2) Excludes Mexico.
Source: U.S. Census Bureau, 2019-2023 American Community Survey 5-Year Estimates

Household Size

Area	Persons in Household (%)							Average Household Size
	One	Two	Three	Four	Five	Six	Seven or More	
City	31.6	31.7	15.5	11.5	6.3	2.3	1.1	2.46
MSA[1]	29.0	33.1	15.7	12.4	6.3	2.3	1.2	2.51
U.S.	28.5	33.8	15.4	12.7	5.9	2.3	1.4	2.54

Note: (1) Figures cover the Oklahoma City, OK Metropolitan Statistical Area
Source: U.S. Census Bureau, 2019-2023 American Community Survey 5-Year Estimates

Household Relationships

Area	House-holder	Opposite-sex Spouse	Same-sex Spouse	Opposite-sex Unmarried Partner	Same-sex Unmarried Partner	Child[2]	Grand-child	Other Relatives	Non-relatives
City	39.4	16.6	0.2	2.6	0.2	29.4	2.3	4.3	3.1
MSA[1]	38.8	17.7	0.2	2.4	0.2	29.0	2.3	3.8	3.1
U.S.	38.3	17.5	0.2	2.5	0.2	28.3	2.4	4.8	3.4

Note: Figures are percent of the total population; (1) Figures cover the Oklahoma City, OK Metropolitan Statistical Area; (2) Includes biological, adopted, and stepchildren of the householder
Source: U.S. Census Bureau, 2020 Census

Gender

Area	Males	Females	Males per 100 Females
City	340,327	348,366	97.7
MSA[1]	714,932	730,190	97.9
U.S.	164,545,087	167,842,453	98.0

Note: (1) Figures cover the Oklahoma City, OK Metropolitan Statistical Area
Source: U.S. Census Bureau, 2019-2023 American Community Survey 5-Year Estimates

Marital Status

Area	Never Married	Now Married[2]	Separated	Widowed	Divorced
City	34.2	46.4	2.1	5.2	12.2
MSA[1]	32.3	48.6	1.8	5.5	11.9
U.S.	34.1	47.9	1.7	5.6	10.7

Note: Figures are percentages and cover the population 15 years of age and older; (1) Figures cover the Oklahoma City, OK Metropolitan Statistical Area; (2) Excludes separated
Source: U.S. Census Bureau, 2019-2023 American Community Survey 5-Year Estimates

Religious Groups by Family

Area	Catholic	Baptist	Methodist	LDS[2]	Pentecostal	Lutheran	Islam	Adventist	Other
MSA[1]	10.0	16.6	6.2	1.3	3.9	0.6	0.6	0.9	21.4
U.S.	18.7	7.3	3.0	2.0	1.8	1.7	1.3	1.3	11.6

Note: Figures are the number of adherents as a percentage of the total population and cover the eight largest religious groups in the U.S; (1) Figures cover the Oklahoma City, OK Metropolitan Statistical Area; (2) Church of Jesus Christ of Latter-day Saints
Sources: 2020 U.S. Religion Census, Association of Statisticians of American Religious Bodies; The Association of Religion Data Archives (ARDA)

Religious Groups by Tradition

Area	Catholic	Evangelical Protestant	Mainline Protestant	Black Protestant	Islam	Judaism	Hinduism	Orthodox	Buddhism
MSA[1]	10.0	38.7	7.1	2.2	0.6	0.1	0.4	0.1	0.4
U.S.	18.7	16.5	5.2	2.3	1.3	0.6	0.4	0.4	0.3

Note: Figures are the number of adherents as a percentage of the total population; (1) Figures cover the Oklahoma City, OK Metropolitan Statistical Area
Sources: 2020 U.S. Religion Census, Association of Statisticians of American Religious Bodies; The Association of Religion Data Archives (ARDA)

ECONOMY

Real Gross Domestic Product (GDP)

Area	2017	2018	2019	2020	2021	2022	2023	Rank[3]
MSA[1]	74.4	77.0	78.4	76.1	76.7	76.3	81.6	46
U.S.[2]	17,619.1	18,160.7	18,642.5	18,238.9	19,387.6	19,896.6	20,436.3	—

Note: Figures are in billions of chained 2017 dollars; (1) Figures cover the Oklahoma City, OK Metropolitan Statistical Area; (2) Figures cover real GDP within metropolitan areas; (3) Rank is based on 2023 data and ranges from 1 to 384
Source: U.S. Bureau of Economic Analysis

Economic Growth

Area	2014	2015	2016	2017	2018	2019	2020	2021	2022	2023
MSA[1]	6.4	4.2	0.3	3.1	3.5	1.7	-2.8	0.7	-0.5	6.9
U.S.[2]	2.6	3.2	2.0	2.7	3.1	2.7	-2.2	6.3	2.6	2.7

Note: Figures are real gross domestic product growth rates and represent percent change from preceding period; (1) Figures cover the Oklahoma City, OK Metropolitan Statistical Area; (2) Figures are the average growth rates within metropolitan areas
Source: U.S. Bureau of Economic Analysis

Metropolitan Area Exports

Area	2018	2019	2020	2021	2022	2023	Rank[2]
MSA[1]	1,489.4	1,434.5	1,326.6	1,773.2	2,019.1	2,277.7	107
U.S.	1,664,056.1	1,645,173.7	1,431,406.6	1,753,941.4	2,062,937.4	2,019,160.5	—

Note: Figures are in millions of dollars; (1) Figures cover the Oklahoma City, OK Metropolitan Statistical Area; (2) Rank is based on 2023 data and ranges from 1 to 386
Source: U.S. Department of Commerce, International Trade Administration, Office of Trade and Economic Analysis, Industry and Analysis, Exports by Metropolitan Area, data extracted April 2, 2025

Building Permits

Area	Single-Family 2023	Single-Family 2024	Single-Family Pct. Chg.	Multi-Family 2023	Multi-Family 2024	Multi-Family Pct. Chg.	Total 2023	Total 2024	Total Pct. Chg.
City	3,339	3,460	3.6	805	938	16.5	4,144	4,398	6.1
MSA[1]	5,573	6,014	7.9	1,163	1,693	45.6	6,736	7,707	14.4
U.S.	920,000	981,900	6.7	591,100	496,100	-16.1	1,511,100	1,478,000	-2.2

Note: (1) Figures cover the Oklahoma City, OK Metropolitan Statistical Area; Figures represent new, privately-owned housing units authorized (unadjusted data)
Source: U.S. Census Bureau, Building Permits Survey (BPS), 2023, 2024

Bankruptcy Filings

Area	Business Filings 2023	Business Filings 2024	% Chg.	Nonbusiness Filings 2023	Nonbusiness Filings 2024	% Chg.
Oklahoma County	46	54	17.4	1,374	1,526	11.1
U.S.	18,926	23,107	22.1	434,064	494,201	13.9

Note: Business filings include Chapter 7, Chapter 9, Chapter 11, Chapter 12, Chapter 13, Chapter 15, and Section 304; Nonbusiness filings include Chapter 7, Chapter 11, and Chapter 13
Source: Administrative Office of the U.S. Courts, Business and Nonbusiness Bankruptcy, County Cases Commenced by Chapter of the Bankruptcy Code, During the 12-Month Period Ending December 31, 2023 and Business and Nonbusiness Bankruptcy, County Cases Commenced by Chapter of the Bankruptcy Code, During the 12-Month Period Ending December 31, 2024

Housing Vacancy Rates

Area	Gross Vacancy Rate[3] (%) 2022	2023	2024	Year-Round Vacancy Rate[4] (%) 2022	2023	2024	Rental Vacancy Rate[5] (%) 2022	2023	2024	Homeowner Vacancy Rate[6] (%) 2022	2023	2024
MSA[1]	8.6	7.8	7.0	8.5	7.6	6.7	10.6	10.6	9.0	0.9	1.6	1.2
U.S.[2]	9.1	9.0	9.1	7.5	7.5	7.6	5.7	6.5	6.8	0.8	0.8	1.0

Note: (1) Figures cover the Oklahoma City, OK Metropolitan Statistical Area; (2) Figures cover the 75 largest Metropolitan Statistical Areas; (3) The percentage of the total housing inventory that is vacant; (4) The percentage of the housing inventory (excluding seasonal units) that is year-round vacant; (5) The percentage of rental inventory that is vacant for rent; (6) The percentage of homeowner inventory that is vacant for sale
Source: U.S. Census Bureau, Housing Vacancies and Homeownership Annual Statistics: 2022, 2023, 2024

INCOME

Income

Area	Per Capita ($)	Median Household ($)	Average Household ($)
City	37,109	66,702	91,131
MSA[1]	38,240	70,499	95,891
U.S.	43,289	78,538	110,491

Note: (1) Figures cover the Oklahoma City, OK Metropolitan Statistical Area
Source: U.S. Census Bureau, 2019-2023 American Community Survey 5-Year Estimates

Household Income Distribution

Area	Percent of Households Earning							
	Under $15,000	$15,000 -$24,999	$25,000 -$34,999	$35,000 -$49,999	$50,000 -$74,999	$75,000 -$99,999	$100,000 -$149,999	$150,000 and up
City	10.0	7.0	7.9	12.4	18.1	13.3	15.9	15.4
MSA[1]	8.9	6.7	7.8	11.9	17.6	13.5	17.0	16.6
U.S.	8.5	6.6	6.8	10.4	15.7	12.7	17.4	21.9

Note: (1) Figures cover the Oklahoma City, OK Metropolitan Statistical Area
Source: U.S. Census Bureau, 2019-2023 American Community Survey 5-Year Estimates

Poverty Rate

Area	All Ages	Under 18 Years Old	18 to 64 Years Old	65 Years and Over
City	15.2	20.6	14.2	9.4
MSA[1]	13.9	18.3	13.3	8.8
U.S.	12.4	16.3	11.6	10.4

Note: Figures are percentage of people whose income during the past 12 months was below the poverty level; (1) Figures cover the Oklahoma City, OK Metropolitan Statistical Area
Source: U.S. Census Bureau, 2019-2023 American Community Survey 5-Year Estimates

EMPLOYMENT

Labor Force and Employment

Area	Civilian Labor Force			Workers Employed		
	Dec. 2023	Dec. 2024	% Chg.	Dec. 2023	Dec. 2024	% Chg.
City	352,331	357,109	1.4	341,478	346,634	1.5
MSA[1]	752,168	762,662	1.4	729,908	740,966	1.5
U.S.	166,661,000	167,746,000	0.7	160,754,000	161,294,000	0.3

Note: Data is not seasonally adjusted and covers workers 16 years of age and older; (1) Figures cover the Oklahoma City, OK Metropolitan Statistical Area
Source: Bureau of Labor Statistics, Local Area Unemployment Statistics

Unemployment Rate

Area	2024											
	Jan.	Feb.	Mar.	Apr.	May	Jun.	Jul.	Aug.	Sep.	Oct.	Nov.	Dec.
City	3.4	3.4	3.1	2.7	3.2	3.4	3.4	3.3	3.1	3.1	3.1	2.9
MSA[1]	3.3	3.4	3.0	2.6	3.0	3.3	3.3	3.2	3.0	3.0	3.0	2.8
U.S.	4.1	4.2	3.9	3.5	3.7	4.3	4.5	4.4	3.9	3.9	4.0	3.8

Note: Data is not seasonally adjusted and covers workers 16 years of age and older; (1) Figures cover the Oklahoma City, OK Metropolitan Statistical Area
Source: Bureau of Labor Statistics, Local Area Unemployment Statistics

Average Wages

Occupation	$/Hr.	Occupation	$/Hr.
Accountants and Auditors	41.96	Maintenance and Repair Workers	21.81
Automotive Mechanics	23.62	Marketing Managers	69.08
Bookkeepers	22.88	Network and Computer Systems Admin.	41.11
Carpenters	25.29	Nurses, Licensed Practical	26.98
Cashiers	13.24	Nurses, Registered	41.29
Computer Programmers	57.04	Nursing Assistants	17.28
Computer Systems Analysts	47.08	Office Clerks, General	19.03
Computer User Support Specialists	26.99	Physical Therapists	48.05
Construction Laborers	20.63	Physicians	113.07
Cooks, Restaurant	17.14	Plumbers, Pipefitters and Steamfitters	27.59
Customer Service Representatives	20.02	Police and Sheriff's Patrol Officers	35.39
Dentists	112.93	Postal Service Mail Carriers	28.83
Electricians	30.47	Real Estate Sales Agents	n/a
Engineers, Electrical	53.72	Retail Salespersons	16.29
Fast Food and Counter Workers	12.18	Sales Representatives, Technical/Scientific	44.00
Financial Managers	71.53	Secretaries, Exc. Legal/Medical/Executive	19.75
First-Line Supervisors of Office Workers	32.48	Security Guards	20.95
General and Operations Managers	52.56	Surgeons	n/a
Hairdressers/Cosmetologists	18.80	Teacher Assistants, Exc. Postsecondary[1]	14.11
Home Health and Personal Care Aides	13.47	Teachers, Secondary School, Exc. Sp. Ed.[1]	27.06
Janitors and Cleaners	15.40	Telemarketers	16.04
Landscaping/Groundskeeping Workers	17.06	Truck Drivers, Heavy/Tractor-Trailer	27.43
Lawyers	59.75	Truck Drivers, Light/Delivery Services	20.70
Maids and Housekeeping Cleaners	13.86	Waiters and Waitresses	14.43

Note: Wage data covers the Oklahoma City, OK Metropolitan Statistical Area; (1) Hourly wages were calculated from annual wage data based on a 40 hour work week
Source: Bureau of Labor Statistics, Metro Area Occupational Employment & Wage Estimates, May 2024

Employment by Industry

Sector	MSA[1] Number of Employees	MSA[1] Percent of Total	U.S. Percent of Total
Construction	36,000	5.0	5.1
Financial Activities	37,500	5.2	5.8
Government	136,600	19.0	14.9
Information	6,600	0.9	1.9
Leisure and Hospitality	81,900	11.4	10.4
Manufacturing	35,500	4.9	8.0
Mining and Logging	10,400	1.4	0.4
Other Services	31,200	4.3	3.7
Private Education and Health Services	119,700	16.7	16.9
Professional and Business Services	90,900	12.7	14.2
Retail Trade	72,900	10.2	10.0
Transportation, Warehousing, and Utilities	33,500	4.7	4.8
Wholesale Trade	25,100	3.5	3.9

Note: Figures are non-farm employment as of December 2024. Figures are not seasonally adjusted and include workers 16 years of age and older; (1) Figures cover the Oklahoma City, OK Metropolitan Statistical Area
Source: Bureau of Labor Statistics, Current Employment Statistics, Employment, Hours, and Earnings

Employment by Occupation

Occupation Classification	City (%)	MSA[1] (%)	U.S. (%)
Management, Business, Science, and Arts	40.6	40.9	42.0
Natural Resources, Construction, and Maintenance	9.8	9.8	8.6
Production, Transportation, and Material Moving	12.5	12.1	13.0
Sales and Office	20.6	21.3	19.9
Service	16.4	15.9	16.5

Note: Figures cover employed civilians 16 years of age and older; (1) Figures cover the Oklahoma City, OK Metropolitan Statistical Area
Source: U.S. Census Bureau, 2019-2023 American Community Survey 5-Year Estimates

Occupations with Greatest Projected Employment Growth: 2022 – 2032

Occupation[1]	2022 Employment	2032 Projected Employment	Numeric Employment Change	Percent Employment Change
Cooks, Restaurant	17,540	22,760	5,220	29.8
Home Health and Personal Care Aides	19,090	23,300	4,210	22.1
Fast Food and Counter Workers	38,730	42,310	3,580	9.2
Stockers and Order Fillers	34,260	37,570	3,310	9.7
General and Operations Managers	44,230	47,300	3,070	6.9
Laborers and Freight, Stock, and Material Movers, Hand	31,840	34,070	2,230	7.0
Heavy and Tractor-Trailer Truck Drivers	28,050	30,090	2,040	7.3
Medical and Health Services Managers	7,420	9,360	1,940	26.1
First-Line Supervisors of Food Preparation and Serving Workers	15,550	17,460	1,910	12.3
Registered Nurses	37,490	39,290	1,800	4.8

Note: Projections cover Oklahoma; (1) Sorted by numeric employment change
Source: www.projectionscentral.org, State Occupational Projections, 2022–2032 Long-Term Projections

Fastest-Growing Occupations: 2022 – 2032

Occupation[1]	2022 Employment	2032 Projected Employment	Numeric Employment Change	Percent Employment Change
Wind Turbine Service Technicians	610	970	360	59.0
Nurse Practitioners	3,030	4,200	1,170	38.6
Data Scientists	2,060	2,710	650	31.6
Cooks, Restaurant	17,540	22,760	5,220	29.8
Information Security Analysts (SOC 2018)	1,010	1,300	290	28.7
Medical and Health Services Managers	7,420	9,360	1,940	26.1
Operations Research Analysts	460	570	110	23.9
Personal Care and Service Workers, All Other	630	780	150	23.8
Taxi Drivers	610	750	140	23.0
Physician Assistants	1,650	2,020	370	22.4

Note: Projections cover Oklahoma; (1) Sorted by percent employment change and excludes occupations with numeric employment change less than 50
Source: www.projectionscentral.org, State Occupational Projections, 2022–2032 Long-Term Projections

CITY FINANCES

City Government Finances

Component	2022 ($000)	2022 ($ per capita)
Total Revenues	1,743,472	2,632
Total Expenditures	1,416,390	2,139
Debt Outstanding	2,382,651	3,597

Source: U.S. Census Bureau, State & Local Government Finances 2022

City Government Revenue by Source

Source	2022 ($000)	2022 ($ per capita)	2022 (%)
General Revenue			
From Federal Government	143,534	217	8.2
From State Government	58,557	88	3.4
From Local Governments	53,615	81	3.1
Taxes			
Property	126,850	192	7.3
Sales and Gross Receipts	695,466	1,050	39.9
Personal Income	0	0	0.0
Corporate Income	0	0	0.0
Motor Vehicle License	0	0	0.0
Other Taxes	78,058	118	4.5
Current Charges	332,367	502	19.1
Liquor Store	0	0	0.0
Utility	209,487	316	12.0

Source: U.S. Census Bureau, State & Local Government Finances 2022

City Government Expenditures by Function

Function	2022 ($000)	2022 ($ per capita)	2022 (%)
General Direct Expenditures			
Air Transportation	57,293	86	4.0
Corrections	0	0	0.0
Education	0	0	0.0
Employment Security Administration	0	0	0.0
Financial Administration	11,385	17	0.8
Fire Protection	169,327	255	12.0
General Public Buildings	0	0	0.0
Governmental Administration, Other	14,523	21	1.0
Health	4,981	7	0.4
Highways	110,502	166	7.8
Hospitals	0	0	0.0
Housing and Community Development	41,676	62	2.9
Interest on General Debt	40,695	61	2.9
Judicial and Legal	16,369	24	1.2
Libraries	0	0	0.0
Parking	3,234	4	0.2
Parks and Recreation	173,399	261	12.2
Police Protection	197,043	297	13.9
Public Welfare	0	0	0.0
Sewerage	71,953	108	5.1
Solid Waste Management	53,952	81	3.8
Veterans' Services	0	0	0.0
Liquor Store	0	0	0.0
Utility	244,993	369	17.3

Source: U.S. Census Bureau, State & Local Government Finances 2022

TAXES

State Corporate Income Tax Rates

State	Tax Rate (%)	Income Brackets ($)	Num. of Brackets	Financial Institution Tax Rate (%)[a]	Federal Income Tax Ded.
Oklahoma	4.0	Flat rate	1	4.0	No

Note: Tax rates for tax year 2024; (a) Rates listed are the corporate income tax rate applied to financial institutions or excise taxes based on income. Some states have other taxes based upon the value of deposits or shares.
Source: Federation of Tax Administrators, State Corporate Income Tax Rates, January 1, 2025

State Individual Income Tax Rates

State	Tax Rate (%)	Income Brackets ($)	Personal Exemptions ($)			Standard Ded. ($)	
			Single	Married	Depend.	Single	Married
Oklahoma	0.25 - 4.75	1,000 - 7,200 (v)	1,000	2,000	1,000	6,350	12,700

Note: Tax rates for tax year 2024; Local- and county-level taxes are not included; Federal income tax is not deductible on state income tax returns; (v) Married and HOH tax brackets are twice Single filing status. Legislature seeking HB 2949 - flat rate 4.25% personal income tax effective 2024. HB1953 eliminates the current standard deductions and changes the personal income taxing framework from a bracket based system to a flat rate system
Source: Federation of Tax Administrators, State Individual Income Tax Rates, January 1, 2025

Various State Sales and Excise Tax Rates

State	State Sales Tax (%)	Gasoline[1] ($/gal.)	Cigarette[2] ($/pack)	Spirits[3] ($/gal.)	Wine[4] ($/gal.)	Beer[5] ($/gal.)	Recreational Marijuana (%)
Oklahoma	4.5	0.20	2.03	5.56	0.72	0.40	Not legal

Note: All tax rates as of January 1, 2025; (1) The American Petroleum Institute has developed a methodology for determining the average tax rate on a gallon of fuel. Rates may include any of the following: excise taxes, environmental fees, storage tank fees, other fees or taxes, general sales tax, and local taxes; (2) The federal excise tax of $1.0066 per pack and local taxes are not included; (3) Rates are those applicable to off-premise sales of 40% alcohol by volume (a.b.v.) distilled spirits in 750ml containers. Local excise taxes are excluded; (4) Rates are those applicable to off-premise sales of 11% a.b.v. non-carbonated wine in 750ml containers; (5) Rates are those applicable to off-premise sales of 4.7% a.b.v. beer in 12 ounce containers.
Source: Tax Foundation, 2025 Facts & Figures: How Does Your State Compare?

State Tax Competitiveness Index

State	Overall Rank	Corporate Tax Rank	Individual Income Tax Rank	Sales Tax Rank	Property Tax Rank	Unemployment Insurance Tax Rank
Oklahoma	21	5	28	32	15	6

Note: The Tax Foundation's State Tax Competitiveness Index enables policymakers, taxpayers, and business leaders to gauge how their states' tax systems compare. A rank of 1 is best, 50 is worst. Rankings do not average to the total. States without a tax rank equally as 1. DC's scores and rankings do not affect other states. The report shows tax systems as of July 1, 2024 (the beginning of Fiscal Year 2025).
Source: Tax Foundation, State Tax Competitiveness Index 2025

TRANSPORTATION

Means of Transportation to Work

Area	Car/Truck/Van		Public Transportation			Bicycle	Walked	Other Means	Worked at Home
	Drove Alone	Car-pooled	Bus	Subway	Railroad				
City	77.0	9.6	0.4	0.0	0.0	0.2	1.4	1.6	9.8
MSA[1]	78.1	9.0	0.3	0.0	0.0	0.2	1.6	1.3	9.5
U.S.	70.2	8.5	1.7	1.3	0.4	0.4	2.4	1.6	13.5

Note: Figures are percentages and cover workers 16 years of age and older; (1) Figures cover the Oklahoma City, OK Metropolitan Statistical Area
Source: U.S. Census Bureau, 2019-2023 American Community Survey 5-Year Estimates

Travel Time to Work

Area	Less Than 10 Minutes	10 to 19 Minutes	20 to 29 Minutes	30 to 44 Minutes	45 to 59 Minutes	60 to 89 Minutes	90 Minutes or More
City	10.4	35.0	28.8	19.2	3.6	1.5	1.6
MSA[1]	12.2	31.4	25.4	21.2	5.6	2.6	1.7
U.S.	12.6	28.6	21.2	20.8	8.1	6.0	2.8

Note: Note: Figures are percentages and include workers 16 years old and over; (1) Figures cover the Oklahoma City, OK Metropolitan Statistical Area
Source: U.S. Census Bureau, 2019-2023 American Community Survey 5-Year Estimates

Key Congestion Measures

Measure	2000	2010	2015	2020	2022
Annual Hours of Delay, Total (000)	22,189	32,864	40,393	30,057	43,749
Annual Hours of Delay, Per Auto Commuter	36	43	47	35	52
Annual Congestion Cost, Per Auto Commuter ($)	691	813	923	733	1,026

Note: Figures cover the Oklahoma City OK urban area
Source: Texas A&M Transportation Institute, 2023 Urban Mobility Report

Freeway Travel Time Index

Measure	1985	1990	1995	2000	2005	2010	2015	2020	2022
Urban Area Index[1]	1.06	1.08	1.11	1.16	1.18	1.18	1.19	1.12	1.19
Urban Area Rank[1,2]	53	62	66	43	41	38	38	10	37

Note: Freeway Travel Time Index—the ratio of travel time in the peak period to the travel time at free-flow conditions. For example, a value of 1.30 indicates a 20-minute free-flow trip takes 26 minutes in the peak (20 minutes x 1.30 = 26 minutes); (1) Covers the Oklahoma City OK urban area; (2) Rank is based on 101 larger urban areas (#1 = highest travel time index)
Source: Texas A&M Transportation Institute, 2023 Urban Mobility Report

Public Transportation

Agency Name / Mode of Transportation	Vehicles Operated in Maximum Service[1]	Annual Unlinked Passenger Trips[2] (in thous.)	Annual Passenger Miles[3] (in thous.)
Central Oklahoma Transportation & Parking Authority (COTPA)			
Bus (directly operated)	49	2,650.0	13,530.9
Demand Response (directly operated)	17	45.2	362.3
Ferryboat (purchased transportation)	1	1.8	3.9
Streetcar Rail (purchased transportation)	4	252.4	561.0
Vanpool (purchased transportation)	2	0.6	5.4

Note: (1) Number of revenue vehicles operated by the given mode and type of service to meet the annual maximum service requirement. This is the revenue vehicle count during the peak season of the year; on the week and day that maximum service is provided. Vehicles operated in maximum service (VOMS) exclude atypical days and one-time special events; (2) Number of passengers who boarded public transportation vehicles. Passengers are counted each time they board a vehicle no matter how many vehicles they use to travel from their origin to their destination. (3) Sum of the distances ridden by all passengers during the entire fiscal year.
Source: Federal Transit Administration, National Transit Database, 2023

Air Transportation

Airport Name and Code / Type of Service	Passenger Airlines[1]	Passenger Enplanements	Freight Carriers[2]	Freight (lbs)
Will Rogers World Airport (OKC)				
Domestic service (U.S. carriers only)	21	2,243,268	11	30,226,082
International service (U.S. carriers only)	2	198	0	0

Note: (1) Includes all U.S.-based major, minor and commuter airlines that carried at least one passenger during the year; (2) Includes all U.S.-based airlines and freight carriers that transported at least one pound of freight during the year.
Source: Bureau of Transportation Statistics, The Intermodal Transportation Database, Air Carriers: T-100 Domestic Market (U.S. carriers only), 2024; Bureau of Transportation Statistics, The Intermodal Transportation Database, Air Carriers: T-100 International Market (U.S. carriers only), 2024

BUSINESSES

Major Business Headquarters

Company Name	Industry	Rankings	
		Fortune[1]	Forbes[2]
Chesapeake Energy	Mining, crude-oil production	440	-
Continental Resources	Mining, crude-oil production	439	59
Devon Energy	Mining, crude-oil production	271	-
Hobby Lobby Stores	Retailing	-	69
Love's Travel Stops & Country Stores	Convenience stores & gas stations	-	11

Note: (1) Companies that produce a 10-K are ranked 1 to 500 based on 2023 revenue; (2) All private companies with at least $2 billion in annual revenue through the end of their most current fiscal year are ranked 1 to 275; companies listed are headquartered in the city; dashes indicate no ranking
Source: Fortune, "Fortune 500," 2024; Forbes, "America's Largest Private Companies," 2024

Fastest-Growing Businesses

According to *Inc.*, Oklahoma City is home to two of America's 500 fastest-growing private companies: **Larken** (#343); **T&T Industrial** (#480). Criteria: must be an independent, privately-held, for-profit, U.S. corporation, proprietorship or partnership as of December 31, 2023; revenues must be at least $100,000 in 2020 and $2 million in 2023; must have four-year operating/sales history. *Inc.*, "America's 500 Fastest-Growing Private Companies," 2024

Living Environment

COST OF LIVING

Cost of Living Index

Composite Index	Groceries	Housing	Utilities	Transportation	Health Care	Misc. Goods/Services
82.2	94.9	60.1	96.8	91.3	103.9	86.0

Note: The Cost of Living Index measures regional differences in the cost of consumer goods and services, excluding taxes and non-consumer expenditures, for professional and managerial households in the top income quintile. It is based on more than 50,000 prices covering almost 60 different items for which prices are collected three times a year by chambers of commerce, economic development organizations or university applied economic centers in each participating urban area. The numbers shown should be read as a percentage above or below the national average of 100. For example, a value of 115.4 in the groceries column indicates that grocery prices are 15.4% higher than the national average. Small differences in the index numbers should not be interpreted as significant; Figures cover the Oklahoma City OK urban area.
Source: The Council for Community and Economic Research, Cost of Living Index, 2024

Grocery Prices

Area[1]	T-Bone Steak ($/pound)	Frying Chicken ($/pound)	Whole Milk ($/half gal.)	Eggs ($/dozen)	Orange Juice ($/64 oz.)	Coffee ($/11.5 oz.)
City[2]	15.34	1.46	4.55	2.97	4.28	5.16
Avg.	15.42	1.55	4.69	3.25	4.41	5.46
Min.	14.50	1.16	4.43	2.75	4.00	4.85
Max.	17.56	2.89	5.49	4.78	5.54	7.89

Note: (1) Values for the local area are compared with the average, minimum and maximum values for all 276 areas in the Cost of Living Index; (2) Figures cover the Oklahoma City OK urban area; **T-Bone Steak** (price per pound); **Frying Chicken** (price per pound, whole fryer); **Whole Milk** (half gallon carton); **Eggs** (price per dozen, Grade A, large); **Orange Juice** (64 oz. Tropicana or Florida Natural); **Coffee** (11.5 oz. can, vacuum-packed, Maxwell House, Hills Bros, or Folgers).
Source: The Council for Community and Economic Research, Cost of Living Index, 2024

Housing and Utility Costs

Area[1]	New Home Price ($)	Apartment Rent ($/month)	All Electric ($/month)	Part Electric ($/month)	Other Energy ($/month)	Telephone ($/month)
City[2]	320,395	811	-	115.46	78.66	197.38
Avg.	515,975	1,550	210.99	123.07	82.07	194.99
Min.	265,375	692	104.33	53.68	36.26	179.42
Max.	2,775,821	5,719	529.02	397.28	361.63	223.33

Note: (1) Values for the local area are compared with the average, minimum and maximum values for all 276 areas in the Cost of Living Index; (2) Figures cover the Oklahoma City OK urban area; **New Home Price** (2,400 sf living area, 8,000 sf lot, in urban area with full utilities); **Apartment Rent** (950 sf 2 bedroom/1.5 or 2 bath, unfurnished, excluding all utilities except water); **All Electric** (average monthly cost for an all-electric home); **Part Electric** (average monthly cost for a part-electric home); **Other Energy** (average monthly cost for natural gas, fuel oil, coal, wood, and any other forms of energy except electricity); **Telephone** (price includes the base monthly rate plus taxes and fees for three lines of mobile phone service).
Source: The Council for Community and Economic Research, Cost of Living Index, 2024

Health Care, Transportation, and Other Costs

Area[1]	Doctor ($/visit)	Dentist ($/visit)	Optometrist ($/visit)	Gasoline ($/gallon)	Beauty Salon ($/visit)	Men's Shirt ($)
City[2]	149.53	124.67	99.96	3.02	51.40	22.45
Avg.	143.77	117.51	129.23	3.32	48.57	38.14
Min.	36.74	58.67	67.33	2.80	24.00	13.41
Max.	270.44	216.82	307.33	5.28	94.00	63.89

Note: (1) Values for the local area are compared with the average, minimum and maximum values for all 276 areas in the Cost of Living Index; (2) Figures cover the Oklahoma City OK urban area; **Doctor** (general practitioners routine exam of an established patient); **Dentist** (adult teeth cleaning and periodic oral examination); **Optometrist** (full vision eye exam for established adult patient); **Gasoline** (one gallon regular unleaded, national brand, including all taxes, cash price at self-service pump if available); **Beauty Salon** (woman's shampoo, trim, and blow-dry); **Men's Shirt** (cotton/polyester dress shirt, pinpoint weave, long sleeves).
Source: The Council for Community and Economic Research, Cost of Living Index, 2024

HOUSING

Homeownership Rate

Area	2017 (%)	2018 (%)	2019 (%)	2020 (%)	2021 (%)	2022 (%)	2023 (%)	2024 (%)
MSA[1]	64.7	64.6	64.3	68.3	61.9	64.8	68.1	65.0
U.S.	63.9	64.4	64.6	66.6	65.5	65.8	65.9	65.6

Note: (1) Figures cover the Oklahoma City, OK Metropolitan Statistical Area
Source: U.S. Census Bureau, Housing Vacancies and Homeownership Annual Statistics: 2017-2024

House Price Index (HPI)

Area	National Ranking[2]	Quarterly Change (%)	One-Year Change (%)	Five-Year Change (%)	Since 1991Q1 (%)
MSA[1]	129	-0.57	5.22	50.62	294.07
U.S.[3]	—	1.43	4.51	57.13	327.82

Note: The HPI is a weighted repeat sales index. It measures average price changes in repeat sales or refinancings on the same properties. This information is obtained by reviewing repeat mortgage transactions on single-family properties whose mortgages have been purchased or securitized by Fannie Mae or Freddie Mac since January 1975; (1) Figures cover the Oklahoma City, OK Metropolitan Statistical Area; (2) Rankings are based on annual percentage change for all metro areas containing at least 15,000 transactions over the last 10 years and ranges from 1 to 241; (3) figures based on a weighted average of Census Division estimates using a seasonally adjusted, purchase-only index; all figures are for the period ending December 31, 2024
Source: Federal Housing Finance Agency, Change in FHFA Metropolitan Area House Price Indexes, All Transactions Index, 2024Q4

Home Value

Area	Under $100,000	$100,000 -$199,999	$200,000 -$299,999	$300,000 -$399,999	$400,000 -$499,999	$500,000 -$999,999	$1,000,000 or more	Median ($)
City	14.8	30.5	27.8	13.1	5.7	6.6	1.6	215,100
MSA[1]	14.4	31.1	26.8	12.7	6.2	7.1	1.7	214,700
U.S.	12.1	17.8	19.5	14.4	10.5	19.1	6.5	303,400

Note: Figures are percentages except for median and cover owner-occupied housing units; (1) Figures cover the Oklahoma City, OK Metropolitan Statistical Area
Source: U.S. Census Bureau, 2019-2023 American Community Survey 5-Year Estimates

Year Housing Structure Built

Area	2020 or Later	2010 -2019	2000 -2009	1990 -1999	1980 -1989	1970 -1979	1960 -1969	1950 -1959	1940 -1949	Before 1940	Median Year
City	1.6	13.7	13.3	9.3	13.4	15.6	11.3	9.2	5.0	7.4	1981
MSA[1]	1.7	13.5	14.4	10.3	13.8	16.5	11.2	8.6	4.3	5.6	1983
U.S.	1.2	8.9	13.6	12.8	13.0	14.4	10.0	9.7	4.5	11.9	1980

Note: Figures are percentages except for Median Year; Note: (1) Figures cover the Oklahoma City, OK Metropolitan Statistical Area
Source: U.S. Census Bureau, 2019-2023 American Community Survey 5-Year Estimates

Gross Monthly Rent

Area	Under $500	$500 -$999	$1,000 -$1,499	$1,500 -$1,999	$2,000 -$2,499	$2,500 -$2,999	$3,000 and up	Median ($)
City	5.3	36.3	40.4	13.3	2.8	1.1	0.7	1,083
MSA[1]	5.3	36.8	39.1	13.4	3.1	1.1	1.1	1,081
U.S.	6.5	22.3	29.5	20.2	10.8	4.8	5.9	1,348

Note: Figures are percentages except for median; Gross rent is the contract rent plus the estimated average monthly cost of utilities (electricity, gas, and water and sewer) and fuels (oil, coal, kerosene, wood, etc.) if these are paid by the renter (or paid for the renter by someone else); (1) Figures cover the Oklahoma City, OK Metropolitan Statistical Area
Source: U.S. Census Bureau, 2019-2023 American Community Survey 5-Year Estimates

HEALTH

Health Risk Factors

Category	MSA[1] (%)	U.S. (%)
Adults aged 18–64 who have any kind of health care coverage	86.4	90.8
Adults who reported being in good or better health	81.5	81.8
Adults who have been told they have high blood cholesterol	38.4	36.9
Adults who have been told they have high blood pressure	36.8	34.0
Adults who are current smokers	13.2	12.1
Adults who currently use e-cigarettes	12.0	7.7
Adults who currently use chewing tobacco, snuff, or snus	4.9	3.2
Adults who are heavy drinkers[2]	4.5	6.1
Adults who are binge drinkers[3]	14.6	15.2
Adults who are overweight (BMI 25.0 - 29.9)	32.0	34.4
Adults who are obese (BMI 30.0 - 99.8)	38.5	34.3
Adults who participated in any physical activities in the past month	72.5	75.8

Note: All figures are crude prevalence; (1) Figures cover the Oklahoma City, OK Metropolitan Statistical Area; (2) Heavy drinkers are classified as adult men having more than 14 drinks per week and adult women having more than 7 drinks per week; (3) Binge drinkers are classified as males having five or more drinks on one occasion or females having four or more drinks on one occasion
Source: Centers for Disease Control and Prevention, Behavioral Risk Factor Surveillance System, SMART: Selected Metropolitan Area Risk Trends, 2023

Acute and Chronic Health Conditions

Category	MSA[1] (%)	U.S. (%)
Adults who have ever been told they had a heart attack	4.1	4.2
Adults who have ever been told they have angina or coronary heart disease	5.0	4.0
Adults who have ever been told they had a stroke	3.6	3.3
Adults who have ever been told they have asthma	15.8	15.7
Adults who have ever been told they have arthritis	27.2	26.3
Adults who have ever been told they have diabetes[2]	12.2	11.5
Adults who have ever been told they had skin cancer	4.6	5.6
Adults who have ever been told they had any other types of cancer	6.8	8.4
Adults who have ever been told they have COPD	5.8	6.4
Adults who have ever been told they have kidney disease	4.0	3.7
Adults who have ever been told they have a form of depression	25.0	22.0

Note: All figures are crude prevalence; (1) Figures cover the Oklahoma City, OK Metropolitan Statistical Area; (2) Figures do not include pregnancy-related, borderline, or pre-diabetes
Source: Centers for Disease Control and Prevention, Behaviorial Risk Factor Surveillance System, SMART: Selected Metropolitan Area Risk Trends, 2023

Health Screening and Vaccination Rates

Category	MSA[1] (%)	U.S. (%)
Adults who have ever been tested for HIV	32.6	37.5
Adults who have had their blood cholesterol checked within the last five years	84.4	87.0
Adults aged 65+ who have had flu shot within the past year	63.2	63.4
Adults aged 65+ who have ever had a pneumonia vaccination	72.0	71.9

Note: All figures are crude prevalence; (1) Figures cover the Oklahoma City, OK Metropolitan Statistical Area.
Source: Centers for Disease Control and Prevention, Behaviorial Risk Factor Surveillance System, SMART: Selected Metropolitan Area Risk Trends, 2023

Disability Status

Category	MSA[1] (%)	U.S. (%)
Adults who reported being deaf	8.4	7.4
Are you blind or have serious difficulty seeing, even when wearing glasses?	6.3	4.9
Do you have difficulty doing errands alone?	9.7	7.8
Do you have difficulty dressing or bathing?	3.9	3.6
Do you have serious difficulty concentrating/remembering/making decisions?	17.4	13.7
Do you have serious difficulty walking or climbing stairs?	16.1	13.2

Note: All figures are crude prevalence; (1) Figures cover the Oklahoma City, OK Metropolitan Statistical Area.
Source: Centers for Disease Control and Prevention, Behaviorial Risk Factor Surveillance System, SMART: Selected Metropolitan Area Risk Trends, 2023

Mortality Rates for the Top 10 Causes of Death in the U.S.

ICD-10[a] Sub-Chapter	ICD-10[a] Code	Crude Mortality Rate[2] per 100,000 population	
		County[3]	U.S.
Malignant neoplasms	C00-C97	184.8	182.7
Ischaemic heart diseases	I20-I25	127.7	109.6
Provisional assignment of new diseases of uncertain etiology[1]	U00-U49	75.0	65.3
Other forms of heart disease	I30-I51	42.4	65.1
Other degenerative diseases of the nervous system	G30-G31	62.3	52.4
Other external causes of accidental injury	W00-X59	68.0	52.3
Cerebrovascular diseases	I60-I69	41.6	49.1
Chronic lower respiratory diseases	J40-J47	57.2	43.5
Hypertensive diseases	I10-I15	78.8	38.9
Organic, including symptomatic, mental disorders	F01-F09	27.1	33.9

Note: (a) ICD-10 = International Classification of Diseases 10th Revision; (1) Includes COVID-19, adverse effects to COVID-19 vaccines, SARS, and vaping-related disorders; (2) Crude mortality rates are a three-year average covering 2021-2023; (3) Figures cover Oklahoma County.
Source: Centers for Disease Control and Prevention, National Center for Health Statistics. National Vital Statistics System, Mortality 2018-2023 on CDC WONDER Online Database

Mortality Rates for Selected Causes of Death

Cause of Death	ICD-10[a] Code	Crude Mortality Rate[1] per 100,000 population	
		County[2]	U.S.
Accidental poisoning and exposure to noxious substances	X40-X49	32.2	30.5
Alzheimer disease	G30	35.0	35.4
Assault	X85-Y09	9.9	7.3
COVID-19	U07.1	75.0	65.3
Diabetes mellitus	E10-E14	37.1	30.0
Diseases of the liver	K70-K76	21.5	20.8
Human immunodeficiency virus (HIV) disease	B20-B24	2.9	1.5
Influenza and pneumonia	J09-J18	10.7	13.4
Intentional self-harm	X60-X84	20.4	14.7
Malnutrition	E40-E46	4.1	6.0
Obesity and other hyperalimentation	E65-E68	2.4	3.1
Renal failure	N17-N19	11.3	16.4
Transport accidents	V01-V99	16.3	14.4

Note: (a) ICD-10 = International Classification of Diseases 10th Revision; (1) Crude mortality rates are a three-year average covering 2021-2023; (2) Figures cover Oklahoma County; Data are suppressed when the data meet the criteria for confidentiality constraints; Crude mortality rates are flagged as unreliable when the rate would be calculated with a numerator of 20 or less.
Source: Centers for Disease Control and Prevention, National Center for Health Statistics. National Vital Statistics System, Mortality 2018-2023 on CDC WONDER Online Database

Health Insurance Coverage

Area	With Health Insurance	With Private Health Insurance	With Public Health Insurance	Without Health Insurance	Population Under Age 19 Without Health Insurance
City	86.0	63.0	34.4	14.0	7.6
MSA[1]	87.7	66.8	33.5	12.3	7.3
U.S.	91.4	67.3	36.3	8.6	5.4

Note: Figures are percentages that cover the civilian noninstitutionalized population; (1) Figures cover the Oklahoma City, OK Metropolitan Statistical Area
Source: U.S. Census Bureau, 2019-2023 American Community Survey 5-Year Estimates

Number of Medical Professionals

Area	MDs[3]	DOs[3,4]	Dentists	Podiatrists	Chiropractors	Optometrists
County[1] (number)	3,472	419	902	39	240	172
County[1] (rate[2])	432.6	52.2	111.5	4.8	29.7	21.3
U.S. (rate[2])	302.5	29.2	74.6	6.4	29.5	18.0

Note: Data as of 2023 unless noted; (1) Data covers Oklahoma County; (2) Number of medical professionals per 100,000 population; (3) Data as of 2022 and includes all active, non-federal physicians; (4) Doctor of Osteopathic Medicine
Source: U.S. Department of Health and Human Services, Health Resources and Services Administration, Bureau of Health Professions, Area Resource File (ARF) 2023-2024

Best Hospitals

According to *U.S. News*, the Oklahoma City, OK metro area is home to one of the best hospitals in the U.S.: **Dean McGee Eye Institute** (1 pediatric specialty). The hospital listed was nationally ranked in at least one of 15 adult or 11 pediatric specialties. The number of specialties shown cover the parent hospital. Only 160 U.S. hospitals performed well enough to be nationally ranked in one or more specialties. Twenty hospitals in the U.S. made the Honor Roll. The Best Hospitals Honor Roll takes both the national rankings and the procedure and condition ratings into account. Hospitals received points if they were nationally ranked in one of the 15 adult specialties—the higher they ranked, the more points they got—and how many ratings of "high performing" they earned in the 20 procedures and conditions. *U.S. News Online, "America's Best Hospitals 2024-25"*

According to *U.S. News*, the Oklahoma City, OK metro area is home to one of the best children's hospitals in the U.S.: **Oklahoma Children's Hospital OU Health** (1 pediatric specialty). The hospital listed was highly ranked in at least one of 11 pediatric specialties. One hundred five children's hospitals in the U.S. were nationally ranked in at least one specialty. Hospitals received points for being ranked in a specialty, and the 10 hospitals with the most points across the 11 specialties make up the Honor Roll. *U.S. News Online, "America's Best Children's Hospitals 2024-25"*

EDUCATION

Public School District Statistics

District Name	Schls	Pupils	Pupil/ Teacher Ratio	Minority Pupils[1] (%)	Total Rev. per Pupil ($)	Total Exp. per Pupil ($)
Epic One On One Charter School	2	27,052	22.7	49.5	6,965	6,980
Oklahoma City	58	32,899	15.4	88.8	15,348	14,864
Santa Fe South Charter	10	4,290	17.2	98.1	10,655	10,404
Western Heights	8	2,888	14.6	84.6	17,475	16,628

Note: Table includes school districts with 2,000 or more students; (1) Percentage of students that are not non-Hispanic white.
Source: U.S. Department of Education, National Center for Education Statistics, Common Core of Data, Local Education Agency (School District) Universe Survey: School Year 2023-2024; U.S. Department of Education, National Center for Education Statistics, Common Core of Data, School District Finance Survey (F-33): School Year 2021–22

Highest Level of Education

Area	Less than H.S.	H.S. Diploma	Some College, No Deg.	Associate Degree	Bachelor's Degree	Master's Degree	Prof. School Degree	Doctorate Degree
City	12.2	24.5	21.3	8.0	21.5	8.5	2.6	1.3
MSA[1]	10.1	26.2	22.3	8.0	21.3	8.4	2.2	1.5
U.S.	10.6	26.2	19.4	8.8	21.3	9.8	2.3	1.6

Note: Figures cover persons age 25 and over; (1) Figures cover the Oklahoma City, OK Metropolitan Statistical Area
Source: U.S. Census Bureau, 2019-2023 American Community Survey 5-Year Estimates

Educational Attainment by Race

Area	High School Graduate or Higher (%)					Bachelor's Degree or Higher (%)				
	Total	White	Black	Asian	Hisp.[2]	Total	White	Black	Asian	Hisp.[2]
City	87.8	91.4	90.7	81.6	61.7	34.0	38.4	26.1	48.0	12.8
MSA[1]	89.9	92.3	91.0	83.8	65.5	33.4	36.0	25.3	50.9	14.8
U.S.	89.4	92.9	88.1	88.0	72.5	35.0	37.7	24.7	57.0	19.9

Note: Figures shown cover persons 25 years old and over; (1) Figures cover the Oklahoma City, OK Metropolitan Statistical Area; (2) People of Hispanic origin can be of any race
Source: U.S. Census Bureau, 2019-2023 American Community Survey 5-Year Estimates

School Enrollment by Grade and Control

Area	Preschool (%)		Kindergarten (%)		Grades 1 - 4 (%)		Grades 5 - 8 (%)		Grades 9 - 12 (%)	
	Public	Private	Public	Private	Public	Private	Public	Private	Public	Private
City	69.7	30.3	86.9	13.1	87.9	12.1	86.4	13.6	86.9	13.1
MSA[1]	70.9	29.1	86.9	13.1	87.7	12.3	87.4	12.6	87.8	12.2
U.S.	58.7	41.3	85.2	14.8	87.2	12.8	87.9	12.1	89.0	11.0

Note: Figures shown cover persons 3 years old and over; (1) Figures cover the Oklahoma City, OK Metropolitan Statistical Area
Source: U.S. Census Bureau, 2019-2023 American Community Survey 5-Year Estimates

Higher Education

Four-Year Colleges			Two-Year Colleges			Medical Schools[1]	Law Schools[2]	Voc/ Tech[3]
Public	Private Non-profit	Private For-profit	Public	Private Non-profit	Private For-profit			
6	6	0	6	0	1	1	2	10

Note: Figures cover institutions located within the Oklahoma City, OK Metropolitan Statistical Area and include main campuses only; (1) includes schools accredited by the Liaison Committee on Medical Education and the American Osteopathic Association's Commission on Osteopathic College Accreditation; (2) includes ABA-accredited schools, schools with provisional ABA accreditation, and state accredited schools; (3) includes all schools with programs that are less than 2 years.
Source: National Center for Education Statistics, Integrated Postsecondary Education System (IPEDS), 2023-24; Wikipedia, List of Medical Schools in the United States, accessed May 2, 2025; Wikipedia, List of Law Schools in the United States, accessed May 2, 2025

According to *U.S. News & World Report*, the Oklahoma City, OK metro area is home to one of the top 200 national universities in the U.S.: **University of Oklahoma** (#132 tie). The indicators used to capture academic quality fall into a number of categories: assessment by administrators at peer institutions; retention of students; faculty resources; student selectivity; financial resources; alumni giving; high school counselor ratings of colleges; and graduation rate. *U.S. News & World Report, "America's Best Colleges 2025"*

According to *U.S. News & World Report*, the Oklahoma City, OK metro area is home to one of the top 100 law schools in the U.S.: **University of Oklahoma** (#59 tie). The rankings are based on a weighted average of 12 measures of quality: peer assessment score; assessment score by lawyers/judges; median LSAT scores; median undergrad GPA; acceptance rate; employment rates for graduates; placement success; bar passage rate; faculty resources; expenditures per student; stu-

EMPLOYERS

Major Employers

Company Name	Industry
AT&T	Telecommunications
Chesapeake Energy Corp	Oil & gas
City of Oklahoma City	Municipal government
Devon Energy Corp	Oil & gas
FAA Mike Monroney Aeronautical Center	Aerospace
Hobby Lobby Stores	Wholesale & retail
INTEGRIS Health	Healthcare
Mercy Health Center	Healthcare
Norman Regional Hospital	Healthcare
OGE Energy Corp	Utilities
Oklahoma City Community College	Education
OU Medical Center	Healthcare
Sonic Corp	Wholesale & retail
SSM Health Care of Oklahoma	Healthcare
State of Oklahoma	State government
The Boeing Company	Aerospace
Tinker Air Force Base	U.S. military
University of Central Oklahoma	Higher education
University of Oklahoma - Norman	Higher education
University of Oklahoma Health Sci Ctr	Higher education

Note: Companies shown are located within the Oklahoma City, OK Metropolitan Statistical Area.
Source: Chambers of Commerce; State Departments of Labor; Wikipedia

Best Companies to Work For

American Fidelity Assurance Company, headquartered in Oklahoma City, is among "Fortune's Best Workplaces for Parents." To pick the best companies, *Fortune* partnered with the Great Place to Work Institute. To be considered for the list, companies must be Great Place To Work-Certified and have at least 50 responses from parents in the US. The survey enables employees to share confidential quantitative and qualitative feedback about their organization's culture by responding to 60 statements on a 5-point scale and answering two open-ended questions. Collectively, these statements describe a great employee experience, defined by high levels of trust, respect, credibility, fairness, pride, and camaraderie. In addition, companies provide organizational data like size, location, industry, demographics, roles, and levels; and provide information about parental leave, adoption, flexible schedule, childcare and dependent health care benefits. *Fortune, "Best Workplaces for Parents," 2024*

180 Medical; American Fidelity Assurance Company, headquartered in Oklahoma City, are among "Fortune's Best Workplaces for Women." To pick the best companies, *Fortune* partnered with the Great Place to Work Institute. To be considered for the list, companies must be Great Place To Work-Certified. Companies must also employ at least 50 women, at least 20% of their non-executive managers must be female, and at least one executive must be female. To determine the Best Workplaces for Women, Great Place To Work measured the differences in women's survey responses to those of their peers and assesses the impact of demographics and roles on the quality and consistency of women's experiences. Great Place To Work also analyzed the gender balance of each workplace, how it compared to each company's industry, and patterns in representation as women rise from front-line positions to the board of directors. *Fortune, "Best Workplaces for Women," 2024*

American Fidelity, headquartered in Oklahoma City, is among the "Best Places to Work in IT." To qualify, companies had to have a minimum of 100 total employees and five IT employees. The best places to work were selected based on DEI (diversity, equity, and inclusion) practices; IT turnover, promotions, and growth; IT retention and engagement programs; remote/hybrid working; benefits and perks (such as elder care and child care, flextime, and reimbursement for college tuition); and training and career development opportunities. *Computerworld, "Best Places to Work in IT," 2025*

PUBLIC SAFETY

Crime Rate

Area	Total Crime Rate	Violent Crime Rate				Property Crime Rate		
		Murder	Rape	Robbery	Aggrav. Assault	Burglary	Larceny-Theft	Motor Vehicle Theft
City	3,571.8	9.0	68.9	88.0	471.6	566.1	1,965.4	402.7
U.S.	2,290.9	5.7	38.0	66.5	264.1	250.7	1,347.2	318.7

Note: Figures are crimes per 100,000 population.
Source: FBI, Table 8, Offenses Known to Law Enforcement, by State by City, 2023

Hate Crimes

Area	Number of Quarters Reported	Number of Incidents per Bias Motivation					
		Race/Ethnicity/Ancestry	Religion	Sexual Orientation	Disability	Gender	Gender Identity
City[1]	4	25	1	3	0	0	1
U.S.	4	5,900	2,699	2,077	187	92	492

Note: (1) Figures include at least one incident reported with more than one bias motivation.
Source: Federal Bureau of Investigation, Hate Crime Statistics 2023

Identity Theft Consumer Reports

Area	Reports	Reports per 100,000 Population	Rank[2]
MSA[1]	2,968	205	148
U.S.	1,135,291	339	-

Note: (1) Figures cover the Oklahoma City, OK Metropolitan Statistical Area; (2) Rank ranges from 1 to 401 where 1 indicates greatest number of identity theft reports per 100,000 population
Source: Federal Trade Commission, Consumer Sentinel Network Data Book 2024

Fraud and Other Consumer Reports

Area	Reports	Reports per 100,000 Population	Rank[2]
MSA[1]	15,385	1,065	181
U.S.	5,360,641	1,601	-

Note: (1) Figures cover the Oklahoma City, OK Metropolitan Statistical Area; (2) Rank ranges from 1 to 401 where 1 indicates greatest number of fraud and other consumer reports per 100,000 population
Source: Federal Trade Commission, Consumer Sentinel Network Data Book 2024

POLITICS

2024 Presidential Election Results

Area	Trump (Rep.)	Harris (Dem.)	Stein (Green)	Kennedy (Ind.)	Oliver (Lib.)	Other
Oklahoma County	49.7	48.0	0.0	1.1	0.8	0.4
U.S.	49.7	48.2	0.6	0.5	0.4	0.6

Note: Results are percentages and may not add to 100% due to rounding
Source: Dave Leip's Atlas of U.S. Presidential Elections

SPORTS

Professional Sports Teams

Team Name	League	Year Established
Oklahoma City Thunder	National Basketball Association (NBA)	2008

Note: Includes teams located in the Oklahoma City, OK Metropolitan Statistical Area.
Source: Wikipedia, Major Professional Sports Teams of the United States and Canada, May 1, 2025

CLIMATE

Average and Extreme Temperatures

Temperature	Jan	Feb	Mar	Apr	May	Jun	Jul	Aug	Sep	Oct	Nov	Dec	Yr.
Extreme High (°F)	80	84	93	100	104	105	109	110	104	96	87	86	110
Average High (°F)	47	52	61	72	79	87	93	92	84	74	60	50	71
Average Temp. (°F)	36	41	50	60	69	77	82	81	73	62	49	40	60
Average Low (°F)	26	30	38	49	58	66	71	70	62	51	38	29	49
Extreme Low (°F)	-4	-3	1	20	32	47	53	51	36	22	11	-8	-8

Note: Figures cover the years 1948-1990
Source: National Climatic Data Center, International Station Meteorological Climate Summary, 9/96

Average Precipitation/Snowfall/Humidity

Precip./Humidity	Jan	Feb	Mar	Apr	May	Jun	Jul	Aug	Sep	Oct	Nov	Dec	Yr.
Avg. Precip. (in.)	1.2	1.5	2.5	2.8	5.6	4.4	2.8	2.5	3.5	3.1	1.6	1.3	32.8
Avg. Snowfall (in.)	3	3	2	Tr	0	0	0	0	0	Tr	1	2	10
Avg. Rel. Hum. 6am (%)	78	78	76	77	84	84	81	81	82	79	78	77	80
Avg. Rel. Hum. 3pm (%)	53	52	47	46	52	51	46	44	47	46	48	52	49

Note: Figures cover the years 1948-1990; Tr = Trace amounts (<0.05 in. of rain; <0.5 in. of snow)
Source: National Climatic Data Center, International Station Meteorological Climate Summary, 9/96

Weather Conditions

Temperature			Daytime Sky			Precipitation		
10°F & below	32°F & below	90°F & above	Clear	Partly cloudy	Cloudy	0.01 inch or more precip.	0.1 inch or more snow/ice	Thunderstorms
5	79	70	124	131	110	80	8	50

Note: Figures are average number of days per year and cover the years 1948-1990
Source: National Climatic Data Center, International Station Meteorological Climate Summary, 9/96

HAZARDOUS WASTE

Superfund Sites

The Oklahoma City, OK metro area is home to three sites on the EPA's Superfund National Priorities List (NPL) or Superfund Alternative Approach (SAA) list: **Eagle Industries** (Final NPL); **Hardage/Criner** (Final NPL); **Tinker Air Force Base (Soldier Creek/Building 3001)** (Final NPL). The Superfund alternative approach uses the same investigation and cleanup process and standards that are used for sites listed on the National Priorities List. The SAA is an alternative to listing a site on the NPL; it is not an alternative to Superfund or the Superfund process. There are a total of 1,445 Superfund sites with a status of proposed or final on both lists in the United States. *U.S. Environmental Protection Agency, National Priorities List, May 1, 2025; U.S. Environmental Protection Agency, Superfund Alternative Approach Sites, May 1, 2025*

AIR QUALITY

Air Quality Trends: Ozone

	1990	1995	2000	2005	2010	2015	2020	2021	2022	2023
MSA[1]	0.080	0.087	0.083	0.077	0.071	0.067	0.066	0.068	0.071	0.072
U.S.	0.087	0.089	0.081	0.080	0.072	0.068	0.066	0.067	0.067	0.070

Note: (1) Data covers the Oklahoma City, OK Metropolitan Statistical Area. The values shown are the composite ozone concentration averages among trend sites based on the highest fourth daily maximum 8-hour concentration in parts per million. These trends are based on sites having an adequate record of monitoring data during the trend period. Data from exceptional events are included.
Source: U.S. Environmental Protection Agency, Air Quality Monitoring Information, "Air Quality Trends by City, 1990-2023"

Air Quality Index

Area	Percent of Days when Air Quality was...[2]					AQI Statistics[2]	
	Good	Moderate	Unhealthy for Sensitive Groups	Unhealthy	Very Unhealthy	Maximum	Median
MSA[1]	35.1	60.8	4.1	0.0	0.0	143	54

Note: (1) Data covers the Oklahoma City, OK Metropolitan Statistical Area; (2) Based on 365 days with AQI data in 2023. Air Quality Index (AQI) is an index for reporting daily air quality. EPA calculates the AQI for five major air pollutants regulated by the Clean Air Act: ground-level ozone, particle pollution (aka particulate matter), carbon monoxide, sulfur dioxide, and nitrogen dioxide. The AQI runs from 0 to 500. The higher the AQI value, the greater the level of air pollution and the greater the health concern. There are six AQI categories: "Good" AQI is between 0 and 50. Air quality is considered satisfactory; "Moderate" AQI is between 51 and 100. Air quality is acceptable; "Unhealthy for Sensitive Groups" When AQI values are between 101 and 150, members of sensitive groups may experience health effects; "Unhealthy" When AQI values are between 151 and 200 everyone may begin to experience health effects; "Very Unhealthy" AQI values between 201 and 300 trigger a health alert; "Hazardous" AQI values over 300 trigger warnings of emergency conditions (not shown).
Source: U.S. Environmental Protection Agency, Air Quality Index Report, 2023

Air Quality Index Pollutants

Area	Percent of Days when AQI Pollutant was...[2]					
	Carbon Monoxide	Nitrogen Dioxide	Ozone	Sulfur Dioxide	Particulate Matter 2.5	Particulate Matter 10
MSA[1]	0.0	2.2	42.7	(3)	54.2	0.8

Note: (1) Data covers the Oklahoma City, OK Metropolitan Statistical Area; (2) Based on 365 days with AQI data in 2023. The Air Quality Index (AQI) is an index for reporting daily air quality. EPA calculates the AQI for five major air pollutants regulated by the Clean Air Act: ground-level ozone, particle pollution (also known as particulate matter), carbon monoxide, sulfur dioxide, and nitrogen dioxide. The AQI runs from 0 to 500. The higher the AQI value, the greater the level of air pollution and the greater the health concern; (3) Sulfur dioxide is no longer included in this table because SO_2 concentrations tend to be very localized and not necessarily representative of broad geographical areas like counties and CBSAs.
Source: U.S. Environmental Protection Agency, Air Quality Index Report, 2023

Maximum Air Pollutant Concentrations: Particulate Matter, Ozone, CO and Lead

	Particulate Matter 10 (ug/m³)	Particulate Matter 2.5 Wtd AM (ug/m³)	Particulate Matter 2.5 24-Hr (ug/m³)	Ozone (ppm)	Carbon Monoxide (ppm)	Lead (ug/m³)
MSA[1] Level	89	9.2	21	0.074	1	n/a
NAAQS[2]	150	15	35	0.075	9	0.15
Met NAAQS[2]	Yes	Yes	Yes	Yes	Yes	n/a

Note: (1) Data covers the Oklahoma City, OK Metropolitan Statistical Area; Data from exceptional events are included; (2) National Ambient Air Quality Standards; ppm = parts per million; ug/m³ = micrograms per cubic meter; n/a not available.
Concentrations: Particulate Matter 10 (coarse particulate)—highest second maximum 24-hour concentration; Particulate Matter 2.5 Wtd AM (fine particulate)—highest weighted annual mean concentration; Particulate Matter 2.5 24-Hour (fine particulate)—highest 98th percentile 24-hour concentration; Ozone—highest fourth daily maximum 8-hour concentration; Carbon Monoxide—highest second maximum non-overlapping 8-hour concentration; Lead—maximum running 3-month average
Source: U.S. Environmental Protection Agency, Air Quality Monitoring Information, "Air Quality Statistics by City, 2023"

Maximum Air Pollutant Concentrations: Nitrogen Dioxide and Sulfur Dioxide

	Nitrogen Dioxide AM (ppb)	Nitrogen Dioxide 1-Hr (ppb)	Sulfur Dioxide AM (ppb)	Sulfur Dioxide 1-Hr (ppb)	Sulfur Dioxide 24-Hr (ppb)
MSA[1] Level	12	29	n/a	1	n/a
NAAQS[2]	53	100	30	75	140
Met NAAQS[2]	Yes	Yes	n/a	Yes	n/a

Note: (1) Data covers the Oklahoma City, OK Metropolitan Statistical Area; Data from exceptional events are included; (2) National Ambient Air Quality Standards; ppm = parts per million; ug/m³ = micrograms per cubic meter; n/a not available.
Concentrations: Nitrogen Dioxide AM—highest arithmetic mean concentration; Nitrogen Dioxide 1-Hr—highest 98th percentile 1-hour daily maximum concentration; Sulfur Dioxide AM—highest annual mean concentration; Sulfur Dioxide 1-Hr—highest 99th percentile 1-hour daily maximum concentration; Sulfur Dioxide 24-Hr—highest second maximum 24-hour concentration
Source: U.S. Environmental Protection Agency, Air Quality Monitoring Information, "Air Quality Statistics by City, 2023"

Omaha, Nebraska

Background

Omaha is centrally located in the heartland of the United States on the western banks of the Missouri River. It's been a significant agricultural and transportation center since its establishment in 1854, established early on as a trading center and "Gateway to the West." From these roots, Omaha has seen steady growth.

The city is home to five Fortune 500 companies, including Mutual of Omaha, Union Pacific Railroad, ConAgra Foods, Peter Kiewit Sons, and Berkshire Hathaway, owned by Warren Buffet, recognized as one of the richest men in the world.

The headquarters of insurance companies, direct response/telemarketing centers and other national and international firms call Omaha home. The city is also a regional service and trade center with these segments comprising nearly 60 percent of metro area employment.

Omaha is large enough to offer a variety of cosmopolitan attractions, yet small enough to provide a relaxed lifestyle. Residents enjoy a variety of recreational activities and a low cost of living, excellent health care and low crime.

The Omaha metropolitan area is served by several public and private school systems, and offers 11 colleges and universities, including Gallup University, whose Riverfront Campus opened in 2013 and houses Gallup Poll Service, Gallup Performance Management Systems, and an international management education program.

The community also has access to excellent cultural programs, including the professional Omaha Symphony, Omaha Theater Ballet, and Opera Omaha. Performances by these groups and other touring companies are held in the magnificent Orpheum Theater, a restored 1920s vaudeville venue. The Bemis Center for Contemporary Arts, the largest urban artist colony in the world, plays host to artists from all over the world.

Omaha is home to world-famous Father Flanagan's Boys and Girls Town, and the award-winning Henry Doorly Zoo and Aquarium, which includes the world's largest indoor rainforest and a collection of rare white tigers. Other attractions include the Strategic Air & Space Museum and the birthplaces of Malcom X and former President Gerald R. Ford.

Around the start of the 21st century, several downtown skyscrapers and cultural institutions were built. One First National Center was completed in 2002, surpassing the Woodmen Tower as the tallest building in Omaha and the state at 634 feet. The creation of the city's new North Downtown included the construction of the CenturyLink Center and the Slowdown/Film Streams development at North 14th and Webster Streets. Construction of TD Ameritrade Park (now known as Charles Schwab Field Omaha), also in the North Downtown area, began in 2009 and was completed in 2011. Charles Schwab Field Omaha is now the home of the College World Series, an event tourists flock to each year. The Union Pacific Center and the Holland Performing Arts Center opened in 2004 and 2005, respectively.

The Midwestern headquarters for the National Park Service is in Omaha, the first building in Nebraska to be rated tops under the Leadership in Energy and Environmental Design system, or LEED. The nearby Riverfront Place is a six-acre urban neighborhood that includes residential units, commercial space, a public plaza, riverfront access, and connections to miles of walking trails.

Omaha's weather shows the usual contrasts of a continental climate, with cold, dry winters and warm summers. Situated between two climatic zones, the humid east and the dry west, fluctuation between these zones results in weather characteristic of either, or combinations of both. Most precipitation falls between April and September in the form of severe thunderstorms or evening lightning shows.

Rankings

General Rankings

- To help military veterans find the best places in which to settle down, *WalletHub* compared the 100 largest U.S. cities across 19 key indicators of livability, affordability and veteran-friendliness. They range from the share of military skill-related jobs to veteran income growth to the availability of VA health facilities. Omaha ranked #48. *Wallethub.com, "Best & Worst Places for Veterans to Live (2025)," November 7, 2024*

- *US News & World Report* conducted a survey of more than 3,500 people and analyzed the 150 largest metropolitan areas to determine what matters most when selecting the next place to live. Omaha ranked #18 out of the top 25 as having the best combination of desirable factors. Criteria: cost of living; quality of life and education; climate; job market; desirability; and other factors. *realestate.usnews.com, "Best Places to Live in the U.S. in 2024-2025," May 21, 2024*

- In their annual survey, Livability.com looked at data for more than 2,000 mid-sized U.S. cities to assign a "Livability Score" for each. The top 100 scoring cities make up Livability's "Top 100 Best Places to Live in the U.S." in 2025. Omaha was placed among the top 100 of the customizable list. Criteria: housing and economy; cost of living; environment; education; health care options; transportation; safety; and community amenities. *Livability.com, "Top 100 Best Places to Live in the U.S. in 2025" April 15, 2025*

Business/Finance Rankings

- The Omaha metro area appeared on the Milken Institute "2025 Best Performing Cities" list. Rank: #97 out of 200 large metro areas (based on performance category). Criteria: job growth; wage growth; high-tech growth and impact; community resilience; housing affordability; household broadband access. *Milken Institute, "Best-Performing Cities 2025," January 14, 2025*

Education Rankings

- Personal finance website *WalletHub* analyzed the 150 largest U.S. metropolitan statistical areas to determine where the most educated Americans are putting their degrees to work. Criteria: education levels; percentage of workers with degrees; education quality and attainment gap; public school quality rankings; quality and enrollment of each metro area's universities. Omaha was ranked #38 (#1 = most educated city). *WalletHub.com, "Most & Least Educated Cities in America, 2025" July 2, 2024*

Health/Fitness Rankings

- For each of the 100 largest cities in the United States, the American Fitness Index®, compiled in partnership between the American College of Sports Medicine and the Elevance Health Foundation, evaluated community infrastructure and more than 30 health behaviors including preventive health, levels of chronic disease conditions, food insecurity, pedestrian safety, air quality, and community/environment resources that support physical activity. Omaha ranked #51 for "community fitness." *americanfitnessindex.org, "2024 ACSM American Fitness Index Summary Report," July 23, 2024*

- The Omaha metro area was identified as one of the worst cities for bed bugs in America by pest control company Orkin. The area ranked #36 out of 50 based on the number of bed bug treatments Orkin performed from December 2022 to November 2023. *Orkin, "Chicago Joins Paris In Global Bed Bug Spotlight Ranking As The Worst City On Orkin's U.S. Bed Bug Cities List," January 22, 2024*

- Omaha was identified as a "2025 Allergy Capital." The area ranked #61 out of the nation's 100 largest metropolitan areas. Three groups of factors were used to identify the most challenging cities for people with allergies: annual tree, grass, and weed pollen scores; over the counter allergy medicine use; number of board-certified allergy specialists. *Asthma and Allergy Foundation of America, "2025 Allergy Capitals: The Most Challenging Places to Live with Allergies," March 18, 2025*

- Omaha was identified as a "2024 Asthma Capital." The area ranked #34 out of the nation's 100 largest metropolitan areas. Criteria: estimated asthma prevalence; asthma-related mortality; and ER visits due to asthma. Risk factors analyzed but not factored in the rankings: annual air quality including pollution and ozone levels; public smoking laws; indoor air quality; access to asthma specialists; rescue and controller medication use; uninsured rate; pollen allergy; poverty rate. *Asthma and Allergy Foundation of America, "Asthma Capitals 2024: The Most Challenging Places to Live With Asthma," September 10, 2024*

Real Estate Rankings

- *WalletHub* compared the most populated U.S. cities to determine which had the best markets for real estate agents. Omaha ranked #42 where demand was high and pay was the best. Criteria: sales per agent; annual median wage for real-estate agents; monthly average starting salary for real estate agents; real estate job density and competition; unemployment rate; home turnover rate; housing-market health index; and other relevant metrics. *WalletHub.com, "2021 Best Places to Be a Real Estate Agent," May 12, 2021*

- Omaha was ranked #52 out of 176 metro areas in terms of cost of housing in 2024 by the National Association of Home Builders (#1 = most affordable). Criteria: the portion of an average family's income necessary to pay the mortgage on a median-priced home. *National Association of Home Builders®, NAHB-Wells Fargo Cost of Housing Index, 4th Quarter 2024*

Safety Rankings

- Allstate ranked the 100 most populous cities in America in terms of driver safety. Omaha ranked #71. Criteria based on anonymized driving behavior data from Allstate's mobile app powered by Arity: high speed driving (over 80 mph), phone handling, and hard braking. The report helps increase the importance of safety and awareness behind the wheel. *Allstate, "16th Allstate America's Best Drivers Report®" July 11, 2024*

Women/Minorities Rankings

- Personal finance website *WalletHub* compared more than 180 U.S. cities across two key dimensions, "Hispanic Business-Friendliness" and "Hispanic Purchasing Power," to arrive at the most favorable conditions for Hispanic entrepreneurs. Omaha was ranked #110 out of 182. Criteria includes: share of Hispanic-Owned Businesses; average growth of Hispanic Business revenues; Small Business-Friendliness score; affordability; and number of Hispanics with at least a bachelor's degree. *WalletHub.com, "Best Cities for Hispanic Entrepreneurs," September 4, 2024*

Miscellaneous Rankings

- *WalletHub* compared 148 of the most populated U.S. cities to determine their operating efficiency. A "Quality of Services" score was constructed for each city and then measured against the total budget per capita to reveal which were managed the best. Omaha ranked #72. Criteria: financial stability; economy; education; safety; health; infrastructure and pollution. *WalletHub.com, "2025's Best- & Worst-Run Cities in America," June 18, 2024*

Business Environment

DEMOGRAPHICS

Population Growth

Area	1990 Census	2000 Census	2010 Census	2020 Census	2023 Estimate[2]	Population Growth 1990-2023 (%)
City	371,972	390,007	408,958	486,051	488,197	31.2
MSA[1]	685,797	767,041	865,350	967,604	972,840	41.9
U.S.	248,709,873	281,421,906	308,745,538	331,449,281	332,387,540	33.6

Note: (1) Figures cover the Omaha, NE-IA Metropolitan Statistical Area; (2) 2019-2023 5-year ACS population estimate
Source: U.S. Census Bureau, 1990 Census, 2000 Census, 2010 Census, 2020 Census, 2019-2023 American Community Survey 5-Year Estimates

Race

Area	White Alone[2] (%)	Black Alone[2] (%)	Asian Alone[2] (%)	AIAN[3] Alone[2] (%)	NHOPI[4] Alone[2] (%)	Other Race Alone[2] (%)	Two or More Races (%)
City	68.8	11.8	4.0	0.8	0.0	5.0	9.7
MSA[1]	77.1	7.4	3.2	0.6	0.1	3.7	7.9
U.S.	63.4	12.4	5.8	0.9	0.2	6.6	10.7

Note: (1) Figures cover the Omaha, NE-IA Metropolitan Statistical Area; (2) Alone is defined as not being in combination with one or more other races; (3) American Indian and Alaska Native; (4) Native Hawaiian and Other Pacific Islander
Source: U.S. Census Bureau, 2019-2023 American Community Survey 5-Year Estimates

Hispanic or Latino Origin

Area	Total (%)	Mexican (%)	Puerto Rican (%)	Cuban (%)	Other (%)
City	15.6	11.4	0.5	0.2	3.5
MSA[1]	11.9	8.7	0.4	0.2	2.6
U.S.	19.0	11.3	1.8	0.7	5.2

Note: Persons of Hispanic or Latino origin can be of any race; (1) Figures cover the Omaha, NE-IA Metropolitan Statistical Area
Source: U.S. Census Bureau, 2019-2023 American Community Survey 5-Year Estimates

Age

Area	Percent of Population									Median Age
	Under Age 5	Age 5–19	Age 20–34	Age 35–44	Age 45–54	Age 55–64	Age 65–74	Age 75–84	Age 85+	
City	6.8	20.5	22.4	13.6	11.2	11.4	8.7	3.9	1.5	35.3
MSA[1]	6.6	21.3	20.0	13.9	11.7	12.0	8.9	4.0	1.6	36.5
U.S.	5.7	19.1	20.2	13.1	12.3	12.8	10.0	4.9	1.9	38.7

Note: (1) Figures cover the Omaha, NE-IA Metropolitan Statistical Area
Source: U.S. Census Bureau, 2019-2023 American Community Survey 5-Year Estimates

Disability by Age

Area	All Ages	Under 18 Years Old	18 to 64 Years Old	65 Years and Over
City	11.1	3.8	9.8	30.2
MSA[1]	11.2	3.8	9.7	31.0
U.S.	13.0	4.7	10.7	32.9

Note: Figures show percent of the civilian noninstitutionalized population that reported having a disability. Disability status is determined from six types of difficulty: vision, hearing, cognitive, ambulatory, self-care, and independent living. For children under 5 years old, hearing and vision difficulty are used to determine disability status. For children between the ages of 5 and 14, disability status is determined from hearing, vision, cognitive, ambulatory, and self-care difficulties. For people aged 15 years and older, they are considered to have a disability if they have difficulty with any one of the six difficulty types; Note: (1) Figures cover the Omaha, NE-IA Metropolitan Statistical Area
Source: U.S. Census Bureau, 2019-2023 American Community Survey 5-Year Estimates

Ancestry

Area	German	Irish	English	American	Italian	Polish	French[2]	European	Scottish
City	24.8	12.8	8.4	2.7	3.7	3.3	1.9	1.6	1.8
MSA[1]	27.8	12.9	9.7	3.5	3.7	3.5	1.8	1.7	1.6
U.S.	12.6	9.4	9.1	5.5	4.9	2.6	2.0	1.6	1.6

Note: Figures are the percentage of the total population reporting a particular ancestry. The nine most commonly reported ancestries in the U.S. are shown. Figures include multiple ancestries (e.g. if a person reported being Irish and Italian, they were included in both columns); (1) Figures cover the Omaha, NE-IA Metropolitan Statistical Area; (2) Excludes Basque
Source: U.S. Census Bureau, 2019-2023 American Community Survey 5-Year Estimates

Foreign-born Population

Area	Percent of Population Born in								
	Any Foreign Country	Asia	Mexico	Europe	Caribbean	Central America[2]	South America	Africa	Canada
City	11.0	3.3	3.4	0.6	0.2	1.5	0.3	1.5	0.2
MSA[1]	7.9	2.6	2.4	0.6	0.2	0.9	0.3	1.0	0.1
U.S.	13.9	4.3	3.3	1.4	1.4	1.2	1.2	0.8	0.2

Note: (1) Figures cover the Omaha, NE-IA Metropolitan Statistical Area; (2) Excludes Mexico.
Source: U.S. Census Bureau, 2019-2023 American Community Survey 5-Year Estimates

Household Size

Area	Persons in Household (%)							Average Household Size
	One	Two	Three	Four	Five	Six	Seven or More	
City	34.5	31.5	13.1	10.7	6.0	2.5	1.7	2.39
MSA[1]	29.6	33.1	14.3	12.3	6.6	2.5	1.5	2.49
U.S.	28.5	33.8	15.4	12.7	5.9	2.3	1.4	2.54

Note: (1) Figures cover the Omaha, NE-IA Metropolitan Statistical Area
Source: U.S. Census Bureau, 2019-2023 American Community Survey 5-Year Estimates

Household Relationships

Area	Householder	Opposite-sex Spouse	Same-sex Spouse	Opposite-sex Unmarried Partner	Same-sex Unmarried Partner	Child[2]	Grandchild	Other Relatives	Non-relatives
City	39.8	16.0	0.2	2.8	0.2	29.6	1.8	3.7	3.6
MSA[1]	38.8	18.4	0.2	2.6	0.1	30.6	1.6	3.1	2.8
U.S.	38.3	17.5	0.2	2.5	0.2	28.3	2.4	4.8	3.4

Note: Figures are percent of the total population; (1) Figures cover the Omaha, NE-IA Metropolitan Statistical Area; (2) Includes biological, adopted, and stepchildren of the householder
Source: U.S. Census Bureau, 2020 Census

Gender

Area	Males	Females	Males per 100 Females
City	242,508	245,689	98.7
MSA[1]	485,489	487,351	99.6
U.S.	164,545,087	167,842,453	98.0

Note: (1) Figures cover the Omaha, NE-IA Metropolitan Statistical Area
Source: U.S. Census Bureau, 2019-2023 American Community Survey 5-Year Estimates

Marital Status

Area	Never Married	Now Married[2]	Separated	Widowed	Divorced
City	37.9	45.3	1.2	4.7	11.0
MSA[1]	32.4	51.2	1.1	4.6	10.8
U.S.	34.1	47.9	1.7	5.6	10.7

Note: Figures are percentages and cover the population 15 years of age and older; (1) Figures cover the Omaha, NE-IA Metropolitan Statistical Area; (2) Excludes separated
Source: U.S. Census Bureau, 2019-2023 American Community Survey 5-Year Estimates

Religious Groups by Family

Area	Catholic	Baptist	Methodist	LDS[2]	Pentecostal	Lutheran	Islam	Adventist	Other
MSA[1]	19.9	2.8	2.8	1.6	1.0	6.1	0.2	1.0	9.0
U.S.	18.7	7.3	3.0	2.0	1.8	1.7	1.3	1.3	11.6

Note: Figures are the number of adherents as a percentage of the total population and cover the eight largest religious groups in the U.S; (1) Figures cover the Omaha, NE-IA Metropolitan Statistical Area; (2) Church of Jesus Christ of Latter-day Saints
Sources: 2020 U.S. Religion Census, Association of Statisticians of American Religious Bodies; The Association of Religion Data Archives (ARDA)

Religious Groups by Tradition

Area	Catholic	Evangelical Protestant	Mainline Protestant	Black Protestant	Islam	Judaism	Hinduism	Orthodox	Buddhism
MSA[1]	19.9	10.8	7.9	1.5	0.2	0.3	1.0	0.2	0.2
U.S.	18.7	16.5	5.2	2.3	1.3	0.6	0.4	0.4	0.3

Note: Figures are the number of adherents as a percentage of the total population; (1) Figures cover the Omaha, NE-IA Metropolitan Statistical Area
Sources: 2020 U.S. Religion Census, Association of Statisticians of American Religious Bodies; The Association of Religion Data Archives (ARDA)

ECONOMY

Real Gross Domestic Product (GDP)

Area	2017	2018	2019	2020	2021	2022	2023	Rank[3]
MSA[1]	64.3	65.7	66.4	65.2	68.9	73.7	75.3	50
U.S.[2]	17,619.1	18,160.7	18,642.5	18,238.9	19,387.6	19,896.6	20,436.3	—

Note: Figures are in billions of chained 2017 dollars; (1) Figures cover the Omaha, NE-IA Metropolitan Statistical Area; (2) Figures cover real GDP within metropolitan areas; (3) Rank is based on 2023 data and ranges from 1 to 384
Source: U.S. Bureau of Economic Analysis

Economic Growth

Area	2014	2015	2016	2017	2018	2019	2020	2021	2022	2023
MSA[1]	6.2	3.3	0.5	4.6	2.1	1.1	-1.8	5.6	7.0	2.2
U.S.[2]	2.6	3.2	2.0	2.7	3.1	2.7	-2.2	6.3	2.6	2.7

Note: Figures are real gross domestic product growth rates and represent percent change from preceding period; (1) Figures cover the Omaha, NE-IA Metropolitan Statistical Area; (2) Figures are the average growth rates within metropolitan areas
Source: U.S. Bureau of Economic Analysis

Metropolitan Area Exports

Area	2018	2019	2020	2021	2022	2023	Rank[2]
MSA[1]	4,371.6	3,725.7	3,852.5	4,595.1	4,585.5	3,411.0	80
U.S.	1,664,056.1	1,645,173.7	1,431,406.6	1,753,941.4	2,062,937.4	2,019,160.5	—

Note: Figures are in millions of dollars; (1) Figures cover the Omaha, NE-IA Metropolitan Statistical Area; (2) Rank is based on 2023 data and ranges from 1 to 386
Source: U.S. Department of Commerce, International Trade Administration, Office of Trade and Economic Analysis, Industry and Analysis, Exports by Metropolitan Area, data extracted April 2, 2025

Building Permits

Area	Single-Family			Multi-Family			Total		
	2023	2024	Pct. Chg.	2023	2024	Pct. Chg.	2023	2024	Pct. Chg.
City	1,294	1,692	30.8	1,756	2,668	51.9	3,050	4,360	43.0
MSA[1]	2,763	3,505	26.9	1,956	3,692	88.8	4,719	7,197	52.5
U.S.	920,000	981,900	6.7	591,100	496,100	-16.1	1,511,100	1,478,000	-2.2

Note: (1) Figures cover the Omaha, NE-IA Metropolitan Statistical Area; Figures represent new, privately-owned housing units authorized (unadjusted data)
Source: U.S. Census Bureau, Building Permits Survey (BPS), 2023, 2024

Bankruptcy Filings

Area	Business Filings			Nonbusiness Filings		
	2023	2024	% Chg.	2023	2024	% Chg.
Douglas County	21	26	23.8	687	802	16.7
U.S.	18,926	23,107	22.1	434,064	494,201	13.9

Note: Business filings include Chapter 7, Chapter 9, Chapter 11, Chapter 12, Chapter 13, Chapter 15, and Section 304; Nonbusiness filings include Chapter 7, Chapter 11, and Chapter 13
Source: Administrative Office of the U.S. Courts, Business and Nonbusiness Bankruptcy, County Cases Commenced by Chapter of the Bankruptcy Code, During the 12-Month Period Ending December 31, 2023 and Business and Nonbusiness Bankruptcy, County Cases Commenced by Chapter of the Bankruptcy Code, During the 12-Month Period Ending December 31, 2024

Housing Vacancy Rates

Area	Gross Vacancy Rate[3] (%)			Year-Round Vacancy Rate[4] (%)			Rental Vacancy Rate[5] (%)			Homeowner Vacancy Rate[6] (%)		
	2022	2023	2024	2022	2023	2024	2022	2023	2024	2022	2023	2024
MSA[1]	5.4	5.4	5.1	5.0	5.1	5.1	4.2	4.3	5.3	0.8	0.9	0.3
U.S.[2]	9.1	9.0	9.1	7.5	7.5	7.6	5.7	6.5	6.8	0.8	0.8	1.0

Note: (1) Figures cover the Omaha, NE-IA Metropolitan Statistical Area; (2) Figures cover the 75 largest Metropolitan Statistical Areas; (3) The percentage of the total housing inventory that is vacant; (4) The percentage of the housing inventory (excluding seasonal units) that is year-round vacant; (5) The percentage of rental inventory that is vacant for rent; (6) The percentage of homeowner inventory that is vacant for sale
Source: U.S. Census Bureau, Housing Vacancies and Homeownership Annual Statistics: 2022, 2023, 2024

INCOME

Income

Area	Per Capita ($)	Median Household ($)	Average Household ($)
City	42,515	72,708	103,010
MSA[1]	44,338	83,023	111,142
U.S.	43,289	78,538	110,491

Note: (1) Figures cover the Omaha, NE-IA Metropolitan Statistical Area
Source: U.S. Census Bureau, 2019-2023 American Community Survey 5-Year Estimates

Household Income Distribution

Area	Percent of Households Earning							
	Under $15,000	$15,000 -$24,999	$25,000 -$34,999	$35,000 -$49,999	$50,000 -$74,999	$75,000 -$99,999	$100,000 -$149,999	$150,000 and up
City	8.8	6.5	7.2	11.4	17.6	13.1	17.1	18.2
MSA[1]	6.9	5.6	6.3	10.1	16.6	13.2	19.6	21.7
U.S.	8.5	6.6	6.8	10.4	15.7	12.7	17.4	21.9

Note: (1) Figures cover the Omaha, NE-IA Metropolitan Statistical Area
Source: U.S. Census Bureau, 2019-2023 American Community Survey 5-Year Estimates

Poverty Rate

Area	All Ages	Under 18 Years Old	18 to 64 Years Old	65 Years and Over
City	12.8	15.9	12.3	9.3
MSA[1]	9.5	11.2	9.1	8.1
U.S.	12.4	16.3	11.6	10.4

Note: Figures are percentage of people whose income during the past 12 months was below the poverty level; (1) Figures cover the Omaha, NE-IA Metropolitan Statistical Area
Source: U.S. Census Bureau, 2019-2023 American Community Survey 5-Year Estimates

EMPLOYMENT

Labor Force and Employment

Area	Civilian Labor Force			Workers Employed		
	Dec. 2023	Dec. 2024	% Chg.	Dec. 2023	Dec. 2024	% Chg.
City	251,851	256,156	1.7	245,154	248,481	1.4
MSA[1]	505,378	514,350	1.8	492,693	499,953	1.5
U.S.	166,661,000	167,746,000	0.7	160,754,000	161,294,000	0.3

Note: Data is not seasonally adjusted and covers workers 16 years of age and older; (1) Figures cover the Omaha, NE-IA Metropolitan Statistical Area
Source: Bureau of Labor Statistics, Local Area Unemployment Statistics

Unemployment Rate

Area	2024											
	Jan.	Feb.	Mar.	Apr.	May	Jun.	Jul.	Aug.	Sep.	Oct.	Nov.	Dec.
City	3.2	3.5	3.2	3.1	3.1	3.5	3.6	3.3	3.0	3.2	3.0	3.0
MSA[1]	3.1	3.2	2.9	2.7	2.9	3.3	3.4	3.1	2.8	3.0	2.9	2.8
U.S.	4.1	4.2	3.9	3.5	3.7	4.3	4.5	4.4	3.9	3.9	4.0	3.8

Note: Data is not seasonally adjusted and covers workers 16 years of age and older; (1) Figures cover the Omaha, NE-IA Metropolitan Statistical Area
Source: Bureau of Labor Statistics, Local Area Unemployment Statistics

Average Wages

Occupation	$/Hr.	Occupation	$/Hr.
Accountants and Auditors	37.98	Maintenance and Repair Workers	25.08
Automotive Mechanics	26.58	Marketing Managers	63.75
Bookkeepers	24.02	Network and Computer Systems Admin.	45.55
Carpenters	26.11	Nurses, Licensed Practical	29.24
Cashiers	14.93	Nurses, Registered	40.84
Computer Programmers	46.38	Nursing Assistants	20.08
Computer Systems Analysts	46.14	Office Clerks, General	19.65
Computer User Support Specialists	29.50	Physical Therapists	45.26
Construction Laborers	23.84	Physicians	132.45
Cooks, Restaurant	18.03	Plumbers, Pipefitters and Steamfitters	34.64
Customer Service Representatives	21.38	Police and Sheriff's Patrol Officers	39.22
Dentists	103.65	Postal Service Mail Carriers	29.45
Electricians	31.36	Real Estate Sales Agents	23.46
Engineers, Electrical	48.89	Retail Salespersons	16.96
Fast Food and Counter Workers	14.83	Sales Representatives, Technical/Scientific	41.73
Financial Managers	75.03	Secretaries, Exc. Legal/Medical/Executive	22.46
First-Line Supervisors of Office Workers	31.66	Security Guards	21.05
General and Operations Managers	51.15	Surgeons	165.50
Hairdressers/Cosmetologists	21.52	Teacher Assistants, Exc. Postsecondary[1]	14.60
Home Health and Personal Care Aides	17.13	Teachers, Secondary School, Exc. Sp. Ed.[1]	29.23
Janitors and Cleaners	17.41	Telemarketers	14.96
Landscaping/Groundskeeping Workers	20.04	Truck Drivers, Heavy/Tractor-Trailer	27.64
Lawyers	68.96	Truck Drivers, Light/Delivery Services	23.61
Maids and Housekeeping Cleaners	16.54	Waiters and Waitresses	19.47

Note: Wage data covers the Omaha, NE-IA Metropolitan Statistical Area; (1) Hourly wages were calculated from annual wage data based on a 40 hour work week
Source: Bureau of Labor Statistics, Metro Area Occupational Employment & Wage Estimates, May 2024

Employment by Industry

Sector	MSA[1] Number of Employees	MSA[1] Percent of Total	U.S. Percent of Total
Construction, Mining, and Logging	32,100	6.2	5.5
Financial Activities	40,100	7.7	5.8
Government	70,100	13.5	14.9
Information	8,600	1.7	1.9
Leisure and Hospitality	55,200	10.7	10.4
Manufacturing	35,900	6.9	8.0
Other Services	17,900	3.5	3.7
Private Education and Health Services	91,200	17.6	16.9
Professional and Business Services	70,700	13.6	14.2
Retail Trade	53,000	10.2	10.0
Transportation, Warehousing, and Utilities	26,800	5.2	4.8
Wholesale Trade	16,500	3.2	3.9

Note: Figures are non-farm employment as of December 2024. Figures are not seasonally adjusted and include workers 16 years of age and older; (1) Figures cover the Omaha, NE-IA Metropolitan Statistical Area
Source: Bureau of Labor Statistics, Current Employment Statistics, Employment, Hours, and Earnings

Employment by Occupation

Occupation Classification	City (%)	MSA[1] (%)	U.S. (%)
Management, Business, Science, and Arts	44.2	44.4	42.0
Natural Resources, Construction, and Maintenance	7.9	8.5	8.6
Production, Transportation, and Material Moving	12.2	11.9	13.0
Sales and Office	20.4	20.5	19.9
Service	15.3	14.6	16.5

Note: Figures cover employed civilians 16 years of age and older; (1) Figures cover the Omaha, NE-IA Metropolitan Statistical Area
Source: U.S. Census Bureau, 2019-2023 American Community Survey 5-Year Estimates

Occupations with Greatest Projected Employment Growth: 2022 – 2032

Occupation[1]	2022 Employment	2032 Projected Employment	Numeric Employment Change	Percent Employment Change
Home Health and Personal Care Aides	10,120	12,360	2,240	22.1
Stockers and Order Fillers	14,130	16,070	1,940	13.7
Software Developers	7,780	9,680	1,900	24.4
Fast Food and Counter Workers	26,230	28,120	1,890	7.2
Heavy and Tractor-Trailer Truck Drivers	27,030	28,840	1,810	6.7
Registered Nurses	22,900	24,670	1,770	7.7
General and Operations Managers	22,330	23,990	1,660	7.4
Laborers and Freight, Stock, and Material Movers, Hand	18,030	19,440	1,410	7.8
Nursing Assistants (SOC 2018)	16,290	17,540	1,250	7.7
Cooks, Restaurant	4,450	5,680	1,230	27.6

Note: Projections cover Nebraska; (1) Sorted by numeric employment change
Source: www.projectionscentral.org, State Occupational Projections, 2022–2032 Long-Term Projections

Fastest-Growing Occupations: 2022 – 2032

Occupation[1]	2022 Employment	2032 Projected Employment	Numeric Employment Change	Percent Employment Change
Gaming Dealers	30	100	70	233.3
Wind Turbine Service Technicians	320	530	210	65.6
Nurse Practitioners	1,790	2,430	640	35.8
Occupational Therapy Assistants	250	330	80	32.0
Data Scientists	1,400	1,830	430	30.7
Physical Therapist Assistants	1,120	1,450	330	29.5
Information Security Analysts (SOC 2018)	670	860	190	28.4
Cooks, Restaurant	4,450	5,680	1,230	27.6
Lodging Managers	480	600	120	25.0
Software Developers	7,780	9,680	1,900	24.4

Note: Projections cover Nebraska; (1) Sorted by percent employment change and excludes occupations with numeric employment change less than 50
Source: www.projectionscentral.org, State Occupational Projections, 2022–2032 Long-Term Projections

CITY FINANCES

City Government Finances

Component	2022 ($000)	2022 ($ per capita)
Total Revenues	871,562	1,822
Total Expenditures	841,274	1,759
Debt Outstanding	1,432,655	2,995

Source: U.S. Census Bureau, State & Local Government Finances 2022

City Government Revenue by Source

Source	2022 ($000)	2022 ($ per capita)	2022 (%)
General Revenue			
From Federal Government	148	0	0.0
From State Government	79,859	167	9.2
From Local Governments	22,898	48	2.6
Taxes			
Property	202,366	423	23.2
Sales and Gross Receipts	183,991	385	21.1
Personal Income	0	0	0.0
Corporate Income	0	0	0.0
Motor Vehicle License	58,682	123	6.7
Other Taxes	59,269	124	6.8
Current Charges	262,317	548	30.1
Liquor Store	0	0	0.0
Utility	0	0	0.0

Source: U.S. Census Bureau, State & Local Government Finances 2022

City Government Expenditures by Function

Function	2022 ($000)	2022 ($ per capita)	2022 (%)
General Direct Expenditures			
Air Transportation	0	0	0.0
Corrections	0	0	0.0
Education	0	0	0.0
Employment Security Administration	0	0	0.0
Financial Administration	0	0	0.0
Fire Protection	105,492	220	12.5
General Public Buildings	76,450	159	9.1
Governmental Administration, Other	9,520	19	1.1
Health	0	0	0.0
Highways	94,391	197	11.2
Hospitals	0	0	0.0
Housing and Community Development	0	0	0.0
Interest on General Debt	45,823	95	5.4
Judicial and Legal	5,208	10	0.6
Libraries	16,911	35	2.0
Parking	8,277	17	1.0
Parks and Recreation	30,815	64	3.7
Police Protection	147,473	308	17.5
Public Welfare	0	0	0.0
Sewerage	142,468	297	16.9
Solid Waste Management	33,862	70	4.0
Veterans' Services	0	0	0.0
Liquor Store	0	0	0.0
Utility	0	0	0.0

Source: U.S. Census Bureau, State & Local Government Finances 2022

TAXES

State Corporate Income Tax Rates

State	Tax Rate (%)	Income Brackets ($)	Num. of Brackets	Financial Institution Tax Rate (%)[a]	Federal Income Tax Ded.
Nebraska	3.99 - 5.2	100,000	2	(a)	No

Note: Tax rates for tax year 2024; (a) Rates listed are the corporate income tax rate applied to financial institutions or excise taxes based on income. Some states have other taxes based upon the value of deposits or shares.
Source: Federation of Tax Administrators, State Corporate Income Tax Rates, January 1, 2025

State Individual Income Tax Rates

State	Tax Rate (%)	Income Brackets ($)	Personal Exemptions ($)			Standard Ded. ($)	
			Single	Married	Depend.	Single	Married
Nebraska (a)	2.46 - 5.84 (bb)	2,399 - 29,000 (b)	157	314	157 (c)	7,900	15,800

Note: Tax rates for tax year 2024; Local- and county-level taxes are not included; Federal income tax is not deductible on state income tax returns; (a) 16 states have statutory provision for automatically adjusting to the rate of inflation the dollar values of the income tax brackets, standard deductions, and/or personal exemptions. Oregon does not index the income brackets for $125,000 and over See: INFL and SPEC above; (b) For joint returns, taxes are twice the tax on half the couple's income. California brackets violate this formula at the two highest tax brackets in 2024; (c) The personal exemption takes the form of a tax credit instead of a deduction; (bb) Louisiana lawmakers repealed the state's throwout rule, ending the taxation of so-called "nowhere income." Iowa is phasing-in a flat rate by 2027, while Nebraska (LB 754 signed into law) and South Carolina is phasing-in a reduced top rate by 2027.
Source: Federation of Tax Administrators, State Individual Income Tax Rates, January 1, 2025

Various State Sales and Excise Tax Rates

State	State Sales Tax (%)	Gasoline[1] ($/gal.)	Cigarette[2] ($/pack)	Spirits[3] ($/gal.)	Wine[4] ($/gal.)	Beer[5] ($/gal.)	Recreational Marijuana (%)
Nebraska	5.5	0.31	0.64	3.75	0.95	0.31	Not legal

Note: All tax rates as of January 1, 2025; (1) The American Petroleum Institute has developed a methodology for determining the average tax rate on a gallon of fuel. Rates may include any of the following: excise taxes, environmental fees, storage tank fees, other fees or taxes, general sales tax, and local taxes; (2) The federal excise tax of $1.0066 per pack and local taxes are not included; (3) Rates are those applicable to off-premise sales of 40% alcohol by volume (a.b.v.) distilled spirits in 750ml containers. Local excise taxes are excluded; (4) Rates are those applicable to off-premise sales of 11% a.b.v. non-carbonated wine in 750ml containers; (5) Rates are those applicable to off-premise sales of 4.7% a.b.v. beer in 12 ounce containers.
Source: Tax Foundation, 2025 Facts & Figures: How Does Your State Compare?

State Tax Competitiveness Index

State	Overall Rank	Corporate Tax Rank	Individual Income Tax Rank	Sales Tax Rank	Property Tax Rank	Unemployment Insurance Tax Rank
Nebraska	24	20	26	13	45	3

Note: The Tax Foundation's State Tax Competitiveness Index enables policymakers, taxpayers, and business leaders to gauge how their states' tax systems compare. A rank of 1 is best, 50 is worst. Rankings do not average to the total. States without a tax rank equally as 1. DC's scores and rankings do not affect other states. The report shows tax systems as of July 1, 2024 (the beginning of Fiscal Year 2025).
Source: Tax Foundation, State Tax Competitiveness Index 2025

TRANSPORTATION

Means of Transportation to Work

Area	Car/Truck/Van		Public Transportation			Bicycle	Walked	Other Means	Worked at Home
	Drove Alone	Car-pooled	Bus	Subway	Railroad				
City	73.3	8.7	1.1	0.0	0.0	0.2	1.8	1.3	13.6
MSA[1]	75.8	7.8	0.6	0.0	0.0	0.1	1.5	1.1	13.0
U.S.	70.2	8.5	1.7	1.3	0.4	0.4	2.4	1.6	13.5

Note: Figures are percentages and cover workers 16 years of age and older; (1) Figures cover the Omaha, NE-IA Metropolitan Statistical Area
Source: U.S. Census Bureau, 2019-2023 American Community Survey 5-Year Estimates

Travel Time to Work

Area	Less Than 10 Minutes	10 to 19 Minutes	20 to 29 Minutes	30 to 44 Minutes	45 to 59 Minutes	60 to 89 Minutes	90 Minutes or More
City	14.6	41.3	26.4	12.4	2.3	1.8	1.2
MSA[1]	14.0	36.2	27.4	15.9	3.5	1.8	1.2
U.S.	12.6	28.6	21.2	20.8	8.1	6.0	2.8

Note: Note: Figures are percentages and include workers 16 years old and over; (1) Figures cover the Omaha, NE-IA Metropolitan Statistical Area
Source: U.S. Census Bureau, 2019-2023 American Community Survey 5-Year Estimates

Key Congestion Measures

Measure	2000	2010	2015	2020	2022
Annual Hours of Delay, Total (000)	9,694	14,864	17,796	9,777	23,559
Annual Hours of Delay, Per Auto Commuter	26	32	36	19	48
Annual Congestion Cost, Per Auto Commuter ($)	552	670	741	421	977

Note: Figures cover the Omaha NE-IA urban area
Source: Texas A&M Transportation Institute, 2023 Urban Mobility Report

Freeway Travel Time Index

Measure	1985	1990	1995	2000	2005	2010	2015	2020	2022
Urban Area Index[1]	1.05	1.08	1.10	1.13	1.15	1.16	1.16	1.05	1.18
Urban Area Rank[1,2]	64	62	72	72	68	54	57	85	40

Note: Freeway Travel Time Index—the ratio of travel time in the peak period to the travel time at free-flow conditions. For example, a value of 1.30 indicates a 20-minute free-flow trip takes 26 minutes in the peak (20 minutes x 1.30 = 26 minutes); (1) Covers the Omaha NE-IA urban area; (2) Rank is based on 101 larger urban areas (#1 = highest travel time index)
Source: Texas A&M Transportation Institute, 2023 Urban Mobility Report

Public Transportation

Agency Name / Mode of Transportation	Vehicles Operated in Maximum Service[1]	Annual Unlinked Passenger Trips[2] (in thous.)	Annual Passenger Miles[3] (in thous.)
Transit Authority of Omaha (MAT)			
Bus (directly operated)	81	3,229.9	10,911.6
Demand Response (directly operated)	28	84.7	483.4

Note: (1) Number of revenue vehicles operated by the given mode and type of service to meet the annual maximum service requirement. This is the revenue vehicle count during the peak season of the year; on the week and day that maximum service is provided. Vehicles operated in maximum service (VOMS) exclude atypical days and one-time special events; (2) Number of passengers who boarded public transportation vehicles. Passengers are counted each time they board a vehicle no matter how many vehicles they use to travel from their origin to their destination. (3) Sum of the distances ridden by all passengers during the entire fiscal year.
Source: Federal Transit Administration, National Transit Database, 2023

Air Transportation

Airport Name and Code / Type of Service	Passenger Airlines[1]	Passenger Enplanements	Freight Carriers[2]	Freight (lbs)
Eppley Airfield (OMA)				
Domestic service (U.S. carriers only)	27	2,580,019	11	45,278,395
International service (U.S. carriers only)	1	12	0	0

Note: (1) Includes all U.S.-based major, minor and commuter airlines that carried at least one passenger during the year; (2) Includes all U.S.-based airlines and freight carriers that transported at least one pound of freight during the year.
Source: Bureau of Transportation Statistics, The Intermodal Transportation Database, Air Carriers: T-100 Domestic Market (U.S. carriers only), 2024; Bureau of Transportation Statistics, The Intermodal Transportation Database, Air Carriers: T-100 International Market (U.S. carriers only), 2024

BUSINESSES

Major Business Headquarters

Company Name	Industry	Rankings Fortune[1]	Rankings Forbes[2]
Berkshire Hathaway	Insurance: property and casualty (stock)	5	-
Kiewit	Construction	-	23
Mutual of Omaha Insurance	Insurance: life, health (mutual)	306	-
Peter Kiewit Sons'	Engineering & construction	239	-
Scoular	Food, drink & tobacco	-	75
Tenaska	Multicompany	-	56
Union Pacific	Railroads	170	-

Note: (1) Companies that produce a 10-K are ranked 1 to 500 based on 2023 revenue; (2) All private companies with at least $2 billion in annual revenue through the end of their most current fiscal year are ranked 1 to 275; companies listed are headquartered in the city; dashes indicate no ranking
Source: Fortune, "Fortune 500," 2024; Forbes, "America's Largest Private Companies," 2024

Fastest-Growing Businesses

According to *Inc.*, Omaha is home to two of America's 500 fastest-growing private companies: **Gordian Staffing** (#29); **CrossMed Healthcare Staffing** (#222). Criteria: must be an independent, privately-held, for-profit, U.S. corporation, proprietorship or partnership as of December 31, 2023; revenues must be at least $100,000 in 2020 and $2 million in 2023; must have four-year operating/sales history. *Inc.*, "America's 500 Fastest-Growing Private Companies," 2024

Living Environment

COST OF LIVING

Cost of Living Index

Composite Index	Groceries	Housing	Utilities	Transportation	Health Care	Misc. Goods/Services
91.9	99.1	82.5	84.2	94.4	94.0	97.5

Note: The Cost of Living Index measures regional differences in the cost of consumer goods and services, excluding taxes and non-consumer expenditures, for professional and managerial households in the top income quintile. It is based on more than 50,000 prices covering almost 60 different items for which prices are collected three times a year by chambers of commerce, economic development organizations or university applied economic centers in each participating urban area. The numbers shown should be read as a percentage above or below the national average of 100. For example, a value of 115.4 in the groceries column indicates that grocery prices are 15.4% higher than the national average. Small differences in the index numbers should not be interpreted as significant; Figures cover the Omaha NE urban area.
Source: The Council for Community and Economic Research, Cost of Living Index, 2024

Grocery Prices

Area[1]	T-Bone Steak ($/pound)	Frying Chicken ($/pound)	Whole Milk ($/half gal.)	Eggs ($/dozen)	Orange Juice ($/64 oz.)	Coffee ($/11.5 oz.)
City[2]	15.51	1.44	4.87	3.22	4.43	5.50
Avg.	15.42	1.55	4.69	3.25	4.41	5.46
Min.	14.50	1.16	4.43	2.75	4.00	4.85
Max.	17.56	2.89	5.49	4.78	5.54	7.89

Note: (1) Values for the local area are compared with the average, minimum and maximum values for all 276 areas in the Cost of Living Index; (2) Figures cover the Omaha NE urban area; **T-Bone Steak** (price per pound); **Frying Chicken** (price per pound, whole fryer); **Whole Milk** (half gallon carton); **Eggs** (price per dozen, Grade A, large); **Orange Juice** (64 oz. Tropicana or Florida Natural); **Coffee** (11.5 oz. can, vacuum-packed, Maxwell House, Hills Bros, or Folgers).
Source: The Council for Community and Economic Research, Cost of Living Index, 2024

Housing and Utility Costs

Area[1]	New Home Price ($)	Apartment Rent ($/month)	All Electric ($/month)	Part Electric ($/month)	Other Energy ($/month)	Telephone ($/month)
City[2]	385,889	1,500	-	93.49	55.47	203.73
Avg.	515,975	1,550	210.99	123.07	82.07	194.99
Min.	265,375	692	104.33	53.68	36.26	179.42
Max.	2,775,821	5,719	529.02	397.28	361.63	223.33

Note: (1) Values for the local area are compared with the average, minimum and maximum values for all 276 areas in the Cost of Living Index; (2) Figures cover the Omaha NE urban area; **New Home Price** (2,400 sf living area, 8,000 sf lot, in urban area with full utilities); **Apartment Rent** (950 sf 2 bedroom/1.5 or 2 bath, unfurnished, excluding all utilities except water); **All Electric** (average monthly cost for an all-electric home); **Part Electric** (average monthly cost for a part-electric home); **Other Energy** (average monthly cost for natural gas, fuel oil, coal, wood, and any other forms of energy except electricity); **Telephone** (price includes the base monthly rate plus taxes and fees for three lines of mobile phone service).
Source: The Council for Community and Economic Research, Cost of Living Index, 2024

Health Care, Transportation, and Other Costs

Area[1]	Doctor ($/visit)	Dentist ($/visit)	Optometrist ($/visit)	Gasoline ($/gallon)	Beauty Salon ($/visit)	Men's Shirt ($)
City[2]	151.64	90.62	117.00	3.08	33.92	35.09
Avg.	143.77	117.51	129.23	3.32	48.57	38.14
Min.	36.74	58.67	67.33	2.80	24.00	13.41
Max.	270.44	216.82	307.33	5.28	94.00	63.89

Note: (1) Values for the local area are compared with the average, minimum and maximum values for all 276 areas in the Cost of Living Index; (2) Figures cover the Omaha NE urban area; **Doctor** (general practitioners routine exam of an established patient); **Dentist** (adult teeth cleaning and periodic oral examination); **Optometrist** (full vision eye exam for established adult patient); **Gasoline** (one gallon regular unleaded, national brand, including all taxes, cash price at self-service pump if available); **Beauty Salon** (woman's shampoo, trim, and blow-dry); **Men's Shirt** (cotton/polyester dress shirt, pinpoint weave, long sleeves).
Source: The Council for Community and Economic Research, Cost of Living Index, 2024

HOUSING

Homeownership Rate

Area	2017 (%)	2018 (%)	2019 (%)	2020 (%)	2021 (%)	2022 (%)	2023 (%)	2024 (%)
MSA[1]	65.5	67.8	66.9	68.6	68.6	67.9	67.0	67.4
U.S.	63.9	64.4	64.6	66.6	65.5	65.8	65.9	65.6

Note: (1) Figures cover the Omaha, NE-IA Metropolitan Statistical Area
Source: U.S. Census Bureau, Housing Vacancies and Homeownership Annual Statistics: 2017-2024

House Price Index (HPI)

Area	National Ranking[2]	Quarterly Change (%)	One-Year Change (%)	Five-Year Change (%)	Since 1991Q1 (%)
MSA[1]	154	0.12	4.63	51.76	295.39
U.S.[3]	–	1.43	4.51	57.13	327.82

Note: The HPI is a weighted repeat sales index. It measures average price changes in repeat sales or refinancings on the same properties. This information is obtained by reviewing repeat mortgage transactions on single-family properties whose mortgages have been purchased or securitized by Fannie Mae or Freddie Mac since January 1975; (1) Figures cover the Omaha-Council Bluffs, NE-IA Metropolitan Statistical Area; (2) Rankings are based on annual percentage change for all metro areas containing at least 15,000 transactions over the last 10 years and ranges from 1 to 241; (3) figures based on a weighted average of Census Division estimates using a seasonally adjusted, purchase-only index; all figures are for the period ending December 31, 2024
Source: Federal Housing Finance Agency, Change in FHFA Metropolitan Area House Price Indexes, All Transactions Index, 2024Q4

Home Value

Area	Under $100,000	$100,000 -$199,999	$200,000 -$299,999	$300,000 -$399,999	$400,000 -$499,999	$500,000 -$999,999	$1,000,000 or more	Median ($)
City	9.8	29.2	31.6	14.2	7.4	6.7	1.2	230,100
MSA[1]	8.7	25.0	29.9	16.9	9.6	8.7	1.3	248,100
U.S.	12.1	17.8	19.5	14.4	10.5	19.1	6.5	303,400

Note: Figures are percentages except for median and cover owner-occupied housing units; (1) Figures cover the Omaha, NE-IA Metropolitan Statistical Area
Source: U.S. Census Bureau, 2019-2023 American Community Survey 5-Year Estimates

Year Housing Structure Built

Area	2020 or Later	2010 -2019	2000 -2009	1990 -1999	1980 -1989	1970 -1979	1960 -1969	1950 -1959	1940 -1949	Before 1940	Median Year
City	0.4	6.4	8.7	11.9	10.8	15.1	13.9	10.5	4.2	18.1	1972
MSA[1]	1.3	10.7	14.3	11.8	9.6	13.9	11.2	8.2	3.4	15.6	1978
U.S.	1.2	8.9	13.6	12.8	13.0	14.4	10.0	9.7	4.5	11.9	1980

Note: Figures are percentages except for Median Year; Note: (1) Figures cover the Omaha, NE-IA Metropolitan Statistical Area
Source: U.S. Census Bureau, 2019-2023 American Community Survey 5-Year Estimates

Gross Monthly Rent

Area	Under $500	$500 -$999	$1,000 -$1,499	$1,500 -$1,999	$2,000 -$2,499	$2,500 -$2,999	$3,000 and up	Median ($)
City	4.4	29.7	43.5	16.1	4.3	0.8	1.3	1,150
MSA[1]	5.0	29.1	42.6	16.6	4.3	0.9	1.5	1,152
U.S.	6.5	22.3	29.5	20.2	10.8	4.8	5.9	1,348

Note: Figures are percentages except for median; Gross rent is the contract rent plus the estimated average monthly cost of utilities (electricity, gas, and water and sewer) and fuels (oil, coal, kerosene, wood, etc.) if these are paid by the renter (or paid for the renter by someone else); (1) Figures cover the Omaha, NE-IA Metropolitan Statistical Area
Source: U.S. Census Bureau, 2019-2023 American Community Survey 5-Year Estimates

HEALTH

Health Risk Factors

Category	MSA[1] (%)	U.S. (%)
Adults aged 18–64 who have any kind of health care coverage	89.9	90.8
Adults who reported being in good or better health	85.5	81.8
Adults who have been told they have high blood cholesterol	34.9	36.9
Adults who have been told they have high blood pressure	32.0	34.0
Adults who are current smokers	12.7	12.1
Adults who currently use e-cigarettes	8.5	7.7
Adults who currently use chewing tobacco, snuff, or snus	3.2	3.2
Adults who are heavy drinkers[2]	6.0	6.1
Adults who are binge drinkers[3]	19.1	15.2
Adults who are overweight (BMI 25.0 - 29.9)	35.5	34.4
Adults who are obese (BMI 30.0 - 99.8)	35.8	34.3
Adults who participated in any physical activities in the past month	78.2	75.8

Note: All figures are crude prevalence; (1) Figures cover the Omaha-Council Bluffs, NE-IA Metropolitan Statistical Area; (2) Heavy drinkers are classified as adult men having more than 14 drinks per week and adult women having more than 7 drinks per week; (3) Binge drinkers are classified as males having five or more drinks on one occasion or females having four or more drinks on one occasion
Source: Centers for Disease Control and Prevention, Behavioral Risk Factor Surveillance System, SMART: Selected Metropolitan Area Risk Trends, 2023

Acute and Chronic Health Conditions

Category	MSA[1] (%)	U.S. (%)
Adults who have ever been told they had a heart attack	3.2	4.2
Adults who have ever been told they have angina or coronary heart disease	3.2	4.0
Adults who have ever been told they had a stroke	2.8	3.3
Adults who have ever been told they have asthma	12.8	15.7
Adults who have ever been told they have arthritis	22.0	26.3
Adults who have ever been told they have diabetes[2]	10.3	11.5
Adults who have ever been told they had skin cancer	4.8	5.6
Adults who have ever been told they had any other types of cancer	7.6	8.4
Adults who have ever been told they have COPD	4.9	6.4
Adults who have ever been told they have kidney disease	3.1	3.7
Adults who have ever been told they have a form of depression	19.5	22.0

Note: All figures are crude prevalence; (1) Figures cover the Omaha-Council Bluffs, NE-IA Metropolitan Statistical Area; (2) Figures do not include pregnancy-related, borderline, or pre-diabetes
Source: Centers for Disease Control and Prevention, Behavioral Risk Factor Surveillance System, SMART: Selected Metropolitan Area Risk Trends, 2023

Health Screening and Vaccination Rates

Category	MSA[1] (%)	U.S. (%)
Adults who have ever been tested for HIV	32.1	37.5
Adults who have had their blood cholesterol checked within the last five years	85.9	87.0
Adults aged 65+ who have had flu shot within the past year	65.5	63.4
Adults aged 65+ who have ever had a pneumonia vaccination	76.4	71.9

Note: All figures are crude prevalence; (1) Figures cover the Omaha-Council Bluffs, NE-IA Metropolitan Statistical Area.
Source: Centers for Disease Control and Prevention, Behavioral Risk Factor Surveillance System, SMART: Selected Metropolitan Area Risk Trends, 2023

Disability Status

Category	MSA[1] (%)	U.S. (%)
Adults who reported being deaf	5.9	7.4
Are you blind or have serious difficulty seeing, even when wearing glasses?	4.1	4.9
Do you have difficulty doing errands alone?	6.3	7.8
Do you have difficulty dressing or bathing?	2.4	3.6
Do you have serious difficulty concentrating/remembering/making decisions?	12.4	13.7
Do you have serious difficulty walking or climbing stairs?	10.3	13.2

Note: All figures are crude prevalence; (1) Figures cover the Omaha-Council Bluffs, NE-IA Metropolitan Statistical Area.
Source: Centers for Disease Control and Prevention, Behavioral Risk Factor Surveillance System, SMART: Selected Metropolitan Area Risk Trends, 2023

Mortality Rates for the Top 10 Causes of Death in the U.S.

ICD-10[a] Sub-Chapter	ICD-10[a] Code	Crude Mortality Rate[2] per 100,000 population	
		County[3]	U.S.
Malignant neoplasms	C00-C97	160.7	182.7
Ischaemic heart diseases	I20-I25	57.4	109.6
Provisional assignment of new diseases of uncertain etiology[1]	U00-U49	36.6	65.3
Other forms of heart disease	I30-I51	56.1	65.1
Other degenerative diseases of the nervous system	G30-G31	51.3	52.4
Other external causes of accidental injury	W00-X59	32.9	52.3
Cerebrovascular diseases	I60-I69	36.9	49.1
Chronic lower respiratory diseases	J40-J47	38.4	43.5
Hypertensive diseases	I10-I15	48.8	38.9
Organic, including symptomatic, mental disorders	F01-F09	25.8	33.9

Note: (a) ICD-10 = International Classification of Diseases 10th Revision; (1) Includes COVID-19, adverse effects to COVID-19 vaccines, SARS, and vaping-related disorders; (2) Crude mortality rates are a three-year average covering 2021-2023; (3) Figures cover Douglas County.
Source: Centers for Disease Control and Prevention, National Center for Health Statistics. National Vital Statistics System, Mortality 2018-2023 on CDC WONDER Online Database

Mortality Rates for Selected Causes of Death

Cause of Death	ICD-10[a] Code	Crude Mortality Rate[1] per 100,000 population	
		County[2]	U.S.
Accidental poisoning and exposure to noxious substances	X40-X49	15.6	30.5
Alzheimer disease	G30	31.7	35.4
Assault	X85-Y09	5.7	7.3
COVID-19	U07.1	36.6	65.3
Diabetes mellitus	E10-E14	26.0	30.0
Diseases of the liver	K70-K76	18.1	20.8
Human immunodeficiency virus (HIV) disease	B20-B24	Unreliable	1.5
Influenza and pneumonia	J09-J18	9.4	13.4
Intentional self-harm	X60-X84	13.7	14.7
Malnutrition	E40-E46	8.5	6.0
Obesity and other hyperalimentation	E65-E68	4.4	3.1
Renal failure	N17-N19	9.9	16.4
Transport accidents	V01-V99	10.3	14.4

Note: (a) ICD-10 = International Classification of Diseases 10th Revision; (1) Crude mortality rates are a three-year average covering 2021-2023; (2) Figures cover Douglas County; Data are suppressed when the data meet the criteria for confidentiality constraints; Crude mortality rates are flagged as unreliable when the rate would be calculated with a numerator of 20 or less.
Source: Centers for Disease Control and Prevention, National Center for Health Statistics. National Vital Statistics System, Mortality 2018-2023 on CDC WONDER Online Database

Health Insurance Coverage

Area	With Health Insurance	With Private Health Insurance	With Public Health Insurance	Without Health Insurance	Population Under Age 19 Without Health Insurance
City	90.3	69.2	31.0	9.7	6.9
MSA[1]	92.9	74.5	29.2	7.1	4.7
U.S.	91.4	67.3	36.3	8.6	5.4

Note: Figures are percentages that cover the civilian noninstitutionalized population; (1) Figures cover the Omaha, NE-IA Metropolitan Statistical Area
Source: U.S. Census Bureau, 2019-2023 American Community Survey 5-Year Estimates

Number of Medical Professionals

Area	MDs[3]	DOs[3,4]	Dentists	Podiatrists	Chiropractors	Optometrists
County[1] (number)	3,518	260	622	32	262	139
County[1] (rate[2])	600.0	44.3	105.5	5.4	44.4	23.6
U.S. (rate[2])	302.5	29.2	74.6	6.4	29.5	18.0

Note: Data as of 2023 unless noted; (1) Data covers Douglas County; (2) Number of medical professionals per 100,000 population; (3) Data as of 2022 and includes all active, non-federal physicians; (4) Doctor of Osteopathic Medicine
Source: U.S. Department of Health and Human Services, Health Resources and Services Administration, Bureau of Health Professions, Area Resource File (ARF) 2023-2024

Best Hospitals

According to *U.S. News*, the Omaha, NE-IA metro area is home to two of the best hospitals in the U.S.: **Fred & Pamela Buffett Cancer Center** (2 adult specialties); **Nebraska Medicine-Nebraska Medical Center** (2 adult specialties). The hospitals listed were nationally ranked in at least one of 15 adult or 11 pediatric specialties. The number of specialties shown cover the parent hospital. Only 160 U.S. hospitals performed well enough to be nationally ranked in one or more specialties. Twenty hospitals in the U.S. made the Honor Roll. The Best Hospitals Honor Roll takes both the national rankings and the procedure and condition ratings into account. Hospitals received points if they were nationally ranked in one of the 15 adult specialties—the higher they ranked, the more points they got—and how many ratings of "high performing" they earned in the 20 procedures and conditions. *U.S. News Online, "America's Best Hospitals 2024-25"*

According to *U.S. News*, the Omaha, NE-IA metro area is home to one of the best children's hospitals in the U.S.: **Children's Nebraska** (2 pediatric specialties). The hospital listed was highly ranked in at least one of 11 pediatric specialties. One hundred five children's hospitals in the U.S. were nationally ranked in at least one specialty. Hospitals received points for being ranked in a specialty, and the 10 hospitals with the most points across the 11 specialties make up the Honor Roll. *U.S. News Online, "America's Best Children's Hospitals 2024-25"*

EDUCATION

Public School District Statistics

District Name	Schls	Pupils	Pupil/ Teacher Ratio	Minority Pupils[1] (%)	Total Rev. per Pupil ($)	Total Exp. per Pupil ($)
Millard Public Schools	36	23,300	15.4	27.4	13,517	13,267
Omaha Public Schools	112	51,693	16.9	78.1	16,364	17,584
Westside Community Schools	14	6,319	14.1	35.0	17,171	15,826

Note: Table includes school districts with 2,000 or more students; (1) Percentage of students that are not non-Hispanic white.
Source: U.S. Department of Education, National Center for Education Statistics, Common Core of Data, Local Education Agency (School District) Universe Survey: School Year 2023-2024; U.S. Department of Education, National Center for Education Statistics, Common Core of Data, School District Finance Survey (F-33): School Year 2021–22

Best High Schools

According to *U.S. News*, Omaha is home to two of the top 500 high schools in the U.S.: **Elkhorn South High School** (#150); **Elkhorn North High School** (#359). Nearly 25,000 public, magnet and charter schools were ranked based on their performance on state assessments and how well they prepare students for college. *U.S. News & World Report, "Best High Schools 2024"*

Highest Level of Education

Area	Less than H.S.	H.S. Diploma	Some College, No Deg.	Associate Degree	Bachelor's Degree	Master's Degree	Prof. School Degree	Doctorate Degree
City	9.5	21.3	21.3	7.7	25.6	9.7	3.2	1.8
MSA[1]	7.3	22.5	21.7	9.4	24.9	10.2	2.5	1.5
U.S.	10.6	26.2	19.4	8.8	21.3	9.8	2.3	1.6

Note: Figures cover persons age 25 and over; (1) Figures cover the Omaha, NE-IA Metropolitan Statistical Area
Source: U.S. Census Bureau, 2019-2023 American Community Survey 5-Year Estimates

Educational Attainment by Race

Area	High School Graduate or Higher (%)					Bachelor's Degree or Higher (%)				
	Total	White	Black	Asian	Hisp.[2]	Total	White	Black	Asian	Hisp.[2]
City	90.5	95.1	86.9	71.7	61.9	40.3	45.7	18.6	50.2	15.0
MSA[1]	92.7	95.6	88.8	74.3	68.3	39.1	41.8	21.4	48.0	18.5
U.S.	89.4	92.9	88.1	88.0	72.5	35.0	37.7	24.7	57.0	19.9

Note: Figures shown cover persons 25 years old and over; (1) Figures cover the Omaha, NE-IA Metropolitan Statistical Area; (2) People of Hispanic origin can be of any race
Source: U.S. Census Bureau, 2019-2023 American Community Survey 5-Year Estimates

School Enrollment by Grade and Control

Area	Preschool (%)		Kindergarten (%)		Grades 1 - 4 (%)		Grades 5 - 8 (%)		Grades 9 - 12 (%)	
	Public	Private	Public	Private	Public	Private	Public	Private	Public	Private
City	54.5	45.5	79.9	20.1	82.7	17.3	82.7	17.3	83.3	16.7
MSA[1]	58.9	41.1	81.9	18.1	84.5	15.5	85.7	14.3	85.5	14.5
U.S.	58.7	41.3	85.2	14.8	87.2	12.8	87.9	12.1	89.0	11.0

Note: Figures shown cover persons 3 years old and over; (1) Figures cover the Omaha, NE-IA Metropolitan Statistical Area
Source: U.S. Census Bureau, 2019-2023 American Community Survey 5-Year Estimates

Higher Education

Four-Year Colleges			Two-Year Colleges			Medical Schools[1]	Law Schools[2]	Voc/ Tech[3]
Public	Private Non-profit	Private For-profit	Public	Private Non-profit	Private For-profit			
2	6	0	2	0	4	2	1	0

Note: Figures cover institutions located within the Omaha, NE-IA Metropolitan Statistical Area and include main campuses only; (1) includes schools accredited by the Liaison Committee on Medical Education and the American Osteopathic Association's Commission on Osteopathic College Accreditation; (2) includes ABA-accredited schools, schools with provisional ABA accreditation, and state accredited schools; (3) includes all schools with programs that are less than 2 years.
Source: National Center for Education Statistics, Integrated Postsecondary Education System (IPEDS), 2023-24; Wikipedia, List of Medical Schools in the United States, accessed May 2, 2025; Wikipedia, List of Law Schools in the United States, accessed May 2, 2025

According to *U.S. News & World Report,* the Omaha, NE-IA metro area is home to one of the top 200 national universities in the U.S.: **Creighton University** (#121 tie). The indicators used to capture academic quality fall into a number of categories: assessment by administrators at peer institutions; retention of students; faculty resources; student selectivity; financial resources; alumni giving; high school counselor ratings of colleges; and graduation rate. *U.S. News & World Report, "America's Best Colleges 2025"*

According to *U.S. News & World Report,* the Omaha, NE-IA metro area is home to one of the top medical schools for research in the U.S.: **University of Nebraska Medical Center** (Tier 2). *U.S. News* placed medical and osteopathic schools into tiers based on their research productivity, faculty and admissions data. Each school's tier was derived from its overall score, calculated by summing the weighted normalized values generated across several factors of academic quality, outlined below. There are four tiers, with tier 1 medical schools as the highest-performing and tier 4 as the lowest-performing. Only tier 1 and 2 schools are shown. Because of the tier presentation, *U.S. News* calculated overall scores based on their percentile performance among all rated schools instead of dividing against the rescaled score of the No. 1-performing schools. Tier 1 included schools with overall scores of 85 to 99. The cutoffs for tiers 2 through 4 were schools scoring 50 to 84, 15 to 49 and 1 to 14, respectively. The rankings are based on a weighted average of the following measures of quality: total research activity; average research activity per faculty member; total NIH research grants at the medical school and its affiliated hospitals; average NIH research grants per faculty; median MCAT total score; median undergraduate GPA; acceptance rate; and faculty resources. *U.S. News & World Report, "America's Best Graduate Schools, Medical, 2025"*

According to *U.S. News & World Report,* the Omaha, NE-IA metro area is home to one of the top medical schools for primary care in the U.S.: **University of Nebraska Medical Center** (Tier 2). *U.S. News* placed medical and osteopathic schools into tiers based on their research productivity, faculty and admissions data. Each school's tier was derived from its overall score, calculated by summing the weighted normalized values generated across several factors of academic quality, outlined below. There are four tiers, with tier 1 medical schools as the highest-performing and tier 4 as the lowest-performing. Only tier 1 and 2 schools are shown. Because of the tier presentation, *U.S. News* calculated overall scores based on their percentile performance among all rated schools instead of dividing against the rescaled score of the No. 1-performing schools. Tier 1 included schools with overall scores of 85 to 99. The cutoffs for tiers 2 through 4 were schools scoring 50 to 84, 15 to 49 and 1 to 14, respectively. The rankings are based on a weighted average of the following measures of quality: graduates practicing in primary care specialties; graduates entering primary care residencies; median MCAT total score; median undergraduate GPA; acceptance rate; and faculty resources. *U.S. News & World Report, "America's Best Graduate Schools, Medical, 2025"*

EMPLOYERS

Major Employers

Company Name	Industry
Alegent Health	General medical & surgical hospitals
City of Omaha	Municipal government
Creighton St. Joseph Reg Healthcare Sys	General medical & surgical hospitals
Creighton University	Colleges & universities
Drivers Management	Truck driver services
First Data Resources	Data processing service
Harveys Iowa Management Company	Casino hotels
Kiewit Offshore Services	Fabricated structural metal
Metropolitan Community College	Community college
Mutual of Omaha Insurance Company	Life insurance
Nebraska Furniture Mart	Furniture stores
Omaha Public Power District	Electric services
The Archbishop Bergan Mercy Hospital	General medical & surgical hospitals
The Nebraska Medical Center	General medical & surgical hospitals
The Pacesetter Corporation	General remodeling, single-family houses
Tyson Foods	Meats & meat products
Valmont Industries	Irrigation equipment, self-propelled

Note: Companies shown are located within the Omaha, NE-IA Metropolitan Statistical Area.
Source: Chambers of Commerce; State Departments of Labor; Wikipedia

Best Companies to Work For

Mutual of Omaha, headquartered in Omaha, is among "Fortune's Best Workplaces for Parents." To pick the best companies, *Fortune* partnered with the Great Place to Work Institute. To be considered for the list, companies must be Great Place To Work-Certified and have at least 50 responses from parents in the US. The survey enables employees to share confidential quantitative and qualitative feedback about their organization's culture by responding to 60 statements on a 5-point scale and answering two open-ended questions. Collectively, these statements describe a great employee experience, defined by high levels of trust, respect, credibility, fairness, pride, and camaraderie. In addition, companies provide organizational data like size, location, industry, demographics, roles, and levels; and provide information about parental leave, adoption, flexible schedule, childcare and dependent health care benefits. *Fortune, "Best Workplaces for Parents," 2024*

Mutual of Omaha; Signature Performance, headquartered in Omaha, are among "Fortune's Best Workplaces for Women." To pick the best companies, *Fortune* partnered with the Great Place to Work Institute. To be considered for the list, companies must be Great Place To Work-Certified. Companies must also employ at least 50 women, at least 20% of their non-executive managers must be female, and at least one executive must be female. To determine the Best Workplaces for Women,

Great Place To Work measured the differences in women's survey responses to those of their peers and assesses the impact of demographics and roles on the quality and consistency of women's experiences. Great Place To Work also analyzed the gender balance of each workplace, how it compared to each company's industry, and patterns in representation as women rise from front-line positions to the board of directors. *Fortune, "Best Workplaces for Women," 2024*

CrossMed Healthcare, headquartered in Omaha, is among "Best Workplaces in Health Care." To determine the Best Workplaces in Health Care list, Great Place To Work analyzed the survey responses of over 185,000 employees from Great Place To Work-Certified companies in the health care industry. Survey data analysis and company-provided datapoints are then factored into a combined score to compare and rank the companies that create the most consistently positive experience for all employees in this industry. *Fortune, "Best Workplaces in Health Care," 2024*

PUBLIC SAFETY

Crime Rate

Area	Total Crime Rate	Violent Crime Rate				Property Crime Rate		
		Murder	Rape	Robbery	Aggrav. Assault	Burglary	Larceny-Theft	Motor Vehicle Theft
City	4,029.5	6.0	61.6	69.5	424.0	259.6	2,514.4	694.4
U.S.	2,362.5	6.5	42.1	67.1	273.0	272.7	1,416.6	284.5

Note: Figures are crimes per 100,000 population and cover 2022. Data for 2023 was not available.
Source: FBI, Table 8, Offenses Known to Law Enforcement, by State by City, 2022

Hate Crimes

Area	Number of Quarters Reported	Number of Incidents per Bias Motivation					
		Race/Ethnicity/Ancestry	Religion	Sexual Orientation	Disability	Gender	Gender Identity
City	3	1	0	5	0	0	1
U.S.	4	5,900	2,699	2,077	187	92	492

Source: Federal Bureau of Investigation, Hate Crime Statistics 2023

Identity Theft Consumer Reports

Area	Reports	Reports per 100,000 Population	Rank[2]
MSA[1]	1,580	162	234
U.S.	1,135,291	339	-

Note: (1) Figures cover the Omaha, NE-IA Metropolitan Statistical Area; (2) Rank ranges from 1 to 401 where 1 indicates greatest number of identity theft reports per 100,000 population
Source: Federal Trade Commission, Consumer Sentinel Network Data Book 2024

Fraud and Other Consumer Reports

Area	Reports	Reports per 100,000 Population	Rank[2]
MSA[1]	11,283	1,160	144
U.S.	5,360,641	1,601	-

Note: (1) Figures cover the Omaha, NE-IA Metropolitan Statistical Area; (2) Rank ranges from 1 to 401 where 1 indicates greatest number of fraud and other consumer reports per 100,000 population
Source: Federal Trade Commission, Consumer Sentinel Network Data Book 2024

POLITICS

2024 Presidential Election Results

Area	Trump (Rep.)	Harris (Dem.)	Stein (Green)	Kennedy (Ind.)	Oliver (Lib.)	Other
Douglas County	43.9	54.1	0.4	0.0	0.6	1.0
U.S.	49.7	48.2	0.6	0.5	0.4	0.6

Note: Results are percentages and may not add to 100% due to rounding
Source: Dave Leip's Atlas of U.S. Presidential Elections

SPORTS

Professional Sports Teams

Team Name	League	Year Established

No teams are located in the metro area
Source: Wikipedia, Major Professional Sports Teams of the United States and Canada, May 1, 2025

CLIMATE

Average and Extreme Temperatures

Temperature	Jan	Feb	Mar	Apr	May	Jun	Jul	Aug	Sep	Oct	Nov	Dec	Yr.
Extreme High (°F)	67	77	89	97	98	105	110	107	103	95	80	69	110
Average High (°F)	31	37	48	64	74	84	88	85	77	66	49	36	62
Average Temp. (°F)	22	27	38	52	63	73	77	75	66	54	39	27	51
Average Low (°F)	11	17	27	40	52	61	66	64	54	42	29	17	40
Extreme Low (°F)	-23	-21	-16	5	27	38	44	43	25	13	-9	-23	-23

Note: Figures cover the years 1948-1992
Source: National Climatic Data Center, International Station Meteorological Climate Summary, 9/96

Average Precipitation/Snowfall/Humidity

Precip./Humidity	Jan	Feb	Mar	Apr	May	Jun	Jul	Aug	Sep	Oct	Nov	Dec	Yr.
Avg. Precip. (in.)	0.8	0.9	2.0	2.8	4.3	4.0	3.7	3.8	3.4	2.1	1.5	0.9	30.1
Avg. Snowfall (in.)	7	6	7	1	Tr	0	0	0	Tr	Tr	3	6	29
Avg. Rel. Hum. 6am (%)	78	80	79	77	80	82	84	86	85	81	79	80	81
Avg. Rel. Hum. 3pm (%)	61	59	54	46	49	50	51	53	51	47	55	61	53

Note: Figures cover the years 1948-1992; Tr = Trace amounts (<0.05 in. of rain; <0.5 in. of snow)
Source: National Climatic Data Center, International Station Meteorological Climate Summary, 9/96

Weather Conditions

Temperature			Daytime Sky			Precipitation		
5°F & below	32°F & below	90°F & above	Clear	Partly cloudy	Cloudy	0.01 inch or more precip.	0.1 inch or more snow/ice	Thunderstorms
23	139	35	100	142	123	97	20	46

Note: Figures are average number of days per year and cover the years 1948-1992
Source: National Climatic Data Center, International Station Meteorological Climate Summary, 9/96

HAZARDOUS WASTE

Superfund Sites

The Omaha, NE-IA metro area is home to four sites on the EPA's Superfund National Priorities List (NPL) or Superfund Alternative Approach (SAA) list: **Nebraska Ordnance Plant (Former)** (Final NPL); **Old Hwy 275 and N 288th Street** (Final NPL); **Omaha Lead** (Final NPL); **PCE - Carriage Cleaners** (Final NPL). The Superfund alternative approach uses the same investigation and cleanup process and standards that are used for sites listed on the National Priorities List. The SAA is an alternative to listing a site on the NPL; it is not an alternative to Superfund or the Superfund process. There are a total of 1,445 Superfund sites with a status of proposed or final on both lists in the United States. *U.S. Environmental Protection Agency, National Priorities List, May 1, 2025; U.S. Environmental Protection Agency, Superfund Alternative Approach Sites, May 1, 2025*

AIR QUALITY

Air Quality Trends: Ozone

	1990	1995	2000	2005	2010	2015	2020	2021	2022	2023
MSA[1]	n/a	n/a	n/a	n/a	n/a	n/a	n/a	n/a	n/a	n/a
U.S.	0.087	0.089	0.081	0.080	0.072	0.068	0.066	0.067	0.067	0.070

Note: (1) Data covers the Omaha, NE-IA Metropolitan Statistical Area; n/a not available. The values shown are the composite ozone concentration averages among trend sites based on the highest fourth daily maximum 8-hour concentration in parts per million. These trends are based on sites having an adequate record of monitoring data during the trend period. Data from exceptional events are included.
Source: U.S. Environmental Protection Agency, Air Quality Monitoring Information, "Air Quality Trends by City, 1990-2023"

Air Quality Index

Area	Percent of Days when Air Quality was...[2]					AQI Statistics[2]	
	Good	Moderate	Unhealthy for Sensitive Groups	Unhealthy	Very Unhealthy	Maximum	Median
MSA[1]	50.4	42.7	6.3	0.5	0.0	169	50

Note: (1) Data covers the Omaha, NE-IA Metropolitan Statistical Area; (2) Based on 365 days with AQI data in 2023. Air Quality Index (AQI) is an index for reporting daily air quality. EPA calculates the AQI for five major air pollutants regulated by the Clean Air Act: ground-level ozone, particle pollution (aka particulate matter), carbon monoxide, sulfur dioxide, and nitrogen dioxide. The AQI runs from 0 to 500. The higher the AQI value, the greater the level of air pollution and the greater the health concern. There are six AQI categories: "Good" AQI is between 0 and 50. Air quality is considered satisfactory; "Moderate" AQI is between 51 and 100. Air quality is acceptable; "Unhealthy for Sensitive Groups" When AQI values are between 101 and 150, members of sensitive groups may experience health effects; "Unhealthy" When AQI values are between 151 and 200 everyone may begin to experience health effects; "Very Unhealthy" AQI values between 201 and 300 trigger a health alert; "Hazardous" AQI values over 300 trigger warnings of emergency conditions (not shown).
Source: U.S. Environmental Protection Agency, Air Quality Index Report, 2023

Air Quality Index Pollutants

Area	Percent of Days when AQI Pollutant was...[2]					
	Carbon Monoxide	Nitrogen Dioxide	Ozone	Sulfur Dioxide	Particulate Matter 2.5	Particulate Matter 10
MSA[1]	0.0	0.0	48.2	(3)	47.4	4.4

Note: (1) Data covers the Omaha, NE-IA Metropolitan Statistical Area; (2) Based on 365 days with AQI data in 2023. The Air Quality Index (AQI) is an index for reporting daily air quality. EPA calculates the AQI for five major air pollutants regulated by the Clean Air Act: ground-level ozone, particle pollution (also known as particulate matter), carbon monoxide, sulfur dioxide, and nitrogen dioxide. The AQI runs from 0 to 500. The higher the AQI value, the greater the level of air pollution and the greater the health concern; (3) Sulfur dioxide is no longer included in this table because SO_2 concentrations tend to be very localized and not necessarily representative of broad geographical areas like counties and CBSAs.
Source: U.S. Environmental Protection Agency, Air Quality Index Report, 2023

Maximum Air Pollutant Concentrations: Particulate Matter, Ozone, CO and Lead

	Particulate Matter 10 (ug/m³)	Particulate Matter 2.5 Wtd AM (ug/m³)	Particulate Matter 2.5 24-Hr (ug/m³)	Ozone (ppm)	Carbon Monoxide (ppm)	Lead (ug/m³)
MSA[1] Level	79	9.7	33	0.082	1	0.06
NAAQS[2]	150	15	35	0.075	9	0.15
Met NAAQS[2]	Yes	Yes	Yes	No	Yes	Yes

Note: (1) Data covers the Omaha, NE-IA Metropolitan Statistical Area; Data from exceptional events are included; (2) National Ambient Air Quality Standards; ppm = parts per million; ug/m³ = micrograms per cubic meter; n/a not available.
Concentrations: Particulate Matter 10 (coarse particulate)—highest second maximum 24-hour concentration; Particulate Matter 2.5 Wtd AM (fine particulate)—highest weighted annual mean concentration; Particulate Matter 2.5 24-Hour (fine particulate)—highest 98th percentile 24-hour concentration; Ozone—highest fourth daily maximum 8-hour concentration; Carbon Monoxide—highest second maximum non-overlapping 8-hour concentration; Lead—maximum running 3-month average
Source: U.S. Environmental Protection Agency, Air Quality Monitoring Information, "Air Quality Statistics by City, 2023"

Maximum Air Pollutant Concentrations: Nitrogen Dioxide and Sulfur Dioxide

	Nitrogen Dioxide AM (ppb)	Nitrogen Dioxide 1-Hr (ppb)	Sulfur Dioxide AM (ppb)	Sulfur Dioxide 1-Hr (ppb)	Sulfur Dioxide 24-Hr (ppb)
MSA[1] Level	n/a	n/a	n/a	39	n/a
NAAQS[2]	53	100	30	75	140
Met NAAQS[2]	n/a	n/a	n/a	Yes	n/a

Note: (1) Data covers the Omaha, NE-IA Metropolitan Statistical Area; Data from exceptional events are included; (2) National Ambient Air Quality Standards; ppm = parts per million; ug/m³ = micrograms per cubic meter; n/a not available.
Concentrations: Nitrogen Dioxide AM—highest arithmetic mean concentration; Nitrogen Dioxide 1-Hr—highest 98th percentile 1-hour daily maximum concentration; Sulfur Dioxide AM—highest annual mean concentration; Sulfur Dioxide 1-Hr—highest 99th percentile 1-hour daily maximum concentration; Sulfur Dioxide 24-Hr—highest second maximum 24-hour concentration
Source: U.S. Environmental Protection Agency, Air Quality Monitoring Information, "Air Quality Statistics by City, 2023"

Rochester, Minnesota

Background

Rochester's early day was as a transportation hub for the wheat markets of southeastern Minnesota. William Mayo arrived from England in 1864, as an examining physician for Civil War draftees, and Rochester's destiny as a medical mecca was determined when a pioneer of medicine, a determined Sister of St. Francis, and a devastating tornado converged on the evening of August 21, 1883. The tornado killed dozens and injuring hundreds, causing the Mayos (father and two sons, Will and Charlie) and other Rochester physicians to call upon the Sisters of St. Francis who worked tirelessly with the Drs. Mayo. In 1889, they established St. Mary's Hospital, in spite of the Mayos' insistence that Rochester was too small for such a hospital. In 1914, St. Mary's Hospital would become the Mayo Clinic which today is a medical model of integrated medicine consisting of teamwork, pooled knowledge, and resources among physicians, used throughout the world. Dr. Mayo personally trained his students, thinking that the best way to learn medicine is by studying large numbers of cases and by hands-on experience, known today as residency training, a standard in medical education.

The Mayo Clinic is still a world pioneer, making Rochester a medical destination, and employing over 42,000 in Rochester alone. Additional Mayo facilities have been established in Arizona and Florida. The Mayo Clinic is the largest not-for-profit medical practice in the world. In 1973, Mayo opened its medical school, the most selective in the country and today, the Mayo Clinic offers history and art tours.

IBM was a mainstay of Rochester's economy for years, employing over 8,000 employees in its heyday. IBM's nickname "Big Blue" was based on the Rochester facility, which is constructed of blue panels designed to reflect the Minnesota sky. The building was dedicated in 1958 and was the largest IBM facility under one roof in the world. In 1990, the National Building Museum acknowledged the facility for its historic significance and innovation. In 2016, IBM consolidated, and in 2018, the property was sold and renamed the Rochester Technology Campus.

The History Center of Olmsted County offers an impressive variety of programs, including research facilities and rare collections. Venues include tours of the historic 38-room, Mayowood Mansion and gardens—once the home of the Mayo family. Much of the architecture was the handiwork of W. W. Mayo himself.

The oldest cultural arts institution in the community, Rochester Symphony Orchestra & Chorale was founded in 1919 as a professional performing arts organization. Its earliest ensemble—the Lawler-Dodge Orchestra—was founded in 1912 as a volunteer orchestra, driven by Daisy Plummer, wife of world-famous Mayo Clinic physician, Dr. Henry Plummer, and directed by Harold Cooke. The Orchestra performed in the former Chateau Theatre where they played background music for silent movies.

The Rochester Downtown Alliance created the Summer Market and Music Festival, and STYLE, the Runway Experience. StyleICE is a unique celebration in which local downtown bars produce an all-ice experience. Everything from glasses to couches is created out of ice and features special lighting effects and live music. In 2019, a new, state-of-the-art movie theater opened its doors in the city.

Minnesota has one of the most extensive state park systems in the nation. Whitewater is the closest state park to Rochester, which has more than 100 city parks over 3500 acres of parkland and more than 85 miles of paved trails, in addition to state trails such as the Douglas State Trail.

Rochester features a humid continental climate with four distinct seasons. Summers are very warm, and winters are very cold. The city sees an annual average of 30 inches of rainfall and 48 inches of snowfall. Significant snow accumulation is common during the winter months. Spring and fall are transitional, with a warming trend during the spring and a cooling trend during the fall. It is not uncommon to see snowfall during early spring and late fall.

Rankings

General Rankings

- In their annual survey, Livability.com looked at data for more than 2,000 mid-sized U.S. cities to assign a "Livability Score"for each. The top 100 scoring cities make up Livability's "Top 100 Best Places to Live in the U.S." in 2025. Rochester was placed among the top 100 of the customizable list. Criteria: housing and economy; cost of living; environment; education; health care options; transportation; safety; and community amenities. *Livability.com, "Top 100 Best Places to Live in the U.S. in 2025" April 15, 2025*

Business/Finance Rankings

- The Rochester metro area appeared on the Milken Institute "2025 Best Performing Cities" list. Rank: #94 out of 203 small metro areas (based on performance category). Criteria: job growth; wage growth; high-tech growth and impact; community resilience; housing affordability; household broadband access. *Milken Institute, "Best-Performing Cities 2025," January 14, 2025*

Seniors/Retirement Rankings

- Rochester made the 2024 *Forbes* list of "25 Best Places to Retire." Criteria, focused on overall affordability as well as quality of life indicators, include: housing/living costs compared to the national average and taxes; air quality; crime rates; median home prices; risk associated with climate-change/natural hazards; availability of medical care; bikeability; walkability; healthy living. *Forbes.com, "The Best Places to Retire in 2024: Las Cruces and Other Unexpected Hot Spots," May 10, 2024*

Business Environment

DEMOGRAPHICS

Population Growth

Area	1990 Census	2000 Census	2010 Census	2020 Census	2023 Estimate[2]	Population Growth 1990-2023 (%)
City	74,151	85,806	106,769	121,395	121,638	64.0
MSA[1]	141,945	163,618	186,011	226,329	227,252	60.1
U.S.	248,709,873	281,421,906	308,745,538	331,449,281	332,387,540	33.6

Note: (1) Figures cover the Rochester, MN Metropolitan Statistical Area; (2) 2019-2023 5-year ACS population estimate
Source: U.S. Census Bureau, 1990 Census, 2000 Census, 2010 Census, 2020 Census, 2019-2023 American Community Survey 5-Year Estimates

Race

Area	White Alone[2] (%)	Black Alone[2] (%)	Asian Alone[2] (%)	AIAN[3] Alone[2] (%)	NHOPI[4] Alone[2] (%)	Other Race Alone[2] (%)	Two or More Races (%)
City	74.3	9.4	8.0	0.2	0.1	2.1	5.9
MSA[1]	83.0	5.4	4.7	0.2	0.1	1.7	4.9
U.S.	63.4	12.4	5.8	0.9	0.2	6.6	10.7

Note: (1) Figures cover the Rochester, MN Metropolitan Statistical Area; (2) Alone is defined as not being in combination with one or more other races; (3) American Indian and Alaska Native; (4) Native Hawaiian and Other Pacific Islander
Source: U.S. Census Bureau, 2019-2023 American Community Survey 5-Year Estimates

Hispanic or Latino Origin

Area	Total (%)	Mexican (%)	Puerto Rican (%)	Cuban (%)	Other (%)
City	6.2	3.9	0.4	0.1	1.8
MSA[1]	5.1	3.2	0.3	0.1	1.5
U.S.	19.0	11.3	1.8	0.7	5.2

Note: Persons of Hispanic or Latino origin can be of any race; (1) Figures cover the Rochester, MN Metropolitan Statistical Area
Source: U.S. Census Bureau, 2019-2023 American Community Survey 5-Year Estimates

Age

Area	Under Age 5	Age 5–19	Age 20–34	Age 35–44	Age 45–54	Age 55–64	Age 65–74	Age 75–84	Age 85+	Median Age
City	6.8	18.9	22.4	14.1	10.3	11.5	8.8	4.9	2.3	36.4
MSA[1]	6.2	20.1	18.7	13.6	11.1	12.9	9.8	5.2	2.3	38.8
U.S.	5.7	19.1	20.2	13.1	12.3	12.8	10.0	4.9	1.9	38.7

Note: (1) Figures cover the Rochester, MN Metropolitan Statistical Area
Source: U.S. Census Bureau, 2019-2023 American Community Survey 5-Year Estimates

Disability by Age

Area	All Ages	Under 18 Years Old	18 to 64 Years Old	65 Years and Over
City	10.1	3.8	7.8	28.9
MSA[1]	10.1	3.6	7.8	27.2
U.S.	13.0	4.7	10.7	32.9

Note: Figures show percent of the civilian noninstitutionalized population that reported having a disability. Disability status is determined from six types of difficulty: vision, hearing, cognitive, ambulatory, self-care, and independent living. For children under 5 years old, hearing and vision difficulty are used to determine disability status. For children between the ages of 5 and 14, disability status is determined from hearing, vision, cognitive, ambulatory, and self-care difficulties. For people aged 15 years and older, they are considered to have a disability if they have difficulty with any one of the six difficulty types; Note: (1) Figures cover the Rochester, MN Metropolitan Statistical Area
Source: U.S. Census Bureau, 2019-2023 American Community Survey 5-Year Estimates

Ancestry

Area	German	Irish	English	American	Italian	Polish	French[2]	European	Scottish
City	28.8	9.8	7.1	2.6	1.8	2.6	1.8	1.6	1.4
MSA[1]	32.8	10.3	7.3	3.6	1.5	2.5	1.7	1.8	1.3
U.S.	12.6	9.4	9.1	5.5	4.9	2.6	2.0	1.6	1.6

Note: Figures are the percentage of the total population reporting a particular ancestry. The nine most commonly reported ancestries in the U.S. are shown. Figures include multiple ancestries (e.g. if a person reported being Irish and Italian, they were included in both columns); (1) Figures cover the Rochester, MN Metropolitan Statistical Area; (2) Excludes Basque
Source: U.S. Census Bureau, 2019-2023 American Community Survey 5-Year Estimates

Foreign-born Population

Area	Percent of Population Born in								
	Any Foreign Country	Asia	Mexico	Europe	Caribbean	Central America[2]	South America	Africa	Canada
City	14.1	5.9	1.0	1.2	0.1	0.3	0.4	4.9	0.2
MSA[1]	8.8	3.5	0.8	0.9	0.1	0.2	0.4	2.7	0.2
U.S.	13.9	4.3	3.3	1.4	1.4	1.2	1.2	0.8	0.2

Note: (1) Figures cover the Rochester, MN Metropolitan Statistical Area; (2) Excludes Mexico.
Source: U.S. Census Bureau, 2019-2023 American Community Survey 5-Year Estimates

Household Size

Area	Persons in Household (%)							Average Household Size
	One	Two	Three	Four	Five	Six	Seven or More	
City	31.6	34.6	13.4	12.5	5.0	1.8	1.1	2.35
MSA[1]	27.9	36.9	13.2	13.3	5.9	1.8	1.1	2.42
U.S.	28.5	33.8	15.4	12.7	5.9	2.3	1.4	2.54

Note: (1) Figures cover the Rochester, MN Metropolitan Statistical Area
Source: U.S. Census Bureau, 2019-2023 American Community Survey 5-Year Estimates

Household Relationships

Area	Householder	Opposite-sex Spouse	Same-sex Spouse	Opposite-sex Unmarried Partner	Same-sex Unmarried Partner	Child[2]	Grandchild	Other Relatives	Non-relatives
City	41.1	18.5	0.2	2.8	0.1	27.8	0.9	2.8	3.3
MSA[1]	40.1	20.5	0.1	2.7	0.1	28.9	1.0	2.2	2.5
U.S.	38.3	17.5	0.2	2.5	0.2	28.3	2.4	4.8	3.4

Note: Figures are percent of the total population; (1) Figures cover the Rochester, MN Metropolitan Statistical Area; (2) Includes biological, adopted, and stepchildren of the householder
Source: U.S. Census Bureau, 2020 Census

Gender

Area	Males	Females	Males per 100 Females
City	59,099	62,539	94.5
MSA[1]	112,416	114,836	97.9
U.S.	164,545,087	167,842,453	98.0

Note: (1) Figures cover the Rochester, MN Metropolitan Statistical Area
Source: U.S. Census Bureau, 2019-2023 American Community Survey 5-Year Estimates

Marital Status

Area	Never Married	Now Married[2]	Separated	Widowed	Divorced
City	34.2	51.3	0.9	4.8	8.8
MSA[1]	29.3	55.9	0.7	4.9	9.1
U.S.	34.1	47.9	1.7	5.6	10.7

Note: Figures are percentages and cover the population 15 years of age and older; (1) Figures cover the Rochester, MN Metropolitan Statistical Area; (2) Excludes separated
Source: U.S. Census Bureau, 2019-2023 American Community Survey 5-Year Estimates

Religious Groups by Family

Area	Catholic	Baptist	Methodist	LDS[2]	Pentecostal	Lutheran	Islam	Adventist	Other
MSA[1]	15.6	0.4	2.8	1.5	1.9	19.3	1.0	0.7	10.1
U.S.	18.7	7.3	3.0	2.0	1.8	1.7	1.3	1.3	11.6

Note: Figures are the number of adherents as a percentage of the total population and cover the eight largest religious groups in the U.S; (1) Figures cover the Rochester, MN Metropolitan Statistical Area; (2) Church of Jesus Christ of Latter-day Saints
Sources: 2020 U.S. Religion Census, Association of Statisticians of American Religious Bodies; The Association of Religion Data Archives (ARDA)

Religious Groups by Tradition

Area	Catholic	Evangelical Protestant	Mainline Protestant	Black Protestant	Islam	Judaism	Hinduism	Orthodox	Buddhism
MSA[1]	15.6	15.0	19.1	n/a	1.0	0.1	0.1	0.2	0.2
U.S.	18.7	16.5	5.2	2.3	1.3	0.6	0.4	0.4	0.3

Note: Figures are the number of adherents as a percentage of the total population; (1) Figures cover the Rochester, MN Metropolitan Statistical Area
Sources: 2020 U.S. Religion Census, Association of Statisticians of American Religious Bodies; The Association of Religion Data Archives (ARDA)

ECONOMY

Real Gross Domestic Product (GDP)

Area	2017	2018	2019	2020	2021	2022	2023	Rank[3]
MSA[1]	13.1	13.6	13.8	13.6	14.1	14.4	14.9	182
U.S.[2]	17,619.1	18,160.7	18,642.5	18,238.9	19,387.6	19,896.6	20,436.3	—

Note: Figures are in billions of chained 2017 dollars; (1) Figures cover the Rochester, MN Metropolitan Statistical Area; (2) Figures cover real GDP within metropolitan areas; (3) Rank is based on 2023 data and ranges from 1 to 384
Source: U.S. Bureau of Economic Analysis

Economic Growth

Area	2014	2015	2016	2017	2018	2019	2020	2021	2022	2023
MSA[1]	1.6	2.9	1.4	3.6	3.5	2.0	-1.6	3.9	2.0	3.2
U.S.[2]	2.6	3.2	2.0	2.7	3.1	2.7	-2.2	6.3	2.6	2.7

Note: Figures are real gross domestic product growth rates and represent percent change from preceding period; (1) Figures cover the Rochester, MN Metropolitan Statistical Area; (2) Figures are the average growth rates within metropolitan areas
Source: U.S. Bureau of Economic Analysis

Metropolitan Area Exports

Area	2018	2019	2020	2021	2022	2023	Rank[2]
MSA[1]	537.6	390.1	194.0	224.9	215.9	258.7	293
U.S.	1,664,056.1	1,645,173.7	1,431,406.6	1,753,941.4	2,062,937.4	2,019,160.5	—

Note: Figures are in millions of dollars; (1) Figures cover the Rochester, MN Metropolitan Statistical Area; (2) Rank is based on 2023 data and ranges from 1 to 386
Source: U.S. Department of Commerce, International Trade Administration, Office of Trade and Economic Analysis, Industry and Analysis, Exports by Metropolitan Area, data extracted April 2, 2025

Building Permits

Area	Single-Family 2023	Single-Family 2024	Pct. Chg.	Multi-Family 2023	Multi-Family 2024	Pct. Chg.	Total 2023	Total 2024	Pct. Chg.
City	241	193	-19.9	551	925	67.9	792	1,118	41.2
MSA[1]	604	491	-18.7	570	993	74.2	1,174	1,484	26.4
U.S.	920,000	981,900	6.7	591,100	496,100	-16.1	1,511,100	1,478,000	-2.2

Note: (1) Figures cover the Rochester, MN Metropolitan Statistical Area; Figures represent new, privately-owned housing units authorized (unadjusted data)
Source: U.S. Census Bureau, Building Permits Survey (BPS), 2023, 2024

Bankruptcy Filings

Area	Business Filings 2023	Business Filings 2024	% Chg.	Nonbusiness Filings 2023	Nonbusiness Filings 2024	% Chg.
Olmsted County	8	6	-25.0	137	161	17.5
U.S.	18,926	23,107	22.1	434,064	494,201	13.9

Note: Business filings include Chapter 7, Chapter 9, Chapter 11, Chapter 12, Chapter 13, Chapter 15, and Section 304; Nonbusiness filings include Chapter 7, Chapter 11, and Chapter 13
Source: Administrative Office of the U.S. Courts, Business and Nonbusiness Bankruptcy, County Cases Commenced by Chapter of the Bankruptcy Code, During the 12-Month Period Ending December 31, 2023 and Business and Nonbusiness Bankruptcy, County Cases Commenced by Chapter of the Bankruptcy Code, During the 12-Month Period Ending December 31, 2024

Housing Vacancy Rates

Area	Gross Vacancy Rate[3] (%) 2022	2023	2024	Year-Round Vacancy Rate[4] (%) 2022	2023	2024	Rental Vacancy Rate[5] (%) 2022	2023	2024	Homeowner Vacancy Rate[6] (%) 2022	2023	2024
MSA[1]	n/a	n/a	n/a	n/a	n/a	n/a	n/a	n/a	n/a	n/a	n/a	n/a
U.S.[2]	9.1	9.0	9.1	7.5	7.5	7.6	5.7	6.5	6.8	0.8	0.8	1.0

Note: (1) Figures cover the Rochester, MN Metropolitan Statistical Area; (2) Figures cover the 75 largest Metropolitan Statistical Areas; (3) The percentage of the total housing inventory that is vacant; (4) The percentage of the housing inventory (excluding seasonal units) that is year-round vacant; (5) The percentage of rental inventory that is vacant for rent; (6) The percentage of homeowner inventory that is vacant for sale; n/a not available
Source: U.S. Census Bureau, Housing Vacancies and Homeownership Annual Statistics: 2022, 2023, 2024

INCOME

Income

Area	Per Capita ($)	Median Household ($)	Average Household ($)
City	49,727	87,767	119,510
MSA[1]	48,977	89,675	120,598
U.S.	43,289	78,538	110,491

Note: (1) Figures cover the Rochester, MN Metropolitan Statistical Area
Source: U.S. Census Bureau, 2019-2023 American Community Survey 5-Year Estimates

Household Income Distribution

Area	Percent of Households Earning							
	Under $15,000	$15,000 -$24,999	$25,000 -$34,999	$35,000 -$49,999	$50,000 -$74,999	$75,000 -$99,999	$100,000 -$149,999	$150,000 and up
City	5.2	5.8	5.7	9.1	16.3	13.5	19.9	24.5
MSA[1]	5.2	5.4	5.6	9.0	16.3	13.4	20.4	24.7
U.S.	8.5	6.6	6.8	10.4	15.7	12.7	17.4	21.9

Note: (1) Figures cover the Rochester, MN Metropolitan Statistical Area
Source: U.S. Census Bureau, 2019-2023 American Community Survey 5-Year Estimates

Poverty Rate

Area	All Ages	Under 18 Years Old	18 to 64 Years Old	65 Years and Over
City	9.1	9.0	9.4	7.6
MSA[1]	7.8	8.3	7.8	7.1
U.S.	12.4	16.3	11.6	10.4

Note: Figures are percentage of people whose income during the past 12 months was below the poverty level; (1) Figures cover the Rochester, MN Metropolitan Statistical Area
Source: U.S. Census Bureau, 2019-2023 American Community Survey 5-Year Estimates

EMPLOYMENT

Labor Force and Employment

Area	Civilian Labor Force			Workers Employed		
	Dec. 2023	Dec. 2024	% Chg.	Dec. 2023	Dec. 2024	% Chg.
City	68,874	73,886	7.3	67,640	72,557	7.3
MSA[1]	128,702	138,168	7.4	126,091	135,339	7.3
U.S.	166,661,000	167,746,000	0.7	160,754,000	161,294,000	0.3

Note: Data is not seasonally adjusted and covers workers 16 years of age and older; (1) Figures cover the Rochester, MN Metropolitan Statistical Area
Source: Bureau of Labor Statistics, Local Area Unemployment Statistics

Unemployment Rate

Area	2024											
	Jan.	Feb.	Mar.	Apr.	May	Jun.	Jul.	Aug.	Sep.	Oct.	Nov.	Dec.
City	2.2	2.5	2.1	2.0	1.9	2.6	2.6	2.5	2.0	1.9	1.9	1.8
MSA[1]	2.8	3.0	2.6	2.2	2.2	2.8	2.7	2.6	2.0	1.8	1.9	2.0
U.S.	4.1	4.2	3.9	3.5	3.7	4.3	4.5	4.4	3.9	3.9	4.0	3.8

Note: Data is not seasonally adjusted and covers workers 16 years of age and older; (1) Figures cover the Rochester, MN Metropolitan Statistical Area
Source: Bureau of Labor Statistics, Local Area Unemployment Statistics

Average Wages

Occupation	$/Hr.	Occupation	$/Hr.
Accountants and Auditors	46.22	Maintenance and Repair Workers	26.25
Automotive Mechanics	27.15	Marketing Managers	80.62
Bookkeepers	27.32	Network and Computer Systems Admin.	52.13
Carpenters	32.24	Nurses, Licensed Practical	29.80
Cashiers	15.88	Nurses, Registered	50.31
Computer Programmers	n/a	Nursing Assistants	21.62
Computer Systems Analysts	n/a	Office Clerks, General	23.84
Computer User Support Specialists	33.24	Physical Therapists	46.20
Construction Laborers	28.42	Physicians	142.26
Cooks, Restaurant	18.68	Plumbers, Pipefitters and Steamfitters	41.69
Customer Service Representatives	23.08	Police and Sheriff's Patrol Officers	38.02
Dentists	122.85	Postal Service Mail Carriers	30.26
Electricians	39.75	Real Estate Sales Agents	32.82
Engineers, Electrical	50.77	Retail Salespersons	18.61
Fast Food and Counter Workers	15.53	Sales Representatives, Technical/Scientific	63.87
Financial Managers	77.53	Secretaries, Exc. Legal/Medical/Executive	25.11
First-Line Supervisors of Office Workers	34.14	Security Guards	23.45
General and Operations Managers	50.21	Surgeons	n/a
Hairdressers/Cosmetologists	22.80	Teacher Assistants, Exc. Postsecondary[1]	18.97
Home Health and Personal Care Aides	17.71	Teachers, Secondary School, Exc. Sp. Ed.[1]	34.45
Janitors and Cleaners	20.40	Telemarketers	n/a
Landscaping/Groundskeeping Workers	21.83	Truck Drivers, Heavy/Tractor-Trailer	30.88
Lawyers	65.23	Truck Drivers, Light/Delivery Services	23.86
Maids and Housekeeping Cleaners	18.18	Waiters and Waitresses	12.89

Note: Wage data covers the Rochester, MN Metropolitan Statistical Area; (1) Hourly wages were calculated from annual wage data based on a 40 hour work week
Source: Bureau of Labor Statistics, Metro Area Occupational Employment & Wage Estimates, May 2024

Employment by Industry

Sector	MSA[1] Number of Employees	MSA[1] Percent of Total	U.S. Percent of Total
Construction, Mining, and Logging	5,300	4.1	5.5
Financial Activities	2,800	2.2	5.8
Government	13,600	10.5	14.9
Information	1,000	0.8	1.9
Leisure and Hospitality	10,700	8.2	10.4
Manufacturing	9,000	6.9	8.0
Other Services	3,900	3.0	3.7
Private Education and Health Services	58,700	45.2	16.9
Professional and Business Services	6,900	5.3	14.2
Retail Trade	12,500	9.6	10.0
Transportation, Warehousing, and Utilities	2,700	2.1	4.8
Wholesale Trade	2,700	2.1	3.9

Note: Figures are non-farm employment as of December 2024. Figures are not seasonally adjusted and include workers 16 years of age and older; (1) Figures cover the Rochester, MN Metropolitan Statistical Area
Source: Bureau of Labor Statistics, Current Employment Statistics, Employment, Hours, and Earnings

Employment by Occupation

Occupation Classification	City (%)	MSA[1] (%)	U.S. (%)
Management, Business, Science, and Arts	56.0	50.3	42.0
Natural Resources, Construction, and Maintenance	4.9	7.6	8.6
Production, Transportation, and Material Moving	8.9	10.8	13.0
Sales and Office	15.1	16.4	19.9
Service	15.2	14.9	16.5

Note: Figures cover employed civilians 16 years of age and older; (1) Figures cover the Rochester, MN Metropolitan Statistical Area
Source: U.S. Census Bureau, 2019-2023 American Community Survey 5-Year Estimates

Occupations with Greatest Projected Employment Growth: 2022 – 2032

Occupation[1]	2022 Employment	2032 Projected Employment	Numeric Employment Change	Percent Employment Change
Home Health and Personal Care Aides	113,680	129,520	15,840	13.9
Software Developers	38,590	47,920	9,330	24.2
General and Operations Managers	76,000	81,170	5,170	6.8
Laborers and Freight, Stock, and Material Movers, Hand	55,000	58,700	3,700	6.7
Registered Nurses	68,040	71,630	3,590	5.3
Stockers and Order Fillers	42,970	46,440	3,470	8.1
Market Research Analysts and Marketing Specialists	23,920	27,220	3,300	13.8
Cooks, Restaurant	26,770	30,010	3,240	12.1
Industrial Engineers	18,230	21,260	3,030	16.6
Medical and Health Services Managers	10,910	13,760	2,850	26.1

Note: Projections cover Minnesota; (1) Sorted by numeric employment change
Source: www.projectionscentral.org, State Occupational Projections, 2022–2032 Long-Term Projections

Fastest-Growing Occupations: 2022 – 2032

Occupation[1]	2022 Employment	2032 Projected Employment	Numeric Employment Change	Percent Employment Change
Wind Turbine Service Technicians	360	540	180	50.0
Nurse Practitioners	5,570	8,010	2,440	43.8
Epidemiologists	260	370	110	42.3
Data Scientists	2,290	3,070	780	34.1
Statisticians	660	860	200	30.3
Information Security Analysts (SOC 2018)	2,910	3,730	820	28.2
Physician Assistants	3,830	4,900	1,070	27.9
Medical and Health Services Managers	10,910	13,760	2,850	26.1
Actuaries	1,150	1,430	280	24.3
Physical Therapist Assistants	1,320	1,640	320	24.2

Note: Projections cover Minnesota; (1) Sorted by percent employment change and excludes occupations with numeric employment change less than 50
Source: www.projectionscentral.org, State Occupational Projections, 2022–2032 Long-Term Projections

CITY FINANCES

City Government Finances

Component	2022 ($000)	2022 ($ per capita)
Total Revenues	531,642	4,435
Total Expenditures	447,384	3,732
Debt Outstanding	354,688	2,959

Source: U.S. Census Bureau, State & Local Government Finances 2022

City Government Revenue by Source

Source	2022 ($000)	2022 ($ per capita)	2022 (%)
General Revenue			
From Federal Government	35,167	293	6.6
From State Government	44,043	367	8.3
From Local Governments	4,529	38	0.9
Taxes			
Property	80,692	673	15.2
Sales and Gross Receipts	30,590	255	5.8
Personal Income	0	0	0.0
Corporate Income	0	0	0.0
Motor Vehicle License	0	0	0.0
Other Taxes	4,611	38	0.9
Current Charges	93,963	784	17.7
Liquor Store	0	0	0.0
Utility	223,778	1,867	42.1

Source: U.S. Census Bureau, State & Local Government Finances 2022

City Government Expenditures by Function

Function	2022 ($000)	2022 ($ per capita)	2022 (%)
General Direct Expenditures			
Air Transportation	14,171	118	3.2
Corrections	0	0	0.0
Education	0	0	0.0
Employment Security Administration	0	0	0.0
Financial Administration	4,886	40	1.1
Fire Protection	20,312	169	4.5
General Public Buildings	0	0	0.0
Governmental Administration, Other	1,042	8	0.2
Health	0	0	0.0
Highways	41,294	344	9.2
Hospitals	0	0	0.0
Housing and Community Development	1,330	11	0.3
Interest on General Debt	11,236	93	2.5
Judicial and Legal	0	0	0.0
Libraries	8,653	72	1.9
Parking	3,463	28	0.8
Parks and Recreation	20,158	168	4.5
Police Protection	38,536	321	8.6
Public Welfare	0	0	0.0
Sewerage	28,200	235	6.3
Solid Waste Management	0	0	0.0
Veterans' Services	0	0	0.0
Liquor Store	0	0	0.0
Utility	189,531	1,581	42.4

Source: U.S. Census Bureau, State & Local Government Finances 2022

TAXES

State Corporate Income Tax Rates

State	Tax Rate (%)	Income Brackets ($)	Num. of Brackets	Financial Institution Tax Rate (%)[a]	Federal Income Tax Ded.
Minnesota	9.8 (l)	Flat rate	1	9.8 (l)	No

Note: Tax rates for tax year 2024; (a) Rates listed are the corporate income tax rate applied to financial institutions or excise taxes based on income. Some states have other taxes based upon the value of deposits or shares; (l) In addition, Minnesota levies a 5.8% tentative minimum tax on Alternative Minimum Taxable Income. Minnesota also imposes a surtax ranging up to $11,570.

Source: Federation of Tax Administrators, State Corporate Income Tax Rates, January 1, 2025

State Individual Income Tax Rates

State	Tax Rate (%)	Income Brackets ($)	Personal Exemptions ($)			Standard Ded. ($)	
			Single	Married	Depend.	Single	Married
Minnesota (a)	5.35 - 9.85	31,690 - 193,240 (n)	(d)	(d)	(d)	5,150	14,575	29,150

Note: Tax rates for tax year 2024; Local- and county-level taxes are not included; Federal income tax is not deductible on state income tax returns; (a) 16 states have statutory provision for automatically adjusting to the rate of inflation the dollar values of the income tax brackets, standard deductions, and/or personal exemptions. Oregon does not index the income brackets for $125,000 and over See: INFL and SPEC above; (d) These states use the personal exemption/standard deduction amounts provided in the federal Internal Revenue Code. Montana personal exemption subject to repeal under Section 15-30-2114; (n) The income brackets reported for Minnesota are for single individuals. For married couples filing jointly, the same tax rates apply to income brackets ranging from $46,331 to $321,450.
Source: Federation of Tax Administrators, State Individual Income Tax Rates, January 1, 2025

Various State Sales and Excise Tax Rates

State	State Sales Tax (%)	Gasoline[1] ($/gal.)	Cigarette[2] ($/pack)	Spirits[3] ($/gal.)	Wine[4] ($/gal.)	Beer[5] ($/gal.)	Recreational Marijuana (%)
Minnesota	6.875	0.32	3.83	8.74	1.25	0.47	(l)

Note: All tax rates as of January 1, 2025; (1) The American Petroleum Institute has developed a methodology for determining the average tax rate on a gallon of fuel. Rates may include any of the following: excise taxes, environmental fees, storage tank fees, other fees or taxes, general sales tax, and local taxes; (2) The federal excise tax of $1.0066 per pack and local taxes are not included; (3) Rates are those applicable to off-premise sales of 40% alcohol by volume (a.b.v.) distilled spirits in 750ml containers. Local excise taxes are excluded; (4) Rates are those applicable to off-premise sales of 11% a.b.v. non-carbonated wine in 750ml containers; (5) Rates are those applicable to off-premise sales of 4.7% a.b.v. beer in 12 ounce containers; (l) 10% excise tax (retail gross receipts)
Source: Tax Foundation, 2025 Facts & Figures: How Does Your State Compare?

State Tax Competitiveness Index

State	Overall Rank	Corporate Tax Rank	Individual Income Tax Rank	Sales Tax Rank	Property Tax Rank	Unemployment Insurance Tax Rank
Minnesota	44	43	44	34	26	42

Note: The Tax Foundation's State Tax Competitiveness Index enables policymakers, taxpayers, and business leaders to gauge how their states' tax systems compare. A rank of 1 is best, 50 is worst. Rankings do not average to the total. States without a tax rank equally as 1. DC's scores and rankings do not affect other states. The report shows tax systems as of July 1, 2024 (the beginning of Fiscal Year 2025).
Source: Tax Foundation, State Tax Competitiveness Index 2025

TRANSPORTATION

Means of Transportation to Work

Area	Car/Truck/Van		Public Transportation			Bicycle	Walked	Other Means	Worked at Home
	Drove Alone	Car-pooled	Bus	Subway	Railroad				
City	65.5	11.1	4.1	0.0	0.0	0.8	4.3	1.3	12.9
MSA[1]	69.6	9.9	2.4	0.0	0.0	0.6	3.5	1.1	12.8
U.S.	70.2	8.5	1.7	1.3	0.4	0.4	2.4	1.6	13.5

Note: Figures are percentages and cover workers 16 years of age and older; (1) Figures cover the Rochester, MN Metropolitan Statistical Area
Source: U.S. Census Bureau, 2019-2023 American Community Survey 5-Year Estimates

Travel Time to Work

Area	Less Than 10 Minutes	10 to 19 Minutes	20 to 29 Minutes	30 to 44 Minutes	45 to 59 Minutes	60 to 89 Minutes	90 Minutes or More
City	18.3	54.5	14.7	6.1	2.8	2.7	0.9
MSA[1]	18.1	41.6	18.7	12.5	4.6	2.9	1.6
U.S.	12.6	28.6	21.2	20.8	8.1	6.0	2.8

Note: Note: Figures are percentages and include workers 16 years old and over; (1) Figures cover the Rochester, MN Metropolitan Statistical Area
Source: U.S. Census Bureau, 2019-2023 American Community Survey 5-Year Estimates

Key Congestion Measures

Measure	2000	2010	2015	2020	2022
Annual Hours of Delay, Total (000)	n/a	n/a	2,253	1,692	2,972
Annual Hours of Delay, Per Auto Commuter	n/a	n/a	19	14	25
Annual Congestion Cost, Per Auto Commuter ($)	n/a	n/a	432	350	619

Note: n/a not available
Source: Texas A&M Transportation Institute, 2023 Urban Mobility Report

Freeway Travel Time Index

Measure	1985	1990	1995	2000	2005	2010	2015	2020	2022
Urban Area Index[1]	n/a	n/a	n/a	n/a	n/a	n/a	1.10	1.07	1.12
Urban Area Rank[1,2]	n/a	n/a	n/a	n/a	n/a	n/a	n/a	n/a	n/a

Note: Freeway Travel Time Index—the ratio of travel time in the peak period to the travel time at free-flow conditions. For example, a value of 1.30 indicates a 20-minute free-flow trip takes 26 minutes in the peak (20 minutes x 1.30 = 26 minutes); (1) Covers the Rochester MN urban area; (2) Rank is based on 101 larger urban areas (#1 = highest travel time index); n/a not available
Source: Texas A&M Transportation Institute, 2023 Urban Mobility Report

Public Transportation

Agency Name / Mode of Transportation	Vehicles Operated in Maximum Service[1]	Annual Unlinked Passenger Trips[2] (in thous.)	Annual Passenger Miles[3] (in thous.)
City of Rochester Public Transportation			
Bus (purchased transportation)	42	705.3	2,337.7
Demand Response (purchased transportation)	9	35.0	195.9
Demand Response - Taxi	4	5.1	24.8

Note: (1) Number of revenue vehicles operated by the given mode and type of service to meet the annual maximum service requirement. This is the revenue vehicle count during the peak season of the year; on the week and day that maximum service is provided. Vehicles operated in maximum service (VOMS) exclude atypical days and one-time special events; (2) Number of passengers who boarded public transportation vehicles. Passengers are counted each time they board a vehicle no matter how many vehicles they use to travel from their origin to their destination. (3) Sum of the distances ridden by all passengers during the entire fiscal year.
Source: Federal Transit Administration, National Transit Database, 2023

Air Transportation

Airport Name and Code / Type of Service	Passenger Airlines[1]	Passenger Enplanements	Freight Carriers[2]	Freight (lbs)
Rochester International Airport (RST)				
Domestic service (U.S. carriers only)	11	98,436	4	7,416,925
International service (U.S. carriers only)	0	0	0	0

Note: (1) Includes all U.S.-based major, minor and commuter airlines that carried at least one passenger during the year; (2) Includes all U.S.-based airlines and freight carriers that transported at least one pound of freight during the year.
Source: Bureau of Transportation Statistics, The Intermodal Transportation Database, Air Carriers: T-100 Domestic Market (U.S. carriers only), 2024; Bureau of Transportation Statistics, The Intermodal Transportation Database, Air Carriers: T-100 International Market (U.S. carriers only), 2024

BUSINESSES

Major Business Headquarters

Company Name	Industry	Rankings Fortune[1]	Rankings Forbes[2]
No companies listed	-	-	-

Note: (1) Companies that produce a 10-K are ranked 1 to 500 based on 2023 revenue; (2) All private companies with at least $2 billion in annual revenue through the end of their most current fiscal year are ranked 1 to 275; companies listed are headquartered in the city; dashes indicate no ranking
Source: Fortune, "Fortune 500," 2024; Forbes, "America's Largest Private Companies," 2024

Living Environment

COST OF LIVING

Cost of Living Index

Composite Index	Groceries	Housing	Utilities	Transportation	Health Care	Misc. Goods/Services
n/a	n/a	n/a	n/a	n/a	n/a	n/a

Note: The Cost of Living Index measures regional differences in the cost of consumer goods and services, excluding taxes and non-consumer expenditures, for professional and managerial households in the top income quintile. It is based on more than 50,000 prices covering almost 60 different items for which prices are collected three times a year by chambers of commerce, economic development organizations or university applied economic centers in each participating urban area. The numbers shown should be read as a percentage above or below the national average of 100. For example, a value of 115.4 in the groceries column indicates that grocery prices are 15.4% higher than the national average. Small differences in the index numbers should not be interpreted as significant; n/a not available.
Source: The Council for Community and Economic Research, Cost of Living Index, 2024

Grocery Prices

Area[1]	T-Bone Steak ($/pound)	Frying Chicken ($/pound)	Whole Milk ($/half gal.)	Eggs ($/dozen)	Orange Juice ($/64 oz.)	Coffee ($/11.5 oz.)
City[2]	n/a	n/a	n/a	n/a	n/a	n/a
Avg.	15.42	1.55	4.69	3.25	4.41	5.46
Min.	14.50	1.16	4.43	2.75	4.00	4.85
Max.	17.56	2.89	5.49	4.78	5.54	7.89

*Note: (1) Values for the local area are compared with the average, minimum and maximum values for all 276 areas in the Cost of Living Index; (2) Figures cover the Rochester MN urban area; n/a not available; **T-Bone Steak** (price per pound); **Frying Chicken** (price per pound, whole fryer); **Whole Milk** (half gallon carton); **Eggs** (price per dozen, Grade A, large); **Orange Juice** (64 oz. Tropicana or Florida Natural); **Coffee** (11.5 oz. can, vacuum-packed, Maxwell House, Hills Bros, or Folgers).*
Source: The Council for Community and Economic Research, Cost of Living Index, 2024

Housing and Utility Costs

Area[1]	New Home Price ($)	Apartment Rent ($/month)	All Electric ($/month)	Part Electric ($/month)	Other Energy ($/month)	Telephone ($/month)
City[2]	n/a	n/a	n/a	n/a	n/a	n/a
Avg.	515,975	1,550	210.99	123.07	82.07	194.99
Min.	265,375	692	104.33	53.68	36.26	179.42
Max.	2,775,821	5,719	529.02	397.28	361.63	223.33

*Note: (1) Values for the local area are compared with the average, minimum and maximum values for all 276 areas in the Cost of Living Index; (2) Figures cover the Rochester MN urban area; n/a not available; **New Home Price** (2,400 sf living area, 8,000 sf lot, in urban area with full utilities); **Apartment Rent** (950 sf 2 bedroom/1.5 or 2 bath, unfurnished, excluding all utilities except water); **All Electric** (average monthly cost for an all-electric home); **Part Electric** (average monthly cost for a part-electric home); **Other Energy** (average monthly cost for natural gas, fuel oil, coal, wood, and any other forms of energy except electricity); **Telephone** (price includes the base monthly rate plus taxes and fees for three lines of mobile phone service).*
Source: The Council for Community and Economic Research, Cost of Living Index, 2024

Health Care, Transportation, and Other Costs

Area[1]	Doctor ($/visit)	Dentist ($/visit)	Optometrist ($/visit)	Gasoline ($/gallon)	Beauty Salon ($/visit)	Men's Shirt ($)
City[2]	n/a	n/a	n/a	n/a	n/a	n/a
Avg.	143.77	117.51	129.23	3.32	48.57	38.14
Min.	36.74	58.67	67.33	2.80	24.00	13.41
Max.	270.44	216.82	307.33	5.28	94.00	63.89

*Note: (1) Values for the local area are compared with the average, minimum and maximum values for all 276 areas in the Cost of Living Index; (2) Figures cover the Rochester MN urban area; n/a not available; **Doctor** (general practitioners routine exam of an established patient); **Dentist** (adult teeth cleaning and periodic oral examination); **Optometrist** (full vision eye exam for established adult patient); **Gasoline** (one gallon regular unleaded, national brand, including all taxes, cash price at self-service pump if available); **Beauty Salon** (woman's shampoo, trim, and blow-dry); **Men's Shirt** (cotton/polyester dress shirt, pinpoint weave, long sleeves).*
Source: The Council for Community and Economic Research, Cost of Living Index, 2024

HOUSING

Homeownership Rate

Area	2017 (%)	2018 (%)	2019 (%)	2020 (%)	2021 (%)	2022 (%)	2023 (%)	2024 (%)
MSA[1]	n/a	n/a	n/a	n/a	n/a	n/a	n/a	n/a
U.S.	63.9	64.4	64.6	66.6	65.5	65.8	65.9	65.6

Note: (1) Figures cover the Rochester, MN Metropolitan Statistical Area; n/a not available
Source: U.S. Census Bureau, Housing Vacancies and Homeownership Annual Statistics: 2017-2024

House Price Index (HPI)

Area	National Ranking[2]	Quarterly Change (%)	One-Year Change (%)	Five-Year Change (%)	Since 1991Q1 (%)
MSA[1]	160	-1.25	4.39	42.16	268.82
U.S.[3]	—	1.43	4.51	57.13	327.82

Note: The HPI is a weighted repeat sales index. It measures average price changes in repeat sales or refinancings on the same properties. This information is obtained by reviewing repeat mortgage transactions on single-family properties whose mortgages have been purchased or securitized by Fannie Mae or Freddie Mac since January 1975; (1) Figures cover the Rochester, MN Metropolitan Statistical Area; (2) Rankings are based on annual percentage change for all metro areas containing at least 15,000 transactions over the last 10 years and ranges from 1 to 241; (3) figures based on a weighted average of Census Division estimates using a seasonally adjusted, purchase-only index; all figures are for the period ending December 31, 2024
Source: Federal Housing Finance Agency, Change in FHFA Metropolitan Area House Price Indexes, All Transactions Index, 2024Q4

Home Value

Area	Under $100,000	$100,000 -$199,999	$200,000 -$299,999	$300,000 -$399,999	$400,000 -$499,999	$500,000 -$999,999	$1,000,000 or more	Median ($)
City	4.4	16.0	33.6	19.2	12.2	13.4	1.1	287,500
MSA[1]	6.7	18.1	29.5	17.4	11.9	14.4	2.0	284,600
U.S.	12.1	17.8	19.5	14.4	10.5	19.1	6.5	303,400

Note: Figures are percentages except for median and cover owner-occupied housing units; (1) Figures cover the Rochester, MN Metropolitan Statistical Area
Source: U.S. Census Bureau, 2019-2023 American Community Survey 5-Year Estimates

Year Housing Structure Built

Area	2020 or Later	2010 -2019	2000 -2009	1990 -1999	1980 -1989	1970 -1979	1960 -1969	1950 -1959	1940 -1949	Before 1940	Median Year
City	1.2	12.9	18.5	14.1	11.1	12.4	9.9	9.0	3.7	7.2	1987
MSA[1]	1.2	10.4	18.3	13.5	10.5	13.0	8.9	7.5	3.4	13.3	1984
U.S.	1.2	8.9	13.6	12.8	13.0	14.4	10.0	9.7	4.5	11.9	1980

Note: Figures are percentages except for Median Year; Note: (1) Figures cover the Rochester, MN Metropolitan Statistical Area
Source: U.S. Census Bureau, 2019-2023 American Community Survey 5-Year Estimates

Gross Monthly Rent

Area	Under $500	$500 -$999	$1,000 -$1,499	$1,500 -$1,999	$2,000 -$2,499	$2,500 -$2,999	$3,000 and up	Median ($)
City	6.3	23.1	32.8	23.3	8.8	1.7	4.0	1,316
MSA[1]	7.9	29.2	31.6	19.9	7.1	1.3	3.0	1,195
U.S.	6.5	22.3	29.5	20.2	10.8	4.8	5.9	1,348

Note: Figures are percentages except for median; Gross rent is the contract rent plus the estimated average monthly cost of utilities (electricity, gas, and water and sewer) and fuels (oil, coal, kerosene, wood, etc.) if these are paid by the renter (or paid for the renter by someone else); (1) Figures cover the Rochester, MN Metropolitan Statistical Area
Source: U.S. Census Bureau, 2019-2023 American Community Survey 5-Year Estimates

HEALTH

Health Risk Factors

Category	MSA[1] (%)	U.S. (%)
Adults aged 18–64 who have any kind of health care coverage	96.9	90.8
Adults who reported being in good or better health	85.5	81.8
Adults who have been told they have high blood cholesterol	34.3	36.9
Adults who have been told they have high blood pressure	29.7	34.0
Adults who are current smokers	10.5	12.1
Adults who currently use e-cigarettes	n/a	7.7
Adults who currently use chewing tobacco, snuff, or snus	2.4	3.2
Adults who are heavy drinkers[2]	3.9	6.1
Adults who are binge drinkers[3]	18.1	15.2
Adults who are overweight (BMI 25.0 - 29.9)	30.1	34.4
Adults who are obese (BMI 30.0 - 99.8)	38.0	34.3
Adults who participated in any physical activities in the past month	78.8	75.8

Note: All figures are crude prevalence; (1) Figures cover the Rochester, MN Metropolitan Statistical Area; (2) Heavy drinkers are classified as adult men having more than 14 drinks per week and adult women having more than 7 drinks per week; (3) Binge drinkers are classified as males having five or more drinks on one occasion or females having four or more drinks on one occasion
Source: Centers for Disease Control and Prevention, Behavioral Risk Factor Surveillance System, SMART: Selected Metropolitan Area Risk Trends, 2023

Acute and Chronic Health Conditions

Category	MSA[1] (%)	U.S. (%)
Adults who have ever been told they had a heart attack	4.0	4.2
Adults who have ever been told they have angina or coronary heart disease	3.4	4.0
Adults who have ever been told they had a stroke	3.4	3.3
Adults who have ever been told they have asthma	17.7	15.7
Adults who have ever been told they have arthritis	22.9	26.3
Adults who have ever been told they have diabetes[2]	9.4	11.5
Adults who have ever been told they had skin cancer	4.3	5.6
Adults who have ever been told they had any other types of cancer	8.2	8.4
Adults who have ever been told they have COPD	3.9	6.4
Adults who have ever been told they have kidney disease	4.3	3.7
Adults who have ever been told they have a form of depression	28.4	22.0

Note: All figures are crude prevalence; (1) Figures cover the Rochester, MN Metropolitan Statistical Area; (2) Figures do not include pregnancy-related, borderline, or pre-diabetes
Source: Centers for Disease Control and Prevention, Behaviorial Risk Factor Surveillance System, SMART: Selected Metropolitan Area Risk Trends, 2023

Health Screening and Vaccination Rates

Category	MSA[1] (%)	U.S. (%)
Adults who have ever been tested for HIV	31.0	37.5
Adults who have had their blood cholesterol checked within the last five years	85.7	87.0
Adults aged 65+ who have had flu shot within the past year	73.8	63.4
Adults aged 65+ who have ever had a pneumonia vaccination	76.5	71.9

Note: All figures are crude prevalence; (1) Figures cover the Rochester, MN Metropolitan Statistical Area.
Source: Centers for Disease Control and Prevention, Behaviorial Risk Factor Surveillance System, SMART: Selected Metropolitan Area Risk Trends, 2023

Disability Status

Category	MSA[1] (%)	U.S. (%)
Adults who reported being deaf	8.0	7.4
Are you blind or have serious difficulty seeing, even when wearing glasses?	3.4	4.9
Do you have difficulty doing errands alone?	5.7	7.8
Do you have difficulty dressing or bathing?	n/a	3.6
Do you have serious difficulty concentrating/remembering/making decisions?	11.4	13.7
Do you have serious difficulty walking or climbing stairs?	10.1	13.2

Note: All figures are crude prevalence; (1) Figures cover the Rochester, MN Metropolitan Statistical Area.
Source: Centers for Disease Control and Prevention, Behaviorial Risk Factor Surveillance System, SMART: Selected Metropolitan Area Risk Trends, 2023

Mortality Rates for the Top 10 Causes of Death in the U.S.

ICD-10[a] Sub-Chapter	ICD-10[a] Code	Crude Mortality Rate[2] per 100,000 population	
		County[3]	U.S.
Malignant neoplasms	C00-C97	162.9	182.7
Ischaemic heart diseases	I20-I25	108.9	109.6
Provisional assignment of new diseases of uncertain etiology[1]	U00-U49	24.8	65.3
Other forms of heart disease	I30-I51	34.7	65.1
Other degenerative diseases of the nervous system	G30-G31	70.1	52.4
Other external causes of accidental injury	W00-X59	51.0	52.3
Cerebrovascular diseases	I60-I69	31.3	49.1
Chronic lower respiratory diseases	J40-J47	29.5	43.5
Hypertensive diseases	I10-I15	41.8	38.9
Organic, including symptomatic, mental disorders	F01-F09	53.6	33.9

Note: (a) ICD-10 = International Classification of Diseases 10th Revision; (1) Includes COVID-19, adverse effects to COVID-19 vaccines, SARS, and vaping-related disorders; (2) Crude mortality rates are a three-year average covering 2021-2023; (3) Figures cover Olmsted County.
Source: Centers for Disease Control and Prevention, National Center for Health Statistics. National Vital Statistics System, Mortality 2018-2023 on CDC WONDER Online Database

Mortality Rates for Selected Causes of Death

Cause of Death	ICD-10[a] Code	Crude Mortality Rate[1] per 100,000 population	
		County[2]	U.S.
Accidental poisoning and exposure to noxious substances	X40-X49	22.8	30.5
Alzheimer disease	G30	50.8	35.4
Assault	X85-Y09	Unreliable	7.3
COVID-19	U07.1	24.8	65.3
Diabetes mellitus	E10-E14	13.4	30.0
Diseases of the liver	K70-K76	15.8	20.8
Human immunodeficiency virus (HIV) disease	B20-B24	Suppressed	1.5
Influenza and pneumonia	J09-J18	4.3	13.4
Intentional self-harm	X60-X84	13.8	14.7
Malnutrition	E40-E46	Unreliable	6.0
Obesity and other hyperalimentation	E65-E68	Unreliable	3.1
Renal failure	N17-N19	Unreliable	16.4
Transport accidents	V01-V99	6.3	14.4

Note: (a) ICD-10 = International Classification of Diseases 10th Revision; (1) Crude mortality rates are a three-year average covering 2021-2023; (2) Figures cover Olmsted County; Data are suppressed when the data meet the criteria for confidentiality constraints; Crude mortality rates are flagged as unreliable when the rate would be calculated with a numerator of 20 or less.
Source: Centers for Disease Control and Prevention, National Center for Health Statistics. National Vital Statistics System, Mortality 2018-2023 on CDC WONDER Online Database

Health Insurance Coverage

Area	With Health Insurance	With Private Health Insurance	With Public Health Insurance	Without Health Insurance	Population Under Age 19 Without Health Insurance
City	95.7	79.7	30.5	4.3	3.7
MSA[1]	95.6	79.5	31.1	4.4	4.0
U.S.	91.4	67.3	36.3	8.6	5.4

Note: Figures are percentages that cover the civilian noninstitutionalized population; (1) Figures cover the Rochester, MN Metropolitan Statistical Area
Source: U.S. Census Bureau, 2019-2023 American Community Survey 5-Year Estimates

Number of Medical Professionals

Area	MDs[3]	DOs[3,4]	Dentists	Podiatrists	Chiropractors	Optometrists
County[1] (number)	4,380	117	226	12	75	41
County[1] (rate[2])	2,670.4	71.3	137.1	7.3	45.5	24.9
U.S. (rate[2])	302.5	29.2	74.6	6.4	29.5	18.0

Note: Data as of 2023 unless noted; (1) Data covers Olmsted County; (2) Number of medical professionals per 100,000 population; (3) Data as of 2022 and includes all active, non-federal physicians; (4) Doctor of Osteopathic Medicine
Source: U.S. Department of Health and Human Services, Health Resources and Services Administration, Bureau of Health Professions, Area Resource File (ARF) 2023-2024

Best Hospitals

According to *U.S. News,* the Rochester, MN metro area is home to one of the best hospitals in the U.S.: **Mayo Clinic-Rochester** (Honor Roll/13 adult specialties and 10 pediatric specialties). The hospital listed was nationally ranked in at least one of 15 adult or 11 pediatric specialties. The number of specialties shown cover the parent hospital. Only 160 U.S. hospitals performed well enough to be nationally ranked in one or more specialties. Twenty hospitals in the U.S. made the Honor Roll. The Best Hospitals Honor Roll takes both the national rankings and the procedure and condition ratings into account. Hospitals received points if they were nationally ranked in one of the 15 adult specialties—the higher they ranked, the more points they got—and how many ratings of "high performing" they earned in the 20 procedures and conditions. *U.S. News Online, "America's Best Hospitals 2024-25"*

According to *U.S. News,* the Rochester, MN metro area is home to two of the best children's hospitals in the U.S.: **Mayo Clinic Children's Center** (10 pediatric specialties); **Mayo Clinic-Children's Minnesota Cardiovascular Collaborative** (10 pediatric specialties). The hospitals listed were highly ranked in at least one of 11 pediatric specialties. One hundred five children's hospitals in the U.S. were nationally ranked in at least one specialty. Hospitals received points for being ranked in a specialty, and the 10 hospitals with the most points across the 11 specialties make up the Honor Roll. *U.S. News Online, "America's Best Children's Hospitals 2024-25"*

EDUCATION

Public School District Statistics

District Name	Schls	Pupils	Pupil/ Teacher Ratio	Minority Pupils[1] (%)	Total Rev. per Pupil ($)	Total Exp. per Pupil ($)
Rochester Public School District	50	17,342	15.4	47.2	17,185	22,548

Note: Table includes school districts with 2,000 or more students; (1) Percentage of students that are not non-Hispanic white.
Source: U.S. Department of Education, National Center for Education Statistics, Common Core of Data, Local Education Agency (School District) Universe Survey: School Year 2023-2024; U.S. Department of Education, National Center for Education Statistics, Common Core of Data, School District Finance Survey (F-33): School Year 2021–22

Highest Level of Education

Area	Less than H.S.	H.S. Diploma	Some College, No Deg.	Associate Degree	Bachelor's Degree	Master's Degree	Prof. School Degree	Doctorate Degree
City	5.5	18.9	14.9	10.6	27.7	13.2	5.2	3.9
MSA[1]	5.2	23.0	17.1	12.5	24.7	10.8	4.1	2.7
U.S.	10.6	26.2	19.4	8.8	21.3	9.8	2.3	1.6

Note: Figures cover persons age 25 and over; (1) Figures cover the Rochester, MN Metropolitan Statistical Area
Source: U.S. Census Bureau, 2019-2023 American Community Survey 5-Year Estimates

Educational Attainment by Race

Area	High School Graduate or Higher (%)					Bachelor's Degree or Higher (%)				
	Total	White	Black	Asian	Hisp.[2]	Total	White	Black	Asian	Hisp.[2]
City	94.5	97.2	73.9	86.1	78.6	50.1	51.6	25.7	61.6	34.9
MSA[1]	94.8	96.5	74.4	85.8	79.8	42.3	42.2	25.1	60.4	33.9
U.S.	89.4	92.9	88.1	88.0	72.5	35.0	37.7	24.7	57.0	19.9

Note: Figures shown cover persons 25 years old and over; (1) Figures cover the Rochester, MN Metropolitan Statistical Area; (2) People of Hispanic origin can be of any race
Source: U.S. Census Bureau, 2019-2023 American Community Survey 5-Year Estimates

School Enrollment by Grade and Control

Area	Preschool (%)		Kindergarten (%)		Grades 1 - 4 (%)		Grades 5 - 8 (%)		Grades 9 - 12 (%)	
	Public	Private	Public	Private	Public	Private	Public	Private	Public	Private
City	43.6	56.4	90.6	9.4	86.3	13.7	84.5	15.5	90.2	9.8
MSA[1]	61.3	38.7	91.0	9.0	88.1	11.9	87.9	12.1	91.8	8.2
U.S.	58.7	41.3	85.2	14.8	87.2	12.8	87.9	12.1	89.0	11.0

Note: Figures shown cover persons 3 years old and over; (1) Figures cover the Rochester, MN Metropolitan Statistical Area
Source: U.S. Census Bureau, 2019-2023 American Community Survey 5-Year Estimates

Higher Education

Four-Year Colleges			Two-Year Colleges			Medical Schools[1]	Law Schools[2]	Voc/ Tech[3]
Public	Private Non-profit	Private For-profit	Public	Private Non-profit	Private For-profit			
1	1	0	1	0	0	1	0	1

Note: Figures cover institutions located within the Rochester, MN Metropolitan Statistical Area and include main campuses only; (1) includes schools accredited by the Liaison Committee on Medical Education and the American Osteopathic Association's Commission on Osteopathic College Accreditation; (2) includes ABA-accredited schools, schools with provisional ABA accreditation, and state accredited schools; (3) includes all schools with programs that are less than 2 years.
Source: National Center for Education Statistics, Integrated Postsecondary Education System (IPEDS), 2023-24; Wikipedia, List of Medical Schools in the United States, accessed May 2, 2025; Wikipedia, List of Law Schools in the United States, accessed May 2, 2025

According to *U.S. News & World Report,* the Rochester, MN metro area is home to one of the top medical schools for research in the U.S.: **Mayo Clinic School of Medicine (Alix)** (Tier 1). *U.S. News* placed medical and osteopathic schools into tiers based on their research productivity, faculty and admissions data. Each school's tier was derived from its overall score, calculated by summing the weighted normalized values generated across several factors of academic quality, outlined below. There are four tiers, with tier 1 medical schools as the highest-performing and tier 4 as the lowest-performing. Only tier 1 and 2 schools are shown. Because of the tier presentation, *U.S. News* calculated overall scores based on their percentile performance among all rated schools instead of dividing against the rescaled score of the No. 1-performing schools. Tier 1 included schools with overall scores of 85 to 99. The cutoffs for tiers 2 through 4 were schools scoring 50 to 84, 15 to 49 and 1 to 14, respectively. The rankings are based on a weighted average of the following measures of quality: total research activity; average research activity per faculty member; total NIH research grants at the medical school and its affiliated hospitals; average NIH research grants per faculty; median MCAT total score; median undergraduate GPA; acceptance rate; and faculty resources. *U.S. News & World Report, "America's Best Graduate Schools, Medical, 2025"*

EMPLOYERS

Major Employers

Company Name	Industry
Benchmark Electronics	Contract mfg/design/engineering
Cardinal of Minnesota	Res. services/dev. disabilities
Charter Communications	Cable & other pay television services
City of Rochester	Municipal government
Crenlo	Fabricated metal
Federal Medical Center	Corrections/medical
Halcon	Furniture manufacturer
Hiawatha Homes	Res. services/dev. disabilities
IBM	Electronics
Interstate Hotels & Resorts	Hotel/restaurant services
Kemps	Food processing
Mayo Clinic	Healthcare
McNeilus Steel	Steel fabrication
McNeilus Truck	Mobile concrete mixers, garbage trucks
Olmstead County	Government
Olmstead Medical Center	Healthcare
Pace Dairy	Food processing
RCTC	Post-secondary education
Reichel Foods	Refrigerated lunch & snacks
Rochester Meat Company	Meat processor

Note: Companies shown are located within the Rochester, MN Metropolitan Statistical Area.
Source: Chambers of Commerce; State Departments of Labor; Wikipedia

PUBLIC SAFETY

Crime Rate

Area	Total Crime Rate	Violent Crime Rate				Property Crime Rate		
		Murder	Rape	Robbery	Aggrav. Assault	Burglary	Larceny-Theft	Motor Vehicle Theft
City	1,754.4	0.8	36.1	22.9	102.4	182.7	1,283.2	126.2
U.S.	2,290.9	5.7	38.0	66.5	264.1	250.7	1,347.2	318.7

Note: Figures are crimes per 100,000 population.
Source: FBI, Table 8, Offenses Known to Law Enforcement, by State by City, 2023

Hate Crimes

Area	Number of Quarters Reported	Number of Incidents per Bias Motivation					
		Race/Ethnicity/Ancestry	Religion	Sexual Orientation	Disability	Gender	Gender Identity
City	4	0	3	0	0	0	2
U.S.	4	5,900	2,699	2,077	187	92	492

Source: Federal Bureau of Investigation, Hate Crime Statistics 2023

Identity Theft Consumer Reports

Area	Reports	Reports per 100,000 Population	Rank[2]
MSA[1]	233	103	377
U.S.	1,135,291	339	-

Note: (1) Figures cover the Rochester, MN Metropolitan Statistical Area; (2) Rank ranges from 1 to 401 where 1 indicates greatest number of identity theft reports per 100,000 population
Source: Federal Trade Commission, Consumer Sentinel Network Data Book 2024

Fraud and Other Consumer Reports

Area	Reports	Reports per 100,000 Population	Rank[2]
MSA[1]	1,818	800	321
U.S.	5,360,641	1,601	-

Note: (1) Figures cover the Rochester, MN Metropolitan Statistical Area; (2) Rank ranges from 1 to 401 where 1 indicates greatest number of fraud and other consumer reports per 100,000 population
Source: Federal Trade Commission, Consumer Sentinel Network Data Book 2024

POLITICS

2024 Presidential Election Results

Area	Trump (Rep.)	Harris (Dem.)	Stein (Green)	Kennedy (Ind.)	Oliver (Lib.)	Other
Olmsted County	43.4	54.0	0.6	0.8	0.5	0.7
U.S.	49.7	48.2	0.6	0.5	0.4	0.6

Note: Results are percentages and may not add to 100% due to rounding
Source: Dave Leip's Atlas of U.S. Presidential Elections

SPORTS

Professional Sports Teams

Team Name	League	Year Established

No teams are located in the metro area
Source: Wikipedia, Major Professional Sports Teams of the United States and Canada, May 1, 2025

CLIMATE

Average and Extreme Temperatures

Temperature	Jan	Feb	Mar	Apr	May	Jun	Jul	Aug	Sep	Oct	Nov	Dec	Yr.
Extreme High (°F)	55	63	79	91	92	101	102	100	97	90	74	62	102
Average High (°F)	21	26	38	55	68	78	82	79	70	59	40	26	54
Average Temp. (°F)	12	18	29	45	57	67	71	69	60	48	32	19	44
Average Low (°F)	3	8	20	34	46	56	60	58	48	38	24	10	34
Extreme Low (°F)	-40	-29	-31	5	21	35	42	35	23	11	-20	-33	-40

Note: Figures cover the years 1948-1995
Source: National Climatic Data Center, International Station Meteorological Climate Summary, 9/96

Average Precipitation/Snowfall/Humidity

Precip./Humidity	Jan	Feb	Mar	Apr	May	Jun	Jul	Aug	Sep	Oct	Nov	Dec	Yr.
Avg. Precip. (in.)	0.8	0.8	1.8	2.8	3.4	4.0	4.2	3.9	3.1	2.0	1.7	1.0	29.4
Avg. Snowfall (in.)	9	8	10	4	Tr	0	0	0	Tr	1	6	10	47
Avg. Rel. Hum. 6am (%)	80	81	82	80	80	82	86	88	87	82	83	83	83
Avg. Rel. Hum. 3pm (%)	72	68	65	54	52	53	56	57	56	54	66	74	61

Note: Figures cover the years 1948-1995; Tr = Trace amounts (<0.05 in. of rain; <0.5 in. of snow)
Source: National Climatic Data Center, International Station Meteorological Climate Summary, 9/96

Weather Conditions

Temperature			Daytime Sky			Precipitation		
5°F & below	32°F & below	90°F & above	Clear	Partly cloudy	Cloudy	0.01 inch or more precip.	0.1 inch or more snow/ice	Thunder-storms
46	165	9	87	126	152	114	40	41

Note: Figures are average number of days per year and cover the years 1948-1995
Source: National Climatic Data Center, International Station Meteorological Climate Summary, 9/96

HAZARDOUS WASTE

Superfund Sites

The Rochester, MN metro area has no sites on the EPA's Superfund Final National Priorities List (NPL) or Superfund Alternative Approach (SAA) list. The Superfund alternative approach uses the same investigation and cleanup process and standards that are used for sites listed on the National Priorities List. The SAA is an alternative to listing a site on the NPL; it is not an alternative to Superfund or the Superfund process. There are a total of 1,445 Superfund sites with a status of proposed or final on both lists in the United States. *U.S. Environmental Protection Agency, National Priorities List, May 1, 2025; U.S. Environmental Protection Agency, Superfund Alternative Approach Sites, May 1, 2025*

AIR QUALITY

Air Quality Trends: Ozone

	1990	1995	2000	2005	2010	2015	2020	2021	2022	2023
MSA[1]	n/a	n/a	n/a	n/a	n/a	n/a	n/a	n/a	n/a	n/a
U.S.	0.087	0.089	0.081	0.080	0.072	0.068	0.066	0.067	0.067	0.070

Note: (1) Data covers the Rochester, MN Metropolitan Statistical Area; n/a not available. The values shown are the composite ozone concentration averages among trend sites based on the highest fourth daily maximum 8-hour concentration in parts per million. These trends are based on sites having an adequate record of monitoring data during the trend period. Data from exceptional events are included.
Source: U.S. Environmental Protection Agency, Air Quality Monitoring Information, "Air Quality Trends by City, 1990-2023"

Air Quality Index

Area	Percent of Days when Air Quality was...[2]					AQI Statistics[2]	
	Good	Moderate	Unhealthy for Sensitive Groups	Unhealthy	Very Unhealthy	Maximum	Median
MSA[1]	51.8	44.1	3.8	0.3	0.0	167	49

Note: (1) Data covers the Rochester, MN Metropolitan Statistical Area; (2) Based on 365 days with AQI data in 2023. Air Quality Index (AQI) is an index for reporting daily air quality. EPA calculates the AQI for five major air pollutants regulated by the Clean Air Act: ground-level ozone, particle pollution (aka particulate matter), carbon monoxide, sulfur dioxide, and nitrogen dioxide. The AQI runs from 0 to 500. The higher the AQI value, the greater the level of air pollution and the greater the health concern. There are six AQI categories: "Good" AQI is between 0 and 50. Air quality is considered satisfactory; "Moderate" AQI is between 51 and 100. Air quality is acceptable; "Unhealthy for Sensitive Groups" When AQI values are between 101 and 150, members of sensitive groups may experience health effects; "Unhealthy" When AQI values are between 151 and 200 everyone may begin to experience health effects; "Very Unhealthy" AQI values between 201 and 300 trigger a health alert; "Hazardous" AQI values over 300 trigger warnings of emergency conditions (not shown).
Source: U.S. Environmental Protection Agency, Air Quality Index Report, 2023

Air Quality Index Pollutants

Area	Percent of Days when AQI Pollutant was...[2]					
	Carbon Monoxide	Nitrogen Dioxide	Ozone	Sulfur Dioxide	Particulate Matter 2.5	Particulate Matter 10
MSA[1]	0.0	0.0	32.6	(3)	67.4	0.0

Note: (1) Data covers the Rochester, MN Metropolitan Statistical Area; (2) Based on 365 days with AQI data in 2023. The Air Quality Index (AQI) is an index for reporting daily air quality. EPA calculates the AQI for five major air pollutants regulated by the Clean Air Act: ground-level ozone, particle pollution (also known as particulate matter), carbon monoxide, sulfur dioxide, and nitrogen dioxide. The AQI runs from 0 to 500. The higher the AQI value, the greater the level of air pollution and the greater the health concern; (3) Sulfur dioxide is no longer included in this table because SO_2 concentrations tend to be very localized and not necessarily representative of broad geographical areas like counties and CBSAs.
Source: U.S. Environmental Protection Agency, Air Quality Index Report, 2023

Maximum Air Pollutant Concentrations: Particulate Matter, Ozone, CO and Lead

	Particulate Matter 10 (ug/m³)	Particulate Matter 2.5 Wtd AM (ug/m³)	Particulate Matter 2.5 24-Hr (ug/m³)	Ozone (ppm)	Carbon Monoxide (ppm)	Lead (ug/m³)
MSA[1] Level	n/a	9.6	33	0.074	n/a	n/a
NAAQS[2]	150	15	35	0.075	9	0.15
Met NAAQS[2]	n/a	Yes	Yes	Yes	n/a	n/a

Note: (1) Data covers the Rochester, MN Metropolitan Statistical Area; Data from exceptional events are included; (2) National Ambient Air Quality Standards; ppm = parts per million; ug/m³ = micrograms per cubic meter; n/a not available.
Concentrations: Particulate Matter 10 (coarse particulate)—highest second maximum 24-hour concentration; Particulate Matter 2.5 Wtd AM (fine particulate)—highest weighted annual mean concentration; Particulate Matter 2.5 24-Hour (fine particulate)—highest 98th percentile 24-hour concentration; Ozone—highest fourth daily maximum 8-hour concentration; Carbon Monoxide—highest second maximum non-overlapping 8-hour concentration; Lead—maximum running 3-month average
Source: U.S. Environmental Protection Agency, Air Quality Monitoring Information, "Air Quality Statistics by City, 2023"

Maximum Air Pollutant Concentrations: Nitrogen Dioxide and Sulfur Dioxide

	Nitrogen Dioxide AM (ppb)	Nitrogen Dioxide 1-Hr (ppb)	Sulfur Dioxide AM (ppb)	Sulfur Dioxide 1-Hr (ppb)	Sulfur Dioxide 24-Hr (ppb)
MSA[1] Level	n/a	n/a	n/a	n/a	n/a
NAAQS[2]	53	100	30	75	140
Met NAAQS[2]	n/a	n/a	n/a	n/a	n/a

Note: (1) Data covers the Rochester, MN Metropolitan Statistical Area; Data from exceptional events are included; (2) National Ambient Air Quality Standards; ppm = parts per million; ug/m³ = micrograms per cubic meter; n/a not available.
Concentrations: Nitrogen Dioxide AM—highest arithmetic mean concentration; Nitrogen Dioxide 1-Hr—highest 98th percentile 1-hour daily maximum concentration; Sulfur Dioxide AM—highest annual mean concentration; Sulfur Dioxide 1-Hr—highest 99th percentile 1-hour daily maximum concentration; Sulfur Dioxide 24-Hr—highest second maximum 24-hour concentration
Source: U.S. Environmental Protection Agency, Air Quality Monitoring Information, "Air Quality Statistics by City, 2023"

Saint Louis, Missouri

Background

St. Louis, the "Gateway to the West," is known for a skyline dominated by the Gateway Arch, which was built in 1965 as a monument to President Thomas Jefferson's vision of a continental United States. The city is situated at the confluence of the Missouri and Mississippi rivers, near the geographical center of the United States.

The city began as an inland river trading post for French settlers from New Orleans. Founder Pierre Laclade was granted exclusive rights by the Louisiana government to trade with the Native American tribes of the region. The site was rich with wildlife, including raccoon, beaver, muskrat, otter, and bear, making for an active fur trade. In 1827, John Jacob Astor started a profitable fur business called the American Fur Company.

After the Civil War, St. Louis experienced an industrial and cultural boom. The city's industries included iron, steel, leather, and food, and it became a center for Hegelian thought, based on German philosopher Hegel, thanks to the large influx of German immigrants.

World War I, the Depression, and Prohibition all contributed to St. Louis's economic decline which started in the 1950s and continued through the 1970s. Since the 1980s, however, St. Louis has been prospering and today, its diverse economy includes the service, manufacturing, trade, transportation, and tourism industries, and it is home to six Fortune 500 companies. Major employers include Edward Jones, BJC Health, Washington University in St. Louis, and Anheuser-Busch.

Major research universities include Saint Louis University and Washington University in St. Louis, and the Washington University Medical Center neighborhood is home to many medical and pharmaceutical institutions, giving the city the nickname Biobelt of the Midwest.

The city's attractions include The St. Louis Walk of Fame honoring its rich musical tradition and legendary sons and daughters Chuck Berry, Tina Turner, Miles Davis, and Scott Joplin. The St. Louis Art Museum houses more than 30,000 pieces of art. The Black World History Museum honors such notable African American Missourians as George Washington Carver, Dred and Harriet Scott, and musician Clark Terry.

Historical sites include the 630-foot, stainless steel Gateway Arch, Daniel Boone's Home, Lewis and Clark State Historic Site, and the Ulysses S. Grant National Historic Site. Children enjoy the St. Louis Zoo, St. Louis Children's Aquarium, St. Louis Science Center, and Worldways Children's Museum with interactive cultural exhibits.

St. Louis operates more than 100 parks and is home to the Missouri Botanical Garden, which is among the top three botanical gardens worldwide. The city also hosts Laumeier Sculpture Park, Gateway International Raceway, and the Soulard Farmers Market and surrounding historical neighborhood offering dining options ranging from Cajun to continental.

St. Louis is home to Major League Baseball's St. Louis Cardinals, the National Hockey League's St. Louis Blues, and Major League Soccer's St. Louis SC (which began play in 2023). The U.S. Chess Championship, which began in 1845, has been held at the St. Louis Chess Club since 2009.

The urban area of St. Louis has a humid subtropical climate, while its metropolitan region to the south offers a hot-summer humid continental climate, the effect of the urban heat island in the city. The city experiences hot, humid summers and chilly to cold winters. It is subject to both cold Arctic air and hot, humid tropical air from the Gulf of Mexico. Annual precipitation averages 42 inches, but can vary widely from year-to-year. St. Louis experiences thunderstorms 48 days a year on average. These storms can often be severe, especially in the spring, with high winds, large hail and tornadoes. Lying within the hotbed of Tornado Alley, St. Louis is one of the most frequently tornado-struck metropolitan areas in the U.S. and has an extensive history of damaging tornadoes. Severe flooding, such as the Great Flood of 1993, may occur in spring and summer; rapid melting of thick snow cover upstream on the Missouri or Mississippi Rivers can contribute to springtime flooding.

Rankings

General Rankings

- To help military veterans find the best places in which to settle down, *WalletHub* compared the 100 largest U.S. cities across 19 key indicators of livability, affordability and veteran-friendliness. They range from the share of military skill-related jobs to veteran income growth to the availability of VA health facilities. Saint Louis ranked #46. *Wallethub.com, "Best & Worst Places for Veterans to Live (2025)," November 7, 2024*

- The human resources consulting firm Mercer ranked 241 major cities worldwide in terms of overall quality of life. Saint Louis ranked #73. Criteria: political and personal safety, social, and economic factors; medical and health considerations; schools and education; public services and transportation; recreation; connectivity; housing and infrastructure; and climate. *Mercer, "Mercer 2024 Quality of Living Survey," December 2024*

- In their annual survey, Livability.com looked at data for more than 2,000 mid-sized U.S. cities to assign a "Livability Score" for each. The top 100 scoring cities make up Livability's "Top 100 Best Places to Live in the U.S." in 2025. Saint Louis was placed among the top 100 of the customizable list. Criteria: housing and economy; cost of living; environment; education; health care options; transportation; safety; and community amenities. *Livability.com, "Top 100 Best Places to Live in the U.S. in 2025" April 15, 2025*

Business/Finance Rankings

- Payscale.com ranked the 32 largest metro areas in terms of wage growth. The Saint Louis metro area ranked #28. Criteria: quarterly changes in private industry employee and education professional wage growth from the previous year. *PayScale, "Wage Trends by Metro Area-4th Quarter," February 4, 2025*

- The Saint Louis metro area appeared on the Milken Institute "2025 Best Performing Cities" list. Rank: #81 out of 200 large metro areas (based on performance category). Criteria: job growth; wage growth; high-tech growth and impact; community resilience; housing affordability; household broadband access. *Milken Institute, "Best-Performing Cities 2025," January 14, 2025*

- Mercer Human Resources Consulting ranked 226 cities worldwide in terms of cost-of-living. Saint Louis ranked #72 (the lower the ranking, the higher the cost-of-living). The survey measured the comparative cost of over 200 items (such as housing, food, clothing, domestic supplies, transportation, and recreation/entertainment) in each location. *Mercer, "2024 Cost of Living City Ranking," June 17, 2024*

Education Rankings

- Personal finance website *WalletHub* analyzed the 150 largest U.S. metropolitan statistical areas to determine where the most educated Americans are putting their degrees to work. Criteria: education levels; percentage of workers with degrees; education quality and attainment gap; public school quality rankings; quality and enrollment of each metro area's universities. Saint Louis was ranked #47 (#1 = most educated city). *WalletHub.com, "Most & Least Educated Cities in America, 2025" July 2, 2024*

Environmental Rankings

- Saint Louis was highlighted as one of the 25 most ozone-polluted metro areas in the U.S. during 2021 through 2023. The area ranked #21. *American Lung Association, "State of the Air 2025," April 23, 2025*

- Saint Louis was highlighted as one of the 25 metro areas most polluted by year-round particle pollution (Annual PM 2.5) in the U.S. during 2021 through 2023. The area ranked #17. *American Lung Association, "State of the Air 2025," April 23, 2025*

Health/Fitness Rankings

- For each of the 100 largest cities in the United States, the American Fitness Index®, compiled in partnership between the American College of Sports Medicine and the Elevance Health Foundation, evaluated community infrastructure and more than 30 health behaviors including preventive health, levels of chronic disease conditions, food insecurity, pedestrian safety, air quality, and community/environment resources that support physical activity. Saint Louis ranked #64 for "community fitness." *americanfitnessindex.org, "2024 ACSM American Fitness Index Summary Report," July 23, 2024*

- The Saint Louis metro area was identified as one of the worst cities for bed bugs in America by pest control company Orkin. The area ranked #19 out of 50 based on the number of bed bug treatments Orkin performed from December 2022 to November 2023. *Orkin, "Chicago Joins Paris In Global Bed Bug Spotlight Ranking As The Worst City On Orkin's U.S. Bed Bug Cities List," January 22, 2024*

- Saint Louis was identified as a "2025 Allergy Capital." The area ranked #67 out of the nation's 100 largest metropolitan areas. Three groups of factors were used to identify the most challenging cities for people with allergies: annual tree, grass, and weed pollen scores; over the counter allergy medicine use; number of board-certified allergy specialists. *Asthma and Allergy Foundation of America, "2025 Allergy Capitals: The Most Challenging Places to Live with Allergies," March 18, 2025*

- Saint Louis was identified as a "2024 Asthma Capital." The area ranked #17 out of the nation's 100 largest metropolitan areas. Criteria: estimated asthma prevalence; asthma-related mortality; and ER visits due to asthma. Risk factors analyzed but not factored in the rankings: annual air quality including pollution and ozone levels; public smoking laws; indoor air quality; access to asthma specialists; rescue and controller medication use; uninsured rate; pollen allergy; poverty rate. *Asthma and Allergy Foundation of America, "Asthma Capitals 2024: The Most Challenging Places to Live With Asthma," September 10, 2024*

Real Estate Rankings

- *WalletHub* compared the most populated U.S. cities to determine which had the best markets for real estate agents. Saint Louis ranked #146 where demand was high and pay was the best. Criteria: sales per agent; annual median wage for real-estate agents; monthly average starting salary for real estate agents; real estate job density and competition; unemployment rate; home turnover rate; housing-market health index; and other relevant metrics. *WalletHub.com, "2021 Best Places to Be a Real Estate Agent," May 12, 2021*

- Saint Louis was ranked #28 out of 176 metro areas in terms of cost of housing in 2024 by the National Association of Home Builders (#1 = most affordable). Criteria: the portion of an average family's income necessary to pay the mortgage on a median-priced home. *National Association of Home Builders®, NAHB-Wells Fargo Cost of Housing Index, 4th Quarter 2024*

Safety Rankings

- To identify the most dangerous cities in America, *24/7 Wall St.* focused on violent crime categories—murder, non-negligent manslaughter, rape, robbery, and aggravated assault—as reported for every 100,000 residents using data from the FBI's 2020 annual Uniform Crime Report. For cities with populations over 25,000, Saint Louis was ranked #5. *247wallst.com, "America's Most Dangerous Cities" November 12, 2021*

- Allstate ranked the 100 most populous cities in America in terms of driver safety. Saint Louis ranked #16. Criteria based on anonymized driving behavior data from Allstate's mobile app powered by Arity: high speed driving (over 80 mph), phone handling, and hard braking. The report helps increase the importance of safety and awareness behind the wheel. *Allstate, "16th Allstate America's Best Drivers Report®" July 11, 2024*

- Saint Louis was identified as one of the most dangerous cities in America by NeighborhoodScout. The city ranked #23 out of 100 (#1 = most dangerous). Criteria: number of violent crimes per 1,000 residents. The editors evaluated cities with 25,000 or more residents. *NeighborhoodScout.com, "2023 Top 100 Most Dangerous Cities in the U.S.," January 12, 2023*

Women/Minorities Rankings

- Personal finance website *WalletHub* compared more than 180 U.S. cities across two key dimensions, "Hispanic Business-Friendliness" and "Hispanic Purchasing Power," to arrive at the most favorable conditions for Hispanic entrepreneurs. Saint Louis was ranked #62 out of 182. Criteria includes: share of Hispanic-Owned Businesses; average growth of Hispanic Business revenues; Small Business-Friendliness score; affordability; and number of Hispanics with at least a bachelor's degree. *WalletHub.com, "Best Cities for Hispanic Entrepreneurs," September 4, 2024*

Miscellaneous Rankings

- *MoveHub* ranked 446 hipster cities across 20 countries, using its new and improved alternative Hipster Index and Saint Louis came out as #34 among the top 50. Criteria: population over 150,000; number of vintage boutiques; density of tattoo parlors; vegan places to eat; coffee shops; and density of vinyl record stores. *MoveHub.com, "The Hipster Index: Brighton Pips Portland to Global Top Spot," July 28, 2021*

- In its roundup of St. Patrick's Day parades, *Gayot* listed the best festivals and parades of all things Irish. The festivities in Saint Louis as among the best in North America. *Gayot.com, "Best St. Patrick's Day Parades," March 2025*

- *WalletHub* compared 148 of the most populated U.S. cities to determine their operating efficiency. A "Quality of Services" score was constructed for each city and then measured against the total budget per capita to reveal which were managed the best. Saint Louis ranked #122. Criteria: financial stability; economy; education; safety; health; infrastructure and pollution. *WalletHub.com, "2025's Best- & Worst-Run Cities in America," June 18, 2024*

Business Environment

DEMOGRAPHICS

Population Growth

Area	1990 Census	2000 Census	2010 Census	2020 Census	2023 Estimate[2]	Population Growth 1990-2023 (%)
City	396,685	348,189	319,294	301,578	293,109	-26.1
MSA[1]	2,580,897	2,698,687	2,812,896	2,820,253	2,809,414	8.9
U.S.	248,709,873	281,421,906	308,745,538	331,449,281	332,387,540	33.6

Note: (1) Figures cover the St. Louis, MO-IL Metropolitan Statistical Area; (2) 2019-2023 5-year ACS population estimate
Source: U.S. Census Bureau, 1990 Census, 2000 Census, 2010 Census, 2020 Census, 2019-2023 American Community Survey 5-Year Estimates

Race

Area	White Alone[2] (%)	Black Alone[2] (%)	Asian Alone[2] (%)	AIAN[3] Alone[2] (%)	NHOPI[4] Alone[2] (%)	Other Race Alone[2] (%)	Two or More Races (%)
City	45.7	43.1	3.4	0.2	0.0	1.6	5.9
MSA[1]	72.1	17.5	2.8	0.1	0.0	1.3	6.1
U.S.	63.4	12.4	5.8	0.9	0.2	6.6	10.7

Note: (1) Figures cover the St. Louis, MO-IL Metropolitan Statistical Area; (2) Alone is defined as not being in combination with one or more other races; (3) American Indian and Alaska Native; (4) Native Hawaiian and Other Pacific Islander
Source: U.S. Census Bureau, 2019-2023 American Community Survey 5-Year Estimates

Hispanic or Latino Origin

Area	Total (%)	Mexican (%)	Puerto Rican (%)	Cuban (%)	Other (%)
City	5.1	3.1	0.3	0.3	1.4
MSA[1]	3.8	2.3	0.3	0.1	1.1
U.S.	19.0	11.3	1.8	0.7	5.2

Note: Persons of Hispanic or Latino origin can be of any race; (1) Figures cover the St. Louis, MO-IL Metropolitan Statistical Area
Source: U.S. Census Bureau, 2019-2023 American Community Survey 5-Year Estimates

Age

Area	Under Age 5	Age 5–19	Age 20–34	Age 35–44	Age 45–54	Age 55–64	Age 65–74	Age 75–84	Age 85+	Median Age
City	5.8	15.0	26.2	14.2	11.1	12.6	9.6	3.7	1.6	36.6
MSA[1]	5.6	18.8	19.2	13.2	12.0	13.8	10.5	4.9	2.0	39.8
U.S.	5.7	19.1	20.2	13.1	12.3	12.8	10.0	4.9	1.9	38.7

Note: (1) Figures cover the St. Louis, MO-IL Metropolitan Statistical Area
Source: U.S. Census Bureau, 2019-2023 American Community Survey 5-Year Estimates

Disability by Age

Area	All Ages	Under 18 Years Old	18 to 64 Years Old	65 Years and Over
City	16.6	6.5	14.4	39.0
MSA[1]	13.3	4.7	11.2	32.1
U.S.	13.0	4.7	10.7	32.9

Note: Figures show percent of the civilian noninstitutionalized population that reported having a disability. Disability status is determined from six types of difficulty: vision, hearing, cognitive, ambulatory, self-care, and independent living. For children under 5 years old, hearing and vision difficulty are used to determine disability status. For children between the ages of 5 and 14, disability status is determined from hearing, vision, cognitive, ambulatory, and self-care difficulties. For people aged 15 years and older, they are considered to have a disability if they have difficulty with any one of the six difficulty types; Note: (1) Figures cover the St. Louis, MO-IL Metropolitan Statistical Area
Source: U.S. Census Bureau, 2019-2023 American Community Survey 5-Year Estimates

Ancestry

Area	German	Irish	English	American	Italian	Polish	French[2]	European	Scottish
City	15.9	9.7	6.4	6.3	4.0	1.7	2.5	1.2	1.3
MSA[1]	25.5	12.6	9.6	5.5	4.5	2.3	2.8	1.6	1.5
U.S.	12.6	9.4	9.1	5.5	4.9	2.6	2.0	1.6	1.6

Note: Figures are the percentage of the total population reporting a particular ancestry. The nine most commonly reported ancestries in the U.S. are shown. Figures include multiple ancestries (e.g. if a person reported being Irish and Italian, they were included in both columns); (1) Figures cover the St. Louis, MO-IL Metropolitan Statistical Area; (2) Excludes Basque
Source: U.S. Census Bureau, 2019-2023 American Community Survey 5-Year Estimates

Foreign-born Population

Area	Percent of Population Born in								
	Any Foreign Country	Asia	Mexico	Europe	Caribbean	Central America[2]	South America	Africa	Canada
City	6.6	2.7	0.8	1.0	0.3	0.3	0.3	0.9	0.1
MSA[1]	5.0	2.3	0.5	1.0	0.1	0.3	0.2	0.5	0.1
U.S.	13.9	4.3	3.3	1.4	1.4	1.2	1.2	0.8	0.2

Note: (1) Figures cover the St. Louis, MO-IL Metropolitan Statistical Area; (2) Excludes Mexico.
Source: U.S. Census Bureau, 2019-2023 American Community Survey 5-Year Estimates

Household Size

Area	Persons in Household (%)							Average Household Size
	One	Two	Three	Four	Five	Six	Seven or More	
City	47.9	30.1	10.3	6.9	3.0	1.0	0.8	1.96
MSA[1]	31.3	34.4	14.6	11.9	5.2	1.6	0.9	2.38
U.S.	28.5	33.8	15.4	12.7	5.9	2.3	1.4	2.54

Note: (1) Figures cover the St. Louis, MO-IL Metropolitan Statistical Area
Source: U.S. Census Bureau, 2019-2023 American Community Survey 5-Year Estimates

Household Relationships

Area	Householder	Opposite-sex Spouse	Same-sex Spouse	Opposite-sex Unmarried Partner	Same-sex Unmarried Partner	Child[2]	Grandchild	Other Relatives	Non-relatives
City	48.0	10.3	0.4	3.7	0.4	22.5	2.6	4.0	4.3
MSA[1]	40.8	18.2	0.2	2.6	0.2	28.5	2.2	3.0	2.4
U.S.	38.3	17.5	0.2	2.5	0.2	28.3	2.4	4.8	3.4

Note: Figures are percent of the total population; (1) Figures cover the St. Louis, MO-IL Metropolitan Statistical Area; (2) Includes biological, adopted, and stepchildren of the householder
Source: U.S. Census Bureau, 2020 Census

Gender

Area	Males	Females	Males per 100 Females
City	142,190	150,919	94.2
MSA[1]	1,370,976	1,438,438	95.3
U.S.	164,545,087	167,842,453	98.0

Note: (1) Figures cover the St. Louis, MO-IL Metropolitan Statistical Area
Source: U.S. Census Bureau, 2019-2023 American Community Survey 5-Year Estimates

Marital Status

Area	Never Married	Now Married[2]	Separated	Widowed	Divorced
City	49.7	30.2	2.7	5.3	12.2
MSA[1]	32.9	48.4	1.6	5.8	11.2
U.S.	34.1	47.9	1.7	5.6	10.7

Note: Figures are percentages and cover the population 15 years of age and older; (1) Figures cover the St. Louis, MO-IL Metropolitan Statistical Area; (2) Excludes separated
Source: U.S. Census Bureau, 2019-2023 American Community Survey 5-Year Estimates

Religious Groups by Family

Area	Catholic	Baptist	Methodist	LDS[2]	Pentecostal	Lutheran	Islam	Adventist	Other
MSA[1]	21.2	8.6	2.9	0.7	1.4	3.2	1.3	0.8	11.1
U.S.	18.7	7.3	3.0	2.0	1.8	1.7	1.3	1.3	11.6

Note: Figures are the number of adherents as a percentage of the total population and cover the eight largest religious groups in the U.S; (1) Figures cover the St. Louis, MO-IL Metropolitan Statistical Area; (2) Church of Jesus Christ of Latter-day Saints
Sources: 2020 U.S. Religion Census, Association of Statisticians of American Religious Bodies; The Association of Religion Data Archives (ARDA)

Religious Groups by Tradition

Area	Catholic	Evangelical Protestant	Mainline Protestant	Black Protestant	Islam	Judaism	Hinduism	Orthodox	Buddhism
MSA[1]	21.2	16.1	5.7	3.9	1.3	0.6	0.2	0.2	0.3
U.S.	18.7	16.5	5.2	2.3	1.3	0.6	0.4	0.4	0.3

Note: Figures are the number of adherents as a percentage of the total population; (1) Figures cover the St. Louis, MO-IL Metropolitan Statistical Area
Sources: 2020 U.S. Religion Census, Association of Statisticians of American Religious Bodies; The Association of Religion Data Archives (ARDA)

ECONOMY

Real Gross Domestic Product (GDP)

Area	2017	2018	2019	2020	2021	2022	2023	Rank[3]
MSA[1]	164.4	166.6	169.5	165.7	175.8	180.2	184.8	24
U.S.[2]	17,619.1	18,160.7	18,642.5	18,238.9	19,387.6	19,896.6	20,436.3	—

Note: Figures are in billions of chained 2017 dollars; (1) Figures cover the St. Louis, MO-IL Metropolitan Statistical Area; (2) Figures cover real GDP within metropolitan areas; (3) Rank is based on 2023 data and ranges from 1 to 384
Source: U.S. Bureau of Economic Analysis

Economic Growth

Area	2014	2015	2016	2017	2018	2019	2020	2021	2022	2023
MSA[1]	1.4	0.8	0.1	-0.4	1.3	1.7	-2.2	6.1	2.5	2.5
U.S.[2]	2.6	3.2	2.0	2.7	3.1	2.7	-2.2	6.3	2.6	2.7

Note: Figures are real gross domestic product growth rates and represent percent change from preceding period; (1) Figures cover the St. Louis, MO-IL Metropolitan Statistical Area; (2) Figures are the average growth rates within metropolitan areas
Source: U.S. Bureau of Economic Analysis

Metropolitan Area Exports

Area	2018	2019	2020	2021	2022	2023	Rank[2]
MSA[1]	10,866.8	10,711.1	9,089.4	10,486.1	14,215.6	13,817.0	30
U.S.	1,664,056.1	1,645,173.7	1,431,406.6	1,753,941.4	2,062,937.4	2,019,160.5	—

Note: Figures are in millions of dollars; (1) Figures cover the St. Louis, MO-IL Metropolitan Statistical Area; (2) Rank is based on 2023 data and ranges from 1 to 386
Source: U.S. Department of Commerce, International Trade Administration, Office of Trade and Economic Analysis, Industry and Analysis, Exports by Metropolitan Area, data extracted April 2, 2025

Building Permits

Area	Single-Family			Multi-Family			Total		
	2023	2024	Pct. Chg.	2023	2024	Pct. Chg.	2023	2024	Pct. Chg.
City	51	56	9.8	227	238	4.8	278	294	5.8
MSA[1]	4,599	4,653	1.2	2,508	2,364	-5.7	7,107	7,017	-1.3
U.S.	920,000	981,900	6.7	591,100	496,100	-16.1	1,511,100	1,478,000	-2.2

Note: (1) Figures cover the St. Louis, MO-IL Metropolitan Statistical Area; Figures represent new, privately-owned housing units authorized (unadjusted data)
Source: U.S. Census Bureau, Building Permits Survey (BPS), 2023, 2024

Bankruptcy Filings

Area	Business Filings			Nonbusiness Filings		
	2023	2024	% Chg.	2023	2024	% Chg.
Saint Louis city County	12	23	91.7	1,497	1,311	-12.4
U.S.	18,926	23,107	22.1	434,064	494,201	13.9

Note: Business filings include Chapter 7, Chapter 9, Chapter 11, Chapter 12, Chapter 13, Chapter 15, and Section 304; Nonbusiness filings include Chapter 7, Chapter 11, and Chapter 13
Source: Administrative Office of the U.S. Courts, Business and Nonbusiness Bankruptcy, County Cases Commenced by Chapter of the Bankruptcy Code, During the 12-Month Period Ending December 31, 2023 and Business and Nonbusiness Bankruptcy, County Cases Commenced by Chapter of the Bankruptcy Code, During the 12-Month Period Ending December 31, 2024

Housing Vacancy Rates

Area	Gross Vacancy Rate[3] (%)			Year-Round Vacancy Rate[4] (%)			Rental Vacancy Rate[5] (%)			Homeowner Vacancy Rate[6] (%)		
	2022	2023	2024	2022	2023	2024	2022	2023	2024	2022	2023	2024
MSA[1]	7.2	7.4	7.7	7.1	7.3	7.6	6.8	7.8	7.9	1.4	0.6	0.9
U.S.[2]	9.1	9.0	9.1	7.5	7.5	7.6	5.7	6.5	6.8	0.8	0.8	1.0

Note: (1) Figures cover the St. Louis, MO-IL Metropolitan Statistical Area; (2) Figures cover the 75 largest Metropolitan Statistical Areas; (3) The percentage of the total housing inventory that is vacant; (4) The percentage of the housing inventory (excluding seasonal units) that is year-round vacant; (5) The percentage of rental inventory that is vacant for rent; (6) The percentage of homeowner inventory that is vacant for sale
Source: U.S. Census Bureau, Housing Vacancies and Homeownership Annual Statistics: 2022, 2023, 2024

INCOME

Income

Area	Per Capita ($)	Median Household ($)	Average Household ($)
City	38,947	55,279	78,097
MSA[1]	44,689	78,225	107,013
U.S.	43,289	78,538	110,491

Note: (1) Figures cover the St. Louis, MO-IL Metropolitan Statistical Area
Source: U.S. Census Bureau, 2019-2023 American Community Survey 5-Year Estimates

Household Income Distribution

Area	Percent of Households Earning							
	Under $15,000	$15,000 -$24,999	$25,000 -$34,999	$35,000 -$49,999	$50,000 -$74,999	$75,000 -$99,999	$100,000 -$149,999	$150,000 and up
City	15.5	8.8	9.1	12.5	17.5	11.3	13.1	12.4
MSA[1]	7.6	6.2	6.8	11.1	16.4	13.1	18.1	20.7
U.S.	8.5	6.6	6.8	10.4	15.7	12.7	17.4	21.9

Note: (1) Figures cover the St. Louis, MO-IL Metropolitan Statistical Area
Source: U.S. Census Bureau, 2019-2023 American Community Survey 5-Year Estimates

Poverty Rate

Area	All Ages	Under 18 Years Old	18 to 64 Years Old	65 Years and Over
City	19.8	26.9	18.2	17.8
MSA[1]	10.3	13.3	9.7	8.7
U.S.	12.4	16.3	11.6	10.4

Note: Figures are percentage of people whose income during the past 12 months was below the poverty level;
(1) Figures cover the St. Louis, MO-IL Metropolitan Statistical Area
Source: U.S. Census Bureau, 2019-2023 American Community Survey 5-Year Estimates

EMPLOYMENT

Labor Force and Employment

Area	Civilian Labor Force			Workers Employed		
	Dec. 2023	Dec. 2024	% Chg.	Dec. 2023	Dec. 2024	% Chg.
City	150,472	152,715	1.5	144,679	146,505	1.3
MSA[1]	1,476,468	1,495,860	1.3	1,428,392	1,447,762	1.4
U.S.	166,661,000	167,746,000	0.7	160,754,000	161,294,000	0.3

Note: Data is not seasonally adjusted and covers workers 16 years of age and older; (1) Figures cover the St. Louis, MO-IL Metropolitan Statistical Area
Source: Bureau of Labor Statistics, Local Area Unemployment Statistics

Unemployment Rate

Area	2024											
	Jan.	Feb.	Mar.	Apr.	May	Jun.	Jul.	Aug.	Sep.	Oct.	Nov.	Dec.
City	4.4	4.8	4.6	3.9	4.3	4.6	4.9	4.8	3.8	4.0	4.0	4.1
MSA[1]	3.9	4.1	3.9	3.4	3.7	4.0	4.2	3.9	3.2	3.3	3.3	3.2
U.S.	4.1	4.2	3.9	3.5	3.7	4.3	4.5	4.4	3.9	3.9	4.0	3.8

Note: Data is not seasonally adjusted and covers workers 16 years of age and older; (1) Figures cover the St. Louis, MO-IL Metropolitan Statistical Area
Source: Bureau of Labor Statistics, Local Area Unemployment Statistics

Average Wages

Occupation	$/Hr.	Occupation	$/Hr.
Accountants and Auditors	40.41	Maintenance and Repair Workers	26.56
Automotive Mechanics	25.56	Marketing Managers	66.03
Bookkeepers	25.12	Network and Computer Systems Admin.	43.67
Carpenters	33.56	Nurses, Licensed Practical	30.72
Cashiers	15.63	Nurses, Registered	40.74
Computer Programmers	48.91	Nursing Assistants	19.04
Computer Systems Analysts	46.89	Office Clerks, General	21.94
Computer User Support Specialists	29.80	Physical Therapists	46.78
Construction Laborers	31.00	Physicians	n/a
Cooks, Restaurant	18.07	Plumbers, Pipefitters and Steamfitters	37.26
Customer Service Representatives	22.36	Police and Sheriff's Patrol Officers	34.71
Dentists	n/a	Postal Service Mail Carriers	28.63
Electricians	36.65	Real Estate Sales Agents	22.92
Engineers, Electrical	56.55	Retail Salespersons	17.47
Fast Food and Counter Workers	15.19	Sales Representatives, Technical/Scientific	49.86
Financial Managers	76.57	Secretaries, Exc. Legal/Medical/Executive	21.95
First-Line Supervisors of Office Workers	34.31	Security Guards	21.78
General and Operations Managers	53.75	Surgeons	n/a
Hairdressers/Cosmetologists	20.57	Teacher Assistants, Exc. Postsecondary[1]	16.42
Home Health and Personal Care Aides	15.72	Teachers, Secondary School, Exc. Sp. Ed.[1]	31.39
Janitors and Cleaners	17.54	Telemarketers	15.91
Landscaping/Groundskeeping Workers	19.80	Truck Drivers, Heavy/Tractor-Trailer	27.24
Lawyers	73.53	Truck Drivers, Light/Delivery Services	23.38
Maids and Housekeeping Cleaners	16.55	Waiters and Waitresses	15.95

Note: Wage data covers the St. Louis, MO-IL Metropolitan Statistical Area; (1) Hourly wages were calculated from annual wage data based on a 40 hour work week
Source: Bureau of Labor Statistics, Metro Area Occupational Employment & Wage Estimates, May 2024

Employment by Industry

Sector	MSA[1] Number of Employees	MSA[1] Percent of Total	U.S. Percent of Total
Construction, Mining, and Logging	77,200	5.4	5.5
Financial Activities	96,400	6.7	5.8
Government	160,800	11.2	14.9
Information	28,500	2.0	1.9
Leisure and Hospitality	139,900	9.7	10.4
Manufacturing	118,600	8.2	8.0
Other Services	51,800	3.6	3.7
Private Education and Health Services	280,500	19.5	16.9
Professional and Business Services	214,800	14.9	14.2
Retail Trade	138,900	9.6	10.0
Transportation, Warehousing, and Utilities	68,600	4.8	4.8
Wholesale Trade	66,100	4.6	3.9

Note: Figures are non-farm employment as of December 2024. Figures are not seasonally adjusted and include workers 16 years of age and older; (1) Figures cover the St. Louis, MO-IL Metropolitan Statistical Area
Source: Bureau of Labor Statistics, Current Employment Statistics, Employment, Hours, and Earnings

Employment by Occupation

Occupation Classification	City (%)	MSA[1] (%)	U.S. (%)
Management, Business, Science, and Arts	48.0	44.7	42.0
Natural Resources, Construction, and Maintenance	4.4	7.5	8.6
Production, Transportation, and Material Moving	11.2	12.3	13.0
Sales and Office	17.6	20.3	19.9
Service	18.7	15.2	16.5

Note: Figures cover employed civilians 16 years of age and older; (1) Figures cover the St. Louis, MO-IL Metropolitan Statistical Area
Source: U.S. Census Bureau, 2019-2023 American Community Survey 5-Year Estimates

Occupations with Greatest Projected Employment Growth: 2022 – 2032

Occupation[1]	2022 Employment	2032 Projected Employment	Numeric Employment Change	Percent Employment Change
Home Health and Personal Care Aides	79,380	91,510	12,130	15.3
Registered Nurses	76,960	84,580	7,620	9.9
Cooks, Restaurant	31,980	39,310	7,330	22.9
General and Operations Managers	97,060	102,780	5,720	5.9
Software Developers	19,530	24,690	5,160	26.4
Stockers and Order Fillers	57,940	62,820	4,880	8.4
Laborers and Freight, Stock, and Material Movers, Hand	43,160	46,620	3,460	8.0
Nurse Practitioners	7,520	10,670	3,150	41.9
Medical and Health Services Managers	9,950	13,050	3,100	31.2
Maintenance and Repair Workers, General	32,440	34,810	2,370	7.3

Note: Projections cover Missouri; (1) Sorted by numeric employment change
Source: www.projectionscentral.org, State Occupational Projections, 2022–2032 Long-Term Projections

Fastest-Growing Occupations: 2022 – 2032

Occupation[1]	2022 Employment	2032 Projected Employment	Numeric Employment Change	Percent Employment Change
Nurse Practitioners	7,520	10,670	3,150	41.9
Data Scientists	4,320	5,950	1,630	37.7
Information Security Analysts (SOC 2018)	3,470	4,640	1,170	33.7
Computer and Information Research Scientists (SOC 2018)	540	710	170	31.5
Medical and Health Services Managers	9,950	13,050	3,100	31.2
Physical Therapist Assistants	2,520	3,240	720	28.6
Occupational Therapy Assistants	1,160	1,490	330	28.4
Veterinary Technologists and Technicians	2,080	2,640	560	26.9
Speech-Language Pathologists	4,030	5,100	1,070	26.6
Software Developers	19,530	24,690	5,160	26.4

Note: Projections cover Missouri; (1) Sorted by percent employment change and excludes occupations with numeric employment change less than 50
Source: www.projectionscentral.org, State Occupational Projections, 2022–2032 Long-Term Projections

CITY FINANCES

City Government Finances

Component	2022 ($000)	2022 ($ per capita)
Total Revenues	1,126,883	3,786
Total Expenditures	1,189,135	3,995
Debt Outstanding	1,537,172	5,164

Source: U.S. Census Bureau, State & Local Government Finances 2022

City Government Revenue by Source

Source	2022 ($000)	2022 ($ per capita)	2022 (%)
General Revenue			
From Federal Government	13,061	44	1.2
From State Government	66,542	224	5.9
From Local Governments	0	0	0.0
Taxes			
Property	115,096	387	10.2
Sales and Gross Receipts	333,646	1,121	29.6
Personal Income	186,734	627	16.6
Corporate Income	40,745	137	3.6
Motor Vehicle License	1,417	5	0.1
Other Taxes	37,527	126	3.3
Current Charges	261,825	880	23.2
Liquor Store	0	0	0.0
Utility	55,266	186	4.9

Source: U.S. Census Bureau, State & Local Government Finances 2022

City Government Expenditures by Function

Function	2022 ($000)	2022 ($ per capita)	2022 (%)
General Direct Expenditures			
Air Transportation	170,037	571	14.3
Corrections	42,044	141	3.5
Education	0	0	0.0
Employment Security Administration	0	0	0.0
Financial Administration	40,465	136	3.4
Fire Protection	81,272	273	6.8
General Public Buildings	15,926	53	1.3
Governmental Administration, Other	27,975	94	2.4
Health	89,004	299	7.5
Highways	63,362	212	5.3
Hospitals	0	0	0.0
Housing and Community Development	44,695	150	3.8
Interest on General Debt	63,584	213	5.3
Judicial and Legal	53,274	179	4.5
Libraries	351	1	0.0
Parking	15,372	51	1.3
Parks and Recreation	38,280	128	3.2
Police Protection	224,630	754	18.9
Public Welfare	0	0	0.0
Sewerage	2,432	8	0.2
Solid Waste Management	16,065	54	1.4
Veterans' Services	0	0	0.0
Liquor Store	0	0	0.0
Utility	98,101	329	8.2

Source: U.S. Census Bureau, State & Local Government Finances 2022

TAXES

State Corporate Income Tax Rates

State	Tax Rate (%)	Income Brackets ($)	Num. of Brackets	Financial Institution Tax Rate (%)[a]	Federal Income Tax Ded.
Missouri	4.0	Flat rate	1	4.48	Yes (h)

Note: Tax rates for tax year 2024; (a) Rates listed are the corporate income tax rate applied to financial institutions or excise taxes based on income. Some states have other taxes based upon the value of deposits or shares; (h) 50% of the federal income tax is deductible.
Source: Federation of Tax Administrators, State Corporate Income Tax Rates, January 1, 2025

State Individual Income Tax Rates

State	Tax Rate (%)	Income Brackets ($)	Personal Exemptions ($)			Standard Ded. ($)	
			Single	Married	Depend.	Single	Married
Missouri (a)	0.0 - 4.8	1,207 - 8,449	(d)	(d)	(d)	14,600	29,200 (d)

Note: Tax rates for tax year 2024; Local- and county-level taxes are not included; The deduction for federal SALT deductions is limited to $5,000 for individuals and $10,000 for joint returns in Missouri and Montana, and to $7,800 for all filers in Oregon; (a) 16 states have statutory provision for automatically adjusting to the rate of inflation the dollar values of the income tax brackets, standard deductions, and/or personal exemptions. Oregon does not index the income brackets for $125,000 and over See: INFL and SPEC above; (d) These states use the personal exemption/standard deduction amounts provided in the federal Internal Revenue Code. Montana personal exemption subject to repeal under Section 15-30-2114.
Source: Federation of Tax Administrators, State Individual Income Tax Rates, January 1, 2025

Various State Sales and Excise Tax Rates

State	State Sales Tax (%)	Gasoline[1] ($/gal.)	Cigarette[2] ($/pack)	Spirits[3] ($/gal.)	Wine[4] ($/gal.)	Beer[5] ($/gal.)	Recreational Marijuana (%)
Missouri	4.225	0.27	0.17	2.00	0.42	0.06	(m)

Note: All tax rates as of January 1, 2025; (1) The American Petroleum Institute has developed a methodology for determining the average tax rate on a gallon of fuel. Rates may include any of the following: excise taxes, environmental fees, storage tank fees, other fees or taxes, general sales tax, and local taxes; (2) The federal excise tax of $1.0066 per pack and local taxes are not included; (3) Rates are those applicable to off-premise sales of 40% alcohol by volume (a.b.v.) distilled spirits in 750ml containers. Local excise taxes are excluded; (4) Rates are those applicable to off-premise sales of 11% a.b.v. non-carbonated wine in 750ml containers; (5) Rates are those applicable to off-premise sales of 4.7% a.b.v. beer in 12 ounce containers; (m) 6% excise tax (retail price)
Source: Tax Foundation, 2025 Facts & Figures: How Does Your State Compare?

State Tax Competitiveness Index

State	Overall Rank	Corporate Tax Rank	Individual Income Tax Rank	Sales Tax Rank	Property Tax Rank	Unemployment Insurance Tax Rank
Missouri	13	4	20	24	11	5

Note: The Tax Foundation's State Tax Competitiveness Index enables policymakers, taxpayers, and business leaders to gauge how their states' tax systems compare. A rank of 1 is best, 50 is worst. Rankings do not average to the total. States without a tax rank equally as 1. DC's scores and rankings do not affect other states. The report shows tax systems as of July 1, 2024 (the beginning of Fiscal Year 2025).
Source: Tax Foundation, State Tax Competitiveness Index 2025

TRANSPORTATION

Means of Transportation to Work

Area	Car/Truck/Van		Public Transportation			Bicycle	Walked	Other Means	Worked at Home
	Drove Alone	Car-pooled	Bus	Subway	Railroad				
City	66.6	6.7	4.4	0.4	0.1	0.9	4.0	1.9	15.0
MSA[1]	75.6	6.6	1.1	0.1	0.0	0.2	1.5	1.1	13.8
U.S.	70.2	8.5	1.7	1.3	0.4	0.4	2.4	1.6	13.5

Note: Figures are percentages and cover workers 16 years of age and older; (1) Figures cover the St. Louis, MO-IL Metropolitan Statistical Area
Source: U.S. Census Bureau, 2019-2023 American Community Survey 5-Year Estimates

Travel Time to Work

Area	Less Than 10 Minutes	10 to 19 Minutes	20 to 29 Minutes	30 to 44 Minutes	45 to 59 Minutes	60 to 89 Minutes	90 Minutes or More
City	9.9	36.2	27.2	19.5	3.2	2.5	1.6
MSA[1]	11.3	28.2	24.6	23.4	7.3	3.5	1.6
U.S.	12.6	28.6	21.2	20.8	8.1	6.0	2.8

Note: Note: Figures are percentages and include workers 16 years old and over; (1) Figures cover the St. Louis, MO-IL Metropolitan Statistical Area
Source: U.S. Census Bureau, 2019-2023 American Community Survey 5-Year Estimates

Key Congestion Measures

Measure	2000	2010	2015	2020	2022
Annual Hours of Delay, Total (000)	47,642	62,483	69,729	51,115	71,765
Annual Hours of Delay, Per Auto Commuter	39	43	45	33	49
Annual Congestion Cost, Per Auto Commuter ($)	963	1,005	1,034	804	1,152

Note: Figures cover the St. Louis MO-IL urban area
Source: Texas A&M Transportation Institute, 2023 Urban Mobility Report

Freeway Travel Time Index

Measure	1985	1990	1995	2000	2005	2010	2015	2020	2022
Urban Area Index[1]	1.07	1.09	1.13	1.15	1.16	1.16	1.15	1.08	1.14
Urban Area Rank[1,2]	48	56	47	53	57	54	67	44	64

Note: Freeway Travel Time Index—the ratio of travel time in the peak period to the travel time at free-flow conditions. For example, a value of 1.30 indicates a 20-minute free-flow trip takes 26 minutes in the peak (20 minutes x 1.30 = 26 minutes); (1) Covers the St. Louis MO-IL urban area; (2) Rank is based on 101 larger urban areas (#1 = highest travel time index)
Source: Texas A&M Transportation Institute, 2023 Urban Mobility Report

Public Transportation

Agency Name / Mode of Transportation	Vehicles Operated in Maximum Service[1]	Annual Unlinked Passenger Trips[2] (in thous.)	Annual Passenger Miles[3] (in thous.)
Bi-State Development Agency (METRO)			
Bus (directly operated)	241	12,508.9	72,681.7
Demand Response (directly operated)	102	296.0	3,534.4
Light Rail (directly operated)	42	6,886.0	45,652.1

Note: (1) Number of revenue vehicles operated by the given mode and type of service to meet the annual maximum service requirement. This is the revenue vehicle count during the peak season of the year; on the week and day that maximum service is provided. Vehicles operated in maximum service (VOMS) exclude atypical days and one-time special events; (2) Number of passengers who boarded public transportation vehicles. Passengers are counted each time they board a vehicle no matter how many vehicles they use to travel from their origin to their destination. (3) Sum of the distances ridden by all passengers during the entire fiscal year.
Source: Federal Transit Administration, National Transit Database, 2023

Air Transportation

Airport Name and Code / Type of Service	Passenger Airlines[1]	Passenger Enplanements	Freight Carriers[2]	Freight (lbs)
Lambert-St. Louis International (STL)				
Domestic service (U.S. carriers only)	27	7,569,385	18	79,285,870
International service (U.S. carriers only)	9	164,004	3	40,754

Note: (1) Includes all U.S.-based major, minor and commuter airlines that carried at least one passenger during the year; (2) Includes all U.S.-based airlines and freight carriers that transported at least one pound of freight during the year.
Source: Bureau of Transportation Statistics, The Intermodal Transportation Database, Air Carriers: T-100 Domestic Market (U.S. carriers only), 2024; Bureau of Transportation Statistics, The Intermodal Transportation Database, Air Carriers: T-100 International Market (U.S. carriers only), 2024

BUSINESSES

Major Business Headquarters

Company Name	Industry	Rankings	
		Fortune[1]	Forbes[2]
Alberici	Construction	-	158
Ameren	Utilities: gas and electric	494	-
Arco Construction	Construction	-	95
Centene	Health care: insurance and managed care	22	-
Clayco Construction	Construction	-	109
Edward Jones	Diversified financials	-	31
Emerson Electric	Industrial machinery	224	-
Enterprise Mobility	Services	-	7
Graybar Electric	Wholesalers: diversified	367	-
Graybar Electric	Capital goods	-	44
McCarthy Holdings	Construction	-	99
Schnuck Markets	Food markets	-	203
World Wide Technology	IT software & services	-	19

Note: (1) Companies that produce a 10-K are ranked 1 to 500 based on 2023 revenue; (2) All private companies with at least $2 billion in annual revenue through the end of their most current fiscal year are ranked 1 to 275; companies listed are headquartered in the city; dashes indicate no ranking
Source: Fortune, "Fortune 500," 2024; Forbes, "America's Largest Private Companies," 2024

Fastest-Growing Businesses

According to *Inc.*, Saint Louis is home to two of America's 500 fastest-growing private companies: **Experience Fresh** (#403); **Orchard** (#450). Criteria: must be an independent, privately-held, for-profit, U.S. corporation, proprietorship or partnership as of December 31, 2023; revenues must be at least $100,000 in 2020 and $2 million in 2023; must have four-year operating/sales history. *Inc.*, "America's 500 Fastest-Growing Private Companies," 2024

According to *Initiative for a Competitive Inner City (ICIC)*, Saint Louis is home to one of America's 100 fastest-growing "inner city" companies: **Clementine's Naughty and Nice Ice Cream** (#42). To be eligible for the IC100, companies have to be independently operated, privately held, for-profit businesses with revenues of at least $50,000 in 2019 and $500,000 in 2023, and headquartered in an under-resourced community. Recognizing that concentrated poverty exists within metropolitan areas outside of big cities (and that poverty overall is suburbanizing), ICIC defines under-resourced communities as large low-income, high-poverty areas located in the urban and suburban parts of all but the smallest metropolitan areas. Companies were ranked overall by revenue growth over the five-year period between 2019 and 2023. *Initiative for a Competitive Inner City (ICIC), "Inner City 100 Companies," 2024*

According to Deloitte, Saint Louis is home to one of North America's 500 fastest-growing high-technology companies: **Benson Hill** (#359). Companies are ranked by percentage growth in revenue over a four-year period. Criteria for inclusion: company must be headquartered within North America; must own proprietary intellectual property or technology that is sold to customers in products that contributes to a significant portion of the company's operating revenue; must have been in business for a minumum of four years with 2020 operating revenues of at least $50,000 USD/CD and 2023 operating revenues of at least $5 million USD/CD. *Deloitte, 2024 Technology Fast 500™*

Saint Louis, Missouri

Living Environment

COST OF LIVING

Cost of Living Index

Composite Index	Groceries	Housing	Utilities	Transportation	Health Care	Misc. Goods/Services
89.1	98.8	78.0	97.9	93.3	87.6	90.9

Note: The Cost of Living Index measures regional differences in the cost of consumer goods and services, excluding taxes and non-consumer expenditures, for professional and managerial households in the top income quintile. It is based on more than 50,000 prices covering almost 60 different items for which prices are collected three times a year by chambers of commerce, economic development organizations or university applied economic centers in each participating urban area. The numbers shown should be read as a percentage above or below the national average of 100. For example, a value of 115.4 in the groceries column indicates that grocery prices are 15.4% higher than the national average. Small differences in the index numbers should not be interpreted as significant; Figures cover the St. Louis MO-IL urban area.
Source: The Council for Community and Economic Research, Cost of Living Index, 2024

Grocery Prices

Area[1]	T-Bone Steak ($/pound)	Frying Chicken ($/pound)	Whole Milk ($/half gal.)	Eggs ($/dozen)	Orange Juice ($/64 oz.)	Coffee ($/11.5 oz.)
City[2]	15.51	1.44	4.67	3.37	4.43	5.05
Avg.	15.42	1.55	4.69	3.25	4.41	5.46
Min.	14.50	1.16	4.43	2.75	4.00	4.85
Max.	17.56	2.89	5.49	4.78	5.54	7.89

Note: (1) Values for the local area are compared with the average, minimum and maximum values for all 276 areas in the Cost of Living Index; (2) Figures cover the St. Louis MO-IL urban area; **T-Bone Steak** (price per pound); **Frying Chicken** (price per pound, whole fryer); **Whole Milk** (half gallon carton); **Eggs** (price per dozen, Grade A, large); **Orange Juice** (64 oz. Tropicana or Florida Natural); **Coffee** (11.5 oz. can, vacuum-packed, Maxwell House, Hills Bros, or Folgers).
Source: The Council for Community and Economic Research, Cost of Living Index, 2024

Housing and Utility Costs

Area[1]	New Home Price ($)	Apartment Rent ($/month)	All Electric ($/month)	Part Electric ($/month)	Other Energy ($/month)	Telephone ($/month)
City[2]	427,558	1,128	-	100.98	92.58	203.68
Avg.	515,975	1,550	210.99	123.07	82.07	194.99
Min.	265,375	692	104.33	53.68	36.26	179.42
Max.	2,775,821	5,719	529.02	397.28	361.63	223.33

Note: (1) Values for the local area are compared with the average, minimum and maximum values for all 276 areas in the Cost of Living Index; (2) Figures cover the St. Louis MO-IL urban area; **New Home Price** (2,400 sf living area, 8,000 sf lot, in urban area with full utilities); **Apartment Rent** (950 sf 2 bedroom/1.5 or 2 bath, unfurnished, excluding all utilities except water); **All Electric** (average monthly cost for an all-electric home); **Part Electric** (average monthly cost for a part-electric home); **Other Energy** (average monthly cost for natural gas, fuel oil, coal, wood, and any other forms of energy except electricity); **Telephone** (price includes the base monthly rate plus taxes and fees for three lines of mobile phone service).
Source: The Council for Community and Economic Research, Cost of Living Index, 2024

Health Care, Transportation, and Other Costs

Area[1]	Doctor ($/visit)	Dentist ($/visit)	Optometrist ($/visit)	Gasoline ($/gallon)	Beauty Salon ($/visit)	Men's Shirt ($)
City[2]	92.32	115.88	95.55	3.38	41.97	28.19
Avg.	143.77	117.51	129.23	3.32	48.57	38.14
Min.	36.74	58.67	67.33	2.80	24.00	13.41
Max.	270.44	216.82	307.33	5.28	94.00	63.89

Note: (1) Values for the local area are compared with the average, minimum and maximum values for all 276 areas in the Cost of Living Index; (2) Figures cover the St. Louis MO-IL urban area; **Doctor** (general practitioners routine exam of an established patient); **Dentist** (adult teeth cleaning and periodic oral examination); **Optometrist** (full vision eye exam for established adult patient); **Gasoline** (one gallon regular unleaded, national brand, including all taxes, cash price at self-service pump if available); **Beauty Salon** (woman's shampoo, trim, and blow-dry); **Men's Shirt** (cotton/polyester dress shirt, pinpoint weave, long sleeves).
Source: The Council for Community and Economic Research, Cost of Living Index, 2024

HOUSING

Homeownership Rate

Area	2017 (%)	2018 (%)	2019 (%)	2020 (%)	2021 (%)	2022 (%)	2023 (%)	2024 (%)
MSA[1]	65.6	65.8	68.1	71.1	73.8	69.9	69.4	68.2
U.S.	63.9	64.4	64.6	66.6	65.5	65.8	65.9	65.6

Note: (1) Figures cover the St. Louis, MO-IL Metropolitan Statistical Area
Source: U.S. Census Bureau, Housing Vacancies and Homeownership Annual Statistics: 2017-2024

House Price Index (HPI)

Area	National Ranking[2]	Quarterly Change (%)	One-Year Change (%)	Five-Year Change (%)	Since 1991Q1 (%)
MSA[1]	92	1.02	6.12	48.75	237.26
U.S.[3]	—	1.43	4.51	57.13	327.82

Note: The HPI is a weighted repeat sales index. It measures average price changes in repeat sales or refinancings on the same properties. This information is obtained by reviewing repeat mortgage transactions on single-family properties whose mortgages have been purchased or securitized by Fannie Mae or Freddie Mac since January 1975; (1) Figures cover the St. Louis, MO-IL Metropolitan Statistical Area; (2) Rankings are based on annual percentage change for all metro areas containing at least 15,000 transactions over the last 10 years and ranges from 1 to 241; (3) figures based on a weighted average of Census Division estimates using a seasonally adjusted, purchase-only index; all figures are for the period ending December 31, 2024
Source: Federal Housing Finance Agency, Change in FHFA Metropolitan Area House Price Indexes, All Transactions Index, 2024Q4

Home Value

Area	Under $100,000	$100,000 -$199,999	$200,000 -$299,999	$300,000 -$399,999	$400,000 -$499,999	$500,000 -$999,999	$1,000,000 or more	Median ($)
City	22.9	31.6	22.8	11.1	5.1	5.2	1.2	185,100
MSA[1]	14.9	26.3	25.0	14.9	8.2	8.9	1.8	232,100
U.S.	12.1	17.8	19.5	14.4	10.5	19.1	6.5	303,400

Note: Figures are percentages except for median and cover owner-occupied housing units; (1) Figures cover the St. Louis, MO-IL Metropolitan Statistical Area
Source: U.S. Census Bureau, 2019-2023 American Community Survey 5-Year Estimates

Year Housing Structure Built

Area	2020 or Later	2010 -2019	2000 -2009	1990 -1999	1980 -1989	1970 -1979	1960 -1969	1950 -1959	1940 -1949	Before 1940	Median Year
City	0.2	3.2	4.0	3.0	3.7	4.3	6.1	9.7	7.6	58.3	1938
MSA[1]	0.8	6.3	11.4	11.6	11.1	12.8	12.2	12.3	5.4	16.1	1973
U.S.	1.2	8.9	13.6	12.8	13.0	14.4	10.0	9.7	4.5	11.9	1980

Note: Figures are percentages except for Median Year; Note: (1) Figures cover the St. Louis, MO-IL Metropolitan Statistical Area
Source: U.S. Census Bureau, 2019-2023 American Community Survey 5-Year Estimates

Gross Monthly Rent

Area	Under $500	$500 -$999	$1,000 -$1,499	$1,500 -$1,999	$2,000 -$2,499	$2,500 -$2,999	$3,000 and up	Median ($)
City	9.1	43.5	33.0	9.9	3.0	0.9	0.7	978
MSA[1]	6.4	36.8	37.9	12.7	3.4	1.2	1.8	1,073
U.S.	6.5	22.3	29.5	20.2	10.8	4.8	5.9	1,348

Note: Figures are percentages except for median; Gross rent is the contract rent plus the estimated average monthly cost of utilities (electricity, gas, and water and sewer) and fuels (oil, coal, kerosene, wood, etc.) if these are paid by the renter (or paid for the renter by someone else); (1) Figures cover the St. Louis, MO-IL Metropolitan Statistical Area
Source: U.S. Census Bureau, 2019-2023 American Community Survey 5-Year Estimates

HEALTH

Health Risk Factors

Category	MSA[1] (%)	U.S. (%)
Adults aged 18–64 who have any kind of health care coverage	94.8	90.8
Adults who reported being in good or better health	82.7	81.8
Adults who have been told they have high blood cholesterol	36.6	36.9
Adults who have been told they have high blood pressure	34.9	34.0
Adults who are current smokers	12.2	12.1
Adults who currently use e-cigarettes	6.4	7.7
Adults who currently use chewing tobacco, snuff, or snus	2.0	3.2
Adults who are heavy drinkers[2]	4.7	6.1
Adults who are binge drinkers[3]	18.4	15.2
Adults who are overweight (BMI 25.0 - 29.9)	34.3	34.4
Adults who are obese (BMI 30.0 - 99.8)	35.7	34.3
Adults who participated in any physical activities in the past month	75.5	75.8

Note: All figures are crude prevalence; (1) Figures cover the St. Louis, MO-IL Metropolitan Statistical Area; (2) Heavy drinkers are classified as adult men having more than 14 drinks per week and adult women having more than 7 drinks per week; (3) Binge drinkers are classified as males having five or more drinks on one occasion or females having four or more drinks on one occasion
Source: Centers for Disease Control and Prevention, Behavioral Risk Factor Surveillance System, SMART: Selected Metropolitan Area Risk Trends, 2023

Acute and Chronic Health Conditions

Category	MSA[1] (%)	U.S. (%)
Adults who have ever been told they had a heart attack	5.2	4.2
Adults who have ever been told they have angina or coronary heart disease	4.4	4.0
Adults who have ever been told they had a stroke	4.6	3.3
Adults who have ever been told they have asthma	15.1	15.7
Adults who have ever been told they have arthritis	28.6	26.3
Adults who have ever been told they have diabetes[2]	11.5	11.5
Adults who have ever been told they had skin cancer	6.0	5.6
Adults who have ever been told they had any other types of cancer	8.6	8.4
Adults who have ever been told they have COPD	7.4	6.4
Adults who have ever been told they have kidney disease	3.6	3.7
Adults who have ever been told they have a form of depression	21.6	22.0

Note: All figures are crude prevalence; (1) Figures cover the St. Louis, MO-IL Metropolitan Statistical Area; (2) Figures do not include pregnancy-related, borderline, or pre-diabetes
Source: Centers for Disease Control and Prevention, Behavioral Risk Factor Surveillance System, SMART: Selected Metropolitan Area Risk Trends, 2023

Health Screening and Vaccination Rates

Category	MSA[1] (%)	U.S. (%)
Adults who have ever been tested for HIV	31.3	37.5
Adults who have had their blood cholesterol checked within the last five years	88.0	87.0
Adults aged 65+ who have had flu shot within the past year	69.8	63.4
Adults aged 65+ who have ever had a pneumonia vaccination	77.2	71.9

Note: All figures are crude prevalence; (1) Figures cover the St. Louis, MO-IL Metropolitan Statistical Area.
Source: Centers for Disease Control and Prevention, Behavioral Risk Factor Surveillance System, SMART: Selected Metropolitan Area Risk Trends, 2023

Disability Status

Category	MSA[1] (%)	U.S. (%)
Adults who reported being deaf	8.1	7.4
Are you blind or have serious difficulty seeing, even when wearing glasses?	5.9	4.9
Do you have difficulty doing errands alone?	7.9	7.8
Do you have difficulty dressing or bathing?	4.2	3.6
Do you have serious difficulty concentrating/remembering/making decisions?	13.2	13.7
Do you have serious difficulty walking or climbing stairs?	15.0	13.2

Note: All figures are crude prevalence; (1) Figures cover the St. Louis, MO-IL Metropolitan Statistical Area.
Source: Centers for Disease Control and Prevention, Behavioral Risk Factor Surveillance System, SMART: Selected Metropolitan Area Risk Trends, 2023

Mortality Rates for the Top 10 Causes of Death in the U.S.

ICD-10[a] Sub-Chapter	ICD-10[a] Code	Crude Mortality Rate[2] per 100,000 population	
		County[3]	U.S.
Malignant neoplasms	C00-C97	186.0	182.7
Ischaemic heart diseases	I20-I25	127.2	109.6
Provisional assignment of new diseases of uncertain etiology[1]	U00-U49	49.0	65.3
Other forms of heart disease	I30-I51	56.6	65.1
Other degenerative diseases of the nervous system	G30-G31	32.5	52.4
Other external causes of accidental injury	W00-X59	127.4	52.3
Cerebrovascular diseases	I60-I69	50.7	49.1
Chronic lower respiratory diseases	J40-J47	34.4	43.5
Hypertensive diseases	I10-I15	68.0	38.9
Organic, including symptomatic, mental disorders	F01-F09	21.1	33.9

Note: (a) ICD-10 = International Classification of Diseases 10th Revision; (1) Includes COVID-19, adverse effects to COVID-19 vaccines, SARS, and vaping-related disorders; (2) Crude mortality rates are a three-year average covering 2021-2023; (3) Figures cover St. Louis city.
Source: Centers for Disease Control and Prevention, National Center for Health Statistics. National Vital Statistics System, Mortality 2018-2023 on CDC WONDER Online Database

Mortality Rates for Selected Causes of Death

Cause of Death	ICD-10[a] Code	Crude Mortality Rate[1] per 100,000 population	
		County[2]	U.S.
Accidental poisoning and exposure to noxious substances	X40-X49	103.6	30.5
Alzheimer disease	G30	25.9	35.4
Assault	X85-Y09	48.9	7.3
COVID-19	U07.1	49.0	65.3
Diabetes mellitus	E10-E14	34.7	30.0
Diseases of the liver	K70-K76	19.6	20.8
Human immunodeficiency virus (HIV) disease	B20-B24	3.4	1.5
Influenza and pneumonia	J09-J18	9.7	13.4
Intentional self-harm	X60-X84	16.2	14.7
Malnutrition	E40-E46	9.3	6.0
Obesity and other hyperalimentation	E65-E68	4.1	3.1
Renal failure	N17-N19	23.6	16.4
Transport accidents	V01-V99	18.7	14.4

Note: (a) ICD-10 = International Classification of Diseases 10th Revision; (1) Crude mortality rates are a three-year average covering 2021-2023; (2) Figures cover St. Louis city; Data are suppressed when the data meet the criteria for confidentiality constraints; Crude mortality rates are flagged as unreliable when the rate would be calculated with a numerator of 20 or less.
Source: Centers for Disease Control and Prevention, National Center for Health Statistics. National Vital Statistics System, Mortality 2018-2023 on CDC WONDER Online Database

Health Insurance Coverage

Area	With Health Insurance	With Private Health Insurance	With Public Health Insurance	Without Health Insurance	Population Under Age 19 Without Health Insurance
City	90.7	63.5	35.7	9.3	3.7
MSA[1]	94.0	73.7	31.5	6.0	3.5
U.S.	91.4	67.3	36.3	8.6	5.4

Note: Figures are percentages that cover the civilian noninstitutionalized population; (1) Figures cover the St. Louis, MO-IL Metropolitan Statistical Area
Source: U.S. Census Bureau, 2019-2023 American Community Survey 5-Year Estimates

Number of Medical Professionals

Area	MDs[3]	DOs[3,4]	Dentists	Podiatrists	Chiropractors	Optometrists
City[1] (number)	4,273	163	200	12	66	61
City[1] (rate[2])	1,491.0	56.9	71.0	4.3	23.4	21.7
U.S. (rate[2])	302.5	29.2	74.6	6.4	29.5	18.0

Note: Data as of 2023 unless noted; (1) Data covers the city of Saint Louis; (2) Number of medical professionals per 100,000 population; (3) Data as of 2022 and includes all active, non-federal physicians; (4) Doctor of Osteopathic Medicine
Source: U.S. Department of Health and Human Services, Health Resources and Services Administration, Bureau of Health Professions, Area Resource File (ARF) 2023-2024

Best Hospitals

According to *U.S. News,* the St. Louis, MO-IL metro area is home to two of the best hospitals in the U.S.: **Barnes-Jewish Hospital** (11 adult specialties); **Siteman Cancer Center at Barnes-Jewish Hospital** (11 adult specialties). The hospitals listed were nationally ranked in at least one of 15 adult or 11 pediatric specialties. The number of specialties shown cover the parent hospital. Only 160 U.S. hospitals performed well enough to be nationally ranked in one or more specialties. Twenty hospitals in the U.S. made the Honor Roll. The Best Hospitals Honor Roll takes both the national rankings and the procedure and condition ratings into account. Hospitals received points if they were nationally ranked in one of the 15 adult specialties—the higher they ranked, the more points they got—and how many ratings of "high performing" they earned in the 20 procedures and conditions. *U.S. News Online, "America's Best Hospitals 2024-25"*

According to *U.S. News,* the St. Louis, MO-IL metro area is home to three of the best children's hospitals in the U.S.: **SSM Health Cardinal Glennon Children's Hospital-St. Louis University** (7 pediatric specialties); **St. Louis Children's Hospital-Washington University** (10 pediatric specialties); **St. Louis Children's Hospital-Washington University/Shriners Children's St. Louis** (10 pediatric specialties). The hospitals listed were highly ranked in at least one of 11 pediatric specialties. One hundred five children's hospitals in the U.S. were nationally ranked in at least one specialty. Hospitals received points for being ranked in a specialty, and the 10 hospitals with the most points across the 11 specialties make up the Honor Roll. *U.S. News Online, "America's Best Children's Hospitals 2024-25"*

EDUCATION

Public School District Statistics

District Name	Schls	Pupils	Pupil/Teacher Ratio	Minority Pupils[1] (%)	Total Rev. per Pupil ($)	Total Exp. per Pupil ($)
Affton 101	4	2,582	14.3	28.6	16,053	15,352
Confluence Academies	6	2,274	10.5	95.3	19,397	17,326
Kipp St Louis Public Schools	6	2,368	10.8	99.4	14,593	16,242
Ladue	8	4,482	13.8	44.8	20,060	26,386
Lindbergh Schools	10	7,497	16.1	17.4	13,726	18,467
Mehlville R-IX	19	10,162	14.2	20.6	13,131	12,288
Normandy Schools Collaborative	7	2,883	19.2	98.4	23,274	24,863
Ritenour	10	6,414	15.2	81.0	12,460	12,381
Riverview Gardens	13	5,100	15.6	99.3	13,741	12,179
St. Louis City	68	18,284	12.6	87.7	22,893	19,285

Note: Table includes school districts with 2,000 or more students; (1) Percentage of students that are not non-Hispanic white.
Source: U.S. Department of Education, National Center for Education Statistics, Common Core of Data, Local Education Agency (School District) Universe Survey: School Year 2023-2024; U.S. Department of Education, National Center for Education Statistics, Common Core of Data, School District Finance Survey (F-33): School Year 2021–22

Best High Schools

According to *U.S. News*, Saint Louis is home to two of the top 500 high schools in the U.S.: **Metro Academic and Classical High School** (#99); **Ladue Horton Watkins High School** (#340). Nearly 25,000 public, magnet and charter schools were ranked based on their performance on state assessments and how well they prepare students for college. *U.S. News & World Report, "Best High Schools 2024"*

Highest Level of Education

Area	Less than H.S.	H.S. Diploma	Some College, No Deg.	Associate Degree	Bachelor's Degree	Master's Degree	Prof. School Degree	Doctorate Degree
City	9.5	24.5	19.7	6.1	22.0	12.1	3.4	2.7
MSA[1]	6.7	25.5	21.0	9.3	22.3	11.2	2.3	1.7
U.S.	10.6	26.2	19.4	8.8	21.3	9.8	2.3	1.6

Note: Figures cover persons age 25 and over; (1) Figures cover the St. Louis, MO-IL Metropolitan Statistical Area
Source: U.S. Census Bureau, 2019-2023 American Community Survey 5-Year Estimates

Educational Attainment by Race

Area	High School Graduate or Higher (%)					Bachelor's Degree or Higher (%)				
	Total	White	Black	Asian	Hisp.[2]	Total	White	Black	Asian	Hisp.[2]
City	90.5	95.0	85.7	86.9	81.7	40.2	56.0	18.1	63.5	35.3
MSA[1]	93.3	94.7	88.8	90.9	82.6	37.6	40.1	22.0	68.6	31.0
U.S.	89.4	92.9	88.1	88.0	72.5	35.0	37.7	24.7	57.0	19.9

Note: Figures shown cover persons 25 years old and over; (1) Figures cover the St. Louis, MO-IL Metropolitan Statistical Area; (2) People of Hispanic origin can be of any race
Source: U.S. Census Bureau, 2019-2023 American Community Survey 5-Year Estimates

School Enrollment by Grade and Control

Area	Preschool (%)		Kindergarten (%)		Grades 1 - 4 (%)		Grades 5 - 8 (%)		Grades 9 - 12 (%)	
	Public	Private	Public	Private	Public	Private	Public	Private	Public	Private
City	56.5	43.5	85.1	14.9	83.3	16.7	82.7	17.3	84.0	16.0
MSA[1]	53.9	46.1	82.1	17.9	82.1	17.9	83.2	16.8	84.7	15.3
U.S.	58.7	41.3	85.2	14.8	87.2	12.8	87.9	12.1	89.0	11.0

Note: Figures shown cover persons 3 years old and over; (1) Figures cover the St. Louis, MO-IL Metropolitan Statistical Area
Source: U.S. Census Bureau, 2019-2023 American Community Survey 5-Year Estimates

Higher Education

Four-Year Colleges			Two-Year Colleges			Medical Schools[1]	Law Schools[2]	Voc/ Tech[3]
Public	Private Non-profit	Private For-profit	Public	Private Non-profit	Private For-profit			
4	23	4	6	0	2	2	2	14

Note: Figures cover institutions located within the St. Louis, MO-IL Metropolitan Statistical Area and include main campuses only; (1) includes schools accredited by the Liaison Committee on Medical Education and the American Osteopathic Association's Commission on Osteopathic College Accreditation; (2) includes ABA-accredited schools, schools with provisional ABA accreditation, and state accredited schools; (3) includes all schools with programs that are less than 2 years.
Source: National Center for Education Statistics, Integrated Postsecondary Education System (IPEDS), 2023-24; Wikipedia, List of Medical Schools in the United States, accessed May 2, 2025; Wikipedia, List of Law Schools in the United States, accessed May 2, 2025

According to *U.S. News & World Report*, the St. Louis, MO-IL metro area is home to two of the top 200 national universities in the U.S.: **Washington University in St. Louis** (#21 tie); **Saint Louis University** (#105 tie). The indicators used to capture academic quality fall into a number of categories: assessment by administrators at peer institutions; retention of students; faculty resources; student selectivity; financial resources; alumni giving; high school counselor ratings of colleges; and graduation rate. *U.S. News & World Report*, "America's Best Colleges 2025"

According to *U.S. News & World Report*, the St. Louis, MO-IL metro area is home to one of the top 100 liberal arts colleges in the U.S.: **Principia College** (#66 tie). The indicators used to capture academic quality fall into a number of categories: assessment by administrators at peer institutions; retention of students; faculty resources; student selectivity; financial resources; alumni giving; high school counselor ratings of colleges; and graduation rate. *U.S. News & World Report*, "America's Best Colleges 2025"

According to *U.S. News & World Report*, the St. Louis, MO-IL metro area is home to two of the top 100 law schools in the U.S.: **Washington University in St. Louis** (#14 tie); **Saint Louis University** (#94 tie). The rankings are based on a weighted average of 12 measures of quality: peer assessment score; assessment score by lawyers/judges; median LSAT scores; median undergrad GPA; acceptance rate; employment rates for graduates; placement success; bar passage rate; faculty resources; expenditures per student; student/faculty ratio; and library resources. *U.S. News & World Report*, "America's Best Graduate Schools, Law, 2025"

According to *U.S. News & World Report*, the St. Louis, MO-IL metro area is home to one of the top medical schools for primary care in the U.S.: **Saint Louis University** (Tier 1). *U.S. News* placed medical and osteopathic schools into tiers based on their research productivity, faculty and admissions data. Each school's tier was derived from its overall score, calculated by summing the weighted normalized values generated across several factors of academic quality, outlined below. There are four tiers, with tier 1 medical schools as the highest-performing and tier 4 as the lowest-performing. Only tier 1 and 2 schools are shown. Because of the tier presentation, *U.S. News* calculated overall scores based on their percentile performance among all rated schools instead of dividing against the rescaled score of the No. 1-performing schools. Tier 1 included schools with overall scores of 85 to 99. The cutoffs for tiers 2 through 4 were schools scoring 50 to 84, 15 to 49 and 1 to 14, respectively. The rankings are based on a weighted average of the following measures of quality: graduates practicing in primary care specialties; graduates entering primary care residencies; median MCAT total score; median undergraduate GPA; acceptance rate; and faculty resources. *U.S. News & World Report*, "America's Best Graduate Schools, Medical, 2025"

According to *U.S. News & World Report*, the St. Louis, MO-IL metro area is home to one of the top 75 business schools in the U.S.: **Washington University in St. Louis (Olin)** (#24 tie). The rankings are based on a weighted average of the following nine measures: quality assessment; peer assessment; recruiter assessment; placement success; mean starting salary and bonus; student selectivity; mean GMAT and GRE scores; mean undergraduate GPA; and acceptance rate. *U.S. News & World Report*, "America's Best Graduate Schools, Business, 2025"

EMPLOYERS

Major Employers

Company Name	Industry
Ameren Corp.	Energy
Barnes Jewish Hospital	Healthcare
BJC Healthcare	Healthcare
Boeing Defense, Space & Security	Defense and aerospace products and services
City of St. Louis	Municipal government
Defense Finance and Accounting Service	Federal government
Edward Jones	Investments; banking
Enterprise Holdings Inc.	Car rentals
General Motors	Automobile manufacturing
Mercy	Healthcare
Schnuck Markets Inc.	Grocery
Scott Air Force Base	Military
Special School District of St. Louis County	Education
SSM Health	Healthcare
St. Louis County Government	Local government
St. Louis University	Colleges & universities
St. Luke's Hospital	Healthcare
University of Missouri-St. Louis	Higher education
Wal-Mart Stores	Retail
Washington University in St. Louis	Colleges & universities

Note: Companies shown are located within the St. Louis, MO-IL Metropolitan Statistical Area.
Source: Chambers of Commerce; State Departments of Labor; Wikipedia

Best Companies to Work For

Edward Jones; World Wide Technology, headquartered in Saint Louis, are among "The 100 Best Companies to Work For." To pick the best companies, *Fortune* partnered with the Great Place to Work Institute. Using their proprietary Trust Index™ survey, the core of what creates great a workplace is measured—key behaviors that drive trust in management, connection with colleagues, and loyalty to the company. To be eligible for the *Fortune* 100 Best Companies to Work For list, employers must have 1,000 or more employees in the U.S. and cannot be a government agency. *Fortune, "The 100 Best Companies to Work For," 2025*

Centene Corporation; Edward Jones, headquartered in Saint Louis, are among "Fortune's Best Workplaces for Women." To pick the best companies, *Fortune* partnered with the Great Place to Work Institute. To be considered for the list, companies must be Great Place To Work-Certified. Companies must also employ at least 50 women, at least 20% of their non-executive managers must be female, and at least one executive must be female. To determine the Best Workplaces for Women, Great Place To Work measured the differences in women's survey responses to those of their peers and assesses the impact of demographics and roles on the quality and consistency of women's experiences. Great Place To Work also analyzed the gender balance of each workplace, how it compared to each company's industry, and patterns in representation as women rise from front-line positions to the board of directors. *Fortune, "Best Workplaces for Women," 2024*

Centene Corporation; Navvis; Private Home Care, headquartered in Saint Louis, are among "Best Workplaces in Health Care." To determine the Best Workplaces in Health Care list, Great Place To Work analyzed the survey responses of over 185,000 employees from Great Place To Work-Certified companies in the health care industry. Survey data analysis and company-provided datapoints are then factored into a combined score to compare and rank the companies that create the most consistently positive experience for all employees in this industry. *Fortune, "Best Workplaces in Health Care," 2024*

PUBLIC SAFETY

Crime Rate

Area	Total Crime Rate	Violent Crime Rate				Property Crime Rate		
		Murder	Rape	Robbery	Aggrav. Assault	Burglary	Larceny-Theft	Motor Vehicle Theft
City	7,844.8	56.4	70.3	260.3	1,058.2	751.1	3,434.0	2,214.5
U.S.	2,290.9	5.7	38.0	66.5	264.1	250.7	1,347.2	318.7

Note: Figures are crimes per 100,000 population.
Source: FBI, Table 8, Offenses Known to Law Enforcement, by State by City, 2023

Hate Crimes

Area	Number of Quarters Reported	Number of Incidents per Bias Motivation					
		Race/Ethnicity/Ancestry	Religion	Sexual Orientation	Disability	Gender	Gender Identity
City[1]	4	11	3	0	0	1	0
U.S.	4	5,900	2,699	2,077	187	92	492

Note: (1) Figures include at least one incident reported with more than one bias motivation.
Source: Federal Bureau of Investigation, Hate Crime Statistics 2023

Identity Theft Consumer Reports

Area	Reports	Reports per 100,000 Population	Rank[2]
MSA[1]	7,242	258	97
U.S.	1,135,291	339	-

Note: (1) Figures cover the St. Louis, MO-IL Metropolitan Statistical Area; (2) Rank ranges from 1 to 401 where 1 indicates greatest number of identity theft reports per 100,000 population
Source: Federal Trade Commission, Consumer Sentinel Network Data Book 2024

Fraud and Other Consumer Reports

Area	Reports	Reports per 100,000 Population	Rank[2]
MSA[1]	42,059	1,497	58
U.S.	5,360,641	1,601	-

Note: (1) Figures cover the St. Louis, MO-IL Metropolitan Statistical Area; (2) Rank ranges from 1 to 401 where 1 indicates greatest number of fraud and other consumer reports per 100,000 population
Source: Federal Trade Commission, Consumer Sentinel Network Data Book 2024

POLITICS

2024 Presidential Election Results

Area	Trump (Rep.)	Harris (Dem.)	Stein (Green)	Kennedy (Ind.)	Oliver (Lib.)	Other
St. Louis City	16.5	80.7	1.2	0.0	0.7	0.8
U.S.	49.7	48.2	0.6	0.5	0.4	0.6

Note: Results are percentages and may not add to 100% due to rounding
Source: Dave Leip's Atlas of U.S. Presidential Elections

SPORTS

Professional Sports Teams

Team Name	League	Year Established
Saint Louis Blues	National Hockey League (NHL)	1967
Saint Louis Cardinals	Major League Baseball (MLB)	1882
St. Louis City SC	Major League Soccer (MLS)	2023

Note: Includes teams located in the St. Louis, MO-IL Metropolitan Statistical Area.
Source: Wikipedia, Major Professional Sports Teams of the United States and Canada, May 1, 2025

CLIMATE

Average and Extreme Temperatures

Temperature	Jan	Feb	Mar	Apr	May	Jun	Jul	Aug	Sep	Oct	Nov	Dec	Yr.
Extreme High (°F)	77	83	89	93	98	105	115	107	104	94	85	76	115
Average High (°F)	39	43	54	67	76	85	89	87	80	69	54	42	66
Average Temp. (°F)	30	34	44	56	66	75	79	78	70	59	45	34	56
Average Low (°F)	21	25	34	46	55	65	69	67	59	48	36	26	46
Extreme Low (°F)	-18	-10	-5	22	31	43	51	47	36	23	1	-16	-18

Note: Figures cover the years 1945-1990
Source: National Climatic Data Center, International Station Meteorological Climate Summary, 9/96

Average Precipitation/Snowfall/Humidity

Precip./Humidity	Jan	Feb	Mar	Apr	May	Jun	Jul	Aug	Sep	Oct	Nov	Dec	Yr.
Avg. Precip. (in.)	1.9	2.2	3.4	3.4	3.8	4.0	3.8	2.9	2.9	2.8	3.0	2.6	36.8
Avg. Snowfall (in.)	6	4	4	Tr	0	0	0	0	0	Tr	1	4	20
Avg. Rel. Hum. 6am (%)	80	81	80	78	81	82	84	86	87	83	81	81	82
Avg. Rel. Hum. 3pm (%)	62	59	54	49	51	51	51	52	50	50	56	63	54

Note: Figures cover the years 1945-1990; Tr = Trace amounts (<0.05 in. of rain; <0.5 in. of snow)
Source: National Climatic Data Center, International Station Meteorological Climate Summary, 9/96

Weather Conditions

Temperature			Daytime Sky			Precipitation		
10°F & below	32°F & below	90°F & above	Clear	Partly cloudy	Cloudy	0.01 inch or more precip.	0.1 inch or more snow/ice	Thunderstorms
13	100	43	97	138	130	109	14	46

Note: Figures are average number of days per year and cover the years 1945-1990
Source: National Climatic Data Center, International Station Meteorological Climate Summary, 9/96

HAZARDOUS WASTE

Superfund Sites

The St. Louis, MO-IL metro area is home to 19 sites on the EPA's Superfund National Priorities List (NPL) or Superfund Alternative Approach (SAA) list: **Alcoa Properties** (SAA); **Chemetco** (Final NPL); **Circle Smelting Corp.** (Proposed NPL); **Ellisville Site** (Final NPL); **Jennison-Wright Corporation** (Final NPL); **Minker/Stout/Romaine Creek** (Final NPL); **NI Industries/Taracorp Lead Smelter** (Final NPL); **Oak Grove Village Well** (Final NPL); **Old American Zinc Plant** (Final NPL); **Riverfront** (Final NPL); **Sauget Area 1** (Proposed NPL); **Sauget Area 2** (Proposed NPL); **Southwest Jefferson County Mining** (Final NPL); **Sporlan Valve Plant #1** (Final NPL); **St. Louis Airport/hazelwood Interim Storage/futura Coatings Co.** (Final NPL); **Valley Park Tce** (Final NPL); **Weldon Spring Former Army Ordnance Works** (Final NPL); **Weldon Spring Quarry/plant/pits (USDOE/ARMY)** (Final NPL); **Westlake Landfill** (Final NPL). The Superfund alternative approach uses the same investigation and cleanup process and standards that are used for sites listed on the National Priorities List. The SAA is an alternative to listing a site on the NPL; it is not an alternative to Superfund or the Superfund process. There are a total of 1,445 Superfund sites with a status of proposed or final on both lists in the United States. *U.S. Environmental Protection Agency, National Priorities List, May 1, 2025; U.S. Environmental Protection Agency, Superfund Alternative Approach Sites, May 1, 2025*

AIR QUALITY

Air Quality Trends: Ozone

	1990	1995	2000	2005	2010	2015	2020	2021	2022	2023
MSA[1]	0.077	0.084	0.074	0.078	0.069	0.067	0.066	0.067	0.070	0.077
U.S.	0.087	0.089	0.081	0.080	0.072	0.068	0.066	0.067	0.067	0.070

Note: (1) Data covers the St. Louis, MO-IL Metropolitan Statistical Area. The values shown are the composite ozone concentration averages among trend sites based on the highest fourth daily maximum 8-hour concentration in parts per million. These trends are based on sites having an adequate record of monitoring data during the trend period. Data from exceptional events are included.
Source: U.S. Environmental Protection Agency, Air Quality Monitoring Information, "Air Quality Trends by City, 1990-2023"

Air Quality Index

Area	Percent of Days when Air Quality was...[2]					AQI Statistics[2]	
	Good	Moderate	Unhealthy for Sensitive Groups	Unhealthy	Very Unhealthy	Maximum	Median
MSA[1]	14.0	79.5	5.8	0.8	0.0	185	60

Note: (1) Data covers the St. Louis, MO-IL Metropolitan Statistical Area; (2) Based on 365 days with AQI data in 2023. Air Quality Index (AQI) is an index for reporting daily air quality. EPA calculates the AQI for five major air pollutants regulated by the Clean Air Act: ground-level ozone, particle pollution (aka particulate matter), carbon monoxide, sulfur dioxide, and nitrogen dioxide. The AQI runs from 0 to 500. The higher the AQI value, the greater the level of air pollution and the greater the health concern. There are six AQI categories: "Good" AQI is between 0 and 50. Air quality is considered satisfactory; "Moderate" AQI is between 51 and 100. Air quality is acceptable; "Unhealthy for Sensitive Groups" When AQI values are between 101 and 150, members of sensitive groups may experience health effects; "Unhealthy" When AQI values are between 151 and 200 everyone may begin to experience health effects; "Very Unhealthy" AQI values between 201 and 300 trigger a health alert; "Hazardous" AQI values over 300 trigger warnings of emergency conditions (not shown).
Source: U.S. Environmental Protection Agency, Air Quality Index Report, 2023

Air Quality Index Pollutants

Area	Percent of Days when AQI Pollutant was...[2]					
	Carbon Monoxide	Nitrogen Dioxide	Ozone	Sulfur Dioxide	Particulate Matter 2.5	Particulate Matter 10
MSA[1]	0.0	0.0	27.7	(3)	67.4	4.9

Note: (1) Data covers the St. Louis, MO-IL Metropolitan Statistical Area; (2) Based on 365 days with AQI data in 2023. The Air Quality Index (AQI) is an index for reporting daily air quality. EPA calculates the AQI for five major air pollutants regulated by the Clean Air Act: ground-level ozone, particle pollution (also known as particulate matter), carbon monoxide, sulfur dioxide, and nitrogen dioxide. The AQI runs from 0 to 500. The higher the AQI value, the greater the level of air pollution and the greater the health concern; (3) Sulfur dioxide is no longer included in this table because SO_2 concentrations tend to be very localized and not necessarily representative of broad geographical areas like counties and CBSAs.
Source: U.S. Environmental Protection Agency, Air Quality Index Report, 2023

Maximum Air Pollutant Concentrations: Particulate Matter, Ozone, CO and Lead

	Particulate Matter 10 (ug/m^3)	Particulate Matter 2.5 Wtd AM (ug/m^3)	Particulate Matter 2.5 24-Hr (ug/m^3)	Ozone (ppm)	Carbon Monoxide (ppm)	Lead (ug/m^3)
MSA[1] Level	160	11.3	26	0.082	2	0.1
NAAQS[2]	150	15	35	0.075	9	0.15
Met NAAQS[2]	No	Yes	Yes	No	Yes	Yes

Note: (1) Data covers the St. Louis, MO-IL Metropolitan Statistical Area; Data from exceptional events are included; (2) National Ambient Air Quality Standards; ppm = parts per million; ug/m^3 = micrograms per cubic meter; n/a not available.
Concentrations: Particulate Matter 10 (coarse particulate)—highest second maximum 24-hour concentration; Particulate Matter 2.5 Wtd AM (fine particulate)—highest weighted annual mean concentration; Particulate Matter 2.5 24-Hour (fine particulate)—highest 98th percentile 24-hour concentration; Ozone—highest fourth daily maximum 8-hour concentration; Carbon Monoxide—highest second maximum non-overlapping 8-hour concentration; Lead—maximum running 3-month average
Source: U.S. Environmental Protection Agency, Air Quality Monitoring Information, "Air Quality Statistics by City, 2023"

Maximum Air Pollutant Concentrations: Nitrogen Dioxide and Sulfur Dioxide

	Nitrogen Dioxide AM (ppb)	Nitrogen Dioxide 1-Hr (ppb)	Sulfur Dioxide AM (ppb)	Sulfur Dioxide 1-Hr (ppb)	Sulfur Dioxide 24-Hr (ppb)
MSA[1] Level	10	43	n/a	38	n/a
NAAQS[2]	53	100	30	75	140
Met NAAQS[2]	Yes	Yes	n/a	Yes	n/a

Note: (1) Data covers the St. Louis, MO-IL Metropolitan Statistical Area; Data from exceptional events are included; (2) National Ambient Air Quality Standards; ppm = parts per million; ug/m^3 = micrograms per cubic meter; n/a not available.
Concentrations: Nitrogen Dioxide AM—highest arithmetic mean concentration; Nitrogen Dioxide 1-Hr—highest 98th percentile 1-hour daily maximum concentration; Sulfur Dioxide AM—highest annual mean concentration; Sulfur Dioxide 1-Hr—highest 99th percentile 1-hour daily maximum concentration; Sulfur Dioxide 24-Hr—highest second maximum 24-hour concentration
Source: U.S. Environmental Protection Agency, Air Quality Monitoring Information, "Air Quality Statistics by City, 2023"

Saint Paul, Minnesota

Background

St. Paul is the capital of Minnesota and the seat of Ramsey County. The city is situated on both sides of the Mississippi River in east-central Minnesota, around the confluence of the Mississippi, Minnesota, and St. Croix Rivers, and shares a border with Minneapolis. Together, St. Paul and Minneapolis constitute the Twin Cities metropolitan area, yet remain distinct in their development, with newer/avant-garde architecture in Minneapolis and St. Paul integrating new building into classical and Victorian styles.

The first inhabitants of the area were Sioux and Ojibwe indigenous people. Europeans visited the region in the mid-1600s, including Jesuit priest Louis Hennepin in 1680, but permanent settlement did not occur until after 1805, when Zebulon Pike and his expedition was sent by President Thomas Jefferson to explore new territory. They purchased current-day St. Paul from the Sioux people. In 1820, Fort Snelling was built at the confluence of the Minnesota and Mississippi Rivers, and the first steamboat arrived in 1823, proving viability of river transportation and encouraging permanent settlement in 1840. The settlement was called St. Paul's Landing for its river access, and then simply St. Paul, which became the state capital in 1849.

Incorporated as a city in 1854, St. Paul grew steadily after the Civil War, becoming a major railway transportation hub for the Midwest. By 1888, two dozen separate rail lines originated or terminated at St. Paul, accounting for a quarter of the rail mileage in the United States. The city was soon established as an economic powerhouse, with a nearby livestock market rivaled only by that in Chicago. By World War II, more than 600 major manufacturing establishments were headquartered in the city, including agricultural processing, printing and publishing, foundries, machine shops, adhesives and abrasives, automobiles, and fur clothing.

Today, St. Paul's dynamic economic legacy is alive and well, leading with manufacturing, healthcare, and real estate major industries, and followed closely by agriculture and financial services. UnitedHealth Group, Target, Best Buy, US Bank, 3M, U.S. Bancorp, and General Mills are among its major employers.

Melvin Carter, mayor since 2018, is the city's first African American mayor. His accomplishments include raising the minimum wage to $15/hour, reestablishing an Affordable Housing Trust Fund, expanding immigrant and refugee support services, and CollegeBound St. Paul, which starts every child born in the city with a $50 college savings account.

In early 2025, the city announced two major renovation projects: The Xcel Energy Century Arena Complex, comprised of the Excel Energy Center, Saint Paul RiverCentre, and Roy Wilkins Auditorium; and a 20-story apartment tower and a six-story building connected by a skyway over the METRO Green Line on undeveloped land in the heart of the city. Construction on both projects is anticipated to begin in 2026.

Minneapolis/St. Paul Airport is the 18th busiest passenger airport in the U.S. It's a base for Sun County Airlines and Delta's second largest hub.

St. Paul's cultural heritage is rich and varied, claiming quaint neighborhoods and family destinations as its cornerstones. Alexander Ramsey House (one of the best-preserved Victorian houses in the country), Cathedral of St. Paul (1915), 100-year-old Como Park Zoo and Conservatory, and Historic Fort Snelling are a few outstanding examples. The city's museums include the renovated Minnesota Museum of American Art, Science Museum of Minnesota, Minnesota Transportation Museum, and Minnesota Children's Museum.

With over 250 parks, St. Paul has something for everyone, including amusement parks and public gardens. The State Capitol Building, Minnesota's third, was designed by architect Cass Gilbert and opened for business in 1905. Sports teams in the Twin Cities include MLB's Minnesota Twins and NFL's Minnesota Vikings.

St. Paul is home to more than a dozen institutions of higher learning, including Hamline University, Bethel College, Macalester College, University of St. Thomas, Concordia University, William Mitchell College of Law, and Metropolitan State University.

Summers in St. Paul are warm and wet; winters are freezing, snowy, and windy. It is partly cloudy year-round. The hottest month is July, with an average high of 82 degrees. The coldest month is January with an average low of 10 degrees. Rainfall in St. Paul occurs primarily between March and December.

Rankings

General Rankings

- To help military veterans find the best places in which to settle down, *WalletHub* compared the 100 largest U.S. cities across 19 key indicators of livability, affordability and veteran-friendliness. They range from the share of military skill-related jobs to veteran income growth to the availability of VA health facilities. Saint Paul ranked #55. *Wallethub.com, "Best & Worst Places for Veterans to Live (2025)," November 7, 2024*

Business/Finance Rankings

- Payscale.com ranked the 32 largest metro areas in terms of wage growth. The Minneapolis metro area ranked #18. Criteria: quarterly changes in private industry employee and education professional wage growth from the previous year. *PayScale, "Wage Trends by Metro Area-4th Quarter," February 4, 2025*

- The Minneapolis metro area appeared on the Milken Institute "2025 Best Performing Cities" list. Rank: #125 out of 200 large metro areas (based on performance category). Criteria: job growth; wage growth; high-tech growth and impact; community resilience; housing affordability; household broadband access. *Milken Institute, "Best-Performing Cities 2025," January 14, 2025*

Education Rankings

- Personal finance website *WalletHub* analyzed the 150 largest U.S. metropolitan statistical areas to determine where the most educated Americans are putting their degrees to work. Criteria: education levels; percentage of workers with degrees; education quality and attainment gap; public school quality rankings; quality and enrollment of each metro area's universities. Minneapolis was ranked #18 (#1 = most educated city). *WalletHub.com, "Most & Least Educated Cities in America, 2025" July 2, 2024*

Environmental Rankings

- Sperling's *BestPlaces* assessed the 50 largest metropolitan areas of the United States for the likelihood of dangerously extreme weather events or earthquakes. In general the Southeast and South-Central regions have the highest risk of weather extremes and earthquakes, while the Pacific Northwest enjoys the lowest risk. Of the least risky metropolitan areas, the Minneapolis metro area was ranked #7. *Bestplaces.net, "Avoid Natural Disasters: BestPlaces Reveals The Top 10 Safest Places to Live," October 25, 2017*

- The U.S. Environmental Protection Agency (EPA) released its list of U.S. metropolitan areas with the most ENERGY STAR certified buildings in 2023. The Minneapolis metro area was ranked #16 out of 25. *U.S. Environmental Protection Agency, "2024 Energy Star Top Cities," May 22, 2024*

Health/Fitness Rankings

- For each of the 100 largest cities in the United States, the American Fitness Index®, compiled in partnership between the American College of Sports Medicine and the Elevance Health Foundation, evaluated community infrastructure and more than 30 health behaviors including preventive health, levels of chronic disease conditions, food insecurity, pedestrian safety, air quality, and community/environment resources that support physical activity. Saint Paul ranked #10 for "community fitness." *americanfitnessindex.org, "2024 ACSM American Fitness Index Summary Report," July 23, 2024*

- The Minneapolis metro area was identified as one of the worst cities for bed bugs in America by pest control company Orkin. The area ranked #47 out of 50 based on the number of bed bug treatments Orkin performed from December 2022 to November 2023. *Orkin, "Chicago Joins Paris In Global Bed Bug Spotlight Ranking As The Worst City On Orkin's U.S. Bed Bug Cities List," January 22, 2024*

- Minneapolis was identified as a "2025 Allergy Capital." The area ranked #90 out of the nation's 100 largest metropolitan areas. Three groups of factors were used to identify the most challenging cities for people with allergies: annual tree, grass, and weed pollen scores; over the counter allergy medicine use; number of board-certified allergy specialists. *Asthma and Allergy Foundation of America, "2025 Allergy Capitals: The Most Challenging Places to Live with Allergies," March 18, 2025*

- Minneapolis was identified as a "2024 Asthma Capital." The area ranked #47 out of the nation's 100 largest metropolitan areas. Criteria: estimated asthma prevalence; asthma-related mortality; and ER visits due to asthma. Risk factors analyzed but not factored in the rankings: annual air quality including pollution and ozone levels; public smoking laws; indoor air quality; access to asthma specialists; rescue and controller medication use; uninsured rate; pollen allergy; poverty rate. *Asthma and Allergy Foundation of America, "Asthma Capitals 2024: The Most Challenging Places to Live With Asthma," September 10, 2024*

Pet Rankings

- Saint Paul was selected by *Sniffspot.com* as one of the most dog-friendly cities in the U.S., ranking #40 out of 50. Criteria: dog parks; hiking; sniffspots; public parks; dog-friendly businesses; housing; dog waste cleanliness; leash laws; dog services; and overall cost. *Sniffspot.com, "The Top 50 Most Dog-Friendly Cities in the U.S.," September 30, 2024*

Real Estate Rankings

- *WalletHub* compared the most populated U.S. cities to determine which had the best markets for real estate agents. Saint Paul ranked #139 where demand was high and pay was the best. Criteria: sales per agent; annual median wage for real-estate agents; monthly average starting salary for real estate agents; real estate job density and competition; unemployment rate; home turnover rate; housing-market health index; and other relevant metrics. *WalletHub.com, "2021 Best Places to Be a Real Estate Agent," May 12, 2021*

- Minneapolis was ranked #62 out of 176 metro areas in terms of cost of housing in 2024 by the National Association of Home Builders (#1 = most affordable). Criteria: the portion of an average family's income necessary to pay the mortgage on a median-priced home. *National Association of Home Builders®, NAHB-Wells Fargo Cost of Housing Index, 4th Quarter 2024*

Safety Rankings

- Statistics drawn from the FBI's Uniform Crime Report were used to rank the cities where violent crime rose the most year over year from 2019 to 2020. Only cities with 25,000 or more residents were included. *24/7 Wall St.* found that Saint Paul placed #39 of those with a notable surge in incidents of violent crime. *247wallst.com, "American Cities Where Crime Is Soaring," March 4, 2022*

Women/Minorities Rankings

- Personal finance website *WalletHub* compared more than 180 U.S. cities across two key dimensions, "Hispanic Business-Friendliness" and "Hispanic Purchasing Power," to arrive at the most favorable conditions for Hispanic entrepreneurs. Saint Paul was ranked #166 out of 182. Criteria includes: share of Hispanic-Owned Businesses; average growth of Hispanic Business revenues; Small Business-Friendliness score; affordability; and number of Hispanics with at least a bachelor's degree. *WalletHub.com, "Best Cities for Hispanic Entrepreneurs," September 4, 2024*

Miscellaneous Rankings

- *WalletHub* compared 148 of the most populated U.S. cities to determine their operating efficiency. A "Quality of Services" score was constructed for each city and then measured against the total budget per capita to reveal which were managed the best. Saint Paul ranked #90. Criteria: financial stability; economy; education; safety; health; infrastructure and pollution. *WalletHub.com, "2025's Best- & Worst-Run Cities in America," June 18, 2024*

Saint Paul, Minnesota

Business Environment

DEMOGRAPHICS

Population Growth

Area	1990 Census	2000 Census	2010 Census	2020 Census	2023 Estimate[2]	Population Growth 1990-2023 (%)
City	272,235	287,151	285,068	311,527	307,762	13.1
MSA[1]	2,538,834	2,968,806	3,279,833	3,690,261	3,693,351	45.5
U.S.	248,709,873	281,421,906	308,745,538	331,449,281	332,387,540	33.6

Note: (1) Figures cover the Minneapolis-St. Paul-Bloomington, MN-WI Metropolitan Statistical Area; (2) 2019-2023 5-year ACS population estimate
Source: U.S. Census Bureau, 1990 Census, 2000 Census, 2010 Census, 2020 Census, 2019-2023 American Community Survey 5-Year Estimates

Race

Area	White Alone[2] (%)	Black Alone[2] (%)	Asian Alone[2] (%)	AIAN[3] Alone[2] (%)	NHOPI[4] Alone[2] (%)	Other Race Alone[2] (%)	Two or More Races (%)
City	53.2	16.2	17.9	0.7	0.0	3.5	8.4
MSA[1]	73.8	8.9	6.9	0.5	0.0	3.0	6.8
U.S.	63.4	12.4	5.8	0.9	0.2	6.6	10.7

Note: (1) Figures cover the Minneapolis-St. Paul-Bloomington, MN-WI Metropolitan Statistical Area; (2) Alone is defined as not being in combination with one or more other races; (3) American Indian and Alaska Native; (4) Native Hawaiian and Other Pacific Islander
Source: U.S. Census Bureau, 2019-2023 American Community Survey 5-Year Estimates

Hispanic or Latino Origin

Area	Total (%)	Mexican (%)	Puerto Rican (%)	Cuban (%)	Other (%)
City	9.1	5.9	0.4	0.2	2.7
MSA[1]	6.7	4.1	0.3	0.1	2.1
U.S.	19.0	11.3	1.8	0.7	5.2

Note: Persons of Hispanic or Latino origin can be of any race; (1) Figures cover the Minneapolis-St. Paul-Bloomington, MN-WI Metropolitan Statistical Area
Source: U.S. Census Bureau, 2019-2023 American Community Survey 5-Year Estimates

Age

Area	Percent of Population									Median Age
	Under Age 5	Age 5–19	Age 20–34	Age 35–44	Age 45–54	Age 55–64	Age 65–74	Age 75–84	Age 85+	
City	6.3	20.3	25.8	13.9	10.7	10.7	7.9	3.0	1.3	33.5
MSA[1]	6.1	19.7	20.0	14.1	12.2	12.8	9.1	4.2	1.7	37.8
U.S.	5.7	19.1	20.2	13.1	12.3	12.8	10.0	4.9	1.9	38.7

Note: (1) Figures cover the Minneapolis-St. Paul-Bloomington, MN-WI Metropolitan Statistical Area
Source: U.S. Census Bureau, 2019-2023 American Community Survey 5-Year Estimates

Disability by Age

Area	All Ages	Under 18 Years Old	18 to 64 Years Old	65 Years and Over
City	12.5	4.7	11.9	31.3
MSA[1]	10.4	4.0	8.6	27.9
U.S.	13.0	4.7	10.7	32.9

Note: Figures show percent of the civilian noninstitutionalized population that reported having a disability. Disability status is determined from six types of difficulty: vision, hearing, cognitive, ambulatory, self-care, and independent living. For children under 5 years old, hearing and vision difficulty are used to determine disability status. For children between the ages of 5 and 14, disability status is determined from hearing, vision, cognitive, ambulatory, and self-care difficulties. For people aged 15 years and older, they are considered to have a disability if they have difficulty with any one of the six difficulty types; Note: (1) Figures cover the Minneapolis-St. Paul-Bloomington, MN-WI Metropolitan Statistical Area
Source: U.S. Census Bureau, 2019-2023 American Community Survey 5-Year Estimates

Ancestry

Area	German	Irish	English	American	Italian	Polish	French[2]	European	Scottish
City	19.5	9.9	5.6	1.9	2.5	2.6	2.6	1.5	1.2
MSA[1]	27.4	10.7	6.9	3.1	2.5	4.0	2.9	2.0	1.2
U.S.	12.6	9.4	9.1	5.5	4.9	2.6	2.0	1.6	1.6

Note: Figures are the percentage of the total population reporting a particular ancestry. The nine most commonly reported ancestries in the U.S. are shown. Figures include multiple ancestries (e.g. if a person reported being Irish and Italian, they were included in both columns); (1) Figures cover the Minneapolis-St. Paul-Bloomington, MN-WI Metropolitan Statistical Area; (2) Excludes Basque
Source: U.S. Census Bureau, 2019-2023 American Community Survey 5-Year Estimates

Foreign-born Population

Area	Percent of Population Born in								
	Any Foreign Country	Asia	Mexico	Europe	Caribbean	Central America[2]	South America	Africa	Canada
City	18.7	9.3	1.8	0.7	0.2	0.9	0.4	4.9	0.3
MSA[1]	10.7	4.0	1.2	1.0	0.2	0.4	0.6	3.1	0.2
U.S.	13.9	4.3	3.3	1.4	1.4	1.2	1.2	0.8	0.2

Note: (1) Figures cover the Minneapolis-St. Paul-Bloomington, MN-WI Metropolitan Statistical Area; (2) Excludes Mexico.
Source: U.S. Census Bureau, 2019-2023 American Community Survey 5-Year Estimates

Household Size

Area	Persons in Household (%)							Average Household Size
	One	Two	Three	Four	Five	Six	Seven or More	
City	37.1	29.8	12.5	9.6	5.1	2.9	3.1	2.42
MSA[1]	28.9	34.2	14.3	13.3	5.8	2.1	1.4	2.49
U.S.	28.5	33.8	15.4	12.7	5.9	2.3	1.4	2.54

Note: (1) Figures cover the Minneapolis-St. Paul-Bloomington, MN-WI Metropolitan Statistical Area
Source: U.S. Census Bureau, 2019-2023 American Community Survey 5-Year Estimates

Household Relationships

Area	Householder	Opposite-sex Spouse	Same-sex Spouse	Opposite-sex Unmarried Partner	Same-sex Unmarried Partner	Child[2]	Grandchild	Other Relatives	Non-relatives
City	38.7	12.7	0.4	3.3	0.3	28.8	1.7	5.6	4.8
MSA[1]	38.9	18.7	0.2	2.8	0.2	29.4	1.2	3.3	3.3
U.S.	38.3	17.5	0.2	2.5	0.2	28.3	2.4	4.8	3.4

Note: Figures are percent of the total population; (1) Figures cover the Minneapolis-St. Paul-Bloomington, MN-WI Metropolitan Statistical Area; (2) Includes biological, adopted, and stepchildren of the householder
Source: U.S. Census Bureau, 2020 Census

Gender

Area	Males	Females	Males per 100 Females
City	151,659	156,103	97.2
MSA[1]	1,842,197	1,851,154	99.5
U.S.	164,545,087	167,842,453	98.0

Note: (1) Figures cover the Minneapolis-St. Paul-Bloomington, MN-WI Metropolitan Statistical Area
Source: U.S. Census Bureau, 2019-2023 American Community Survey 5-Year Estimates

Marital Status

Area	Never Married	Now Married[2]	Separated	Widowed	Divorced
City	46.4	37.8	1.5	3.6	10.6
MSA[1]	34.1	50.7	0.9	4.3	10.0
U.S.	34.1	47.9	1.7	5.6	10.7

Note: Figures are percentages and cover the population 15 years of age and older; (1) Figures cover the Minneapolis-St. Paul-Bloomington, MN-WI Metropolitan Statistical Area; (2) Excludes separated
Source: U.S. Census Bureau, 2019-2023 American Community Survey 5-Year Estimates

Religious Groups by Family

Area	Catholic	Baptist	Methodist	LDS[2]	Pentecostal	Lutheran	Islam	Adventist	Other
MSA[1]	19.8	0.8	1.4	0.5	2.5	10.7	2.9	0.7	7.4
U.S.	18.7	7.3	3.0	2.0	1.8	1.7	1.3	1.3	11.6

Note: Figures are the number of adherents as a percentage of the total population and cover the eight largest religious groups in the U.S; (1) Figures cover the Minneapolis-St. Paul-Bloomington, MN-WI Metropolitan Statistical Area; (2) Church of Jesus Christ of Latter-day Saints
Sources: 2020 U.S. Religion Census, Association of Statisticians of American Religious Bodies; The Association of Religion Data Archives (ARDA)

Religious Groups by Tradition

Area	Catholic	Evangelical Protestant	Mainline Protestant	Black Protestant	Islam	Judaism	Hinduism	Orthodox	Buddhism
MSA[1]	19.8	10.6	10.3	0.5	2.9	0.6	0.2	0.3	0.3
U.S.	18.7	16.5	5.2	2.3	1.3	0.6	0.4	0.4	0.3

Note: Figures are the number of adherents as a percentage of the total population; (1) Figures cover the Minneapolis-St. Paul-Bloomington, MN-WI Metropolitan Statistical Area
Sources: 2020 U.S. Religion Census, Association of Statisticians of American Religious Bodies; The Association of Religion Data Archives (ARDA)

ECONOMY

Real Gross Domestic Product (GDP)

Area	2017	2018	2019	2020	2021	2022	2023	Rank[3]
MSA[1]	257.8	265.7	270.1	260.6	275.7	281.3	286.7	15
U.S.[2]	17,619.1	18,160.7	18,642.5	18,238.9	19,387.6	19,896.6	20,436.3	—

Note: Figures are in billions of chained 2017 dollars; (1) Figures cover the Minneapolis-St. Paul-Bloomington, MN-WI Metropolitan Statistical Area; (2) Figures cover real GDP within metropolitan areas; (3) Rank is based on 2023 data and ranges from 1 to 384
Source: U.S. Bureau of Economic Analysis

Economic Growth

Area	2014	2015	2016	2017	2018	2019	2020	2021	2022	2023
MSA[1]	3.8	2.2	1.6	1.9	3.1	1.6	-3.5	5.8	2.0	2.0
U.S.[2]	2.6	3.2	2.0	2.7	3.1	2.7	-2.2	6.3	2.6	2.7

Note: Figures are real gross domestic product growth rates and represent percent change from preceding period; (1) Figures cover the Minneapolis-St. Paul-Bloomington, MN-WI Metropolitan Statistical Area; (2) Figures are the average growth rates within metropolitan areas
Source: U.S. Bureau of Economic Analysis

Metropolitan Area Exports

Area	2018	2019	2020	2021	2022	2023	Rank[2]
MSA[1]	20,016.2	18,633.0	17,109.5	21,098.8	21,964.3	22,209.4	23
U.S.	1,664,056.1	1,645,173.7	1,431,406.6	1,753,941.4	2,062,937.4	2,019,160.5	—

Note: Figures are in millions of dollars; (1) Figures cover the Minneapolis-St. Paul-Bloomington, MN-WI Metropolitan Statistical Area; (2) Rank is based on 2023 data and ranges from 1 to 386
Source: U.S. Department of Commerce, International Trade Administration, Office of Trade and Economic Analysis, Industry and Analysis, Exports by Metropolitan Area, data extracted April 2, 2025

Building Permits

Area	Single-Family			Multi-Family			Total		
	2023	2024	Pct. Chg.	2023	2024	Pct. Chg.	2023	2024	Pct. Chg.
City	48	75	56.3	1,156	329	-71.5	1,204	404	-66.4
MSA[1]	8,245	9,300	12.8	10,388	4,722	-54.5	18,633	14,022	-24.7
U.S.	920,000	981,900	6.7	591,100	496,100	-16.1	1,511,100	1,478,000	-2.2

Note: (1) Figures cover the Minneapolis-St. Paul-Bloomington, MN-WI Metropolitan Statistical Area; Figures represent new, privately-owned housing units authorized (unadjusted data)
Source: U.S. Census Bureau, Building Permits Survey (BPS), 2023, 2024

Bankruptcy Filings

Area	Business Filings			Nonbusiness Filings		
	2023	2024	% Chg.	2023	2024	% Chg.
Ramsey County	20	19	-5.0	694	840	21.0
U.S.	18,926	23,107	22.1	434,064	494,201	13.9

Note: Business filings include Chapter 7, Chapter 9, Chapter 11, Chapter 12, Chapter 13, Chapter 15, and Section 304; Nonbusiness filings include Chapter 7, Chapter 11, and Chapter 13
Source: Administrative Office of the U.S. Courts, Business and Nonbusiness Bankruptcy, County Cases Commenced by Chapter of the Bankruptcy Code, During the 12-Month Period Ending December 31, 2023 and Business and Nonbusiness Bankruptcy, County Cases Commenced by Chapter of the Bankruptcy Code, During the 12-Month Period Ending December 31, 2024

Housing Vacancy Rates

Area	Gross Vacancy Rate[3] (%)			Year-Round Vacancy Rate[4] (%)			Rental Vacancy Rate[5] (%)			Homeowner Vacancy Rate[6] (%)		
	2022	2023	2024	2022	2023	2024	2022	2023	2024	2022	2023	2024
MSA[1]	4.8	5.5	4.9	4.5	5.3	4.6	6.7	8.1	5.2	0.8	0.5	0.4
U.S.[2]	9.1	9.0	9.1	7.5	7.5	7.6	5.7	6.5	6.8	0.8	0.8	1.0

Note: (1) Figures cover the Minneapolis-St. Paul-Bloomington, MN-WI Metropolitan Statistical Area; (2) Figures cover the 75 largest Metropolitan Statistical Areas; (3) The percentage of the total housing inventory that is vacant; (4) The percentage of the housing inventory (excluding seasonal units) that is year-round vacant; (5) The percentage of rental inventory that is vacant for rent; (6) The percentage of homeowner inventory that is vacant for sale
Source: U.S. Census Bureau, Housing Vacancies and Homeownership Annual Statistics: 2022, 2023, 2024

INCOME

Income

Area	Per Capita ($)	Median Household ($)	Average Household ($)
City	41,594	73,055	102,197
MSA[1]	51,500	98,180	128,647
U.S.	43,289	78,538	110,491

Note: (1) Figures cover the Minneapolis-St. Paul-Bloomington, MN-WI Metropolitan Statistical Area
Source: U.S. Census Bureau, 2019-2023 American Community Survey 5-Year Estimates

Household Income Distribution

Area	Percent of Households Earning							
	Under $15,000	$15,000 -$24,999	$25,000 -$34,999	$35,000 -$49,999	$50,000 -$74,999	$75,000 -$99,999	$100,000 -$149,999	$150,000 and up
City	9.0	6.6	6.9	10.4	18.4	13.2	16.1	19.4
MSA[1]	5.5	4.5	4.9	8.5	14.5	13.0	20.3	28.9
U.S.	8.5	6.6	6.8	10.4	15.7	12.7	17.4	21.9

Note: (1) Figures cover the Minneapolis-St. Paul-Bloomington, MN-WI Metropolitan Statistical Area
Source: U.S. Census Bureau, 2019-2023 American Community Survey 5-Year Estimates

Poverty Rate

Area	All Ages	Under 18 Years Old	18 to 64 Years Old	65 Years and Over
City	15.7	22.9	13.8	11.7
MSA[1]	8.2	9.6	7.7	7.7
U.S.	12.4	16.3	11.6	10.4

Note: Figures are percentage of people whose income during the past 12 months was below the poverty level; (1) Figures cover the Minneapolis-St. Paul-Bloomington, MN-WI Metropolitan Statistical Area
Source: U.S. Census Bureau, 2019-2023 American Community Survey 5-Year Estimates

EMPLOYMENT

Labor Force and Employment

Area	Civilian Labor Force			Workers Employed		
	Dec. 2023	Dec. 2024	% Chg.	Dec. 2023	Dec. 2024	% Chg.
City	156,382	157,144	0.5	152,569	153,219	0.4
MSA[1]	2,005,284	2,015,070	0.5	1,956,084	1,964,999	0.5
U.S.	166,661,000	167,746,000	0.7	160,754,000	161,294,000	0.3

Note: Data is not seasonally adjusted and covers workers 16 years of age and older; (1) Figures cover the Minneapolis-St. Paul-Bloomington, MN-WI Metropolitan Statistical Area
Source: Bureau of Labor Statistics, Local Area Unemployment Statistics

Unemployment Rate

Area	2024											
	Jan.	Feb.	Mar.	Apr.	May	Jun.	Jul.	Aug.	Sep.	Oct.	Nov.	Dec.
City	3.0	3.3	3.1	2.8	2.7	3.6	3.7	3.7	3.1	2.8	2.6	2.5
MSA[1]	3.1	3.3	3.1	2.7	2.6	3.5	3.4	3.4	2.7	2.4	2.4	2.5
U.S.	4.1	4.2	3.9	3.5	3.7	4.3	4.5	4.4	3.9	3.9	4.0	3.8

Note: Data is not seasonally adjusted and covers workers 16 years of age and older; (1) Figures cover the Minneapolis-St. Paul-Bloomington, MN-WI Metropolitan Statistical Area
Source: Bureau of Labor Statistics, Local Area Unemployment Statistics

Average Wages

Occupation	$/Hr.	Occupation	$/Hr.
Accountants and Auditors	45.40	Maintenance and Repair Workers	28.72
Automotive Mechanics	29.52	Marketing Managers	85.36
Bookkeepers	26.89	Network and Computer Systems Admin.	48.14
Carpenters	35.62	Nurses, Licensed Practical	30.75
Cashiers	16.35	Nurses, Registered	49.42
Computer Programmers	50.83	Nursing Assistants	22.60
Computer Systems Analysts	53.62	Office Clerks, General	24.20
Computer User Support Specialists	33.76	Physical Therapists	47.65
Construction Laborers	30.67	Physicians	159.99
Cooks, Restaurant	20.11	Plumbers, Pipefitters and Steamfitters	42.95
Customer Service Representatives	24.54	Police and Sheriff's Patrol Officers	42.99
Dentists	108.57	Postal Service Mail Carriers	29.62
Electricians	41.70	Real Estate Sales Agents	34.01
Engineers, Electrical	54.81	Retail Salespersons	18.56
Fast Food and Counter Workers	16.17	Sales Representatives, Technical/Scientific	50.40
Financial Managers	85.12	Secretaries, Exc. Legal/Medical/Executive	25.28
First-Line Supervisors of Office Workers	37.88	Security Guards	24.99
General and Operations Managers	59.75	Surgeons	180.26
Hairdressers/Cosmetologists	22.01	Teacher Assistants, Exc. Postsecondary[1]	20.05
Home Health and Personal Care Aides	17.88	Teachers, Secondary School, Exc. Sp. Ed.[1]	35.70
Janitors and Cleaners	19.66	Telemarketers	22.16
Landscaping/Groundskeeping Workers	22.32	Truck Drivers, Heavy/Tractor-Trailer	31.39
Lawyers	79.57	Truck Drivers, Light/Delivery Services	25.01
Maids and Housekeeping Cleaners	19.15	Waiters and Waitresses	13.95

Note: Wage data covers the Minneapolis-St. Paul-Bloomington, MN-WI Metropolitan Statistical Area; (1) Hourly wages were calculated from annual wage data based on a 40 hour work week
Source: Bureau of Labor Statistics, Metro Area Occupational Employment & Wage Estimates, May 2024

Employment by Industry

Sector	MSA[1] Number of Employees	MSA[1] Percent of Total	U.S. Percent of Total
Construction, Mining, and Logging	85,600	4.3	5.5
Financial Activities	143,800	7.2	5.8
Government	262,700	13.2	14.9
Information	27,500	1.4	1.9
Leisure and Hospitality	176,800	8.9	10.4
Manufacturing	199,500	10.0	8.0
Other Services	76,900	3.9	3.7
Private Education and Health Services	378,700	19.0	16.9
Professional and Business Services	287,200	14.4	14.2
Retail Trade	183,200	9.2	10.0
Transportation, Warehousing, and Utilities	87,100	4.4	4.8
Wholesale Trade	84,000	4.2	3.9

Note: Figures are non-farm employment as of December 2024. Figures are not seasonally adjusted and include workers 16 years of age and older; (1) Figures cover the Minneapolis-St. Paul-Bloomington, MN-WI Metropolitan Statistical Area
Source: Bureau of Labor Statistics, Current Employment Statistics, Employment, Hours, and Earnings

Employment by Occupation

Occupation Classification	City (%)	MSA[1] (%)	U.S. (%)
Management, Business, Science, and Arts	45.9	48.6	42.0
Natural Resources, Construction, and Maintenance	4.8	6.4	8.6
Production, Transportation, and Material Moving	14.0	12.3	13.0
Sales and Office	17.7	18.8	19.9
Service	17.5	14.0	16.5

Note: Figures cover employed civilians 16 years of age and older; (1) Figures cover the Minneapolis-St. Paul-Bloomington, MN-WI Metropolitan Statistical Area
Source: U.S. Census Bureau, 2019-2023 American Community Survey 5-Year Estimates

Occupations with Greatest Projected Employment Growth: 2022 – 2032

Occupation[1]	2022 Employment	2032 Projected Employment	Numeric Employment Change	Percent Employment Change
Home Health and Personal Care Aides	113,680	129,520	15,840	13.9
Software Developers	38,590	47,920	9,330	24.2
General and Operations Managers	76,000	81,170	5,170	6.8
Laborers and Freight, Stock, and Material Movers, Hand	55,000	58,700	3,700	6.7
Registered Nurses	68,040	71,630	3,590	5.3
Stockers and Order Fillers	42,970	46,440	3,470	8.1
Market Research Analysts and Marketing Specialists	23,920	27,220	3,300	13.8
Cooks, Restaurant	26,770	30,010	3,240	12.1
Industrial Engineers	18,230	21,260	3,030	16.6
Medical and Health Services Managers	10,910	13,760	2,850	26.1

Note: Projections cover Minnesota; (1) Sorted by numeric employment change
Source: www.projectionscentral.org, State Occupational Projections, 2022–2032 Long-Term Projections

Fastest-Growing Occupations: 2022 – 2032

Occupation[1]	2022 Employment	2032 Projected Employment	Numeric Employment Change	Percent Employment Change
Wind Turbine Service Technicians	360	540	180	50.0
Nurse Practitioners	5,570	8,010	2,440	43.8
Epidemiologists	260	370	110	42.3
Data Scientists	2,290	3,070	780	34.1
Statisticians	660	860	200	30.3
Information Security Analysts (SOC 2018)	2,910	3,730	820	28.2
Physician Assistants	3,830	4,900	1,070	27.9
Medical and Health Services Managers	10,910	13,760	2,850	26.1
Actuaries	1,150	1,430	280	24.3
Physical Therapist Assistants	1,320	1,640	320	24.2

Note: Projections cover Minnesota; (1) Sorted by percent employment change and excludes occupations with numeric employment change less than 50
Source: www.projectionscentral.org, State Occupational Projections, 2022–2032 Long-Term Projections

Saint Paul, Minnesota

CITY FINANCES

City Government Finances

Component	2022 ($000)	2022 ($ per capita)
Total Revenues	845,549	2,757
Total Expenditures	849,562	2,770
Debt Outstanding	785,898	2,562

Source: U.S. Census Bureau, State & Local Government Finances 2022

City Government Revenue by Source

Source	2022 ($000)	2022 ($ per capita)	2022 (%)
General Revenue			
From Federal Government	126,907	414	15.0
From State Government	105,298	343	12.5
From Local Governments	13,311	43	1.6
Taxes			
Property	191,199	623	22.6
Sales and Gross Receipts	49,759	162	5.9
Personal Income	0	0	0.0
Corporate Income	0	0	0.0
Motor Vehicle License	0	0	0.0
Other Taxes	16,649	54	2.0
Current Charges	205,398	670	24.3
Liquor Store	0	0	0.0
Utility	84,821	277	10.0

Source: U.S. Census Bureau, State & Local Government Finances 2022

City Government Expenditures by Function

Function	2022 ($000)	2022 ($ per capita)	2022 (%)
General Direct Expenditures			
Air Transportation	0	0	0.0
Corrections	0	0	0.0
Education	0	0	0.0
Employment Security Administration	0	0	0.0
Financial Administration	11,866	38	1.4
Fire Protection	75,038	244	8.8
General Public Buildings	0	0	0.0
Governmental Administration, Other	5,791	18	0.7
Health	1,613	5	0.2
Highways	64,203	209	7.6
Hospitals	0	0	0.0
Housing and Community Development	103,907	338	12.2
Interest on General Debt	52,656	171	6.2
Judicial and Legal	0	0	0.0
Libraries	20,285	66	2.4
Parking	5,443	17	0.6
Parks and Recreation	74,844	244	8.8
Police Protection	143,993	469	16.9
Public Welfare	0	0	0.0
Sewerage	63,181	206	7.4
Solid Waste Management	9,332	30	1.1
Veterans' Services	0	0	0.0
Liquor Store	0	0	0.0
Utility	78,763	256	9.3

Source: U.S. Census Bureau, State & Local Government Finances 2022

TAXES

State Corporate Income Tax Rates

State	Tax Rate (%)	Income Brackets ($)	Num. of Brackets	Financial Institution Tax Rate (%)[a]	Federal Income Tax Ded.
Minnesota	9.8 (l)	Flat rate	1	9.8 (l)	No

Note: Tax rates for tax year 2024; (a) Rates listed are the corporate income tax rate applied to financial institutions or excise taxes based on income. Some states have other taxes based upon the value of deposits or shares; (l) In addition, Minnesota levies a 5.8% tentative minimum tax on Alternative Minimum Taxable Income. Minnesota also imposes a surtax ranging up to $11,570.
Source: Federation of Tax Administrators, State Corporate Income Tax Rates, January 1, 2025

State Individual Income Tax Rates

State	Tax Rate (%)	Income Brackets ($)	Personal Exemptions ($)			Standard Ded. ($)	
			Single	Married	Depend.	Single	Married
Minnesota (a)	5.35 - 9.85	31,690 - 193,240 (n)	(d)	(d)	5,150	14,575	29,150

Note: Tax rates for tax year 2024; Local- and county-level taxes are not included; Federal income tax is not deductible on state income tax returns; (a) 16 states have statutory provision for automatically adjusting to the rate of inflation the dollar values of the income tax brackets, standard deductions, and/or personal exemptions. Oregon does not index the income brackets for $125,000 and over See: INFL and SPEC above; (d) These states use the personal exemption/standard deduction amounts provided in the federal Internal Revenue Code. Montana personal exemption subject to repeal under Section 15-30-2114; (n) The income brackets reported for Minnesota are for single individuals. For married couples filing jointly, the same tax rates apply to income brackets ranging from $46,331 to $321,450.
Source: Federation of Tax Administrators, State Individual Income Tax Rates, January 1, 2025

Various State Sales and Excise Tax Rates

State	State Sales Tax (%)	Gasoline[1] ($/gal.)	Cigarette[2] ($/pack)	Spirits[3] ($/gal.)	Wine[4] ($/gal.)	Beer[5] ($/gal.)	Recreational Marijuana (%)
Minnesota	6.875	0.32	3.83	8.74	1.25	0.47	(l)

Note: All tax rates as of January 1, 2025; (1) The American Petroleum Institute has developed a methodology for determining the average tax rate on a gallon of fuel. Rates may include any of the following: excise taxes, environmental fees, storage tank fees, other fees or taxes, general sales tax, and local taxes; (2) The federal excise tax of $1.0066 per pack and local taxes are not included; (3) Rates are those applicable to off-premise sales of 40% alcohol by volume (a.b.v.) distilled spirits in 750ml containers. Local excise taxes are excluded; (4) Rates are those applicable to off-premise sales of 11% a.b.v. non-carbonated wine in 750ml containers; (5) Rates are those applicable to off-premise sales of 4.7% a.b.v. beer in 12 ounce containers; (l) 10% excise tax (retail gross receipts)
Source: Tax Foundation, 2025 Facts & Figures: How Does Your State Compare?

State Tax Competitiveness Index

State	Overall Rank	Corporate Tax Rank	Individual Income Tax Rank	Sales Tax Rank	Property Tax Rank	Unemployment Insurance Tax Rank
Minnesota	44	43	44	34	26	42

Note: The Tax Foundation's State Tax Competitiveness Index enables policymakers, taxpayers, and business leaders to gauge how their states' tax systems compare. A rank of 1 is best, 50 is worst. Rankings do not average to the total. States without a tax rank equally as 1. DC's scores and rankings do not affect other states. The report shows tax systems as of July 1, 2024 (the beginning of Fiscal Year 2025).
Source: Tax Foundation, State Tax Competitiveness Index 2025

TRANSPORTATION

Means of Transportation to Work

Area	Car/Truck/Van		Public Transportation			Bicycle	Walked	Other Means	Worked at Home
	Drove Alone	Car-pooled	Bus	Subway	Railroad				
City	59.3	10.0	5.0	0.1	0.0	0.8	3.7	2.7	18.3
MSA[1]	67.7	7.1	2.2	0.0	0.0	0.5	2.0	1.4	19.0
U.S.	70.2	8.5	1.7	1.3	0.4	0.4	2.4	1.6	13.5

Note: Figures are percentages and cover workers 16 years of age and older; (1) Figures cover the Minneapolis-St. Paul-Bloomington, MN-WI Metropolitan Statistical Area
Source: U.S. Census Bureau, 2019-2023 American Community Survey 5-Year Estimates

Travel Time to Work

Area	Less Than 10 Minutes	10 to 19 Minutes	20 to 29 Minutes	30 to 44 Minutes	45 to 59 Minutes	60 to 89 Minutes	90 Minutes or More
City	10.5	35.0	27.6	19.0	4.4	2.1	1.4
MSA[1]	11.1	29.6	25.3	22.3	6.9	3.5	1.4
U.S.	12.6	28.6	21.2	20.8	8.1	6.0	2.8

Note: Note: Figures are percentages and include workers 16 years old and over; (1) Figures cover the Minneapolis-St. Paul-Bloomington, MN-WI Metropolitan Statistical Area
Source: U.S. Census Bureau, 2019-2023 American Community Survey 5-Year Estimates

Key Congestion Measures

Measure	2000	2010	2015	2020	2022
Annual Hours of Delay, Total (000)	68,767	84,317	99,730	59,835	103,024
Annual Hours of Delay, Per Auto Commuter	47	47	53	32	59
Annual Congestion Cost, Per Auto Commuter ($)	1,045	1,017	1,112	693	1,208

Note: Figures cover the Minneapolis-St. Paul MN-WI urban area
Source: Texas A&M Transportation Institute, 2023 Urban Mobility Report

Saint Paul, Minnesota

Freeway Travel Time Index

Measure	1985	1990	1995	2000	2005	2010	2015	2020	2022
Urban Area Index[1]	1.10	1.14	1.21	1.27	1.28	1.25	1.25	1.11	1.24
Urban Area Rank[1,2]	27	26	16	10	14	21	24	20	22

Note: Freeway Travel Time Index—the ratio of travel time in the peak period to the travel time at free-flow conditions. For example, a value of 1.30 indicates a 20-minute free-flow trip takes 26 minutes in the peak (20 minutes x 1.30 = 26 minutes); (1) Covers the Minneapolis-St. Paul MN-WI urban area; (2) Rank is based on 101 larger urban areas (#1 = highest travel time index)
Source: Texas A&M Transportation Institute, 2023 Urban Mobility Report

Public Transportation

Agency Name / Mode of Transportation	Vehicles Operated in Maximum Service[1]	Annual Unlinked Passenger Trips[2] (in thous.)	Annual Passenger Miles[3] (in thous.)
Metropolitan Council			
Bus (purchased transportation)	67	1,566.9	6,819.1
Demand Response (purchased transportation)	590	2,211.4	24,524.9
Vanpool (purchased transportation)	53	94.7	2,821.2

Note: (1) Number of revenue vehicles operated by the given mode and type of service to meet the annual maximum service requirement. This is the revenue vehicle count during the peak season of the year; on the week and day that maximum service is provided. Vehicles operated in maximum service (VOMS) exclude atypical days and one-time special events; (2) Number of passengers who boarded public transportation vehicles. Passengers are counted each time they board a vehicle no matter how many vehicles they use to travel from their origin to their destination. (3) Sum of the distances ridden by all passengers during the entire fiscal year.
Source: Federal Transit Administration, National Transit Database, 2023

Air Transportation

Airport Name and Code / Type of Service	Passenger Airlines[1]	Passenger Enplanements	Freight Carriers[2]	Freight (lbs)
Minneapolis-St. Paul International (MSP)				
Domestic service (U.S. carriers only)	33	16,321,623	18	158,998,803
International service (U.S. carriers only)	7	1,411,075	3	26,482,102

Note: (1) Includes all U.S.-based major, minor and commuter airlines that carried at least one passenger during the year; (2) Includes all U.S.-based airlines and freight carriers that transported at least one pound of freight during the year.
Source: Bureau of Transportation Statistics, The Intermodal Transportation Database, Air Carriers: T-100 Domestic Market (U.S. carriers only), 2024; Bureau of Transportation Statistics, The Intermodal Transportation Database, Air Carriers: T-100 International Market (U.S. carriers only), 2024

BUSINESSES

Major Business Headquarters

Company Name	Industry	Rankings	
		Fortune[1]	Forbes[2]
3M	Chemicals	134	-
Ecolab	Chemicals	269	-
Johnson Brothers Liquor	Food, drink & tobacco	-	192
Securian Financial Group	Insurance: life, health (stock)	462	-

Note: (1) Companies that produce a 10-K are ranked 1 to 500 based on 2023 revenue; (2) All private companies with at least $2 billion in annual revenue through the end of their most current fiscal year are ranked 1 to 275; companies listed are headquartered in the city; dashes indicate no ranking
Source: Fortune, "Fortune 500," 2024; Forbes, "America's Largest Private Companies," 2024

Living Environment

COST OF LIVING

Cost of Living Index

Composite Index	Groceries	Housing	Utilities	Transportation	Health Care	Misc. Goods/Services
94.0	105.2	81.3	95.6	96.0	96.7	98.1

Note: The Cost of Living Index measures regional differences in the cost of consumer goods and services, excluding taxes and non-consumer expenditures, for professional and managerial households in the top income quintile. It is based on more than 50,000 prices covering almost 60 different items for which prices are collected three times a year by chambers of commerce, economic development organizations or university applied economic centers in each participating urban area. The numbers shown should be read as a percentage above or below the national average of 100. For example, a value of 115.4 in the groceries column indicates that grocery prices are 15.4% higher than the national average. Small differences in the index numbers should not be interpreted as significant; Figures cover the St Paul MN urban area.
Source: The Council for Community and Economic Research, Cost of Living Index, 2024

Grocery Prices

Area[1]	T-Bone Steak ($/pound)	Frying Chicken ($/pound)	Whole Milk ($/half gal.)	Eggs ($/dozen)	Orange Juice ($/64 oz.)	Coffee ($/11.5 oz.)
City[2]	15.52	1.44	4.64	3.81	4.58	5.13
Avg.	15.42	1.55	4.69	3.25	4.41	5.46
Min.	14.50	1.16	4.43	2.75	4.00	4.85
Max.	17.56	2.89	5.49	4.78	5.54	7.89

Note: (1) Values for the local area are compared with the average, minimum and maximum values for all 276 areas in the Cost of Living Index; (2) Figures cover the St Paul MN urban area; **T-Bone Steak** (price per pound); **Frying Chicken** (price per pound, whole fryer); **Whole Milk** (half gallon carton); **Eggs** (price per dozen, Grade A, large); **Orange Juice** (64 oz. Tropicana or Florida Natural); **Coffee** (11.5 oz. can, vacuum-packed, Maxwell House, Hills Bros, or Folgers).
Source: The Council for Community and Economic Research, Cost of Living Index, 2024

Housing and Utility Costs

Area[1]	New Home Price ($)	Apartment Rent ($/month)	All Electric ($/month)	Part Electric ($/month)	Other Energy ($/month)	Telephone ($/month)
City[2]	404,109	1,358	-	92.16	101.15	192.06
Avg.	515,975	1,550	210.99	123.07	82.07	194.99
Min.	265,375	692	104.33	53.68	36.26	179.42
Max.	2,775,821	5,719	529.02	397.28	361.63	223.33

Note: (1) Values for the local area are compared with the average, minimum and maximum values for all 276 areas in the Cost of Living Index; (2) Figures cover the St Paul MN urban area; **New Home Price** (2,400 sf living area, 8,000 sf lot, in urban area with full utilities); **Apartment Rent** (950 sf 2 bedroom/1.5 or 2 bath, unfurnished, excluding all utilities except water); **All Electric** (average monthly cost for an all-electric home); **Part Electric** (average monthly cost for a part-electric home); **Other Energy** (average monthly cost for natural gas, fuel oil, coal, wood, and any other forms of energy except electricity); **Telephone** (price includes the base monthly rate plus taxes and fees for three lines of mobile phone service).
Source: The Council for Community and Economic Research, Cost of Living Index, 2024

Health Care, Transportation, and Other Costs

Area[1]	Doctor ($/visit)	Dentist ($/visit)	Optometrist ($/visit)	Gasoline ($/gallon)	Beauty Salon ($/visit)	Men's Shirt ($)
City[2]	169.08	101.40	118.46	3.16	41.44	42.25
Avg.	143.77	117.51	129.23	3.32	48.57	38.14
Min.	36.74	58.67	67.33	2.80	24.00	13.41
Max.	270.44	216.82	307.33	5.28	94.00	63.89

Note: (1) Values for the local area are compared with the average, minimum and maximum values for all 276 areas in the Cost of Living Index; (2) Figures cover the St Paul MN urban area; **Doctor** (general practitioners routine exam of an established patient); **Dentist** (adult teeth cleaning and periodic oral examination); **Optometrist** (full vision eye exam for established adult patient); **Gasoline** (one gallon regular unleaded, national brand, including all taxes, cash price at self-service pump if available); **Beauty Salon** (woman's shampoo, trim, and blow-dry); **Men's Shirt** (cotton/polyester dress shirt, pinpoint weave, long sleeves).
Source: The Council for Community and Economic Research, Cost of Living Index, 2024

HOUSING

Homeownership Rate

Area	2017 (%)	2018 (%)	2019 (%)	2020 (%)	2021 (%)	2022 (%)	2023 (%)	2024 (%)
MSA[1]	70.1	67.8	70.2	73.0	75.0	73.0	72.0	67.8
U.S.	63.9	64.4	64.6	66.6	65.5	65.8	65.9	65.6

Note: (1) Figures cover the Minneapolis-St. Paul-Bloomington, MN-WI Metropolitan Statistical Area
Source: U.S. Census Bureau, Housing Vacancies and Homeownership Annual Statistics: 2017-2024

House Price Index (HPI)

Area	National Ranking[2]	Quarterly Change (%)	One-Year Change (%)	Five-Year Change (%)	Since 1991Q1 (%)
MSA[1]	153	0.20	4.68	37.75	302.55
U.S.[3]	–	1.43	4.51	57.13	327.82

Note: The HPI is a weighted repeat sales index. It measures average price changes in repeat sales or refinancings on the same properties. This information is obtained by reviewing repeat mortgage transactions on single-family properties whose mortgages have been purchased or securitized by Fannie Mae or Freddie Mac since January 1975; (1) Figures cover the Minneapolis-St. Paul-Bloomington, MN-WI Metropolitan Statistical Area; (2) Rankings are based on annual percentage change for all metro areas containing at least 15,000 transactions over the last 10 years and ranges from 1 to 241; (3) figures based on a weighted average of Census Division estimates using a seasonally adjusted, purchase-only index; all figures are for the period ending December 31, 2024
Source: Federal Housing Finance Agency, Change in FHFA Metropolitan Area House Price Indexes, All Transactions Index, 2024Q4

Home Value

Area	Under $100,000	$100,000 -$199,999	$200,000 -$299,999	$300,000 -$399,999	$400,000 -$499,999	$500,000 -$999,999	$1,000,000 or more	Median ($)
City	3.5	15.9	37.6	19.5	9.9	11.4	2.0	280,300
MSA[1]	4.0	7.4	24.9	25.1	16.1	19.6	2.9	354,400
U.S.	12.1	17.8	19.5	14.4	10.5	19.1	6.5	303,400

Note: Figures are percentages except for median and cover owner-occupied housing units; (1) Figures cover the Minneapolis-St. Paul-Bloomington, MN-WI Metropolitan Statistical Area
Source: U.S. Census Bureau, 2019-2023 American Community Survey 5-Year Estimates

Year Housing Structure Built

Area	2020 or Later	2010 -2019	2000 -2009	1990 -1999	1980 -1989	1970 -1979	1960 -1969	1950 -1959	1940 -1949	Before 1940	Median Year
City	0.7	4.5	5.1	3.5	7.3	9.8	9.4	11.7	6.7	41.2	1952
MSA[1]	1.3	8.6	13.3	13.4	13.8	13.9	9.3	9.1	3.6	13.6	1980
U.S.	1.2	8.9	13.6	12.8	13.0	14.4	10.0	9.7	4.5	11.9	1980

Note: Figures are percentages except for Median Year; Note: (1) Figures cover the Minneapolis-St. Paul-Bloomington, MN-WI Metropolitan Statistical Area
Source: U.S. Census Bureau, 2019-2023 American Community Survey 5-Year Estimates

Gross Monthly Rent

Area	Under $500	$500 -$999	$1,000 -$1,499	$1,500 -$1,999	$2,000 -$2,499	$2,500 -$2,999	$3,000 and up	Median ($)
City	9.5	16.7	41.4	20.1	9.0	1.6	1.7	1,248
MSA[1]	6.6	14.0	36.6	25.6	10.8	3.3	3.2	1,396
U.S.	6.5	22.3	29.5	20.2	10.8	4.8	5.9	1,348

Note: Figures are percentages except for median; Gross rent is the contract rent plus the estimated average monthly cost of utilities (electricity, gas, and water and sewer) and fuels (oil, coal, kerosene, wood, etc.) if these are paid by the renter (or paid for the renter by someone else); (1) Figures cover the Minneapolis-St. Paul-Bloomington, MN-WI Metropolitan Statistical Area
Source: U.S. Census Bureau, 2019-2023 American Community Survey 5-Year Estimates

HEALTH

Health Risk Factors

Category	MSA[1] (%)	U.S. (%)
Adults aged 18–64 who have any kind of health care coverage	93.3	90.8
Adults who reported being in good or better health	84.5	81.8
Adults who have been told they have high blood cholesterol	34.0	36.9
Adults who have been told they have high blood pressure	30.6	34.0
Adults who are current smokers	10.5	12.1
Adults who currently use e-cigarettes	6.7	7.7
Adults who currently use chewing tobacco, snuff, or snus	2.6	3.2
Adults who are heavy drinkers[2]	5.5	6.1
Adults who are binge drinkers[3]	16.3	15.2
Adults who are overweight (BMI 25.0 - 29.9)	34.6	34.4
Adults who are obese (BMI 30.0 - 99.8)	31.3	34.3
Adults who participated in any physical activities in the past month	78.5	75.8

Note: All figures are crude prevalence; (1) Figures cover the Minneapolis-St. Paul-Bloomington, MN-WI Metropolitan Statistical Area; (2) Heavy drinkers are classified as adult men having more than 14 drinks per week and adult women having more than 7 drinks per week; (3) Binge drinkers are classified as males having five or more drinks on one occasion or females having four or more drinks on one occasion
Source: Centers for Disease Control and Prevention, Behavioral Risk Factor Surveillance System, SMART: Selected Metropolitan Area Risk Trends, 2023

Acute and Chronic Health Conditions

Category	MSA[1] (%)	U.S. (%)
Adults who have ever been told they had a heart attack	3.4	4.2
Adults who have ever been told they have angina or coronary heart disease	3.4	4.0
Adults who have ever been told they had a stroke	2.9	3.3
Adults who have ever been told they have asthma	13.9	15.7
Adults who have ever been told they have arthritis	20.4	26.3
Adults who have ever been told they have diabetes[2]	10.0	11.5
Adults who have ever been told they had skin cancer	5.1	5.6
Adults who have ever been told they had any other types of cancer	7.9	8.4
Adults who have ever been told they have COPD	3.9	6.4
Adults who have ever been told they have kidney disease	3.3	3.7
Adults who have ever been told they have a form of depression	23.3	22.0

Note: All figures are crude prevalence; (1) Figures cover the Minneapolis-St. Paul-Bloomington, MN-WI Metropolitan Statistical Area; (2) Figures do not include pregnancy-related, borderline, or pre-diabetes
Source: Centers for Disease Control and Prevention, Behavioral Risk Factor Surveillance System, SMART: Selected Metropolitan Area Risk Trends, 2023

Health Screening and Vaccination Rates

Category	MSA[1] (%)	U.S. (%)
Adults who have ever been tested for HIV	36.3	37.5
Adults who have had their blood cholesterol checked within the last five years	86.7	87.0
Adults aged 65+ who have had flu shot within the past year	69.0	63.4
Adults aged 65+ who have ever had a pneumonia vaccination	72.7	71.9

Note: All figures are crude prevalence; (1) Figures cover the Minneapolis-St. Paul-Bloomington, MN-WI Metropolitan Statistical Area.
Source: Centers for Disease Control and Prevention, Behavioral Risk Factor Surveillance System, SMART: Selected Metropolitan Area Risk Trends, 2023

Disability Status

Category	MSA[1] (%)	U.S. (%)
Adults who reported being deaf	5.6	7.4
Are you blind or have serious difficulty seeing, even when wearing glasses?	3.7	4.9
Do you have difficulty doing errands alone?	7.2	7.8
Do you have difficulty dressing or bathing?	3.0	3.6
Do you have serious difficulty concentrating/remembering/making decisions?	11.7	13.7
Do you have serious difficulty walking or climbing stairs?	10.4	13.2

Note: All figures are crude prevalence; (1) Figures cover the Minneapolis-St. Paul-Bloomington, MN-WI Metropolitan Statistical Area.
Source: Centers for Disease Control and Prevention, Behavioral Risk Factor Surveillance System, SMART: Selected Metropolitan Area Risk Trends, 2023

Mortality Rates for the Top 10 Causes of Death in the U.S.

ICD-10[a] Sub-Chapter	ICD-10[a] Code	Crude Mortality Rate[2] per 100,000 population	
		County[3]	U.S.
Malignant neoplasms	C00-C97	170.7	182.7
Ischaemic heart diseases	I20-I25	68.8	109.6
Provisional assignment of new diseases of uncertain etiology[1]	U00-U49	41.9	65.3
Other forms of heart disease	I30-I51	56.6	65.1
Other degenerative diseases of the nervous system	G30-G31	46.5	52.4
Other external causes of accidental injury	W00-X59	77.2	52.3
Cerebrovascular diseases	I60-I69	47.8	49.1
Chronic lower respiratory diseases	J40-J47	32.1	43.5
Hypertensive diseases	I10-I15	33.0	38.9
Organic, including symptomatic, mental disorders	F01-F09	46.9	33.9

Note: (a) ICD-10 = International Classification of Diseases 10th Revision; (1) Includes COVID-19, adverse effects to COVID-19 vaccines, SARS, and vaping-related disorders; (2) Crude mortality rates are a three-year average covering 2021-2023; (3) Figures cover Ramsey County.
Source: Centers for Disease Control and Prevention, National Center for Health Statistics. National Vital Statistics System, Mortality 2018-2023 on CDC WONDER Online Database

Mortality Rates for Selected Causes of Death

Cause of Death	ICD-10[a] Code	Crude Mortality Rate[1] per 100,000 population	
		County[2]	U.S.
Accidental poisoning and exposure to noxious substances	X40-X49	39.6	30.5
Alzheimer disease	G30	39.8	35.4
Assault	X85-Y09	7.9	7.3
COVID-19	U07.1	41.9	65.3
Diabetes mellitus	E10-E14	33.5	30.0
Diseases of the liver	K70-K76	20.7	20.8
Human immunodeficiency virus (HIV) disease	B20-B24	Unreliable	1.5
Influenza and pneumonia	J09-J18	7.4	13.4
Intentional self-harm	X60-X84	13.1	14.7
Malnutrition	E40-E46	4.6	6.0
Obesity and other hyperalimentation	E65-E68	3.5	3.1
Renal failure	N17-N19	11.0	16.4
Transport accidents	V01-V99	8.1	14.4

Note: (a) ICD-10 = International Classification of Diseases 10th Revision; (1) Crude mortality rates are a three-year average covering 2021-2023; (2) Figures cover Ramsey County; Data are suppressed when the data meet the criteria for confidentiality constraints; Crude mortality rates are flagged as unreliable when the rate would be calculated with a numerator of 20 or less.
Source: Centers for Disease Control and Prevention, National Center for Health Statistics. National Vital Statistics System, Mortality 2018-2023 on CDC WONDER Online Database

Health Insurance Coverage

Area	With Health Insurance	With Private Health Insurance	With Public Health Insurance	Without Health Insurance	Population Under Age 19 Without Health Insurance
City	93.6	62.5	41.0	6.4	4.5
MSA[1]	95.7	77.3	30.9	4.3	2.7
U.S.	91.4	67.3	36.3	8.6	5.4

Note: Figures are percentages that cover the civilian noninstitutionalized population; (1) Figures cover the Minneapolis-St. Paul-Bloomington, MN-WI Metropolitan Statistical Area
Source: U.S. Census Bureau, 2019-2023 American Community Survey 5-Year Estimates

Number of Medical Professionals

Area	MDs[3]	DOs[3,4]	Dentists	Podiatrists	Chiropractors	Optometrists
County[1] (number)	2,036	92	513	31	383	79
County[1] (rate[2])	379.6	17.2	95.7	5.8	71.4	14.7
U.S. (rate[2])	302.5	29.2	74.6	6.4	29.5	18.0

Note: Data as of 2023 unless noted; (1) Data covers Ramsey County; (2) Number of medical professionals per 100,000 population; (3) Data as of 2022 and includes all active, non-federal physicians; (4) Doctor of Osteopathic Medicine
Source: U.S. Department of Health and Human Services, Health Resources and Services Administration, Bureau of Health Professions, Area Resource File (ARF) 2023-2024

Best Hospitals

According to *U.S. News,* the Minneapolis-St. Paul-Bloomington, MN-WI metro area is home to two of the best hospitals in the U.S.: **Courage Kenny Rehabilitation Institute at Abbott Northwestern Hospital** (1 adult specialty); **M Health Fairview University of Minnesota Medical Center** (3 pediatric specialties). The hospitals listed were nationally ranked in at least one of 15 adult or 11 pediatric specialties. The number of specialties shown cover the parent hospital. Only 160 U.S. hospitals performed well enough to be nationally ranked in one or more specialties. Twenty hospitals in the U.S. made the Honor Roll. The Best Hospitals Honor Roll takes both the national rankings and the procedure and condition ratings into account. Hospitals received points if they were nationally ranked in one of the 15 adult specialties—the higher they ranked, the more points they got—and how many ratings of "high performing" they earned in the 20 procedures and conditions. *U.S. News Online, "America's Best Hospitals 2024-25"*

According to *U.S. News,* the Minneapolis-St. Paul-Bloomington, MN-WI metro area is home to two of the best children's hospitals in the U.S.: **M Health Fairview Masonic Children's Hospital** (3 pediatric specialties); **M Health Fairview Masonic Children's Hospital-Children's Minnesota** (3 pediatric specialties). The hospitals listed were highly ranked in at least one of 11 pediatric specialties. One hundred five children's hospitals in the U.S. were nationally ranked in at least one specialty. Hospitals received points for being ranked in a specialty, and the 10 hospitals with the most points across the 11 specialties make up the Honor Roll. *U.S. News Online, "America's Best Children's Hospitals 2024-25"*

EDUCATION

Public School District Statistics

District Name	Schls	Pupils	Pupil/ Teacher Ratio	Minority Pupils[1] (%)	Total Rev. per Pupil ($)	Total Exp. per Pupil ($)
St. Paul Public Schools	102	32,145	13.7	77.4	25,042	24,161

Note: Table includes school districts with 2,000 or more students; (1) Percentage of students that are not non-Hispanic white.
Source: U.S. Department of Education, National Center for Education Statistics, Common Core of Data, Local Education Agency (School District) Universe Survey: School Year 2023-2024; U.S. Department of Education, National Center for Education Statistics, Common Core of Data, School District Finance Survey (F-33): School Year 2021–22

Best High Schools

According to *U.S. News*, Saint Paul is home to one of the top 500 high schools in the U.S.: **Nova Classical Academy Upper School** (#179). Nearly 25,000 public, magnet and charter schools were ranked based on their performance on state assessments and how well they prepare students for college. *U.S. News & World Report, "Best High Schools 2024"*

Highest Level of Education

Area	Less than H.S.	H.S. Diploma	Some College, No Deg.	Associate Degree	Bachelor's Degree	Master's Degree	Prof. School Degree	Doctorate Degree
City	11.1	20.8	16.9	7.7	25.2	12.3	3.3	2.8
MSA[1]	5.8	20.2	18.7	10.5	29.1	11.3	2.7	1.9
U.S.	10.6	26.2	19.4	8.8	21.3	9.8	2.3	1.6

Note: Figures cover persons age 25 and over; (1) Figures cover the Minneapolis-St. Paul-Bloomington, MN-WI Metropolitan Statistical Area
Source: U.S. Census Bureau, 2019-2023 American Community Survey 5-Year Estimates

Educational Attainment by Race

Area	High School Graduate or Higher (%)					Bachelor's Degree or Higher (%)				
	Total	White	Black	Asian	Hisp.[2]	Total	White	Black	Asian	Hisp.[2]
City	88.9	96.6	81.4	67.4	73.7	43.5	55.6	21.2	23.6	24.2
MSA[1]	94.2	97.0	84.0	83.5	76.4	44.9	47.7	25.1	47.6	27.2
U.S.	89.4	92.9	88.1	88.0	72.5	35.0	37.7	24.7	57.0	19.9

Note: Figures shown cover persons 25 years old and over; (1) Figures cover the Minneapolis-St. Paul-Bloomington, MN-WI Metropolitan Statistical Area; (2) People of Hispanic origin can be of any race
Source: U.S. Census Bureau, 2019-2023 American Community Survey 5-Year Estimates

School Enrollment by Grade and Control

Area	Preschool (%)		Kindergarten (%)		Grades 1 - 4 (%)		Grades 5 - 8 (%)		Grades 9 - 12 (%)	
	Public	Private	Public	Private	Public	Private	Public	Private	Public	Private
City	64.7	35.3	82.1	17.9	89.2	10.8	87.3	12.7	90.7	9.3
MSA[1]	60.7	39.3	85.8	14.2	88.3	11.7	88.7	11.3	91.5	8.5
U.S.	58.7	41.3	85.2	14.8	87.2	12.8	87.9	12.1	89.0	11.0

Note: Figures shown cover persons 3 years old and over; (1) Figures cover the Minneapolis-St. Paul-Bloomington, MN-WI Metropolitan Statistical Area
Source: U.S. Census Bureau, 2019-2023 American Community Survey 5-Year Estimates

Higher Education

Four-Year Colleges			Two-Year Colleges			Medical Schools[1]	Law Schools[2]	Voc/ Tech[3]
Public	Private Non-profit	Private For-profit	Public	Private Non-profit	Private For-profit			
3	21	4	10	0	0	0	3	8

Note: Figures cover institutions located within the Minneapolis-St. Paul-Bloomington, MN-WI Metropolitan Statistical Area and include main campuses only; (1) includes schools accredited by the Liaison Committee on Medical Education and the American Osteopathic Association's Commission on Osteopathic College Accreditation; (2) includes ABA-accredited schools, schools with provisional ABA accreditation, and state accredited schools; (3) includes all schools with programs that are less than 2 years.
Source: National Center for Education Statistics, Integrated Postsecondary Education System (IPEDS), 2023-24; Wikipedia, List of Medical Schools in the United States, accessed May 2, 2025; Wikipedia, List of Law Schools in the United States, accessed May 2, 2025

According to *U.S. News & World Report,* the Minneapolis-St. Paul-Bloomington, MN-WI metro area is home to two of the top 200 national universities in the U.S.: **University of Minnesota—Twin Cities** (#54 tie); **University of St. Thomas (MN)** (#148 tie). The indicators used to capture academic quality fall into a number of categories: assessment by administrators at peer institutions; retention of students; faculty resources; student selectivity; financial resources; alumni giving; high school counselor ratings of colleges; and graduation rate. *U.S. News & World Report, "America's Best Colleges 2025"*

According to *U.S. News & World Report,* the Minneapolis-St. Paul-Bloomington, MN-WI metro area is home to one of the top 100 liberal arts colleges in the U.S.: **Macalester College** (#26 tie). The indicators used to capture academic quality fall into a number of categories: assessment by administrators at peer institutions; retention of students; faculty resources; student selectivity; financial resources; alumni giving; high school counselor ratings of colleges; and graduation rate. *U.S. News & World Report, "America's Best Colleges 2025"*

According to *U.S. News & World Report,* the Minneapolis-St. Paul-Bloomington, MN-WI metro area is home to two of the top 100 law schools in the U.S.: **University of Minnesota** (#20 tie); **University of St. Thomas** (#94 tie). The rankings are based on a weighted average of 12 measures of quality: peer assessment score; assessment score by lawyers/judges; median LSAT scores; median undergrad GPA; acceptance rate; employment rates for graduates; placement success; bar passage rate; faculty resources; expenditures per student; student/faculty ratio; and library resources. *U.S. News & World Report, "America's Best Graduate Schools, Law, 2025"*

According to *U.S. News & World Report,* the Minneapolis-St. Paul-Bloomington, MN-WI metro area is home to one of the top medical schools for research in the U.S.: **University of Minnesota** (Tier 2). *U.S. News* placed medical and osteopathic schools into tiers based on their research productivity, faculty and admissions data. Each school's tier was derived from its overall score, calculated by summing the weighted normalized values generated across several factors of academic quality, outlined below. There are four tiers, with tier 1 medical schools as the highest-performing and tier 4 as the lowest-performing. Only tier 1 and 2 schools are shown. Because of the tier presentation, *U.S. News* calculated overall scores based on their percentile performance among all rated schools instead of dividing against the rescaled score of the No. 1-performing schools. Tier 1 included schools with overall scores of 85 to 99. The cutoffs for tiers 2 through 4 were schools scoring 50 to 84, 15 to 49 and 1 to 14, respectively. The rankings are based on a weighted average of the following measures of quality: total research activity; average research activity per faculty member; total NIH research grants at the medical school and its affiliated hospitals; average NIH research grants per faculty; median MCAT total score; median undergraduate GPA; acceptance rate; and faculty resources. *U.S. News & World Report, "America's Best Graduate Schools, Medical, 2025"*

According to *U.S. News & World Report,* the Minneapolis-St. Paul-Bloomington, MN-WI metro area is home to one of the top medical schools for primary care in the U.S.: **University of Minnesota** (Tier 1). *U.S. News* placed medical and osteopathic schools into tiers based on their research productivity, faculty and admissions data. Each school's tier was derived from its overall score, calculated by summing the weighted normalized values generated across several factors of academic quality, outlined below. There are four tiers, with tier 1 medical schools as the highest-performing and tier 4 as the lowest-performing. Only tier 1 and 2 schools are shown. Because of the tier presentation, *U.S. News* calculated overall scores based on their percentile performance among all rated schools instead of dividing against the rescaled score of the No. 1-performing schools. Tier 1 included schools with overall scores of 85 to 99. The cutoffs for tiers 2 through 4 were schools scoring 50 to 84, 15 to 49 and 1 to 14, respectively. The rankings are based on a weighted average of the following measures of quality: graduates practicing in primary care specialties; graduates entering primary care residencies; median MCAT total score; median undergraduate GPA; acceptance rate; and faculty resources. *U.S. News & World Report, "America's Best Graduate Schools, Medical, 2025"*

According to *U.S. News & World Report,* the Minneapolis-St. Paul-Bloomington, MN-WI metro area is home to one of the top 75 business schools in the U.S.: **University of Minnesota—Twin Cities (Carlson)** (#35 tie). The rankings are based on a weighted average of the following nine measures: quality assessment; peer assessment; recruiter assessment; placement success; mean starting salary and bonus; student selectivity; mean GMAT and GRE scores; mean undergraduate GPA; and acceptance rate. *U.S. News & World Report, "America's Best Graduate Schools, Business, 2025"*

EMPLOYERS

Major Employers

Company Name	Industry
3M Company	Adhesives, sealants
Ameriprise Financial	Investment advice
Anderson Corporation	Millwork
Aware Integrated	Hospital & medical services plans
Bethesda Healtheast Hospital	General medical & surgical hospitals
Carlson Holdings	Hotels & motels
City of Minneapolis	Municipal government
County of Hennepin	County government
Hennepin County	County government
Honeywell International	Aircraft engines & engine parts
Lawson Software	Application computer software
Medtronic	Electromedical equipment
Minnesota Department of Human Services	Family services agency
Minnesota Department of Transportation	Regulation, administration of transportation
North Memorial Hospital	General medical & surgical hospitals
Regents of the University of Minnesota	Specialty outpatient clinics
Rosemount Apple Valley and Eagan	Personal service agents, brokers, & bureaus
St. Paul Fire & Marine Insurance Company	Fire, marine, & casualty insurance
Thomson Legal Regulatory	Books, publishing & printing
United Parcel Service	Package delivery services

Note: Companies shown are located within the Minneapolis-St. Paul-Bloomington, MN-WI Metropolitan Statistical Area.
Source: Chambers of Commerce; State Departments of Labor; Wikipedia

PUBLIC SAFETY

Crime Rate

Area	Total Crime Rate	Violent Crime Rate				Property Crime Rate		
		Murder	Rape	Robbery	Aggrav. Assault	Burglary	Larceny-Theft	Motor Vehicle Theft
City	3,714.1	9.0	67.3	126.8	420.8	434.5	1,962.9	692.8
U.S.	2,290.9	5.7	38.0	66.5	264.1	250.7	1,347.2	318.7

Note: Figures are crimes per 100,000 population.
Source: FBI, Table 8, Offenses Known to Law Enforcement, by State by City, 2023

Hate Crimes

Area	Number of Quarters Reported	Number of Incidents per Bias Motivation					
		Race/Ethnicity/Ancestry	Religion	Sexual Orientation	Disability	Gender	Gender Identity
City[1]	4	13	8	6	1	0	2
U.S.	4	5,900	2,699	2,077	187	92	492

Note: (1) Figures include at least one incident reported with more than one bias motivation.
Source: Federal Bureau of Investigation, Hate Crime Statistics 2023

Identity Theft Consumer Reports

Area	Reports	Reports per 100,000 Population	Rank[2]
MSA[1]	5,552	150	262
U.S.	1,135,291	339	-

Note: (1) Figures cover the Minneapolis-St. Paul-Bloomington, MN-WI Metropolitan Statistical Area; (2) Rank ranges from 1 to 401 where 1 indicates greatest number of identity theft reports per 100,000 population
Source: Federal Trade Commission, Consumer Sentinel Network Data Book 2024

Fraud and Other Consumer Reports

Area	Reports	Reports per 100,000 Population	Rank[2]
MSA[1]	38,139	1,033	191
U.S.	5,360,641	1,601	-

Note: (1) Figures cover the Minneapolis-St. Paul-Bloomington, MN-WI Metropolitan Statistical Area; (2) Rank ranges from 1 to 401 where 1 indicates greatest number of fraud and other consumer reports per 100,000 population
Source: Federal Trade Commission, Consumer Sentinel Network Data Book 2024

POLITICS

2024 Presidential Election Results

Area	Trump (Rep.)	Harris (Dem.)	Stein (Green)	Kennedy (Ind.)	Oliver (Lib.)	Other
Ramsey County	27.1	70.2	0.8	0.5	0.5	0.9
U.S.	49.7	48.2	0.6	0.5	0.4	0.6

Note: Results are percentages and may not add to 100% due to rounding
Source: Dave Leip's Atlas of U.S. Presidential Elections

SPORTS

Professional Sports Teams

Team Name	League	Year Established
Minnesota Timberwolves	National Basketball Association (NBA)	1989
Minnesota Twins	Major League Baseball (MLB)	1961
Minnesota United FC	Major League Soccer (MLS)	2017
Minnesota Vikings	National Football League (NFL)	1961
Minnesota Wild	National Hockey League (NHL)	2000

Note: Includes teams located in the Minneapolis-St. Paul-Bloomington, MN-WI Metropolitan Statistical Area.
Source: Wikipedia, Major Professional Sports Teams of the United States and Canada, May 1, 2025

CLIMATE

Average and Extreme Temperatures

Temperature	Jan	Feb	Mar	Apr	May	Jun	Jul	Aug	Sep	Oct	Nov	Dec	Yr.
Extreme High (°F)	57	60	83	95	96	102	105	101	98	89	74	63	105
Average High (°F)	21	27	38	56	69	79	84	81	71	59	41	26	54
Average Temp. (°F)	12	18	30	46	59	69	74	71	61	50	33	19	45
Average Low (°F)	3	9	21	36	48	58	63	61	50	39	25	11	35
Extreme Low (°F)	-34	-28	-32	2	18	37	43	39	26	15	-17	-29	-34

Note: Figures cover the years 1948-1990
Source: National Climatic Data Center, International Station Meteorological Climate Summary, 9/96

Average Precipitation/Snowfall/Humidity

Precip./Humidity	Jan	Feb	Mar	Apr	May	Jun	Jul	Aug	Sep	Oct	Nov	Dec	Yr.
Avg. Precip. (in.)	0.8	0.8	1.9	2.2	3.1	4.0	3.8	3.6	2.5	1.9	1.4	1.0	27.1
Avg. Snowfall (in.)	11	9	12	3	Tr	0	0	0	Tr	Tr	7	10	52
Avg. Rel. Hum. 6am (%)	75	76	77	75	75	79	81	84	85	81	80	79	79
Avg. Rel. Hum. 3pm (%)	64	62	58	48	47	50	50	52	53	52	62	68	55

Note: Figures cover the years 1948-1990; Tr = Trace amounts (<0.05 in. of rain; <0.5 in. of snow)
Source: National Climatic Data Center, International Station Meteorological Climate Summary, 9/96

Weather Conditions

Temperature			Daytime Sky			Precipitation		
5°F & below	32°F & below	90°F & above	Clear	Partly cloudy	Cloudy	0.01 inch or more precip.	0.1 inch or more snow/ice	Thunder-storms
45	156	16	93	125	147	113	41	37

Note: Figures are average number of days per year and cover the years 1948-1990
Source: National Climatic Data Center, International Station Meteorological Climate Summary, 9/96

HAZARDOUS WASTE

Superfund Sites

The Minneapolis-St. Paul-Bloomington, MN-WI metro area is home to 17 sites on the EPA's Superfund National Priorities List (NPL) or Superfund Alternative Approach (SAA) list: **Baytown Township Ground Water Plume** (Final NPL); **FMC Corp. (Fridley Plant)** (Final NPL); **Freeway Sanitary Landfill** (Final NPL); **General Mills/Henkel Corp.** (Final NPL); **Highway 100 and County Road 3 Groundwater Plume** (Final NPL); **Joslyn Manufacturing & Supply Co.** (Final NPL); **Koppers Coke** (Final NPL); **Kurt Manufacturing Co.** (Final NPL); **Macgillis & Gibbs Co./Bell Lumber & Pole Co.** (Final NPL); **Naval Industrial Reserve Ordnance Plant** (Final NPL); **New Brighton/Arden Hills/Tcaap (USARMY)** (Final NPL); **Oakdale Dump** (Final NPL); **Reilly Tar & Chemical Corp. (Saint Louis Park Plant)** (Final NPL); **South Andover Site** (Final NPL); **South Minneapolis Residential Soil Contamination** (Final NPL); **Southeast Hennepin Area Groundwater and Vapor** (Final NPL); **Spring Park Municipal Well Field** (Final NPL). The Superfund alternative approach uses the same investigation and cleanup process and standards that are used for sites listed on the National Priorities List. The SAA is an alternative to listing a site on the NPL; it is not an alternative to Superfund or the Superfund process. There are a total of 1,445 Superfund sites with a status of proposed or final on both lists in the United States. *U.S. Environmental Protection Agency, National Priorities List, May 1, 2025; U.S. Environmental Protection Agency, Superfund Alternative Approach Sites, May 1, 2025*

AIR QUALITY

Air Quality Trends: Ozone

	1990	1995	2000	2005	2010	2015	2020	2021	2022	2023
MSA[1]	0.068	0.084	0.065	0.074	0.066	0.061	0.060	0.067	0.057	0.077
U.S.	0.087	0.089	0.081	0.080	0.072	0.068	0.066	0.067	0.067	0.070

Note: (1) Data covers the Minneapolis-St. Paul-Bloomington, MN-WI Metropolitan Statistical Area. The values shown are the composite ozone concentration averages among trend sites based on the highest fourth daily maximum 8-hour concentration in parts per million. These trends are based on sites having an adequate record of monitoring data during the trend period. Data from exceptional events are included.
Source: U.S. Environmental Protection Agency, Air Quality Monitoring Information, "Air Quality Trends by City, 1990-2023"

Air Quality Index

Area	Percent of Days when Air Quality was...[2]					AQI Statistics[2]	
	Good	Moderate	Unhealthy for Sensitive Groups	Unhealthy	Very Unhealthy	Maximum	Median
MSA[1]	36.7	55.1	6.6	1.6	0.0	190	55

Note: (1) Data covers the Minneapolis-St. Paul-Bloomington, MN-WI Metropolitan Statistical Area; (2) Based on 365 days with AQI data in 2023. Air Quality Index (AQI) is an index for reporting daily air quality. EPA calculates the AQI for five major air pollutants regulated by the Clean Air Act: ground-level ozone, particle pollution (aka particulate matter), carbon monoxide, sulfur dioxide, and nitrogen dioxide. The AQI runs from 0 to 500. The higher the AQI value, the greater the level of air pollution and the greater the health concern. There are six AQI categories: "Good" AQI is between 0 and 50. Air quality is considered satisfactory; "Moderate" AQI is between 51 and 100. Air quality is acceptable; "Unhealthy for Sensitive Groups" When AQI values are between 101 and 150, members of sensitive groups may experience health effects; "Unhealthy" When AQI values are between 151 and 200 everyone may begin to experience health effects; "Very Unhealthy" AQI values between 201 and 300 trigger a health alert; "Hazardous" AQI values over 300 trigger warnings of emergency conditions (not shown).
Source: U.S. Environmental Protection Agency, Air Quality Index Report, 2023

Air Quality Index Pollutants

Area	Percent of Days when AQI Pollutant was...[2]					
	Carbon Monoxide	Nitrogen Dioxide	Ozone	Sulfur Dioxide	Particulate Matter 2.5	Particulate Matter 10
MSA[1]	0.3	0.8	33.4	(3)	61.1	4.4

Note: (1) Data covers the Minneapolis-St. Paul-Bloomington, MN-WI Metropolitan Statistical Area; (2) Based on 365 days with AQI data in 2023. The Air Quality Index (AQI) is an index for reporting daily air quality. EPA calculates the AQI for five major air pollutants regulated by the Clean Air Act: ground-level ozone, particle pollution (also known as particulate matter), carbon monoxide, sulfur dioxide, and nitrogen dioxide. The AQI runs from 0 to 500. The higher the AQI value, the greater the level of air pollution and the greater the health concern; (3) Sulfur dioxide is no longer included in this table because SO_2 concentrations tend to be very localized and not necessarily representative of broad geographical areas like counties and CBSAs.
Source: U.S. Environmental Protection Agency, Air Quality Index Report, 2023

Maximum Air Pollutant Concentrations: Particulate Matter, Ozone, CO and Lead

	Particulate Matter 10 (ug/m^3)	Particulate Matter 2.5 Wtd AM (ug/m^3)	Particulate Matter 2.5 24-Hr (ug/m^3)	Ozone (ppm)	Carbon Monoxide (ppm)	Lead (ug/m^3)
MSA[1] Level	118	10.6	41	0.079	4	0.46
NAAQS[2]	150	15	35	0.075	9	0.15
Met NAAQS[2]	Yes	Yes	No	No	Yes	No

Note: (1) Data covers the Minneapolis-St. Paul-Bloomington, MN-WI Metropolitan Statistical Area; Data from exceptional events are included; (2) National Ambient Air Quality Standards; ppm = parts per million; ug/m^3 = micrograms per cubic meter; n/a not available.
Concentrations: Particulate Matter 10 (coarse particulate)—highest second maximum 24-hour concentration; Particulate Matter 2.5 Wtd AM (fine particulate)—highest weighted annual mean concentration; Particulate Matter 2.5 24-Hour (fine particulate)—highest 98th percentile 24-hour concentration; Ozone—highest fourth daily maximum 8-hour concentration; Carbon Monoxide—highest second maximum non-overlapping 8-hour concentration; Lead—maximum running 3-month average
Source: U.S. Environmental Protection Agency, Air Quality Monitoring Information, "Air Quality Statistics by City, 2023"

Maximum Air Pollutant Concentrations: Nitrogen Dioxide and Sulfur Dioxide

	Nitrogen Dioxide AM (ppb)	Nitrogen Dioxide 1-Hr (ppb)	Sulfur Dioxide AM (ppb)	Sulfur Dioxide 1-Hr (ppb)	Sulfur Dioxide 24-Hr (ppb)
MSA[1] Level	12	45	n/a	14	n/a
NAAQS[2]	53	100	30	75	140
Met NAAQS[2]	Yes	Yes	n/a	Yes	n/a

Note: (1) Data covers the Minneapolis-St. Paul-Bloomington, MN-WI Metropolitan Statistical Area; Data from exceptional events are included; (2) National Ambient Air Quality Standards; ppm = parts per million; ug/m^3 = micrograms per cubic meter; n/a not available.
Concentrations: Nitrogen Dioxide AM—highest arithmetic mean concentration; Nitrogen Dioxide 1-Hr—highest 98th percentile 1-hour daily maximum concentration; Sulfur Dioxide AM—highest annual mean concentration; Sulfur Dioxide 1-Hr—highest 99th percentile 1-hour daily maximum concentration; Sulfur Dioxide 24-Hr—highest second maximum 24-hour concentration
Source: U.S. Environmental Protection Agency, Air Quality Monitoring Information, "Air Quality Statistics by City, 2023"

Sioux Falls, South Dakota

Background

Sioux Falls in southeastern South Dakota on the Big Sioux River, is named for the river falls. This Great Plain city is the seat of Minnehaha County and is rich in history and scenic attractions, a dynamic economic center, and a splendid family town, offering an extensive range of outdoor activities.

The city was founded prior to the Civil War by settlers who were attracted by the nearby stone quarries and the possibility of harnessing the river for waterpower. Many Scottish, English, and Norwegian immigrants came to the area and used their skills as stonecutters. The community was incorporated as a village in 1877 and as a city in 1883.

At the city's popular Falls Park, the remains of a water-driven mill testify to the importance of the river. The city has preserved much of its early architectural charm; it boasts five separate historical districts with buildings of considerable interest, including the R.F. Pettigrew home, residence of the state's first U.S. senator, and the Minnehaha County Courthouse.

Sioux Falls' restoration "Phillips to the Falls" program connected the park to the rest of downtown by extending Phillips Avenue north to Falls Park and expanding the park to the south.

Sioux Falls offers one of the Midwest's most dynamic business environments, partly due to the lack of a state corporate income tax, and is home to industry leaders in agri-business, distribution and trade, financial services, high-tech manufacturing, health care, retail, and tourism. The city embarked on a 2022-2026 capital program to replace, rehabilitate, and expand street and utility infrastructure and invest in the park system and entertainment venues, at a cost of $812 million.

The city is at the heart of a large agricultural and stock-raising area, producing corn and soybeans, and serving as a regional center for stockyards and meat-packing plants. Industries in Sioux Falls also produce computer components, electronics, and artificial flowers. Some of the nation's leading credit card operations are based in the city, including Wells Fargo, First Premier Bank Bankcard, and Citibank. Top employers include Hy-Vee, Avera Health, and Smithfield Foods and the city's unemployment rate is generally half that of the state.

Amazon's new five-story, 3-million-square-foot distribution center opened in the city in 2022, today employing 2,000.

Air travel is available through the Sioux Falls Regional Airport, which connects conveniently to major air hubs.

Sioux Falls is an important center of higher education, home to the University of South Dakota, Dakota State University, South Dakota State University, Northern State University, Augustana College, National American University, Colorado Technical University at Sioux Falls, and Southeast Technical Institute. The Federal Earth Resource Observation System operates a major data collection and analysis site nearby.

The city and its environs are home to a variety of recreation, such as the Catfish Bay Water Ski & Stage Show, Empire Golf Sport Dome, Great Bear Recreation Park, Huset's Speedway, and Wild Water West, the state's largest water and amusement park. The Downtown River Greenway Project connects its riverfront trail to Chris Larsen Park, providing users with over 12 miles of continuous trail. The city operates over 80 parks.

The modern Washington Pavilion of Arts and Science in the Sioux Falls historic downtown district features a performing arts space, a domed Omni theater, a science museum, and display areas for the city's Fine Arts Center. The Sioux Falls Jazz and Blues Festival celebrated its 34th anniversary in 2025.

The climate is continental with frequent weather changes, a result of differing, usually cold, air masses, which move in rapidly. During the late fall and winter, cold fronts accompanied by strong, gusty winds can cause temperatures to drop significantly during a 24-hour period. Rainfall is heavier during the spring and summer, and thunderstorms are frequent. Summer daytime temperatures can be high, but the nights are usually comfortable.

Rankings

General Rankings

- In their annual survey, Livability.com looked at data for more than 2,000 mid-sized U.S. cities to assign a "Livability Score"for each. The top 100 scoring cities make up Livability's "Top 100 Best Places to Live in the U.S." in 2025. Sioux Falls was placed among the top 100 of the customizable list. Criteria: housing and economy; cost of living; environment; education; health care options; transportation; safety; and community amenities. *Livability.com, "Top 100 Best Places to Live in the U.S. in 2025" April 15, 2025*

Business/Finance Rankings

- Sioux Falls was cited as one of America's top metros for total major capital investment facility projects in 2024. The area ranked #1 in the Tier 2 (mid-sized) metro area category (population 200,000 to 1 million). *Site Selection, "Top Metros of 2024," March 2025*
- The Sioux Falls metro area appeared on the Milken Institute "2025 Best Performing Cities" list. Rank: #56 out of 200 large metro areas (based on performance category). Criteria: job growth; wage growth; high-tech growth and impact; community resilience; housing affordability; household broadband access. *Milken Institute, "Best-Performing Cities 2025," January 14, 2025*

Real Estate Rankings

- *WalletHub* compared the most populated U.S. cities to determine which had the best markets for real estate agents. Sioux Falls ranked #23 where demand was high and pay was the best. Criteria: sales per agent; annual median wage for real-estate agents; monthly average starting salary for real estate agents; real estate job density and competition; unemployment rate; home turnover rate; housing-market health index; and other relevant metrics. *WalletHub.com, "2021 Best Places to Be a Real Estate Agent," May 12, 2021*
- Sioux Falls was ranked #62 out of 176 metro areas in terms of cost of housing in 2024 by the National Association of Home Builders (#1 = most affordable). Criteria: the portion of an average family's income necessary to pay the mortgage on a median-priced home. *National Association of Home Builders®, NAHB-Wells Fargo Cost of Housing Index, 4th Quarter 2024*

Seniors/Retirement Rankings

- Sioux Falls made the 2024 *Forbes* list of "25 Best Places to Retire." Criteria, focused on overall affordability as well as quality of life indicators, include: housing/living costs compared to the national average and taxes; air quality; crime rates; median home prices; risk associated with climate-change/natural hazards; availability of medical care; bikeability; walkability; healthy living. *Forbes.com, "The Best Places to Retire in 2024: Las Cruces and Other Unexpected Hot Spots," May 10, 2024*

Women/Minorities Rankings

- Personal finance website *WalletHub* compared more than 180 U.S. cities across two key dimensions, "Hispanic Business-Friendliness" and "Hispanic Purchasing Power," to arrive at the most favorable conditions for Hispanic entrepreneurs. Sioux Falls was ranked #22 out of 182. Criteria includes: share of Hispanic-Owned Businesses; average growth of Hispanic Business revenues; Small Business-Friendliness score; affordability; and number of Hispanics with at least a bachelor's degree. *WalletHub.com, "Best Cities for Hispanic Entrepreneurs," September 4, 2024*

Miscellaneous Rankings

- The financial planning site *SmartAsset* has compiled its annual study on the best places for Halloween in the U.S. for 2022. 146 cities were compared to determine that Sioux Falls ranked #19 out of 35 for still being able to enjoy the festivities despite COVID-19. Metrics included: safety, family-friendliness, percentage of children in the population, concentration of candy and costume shops, weather and COVID infection rates. *SmartAsset.com, "2022 Edition-Best Places to Celebrate Halloween," October 19, 2022*
- *WalletHub* compared 148 of the most populated U.S. cities to determine their operating efficiency. A "Quality of Services" score was constructed for each city and then measured against the total budget per capita to reveal which were managed the best. Sioux Falls ranked #9. Criteria: financial stability; economy; education; safety; health; infrastructure and pollution. *WalletHub.com, "2025's Best- & Worst-Run Cities in America," June 18, 2024*

Business Environment

DEMOGRAPHICS

Population Growth

Area	1990 Census	2000 Census	2010 Census	2020 Census	2023 Estimate[2]	Population Growth 1990-2023 (%)
City	102,262	123,975	153,888	192,517	197,642	93.3
MSA[1]	153,500	187,093	228,261	276,730	293,107	90.9
U.S.	248,709,873	281,421,906	308,745,538	331,449,281	332,387,540	33.6

Note: (1) Figures cover the Sioux Falls, SD-MN Metropolitan Statistical Area; (2) 2019-2023 5-year ACS population estimate
Source: U.S. Census Bureau, 1990 Census, 2000 Census, 2010 Census, 2020 Census, 2019-2023 American Community Survey 5-Year Estimates

Race

Area	White Alone[2] (%)	Black Alone[2] (%)	Asian Alone[2] (%)	AIAN[3] Alone[2] (%)	NHOPI[4] Alone[2] (%)	Other Race Alone[2] (%)	Two or More Races (%)
City	79.9	7.0	2.3	1.9	0.0	2.0	7.0
MSA[1]	84.2	5.1	1.6	1.5	0.0	1.6	6.0
U.S.	63.4	12.4	5.8	0.9	0.2	6.6	10.7

Note: (1) Figures cover the Sioux Falls, SD-MN Metropolitan Statistical Area; (2) Alone is defined as not being in combination with one or more other races; (3) American Indian and Alaska Native; (4) Native Hawaiian and Other Pacific Islander
Source: U.S. Census Bureau, 2019-2023 American Community Survey 5-Year Estimates

Hispanic or Latino Origin

Area	Total (%)	Mexican (%)	Puerto Rican (%)	Cuban (%)	Other (%)
City	6.4	2.7	0.3	0.1	3.3
MSA[1]	5.3	2.4	0.2	0.1	2.6
U.S.	19.0	11.3	1.8	0.7	5.2

Note: Persons of Hispanic or Latino origin can be of any race; (1) Figures cover the Sioux Falls, SD-MN Metropolitan Statistical Area
Source: U.S. Census Bureau, 2019-2023 American Community Survey 5-Year Estimates

Age

Area	Under Age 5	Age 5–19	Age 20–34	Age 35–44	Age 45–54	Age 55–64	Age 65–74	Age 75–84	Age 85+	Median Age
City	7.0	20.0	22.8	14.4	10.8	11.4	8.8	3.4	1.4	35.1
MSA[1]	6.9	21.1	20.4	14.3	11.2	11.8	9.1	3.7	1.5	36.1
U.S.	5.7	19.1	20.2	13.1	12.3	12.8	10.0	4.9	1.9	38.7

Note: (1) Figures cover the Sioux Falls, SD-MN Metropolitan Statistical Area
Source: U.S. Census Bureau, 2019-2023 American Community Survey 5-Year Estimates

Disability by Age

Area	All Ages	Under 18 Years Old	18 to 64 Years Old	65 Years and Over
City	10.0	3.4	8.7	28.4
MSA[1]	9.9	3.3	8.5	28.5
U.S.	13.0	4.7	10.7	32.9

Note: Figures show percent of the civilian noninstitutionalized population that reported having a disability. Disability status is determined from six types of difficulty: vision, hearing, cognitive, ambulatory, self-care, and independent living. For children under 5 years old, hearing and vision difficulty are used to determine disability status. For children between the ages of 5 and 14, disability status is determined from hearing, vision, cognitive, ambulatory, and self-care difficulties. For people aged 15 years and older, they are considered to have a disability if they have difficulty with any one of the six difficulty types; Note: (1) Figures cover the Sioux Falls, SD-MN Metropolitan Statistical Area
Source: U.S. Census Bureau, 2019-2023 American Community Survey 5-Year Estimates

Ancestry

Area	German	Irish	English	American	Italian	Polish	French[2]	European	Scottish
City	31.7	10.1	7.4	4.3	1.5	1.4	1.6	1.3	0.8
MSA[1]	33.6	9.6	6.6	5.0	1.4	1.3	1.5	1.3	0.8
U.S.	12.6	9.4	9.1	5.5	4.9	2.6	2.0	1.6	1.6

Note: Figures are the percentage of the total population reporting a particular ancestry. The nine most commonly reported ancestries in the U.S. are shown. Figures include multiple ancestries (e.g. if a person reported being Irish and Italian, they were included in both columns); (1) Figures cover the Sioux Falls, SD-MN Metropolitan Statistical Area; (2) Excludes Basque
Source: U.S. Census Bureau, 2019-2023 American Community Survey 5-Year Estimates

Foreign-born Population

Area	Percent of Population Born in								
	Any Foreign Country	Asia	Mexico	Europe	Caribbean	Central America[2]	South America	Africa	Canada
City	9.0	2.0	0.6	1.1	0.1	1.7	0.2	3.2	0.1
MSA[1]	6.7	1.5	0.5	0.9	0.1	1.2	0.1	2.2	0.1
U.S.	13.9	4.3	3.3	1.4	1.4	1.2	1.2	0.8	0.2

Note: (1) Figures cover the Sioux Falls, SD-MN Metropolitan Statistical Area; (2) Excludes Mexico.
Source: U.S. Census Bureau, 2019-2023 American Community Survey 5-Year Estimates

Household Size

Area	Persons in Household (%)							Average Household Size
	One	Two	Three	Four	Five	Six	Seven or More	
City	33.9	33.0	12.9	10.3	6.9	1.8	1.2	2.32
MSA[1]	30.0	34.4	13.6	11.4	7.3	2.1	1.2	2.41
U.S.	28.5	33.8	15.4	12.7	5.9	2.3	1.4	2.54

Note: (1) Figures cover the Sioux Falls, SD-MN Metropolitan Statistical Area
Source: U.S. Census Bureau, 2019-2023 American Community Survey 5-Year Estimates

Household Relationships

Area	Householder	Opposite-sex Spouse	Same-sex Spouse	Opposite-sex Unmarried Partner	Same-sex Unmarried Partner	Child[2]	Grandchild	Other Relatives	Non-relatives
City	40.7	18.0	0.1	3.2	0.1	28.4	1.1	2.7	3.1
MSA[1]	39.5	19.4	0.1	2.9	0.1	29.8	1.1	2.3	2.6
U.S.	38.3	17.5	0.2	2.5	0.2	28.3	2.4	4.8	3.4

Note: Figures are percent of the total population; (1) Figures cover the Sioux Falls, SD-MN Metropolitan Statistical Area; (2) Includes biological, adopted, and stepchildren of the householder
Source: U.S. Census Bureau, 2020 Census

Gender

Area	Males	Females	Males per 100 Females
City	99,791	97,851	102.0
MSA[1]	148,246	144,861	102.3
U.S.	164,545,087	167,842,453	98.0

Note: (1) Figures cover the Sioux Falls, SD-MN Metropolitan Statistical Area
Source: U.S. Census Bureau, 2019-2023 American Community Survey 5-Year Estimates

Marital Status

Area	Never Married	Now Married[2]	Separated	Widowed	Divorced
City	34.5	48.4	1.4	4.3	11.4
MSA[1]	30.7	53.1	1.1	4.3	10.8
U.S.	34.1	47.9	1.7	5.6	10.7

Note: Figures are percentages and cover the population 15 years of age and older; (1) Figures cover the Sioux Falls, SD-MN Metropolitan Statistical Area; (2) Excludes separated
Source: U.S. Census Bureau, 2019-2023 American Community Survey 5-Year Estimates

Religious Groups by Family

Area	Catholic	Baptist	Methodist	LDS[2]	Pentecostal	Lutheran	Islam	Adventist	Other
MSA[1]	13.1	0.7	2.9	0.7	1.7	16.4	0.1	0.6	20.3
U.S.	18.7	7.3	3.0	2.0	1.8	1.7	1.3	1.3	11.6

Note: Figures are the number of adherents as a percentage of the total population and cover the eight largest religious groups in the U.S; (1) Figures cover the Sioux Falls, SD-MN Metropolitan Statistical Area; (2) Church of Jesus Christ of Latter-day Saints
Sources: 2020 U.S. Religion Census, Association of Statisticians of American Religious Bodies; The Association of Religion Data Archives (ARDA)

Religious Groups by Tradition

Area	Catholic	Evangelical Protestant	Mainline Protestant	Black Protestant	Islam	Judaism	Hinduism	Orthodox	Buddhism
MSA[1]	13.1	21.0	20.2	0.1	0.1	n/a	n/a	0.8	<0.1
U.S.	18.7	16.5	5.2	2.3	1.3	0.6	0.4	0.4	0.3

Note: Figures are the number of adherents as a percentage of the total population; (1) Figures cover the Sioux Falls, SD-MN Metropolitan Statistical Area
Sources: 2020 U.S. Religion Census, Association of Statisticians of American Religious Bodies; The Association of Religion Data Archives (ARDA)

ECONOMY

Real Gross Domestic Product (GDP)

Area	2017	2018	2019	2020	2021	2022	2023	Rank[3]
MSA[1]	22.2	21.9	22.8	22.0	23.2	22.8	23.2	128
U.S.[2]	17,619.1	18,160.7	18,642.5	18,238.9	19,387.6	19,896.6	20,436.3	—

Note: Figures are in billions of chained 2017 dollars; (1) Figures cover the Sioux Falls, SD-MN Metropolitan Statistical Area; (2) Figures cover real GDP within metropolitan areas; (3) Rank is based on 2023 data and ranges from 1 to 384
Source: U.S. Bureau of Economic Analysis

Economic Growth

Area	2014	2015	2016	2017	2018	2019	2020	2021	2022	2023
MSA[1]	5.5	1.3	1.4	1.5	-1.2	4.3	-3.5	5.4	-2.0	2.0
U.S.[2]	2.6	3.2	2.0	2.7	3.1	2.7	-2.2	6.3	2.6	2.7

Note: Figures are real gross domestic product growth rates and represent percent change from preceding period; (1) Figures cover the Sioux Falls, SD-MN Metropolitan Statistical Area; (2) Figures are the average growth rates within metropolitan areas
Source: U.S. Bureau of Economic Analysis

Metropolitan Area Exports

Area	2018	2019	2020	2021	2022	2023	Rank[2]
MSA[1]	400.0	431.5	524.9	547.3	371.3	510.9	224
U.S.	1,664,056.1	1,645,173.7	1,431,406.6	1,753,941.4	2,062,937.4	2,019,160.5	—

Note: Figures are in millions of dollars; (1) Figures cover the Sioux Falls, SD-MN Metropolitan Statistical Area; (2) Rank is based on 2023 data and ranges from 1 to 386
Source: U.S. Department of Commerce, International Trade Administration, Office of Trade and Economic Analysis, Industry and Analysis, Exports by Metropolitan Area, data extracted April 2, 2025

Building Permits

Area	Single-Family			Multi-Family			Total		
	2023	2024	Pct. Chg.	2023	2024	Pct. Chg.	2023	2024	Pct. Chg.
City	750	880	17.3	1,986	1,239	-37.6	2,736	2,119	-22.6
MSA[1]	1,155	1,270	10.0	2,284	1,532	-32.9	3,439	2,802	-18.5
U.S.	920,000	981,900	6.7	591,100	496,100	-16.1	1,511,100	1,478,000	-2.2

Note: (1) Figures cover the Sioux Falls, SD-MN Metropolitan Statistical Area; Figures represent new, privately-owned housing units authorized (unadjusted data)
Source: U.S. Census Bureau, Building Permits Survey (BPS), 2023, 2024

Bankruptcy Filings

Area	Business Filings			Nonbusiness Filings		
	2023	2024	% Chg.	2023	2024	% Chg.
Minnehaha County	10	8	-20.0	220	220	0.0
U.S.	18,926	23,107	22.1	434,064	494,201	13.9

Note: Business filings include Chapter 7, Chapter 9, Chapter 11, Chapter 12, Chapter 13, Chapter 15, and Section 304; Nonbusiness filings include Chapter 7, Chapter 11, and Chapter 13
Source: Administrative Office of the U.S. Courts, Business and Nonbusiness Bankruptcy, County Cases Commenced by Chapter of the Bankruptcy Code, During the 12-Month Period Ending December 31, 2023 and Business and Nonbusiness Bankruptcy, County Cases Commenced by Chapter of the Bankruptcy Code, During the 12-Month Period Ending December 31, 2024

Housing Vacancy Rates

Area	Gross Vacancy Rate[3] (%)			Year-Round Vacancy Rate[4] (%)			Rental Vacancy Rate[5] (%)			Homeowner Vacancy Rate[6] (%)		
	2022	2023	2024	2022	2023	2024	2022	2023	2024	2022	2023	2024
MSA[1]	n/a	n/a	n/a	n/a	n/a	n/a	n/a	n/a	n/a	n/a	n/a	n/a
U.S.[2]	9.1	9.0	9.1	7.5	7.5	7.6	5.7	6.5	6.8	0.8	0.8	1.0

Note: (1) Figures cover the Sioux Falls, SD-MN Metropolitan Statistical Area; (2) Figures cover the 75 largest Metropolitan Statistical Areas; (3) The percentage of the total housing inventory that is vacant; (4) The percentage of the housing inventory (excluding seasonal units) that is year-round vacant; (5) The percentage of rental inventory that is vacant for rent; (6) The percentage of homeowner inventory that is vacant for sale; n/a not available
Source: U.S. Census Bureau, Housing Vacancies and Homeownership Annual Statistics: 2022, 2023, 2024

INCOME

Income

Area	Per Capita ($)	Median Household ($)	Average Household ($)
City	43,231	74,714	102,058
MSA[1]	43,434	81,418	106,253
U.S.	43,289	78,538	110,491

Note: (1) Figures cover the Sioux Falls, SD-MN Metropolitan Statistical Area
Source: U.S. Census Bureau, 2019-2023 American Community Survey 5-Year Estimates

Household Income Distribution

Area	Percent of Households Earning							
	Under $15,000	$15,000 -$24,999	$25,000 -$34,999	$35,000 -$49,999	$50,000 -$74,999	$75,000 -$99,999	$100,000 -$149,999	$150,000 and up
City	6.0	5.5	7.5	12.3	18.8	14.3	18.6	16.9
MSA[1]	5.4	5.2	6.6	11.6	17.7	14.7	20.0	18.9
U.S.	8.5	6.6	6.8	10.4	15.7	12.7	17.4	21.9

Note: (1) Figures cover the Sioux Falls, SD-MN Metropolitan Statistical Area
Source: U.S. Census Bureau, 2019-2023 American Community Survey 5-Year Estimates

Poverty Rate

Area	All Ages	Under 18 Years Old	18 to 64 Years Old	65 Years and Over
City	9.6	12.3	9.1	7.1
MSA[1]	8.1	9.7	7.7	6.8
U.S.	12.4	16.3	11.6	10.4

Note: Figures are percentage of people whose income during the past 12 months was below the poverty level; (1) Figures cover the Sioux Falls, SD-MN Metropolitan Statistical Area
Source: U.S. Census Bureau, 2019-2023 American Community Survey 5-Year Estimates

EMPLOYMENT

Labor Force and Employment

Area	Civilian Labor Force			Workers Employed		
	Dec. 2023	Dec. 2024	% Chg.	Dec. 2023	Dec. 2024	% Chg.
City	113,602	115,243	1.4	111,615	112,947	1.2
MSA[1]	171,226	173,604	1.4	168,466	170,431	1.2
U.S.	166,661,000	167,746,000	0.7	160,754,000	161,294,000	0.3

Note: Data is not seasonally adjusted and covers workers 16 years of age and older; (1) Figures cover the Sioux Falls, SD-MN Metropolitan Statistical Area
Source: Bureau of Labor Statistics, Local Area Unemployment Statistics

Unemployment Rate

Area	2024											
	Jan.	Feb.	Mar.	Apr.	May	Jun.	Jul.	Aug.	Sep.	Oct.	Nov.	Dec.
City	1.9	2.2	1.7	1.7	1.6	1.8	1.6	1.8	1.4	1.6	1.6	2.0
MSA[1]	1.8	2.1	1.6	1.6	1.6	1.8	1.5	1.8	1.3	1.5	1.5	1.8
U.S.	4.1	4.2	3.9	3.5	3.7	4.3	4.5	4.4	3.9	3.9	4.0	3.8

Note: Data is not seasonally adjusted and covers workers 16 years of age and older; (1) Figures cover the Sioux Falls, SD-MN Metropolitan Statistical Area
Source: Bureau of Labor Statistics, Local Area Unemployment Statistics

Average Wages

Occupation	$/Hr.	Occupation	$/Hr.
Accountants and Auditors	40.80	Maintenance and Repair Workers	23.21
Automotive Mechanics	28.20	Marketing Managers	78.00
Bookkeepers	21.98	Network and Computer Systems Admin.	37.26
Carpenters	23.96	Nurses, Licensed Practical	24.52
Cashiers	14.91	Nurses, Registered	34.16
Computer Programmers	n/a	Nursing Assistants	18.18
Computer Systems Analysts	48.25	Office Clerks, General	18.51
Computer User Support Specialists	23.81	Physical Therapists	42.66
Construction Laborers	20.75	Physicians	n/a
Cooks, Restaurant	17.44	Plumbers, Pipefitters and Steamfitters	27.31
Customer Service Representatives	21.01	Police and Sheriff's Patrol Officers	37.35
Dentists	89.53	Postal Service Mail Carriers	29.60
Electricians	28.14	Real Estate Sales Agents	44.83
Engineers, Electrical	48.75	Retail Salespersons	20.29
Fast Food and Counter Workers	15.01	Sales Representatives, Technical/Scientific	72.14
Financial Managers	86.95	Secretaries, Exc. Legal/Medical/Executive	19.77
First-Line Supervisors of Office Workers	31.03	Security Guards	19.11
General and Operations Managers	76.69	Surgeons	n/a
Hairdressers/Cosmetologists	23.12	Teacher Assistants, Exc. Postsecondary[1]	13.44
Home Health and Personal Care Aides	18.16	Teachers, Secondary School, Exc. Sp. Ed.[1]	24.78
Janitors and Cleaners	16.68	Telemarketers	n/a
Landscaping/Groundskeeping Workers	17.48	Truck Drivers, Heavy/Tractor-Trailer	28.36
Lawyers	64.81	Truck Drivers, Light/Delivery Services	21.88
Maids and Housekeeping Cleaners	15.77	Waiters and Waitresses	15.30

Note: Wage data covers the Sioux Falls, SD-MN Metropolitan Statistical Area; (1) Hourly wages were calculated from annual wage data based on a 40 hour work week
Source: Bureau of Labor Statistics, Metro Area Occupational Employment & Wage Estimates, May 2024

Employment by Industry

Sector	MSA[1]		U.S.
	Number of Employees	Percent of Total	Percent of Total
Construction, Mining, and Logging	12,200	6.8	5.5
Financial Activities	14,800	8.2	5.8
Government	17,000	9.5	14.9
Information	2,700	1.5	1.9
Leisure and Hospitality	16,300	9.1	10.4
Manufacturing	15,600	8.7	8.0
Other Services	6,700	3.7	3.7
Private Education and Health Services	38,700	21.6	16.9
Professional and Business Services	17,500	9.7	14.2
Retail Trade	20,400	11.4	10.0
Transportation, Warehousing, and Utilities	8,200	4.6	4.8
Wholesale Trade	9,400	5.2	3.9

Note: Figures are non-farm employment as of December 2024. Figures are not seasonally adjusted and include workers 16 years of age and older; (1) Figures cover the Sioux Falls, SD-MN Metropolitan Statistical Area
Source: Bureau of Labor Statistics, Current Employment Statistics, Employment, Hours, and Earnings

Employment by Occupation

Occupation Classification	City (%)	MSA[1] (%)	U.S. (%)
Management, Business, Science, and Arts	41.1	41.5	42.0
Natural Resources, Construction, and Maintenance	8.1	9.2	8.6
Production, Transportation, and Material Moving	14.5	14.1	13.0
Sales and Office	20.4	20.0	19.9
Service	15.8	15.2	16.5

Note: Figures cover employed civilians 16 years of age and older; (1) Figures cover the Sioux Falls, SD-MN Metropolitan Statistical Area
Source: U.S. Census Bureau, 2019-2023 American Community Survey 5-Year Estimates

Occupations with Greatest Projected Employment Growth: 2022 – 2032

Occupation[1]	2022 Employment	2032 Projected Employment	Numeric Employment Change	Percent Employment Change
Registered Nurses	14,590	16,510	1,920	13.2
Fast Food and Counter Workers	14,570	16,170	1,600	11.0
Farmers, Ranchers, and Other Agricultural Managers	21,350	22,750	1,400	6.6
Stockers and Order Fillers	9,190	10,380	1,190	12.9
Retail Salespersons	13,960	15,050	1,090	7.8
Janitors and Cleaners, Except Maids and Housekeeping Cleaners	9,540	10,440	900	9.4
Heavy and Tractor-Trailer Truck Drivers	7,560	8,300	740	9.8
Home Health and Personal Care Aides	4,620	5,340	720	15.6
Carpenters	6,120	6,780	660	10.8
Accountants and Auditors	6,180	6,830	650	10.5

Note: Projections cover South Dakota; (1) Sorted by numeric employment change
Source: www.projectionscentral.org, State Occupational Projections, 2022–2032 Long-Term Projections

Fastest-Growing Occupations: 2022 – 2032

Occupation[1]	2022 Employment	2032 Projected Employment	Numeric Employment Change	Percent Employment Change
Nurse Practitioners	820	1,280	460	56.1
Wind Turbine Service Technicians	160	240	80	50.0
Information Security Analysts (SOC 2018)	710	980	270	38.0
Physician Assistants	590	790	200	33.9
Physical Therapist Assistants	340	450	110	32.4
Cooks, Restaurant	1,590	2,090	500	31.4
Medical and Health Services Managers	1,000	1,280	280	28.0
Nurse Anesthetists	360	460	100	27.8
Medical Equipment Repairers	330	420	90	27.3
Industrial Machinery Mechanics	1,250	1,590	340	27.2

Note: Projections cover South Dakota; (1) Sorted by percent employment change and excludes occupations with numeric employment change less than 50
Source: www.projectionscentral.org, State Occupational Projections, 2022–2032 Long-Term Projections

CITY FINANCES

City Government Finances

Component	2022 ($000)	2022 ($ per capita)
Total Revenues	433,506	2,308
Total Expenditures	372,929	1,986
Debt Outstanding	287,189	1,529

Source: U.S. Census Bureau, State & Local Government Finances 2022

City Government Revenue by Source

Source	2022 ($000)	2022 ($ per capita)	2022 (%)
General Revenue			
From Federal Government	46,480	247	10.7
From State Government	10,304	55	2.4
From Local Governments	71	0	0.0
Taxes			
Property	74,350	396	17.2
Sales and Gross Receipts	176,651	941	40.7
Personal Income	0	0	0.0
Corporate Income	0	0	0.0
Motor Vehicle License	0	0	0.0
Other Taxes	7,002	37	1.6
Current Charges	62,371	332	14.4
Liquor Store	0	0	0.0
Utility	50,622	270	11.7

Source: U.S. Census Bureau, State & Local Government Finances 2022

City Government Expenditures by Function

Function	2022 ($000)	2022 ($ per capita)	2022 (%)
General Direct Expenditures			
Air Transportation	0	0	0.0
Corrections	0	0	0.0
Education	0	0	0.0
Employment Security Administration	0	0	0.0
Financial Administration	3,203	17	0.9
Fire Protection	37,918	201	10.2
General Public Buildings	2,342	12	0.6
Governmental Administration, Other	4,001	21	1.1
Health	14,659	78	3.9
Highways	83,293	443	22.3
Hospitals	0	0	0.0
Housing and Community Development	14,587	77	3.9
Interest on General Debt	8,360	44	2.2
Judicial and Legal	1,975	10	0.5
Libraries	9,682	51	2.6
Parking	1,198	6	0.3
Parks and Recreation	32,317	172	8.7
Police Protection	42,916	228	11.5
Public Welfare	0	0	0.0
Sewerage	42,732	227	11.5
Solid Waste Management	9,931	52	2.7
Veterans' Services	0	0	0.0
Liquor Store	0	0	0.0
Utility	54,384	289	14.6

Source: U.S. Census Bureau, State & Local Government Finances 2022

TAXES

State Corporate Income Tax Rates

State	Tax Rate (%)	Income Brackets ($)	Num. of Brackets	Financial Institution Tax Rate (%)[a]	Federal Income Tax Ded.
South Dakota	None	–	–	6.0-0.25 (b)	No

Note: Tax rates for tax year 2024; (a) Rates listed are the corporate income tax rate applied to financial institutions or excise taxes based on income. Some states have other taxes based upon the value of deposits or shares; (b) Minimum tax is $800 in California, $250 in District of Columbia, $50 in Arizona and North Dakota (banks), $400 ($100 banks) in Rhode Island, $200 per location in South Dakota (banks), $100 in Utah, in Vermont, simplified entity business tax for residents only at $250, otherwise minimum tax ($100 - $100,000) is based upon gross receipts.

Source: Federation of Tax Administrators, State Corporate Income Tax Rates, January 1, 2025

State Individual Income Tax Rates

State	Tax Rate (%)	Income Brackets ($)	Personal Exemptions ($)			Standard Ded. ($)	
			Single	Married	Depend.	Single	Married
South Dakota					– No state income tax –		

Note: Tax rates for tax year 2024; Local- and county-level taxes are not included
Source: Federation of Tax Administrators, State Individual Income Tax Rates, January 1, 2025

Various State Sales and Excise Tax Rates

State	State Sales Tax (%)	Gasoline[1] ($/gal.)	Cigarette[2] ($/pack)	Spirits[3] ($/gal.)	Wine[4] ($/gal.)	Beer[5] ($/gal.)	Recreational Marijuana (%)
South Dakota	4.2	0.30	1.53	4.93	1.44	0.27	Not legal

Note: All tax rates as of January 1, 2025; (1) The American Petroleum Institute has developed a methodology for determining the average tax rate on a gallon of fuel. Rates may include any of the following: excise taxes, environmental fees, storage tank fees, other fees or taxes, general sales tax, and local taxes; (2) The federal excise tax of $1.0066 per pack and local taxes are not included; (3) Rates are those applicable to off-premise sales of 40% alcohol by volume (a.b.v.) distilled spirits in 750ml containers. Local excise taxes are excluded; (4) Rates are those applicable to off-premise sales of 11% a.b.v. non-carbonated wine in 750ml containers; (5) Rates are those applicable to off-premise sales of 4.7% a.b.v. beer in 12 ounce containers.
Source: Tax Foundation, 2025 Facts & Figures: How Does Your State Compare?

State Tax Competitiveness Index

State	Overall Rank	Corporate Tax Rank	Individual Income Tax Rank	Sales Tax Rank	Property Tax Rank	Unemployment Insurance Tax Rank
South Dakota	2	1	1	31	10	22

Note: The Tax Foundation's State Tax Competitiveness Index enables policymakers, taxpayers, and business leaders to gauge how their states' tax systems compare. A rank of 1 is best, 50 is worst. Rankings do not average to the total. States without a tax rank equally as 1. DC's scores and rankings do not affect other states. The report shows tax systems as of July 1, 2024 (the beginning of Fiscal Year 2025).
Source: Tax Foundation, State Tax Competitiveness Index 2025

TRANSPORTATION

Means of Transportation to Work

Area	Car/Truck/Van		Public Transportation			Bicycle	Walked	Other Means	Worked at Home
	Drove Alone	Car-pooled	Bus	Subway	Railroad				
City	79.4	7.7	0.7	0.0	0.0	0.2	1.9	0.9	9.4
MSA[1]	79.3	7.2	0.5	0.0	0.0	0.1	2.0	0.8	10.1
U.S.	70.2	8.5	1.7	1.3	0.4	0.4	2.4	1.6	13.5

Note: Figures are percentages and cover workers 16 years of age and older; (1) Figures cover the Sioux Falls, SD-MN Metropolitan Statistical Area
Source: U.S. Census Bureau, 2019-2023 American Community Survey 5-Year Estimates

Travel Time to Work

Area	Less Than 10 Minutes	10 to 19 Minutes	20 to 29 Minutes	30 to 44 Minutes	45 to 59 Minutes	60 to 89 Minutes	90 Minutes or More
City	15.9	52.2	22.0	6.2	1.5	1.0	1.2
MSA[1]	17.3	43.1	23.9	10.5	2.5	1.3	1.3
U.S.	12.6	28.6	21.2	20.8	8.1	6.0	2.8

Note: Note: Figures are percentages and include workers 16 years old and over; (1) Figures cover the Sioux Falls, SD-MN Metropolitan Statistical Area
Source: U.S. Census Bureau, 2019-2023 American Community Survey 5-Year Estimates

Key Congestion Measures

Measure	2000	2010	2015	2020	2022
Annual Hours of Delay, Total (000)	n/a	n/a	3,176	1,708	3,159
Annual Hours of Delay, Per Auto Commuter	n/a	n/a	18	9	17
Annual Congestion Cost, Per Auto Commuter ($)	n/a	n/a	409	230	409

Note: n/a not available
Source: Texas A&M Transportation Institute, 2023 Urban Mobility Report

Freeway Travel Time Index

Measure	1985	1990	1995	2000	2005	2010	2015	2020	2022
Urban Area Index[1]	n/a	n/a	n/a	n/a	n/a	n/a	1.05	1.03	1.08
Urban Area Rank[1,2]	n/a	n/a	n/a	n/a	n/a	n/a	n/a	n/a	n/a

Note: Freeway Travel Time Index—the ratio of travel time in the peak period to the travel time at free-flow conditions. For example, a value of 1.30 indicates a 20-minute free-flow trip takes 26 minutes in the peak (20 minutes x 1.30 = 26 minutes); (1) Covers the Sioux Falls SD urban area; (2) Rank is based on 101 larger urban areas (#1 = highest travel time index); n/a not available
Source: Texas A&M Transportation Institute, 2023 Urban Mobility Report

Public Transportation

Agency Name / Mode of Transportation	Vehicles Operated in Maximum Service[1]	Annual Unlinked Passenger Trips[2] (in thous.)	Annual Passenger Miles[3] (in thous.)
Sioux Falls Transit			
Bus (directly operated)	16	499.7	1,731.1
Demand Response (directly operated)	15	55.0	316.7

Note: (1) Number of revenue vehicles operated by the given mode and type of service to meet the annual maximum service requirement. This is the revenue vehicle count during the peak season of the year; on the week and day that maximum service is provided. Vehicles operated in maximum service (VOMS) exclude atypical days and one-time special events; (2) Number of passengers who boarded public transportation vehicles. Passengers are counted each time they board a vehicle no matter how many vehicles they use to travel from their origin to their destination. (3) Sum of the distances ridden by all passengers during the entire fiscal year.
Source: Federal Transit Administration, National Transit Database, 2023

Air Transportation

Airport Name and Code / Type of Service	Passenger Airlines[1]	Passenger Enplanements	Freight Carriers[2]	Freight (lbs)
Joe Foss Field (FSD)				
Domestic service (U.S. carriers only)	19	700,851	8	39,795,889
International service (U.S. carriers only)	2	161	1	19,840,430

Note: (1) Includes all U.S.-based major, minor and commuter airlines that carried at least one passenger during the year; (2) Includes all U.S.-based airlines and freight carriers that transported at least one pound of freight during the year.
Source: Bureau of Transportation Statistics, The Intermodal Transportation Database, Air Carriers: T-100 Domestic Market (U.S. carriers only), 2024; Bureau of Transportation Statistics, The Intermodal Transportation Database, Air Carriers: T-100 International Market (U.S. carriers only), 2024

BUSINESSES

Major Business Headquarters

Company Name	Industry	Rankings	
		Fortune[1]	Forbes[2]
No companies listed	-	-	-

Note: (1) Companies that produce a 10-K are ranked 1 to 500 based on 2023 revenue; (2) All private companies with at least $2 billion in annual revenue through the end of their most current fiscal year are ranked 1 to 275; companies listed are headquartered in the city; dashes indicate no ranking
Source: Fortune, "Fortune 500," 2024; Forbes, "America's Largest Private Companies," 2024

Living Environment

COST OF LIVING

Cost of Living Index

Composite Index	Groceries	Housing	Utilities	Trans-portation	Health Care	Misc. Goods/Services
91.0	96.4	88.5	91.3	89.9	92.6	90.7

Note: The Cost of Living Index measures regional differences in the cost of consumer goods and services, excluding taxes and non-consumer expenditures, for professional and managerial households in the top income quintile. It is based on more than 50,000 prices covering almost 60 different items for which prices are collected three times a year by chambers of commerce, economic development organizations or university applied economic centers in each participating urban area. The numbers shown should be read as a percentage above or below the national average of 100. For example, a value of 115.4 in the groceries column indicates that grocery prices are 15.4% higher than the national average. Small differences in the index numbers should not be interpreted as significant; Figures cover the Sioux Falls SD urban area.
Source: The Council for Community and Economic Research, Cost of Living Index, 2024

Grocery Prices

Area[1]	T-Bone Steak ($/pound)	Frying Chicken ($/pound)	Whole Milk ($/half gal.)	Eggs ($/dozen)	Orange Juice ($/64 oz.)	Coffee ($/11.5 oz.)
City[2]	15.53	1.49	4.52	3.10	4.37	5.10
Avg.	15.42	1.55	4.69	3.25	4.41	5.46
Min.	14.50	1.16	4.43	2.75	4.00	4.85
Max.	17.56	2.89	4.78	5.49	5.54	7.89

Note: (1) Values for the local area are compared with the average, minimum and maximum values for all 276 areas in the Cost of Living Index; (2) Figures cover the Sioux Falls SD urban area; **T-Bone Steak** (price per pound); **Frying Chicken** (price per pound, whole fryer); **Whole Milk** (half gallon carton); **Eggs** (price per dozen, Grade A, large); **Orange Juice** (64 oz. Tropicana or Florida Natural); **Coffee** (11.5 oz. can, vacuum-packed, Maxwell House, Hills Bros, or Folgers).
Source: The Council for Community and Economic Research, Cost of Living Index, 2024

Housing and Utility Costs

Area[1]	New Home Price ($)	Apartment Rent ($/month)	All Electric ($/month)	Part Electric ($/month)	Other Energy ($/month)	Telephone ($/month)
City[2]	509,371	977	-	103.68	71.55	198.68
Avg.	515,975	1,550	210.99	123.07	82.07	194.99
Min.	265,375	692	104.33	53.68	36.26	179.42
Max.	2,775,821	5,719	529.02	397.28	361.63	223.33

Note: (1) Values for the local area are compared with the average, minimum and maximum values for all 276 areas in the Cost of Living Index; (2) Figures cover the Sioux Falls SD urban area; **New Home Price** (2,400 sf living area, 8,000 sf lot, in urban area with full utilities); **Apartment Rent** (950 sf 2 bedroom/1.5 or 2 bath, unfurnished, excluding all utilities except water); **All Electric** (average monthly cost for an all-electric home); **Part Electric** (average monthly cost for a part-electric home); **Other Energy** (average monthly cost for natural gas, fuel oil, coal, wood, and any other forms of energy except electricity); **Telephone** (price includes the base monthly rate plus taxes and fees for three lines of mobile phone service).
Source: The Council for Community and Economic Research, Cost of Living Index, 2024

Health Care, Transportation, and Other Costs

Area[1]	Doctor ($/visit)	Dentist ($/visit)	Optometrist ($/visit)	Gasoline ($/gallon)	Beauty Salon ($/visit)	Men's Shirt ($)
City[2]	116.42	116.32	140.94	3.04	40.11	30.74
Avg.	143.77	117.51	129.23	3.32	48.57	38.14
Min.	36.74	58.67	67.33	2.80	24.00	13.41
Max.	270.44	216.82	307.33	5.28	94.00	63.89

Note: (1) Values for the local area are compared with the average, minimum and maximum values for all 276 areas in the Cost of Living Index; (2) Figures cover the Sioux Falls SD urban area; **Doctor** (general practitioners routine exam of an established patient); **Dentist** (adult teeth cleaning and periodic oral examination); **Optometrist** (full vision eye exam for established adult patient); **Gasoline** (one gallon regular unleaded, national brand, including all taxes, cash price at self-service pump if available); **Beauty Salon** (woman's shampoo, trim, and blow-dry); **Men's Shirt** (cotton/polyester dress shirt, pinpoint weave, long sleeves).
Source: The Council for Community and Economic Research, Cost of Living Index, 2024

HOUSING

Homeownership Rate

Area	2017 (%)	2018 (%)	2019 (%)	2020 (%)	2021 (%)	2022 (%)	2023 (%)	2024 (%)
MSA[1]	n/a	n/a	n/a	n/a	n/a	n/a	n/a	n/a
U.S.	63.9	64.4	64.6	66.6	65.5	65.8	65.9	65.6

Note: (1) Figures cover the Sioux Falls, SD-MN Metropolitan Statistical Area; n/a not available
Source: U.S. Census Bureau, Housing Vacancies and Homeownership Annual Statistics: 2017-2024

House Price Index (HPI)

Area	National Ranking[2]	Quarterly Change (%)	One-Year Change (%)	Five-Year Change (%)	Since 1991Q1 (%)
MSA[1]	224	0.06	2.21	52.27	347.79
U.S.[3]	—	1.43	4.51	57.13	327.82

Note: The HPI is a weighted repeat sales index. It measures average price changes in repeat sales or refinancings on the same properties. This information is obtained by reviewing repeat mortgage transactions on single-family properties whose mortgages have been purchased or securitized by Fannie Mae or Freddie Mac since January 1975; (1) Figures cover the Sioux Falls, SD Metropolitan Statistical Area; (2) Rankings are based on annual percentage change for all metro areas containing at least 15,000 transactions over the last 10 years and ranges from 1 to 241; (3) figures based on a weighted average of Census Division estimates using a seasonally adjusted, purchase-only index; all figures are for the period ending December 31, 2024
Source: Federal Housing Finance Agency, Change in FHFA Metropolitan Area House Price Indexes, All Transactions Index, 2024Q4

Home Value

Area	Under $100,000	$100,000 -$199,999	$200,000 -$299,999	$300,000 -$399,999	$400,000 -$499,999	$500,000 -$999,999	$1,000,000 or more	Median ($)
City	7.9	18.0	32.8	18.7	10.0	10.5	2.2	271,400
MSA[1]	8.4	18.3	30.7	18.5	10.4	11.8	1.9	274,800
U.S.	12.1	17.8	19.5	14.4	10.5	19.1	6.5	303,400

Note: Figures are percentages except for median and cover owner-occupied housing units; (1) Figures cover the Sioux Falls, SD-MN Metropolitan Statistical Area
Source: U.S. Census Bureau, 2019-2023 American Community Survey 5-Year Estimates

Year Housing Structure Built

Area	2020 or Later	2010 -2019	2000 -2009	1990 -1999	1980 -1989	1970 -1979	1960 -1969	1950 -1959	1940 -1949	Before 1940	Median Year
City	2.0	19.1	18.4	13.3	10.6	10.4	6.5	8.0	3.0	8.6	1992
MSA[1]	1.9	17.3	17.9	13.6	9.2	11.2	6.3	7.4	3.1	12.2	1990
U.S.	1.2	8.9	13.6	12.8	13.0	14.4	10.0	9.7	4.5	11.9	1980

Note: Figures are percentages except for Median Year; Note: (1) Figures cover the Sioux Falls, SD-MN Metropolitan Statistical Area
Source: U.S. Census Bureau, 2019-2023 American Community Survey 5-Year Estimates

Gross Monthly Rent

Area	Under $500	$500 -$999	$1,000 -$1,499	$1,500 -$1,999	$2,000 -$2,499	$2,500 -$2,999	$3,000 and up	Median ($)
City	4.5	46.5	36.9	8.1	2.4	0.3	1.2	993
MSA[1]	5.6	46.3	36.0	8.1	2.6	0.3	1.1	987
U.S.	6.5	22.3	29.5	20.2	10.8	4.8	5.9	1,348

Note: Figures are percentages except for median; Gross rent is the contract rent plus the estimated average monthly cost of utilities (electricity, gas, and water and sewer) and fuels (oil, coal, kerosene, wood, etc.) if these are paid by the renter (or paid for the renter by someone else); (1) Figures cover the Sioux Falls, SD-MN Metropolitan Statistical Area
Source: U.S. Census Bureau, 2019-2023 American Community Survey 5-Year Estimates

HEALTH

Health Risk Factors

Category	MSA[1] (%)	U.S. (%)
Adults aged 18–64 who have any kind of health care coverage	89.5	90.8
Adults who reported being in good or better health	84.7	81.8
Adults who have been told they have high blood cholesterol	31.5	36.9
Adults who have been told they have high blood pressure	32.0	34.0
Adults who are current smokers	9.5	12.1
Adults who currently use e-cigarettes	7.6	7.7
Adults who currently use chewing tobacco, snuff, or snus	1.8	3.2
Adults who are heavy drinkers[2]	8.7	6.1
Adults who are binge drinkers[3]	21.9	15.2
Adults who are overweight (BMI 25.0 - 29.9)	32.2	34.4
Adults who are obese (BMI 30.0 - 99.8)	36.6	34.3
Adults who participated in any physical activities in the past month	76.3	75.8

Note: All figures are crude prevalence; (1) Figures cover the Sioux Falls, SD Metropolitan Statistical Area; (2) Heavy drinkers are classified as adult men having more than 14 drinks per week and adult women having more than 7 drinks per week; (3) Binge drinkers are classified as males having five or more drinks on one occasion or females having four or more drinks on one occasion
Source: Centers for Disease Control and Prevention, Behavioral Risk Factor Surveillance System, SMART: Selected Metropolitan Area Risk Trends, 2023

Acute and Chronic Health Conditions

Category	MSA[1] (%)	U.S. (%)
Adults who have ever been told they had a heart attack	3.8	4.2
Adults who have ever been told they have angina or coronary heart disease	2.9	4.0
Adults who have ever been told they had a stroke	1.8	3.3
Adults who have ever been told they have asthma	12.4	15.7
Adults who have ever been told they have arthritis	22.4	26.3
Adults who have ever been told they have diabetes[2]	11.3	11.5
Adults who have ever been told they had skin cancer	4.6	5.6
Adults who have ever been told they had any other types of cancer	8.5	8.4
Adults who have ever been told they have COPD	5.3	6.4
Adults who have ever been told they have kidney disease	2.8	3.7
Adults who have ever been told they have a form of depression	22.9	22.0

Note: All figures are crude prevalence; (1) Figures cover the Sioux Falls, SD Metropolitan Statistical Area; (2) Figures do not include pregnancy-related, borderline, or pre-diabetes
Source: Centers for Disease Control and Prevention, Behaviorial Risk Factor Surveillance System, SMART: Selected Metropolitan Area Risk Trends, 2023

Health Screening and Vaccination Rates

Category	MSA[1] (%)	U.S. (%)
Adults who have ever been tested for HIV	32.3	37.5
Adults who have had their blood cholesterol checked within the last five years	87.1	87.0
Adults aged 65+ who have had flu shot within the past year	73.1	63.4
Adults aged 65+ who have ever had a pneumonia vaccination	80.4	71.9

Note: All figures are crude prevalence; (1) Figures cover the Sioux Falls, SD Metropolitan Statistical Area.
Source: Centers for Disease Control and Prevention, Behaviorial Risk Factor Surveillance System, SMART: Selected Metropolitan Area Risk Trends, 2023

Disability Status

Category	MSA[1] (%)	U.S. (%)
Adults who reported being deaf	5.5	7.4
Are you blind or have serious difficulty seeing, even when wearing glasses?	2.9	4.9
Do you have difficulty doing errands alone?	8.1	7.8
Do you have difficulty dressing or bathing?	n/a	3.6
Do you have serious difficulty concentrating/remembering/making decisions?	14.6	13.7
Do you have serious difficulty walking or climbing stairs?	11.6	13.2

Note: All figures are crude prevalence; (1) Figures cover the Sioux Falls, SD Metropolitan Statistical Area.
Source: Centers for Disease Control and Prevention, Behaviorial Risk Factor Surveillance System, SMART: Selected Metropolitan Area Risk Trends, 2023

Mortality Rates for the Top 10 Causes of Death in the U.S.

ICD-10[a] Sub-Chapter	ICD-10[a] Code	Crude Mortality Rate[2] per 100,000 population	
		County[3]	U.S.
Malignant neoplasms	C00-C97	174.1	182.7
Ischaemic heart diseases	I20-I25	81.1	109.6
Provisional assignment of new diseases of uncertain etiology[1]	U00-U49	39.0	65.3
Other forms of heart disease	I30-I51	30.1	65.1
Other degenerative diseases of the nervous system	G30-G31	49.8	52.4
Other external causes of accidental injury	W00-X59	42.1	52.3
Cerebrovascular diseases	I60-I69	40.1	49.1
Chronic lower respiratory diseases	J40-J47	34.9	43.5
Hypertensive diseases	I10-I15	55.4	38.9
Organic, including symptomatic, mental disorders	F01-F09	20.6	33.9

Note: (a) ICD-10 = International Classification of Diseases 10th Revision; (1) Includes COVID-19, adverse effects to COVID-19 vaccines, SARS, and vaping-related disorders; (2) Crude mortality rates are a three-year average covering 2021-2023; (3) Figures cover Minnehaha County.
Source: Centers for Disease Control and Prevention, National Center for Health Statistics. National Vital Statistics System, Mortality 2018-2023 on CDC WONDER Online Database

Mortality Rates for Selected Causes of Death

Cause of Death	ICD-10[a] Code	Crude Mortality Rate[1] per 100,000 population	
		County[2]	U.S.
Accidental poisoning and exposure to noxious substances	X40-X49	14.1	30.5
Alzheimer disease	G30	35.7	35.4
Assault	X85-Y09	Unreliable	7.3
COVID-19	U07.1	39.0	65.3
Diabetes mellitus	E10-E14	21.1	30.0
Diseases of the liver	K70-K76	26.4	20.8
Human immunodeficiency virus (HIV) disease	B20-B24	Suppressed	1.5
Influenza and pneumonia	J09-J18	11.1	13.4
Intentional self-harm	X60-X84	16.7	14.7
Malnutrition	E40-E46	10.5	6.0
Obesity and other hyperalimentation	E65-E68	Suppressed	3.1
Renal failure	N17-N19	7.7	16.4
Transport accidents	V01-V99	12.9	14.4

Note: (a) ICD-10 = International Classification of Diseases 10th Revision; (1) Crude mortality rates are a three-year average covering 2021-2023; (2) Figures cover Minnehaha County; Data are suppressed when the data meet the criteria for confidentiality constraints; Crude mortality rates are flagged as unreliable when the rate would be calculated with a numerator of 20 or less.
Source: Centers for Disease Control and Prevention, National Center for Health Statistics. National Vital Statistics System, Mortality 2018-2023 on CDC WONDER Online Database

Health Insurance Coverage

Area	With Health Insurance	With Private Health Insurance	With Public Health Insurance	Without Health Insurance	Population Under Age 19 Without Health Insurance
City	92.2	77.7	25.8	7.8	5.6
MSA[1]	93.1	79.1	25.6	6.9	4.8
U.S.	91.4	67.3	36.3	8.6	5.4

Note: Figures are percentages that cover the civilian noninstitutionalized population; (1) Figures cover the Sioux Falls, SD-MN Metropolitan Statistical Area
Source: U.S. Census Bureau, 2019-2023 American Community Survey 5-Year Estimates

Number of Medical Professionals

Area	MDs[3]	DOs[3,4]	Dentists	Podiatrists	Chiropractors	Optometrists
County[1] (number)	807	64	116	12	119	38
County[1] (rate[2])	395.6	31.4	56.1	5.8	57.5	18.4
U.S. (rate[2])	302.5	29.2	74.6	6.4	29.5	18.0

Note: Data as of 2023 unless noted; (1) Data covers Minnehaha County; (2) Number of medical professionals per 100,000 population; (3) Data as of 2022 and includes all active, non-federal physicians; (4) Doctor of Osteopathic Medicine
Source: U.S. Department of Health and Human Services, Health Resources and Services Administration, Bureau of Health Professions, Area Resource File (ARF) 2023-2024

EDUCATION

Public School District Statistics

District Name	Schls	Pupils	Pupil/Teacher Ratio	Minority Pupils[1] (%)	Total Rev. per Pupil ($)	Total Exp. per Pupil ($)
Sioux Falls School District 49-5	44	25,216	14.8	43.9	13,283	12,493

Note: Table includes school districts with 2,000 or more students; (1) Percentage of students that are not non-Hispanic white.
Source: U.S. Department of Education, National Center for Education Statistics, Common Core of Data, Local Education Agency (School District) Universe Survey: School Year 2023-2024; U.S. Department of Education, National Center for Education Statistics, Common Core of Data, School District Finance Survey (F-33): School Year 2021–22

Highest Level of Education

Area	Less than H.S.	H.S. Diploma	Some College, No Deg.	Associate Degree	Bachelor's Degree	Master's Degree	Prof. School Degree	Doctorate Degree
City	6.9	24.3	20.1	11.2	25.4	8.2	2.5	1.3
MSA[1]	6.3	25.7	19.7	12.6	24.8	7.7	2.0	1.2
U.S.	10.6	26.2	19.4	8.8	21.3	9.8	2.3	1.6

Note: Figures cover persons age 25 and over; (1) Figures cover the Sioux Falls, SD-MN Metropolitan Statistical Area
Source: U.S. Census Bureau, 2019-2023 American Community Survey 5-Year Estimates

Educational Attainment by Race

Area	High School Graduate or Higher (%)					Bachelor's Degree or Higher (%)				
	Total	White	Black	Asian	Hisp.[2]	Total	White	Black	Asian	Hisp.[2]
City	93.1	95.7	83.0	76.0	64.7	37.4	40.0	21.0	42.2	14.8
MSA[1]	93.7	95.6	83.4	76.1	66.5	35.7	37.4	20.1	40.3	16.0
U.S.	89.4	92.9	88.1	88.0	72.5	35.0	37.7	24.7	57.0	19.9

Note: Figures shown cover persons 25 years old and over; (1) Figures cover the Sioux Falls, SD-MN Metropolitan Statistical Area; (2) People of Hispanic origin can be of any race
Source: U.S. Census Bureau, 2019-2023 American Community Survey 5-Year Estimates

School Enrollment by Grade and Control

Area	Preschool (%)		Kindergarten (%)		Grades 1 - 4 (%)		Grades 5 - 8 (%)		Grades 9 - 12 (%)	
	Public	Private	Public	Private	Public	Private	Public	Private	Public	Private
City	59.5	40.5	86.0	14.0	85.9	14.1	86.2	13.8	86.7	13.3
MSA[1]	64.5	35.5	86.8	13.2	86.8	13.2	87.8	12.2	87.7	12.3
U.S.	58.7	41.3	85.2	14.8	87.2	12.8	87.9	12.1	89.0	11.0

Note: Figures shown cover persons 3 years old and over; (1) Figures cover the Sioux Falls, SD-MN Metropolitan Statistical Area
Source: U.S. Census Bureau, 2019-2023 American Community Survey 5-Year Estimates

Higher Education

Four-Year Colleges			Two-Year Colleges			Medical Schools[1]	Law Schools[2]	Voc/Tech[3]
Public	Private Non-profit	Private For-profit	Public	Private Non-profit	Private For-profit			
0	3	1	1	2	0	1	0	1

Note: Figures cover institutions located within the Sioux Falls, SD-MN Metropolitan Statistical Area and include main campuses only; (1) includes schools accredited by the Liaison Committee on Medical Education and the American Osteopathic Association's Commission on Osteopathic College Accreditation; (2) includes ABA-accredited schools, schools with provisional ABA accreditation, and state accredited schools; (3) includes all schools with programs that are less than 2 years.
Source: National Center for Education Statistics, Integrated Postsecondary Education System (IPEDS), 2023-24; Wikipedia, List of Medical Schools in the United States, accessed May 2, 2025; Wikipedia, List of Law Schools in the United States, accessed May 2, 2025

EMPLOYERS

Major Employers

Company Name	Industry
Avera Health	Healthcare
Billion Automotive	Auto dealership
Capital One	Financial/credit card processing
CIGNA	Mail order pharmacy
Citi	Credit card processing
City of Sioux Falls	Municipal government
Department of Veterans Affairs	Government medical facilities
Esurance	Insurance service center
Evangelical Lutheran Good Samaritan	Healthcare
First Premier Bank/Premier Bankcard	Financial/credit card processing
Hy-Vee Food Stores	Retail grocery
John Morrell & Co.	Meat processing
Lewis Drug	Retail pharmacy
LifeScape	Healthcare
Midcontinent Communications	Telecommunications/cable services
Minnehaha County	Government
Raven Industries	Manufacturing
Sammons Financial Group/Midland National	Insurance
Sanford Health	Healthcare
Sioux Falls School District 49-5	Education

Note: Companies shown are located within the Sioux Falls, SD-MN Metropolitan Statistical Area.
Source: Chambers of Commerce; State Departments of Labor; Wikipedia

PUBLIC SAFETY

Crime Rate

Area	Total Crime Rate	Violent Crime Rate				Property Crime Rate		
		Murder	Rape	Robbery	Aggrav. Assault	Burglary	Larceny-Theft	Motor Vehicle Theft
City	2,864.1	0.5	16.9	32.4	385.4	287.6	1,635.4	505.9
U.S.	2,290.9	5.7	38.0	66.5	264.1	250.7	1,347.2	318.7

Note: Figures are crimes per 100,000 population.
Source: FBI, Table 8, Offenses Known to Law Enforcement, by State by City, 2023

Hate Crimes

Area	Number of Quarters Reported	Number of Incidents per Bias Motivation					
		Race/Ethnicity/Ancestry	Religion	Sexual Orientation	Disability	Gender	Gender Identity
City	4	0	0	1	0	0	0
U.S.	4	5,900	2,699	2,077	187	92	492

Source: Federal Bureau of Investigation, Hate Crime Statistics 2023

Identity Theft Consumer Reports

Area	Reports	Reports per 100,000 Population	Rank[2]
MSA[1]	352	120	334
U.S.	1,135,291	339	-

Note: (1) Figures cover the Sioux Falls, SD-MN Metropolitan Statistical Area; (2) Rank ranges from 1 to 401 where 1 indicates greatest number of identity theft reports per 100,000 population
Source: Federal Trade Commission, Consumer Sentinel Network Data Book 2024

Fraud and Other Consumer Reports

Area	Reports	Reports per 100,000 Population	Rank[2]
MSA[1]	2,266	773	336
U.S.	5,360,641	1,601	-

Note: (1) Figures cover the Sioux Falls, SD-MN Metropolitan Statistical Area; (2) Rank ranges from 1 to 401 where 1 indicates greatest number of fraud and other consumer reports per 100,000 population
Source: Federal Trade Commission, Consumer Sentinel Network Data Book 2024

POLITICS

2024 Presidential Election Results

Area	Trump (Rep.)	Harris (Dem.)	Stein (Green)	Kennedy (Ind.)	Oliver (Lib.)	Other
Minnehaha County	55.2	42.5	0.0	1.6	0.7	0.0
U.S.	49.7	48.2	0.6	0.5	0.4	0.6

Note: Results are percentages and may not add to 100% due to rounding
Source: Dave Leip's Atlas of U.S. Presidential Elections

SPORTS

Professional Sports Teams

Team Name	League	Year Established
No teams are located in the metro area		

Source: Wikipedia, Major Professional Sports Teams of the United States and Canada, May 1, 2025

CLIMATE

Average and Extreme Temperatures

Temperature	Jan	Feb	Mar	Apr	May	Jun	Jul	Aug	Sep	Oct	Nov	Dec	Yr.
Extreme High (°F)	66	70	88	94	104	110	110	109	104	94	76	62	110
Average High (°F)	25	30	41	59	71	80	86	84	74	62	43	29	57
Average Temp. (°F)	15	20	32	47	59	69	75	72	62	50	33	20	46
Average Low (°F)	5	10	22	35	47	57	62	60	49	38	23	10	35
Extreme Low (°F)	-36	-31	-23	4	17	33	38	34	22	9	-17	-28	-36

Note: Figures cover the years 1932-1990
Source: National Climatic Data Center, International Station Meteorological Climate Summary, 9/96

Average Precipitation/Snowfall/Humidity

Precip./Humidity	Jan	Feb	Mar	Apr	May	Jun	Jul	Aug	Sep	Oct	Nov	Dec	Yr.
Avg. Precip. (in.)	0.6	0.8	1.6	2.4	3.3	3.9	2.8	3.2	2.8	1.5	1.0	0.7	24.6
Avg. Snowfall (in.)	7	8	9	2	Tr	0	0	0	Tr	Tr	5	7	38
Avg. Rel. Hum. 6am (%)	n/a	n/a	n/a	n/a	n/a	n/a	n/a	n/a	n/a	n/a	n/a	n/a	n/a
Avg. Rel. Hum. 3pm (%)	n/a	n/a	n/a	n/a	n/a	n/a	n/a	n/a	n/a	n/a	n/a	n/a	n/a

Note: Figures cover the years 1932-1990; Tr = Trace amounts (<0.05 in. of rain; <0.5 in. of snow)
Source: National Climatic Data Center, International Station Meteorological Climate Summary, 9/96

Weather Conditions

Temperature			Daytime Sky			Precipitation		
5°F & below	32°F & below	90°F & above	Clear	Partly cloudy	Cloudy	0.01 inch or more precip.	0.1 inch or more snow/ice	Thunder-storms
n/a	n/a	n/a	95	136	134	n/a	n/a	n/a

Note: Figures are average number of days per year and cover the years 1932-1990
Source: National Climatic Data Center, International Station Meteorological Climate Summary, 9/96

HAZARDOUS WASTE

Superfund Sites

The Sioux Falls, SD-MN metro area has no sites on the EPA's Superfund Final National Priorities List (NPL) or Superfund Alternative Approach (SAA) list. The Superfund alternative approach uses the same investigation and cleanup process and standards that are used for sites listed on the National Priorities List. The SAA is an alternative to listing a site on the NPL; it is not an alternative to Superfund or the Superfund process. There are a total of 1,445 Superfund sites with a status of proposed or final on both lists in the United States. *U.S. Environmental Protection Agency, National Priorities List, May 1, 2025; U.S. Environmental Protection Agency, Superfund Alternative Approach Sites, May 1, 2025*

AIR QUALITY

Air Quality Trends: Ozone

	1990	1995	2000	2005	2010	2015	2020	2021	2022	2023
MSA[1]	n/a	n/a	n/a	n/a	n/a	n/a	n/a	n/a	n/a	n/a
U.S.	0.087	0.089	0.081	0.080	0.072	0.068	0.066	0.067	0.067	0.070

Note: (1) Data covers the Sioux Falls, SD-MN Metropolitan Statistical Area; n/a not available. The values shown are the composite ozone concentration averages among trend sites based on the highest fourth daily maximum 8-hour concentration in parts per million. These trends are based on sites having an adequate record of monitoring data during the trend period. Data from exceptional events are included.
Source: U.S. Environmental Protection Agency, Air Quality Monitoring Information, "Air Quality Trends by City, 1990-2023"

Air Quality Index

Area	Percent of Days when Air Quality was...[2]					AQI Statistics[2]	
	Good	Moderate	Unhealthy for Sensitive Groups	Unhealthy	Very Unhealthy	Maximum	Median
MSA[1]	64.4	28.2	6.3	1.1	0.0	181	44

Note: (1) Data covers the Sioux Falls, SD-MN Metropolitan Statistical Area; (2) Based on 365 days with AQI data in 2023. Air Quality Index (AQI) is an index for reporting daily air quality. EPA calculates the AQI for five major air pollutants regulated by the Clean Air Act: ground-level ozone, particle pollution (aka particulate matter), carbon monoxide, sulfur dioxide, and nitrogen dioxide. The AQI runs from 0 to 500. The higher the AQI value, the greater the level of air pollution and the greater the health concern. There are six AQI categories: "Good" AQI is between 0 and 50. Air quality is considered satisfactory; "Moderate" AQI is between 51 and 100. Air quality is acceptable; "Unhealthy for Sensitive Groups" When AQI values are between 101 and 150, members of sensitive groups may experience health effects; "Unhealthy" When AQI values are between 151 and 200 everyone may begin to experience health effects; "Very Unhealthy" AQI values between 201 and 300 trigger a health alert; "Hazardous" AQI values over 300 trigger warnings of emergency conditions (not shown).
Source: U.S. Environmental Protection Agency, Air Quality Index Report, 2023

Air Quality Index Pollutants

Area	Percent of Days when AQI Pollutant was...[2]					
	Carbon Monoxide	Nitrogen Dioxide	Ozone	Sulfur Dioxide	Particulate Matter 2.5	Particulate Matter 10
MSA[1]	0.0	1.6	69.6	(3)	26.3	2.5

Note: (1) Data covers the Sioux Falls, SD-MN Metropolitan Statistical Area; (2) Based on 365 days with AQI data in 2023. The Air Quality Index (AQI) is an index for reporting daily air quality. EPA calculates the AQI for five major air pollutants regulated by the Clean Air Act: ground-level ozone, particle pollution (also known as particulate matter), carbon monoxide, sulfur dioxide, and nitrogen dioxide. The AQI runs from 0 to 500. The higher the AQI value, the greater the level of air pollution and the greater the health concern; (3) Sulfur dioxide is no longer included in this table because SO_2 concentrations tend to be very localized and not necessarily representative of broad geographical areas like counties and CBSAs.
Source: U.S. Environmental Protection Agency, Air Quality Index Report, 2023

Maximum Air Pollutant Concentrations: Particulate Matter, Ozone, CO and Lead

	Particulate Matter 10 (ug/m³)	Particulate Matter 2.5 Wtd AM (ug/m³)	Particulate Matter 2.5 24-Hr (ug/m³)	Ozone (ppm)	Carbon Monoxide (ppm)	Lead (ug/m³)
MSA[1] Level	80	n/a	n/a	0.082	n/a	n/a
NAAQS[2]	150	15	35	0.075	9	0.15
Met NAAQS[2]	Yes	n/a	n/a	No	n/a	n/a

Note: (1) Data covers the Sioux Falls, SD-MN Metropolitan Statistical Area; Data from exceptional events are included; (2) National Ambient Air Quality Standards; ppm = parts per million; ug/m³ = micrograms per cubic meter; n/a not available.
Concentrations: Particulate Matter 10 (coarse particulate)—highest second maximum 24-hour concentration; Particulate Matter 2.5 Wtd AM (fine particulate)—highest weighted annual mean concentration; Particulate Matter 2.5 24-Hour (fine particulate)—highest 98th percentile 24-hour concentration; Ozone—highest fourth daily maximum 8-hour concentration; Carbon Monoxide—highest second maximum non-overlapping 8-hour concentration; Lead—maximum running 3-month average
Source: U.S. Environmental Protection Agency, Air Quality Monitoring Information, "Air Quality Statistics by City, 2023"

Maximum Air Pollutant Concentrations: Nitrogen Dioxide and Sulfur Dioxide

	Nitrogen Dioxide AM (ppb)	Nitrogen Dioxide 1-Hr (ppb)	Sulfur Dioxide AM (ppb)	Sulfur Dioxide 1-Hr (ppb)	Sulfur Dioxide 24-Hr (ppb)
MSA[1] Level	5	40	n/a	1	n/a
NAAQS[2]	53	100	30	75	140
Met NAAQS[2]	Yes	Yes	n/a	Yes	n/a

Note: (1) Data covers the Sioux Falls, SD-MN Metropolitan Statistical Area; Data from exceptional events are included; (2) National Ambient Air Quality Standards; ppm = parts per million; ug/m^3 = micrograms per cubic meter; n/a not available.
Concentrations: Nitrogen Dioxide AM—highest arithmetic mean concentration; Nitrogen Dioxide 1-Hr—highest 98th percentile 1-hour daily maximum concentration; Sulfur Dioxide AM—highest annual mean concentration; Sulfur Dioxide 1-Hr—highest 99th percentile 1-hour daily maximum concentration; Sulfur Dioxide 24-Hr—highest second maximum 24-hour concentration
Source: U.S. Environmental Protection Agency, Air Quality Monitoring Information, "Air Quality Statistics by City, 2023"

Tulsa, Oklahoma

Background

The city of Tulsa sits at the intersection of Tulsa, Osage, Rogers, and Wagoner counties, in northeast Oklahoma on the Arkansas River, between the Osage Hills and the foothills of the Ozark Mountains.

Tulsa was first settled by Creek Indians in 1828. In 1848, Lewis Perryman established the first trading post at the new settlement, and his son George developed a regular mail station at the site in 1878, which came to be called Tulsa, likely from the Talsi (or Talasi) branch of the Creek Native Americans. In 2020, the U.S. Supreme Court ruled that that city was indeed Native American land.

Originally a cattle and dry goods trading center used by ranchers scattered throughout the area, Tulsa was integrated into a wider trade area in 1882 when the Frisco Railroad brought a line into the town. This facilitated new settlers to move into the area and allowed "Tulsey Town," as it was called, to transport cattle throughout the nation. Tulsa was incorporated as a town on January 18, 1898.

Oil was first discovered in the area in 1901 at Red Fork and in 1905 in Glenn Pool, both suburbs of Tulsa. Since then, Tulsa's fortune has been tied to the oil industry. Oklahoma achieved statehood two years after the Glenn Pool strike, the largest at the time, and by 1920 the city was well-known as the "Oil Capital of the World." During this boom period, many of Tulsa's historic buildings were constructed, which explains the city's extraordinary art deco influence in its downtown architecture. The influx of wealthy easterners left parts of the city resembling New York and Philadelphia.

Oil naturally fueled the growth of aviation, and Tulsa was an early aviation center. By the beginning of the Second World War, many of the nation's pilots were being trained at Spartan School of Aeronautics in the city, and Douglas Aircraft in 1942 sited a major plant there. In later years, both McDonnell-Douglas and Rockwell International based aviation and space technology operations in Tulsa.

Today, Tulsa is home to American Airlines' Maintenance & Engineering Center, one of the world's largest such commercial centers. Work began in 2021 on a $550 million major renovation to the center which will be complete in 2028. A new hangar and base support building were the first to be completed.

The city is home to Lufthansa Technik and major employers Saint Francis Health System, Helmerich & Payne, Quik Trip, and Williams Companies.

The city is a hub for logistics, with its busy Tulsa International Airport and Tulsa Port of Catoosa, a 445-mile navigation system that links Tulsa to the Mississippi, making Tulsa a major inland ice-free port, with a designated foreign trade zone, and a 2,000-acre industrial park that includes an Amazon distribution center.

Tulsa is part of the Oklahoma-South Kansas Unmanned Aerial Systems (drone) industry cluster. It is ranked as the third most drone-friendly state. In 2021, Tulsa launched Geeenwood Entrepreneurship Incubator at Moton, providing financing, space, training, networking, and resources for aspiring entrepreneurs that received a $3 million federal grant in 2024.

The city hosts a broad range of cultural and recreational activities, including the Gilcrease Museum, with the world's largest collection of art and artifacts of the American West, and Philbrook Museum of Art. Many cultural activities are sponsored by the city's several universities, including a branch of Oklahoma State University. Discovery Lab, a children's museum, housed in a 50,000-sq-ft. facility with state-of-the-art exhibit experiences, education opportunities with on-site educators.

The city's Cox Business Convention Center includes an assembly hall, the state's largest ballroom, and 34 meeting rooms. The BOK (Bank of Oklahoma) Center is a multi-purpose arena that plays host to the Tulsa Oilers ice hockey team. Minor league baseball team, Tulsa Drillers, play in ONEOK Field, as do the Tulsa Roughnecks FC soccer team. The University of Tulsa's men's basketball team hosts the competitive Golden Hurricane team, and Oral Roberts University's boasts men's basketball team, the Golden Eagles.

Tulsa's weather is humid and subtropical, characterized by hot, humid summers and mild, wet winters with occasional snow. The city is prone to severe weather, including tornadoes and thunderstorms. The city's average yearly temperature is 61 degrees.

Rankings

General Rankings

- To help military veterans find the best places in which to settle down, *WalletHub* compared the 100 largest U.S. cities across 19 key indicators of livability, affordability and veteran-friendliness. They range from the share of military skill-related jobs to veteran income growth to the availability of VA health facilities. Tulsa ranked #54. *Wallethub.com, "Best & Worst Places for Veterans to Live (2025)," November 7, 2024*

- Tulsa was selected as one of the best places to live in the United States by *Money* magazine. The city placed among the top 50. This year's list focused on cities built around community spirit, thoughtful policy and civic engagement. Instead of relying on a predetermined dataset, the cities and towns were grouped according to their strengths and chosen due their affordability, good schools and strong job markets. *Money, "The 50 Best Places to Live in the U.S., 2024" April 8, 2024*

- In their annual survey, Livability.com looked at data for more than 2,000 mid-sized U.S. cities to assign a "Livability Score"for each. The top 100 scoring cities make up Livability's "Top 100 Best Places to Live in the U.S." in 2025. Tulsa was placed among the top 100 of the customizable list. Criteria: housing and economy; cost of living; environment; education; health care options; transportation; safety; and community amenities. *Livability.com, "Top 100 Best Places to Live in the U.S. in 2025" April 15, 2025*

Business/Finance Rankings

- For its annual survey of the "Cheapest U.S. Cities to Live In," Kiplinger applied Cost of Living Index statistics developed by the Council for Community and Economic Research to U.S. Census Bureau population and median household income data for 265 urban areas. Only areas with at least 50,000 residents were considered. In the resulting ranking, Tulsa ranked #17. *Kiplinger.com, "The 25 Cheapest Places to Live: U.S. Cities Edition," January 19, 2025*

- The Tulsa metro area appeared on the Milken Institute "2025 Best Performing Cities" list. Rank: #86 out of 200 large metro areas (based on performance category). Criteria: job growth; wage growth; high-tech growth and impact; community resilience; housing affordability; household broadband access. *Milken Institute, "Best-Performing Cities 2025," January 14, 2025*

Culture/Performing Arts Rankings

- Tulsa was selected as one of the 25 best cities for moviemakers in North America. Great film cities are places where filmmaking dreams can come true, that offer more creative space, lower costs, and great outdoor locations. NYC & LA were intentionally excluded. Criteria: film industry presence and culture; tax incentives; affordability; and proximity of festivals and schools. The city was ranked #15. *MovieMaker Magazine, "Best Places to Live and Work as a Moviemaker, 2025," January 29, 2025*

Education Rankings

- Personal finance website *WalletHub* analyzed the 150 largest U.S. metropolitan statistical areas to determine where the most educated Americans are putting their degrees to work. Criteria: education levels; percentage of workers with degrees; education quality and attainment gap; public school quality rankings; quality and enrollment of each metro area's universities. Tulsa was ranked #111 (#1 = most educated city). *WalletHub.com, "Most & Least Educated Cities in America, 2025" July 2, 2024*

Environmental Rankings

- The U.S. Environmental Protection Agency (EPA) released its list of mid-size U.S. metropolitan areas with the most ENERGY STAR certified buildings in 2023. The Tulsa metro area was ranked #5 out of 10. *U.S. Environmental Protection Agency, "2024 Energy Star Top Cities," May 22, 2024*

- Tulsa was highlighted as one of the 25 most ozone-polluted metro areas in the U.S. during 2021 through 2023. The area ranked #19. *American Lung Association, "State of the Air 2025," April 23, 2025*

Health/Fitness Rankings

- For each of the 100 largest cities in the United States, the American Fitness Index®, compiled in partnership between the American College of Sports Medicine and the Elevance Health Foundation, evaluated community infrastructure and more than 30 health behaviors including preventive health, levels of chronic disease conditions, food insecurity, pedestrian safety, air quality, and community/environment resources that support physical activity. Tulsa ranked #95 for "community fitness." *americanfitnessindex.org, "2024 ACSM American Fitness Index Summary Report," July 23, 2024*

- Tulsa was identified as a "2025 Allergy Capital." The area ranked #4 out of the nation's 100 largest metropolitan areas. Three groups of factors were used to identify the most challenging cities for people with allergies: annual tree, grass, and weed pollen scores; over the counter allergy medicine use; number of board-certified allergy specialists. *Asthma and Allergy Foundation of America, "2025 Allergy Capitals: The Most Challenging Places to Live with Allergies," March 18, 2025*

- Tulsa was identified as a "2024 Asthma Capital." The area ranked #82 out of the nation's 100 largest metropolitan areas. Criteria: estimated asthma prevalence; asthma-related mortality; and ER visits due to asthma. Risk factors analyzed but not factored in the rankings: annual air quality including pollution and ozone levels; public smoking laws; indoor air quality; access to asthma specialists; rescue and controller medication use; uninsured rate; pollen allergy; poverty rate. *Asthma and Allergy Foundation of America, "Asthma Capitals 2024: The Most Challenging Places to Live With Asthma," September 10, 2024*

Real Estate Rankings

- *WalletHub* compared the most populated U.S. cities to determine which had the best markets for real estate agents. Tulsa ranked #66 where demand was high and pay was the best. Criteria: sales per agent; annual median wage for real-estate agents; monthly average starting salary for real estate agents; real estate job density and competition; unemployment rate; home turnover rate; housing-market health index; and other relevant metrics. *WalletHub.com, "2021 Best Places to Be a Real Estate Agent," May 12, 2021*

- The Tulsa metro area was identified as one of the top 16 housing markets to invest in for 2025 by *Forbes*. Criteria: stable local economies with good population growth and increase in jobs providing good support for home prices and rents. *Forbes.com, "Best Local Markets For Real Estate Investing In 2025," November 6, 2024*

- Tulsa was ranked #52 out of 176 metro areas in terms of cost of housing in 2024 by the National Association of Home Builders (#1 = most affordable). Criteria: the portion of an average family's income necessary to pay the mortgage on a median-priced home. *National Association of Home Builders®, NAHB-Wells Fargo Cost of Housing Index, 4th Quarter 2024*

Safety Rankings

- Allstate ranked the 100 most populous cities in America in terms of driver safety. Tulsa ranked #39. Criteria based on anonymized driving behavior data from Allstate's mobile app powered by Arity: high speed driving (over 80 mph), phone handling, and hard braking. The report helps increase the importance of safety and awareness behind the wheel. *Allstate, "16th Allstate America's Best Drivers Report®" July 11, 2024*

- Tulsa was identified as one of the most dangerous cities in America by NeighborhoodScout. The city ranked #66 out of 100 (#1 = most dangerous). Criteria: number of violent crimes per 1,000 residents. The editors evaluated cities with 25,000 or more residents. *NeighborhoodScout.com, "2023 Top 100 Most Dangerous Cities in the U.S.," January 12, 2023*

Women/Minorities Rankings

- Personal finance website *WalletHub* compared more than 180 U.S. cities across two key dimensions, "Hispanic Business-Friendliness" and "Hispanic Purchasing Power," to arrive at the most favorable conditions for Hispanic entrepreneurs. Tulsa was ranked #42 out of 182. Criteria includes: share of Hispanic-Owned Businesses; average growth of Hispanic Business revenues; Small Business-Friendliness score; affordability; and number of Hispanics with at least a bachelor's degree. *WalletHub.com, "Best Cities for Hispanic Entrepreneurs," September 4, 2024*

Miscellaneous Rankings

- Despite a wide range of popular international destinations, plugged-in travel influencers and experts continue to rediscover their local regions. Tulsa appeared on a *Forbes Advisor* list of places in the U.S. designed to showcase a large variety of destinations. Whether it be discovery of hidden gems, delicious food, or outdoor exploring and daytrips, these places are a must-see. *Forbes.com, "Top 18 Places To Travel In the U.S. In 2024," February 7, 2024*

- *WalletHub* compared 148 of the most populated U.S. cities to determine their operating efficiency. A "Quality of Services" score was constructed for each city and then measured against the total budget per capita to reveal which were managed the best. Tulsa ranked #29. Criteria: financial stability; economy; education; safety; health; infrastructure and pollution. *WalletHub.com, "2025's Best- & Worst-Run Cities in America," June 18, 2024*

Business Environment

DEMOGRAPHICS

Population Growth

Area	1990 Census	2000 Census	2010 Census	2020 Census	2023 Estimate[2]	Population Growth 1990-2023 (%)
City	367,241	393,049	391,906	413,066	412,322	12.3
MSA[1]	761,019	859,532	937,478	1,015,331	1,026,209	34.8
U.S.	248,709,873	281,421,906	308,745,538	331,449,281	332,387,540	33.6

Note: (1) Figures cover the Tulsa, OK Metropolitan Statistical Area; (2) 2019-2023 5-year ACS population estimate
Source: U.S. Census Bureau, 1990 Census, 2000 Census, 2010 Census, 2020 Census, 2019-2023 American Community Survey 5-Year Estimates

Race

Area	White Alone[2] (%)	Black Alone[2] (%)	Asian Alone[2] (%)	AIAN[3] Alone[2] (%)	NHOPI[4] Alone[2] (%)	Other Race Alone[2] (%)	Two or More Races (%)
City	57.0	14.2	3.5	4.3	0.2	5.9	14.9
MSA[1]	65.3	7.6	2.8	7.2	0.1	3.5	13.4
U.S.	63.4	12.4	5.8	0.9	0.2	6.6	10.7

Note: (1) Figures cover the Tulsa, OK Metropolitan Statistical Area; (2) Alone is defined as not being in combination with one or more other races; (3) American Indian and Alaska Native; (4) Native Hawaiian and Other Pacific Islander
Source: U.S. Census Bureau, 2019-2023 American Community Survey 5-Year Estimates

Hispanic or Latino Origin

Area	Total (%)	Mexican (%)	Puerto Rican (%)	Cuban (%)	Other (%)
City	19.2	14.5	0.7	0.1	4.0
MSA[1]	12.0	8.9	0.5	0.1	2.5
U.S.	19.0	11.3	1.8	0.7	5.2

Note: Persons of Hispanic or Latino origin can be of any race; (1) Figures cover the Tulsa, OK Metropolitan Statistical Area
Source: U.S. Census Bureau, 2019-2023 American Community Survey 5-Year Estimates

Age

Area	Under Age 5	Age 5–19	Age 20–34	Age 35–44	Age 45–54	Age 55–64	Age 65–74	Age 75–84	Age 85+	Median Age
City	6.7	20.3	22.3	13.2	11.2	11.3	9.1	4.2	1.7	35.5
MSA[1]	6.3	20.7	19.9	13.1	11.9	12.2	9.6	4.7	1.7	37.3
U.S.	5.7	19.1	20.2	13.1	12.3	12.8	10.0	4.9	1.9	38.7

Note: (1) Figures cover the Tulsa, OK Metropolitan Statistical Area
Source: U.S. Census Bureau, 2019-2023 American Community Survey 5-Year Estimates

Disability by Age

Area	All Ages	Under 18 Years Old	18 to 64 Years Old	65 Years and Over
City	14.4	5.3	13.3	34.2
MSA[1]	15.0	5.2	13.4	37.0
U.S.	13.0	4.7	10.7	32.9

Note: Figures show percent of the civilian noninstitutionalized population that reported having a disability. Disability status is determined from six types of difficulty: vision, hearing, cognitive, ambulatory, self-care, and independent living. For children under 5 years old, hearing and vision difficulty are used to determine disability status. For children between the ages of 5 and 14, disability status is determined from hearing, vision, cognitive, ambulatory, and self-care difficulties. For people aged 15 years and older, they are considered to have a disability if they have difficulty with any one of the six difficulty types; Note: (1) Figures cover the Tulsa, OK Metropolitan Statistical Area
Source: U.S. Census Bureau, 2019-2023 American Community Survey 5-Year Estimates

Ancestry

Area	German	Irish	English	American	Italian	Polish	French[2]	European	Scottish
City	10.4	8.5	10.6	6.0	2.0	0.9	1.6	1.6	2.1
MSA[1]	12.4	10.2	11.7	5.6	1.9	0.9	1.7	1.7	2.1
U.S.	12.6	9.4	9.1	5.5	4.9	2.6	2.0	1.6	1.6

Note: Figures are the percentage of the total population reporting a particular ancestry. The nine most commonly reported ancestries in the U.S. are shown. Figures include multiple ancestries (e.g. if a person reported being Irish and Italian, they were included in both columns); (1) Figures cover the Tulsa, OK Metropolitan Statistical Area; (2) Excludes Basque
Source: U.S. Census Bureau, 2019-2023 American Community Survey 5-Year Estimates

Foreign-born Population

Area	Percent of Population Born in								
	Any Foreign Country	Asia	Mexico	Europe	Caribbean	Central America[2]	South America	Africa	Canada
City	12.0	2.6	5.5	0.7	0.3	1.3	0.7	0.6	0.1
MSA[1]	7.2	2.0	2.9	0.6	0.2	0.7	0.4	0.4	0.1
U.S.	13.9	4.3	3.3	1.4	1.4	1.2	1.2	0.8	0.2

Note: (1) Figures cover the Tulsa, OK Metropolitan Statistical Area; (2) Excludes Mexico.
Source: U.S. Census Bureau, 2019-2023 American Community Survey 5-Year Estimates

Household Size

Area	Persons in Household (%)							Average Household Size
	One	Two	Three	Four	Five	Six	Seven or More	
City	35.9	31.9	13.4	10.3	4.9	2.4	1.3	2.36
MSA[1]	29.2	33.6	15.2	12.3	5.9	2.5	1.4	2.53
U.S.	28.5	33.8	15.4	12.7	5.9	2.3	1.4	2.54

Note: (1) Figures cover the Tulsa, OK Metropolitan Statistical Area
Source: U.S. Census Bureau, 2019-2023 American Community Survey 5-Year Estimates

Household Relationships

Area	Householder	Opposite-sex Spouse	Same-sex Spouse	Opposite-sex Unmarried Partner	Same-sex Unmarried Partner	Child[2]	Grandchild	Other Relatives	Non-relatives
City	41.6	14.8	0.2	2.9	0.2	27.8	2.3	4.3	3.4
MSA[1]	39.1	18.2	0.2	2.4	0.1	29.0	2.6	3.9	2.7
U.S.	38.3	17.5	0.2	2.5	0.2	28.3	2.4	4.8	3.4

Note: Figures are percent of the total population; (1) Figures cover the Tulsa, OK Metropolitan Statistical Area; (2) Includes biological, adopted, and stepchildren of the householder
Source: U.S. Census Bureau, 2020 Census

Gender

Area	Males	Females	Males per 100 Females
City	201,524	210,798	95.6
MSA[1]	506,779	519,430	97.6
U.S.	164,545,087	167,842,453	98.0

Note: (1) Figures cover the Tulsa, OK Metropolitan Statistical Area
Source: U.S. Census Bureau, 2019-2023 American Community Survey 5-Year Estimates

Marital Status

Area	Never Married	Now Married[2]	Separated	Widowed	Divorced
City	36.5	41.7	2.4	5.5	14.0
MSA[1]	29.9	49.5	1.8	6.1	12.7
U.S.	34.1	47.9	1.7	5.6	10.7

Note: Figures are percentages and cover the population 15 years of age and older; (1) Figures cover the Tulsa, OK Metropolitan Statistical Area; (2) Excludes separated
Source: U.S. Census Bureau, 2019-2023 American Community Survey 5-Year Estimates

Religious Groups by Family

Area	Catholic	Baptist	Methodist	LDS[2]	Pentecostal	Lutheran	Islam	Adventist	Other
MSA[1]	5.6	15.5	7.7	1.2	2.5	0.5	0.5	1.2	22.2
U.S.	18.7	7.3	3.0	2.0	1.8	1.7	1.3	1.3	11.6

Note: Figures are the number of adherents as a percentage of the total population and cover the eight largest religious groups in the U.S; (1) Figures cover the Tulsa, OK Metropolitan Statistical Area; (2) Church of Jesus Christ of Latter-day Saints
Sources: 2020 U.S. Religion Census, Association of Statisticians of American Religious Bodies; The Association of Religion Data Archives (ARDA)

Religious Groups by Tradition

Area	Catholic	Evangelical Protestant	Mainline Protestant	Black Protestant	Islam	Judaism	Hinduism	Orthodox	Buddhism
MSA[1]	5.6	37.8	8.6	1.7	0.5	0.2	0.1	0.1	<0.1
U.S.	18.7	16.5	5.2	2.3	1.3	0.6	0.4	0.4	0.3

Note: Figures are the number of adherents as a percentage of the total population; (1) Figures cover the Tulsa, OK Metropolitan Statistical Area
Sources: 2020 U.S. Religion Census, Association of Statisticians of American Religious Bodies; The Association of Religion Data Archives (ARDA)

ECONOMY

Real Gross Domestic Product (GDP)

Area	2017	2018	2019	2020	2021	2022	2023	Rank[3]
MSA[1]	51.6	53.1	52.0	49.2	51.1	51.6	53.9	61
U.S.[2]	17,619.1	18,160.7	18,642.5	18,238.9	19,387.6	19,896.6	20,436.3	—

Note: Figures are in billions of chained 2017 dollars; (1) Figures cover the Tulsa, OK Metropolitan Statistical Area; (2) Figures cover real GDP within metropolitan areas; (3) Rank is based on 2023 data and ranges from 1 to 384
Source: U.S. Bureau of Economic Analysis

Economic Growth

Area	2014	2015	2016	2017	2018	2019	2020	2021	2022	2023
MSA[1]	5.4	1.7	-5.9	3.5	2.9	-2.1	-5.4	3.9	1.0	4.4
U.S.[2]	2.6	3.2	2.0	2.7	3.1	2.7	-2.2	6.3	2.6	2.7

Note: Figures are real gross domestic product growth rates and represent percent change from preceding period; (1) Figures cover the Tulsa, OK Metropolitan Statistical Area; (2) Figures are the average growth rates within metropolitan areas
Source: U.S. Bureau of Economic Analysis

Metropolitan Area Exports

Area	2018	2019	2020	2021	2022	2023	Rank[2]
MSA[1]	3,351.7	3,399.2	2,567.8	3,064.8	3,379.2	3,234.5	84
U.S.	1,664,056.1	1,645,173.7	1,431,406.6	1,753,941.4	2,062,937.4	2,019,160.5	—

Note: Figures are in millions of dollars; (1) Figures cover the Tulsa, OK Metropolitan Statistical Area; (2) Rank is based on 2023 data and ranges from 1 to 386
Source: U.S. Department of Commerce, International Trade Administration, Office of Trade and Economic Analysis, Industry and Analysis, Exports by Metropolitan Area, data extracted April 2, 2025

Building Permits

Area	Single-Family			Multi-Family			Total		
	2023	2024	Pct. Chg.	2023	2024	Pct. Chg.	2023	2024	Pct. Chg.
City	524	424	-19.1	352	299	-15.1	876	723	-17.5
MSA[1]	3,393	3,602	6.2	1,616	709	-56.1	5,009	4,311	-13.9
U.S.	920,000	981,900	6.7	591,100	496,100	-16.1	1,511,100	1,478,000	-2.2

Note: (1) Figures cover the Tulsa, OK Metropolitan Statistical Area; Figures represent new, privately-owned housing units authorized (unadjusted data)
Source: U.S. Census Bureau, Building Permits Survey (BPS), 2023, 2024

Bankruptcy Filings

Area	Business Filings			Nonbusiness Filings		
	2023	2024	% Chg.	2023	2024	% Chg.
Tulsa County	46	44	-4.3	867	1,065	22.8
U.S.	18,926	23,107	22.1	434,064	494,201	13.9

Note: Business filings include Chapter 7, Chapter 9, Chapter 11, Chapter 12, Chapter 13, Chapter 15, and Section 304; Nonbusiness filings include Chapter 7, Chapter 11, and Chapter 13
Source: Administrative Office of the U.S. Courts, Business and Nonbusiness Bankruptcy, County Cases Commenced by Chapter of the Bankruptcy Code, During the 12-Month Period Ending December 31, 2023 and Business and Nonbusiness Bankruptcy, County Cases Commenced by Chapter of the Bankruptcy Code, During the 12-Month Period Ending December 31, 2024

Housing Vacancy Rates

Area	Gross Vacancy Rate[3] (%)			Year-Round Vacancy Rate[4] (%)			Rental Vacancy Rate[5] (%)			Homeowner Vacancy Rate[6] (%)		
	2022	2023	2024	2022	2023	2024	2022	2023	2024	2022	2023	2024
MSA[1]	8.9	8.3	7.5	8.5	7.9	6.8	5.6	6.7	7.2	0.7	0.8	0.7
U.S.[2]	9.1	9.0	9.1	7.5	7.5	7.6	5.7	6.5	6.8	0.8	0.8	1.0

Note: (1) Figures cover the Tulsa, OK Metropolitan Statistical Area; (2) Figures cover the 75 largest Metropolitan Statistical Areas; (3) The percentage of the total housing inventory that is vacant; (4) The percentage of the housing inventory (excluding seasonal units) that is year-round vacant; (5) The percentage of rental inventory that is vacant for rent; (6) The percentage of homeowner inventory that is vacant for sale
Source: U.S. Census Bureau, Housing Vacancies and Homeownership Annual Statistics: 2022, 2023, 2024

INCOME

Income

Area	Per Capita ($)	Median Household ($)	Average Household ($)
City	37,533	58,407	88,998
MSA[1]	37,865	67,823	94,114
U.S.	43,289	78,538	110,491

Note: (1) Figures cover the Tulsa, OK Metropolitan Statistical Area
Source: U.S. Census Bureau, 2019-2023 American Community Survey 5-Year Estimates

Household Income Distribution

Area	Percent of Households Earning							
	Under $15,000	$15,000 -$24,999	$25,000 -$34,999	$35,000 -$49,999	$50,000 -$74,999	$75,000 -$99,999	$100,000 -$149,999	$150,000 and up
City	11.9	7.6	10.1	13.5	17.8	11.5	13.4	14.2
MSA[1]	8.9	7.1	8.4	12.3	17.8	12.9	16.9	15.8
U.S.	8.5	6.6	6.8	10.4	15.7	12.7	17.4	21.9

Note: (1) Figures cover the Tulsa, OK Metropolitan Statistical Area
Source: U.S. Census Bureau, 2019-2023 American Community Survey 5-Year Estimates

Poverty Rate

Area	All Ages	Under 18 Years Old	18 to 64 Years Old	65 Years and Over
City	18.6	27.0	17.3	10.4
MSA[1]	13.7	18.9	12.9	8.9
U.S.	12.4	16.3	11.6	10.4

Note: Figures are percentage of people whose income during the past 12 months was below the poverty level; (1) Figures cover the Tulsa, OK Metropolitan Statistical Area
Source: U.S. Census Bureau, 2019-2023 American Community Survey 5-Year Estimates

EMPLOYMENT

Labor Force and Employment

Area	Civilian Labor Force			Workers Employed		
	Dec. 2023	Dec. 2024	% Chg.	Dec. 2023	Dec. 2024	% Chg.
City	206,897	209,496	1.3	199,811	203,133	1.7
MSA[1]	510,676	517,614	1.4	494,038	502,372	1.7
U.S.	166,661,000	167,746,000	0.7	160,754,000	161,294,000	0.3

Note: Data is not seasonally adjusted and covers workers 16 years of age and older; (1) Figures cover the Tulsa, OK Metropolitan Statistical Area
Source: Bureau of Labor Statistics, Local Area Unemployment Statistics

Unemployment Rate

Area	2024											
	Jan.	Feb.	Mar.	Apr.	May	Jun.	Jul.	Aug.	Sep.	Oct.	Nov.	Dec.
City	4.0	4.0	3.3	3.0	3.5	3.7	3.7	3.6	3.2	3.3	3.3	3.0
MSA[1]	3.8	3.8	3.2	2.8	3.3	3.6	3.5	3.4	3.1	3.2	3.2	2.9
U.S.	4.1	4.2	3.9	3.5	3.7	4.3	4.5	4.4	3.9	3.9	4.0	3.8

Note: Data is not seasonally adjusted and covers workers 16 years of age and older; (1) Figures cover the Tulsa, OK Metropolitan Statistical Area
Source: Bureau of Labor Statistics, Local Area Unemployment Statistics

Average Wages

Occupation	$/Hr.	Occupation	$/Hr.
Accountants and Auditors	40.70	Maintenance and Repair Workers	22.39
Automotive Mechanics	24.36	Marketing Managers	70.25
Bookkeepers	23.49	Network and Computer Systems Admin.	51.21
Carpenters	24.64	Nurses, Licensed Practical	27.71
Cashiers	13.45	Nurses, Registered	43.20
Computer Programmers	47.67	Nursing Assistants	17.41
Computer Systems Analysts	55.21	Office Clerks, General	19.08
Computer User Support Specialists	27.43	Physical Therapists	46.55
Construction Laborers	21.54	Physicians	83.29
Cooks, Restaurant	16.20	Plumbers, Pipefitters and Steamfitters	28.27
Customer Service Representatives	19.80	Police and Sheriff's Patrol Officers	31.70
Dentists	97.17	Postal Service Mail Carriers	29.17
Electricians	30.23	Real Estate Sales Agents	29.25
Engineers, Electrical	53.92	Retail Salespersons	16.41
Fast Food and Counter Workers	12.63	Sales Representatives, Technical/Scientific	43.73
Financial Managers	71.47	Secretaries, Exc. Legal/Medical/Executive	19.75
First-Line Supervisors of Office Workers	31.71	Security Guards	19.04
General and Operations Managers	53.60	Surgeons	n/a
Hairdressers/Cosmetologists	17.42	Teacher Assistants, Exc. Postsecondary[1]	13.50
Home Health and Personal Care Aides	13.24	Teachers, Secondary School, Exc. Sp. Ed.[1]	28.84
Janitors and Cleaners	15.65	Telemarketers	16.76
Landscaping/Groundskeeping Workers	17.01	Truck Drivers, Heavy/Tractor-Trailer	27.89
Lawyers	57.59	Truck Drivers, Light/Delivery Services	20.63
Maids and Housekeeping Cleaners	13.86	Waiters and Waitresses	14.21

Note: Wage data covers the Tulsa, OK Metropolitan Statistical Area; (1) Hourly wages were calculated from annual wage data based on a 40 hour work week
Source: Bureau of Labor Statistics, Metro Area Occupational Employment & Wage Estimates, May 2024

Employment by Industry

Sector	MSA[1] Number of Employees	MSA[1] Percent of Total	U.S. Percent of Total
Construction	27,600	5.7	5.1
Financial Activities	25,000	5.1	5.8
Government	64,200	13.2	14.9
Information	4,900	1.0	1.9
Leisure and Hospitality	48,000	9.9	10.4
Manufacturing	54,100	11.1	8.0
Mining and Logging	3,300	0.7	0.4
Other Services	21,900	4.5	3.7
Private Education and Health Services	82,600	17.0	16.9
Professional and Business Services	64,100	13.2	14.2
Retail Trade	50,100	10.3	10.0
Transportation, Warehousing, and Utilities	22,400	4.6	4.8
Wholesale Trade	17,900	3.7	3.9

Note: Figures are non-farm employment as of December 2024. Figures are not seasonally adjusted and include workers 16 years of age and older; (1) Figures cover the Tulsa, OK Metropolitan Statistical Area
Source: Bureau of Labor Statistics, Current Employment Statistics, Employment, Hours, and Earnings

Employment by Occupation

Occupation Classification	City (%)	MSA[1] (%)	U.S. (%)
Management, Business, Science, and Arts	38.5	38.7	42.0
Natural Resources, Construction, and Maintenance	9.4	9.9	8.6
Production, Transportation, and Material Moving	13.7	14.1	13.0
Sales and Office	21.0	21.4	19.9
Service	17.5	15.9	16.5

Note: Figures cover employed civilians 16 years of age and older; (1) Figures cover the Tulsa, OK Metropolitan Statistical Area
Source: U.S. Census Bureau, 2019-2023 American Community Survey 5-Year Estimates

Occupations with Greatest Projected Employment Growth: 2022 – 2032

Occupation[1]	2022 Employment	2032 Projected Employment	Numeric Employment Change	Percent Employment Change
Cooks, Restaurant	17,540	22,760	5,220	29.8
Home Health and Personal Care Aides	19,090	23,300	4,210	22.1
Fast Food and Counter Workers	38,730	42,310	3,580	9.2
Stockers and Order Fillers	34,260	37,570	3,310	9.7
General and Operations Managers	44,230	47,300	3,070	6.9
Laborers and Freight, Stock, and Material Movers, Hand	31,840	34,070	2,230	7.0
Heavy and Tractor-Trailer Truck Drivers	28,050	30,090	2,040	7.3
Medical and Health Services Managers	7,420	9,360	1,940	26.1
First-Line Supervisors of Food Preparation and Serving Workers	15,550	17,460	1,910	12.3
Registered Nurses	37,490	39,290	1,800	4.8

Note: Projections cover Oklahoma; (1) Sorted by numeric employment change
Source: www.projectionscentral.org, State Occupational Projections, 2022–2032 Long-Term Projections

Fastest-Growing Occupations: 2022 – 2032

Occupation[1]	2022 Employment	2032 Projected Employment	Numeric Employment Change	Percent Employment Change
Wind Turbine Service Technicians	610	970	360	59.0
Nurse Practitioners	3,030	4,200	1,170	38.6
Data Scientists	2,060	2,710	650	31.6
Cooks, Restaurant	17,540	22,760	5,220	29.8
Information Security Analysts (SOC 2018)	1,010	1,300	290	28.7
Medical and Health Services Managers	7,420	9,360	1,940	26.1
Operations Research Analysts	460	570	110	23.9
Personal Care and Service Workers, All Other	630	780	150	23.8
Taxi Drivers	610	750	140	23.0
Physician Assistants	1,650	2,020	370	22.4

Note: Projections cover Oklahoma; (1) Sorted by percent employment change and excludes occupations with numeric employment change less than 50
Source: www.projectionscentral.org, State Occupational Projections, 2022–2032 Long-Term Projections

CITY FINANCES

City Government Finances

Component	2022 ($000)	2022 ($ per capita)
Total Revenues	1,156,826	2,869
Total Expenditures	1,036,107	2,570
Debt Outstanding	1,305,432	3,238

Source: U.S. Census Bureau, State & Local Government Finances 2022

City Government Revenue by Source

Source	2022 ($000)	2022 ($ per capita)	2022 (%)
General Revenue			
From Federal Government	72,184	179	6.2
From State Government	14,068	35	1.2
From Local Governments	22,669	56	2.0
Taxes			
Property	83,771	208	7.2
Sales and Gross Receipts	422,120	1,047	36.5
Personal Income	0	0	0.0
Corporate Income	0	0	0.0
Motor Vehicle License	0	0	0.0
Other Taxes	12,032	30	1.0
Current Charges	288,510	716	24.9
Liquor Store	0	0	0.0
Utility	128,687	319	11.1

Source: U.S. Census Bureau, State & Local Government Finances 2022

City Government Expenditures by Function

Function	2022 ($000)	2022 ($ per capita)	2022 (%)
General Direct Expenditures			
Air Transportation	44,219	109	4.3
Corrections	0	0	0.0
Education	0	0	0.0
Employment Security Administration	0	0	0.0
Financial Administration	17,620	43	1.7
Fire Protection	92,068	228	8.9
General Public Buildings	0	0	0.0
Governmental Administration, Other	32,087	79	3.1
Health	86,570	214	8.4
Highways	173,446	430	16.7
Hospitals	0	0	0.0
Housing and Community Development	34,072	84	3.3
Interest on General Debt	67	<1	<0.1
Judicial and Legal	6,357	15	0.6
Libraries	0	0	0.0
Parking	20	<1	<0.1
Parks and Recreation	44,722	110	4.3
Police Protection	127,076	315	12.3
Public Welfare	25,813	64	2.5
Sewerage	167,019	414	16.1
Solid Waste Management	25,799	64	2.5
Veterans' Services	0	0	0.0
Liquor Store	0	0	0.0
Utility	145,757	361	14.1

Source: U.S. Census Bureau, State & Local Government Finances 2022

TAXES

State Corporate Income Tax Rates

State	Tax Rate (%)	Income Brackets ($)	Num. of Brackets	Financial Institution Tax Rate (%)[a]	Federal Income Tax Ded.
Oklahoma	4.0	Flat rate	1	4.0	No

Note: Tax rates for tax year 2024; (a) Rates listed are the corporate income tax rate applied to financial institutions or excise taxes based on income. Some states have other taxes based upon the value of deposits or shares.
Source: Federation of Tax Administrators, State Corporate Income Tax Rates, January 1, 2025

State Individual Income Tax Rates

State	Tax Rate (%)	Income Brackets ($)	Personal Exemptions ($)			Standard Ded. ($)	
			Single	Married	Depend.	Single	Married
Oklahoma	0.25 - 4.75	1,000 - 7,200 (v)	1,000	2,000	1,000	6,350	12,700

Note: Tax rates for tax year 2024; Local- and county-level taxes are not included; Federal income tax is not deductible on state income tax returns; (v) Married and HOH tax brackets are twice Single filing status. Legislature seeking HB 2949 - flat rate 4.25% personal income tax effective 2024. HB1953 eliminates the current standard deductions and changes the personal income taxing framework from a bracket based system to a flat rate system
Source: Federation of Tax Administrators, State Individual Income Tax Rates, January 1, 2025

Various State Sales and Excise Tax Rates

State	State Sales Tax (%)	Gasoline[1] ($/gal.)	Cigarette[2] ($/pack)	Spirits[3] ($/gal.)	Wine[4] ($/gal.)	Beer[5] ($/gal.)	Recreational Marijuana (%)
Oklahoma	4.5	0.20	2.03	5.56	0.72	0.40	Not legal

Note: All tax rates as of January 1, 2025; (1) The American Petroleum Institute has developed a methodology for determining the average tax rate on a gallon of fuel. Rates may include any of the following: excise taxes, environmental fees, storage tank fees, other fees or taxes, general sales tax, and local taxes; (2) The federal excise tax of $1.0066 per pack and local taxes are not included; (3) Rates are those applicable to off-premise sales of 40% alcohol by volume (a.b.v.) distilled spirits in 750ml containers. Local excise taxes are excluded; (4) Rates are those applicable to off-premise sales of 11% a.b.v. non-carbonated wine in 750ml containers; (5) Rates are those applicable to off-premise sales of 4.7% a.b.v. beer in 12 ounce containers.
Source: Tax Foundation, 2025 Facts & Figures: How Does Your State Compare?

State Tax Competitiveness Index

State	Overall Rank	Corporate Tax Rank	Individual Income Tax Rank	Sales Tax Rank	Property Tax Rank	Unemployment Insurance Tax Rank
Oklahoma	21	5	28	32	15	6

Note: The Tax Foundation's State Tax Competitiveness Index enables policymakers, taxpayers, and business leaders to gauge how their states' tax systems compare. A rank of 1 is best, 50 is worst. Rankings do not average to the total. States without a tax rank equally as 1. DC's scores and rankings do not affect other states. The report shows tax systems as of July 1, 2024 (the beginning of Fiscal Year 2025).
Source: Tax Foundation, State Tax Competitiveness Index 2025

TRANSPORTATION

Means of Transportation to Work

Area	Car/Truck/Van		Public Transportation			Bicycle	Walked	Other Means	Worked at Home
	Drove Alone	Car-pooled	Bus	Subway	Railroad				
City	75.4	10.2	0.5	0.0	0.0	0.3	1.7	1.8	10.1
MSA[1]	78.2	9.0	0.3	0.0	0.0	0.2	1.2	1.2	9.8
U.S.	70.2	8.5	1.7	1.3	0.4	0.4	2.4	1.6	13.5

Note: Figures are percentages and cover workers 16 years of age and older; (1) Figures cover the Tulsa, OK Metropolitan Statistical Area
Source: U.S. Census Bureau, 2019-2023 American Community Survey 5-Year Estimates

Travel Time to Work

Area	Less Than 10 Minutes	10 to 19 Minutes	20 to 29 Minutes	30 to 44 Minutes	45 to 59 Minutes	60 to 89 Minutes	90 Minutes or More
City	14.0	46.0	25.7	9.8	1.8	1.4	1.3
MSA[1]	13.4	34.0	26.6	17.7	4.7	2.2	1.5
U.S.	12.6	28.6	21.2	20.8	8.1	6.0	2.8

Note: Note: Figures are percentages and include workers 16 years old and over; (1) Figures cover the Tulsa, OK Metropolitan Statistical Area
Source: U.S. Census Bureau, 2019-2023 American Community Survey 5-Year Estimates

Key Congestion Measures

Measure	2000	2010	2015	2020	2022
Annual Hours of Delay, Total (000)	14,079	20,116	23,868	14,440	20,658
Annual Hours of Delay, Per Auto Commuter	34	35	42	27	41
Annual Congestion Cost, Per Auto Commuter ($)	657	747	819	536	756

Note: Figures cover the Tulsa OK urban area
Source: Texas A&M Transportation Institute, 2023 Urban Mobility Report

Freeway Travel Time Index

Measure	1985	1990	1995	2000	2005	2010	2015	2020	2022
Urban Area Index[1]	1.06	1.08	1.11	1.13	1.16	1.16	1.15	1.08	1.12
Urban Area Rank[1,2]	53	62	66	72	57	54	67	44	81

Note: Freeway Travel Time Index—the ratio of travel time in the peak period to the travel time at free-flow conditions. For example, a value of 1.30 indicates a 20-minute free-flow trip takes 26 minutes in the peak (20 minutes x 1.30 = 26 minutes); (1) Covers the Tulsa OK urban area; (2) Rank is based on 101 larger urban areas (#1 = highest travel time index)
Source: Texas A&M Transportation Institute, 2023 Urban Mobility Report

Public Transportation

Agency Name / Mode of Transportation	Vehicles Operated in Maximum Service[1]	Annual Unlinked Passenger Trips[2] (in thous.)	Annual Passenger Miles[3] (in thous.)
Metropolitan Tulsa Transit Authority (MTTA)			
Bus (directly operated)	43	1,854.6	10,497.2
Bus (purchased transportation)	14	46.1	194.5
Demand Response (purchased transportation)	25	91.2	820.7

Note: (1) Number of revenue vehicles operated by the given mode and type of service to meet the annual maximum service requirement. This is the revenue vehicle count during the peak season of the year; on the week and day that maximum service is provided. Vehicles operated in maximum service (VOMS) exclude atypical days and one-time special events; (2) Number of passengers who boarded public transportation vehicles. Passengers are counted each time they board a vehicle no matter how many vehicles they use to travel from their origin to their destination. (3) Sum of the distances ridden by all passengers during the entire fiscal year.
Source: Federal Transit Administration, National Transit Database, 2023

Air Transportation

Airport Name and Code / Type of Service	Passenger Airlines[1]	Passenger Enplanements	Freight Carriers[2]	Freight (lbs)
Tulsa International (TUL)				
Domestic service (U.S. carriers only)	21	1,625,731	14	51,350,273
International service (U.S. carriers only)	1	2	0	0

Note: (1) Includes all U.S.-based major, minor and commuter airlines that carried at least one passenger during the year; (2) Includes all U.S.-based airlines and freight carriers that transported at least one pound of freight during the year.
Source: Bureau of Transportation Statistics, The Intermodal Transportation Database, Air Carriers: T-100 Domestic Market (U.S. carriers only), 2024; Bureau of Transportation Statistics, The Intermodal Transportation Database, Air Carriers: T-100 International Market (U.S. carriers only), 2024

BUSINESSES

Major Business Headquarters

Company Name	Industry	Rankings Fortune[1]	Rankings Forbes[2]
NGL Energy Partners	Pipelines	442	-
Oneok	Pipelines	232	-
QuikTrip	Convenience stores & gas stations	-	20
Williams	Pipelines	371	-

Note: (1) Companies that produce a 10-K are ranked 1 to 500 based on 2023 revenue; (2) All private companies with at least $2 billion in annual revenue through the end of their most current fiscal year are ranked 1 to 275; companies listed are headquartered in the city; dashes indicate no ranking
Source: Fortune, "Fortune 500," 2024; Forbes, "America's Largest Private Companies," 2024

Living Environment

COST OF LIVING

Cost of Living Index

Composite Index	Groceries	Housing	Utilities	Transportation	Health Care	Misc. Goods/Services
84.7	95.9	65.1	98.3	88.4	93.5	90.3

Note: The Cost of Living Index measures regional differences in the cost of consumer goods and services, excluding taxes and non-consumer expenditures, for professional and managerial households in the top income quintile. It is based on more than 50,000 prices covering almost 60 different items for which prices are collected three times a year by chambers of commerce, economic development organizations or university applied economic centers in each participating urban area. The numbers shown should be read as a percentage above or below the national average of 100. For example, a value of 115.4 in the groceries column indicates that grocery prices are 15.4% higher than the national average. Small differences in the index numbers should not be interpreted as significant; Figures cover the Tulsa OK urban area.
Source: The Council for Community and Economic Research, Cost of Living Index, 2024

Grocery Prices

Area[1]	T-Bone Steak ($/pound)	Frying Chicken ($/pound)	Whole Milk ($/half gal.)	Eggs ($/dozen)	Orange Juice ($/64 oz.)	Coffee ($/11.5 oz.)
City[2]	15.52	1.45	4.59	2.97	4.32	5.06
Avg.	15.42	1.55	4.69	3.25	4.41	5.46
Min.	14.50	1.16	4.43	2.75	4.00	4.85
Max.	17.56	2.89	5.49	4.78	5.54	7.89

*Note: (1) Values for the local area are compared with the average, minimum and maximum values for all 276 areas in the Cost of Living Index; (2) Figures cover the Tulsa OK urban area; **T-Bone Steak** (price per pound); **Frying Chicken** (price per pound, whole fryer); **Whole Milk** (half gallon carton); **Eggs** (price per dozen, Grade A, large); **Orange Juice** (64 oz. Tropicana or Florida Natural); **Coffee** (11.5 oz. can, vacuum-packed, Maxwell House, Hills Bros, or Folgers).*
Source: The Council for Community and Economic Research, Cost of Living Index, 2024

Housing and Utility Costs

Area[1]	New Home Price ($)	Apartment Rent ($/month)	All Electric ($/month)	Part Electric ($/month)	Other Energy ($/month)	Telephone ($/month)
City[2]	339,822	935	-	118.37	80.52	197.22
Avg.	515,975	1,550	210.99	123.07	82.07	194.99
Min.	265,375	692	104.33	53.68	36.26	179.42
Max.	2,775,821	5,719	529.02	397.28	361.63	223.33

*Note: (1) Values for the local area are compared with the average, minimum and maximum values for all 276 areas in the Cost of Living Index; (2) Figures cover the Tulsa OK urban area; **New Home Price** (2,400 sf living area, 8,000 sf lot, in urban area with full utilities); **Apartment Rent** (950 sf 2 bedroom/1.5 or 2 bath, unfurnished, excluding all utilities except water); **All Electric** (average monthly cost for an all-electric home); **Part Electric** (average monthly cost for a part-electric home); **Other Energy** (average monthly cost for natural gas, fuel oil, coal, wood, and any other forms of energy except electricity); **Telephone** (price includes the base monthly rate plus taxes and fees for three lines of mobile phone service).*
Source: The Council for Community and Economic Research, Cost of Living Index, 2024

Health Care, Transportation, and Other Costs

Area[1]	Doctor ($/visit)	Dentist ($/visit)	Optometrist ($/visit)	Gasoline ($/gallon)	Beauty Salon ($/visit)	Men's Shirt ($)
City[2]	109.57	109.83	111.11	2.95	35.40	29.28
Avg.	143.77	117.51	129.23	3.32	48.57	38.14
Min.	36.74	58.67	67.33	2.80	24.00	13.41
Max.	270.44	216.82	307.33	5.28	94.00	63.89

*Note: (1) Values for the local area are compared with the average, minimum and maximum values for all 276 areas in the Cost of Living Index; (2) Figures cover the Tulsa OK urban area; **Doctor** (general practitioners routine exam of an established patient); **Dentist** (adult teeth cleaning and periodic oral examination); **Optometrist** (full vision eye exam for established adult patient); **Gasoline** (one gallon regular unleaded, national brand, including all taxes, cash price at self-service pump if available); **Beauty Salon** (woman's shampoo, trim, and blow-dry); **Men's Shirt** (cotton/polyester dress shirt, pinpoint weave, long sleeves).*
Source: The Council for Community and Economic Research, Cost of Living Index, 2024

HOUSING

Homeownership Rate

Area	2017 (%)	2018 (%)	2019 (%)	2020 (%)	2021 (%)	2022 (%)	2023 (%)	2024 (%)
MSA[1]	66.8	68.3	70.5	70.1	63.8	63.7	62.8	65.3
U.S.	63.9	64.4	64.6	66.6	65.5	65.8	65.9	65.6

Note: (1) Figures cover the Tulsa, OK Metropolitan Statistical Area
Source: U.S. Census Bureau, Housing Vacancies and Homeownership Annual Statistics: 2017-2024

House Price Index (HPI)

Area	National Ranking[2]	Quarterly Change (%)	One-Year Change (%)	Five-Year Change (%)	Since 1991Q1 (%)
MSA[1]	116	1.84	5.52	56.84	272.73
U.S.[3]	—	1.43	4.51	57.13	327.82

Note: The HPI is a weighted repeat sales index. It measures average price changes in repeat sales or refinancings on the same properties. This information is obtained by reviewing repeat mortgage transactions on single-family properties whose mortgages have been purchased or securitized by Fannie Mae or Freddie Mac since January 1975; (1) Figures cover the Tulsa, OK Metropolitan Statistical Area; (2) Rankings are based on annual percentage change for all metro areas containing at least 15,000 transactions over the last 10 years and ranges from 1 to 241; (3) figures based on a weighted average of Census Division estimates using a seasonally adjusted, purchase-only index; all figures are for the period ending December 31, 2024
Source: Federal Housing Finance Agency, Change in FHFA Metropolitan Area House Price Indexes, All Transactions Index, 2024Q4

Home Value

Area	Under $100,000	$100,000 -$199,999	$200,000 -$299,999	$300,000 -$399,999	$400,000 -$499,999	$500,000 -$999,999	$1,000,000 or more	Median ($)
City	20.0	33.1	20.0	10.7	5.6	8.3	2.3	189,600
MSA[1]	17.5	31.2	25.4	12.1	5.9	6.5	1.4	204,400
U.S.	12.1	17.8	19.5	14.4	10.5	19.1	6.5	303,400

Note: Figures are percentages except for median and cover owner-occupied housing units; (1) Figures cover the Tulsa, OK Metropolitan Statistical Area
Source: U.S. Census Bureau, 2019-2023 American Community Survey 5-Year Estimates

Year Housing Structure Built

Area	2020 or Later	2010 -2019	2000 -2009	1990 -1999	1980 -1989	1970 -1979	1960 -1969	1950 -1959	1940 -1949	Before 1940	Median Year
City	0.4	6.0	6.5	8.2	13.8	20.0	14.5	15.5	6.2	8.9	1972
MSA[1]	1.2	11.0	13.9	11.1	13.9	18.2	10.3	9.8	4.1	6.7	1981
U.S.	1.2	8.9	13.6	12.8	13.0	14.4	10.0	9.7	4.5	11.9	1980

Note: Figures are percentages except for Median Year; Note: (1) Figures cover the Tulsa, OK Metropolitan Statistical Area
Source: U.S. Census Bureau, 2019-2023 American Community Survey 5-Year Estimates

Gross Monthly Rent

Area	Under $500	$500 -$999	$1,000 -$1,499	$1,500 -$1,999	$2,000 -$2,499	$2,500 -$2,999	$3,000 and up	Median ($)
City	7.3	42.9	36.4	9.1	2.1	1.0	1.2	998
MSA[1]	7.1	39.7	37.8	10.4	2.9	1.0	1.1	1,034
U.S.	6.5	22.3	29.5	20.2	10.8	4.8	5.9	1,348

Note: Figures are percentages except for median; Gross rent is the contract rent plus the estimated average monthly cost of utilities (electricity, gas, and water and sewer) and fuels (oil, coal, kerosene, wood, etc.) if these are paid by the renter (or paid for the renter by someone else); (1) Figures cover the Tulsa, OK Metropolitan Statistical Area
Source: U.S. Census Bureau, 2019-2023 American Community Survey 5-Year Estimates

HEALTH

Health Risk Factors

Category	MSA[1] (%)	U.S. (%)
Adults aged 18–64 who have any kind of health care coverage	87.2	90.8
Adults who reported being in good or better health	79.9	81.8
Adults who have been told they have high blood cholesterol	35.8	36.9
Adults who have been told they have high blood pressure	36.1	34.0
Adults who are current smokers	14.5	12.1
Adults who currently use e-cigarettes	11.4	7.7
Adults who currently use chewing tobacco, snuff, or snus	4.6	3.2
Adults who are heavy drinkers[2]	4.4	6.1
Adults who are binge drinkers[3]	13.2	15.2
Adults who are overweight (BMI 25.0 - 29.9)	32.1	34.4
Adults who are obese (BMI 30.0 - 99.8)	35.6	34.3
Adults who participated in any physical activities in the past month	70.0	75.8

Note: All figures are crude prevalence; (1) Figures cover the Tulsa, OK Metropolitan Statistical Area; (2) Heavy drinkers are classified as adult men having more than 14 drinks per week and adult women having more than 7 drinks per week; (3) Binge drinkers are classified as males having five or more drinks on one occasion or females having four or more drinks on one occasion
Source: Centers for Disease Control and Prevention, Behavioral Risk Factor Surveillance System, SMART: Selected Metropolitan Area Risk Trends, 2023

Acute and Chronic Health Conditions

Category	MSA[1] (%)	U.S. (%)
Adults who have ever been told they had a heart attack	5.2	4.2
Adults who have ever been told they have angina or coronary heart disease	4.7	4.0
Adults who have ever been told they had a stroke	3.5	3.3
Adults who have ever been told they have asthma	17.4	15.7
Adults who have ever been told they have arthritis	26.7	26.3
Adults who have ever been told they have diabetes[2]	11.5	11.5
Adults who have ever been told they had skin cancer	5.6	5.6
Adults who have ever been told they had any other types of cancer	7.8	8.4
Adults who have ever been told they have COPD	7.5	6.4
Adults who have ever been told they have kidney disease	4.3	3.7
Adults who have ever been told they have a form of depression	26.6	22.0

Note: All figures are crude prevalence; (1) Figures cover the Tulsa, OK Metropolitan Statistical Area; (2) Figures do not include pregnancy-related, borderline, or pre-diabetes
Source: Centers for Disease Control and Prevention, Behaviorial Risk Factor Surveillance System, SMART: Selected Metropolitan Area Risk Trends, 2023

Health Screening and Vaccination Rates

Category	MSA[1] (%)	U.S. (%)
Adults who have ever been tested for HIV	34.4	37.5
Adults who have had their blood cholesterol checked within the last five years	85.4	87.0
Adults aged 65+ who have had flu shot within the past year	62.5	63.4
Adults aged 65+ who have ever had a pneumonia vaccination	76.6	71.9

Note: All figures are crude prevalence; (1) Figures cover the Tulsa, OK Metropolitan Statistical Area.
Source: Centers for Disease Control and Prevention, Behaviorial Risk Factor Surveillance System, SMART: Selected Metropolitan Area Risk Trends, 2023

Disability Status

Category	MSA[1] (%)	U.S. (%)
Adults who reported being deaf	9.7	7.4
Are you blind or have serious difficulty seeing, even when wearing glasses?	6.8	4.9
Do you have difficulty doing errands alone?	10.5	7.8
Do you have difficulty dressing or bathing?	3.9	3.6
Do you have serious difficulty concentrating/remembering/making decisions?	18.5	13.7
Do you have serious difficulty walking or climbing stairs?	16.2	13.2

Note: All figures are crude prevalence; (1) Figures cover the Tulsa, OK Metropolitan Statistical Area.
Source: Centers for Disease Control and Prevention, Behaviorial Risk Factor Surveillance System, SMART: Selected Metropolitan Area Risk Trends, 2023

Mortality Rates for the Top 10 Causes of Death in the U.S.

ICD-10[a] Sub-Chapter	ICD-10[a] Code	Crude Mortality Rate[2] per 100,000 population	
		County[3]	U.S.
Malignant neoplasms	C00-C97	179.2	182.7
Ischaemic heart diseases	I20-I25	78.9	109.6
Provisional assignment of new diseases of uncertain etiology[1]	U00-U49	83.2	65.3
Other forms of heart disease	I30-I51	38.7	65.1
Other degenerative diseases of the nervous system	G30-G31	50.8	52.4
Other external causes of accidental injury	W00-X59	64.0	52.3
Cerebrovascular diseases	I60-I69	49.2	49.1
Chronic lower respiratory diseases	J40-J47	54.5	43.5
Hypertensive diseases	I10-I15	181.5	38.9
Organic, including symptomatic, mental disorders	F01-F09	27.9	33.9

Note: (a) ICD-10 = International Classification of Diseases 10th Revision; (1) Includes COVID-19, adverse effects to COVID-19 vaccines, SARS, and vaping-related disorders; (2) Crude mortality rates are a three-year average covering 2021-2023; (3) Figures cover Tulsa County.
Source: Centers for Disease Control and Prevention, National Center for Health Statistics. National Vital Statistics System, Mortality 2018-2023 on CDC WONDER Online Database

Mortality Rates for Selected Causes of Death

Cause of Death	ICD-10[a] Code	Crude Mortality Rate[1] per 100,000 population	
		County[2]	U.S.
Accidental poisoning and exposure to noxious substances	X40-X49	38.0	30.5
Alzheimer disease	G30	37.0	35.4
Assault	X85-Y09	10.0	7.3
COVID-19	U07.1	83.2	65.3
Diabetes mellitus	E10-E14	25.9	30.0
Diseases of the liver	K70-K76	24.6	20.8
Human immunodeficiency virus (HIV) disease	B20-B24	1.9	1.5
Influenza and pneumonia	J09-J18	14.3	13.4
Intentional self-harm	X60-X84	22.1	14.7
Malnutrition	E40-E46	3.6	6.0
Obesity and other hyperalimentation	E65-E68	1.5	3.1
Renal failure	N17-N19	8.8	16.4
Transport accidents	V01-V99	17.1	14.4

Note: (a) ICD-10 = International Classification of Diseases 10th Revision; (1) Crude mortality rates are a three-year average covering 2021-2023; (2) Figures cover Tulsa County; Data are suppressed when the data meet the criteria for confidentiality constraints; Crude mortality rates are flagged as unreliable when the rate would be calculated with a numerator of 20 or less.
Source: Centers for Disease Control and Prevention, National Center for Health Statistics. National Vital Statistics System, Mortality 2018-2023 on CDC WONDER Online Database

Health Insurance Coverage

Area	With Health Insurance	With Private Health Insurance	With Public Health Insurance	Without Health Insurance	Population Under Age 19 Without Health Insurance
City	83.5	56.6	37.7	16.5	8.4
MSA[1]	86.8	63.7	35.3	13.2	7.6
U.S.	91.4	67.3	36.3	8.6	5.4

Note: Figures are percentages that cover the civilian noninstitutionalized population; (1) Figures cover the Tulsa, OK Metropolitan Statistical Area
Source: U.S. Census Bureau, 2019-2023 American Community Survey 5-Year Estimates

Number of Medical Professionals

Area	MDs[3]	DOs[3,4]	Dentists	Podiatrists	Chiropractors	Optometrists
County[1] (number)	1,798	1,037	490	29	274	171
County[1] (rate[2])	265.4	153.1	71.8	4.2	40.1	25.0
U.S. (rate[2])	302.5	29.2	74.6	6.4	29.5	18.0

Note: Data as of 2023 unless noted; (1) Data covers Tulsa County; (2) Number of medical professionals per 100,000 population; (3) Data as of 2022 and includes all active, non-federal physicians; (4) Doctor of Osteopathic Medicine
Source: U.S. Department of Health and Human Services, Health Resources and Services Administration, Bureau of Health Professions, Area Resource File (ARF) 2023-2024

EDUCATION

Public School District Statistics

District Name	Schls	Pupils	Pupil/Teacher Ratio	Minority Pupils[1] (%)	Total Rev. per Pupil ($)	Total Exp. per Pupil ($)
Tulsa	69	33,562	18.4	79.1	15,218	15,015
Union	17	14,974	17.5	77.0	14,187	12,490

Note: Table includes school districts with 2,000 or more students; (1) Percentage of students that are not non-Hispanic white.
Source: U.S. Department of Education, National Center for Education Statistics, Common Core of Data, Local Education Agency (School District) Universe Survey: School Year 2023-2024; U.S. Department of Education, National Center for Education Statistics, Common Core of Data, School District Finance Survey (F-33): School Year 2021–22

Highest Level of Education

Area	Less than H.S.	H.S. Diploma	Some College, No Deg.	Associate Degree	Bachelor's Degree	Master's Degree	Prof. School Degree	Doctorate Degree
City	12.4	25.0	21.2	8.2	20.8	8.0	3.0	1.5
MSA[1]	9.9	28.6	22.4	9.4	19.7	7.0	1.9	1.1
U.S.	10.6	26.2	19.4	8.8	21.3	9.8	2.3	1.6

Note: Figures cover persons age 25 and over; (1) Figures cover the Tulsa, OK Metropolitan Statistical Area
Source: U.S. Census Bureau, 2019-2023 American Community Survey 5-Year Estimates

Educational Attainment by Race

Area	High School Graduate or Higher (%)					Bachelor's Degree or Higher (%)				
	Total	White	Black	Asian	Hisp.[2]	Total	White	Black	Asian	Hisp.[2]
City	87.6	92.1	90.0	77.0	59.5	33.3	39.7	19.7	38.0	12.4
MSA[1]	90.1	92.7	90.7	77.9	66.0	29.8	32.6	21.1	33.6	15.1
U.S.	89.4	92.9	88.1	88.0	72.5	35.0	37.7	24.7	57.0	19.9

Note: Figures shown cover persons 25 years old and over; (1) Figures cover the Tulsa, OK Metropolitan Statistical Area; (2) People of Hispanic origin can be of any race
Source: U.S. Census Bureau, 2019-2023 American Community Survey 5-Year Estimates

School Enrollment by Grade and Control

Area	Preschool (%)		Kindergarten (%)		Grades 1 - 4 (%)		Grades 5 - 8 (%)		Grades 9 - 12 (%)	
	Public	Private	Public	Private	Public	Private	Public	Private	Public	Private
City	65.1	34.9	83.2	16.8	82.9	17.1	82.2	17.8	82.6	17.4
MSA[1]	67.2	32.8	84.6	15.4	84.2	15.8	85.3	14.7	85.5	14.5
U.S.	58.7	41.3	85.2	14.8	87.2	12.8	87.9	12.1	89.0	11.0

Note: Figures shown cover persons 3 years old and over; (1) Figures cover the Tulsa, OK Metropolitan Statistical Area
Source: U.S. Census Bureau, 2019-2023 American Community Survey 5-Year Estimates

Higher Education

Four-Year Colleges			Two-Year Colleges			Medical Schools[1]	Law Schools[2]	Voc/ Tech[3]
Public	Private Non-profit	Private For-profit	Public	Private Non-profit	Private For-profit			
3	3	1	3	3	3	1	1	6

Note: Figures cover institutions located within the Tulsa, OK Metropolitan Statistical Area and include main campuses only; (1) includes schools accredited by the Liaison Committee on Medical Education and the American Osteopathic Association's Commission on Osteopathic College Accreditation; (2) includes ABA-accredited schools, schools with provisional ABA accreditation, and state accredited schools; (3) includes all schools with programs that are less than 2 years.
Source: National Center for Education Statistics, Integrated Postsecondary Education System (IPEDS), 2023-24; Wikipedia, List of Medical Schools in the United States, accessed May 2, 2025; Wikipedia, List of Law Schools in the United States, accessed May 2, 2025

According to *U.S. News & World Report,* the Tulsa, OK metro area is home to one of the top 200 national universities in the U.S.: **University of Tulsa** (#179 tie). The indicators used to capture academic quality fall into a number of categories: assessment by administrators at peer institutions; retention of students; faculty resources; student selectivity; financial resources; alumni giving; high school counselor ratings of colleges; and graduation rate. *U.S. News & World Report, "America's Best Colleges 2025"*

EMPLOYERS

Major Employers

Company Name	Industry
AHS Hillcrest Medical Center	General medical & surgical hospitals
American Airlines	Airports, flying fields, & services
BlueCross BlueShield of Oklahoma	Hospital & medical services plans
Caprock Pipeline Company	Pipelines, natural gas
City of Tulsa	Local government
County of Tulsa	County government
Dollar Thrifty Automotive Group	Passenger car rental
GHS Health Maintenance Organization	Health insurance carriers
IC of Oklahoma	Truck & bus bodies
Matrix Service	Oil & gas pipeline construction
ONEOK	Natural gas transmission
Saint Francis Health System	General medical & surgical hospitals
St. John Medical Center	General medical & surgical hospitals
State Farm Fire and Casualty Company	Fire, marine, & casualty insurance
The Bama Companies	Bread, cake & related products
The Boeing Company	Missile guidance systems & equipment
The NORDAM Group	Aircraft parts & equipment
The Williams Companies	Natural gas transmission
Tulsa Public Schools	Education
Wal-Mart Stores	Retail

Note: Companies shown are located within the Tulsa, OK Metropolitan Statistical Area.
Source: Chambers of Commerce; State Departments of Labor; Wikipedia

Best Companies to Work For

Craft Health, headquartered in Tulsa, is among "Best Workplaces in Health Care." To determine the Best Workplaces in Health Care list, Great Place To Work analyzed the survey responses of over 185,000 employees from Great Place To Work-Certified companies in the health care industry. Survey data analysis and company-provided datapoints are then factored into a combined score to compare and rank the companies that create the most consistently positive experience for all employees in this industry. *Fortune, "Best Workplaces in Health Care," 2024*

PUBLIC SAFETY

Crime Rate

Area	Total Crime Rate	Violent Crime Rate				Property Crime Rate		
		Murder	Rape	Robbery	Aggrav. Assault	Burglary	Larceny-Theft	Motor Vehicle Theft
City	4,850.8	8.8	101.5	100.0	702.2	878.8	2,486.1	573.5
U.S.	2,290.9	5.7	38.0	66.5	264.1	250.7	1,347.2	318.7

Note: Figures are crimes per 100,000 population.
Source: FBI, Table 8, Offenses Known to Law Enforcement, by State by City, 2023

Hate Crimes

Area	Number of Quarters Reported	Number of Incidents per Bias Motivation					
		Race/Ethnicity/Ancestry	Religion	Sexual Orientation	Disability	Gender	Gender Identity
City	4	2	0	0	0	0	0
U.S.	4	5,900	2,699	2,077	187	92	492

Source: Federal Bureau of Investigation, Hate Crime Statistics 2023

Identity Theft Consumer Reports

Area	Reports	Reports per 100,000 Population	Rank[2]
MSA[1]	1,935	189	181
U.S.	1,135,291	339	-

Note: (1) Figures cover the Tulsa, OK Metropolitan Statistical Area; (2) Rank ranges from 1 to 401 where 1 indicates greatest number of identity theft reports per 100,000 population
Source: Federal Trade Commission, Consumer Sentinel Network Data Book 2024

Fraud and Other Consumer Reports

Area	Reports	Reports per 100,000 Population	Rank[2]
MSA[1]	10,338	1,007	203
U.S.	5,360,641	1,601	-

Note: (1) Figures cover the Tulsa, OK Metropolitan Statistical Area; (2) Rank ranges from 1 to 401 where 1 indicates greatest number of fraud and other consumer reports per 100,000 population
Source: Federal Trade Commission, Consumer Sentinel Network Data Book 2024

POLITICS

2024 Presidential Election Results

Area	Trump (Rep.)	Harris (Dem.)	Stein (Green)	Kennedy (Ind.)	Oliver (Lib.)	Other
Tulsa County	56.5	41.3	0.0	1.1	0.7	0.4
U.S.	49.7	48.2	0.6	0.5	0.4	0.6

Note: Results are percentages and may not add to 100% due to rounding
Source: Dave Leip's Atlas of U.S. Presidential Elections

SPORTS

Professional Sports Teams

Team Name	League	Year Established

No teams are located in the metro area
Source: Wikipedia, Major Professional Sports Teams of the United States and Canada, May 1, 2025

CLIMATE

Average and Extreme Temperatures

Temperature	Jan	Feb	Mar	Apr	May	Jun	Jul	Aug	Sep	Oct	Nov	Dec	Yr.
Extreme High (°F)	79	86	96	102	96	103	112	110	105	98	85	80	112
Average High (°F)	46	52	61	72	80	88	93	93	85	74	61	50	71
Average Temp. (°F)	36	41	50	61	69	78	83	82	74	63	50	40	61
Average Low (°F)	25	30	38	50	59	68	72	70	63	51	39	29	50
Extreme Low (°F)	-6	-7	-3	22	35	49	51	52	35	26	10	-8	-8

Note: Figures cover the years 1948-1990
Source: National Climatic Data Center, International Station Meteorological Climate Summary, 9/96

Average Precipitation/Snowfall/Humidity

Precip./Humidity	Jan	Feb	Mar	Apr	May	Jun	Jul	Aug	Sep	Oct	Nov	Dec	Yr.
Avg. Precip. (in.)	1.6	1.9	3.2	3.7	5.6	4.3	3.4	3.0	4.1	3.5	2.6	1.9	38.9
Avg. Snowfall (in.)	3	2	2	Tr	0	0	0	0	0	Tr	1	2	10
Avg. Rel. Hum. 6am (%)	78	78	76	77	85	85	82	84	85	82	78	78	81
Avg. Rel. Hum. 3pm (%)	53	51	47	46	54	53	48	46	49	46	48	52	49

Note: Figures cover the years 1948-1990; Tr = Trace amounts (<0.05 in. of rain; <0.5 in. of snow)
Source: National Climatic Data Center, International Station Meteorological Climate Summary, 9/96

Weather Conditions

Temperature			Daytime Sky			Precipitation		
10°F & below	32°F & below	90°F & above	Clear	Partly cloudy	Cloudy	0.01 inch or more precip.	0.1 inch or more snow/ice	Thunder-storms
6	78	74	117	141	107	88	8	50

Note: Figures are average number of days per year and cover the years 1948-1990
Source: National Climatic Data Center, International Station Meteorological Climate Summary, 9/96

HAZARDOUS WASTE

Superfund Sites

The Tulsa, OK metro area is home to two sites on the EPA's Superfund National Priorities List (NPL) or Superfund Alternative Approach (SAA) list: **Henryetta Iron and Metal** (Final NPL); **Wilcox Oil Company** (Final NPL). The Superfund alternative approach uses the same investigation and cleanup process and standards that are used for sites listed on the National Priorities List. The SAA is an alternative to listing a site on the NPL; it is not an alternative to Superfund or the Superfund process. There are a total of 1,445 Superfund sites with a status of proposed or final on both lists in the United States. *U.S. Environmental Protection Agency, National Priorities List, May 1, 2025; U.S. Environmental Protection Agency, Superfund Alternative Approach Sites, May 1, 2025*

AIR QUALITY

Air Quality Trends: Ozone

	1990	1995	2000	2005	2010	2015	2020	2021	2022	2023
MSA[1]	0.086	0.091	0.081	0.072	0.069	0.061	0.061	0.063	0.070	0.072
U.S.	0.087	0.089	0.081	0.080	0.072	0.068	0.066	0.067	0.067	0.070

Note: (1) Data covers the Tulsa, OK Metropolitan Statistical Area. The values shown are the composite ozone concentration averages among trend sites based on the highest fourth daily maximum 8-hour concentration in parts per million. These trends are based on sites having an adequate record of monitoring data during the trend period. Data from exceptional events are included.
Source: U.S. Environmental Protection Agency, Air Quality Monitoring Information, "Air Quality Trends by City, 1990-2023"

Air Quality Index

Area	Percent of Days when Air Quality was...[2]					AQI Statistics[2]	
	Good	Moderate	Unhealthy for Sensitive Groups	Unhealthy	Very Unhealthy	Maximum	Median
MSA[1]	37.8	56.7	4.9	0.5	0.0	197	53

Note: (1) Data covers the Tulsa, OK Metropolitan Statistical Area; (2) Based on 365 days with AQI data in 2023. Air Quality Index (AQI) is an index for reporting daily air quality. EPA calculates the AQI for five major air pollutants regulated by the Clean Air Act: ground-level ozone, particle pollution (aka particulate matter), carbon monoxide, sulfur dioxide, and nitrogen dioxide. The AQI runs from 0 to 500. The higher the AQI value, the greater the level of air pollution and the greater the health concern. There are six AQI categories: "Good" AQI is between 0 and 50. Air quality is considered satisfactory; "Moderate" AQI is between 51 and 100. Air quality is acceptable; "Unhealthy for Sensitive Groups" When AQI values are between 101 and 150, members of sensitive groups may experience health effects; "Unhealthy" When AQI values are between 151 and 200 everyone may begin to experience health effects; "Very Unhealthy" AQI values between 201 and 300 trigger a health alert; "Hazardous" AQI values over 300 trigger warnings of emergency conditions (not shown).
Source: U.S. Environmental Protection Agency, Air Quality Index Report, 2023

Air Quality Index Pollutants

Area	Percent of Days when AQI Pollutant was...[2]					
	Carbon Monoxide	Nitrogen Dioxide	Ozone	Sulfur Dioxide	Particulate Matter 2.5	Particulate Matter 10
MSA[1]	0.0	0.0	45.2	(3)	52.9	1.9

Note: (1) Data covers the Tulsa, OK Metropolitan Statistical Area; (2) Based on 365 days with AQI data in 2023. The Air Quality Index (AQI) is an index for reporting daily air quality. EPA calculates the AQI for five major air pollutants regulated by the Clean Air Act: ground-level ozone, particle pollution (also known as particulate matter), carbon monoxide, sulfur dioxide, and nitrogen dioxide. The AQI runs from 0 to 500. The higher the AQI value, the greater the level of air pollution and the greater the health concern; (3) Sulfur dioxide is no longer included in this table because SO_2 concentrations tend to be very localized and not necessarily representative of broad geographical areas like counties and CBSAs.
Source: U.S. Environmental Protection Agency, Air Quality Index Report, 2023

Maximum Air Pollutant Concentrations: Particulate Matter, Ozone, CO and Lead

	Particulate Matter 10 (ug/m^3)	Particulate Matter 2.5 Wtd AM (ug/m^3)	Particulate Matter 2.5 24-Hr (ug/m^3)	Ozone (ppm)	Carbon Monoxide (ppm)	Lead (ug/m^3)
MSA[1] Level	101	9.3	20	0.078	1	n/a
NAAQS[2]	150	15	35	0.075	9	0.15
Met NAAQS[2]	Yes	Yes	Yes	No	Yes	n/a

Note: (1) Data covers the Tulsa, OK Metropolitan Statistical Area; Data from exceptional events are included; (2) National Ambient Air Quality Standards; ppm = parts per million; ug/m^3 = micrograms per cubic meter; n/a not available.
Concentrations: Particulate Matter 10 (coarse particulate)—highest second maximum 24-hour concentration; Particulate Matter 2.5 Wtd AM (fine particulate)—highest weighted annual mean concentration; Particulate Matter 2.5 24-Hour (fine particulate)—highest 98th percentile 24-hour concentration; Ozone—highest fourth daily maximum 8-hour concentration; Carbon Monoxide—highest second maximum non-overlapping 8-hour concentration; Lead—maximum running 3-month average
Source: U.S. Environmental Protection Agency, Air Quality Monitoring Information, "Air Quality Statistics by City, 2023"

Maximum Air Pollutant Concentrations: Nitrogen Dioxide and Sulfur Dioxide

	Nitrogen Dioxide AM (ppb)	Nitrogen Dioxide 1-Hr (ppb)	Sulfur Dioxide AM (ppb)	Sulfur Dioxide 1-Hr (ppb)	Sulfur Dioxide 24-Hr (ppb)
MSA[1] Level	6	33	n/a	3	n/a
NAAQS[2]	53	100	30	75	140
Met NAAQS[2]	Yes	Yes	n/a	Yes	n/a

Note: (1) Data covers the Tulsa, OK Metropolitan Statistical Area; Data from exceptional events are included; (2) National Ambient Air Quality Standards; ppm = parts per million; ug/m^3 = micrograms per cubic meter; n/a not available.
Concentrations: Nitrogen Dioxide AM—highest arithmetic mean concentration; Nitrogen Dioxide 1-Hr—highest 98th percentile 1-hour daily maximum concentration; Sulfur Dioxide AM—highest annual mean concentration; Sulfur Dioxide 1-Hr—highest 99th percentile 1-hour daily maximum concentration; Sulfur Dioxide 24-Hr—highest second maximum 24-hour concentration
Source: U.S. Environmental Protection Agency, Air Quality Monitoring Information, "Air Quality Statistics by City, 2023"

Wichita, Kansas

Background

Wichita lies in the southeastern plains of Kansas, named for a local Native American tribe. In 1864, two white entrepreneurs, Jesse Chisholm and James R. Mead, struck up a lively trade in the area with Native Americans. After the tribe was relocated to Indian Territory in Oklahoma in 1867, white settlers planted roots in the area, and cowboys used a trail that Chisholm laid out from the town's trading post to Texas, to drive Longhorn cattle to the railhead of the Wichita and Southwestern Railroad.

In the 1880s, like many Plains-area cattle-shipping points, Wichita hosted dance halls, gambling, and saloons. Wyatt Earp served there as a lawman for a time. In 1886, the town officially became a city, having grown to over 20,000 in population, much of it due to eager speculation in prairie lands.

After the turn of the century, oil was discovered in the area, luring more people, and the city swelled to over 100,000 by 1930. Shortly after World War I, which saw great advancements in aviation, Wichita's first airplane factory was built, and the city became the country's leading manufacturer of aircraft. Walter H. Beech, Clyde V. Cessna, and Lloyd C. Stearman became famous members of the community for their early leadership in the industry.

Wichita is the largest and most dominant industrial city in the state of Kansas. Oil rigs and aircraft factories shielded the worst of the Great Depression from Wichita, while much of Kansas was consumed by the Dust Bowl. During World War II, more airplanes rolled off the city's three assembly lines than in any other city in America. Steady aircraft industry growth continued until the 1980s, when a slump occurred. By the late 1990s, a revival of the industry was in full swing until major layoffs of the early 2000s. In 2013, Boeing closed its Wichita plant, but the void was filled by Spirit AeroSystems, and the city remains a major manufacturer of private and military aircraft, with Spirit, Textron Aviation (Cessna and Beechcraft), and Bombardier Learjet operating there.

A global company with headquarters in Wichita is Koch Industries, which deals in chemicals, energy, and gas liquids. The city is also headquarters to Cargill Beef. Other major industries in Wichita are healthcare and manufacturing.

Transportation to and from Wichita is provided by the Wichita Dwight D. Eisenhower Airport, the largest in the state, and Colonel James Jabara Airport. Two railroad lines run freight service through the city and Wichita Bicycle Master Plan oversees the city's 149-mile Priority Bicycle Network.

Wichita State University, a public research institution, is the largest of the city's three universities and the third largest in the state, competing at the Division I level. Wichita is also home to several minor league teams, including the Wind Surge (baseball), the Thunder (ice hockey), and the Force (indoor football).

Wichita's cultural institutions include the Wichita Museum of Art with a permanent collection of 7,000 objects, Ulrich Museum of Art at Wichita State, and Wichita Symphony Orchestra, the oldest professional symphony orchestra in Kansas. The River Festival and the Wichita Black Arts Festival are popular annual events.

The climate in Wichita is continental but generally mild, punctuated occasionally by more intemperate weather conditions. Summers are usually warm and humid. Winters are usually mild, with brief periods of cold weather. Snowfall is light to moderate, with the ground rarely being covered for more than three days. Thunderstorms, occasionally severe, occur through the spring and summer months. The city experienced a destructive supercell in April 2024

Rankings

General Rankings

- To help military veterans find the best places in which to settle down, *WalletHub* compared the 100 largest U.S. cities across 19 key indicators of livability, affordability and veteran-friendliness. They range from the share of military skill-related jobs to veteran income growth to the availability of VA health facilities. Wichita ranked #80. *Wallethub.com, "Best & Worst Places for Veterans to Live (2025)," November 7, 2024*

- In their annual survey, Livability.com looked at data for more than 2,000 mid-sized U.S. cities to assign a "Livability Score"for each. The top 100 scoring cities make up Livability's "Top 100 Best Places to Live in the U.S." in 2025. Wichita was placed among the top 100 of the customizable list. Criteria: housing and economy; cost of living; environment; education; health care options; transportation; safety; and community amenities. *Livability.com, "Top 100 Best Places to Live in the U.S. in 2025" April 15, 2025*

Business/Finance Rankings

- The Wichita metro area appeared on the Milken Institute "2025 Best Performing Cities" list. Rank: #43 out of 200 large metro areas (based on performance category). Criteria: job growth; wage growth; high-tech growth and impact; community resilience; housing affordability; household broadband access. *Milken Institute, "Best-Performing Cities 2025," January 14, 2025*

Education Rankings

- Personal finance website *WalletHub* analyzed the 150 largest U.S. metropolitan statistical areas to determine where the most educated Americans are putting their degrees to work. Criteria: education levels; percentage of workers with degrees; education quality and attainment gap; public school quality rankings; quality and enrollment of each metro area's universities. Wichita was ranked #99 (#1 = most educated city). *WalletHub.com, "Most & Least Educated Cities in America, 2025" July 2, 2024*

Health/Fitness Rankings

- For each of the 100 largest cities in the United States, the American Fitness Index®, compiled in partnership between the American College of Sports Medicine and the Elevance Health Foundation, evaluated community infrastructure and more than 30 health behaviors including preventive health, levels of chronic disease conditions, food insecurity, pedestrian safety, air quality, and community/environment resources that support physical activity. Wichita ranked #97 for "community fitness." *americanfitnessindex.org, "2024 ACSM American Fitness Index Summary Report," July 23, 2024*

- Wichita was identified as a "2025 Allergy Capital." The area ranked #1 out of the nation's 100 largest metropolitan areas. Three groups of factors were used to identify the most challenging cities for people with allergies: annual tree, grass, and weed pollen scores; over the counter allergy medicine use; number of board-certified allergy specialists. *Asthma and Allergy Foundation of America, "2025 Allergy Capitals: The Most Challenging Places to Live with Allergies," March 18, 2025*

- Wichita was identified as a "2024 Asthma Capital." The area ranked #67 out of the nation's 100 largest metropolitan areas. Criteria: estimated asthma prevalence; asthma-related mortality; and ER visits due to asthma. Risk factors analyzed but not factored in the rankings: annual air quality including pollution and ozone levels; public smoking laws; indoor air quality; access to asthma specialists; rescue and controller medication use; uninsured rate; pollen allergy; poverty rate. *Asthma and Allergy Foundation of America, "Asthma Capitals 2024: The Most Challenging Places to Live With Asthma," September 10, 2024*

Real Estate Rankings

- *WalletHub* compared the most populated U.S. cities to determine which had the best markets for real estate agents. Wichita ranked #95 where demand was high and pay was the best. Criteria: sales per agent; annual median wage for real-estate agents; monthly average starting salary for real estate agents; real estate job density and competition; unemployment rate; home turnover rate; housing-market health index; and other relevant metrics. *WalletHub.com, "2021 Best Places to Be a Real Estate Agent," May 12, 2021*

- Wichita was ranked #28 out of 176 metro areas in terms of cost of housing in 2024 by the National Association of Home Builders (#1 = most affordable). Criteria: the portion of an average family's income necessary to pay the mortgage on a median-priced home. *National Association of Home Builders®, NAHB-Wells Fargo Cost of Housing Index, 4th Quarter 2024*

Safety Rankings

- Allstate ranked the 100 most populous cities in America in terms of driver safety. Wichita ranked #21. Criteria based on anonymized driving behavior data from Allstate's mobile app powered by Arity: high speed driving (over 80 mph), phone handling, and hard braking. The report helps increase the importance of safety and awareness behind the wheel. *Allstate, "16th Allstate America's Best Drivers Report®," July 11, 2024*

- Wichita was identified as one of the most dangerous cities in America by NeighborhoodScout. The city ranked #54 out of 100 (#1 = most dangerous). Criteria: number of violent crimes per 1,000 residents. The editors evaluated cities with 25,000 or more residents. *NeighborhoodScout.com, "2023 Top 100 Most Dangerous Cities in the U.S.," January 12, 2023*

Women/Minorities Rankings

- Personal finance website *WalletHub* compared more than 180 U.S. cities across two key dimensions, "Hispanic Business-Friendliness" and "Hispanic Purchasing Power," to arrive at the most favorable conditions for Hispanic entrepreneurs. Wichita was ranked #112 out of 182. Criteria includes: share of Hispanic-Owned Businesses; average growth of Hispanic Business revenues; Small Business-Friendliness score; affordability; and number of Hispanics with at least a bachelor's degree. *WalletHub.com, "Best Cities for Hispanic Entrepreneurs," September 4, 2024*

Miscellaneous Rankings

- Wichita was selected as a 2024 Digital Cities Survey winner. The city ranked #4 in the large city (250,000 to 499,999 population) category. The survey examined and assessed how city governments are utilizing new technology and modernized applications to provide residents an array of contactless services and conveniences. Survey questions focused on ten initiatives: cybersecurity; citizen experience; disaster recovery; business intelligence; IT personnel retention; data governance; business automation; AI/machine learning; application modernization; and IT collaboration. *Center for Digital Government, "2024 Digital Cities Survey," November 5, 2024*

- The financial planning site *SmartAsset* has compiled its annual study on the best places for Halloween in the U.S. for 2022. 146 cities were compared to determine that Wichita ranked #29 out of 35 for still being able to enjoy the festivities despite COVID-19. Metrics included: safety, family-friendliness, percentage of children in the population, concentration of candy and costume shops, weather and COVID infection rates. *SmartAsset.com, "2022 Edition-Best Places to Celebrate Halloween," October 19, 2022*

- *WalletHub* compared 148 of the most populated U.S. cities to determine their operating efficiency. A "Quality of Services" score was constructed for each city and then measured against the total budget per capita to reveal which were managed the best. Wichita ranked #10. Criteria: financial stability; economy; education; safety; health; infrastructure and pollution. *WalletHub.com, "2025's Best- & Worst-Run Cities in America," June 18, 2024*

Business Environment

DEMOGRAPHICS

Population Growth

Area	1990 Census	2000 Census	2010 Census	2020 Census	2023 Estimate[2]	Population Growth 1990-2023 (%)
City	313,693	344,284	382,368	397,532	396,488	26.4
MSA[1]	511,111	571,166	623,061	647,610	648,935	27.0
U.S.	248,709,873	281,421,906	308,745,538	331,449,281	332,387,540	33.6

Note: (1) Figures cover the Wichita, KS Metropolitan Statistical Area; (2) 2019-2023 5-year ACS population estimate
Source: U.S. Census Bureau, 1990 Census, 2000 Census, 2010 Census, 2020 Census, 2019-2023 American Community Survey 5-Year Estimates

Race

Area	White Alone[2] (%)	Black Alone[2] (%)	Asian Alone[2] (%)	AIAN[3] Alone[2] (%)	NHOPI[4] Alone[2] (%)	Other Race Alone[2] (%)	Two or More Races (%)
City	66.6	9.7	4.9	0.9	0.0	5.5	12.4
MSA[1]	74.4	6.7	3.7	0.8	0.1	4.3	10.1
U.S.	63.4	12.4	5.8	0.9	0.2	6.6	10.7

Note: (1) Figures cover the Wichita, KS Metropolitan Statistical Area; (2) Alone is defined as not being in combination with one or more other races; (3) American Indian and Alaska Native; (4) Native Hawaiian and Other Pacific Islander
Source: U.S. Census Bureau, 2019-2023 American Community Survey 5-Year Estimates

Hispanic or Latino Origin

Area	Total (%)	Mexican (%)	Puerto Rican (%)	Cuban (%)	Other (%)
City	18.4	15.1	0.8	0.1	2.5
MSA[1]	14.5	11.8	0.6	0.1	2.0
U.S.	19.0	11.3	1.8	0.7	5.2

Note: Persons of Hispanic or Latino origin can be of any race; (1) Figures cover the Wichita, KS Metropolitan Statistical Area
Source: U.S. Census Bureau, 2019-2023 American Community Survey 5-Year Estimates

Age

Area	Percent of Population									Median Age
	Under Age 5	Age 5–19	Age 20–34	Age 35–44	Age 45–54	Age 55–64	Age 65–74	Age 75–84	Age 85+	
City	6.3	20.7	22.0	12.9	11.0	11.7	9.4	4.1	1.9	35.7
MSA[1]	6.3	21.5	20.2	12.8	11.2	12.3	9.6	4.3	2.0	36.6
U.S.	5.7	19.1	20.2	13.1	12.3	12.8	10.0	4.9	1.9	38.7

Note: (1) Figures cover the Wichita, KS Metropolitan Statistical Area
Source: U.S. Census Bureau, 2019-2023 American Community Survey 5-Year Estimates

Disability by Age

Area	All Ages	Under 18 Years Old	18 to 64 Years Old	65 Years and Over
City	14.9	5.9	13.6	34.7
MSA[1]	14.6	5.6	13.0	35.1
U.S.	13.0	4.7	10.7	32.9

Note: Figures show percent of the civilian noninstitutionalized population that reported having a disability. Disability status is determined from six types of difficulty: vision, hearing, cognitive, ambulatory, self-care, and independent living. For children under 5 years old, hearing and vision difficulty are used to determine disability status. For children between the ages of 5 and 14, disability status is determined from hearing, vision, cognitive, ambulatory, and self-care difficulties. For people aged 15 years and older, they are considered to have a disability if they have difficulty with any one of the six difficulty types; Note: (1) Figures cover the Wichita, KS Metropolitan Statistical Area
Source: U.S. Census Bureau, 2019-2023 American Community Survey 5-Year Estimates

Ancestry

Area	German	Irish	English	American	Italian	Polish	French[2]	European	Scottish
City	19.2	9.8	10.4	4.8	1.7	0.9	1.8	1.6	1.6
MSA[1]	21.4	9.8	11.1	5.5	1.8	0.9	1.8	1.9	1.8
U.S.	12.6	9.4	9.1	5.5	4.9	2.6	2.0	1.6	1.6

Note: Figures are the percentage of the total population reporting a particular ancestry. The nine most commonly reported ancestries in the U.S. are shown. Figures include multiple ancestries (e.g. if a person reported being Irish and Italian, they were included in both columns); (1) Figures cover the Wichita, KS Metropolitan Statistical Area; (2) Excludes Basque
Source: U.S. Census Bureau, 2019-2023 American Community Survey 5-Year Estimates

Foreign-born Population

Area	Percent of Population Born in								
	Any Foreign Country	Asia	Mexico	Europe	Caribbean	Central America[2]	South America	Africa	Canada
City	10.0	3.5	4.4	0.5	0.1	0.5	0.4	0.6	0.1
MSA[1]	7.4	2.6	3.1	0.5	0.1	0.4	0.3	0.4	0.1
U.S.	13.9	4.3	3.3	1.4	1.4	1.2	1.2	0.8	0.2

Note: (1) Figures cover the Wichita, KS Metropolitan Statistical Area; (2) Excludes Mexico.
Source: U.S. Census Bureau, 2019-2023 American Community Survey 5-Year Estimates

Household Size

Area	Persons in Household (%)							Average Household Size
	One	Two	Three	Four	Five	Six	Seven or More	
City	33.2	32.6	13.2	10.8	5.7	2.7	1.7	2.47
MSA[1]	30.1	33.6	14.0	11.7	6.2	2.8	1.7	2.52
U.S.	28.5	33.8	15.4	12.7	5.9	2.3	1.4	2.54

Note: (1) Figures cover the Wichita, KS Metropolitan Statistical Area
Source: U.S. Census Bureau, 2019-2023 American Community Survey 5-Year Estimates

Household Relationships

Area	Householder	Opposite-sex Spouse	Same-sex Spouse	Opposite-sex Unmarried Partner	Same-sex Unmarried Partner	Child[2]	Grandchild	Other Relatives	Non-relatives
City	40.0	16.4	0.2	2.7	0.2	29.1	2.2	3.7	3.1
MSA[1]	39.0	18.2	0.1	2.4	0.1	29.8	2.1	3.2	2.6
U.S.	38.3	17.5	0.2	2.5	0.2	28.3	2.4	4.8	3.4

Note: Figures are percent of the total population; (1) Figures cover the Wichita, KS Metropolitan Statistical Area; (2) Includes biological, adopted, and stepchildren of the householder
Source: U.S. Census Bureau, 2020 Census

Gender

Area	Males	Females	Males per 100 Females
City	197,295	199,193	99.0
MSA[1]	323,191	325,744	99.2
U.S.	164,545,087	167,842,453	98.0

Note: (1) Figures cover the Wichita, KS Metropolitan Statistical Area
Source: U.S. Census Bureau, 2019-2023 American Community Survey 5-Year Estimates

Marital Status

Area	Never Married	Now Married[2]	Separated	Widowed	Divorced
City	35.0	45.2	1.8	5.2	12.8
MSA[1]	31.2	50.0	1.4	5.4	12.0
U.S.	34.1	47.9	1.7	5.6	10.7

Note: Figures are percentages and cover the population 15 years of age and older; (1) Figures cover the Wichita, KS Metropolitan Statistical Area; (2) Excludes separated
Source: U.S. Census Bureau, 2019-2023 American Community Survey 5-Year Estimates

Religious Groups by Family

Area	Catholic	Baptist	Methodist	LDS[2]	Pentecostal	Lutheran	Islam	Adventist	Other
MSA[1]	12.7	23.5	4.5	1.5	1.4	1.3	0.1	1.1	15.0
U.S.	18.7	7.3	3.0	2.0	1.8	1.7	1.3	1.3	11.6

Note: Figures are the number of adherents as a percentage of the total population and cover the eight largest religious groups in the U.S; (1) Figures cover the Wichita, KS Metropolitan Statistical Area; (2) Church of Jesus Christ of Latter-day Saints
Sources: 2020 U.S. Religion Census, Association of Statisticians of American Religious Bodies; The Association of Religion Data Archives (ARDA)

Religious Groups by Tradition

Area	Catholic	Evangelical Protestant	Mainline Protestant	Black Protestant	Islam	Judaism	Hinduism	Orthodox	Buddhism
MSA[1]	12.7	19.4	23.2	2.6	0.1	<0.1	0.1	0.2	0.5
U.S.	18.7	16.5	5.2	2.3	1.3	0.6	0.4	0.4	0.3

Note: Figures are the number of adherents as a percentage of the total population; (1) Figures cover the Wichita, KS Metropolitan Statistical Area
Sources: 2020 U.S. Religion Census, Association of Statisticians of American Religious Bodies; The Association of Religion Data Archives (ARDA)

ECONOMY

Real Gross Domestic Product (GDP)

Area	2017	2018	2019	2020	2021	2022	2023	Rank[3]
MSA[1]	35.9	35.8	35.8	34.7	35.7	36.7	37.7	89
U.S.[2]	17,619.1	18,160.7	18,642.5	18,238.9	19,387.6	19,896.6	20,436.3	—

Note: Figures are in billions of chained 2017 dollars; (1) Figures cover the Wichita, KS Metropolitan Statistical Area; (2) Figures cover real GDP within metropolitan areas; (3) Rank is based on 2023 data and ranges from 1 to 384
Source: U.S. Bureau of Economic Analysis

Economic Growth

Area	2014	2015	2016	2017	2018	2019	2020	2021	2022	2023
MSA[1]	6.2	5.6	8.2	0.4	-0.1	-0.2	-2.9	2.8	2.9	2.8
U.S.[2]	2.6	3.2	2.0	2.7	3.1	2.7	-2.2	6.3	2.6	2.7

Note: Figures are real gross domestic product growth rates and represent percent change from preceding period; (1) Figures cover the Wichita, KS Metropolitan Statistical Area; (2) Figures are the average growth rates within metropolitan areas
Source: U.S. Bureau of Economic Analysis

Metropolitan Area Exports

Area	2018	2019	2020	2021	2022	2023	Rank[2]
MSA[1]	3,817.0	3,494.7	2,882.1	3,615.3	4,550.4	4,475.1	69
U.S.	1,664,056.1	1,645,173.7	1,431,406.6	1,753,941.4	2,062,937.4	2,019,160.5	—

Note: Figures are in millions of dollars; (1) Figures cover the Wichita, KS Metropolitan Statistical Area; (2) Rank is based on 2023 data and ranges from 1 to 386
Source: U.S. Department of Commerce, International Trade Administration, Office of Trade and Economic Analysis, Industry and Analysis, Exports by Metropolitan Area, data extracted April 2, 2025

Building Permits

Area	Single-Family			Multi-Family			Total		
	2023	2024	Pct. Chg.	2023	2024	Pct. Chg.	2023	2024	Pct. Chg.
City	605	558	-7.8	1,173	742	-36.7	1,778	1,300	-26.9
MSA[1]	1,470	1,479	0.6	2,063	1,560	-24.4	3,533	3,039	-14.0
U.S.	920,000	981,900	6.7	591,100	496,100	-16.1	1,511,100	1,478,000	-2.2

Note: (1) Figures cover the Wichita, KS Metropolitan Statistical Area; Figures represent new, privately-owned housing units authorized (unadjusted data)
Source: U.S. Census Bureau, Building Permits Survey (BPS), 2023, 2024

Bankruptcy Filings

Area	Business Filings			Nonbusiness Filings		
	2023	2024	% Chg.	2023	2024	% Chg.
Sedgwick County	24	27	12.5	757	777	2.6
U.S.	18,926	23,107	22.1	434,064	494,201	13.9

Note: Business filings include Chapter 7, Chapter 9, Chapter 11, Chapter 12, Chapter 13, Chapter 15, and Section 304; Nonbusiness filings include Chapter 7, Chapter 11, and Chapter 13
Source: Administrative Office of the U.S. Courts, Business and Nonbusiness Bankruptcy, County Cases Commenced by Chapter of the Bankruptcy Code, During the 12-Month Period Ending December 31, 2023 and Business and Nonbusiness Bankruptcy, County Cases Commenced by Chapter of the Bankruptcy Code, During the 12-Month Period Ending December 31, 2024

Housing Vacancy Rates

Area	Gross Vacancy Rate[3] (%)			Year-Round Vacancy Rate[4] (%)			Rental Vacancy Rate[5] (%)			Homeowner Vacancy Rate[6] (%)		
	2022	2023	2024	2022	2023	2024	2022	2023	2024	2022	2023	2024
MSA[1]	n/a	n/a	n/a	n/a	n/a	n/a	n/a	n/a	n/a	n/a	n/a	n/a
U.S.[2]	9.1	9.0	9.1	7.5	7.5	7.6	5.7	6.5	6.8	0.8	0.8	1.0

Note: (1) Figures cover the Wichita, KS Metropolitan Statistical Area; (2) Figures cover the 75 largest Metropolitan Statistical Areas; (3) The percentage of the total housing inventory that is vacant; (4) The percentage of the housing inventory (excluding seasonal units) that is year-round vacant; (5) The percentage of rental inventory that is vacant for rent; (6) The percentage of homeowner inventory that is vacant for sale; n/a not available
Source: U.S. Census Bureau, Housing Vacancies and Homeownership Annual Statistics: 2022, 2023, 2024

INCOME

Income

Area	Per Capita ($)	Median Household ($)	Average Household ($)
City	35,958	63,072	87,820
MSA[1]	36,529	68,930	91,559
U.S.	43,289	78,538	110,491

Note: (1) Figures cover the Wichita, KS Metropolitan Statistical Area
Source: U.S. Census Bureau, 2019-2023 American Community Survey 5-Year Estimates

Household Income Distribution

Area	Percent of Households Earning							
	Under $15,000	$15,000 -$24,999	$25,000 -$34,999	$35,000 -$49,999	$50,000 -$74,999	$75,000 -$99,999	$100,000 -$149,999	$150,000 and up
City	9.5	7.6	9.6	13.0	18.1	13.3	15.6	13.3
MSA[1]	8.3	6.6	8.7	12.2	18.3	13.9	17.0	14.8
U.S.	8.5	6.6	6.8	10.4	15.7	12.7	17.4	21.9

Note: (1) Figures cover the Wichita, KS Metropolitan Statistical Area
Source: U.S. Census Bureau, 2019-2023 American Community Survey 5-Year Estimates

Poverty Rate

Area	All Ages	Under 18 Years Old	18 to 64 Years Old	65 Years and Over
City	15.9	21.6	15.0	10.3
MSA[1]	13.1	17.4	12.4	8.8
U.S.	12.4	16.3	11.6	10.4

Note: Figures are percentage of people whose income during the past 12 months was below the poverty level; (1) Figures cover the Wichita, KS Metropolitan Statistical Area
Source: U.S. Census Bureau, 2019-2023 American Community Survey 5-Year Estimates

EMPLOYMENT

Labor Force and Employment

Area	Civilian Labor Force			Workers Employed		
	Dec. 2023	Dec. 2024	% Chg.	Dec. 2023	Dec. 2024	% Chg.
City	194,170	197,795	1.9	188,497	190,038	0.8
MSA[1]	320,952	326,697	1.8	311,687	314,280	0.8
U.S.	166,661,000	167,746,000	0.7	160,754,000	161,294,000	0.3

Note: Data is not seasonally adjusted and covers workers 16 years of age and older; (1) Figures cover the Wichita, KS Metropolitan Statistical Area
Source: Bureau of Labor Statistics, Local Area Unemployment Statistics

Unemployment Rate

Area	2024											
	Jan.	Feb.	Mar.	Apr.	May	Jun.	Jul.	Aug.	Sep.	Oct.	Nov.	Dec.
City	3.7	4.1	3.9	3.5	3.9	4.4	5.1	4.7	3.9	4.4	4.5	3.9
MSA[1]	3.6	3.8	3.7	3.4	3.7	4.2	5.0	4.6	3.8	4.2	4.3	3.8
U.S.	4.1	4.2	3.9	3.5	3.7	4.3	4.5	4.4	3.9	3.9	4.0	3.8

Note: Data is not seasonally adjusted and covers workers 16 years of age and older; (1) Figures cover the Wichita, KS Metropolitan Statistical Area
Source: Bureau of Labor Statistics, Local Area Unemployment Statistics

Average Wages

Occupation	$/Hr.	Occupation	$/Hr.
Accountants and Auditors	37.74	Maintenance and Repair Workers	22.57
Automotive Mechanics	24.13	Marketing Managers	67.18
Bookkeepers	21.79	Network and Computer Systems Admin.	39.93
Carpenters	25.64	Nurses, Licensed Practical	27.76
Cashiers	13.10	Nurses, Registered	36.06
Computer Programmers	50.82	Nursing Assistants	17.82
Computer Systems Analysts	48.92	Office Clerks, General	16.54
Computer User Support Specialists	24.62	Physical Therapists	46.81
Construction Laborers	20.29	Physicians	100.27
Cooks, Restaurant	15.63	Plumbers, Pipefitters and Steamfitters	29.54
Customer Service Representatives	19.26	Police and Sheriff's Patrol Officers	28.31
Dentists	82.76	Postal Service Mail Carriers	28.32
Electricians	31.51	Real Estate Sales Agents	n/a
Engineers, Electrical	46.39	Retail Salespersons	16.72
Fast Food and Counter Workers	12.56	Sales Representatives, Technical/Scientific	58.23
Financial Managers	75.40	Secretaries, Exc. Legal/Medical/Executive	19.03
First-Line Supervisors of Office Workers	30.36	Security Guards	18.73
General and Operations Managers	48.65	Surgeons	n/a
Hairdressers/Cosmetologists	17.46	Teacher Assistants, Exc. Postsecondary[1]	14.38
Home Health and Personal Care Aides	14.72	Teachers, Secondary School, Exc. Sp. Ed.[1]	28.72
Janitors and Cleaners	15.77	Telemarketers	n/a
Landscaping/Groundskeeping Workers	18.31	Truck Drivers, Heavy/Tractor-Trailer	26.88
Lawyers	60.10	Truck Drivers, Light/Delivery Services	19.57
Maids and Housekeeping Cleaners	14.70	Waiters and Waitresses	17.67

Note: Wage data covers the Wichita, KS Metropolitan Statistical Area; (1) Hourly wages were calculated from annual wage data based on a 40 hour work week
Source: Bureau of Labor Statistics, Metro Area Occupational Employment & Wage Estimates, May 2024

Employment by Industry

Sector	MSA[1] Number of Employees	MSA[1] Percent of Total	U.S. Percent of Total
Construction, Mining, and Logging	17,400	5.5	5.5
Financial Activities	12,900	4.1	5.8
Government	44,100	14.0	14.9
Information	3,500	1.1	1.9
Leisure and Hospitality	32,300	10.2	10.4
Manufacturing	52,600	16.7	8.0
Other Services	12,500	4.0	3.7
Private Education and Health Services	50,300	15.9	16.9
Professional and Business Services	34,100	10.8	14.2
Retail Trade	31,900	10.1	10.0
Transportation, Warehousing, and Utilities	13,800	4.4	4.8
Wholesale Trade	10,100	3.2	3.9

Note: Figures are non-farm employment as of December 2024. Figures are not seasonally adjusted and include workers 16 years of age and older; (1) Figures cover the Wichita, KS Metropolitan Statistical Area
Source: Bureau of Labor Statistics, Current Employment Statistics, Employment, Hours, and Earnings

Employment by Occupation

Occupation Classification	City (%)	MSA[1] (%)	U.S. (%)
Management, Business, Science, and Arts	36.4	38.2	42.0
Natural Resources, Construction, and Maintenance	10.1	10.3	8.6
Production, Transportation, and Material Moving	15.6	15.2	13.0
Sales and Office	20.8	20.2	19.9
Service	17.1	16.1	16.5

Note: Figures cover employed civilians 16 years of age and older; (1) Figures cover the Wichita, KS Metropolitan Statistical Area
Source: U.S. Census Bureau, 2019-2023 American Community Survey 5-Year Estimates

Occupations with Greatest Projected Employment Growth: 2022 – 2032

Occupation[1]	2022 Employment	2032 Projected Employment	Numeric Employment Change	Percent Employment Change
Home Health and Personal Care Aides	27,140	32,990	5,850	21.6
Cooks, Restaurant	11,800	14,850	3,050	25.8
Software Developers	12,550	15,460	2,910	23.2
Fast Food and Counter Workers	35,020	37,000	1,980	5.7
Stockers and Order Fillers	28,280	30,170	1,890	6.7
Registered Nurses	32,310	33,910	1,600	5.0
Medical and Health Services Managers	5,110	6,550	1,440	28.2
Nurse Practitioners	3,240	4,630	1,390	42.9
Nursing Assistants (SOC 2018)	22,100	23,450	1,350	6.1
Heavy and Tractor-Trailer Truck Drivers	25,400	26,700	1,300	5.1

Note: Projections cover Kansas; (1) Sorted by numeric employment change
Source: www.projectionscentral.org, State Occupational Projections, 2022–2032 Long-Term Projections

Fastest-Growing Occupations: 2022 – 2032

Occupation[1]	2022 Employment	2032 Projected Employment	Numeric Employment Change	Percent Employment Change
Nurse Practitioners	3,240	4,630	1,390	42.9
Data Scientists	320	430	110	34.4
Wind Turbine Service Technicians	620	830	210	33.9
Logisticians	2,230	2,890	660	29.6
Taxi Drivers	1,020	1,310	290	28.4
Medical and Health Services Managers	5,110	6,550	1,440	28.2
Physician Assistants	900	1,140	240	26.7
Cooks, Restaurant	11,800	14,850	3,050	25.8
Electrical, Electronic, and Electromechanical Assemblers, Except Coil Winders, Tapers, and Fini	3,380	4,210	830	24.6
Information Security Analysts (SOC 2018)	1,280	1,590	310	24.2

Note: Projections cover Kansas; (1) Sorted by percent employment change and excludes occupations with numeric employment change less than 50
Source: www.projectionscentral.org, State Occupational Projections, 2022–2032 Long-Term Projections

CITY FINANCES

City Government Finances

Component	2022 ($000)	2022 ($ per capita)
Total Revenues	603,538	1,541
Total Expenditures	415,699	1,061
Debt Outstanding	1,216,782	3,106

Source: U.S. Census Bureau, State & Local Government Finances 2022

City Government Revenue by Source

Source	2022 ($000)	2022 ($ per capita)	2022 (%)
General Revenue			
From Federal Government	0	0	0.0
From State Government	38,479	98	6.4
From Local Governments	0	0	0.0
Taxes			
Property	147,638	377	24.5
Sales and Gross Receipts	126,410	323	20.9
Personal Income	0	0	0.0
Corporate Income	0	0	0.0
Motor Vehicle License	0	0	0.0
Other Taxes	2,178	6	0.4
Current Charges	131,157	335	21.7
Liquor Store	0	0	0.0
Utility	113,131	289	18.7

Source: U.S. Census Bureau, State & Local Government Finances 2022

City Government Expenditures by Function

Function	2022 ($000)	2022 ($ per capita)	2022 (%)
General Direct Expenditures			
Air Transportation	20,460	52	4.9
Corrections	0	0	0.0
Education	0	0	0.0
Employment Security Administration	0	0	0.0
Financial Administration	5,657	14	1.4
Fire Protection	51,902	132	12.5
General Public Buildings	1,090	2	0.3
Governmental Administration, Other	11,770	30	2.8
Health	2,222	5	0.5
Highways	33,522	85	8.1
Hospitals	0	0	0.0
Housing and Community Development	0	0	0.0
Interest on General Debt	16,764	42	4.0
Judicial and Legal	10,005	25	2.4
Libraries	9,178	23	2.2
Parking	1,437	3	0.3
Parks and Recreation	25,781	65	6.2
Police Protection	98,942	252	23.8
Public Welfare	343	< 1	< 0.1
Sewerage	43,828	111	10.5
Solid Waste Management	3,221	8	0.8
Veterans' Services	0	0	0.0
Liquor Store	0	0	0.0
Utility	59,622	152	14.3

Source: U.S. Census Bureau, State & Local Government Finances 2022

TAXES

State Corporate Income Tax Rates

State	Tax Rate (%)	Income Brackets ($)	Num. of Brackets	Financial Institution Tax Rate (%)[a]	Federal Income Tax Ded.
Kansas	3.5 (i)	Flat rate	1	2.25 (j)	No

Note: Tax rates for tax year 2024; (a) Rates listed are the corporate income tax rate applied to financial institutions or excise taxes based on income. Some states have other taxes based upon the value of deposits or shares; (i) In addition to the flat 3.5% corporate income tax, Kansas levies a 3.0% surtax on taxable income over $50,000. Banks pay a privilege tax of 2.25% of net income, plus a surtax of 2.125% (2.25% for savings and loans, trust companies, and federallychartered savings banks) on net income in excess of $25,000; (j) The state franchise tax on financial institutions is either (1) the sum of 1% of the Maine net income of the financial institution for the taxable year, plus 8¢ per $1,000 of the institution's Maine assets as of the end of its taxable year, or (2)39¢ per $1,000 of the institution's Maine assets as of the end of its taxable year.
Source: Federation of Tax Administrators, State Corporate Income Tax Rates, January 1, 2025

State Individual Income Tax Rates

State	Tax Rate (%)	Income Brackets ($)	Personal Exemptions ($)			Standard Ded. ($)	
			Single	Married	Depend.	Single	Married
Kansas	0.0 - 5.7	15,000 - 30,000 (b)	3,500	8,000	2,250	3,500	8,000

Note: Tax rates for tax year 2024; Local- and county-level taxes are not included; Federal income tax is not deductible on state income tax returns; (b) For joint returns, taxes are twice the tax on half the couple's income. California brackets violate this formula at the two highest tax brackets in 2024.
Source: Federation of Tax Administrators, State Individual Income Tax Rates, January 1, 2025

Various State Sales and Excise Tax Rates

State	State Sales Tax (%)	Gasoline[1] ($/gal.)	Cigarette[2] ($/pack)	Spirits[3] ($/gal.)	Wine[4] ($/gal.)	Beer[5] ($/gal.)	Recreational Marijuana (%)
Kansas	6.5	0.25	1.29	2.50	0.30	0.18	Not legal

Note: All tax rates as of January 1, 2025; (1) The American Petroleum Institute has developed a methodology for determining the average tax rate on a gallon of fuel. Rates may include any of the following: excise taxes, environmental fees, storage tank fees, other fees or taxes, general sales tax, and local taxes; (2) The federal excise tax of $1.0066 per pack and local taxes are not included; (3) Rates are those applicable to off-premise sales of 40% alcohol by volume (a.b.v.) distilled spirits in 750ml containers. Local excise taxes are excluded; (4) Rates are those applicable to off-premise sales of 11% a.b.v. non-carbonated wine in 750ml containers; (5) Rates are those applicable to off-premise sales of 4.7% a.b.v. beer in 12 ounce containers.
Source: Tax Foundation, 2025 Facts & Figures: How Does Your State Compare?

State Tax Competitiveness Index

State	Overall Rank	Corporate Tax Rank	Individual Income Tax Rank	Sales Tax Rank	Property Tax Rank	Unemployment Insurance Tax Rank
Kansas	25	27	27	30	29	4

Note: The Tax Foundation's State Tax Competitiveness Index enables policymakers, taxpayers, and business leaders to gauge how their states' tax systems compare. A rank of 1 is best, 50 is worst. Rankings do not average to the total. States without a tax rank equally as 1. DC's scores and rankings do not affect other states. The report shows tax systems as of July 1, 2024 (the beginning of Fiscal Year 2025).
Source: Tax Foundation, State Tax Competitiveness Index 2025

TRANSPORTATION

Means of Transportation to Work

Area	Car/Truck/Van		Public Transportation			Bicycle	Walked	Other Means	Worked at Home
	Drove Alone	Car-pooled	Bus	Subway	Railroad				
City	80.0	9.6	0.6	0.0	0.0	0.4	0.9	1.5	6.9
MSA[1]	80.6	8.6	0.4	0.0	0.0	0.3	1.4	1.3	7.3
U.S.	70.2	8.5	1.7	1.3	0.4	0.4	2.4	1.6	13.5

Note: Figures are percentages and cover workers 16 years of age and older; (1) Figures cover the Wichita, KS Metropolitan Statistical Area
Source: U.S. Census Bureau, 2019-2023 American Community Survey 5-Year Estimates

Travel Time to Work

Area	Less Than 10 Minutes	10 to 19 Minutes	20 to 29 Minutes	30 to 44 Minutes	45 to 59 Minutes	60 to 89 Minutes	90 Minutes or More
City	14.0	46.0	25.9	9.5	1.8	1.4	1.4
MSA[1]	15.7	38.0	25.6	14.9	2.8	1.6	1.4
U.S.	12.6	28.6	21.2	20.8	8.1	6.0	2.8

Note: Note: Figures are percentages and include workers 16 years old and over; (1) Figures cover the Wichita, KS Metropolitan Statistical Area
Source: U.S. Census Bureau, 2019-2023 American Community Survey 5-Year Estimates

Key Congestion Measures

Measure	2000	2010	2015	2020	2022
Annual Hours of Delay, Total (000)	5,994	8,917	10,498	7,423	11,836
Annual Hours of Delay, Per Auto Commuter	28	29	34	25	40
Annual Congestion Cost, Per Auto Commuter ($)	439	519	565	421	641

Note: Figures cover the Wichita KS urban area
Source: Texas A&M Transportation Institute, 2023 Urban Mobility Report

Freeway Travel Time Index

Measure	1985	1990	1995	2000	2005	2010	2015	2020	2022
Urban Area Index[1]	1.08	1.11	1.13	1.14	1.16	1.14	1.14	1.09	1.15
Urban Area Rank[1,2]	40	42	47	62	57	71	79	40	54

Note: Freeway Travel Time Index—the ratio of travel time in the peak period to the travel time at free-flow conditions. For example, a value of 1.30 indicates a 20-minute free-flow trip takes 26 minutes in the peak (20 minutes x 1.30 = 26 minutes); (1) Covers the Wichita KS urban area; (2) Rank is based on 101 larger urban areas (#1 = highest travel time index)
Source: Texas A&M Transportation Institute, 2023 Urban Mobility Report

Public Transportation

Agency Name / Mode of Transportation	Vehicles Operated in Maximum Service[1]	Annual Unlinked Passenger Trips[2] (in thous.)	Annual Passenger Miles[3] (in thous.)
Wichita Transit (WT)			
Bus (directly operated)	43	1,169.7	6,532.9
Demand Response (directly operated)	23	80.4	544.4

Note: (1) Number of revenue vehicles operated by the given mode and type of service to meet the annual maximum service requirement. This is the revenue vehicle count during the peak season of the year; on the week and day that maximum service is provided. Vehicles operated in maximum service (VOMS) exclude atypical days and one-time special events; (2) Number of passengers who boarded public transportation vehicles. Passengers are counted each time they board a vehicle no matter how many vehicles they use to travel from their origin to their destination. (3) Sum of the distances ridden by all passengers during the entire fiscal year.
Source: Federal Transit Administration, National Transit Database, 2023

Air Transportation

Airport Name and Code / Type of Service	Passenger Airlines[1]	Passenger Enplanements	Freight Carriers[2]	Freight (lbs)
Wichita Mid-Continent Airport (ICT)				
Domestic service (U.S. carriers only)	21	885,566	12	19,087,269
International service (U.S. carriers only)	0	0	0	0

Note: (1) Includes all U.S.-based major, minor and commuter airlines that carried at least one passenger during the year; (2) Includes all U.S.-based airlines and freight carriers that transported at least one pound of freight during the year.
Source: Bureau of Transportation Statistics, The Intermodal Transportation Database, Air Carriers: T-100 Domestic Market (U.S. carriers only), 2024; Bureau of Transportation Statistics, The Intermodal Transportation Database, Air Carriers: T-100 International Market (U.S. carriers only), 2024

BUSINESSES

Major Business Headquarters

Company Name	Industry	Rankings	
		Fortune[1]	Forbes[2]
Koch	Multicompany	-	2

Note: (1) Companies that produce a 10-K are ranked 1 to 500 based on 2023 revenue; (2) All private companies with at least $2 billion in annual revenue through the end of their most current fiscal year are ranked 1 to 275; companies listed are headquartered in the city; dashes indicate no ranking
Source: Fortune, "Fortune 500," 2024; Forbes, "America's Largest Private Companies," 2024

Living Environment

COST OF LIVING

Cost of Living Index

Composite Index	Groceries	Housing	Utilities	Transportation	Health Care	Misc. Goods/Services
88.8	94.9	65.9	98.2	97.5	94.3	99.6

Note: The Cost of Living Index measures regional differences in the cost of consumer goods and services, excluding taxes and non-consumer expenditures, for professional and managerial households in the top income quintile. It is based on more than 50,000 prices covering almost 60 different items for which prices are collected three times a year by chambers of commerce, economic development organizations or university applied economic centers in each participating urban area. The numbers shown should be read as a percentage above or below the national average of 100. For example, a value of 115.4 in the groceries column indicates that grocery prices are 15.4% higher than the national average. Small differences in the index numbers should not be interpreted as significant; Figures cover the Wichita KS urban area.
Source: The Council for Community and Economic Research, Cost of Living Index, 2024

Grocery Prices

Area[1]	T-Bone Steak ($/pound)	Frying Chicken ($/pound)	Whole Milk ($/half gal.)	Eggs ($/dozen)	Orange Juice ($/64 oz.)	Coffee ($/11.5 oz.)
City[2]	15.50	1.43	4.66	3.16	4.30	5.36
Avg.	15.42	1.55	4.69	3.25	4.41	5.46
Min.	14.50	1.16	4.43	2.75	4.00	4.85
Max.	17.56	2.89	5.49	4.78	5.54	7.89

Note: (1) Values for the local area are compared with the average, minimum and maximum values for all 276 areas in the Cost of Living Index; (2) Figures cover the Wichita KS urban area; **T-Bone Steak** (price per pound); **Frying Chicken** (price per pound, whole fryer); **Whole Milk** (half gallon carton); **Eggs** (price per dozen, Grade A, large); **Orange Juice** (64 oz. Tropicana or Florida Natural); **Coffee** (11.5 oz. can, vacuum-packed, Maxwell House, Hills Bros, or Folgers).
Source: The Council for Community and Economic Research, Cost of Living Index, 2024

Housing and Utility Costs

Area[1]	New Home Price ($)	Apartment Rent ($/month)	All Electric ($/month)	Part Electric ($/month)	Other Energy ($/month)	Telephone ($/month)
City[2]	334,425	1,007	-	113.92	81.43	202.42
Avg.	515,975	1,550	210.99	123.07	82.07	194.99
Min.	265,375	692	104.33	53.68	36.26	179.42
Max.	2,775,821	5,719	529.02	397.28	361.63	223.33

Note: (1) Values for the local area are compared with the average, minimum and maximum values for all 276 areas in the Cost of Living Index; (2) Figures cover the Wichita KS urban area; **New Home Price** (2,400 sf living area, 8,000 sf lot, in urban area with full utilities); **Apartment Rent** (950 sf 2 bedroom/1.5 or 2 bath, unfurnished, excluding all utilities except water); **All Electric** (average monthly cost for an all-electric home); **Part Electric** (average monthly cost for a part-electric home); **Other Energy** (average monthly cost for natural gas, fuel oil, coal, wood, and any other forms of energy except electricity); **Telephone** (price includes the base monthly rate plus taxes and fees for three lines of mobile phone service).
Source: The Council for Community and Economic Research, Cost of Living Index, 2024

Health Care, Transportation, and Other Costs

Area[1]	Doctor ($/visit)	Dentist ($/visit)	Optometrist ($/visit)	Gasoline ($/gallon)	Beauty Salon ($/visit)	Men's Shirt ($)
City[2]	111.32	102.90	144.60	3.09	48.13	54.27
Avg.	143.77	117.51	129.23	3.32	48.57	38.14
Min.	36.74	58.67	67.33	2.80	24.00	13.41
Max.	270.44	216.82	307.33	5.28	94.00	63.89

Note: (1) Values for the local area are compared with the average, minimum and maximum values for all 276 areas in the Cost of Living Index; (2) Figures cover the Wichita KS urban area; **Doctor** (general practitioners routine exam of an established patient); **Dentist** (adult teeth cleaning and periodic oral examination); **Optometrist** (full vision eye exam for established adult patient); **Gasoline** (one gallon regular unleaded, national brand, including all taxes, cash price at self-service pump if available); **Beauty Salon** (woman's shampoo, trim, and blow-dry); **Men's Shirt** (cotton/polyester dress shirt, pinpoint weave, long sleeves).
Source: The Council for Community and Economic Research, Cost of Living Index, 2024

HOUSING

Homeownership Rate

Area	2017 (%)	2018 (%)	2019 (%)	2020 (%)	2021 (%)	2022 (%)	2023 (%)	2024 (%)
MSA[1]	n/a	n/a	n/a	n/a	n/a	n/a	n/a	n/a
U.S.	63.9	64.4	64.6	66.6	65.5	65.8	65.9	65.6

Note: (1) Figures cover the Wichita, KS Metropolitan Statistical Area; n/a not available
Source: U.S. Census Bureau, Housing Vacancies and Homeownership Annual Statistics: 2017-2024

House Price Index (HPI)

Area	National Ranking[2]	Quarterly Change (%)	One-Year Change (%)	Five-Year Change (%)	Since 1991Q1 (%)
MSA[1]	170	-0.42	4.15	57.02	241.93
U.S.[3]	–	1.43	4.51	57.13	327.82

Note: The HPI is a weighted repeat sales index. It measures average price changes in repeat sales or refinancings on the same properties. This information is obtained by reviewing repeat mortgage transactions on single-family properties whose mortgages have been purchased or securitized by Fannie Mae or Freddie Mac since January 1975; (1) Figures cover the Wichita, KS Metropolitan Statistical Area; (2) Rankings are based on annual percentage change for all metro areas containing at least 15,000 transactions over the last 10 years and ranges from 1 to 241; (3) figures based on a weighted average of Census Division estimates using a seasonally adjusted, purchase-only index; all figures are for the period ending December 31, 2024
Source: Federal Housing Finance Agency, Change in FHFA Metropolitan Area House Price Indexes, All Transactions Index, 2024Q4

Home Value

Area	Under $100,000	$100,000 -$199,999	$200,000 -$299,999	$300,000 -$399,999	$400,000 -$499,999	$500,000 -$999,999	$1,000,000 or more	Median ($)
City	21.6	34.9	24.3	9.6	4.5	4.2	0.9	179,500
MSA[1]	20.1	33.8	25.4	10.2	4.8	4.9	0.8	188,200
U.S.	12.1	17.8	19.5	14.4	10.5	19.1	6.5	303,400

Note: Figures are percentages except for median and cover owner-occupied housing units; (1) Figures cover the Wichita, KS Metropolitan Statistical Area
Source: U.S. Census Bureau, 2019-2023 American Community Survey 5-Year Estimates

Year Housing Structure Built

Area	2020 or Later	2010 -2019	2000 -2009	1990 -1999	1980 -1989	1970 -1979	1960 -1969	1950 -1959	1940 -1949	Before 1940	Median Year
City	0.7	6.9	10.1	11.2	12.8	13.3	9.1	18.0	7.7	10.3	1974
MSA[1]	0.9	7.8	12.0	12.8	12.5	13.0	8.1	15.9	6.1	10.7	1977
U.S.	1.2	8.9	13.6	12.8	13.0	14.4	10.0	9.7	4.5	11.9	1980

Note: Figures are percentages except for Median Year; Note: (1) Figures cover the Wichita, KS Metropolitan Statistical Area
Source: U.S. Census Bureau, 2019-2023 American Community Survey 5-Year Estimates

Gross Monthly Rent

Area	Under $500	$500 -$999	$1,000 -$1,499	$1,500 -$1,999	$2,000 -$2,499	$2,500 -$2,999	$3,000 and up	Median ($)
City	4.8	50.2	34.2	7.8	2.1	0.3	0.7	960
MSA[1]	5.7	48.1	34.1	8.5	2.5	0.5	0.6	969
U.S.	6.5	22.3	29.5	20.2	10.8	4.8	5.9	1,348

Note: Figures are percentages except for median; Gross rent is the contract rent plus the estimated average monthly cost of utilities (electricity, gas, and water and sewer) and fuels (oil, coal, kerosene, wood, etc.) if these are paid by the renter (or paid for the renter by someone else); (1) Figures cover the Wichita, KS Metropolitan Statistical Area
Source: U.S. Census Bureau, 2019-2023 American Community Survey 5-Year Estimates

HEALTH

Health Risk Factors

Category	MSA[1] (%)	U.S. (%)
Adults aged 18–64 who have any kind of health care coverage	87.2	90.8
Adults who reported being in good or better health	80.0	81.8
Adults who have been told they have high blood cholesterol	38.4	36.9
Adults who have been told they have high blood pressure	35.3	34.0
Adults who are current smokers	14.2	12.1
Adults who currently use e-cigarettes	10.1	7.7
Adults who currently use chewing tobacco, snuff, or snus	4.0	3.2
Adults who are heavy drinkers[2]	6.4	6.1
Adults who are binge drinkers[3]	16.0	15.2
Adults who are overweight (BMI 25.0 - 29.9)	31.8	34.4
Adults who are obese (BMI 30.0 - 99.8)	38.4	34.3
Adults who participated in any physical activities in the past month	75.7	75.8

Note: All figures are crude prevalence; (1) Figures cover the Wichita, KS Metropolitan Statistical Area; (2) Heavy drinkers are classified as adult men having more than 14 drinks per week and adult women having more than 7 drinks per week; (3) Binge drinkers are classified as males having five or more drinks on one occasion or females having four or more drinks on one occasion
Source: Centers for Disease Control and Prevention, Behaviorial Risk Factor Surveillance System, SMART: Selected Metropolitan Area Risk Trends, 2023

Acute and Chronic Health Conditions

Category	MSA[1] (%)	U.S. (%)
Adults who have ever been told they had a heart attack	4.2	4.2
Adults who have ever been told they have angina or coronary heart disease	4.1	4.0
Adults who have ever been told they had a stroke	3.5	3.3
Adults who have ever been told they have asthma	15.1	15.7
Adults who have ever been told they have arthritis	25.5	26.3
Adults who have ever been told they have diabetes[2]	13.5	11.5
Adults who have ever been told they had skin cancer	5.0	5.6
Adults who have ever been told they had any other types of cancer	8.8	8.4
Adults who have ever been told they have COPD	8.2	6.4
Adults who have ever been told they have kidney disease	3.6	3.7
Adults who have ever been told they have a form of depression	24.2	22.0

Note: All figures are crude prevalence; (1) Figures cover the Wichita, KS Metropolitan Statistical Area; (2) Figures do not include pregnancy-related, borderline, or pre-diabetes
Source: Centers for Disease Control and Prevention, Behavioral Risk Factor Surveillance System, SMART: Selected Metropolitan Area Risk Trends, 2023

Health Screening and Vaccination Rates

Category	MSA[1] (%)	U.S. (%)
Adults who have ever been tested for HIV	33.5	37.5
Adults who have had their blood cholesterol checked within the last five years	82.7	87.0
Adults aged 65+ who have had flu shot within the past year	62.5	63.4
Adults aged 65+ who have ever had a pneumonia vaccination	74.0	71.9

Note: All figures are crude prevalence; (1) Figures cover the Wichita, KS Metropolitan Statistical Area.
Source: Centers for Disease Control and Prevention, Behavioral Risk Factor Surveillance System, SMART: Selected Metropolitan Area Risk Trends, 2023

Disability Status

Category	MSA[1] (%)	U.S. (%)
Adults who reported being deaf	7.5	7.4
Are you blind or have serious difficulty seeing, even when wearing glasses?	5.0	4.9
Do you have difficulty doing errands alone?	8.2	7.8
Do you have difficulty dressing or bathing?	3.9	3.6
Do you have serious difficulty concentrating/remembering/making decisions?	14.6	13.7
Do you have serious difficulty walking or climbing stairs?	13.7	13.2

Note: All figures are crude prevalence; (1) Figures cover the Wichita, KS Metropolitan Statistical Area.
Source: Centers for Disease Control and Prevention, Behavioral Risk Factor Surveillance System, SMART: Selected Metropolitan Area Risk Trends, 2023

Mortality Rates for the Top 10 Causes of Death in the U.S.

ICD-10[a] Sub-Chapter	ICD-10[a] Code	Crude Mortality Rate[2] per 100,000 population	
		County[3]	U.S.
Malignant neoplasms	C00-C97	179.1	182.7
Ischaemic heart diseases	I20-I25	129.1	109.6
Provisional assignment of new diseases of uncertain etiology[1]	U00-U49	69.6	65.3
Other forms of heart disease	I30-I51	58.9	65.1
Other degenerative diseases of the nervous system	G30-G31	62.4	52.4
Other external causes of accidental injury	W00-X59	65.0	52.3
Cerebrovascular diseases	I60-I69	43.4	49.1
Chronic lower respiratory diseases	J40-J47	52.4	43.5
Hypertensive diseases	I10-I15	40.1	38.9
Organic, including symptomatic, mental disorders	F01-F09	38.3	33.9

Note: (a) ICD-10 = International Classification of Diseases 10th Revision; (1) Includes COVID-19, adverse effects to COVID-19 vaccines, SARS, and vaping-related disorders; (2) Crude mortality rates are a three-year average covering 2021-2023; (3) Figures cover Sedgwick County.
Source: Centers for Disease Control and Prevention, National Center for Health Statistics. National Vital Statistics System, Mortality 2018-2023 on CDC WONDER Online Database

Mortality Rates for Selected Causes of Death

Cause of Death	ICD-10[a] Code	Crude Mortality Rate[1] per 100,000 population	
		County[2]	U.S.
Accidental poisoning and exposure to noxious substances	X40-X49	42.1	30.5
Alzheimer disease	G30	20.0	35.4
Assault	X85-Y09	8.6	7.3
COVID-19	U07.1	69.6	65.3
Diabetes mellitus	E10-E14	29.8	30.0
Diseases of the liver	K70-K76	24.4	20.8
Human immunodeficiency virus (HIV) disease	B20-B24	Unreliable	1.5
Influenza and pneumonia	J09-J18	11.2	13.4
Intentional self-harm	X60-X84	19.5	14.7
Malnutrition	E40-E46	5.0	6.0
Obesity and other hyperalimentation	E65-E68	2.2	3.1
Renal failure	N17-N19	19.9	16.4
Transport accidents	V01-V99	15.0	14.4

Note: (a) ICD-10 = International Classification of Diseases 10th Revision; (1) Crude mortality rates are a three-year average covering 2021-2023; (2) Figures cover Sedgwick County; Data are suppressed when the data meet the criteria for confidentiality constraints; Crude mortality rates are flagged as unreliable when the rate would be calculated with a numerator of 20 or less.
Source: Centers for Disease Control and Prevention, National Center for Health Statistics. National Vital Statistics System, Mortality 2018-2023 on CDC WONDER Online Database

Health Insurance Coverage

Area	With Health Insurance	With Private Health Insurance	With Public Health Insurance	Without Health Insurance	Population Under Age 19 Without Health Insurance
City	87.6	65.3	34.1	12.4	6.1
MSA[1]	89.7	69.9	32.5	10.3	5.3
U.S.	91.4	67.3	36.3	8.6	5.4

Note: Figures are percentages that cover the civilian noninstitutionalized population; (1) Figures cover the Wichita, KS Metropolitan Statistical Area
Source: U.S. Census Bureau, 2019-2023 American Community Survey 5-Year Estimates

Number of Medical Professionals

Area	MDs[3]	DOs[3,4]	Dentists	Podiatrists	Chiropractors	Optometrists
County[1] (number)	1,398	221	377	10	232	153
County[1] (rate[2])	266.0	42.1	71.3	1.9	43.9	29.0
U.S. (rate[2])	302.5	29.2	74.6	6.4	29.5	18.0

Note: Data as of 2023 unless noted; (1) Data covers Sedgwick County; (2) Number of medical professionals per 100,000 population; (3) Data as of 2022 and includes all active, non-federal physicians; (4) Doctor of Osteopathic Medicine
Source: U.S. Department of Health and Human Services, Health Resources and Services Administration, Bureau of Health Professions, Area Resource File (ARF) 2023-2024

EDUCATION

Public School District Statistics

District Name	Schls	Pupils	Pupil/Teacher Ratio	Minority Pupils[1] (%)	Total Rev. per Pupil ($)	Total Exp. per Pupil ($)
Wichita	87	46,516	10.7	71.0	16,795	17,357

Note: Table includes school districts with 2,000 or more students; (1) Percentage of students that are not non-Hispanic white.
Source: U.S. Department of Education, National Center for Education Statistics, Common Core of Data, Local Education Agency (School District) Universe Survey: School Year 2023-2024; U.S. Department of Education, National Center for Education Statistics, Common Core of Data, School District Finance Survey (F-33): School Year 2021–22

Highest Level of Education

Area	Less than H.S.	H.S. Diploma	Some College, No Deg.	Associate Degree	Bachelor's Degree	Master's Degree	Prof. School Degree	Doctorate Degree
City	12.0	26.0	23.0	8.1	19.7	8.5	1.6	1.1
MSA[1]	9.7	26.4	23.4	9.0	20.2	8.8	1.5	1.0
U.S.	10.6	26.2	19.4	8.8	21.3	9.8	2.3	1.6

Note: Figures cover persons age 25 and over; (1) Figures cover the Wichita, KS Metropolitan Statistical Area
Source: U.S. Census Bureau, 2019-2023 American Community Survey 5-Year Estimates

Educational Attainment by Race

Area	High School Graduate or Higher (%)					Bachelor's Degree or Higher (%)				
	Total	White	Black	Asian	Hisp.[2]	Total	White	Black	Asian	Hisp.[2]
City	88.0	92.3	87.4	74.0	63.9	30.9	34.8	19.0	31.6	14.7
MSA[1]	90.3	93.5	87.6	75.1	67.1	31.5	34.2	19.0	32.5	16.4
U.S.	89.4	92.9	88.1	88.0	72.5	35.0	37.7	24.7	57.0	19.9

Note: Figures shown cover persons 25 years old and over; (1) Figures cover the Wichita, KS Metropolitan Statistical Area; (2) People of Hispanic origin can be of any race
Source: U.S. Census Bureau, 2019-2023 American Community Survey 5-Year Estimates

School Enrollment by Grade and Control

Area	Preschool (%)		Kindergarten (%)		Grades 1 - 4 (%)		Grades 5 - 8 (%)		Grades 9 - 12 (%)	
	Public	Private	Public	Private	Public	Private	Public	Private	Public	Private
City	61.8	38.2	82.0	18.0	84.6	15.4	84.4	15.6	86.3	13.7
MSA[1]	63.2	36.8	80.5	19.5	85.1	14.9	86.3	13.7	87.5	12.5
U.S.	58.7	41.3	85.2	14.8	87.2	12.8	87.9	12.1	89.0	11.0

Note: Figures shown cover persons 3 years old and over; (1) Figures cover the Wichita, KS Metropolitan Statistical Area
Source: U.S. Census Bureau, 2019-2023 American Community Survey 5-Year Estimates

Higher Education

Four-Year Colleges			Two-Year Colleges			Medical Schools[1]	Law Schools[2]	Voc/ Tech[3]
Public	Private Non-profit	Private For-profit	Public	Private Non-profit	Private For-profit			
1	5	0	2	0	2	1	0	7

Note: Figures cover institutions located within the Wichita, KS Metropolitan Statistical Area and include main campuses only; (1) includes schools accredited by the Liaison Committee on Medical Education and the American Osteopathic Association's Commission on Osteopathic College Accreditation; (2) includes ABA-accredited schools, schools with provisional ABA accreditation, and state accredited schools; (3) includes all schools with programs that are less than 2 years.
Source: National Center for Education Statistics, Integrated Postsecondary Education System (IPEDS), 2023-24; Wikipedia, List of Medical Schools in the United States, accessed May 2, 2025; Wikipedia, List of Law Schools in the United States, accessed May 2, 2025

EMPLOYERS

Major Employers

Company Name	Industry
AGCO Corporation	Agricultural equipment
Ascension via Christi Health	Healthcare
Beechcraft Corp.	Aircraft
Boeing Defense, Space & Security	Aircraft modification
Bombardier Learjet	Aircraft
Cargill Meat Solutions	Meat products
Cessna Aircraft Company	Manufacturing
City of Wichita	Municipal government
Cox Communications	Broadband communications & entertainment company
Dillons Food Stores	Grocery stores
Koch Industries	Manufacturing, energy & commodities
McConnell Air Force Base	U.S. military
Robert J. Dole VA Medical Center	Veterans medical center
Sedgwick County	County government
Spirit AeroSystems	Manufacturing
State of Kansas	State government
Textron Aviation	Aircraft manufacturer
U.S. Postal Service	Federal mail delivery service
Wichita Public Schools USD 259	Public school district
Wichita State University	Higher education

Note: Companies shown are located within the Wichita, KS Metropolitan Statistical Area.
Source: Chambers of Commerce; State Departments of Labor; Wikipedia

PUBLIC SAFETY

Crime Rate

Area	Total Crime Rate	Violent Crime Rate				Property Crime Rate		
		Murder	Rape	Robbery	Aggrav. Assault	Burglary	Larceny -Theft	Motor Vehicle Theft
City	5,864.8	9.9	87.8	104.7	930.0	548.2	3,662.4	521.9
U.S.	2,290.9	5.7	38.0	66.5	264.1	250.7	1,347.2	318.7

Note: Figures are crimes per 100,000 population.
Source: FBI, Table 8, Offenses Known to Law Enforcement, by State by City, 2023

Hate Crimes

Area	Number of Quarters Reported	Number of Incidents per Bias Motivation					
		Race/Ethnicity/Ancestry	Religion	Sexual Orientation	Disability	Gender	Gender Identity
City[1]	4	8	0	3	0	0	0
U.S.	4	5,900	2,699	2,077	187	92	492

Note: (1) Figures include at least one incident reported with more than one bias motivation.
Source: Federal Bureau of Investigation, Hate Crime Statistics 2023

Identity Theft Consumer Reports

Area	Reports	Reports per 100,000 Population	Rank[2]
MSA[1]	1,085	167	224
U.S.	1,135,291	339	-

Note: (1) Figures cover the Wichita, KS Metropolitan Statistical Area; (2) Rank ranges from 1 to 401 where 1 indicates greatest number of identity theft reports per 100,000 population
Source: Federal Trade Commission, Consumer Sentinel Network Data Book 2024

Fraud and Other Consumer Reports

Area	Reports	Reports per 100,000 Population	Rank[2]
MSA[1]	5,811	895	273
U.S.	5,360,641	1,601	-

Note: (1) Figures cover the Wichita, KS Metropolitan Statistical Area; (2) Rank ranges from 1 to 401 where 1 indicates greatest number of fraud and other consumer reports per 100,000 population
Source: Federal Trade Commission, Consumer Sentinel Network Data Book 2024

POLITICS

2024 Presidential Election Results

Area	Trump (Rep.)	Harris (Dem.)	Stein (Green)	Kennedy (Ind.)	Oliver (Lib.)	Other
Sedgwick County	55.7	42.0	0.1	1.1	0.6	0.5
U.S.	49.7	48.2	0.6	0.5	0.4	0.6

Note: Results are percentages and may not add to 100% due to rounding
Source: Dave Leip's Atlas of U.S. Presidential Elections

SPORTS

Professional Sports Teams

Team Name	League	Year Established

No teams are located in the metro area
Source: Wikipedia, Major Professional Sports Teams of the United States and Canada, May 1, 2025

CLIMATE

Average and Extreme Temperatures

Temperature	Jan	Feb	Mar	Apr	May	Jun	Jul	Aug	Sep	Oct	Nov	Dec	Yr.
Extreme High (°F)	75	84	89	96	100	110	113	110	107	95	87	83	113
Average High (°F)	40	46	56	68	77	87	92	91	82	71	55	44	68
Average Temp. (°F)	30	35	45	57	66	76	81	80	71	59	45	34	57
Average Low (°F)	20	24	33	45	55	65	70	68	59	47	34	24	45
Extreme Low (°F)	-12	-21	-3	15	31	43	51	47	31	21	1	-16	-21

Note: Figures cover the years 1948-1990
Source: National Climatic Data Center, International Station Meteorological Climate Summary, 9/96

Average Precipitation/Snowfall/Humidity

Precip./Humidity	Jan	Feb	Mar	Apr	May	Jun	Jul	Aug	Sep	Oct	Nov	Dec	Yr.
Avg. Precip. (in.)	0.9	1.0	2.3	2.3	3.9	4.3	3.7	3.0	3.2	2.3	1.4	1.0	29.3
Avg. Snowfall (in.)	5	4	3	Tr	0	0	0	0	0	Tr	2	3	17
Avg. Rel. Hum. 6am (%)	78	79	77	78	83	83	78	79	82	80	79	79	80
Avg. Rel. Hum. 3pm (%)	56	54	48	46	51	47	42	43	47	47	51	56	49

Note: Figures cover the years 1948-1990; Tr = Trace amounts (<0.05 in. of rain; <0.5 in. of snow)
Source: National Climatic Data Center, International Station Meteorological Climate Summary, 9/96

Weather Conditions

Temperature			Daytime Sky			Precipitation		
10°F & below	32°F & below	90°F & above	Clear	Partly cloudy	Cloudy	0.01 inch or more precip.	0.1 inch or more snow/ice	Thunderstorms
13	110	63	117	132	116	87	13	54

Note: Figures are average number of days per year and cover the years 1948-1990
Source: National Climatic Data Center, International Station Meteorological Climate Summary, 9/96

HAZARDOUS WASTE

Superfund Sites

The Wichita, KS metro area is home to two sites on the EPA's Superfund National Priorities List (NPL) or Superfund Alternative Approach (SAA) list: **57th and North Broadway Streets Site** (Final NPL); **Pester Refinery Co.** (Final NPL). The Superfund alternative approach uses the same investigation and cleanup process and standards that are used for sites listed on the National Priorities List. The SAA is an alternative to listing a site on the NPL; it is not an alternative to Superfund or the Superfund process. There are a total of 1,445 Superfund sites with a status of proposed or final on both lists in the United States. *U.S. Environmental Protection Agency, National Priorities List, May 1, 2025; U.S. Environmental Protection Agency, Superfund Alternative Approach Sites, May 1, 2025*

AIR QUALITY

Air Quality Trends: Ozone

	1990	1995	2000	2005	2010	2015	2020	2021	2022	2023
MSA[1]	0.077	0.069	0.080	0.074	0.075	0.064	0.059	0.061	0.072	0.066
U.S.	0.087	0.089	0.081	0.080	0.072	0.068	0.066	0.067	0.067	0.070

Note: (1) Data covers the Wichita, KS Metropolitan Statistical Area. The values shown are the composite ozone concentration averages among trend sites based on the highest fourth daily maximum 8-hour concentration in parts per million. These trends are based on sites having an adequate record of monitoring data during the trend period. Data from exceptional events are included.
Source: U.S. Environmental Protection Agency, Air Quality Monitoring Information, "Air Quality Trends by City, 1990-2023"

Air Quality Index

Area	Percent of Days when Air Quality was...[2]					AQI Statistics[2]	
	Good	Moderate	Unhealthy for Sensitive Groups	Unhealthy	Very Unhealthy	Maximum	Median
MSA[1]	44.7	54.0	1.1	0.3	0.0	157	52

Note: (1) Data covers the Wichita, KS Metropolitan Statistical Area; (2) Based on 365 days with AQI data in 2023. Air Quality Index (AQI) is an index for reporting daily air quality. EPA calculates the AQI for five major air pollutants regulated by the Clean Air Act: ground-level ozone, particle pollution (aka particulate matter), carbon monoxide, sulfur dioxide, and nitrogen dioxide. The AQI runs from 0 to 500. The higher the AQI value, the greater the level of air pollution and the greater the health concern. There are six AQI categories: "Good" AQI is between 0 and 50. Air quality is considered satisfactory; "Moderate" AQI is between 51 and 100. Air quality is acceptable; "Unhealthy for Sensitive Groups" When AQI values are between 101 and 150, members of sensitive groups may experience health effects; "Unhealthy" When AQI values are between 151 and 200 everyone may begin to experience health effects; "Very Unhealthy" AQI values between 201 and 300 trigger a health alert; "Hazardous" AQI values over 300 trigger warnings of emergency conditions (not shown).
Source: U.S. Environmental Protection Agency, Air Quality Index Report, 2023

Air Quality Index Pollutants

Area	Percent of Days when AQI Pollutant was...[2]					
	Carbon Monoxide	Nitrogen Dioxide	Ozone	Sulfur Dioxide	Particulate Matter 2.5	Particulate Matter 10
MSA[1]	0.0	0.5	45.2	(3)	51.2	3.0

Note: (1) Data covers the Wichita, KS Metropolitan Statistical Area; (2) Based on 365 days with AQI data in 2023. The Air Quality Index (AQI) is an index for reporting daily air quality. EPA calculates the AQI for five major air pollutants regulated by the Clean Air Act: ground-level ozone, particle pollution (also known as particulate matter), carbon monoxide, sulfur dioxide, and nitrogen dioxide. The AQI runs from 0 to 500. The higher the AQI value, the greater the level of air pollution and the greater the health concern; (3) Sulfur dioxide is no longer included in this table because SO_2 concentrations tend to be very localized and not necessarily representative of broad geographical areas like counties and CBSAs.
Source: U.S. Environmental Protection Agency, Air Quality Index Report, 2023

Maximum Air Pollutant Concentrations: Particulate Matter, Ozone, CO and Lead

	Particulate Matter 10 (ug/m³)	Particulate Matter 2.5 Wtd AM (ug/m³)	Particulate Matter 2.5 24-Hr (ug/m³)	Ozone (ppm)	Carbon Monoxide (ppm)	Lead (ug/m³)
MSA[1] Level	99	n/a	n/a	0.068	n/a	n/a
NAAQS[2]	150	15	35	0.075	9	0.15
Met NAAQS[2]	Yes	n/a	Yes	Yes	n/a	n/a

Note: (1) Data covers the Wichita, KS Metropolitan Statistical Area; Data from exceptional events are included; (2) National Ambient Air Quality Standards; ppm = parts per million; ug/m³ = micrograms per cubic meter; n/a not available.
Concentrations: Particulate Matter 10 (coarse particulate)—highest second maximum 24-hour concentration; Particulate Matter 2.5 Wtd AM (fine particulate)—highest weighted annual mean concentration; Particulate Matter 2.5 24-Hour (fine particulate)—highest 98th percentile 24-hour concentration; Ozone—highest fourth daily maximum 8-hour concentration; Carbon Monoxide—highest second maximum non-overlapping 8-hour concentration; Lead—maximum running 3-month average
Source: U.S. Environmental Protection Agency, Air Quality Monitoring Information, "Air Quality Statistics by City, 2023"

Maximum Air Pollutant Concentrations: Nitrogen Dioxide and Sulfur Dioxide

	Nitrogen Dioxide AM (ppb)	Nitrogen Dioxide 1-Hr (ppb)	Sulfur Dioxide AM (ppb)	Sulfur Dioxide 1-Hr (ppb)	Sulfur Dioxide 24-Hr (ppb)
MSA[1] Level	6	23	n/a	2	n/a
NAAQS[2]	53	100	30	75	140
Met NAAQS[2]	Yes	Yes	n/a	Yes	n/a

Note: (1) Data covers the Wichita, KS Metropolitan Statistical Area; Data from exceptional events are included; (2) National Ambient Air Quality Standards; ppm = parts per million; ug/m³ = micrograms per cubic meter; n/a not available.
Concentrations: Nitrogen Dioxide AM—highest arithmetic mean concentration; Nitrogen Dioxide 1-Hr—highest 98th percentile 1-hour daily maximum concentration; Sulfur Dioxide AM—highest annual mean concentration; Sulfur Dioxide 1-Hr—highest 99th percentile 1-hour daily maximum concentration; Sulfur Dioxide 24-Hr—highest second maximum 24-hour concentration
Source: U.S. Environmental Protection Agency, Air Quality Monitoring Information, "Air Quality Statistics by City, 2023"

Appendixes

Appendixes

Appendix A: Comparative Statistics

Table of Contents

Demographics
- Population Growth: City A-4
- Population Growth: Metro Area A-6
- Male/Female Ratio: City A-8
- Male/Female Ratio: Metro Area A-10
- Race: City A-12
- Race: Metro Area A-14
- Hispanic Origin: City A-16
- Hispanic Origin: Metro Area A-18
- Household Size: City A-20
- Household Size: Metro Area A-22
- Household Relationships: City A-24
- Household Relationships: Metro Area A-26
- Age: City A-28
- Age: Metro Area A-30
- Ancestry: City A-32
- Ancestry: Metro Area A-34
- Foreign-born Population: City A-36
- Foreign-born Population: Metro Area A-38
- Marital Status: City A-40
- Marital Status: Metro Area A-42
- Disability by Age: City A-44
- Disability by Age: Metro Area A-46
- Religious Groups by Family A-48
- Religious Groups by Tradition A-50

Economy
- Gross Metropolitan Product A-52
- Economic Growth A-54
- Metropolitan Area Exports A-56
- Building Permits: City A-58
- Building Permits: Metro Area A-60
- Housing Vacancy Rates A-62
- Bankruptcy Filings A-64

Income and Poverty
- Income: City A-66
- Income: Metro Area A-68
- Household Income Distribution: City A-70
- Household Income Distribution: Metro Area A-72
- Poverty Rate: City A-74
- Poverty Rate: Metro Area A-76

Employment and Earnings
- Employment by Industry A-78
- Labor Force, Employment and Job Growth: City A-80
- Labor Force, Employment and Job Growth: Metro Area . A-82
- Unemployment Rate: City A-84
- Unemployment Rate: Metro Area A-86
- Average Hourly Wages: Occupations A - C A-88
- Average Hourly Wages: Occupations C - E A-90
- Average Hourly Wages: Occupations F - J A-92
- Average Hourly Wages: Occupations L - N A-94
- Average Hourly Wages: Occupations N - P A-96

- Average Hourly Wages: Occupations P - S A-98
- Average Hourly Wages: Occupations T - W A-100
- Means of Transportation to Work: City A-102
- Means of Transportation to Work: Metro Area A-104
- Travel Time to Work: City A-106
- Travel Time to Work: Metro Area A-108

Election Results
- 2020 Presidential Election Results A-110

Housing
- House Price Index (HPI) A-112
- Home Value: City A-114
- Home Value: Metro Area A-116
- Homeownership Rate A-118
- Year Housing Structure Built: City A-120
- Year Housing Structure Built: Metro Area A-122
- Gross Monthly Rent: City A-124
- Gross Monthly Rent: Metro Area A-126

Education
- Highest Level of Education: City A-128
- Highest Level of Education: Metro Area A-130
- School Enrollment by Grade and Control: City A-132
- School Enrollment by Grade and Control: Metro Area A-134
- Educational Attainment by Race: City A-136
- Educational Attainment by Race: Metro Area A-138

Cost of Living
- Cost of Living Index A-140
- Grocery Prices A-142
- Housing and Utility Costs A-144
- Health Care, Transportation, and Other Costs A-146

Health Care
- Number of Medical Professionals A-148
- Health Insurance Coverage: City A-150
- Health Insurance Coverage: Metro Area A-152

Public Safety
- Crime Rate A-154

Climate
- Temperature & Precipitation: Yearly Averages
  and Extremes A-156
- Weather Conditions A-158

Air Quality
- Air Quality Index A-160
- Air Quality Index Pollutants A-162
- Air Quality Trends: Ozone A-164
- Maximum Air Pollutant Concentrations:
  Particulate Matter, Ozone, CO and Lead A-166
- Maximum Air Pollutant Concentrations:
  Nitrogen Dioxide and Sulfur Dioxide A-168

Appendix A: Comparative Statistics

Population Growth: City

City	1990 Census	2000 Census	2010 Census	2020 Census	Current Estimate[1]	Population Growth 1990-2023 (%)
Albuquerque, NM	388,375	448,607	545,852	564,559	562,488	44.8
Anchorage, AK	226,338	260,283	291,826	291,247	289,069	27.7
Ann Arbor, MI	111,018	114,024	113,934	123,851	121,179	9.2
Athens, GA	86,561	100,266	115,452	127,315	126,987	46.7
Atlanta, GA	394,092	416,474	420,003	498,715	499,287	26.7
Austin, TX	499,053	656,562	790,390	961,855	967,862	93.9
Baltimore, MD	736,014	651,154	620,961	585,708	577,193	-21.6
Billings, MT	81,812	89,847	104,170	117,116	118,321	44.6
Boise City, ID	144,317	185,787	205,671	235,684	235,701	63.3
Boston, MA	574,283	589,141	617,594	675,647	663,972	15.6
Boulder, CO	87,737	94,673	97,385	108,250	106,274	21.1
Cape Coral, FL	75,507	102,286	154,305	194,016	206,387	173.3
Cedar Rapids, IA	110,829	120,758	126,326	137,710	136,859	23.5
Charleston, SC	96,102	96,650	120,083	150,227	152,014	58.2
Charlotte, NC	428,283	540,828	731,424	874,579	886,283	106.9
Chicago, IL	2,783,726	2,896,016	2,695,598	2,746,388	2,707,648	-2.7
Cincinnati, OH	363,974	331,285	296,943	309,317	309,595	-14.9
Clarksville, TN	78,569	103,455	132,929	166,722	171,897	118.8
Cleveland, OH	505,333	478,403	396,815	372,624	367,523	-27.3
College Station, TX	53,318	67,890	93,857	120,511	122,280	129.3
Colorado Springs, CO	283,798	360,890	416,427	478,961	483,099	70.2
Columbia, MO	71,069	84,531	108,500	126,254	127,200	79.0
Columbia, SC	115,475	116,278	129,272	136,632	138,019	19.5
Columbus, OH	648,656	711,470	787,033	905,748	906,480	39.7
Dallas, TX	1,006,971	1,188,580	1,197,816	1,304,379	1,299,553	29.1
Davenport, IA	95,705	98,359	99,685	101,724	101,083	5.6
Denver, CO	467,153	554,636	600,158	715,522	713,734	52.8
Des Moines, IA	193,569	198,682	203,433	214,133	212,464	9.8
Detroit, MI	1,027,974	951,270	713,777	639,111	636,644	-38.1
Durham, NC	151,737	187,035	228,330	283,506	288,465	90.1
El Paso, TX	515,541	563,662	649,121	678,815	678,147	31.5
Eugene, OR	118,073	137,893	156,185	176,654	177,520	50.3
Fargo, ND	74,372	90,599	105,549	125,990	129,064	73.5
Fort Collins, CO	89,555	118,652	143,986	169,810	169,705	89.5
Fort Wayne, IN	205,671	205,727	253,691	263,886	266,235	29.4
Fort Worth, TX	448,311	534,694	741,206	918,915	941,311	110.0
Gainesville, FL	90,519	95,447	124,354	141,085	143,611	58.7
Green Bay, WI	96,466	102,313	104,057	107,395	106,585	10.5
Greensboro, NC	193,389	223,891	269,666	299,035	298,564	54.4
Honolulu, HI	376,465	371,657	337,256	350,964	346,323	-8.0
Houston, TX	1,697,610	1,953,631	2,099,451	2,304,580	2,300,419	35.5
Huntsville, AL	161,842	158,216	180,105	215,006	218,814	35.2
Indianapolis, IN	730,993	781,870	820,445	887,642	882,043	20.7
Jacksonville, FL	635,221	735,617	821,784	949,611	961,739	51.4
Kansas City, MO	434,967	441,545	459,787	508,090	508,233	16.8
Lafayette, LA	104,735	110,257	120,623	121,374	121,537	16.0
Las Vegas, NV	261,374	478,434	583,756	641,903	650,873	149.0
Lexington, KY	225,366	260,512	295,803	322,570	321,122	42.5
Lincoln, NE	193,629	225,581	258,379	291,082	291,932	50.8
Little Rock, AR	177,519	183,133	193,524	202,591	202,739	14.2
Los Angeles, CA	3,487,671	3,694,820	3,792,621	3,898,747	3,857,897	10.6
Louisville, KY	269,160	256,231	597,337	386,884	627,210	133.0
Madison, WI	193,451	208,054	233,209	269,840	275,568	42.4
Manchester, NH	99,567	107,006	109,565	115,644	115,415	15.9
McAllen, TX	86,145	106,414	129,877	142,210	143,789	66.9

Table continued on following page.

City	1990 Census	2000 Census	2010 Census	2020 Census	Current Estimate[1]	Population Growth 1990-2023 (%)
Memphis, TN	660,536	650,100	646,889	633,104	629,063	-4.8
Miami, FL	358,843	362,470	399,457	442,241	446,663	24.5
Midland, TX	89,358	94,996	111,147	132,524	133,998	50.0
Milwaukee, WI	628,095	596,974	594,833	577,222	569,756	-9.3
Minneapolis, MN	368,383	382,618	382,578	429,954	426,845	15.9
Nashville, TN	488,364	545,524	601,222	689,447	684,298	40.1
New Orleans, LA	496,938	484,674	343,829	383,997	376,035	-24.3
New York, NY	7,322,552	8,008,278	8,175,133	8,804,190	8,516,202	16.3
Oklahoma City, OK	445,065	506,132	579,999	681,054	688,693	54.7
Omaha, NE	371,972	390,007	408,958	486,051	488,197	31.2
Orlando, FL	161,172	185,951	238,300	307,573	311,732	93.4
Philadelphia, PA	1,585,577	1,517,550	1,526,006	1,603,797	1,582,432	-0.2
Phoenix, AZ	989,873	1,321,045	1,445,632	1,608,139	1,624,832	64.1
Pittsburgh, PA	369,785	334,563	305,704	302,971	303,620	-17.9
Portland, OR	485,833	529,121	583,776	652,503	642,715	32.3
Providence, RI	160,734	173,618	178,042	190,934	190,214	18.3
Provo, UT	87,148	105,166	112,488	115,162	114,303	31.2
Raleigh, NC	226,841	276,093	403,892	467,665	470,763	107.5
Reno, NV	139,950	180,480	225,221	264,165	268,959	92.2
Richmond, VA	202,783	197,790	204,214	226,610	227,595	12.2
Rochester, MN	74,151	85,806	106,769	121,395	121,638	64.0
Sacramento, CA	368,923	407,018	466,488	524,943	524,802	42.3
Saint Louis, MO	396,685	348,189	319,294	301,578	293,109	-26.1
Saint Paul, MN	272,235	287,151	285,068	311,527	307,762	13.1
Salem, OR	112,046	136,924	154,637	175,535	176,666	57.7
Salt Lake City, UT	159,796	181,743	186,440	199,723	203,888	27.6
San Antonio, TX	997,258	1,144,646	1,327,407	1,434,625	1,458,954	46.3
San Diego, CA	1,111,048	1,223,400	1,307,402	1,386,932	1,385,061	24.7
San Francisco, CA	723,959	776,733	805,235	873,965	836,321	15.5
San Jose, CA	784,324	894,943	945,942	1,013,240	990,054	26.2
Santa Rosa, CA	123,297	147,595	167,815	178,127	177,216	43.7
Savannah, GA	138,038	131,510	136,286	147,780	147,546	6.9
Seattle, WA	516,262	563,374	608,660	737,015	741,440	43.6
Sioux Falls, SD	102,262	123,975	153,888	192,517	197,642	93.3
Tampa, FL	279,960	303,447	335,709	384,959	393,389	40.5
Tucson, AZ	417,942	486,699	520,116	542,629	543,348	30.0
Tulsa, OK	367,241	393,049	391,906	413,066	412,322	12.3
Virginia Beach, VA	393,069	425,257	437,994	459,470	457,066	16.3
Washington, DC	606,900	572,059	601,723	689,545	672,079	10.7
Wichita, KS	313,693	344,284	382,368	397,532	396,488	26.4
Wilmington, NC	64,609	75,838	106,476	115,451	118,578	83.5
Winston-Salem, NC	168,139	185,776	229,617	249,545	250,887	49.2
U.S.	248,709,873	281,421,906	308,745,538	331,449,281	332,387,540	33.6

Note: (1) 2019-2023 5-year estimated population
Source: U.S. Census Bureau: 1990 Census, Census 2000, Census 2010, Census 2020, 2019-2023 American Community Survey 5-Year Estimates

Population Growth: Metro Area

Metro Area	1990 Census	2000 Census	2010 Census	2020 Census	Current Estimate[1]	Population Growth 1990-2023 (%)
Albuquerque, NM	599,416	729,649	887,077	916,528	918,567	53.2
Anchorage, AK	266,021	319,605	380,821	398,328	399,746	50.3
Ann Arbor, MI	282,937	322,895	344,791	372,258	368,394	30.2
Athens, GA	136,025	166,079	192,541	215,415	218,190	60.4
Atlanta, GA	3,069,411	4,247,981	5,268,860	6,089,815	6,176,937	101.2
Austin, TX	846,217	1,249,763	1,716,289	2,283,371	2,357,497	178.6
Baltimore, MD	2,382,172	2,552,994	2,710,489	2,844,510	2,839,409	19.2
Billings, MT	121,499	138,904	158,050	184,167	187,269	54.1
Boise City, ID	319,596	464,840	616,561	764,718	790,640	147.4
Boston, MA	4,133,895	4,391,344	4,552,402	4,941,632	4,917,661	19.0
Boulder, CO	208,898	269,758	294,567	330,758	328,317	57.2
Cape Coral, FL	335,113	440,888	618,754	760,822	792,692	136.5
Cedar Rapids, IA	210,640	237,230	257,940	276,520	275,960	31.0
Charleston, SC	506,875	549,033	664,607	799,636	817,756	61.3
Charlotte, NC	1,024,331	1,330,448	1,758,038	2,660,329	2,712,818	164.8
Chicago, IL	8,182,076	9,098,316	9,461,105	9,618,502	9,359,555	14.4
Cincinnati, OH	1,844,917	2,009,632	2,130,151	2,256,884	2,255,257	22.2
Clarksville, TN	189,277	232,000	273,949	320,535	328,626	73.6
Cleveland, OH	2,102,219	2,148,143	2,077,240	2,088,251	2,171,978	3.3
College Station, TX	150,998	184,885	228,660	268,248	273,280	81.0
Colorado Springs, CO	409,482	537,484	645,613	755,105	760,782	85.8
Columbia, MO	122,010	145,666	172,786	210,864	212,850	74.5
Columbia, SC	548,325	647,158	767,598	829,470	839,868	53.2
Columbus, OH	1,405,176	1,612,694	1,836,536	2,138,926	2,151,847	53.1
Dallas, TX	3,989,294	5,161,544	6,371,773	7,637,387	7,807,555	95.7
Davenport, IA	368,151	376,019	379,690	384,324	381,864	3.7
Denver, CO	1,666,935	2,179,296	2,543,482	2,963,821	2,977,085	78.6
Des Moines, IA	416,346	481,394	569,633	709,466	720,331	73.0
Detroit, MI	4,248,699	4,452,557	4,296,250	4,392,041	4,367,620	2.8
Durham, NC	344,646	426,493	504,357	649,903	594,291	72.4
El Paso, TX	591,610	679,622	800,647	868,859	869,606	47.0
Eugene, OR	282,912	322,959	351,715	382,971	382,628	35.2
Fargo, ND	153,296	174,367	208,777	249,843	254,914	66.3
Fort Collins, CO	186,136	251,494	299,630	359,066	363,561	95.3
Fort Wayne, IN	354,435	390,156	416,257	419,601	451,440	27.4
Fort Worth, TX	3,989,294	5,161,544	6,371,773	7,637,387	7,807,555	95.7
Gainesville, FL	191,263	232,392	264,275	339,247	344,521	80.1
Green Bay, WI	243,698	282,599	306,241	328,268	329,375	35.2
Greensboro, NC	540,257	643,430	723,801	776,566	779,894	44.4
Honolulu, HI	836,231	876,156	953,207	1,016,508	1,003,666	20.0
Houston, TX	3,767,335	4,715,407	5,946,800	7,122,240	7,274,714	93.1
Huntsville, AL	293,047	342,376	417,593	491,723	504,712	72.2
Indianapolis, IN	1,294,217	1,525,104	1,756,241	2,111,040	2,106,327	62.7
Jacksonville, FL	925,213	1,122,750	1,345,596	1,605,848	1,645,707	77.9
Kansas City, MO	1,636,528	1,836,038	2,035,334	2,192,035	2,202,006	34.6
Lafayette, LA	208,740	239,086	273,738	478,384	410,883	96.8
Las Vegas, NV	741,459	1,375,765	1,951,269	2,265,461	2,293,764	209.4
Lexington, KY	348,428	408,326	472,099	516,811	517,378	48.5
Lincoln, NE	229,091	266,787	302,157	340,217	341,309	49.0
Little Rock, AR	535,034	610,518	699,757	748,031	753,605	40.9
Los Angeles, CA	11,273,720	12,365,627	12,828,837	13,200,998	13,012,469	15.4
Louisville, KY	1,055,973	1,161,975	1,283,566	1,285,439	1,361,847	29.0
Madison, WI	432,323	501,774	568,593	680,796	683,967	58.2
Manchester, NH	336,073	380,841	400,721	422,937	424,732	26.4
McAllen, TX	383,545	569,463	774,769	870,781	880,921	129.7

Table continued on following page.

Metro Area	1990 Census	2000 Census	2010 Census	2020 Census	Current Estimate[1]	Population Growth 1990-2023 (%)
Memphis, TN	1,067,263	1,205,204	1,316,100	1,337,779	1,341,606	25.7
Miami, FL	4,056,100	5,007,564	5,564,635	6,138,333	6,138,876	51.3
Midland, TX	106,611	116,009	136,872	175,220	176,726	65.8
Milwaukee, WI	1,432,149	1,500,741	1,555,908	1,574,731	1,566,361	9.4
Minneapolis, MN	2,538,834	2,968,806	3,279,833	3,690,261	3,693,351	45.5
Nashville, TN	1,048,218	1,311,789	1,589,934	1,989,519	2,043,713	95.0
New Orleans, LA	1,264,391	1,316,510	1,167,764	1,271,845	988,763	-21.8
New York, NY	16,845,992	18,323,002	18,897,109	20,140,470	19,756,722	17.3
Oklahoma City, OK	971,042	1,095,421	1,252,987	1,425,695	1,445,122	48.8
Omaha, NE	685,797	767,041	865,350	967,604	972,840	41.9
Orlando, FL	1,224,852	1,644,561	2,134,411	2,673,376	2,721,022	122.2
Philadelphia, PA	5,435,470	5,687,147	5,965,343	6,245,051	6,241,882	14.8
Phoenix, AZ	2,238,480	3,251,876	4,192,887	4,845,832	4,941,206	120.7
Pittsburgh, PA	2,468,289	2,431,087	2,356,285	2,370,930	2,443,921	-1.0
Portland, OR	1,523,741	1,927,881	2,226,009	2,512,859	2,510,529	64.8
Providence, RI	1,509,789	1,582,997	1,600,852	1,676,579	1,673,807	10.9
Provo, UT	269,407	376,774	526,810	671,185	695,895	158.3
Raleigh, NC	541,081	797,071	1,130,490	1,413,982	1,449,594	167.9
Reno, NV	257,193	342,885	425,417	490,596	556,539	116.4
Richmond, VA	949,244	1,096,957	1,258,251	1,314,434	1,327,321	39.8
Rochester, MN	141,945	163,618	186,011	226,329	227,252	60.1
Sacramento, CA	1,481,126	1,796,857	2,149,127	2,397,382	2,406,563	62.5
Saint Louis, MO	2,580,897	2,698,687	2,812,896	2,820,253	2,809,414	8.9
Saint Paul, MN	2,538,834	2,968,806	3,279,833	3,690,261	3,693,351	45.5
Salem, OR	278,024	347,214	390,738	433,353	435,085	56.5
Salt Lake City, UT	768,075	968,858	1,124,197	1,257,936	1,261,337	64.2
San Antonio, TX	1,407,745	1,711,703	2,142,508	2,558,143	2,612,802	85.6
San Diego, CA	2,498,016	2,813,833	3,095,313	3,298,634	3,282,782	31.4
San Francisco, CA	3,686,592	4,123,740	4,335,391	4,749,008	4,653,593	26.2
San Jose, CA	1,534,280	1,735,819	1,836,911	2,000,468	1,969,353	28.4
Santa Rosa, CA	388,222	458,614	483,878	488,863	485,642	25.1
Savannah, GA	258,060	293,000	347,611	404,798	412,089	59.7
Seattle, WA	2,559,164	3,043,878	3,439,809	4,018,762	4,021,467	57.1
Sioux Falls, SD	153,500	187,093	228,261	276,730	293,107	90.9
Tampa, FL	2,067,959	2,395,997	2,783,243	3,175,275	3,240,469	56.7
Tucson, AZ	666,880	843,746	980,263	1,043,433	1,049,947	57.4
Tulsa, OK	761,019	859,532	937,478	1,015,331	1,026,209	34.8
Virginia Beach, VA	1,449,389	1,576,370	1,671,683	1,799,674	1,782,590	23.0
Washington, DC	4,122,914	4,796,183	5,582,170	6,385,162	6,263,796	51.9
Wichita, KS	511,111	571,166	623,061	647,610	648,935	27.0
Wilmington, NC	200,124	274,532	362,315	285,905	440,578	120.2
Winston-Salem, NC	361,091	421,961	477,717	675,966	683,637	89.3
U.S.	248,709,873	281,421,906	308,745,538	331,449,281	332,387,540	33.6

Note: (1) 2019-2023 5-year estimated population; Figures cover the Metropolitan Statistical Area (MSA)
Source: U.S. Census Bureau: 1990 Census, Census 2000, Census 2010, Census 2020, 2019-2023 American Community Survey 5-Year Estimates

Male/Female Ratio: City

City	Males	Females	Males per 100 Females
Albuquerque, NM	275,413	287,075	95.9
Anchorage, AK	147,620	141,449	104.4
Ann Arbor, MI	60,397	60,782	99.4
Athens, GA	60,237	66,750	90.2
Atlanta, GA	242,994	256,293	94.8
Austin, TX	495,563	472,299	104.9
Baltimore, MD	268,932	308,261	87.2
Billings, MT	58,615	59,706	98.2
Boise City, ID	118,294	117,407	100.8
Boston, MA	319,182	344,790	92.6
Boulder, CO	55,022	51,252	107.4
Cape Coral, FL	103,313	103,074	100.2
Cedar Rapids, IA	67,551	69,308	97.5
Charleston, SC	72,280	79,734	90.7
Charlotte, NC	427,869	458,414	93.3
Chicago, IL	1,314,256	1,393,392	94.3
Cincinnati, OH	148,944	160,651	92.7
Clarksville, TN	86,129	85,768	100.4
Cleveland, OH	177,863	189,660	93.8
College Station, TX	62,870	59,410	105.8
Colorado Springs, CO	241,781	241,318	100.2
Columbia, MO	61,139	66,061	92.5
Columbia, SC	68,245	69,774	97.8
Columbus, OH	445,564	460,916	96.7
Dallas, TX	647,372	652,181	99.3
Davenport, IA	50,102	50,981	98.3
Denver, CO	359,969	353,765	101.8
Des Moines, IA	105,131	107,333	97.9
Detroit, MI	302,503	334,141	90.5
Durham, NC	136,368	152,097	89.7
El Paso, TX	333,802	344,345	96.9
Eugene, OR	87,095	90,425	96.3
Fargo, ND	65,129	63,935	101.9
Fort Collins, CO	84,686	85,019	99.6
Fort Wayne, IN	129,959	136,276	95.4
Fort Worth, TX	461,317	479,994	96.1
Gainesville, FL	68,593	75,018	91.4
Green Bay, WI	52,829	53,756	98.3
Greensboro, NC	138,079	160,485	86.0
Honolulu, HI	173,028	173,295	99.8
Houston, TX	1,138,504	1,161,915	98.0
Huntsville, AL	107,036	111,778	95.8
Indianapolis, IN	428,660	453,383	94.5
Jacksonville, FL	466,421	495,318	94.2
Kansas City, MO	245,780	262,453	93.6
Lafayette, LA	58,993	62,544	94.3
Las Vegas, NV	325,629	325,244	100.1
Lexington, KY	158,152	162,970	97.0
Lincoln, NE	146,855	145,077	101.2
Little Rock, AR	95,597	107,142	89.2
Los Angeles, CA	1,921,735	1,936,162	99.3
Louisville, KY	305,342	321,868	94.9
Madison, WI	137,655	137,913	99.8
Manchester, NH	57,084	58,331	97.9
McAllen, TX	71,212	72,577	98.1

Table continued on following page.

City	Males	Females	Males per 100 Females
Memphis, TN	298,855	330,208	90.5
Miami, FL	226,349	220,314	102.7
Midland, TX	68,527	65,471	104.7
Milwaukee, WI	275,637	294,119	93.7
Minneapolis, MN	218,753	208,092	105.1
Nashville, TN	331,646	352,652	94.0
New Orleans, LA	177,299	198,736	89.2
New York, NY	4,088,026	4,428,176	92.3
Oklahoma City, OK	340,327	348,366	97.7
Omaha, NE	242,508	245,689	98.7
Orlando, FL	153,714	158,018	97.3
Philadelphia, PA	749,410	833,022	90.0
Phoenix, AZ	815,308	809,524	100.7
Pittsburgh, PA	149,240	154,380	96.7
Portland, OR	319,454	323,261	98.8
Providence, RI	93,138	97,076	95.9
Provo, UT	56,107	58,196	96.4
Raleigh, NC	228,452	242,311	94.3
Reno, NV	136,341	132,618	102.8
Richmond, VA	108,090	119,505	90.4
Rochester, MN	59,099	62,539	94.5
Sacramento, CA	260,163	264,639	98.3
Saint Louis, MO	142,190	150,919	94.2
Saint Paul, MN	151,659	156,103	97.2
Salem, OR	89,295	87,371	102.2
Salt Lake City, UT	105,049	98,839	106.3
San Antonio, TX	722,875	736,079	98.2
San Diego, CA	703,091	681,970	103.1
San Francisco, CA	429,837	406,484	105.7
San Jose, CA	504,179	485,875	103.8
Santa Rosa, CA	86,188	91,028	94.7
Savannah, GA	69,345	78,201	88.7
Seattle, WA	378,278	363,162	104.2
Sioux Falls, SD	99,791	97,851	102.0
Tampa, FL	197,565	195,824	100.9
Tucson, AZ	270,198	273,150	98.9
Tulsa, OK	201,524	210,798	95.6
Virginia Beach, VA	224,463	232,603	96.5
Washington, DC	320,001	352,078	90.9
Wichita, KS	197,295	199,193	99.0
Wilmington, NC	55,595	62,983	88.3
Winston-Salem, NC	116,981	133,906	87.4
U.S.	164,545,087	167,842,453	98.0

Source: U.S. Census Bureau, 2019-2023 American Community Survey 5-Year Estimates

Male/Female Ratio: Metro Area

Metro Area	Males	Females	Males per 100 Females
Albuquerque, NM	452,929	465,638	97.3
Anchorage, AK	205,511	194,235	105.8
Ann Arbor, MI	183,761	184,633	99.5
Athens, GA	105,119	113,071	93.0
Atlanta, GA	2,998,312	3,178,625	94.3
Austin, TX	1,190,277	1,167,220	102.0
Baltimore, MD	1,371,348	1,468,061	93.4
Billings, MT	92,957	94,312	98.6
Boise City, ID	397,370	393,270	101.0
Boston, MA	2,405,154	2,512,507	95.7
Boulder, CO	165,677	162,640	101.9
Cape Coral, FL	389,853	402,839	96.8
Cedar Rapids, IA	137,287	138,673	99.0
Charleston, SC	400,382	417,374	95.9
Charlotte, NC	1,323,612	1,389,206	95.3
Chicago, IL	4,607,366	4,752,189	97.0
Cincinnati, OH	1,113,237	1,142,020	97.5
Clarksville, TN	165,784	162,842	101.8
Cleveland, OH	1,057,990	1,113,988	95.0
College Station, TX	137,218	136,062	100.8
Colorado Springs, CO	386,799	373,983	103.4
Columbia, MO	103,590	109,260	94.8
Columbia, SC	407,291	432,577	94.2
Columbus, OH	1,066,090	1,085,757	98.2
Dallas, TX	3,864,152	3,943,403	98.0
Davenport, IA	189,025	192,839	98.0
Denver, CO	1,499,649	1,477,436	101.5
Des Moines, IA	359,219	361,112	99.5
Detroit, MI	2,140,962	2,226,658	96.2
Durham, NC	285,396	308,895	92.4
El Paso, TX	432,470	437,136	98.9
Eugene, OR	189,067	193,561	97.7
Fargo, ND	128,561	126,353	101.7
Fort Collins, CO	181,725	181,836	99.9
Fort Wayne, IN	222,504	228,936	97.2
Fort Worth, TX	3,864,152	3,943,403	98.0
Gainesville, FL	166,988	177,533	94.1
Green Bay, WI	165,274	164,101	100.7
Greensboro, NC	374,844	405,050	92.5
Honolulu, HI	507,355	496,311	102.2
Houston, TX	3,616,570	3,658,144	98.9
Huntsville, AL	249,354	255,358	97.6
Indianapolis, IN	1,034,791	1,071,536	96.6
Jacksonville, FL	804,019	841,688	95.5
Kansas City, MO	1,087,932	1,114,074	97.7
Lafayette, LA	200,575	210,308	95.4
Las Vegas, NV	1,148,112	1,145,652	100.2
Lexington, KY	254,019	263,359	96.5
Lincoln, NE	172,052	169,257	101.7
Little Rock, AR	365,071	388,534	94.0
Los Angeles, CA	6,447,486	6,564,983	98.2
Louisville, KY	669,908	691,939	96.8
Madison, WI	343,409	340,558	100.8
Manchester, NH	212,913	211,819	100.5
McAllen, TX	434,784	446,137	97.5

Table continued on following page.

Metro Area	Males	Females	Males per 100 Females
Memphis, TN	642,599	699,007	91.9
Miami, FL	3,005,200	3,133,676	95.9
Midland, TX	90,328	86,398	104.5
Milwaukee, WI	768,160	798,201	96.2
Minneapolis, MN	1,842,197	1,851,154	99.5
Nashville, TN	1,004,473	1,039,240	96.7
New Orleans, LA	476,985	511,778	93.2
New York, NY	9,622,708	10,134,014	95.0
Oklahoma City, OK	714,932	730,190	97.9
Omaha, NE	485,489	487,351	99.6
Orlando, FL	1,336,264	1,384,758	96.5
Philadelphia, PA	3,031,854	3,210,028	94.4
Phoenix, AZ	2,466,995	2,474,211	99.7
Pittsburgh, PA	1,200,522	1,243,399	96.6
Portland, OR	1,251,055	1,259,474	99.3
Providence, RI	819,607	854,200	96.0
Provo, UT	353,303	342,592	103.1
Raleigh, NC	711,279	738,315	96.3
Reno, NV	283,387	273,152	103.7
Richmond, VA	645,193	682,128	94.6
Rochester, MN	112,416	114,836	97.9
Sacramento, CA	1,184,908	1,221,655	97.0
Saint Louis, MO	1,370,976	1,438,438	95.3
Saint Paul, MN	1,842,197	1,851,154	99.5
Salem, OR	217,233	217,852	99.7
Salt Lake City, UT	637,671	623,666	102.2
San Antonio, TX	1,298,427	1,314,375	98.8
San Diego, CA	1,660,156	1,622,626	102.3
San Francisco, CA	2,318,841	2,334,752	99.3
San Jose, CA	1,003,282	966,071	103.9
Santa Rosa, CA	238,817	246,825	96.8
Savannah, GA	200,060	212,029	94.4
Seattle, WA	2,031,168	1,990,299	102.1
Sioux Falls, SD	148,246	144,861	102.3
Tampa, FL	1,583,138	1,657,331	95.5
Tucson, AZ	518,998	530,949	97.7
Tulsa, OK	506,779	519,430	97.6
Virginia Beach, VA	875,910	906,680	96.6
Washington, DC	3,081,518	3,182,278	96.8
Wichita, KS	323,191	325,744	99.2
Wilmington, NC	212,689	227,889	93.3
Winston-Salem, NC	330,177	353,460	93.4
U.S.	164,545,087	167,842,453	98.0

Note: Figures cover the Metropolitan Statistical Area (MSA)
Source: U.S. Census Bureau, 2019-2023 American Community Survey 5-Year Estimates

Race: City

City	White Alone[1] (%)	Black Alone[1] (%)	Asian Alone[1] (%)	AIAN[2] Alone[1] (%)	NHOPI[3] Alone[1] (%)	Other Race Alone[1] (%)	Two or More Races (%)
Albuquerque, NM	55.3	3.3	3.3	5.0	0.1	11.1	21.9
Anchorage, AK	58.3	5.3	9.8	7.3	3.1	3.1	13.1
Ann Arbor, MI	68.8	7.2	15.2	0.3	0.0	1.2	7.3
Athens, GA	57.6	26.2	4.3	0.4	0.0	3.4	8.1
Atlanta, GA	39.9	46.9	5.0	0.3	0.1	2.1	5.8
Austin, TX	59.9	7.5	8.6	0.7	0.1	7.7	15.5
Baltimore, MD	27.4	60.0	2.5	0.4	0.0	4.4	5.2
Billings, MT	86.3	1.0	0.9	4.4	0.1	1.4	6.1
Boise City, ID	83.6	1.4	3.3	0.7	0.3	3.0	7.6
Boston, MA	47.8	21.5	10.0	0.3	0.1	7.1	13.2
Boulder, CO	81.8	1.1	5.8	0.3	0.1	1.8	9.2
Cape Coral, FL	72.9	4.5	1.5	0.1	0.0	4.1	16.9
Cedar Rapids, IA	79.7	8.5	2.6	0.2	0.0	1.4	7.6
Charleston, SC	72.9	17.4	2.2	0.6	0.2	1.9	5.0
Charlotte, NC	41.5	34.1	6.4	0.4	0.0	8.8	8.9
Chicago, IL	39.0	28.4	7.1	0.9	0.1	12.4	12.0
Cincinnati, OH	49.4	38.7	2.8	0.1	0.0	2.0	7.0
Clarksville, TN	59.4	23.0	2.5	0.4	0.3	2.8	11.7
Cleveland, OH	36.7	46.8	2.3	0.4	0.0	4.6	9.2
College Station, TX	67.0	8.8	9.6	0.3	0.1	3.3	10.9
Colorado Springs, CO	72.3	5.8	3.0	1.0	0.2	4.9	12.8
Columbia, MO	74.3	12.1	6.1	0.1	0.1	1.2	6.1
Columbia, SC	49.9	39.5	2.7	0.2	0.2	1.7	5.9
Columbus, OH	53.3	29.0	5.8	0.3	0.0	3.4	8.2
Dallas, TX	41.9	23.7	3.7	0.8	0.1	12.5	17.3
Davenport, IA	75.9	11.2	2.0	0.3	0.1	2.1	8.5
Denver, CO	62.9	8.8	3.6	0.9	0.1	8.2	15.5
Des Moines, IA	66.9	12.0	6.2	0.5	0.0	5.2	9.1
Detroit, MI	11.7	76.8	1.6	0.4	0.0	4.6	4.8
Durham, NC	43.9	34.4	5.6	0.5	0.1	6.8	8.6
El Paso, TX	39.3	3.6	1.5	0.9	0.2	16.0	38.6
Eugene, OR	78.9	1.8	3.9	0.8	0.4	3.8	10.5
Fargo, ND	80.8	8.3	3.9	1.0	0.0	1.1	5.0
Fort Collins, CO	81.7	1.4	3.3	0.8	0.1	2.2	10.5
Fort Wayne, IN	66.4	14.6	5.8	0.4	0.0	4.3	8.4
Fort Worth, TX	47.7	19.5	5.2	0.6	0.1	10.4	16.4
Gainesville, FL	59.2	21.6	6.2	0.2	0.1	3.0	9.7
Green Bay, WI	69.9	3.8	4.1	3.3	0.0	7.1	11.8
Greensboro, NC	40.4	42.2	5.0	0.5	0.0	4.5	7.5
Honolulu, HI	17.0	1.8	52.9	0.2	8.5	1.2	18.4
Houston, TX	35.5	22.9	6.9	0.9	0.1	14.6	19.2
Huntsville, AL	58.4	29.7	2.0	0.6	0.1	2.9	6.2
Indianapolis, IN	53.6	28.1	4.1	0.5	0.0	5.7	8.0
Jacksonville, FL	51.2	30.1	4.9	0.2	0.1	3.9	9.6
Kansas City, MO	57.8	25.8	2.7	0.4	0.3	4.5	8.6
Lafayette, LA	59.1	28.6	2.1	0.1	0.1	1.2	8.8
Las Vegas, NV	49.2	11.9	6.9	1.1	0.8	13.9	16.2
Lexington, KY	69.9	14.4	4.2	0.2	0.0	3.5	7.8
Lincoln, NE	80.9	4.2	4.5	0.7	0.1	2.3	7.4
Little Rock, AR	46.3	39.4	3.0	0.3	0.1	4.2	6.6
Los Angeles, CA	37.3	8.5	12.0	1.2	0.1	25.1	15.7
Louisville, KY	63.1	23.7	2.6	0.1	0.0	2.1	8.4
Madison, WI	73.0	7.1	8.0	0.4	0.0	2.1	9.4
Manchester, NH	76.7	5.3	4.6	0.2	0.0	3.2	10.0

Table continued on following page.

City	White Alone[1] (%)	Black Alone[1] (%)	Asian Alone[1] (%)	AIAN[2] Alone[1] (%)	NHOPI[3] Alone[1] (%)	Other Race Alone[1] (%)	Two or More Races (%)
McAllen, TX	43.1	0.9	2.9	0.6	0.0	17.5	35.1
Memphis, TN	25.0	62.9	1.7	0.5	0.1	5.1	4.6
Miami, FL	34.2	13.7	1.6	0.4	0.0	7.5	42.6
Midland, TX	58.8	8.6	2.1	0.7	0.0	12.0	17.9
Milwaukee, WI	36.5	38.6	4.8	0.7	0.0	6.9	12.4
Minneapolis, MN	61.6	18.3	5.2	1.1	0.1	4.9	8.9
Nashville, TN	56.5	25.5	3.5	0.3	0.1	4.9	9.2
New Orleans, LA	31.6	55.2	2.8	0.3	0.0	2.8	7.3
New York, NY	35.9	22.7	14.6	0.7	0.1	15.5	10.5
Oklahoma City, OK	58.4	13.4	4.5	3.4	0.1	5.8	14.4
Omaha, NE	68.8	11.8	4.0	0.8	0.0	5.0	9.7
Orlando, FL	43.2	22.9	4.4	0.1	0.1	8.4	21.0
Philadelphia, PA	36.1	39.9	7.8	0.4	0.1	8.4	7.3
Phoenix, AZ	53.7	7.8	3.9	2.3	0.2	11.4	20.8
Pittsburgh, PA	63.7	22.5	5.8	0.2	0.0	1.6	6.2
Portland, OR	70.1	5.8	8.1	0.8	0.5	3.3	11.3
Providence, RI	40.7	13.3	5.9	1.0	0.1	20.4	18.7
Provo, UT	78.6	1.1	2.2	1.0	1.4	5.4	10.2
Raleigh, NC	53.8	27.5	4.7	0.4	0.0	5.5	8.0
Reno, NV	63.5	3.2	7.0	1.0	0.7	11.1	13.5
Richmond, VA	43.2	42.0	2.1	0.2	0.0	5.3	7.1
Rochester, MN	74.3	9.4	8.0	0.2	0.1	2.1	5.9
Sacramento, CA	36.8	12.4	19.7	1.0	1.7	13.4	15.0
Saint Louis, MO	45.7	43.1	3.4	0.2	0.0	1.6	5.9
Saint Paul, MN	53.2	16.2	17.9	0.7	0.0	3.5	8.4
Salem, OR	69.8	1.6	3.5	1.2	1.6	8.2	14.1
Salt Lake City, UT	70.5	2.7	5.4	1.2	1.4	9.2	9.6
San Antonio, TX	48.3	6.9	3.1	1.1	0.1	10.9	29.6
San Diego, CA	50.4	5.7	17.6	0.7	0.5	9.5	15.6
San Francisco, CA	40.5	5.1	35.0	0.7	0.4	7.7	10.7
San Jose, CA	29.0	2.9	38.6	1.0	0.5	13.6	14.4
Santa Rosa, CA	56.2	1.9	6.5	1.4	0.6	20.0	13.4
Savannah, GA	37.2	52.2	2.9	0.2	0.2	2.0	5.4
Seattle, WA	61.8	6.6	17.2	0.6	0.3	3.0	10.5
Sioux Falls, SD	79.9	7.0	2.3	1.9	0.0	2.0	7.0
Tampa, FL	51.8	21.3	4.8	0.3	0.1	4.8	17.0
Tucson, AZ	58.2	5.0	3.1	2.7	0.2	11.6	19.1
Tulsa, OK	57.0	14.2	3.5	4.3	0.2	5.9	14.9
Virginia Beach, VA	61.6	18.9	7.3	0.2	0.2	2.4	9.4
Washington, DC	39.1	43.3	4.1	0.3	0.1	4.8	8.4
Wichita, KS	66.6	9.7	4.9	0.9	0.0	5.5	12.4
Wilmington, NC	72.9	14.9	1.3	0.3	0.0	4.8	5.9
Winston-Salem, NC	48.7	32.4	2.3	0.5	0.0	7.3	8.8
U.S.	63.4	12.4	5.8	0.9	0.2	6.6	10.7

Note: (1) Alone is defined as not being in combination with one or more other races; (2) American Indian and Alaska Native; (3) Native Hawaiian and Other Pacific Islander
Source: U.S. Census Bureau, 2019-2023 American Community Survey 5-Year Estimates

Race: Metro Area

Metro Area	White Alone[1] (%)	Black Alone[1] (%)	Asian Alone[1] (%)	AIAN[2] Alone[1] (%)	NHOPI[3] Alone[1] (%)	Other Race Alone[1] (%)	Two or More Races (%)
Albuquerque, NM	55.2	2.7	2.5	6.2	0.1	10.9	22.3
Anchorage, AK	63.8	4.2	7.6	6.9	2.4	2.7	12.5
Ann Arbor, MI	69.9	11.6	8.9	0.3	0.0	1.6	7.7
Athens, GA	67.1	18.6	3.7	0.4	0.2	3.0	7.1
Atlanta, GA	46.3	34.0	6.4	0.4	0.1	4.9	7.9
Austin, TX	61.4	7.2	6.9	0.7	0.1	7.3	16.5
Baltimore, MD	54.8	29.0	5.8	0.3	0.0	3.6	6.4
Billings, MT	87.5	0.8	0.8	3.6	0.0	1.6	5.7
Boise City, ID	81.5	1.0	1.9	0.8	0.2	5.6	9.0
Boston, MA	69.2	7.5	8.5	0.2	0.0	5.5	9.1
Boulder, CO	80.7	0.8	4.7	0.3	0.1	2.9	10.6
Cape Coral, FL	70.5	8.0	1.7	0.6	0.0	4.3	15.0
Cedar Rapids, IA	86.2	5.0	2.0	0.3	0.0	1.1	5.5
Charleston, SC	64.6	23.9	2.0	0.4	0.2	3.3	5.7
Charlotte, NC	60.2	22.2	4.2	0.4	0.0	5.5	7.5
Chicago, IL	55.7	16.2	7.1	0.6	0.0	9.5	10.8
Cincinnati, OH	78.0	11.9	2.9	0.1	0.1	1.7	5.5
Clarksville, TN	67.3	18.5	2.1	0.3	0.3	2.2	9.5
Cleveland, OH	70.5	18.6	2.3	0.2	0.0	1.9	6.4
College Station, TX	66.6	11.4	5.1	0.6	0.1	4.4	11.8
Colorado Springs, CO	73.1	5.8	2.8	0.9	0.3	4.3	12.8
Columbia, MO	79.2	9.0	4.1	0.2	0.1	1.3	6.1
Columbia, SC	55.4	33.3	2.3	0.2	0.1	2.7	5.9
Columbus, OH	70.3	15.8	4.8	0.2	0.0	2.2	6.7
Dallas, TX	52.7	16.2	7.8	0.6	0.1	8.0	14.5
Davenport, IA	79.4	7.7	2.4	0.2	0.1	2.8	7.5
Denver, CO	69.1	5.6	4.3	0.9	0.2	6.4	13.6
Des Moines, IA	81.5	5.7	4.2	0.3	0.0	2.5	5.8
Detroit, MI	65.6	21.5	4.8	0.2	0.0	1.9	5.9
Durham, NC	56.6	24.0	5.1	0.5	0.0	5.9	7.8
El Paso, TX	39.2	3.3	1.3	0.9	0.2	16.3	38.9
Eugene, OR	82.0	1.2	2.6	1.0	0.2	3.6	9.5
Fargo, ND	84.2	6.1	2.7	0.9	0.1	0.9	5.1
Fort Collins, CO	84.1	1.0	2.1	0.6	0.1	2.6	9.5
Fort Wayne, IN	75.6	9.5	4.3	0.3	0.0	3.2	7.1
Fort Worth, TX	52.7	16.2	7.8	0.6	0.1	8.0	14.5
Gainesville, FL	66.6	17.1	4.9	0.2	0.0	2.5	8.7
Green Bay, WI	82.9	2.2	2.7	1.7	0.0	3.3	7.1
Greensboro, NC	57.7	26.9	3.8	0.4	0.0	4.3	6.9
Honolulu, HI	18.8	2.4	42.6	0.2	9.9	1.6	24.4
Houston, TX	45.3	17.3	8.2	0.7	0.1	10.7	17.8
Huntsville, AL	66.6	21.8	2.4	0.7	0.1	2.2	6.2
Indianapolis, IN	70.8	15.1	3.8	0.3	0.0	3.4	6.5
Jacksonville, FL	62.8	20.7	4.0	0.2	0.1	3.2	9.0
Kansas City, MO	73.0	11.9	2.9	0.4	0.2	3.7	7.8
Lafayette, LA	68.0	22.7	1.5	0.2	0.1	1.1	6.4
Las Vegas, NV	47.1	12.1	10.5	1.1	0.8	12.9	15.5
Lexington, KY	76.6	10.6	2.9	0.2	0.0	2.9	6.7
Lincoln, NE	83.0	3.6	3.9	0.7	0.1	2.0	6.8
Little Rock, AR	65.9	23.5	1.6	0.3	0.0	2.8	5.8
Los Angeles, CA	38.1	6.3	16.7	1.1	0.2	21.2	16.2
Louisville, KY	75.2	14.2	2.1	0.1	0.0	1.6	6.7
Madison, WI	81.4	4.5	5.0	0.3	0.1	1.7	7.1
Manchester, NH	83.3	2.6	4.2	0.1	0.0	2.1	7.7

Table continued on following page.

Metro Area	White Alone[1] (%)	Black Alone[1] (%)	Asian Alone[1] (%)	AIAN[2] Alone[1] (%)	NHOPI[3] Alone[1] (%)	Other Race Alone[1] (%)	Two or More Races (%)
McAllen, TX	39.5	0.7	1.0	0.4	0.0	10.8	47.6
Memphis, TN	42.5	46.8	2.2	0.3	0.1	3.4	4.7
Miami, FL	43.7	20.3	2.6	0.2	0.0	6.6	26.6
Midland, TX	60.4	7.1	2.1	0.6	0.0	12.8	17.1
Milwaukee, WI	67.4	16.1	4.0	0.4	0.0	3.8	8.3
Minneapolis, MN	73.8	8.9	6.9	0.5	0.0	3.0	6.8
Nashville, TN	71.6	14.3	2.9	0.2	0.1	3.4	7.6
New Orleans, LA	45.0	38.5	3.2	0.6	0.0	4.4	8.4
New York, NY	48.4	16.3	11.8	0.5	0.0	12.3	10.6
Oklahoma City, OK	66.5	9.8	3.3	3.6	0.1	3.9	12.8
Omaha, NE	77.1	7.4	3.2	0.6	0.1	3.7	7.9
Orlando, FL	52.5	16.0	4.5	0.3	0.1	9.5	17.2
Philadelphia, PA	61.4	20.2	6.3	0.2	0.0	4.9	6.9
Phoenix, AZ	63.2	5.7	4.1	2.2	0.2	8.4	16.1
Pittsburgh, PA	84.1	7.9	2.5	0.1	0.0	0.8	4.6
Portland, OR	73.0	3.0	7.0	0.8	0.5	4.5	11.2
Providence, RI	74.5	5.3	3.1	0.4	0.1	6.6	10.0
Provo, UT	83.9	0.7	1.4	0.6	0.8	4.0	8.6
Raleigh, NC	60.7	19.1	6.6	0.4	0.0	5.4	7.8
Reno, NV	66.9	2.3	5.1	1.4	0.6	10.0	13.7
Richmond, VA	56.8	28.5	4.1	0.3	0.1	4.0	6.2
Rochester, MN	83.0	5.4	4.7	0.2	0.1	1.7	4.9
Sacramento, CA	54.8	6.9	14.8	0.8	0.8	8.7	13.2
Saint Louis, MO	72.1	17.5	2.8	0.1	0.0	1.3	6.1
Saint Paul, MN	73.8	8.9	6.9	0.5	0.0	3.0	6.8
Salem, OR	71.3	1.1	2.0	1.4	1.0	9.3	14.0
Salt Lake City, UT	73.6	1.7	3.9	0.9	1.5	8.7	9.6
San Antonio, TX	53.5	7.0	2.8	0.9	0.1	9.5	26.2
San Diego, CA	53.0	4.7	12.2	0.9	0.4	10.6	18.1
San Francisco, CA	39.9	7.0	27.6	0.9	0.6	11.8	12.2
San Jose, CA	33.6	2.3	38.3	0.8	0.4	10.7	13.9
Santa Rosa, CA	64.5	1.6	4.4	1.3	0.4	14.1	13.7
Savannah, GA	55.2	32.4	2.5	0.2	0.1	3.1	6.5
Seattle, WA	60.9	6.1	15.4	0.8	0.9	4.6	11.4
Sioux Falls, SD	84.2	5.1	1.6	1.5	0.0	1.6	6.0
Tampa, FL	66.0	11.8	3.8	0.3	0.1	4.8	13.2
Tucson, AZ	63.2	3.6	3.0	3.1	0.2	9.9	17.0
Tulsa, OK	65.3	7.6	2.8	7.2	0.1	3.5	13.4
Virginia Beach, VA	55.0	29.7	4.1	0.3	0.1	2.4	8.4
Washington, DC	45.5	24.9	10.7	0.5	0.0	8.3	10.1
Wichita, KS	74.4	6.7	3.7	0.8	0.1	4.3	10.1
Wilmington, NC	78.8	10.4	1.0	0.3	0.0	3.5	5.9
Winston-Salem, NC	68.8	17.4	1.8	0.3	0.0	4.4	7.3
U.S.	63.4	12.4	5.8	0.9	0.2	6.6	10.7

Note: Figures cover the Metropolitan Statistical Area (MSA); (1) Alone is defined as not being in combination with one or more other races; (2) American Indian and Alaska Native; (3) Native Hawaiian & Other Pacific Islander
Source: U.S. Census Bureau, 2019-2023 American Community Survey 5-Year Estimates

Hispanic Origin: City

City	Hispanic or Latino (%)	Mexican (%)	Puerto Rican (%)	Cuban (%)	Other Hispanic or Latino (%)
Albuquerque, NM	47.9	28.9	0.7	0.5	17.9
Anchorage, AK	9.3	4.2	1.4	0.5	3.1
Ann Arbor, MI	5.4	2.3	0.7	0.2	2.3
Athens, GA	11.5	6.1	0.4	0.7	4.2
Atlanta, GA	6.3	2.0	0.9	0.3	3.0
Austin, TX	32.2	23.7	1.0	0.9	6.7
Baltimore, MD	7.9	1.6	1.0	0.4	4.8
Billings, MT	7.2	5.0	0.3	0.2	1.8
Boise City, ID	9.5	7.0	0.4	0.1	2.1
Boston, MA	18.9	1.2	4.4	0.4	13.0
Boulder, CO	11.2	6.6	0.3	0.5	3.8
Cape Coral, FL	25.0	1.9	4.9	10.7	7.5
Cedar Rapids, IA	5.1	3.5	0.4	0.1	1.2
Charleston, SC	5.9	2.6	0.7	0.2	2.4
Charlotte, NC	17.0	6.0	1.2	0.5	9.3
Chicago, IL	29.6	21.6	3.5	0.4	4.2
Cincinnati, OH	5.4	1.6	0.9	0.2	2.6
Clarksville, TN	12.5	6.0	3.0	0.3	3.2
Cleveland, OH	12.8	1.7	8.8	0.2	2.2
College Station, TX	18.4	12.9	0.7	0.5	4.3
Colorado Springs, CO	18.7	12.0	1.2	0.2	5.3
Columbia, MO	4.3	2.5	0.2	0.2	1.3
Columbia, SC	5.7	2.0	1.3	0.2	2.2
Columbus, OH	7.9	3.7	1.1	0.1	3.0
Dallas, TX	41.9	33.6	0.6	0.4	7.4
Davenport, IA	9.1	8.0	0.4	0.1	0.6
Denver, CO	27.9	20.9	0.7	0.3	6.1
Des Moines, IA	16.0	11.4	0.6	0.3	3.8
Detroit, MI	8.0	5.5	0.9	0.2	1.3
Durham, NC	14.7	6.6	0.9	0.5	6.7
El Paso, TX	81.3	76.1	1.1	0.2	3.9
Eugene, OR	11.4	8.0	0.4	0.2	2.8
Fargo, ND	3.7	2.2	0.6	0.0	0.8
Fort Collins, CO	12.3	8.2	0.7	0.2	3.3
Fort Wayne, IN	10.5	7.7	0.7	0.1	2.2
Fort Worth, TX	34.6	28.7	1.3	0.4	4.2
Gainesville, FL	13.4	1.3	2.9	2.9	6.3
Green Bay, WI	18.1	13.8	2.3	0.1	1.9
Greensboro, NC	10.5	4.5	1.7	0.2	4.1
Honolulu, HI	6.6	2.3	1.8	0.1	2.4
Houston, TX	44.1	28.5	0.8	0.8	14.0
Huntsville, AL	8.1	4.3	1.0	0.2	2.5
Indianapolis, IN	13.3	8.7	0.8	0.3	3.5
Jacksonville, FL	12.0	2.0	3.9	1.8	4.3
Kansas City, MO	12.3	8.3	0.6	0.4	3.0
Lafayette, LA	7.6	1.9	0.4	0.5	4.8
Las Vegas, NV	34.1	24.7	1.2	1.6	6.6
Lexington, KY	9.2	5.9	0.7	0.3	2.4
Lincoln, NE	8.8	5.7	0.4	0.2	2.5
Little Rock, AR	10.4	6.8	0.2	0.1	3.3
Los Angeles, CA	47.2	30.0	0.5	0.4	16.3
Louisville, KY	8.6	2.9	0.4	3.4	1.9
Madison, WI	9.3	5.7	0.7	0.2	2.8
Manchester, NH	13.4	1.5	4.4	0.1	7.4
McAllen, TX	86.5	81.1	0.5	0.1	4.8

Table continued on following page.

City	Hispanic or Latino (%)	Mexican (%)	Puerto Rican (%)	Cuban (%)	Other Hispanic or Latino (%)
Memphis, TN	10.2	5.7	0.3	0.2	3.9
Miami, FL	71.2	2.2	3.3	31.0	34.8
Midland, TX	44.3	38.1	0.6	1.3	4.3
Milwaukee, WI	20.7	13.7	4.9	0.1	1.9
Minneapolis, MN	10.5	5.9	0.4	0.2	4.0
Nashville, TN	13.8	6.8	0.7	0.6	5.7
New Orleans, LA	7.9	1.5	0.4	0.8	5.3
New York, NY	28.4	3.9	7.1	0.5	17.0
Oklahoma City, OK	21.7	17.3	0.5	0.1	3.8
Omaha, NE	15.6	11.4	0.5	0.2	3.5
Orlando, FL	35.6	2.0	15.2	2.6	15.8
Philadelphia, PA	15.2	1.4	8.4	0.2	5.2
Phoenix, AZ	41.8	36.7	0.7	0.4	4.0
Pittsburgh, PA	4.2	1.4	0.8	0.1	2.0
Portland, OR	11.3	7.6	0.5	0.4	2.8
Providence, RI	44.3	1.6	6.8	0.3	35.6
Provo, UT	18.9	11.4	0.7	0.2	6.6
Raleigh, NC	12.7	5.0	1.4	0.4	5.9
Reno, NV	24.6	17.9	0.7	0.3	5.7
Richmond, VA	10.3	2.1	1.1	0.3	6.8
Rochester, MN	6.2	3.9	0.4	0.1	1.8
Sacramento, CA	29.5	24.1	0.9	0.1	4.4
Saint Louis, MO	5.1	3.1	0.3	0.3	1.4
Saint Paul, MN	9.1	5.9	0.4	0.2	2.7
Salem, OR	23.4	20.0	0.4	0.1	2.9
Salt Lake City, UT	20.8	15.2	0.5	0.3	4.8
San Antonio, TX	64.4	54.1	1.4	0.4	8.6
San Diego, CA	29.6	24.9	0.8	0.3	3.6
San Francisco, CA	15.9	7.8	0.7	0.2	7.2
San Jose, CA	31.0	25.4	0.5	0.2	4.9
Santa Rosa, CA	35.8	30.3	0.5	0.1	4.9
Savannah, GA	7.1	2.2	2.0	0.5	2.4
Seattle, WA	8.2	4.8	0.4	0.2	2.8
Sioux Falls, SD	6.4	2.7	0.3	0.1	3.3
Tampa, FL	26.2	3.2	6.1	7.8	9.1
Tucson, AZ	42.7	38.1	0.8	0.3	3.5
Tulsa, OK	19.2	14.5	0.7	0.1	4.0
Virginia Beach, VA	8.9	2.8	2.5	0.3	3.3
Washington, DC	11.6	2.1	0.8	0.4	8.2
Wichita, KS	18.4	15.1	0.8	0.1	2.5
Wilmington, NC	8.9	3.6	1.4	0.4	3.5
Winston-Salem, NC	17.9	10.1	1.7	0.3	5.8
U.S.	19.0	11.3	1.8	0.7	5.2

Note: Persons of Hispanic or Latino origin can be of any race
Source: U.S. Census Bureau, 2019-2023 American Community Survey 5-Year Estimates

Hispanic Origin: Metro Area

Metro Area	Hispanic or Latino (%)	Mexican (%)	Puerto Rican (%)	Cuban (%)	Other Hispanic or Latino (%)
Albuquerque, NM	48.3	28.5	0.7	0.4	18.6
Anchorage, AK	8.2	3.8	1.2	0.4	2.8
Ann Arbor, MI	5.6	2.8	0.6	0.2	2.1
Athens, GA	9.3	5.1	0.4	0.5	3.3
Atlanta, GA	12.1	5.7	1.2	0.4	4.7
Austin, TX	32.0	24.8	1.0	0.6	5.6
Baltimore, MD	7.8	1.6	1.2	0.3	4.7
Billings, MT	6.1	4.4	0.2	0.1	1.3
Boise City, ID	14.7	11.8	0.4	0.1	2.4
Boston, MA	12.0	0.8	2.7	0.3	8.3
Boulder, CO	14.6	9.8	0.5	0.3	3.9
Cape Coral, FL	23.6	4.7	4.5	6.7	7.8
Cedar Rapids, IA	3.7	2.6	0.2	0.0	0.8
Charleston, SC	7.5	3.5	1.1	0.3	2.7
Charlotte, NC	12.0	4.9	1.1	0.4	5.6
Chicago, IL	23.8	18.3	2.3	0.3	2.9
Cincinnati, OH	4.3	1.8	0.5	0.2	1.9
Clarksville, TN	9.7	5.0	2.3	0.2	2.2
Cleveland, OH	6.5	1.5	3.6	0.1	1.3
College Station, TX	26.4	21.9	0.5	0.5	3.6
Colorado Springs, CO	18.0	10.8	1.5	0.3	5.3
Columbia, MO	4.1	2.7	0.2	0.1	1.0
Columbia, SC	6.8	3.2	1.1	0.3	2.3
Columbus, OH	5.3	2.5	0.8	0.1	2.0
Dallas, TX	29.4	23.1	0.9	0.4	5.1
Davenport, IA	9.5	8.3	0.4	0.1	0.8
Denver, CO	23.6	17.5	0.7	0.2	5.3
Des Moines, IA	8.4	5.7	0.4	0.1	2.2
Detroit, MI	5.1	3.4	0.6	0.1	1.0
Durham, NC	13.2	6.3	0.8	0.4	5.8
El Paso, TX	82.6	77.5	1.0	0.2	4.0
Eugene, OR	10.2	7.3	0.4	0.2	2.3
Fargo, ND	3.8	2.5	0.4	0.0	0.8
Fort Collins, CO	12.7	9.0	0.5	0.2	3.0
Fort Wayne, IN	8.0	5.7	0.6	0.1	1.7
Fort Worth, TX	29.4	23.1	0.9	0.4	5.1
Gainesville, FL	11.6	1.8	2.8	2.1	4.9
Green Bay, WI	8.7	6.2	1.0	0.1	1.3
Greensboro, NC	10.2	5.9	1.2	0.2	2.8
Honolulu, HI	9.3	3.1	3.1	0.2	3.0
Houston, TX	37.8	26.1	0.8	0.8	10.1
Huntsville, AL	6.7	3.6	0.9	0.2	1.9
Indianapolis, IN	8.6	5.4	0.6	0.2	2.4
Jacksonville, FL	10.6	1.8	3.3	1.5	4.0
Kansas City, MO	10.6	7.5	0.5	0.3	2.3
Lafayette, LA	5.3	1.9	0.2	0.2	3.0
Las Vegas, NV	31.4	22.7	1.1	1.5	6.1
Lexington, KY	7.8	4.9	0.5	0.3	2.0
Lincoln, NE	8.0	5.2	0.4	0.2	2.2
Little Rock, AR	7.1	4.6	0.3	0.1	2.1
Los Angeles, CA	44.8	33.8	0.5	0.4	10.2
Louisville, KY	6.5	2.7	0.5	1.8	1.5
Madison, WI	6.9	4.2	0.6	0.1	1.9
Manchester, NH	8.3	1.2	2.6	0.2	4.2
McAllen, TX	91.9	87.6	0.3	0.1	3.9

Table continued on following page.

Metro Area	Hispanic or Latino (%)	Mexican (%)	Puerto Rican (%)	Cuban (%)	Other Hispanic or Latino (%)
Memphis, TN	7.2	4.2	0.3	0.2	2.5
Miami, FL	46.0	2.5	3.7	18.4	21.5
Midland, TX	44.8	39.3	0.6	1.2	3.8
Milwaukee, WI	11.8	7.7	2.6	0.1	1.4
Minneapolis, MN	6.7	4.1	0.3	0.1	2.1
Nashville, TN	9.7	5.1	0.7	0.4	3.5
New Orleans, LA	12.6	2.0	0.7	0.9	9.1
New York, NY	25.4	3.0	5.6	0.8	16.0
Oklahoma City, OK	15.3	11.9	0.5	0.1	2.8
Omaha, NE	11.9	8.7	0.4	0.2	2.6
Orlando, FL	32.5	2.7	14.3	2.6	12.9
Philadelphia, PA	10.4	2.0	4.6	0.3	3.6
Phoenix, AZ	30.8	26.2	0.7	0.3	3.6
Pittsburgh, PA	2.3	0.8	0.5	0.1	0.9
Portland, OR	13.5	10.2	0.4	0.2	2.6
Providence, RI	14.6	1.0	4.3	0.2	9.1
Provo, UT	13.7	8.1	0.4	0.1	5.1
Raleigh, NC	12.1	6.0	1.4	0.4	4.4
Reno, NV	24.7	18.9	0.6	0.3	5.0
Richmond, VA	8.1	1.9	1.2	0.3	4.7
Rochester, MN	5.1	3.2	0.3	0.1	1.5
Sacramento, CA	22.6	17.9	0.7	0.2	3.8
Saint Louis, MO	3.8	2.3	0.3	0.1	1.1
Saint Paul, MN	6.7	4.1	0.3	0.1	2.1
Salem, OR	25.6	22.2	0.3	0.2	3.0
Salt Lake City, UT	19.6	13.7	0.4	0.1	5.3
San Antonio, TX	54.5	45.5	1.5	0.3	7.2
San Diego, CA	34.3	29.6	0.8	0.2	3.6
San Francisco, CA	23.0	14.5	0.7	0.2	7.6
San Jose, CA	26.3	21.2	0.4	0.2	4.5
Santa Rosa, CA	29.4	23.7	0.4	0.2	5.1
Savannah, GA	7.7	2.9	1.9	0.5	2.4
Seattle, WA	11.4	7.7	0.6	0.2	2.9
Sioux Falls, SD	5.3	2.4	0.2	0.1	2.6
Tampa, FL	21.1	3.7	6.0	4.5	6.9
Tucson, AZ	36.1	32.1	0.9	0.2	3.0
Tulsa, OK	12.0	8.9	0.5	0.1	2.5
Virginia Beach, VA	7.8	2.6	2.2	0.3	2.8
Washington, DC	17.6	2.5	1.2	0.3	13.6
Wichita, KS	14.5	11.8	0.6	0.1	2.0
Wilmington, NC	7.1	3.4	0.9	0.3	2.5
Winston-Salem, NC	11.8	7.0	1.1	0.3	3.4
U.S.	19.0	11.3	1.8	0.7	5.2

Note: Persons of Hispanic or Latino origin can be of any race; Figures cover the Metropolitan Statistical Area (MSA)
Source: U.S. Census Bureau, 2019-2023 American Community Survey 5-Year Estimates

Household Size: City

City	Persons in Household (%)							Average Household Size
	One	Two	Three	Four	Five	Six	Seven or More	
Albuquerque, NM	37.3	32.4	13.7	9.8	4.6	1.4	0.8	2.29
Anchorage, AK	28.5	33.7	14.8	13.5	5.4	2.3	1.8	2.61
Ann Arbor, MI	34.0	35.9	14.5	9.9	3.2	1.8	0.7	2.19
Athens, GA	33.6	35.1	15.3	10.6	4.0	0.9	0.6	2.18
Atlanta, GA	47.0	32.0	10.6	6.5	2.3	1.0	0.6	2.01
Austin, TX	36.9	34.0	13.4	10.0	3.4	1.5	0.7	2.14
Baltimore, MD	43.4	29.6	13.4	7.7	3.7	1.3	1.0	2.22
Billings, MT	34.0	35.0	13.2	10.8	4.7	1.2	1.1	2.29
Boise City, ID	30.1	37.7	15.0	10.9	4.2	1.5	0.7	2.30
Boston, MA	36.9	33.2	14.6	8.9	4.0	1.5	0.9	2.22
Boulder, CO	34.9	36.6	13.9	10.9	2.5	0.6	0.7	2.16
Cape Coral, FL	24.2	44.1	13.7	10.3	5.5	1.3	0.8	2.59
Cedar Rapids, IA	34.4	35.4	13.5	9.4	5.0	1.1	1.3	2.27
Charleston, SC	34.5	40.1	12.4	8.7	3.2	0.8	0.3	2.20
Charlotte, NC	35.1	31.7	14.8	11.2	4.7	1.5	1.0	2.42
Chicago, IL	39.2	29.4	13.1	9.9	4.8	2.1	1.5	2.32
Cincinnati, OH	44.9	30.5	10.7	8.5	3.0	1.4	1.0	2.07
Clarksville, TN	25.7	33.0	18.0	13.6	5.5	2.5	1.6	2.59
Cleveland, OH	46.4	28.4	11.9	7.4	3.4	1.7	0.9	2.11
College Station, TX	31.1	32.3	15.1	15.1	3.5	2.4	0.6	2.42
Colorado Springs, CO	28.2	36.1	15.4	11.8	5.3	2.2	1.0	2.39
Columbia, MO	34.5	33.8	13.4	12.2	4.6	1.0	0.5	2.29
Columbia, SC	39.3	33.0	14.2	8.3	3.7	1.2	0.3	2.16
Columbus, OH	36.5	32.2	13.4	9.7	4.9	2.0	1.3	2.29
Dallas, TX	37.1	29.7	12.7	10.1	6.1	2.6	1.6	2.43
Davenport, IA	34.9	35.3	13.1	9.5	5.1	1.4	0.7	2.25
Denver, CO	40.0	33.5	11.4	9.0	3.7	1.5	1.0	2.12
Des Moines, IA	37.1	30.7	13.2	10.3	4.8	2.1	1.8	2.30
Detroit, MI	42.5	25.3	13.8	8.9	4.8	2.7	1.9	2.47
Durham, NC	36.1	34.1	13.9	9.9	4.0	1.4	0.6	2.25
El Paso, TX	25.8	28.2	18.0	15.5	8.0	2.8	1.7	2.77
Eugene, OR	34.3	35.7	13.6	10.6	4.0	1.2	0.5	2.23
Fargo, ND	41.1	33.0	11.6	9.3	3.4	1.1	0.5	2.10
Fort Collins, CO	26.6	37.8	17.6	12.5	4.1	1.0	0.4	2.27
Fort Wayne, IN	33.5	33.1	13.3	10.7	5.4	2.5	1.4	2.39
Fort Worth, TX	27.7	29.8	15.6	14.1	7.6	3.1	2.0	2.76
Gainesville, FL	39.2	33.2	14.6	8.8	3.1	0.5	0.6	2.17
Green Bay, WI	35.7	32.4	12.0	11.7	4.8	2.0	1.3	2.35
Greensboro, NC	36.4	30.7	15.3	9.8	4.8	1.5	1.5	2.33
Honolulu, HI	35.0	31.1	14.6	9.7	4.5	2.1	3.0	2.47
Houston, TX	34.1	29.2	15.6	11.6	5.7	2.3	1.5	2.47
Huntsville, AL	36.9	35.6	13.6	8.6	3.8	1.2	0.4	2.21
Indianapolis, IN	36.6	31.9	13.1	9.8	5.4	1.9	1.3	2.41
Jacksonville, FL	32.2	33.3	16.2	10.6	5.0	1.8	0.9	2.44
Kansas City, MO	37.7	31.3	12.3	10.8	4.7	2.1	1.0	2.28
Lafayette, LA	33.8	36.5	13.4	9.1	5.0	1.4	0.9	2.25
Las Vegas, NV	30.3	31.2	15.8	11.9	6.3	2.7	1.9	2.63
Lexington, KY	34.8	33.4	14.3	10.8	4.0	1.7	0.9	2.24
Lincoln, NE	32.7	34.1	13.7	11.0	4.9	2.5	1.0	2.31
Little Rock, AR	39.4	31.1	13.5	9.1	4.3	1.4	1.1	2.28
Los Angeles, CA	31.5	28.9	15.5	12.5	6.4	2.6	2.5	2.64
Louisville, KY	34.5	32.8	15.3	10.3	4.6	1.7	0.9	2.34
Madison, WI	39.0	35.2	12.0	9.1	3.3	0.8	0.7	2.09
Manchester, NH	34.5	34.2	14.7	10.7	3.7	1.7	0.5	2.27

Table continued on following page.

City	Persons in Household (%)							Average Household Size
	One	Two	Three	Four	Five	Six	Seven or More	
McAllen, TX	21.4	28.2	18.3	16.3	10.9	2.4	2.5	2.96
Memphis, TN	38.9	29.6	14.5	9.4	4.3	1.8	1.5	2.42
Miami, FL	36.5	32.1	15.8	9.5	3.8	1.1	1.2	2.30
Midland, TX	29.9	27.2	15.3	16.3	7.6	2.6	1.1	2.51
Milwaukee, WI	38.7	29.0	13.7	9.4	5.6	2.1	1.6	2.40
Minneapolis, MN	42.0	30.8	11.5	9.2	3.5	1.5	1.4	2.16
Nashville, TN	36.9	33.0	13.6	9.2	4.6	1.5	1.2	2.19
New Orleans, LA	44.7	29.3	13.2	8.0	3.3	1.0	0.5	2.34
New York, NY	33.4	28.8	16.1	11.7	5.6	2.5	1.9	2.51
Oklahoma City, OK	31.6	31.7	15.5	11.5	6.3	2.3	1.1	2.46
Omaha, NE	34.5	31.5	13.1	10.7	6.0	2.5	1.7	2.39
Orlando, FL	32.4	33.5	15.9	11.2	4.5	1.4	1.1	2.44
Philadelphia, PA	37.6	29.9	14.9	9.6	4.8	1.7	1.4	2.29
Phoenix, AZ	28.3	30.6	15.2	12.8	7.3	3.3	2.5	2.66
Pittsburgh, PA	43.9	33.0	11.6	7.1	2.9	0.8	0.7	2.03
Portland, OR	36.4	34.8	13.8	9.9	3.2	1.1	0.7	2.18
Providence, RI	33.8	28.4	15.4	11.7	7.0	2.3	1.4	2.48
Provo, UT	14.0	36.9	17.7	14.4	7.6	6.5	3.0	2.98
Raleigh, NC	35.3	33.7	13.8	11.4	4.2	1.1	0.5	2.30
Reno, NV	31.9	34.1	14.9	12.1	4.5	1.3	1.2	2.35
Richmond, VA	42.9	32.7	12.2	7.7	2.6	1.2	0.6	2.13
Rochester, MN	31.6	34.6	13.4	12.5	5.0	1.8	1.1	2.35
Sacramento, CA	31.7	29.8	14.4	12.4	6.6	2.6	2.5	2.58
Saint Louis, MO	47.9	30.1	10.3	6.9	3.0	1.0	0.8	1.96
Saint Paul, MN	37.1	29.8	12.5	9.6	5.1	2.9	3.1	2.42
Salem, OR	29.2	33.2	15.5	11.5	5.8	3.0	1.8	2.51
Salt Lake City, UT	39.3	34.1	11.6	8.2	3.8	1.8	1.3	2.19
San Antonio, TX	31.3	29.4	15.5	12.5	6.7	2.8	1.8	2.62
San Diego, CA	28.8	34.2	15.5	12.8	5.4	2.0	1.4	2.55
San Francisco, CA	38.0	32.3	13.4	9.9	3.5	1.6	1.2	2.24
San Jose, CA	20.7	29.4	18.8	17.6	7.6	3.0	2.9	2.98
Santa Rosa, CA	28.0	33.1	16.1	13.7	5.7	2.2	1.2	2.54
Savannah, GA	35.4	34.5	14.8	9.4	3.7	1.1	1.1	2.35
Seattle, WA	41.3	35.4	11.2	8.5	2.5	0.7	0.5	2.03
Sioux Falls, SD	33.9	33.0	12.9	10.3	6.9	1.8	1.2	2.32
Tampa, FL	35.7	32.1	15.4	10.9	4.1	1.4	0.5	2.35
Tucson, AZ	36.3	31.0	13.7	10.7	5.2	2.0	1.1	2.30
Tulsa, OK	35.9	31.9	13.4	10.3	4.9	2.4	1.3	2.36
Virginia Beach, VA	26.1	35.6	17.3	12.7	5.9	1.7	0.8	2.50
Washington, DC	46.7	30.2	11.1	7.4	2.8	1.2	0.7	1.99
Wichita, KS	33.2	32.6	13.2	10.8	5.7	2.7	1.7	2.47
Wilmington, NC	38.5	38.5	12.3	6.8	2.8	0.8	0.3	2.06
Winston-Salem, NC	35.2	32.7	14.2	9.8	4.8	2.3	1.0	2.40
U.S.	28.5	33.8	15.4	12.7	5.9	2.3	1.4	2.54

U.S. Census Bureau, 2019-2023 American Community Survey 5-Year Estimates

Household Size: Metro Area

Metro Area	Persons in Household (%)							Average Household Size
	One	Two	Three	Four	Five	Six	Seven or More	
Albuquerque, NM	33.0	33.6	14.6	10.8	5.0	1.9	1.2	2.44
Anchorage, AK	27.2	33.9	14.5	13.6	6.1	2.7	2.1	2.64
Ann Arbor, MI	30.6	36.1	14.9	11.5	4.2	1.9	0.9	2.34
Athens, GA	28.1	35.1	16.5	12.8	5.1	1.7	0.7	2.43
Atlanta, GA	27.1	32.0	17.0	13.7	6.2	2.4	1.5	2.67
Austin, TX	28.7	33.8	15.6	13.2	5.3	2.3	1.1	2.44
Baltimore, MD	30.0	32.8	15.7	13.0	5.3	2.1	1.2	2.51
Billings, MT	31.0	36.9	13.2	11.3	4.8	1.5	1.3	2.36
Boise City, ID	23.2	36.6	15.4	13.4	6.5	3.3	1.7	2.62
Boston, MA	28.0	33.2	16.7	14.0	5.5	1.7	0.9	2.47
Boulder, CO	29.8	37.0	14.5	12.6	4.2	1.3	0.6	2.33
Cape Coral, FL	28.3	44.7	11.6	8.8	4.4	1.5	0.7	2.44
Cedar Rapids, IA	29.8	37.2	13.8	11.3	5.4	1.4	1.1	2.38
Charleston, SC	29.3	36.3	15.3	11.8	5.0	1.6	0.7	2.45
Charlotte, NC	28.0	34.2	15.9	13.2	5.6	1.9	1.1	2.55
Chicago, IL	29.9	31.0	15.4	13.5	6.4	2.3	1.5	2.55
Cincinnati, OH	29.7	34.2	14.5	12.8	5.6	2.1	1.2	2.46
Clarksville, TN	26.0	33.6	17.5	12.8	5.8	2.4	1.9	2.63
Cleveland, OH	35.3	33.7	13.6	10.5	4.4	1.6	0.9	2.29
College Station, TX	30.3	32.8	14.7	13.5	5.3	2.3	1.1	2.48
Colorado Springs, CO	24.8	36.1	16.2	13.0	6.1	2.4	1.4	2.51
Columbia, MO	31.1	36.1	13.7	12.2	5.0	1.2	0.8	2.37
Columbia, SC	30.6	34.0	15.5	11.9	5.2	1.9	0.9	2.42
Columbus, OH	29.4	33.6	15.1	12.7	5.8	2.2	1.2	2.46
Dallas, TX	25.9	30.9	16.4	14.7	7.5	2.9	1.7	2.73
Davenport, IA	31.5	35.8	13.6	11.3	5.3	1.8	0.8	2.32
Denver, CO	29.2	34.9	14.8	12.7	5.0	2.2	1.2	2.45
Des Moines, IA	29.6	33.9	14.0	12.8	6.4	2.1	1.1	2.44
Detroit, MI	31.9	32.8	15.0	11.9	5.3	1.9	1.2	2.46
Durham, NC	31.7	35.8	14.8	10.9	4.6	1.5	0.6	2.33
El Paso, TX	23.9	27.3	18.2	16.3	9.0	3.5	1.8	2.88
Eugene, OR	29.5	38.4	14.1	10.8	4.8	1.5	0.9	2.34
Fargo, ND	35.2	33.4	13.1	11.0	5.0	1.5	0.8	2.28
Fort Collins, CO	25.5	39.2	16.4	12.1	4.5	1.4	0.9	2.33
Fort Wayne, IN	29.7	34.7	13.4	11.7	6.1	2.7	1.6	2.48
Fort Worth, TX	25.9	30.9	16.4	14.7	7.5	2.9	1.7	2.73
Gainesville, FL	32.9	35.5	15.3	10.3	3.9	1.2	0.9	2.36
Green Bay, WI	29.3	37.6	13.1	12.1	5.2	1.8	0.8	2.38
Greensboro, NC	31.0	33.8	15.5	11.4	5.2	2.0	1.1	2.42
Honolulu, HI	24.9	30.8	16.7	13.1	6.8	3.5	4.1	2.88
Houston, TX	24.8	29.9	17.2	15.3	8.0	3.0	1.8	2.76
Huntsville, AL	29.4	36.4	15.1	12.1	4.8	1.5	0.6	2.42
Indianapolis, IN	29.6	33.8	14.7	12.7	6.1	1.9	1.1	2.50
Jacksonville, FL	27.8	35.6	16.4	11.8	5.5	1.9	1.0	2.51
Kansas City, MO	29.8	34.3	14.1	12.6	5.8	2.3	1.2	2.46
Lafayette, LA	29.1	33.5	16.1	12.4	5.4	2.1	1.2	2.49
Las Vegas, NV	28.0	32.7	15.8	12.3	6.8	2.8	1.8	2.68
Lexington, KY	31.6	34.5	15.2	11.6	4.3	1.9	0.9	2.35
Lincoln, NE	30.8	35.3	13.6	11.4	5.2	2.5	1.1	2.35
Little Rock, AR	31.7	34.1	15.2	11.0	5.3	1.7	1.0	2.41
Los Angeles, CA	25.1	29.0	17.0	15.1	7.7	3.2	2.8	2.86
Louisville, KY	30.6	34.4	15.5	11.8	5.1	1.8	0.9	2.43
Madison, WI	32.9	36.5	13.2	11.1	4.3	1.4	0.7	2.25
Manchester, NH	27.2	35.8	16.5	13.1	4.9	1.7	0.8	2.48

Table continued on following page.

Metro Area	Persons in Household (%)							Average Household Size
	One	Two	Three	Four	Five	Six	Seven or More	
McAllen, TX	18.5	25.1	16.9	17.1	12.2	5.6	4.5	3.30
Memphis, TN	31.2	31.7	16.4	11.7	5.5	2.0	1.5	2.55
Miami, FL	27.9	32.2	17.3	13.3	6.0	2.1	1.3	2.62
Midland, TX	28.9	27.1	15.8	16.0	8.2	2.7	1.4	2.53
Milwaukee, WI	33.0	34.4	13.7	11.3	5.1	1.7	0.9	2.37
Minneapolis, MN	28.9	34.2	14.3	13.3	5.8	2.1	1.4	2.49
Nashville, TN	28.0	34.5	16.1	12.7	5.7	1.9	1.1	2.49
New Orleans, LA	36.4	30.5	15.4	10.8	4.4	1.6	0.9	2.44
New York, NY	28.6	29.6	16.8	14.1	6.3	2.6	1.9	2.63
Oklahoma City, OK	29.0	33.1	15.7	12.4	6.3	2.3	1.2	2.51
Omaha, NE	29.6	33.1	14.3	12.3	6.6	2.5	1.5	2.49
Orlando, FL	24.5	34.1	17.0	14.3	6.5	2.2	1.3	2.71
Philadelphia, PA	29.7	32.3	16.0	13.2	5.7	1.9	1.1	2.49
Phoenix, AZ	26.0	34.8	14.8	12.6	6.7	3.0	2.1	2.62
Pittsburgh, PA	34.1	35.8	13.7	10.6	4.1	1.2	0.6	2.25
Portland, OR	27.6	35.7	15.6	12.8	5.2	1.9	1.2	2.47
Providence, RI	29.5	33.7	16.3	12.9	5.1	1.6	0.9	2.41
Provo, UT	12.3	29.0	16.2	16.6	12.5	8.1	5.3	3.40
Raleigh, NC	25.9	34.7	16.1	14.5	6.0	1.9	0.9	2.57
Reno, NV	27.5	35.2	15.5	12.9	5.6	2.1	1.3	2.49
Richmond, VA	29.5	34.7	15.8	12.2	5.1	1.8	1.0	2.47
Rochester, MN	27.9	36.9	13.2	13.3	5.9	1.8	1.1	2.42
Sacramento, CA	25.1	32.7	16.0	14.5	7.1	2.7	2.0	2.70
Saint Louis, MO	31.3	34.4	14.6	11.9	5.2	1.6	0.9	2.38
Saint Paul, MN	28.9	34.2	14.3	13.3	5.8	2.1	1.4	2.49
Salem, OR	25.5	33.8	15.8	12.5	6.7	3.3	2.3	2.67
Salt Lake City, UT	24.0	31.1	15.7	13.9	7.9	4.4	3.0	2.83
San Antonio, TX	26.8	31.1	16.3	13.8	7.3	2.8	1.9	2.71
San Diego, CA	24.5	33.0	16.7	14.6	6.7	2.6	1.8	2.74
San Francisco, CA	27.2	31.8	16.7	14.5	5.9	2.3	1.6	2.63
San Jose, CA	21.4	31.1	18.8	17.2	6.9	2.6	2.1	2.86
Santa Rosa, CA	27.5	35.1	15.1	13.5	5.5	2.0	1.2	2.50
Savannah, GA	28.1	36.4	15.7	12.1	5.2	1.5	1.1	2.52
Seattle, WA	28.0	34.0	15.8	13.6	5.4	1.9	1.3	2.49
Sioux Falls, SD	30.0	34.4	13.6	11.4	7.3	2.1	1.2	2.41
Tampa, FL	30.8	36.3	15.0	10.9	4.6	1.6	0.8	2.44
Tucson, AZ	31.8	35.4	13.2	11.1	5.1	2.3	1.2	2.37
Tulsa, OK	29.2	33.6	15.2	12.3	5.9	2.5	1.4	2.53
Virginia Beach, VA	28.6	34.6	16.5	12.2	5.5	1.9	0.9	2.46
Washington, DC	28.6	30.4	15.9	14.3	6.5	2.6	1.7	2.62
Wichita, KS	30.1	33.6	14.0	11.7	6.2	2.8	1.7	2.52
Wilmington, NC	29.9	42.0	14.0	8.9	3.6	1.2	0.4	2.26
Winston-Salem, NC	30.3	35.6	15.4	11.1	4.7	2.0	0.9	2.43
U.S.	28.5	33.8	15.4	12.7	5.9	2.3	1.4	2.54

Note: Figures cover the Metropolitan Statistical Area (MSA)
Source: U.S. Census Bureau, 2019-2023 American Community Survey 5-Year Estimates

Household Relationships: City

City	House-holder	Opposite-sex Spouse	Same-sex Spouse	Opposite-sex Unmarried Partner	Same-sex Unmarried Partner	Child[1]	Grand-child	Other Relatives	Non-relatives
Albuquerque, NM	42.1	15.1	0.3	3.4	0.3	27.0	2.5	4.6	3.2
Anchorage, AK	37.5	17.0	0.2	3.0	0.2	28.3	1.9	4.6	4.2
Ann Arbor, MI	40.3	13.3	0.3	2.4	0.2	17.1	0.5	1.6	11.5
Athens, GA	40.1	11.6	0.2	2.7	0.2	20.8	2.0	3.7	10.7
Atlanta, GA	45.7	10.4	0.5	3.1	0.6	20.7	2.1	3.9	5.9
Austin, TX	42.7	14.5	0.4	3.6	0.4	23.2	1.5	4.1	6.4
Baltimore, MD	42.9	9.6	0.3	3.3	0.3	24.9	3.7	5.8	6.1
Billings, MT	42.2	17.7	0.2	3.1	0.1	26.0	1.7	2.5	3.5
Boise City, ID	41.4	17.8	0.2	3.2	0.2	24.7	1.3	2.9	5.4
Boston, MA	41.4	10.4	0.5	3.1	0.4	20.6	1.7	5.3	9.7
Boulder, CO	40.2	13.0	0.3	3.1	0.2	16.4	0.3	1.6	12.3
Cape Coral, FL	39.5	21.2	0.3	3.2	0.1	25.5	2.1	4.8	2.8
Cedar Rapids, IA	42.2	16.7	0.2	3.5	0.2	26.8	1.3	2.9	3.4
Charleston, SC	45.0	17.0	0.3	3.1	0.2	21.8	1.4	2.7	5.3
Charlotte, NC	40.6	15.2	0.2	2.8	0.2	28.0	2.1	4.9	4.2
Chicago, IL	41.6	12.2	0.3	3.0	0.3	26.6	3.0	6.4	4.8
Cincinnati, OH	45.1	10.2	0.3	3.4	0.3	24.6	2.2	3.4	5.3
Clarksville, TN	36.6	16.9	0.2	2.5	0.1	31.2	2.4	3.9	3.5
Cleveland, OH	45.0	8.5	0.2	3.5	0.3	27.0	3.3	5.0	3.8
College Station, TX	35.2	11.2	0.2	1.8	0.1	19.7	0.7	2.7	13.7
Colorado Springs, CO	39.7	18.3	0.3	2.6	0.2	27.5	1.9	3.6	4.3
Columbia, MO	40.5	14.1	0.2	2.8	0.2	22.4	1.0	2.5	7.8
Columbia, SC	39.2	10.5	0.2	2.1	0.2	19.5	1.6	2.8	5.8
Columbus, OH	42.2	12.9	0.3	3.6	0.3	26.2	2.1	4.4	5.2
Dallas, TX	40.1	13.4	0.4	2.6	0.3	28.6	3.2	6.2	4.0
Davenport, IA	41.9	15.9	0.2	3.7	0.2	27.0	2.0	3.0	3.2
Denver, CO	44.4	14.0	0.5	4.1	0.4	22.3	1.9	4.4	5.9
Des Moines, IA	41.1	14.2	0.3	3.5	0.2	27.9	2.0	4.4	3.9
Detroit, MI	39.8	7.3	0.1	2.9	0.2	32.0	4.8	7.3	3.9
Durham, NC	42.0	14.8	0.4	2.9	0.3	24.6	1.8	4.4	4.6
El Paso, TX	35.9	15.8	0.2	1.8	0.1	32.7	3.9	6.4	2.0
Eugene, OR	41.6	14.7	0.3	3.8	0.3	20.7	1.1	2.7	8.3
Fargo, ND	44.5	15.5	0.1	3.6	0.2	23.5	0.7	2.5	5.0
Fort Collins, CO	39.9	16.0	0.2	3.3	0.2	22.1	0.9	2.4	9.0
Fort Wayne, IN	40.7	15.6	0.2	3.1	0.2	29.7	2.0	3.4	3.0
Fort Worth, TX	35.2	15.8	0.2	2.1	0.1	33.0	3.1	5.6	3.0
Gainesville, FL	41.0	9.4	0.3	3.0	0.3	17.0	1.5	3.4	12.5
Green Bay, WI	40.7	15.2	0.2	4.0	0.2	28.6	1.6	3.4	3.0
Greensboro, NC	40.9	13.6	0.2	2.6	0.2	26.4	2.0	4.1	3.6
Honolulu, HI	39.1	15.0	0.3	2.4	0.2	22.2	3.1	9.1	5.6
Houston, TX	38.9	14.0	0.3	2.4	0.2	29.5	2.9	6.5	3.6
Huntsville, AL	42.8	16.5	0.2	2.2	0.2	25.1	2.1	3.5	3.1
Indianapolis, IN	40.7	14.0	0.3	3.4	0.3	28.6	2.5	4.5	3.9
Jacksonville, FL	39.9	15.6	0.2	2.8	0.2	27.7	2.8	4.9	3.6
Kansas City, MO	42.6	14.5	0.3	3.3	0.3	27.2	2.3	4.0	3.8
Lafayette, LA	43.0	15.3	0.2	2.8	0.2	27.0	2.3	3.5	3.8
Las Vegas, NV	37.5	15.2	0.3	2.9	0.2	29.3	2.7	6.7	4.3
Lexington, KY	41.7	16.0	0.3	2.9	0.3	25.3	1.6	3.4	4.4
Lincoln, NE	40.1	16.9	0.2	2.8	0.1	26.6	1.1	2.7	4.6
Little Rock, AR	43.5	14.5	0.3	2.4	0.3	27.1	2.3	3.9	3.1
Los Angeles, CA	36.2	13.1	0.3	2.8	0.3	26.5	2.8	9.0	6.3
Louisville, KY	40.0	18.0	0.2	2.9	0.2	28.8	2.6	4.2	2.7
Madison, WI	44.8	14.5	0.4	3.8	0.3	19.7	0.7	2.4	8.2
Manchester, NH	42.5	14.9	0.3	4.3	0.2	24.3	1.6	4.3	4.7
McAllen, TX	34.3	16.0	0.1	1.7	0.1	34.6	3.5	6.8	2.0

Table continued on following page.

City	House-holder	Opposite-sex Spouse	Same-sex Spouse	Opposite-sex Unmarried Partner	Same-sex Unmarried Partner	Child[1]	Grand-child	Other Relatives	Non-relatives
Memphis, TN	40.4	10.9	0.2	2.7	0.2	29.7	4.3	6.1	3.7
Miami, FL	42.4	12.6	0.5	3.3	0.3	22.5	2.4	8.7	5.8
Midland, TX	36.4	18.5	0.1	2.1	0.1	31.9	3.0	4.2	2.5
Milwaukee, WI	40.8	10.2	0.2	3.6	0.2	30.2	2.7	4.9	4.4
Minneapolis, MN	43.7	12.0	0.6	3.9	0.5	22.1	1.1	3.5	8.0
Nashville, TN	42.1	14.3	0.3	3.0	0.3	24.0	1.9	4.7	5.7
New Orleans, LA	43.0	11.0	0.3	3.1	0.4	26.1	3.2	4.6	4.3
New York, NY	38.3	12.7	0.3	2.2	0.2	27.6	2.5	8.3	5.3
Oklahoma City, OK	39.4	16.6	0.2	2.6	0.2	29.4	2.3	4.3	3.1
Omaha, NE	39.8	16.0	0.2	2.8	0.2	29.6	1.8	3.7	3.6
Orlando, FL	41.7	13.7	0.5	3.5	0.4	26.1	2.0	5.9	5.0
Philadelphia, PA	41.0	10.9	0.3	3.1	0.3	26.8	3.6	5.9	5.2
Phoenix, AZ	36.3	14.4	0.3	3.1	0.3	30.2	2.9	6.6	4.2
Pittsburgh, PA	46.1	11.5	0.3	3.6	0.4	19.3	1.7	3.1	6.7
Portland, OR	43.2	14.9	0.7	4.4	0.6	21.2	1.1	3.7	7.2
Providence, RI	36.5	10.5	0.3	2.9	0.3	27.3	1.9	5.7	6.1
Provo, UT	29.6	15.9	0.1	0.6	0.0	25.7	1.6	4.0	12.7
Raleigh, NC	41.8	15.1	0.2	2.9	0.2	25.5	1.4	3.9	5.0
Reno, NV	41.1	15.2	0.3	3.8	0.2	24.8	1.7	4.7	5.7
Richmond, VA	45.2	10.4	0.4	4.0	0.4	20.8	2.1	4.3	7.4
Rochester, MN	41.1	18.5	0.2	2.8	0.1	27.8	0.9	2.8	3.3
Sacramento, CA	36.7	13.5	0.4	3.0	0.3	28.0	2.6	7.5	4.7
Saint Louis, MO	48.0	10.3	0.4	3.7	0.4	22.5	2.6	4.0	4.3
Saint Paul, MN	38.7	12.7	0.4	3.3	0.3	28.8	1.7	5.6	4.8
Salem, OR	36.6	16.0	0.2	3.1	0.2	28.1	1.9	4.6	4.2
Salt Lake City, UT	42.3	13.9	0.5	3.4	0.4	22.1	1.7	4.2	7.6
San Antonio, TX	37.5	14.7	0.3	2.7	0.2	30.3	3.8	5.5	3.2
San Diego, CA	37.2	15.7	0.4	2.6	0.3	25.0	2.0	6.2	6.1
San Francisco, CA	42.6	13.6	0.8	3.3	0.6	17.6	1.3	6.8	10.3
San Jose, CA	32.4	17.1	0.2	1.9	0.1	28.6	2.3	9.8	6.1
Santa Rosa, CA	37.6	16.2	0.4	3.0	0.2	27.3	1.8	6.2	5.5
Savannah, GA	39.9	11.2	0.3	2.7	0.3	24.9	3.2	4.4	5.0
Seattle, WA	46.9	15.2	0.8	4.3	0.6	17.5	0.7	2.8	7.3
Sioux Falls, SD	40.7	18.0	0.1	3.2	0.1	28.4	1.1	2.7	3.1
Tampa, FL	40.9	13.8	0.3	3.2	0.3	25.8	2.3	4.9	4.5
Tucson, AZ	41.1	13.3	0.3	3.3	0.3	25.4	2.8	4.8	4.5
Tulsa, OK	41.6	14.8	0.2	2.9	0.2	27.8	2.3	4.3	3.4
Virginia Beach, VA	38.8	18.6	0.2	2.4	0.1	28.7	2.2	4.0	3.5
Washington, DC	45.3	10.3	0.6	3.1	0.5	20.4	2.4	4.2	7.1
Wichita, KS	40.0	16.4	0.2	2.7	0.2	29.1	2.2	3.7	3.1
Wilmington, NC	45.7	14.9	0.3	3.4	0.3	21.2	1.5	3.0	5.9
Winston-Salem, NC	40.9	14.6	0.2	2.5	0.2	28.1	2.4	4.3	2.7
U.S.	38.3	17.5	0.2	2.5	0.2	28.3	2.4	4.8	3.4

Note: Figures are percent of the total population; (1) Includes biological, adopted, and stepchildren of the householder
Source: U.S. Census Bureau, 2020 Census

Household Relationships: Metro Area

Metro Area	House-holder	Opposite-sex Spouse	Same-sex Spouse	Opposite-sex Unmarried Partner	Same-sex Unmarried Partner	Child[1]	Grand-child	Other Relatives	Non-relatives
Albuquerque, NM	40.1	16.3	0.3	3.1	0.3	27.7	3.1	4.6	2.9
Anchorage, AK	37.1	17.6	0.2	2.9	0.1	29.1	1.9	4.2	4.0
Ann Arbor, MI	39.7	17.0	0.3	2.4	0.2	24.3	1.3	2.5	5.8
Athens, GA	38.6	15.6	0.2	2.3	0.2	25.1	2.3	3.7	7.3
Atlanta, GA	37.1	16.7	0.2	2.1	0.2	30.4	2.7	5.7	3.5
Austin, TX	38.6	17.3	0.3	2.7	0.3	27.8	1.9	4.4	4.6
Baltimore, MD	38.7	16.8	0.2	2.4	0.2	28.7	2.5	4.8	3.5
Billings, MT	41.3	19.5	0.1	2.8	0.1	26.5	1.8	2.5	3.1
Boise City, ID	36.6	19.5	0.2	2.5	0.1	29.7	1.9	3.5	3.8
Boston, MA	38.7	17.4	0.3	2.5	0.2	27.1	1.6	4.5	4.4
Boulder, CO	40.1	18.0	0.3	2.8	0.2	23.8	1.0	2.6	6.8
Cape Coral, FL	41.8	20.9	0.3	3.0	0.2	22.4	1.8	4.4	3.3
Cedar Rapids, IA	40.9	19.3	0.1	3.0	0.1	27.9	1.2	2.3	2.5
Charleston, SC	39.9	18.1	0.2	2.4	0.1	27.3	2.6	3.8	3.5
Charlotte, NC	38.9	18.3	0.2	2.4	0.2	29.2	2.4	4.2	2.8
Chicago, IL	38.2	17.1	0.2	2.3	0.1	30.3	2.4	5.1	2.8
Cincinnati, OH	39.5	18.1	0.2	2.7	0.1	28.9	2.3	3.2	2.9
Clarksville, TN	36.7	18.2	0.2	2.2	0.1	30.5	2.5	3.6	3.0
Cleveland, OH	42.5	17.1	0.1	2.7	0.1	27.7	2.1	3.3	2.3
College Station, TX	36.9	14.6	0.1	2.0	0.1	24.7	1.9	3.5	8.3
Colorado Springs, CO	37.5	19.3	0.2	2.2	0.1	28.5	2.0	3.6	3.8
Columbia, MO	39.8	16.5	0.2	2.8	0.2	24.9	1.4	2.5	5.7
Columbia, SC	39.9	17.0	0.2	2.1	0.2	27.5	2.7	3.8	3.0
Columbus, OH	39.4	17.4	0.2	2.9	0.2	28.5	2.0	3.5	3.3
Dallas, TX	36.2	17.6	0.2	2.0	0.2	31.7	2.7	5.5	2.9
Davenport, IA	41.4	18.8	0.2	2.9	0.1	27.9	1.8	2.5	2.2
Denver, CO	39.4	17.9	0.3	2.9	0.2	27.4	1.9	4.4	4.3
Des Moines, IA	39.6	19.2	0.2	2.7	0.1	29.6	1.3	2.8	2.6
Detroit, MI	40.1	17.2	0.1	2.5	0.1	30.1	2.3	4.2	2.4
Durham, NC	40.3	17.2	0.3	2.5	0.2	25.1	1.9	3.8	3.9
El Paso, TX	34.2	15.8	0.2	1.7	0.1	33.5	4.2	6.5	1.8
Eugene, OR	40.9	17.0	0.3	3.7	0.2	22.7	1.8	3.5	6.6
Fargo, ND	41.5	17.7	0.1	3.2	0.1	27.0	0.7	2.2	3.9
Fort Collins, CO	40.2	19.4	0.2	2.8	0.2	24.0	1.2	2.7	6.0
Fort Wayne, IN	39.5	18.0	0.2	2.7	0.1	30.5	1.9	2.9	2.5
Fort Worth, TX	36.2	17.6	0.2	2.0	0.2	31.7	2.7	5.5	2.9
Gainesville, FL	40.4	14.9	0.2	2.8	0.2	22.9	2.2	3.9	6.9
Green Bay, WI	40.5	19.8	0.1	3.3	0.1	28.1	1.2	2.2	2.2
Greensboro, NC	40.2	17.1	0.2	2.4	0.2	27.4	2.3	3.9	2.6
Honolulu, HI	33.1	16.3	0.2	1.9	0.1	26.2	4.5	9.2	4.9
Houston, TX	35.2	17.1	0.2	2.0	0.1	32.7	2.8	6.1	2.6
Huntsville, AL	40.1	19.3	0.1	1.9	0.1	27.8	2.3	3.4	2.3
Indianapolis, IN	39.2	17.9	0.2	2.8	0.2	29.6	2.1	3.5	2.8
Jacksonville, FL	39.1	17.9	0.2	2.6	0.2	28.0	2.6	4.3	3.2
Kansas City, MO	39.6	18.4	0.2	2.6	0.2	29.4	2.0	3.3	2.7
Lafayette, LA	39.5	17.1	0.2	2.7	0.2	30.4	2.9	3.5	2.5
Las Vegas, NV	37.3	15.5	0.3	3.0	0.2	28.7	2.6	7.0	4.4
Lexington, KY	40.5	17.4	0.2	2.8	0.2	26.5	2.0	3.4	3.7
Lincoln, NE	39.5	17.9	0.2	2.6	0.1	27.2	1.1	2.6	4.1
Little Rock, AR	40.8	17.7	0.2	2.3	0.2	27.9	2.6	3.6	2.7
Los Angeles, CA	34.0	15.2	0.2	2.3	0.2	29.0	3.0	9.1	5.1
Louisville, KY	40.5	17.7	0.2	2.8	0.2	27.6	2.5	3.6	2.9
Madison, WI	42.2	18.6	0.3	3.3	0.2	25.0	0.8	2.1	4.5
Manchester, NH	39.7	19.2	0.3	3.2	0.1	27.2	1.6	3.5	3.2
McAllen, TX	29.7	15.0	0.1	1.6	0.1	38.3	5.2	7.5	1.6

Table continued on following page.

Metro Area	House-holder	Opposite-sex Spouse	Same-sex Spouse	Opposite-sex Unmarried Partner	Same-sex Unmarried Partner	Child[1]	Grand-child	Other Relatives	Non-relatives
Memphis, TN	38.6	15.1	0.1	2.2	0.1	30.4	3.9	5.2	2.7
Miami, FL	38.0	16.0	0.3	2.6	0.2	27.6	2.5	7.8	3.7
Midland, TX	35.8	18.6	0.1	2.0	0.1	32.3	3.2	4.4	2.6
Milwaukee, WI	41.3	17.5	0.2	2.9	0.2	28.7	1.6	3.1	2.7
Minneapolis, MN	38.9	18.7	0.2	2.8	0.2	29.4	1.2	3.3	3.3
Nashville, TN	38.8	18.2	0.2	2.4	0.2	28.1	2.2	4.1	3.8
New Orleans, LA	40.3	15.3	0.2	2.7	0.2	28.8	3.1	4.6	2.9
New York, NY	36.8	15.8	0.2	2.0	0.2	29.7	2.1	7.1	4.1
Oklahoma City, OK	38.8	17.7	0.2	2.4	0.2	29.0	2.3	3.8	3.1
Omaha, NE	38.8	18.4	0.2	2.6	0.1	30.6	1.6	3.1	2.8
Orlando, FL	37.0	17.0	0.3	2.7	0.2	28.4	2.4	6.0	4.2
Philadelphia, PA	38.7	16.9	0.2	2.5	0.2	29.2	2.5	4.4	3.0
Phoenix, AZ	36.9	17.2	0.2	2.8	0.2	29.0	2.5	5.4	3.7
Pittsburgh, PA	43.2	19.0	0.2	2.8	0.2	25.6	1.6	2.6	2.4
Portland, OR	39.0	18.1	0.4	3.2	0.3	26.7	1.6	4.2	4.9
Providence, RI	40.0	16.9	0.2	3.0	0.2	27.2	1.9	4.1	3.0
Provo, UT	28.0	18.8	0.1	0.7	0.0	39.0	2.1	4.0	4.8
Raleigh, NC	38.4	19.2	0.2	2.2	0.2	30.0	1.5	3.7	3.0
Reno, NV	39.5	17.2	0.2	3.4	0.2	26.1	2.1	5.0	4.9
Richmond, VA	39.5	17.3	0.2	2.5	0.2	27.7	2.4	4.0	3.3
Rochester, MN	40.1	20.5	0.1	2.7	0.1	28.9	1.0	2.2	2.5
Sacramento, CA	36.2	17.1	0.3	2.4	0.2	29.4	2.2	6.0	4.2
Saint Louis, MO	40.8	18.2	0.2	2.6	0.2	28.5	2.2	3.0	2.4
Saint Paul, MN	38.9	18.7	0.2	2.8	0.2	29.4	1.2	3.3	3.3
Salem, OR	35.7	17.6	0.2	2.7	0.1	29.3	2.3	5.0	4.1
Salt Lake City, UT	34.0	17.4	0.3	2.1	0.2	32.4	2.5	5.3	4.4
San Antonio, TX	36.2	16.9	0.2	2.3	0.2	31.0	3.5	5.1	2.8
San Diego, CA	35.1	16.9	0.3	2.3	0.2	27.8	2.3	6.6	5.1
San Francisco, CA	36.7	17.0	0.4	2.3	0.3	26.3	1.8	6.9	5.9
San Jose, CA	33.8	18.4	0.2	1.8	0.1	28.3	1.9	7.9	5.6
Santa Rosa, CA	38.4	17.6	0.4	2.9	0.2	26.1	1.9	5.2	5.5
Savannah, GA	38.7	16.6	0.2	2.4	0.2	28.0	2.8	4.1	3.4
Seattle, WA	38.9	18.3	0.3	2.9	0.2	26.7	1.5	4.6	4.7
Sioux Falls, SD	39.5	19.4	0.1	2.9	0.1	29.8	1.1	2.3	2.6
Tampa, FL	41.2	17.6	0.3	3.1	0.2	25.5	2.2	4.6	3.4
Tucson, AZ	40.9	17.2	0.3	2.9	0.2	25.5	2.6	4.4	3.4
Tulsa, OK	39.1	18.2	0.2	2.4	0.1	29.0	2.6	3.9	2.7
Virginia Beach, VA	39.0	17.4	0.2	2.3	0.1	27.7	2.5	4.0	3.3
Washington, DC	37.0	17.3	0.3	2.0	0.2	29.3	2.0	5.9	4.4
Wichita, KS	39.0	18.2	0.1	2.4	0.1	29.8	2.1	3.2	2.6
Wilmington, NC	42.3	18.7	0.2	2.9	0.2	24.4	1.9	3.1	3.9
Winston-Salem, NC	40.9	18.6	0.2	2.3	0.1	27.5	2.4	3.7	2.2
U.S.	38.3	17.5	0.2	2.5	0.2	28.3	2.4	4.8	3.4

Note: Figures are percent of the total population; Figures cover the Metropolitan Statistical Area (MSA); (1) Includes biological, adopted, and stepchildren of the householder
Source: U.S. Census Bureau, 2020 Census

Age: City

City	Percent of Population									Median Age
	Under Age 5	Age 5–19	Age 20–34	Age 35–44	Age 45–54	Age 55–64	Age 65–74	Age 75–84	Age 85+	
Albuquerque, NM	5.1	18.0	21.5	13.9	11.7	12.5	10.4	4.7	2.1	38.7
Anchorage, AK	6.5	19.6	24.0	14.2	11.6	11.6	8.2	3.4	0.9	34.9
Ann Arbor, MI	3.8	18.7	38.6	10.1	8.2	7.9	7.3	4.0	1.4	27.7
Athens, GA	4.8	19.9	33.9	11.5	9.1	8.9	7.4	3.5	1.1	29.2
Atlanta, GA	5.1	15.7	31.0	14.7	11.4	9.8	7.5	3.5	1.3	34.0
Austin, TX	5.4	15.7	29.9	17.3	12.0	9.6	6.4	2.6	1.1	34.5
Baltimore, MD	6.1	17.5	24.5	13.7	10.7	12.5	9.3	4.0	1.6	36.1
Billings, MT	5.9	18.9	21.1	14.0	10.2	11.6	10.3	5.4	2.6	38.1
Boise City, ID	4.4	17.8	23.2	14.2	12.6	12.5	9.2	4.6	1.6	38.2
Boston, MA	4.6	15.3	33.4	13.3	10.2	10.5	7.6	3.4	1.7	33.2
Boulder, CO	2.0	20.2	36.8	10.3	10.0	8.4	7.4	3.2	1.8	28.8
Cape Coral, FL	4.5	14.5	15.7	10.8	13.4	15.9	14.6	7.9	2.5	48.7
Cedar Rapids, IA	5.7	18.7	22.7	13.5	11.4	11.8	9.3	4.7	2.3	36.9
Charleston, SC	5.1	15.6	27.7	14.1	10.2	11.3	9.5	4.5	2.1	36.1
Charlotte, NC	6.5	19.1	25.5	14.8	12.8	10.7	6.7	2.8	1.2	34.4
Chicago, IL	5.6	16.6	26.7	14.6	11.8	11.2	8.1	3.9	1.7	35.7
Cincinnati, OH	6.3	18.7	28.1	12.5	10.0	11.1	8.2	3.4	1.7	33.0
Clarksville, TN	8.5	21.0	29.2	14.0	9.6	9.0	5.8	2.3	0.7	30.4
Cleveland, OH	5.6	18.2	24.4	12.2	11.2	13.4	9.3	4.1	1.6	36.3
College Station, TX	4.8	25.3	40.0	10.3	6.8	6.2	4.2	1.9	0.6	22.9
Colorado Springs, CO	5.9	18.5	24.7	13.7	11.2	11.2	8.7	4.3	1.7	35.6
Columbia, MO	5.4	20.7	32.4	12.5	8.9	8.8	6.4	3.3	1.6	29.2
Columbia, SC	5.4	21.9	32.9	10.9	9.5	8.4	6.8	3.2	1.0	28.7
Columbus, OH	6.7	18.6	28.6	13.8	10.9	10.5	6.9	2.9	1.2	33.0
Dallas, TX	7.0	19.5	26.0	13.8	11.6	10.7	7.0	3.1	1.3	33.4
Davenport, IA	6.1	17.9	22.1	13.4	11.1	12.9	9.8	4.6	2.2	37.8
Denver, CO	5.5	14.8	29.4	16.9	11.7	9.5	7.6	3.3	1.4	35.2
Des Moines, IA	6.8	19.2	24.7	13.0	11.8	11.9	7.7	3.3	1.5	34.6
Detroit, MI	6.8	20.8	22.2	11.8	11.8	11.8	9.0	4.1	1.7	35.1
Durham, NC	6.1	17.6	26.8	14.3	11.5	10.7	8.1	3.5	1.4	34.8
El Paso, TX	6.5	21.6	23.2	12.5	11.5	10.8	8.1	4.1	1.8	34.1
Eugene, OR	3.9	17.1	28.5	12.4	10.4	10.1	10.4	5.2	2.1	35.4
Fargo, ND	6.0	18.4	30.1	12.8	9.0	10.1	7.9	3.9	1.8	32.2
Fort Collins, CO	3.9	18.9	33.6	12.6	9.4	9.4	7.3	3.3	1.6	30.6
Fort Wayne, IN	7.0	20.0	22.9	12.5	11.4	11.3	8.8	4.1	2.0	35.0
Fort Worth, TX	7.3	22.1	23.3	14.4	12.0	10.3	6.5	2.9	1.0	33.4
Gainesville, FL	3.7	19.7	40.6	9.6	7.3	7.3	6.7	3.3	1.7	26.5
Green Bay, WI	6.5	20.5	21.8	13.5	11.6	12.2	8.3	3.7	1.7	35.7
Greensboro, NC	5.7	21.4	24.2	12.4	11.6	10.8	8.2	3.9	1.9	34.1
Honolulu, HI	4.5	13.9	20.6	13.8	12.8	12.7	11.5	6.5	3.6	42.9
Houston, TX	6.7	19.4	25.1	14.5	11.7	10.6	7.3	3.4	1.3	34.3
Huntsville, AL	5.6	17.5	24.7	12.3	10.9	12.5	9.2	5.2	2.1	36.4
Indianapolis, IN	7.0	20.5	23.8	13.2	11.2	11.4	8.1	3.3	1.5	34.1
Jacksonville, FL	6.5	18.7	22.6	13.4	11.8	12.5	9.0	4.1	1.6	36.4
Kansas City, MO	6.2	18.7	24.1	13.7	11.4	11.8	8.8	3.6	1.7	35.7
Lafayette, LA	6.1	18.0	22.9	12.8	10.2	12.9	10.9	4.5	1.8	37.1
Las Vegas, NV	5.8	19.1	20.4	13.7	13.0	12.4	9.3	4.8	1.5	38.5
Lexington, KY	5.7	18.8	25.1	13.1	11.6	11.2	8.8	4.2	1.4	35.2
Lincoln, NE	5.9	20.0	26.1	12.8	10.4	10.4	8.8	4.0	1.7	33.4
Little Rock, AR	6.7	19.9	21.8	13.4	12.1	11.0	9.2	4.0	2.0	36.4
Los Angeles, CA	5.2	16.8	24.8	14.8	13.0	11.6	8.1	3.8	1.9	36.9
Louisville, KY	6.2	18.8	21.1	13.1	12.1	12.8	9.9	4.5	1.6	37.7
Madison, WI	4.8	16.9	33.7	12.8	9.6	9.5	7.7	3.6	1.4	31.8
Manchester, NH	4.9	15.1	25.7	13.8	11.6	13.7	8.7	4.6	2.0	37.9

Table continued on following page.

City	Percent of Population									Median Age
	Under Age 5	Age 5–19	Age 20–34	Age 35–44	Age 45–54	Age 55–64	Age 65–74	Age 75–84	Age 85+	
McAllen, TX	7.0	23.3	21.2	13.3	12.4	9.4	8.1	3.8	1.5	34.0
Memphis, TN	7.2	20.2	23.7	12.1	11.1	11.6	8.9	3.9	1.3	34.3
Miami, FL	5.3	12.8	23.8	15.4	13.5	12.8	8.5	5.2	2.6	39.7
Midland, TX	8.8	22.6	24.9	14.7	9.6	8.9	6.0	2.9	1.6	31.6
Milwaukee, WI	6.9	22.2	25.1	13.0	10.6	10.4	7.4	3.0	1.4	32.2
Minneapolis, MN	5.7	17.1	30.9	14.9	10.7	9.9	7.0	2.7	1.1	33.0
Nashville, TN	6.6	16.9	27.6	14.5	11.2	10.8	7.9	3.4	1.2	34.4
New Orleans, LA	5.5	16.9	22.0	14.9	11.5	12.7	10.4	4.3	1.7	38.4
New York, NY	5.9	16.7	22.9	13.9	12.4	12.2	9.2	4.8	2.0	38.0
Oklahoma City, OK	6.8	20.5	22.6	14.2	11.4	11.1	8.3	3.8	1.2	35.0
Omaha, NE	6.8	20.5	22.4	13.6	11.2	11.4	8.7	3.9	1.5	35.3
Orlando, FL	6.2	16.8	26.7	16.5	12.4	10.2	6.6	3.2	1.3	35.1
Philadelphia, PA	6.1	18.4	25.5	13.4	10.9	11.6	8.6	4.1	1.6	35.1
Phoenix, AZ	6.1	20.7	23.4	14.1	12.5	11.2	7.4	3.2	1.2	34.8
Pittsburgh, PA	4.4	16.1	32.1	12.5	9.0	10.8	9.0	4.0	2.0	33.5
Portland, OR	4.3	14.5	24.5	18.0	13.8	10.7	8.8	3.9	1.5	38.6
Providence, RI	5.4	20.3	28.3	12.6	11.9	10.0	6.8	3.3	1.5	32.9
Provo, UT	5.8	20.1	48.3	8.2	5.7	5.3	3.7	1.9	0.9	23.7
Raleigh, NC	5.7	17.8	27.0	14.4	13.0	10.4	7.1	3.3	1.3	34.7
Reno, NV	5.3	17.2	23.9	13.8	11.0	12.3	10.1	4.6	1.6	37.3
Richmond, VA	5.9	15.4	29.6	13.5	10.1	11.9	8.7	3.5	1.4	34.5
Rochester, MN	6.8	18.9	22.4	14.1	10.3	11.5	8.8	4.9	2.3	36.4
Sacramento, CA	5.9	18.4	24.4	14.7	11.6	11.0	8.5	3.8	1.7	35.7
Saint Louis, MO	5.8	15.0	26.2	14.2	11.1	12.6	9.6	3.7	1.6	36.6
Saint Paul, MN	6.3	20.3	25.8	13.9	10.7	10.7	7.9	3.0	1.3	33.5
Salem, OR	5.9	20.2	22.9	13.6	11.4	10.8	8.9	4.7	1.7	35.7
Salt Lake City, UT	4.9	15.8	32.5	14.0	10.9	9.6	7.5	3.3	1.3	33.0
San Antonio, TX	6.3	20.5	23.7	13.8	11.8	10.7	7.9	3.7	1.6	34.6
San Diego, CA	5.3	16.6	26.4	14.7	12.0	10.9	8.2	4.3	1.7	36.0
San Francisco, CA	4.2	11.0	26.1	16.3	13.2	12.0	9.8	4.8	2.6	39.7
San Jose, CA	5.2	18.3	21.9	14.6	13.8	12.1	8.2	4.1	1.8	38.1
Santa Rosa, CA	4.9	17.9	19.3	14.1	12.9	12.1	11.2	5.1	2.4	40.5
Savannah, GA	6.1	18.1	28.1	11.9	10.3	11.4	8.1	4.5	1.4	33.7
Seattle, WA	4.2	12.2	32.7	16.3	12.2	9.7	7.7	3.4	1.6	35.5
Sioux Falls, SD	7.0	20.0	22.8	14.4	10.8	11.4	8.8	3.4	1.4	35.1
Tampa, FL	5.8	18.5	24.6	14.2	12.5	11.2	7.8	4.1	1.3	35.6
Tucson, AZ	5.3	18.5	26.7	12.2	10.4	11.0	9.0	4.8	2.0	34.6
Tulsa, OK	6.7	20.3	22.3	13.2	11.2	11.3	9.1	4.2	1.7	35.5
Virginia Beach, VA	6.0	18.3	22.1	14.1	11.7	12.6	9.2	4.5	1.6	37.4
Washington, DC	6.1	15.2	29.0	16.4	10.7	9.8	7.4	3.8	1.5	34.9
Wichita, KS	6.3	20.7	22.0	12.9	11.0	11.7	9.4	4.1	1.9	35.7
Wilmington, NC	4.3	17.0	25.9	11.7	10.8	12.6	10.2	5.3	2.3	37.5
Winston-Salem, NC	5.9	21.7	21.6	12.1	11.9	12.0	8.5	4.3	1.9	35.6
U.S.	5.7	19.1	20.2	13.1	12.3	12.8	10.0	4.9	1.9	38.7

Source: U.S. Census Bureau, 2019-2023 American Community Survey 5-Year Estimates

Age: Metro Area

Metro Area	Under Age 5	Age 5–19	Age 20–34	Age 35–44	Age 45–54	Age 55–64	Age 65–74	Age 75–84	Age 85+	Median Age
Albuquerque, NM	5.0	18.5	20.0	13.4	11.8	12.9	11.1	5.1	2.0	39.6
Anchorage, AK	6.5	20.2	22.8	14.2	11.7	11.9	8.5	3.3	0.9	35.4
Ann Arbor, MI	4.6	19.1	26.4	11.9	11.3	11.3	9.2	4.5	1.5	34.8
Athens, GA	5.0	20.7	26.4	12.2	11.0	10.6	8.8	4.1	1.3	33.2
Atlanta, GA	5.9	20.6	20.5	13.9	13.7	12.2	8.2	3.7	1.2	37.0
Austin, TX	5.8	19.0	23.8	16.3	13.0	10.5	7.5	3.1	1.1	35.9
Baltimore, MD	5.8	18.8	19.8	13.5	12.3	13.4	9.7	4.7	1.9	38.9
Billings, MT	5.5	19.3	18.9	13.2	11.4	12.9	11.3	5.2	2.2	39.7
Boise City, ID	5.7	20.8	19.9	13.9	12.2	11.8	9.6	4.6	1.4	37.4
Boston, MA	5.1	17.2	21.6	13.2	12.6	13.5	9.8	4.7	2.1	39.3
Boulder, CO	4.0	19.1	23.8	12.6	12.6	12.2	9.8	4.2	1.8	37.5
Cape Coral, FL	4.5	14.9	15.7	10.6	11.3	14.2	15.4	10.2	3.3	49.3
Cedar Rapids, IA	5.8	19.3	19.1	13.2	12.1	13.1	10.1	5.1	2.2	39.3
Charleston, SC	5.9	18.2	21.0	14.1	12.0	12.6	10.0	4.5	1.6	38.1
Charlotte, NC	5.9	19.9	20.1	13.9	13.7	12.2	8.7	4.1	1.4	37.9
Chicago, IL	5.6	19.2	20.4	13.6	12.8	12.7	9.3	4.4	1.8	38.4
Cincinnati, OH	6.0	20.0	19.7	12.8	12.1	13.1	9.9	4.5	1.8	38.2
Clarksville, TN	8.1	21.2	25.9	13.1	10.3	10.0	7.1	3.3	1.1	31.9
Cleveland, OH	5.3	17.9	18.9	12.1	12.2	14.2	11.5	5.6	2.4	41.6
College Station, TX	5.6	22.3	30.9	11.6	9.2	9.0	6.9	3.0	1.4	28.4
Colorado Springs, CO	6.1	19.7	23.6	13.5	11.3	11.7	8.7	3.9	1.4	35.4
Columbia, MO	5.5	20.2	26.9	12.3	10.3	10.9	8.5	3.9	1.5	33.1
Columbia, SC	5.6	20.1	21.2	12.8	12.1	12.5	9.8	4.5	1.5	37.5
Columbus, OH	6.3	19.8	21.6	14.0	12.4	11.9	8.7	3.9	1.5	36.6
Dallas, TX	6.4	21.6	21.3	14.4	13.0	11.4	7.4	3.3	1.1	35.5
Davenport, IA	5.7	19.6	17.9	12.9	11.8	13.2	11.1	5.6	2.3	40.2
Denver, CO	5.5	18.2	22.7	15.4	12.8	11.6	8.6	3.8	1.4	37.2
Des Moines, IA	6.5	20.7	20.4	14.4	12.1	11.7	8.6	4.0	1.7	36.7
Detroit, MI	5.6	18.4	19.6	12.2	12.9	14.0	10.5	4.8	2.0	40.2
Durham, NC	5.3	18.5	22.6	13.0	12.2	12.1	10.0	4.7	1.7	37.6
El Paso, TX	6.8	22.6	23.1	12.8	11.4	10.4	7.6	3.7	1.6	33.3
Eugene, OR	4.4	16.8	22.2	12.5	11.2	12.5	12.5	5.8	2.2	40.2
Fargo, ND	6.5	20.6	26.1	13.8	10.0	9.9	7.7	3.6	1.7	33.0
Fort Collins, CO	4.5	18.2	24.9	12.9	11.0	11.7	10.5	4.5	1.8	36.6
Fort Wayne, IN	6.7	21.0	20.2	12.6	11.7	12.1	9.5	4.3	1.9	36.8
Fort Worth, TX	6.4	21.6	21.3	14.4	13.0	11.4	7.4	3.3	1.1	35.5
Gainesville, FL	4.9	18.6	27.4	11.4	10.1	11.2	9.9	4.7	2.0	34.3
Green Bay, WI	5.7	19.6	18.8	12.9	12.1	13.9	10.4	4.8	1.7	39.2
Greensboro, NC	5.6	20.1	19.7	12.0	12.9	13.0	9.9	4.8	1.9	38.9
Honolulu, HI	5.8	17.0	21.0	13.3	11.8	12.0	10.3	5.8	3.0	39.4
Houston, TX	6.7	22.0	20.8	14.5	12.8	11.1	7.7	3.3	1.1	35.3
Huntsville, AL	5.6	18.9	20.4	13.1	12.5	14.0	9.2	4.7	1.5	38.8
Indianapolis, IN	6.3	20.6	20.5	13.7	12.4	12.2	8.8	3.9	1.6	36.7
Jacksonville, FL	5.8	18.7	19.8	13.3	12.4	13.2	10.2	4.8	1.7	39.1
Kansas City, MO	6.1	20.1	19.9	13.7	12.2	12.6	9.4	4.4	1.8	37.8
Lafayette, LA	6.6	20.1	20.1	13.6	11.7	12.8	9.5	4.2	1.4	37.2
Las Vegas, NV	5.8	19.0	20.5	14.1	13.0	12.1	9.5	4.7	1.3	38.3
Lexington, KY	5.8	19.3	22.7	12.9	12.1	11.9	9.2	4.4	1.5	36.6
Lincoln, NE	5.9	20.6	24.1	12.8	10.7	10.9	9.3	4.0	1.7	34.4
Little Rock, AR	6.1	19.8	20.8	13.3	11.9	12.2	9.7	4.6	1.7	37.4
Los Angeles, CA	5.3	18.2	21.9	13.8	13.3	12.6	8.7	4.3	2.0	38.2
Louisville, KY	5.9	18.8	19.6	13.1	12.6	13.4	10.3	4.7	1.7	39.3
Madison, WI	5.2	18.3	23.8	13.6	11.6	12.0	9.6	4.2	1.7	36.9
Manchester, NH	5.1	17.1	20.1	12.9	13.2	15.0	10.1	4.8	1.8	41.0

Table continued on following page.

Appendix A: Comparative Statistics

Metro Area	Percent of Population									Median Age
	Under Age 5	Age 5–19	Age 20–34	Age 35–44	Age 45–54	Age 55–64	Age 65–74	Age 75–84	Age 85+	
McAllen, TX	8.0	26.8	21.3	12.3	11.4	8.6	6.5	3.8	1.2	30.3
Memphis, TN	6.5	20.8	20.4	12.9	12.2	12.4	9.3	4.1	1.4	36.7
Miami, FL	5.4	16.9	18.5	13.2	13.6	13.4	10.2	6.1	2.7	41.9
Midland, TX	8.3	23.1	22.7	15.3	10.2	9.9	6.5	2.7	1.4	32.7
Milwaukee, WI	5.9	19.3	19.8	13.1	11.9	13.2	10.0	4.5	2.1	38.5
Minneapolis, MN	6.1	19.7	20.0	14.1	12.2	12.8	9.1	4.2	1.7	37.8
Nashville, TN	6.1	19.3	21.9	14.2	12.6	12.1	8.6	4.0	1.2	36.8
New Orleans, LA	5.9	18.1	20.2	13.9	11.8	13.3	10.5	4.5	1.9	38.9
New York, NY	5.8	17.9	20.4	13.3	12.9	13.2	9.6	4.9	2.1	39.4
Oklahoma City, OK	6.3	21.0	21.7	13.7	11.4	11.5	8.9	4.2	1.4	35.8
Omaha, NE	6.6	21.3	20.0	13.9	11.7	12.0	8.9	4.0	1.6	36.5
Orlando, FL	5.5	18.5	21.4	14.2	12.9	12.0	9.1	4.7	1.8	38.3
Philadelphia, PA	5.5	18.6	20.2	13.1	12.3	13.4	10.0	4.8	2.0	39.1
Phoenix, AZ	5.7	19.6	20.9	13.3	12.3	11.8	9.5	5.2	1.8	37.7
Pittsburgh, PA	4.9	16.6	18.7	12.4	12.0	14.5	12.4	5.9	2.8	42.8
Portland, OR	5.1	17.7	20.9	15.2	13.2	12.0	9.8	4.4	1.7	39.1
Providence, RI	5.0	17.6	20.1	12.6	12.6	14.2	10.6	5.2	2.2	40.6
Provo, UT	8.7	27.7	27.3	12.5	9.2	6.7	4.8	2.3	0.8	25.6
Raleigh, NC	5.9	20.4	20.2	14.8	14.1	11.9	8.0	3.6	1.3	37.5
Reno, NV	5.4	17.8	20.9	13.0	11.8	13.1	11.3	5.1	1.6	39.4
Richmond, VA	5.7	18.4	20.5	13.5	12.4	13.1	10.0	4.6	1.7	38.7
Rochester, MN	6.2	20.1	18.7	13.6	11.1	12.9	9.8	5.2	2.3	38.8
Sacramento, CA	5.6	19.3	20.3	13.8	12.2	12.3	9.7	4.6	2.0	38.3
Saint Louis, MO	5.6	18.8	19.2	13.2	12.0	13.8	10.5	4.9	2.0	39.8
Saint Paul, MN	6.1	19.7	20.0	14.1	12.2	12.8	9.1	4.2	1.7	37.8
Salem, OR	5.9	20.5	20.5	13.0	11.6	11.6	10.1	4.9	1.9	37.3
Salt Lake City, UT	6.6	22.3	23.3	14.9	11.7	9.9	7.2	3.1	1.2	33.7
San Antonio, TX	6.3	21.1	21.5	14.1	12.2	11.2	8.3	3.8	1.5	35.7
San Diego, CA	5.7	18.2	23.0	14.1	12.1	11.8	8.9	4.4	1.8	37.1
San Francisco, CA	5.1	16.5	20.6	15.0	13.5	12.7	9.6	4.8	2.1	40.0
San Jose, CA	5.4	18.3	22.1	14.4	13.4	12.1	8.1	4.3	2.0	37.8
Santa Rosa, CA	4.7	17.1	17.8	13.2	12.4	14.0	12.8	5.8	2.4	42.7
Savannah, GA	6.1	19.5	22.0	13.8	11.7	11.8	9.2	4.4	1.5	36.7
Seattle, WA	5.7	17.5	22.8	15.4	12.7	11.9	8.6	3.8	1.6	37.4
Sioux Falls, SD	6.9	21.1	20.4	14.3	11.2	11.8	9.1	3.7	1.5	36.1
Tampa, FL	5.0	16.7	18.7	12.9	12.8	13.7	11.4	6.4	2.4	42.2
Tucson, AZ	5.0	18.0	21.4	11.6	10.8	12.2	12.0	6.8	2.4	39.7
Tulsa, OK	6.3	20.7	19.9	13.1	11.9	12.2	9.6	4.7	1.7	37.3
Virginia Beach, VA	6.0	18.8	22.1	13.3	11.3	12.8	9.4	4.6	1.6	37.2
Washington, DC	6.1	19.2	20.3	14.8	13.4	12.3	8.3	4.0	1.5	37.9
Wichita, KS	6.3	21.5	20.2	12.8	11.2	12.3	9.6	4.3	2.0	36.6
Wilmington, NC	4.5	15.5	18.1	11.8	11.8	14.9	14.8	6.6	2.0	45.1
Winston-Salem, NC	5.5	19.2	18.7	11.8	13.0	13.8	10.7	5.4	2.0	40.6
U.S.	5.7	19.1	20.2	13.1	12.3	12.8	10.0	4.9	1.9	38.7

Note: Figures cover the Metropolitan Statistical Area (MSA)
Source: U.S. Census Bureau, 2019-2023 American Community Survey 5-Year Estimates

Ancestry: City

City	German	Irish	English	American	Italian	Polish	French[1]	European	Scottish
Albuquerque, NM	9.8	7.9	9.1	3.1	3.4	1.4	1.8	1.6	1.5
Anchorage, AK	13.5	9.0	9.9	3.6	3.1	1.9	1.9	2.1	1.8
Ann Arbor, MI	16.5	10.7	9.7	2.1	4.5	6.2	2.2	2.7	2.3
Athens, GA	9.0	8.9	12.2	3.9	3.1	1.8	1.6	2.7	2.7
Atlanta, GA	7.1	6.4	9.3	3.8	2.9	1.4	1.7	1.7	1.4
Austin, TX	11.5	8.7	10.2	2.8	3.2	1.9	2.4	2.4	2.2
Baltimore, MD	5.8	5.7	3.7	2.7	2.9	2.0	0.9	0.7	0.7
Billings, MT	27.7	13.2	13.3	3.7	3.1	1.7	2.6	2.0	2.8
Boise City, ID	18.2	11.5	17.8	3.9	4.2	1.7	2.4	3.7	3.1
Boston, MA	4.8	13.2	5.4	2.2	7.3	2.2	1.7	1.1	1.1
Boulder, CO	16.0	11.3	11.4	2.6	5.2	3.4	2.4	4.2	3.2
Cape Coral, FL	13.4	11.5	8.5	10.4	9.2	3.3	2.2	1.5	1.3
Cedar Rapids, IA	26.8	13.3	10.4	3.3	1.7	1.4	1.8	1.5	1.6
Charleston, SC	11.7	11.0	13.6	13.0	4.8	2.4	2.8	1.9	2.4
Charlotte, NC	7.4	6.7	7.7	4.7	3.5	1.5	1.2	1.1	1.6
Chicago, IL	7.4	7.2	3.2	2.0	3.8	5.0	0.9	0.9	0.7
Cincinnati, OH	17.5	9.8	6.9	3.0	3.7	1.4	1.2	1.2	1.0
Clarksville, TN	12.5	8.8	8.3	6.0	3.6	1.0	1.6	3.7	1.5
Cleveland, OH	9.4	8.4	3.5	2.5	4.4	3.7	0.8	0.5	0.7
College Station, TX	14.8	8.0	9.8	3.2	3.3	2.3	1.9	1.8	1.6
Colorado Springs, CO	17.8	11.4	12.8	4.2	4.7	2.6	2.4	2.9	2.6
Columbia, MO	24.0	12.1	13.5	5.1	3.4	1.6	1.9	2.2	2.3
Columbia, SC	9.0	7.2	8.8	5.3	3.0	1.1	1.7	1.9	2.0
Columbus, OH	14.9	10.0	8.0	3.4	4.6	2.1	1.3	1.5	1.6
Dallas, TX	5.4	4.4	6.0	3.8	1.7	0.8	1.2	1.2	1.1
Davenport, IA	28.1	14.7	8.7	3.0	2.6	1.9	1.3	1.1	1.8
Denver, CO	14.0	10.9	10.4	3.0	5.5	2.8	2.1	2.5	2.0
Des Moines, IA	19.1	12.4	9.2	3.1	3.5	1.0	1.4	1.5	1.3
Detroit, MI	1.8	1.6	1.1	4.4	0.8	1.1	0.5	0.2	0.3
Durham, NC	8.2	6.7	10.0	3.8	3.4	1.8	1.5	1.7	1.8
El Paso, TX	3.8	2.4	2.2	2.2	1.3	0.5	0.6	0.5	0.4
Eugene, OR	18.4	12.9	14.5	3.1	5.2	1.9	3.1	3.8	3.9
Fargo, ND	32.9	8.1	5.2	2.9	1.3	2.2	3.4	0.8	1.4
Fort Collins, CO	23.1	12.3	14.9	3.2	5.6	3.4	3.1	3.6	3.5
Fort Wayne, IN	22.5	9.0	9.2	5.0	2.1	1.9	2.4	2.3	1.9
Fort Worth, TX	7.1	6.0	7.4	3.7	1.8	0.8	1.3	1.4	1.5
Gainesville, FL	10.6	8.9	10.5	3.4	5.1	2.5	1.6	1.3	2.6
Green Bay, WI	26.6	8.2	4.6	3.6	2.0	7.2	3.0	1.6	1.0
Greensboro, NC	6.5	5.3	9.4	4.5	2.4	0.8	1.2	1.6	1.7
Honolulu, HI	4.5	3.4	3.6	1.4	1.3	0.9	1.0	0.5	0.7
Houston, TX	5.0	3.6	5.0	3.1	1.6	0.9	1.4	1.0	0.9
Huntsville, AL	9.2	8.5	13.0	10.2	2.4	1.3	1.8	2.2	2.1
Indianapolis, IN	12.8	7.9	8.0	4.5	2.0	1.4	1.4	1.4	1.5
Jacksonville, FL	7.8	7.7	7.6	6.3	3.6	1.4	1.4	2.2	1.6
Kansas City, MO	15.2	10.0	9.5	4.1	3.7	1.6	1.5	2.3	1.4
Lafayette, LA	9.2	5.6	6.7	5.2	3.8	0.5	16.7	0.7	1.1
Las Vegas, NV	8.0	7.2	7.2	2.9	4.9	1.8	1.5	1.6	1.3
Lexington, KY	12.7	10.8	13.8	7.7	2.7	1.4	1.6	2.4	2.4
Lincoln, NE	30.2	11.0	9.3	3.4	1.9	2.2	1.7	1.8	1.4
Little Rock, AR	7.5	6.5	10.4	4.6	1.2	0.7	1.3	1.7	1.7
Los Angeles, CA	3.9	3.7	3.5	3.8	2.7	1.3	1.1	1.3	0.7
Louisville, KY	14.8	11.3	10.8	5.8	2.5	1.1	1.5	1.6	1.6
Madison, WI	28.4	12.2	9.2	1.9	4.0	5.5	2.0	2.0	1.9
Manchester, NH	6.5	18.5	10.0	3.0	8.7	3.6	10.5	0.8	2.3
McAllen, TX	2.6	1.6	1.9	3.1	0.9	0.4	1.0	0.3	0.2
Memphis, TN	3.3	3.6	4.9	3.3	1.5	0.5	0.7	1.6	0.9

Table continued on following page.

City	German	Irish	English	American	Italian	Polish	French[1]	European	Scottish
Miami, FL	1.9	1.3	1.3	2.6	3.0	0.7	0.9	0.6	0.2
Midland, TX	6.6	6.1	7.8	4.6	0.9	0.4	1.3	1.1	1.5
Milwaukee, WI	15.1	5.4	2.2	1.4	2.4	5.5	1.2	1.0	0.5
Minneapolis, MN	21.0	10.7	7.4	1.7	2.6	3.9	2.7	2.0	1.4
Nashville, TN	8.7	7.9	10.2	5.9	2.7	1.4	1.5	1.7	1.9
New Orleans, LA	6.4	6.0	5.3	2.3	4.0	0.9	5.4	1.2	1.1
New York, NY	2.9	4.4	2.1	3.7	5.8	2.1	0.8	0.9	0.5
Oklahoma City, OK	10.1	7.8	9.5	5.3	1.5	0.7	1.2	1.9	1.7
Omaha, NE	24.8	12.8	8.4	2.7	3.7	3.3	1.9	1.6	1.8
Orlando, FL	6.4	5.4	5.9	6.1	4.5	1.6	1.5	0.8	0.9
Philadelphia, PA	7.0	9.6	3.2	2.2	6.7	3.0	0.7	0.7	0.7
Phoenix, AZ	9.6	7.4	6.8	2.7	3.9	1.8	1.4	1.5	1.3
Pittsburgh, PA	17.1	13.2	6.1	2.7	11.4	6.6	1.2	1.2	1.4
Portland, OR	15.2	11.6	12.9	4.3	4.5	2.4	2.6	4.4	3.1
Providence, RI	3.3	8.1	4.4	2.4	6.9	1.7	2.7	0.7	0.9
Provo, UT	10.4	4.9	28.2	2.2	2.2	0.7	1.3	4.0	3.6
Raleigh, NC	9.2	8.5	11.8	5.7	3.8	1.9	1.7	1.6	2.2
Reno, NV	12.3	11.0	11.1	4.4	5.9	1.6	2.2	2.6	2.0
Richmond, VA	8.2	7.9	9.9	3.9	3.8	1.4	1.5	1.3	1.8
Rochester, MN	28.8	9.8	7.1	2.6	1.8	2.6	1.8	1.6	1.4
Sacramento, CA	6.5	5.8	6.0	2.3	3.4	1.0	1.4	1.4	1.0
Saint Louis, MO	15.9	9.7	6.4	6.3	4.0	1.7	2.5	1.2	1.3
Saint Paul, MN	19.5	9.9	5.6	1.9	2.5	2.6	2.6	1.5	1.2
Salem, OR	16.3	8.2	12.7	4.1	2.9	1.2	2.3	4.2	2.5
Salt Lake City, UT	11.5	7.7	19.4	3.1	4.0	1.4	2.1	3.0	3.4
San Antonio, TX	7.2	4.6	4.7	3.4	2.0	0.9	1.2	0.8	0.9
San Diego, CA	8.7	7.3	7.0	2.3	4.2	1.8	1.7	1.7	1.3
San Francisco, CA	7.1	7.5	6.0	2.1	4.5	1.8	2.2	2.1	1.3
San Jose, CA	4.4	4.0	4.0	1.5	3.2	0.8	1.0	1.2	0.7
Santa Rosa, CA	11.1	10.1	10.4	2.2	6.3	1.6	2.4	2.4	1.9
Savannah, GA	6.6	7.3	6.3	3.8	3.2	1.1	1.3	0.8	1.4
Seattle, WA	14.0	10.8	12.2	2.4	4.7	2.6	2.8	3.9	2.7
Sioux Falls, SD	31.7	10.1	7.4	4.3	1.5	1.4	1.6	1.3	0.8
Tampa, FL	8.8	7.6	7.6	6.2	6.2	2.0	1.6	1.1	1.4
Tucson, AZ	11.5	8.4	8.0	2.9	3.7	1.9	1.8	1.5	1.7
Tulsa, OK	10.4	8.5	10.6	6.0	2.0	0.9	1.6	1.6	2.1
Virginia Beach, VA	11.2	10.5	11.3	7.5	5.5	2.3	1.9	1.6	2.2
Washington, DC	7.7	7.8	6.8	2.8	4.5	2.2	1.7	1.7	1.4
Wichita, KS	19.2	9.8	10.4	4.8	1.7	0.9	1.8	1.6	1.6
Wilmington, NC	10.8	10.8	13.8	4.7	5.6	2.2	2.1	2.3	2.7
Winston-Salem, NC	7.9	6.3	9.5	5.3	2.5	0.8	1.0	1.7	1.9
U.S.	12.6	9.4	9.1	5.5	4.9	2.6	2.0	1.6	1.6

Note: Figures are the percentage of the total population reporting a particular ancestry. The nine most commonly reported ancestries in the U.S. are shown. Figures include multiple ancestries (e.g. if a person reported being Irish and Italian, they were included in both columns); (1) Excludes Basque
Source: U.S. Census Bureau, 2019-2023 American Community Survey 5-Year Estimates

Ancestry: Metro Area

Metro Area	German	Irish	English	American	Italian	Polish	French[1]	European	Scottish
Albuquerque, NM	9.7	7.6	8.9	3.7	3.3	1.4	1.8	1.6	1.7
Anchorage, AK	14.5	9.7	10.1	4.2	2.9	1.9	1.9	2.1	1.9
Ann Arbor, MI	17.8	10.2	11.1	5.1	4.5	6.2	2.5	2.3	2.8
Athens, GA	8.8	10.4	13.5	6.1	2.8	1.4	1.5	2.4	2.5
Atlanta, GA	6.3	6.3	9.1	6.8	2.5	1.2	1.2	1.5	1.6
Austin, TX	12.4	8.3	10.4	3.6	2.9	1.7	2.3	2.4	2.2
Baltimore, MD	13.7	10.9	8.6	4.4	5.5	3.6	1.3	1.4	1.4
Billings, MT	29.0	13.1	12.6	4.2	3.2	1.5	2.6	2.1	2.6
Boise City, ID	17.0	10.2	18.2	4.8	3.5	1.4	2.4	3.1	3.1
Boston, MA	5.7	19.8	10.0	3.2	12.0	3.0	3.9	1.3	2.0
Boulder, CO	18.0	12.1	14.5	3.0	5.1	3.0	2.8	3.2	2.9
Cape Coral, FL	13.1	10.6	9.0	10.2	7.9	3.1	2.0	1.4	1.6
Cedar Rapids, IA	31.4	14.1	10.6	4.0	1.6	1.2	1.8	1.7	1.8
Charleston, SC	10.5	9.6	12.6	8.7	4.1	1.8	2.1	1.8	2.2
Charlotte, NC	10.2	8.4	10.3	8.3	3.9	1.7	1.4	1.5	2.0
Chicago, IL	12.9	10.2	4.8	2.5	6.1	8.0	1.2	1.2	0.9
Cincinnati, OH	25.7	12.9	11.4	5.6	3.9	1.6	1.6	1.6	1.8
Clarksville, TN	11.5	8.6	9.9	7.4	2.8	1.0	1.5	3.5	1.7
Cleveland, OH	18.5	13.3	8.6	4.1	9.1	6.9	1.4	1.1	1.5
College Station, TX	13.5	7.5	9.3	3.8	2.6	2.0	2.1	1.5	1.6
Colorado Springs, CO	17.6	11.0	12.3	4.5	4.5	2.4	2.3	3.0	2.7
Columbia, MO	24.4	11.8	13.9	6.4	2.8	1.4	1.9	2.2	2.1
Columbia, SC	9.5	7.3	9.5	6.5	2.5	1.3	1.5	1.6	1.9
Columbus, OH	20.0	12.4	11.1	5.3	5.1	2.2	1.6	1.8	2.1
Dallas, TX	8.1	6.4	8.7	5.3	2.2	1.0	1.4	1.4	1.5
Davenport, IA	25.2	13.0	9.4	3.8	2.5	1.9	1.5	1.5	1.5
Denver, CO	16.9	11.0	11.7	3.3	5.2	2.5	2.2	2.6	2.2
Des Moines, IA	25.8	13.5	11.3	3.8	3.1	1.2	1.6	2.3	1.7
Detroit, MI	14.3	9.1	7.9	4.0	5.8	8.9	2.8	1.5	2.0
Durham, NC	9.3	8.2	12.5	5.0	3.7	1.9	1.7	1.9	2.3
El Paso, TX	3.5	2.2	2.0	2.3	1.2	0.4	0.5	0.5	0.3
Eugene, OR	18.3	13.1	14.6	3.9	4.4	1.6	3.3	3.4	3.3
Fargo, ND	33.8	7.6	5.1	2.5	1.4	2.2	3.2	0.9	1.3
Fort Collins, CO	24.4	12.6	16.0	4.2	5.1	2.9	3.2	3.5	3.5
Fort Wayne, IN	26.1	9.0	9.8	5.8	2.2	2.0	2.8	2.6	1.8
Fort Worth, TX	8.1	6.4	8.7	5.3	2.2	1.0	1.4	1.4	1.5
Gainesville, FL	11.6	10.3	12.1	4.6	4.5	2.1	2.0	1.7	2.9
Green Bay, WI	33.7	9.3	4.9	4.0	2.2	9.4	3.5	1.6	0.7
Greensboro, NC	8.4	6.9	11.0	7.4	2.4	1.0	1.3	1.8	2.1
Honolulu, HI	5.2	4.0	4.1	1.3	1.8	0.8	1.0	0.6	0.7
Houston, TX	7.1	5.0	6.6	3.6	2.0	1.1	1.8	1.2	1.1
Huntsville, AL	9.4	9.3	13.8	11.4	2.3	1.2	1.5	2.2	2.1
Indianapolis, IN	16.6	9.4	10.9	7.3	2.5	1.7	1.5	1.7	1.8
Jacksonville, FL	9.6	9.6	10.2	7.5	4.5	1.8	1.8	2.1	2.0
Kansas City, MO	19.5	11.8	12.5	4.6	3.0	1.5	1.9	3.4	1.8
Lafayette, LA	7.1	4.5	5.3	6.2	3.0	0.6	17.1	0.7	0.7
Las Vegas, NV	7.9	6.8	7.0	2.9	4.7	1.7	1.4	1.3	1.2
Lexington, KY	12.3	11.3	14.6	10.4	2.5	1.3	1.5	2.3	2.3
Lincoln, NE	32.0	10.9	9.3	3.6	1.8	2.1	1.6	1.7	1.3
Little Rock, AR	8.5	8.4	11.7	6.6	1.4	0.8	1.4	1.6	1.8
Los Angeles, CA	5.1	4.3	4.5	3.5	2.8	1.1	1.1	1.2	0.8
Louisville, KY	16.6	12.4	12.6	7.6	2.6	1.1	1.7	1.7	1.9
Madison, WI	34.3	12.8	9.8	2.6	3.5	5.0	2.3	1.9	1.7
Manchester, NH	8.0	20.6	14.5	3.4	9.9	3.8	10.8	1.3	3.0
McAllen, TX	1.7	1.0	1.1	2.1	0.4	0.2	0.4	0.2	0.2
Memphis, TN	5.1	5.9	7.7	6.6	2.0	0.7	1.0	1.6	1.2

Table continued on following page.

Metro Area	German	Irish	English	American	Italian	Polish	French[1]	European	Scottish
Miami, FL	4.2	4.1	3.1	5.6	4.9	1.8	1.1	0.9	0.6
Midland, TX	7.0	5.8	7.6	5.2	0.9	0.3	1.3	1.0	1.4
Milwaukee, WI	31.6	9.3	5.0	2.4	4.3	9.8	2.1	1.4	0.9
Minneapolis, MN	27.4	10.7	6.9	3.1	2.5	4.0	2.9	2.0	1.2
Nashville, TN	9.6	8.9	12.9	10.5	2.6	1.2	1.6	2.3	2.2
New Orleans, LA	8.2	6.6	5.2	3.8	6.7	0.6	9.1	0.9	0.8
New York, NY	5.7	8.6	3.0	3.9	11.0	3.4	0.8	0.9	0.6
Oklahoma City, OK	11.8	9.0	11.2	6.2	1.7	0.8	1.5	2.0	1.9
Omaha, NE	27.8	12.9	9.7	3.5	3.7	3.5	1.8	1.7	1.6
Orlando, FL	8.2	7.2	7.1	9.1	5.0	1.7	1.6	1.1	1.2
Philadelphia, PA	13.7	16.9	7.8	3.2	12.2	4.6	1.2	1.0	1.2
Phoenix, AZ	12.6	8.7	9.5	4.2	4.5	2.2	1.8	1.8	1.6
Pittsburgh, PA	24.5	16.9	9.2	3.3	15.1	7.8	1.4	1.1	1.8
Portland, OR	16.0	10.5	12.8	4.4	3.5	1.7	2.4	3.8	2.8
Providence, RI	4.5	16.5	10.8	3.4	12.8	3.2	7.9	0.7	1.5
Provo, UT	10.0	4.9	32.1	4.1	2.1	0.5	1.4	4.8	4.1
Raleigh, NC	9.7	8.8	12.8	6.8	4.6	2.0	1.8	2.0	2.3
Reno, NV	12.7	10.9	11.6	4.0	6.0	1.6	2.3	3.5	2.0
Richmond, VA	9.1	8.2	12.7	6.6	3.7	1.5	1.4	1.7	1.8
Rochester, MN	32.8	10.3	7.3	3.6	1.5	2.5	1.7	1.8	1.3
Sacramento, CA	10.1	8.0	9.4	2.6	4.5	1.2	1.8	2.4	1.7
Saint Louis, MO	25.5	12.6	9.6	5.5	4.5	2.3	2.8	1.6	1.5
Saint Paul, MN	27.4	10.7	6.9	3.1	2.5	4.0	2.9	2.0	1.2
Salem, OR	16.6	8.4	12.1	3.9	2.6	1.4	2.3	3.6	2.6
Salt Lake City, UT	9.9	6.1	23.6	3.8	3.0	0.9	1.7	3.3	3.6
San Antonio, TX	10.0	5.8	6.6	3.8	2.2	1.4	1.5	1.1	1.3
San Diego, CA	9.0	7.5	7.6	2.6	4.1	1.6	1.8	1.9	1.5
San Francisco, CA	7.1	6.8	6.6	2.2	4.2	1.4	1.7	2.0	1.3
San Jose, CA	5.6	4.6	4.9	1.8	3.5	1.0	1.2	1.6	0.9
Santa Rosa, CA	12.4	12.2	11.8	2.4	7.9	1.8	2.9	3.7	2.5
Savannah, GA	9.4	9.4	10.2	6.8	3.7	1.2	1.5	1.2	1.8
Seattle, WA	13.2	9.0	10.9	2.9	3.4	1.7	2.4	3.2	2.3
Sioux Falls, SD	33.6	9.6	6.6	5.0	1.4	1.3	1.5	1.3	0.8
Tampa, FL	11.3	9.8	9.2	8.6	7.2	2.8	2.1	1.3	1.6
Tucson, AZ	13.2	9.0	10.1	3.5	4.1	2.2	2.1	1.7	2.0
Tulsa, OK	12.4	10.2	11.7	5.6	1.9	0.9	1.7	1.7	2.1
Virginia Beach, VA	9.4	8.6	10.8	8.0	4.1	1.7	1.7	1.6	1.8
Washington, DC	8.8	8.1	8.0	3.7	4.1	2.1	1.4	1.8	1.5
Wichita, KS	21.4	9.8	11.1	5.5	1.8	0.9	1.8	1.9	1.8
Wilmington, NC	12.2	12.4	14.8	5.9	5.9	2.4	2.1	1.8	2.8
Winston-Salem, NC	10.9	8.3	13.1	7.8	2.6	1.0	1.1	1.7	2.1
U.S.	12.6	9.4	9.1	5.5	4.9	2.6	2.0	1.6	1.6

Note: Figures are the percentage of the total population reporting a particular ancestry. The nine most commonly reported ancestries in the U.S. are shown. Figures include multiple ancestries (e.g. if a person reported being Irish and Italian, they were included in both columns); Figures cover the Metropolitan Statistical Area (MSA); (1) Excludes Basque
Source: U.S. Census Bureau, 2019-2023 American Community Survey 5-Year Estimates

Foreign-born Population: City

City	Percent of Population Born in								
	Any Foreign Country	Asia	Mexico	Europe	Caribbean	Central America[1]	South America	Africa	Canada
Albuquerque, NM	10.4	2.7	5.0	1.0	0.4	0.2	0.5	0.4	0.1
Anchorage, AK	10.9	6.0	0.6	1.2	0.5	0.2	0.6	0.5	0.4
Ann Arbor, MI	18.7	11.8	0.5	2.9	0.1	0.3	0.6	1.6	0.7
Athens, GA	9.8	3.2	2.3	0.9	0.4	1.3	0.8	0.7	0.2
Atlanta, GA	8.6	3.1	0.7	1.3	0.9	0.3	0.9	1.1	0.3
Austin, TX	18.1	6.2	5.2	1.6	0.8	2.0	0.9	1.0	0.3
Baltimore, MD	8.8	2.1	0.4	0.9	1.3	1.6	0.6	1.7	0.1
Billings, MT	2.0	0.7	0.2	0.6	0.0	0.0	0.1	0.0	0.3
Boise City, ID	7.2	3.0	1.3	1.3	0.1	0.1	0.3	0.6	0.5
Boston, MA	27.5	7.8	0.4	3.0	8.1	2.3	2.3	3.0	0.4
Boulder, CO	10.2	4.2	1.0	3.0	0.2	0.4	0.6	0.3	0.6
Cape Coral, FL	17.9	1.3	0.4	2.2	9.2	1.2	2.8	0.1	0.7
Cedar Rapids, IA	7.1	2.6	0.7	0.5	0.1	0.3	0.2	2.5	0.1
Charleston, SC	5.4	1.6	0.6	1.2	0.3	0.3	0.8	0.3	0.2
Charlotte, NC	18.1	4.9	2.7	1.5	1.2	3.8	1.7	2.1	0.2
Chicago, IL	20.7	5.2	8.2	3.3	0.4	0.9	1.4	1.1	0.2
Cincinnati, OH	7.1	2.1	0.3	0.7	0.2	1.0	0.3	2.2	0.1
Clarksville, TN	6.8	1.9	1.2	1.0	0.6	0.6	0.6	0.6	0.2
Cleveland, OH	6.1	2.3	0.4	1.1	0.5	0.5	0.3	0.9	0.1
College Station, TX	12.3	7.1	1.5	0.9	0.1	1.0	1.0	0.5	0.1
Colorado Springs, CO	7.4	2.0	1.7	1.5	0.2	0.6	0.4	0.5	0.3
Columbia, MO	8.1	4.9	0.6	0.4	0.3	0.2	0.5	1.1	0.0
Columbia, SC	5.1	2.0	0.2	0.7	0.8	0.3	0.5	0.4	0.1
Columbus, OH	14.4	4.7	1.3	0.8	0.7	0.9	0.7	5.1	0.1
Dallas, TX	23.4	2.9	12.8	0.8	0.4	3.3	1.0	2.0	0.1
Davenport, IA	4.6	1.5	1.5	0.5	0.0	0.1	0.0	0.6	0.2
Denver, CO	13.8	2.7	5.8	1.5	0.3	0.5	1.2	1.5	0.3
Des Moines, IA	14.0	4.4	3.6	0.8	0.2	1.6	0.1	3.2	0.1
Detroit, MI	6.0	2.4	1.7	0.2	0.3	0.5	0.1	0.5	0.2
Durham, NC	15.3	4.1	2.8	1.4	0.8	3.4	0.8	1.7	0.3
El Paso, TX	22.3	1.0	19.5	0.6	0.2	0.3	0.2	0.3	0.1
Eugene, OR	6.8	2.7	1.5	1.2	0.1	0.4	0.2	0.4	0.3
Fargo, ND	9.7	3.2	0.1	0.6	0.1	0.0	0.1	4.9	0.4
Fort Collins, CO	6.6	2.5	1.2	1.3	0.1	0.3	0.6	0.3	0.2
Fort Wayne, IN	9.0	4.4	2.1	0.5	0.2	1.0	0.2	0.5	0.2
Fort Worth, TX	17.0	4.1	8.9	0.5	0.3	0.8	0.6	1.6	0.1
Gainesville, FL	12.1	4.6	0.2	1.7	1.7	0.4	2.3	0.8	0.4
Green Bay, WI	8.8	2.1	4.5	0.4	0.2	0.5	0.3	0.6	0.2
Greensboro, NC	12.7	4.0	1.9	1.0	0.6	0.9	0.8	3.4	0.2
Honolulu, HI	27.8	22.9	0.2	1.0	0.1	0.1	0.3	0.2	0.2
Houston, TX	28.8	5.7	9.9	1.2	1.0	6.8	1.9	2.0	0.2
Huntsville, AL	6.6	1.7	1.6	0.8	0.7	0.5	0.3	0.5	0.2
Indianapolis, IN	11.6	3.1	3.2	0.5	0.7	1.3	0.6	2.2	0.1
Jacksonville, FL	12.2	4.1	0.5	1.7	2.5	0.8	1.7	0.8	0.1
Kansas City, MO	8.5	2.2	2.2	0.6	0.5	0.9	0.4	1.5	0.1
Lafayette, LA	6.6	2.1	0.5	0.4	0.2	1.8	0.8	0.4	0.1
Las Vegas, NV	20.9	5.3	8.5	1.6	1.3	2.2	1.0	0.4	0.4
Lexington, KY	11.0	3.8	2.3	1.0	0.4	0.8	0.5	2.0	0.2
Lincoln, NE	9.2	4.9	1.3	0.9	0.4	0.6	0.3	0.8	0.1
Little Rock, AR	7.9	2.7	2.1	0.6	0.1	1.6	0.3	0.4	0.1
Los Angeles, CA	35.8	11.2	11.2	2.4	0.3	8.3	1.2	0.7	0.4
Louisville, KY	9.8	2.5	1.0	0.8	2.8	0.6	0.4	1.6	0.1
Madison, WI	11.6	5.5	1.9	1.4	0.2	0.2	1.1	1.0	0.2
Manchester, NH	14.7	3.8	0.4	2.2	2.0	2.1	1.0	2.1	1.0

Table continued on following page.

City	Percent of Population Born in							
	Any Foreign Country	Asia	Mexico	Europe	Caribbean	Central America[1]	South America	Africa	Canada
McAllen, TX	25.7	2.2	22.0	0.2	0.3	0.5	0.4	0.1	0.0
Memphis, TN	7.4	1.3	2.3	0.3	0.3	1.9	0.5	0.7	0.1
Miami, FL	57.7	1.5	1.2	2.2	28.5	11.8	11.9	0.4	0.2
Midland, TX	13.7	2.0	7.1	0.4	1.0	0.5	1.1	1.0	0.6
Milwaukee, WI	10.8	2.8	5.1	0.6	0.3	0.4	0.3	1.0	0.1
Minneapolis, MN	14.1	3.2	1.8	1.0	0.2	0.3	1.5	5.7	0.3
Nashville, TN	15.1	3.6	3.1	0.8	0.6	3.1	0.6	2.9	0.3
New Orleans, LA	6.6	2.0	0.4	0.6	0.6	1.9	0.5	0.3	0.2
New York, NY	36.5	11.0	1.8	5.1	9.7	1.4	5.1	1.9	0.3
Oklahoma City, OK	12.0	3.1	5.4	0.5	0.2	1.3	0.5	0.7	0.2
Omaha, NE	11.0	3.3	3.4	0.6	0.2	1.5	0.3	1.5	0.2
Orlando, FL	24.1	3.0	0.8	1.8	6.5	1.2	10.1	0.5	0.2
Philadelphia, PA	14.6	5.6	0.5	2.2	2.8	0.7	1.0	1.7	0.1
Phoenix, AZ	19.0	3.1	11.3	1.3	0.4	0.9	0.4	1.1	0.3
Pittsburgh, PA	9.3	4.5	0.3	1.8	0.4	0.2	0.6	1.0	0.3
Portland, OR	12.4	5.5	2.0	2.3	0.2	0.4	0.3	0.8	0.5
Providence, RI	32.8	3.9	0.5	2.2	15.3	5.9	1.2	3.4	0.3
Provo, UT	12.2	1.6	3.8	0.7	0.4	1.0	3.3	0.5	0.4
Raleigh, NC	13.6	3.8	2.4	1.3	1.1	1.4	1.1	2.2	0.2
Reno, NV	16.1	5.4	5.3	1.4	0.3	2.2	0.4	0.5	0.3
Richmond, VA	8.6	1.5	0.9	0.8	0.7	3.5	0.4	0.6	0.1
Rochester, MN	14.1	5.9	1.0	1.2	0.1	0.3	0.4	4.9	0.2
Sacramento, CA	21.3	10.6	5.5	1.6	0.1	0.9	0.4	0.6	0.2
Saint Louis, MO	6.6	2.7	0.8	1.0	0.3	0.3	0.3	0.9	0.1
Saint Paul, MN	18.7	9.3	1.8	0.7	0.2	0.9	0.4	4.9	0.3
Salem, OR	12.2	2.5	6.2	1.0	0.0	0.8	0.2	0.4	0.2
Salt Lake City, UT	15.4	4.2	5.1	1.8	0.2	0.7	1.4	1.0	0.3
San Antonio, TX	14.3	2.6	8.8	0.6	0.3	1.0	0.6	0.4	0.1
San Diego, CA	24.8	11.8	7.5	2.3	0.2	0.5	0.9	1.0	0.4
San Francisco, CA	34.2	21.9	2.4	4.4	0.1	2.4	1.3	0.6	0.7
San Jose, CA	41.6	27.3	8.4	2.2	0.1	1.3	1.0	0.7	0.3
Santa Rosa, CA	20.8	4.7	11.5	1.5	0.1	1.4	0.3	0.6	0.3
Savannah, GA	6.7	2.6	0.8	0.8	0.9	0.7	0.5	0.4	0.2
Seattle, WA	19.9	11.4	1.4	2.5	0.2	0.4	0.7	2.1	1.1
Sioux Falls, SD	9.0	2.0	0.6	1.1	0.1	1.7	0.2	3.2	0.1
Tampa, FL	19.0	4.0	1.1	1.8	7.4	1.3	2.4	0.6	0.3
Tucson, AZ	13.7	2.4	8.3	1.0	0.1	0.4	0.3	0.8	0.2
Tulsa, OK	12.0	2.6	5.5	0.7	0.3	1.3	0.7	0.6	0.1
Virginia Beach, VA	9.1	5.0	0.3	1.4	0.5	0.4	0.8	0.5	0.2
Washington, DC	13.3	2.8	0.6	2.3	1.2	2.2	1.7	2.2	0.3
Wichita, KS	10.0	3.5	4.4	0.5	0.1	0.5	0.4	0.6	0.1
Wilmington, NC	5.7	1.2	1.5	1.0	0.2	0.8	0.7	0.2	0.1
Winston-Salem, NC	10.7	2.0	4.1	0.6	0.6	1.7	1.0	0.6	0.1
U.S.	13.9	4.3	3.3	1.4	1.4	1.2	1.2	0.8	0.2

Note: (1) Excludes Mexico
Source: U.S. Census Bureau, 2019-2023 American Community Survey 5-Year Estimates

Appendix A: Comparative Statistics

Foreign-born Population: Metro Area

Metro Area	Any Foreign Country	Asia	Mexico	Europe	Caribbean	Central America[1]	South America	Africa	Canada
Albuquerque, NM	9.2	2.0	4.9	0.8	0.3	0.2	0.4	0.4	0.1
Anchorage, AK	8.7	4.6	0.5	1.2	0.4	0.2	0.5	0.4	0.3
Ann Arbor, MI	12.8	7.3	0.7	2.2	0.1	0.5	0.4	0.9	0.5
Athens, GA	8.0	2.7	1.7	0.7	0.2	1.1	0.5	0.7	0.2
Atlanta, GA	14.8	4.8	2.3	1.1	1.7	1.4	1.4	1.8	0.2
Austin, TX	15.5	5.1	5.1	1.3	0.5	1.4	0.8	0.8	0.3
Baltimore, MD	11.2	4.4	0.4	1.2	0.8	1.5	0.7	2.1	0.1
Billings, MT	1.8	0.5	0.2	0.5	0.0	0.0	0.1	0.1	0.2
Boise City, ID	6.6	1.5	2.6	1.1	0.0	0.3	0.3	0.3	0.3
Boston, MA	19.7	6.4	0.2	3.1	3.5	1.7	2.5	1.8	0.4
Boulder, CO	10.0	3.4	2.0	2.5	0.1	0.4	0.7	0.3	0.5
Cape Coral, FL	17.9	1.4	1.7	1.9	7.0	2.4	2.2	0.2	1.0
Cedar Rapids, IA	4.5	1.8	0.5	0.4	0.1	0.2	0.1	1.3	0.1
Charleston, SC	6.3	1.5	1.1	1.1	0.4	0.7	1.0	0.3	0.2
Charlotte, NC	11.4	3.2	2.0	1.2	0.7	1.8	1.2	1.0	0.2
Chicago, IL	18.3	5.4	6.5	3.7	0.3	0.6	0.8	0.7	0.2
Cincinnati, OH	5.7	2.3	0.5	0.7	0.2	0.6	0.2	0.9	0.2
Clarksville, TN	5.4	1.6	0.9	0.8	0.4	0.4	0.4	0.6	0.2
Cleveland, OH	5.8	2.2	0.3	2.0	0.2	0.2	0.3	0.5	0.2
College Station, TX	11.7	3.8	4.9	0.7	0.2	0.9	0.7	0.4	0.1
Colorado Springs, CO	6.7	1.8	1.5	1.4	0.3	0.5	0.4	0.4	0.3
Columbia, MO	5.8	3.4	0.6	0.4	0.2	0.1	0.3	0.7	0.0
Columbia, SC	5.6	1.8	1.0	0.7	0.5	0.7	0.5	0.3	0.1
Columbus, OH	9.5	3.8	0.8	0.7	0.4	0.5	0.4	2.7	0.1
Dallas, TX	19.0	6.0	7.4	0.8	0.3	1.7	0.8	1.7	0.2
Davenport, IA	5.4	1.8	1.7	0.4	0.1	0.1	0.1	1.1	0.1
Denver, CO	12.1	3.1	4.5	1.4	0.2	0.5	0.8	1.2	0.3
Des Moines, IA	8.6	3.1	1.6	1.0	0.1	0.8	0.3	1.6	0.1
Detroit, MI	10.3	6.0	0.8	1.9	0.2	0.2	0.2	0.4	0.5
Durham, NC	13.2	3.7	2.7	1.6	0.5	2.4	0.8	1.1	0.2
El Paso, TX	23.1	0.9	20.6	0.5	0.2	0.4	0.2	0.3	0.1
Eugene, OR	5.4	1.7	1.6	0.8	0.1	0.2	0.1	0.3	0.4
Fargo, ND	6.9	2.4	0.2	0.5	0.1	0.0	0.1	3.2	0.3
Fort Collins, CO	5.4	1.6	1.4	1.1	0.1	0.3	0.4	0.2	0.2
Fort Wayne, IN	6.9	3.3	1.4	0.5	0.1	0.7	0.2	0.4	0.2
Fort Worth, TX	19.0	6.0	7.4	0.8	0.3	1.7	0.8	1.7	0.2
Gainesville, FL	10.2	3.7	0.5	1.5	1.3	0.6	1.7	0.5	0.4
Green Bay, WI	4.8	1.5	1.9	0.5	0.1	0.3	0.2	0.2	0.1
Greensboro, NC	9.5	2.9	2.3	0.7	0.4	0.7	0.5	1.7	0.1
Honolulu, HI	19.6	15.7	0.2	0.7	0.1	0.1	0.2	0.1	0.3
Houston, TX	23.8	6.2	8.0	1.0	1.0	3.9	1.8	1.6	0.3
Huntsville, AL	5.4	1.8	1.1	0.8	0.4	0.4	0.3	0.3	0.2
Indianapolis, IN	8.4	2.8	1.8	0.6	0.4	0.7	0.5	1.5	0.1
Jacksonville, FL	10.0	3.2	0.5	1.7	1.8	0.6	1.4	0.5	0.2
Kansas City, MO	7.2	2.2	2.0	0.6	0.3	0.8	0.3	0.8	0.1
Lafayette, LA	3.8	1.2	0.5	0.2	0.2	1.0	0.4	0.1	0.0
Las Vegas, NV	21.7	7.4	7.3	1.6	1.3	1.8	0.9	0.9	0.4
Lexington, KY	8.2	2.6	1.8	0.9	0.3	0.7	0.4	1.3	0.2
Lincoln, NE	8.1	4.3	1.1	0.8	0.3	0.5	0.3	0.7	0.1
Little Rock, AR	4.6	1.3	1.4	0.4	0.1	0.9	0.2	0.2	0.1
Los Angeles, CA	32.5	13.0	11.1	1.7	0.3	4.3	1.0	0.6	0.3
Louisville, KY	6.7	1.9	0.9	0.6	1.5	0.4	0.3	1.0	0.1
Madison, WI	7.6	3.3	1.3	1.0	0.1	0.2	0.8	0.6	0.2
Manchester, NH	10.4	3.4	0.4	1.7	1.4	0.8	0.9	0.9	0.8

Table continued on following page.

Appendix A: Comparative Statistics

Metro Area	Percent of Population Born in								
	Any Foreign Country	Asia	Mexico	Europe	Caribbean	Central America[1]	South America	Africa	Canada
McAllen, TX	26.0	0.8	24.1	0.1	0.1	0.5	0.2	0.1	0.1
Memphis, TN	6.1	1.7	1.6	0.4	0.2	1.0	0.4	0.6	0.1
Miami, FL	41.9	2.2	1.1	2.4	20.6	4.3	10.2	0.4	0.5
Midland, TX	13.0	1.9	7.2	0.3	0.9	0.4	0.9	0.8	0.5
Milwaukee, WI	7.6	2.7	2.4	1.1	0.2	0.2	0.3	0.6	0.1
Minneapolis, MN	10.7	4.0	1.2	1.0	0.2	0.4	0.6	3.1	0.2
Nashville, TN	9.4	2.4	2.1	0.7	0.4	1.6	0.5	1.4	0.3
New Orleans, LA	9.5	2.4	0.6	0.5	1.1	3.9	0.5	0.4	0.1
New York, NY	29.8	8.9	1.4	4.2	6.8	2.0	4.7	1.5	0.3
Oklahoma City, OK	8.2	2.3	3.4	0.5	0.1	0.8	0.4	0.5	0.2
Omaha, NE	7.9	2.6	2.4	0.6	0.2	0.9	0.3	1.0	0.1
Orlando, FL	20.3	3.1	0.9	1.6	5.9	1.2	6.8	0.6	0.3
Philadelphia, PA	11.5	4.7	0.8	1.8	1.5	0.5	0.8	1.2	0.2
Phoenix, AZ	13.9	3.3	6.6	1.3	0.3	0.6	0.4	0.7	0.6
Pittsburgh, PA	4.1	2.0	0.2	0.9	0.2	0.1	0.2	0.4	0.1
Portland, OR	12.5	5.0	3.0	2.3	0.2	0.5	0.4	0.6	0.4
Providence, RI	14.4	2.3	0.3	3.8	2.9	1.7	1.3	1.7	0.2
Provo, UT	7.7	1.0	2.5	0.5	0.2	0.6	2.0	0.3	0.3
Raleigh, NC	13.1	5.0	2.5	1.3	0.8	1.0	0.8	1.3	0.3
Reno, NV	13.4	3.6	5.5	1.1	0.2	1.6	0.4	0.3	0.3
Richmond, VA	8.7	3.2	0.7	1.0	0.5	1.8	0.7	0.8	0.1
Rochester, MN	8.8	3.5	0.8	0.9	0.1	0.2	0.4	2.7	0.2
Sacramento, CA	18.9	9.4	4.2	2.8	0.1	0.7	0.4	0.5	0.3
Saint Louis, MO	5.0	2.3	0.5	1.0	0.1	0.3	0.2	0.5	0.1
Saint Paul, MN	10.7	4.0	1.2	1.0	0.2	0.4	0.6	3.1	0.2
Salem, OR	12.0	1.5	7.4	1.0	0.1	0.8	0.2	0.3	0.2
Salt Lake City, UT	12.4	3.0	4.2	1.2	0.1	0.6	1.9	0.6	0.2
San Antonio, TX	11.8	2.2	6.8	0.6	0.3	0.8	0.5	0.4	0.1
San Diego, CA	22.5	8.9	9.1	1.9	0.2	0.6	0.7	0.6	0.4
San Francisco, CA	31.6	18.0	4.9	2.8	0.2	2.7	1.2	0.9	0.5
San Jose, CA	40.3	27.1	6.5	3.0	0.1	1.0	1.1	0.7	0.5
Santa Rosa, CA	16.6	3.1	9.1	1.8	0.1	1.0	0.5	0.4	0.4
Savannah, GA	6.9	2.1	1.1	0.9	0.8	0.6	0.7	0.5	0.2
Seattle, WA	20.4	11.0	2.4	2.8	0.2	0.6	0.7	1.7	0.7
Sioux Falls, SD	6.7	1.5	0.5	0.9	0.1	1.2	0.1	2.2	0.1
Tampa, FL	15.0	2.9	1.2	2.2	4.3	0.8	2.4	0.5	0.6
Tucson, AZ	11.9	2.3	6.6	1.3	0.2	0.3	0.3	0.6	0.3
Tulsa, OK	7.2	2.0	2.9	0.6	0.2	0.7	0.4	0.4	0.1
Virginia Beach, VA	6.8	2.9	0.4	1.1	0.6	0.6	0.4	0.5	0.2
Washington, DC	24.0	8.4	0.9	1.8	1.1	5.2	2.5	3.8	0.2
Wichita, KS	7.4	2.6	3.1	0.5	0.1	0.4	0.3	0.4	0.1
Wilmington, NC	4.9	0.9	1.2	1.0	0.1	0.7	0.7	0.2	0.2
Winston-Salem, NC	7.3	1.4	2.8	0.7	0.3	1.0	0.7	0.3	0.1
U.S.	13.9	4.3	3.3	1.4	1.4	1.2	1.2	0.8	0.2

Note: Figures cover the Metropolitan Statistical Area (MSA); (1) Excludes Mexico
Source: U.S. Census Bureau, 2019-2023 American Community Survey 5-Year Estimates

Marital Status: City

City	Never Married	Now Married[1]	Separated	Widowed	Divorced
Albuquerque, NM	38.6	39.4	1.5	5.5	15.1
Anchorage, AK	34.6	47.7	1.9	3.5	12.2
Ann Arbor, MI	55.4	35.4	0.6	2.3	6.3
Athens, GA	53.9	31.2	1.3	4.3	9.3
Atlanta, GA	55.0	28.9	1.5	4.1	10.5
Austin, TX	44.0	41.7	1.3	3.0	9.9
Baltimore, MD	52.7	27.1	2.9	5.9	11.4
Billings, MT	31.9	47.2	1.0	5.6	14.3
Boise City, ID	35.2	46.8	1.0	4.3	12.7
Boston, MA	55.7	31.0	2.2	3.8	7.4
Boulder, CO	57.8	30.4	0.5	2.2	9.0
Cape Coral, FL	24.7	52.6	1.5	7.8	13.4
Cedar Rapids, IA	36.8	44.3	1.5	5.0	12.3
Charleston, SC	39.4	44.3	1.6	4.8	10.0
Charlotte, NC	42.9	41.1	2.1	3.8	10.1
Chicago, IL	49.1	35.6	2.2	5.0	8.1
Cincinnati, OH	53.4	29.8	1.8	4.5	10.6
Clarksville, TN	30.0	50.9	2.2	4.2	12.7
Cleveland, OH	53.7	23.7	2.8	6.1	13.7
College Station, TX	60.3	31.2	1.2	2.4	5.0
Colorado Springs, CO	30.7	50.8	1.5	4.5	12.5
Columbia, MO	49.8	37.9	1.0	3.4	8.0
Columbia, SC	55.8	29.7	2.0	3.9	8.6
Columbus, OH	45.8	36.3	2.0	4.2	11.7
Dallas, TX	43.0	40.2	2.5	4.0	10.2
Davenport, IA	37.3	44.0	1.0	5.6	12.0
Denver, CO	44.4	39.3	1.3	3.4	11.5
Des Moines, IA	40.8	38.8	2.3	5.7	12.5
Detroit, MI	57.0	22.0	2.9	6.3	11.9
Durham, NC	44.1	40.5	1.8	3.7	9.8
El Paso, TX	35.5	44.8	3.3	5.6	10.9
Eugene, OR	44.6	37.5	1.3	4.2	12.4
Fargo, ND	44.3	41.2	1.0	3.8	9.6
Fort Collins, CO	46.5	41.1	0.7	3.0	8.8
Fort Wayne, IN	37.2	42.9	1.5	5.9	12.5
Fort Worth, TX	35.8	46.5	2.2	4.6	10.7
Gainesville, FL	62.8	24.3	1.3	2.9	8.8
Green Bay, WI	39.4	41.0	1.1	4.9	13.5
Greensboro, NC	45.1	36.4	2.4	5.8	10.3
Honolulu, HI	38.0	44.0	1.2	6.6	10.1
Houston, TX	42.2	40.5	2.8	4.4	10.0
Huntsville, AL	37.9	42.7	1.9	6.0	11.6
Indianapolis, IN	41.1	40.4	1.7	4.8	12.0
Jacksonville, FL	36.2	42.5	2.1	5.5	13.6
Kansas City, MO	39.5	40.6	1.9	4.8	13.2
Lafayette, LA	40.0	42.8	2.2	5.1	9.9
Las Vegas, NV	36.4	42.8	1.8	5.3	13.5
Lexington, KY	38.8	43.1	1.4	4.6	12.0
Lincoln, NE	39.6	45.4	0.8	4.2	10.0
Little Rock, AR	38.6	41.0	1.5	5.5	13.4
Los Angeles, CA	46.5	38.6	2.3	4.5	8.0
Louisville, KY	37.2	41.9	2.0	6.1	12.8
Madison, WI	50.7	37.5	0.8	3.0	8.0
Manchester, NH	39.0	39.6	1.6	5.5	14.3
McAllen, TX	35.1	48.8	2.1	5.6	8.4
Memphis, TN	48.1	30.9	3.3	5.9	11.7

Table continued on following page.

City	Never Married	Now Married[1]	Separated	Widowed	Divorced
Miami, FL	40.4	37.0	3.3	5.7	13.5
Midland, TX	29.3	54.5	1.9	4.8	9.6
Milwaukee, WI	54.7	29.2	1.9	4.3	9.9
Minneapolis, MN	52.0	33.9	1.2	2.9	9.9
Nashville, TN	41.6	41.4	1.7	4.3	11.0
New Orleans, LA	49.2	30.8	2.3	5.2	12.5
New York, NY	44.0	39.8	2.8	5.2	8.2
Oklahoma City, OK	34.2	46.4	2.1	5.2	12.2
Omaha, NE	37.9	45.3	1.2	4.7	11.0
Orlando, FL	42.9	38.6	2.4	3.7	12.5
Philadelphia, PA	50.7	31.9	2.8	5.5	9.1
Phoenix, AZ	40.2	42.0	1.9	4.0	11.9
Pittsburgh, PA	54.4	30.6	1.7	5.0	8.3
Portland, OR	42.9	39.8	1.3	3.5	12.6
Providence, RI	53.4	32.1	2.0	4.1	8.5
Provo, UT	49.3	43.5	0.7	2.2	4.3
Raleigh, NC	43.1	40.5	1.9	3.9	10.6
Reno, NV	37.7	41.7	1.5	4.9	14.2
Richmond, VA	51.4	30.0	2.7	4.6	11.2
Rochester, MN	34.2	51.3	0.9	4.8	8.8
Sacramento, CA	41.5	40.8	2.3	4.7	10.7
Saint Louis, MO	49.7	30.2	2.7	5.3	12.2
Saint Paul, MN	46.4	37.8	1.5	3.6	10.6
Salem, OR	35.6	44.6	1.4	5.3	13.1
Salt Lake City, UT	45.4	39.1	1.6	2.9	10.9
San Antonio, TX	39.1	40.8	2.9	5.3	12.0
San Diego, CA	40.5	44.7	1.6	3.9	9.2
San Francisco, CA	45.6	40.7	1.4	4.5	7.8
San Jose, CA	37.2	49.3	1.6	4.4	7.5
Santa Rosa, CA	34.6	45.9	2.0	5.6	12.0
Savannah, GA	48.6	31.4	2.6	5.4	12.0
Seattle, WA	46.1	40.3	1.1	3.0	9.5
Sioux Falls, SD	34.5	48.4	1.4	4.3	11.4
Tampa, FL	43.1	38.1	2.2	4.7	11.8
Tucson, AZ	42.9	36.0	1.8	5.2	14.1
Tulsa, OK	36.5	41.7	2.4	5.5	14.0
Virginia Beach, VA	31.2	50.6	2.0	5.0	11.2
Washington, DC	55.2	31.5	1.4	3.4	8.5
Wichita, KS	35.0	45.2	1.8	5.2	12.8
Wilmington, NC	42.2	38.8	2.3	5.3	11.4
Winston-Salem, NC	42.5	39.6	2.4	5.2	10.3
U.S.	34.1	47.9	1.7	5.6	10.7

Note: Figures are percentages and cover the population 15 years of age and older; (1) Excludes separated
Source: U.S. Census Bureau, 2019-2023 American Community Survey 5-Year Estimates

Marital Status: Metro Area

Metro Area	Never Married	Now Married[1]	Separated	Widowed	Divorced
Albuquerque, NM	36.1	43.1	1.4	5.4	13.9
Anchorage, AK	33.3	49.3	1.8	3.7	11.9
Ann Arbor, MI	42.3	44.6	0.9	3.8	8.4
Athens, GA	43.0	41.4	1.3	4.7	9.5
Atlanta, GA	36.2	47.1	1.7	4.4	10.6
Austin, TX	35.9	49.4	1.3	3.5	9.8
Baltimore, MD	36.4	46.2	1.8	5.7	9.9
Billings, MT	28.7	51.5	1.0	5.5	13.3
Boise City, ID	28.9	54.0	1.0	4.4	11.8
Boston, MA	37.5	47.6	1.5	4.9	8.6
Boulder, CO	39.2	45.4	0.7	3.7	11.1
Cape Coral, FL	26.5	51.8	1.5	7.8	12.3
Cedar Rapids, IA	30.9	51.1	1.3	5.2	11.5
Charleston, SC	33.2	48.9	2.0	5.4	10.5
Charlotte, NC	33.6	49.4	2.0	4.9	10.0
Chicago, IL	37.6	46.7	1.6	5.3	8.8
Cincinnati, OH	33.2	49.0	1.3	5.5	11.0
Clarksville, TN	29.2	51.6	1.9	5.2	12.0
Cleveland, OH	35.7	44.2	1.5	6.4	12.1
College Station, TX	46.7	39.5	1.6	4.3	7.9
Colorado Springs, CO	29.4	53.8	1.3	4.1	11.5
Columbia, MO	41.1	44.4	1.1	4.3	9.2
Columbia, SC	36.0	45.7	2.3	5.7	10.2
Columbus, OH	35.0	47.4	1.6	4.8	11.2
Dallas, TX	33.4	50.6	1.7	4.2	10.0
Davenport, IA	31.1	50.1	1.2	6.2	11.5
Denver, CO	34.5	49.4	1.3	3.7	11.0
Des Moines, IA	31.7	51.3	1.3	5.0	10.7
Detroit, MI	35.9	45.7	1.2	6.0	11.2
Durham, NC	38.3	46.2	1.7	4.5	9.3
El Paso, TX	35.5	45.7	3.2	5.4	10.2
Eugene, OR	35.8	44.3	1.3	5.4	13.2
Fargo, ND	38.8	47.3	0.9	3.9	9.1
Fort Collins, CO	35.3	50.3	0.8	3.9	9.7
Fort Wayne, IN	31.8	49.9	1.3	5.5	11.5
Fort Worth, TX	33.4	50.6	1.7	4.2	10.0
Gainesville, FL	43.5	39.6	1.3	5.1	10.4
Green Bay, WI	31.8	51.2	0.6	5.2	11.1
Greensboro, NC	35.2	45.3	2.3	6.2	11.0
Honolulu, HI	34.6	49.5	1.1	6.0	8.7
Houston, TX	34.3	50.1	2.1	4.3	9.2
Huntsville, AL	30.6	51.3	1.4	5.5	11.2
Indianapolis, IN	32.7	49.7	1.2	4.9	11.5
Jacksonville, FL	31.4	48.4	1.8	5.6	12.7
Kansas City, MO	31.3	50.3	1.5	5.1	11.8
Lafayette, LA	33.9	47.8	2.0	5.4	10.9
Las Vegas, NV	35.6	44.3	2.0	5.1	13.1
Lexington, KY	34.4	46.7	1.5	5.1	12.3
Lincoln, NE	37.2	48.2	0.8	4.2	9.6
Little Rock, AR	31.5	48.0	1.7	5.9	12.9
Los Angeles, CA	40.7	44.3	2.0	4.7	8.3
Louisville, KY	31.8	47.6	1.7	6.0	12.9
Madison, WI	37.6	48.1	0.7	4.1	9.5
Manchester, NH	32.0	49.8	1.1	5.2	11.8
McAllen, TX	36.7	47.8	3.0	4.9	7.6
Memphis, TN	38.5	42.0	2.5	5.9	11.1

Table continued on following page.

Metro Area	Never Married	Now Married[1]	Separated	Widowed	Divorced
Miami, FL	34.0	44.7	2.4	6.1	12.8
Midland, TX	28.6	55.2	1.6	4.9	9.8
Milwaukee, WI	37.7	45.9	1.2	5.1	10.1
Minneapolis, MN	34.1	50.7	0.9	4.3	10.0
Nashville, TN	32.8	50.3	1.4	4.9	10.6
New Orleans, LA	40.3	38.9	2.3	6.0	12.4
New York, NY	38.3	46.0	2.1	5.4	8.1
Oklahoma City, OK	32.3	48.6	1.8	5.5	11.9
Omaha, NE	32.4	51.2	1.1	4.6	10.8
Orlando, FL	35.1	47.0	1.8	4.9	11.2
Philadelphia, PA	37.7	45.7	1.8	5.6	9.1
Phoenix, AZ	34.3	47.9	1.4	4.9	11.5
Pittsburgh, PA	33.1	48.4	1.5	7.0	10.0
Portland, OR	33.7	48.9	1.3	4.3	11.8
Providence, RI	36.7	45.0	1.5	5.8	11.0
Provo, UT	33.4	57.7	0.8	2.6	5.5
Raleigh, NC	32.4	52.4	1.8	4.2	9.3
Reno, NV	32.6	47.1	1.4	5.1	13.8
Richmond, VA	35.0	47.0	2.0	5.5	10.4
Rochester, MN	29.3	55.9	0.7	4.9	9.1
Sacramento, CA	34.2	48.5	1.8	4.9	10.5
Saint Louis, MO	32.9	48.4	1.6	5.8	11.2
Saint Paul, MN	34.1	50.7	0.9	4.3	10.0
Salem, OR	32.4	48.5	1.6	5.4	12.1
Salt Lake City, UT	33.6	51.2	1.5	3.6	10.2
San Antonio, TX	34.3	47.2	2.3	5.1	11.1
San Diego, CA	36.3	48.1	1.6	4.4	9.6
San Francisco, CA	36.8	48.8	1.4	4.6	8.4
San Jose, CA	35.5	51.7	1.4	4.2	7.1
Santa Rosa, CA	32.7	48.5	1.4	5.2	12.2
Savannah, GA	35.8	45.9	2.1	5.1	11.2
Seattle, WA	33.8	50.4	1.3	4.0	10.5
Sioux Falls, SD	30.7	53.1	1.1	4.3	10.8
Tampa, FL	32.1	46.3	1.8	6.8	13.1
Tucson, AZ	35.1	44.8	1.5	5.8	12.9
Tulsa, OK	29.9	49.5	1.8	6.1	12.7
Virginia Beach, VA	33.7	47.7	2.2	5.5	10.8
Washington, DC	36.7	48.8	1.6	4.2	8.7
Wichita, KS	31.2	50.0	1.4	5.4	12.0
Wilmington, NC	28.5	52.5	1.9	6.2	10.9
Winston-Salem, NC	31.7	48.8	2.2	6.3	11.1
U.S.	34.1	47.9	1.7	5.6	10.7

Note: Figures are percentages and cover the population 15 years of age and older; Figures cover the Metropolitan Statistical Area (MSA); (1) Excludes separated
Source: U.S. Census Bureau, 2019-2023 American Community Survey 5-Year Estimates

Disability by Age: City

City	All Ages	Under 18 Years Old	18 to 64 Years Old	65 Years and Over
Albuquerque, NM	15.2	4.8	13.2	35.2
Anchorage, AK	12.2	4.9	10.7	33.7
Ann Arbor, MI	8.1	4.7	6.1	23.8
Athens, GA	12.2	5.9	10.1	34.0
Atlanta, GA	11.6	5.4	9.6	32.3
Austin, TX	9.5	3.8	8.4	28.3
Baltimore, MD	16.5	5.7	14.6	40.0
Billings, MT	14.5	4.4	11.8	36.3
Boise City, ID	12.1	5.3	10.2	29.4
Boston, MA	12.1	5.8	9.1	37.2
Boulder, CO	7.5	2.9	6.1	20.9
Cape Coral, FL	14.0	3.8	10.0	30.5
Cedar Rapids, IA	11.6	4.9	10.0	27.3
Charleston, SC	9.7	3.2	6.7	29.6
Charlotte, NC	8.3	2.8	7.0	28.3
Chicago, IL	11.9	3.8	9.6	35.4
Cincinnati, OH	13.6	6.0	12.6	31.7
Clarksville, TN	14.8	5.7	15.1	41.8
Cleveland, OH	19.9	9.8	18.5	40.7
College Station, TX	8.2	6.2	6.8	29.3
Colorado Springs, CO	13.2	5.7	11.9	30.1
Columbia, MO	11.9	5.4	10.5	32.2
Columbia, SC	12.7	3.9	10.7	38.0
Columbus, OH	12.2	5.3	10.9	34.7
Dallas, TX	11.4	4.7	9.8	34.9
Davenport, IA	13.9	5.5	11.8	33.3
Denver, CO	10.1	3.3	8.3	30.7
Des Moines, IA	14.3	5.8	13.4	35.2
Detroit, MI	19.6	6.0	19.7	42.6
Durham, NC	9.9	3.6	8.0	29.6
El Paso, TX	14.3	5.5	12.0	40.2
Eugene, OR	15.1	4.8	13.2	31.7
Fargo, ND	11.4	5.4	9.0	32.6
Fort Collins, CO	8.9	3.0	7.7	24.0
Fort Wayne, IN	13.6	5.3	12.5	32.5
Fort Worth, TX	10.2	3.7	9.0	34.4
Gainesville, FL	10.5	3.9	8.3	33.6
Green Bay, WI	15.0	7.1	13.9	34.3
Greensboro, NC	11.8	5.4	9.9	31.4
Honolulu, HI	12.5	3.9	7.9	32.1
Houston, TX	11.0	4.7	8.9	35.1
Huntsville, AL	14.3	5.4	11.8	34.8
Indianapolis, IN	13.5	5.1	12.6	34.6
Jacksonville, FL	13.5	5.0	11.8	34.1
Kansas City, MO	12.8	3.7	11.6	33.3
Lafayette, LA	12.9	3.5	10.3	33.9
Las Vegas, NV	13.3	4.5	11.3	34.2
Lexington, KY	12.8	4.9	11.0	32.4
Lincoln, NE	12.0	4.8	10.6	29.5
Little Rock, AR	13.9	6.8	12.0	33.8
Los Angeles, CA	11.1	3.5	8.3	36.3
Louisville, KY	14.7	5.3	13.3	34.1
Madison, WI	9.1	4.1	7.5	24.6
Manchester, NH	13.6	7.4	11.5	31.1
McAllen, TX	13.0	6.1	9.4	43.8

Table continued on following page.

City	All Ages	Under 18 Years Old	18 to 64 Years Old	65 Years and Over
Memphis, TN	13.6	4.6	12.5	34.6
Miami, FL	11.5	3.7	7.0	38.2
Midland, TX	10.4	3.4	8.7	40.3
Milwaukee, WI	13.2	4.8	12.5	35.3
Minneapolis, MN	11.6	4.8	10.7	30.5
Nashville, TN	11.0	4.5	8.8	33.8
New Orleans, LA	14.1	5.7	11.6	34.2
New York, NY	11.7	3.9	8.5	34.6
Oklahoma City, OK	13.9	5.6	12.5	36.6
Omaha, NE	11.1	3.8	9.8	30.2
Orlando, FL	10.3	5.2	8.3	33.4
Philadelphia, PA	17.4	7.7	15.6	40.8
Phoenix, AZ	11.5	4.6	10.2	32.5
Pittsburgh, PA	14.2	7.4	11.5	34.3
Portland, OR	13.2	4.9	10.9	34.3
Providence, RI	13.7	6.0	12.4	37.3
Provo, UT	10.2	4.2	8.9	42.2
Raleigh, NC	9.6	4.4	7.9	29.1
Reno, NV	12.1	4.0	9.8	31.2
Richmond, VA	14.0	7.0	12.0	33.1
Rochester, MN	10.1	3.8	7.8	28.9
Sacramento, CA	12.4	4.0	10.1	35.8
Saint Louis, MO	16.6	6.5	14.4	39.0
Saint Paul, MN	12.5	4.7	11.9	31.3
Salem, OR	15.4	5.9	13.7	36.8
Salt Lake City, UT	12.1	5.0	9.9	34.9
San Antonio, TX	15.5	6.7	13.5	41.8
San Diego, CA	10.0	3.4	7.3	31.2
San Francisco, CA	11.2	2.7	7.3	34.1
San Jose, CA	9.6	3.6	6.3	34.3
Santa Rosa, CA	12.7	4.3	10.3	30.0
Savannah, GA	15.9	7.0	13.5	40.7
Seattle, WA	10.0	2.8	8.0	30.3
Sioux Falls, SD	10.0	3.4	8.7	28.4
Tampa, FL	11.9	4.1	9.3	38.0
Tucson, AZ	15.5	6.1	13.2	36.8
Tulsa, OK	14.4	5.3	13.3	34.2
Virginia Beach, VA	11.7	4.4	10.1	28.7
Washington, DC	11.0	4.5	8.8	32.3
Wichita, KS	14.9	5.9	13.6	34.7
Wilmington, NC	12.9	3.7	10.4	31.1
Winston-Salem, NC	12.6	4.7	10.9	32.8
U.S.	13.0	4.7	10.7	32.9

Note: Figures show percent of the civilian noninstitutionalized population that reported having a disability. Disability status is determined from from six types of difficulty: vision, hearing, cognitive, ambulatory, self-care, and independent living. For children under 5 years old, hearing and vision difficulty are used to determine disability status. For children between the ages of 5 and 14, disability status is determined from hearing, vision, cognitive, ambulatory, and self-care difficulties. For people aged 15 years and older, they are considered to have a disability if they have difficulty with any one of the six difficulty types.
Source: U.S. Census Bureau, 2019-2023 American Community Survey 5-Year Estimates

Disability by Age: Metro Area

Metro Area	All Ages	Under 18 Years Old	18 to 64 Years Old	65 Years and Over
Albuquerque, NM	16.1	4.7	14.1	36.3
Anchorage, AK	12.6	4.8	11.3	34.0
Ann Arbor, MI	10.3	4.1	8.3	26.9
Athens, GA	12.8	4.9	11.0	32.7
Atlanta, GA	10.8	4.5	9.0	31.3
Austin, TX	10.0	4.3	8.5	29.1
Baltimore, MD	12.0	4.5	9.8	30.7
Billings, MT	14.3	4.4	11.6	35.1
Boise City, ID	12.7	4.9	11.0	31.0
Boston, MA	10.9	4.5	8.2	29.6
Boulder, CO	8.8	2.9	6.9	23.8
Cape Coral, FL	13.7	4.0	9.6	27.1
Cedar Rapids, IA	11.5	5.0	9.5	27.3
Charleston, SC	12.1	4.5	9.8	31.5
Charlotte, NC	10.6	3.4	8.7	31.0
Chicago, IL	10.7	3.6	8.4	30.2
Cincinnati, OH	12.7	5.1	10.8	31.5
Clarksville, TN	16.4	6.5	16.1	41.9
Cleveland, OH	14.6	5.6	12.2	32.1
College Station, TX	10.9	5.5	8.8	33.8
Colorado Springs, CO	12.5	5.4	11.3	29.7
Columbia, MO	13.0	5.3	11.5	31.9
Columbia, SC	14.3	5.1	12.3	35.3
Columbus, OH	12.1	5.0	10.4	32.3
Dallas, TX	10.1	4.0	8.5	32.0
Davenport, IA	13.5	5.7	10.9	30.9
Denver, CO	10.2	3.7	8.4	29.1
Des Moines, IA	10.8	3.8	9.3	29.8
Detroit, MI	14.0	4.6	11.9	33.5
Durham, NC	10.4	3.7	8.1	28.1
El Paso, TX	13.9	5.5	11.7	41.5
Eugene, OR	17.1	6.2	15.0	33.4
Fargo, ND	11.0	4.1	9.3	32.1
Fort Collins, CO	10.3	3.3	8.2	26.6
Fort Wayne, IN	12.4	4.7	11.1	30.4
Fort Worth, TX	10.1	4.0	8.5	32.0
Gainesville, FL	13.3	5.4	10.2	34.6
Green Bay, WI	12.0	4.4	10.6	27.3
Greensboro, NC	13.4	4.9	11.2	32.9
Honolulu, HI	12.2	3.6	8.5	32.8
Houston, TX	10.4	4.3	8.6	32.8
Huntsville, AL	13.5	4.5	11.5	34.9
Indianapolis, IN	12.4	5.0	10.9	32.1
Jacksonville, FL	13.1	4.8	11.1	31.8
Kansas City, MO	12.0	4.4	10.3	31.1
Lafayette, LA	14.5	4.7	12.9	37.2
Las Vegas, NV	13.0	4.4	10.7	34.3
Lexington, KY	13.9	5.4	12.2	33.8
Lincoln, NE	11.8	4.5	10.2	29.6
Little Rock, AR	15.5	5.7	13.6	37.4
Los Angeles, CA	10.5	3.5	7.7	32.8
Louisville, KY	14.4	5.0	12.5	34.4
Madison, WI	9.4	3.8	7.6	24.3
Manchester, NH	11.7	4.7	9.6	28.3
McAllen, TX	12.5	5.5	9.7	45.5

Table continued on following page.

Metro Area	All Ages	Under 18 Years Old	18 to 64 Years Old	65 Years and Over
Memphis, TN	13.5	5.0	12.1	34.6
Miami, FL	11.0	4.0	7.2	30.9
Midland, TX	10.9	3.5	9.3	40.7
Milwaukee, WI	11.3	4.0	9.4	28.9
Minneapolis, MN	10.4	4.0	8.6	27.9
Nashville, TN	11.4	4.2	9.4	32.9
New Orleans, LA	15.3	6.1	12.9	36.3
New York, NY	10.6	3.5	7.7	30.9
Oklahoma City, OK	14.7	5.2	13.0	38.3
Omaha, NE	11.2	3.8	9.7	31.0
Orlando, FL	12.3	5.6	9.5	33.1
Philadelphia, PA	13.2	5.5	11.0	31.5
Phoenix, AZ	12.3	4.9	10.1	31.1
Pittsburgh, PA	14.7	5.7	11.7	31.9
Portland, OR	12.9	4.5	10.8	32.6
Providence, RI	13.9	5.6	11.7	31.4
Provo, UT	8.7	3.9	8.3	31.3
Raleigh, NC	10.0	3.9	8.3	30.1
Reno, NV	13.0	4.7	10.4	31.7
Richmond, VA	12.8	5.3	10.7	30.4
Rochester, MN	10.1	3.6	7.8	27.2
Sacramento, CA	12.3	4.0	9.6	33.8
Saint Louis, MO	13.3	4.7	11.2	32.1
Saint Paul, MN	10.4	4.0	8.6	27.9
Salem, OR	15.8	5.8	13.8	36.9
Salt Lake City, UT	10.2	4.4	9.1	29.8
San Antonio, TX	14.6	6.3	12.6	39.1
San Diego, CA	10.7	3.6	8.2	31.3
San Francisco, CA	10.3	3.2	7.3	30.4
San Jose, CA	8.8	3.1	5.7	31.3
Santa Rosa, CA	12.1	4.0	9.1	28.2
Savannah, GA	14.5	5.3	12.8	35.7
Seattle, WA	11.4	4.2	9.2	32.6
Sioux Falls, SD	9.9	3.3	8.5	28.5
Tampa, FL	14.4	5.3	11.1	33.5
Tucson, AZ	15.1	5.6	12.2	32.3
Tulsa, OK	15.0	5.2	13.4	37.0
Virginia Beach, VA	13.6	5.4	11.6	32.5
Washington, DC	9.1	3.5	7.0	27.9
Wichita, KS	14.6	5.6	13.0	35.1
Wilmington, NC	13.5	5.5	10.7	26.6
Winston-Salem, NC	14.2	4.9	12.0	33.1
U.S.	13.0	4.7	10.7	32.9

Note: Figures show percent of the civilian noninstitutionalized population that reported having a disability. Disability status is determined from from six types of difficulty: vision, hearing, cognitive, ambulatory, self-care, and independent living. For children under 5 years old, hearing and vision difficulty are used to determine disability status. For children between the ages of 5 and 14, disability status is determined from hearing, vision, cognitive, ambulatory, and self-care difficulties. For people aged 15 years and older, they are considered to have a disability if they have difficulty with any one of the six difficulty types; Figures cover the Metropolitan Statistical Area (MSA)
Source: U.S. Census Bureau, 2019-2023 American Community Survey 5-Year Estimates

Religious Groups by Family

Metro Area	Catholic	Baptist	Methodist	LDS[1]	Pentecostal	Lutheran	Islam	Adventist	Other
Albuquerque, NM	32.6	3.2	0.9	2.7	1.7	0.4	0.7	1.5	10.8
Anchorage, AK	4.9	3.4	1.0	5.1	1.7	1.5	0.1	1.7	16.3
Ann Arbor, MI	9.7	2.0	2.4	0.8	1.5	2.3	2.2	0.9	10.0
Athens, GA	6.4	12.8	5.7	1.0	2.4	0.3	0.2	1.3	7.9
Atlanta, GA	10.7	14.7	6.7	0.8	2.0	0.4	1.9	1.9	12.4
Austin, TX	18.8	6.5	2.2	1.3	0.7	1.1	1.0	1.0	9.9
Baltimore, MD	12.4	3.2	4.4	0.6	1.2	1.4	3.3	1.2	11.7
Billings, MT	7.4	1.9	1.1	5.2	3.6	4.9	n/a	1.2	7.8
Boise City, ID	13.0	0.8	2.5	15.0	1.6	0.8	0.3	1.7	10.0
Boston, MA	37.0	1.0	0.7	0.5	0.7	0.2	2.2	0.9	7.1
Boulder, CO	16.0	0.3	0.7	0.7	0.5	1.7	0.4	0.9	15.2
Cape Coral, FL	18.8	2.5	1.7	0.6	3.0	0.7	0.2	2.0	12.2
Cedar Rapids, IA	16.8	1.0	5.3	1.0	1.3	8.1	1.3	0.6	9.6
Charleston, SC	11.5	7.7	8.0	0.8	1.9	0.7	0.2	1.0	12.8
Charlotte, NC	12.1	13.9	7.0	0.7	2.2	1.1	1.7	1.4	15.9
Chicago, IL	28.6	3.4	1.4	0.3	1.5	2.1	4.7	1.1	9.2
Cincinnati, OH	17.0	5.7	2.3	0.6	1.5	0.8	1.1	0.7	21.8
Clarksville, TN	4.6	23.2	4.4	1.4	3.2	0.5	0.1	0.8	12.4
Cleveland, OH	26.1	4.3	2.3	0.4	1.5	1.8	1.1	1.3	16.8
College Station, TX	17.2	10.6	4.3	1.7	0.5	1.1	0.6	0.5	6.8
Colorado Springs, CO	16.4	2.6	1.3	3.0	1.0	1.2	0.1	1.0	16.2
Columbia, MO	7.1	9.0	3.5	1.7	1.1	1.6	1.4	1.2	12.4
Columbia, SC	6.6	15.1	8.5	1.2	3.8	2.3	0.3	1.3	15.4
Columbus, OH	11.7	3.4	3.0	0.8	1.9	1.7	2.1	0.9	17.5
Dallas, TX	14.2	14.3	4.7	1.4	2.2	0.5	1.8	1.3	13.8
Davenport, IA	13.2	3.2	3.6	0.8	1.5	6.6	0.7	0.8	6.7
Denver, CO	16.1	1.5	1.0	2.1	0.6	1.4	0.3	1.1	10.4
Des Moines, IA	12.1	1.8	4.0	0.9	2.5	6.6	1.6	0.8	8.7
Detroit, MI	18.6	4.8	1.7	0.3	2.1	2.2	4.5	1.0	8.5
Durham, NC	8.5	12.3	6.5	0.9	1.3	0.3	1.5	1.1	13.7
El Paso, TX	47.9	2.5	0.4	1.2	1.1	0.2	0.1	2.1	6.9
Eugene, OR	5.6	0.7	0.5	2.8	2.5	0.8	<0.1	2.0	9.0
Fargo, ND	14.2	0.2	1.0	0.6	1.3	24.0	<0.1	0.6	8.1
Fort Collins, CO	9.9	1.2	1.3	4.0	2.7	2.5	<0.1	1.2	12.1
Fort Wayne, IN	13.1	8.1	3.9	0.4	1.1	7.1	1.0	0.9	17.6
Fort Worth, TX	14.2	14.3	4.7	1.4	2.2	0.5	1.8	1.3	13.8
Gainesville, FL	8.5	10.6	4.8	1.4	3.2	0.3	0.4	1.3	14.5
Green Bay, WI	31.8	0.3	1.4	0.5	1.1	10.8	0.4	0.9	7.0
Greensboro, NC	7.9	10.0	8.0	0.7	2.8	0.4	1.5	1.4	17.8
Honolulu, HI	18.0	1.4	0.5	4.1	2.6	0.2	<0.1	1.9	9.8
Houston, TX	18.3	13.1	3.7	1.2	1.6	0.7	1.7	1.5	13.1
Huntsville, AL	7.5	23.6	6.6	1.4	1.2	0.4	0.8	2.7	17.5
Indianapolis, IN	11.5	6.2	3.3	0.7	1.3	1.1	1.1	1.0	17.4
Jacksonville, FL	13.0	14.5	3.0	1.0	1.4	0.4	0.6	1.3	20.5
Kansas City, MO	11.3	9.1	5.0	1.6	2.7	1.7	1.0	1.0	12.1
Lafayette, LA	44.3	9.3	2.0	0.4	1.8	0.1	0.1	0.8	7.0
Las Vegas, NV	26.2	1.9	0.3	5.8	1.5	0.6	0.3	1.3	5.5
Lexington, KY	5.8	14.9	5.5	1.2	1.6	0.3	0.5	1.2	16.6
Lincoln, NE	13.2	1.0	5.7	1.2	3.1	9.1	0.1	1.8	10.0
Little Rock, AR	4.9	23.5	6.2	0.8	3.7	0.4	0.4	1.0	13.6
Los Angeles, CA	31.1	2.6	0.8	1.5	2.4	0.4	1.4	1.5	9.1
Louisville, KY	11.9	14.5	3.2	0.8	0.9	0.5	1.0	1.0	12.4
Madison, WI	14.4	0.5	2.0	0.7	0.2	9.2	1.2	0.7	8.4
Manchester, NH	16.3	0.6	0.6	0.6	0.3	0.3	0.1	0.8	8.1
McAllen, TX	46.6	2.2	0.8	1.2	1.0	0.3	0.2	3.2	6.0
Memphis, TN	4.8	26.6	6.0	0.7	5.1	0.3	1.3	1.3	18.4

Table continued on following page.

Metro Area	Catholic	Baptist	Methodist	LDS[1]	Pentecostal	Lutheran	Islam	Adventist	Other
Miami, FL	23.8	5.1	0.9	0.5	1.3	0.3	0.8	2.4	11.1
Midland, TX	15.4	25.5	2.5	2.0	1.2	0.3	0.4	1.3	16.5
Milwaukee, WI	24.5	3.0	1.0	0.4	2.8	9.1	2.8	0.9	10.7
Minneapolis, MN	19.8	0.8	1.4	0.5	2.5	10.7	2.9	0.7	7.4
Nashville, TN	6.2	16.4	4.8	0.9	1.6	0.4	0.8	1.3	19.4
New Orleans, LA	42.1	9.3	2.5	0.5	2.1	0.5	1.4	1.0	8.0
New York, NY	32.5	1.7	1.2	0.3	0.9	0.5	4.5	1.4	10.6
Oklahoma City, OK	10.0	16.6	6.2	1.3	3.9	0.6	0.6	0.9	21.4
Omaha, NE	19.9	2.8	2.8	1.6	1.0	6.1	0.2	1.0	9.0
Orlando, FL	17.6	5.7	2.1	0.9	2.7	0.6	1.3	2.8	14.6
Philadelphia, PA	26.8	3.3	2.4	0.3	1.0	1.2	2.6	1.0	10.5
Phoenix, AZ	22.9	1.7	0.6	6.2	1.5	1.0	1.9	1.5	9.3
Pittsburgh, PA	30.6	1.9	4.3	0.4	1.3	2.5	0.6	0.6	12.5
Portland, OR	11.8	0.8	0.6	3.3	1.4	1.1	0.2	2.0	14.4
Providence, RI	37.9	0.9	0.6	0.3	0.6	0.3	0.5	0.9	6.1
Provo, UT	4.9	0.1	<0.1	82.6	0.1	<0.1	0.3	0.3	0.4
Raleigh, NC	12.4	9.8	5.4	1.2	1.9	0.7	3.2	1.5	12.8
Reno, NV	24.4	1.4	0.5	4.0	0.9	0.5	0.3	1.4	5.3
Richmond, VA	12.3	14.2	4.8	0.9	3.2	0.5	2.1	1.2	14.8
Rochester, MN	15.6	0.4	2.8	1.5	1.9	19.3	1.0	0.7	10.1
Sacramento, CA	17.1	1.9	1.1	3.1	2.2	0.6	1.9	1.9	8.2
Saint Louis, MO	21.2	8.6	2.9	0.7	1.4	3.2	1.3	0.8	11.1
Saint Paul, MN	19.8	0.8	1.4	0.5	2.5	10.7	2.9	0.7	7.4
Salem, OR	19.5	0.5	0.6	3.8	2.9	1.2	n/a	2.5	10.7
Salt Lake City, UT	9.0	0.6	0.2	52.0	0.7	0.2	1.6	0.7	2.6
San Antonio, TX	27.3	6.4	2.1	1.4	1.6	1.1	0.5	1.5	11.0
San Diego, CA	22.9	1.5	0.6	2.1	1.0	0.6	1.5	1.9	9.4
San Francisco, CA	21.5	2.2	0.9	1.5	1.4	0.4	2.0	1.0	7.7
San Jose, CA	27.2	1.2	0.6	1.4	0.9	0.4	2.0	1.3	11.4
Santa Rosa, CA	23.5	1.1	0.5	1.4	0.5	0.5	0.2	1.8	6.9
Savannah, GA	5.5	11.9	4.8	0.8	1.5	1.1	0.2	1.4	12.3
Seattle, WA	11.0	1.0	0.7	2.6	2.8	1.2	0.6	1.4	19.8
Sioux Falls, SD	13.1	0.7	2.9	0.7	1.7	16.4	0.1	0.6	20.3
Tampa, FL	23.1	6.3	2.9	0.5	1.9	0.6	0.7	1.8	12.1
Tucson, AZ	18.9	1.9	0.6	2.8	1.3	1.1	1.0	1.4	9.7
Tulsa, OK	5.6	15.5	7.7	1.2	2.5	0.5	0.5	1.2	22.2
Virginia Beach, VA	8.3	9.5	4.8	0.7	2.0	0.5	1.0	0.9	16.1
Washington, DC	16.1	6.0	4.1	1.1	1.3	0.8	3.3	1.5	12.6
Wichita, KS	12.7	23.5	4.5	1.5	1.4	1.3	0.1	1.1	15.0
Wilmington, NC	13.2	9.9	8.1	1.0	1.0	0.7	0.7	1.4	12.6
Winston-Salem, NC	9.3	12.8	11.4	0.5	1.0	0.6	0.8	1.4	22.5
U.S.	18.7	7.3	3.0	2.0	1.8	1.7	1.3	1.3	11.6

Note: Figures are the number of adherents as a percentage of the total population; Figures cover the Metropolitan Statistical Area (MSA);
(1) Church of Jesus Christ of Latter-day Saints
Source: 2020 U.S. Religion Census, Association of Statisticians of American Religious Bodies; The Association of Religion Data Archives

Religious Groups by Tradition

Metro Area	Catholic	Evangelical Protestant	Mainline Protestant	Black Protestant	Islam	Judaism	Hinduism	Orthodox	Buddhism
Albuquerque, NM	32.6	13.4	2.2	0.5	0.7	0.2	0.2	0.1	0.6
Anchorage, AK	4.9	19.2	2.4	0.9	0.1	0.1	0.1	0.5	1.3
Ann Arbor, MI	9.7	8.1	5.6	2.5	2.2	0.8	0.5	0.4	0.3
Athens, GA	6.4	19.1	7.2	2.6	0.2	0.2	0.2	0.1	<0.1
Atlanta, GA	10.7	22.3	7.4	5.3	1.9	0.5	0.7	0.3	0.2
Austin, TX	18.8	13.5	4.0	1.7	1.0	0.2	0.6	0.2	0.3
Baltimore, MD	12.4	10.6	5.9	3.3	3.3	1.7	0.1	0.5	0.1
Billings, MT	7.4	13.9	5.2	0.1	n/a	n/a	n/a	0.1	n/a
Boise City, ID	13.0	11.9	3.9	<0.1	0.3	0.1	0.2	0.1	0.1
Boston, MA	37.0	3.4	3.2	0.3	2.2	1.1	0.3	0.9	0.4
Boulder, CO	16.0	12.7	3.4	n/a	0.4	0.7	0.5	0.2	1.0
Cape Coral, FL	18.8	16.4	3.0	0.6	0.2	0.2	0.2	0.1	0.1
Cedar Rapids, IA	16.8	11.9	12.2	0.4	1.3	0.1	0.7	0.1	<0.1
Charleston, SC	11.5	17.1	6.8	6.6	0.2	0.4	<0.1	0.2	n/a
Charlotte, NC	12.1	26.4	9.5	3.4	1.7	0.2	0.2	0.4	0.1
Chicago, IL	28.6	8.2	3.7	3.6	4.7	0.7	0.4	0.7	0.4
Cincinnati, OH	17.0	24.9	4.1	2.0	1.1	0.4	0.3	0.3	0.1
Clarksville, TN	4.6	35.7	4.8	3.4	0.1	n/a	n/a	0.1	n/a
Cleveland, OH	26.1	15.1	5.6	3.5	1.1	1.3	0.3	0.8	0.2
College Station, TX	17.2	16.1	5.3	1.8	0.6	n/a	0.1	0.1	n/a
Colorado Springs, CO	16.4	18.3	2.9	0.9	0.1	<0.1	<0.1	0.1	0.3
Columbia, MO	7.1	19.4	6.3	1.9	1.4	0.2	0.1	0.1	<0.1
Columbia, SC	6.6	27.9	10.7	5.6	0.3	0.2	0.4	0.1	0.3
Columbus, OH	11.7	18.1	6.8	1.5	2.1	0.4	0.4	0.5	0.2
Dallas, TX	14.2	25.4	5.9	3.3	1.8	0.3	0.5	0.3	0.2
Davenport, IA	13.2	8.5	10.6	1.9	0.7	0.1	0.2	0.1	n/a
Denver, CO	16.1	9.6	2.8	0.6	0.3	0.4	0.5	0.4	0.5
Des Moines, IA	12.1	10.3	12.2	1.0	1.6	<0.1	0.2	0.1	0.1
Detroit, MI	18.6	9.1	3.3	5.1	4.5	0.8	0.3	0.8	0.2
Durham, NC	8.5	20.0	8.8	4.3	1.5	0.5	0.1	0.3	0.1
El Paso, TX	47.9	9.9	0.6	0.4	0.1	0.2	<0.1	<0.1	0.2
Eugene, OR	5.6	10.3	2.3	0.1	<0.1	0.4	0.3	0.1	0.5
Fargo, ND	14.2	11.1	23.4	n/a	<0.1	<0.1	n/a	0.1	n/a
Fort Collins, CO	9.9	15.6	3.3	0.4	<0.1	n/a	0.1	0.1	0.1
Fort Wayne, IN	13.1	24.7	6.1	6.5	1.0	0.1	0.1	0.2	0.4
Fort Worth, TX	14.2	25.4	5.9	3.3	1.8	0.3	0.5	0.3	0.2
Gainesville, FL	8.5	25.3	5.4	2.0	0.4	0.3	0.3	<0.1	0.3
Green Bay, WI	31.8	14.6	6.2	<0.1	0.4	n/a	n/a	<0.1	<0.1
Greensboro, NC	7.9	24.9	10.1	3.5	1.5	0.3	0.3	0.1	0.1
Honolulu, HI	18.0	8.1	2.3	0.2	<0.1	0.1	0.2	<0.1	4.0
Houston, TX	18.3	23.8	4.7	2.3	1.7	0.3	0.7	0.3	0.3
Huntsville, AL	7.5	34.8	8.2	7.2	0.8	0.1	0.9	0.1	0.1
Indianapolis, IN	11.5	16.8	7.6	4.2	1.1	0.4	0.2	0.3	0.1
Jacksonville, FL	13.0	29.8	3.5	5.6	0.6	0.3	0.3	0.3	0.2
Kansas City, MO	11.3	19.1	7.1	3.6	1.0	0.3	0.4	0.1	0.2
Lafayette, LA	44.3	12.6	2.4	5.0	0.1	n/a	<0.1	<0.1	0.1
Las Vegas, NV	26.2	6.6	1.0	0.5	0.3	0.3	0.2	0.6	0.7
Lexington, KY	5.8	26.9	8.1	3.5	0.5	0.3	0.1	0.2	<0.1
Lincoln, NE	13.2	16.6	12.9	0.3	0.1	0.1	0.1	0.1	0.1
Little Rock, AR	4.9	32.1	6.6	8.5	0.4	0.1	<0.1	0.1	0.1
Los Angeles, CA	31.1	9.3	1.5	1.7	1.4	0.8	0.4	0.9	0.9
Louisville, KY	11.9	21.1	5.0	4.6	1.0	0.2	0.4	0.2	0.2
Madison, WI	14.4	8.0	10.6	0.2	1.2	0.4	0.1	0.1	0.9
Manchester, NH	16.3	5.8	2.7	n/a	0.1	0.3	<0.1	0.9	n/a
McAllen, TX	46.6	10.0	1.1	0.1	0.2	<0.1	<0.1	<0.1	n/a

Table continued on following page.

Metro Area	Catholic	Evangelical Protestant	Mainline Protestant	Black Protestant	Islam	Judaism	Hinduism	Orthodox	Buddhism
Memphis, TN	4.8	32.4	5.8	17.2	1.3	0.6	0.4	0.1	0.1
Miami, FL	23.8	13.7	1.6	2.2	0.8	1.2	0.3	0.2	0.3
Midland, TX	15.4	35.5	3.0	7.6	0.4	n/a	0.2	n/a	n/a
Milwaukee, WI	24.5	16.3	5.4	3.3	2.8	0.4	0.4	0.5	0.4
Minneapolis, MN	19.8	10.6	10.3	0.5	2.9	0.6	0.2	0.3	0.3
Nashville, TN	6.2	30.1	6.0	5.2	0.8	0.2	0.4	1.1	0.2
New Orleans, LA	42.1	13.5	3.0	4.9	1.4	0.4	0.3	0.1	0.3
New York, NY	32.5	4.4	3.0	1.5	4.5	4.4	1.0	0.8	0.3
Oklahoma City, OK	10.0	38.7	7.1	2.2	0.6	0.1	0.4	0.1	0.4
Omaha, NE	19.9	10.8	7.9	1.5	0.2	0.3	1.0	0.2	0.2
Orlando, FL	17.6	20.6	2.5	2.7	1.3	0.2	0.5	0.3	0.3
Philadelphia, PA	26.8	7.3	6.6	2.2	2.6	1.1	0.6	0.4	0.4
Phoenix, AZ	22.9	11.0	1.6	0.3	1.9	0.3	0.5	0.4	0.2
Pittsburgh, PA	30.6	8.8	10.1	1.3	0.6	0.6	1.2	0.6	0.1
Portland, OR	11.8	14.6	2.3	0.4	0.2	0.3	0.7	0.3	0.4
Providence, RI	37.9	4.0	3.2	0.1	0.5	0.6	0.1	0.5	0.2
Provo, UT	4.9	0.4	<0.1	n/a	0.3	n/a	0.1	n/a	n/a
Raleigh, NC	12.4	19.3	7.4	2.8	3.2	0.2	0.4	0.3	0.4
Reno, NV	24.4	6.8	1.3	0.2	0.3	0.1	0.1	0.1	0.2
Richmond, VA	12.3	23.1	9.3	3.1	2.1	0.3	1.3	0.4	0.2
Rochester, MN	15.6	15.0	19.1	n/a	1.0	0.1	0.1	0.2	0.2
Sacramento, CA	17.1	10.4	1.4	1.1	1.9	0.2	0.4	0.3	0.5
Saint Louis, MO	21.2	16.1	5.7	3.9	1.3	0.6	0.2	0.2	0.3
Saint Paul, MN	19.8	10.6	10.3	0.5	2.9	0.6	0.2	0.3	0.3
Salem, OR	19.5	14.4	2.0	0.2	n/a	0.1	<0.1	<0.1	<0.1
Salt Lake City, UT	9.0	2.4	0.7	0.1	1.6	0.1	0.3	0.4	0.3
San Antonio, TX	27.3	17.7	3.1	0.8	0.5	0.2	0.1	0.1	0.3
San Diego, CA	22.9	9.5	1.5	0.6	1.5	0.4	0.3	0.4	0.7
San Francisco, CA	21.5	5.2	2.2	1.8	2.0	0.7	1.1	0.7	1.1
San Jose, CA	27.2	8.4	1.4	0.3	2.0	0.6	2.4	0.6	1.2
Santa Rosa, CA	23.5	5.3	1.5	<0.1	0.2	0.4	0.3	0.4	1.7
Savannah, GA	5.5	19.0	5.7	5.9	0.2	0.7	0.5	0.1	n/a
Seattle, WA	11.0	19.5	2.7	0.6	0.6	0.4	0.4	0.6	1.6
Sioux Falls, SD	13.1	21.0	20.2	0.1	0.1	n/a	n/a	0.8	<0.1
Tampa, FL	23.1	16.9	3.8	1.7	0.7	0.4	0.3	0.8	0.4
Tucson, AZ	18.9	10.4	2.4	0.6	1.0	0.4	0.4	0.2	0.3
Tulsa, OK	5.6	37.8	8.6	1.7	0.5	0.2	0.1	0.1	<0.1
Virginia Beach, VA	8.3	21.3	6.9	3.7	1.0	0.3	0.2	0.3	0.3
Washington, DC	16.1	12.3	6.5	3.3	3.3	1.0	0.9	0.9	0.5
Wichita, KS	12.7	19.4	23.2	2.6	0.1	<0.1	0.1	0.2	0.5
Wilmington, NC	13.2	17.9	9.3	4.6	0.7	0.3	0.1	0.3	n/a
Winston-Salem, NC	9.3	31.4	13.6	3.4	0.8	n/a	<0.1	0.3	0.1
U.S.	18.7	16.5	5.2	2.3	1.3	0.6	0.4	0.4	0.3

Note: Figures are the number of adherents as a percentage of the total population; Figures cover the Metropolitan Statistical Area (MSA)
Source: 2020 U.S. Religion Census, Association of Statisticians of American Religious Bodies; The Association of Religion Data Archives

Real Gross Domestic Product (GDP)

Metro Area	2017	2018	2019	2020	2021	2022	2023	Rank[1]
Albuquerque, NM	41.9	42.7	43.9	43.3	45.7	47.4	48.6	70
Anchorage, AK	25.8	26.0	26.0	25.3	25.9	26.3	27.3	116
Ann Arbor, MI	24.0	24.6	25.6	25.0	26.3	27.0	27.8	114
Athens, GA	10.0	10.3	10.3	9.8	10.4	10.8	11.0	211
Atlanta, GA	398.2	413.0	429.7	416.6	444.7	462.0	471.7	10
Austin, TX	141.1	149.3	159.1	163.6	181.1	198.5	207.5	20
Baltimore, MD	198.3	200.4	201.6	194.8	204.8	210.2	213.5	19
Billings, MT	10.2	10.3	10.0	9.8	10.5	10.5	10.9	215
Boise City, ID	32.3	34.8	36.4	37.0	40.4	43.4	44.6	76
Boston, MA	433.8	451.3	467.4	463.3	495.9	507.8	515.4	8
Boulder, CO	26.3	27.2	29.7	29.1	31.3	31.9	32.9	100
Cape Coral, FL	31.3	32.6	33.3	33.2	36.0	38.8	40.4	84
Cedar Rapids, IA	18.3	18.7	18.3	18.0	19.2	19.0	18.8	155
Charleston, SC	41.7	43.4	45.5	44.2	46.6	49.6	52.1	65
Charlotte, NC	168.1	171.6	177.5	179.1	190.5	197.3	206.5	21
Chicago, IL	674.6	691.2	697.5	659.6	698.0	715.6	725.7	3
Cincinnati, OH	145.2	145.3	152.3	149.5	155.9	157.4	160.1	29
Clarksville, TN	12.3	12.4	12.7	12.9	13.6	13.9	14.2	189
Cleveland, OH	128.6	130.6	134.0	129.2	136.3	139.1	139.9	36
College Station, TX	12.5	13.0	13.6	13.5	14.2	14.7	15.8	171
Colorado Springs, CO	35.1	36.2	37.7	38.8	41.1	41.8	43.6	79
Columbia, MO	10.0	10.0	10.4	10.1	10.6	10.7	11.0	213
Columbia, SC	41.0	41.7	42.7	42.2	44.6	45.5	47.0	73
Columbus, OH	129.9	131.5	135.7	134.2	143.6	145.5	148.0	34
Dallas, TX	483.7	506.2	526.2	520.2	562.1	594.5	613.4	5
Davenport, IA	21.6	21.4	21.6	21.0	21.6	22.0	22.4	136
Denver, CO	202.2	211.2	222.5	222.8	239.1	250.3	259.0	18
Des Moines, IA	51.8	51.9	54.2	55.6	60.7	59.8	60.4	57
Detroit, MI	256.2	261.5	262.7	249.7	263.7	271.7	276.5	16
Durham, NC	46.4	48.7	50.1	51.5	55.1	57.0	59.0	58
El Paso, TX	30.4	31.4	33.1	32.9	35.3	35.9	38.1	87
Eugene, OR	15.9	16.3	16.4	16.3	17.4	17.7	18.1	157
Fargo, ND	15.0	15.1	15.4	14.9	15.7	15.8	16.3	167
Fort Collins, CO	18.6	19.5	20.3	20.2	21.3	21.7	22.0	139
Fort Wayne, IN	22.4	23.3	23.5	21.8	23.4	24.3	24.7	120
Fort Worth, TX	483.7	506.2	526.2	520.2	562.1	594.5	613.4	5
Gainesville, FL	14.5	15.0	15.4	15.4	16.4	17.0	17.7	159
Green Bay, WI	20.0	20.6	20.7	20.1	20.5	20.8	21.1	144
Greensboro, NC	41.2	41.4	41.0	39.5	41.1	42.2	42.5	80
Honolulu, HI	65.8	66.0	65.6	60.1	62.8	64.5	66.0	55
Houston, TX	470.7	491.2	486.9	478.0	501.2	522.6	550.8	7
Huntsville, AL	27.5	28.6	30.2	30.7	32.6	34.1	36.1	92
Indianapolis, IN	135.9	140.7	143.8	142.8	152.5	158.8	161.8	28
Jacksonville, FL	80.3	83.0	86.5	87.7	94.4	100.4	104.7	40
Kansas City, MO	133.8	136.4	139.5	136.8	141.7	148.9	152.8	32
Lafayette, LA	21.1	22.0	21.8	20.8	21.8	21.8	22.6	132
Las Vegas, NV	116.3	122.7	128.2	117.3	130.1	138.5	142.8	35
Lexington, KY	28.7	29.5	30.0	28.7	29.6	30.6	31.4	105
Lincoln, NE	19.6	19.9	20.3	20.2	21.1	22.1	22.8	130
Little Rock, AR	36.5	37.1	37.4	37.7	39.4	39.9	41.3	82
Los Angeles, CA	965.3	991.3	1,026.5	982.0	1,041.7	1,065.3	1,075.1	2
Louisville, KY	70.8	71.6	74.3	72.8	76.4	77.9	79.2	49
Madison, WI	47.4	49.3	50.6	49.4	52.3	53.4	55.1	59
Manchester, NH	26.0	26.5	27.2	27.0	29.5	30.0	30.5	108
McAllen, TX	20.7	21.2	22.0	21.5	22.7	23.1	24.0	124
Memphis, TN	75.3	76.0	76.6	75.7	79.9	79.7	81.2	47

Table continued on following page.

Metro Area	2017	2018	2019	2020	2021	2022	2023	Rank[1]
Miami, FL	347.0	359.9	367.6	353.8	391.4	415.2	431.9	12
Midland, TX	21.9	27.6	33.1	31.1	31.7	31.0	44.2	78
Milwaukee, WI	99.3	100.8	102.3	98.2	102.4	105.2	106.6	39
Minneapolis, MN	257.8	265.7	270.1	260.6	275.7	281.3	286.7	15
Nashville, TN	130.5	134.6	139.3	138.4	154.0	163.2	168.2	27
New Orleans, LA	78.2	78.1	79.8	73.4	76.8	75.7	79.6	48
New York, NY	1,714.1	1,766.3	1,801.1	1,744.7	1,834.5	1,875.1	1,905.2	1
Oklahoma City, OK	74.4	77.0	78.4	76.1	76.7	76.3	81.6	46
Omaha, NE	64.3	65.7	66.4	65.2	68.9	73.7	75.3	50
Orlando, FL	136.2	141.2	146.8	140.3	156.9	167.8	175.3	26
Philadelphia, PA	425.4	432.3	437.0	420.4	438.8	450.2	459.5	11
Phoenix, AZ	246.1	257.4	269.4	274.6	299.1	313.6	322.8	14
Pittsburgh, PA	150.7	154.3	155.9	147.7	153.2	155.0	159.6	30
Portland, OR	155.8	162.7	166.7	164.9	174.8	178.8	182.0	25
Providence, RI	84.6	84.7	86.8	84.2	88.5	89.3	90.4	45
Provo, UT	25.5	27.6	30.1	31.5	34.1	35.8	37.4	90
Raleigh, NC	84.9	89.5	92.3	92.4	101.0	105.8	110.6	38
Reno, NV	29.4	28.8	29.9	30.1	33.2	33.6	34.1	96
Richmond, VA	84.5	86.5	88.6	87.2	91.8	93.9	94.8	44
Rochester, MN	13.1	13.6	13.8	13.6	14.1	14.4	14.9	182
Sacramento, CA	131.2	136.9	141.9	138.9	147.4	150.4	153.8	31
Saint Louis, MO	164.4	166.6	169.5	165.7	175.8	180.2	184.8	24
Saint Paul, MN	257.8	265.7	270.1	260.6	275.7	281.3	286.7	15
Salem, OR	17.1	18.0	18.6	18.6	19.8	20.1	20.6	147
Salt Lake City, UT	92.0	97.2	103.0	102.5	111.3	114.3	118.0	37
San Antonio, TX	118.9	124.5	129.0	127.4	134.2	143.7	150.3	33
San Diego, CA	224.8	230.5	236.6	233.3	250.4	258.0	261.7	17
San Francisco, CA	526.6	560.6	594.3	596.5	662.4	659.3	681.9	4
San Jose, CA	282.7	304.6	319.4	339.4	381.6	379.7	392.5	13
Santa Rosa, CA	28.9	30.2	30.5	29.6	31.7	31.0	31.0	106
Savannah, GA	21.2	21.5	22.3	22.2	23.9	24.5	25.7	118
Seattle, WA	368.2	395.7	417.4	418.4	449.5	459.5	487.8	9
Sioux Falls, SD	22.2	21.9	22.8	22.0	23.2	22.8	23.2	128
Tampa, FL	152.7	158.0	163.9	165.5	180.0	190.7	198.9	23
Tucson, AZ	42.3	43.9	45.4	45.3	47.9	48.6	50.8	68
Tulsa, OK	51.6	53.1	52.0	49.2	51.1	51.6	53.9	61
Virginia Beach, VA	94.9	93.9	94.9	94.3	99.0	100.9	104.0	41
Washington, DC	528.9	542.4	551.9	543.4	571.1	584.2	600.2	6
Wichita, KS	35.9	35.8	35.8	34.7	35.7	36.7	37.7	89
Wilmington, NC	14.1	14.5	15.1	15.1	16.5	17.1	17.7	160
Winston-Salem, NC	34.9	34.2	34.7	32.6	34.8	35.7	36.1	91
U.S.[2]	17,619.1	18,160.7	18,642.5	18,238.9	19,387.6	19,896.6	20,436.3	–

Note: Figures are in billions of chained 2017 dollars; Figures cover the Metropolitan Statistical Area (MSA); (1) Rank is based on 2023 data and ranges from 1 to 384; (2) Figures cover real GDP within metropolitan areas
Source: U.S. Bureau of Economic Analysis

Economic Growth

Metro Area	2014	2015	2016	2017	2018	2019	2020	2021	2022	2023
Albuquerque, NM	2.0	1.2	1.7	0.4	1.9	2.9	-1.3	5.4	3.9	2.4
Anchorage, AK	0.3	4.3	1.2	-1.5	0.7	-0.3	-2.6	2.6	1.4	3.7
Ann Arbor, MI	1.7	3.7	2.2	3.3	2.5	4.0	-2.5	5.2	2.6	2.9
Athens, GA	2.4	4.3	2.2	5.7	3.5	-0.7	-4.3	5.7	4.5	1.5
Atlanta, GA	4.6	5.3	5.3	4.8	3.7	4.0	-3.0	6.7	3.9	2.1
Austin, TX	5.7	7.7	4.2	4.5	5.8	6.5	2.8	10.7	9.6	4.5
Baltimore, MD	1.6	2.0	3.4	2.1	1.0	0.6	-3.4	5.1	2.6	1.6
Billings, MT	5.4	4.6	-5.8	7.2	0.6	-2.4	-2.3	7.3	0.1	3.5
Boise City, ID	4.5	1.6	4.2	5.5	7.8	4.7	1.6	9.1	7.5	2.9
Boston, MA	2.1	4.0	1.7	2.3	4.0	3.6	-0.9	7.0	2.4	1.5
Boulder, CO	3.3	3.9	3.5	4.9	3.7	9.0	-1.9	7.5	1.9	3.4
Cape Coral, FL	5.0	6.1	7.5	0.6	4.1	2.4	-0.5	8.5	7.8	4.2
Cedar Rapids, IA	4.4	4.0	3.1	0.1	1.8	-1.9	-1.8	6.7	-1.0	-0.9
Charleston, SC	2.8	4.7	5.6	2.0	4.0	4.8	-2.7	5.4	6.4	5.2
Charlotte, NC	3.3	4.2	3.0	3.7	2.1	3.4	0.9	6.4	3.6	4.7
Chicago, IL	2.3	2.4	0.8	1.4	2.5	0.9	-5.4	5.8	2.5	1.4
Cincinnati, OH	3.6	2.9	3.7	3.1	0.0	4.8	-1.8	4.3	1.0	1.7
Clarksville, TN	-1.2	0.5	-1.0	0.0	1.1	2.0	1.4	5.9	2.1	1.9
Cleveland, OH	2.3	0.8	0.1	2.4	1.6	2.6	-3.6	5.5	2.1	0.6
College Station, TX	6.3	6.2	-0.3	1.7	4.3	4.5	-0.2	4.6	4.0	7.4
Colorado Springs, CO	0.9	1.1	2.0	4.2	3.3	4.2	2.9	5.8	1.7	4.4
Columbia, MO	0.4	2.1	0.4	2.4	0.6	4.0	-2.9	5.1	0.5	2.8
Columbia, SC	3.6	2.9	2.9	0.3	1.6	2.4	-1.0	5.6	2.0	3.4
Columbus, OH	3.6	2.1	2.1	4.4	1.2	3.2	-1.1	7.0	1.3	1.8
Dallas, TX	3.8	4.8	2.3	3.6	4.6	3.9	-1.1	8.1	5.8	3.2
Davenport, IA	0.4	-1.4	-0.7	1.0	-0.7	0.8	-2.4	2.8	1.6	2.1
Denver, CO	4.5	5.3	2.2	3.8	4.4	5.3	0.1	7.3	4.7	3.5
Des Moines, IA	12.6	8.5	3.8	-1.3	0.2	4.3	2.6	9.3	-1.5	1.0
Detroit, MI	1.4	1.7	1.9	0.9	2.1	0.4	-4.9	5.6	3.0	1.8
Durham, NC	-1.9	-1.7	-0.7	-0.5	4.9	2.8	2.8	7.0	3.4	3.5
El Paso, TX	-1.5	1.5	0.9	2.1	3.1	5.4	-0.5	7.2	1.9	6.1
Eugene, OR	1.5	5.0	3.0	3.8	2.7	0.4	-0.7	7.0	1.9	2.3
Fargo, ND	7.0	3.5	-0.3	3.3	0.7	2.5	-3.4	5.3	0.4	3.6
Fort Collins, CO	5.3	4.6	4.0	7.7	4.8	4.4	-0.9	5.8	1.9	1.3
Fort Wayne, IN	7.7	4.3	3.2	3.8	3.8	0.7	-7.1	7.2	4.2	1.4
Fort Worth, TX	3.8	4.8	2.3	3.6	4.6	3.9	-1.1	8.1	5.8	3.2
Gainesville, FL	3.2	1.9	2.1	3.8	3.3	2.9	0.1	6.5	3.4	4.5
Green Bay, WI	6.3	2.8	1.0	-0.2	3.2	0.4	-2.8	1.9	1.4	1.3
Greensboro, NC	-0.4	2.5	-1.1	0.5	0.5	-1.1	-3.6	4.0	2.8	0.5
Honolulu, HI	0.9	2.7	1.9	2.1	0.4	-0.6	-8.5	4.5	2.6	2.4
Houston, TX	1.7	5.5	-2.1	0.7	4.4	-0.9	-1.8	4.8	4.3	5.4
Huntsville, AL	0.3	1.8	3.1	3.8	3.9	5.7	1.6	6.0	4.6	6.0
Indianapolis, IN	2.1	-2.5	2.4	2.4	3.6	2.2	-0.7	6.8	4.1	1.9
Jacksonville, FL	2.4	4.2	3.8	4.5	3.3	4.3	1.3	7.7	6.3	4.3
Kansas City, MO	2.7	3.8	0.5	3.3	2.0	2.3	-1.9	3.6	5.0	2.7
Lafayette, LA	1.4	-7.6	-9.3	0.0	4.4	-1.0	-4.5	4.6	0.1	3.8
Las Vegas, NV	1.5	4.4	3.2	3.6	5.5	4.5	-8.5	10.9	6.4	3.2
Lexington, KY	2.6	3.9	2.2	1.2	2.8	1.9	-4.5	3.1	3.6	2.7
Lincoln, NE	4.9	3.5	1.7	5.3	2.0	1.9	-0.7	4.5	4.6	3.3
Little Rock, AR	1.1	1.4	1.1	-0.8	1.5	0.8	0.8	4.6	1.1	3.5
Los Angeles, CA	2.7	4.3	1.8	3.7	2.7	3.6	-4.3	6.1	2.3	0.9
Louisville, KY	1.3	2.6	1.9	1.7	1.2	3.8	-2.0	4.9	2.0	1.6
Madison, WI	5.0	3.7	3.3	1.5	3.9	2.7	-2.4	5.9	2.2	3.2
Manchester, NH	2.2	3.4	1.6	0.4	1.9	3.0	-0.9	9.3	1.7	1.6
McAllen, TX	1.7	1.1	-0.4	0.5	2.2	3.8	-2.1	5.4	1.9	3.8
Memphis, TN	-0.2	2.0	1.3	1.8	0.8	0.9	-1.2	5.5	-0.2	1.9

Table continued on following page.

Metro Area	2014	2015	2016	2017	2018	2019	2020	2021	2022	2023
Miami, FL	3.4	4.4	3.1	4.5	3.7	2.1	-3.7	10.6	6.1	4.0
Midland, TX	9.0	9.5	-1.7	14.0	25.9	20.3	-6.1	1.8	-2.3	42.9
Milwaukee, WI	0.6	1.2	0.5	1.5	1.6	1.5	-4.0	4.3	2.7	1.4
Minneapolis, MN	3.8	2.2	1.6	1.9	3.1	1.6	-3.5	5.8	2.0	2.0
Nashville, TN	4.6	6.7	3.7	4.6	3.1	3.6	-0.7	11.3	6.0	3.1
New Orleans, LA	1.2	0.3	0.8	5.8	-0.1	2.1	-8.0	4.6	-1.3	5.0
New York, NY	1.9	2.2	1.7	2.0	3.0	2.0	-3.1	5.1	2.2	1.6
Oklahoma City, OK	6.4	4.2	0.3	3.1	3.5	1.7	-2.8	0.7	-0.5	6.9
Omaha, NE	6.2	3.3	0.5	4.6	2.1	1.1	-1.8	5.6	7.0	2.2
Orlando, FL	3.8	5.5	3.8	5.5	3.7	4.0	-4.4	11.9	6.9	4.5
Philadelphia, PA	2.5	1.7	1.4	-0.3	1.6	1.1	-3.8	4.4	2.6	2.1
Phoenix, AZ	1.6	3.1	3.6	4.6	4.6	4.7	1.9	8.9	4.8	2.9
Pittsburgh, PA	1.8	3.1	0.2	4.4	2.4	1.0	-5.3	3.7	1.2	2.9
Portland, OR	3.4	5.7	4.7	5.7	4.4	2.5	-1.1	6.0	2.3	1.8
Providence, RI	1.6	2.5	0.2	0.5	0.1	2.4	-3.0	5.1	0.9	1.2
Provo, UT	4.7	8.2	7.0	6.8	8.3	9.1	4.6	8.3	4.9	4.4
Raleigh, NC	6.1	7.4	6.5	4.6	5.4	3.1	0.2	9.3	4.7	4.6
Reno, NV	0.4	7.7	4.1	7.1	-2.0	3.9	0.8	10.2	1.4	1.4
Richmond, VA	1.2	3.9	1.5	1.8	2.4	2.4	-1.6	5.3	2.3	1.0
Rochester, MN	1.6	2.9	1.4	3.6	3.5	2.0	-1.6	3.9	2.0	3.2
Sacramento, CA	2.8	4.3	2.1	2.9	4.4	3.6	-2.1	6.1	2.1	2.2
Saint Louis, MO	1.4	0.8	0.1	-0.4	1.3	1.7	-2.2	6.1	2.5	2.5
Saint Paul, MN	3.8	2.2	1.6	1.9	3.1	1.6	-3.5	5.8	2.0	2.0
Salem, OR	3.4	5.4	5.1	4.5	5.6	3.2	-0.3	6.4	1.7	2.6
Salt Lake City, UT	3.2	3.4	4.7	5.2	5.7	6.0	-0.5	8.6	2.7	3.2
San Antonio, TX	5.3	5.7	0.9	0.3	4.7	3.6	-1.3	5.4	7.1	4.6
San Diego, CA	3.1	3.3	1.3	3.7	2.6	2.7	-1.4	7.3	3.1	1.4
San Francisco, CA	6.1	6.0	5.7	9.3	6.5	6.0	0.4	11.0	-0.5	3.4
San Jose, CA	7.2	8.9	6.1	4.9	7.8	4.8	6.3	12.4	-0.5	3.4
Santa Rosa, CA	4.1	4.8	2.5	1.6	4.7	0.9	-3.0	7.0	-2.2	0.2
Savannah, GA	4.3	3.0	3.9	2.5	1.4	4.0	-0.5	7.7	2.6	4.9
Seattle, WA	4.9	4.6	4.1	8.2	7.5	5.5	0.2	7.4	2.2	6.2
Sioux Falls, SD	5.5	1.3	1.4	1.5	-1.2	4.3	-3.5	5.4	-2.0	2.0
Tampa, FL	2.0	4.2	3.3	2.1	3.5	3.7	1.0	8.8	5.9	4.3
Tucson, AZ	0.2	-0.5	3.4	3.5	3.7	3.5	-0.3	5.7	1.4	4.6
Tulsa, OK	5.4	1.7	-5.9	3.5	2.9	-2.1	-5.4	3.9	1.0	4.4
Virginia Beach, VA	-1.0	1.7	1.1	0.7	-1.2	1.2	-0.7	5.0	1.9	3.2
Washington, DC	1.2	2.1	2.5	2.4	2.5	1.8	-1.6	5.1	2.3	2.7
Wichita, KS	6.2	5.6	8.2	0.4	-0.1	-0.2	-2.9	2.8	2.9	2.8
Wilmington, NC	4.1	1.5	5.1	0.6	3.0	4.2	0.1	9.2	3.6	3.5
Winston-Salem, NC	2.6	1.0	1.4	2.6	-2.1	1.4	-6.0	6.9	2.5	1.3
U.S.[1]	2.6	3.2	2.0	2.7	3.1	2.7	-2.2	6.3	2.6	2.7

Note: Figures are real gross domestic product growth rates and represent percent change from preceding period; Figures cover the Metropolitan Statistical Area (MSA); (1) Figures are the average growth rates within metropolitan areas
Source: U.S. Bureau of Economic Analysis

Metropolitan Area Exports

Metro Area	2018	2019	2020	2021	2022	2023	Rank[1]
Albuquerque, NM	771.5	1,629.7	1,265.3	2,215.0	939.7	789.4	195
Anchorage, AK	1,510.8	1,348.0	990.9	n/a	n/a	n/a	n/a
Ann Arbor, MI	1,538.7	1,432.7	1,183.1	1,230.7	1,334.2	1,196.2	156
Athens, GA	378.1	442.1	338.7	448.1	489.9	533.9	217
Atlanta, GA	24,091.6	25,800.8	25,791.0	28,116.4	30,833.1	32,336.4	13
Austin, TX	12,929.9	12,509.0	13,041.5	15,621.9	17,290.7	17,251.5	27
Baltimore, MD	6,039.2	7,081.8	6,084.6	8,200.6	7,820.0	10,196.2	43
Billings, MT	114.3	141.9	116.0	173.8	156.0	119.2	349
Boise City, ID	2,771.7	2,062.8	1,632.9	1,937.1	2,156.7	1,922.6	121
Boston, MA	24,450.1	23,505.8	23,233.8	32,084.2	33,101.8	34,519.4	12
Boulder, CO	1,044.1	1,014.9	1,110.4	1,078.0	1,201.9	1,213.1	153
Cape Coral, FL	668.0	694.9	654.8	797.5	886.9	935.4	177
Cedar Rapids, IA	1,025.0	1,028.4	832.0	980.0	1,018.7	1,175.4	159
Charleston, SC	10,943.2	16,337.9	6,110.5	3,381.6	4,256.0	9,497.6	44
Charlotte, NC	14,083.2	13,892.4	8,225.6	10,554.3	12,223.1	11,470.3	34
Chicago, IL	47,287.8	42,438.8	41,279.4	54,498.1	63,374.6	56,656.6	5
Cincinnati, OH	27,396.3	28,778.3	21,002.2	23,198.7	29,285.0	31,216.2	14
Clarksville, TN	435.5	341.8	246.8	288.7	376.7	445.6	236
Cleveland, OH	9,382.9	8,829.9	7,415.8	8,560.4	9,561.2	10,206.2	42
College Station, TX	153.0	160.5	114.9	110.3	136.2	180.0	323
Colorado Springs, CO	850.6	864.2	979.2	866.9	1,209.5	1,425.7	137
Columbia, MO	238.6	291.4	256.2	335.4	368.7	474.1	230
Columbia, SC	2,083.8	2,184.6	2,058.8	2,100.2	2,351.3	2,160.3	112
Columbus, OH	7,529.5	7,296.6	6,304.8	6,557.9	7,597.3	8,418.9	47
Dallas, TX	36,260.9	39,474.0	35,642.0	43,189.0	50,632.9	51,863.7	6
Davenport, IA	6,761.9	6,066.3	5,097.5	6,341.0	8,173.6	6,050.0	57
Denver, CO	4,544.3	4,555.6	4,604.4	4,670.8	5,761.7	5,724.2	59
Des Moines, IA	1,293.7	1,437.8	1,414.0	1,706.6	1,706.8	2,175.7	110
Detroit, MI	44,131.4	41,070.4	30,715.1	35,433.2	40,395.3	45,591.4	7
Durham, NC	3,945.8	4,452.9	3,359.3	3,326.4	4,071.8	4,898.7	65
El Paso, TX	30,052.0	32,749.6	27,154.4	32,397.9	36,488.3	35,223.0	11
Eugene, OR	400.1	360.0	340.6	426.7	434.9	415.2	241
Fargo, ND	553.5	515.0	438.3	539.4	518.7	880.1	185
Fort Collins, CO	1,021.8	1,060.0	1,092.5	1,132.5	1,178.8	1,180.5	157
Fort Wayne, IN	1,593.3	1,438.5	1,144.6	1,592.7	1,787.5	2,032.1	115
Fort Worth, TX	36,260.9	39,474.0	35,642.0	43,189.0	50,632.9	51,863.7	6
Gainesville, FL	370.2	297.2	260.9	320.7	307.2	306.6	274
Green Bay, WI	1,044.3	928.2	736.4	765.6	855.1	835.1	190
Greensboro, NC	3,053.5	2,561.8	2,007.3	2,356.2	2,375.6	2,239.4	108
Honolulu, HI	438.9	308.6	169.0	164.3	258.8	450.6	234
Houston, TX	120,714.3	129,656.0	104,538.2	140,750.4	191,846.9	175,470.1	1
Huntsville, AL	1,608.7	1,534.2	1,263.0	1,579.5	1,558.7	1,762.1	125
Indianapolis, IN	11,069.9	11,148.7	11,100.4	12,740.4	14,671.5	23,080.6	20
Jacksonville, FL	2,406.7	2,975.5	2,473.3	2,683.7	3,007.8	2,730.8	92
Kansas City, MO	7,316.9	7,652.6	7,862.7	9,177.6	9,623.5	10,627.2	40
Lafayette, LA	1,001.7	1,086.2	946.2	895.7	911.8	836.2	189
Las Vegas, NV	2,240.6	2,430.8	1,705.9	1,866.2	2,116.3	2,762.3	91
Lexington, KY	2,148.0	2,093.8	1,586.3	1,880.0	2,677.2	3,343.3	81
Lincoln, NE	885.6	807.0	726.3	872.6	1,161.3	1,082.2	165
Little Rock, AR	1,607.4	1,642.5	n/a	1,370.6	1,373.7	1,464.0	134
Los Angeles, CA	64,814.6	61,041.1	50,185.4	58,588.4	60,979.7	59,561.6	4
Louisville, KY	8,987.0	9,105.5	8,360.3	10,262.8	10,618.7	11,072.0	37
Madison, WI	2,460.2	2,337.6	2,450.5	2,756.3	2,893.8	2,822.9	90
Manchester, NH	1,651.4	1,587.1	1,704.9	2,077.6	2,349.8	2,416.7	101
McAllen, TX	6,627.9	5,234.1	4,087.6	5,164.6	5,677.1	7,072.4	51
Memphis, TN	12,695.4	13,751.7	13,350.3	16,761.5	17,835.3	17,853.5	25

Table continued on following page.

Metro Area	2018	2019	2020	2021	2022	2023	Rank[1]
Miami, FL	35,650.2	35,498.9	29,112.1	36,011.3	41,517.8	44,256.4	8
Midland, TX	63.6	63.7	57.7	49.9	76.2	72.4	365
Milwaukee, WI	7,337.6	6,896.3	6,624.0	7,282.8	8,742.5	9,352.5	45
Minneapolis, MN	20,016.2	18,633.0	17,109.5	21,098.8	21,964.3	22,209.4	23
Nashville, TN	8,723.7	7,940.7	6,569.9	8,256.1	9,347.5	10,385.4	41
New Orleans, LA	36,570.4	34,109.6	31,088.4	35,773.5	52,912.9	38,978.6	9
New York, NY	97,692.4	87,365.7	75,745.4	103,930.9	120,643.7	106,209.0	2
Oklahoma City, OK	1,489.4	1,434.5	1,326.6	1,773.2	2,019.1	2,277.7	107
Omaha, NE	4,371.6	3,725.7	3,852.5	4,595.1	4,585.5	3,411.0	80
Orlando, FL	3,131.7	3,363.9	2,849.8	3,313.6	4,096.9	4,443.5	71
Philadelphia, PA	23,663.2	24,721.3	23,022.1	28,724.4	29,352.1	28,760.2	16
Phoenix, AZ	13,614.9	15,136.6	11,073.9	14,165.1	16,658.8	17,553.6	26
Pittsburgh, PA	9,824.2	9,672.9	7,545.1	9,469.6	11,188.3	11,538.4	33
Portland, OR	21,442.9	23,761.9	27,824.7	33,787.5	34,368.0	26,973.2	18
Providence, RI	6,236.6	7,424.8	6,685.2	6,708.2	7,179.7	6,517.8	53
Provo, UT	1,788.1	1,783.7	1,888.5	2,053.8	1,318.4	1,416.7	140
Raleigh, NC	3,193.2	3,546.8	3,372.0	3,962.7	4,714.1	5,965.8	58
Reno, NV	2,631.7	2,598.3	4,553.3	4,503.0	3,864.0	3,434.1	78
Richmond, VA	3,535.0	3,203.2	2,719.1	3,010.7	3,283.5	2,579.8	95
Rochester, MN	537.6	390.1	194.0	224.9	215.9	258.7	293
Sacramento, CA	6,222.8	5,449.2	4,980.9	5,682.3	5,716.7	7,586.6	50
Saint Louis, MO	10,866.8	10,711.1	9,089.4	10,486.1	14,215.6	13,817.0	30
Saint Paul, MN	20,016.2	18,633.0	17,109.5	21,098.8	21,964.3	22,209.4	23
Salem, OR	410.2	405.7	350.5	372.0	422.3	404.8	244
Salt Lake City, UT	9,748.6	13,273.9	13,565.5	13,469.1	12,340.1	12,775.2	32
San Antonio, TX	11,678.1	11,668.0	10,987.9	13,086.4	13,173.6	12,821.8	31
San Diego, CA	20,156.8	19,774.1	18,999.7	23,687.8	24,657.9	22,975.3	22
San Francisco, CA	27,417.0	28,003.8	23,864.5	29,972.0	30,649.0	24,253.0	19
San Jose, CA	22,224.2	20,909.4	19,534.5	22,293.6	24,342.2	22,985.4	21
Santa Rosa, CA	1,231.7	1,234.5	1,131.4	1,301.8	1,297.3	1,121.8	161
Savannah, GA	5,407.8	4,925.5	4,557.0	5,520.5	6,171.2	6,206.1	56
Seattle, WA	59,742.9	41,249.0	23,851.0	28,866.7	34,159.9	36,267.3	10
Sioux Falls, SD	400.0	431.5	524.9	547.3	371.3	510.9	224
Tampa, FL	4,966.7	6,219.7	5,082.2	5,754.7	9,588.2	7,923.6	49
Tucson, AZ	2,824.8	2,943.7	2,640.7	2,846.1	3,779.4	4,503.0	68
Tulsa, OK	3,351.7	3,399.2	2,567.8	3,064.8	3,379.2	3,234.5	84
Virginia Beach, VA	3,950.6	3,642.4	4,284.3	4,566.3	5,750.1	6,338.3	54
Washington, DC	13,602.7	14,563.8	13,537.3	12,210.8	14,001.9	14,758.9	29
Wichita, KS	3,817.0	3,494.7	2,882.1	3,615.3	4,550.4	4,475.1	69
Wilmington, NC	634.4	526.4	553.6	497.8	593.6	671.5	206
Winston-Salem, NC	1,107.5	1,209.1	913.1	918.2	1,012.1	1,071.1	166
U.S.	1,664,056.1	1,645,173.7	1,431,406.6	1,753,941.4	2,062,937.4	2,019,160.5	--

Note: Figures are in millions of dollars; Figures cover the Metropolitan Statistical Area (MSA); (1) Rank is based on 2023 data and ranges from 1 to 386
Source: U.S. Department of Commerce, International Trade Administration, Office of Trade and Economic Analysis, Industry and Analysis, Exports by Metropolitan Area, data extracted April 2, 2025

Building Permits: City

City	Single-Family			Multi-Family			Total		
	2023	2024	Pct. Chg.	2023	2024	Pct. Chg.	2023	2024	Pct. Chg.
Albuquerque, NM	587	525	-10.6	512	574	12.1	1,099	1,099	0.0
Anchorage, AK	271	161	-40.6	28	180	542.9	299	341	14.0
Ann Arbor, MI	161	28	-82.6	61	266	336.1	222	294	32.4
Athens, GA	168	212	26.2	238	960	303.4	406	1,172	188.7
Atlanta, GA	1,139	791	-30.6	6,482	7,318	12.9	7,621	8,109	6.4
Austin, TX	1,799	1,946	8.2	11,885	7,498	-36.9	13,684	9,444	-31.0
Baltimore, MD	92	165	79.3	1,751	1,108	-36.7	1,843	1,273	-30.9
Billings, MT	259	327	26.3	0	328	—	259	655	152.9
Boise City, ID	447	468	4.7	1,450	273	-81.2	1,897	741	-60.9
Boston, MA	108	72	-33.3	1,943	1,717	-11.6	2,051	1,789	-12.8
Boulder, CO	30	35	16.7	225	371	64.9	255	406	59.2
Cape Coral, FL	2,023	2,671	32.0	1,972	726	-63.2	3,995	3,397	-15.0
Cedar Rapids, IA	145	143	-1.4	229	465	103.1	374	608	62.6
Charleston, SC	891	878	-1.5	363	266	-26.7	1,254	1,144	-8.8
Charlotte, NC	n/a	n/a	n/a	n/a	n/a	n/a	n/a	n/a	n/a
Chicago, IL	290	325	12.1	3,326	4,046	21.6	3,616	4,371	20.9
Cincinnati, OH	117	110	-6.0	514	114	-77.8	631	224	-64.5
Clarksville, TN	805	1,366	69.7	1,455	703	-51.7	2,260	2,069	-8.5
Cleveland, OH	161	234	45.3	644	662	2.8	805	896	11.3
College Station, TX	448	650	45.1	293	462	57.7	741	1,112	50.1
Colorado Springs, CO	n/a	n/a	n/a	n/a	n/a	n/a	n/a	n/a	n/a
Columbia, MO	314	461	46.8	56	549	880.4	370	1,010	173.0
Columbia, SC	883	833	-5.7	718	1,315	83.1	1,601	2,148	34.2
Columbus, OH	943	828	-12.2	4,340	5,256	21.1	5,283	6,084	15.2
Dallas, TX	1,995	1,957	-1.9	4,429	4,081	-7.9	6,424	6,038	-6.0
Davenport, IA	94	149	58.5	121	162	33.9	215	311	44.7
Denver, CO	1,174	872	-25.7	4,551	3,122	-31.4	5,725	3,994	-30.2
Des Moines, IA	248	218	-12.1	321	400	24.6	569	618	8.6
Detroit, MI	397	483	21.7	828	1,436	73.4	1,225	1,919	56.7
Durham, NC	1,687	1,822	8.0	2,678	971	-63.7	4,365	2,793	-36.0
El Paso, TX	1,572	1,644	4.6	280	243	-13.2	1,852	1,887	1.9
Eugene, OR	171	309	80.7	422	693	64.2	593	1,002	69.0
Fargo, ND	292	241	-17.5	980	410	-58.2	1,272	651	-48.8
Fort Collins, CO	372	371	-0.3	631	314	-50.2	1,003	685	-31.7
Fort Wayne, IN	n/a	n/a	n/a	n/a	n/a	n/a	n/a	n/a	n/a
Fort Worth, TX	6,631	6,257	-5.6	3,429	6,891	101.0	10,060	13,148	30.7
Gainesville, FL	236	296	25.4	544	922	69.5	780	1,218	56.2
Green Bay, WI	37	42	13.5	0	434	—	37	476	1,186.5
Greensboro, NC	704	618	-12.2	1,063	1,336	25.7	1,767	1,954	10.6
Honolulu, HI	n/a	n/a	n/a	n/a	n/a	n/a	n/a	n/a	n/a
Houston, TX	6,609	6,808	3.0	9,821	5,090	-48.2	16,430	11,898	-27.6
Huntsville, AL	1,403	1,245	-11.3	1,197	240	-79.9	2,600	1,485	-42.9
Indianapolis, IN	896	1,170	30.6	1,517	653	-57.0	2,413	1,823	-24.5
Jacksonville, FL	4,223	5,037	19.3	5,485	1,361	-75.2	9,708	6,398	-34.1
Kansas City, MO	776	429	-44.7	458	2,449	434.7	1,234	2,878	133.2
Lafayette, LA	n/a	n/a	n/a	n/a	n/a	n/a	n/a	n/a	n/a
Las Vegas, NV	2,590	2,655	2.5	1,026	935	-8.9	3,616	3,590	-0.7
Lexington, KY	624	492	-21.2	774	544	-29.7	1,398	1,036	-25.9
Lincoln, NE	699	937	34.0	1,282	793	-38.1	1,981	1,730	-12.7
Little Rock, AR	703	468	-33.4	230	18	-92.2	933	486	-47.9
Los Angeles, CA	2,918	3,041	4.2	10,236	7,447	-27.2	13,154	10,488	-20.3
Louisville, KY	1,014	1,168	15.2	2,686	1,690	-37.1	3,700	2,858	-22.8
Madison, WI	332	250	-24.7	2,288	2,562	12.0	2,620	2,812	7.3
Manchester, NH	99	26	-73.7	280	167	-40.4	379	193	-49.1

Table continued on following page.

City	Single-Family			Multi-Family			Total		
	2023	2024	Pct. Chg.	2023	2024	Pct. Chg.	2023	2024	Pct. Chg.
McAllen, TX	428	669	56.3	753	1,053	39.8	1,181	1,722	45.8
Memphis, TN	n/a	n/a	n/a	n/a	n/a	n/a	n/a	n/a	n/a
Miami, FL	113	145	28.3	5,307	5,878	10.8	5,420	6,023	11.1
Midland, TX	805	1,504	86.8	0	0	0.0	805	1,504	86.8
Milwaukee, WI	61	72	18.0	36	164	355.6	97	236	143.3
Minneapolis, MN	70	65	-7.1	1,458	387	-73.5	1,528	452	-70.4
Nashville, TN	3,106	2,662	-14.3	8,052	4,137	-48.6	11,158	6,799	-39.1
New Orleans, LA	249	202	-18.9	818	508	-37.9	1,067	710	-33.5
New York, NY	232	197	-15.1	31,733	27,044	-14.8	31,965	27,241	-14.8
Oklahoma City, OK	3,339	3,460	3.6	805	938	16.5	4,144	4,398	6.1
Omaha, NE	1,294	1,692	30.8	1,756	2,668	51.9	3,050	4,360	43.0
Orlando, FL	887	914	3.0	1,514	1,056	-30.3	2,401	1,970	-18.0
Philadelphia, PA	405	539	33.1	3,458	2,423	-29.9	3,863	2,962	-23.3
Phoenix, AZ	4,200	4,062	-3.3	10,268	4,935	-51.9	14,468	8,997	-37.8
Pittsburgh, PA	229	229	0.0	2,283	1,435	-37.1	2,512	1,664	-33.8
Portland, OR	877	815	-7.1	2,212	885	-60.0	3,089	1,700	-45.0
Providence, RI	0	31	–	5	238	4,660.0	5	269	5,280.0
Provo, UT	147	133	-9.5	80	153	91.3	227	286	26.0
Raleigh, NC	1,762	1,653	-6.2	4,626	3,391	-26.7	6,388	5,044	-21.0
Reno, NV	1,059	1,087	2.6	2,176	1,636	-24.8	3,235	2,723	-15.8
Richmond, VA	387	380	-1.8	1,896	2,160	13.9	2,283	2,540	11.3
Rochester, MN	241	193	-19.9	551	925	67.9	792	1,118	41.2
Sacramento, CA	653	708	8.4	1,864	1,335	-28.4	2,517	2,043	-18.8
Saint Louis, MO	51	56	9.8	227	238	4.8	278	294	5.8
Saint Paul, MN	48	75	56.3	1,156	329	-71.5	1,204	404	-66.4
Salem, OR	360	392	8.9	326	513	57.4	686	905	31.9
Salt Lake City, UT	243	397	63.4	2,929	886	-69.8	3,172	1,283	-59.6
San Antonio, TX	4,299	5,000	16.3	4,860	1,258	-74.1	9,159	6,258	-31.7
San Diego, CA	516	775	50.2	5,249	5,840	11.3	5,765	6,615	14.7
San Francisco, CA	29	27	-6.9	1,107	743	-32.9	1,136	770	-32.2
San Jose, CA	581	642	10.5	2,069	1,356	-34.5	2,650	1,998	-24.6
Santa Rosa, CA	441	292	-33.8	905	0	-100.0	1,346	292	-78.3
Savannah, GA	589	565	-4.1	12	14	16.7	601	579	-3.7
Seattle, WA	473	405	-14.4	4,826	5,490	13.8	5,299	5,895	11.2
Sioux Falls, SD	750	880	17.3	1,986	1,239	-37.6	2,736	2,119	-22.6
Tampa, FL	738	912	23.6	2,415	1,634	-32.3	3,153	2,546	-19.3
Tucson, AZ	839	923	10.0	829	582	-29.8	1,668	1,505	-9.8
Tulsa, OK	524	424	-19.1	352	299	-15.1	876	723	-17.5
Virginia Beach, VA	201	319	58.7	341	347	1.8	542	666	22.9
Washington, DC	166	146	-12.0	2,854	1,591	-44.3	3,020	1,737	-42.5
Wichita, KS	605	558	-7.8	1,173	742	-36.7	1,778	1,300	-26.9
Wilmington, NC	n/a	n/a	n/a	n/a	n/a	n/a	n/a	n/a	n/a
Winston-Salem, NC	860	1,168	35.8	1,281	966	-24.6	2,141	2,134	-0.3
U.S.	920,000	981,900	6.7	591,100	496,100	-16.1	1,511,100	1,478,000	-2.2

Note: Figures represent new, privately-owned housing units authorized (unadjusted data)
Source: U.S. Census Bureau, Building Permits Survey (BPS), 2023, 2024

Building Permits: Metro Area

Metro Area	Single-Family			Multi-Family			Total		
	2023	2024	Pct. Chg.	2023	2024	Pct. Chg.	2023	2024	Pct. Chg.
Albuquerque, NM	2,057	2,064	0.3	777	812	4.5	2,834	2,876	1.5
Anchorage, AK	338	198	-41.4	119	228	91.6	457	426	-6.8
Ann Arbor, MI	485	557	14.8	1,112	636	-42.8	1,597	1,193	-25.3
Athens, GA	776	863	11.2	250	972	288.8	1,026	1,835	78.8
Atlanta, GA	24,022	25,773	7.3	14,617	14,914	2.0	38,639	40,687	5.3
Austin, TX	16,532	16,435	-0.6	22,241	15,859	-28.7	38,773	32,294	-16.7
Baltimore, MD	3,798	3,849	1.3	3,741	2,435	-34.9	7,539	6,284	-16.6
Billings, MT	343	896	161.2	6	629	10,383.3	349	1,525	337.0
Boise City, ID	6,508	8,252	26.8	3,383	811	-76.0	9,891	9,063	-8.4
Boston, MA	3,396	3,734	10.0	7,426	7,501	1.0	10,822	11,235	3.8
Boulder, CO	791	441	-44.2	851	1,239	45.6	1,642	1,680	2.3
Cape Coral, FL	8,654	10,554	22.0	4,902	4,857	-0.9	13,556	15,411	13.7
Cedar Rapids, IA	467	494	5.8	301	593	97.0	768	1,087	41.5
Charleston, SC	6,184	6,817	10.2	2,389	1,697	-29.0	8,573	8,514	-0.7
Charlotte, NC	19,146	18,954	-1.0	10,273	6,981	-32.0	29,419	25,935	-11.8
Chicago, IL	8,452	9,509	12.5	6,576	8,555	30.1	15,028	18,064	20.2
Cincinnati, OH	3,714	4,025	8.4	2,527	3,064	21.3	6,241	7,089	13.6
Clarksville, TN	1,385	1,975	42.6	1,554	823	-47.0	2,939	2,798	-4.8
Cleveland, OH	2,500	2,980	19.2	991	1,309	32.1	3,491	4,289	22.9
College Station, TX	1,155	1,482	28.3	307	839	173.3	1,462	2,321	58.8
Colorado Springs, CO	2,670	2,878	7.8	2,607	1,116	-57.2	5,277	3,994	-24.3
Columbia, MO	609	763	25.3	72	568	688.9	681	1,331	95.4
Columbia, SC	4,634	4,469	-3.6	831	1,423	71.2	5,465	5,892	7.8
Columbus, OH	5,364	6,094	13.6	6,076	7,868	29.5	11,440	13,962	22.0
Dallas, TX	44,366	46,440	4.7	23,663	25,348	7.1	68,029	71,788	5.5
Davenport, IA	366	401	9.6	248	564	127.4	614	965	57.2
Denver, CO	9,012	9,012	0.0	11,638	6,558	-43.7	20,650	15,570	-24.6
Des Moines, IA	3,689	3,717	0.8	1,311	1,347	2.7	5,000	5,064	1.3
Detroit, MI	4,541	4,878	7.4	2,193	2,826	28.9	6,734	7,704	14.4
Durham, NC	3,127	2,815	-10.0	4,083	1,043	-74.5	7,210	3,858	-46.5
El Paso, TX	1,967	2,077	5.6	280	243	-13.2	2,247	2,320	3.2
Eugene, OR	732	799	9.2	507	1,015	100.2	1,239	1,814	46.4
Fargo, ND	885	832	-6.0	1,204	660	-45.2	2,089	1,492	-28.6
Fort Collins, CO	1,289	1,370	6.3	1,397	416	-70.2	2,686	1,786	-33.5
Fort Wayne, IN	1,680	1,409	-16.1	756	625	-17.3	2,436	2,034	-16.5
Fort Worth, TX	44,366	46,440	4.7	23,663	25,348	7.1	68,029	71,788	5.5
Gainesville, FL	1,247	1,115	-10.6	698	928	33.0	1,945	2,043	5.0
Green Bay, WI	578	717	24.0	415	1,108	167.0	993	1,825	83.8
Greensboro, NC	2,368	2,337	-1.3	1,139	2,639	131.7	3,507	4,976	41.9
Honolulu, HI	657	706	7.5	1,194	932	-21.9	1,851	1,638	-11.5
Houston, TX	50,444	52,703	4.5	18,311	13,044	-28.8	68,755	65,747	-4.4
Huntsville, AL	3,908	3,972	1.6	2,032	1,234	-39.3	5,940	5,206	-12.4
Indianapolis, IN	7,252	9,168	26.4	5,302	2,620	-50.6	12,554	11,788	-6.1
Jacksonville, FL	12,479	12,936	3.7	7,847	2,066	-73.7	20,326	15,002	-26.2
Kansas City, MO	4,299	4,875	13.4	3,215	4,273	32.9	7,514	9,148	21.7
Lafayette, LA	2,008	2,001	-0.3	378	18	-95.2	2,386	2,019	-15.4
Las Vegas, NV	10,087	12,277	21.7	2,986	2,477	-17.0	13,073	14,754	12.9
Lexington, KY	1,319	1,392	5.5	1,123	809	-28.0	2,442	2,201	-9.9
Lincoln, NE	849	1,077	26.9	1,288	959	-25.5	2,137	2,036	-4.7
Little Rock, AR	1,932	2,055	6.4	732	551	-24.7	2,664	2,606	-2.2
Los Angeles, CA	12,035	11,777	-2.1	18,732	15,004	-19.9	30,767	26,781	-13.0
Louisville, KY	2,914	3,690	26.6	3,817	2,106	-44.8	6,731	5,796	-13.9
Madison, WI	1,534	1,679	9.5	3,827	4,159	8.7	5,361	5,838	8.9
Manchester, NH	532	427	-19.7	850	445	-47.6	1,382	872	-36.9

Table continued on following page.

	Single-Family			Multi-Family			Total		
Metro Area	2023	2024	Pct. Chg.	2023	2024	Pct. Chg.	2023	2024	Pct. Chg.
McAllen, TX	4,143	4,336	4.7	2,756	2,956	7.3	6,899	7,292	5.7
Memphis, TN	3,062	2,773	-9.4	996	1,467	47.3	4,058	4,240	4.5
Miami, FL	5,512	5,825	5.7	15,808	10,527	-33.4	21,320	16,352	-23.3
Midland, TX	810	1,505	85.8	8	4	-50.0	818	1,509	84.5
Milwaukee, WI	1,408	1,712	21.6	1,436	2,346	63.4	2,844	4,058	42.7
Minneapolis, MN	8,245	9,300	12.8	10,388	4,722	-54.5	18,633	14,022	-24.7
Nashville, TN	13,842	14,465	4.5	9,716	5,573	-42.6	23,558	20,038	-14.9
New Orleans, LA	1,865	1,007	-46.0	1,207	604	-50.0	3,072	1,611	-47.6
New York, NY	11,734	12,530	6.8	51,296	45,399	-11.5	63,030	57,929	-8.1
Oklahoma City, OK	5,573	6,014	7.9	1,163	1,693	45.6	6,736	7,707	14.4
Omaha, NE	2,763	3,505	26.9	1,956	3,692	88.8	4,719	7,197	52.5
Orlando, FL	17,049	15,364	-9.9	8,366	8,771	4.8	25,415	24,135	-5.0
Philadelphia, PA	6,255	8,324	33.1	5,764	5,890	2.2	12,019	14,214	18.3
Phoenix, AZ	24,708	30,277	22.5	20,908	15,607	-25.4	45,616	45,884	0.6
Pittsburgh, PA	3,332	3,530	5.9	2,962	1,882	-36.5	6,294	5,412	-14.0
Portland, OR	6,326	6,345	0.3	5,056	3,108	-38.5	11,382	9,453	-16.9
Providence, RI	1,255	1,339	6.7	675	1,281	89.8	1,930	2,620	35.8
Provo, UT	4,663	5,246	12.5	1,518	1,182	-22.1	6,181	6,428	4.0
Raleigh, NC	12,147	13,343	9.8	8,472	5,636	-33.5	20,619	18,979	-8.0
Reno, NV	1,992	2,474	24.2	2,279	1,917	-15.9	4,271	4,391	2.8
Richmond, VA	4,590	5,023	9.4	5,383	3,619	-32.8	9,973	8,642	-13.3
Rochester, MN	604	491	-18.7	570	993	74.2	1,174	1,484	26.4
Sacramento, CA	7,931	8,579	8.2	4,010	3,034	-24.3	11,941	11,613	-2.7
Saint Louis, MO	4,599	4,653	1.2	2,508	2,364	-5.7	7,107	7,017	-1.3
Saint Paul, MN	8,245	9,300	12.8	10,388	4,722	-54.5	18,633	14,022	-24.7
Salem, OR	826	994	20.3	1,140	865	-24.1	1,966	1,859	-5.4
Salt Lake City, UT	3,163	3,525	11.4	6,072	1,922	-68.3	9,235	5,447	-41.0
San Antonio, TX	8,718	10,999	26.2	7,767	3,858	-50.3	16,485	14,857	-9.9
San Diego, CA	3,049	3,377	10.8	8,420	8,195	-2.7	11,469	11,572	0.9
San Francisco, CA	3,015	2,776	-7.9	4,515	3,138	-30.5	7,530	5,914	-21.5
San Jose, CA	2,037	2,207	8.3	4,190	1,908	-54.5	6,227	4,115	-33.9
Santa Rosa, CA	1,020	832	-18.4	1,333	180	-86.5	2,353	1,012	-57.0
Savannah, GA	2,620	2,936	12.1	768	1,101	43.4	3,388	4,037	19.2
Seattle, WA	6,296	6,489	3.1	10,927	11,431	4.6	17,223	17,920	4.0
Sioux Falls, SD	1,155	1,270	10.0	2,284	1,532	-32.9	3,439	2,802	-18.5
Tampa, FL	14,852	13,205	-11.1	10,534	7,745	-26.5	25,386	20,950	-17.5
Tucson, AZ	3,688	4,150	12.5	1,567	1,100	-29.8	5,255	5,250	-0.1
Tulsa, OK	3,393	3,602	6.2	1,616	709	-56.1	5,009	4,311	-13.9
Virginia Beach, VA	3,393	3,544	4.5	2,721	862	-68.3	6,114	4,406	-27.9
Washington, DC	10,936	11,743	7.4	12,557	9,744	-22.4	23,493	21,487	-8.5
Wichita, KS	1,470	1,479	0.6	2,063	1,560	-24.4	3,533	3,039	-14.0
Wilmington, NC	2,228	7,263	226.0	1,737	2,355	35.6	3,965	9,618	142.6
Winston-Salem, NC	3,567	4,010	12.4	1,507	1,446	-4.0	5,074	5,456	7.5
U.S.	920,000	981,900	6.7	591,100	496,100	-16.1	1,511,100	1,478,000	-2.2

Note: Figures cover the Metropolitan Statistical Area (MSA); Figures represent new, privately-owned housing units authorized (unadjusted data)
Source: U.S. Census Bureau, Building Permits Survey (BPS), 2023, 2024

Housing Vacancy Rates

Metro Area	Gross Vacancy Rate[1] (%)			Year-Round Vacancy Rate[2] (%)			Rental Vacancy Rate[3] (%)			Homeowner Vacancy Rate[4] (%)		
	2022	2023	2024	2022	2023	2024	2022	2023	2024	2022	2023	2024
Albuquerque, NM	5.3	5.6	6.4	5.1	5.4	6.1	5.5	6.1	6.7	1.0	0.7	1.6
Anchorage, AK	n/a	n/a	n/a	n/a	n/a	n/a	n/a	n/a	n/a	n/a	n/a	n/a
Ann Arbor, MI	n/a	n/a	n/a	n/a	n/a	n/a	n/a	n/a	n/a	n/a	n/a	n/a
Athens, GA	n/a	n/a	n/a	n/a	n/a	n/a	n/a	n/a	n/a	n/a	n/a	n/a
Atlanta, GA	5.9	6.6	6.8	5.7	6.4	6.6	6.7	8.7	9.3	0.8	1.2	0.9
Austin, TX	5.5	8.5	8.6	4.9	8.2	8.3	5.6	9.0	8.2	0.6	1.3	1.7
Baltimore, MD	5.9	6.6	7.0	5.7	6.5	6.5	5.3	9.4	6.1	0.5	0.6	0.9
Billings, MT	n/a	n/a	n/a	n/a	n/a	n/a	n/a	n/a	n/a	n/a	n/a	n/a
Boise City, ID	n/a	n/a	n/a	n/a	n/a	n/a	n/a	n/a	n/a	n/a	n/a	n/a
Boston, MA	6.2	6.1	5.7	5.4	5.3	4.8	2.5	2.5	3.0	0.7	0.6	0.6
Boulder, CO	n/a	n/a	n/a	n/a	n/a	n/a	n/a	n/a	n/a	n/a	n/a	n/a
Cape Coral, FL	38.2	38.7	34.1	16.9	16.1	14.7	11.6	15.3	10.1	3.9	2.3	3.0
Cedar Rapids, IA	n/a	n/a	n/a	n/a	n/a	n/a	n/a	n/a	n/a	n/a	n/a	n/a
Charleston, SC	10.6	12.6	11.9	7.5	10.2	9.8	8.8	12.0	12.8	0.4	0.5	0.9
Charlotte, NC	7.4	7.6	8.1	7.0	7.4	7.7	5.9	6.6	6.7	0.7	0.4	0.9
Chicago, IL	7.3	6.0	5.8	7.1	5.8	5.6	6.1	5.6	5.1	1.1	0.5	0.6
Cincinnati, OH	6.8	5.4	5.8	6.3	5.2	5.5	6.3	7.2	6.1	0.3	0.2	0.8
Clarksville, TN	n/a	n/a	n/a	n/a	n/a	n/a	n/a	n/a	n/a	n/a	n/a	n/a
Cleveland, OH	7.0	7.6	7.5	6.8	7.2	7.4	3.2	4.7	5.8	1.0	0.5	0.4
College Station, TX	n/a	n/a	n/a	n/a	n/a	n/a	n/a	n/a	n/a	n/a	n/a	n/a
Colorado Springs, CO	n/a	n/a	n/a	n/a	n/a	n/a	n/a	n/a	n/a	n/a	n/a	n/a
Columbia, MO	n/a	n/a	n/a	n/a	n/a	n/a	n/a	n/a	n/a	n/a	n/a	n/a
Columbia, SC	12.0	12.7	8.8	12.0	12.6	8.8	6.1	8.5	6.8	0.6	1.0	0.5
Columbus, OH	5.6	6.6	7.4	5.4	6.5	7.3	3.8	5.8	7.3	0.8	0.8	0.3
Dallas, TX	6.6	7.6	7.9	6.3	7.2	7.6	6.8	8.4	8.9	0.7	0.8	1.3
Davenport, IA	n/a	n/a	n/a	n/a	n/a	n/a	n/a	n/a	n/a	n/a	n/a	n/a
Denver, CO	5.8	6.0	4.9	5.2	5.5	4.4	5.1	5.3	4.7	0.3	0.7	0.7
Des Moines, IA	n/a	n/a	n/a	n/a	n/a	n/a	n/a	n/a	n/a	n/a	n/a	n/a
Detroit, MI	7.1	9.0	9.4	6.6	8.7	9.3	4.5	9.3	8.7	0.9	1.0	1.1
Durham, NC	n/a	n/a	n/a	n/a	n/a	n/a	n/a	n/a	n/a	n/a	n/a	n/a
El Paso, TX	n/a	n/a	n/a	n/a	n/a	n/a	n/a	n/a	n/a	n/a	n/a	n/a
Eugene, OR	n/a	n/a	n/a	n/a	n/a	n/a	n/a	n/a	n/a	n/a	n/a	n/a
Fargo, ND	n/a	n/a	n/a	n/a	n/a	n/a	n/a	n/a	n/a	n/a	n/a	n/a
Fort Collins, CO	n/a	n/a	n/a	n/a	n/a	n/a	n/a	n/a	n/a	n/a	n/a	n/a
Fort Wayne, IN	n/a	n/a	n/a	n/a	n/a	n/a	n/a	n/a	n/a	n/a	n/a	n/a
Fort Worth, TX	6.6	7.6	7.9	6.3	7.2	7.6	6.8	8.4	8.9	0.7	0.8	1.3
Gainesville, FL	n/a	n/a	n/a	n/a	n/a	n/a	n/a	n/a	n/a	n/a	n/a	n/a
Green Bay, WI	n/a	n/a	n/a	n/a	n/a	n/a	n/a	n/a	n/a	n/a	n/a	n/a
Greensboro, NC	8.7	6.1	7.8	8.7	5.7	6.0	10.2	5.7	5.5	0.7	0.1	0.5
Honolulu, HI	10.6	11.5	11.9	10.0	10.7	11.1	5.7	6.8	6.2	0.6	0.5	0.9
Houston, TX	6.9	7.9	7.8	6.3	7.3	7.2	8.9	10.9	9.8	0.6	1.4	1.2
Huntsville, AL	n/a	n/a	n/a	n/a	n/a	n/a	n/a	n/a	n/a	n/a	n/a	n/a
Indianapolis, IN	7.7	6.2	6.7	7.2	5.6	5.8	11.0	8.8	9.2	1.0	0.8	0.8
Jacksonville, FL	8.9	8.6	9.2	7.7	7.8	8.5	6.2	9.4	8.8	1.7	0.7	1.0
Kansas City, MO	7.1	7.0	6.9	7.1	6.6	6.3	7.8	7.6	8.9	0.6	1.2	0.9
Lafayette, LA	n/a	n/a	n/a	n/a	n/a	n/a	n/a	n/a	n/a	n/a	n/a	n/a
Las Vegas, NV	9.2	9.6	9.7	8.3	8.8	9.3	5.7	7.2	8.3	0.9	1.1	1.1
Lexington, KY	n/a	n/a	n/a	n/a	n/a	n/a	n/a	n/a	n/a	n/a	n/a	n/a
Lincoln, NE	n/a	n/a	n/a	n/a	n/a	n/a	n/a	n/a	n/a	n/a	n/a	n/a
Little Rock, AR	9.4	10.1	10.7	9.2	9.8	9.9	11.4	10.8	11.7	0.7	0.9	0.6
Los Angeles, CA	5.9	5.8	6.2	5.5	5.7	6.1	4.1	4.0	4.8	0.5	0.6	0.7
Louisville, KY	5.7	6.3	6.7	5.7	6.2	6.5	5.3	3.6	7.1	0.5	0.4	1.2
Madison, WI	n/a	n/a	n/a	n/a	n/a	n/a	n/a	n/a	n/a	n/a	n/a	n/a
Manchester, NH	n/a	n/a	n/a	n/a	n/a	n/a	n/a	n/a	n/a	n/a	n/a	n/a

Table continued on following page.

Metro Area	Gross Vacancy Rate[1] (%)			Year-Round Vacancy Rate[2] (%)			Rental Vacancy Rate[3] (%)			Homeowner Vacancy Rate[4] (%)		
	2022	2023	2024	2022	2023	2024	2022	2023	2024	2022	2023	2024
McAllen, TX	n/a	n/a	n/a	n/a	n/a	n/a	n/a	n/a	n/a	n/a	n/a	n/a
Memphis, TN	6.2	7.0	7.4	6.1	6.9	7.2	6.4	11.4	12.0	0.4	0.4	0.9
Miami, FL	12.6	14.7	14.8	7.5	8.9	9.3	6.3	8.4	9.5	1.1	0.9	1.4
Midland, TX	n/a	n/a	n/a	n/a	n/a	n/a	n/a	n/a	n/a	n/a	n/a	n/a
Milwaukee, WI	5.2	6.7	5.6	5.1	6.6	5.1	5.9	4.1	4.8	0.1	0.8	0.4
Minneapolis, MN	4.8	5.5	4.9	4.5	5.3	4.6	6.7	8.1	5.2	0.8	0.5	0.4
Nashville, TN	7.6	7.5	7.0	7.1	7.0	6.4	6.4	9.3	8.6	0.9	0.9	1.5
New Orleans, LA	13.4	10.9	11.9	11.5	9.8	10.8	6.6	9.2	9.1	1.6	1.6	1.4
New York, NY	8.2	7.8	8.3	7.0	6.7	7.4	3.5	3.9	4.7	1.0	0.9	1.0
Oklahoma City, OK	8.6	7.8	7.0	8.5	7.6	6.7	10.6	10.6	9.0	0.9	1.6	1.2
Omaha, NE	5.4	5.4	5.1	5.0	5.1	5.1	4.2	4.3	5.3	0.8	0.9	0.3
Orlando, FL	9.6	9.5	9.8	7.4	7.6	8.4	6.5	7.0	9.4	1.4	1.1	1.5
Philadelphia, PA	5.5	5.3	5.3	5.4	5.2	5.2	4.2	5.2	6.3	1.0	0.9	0.5
Phoenix, AZ	10.9	11.0	12.6	6.7	7.2	7.9	6.4	8.0	7.9	0.9	0.7	1.0
Pittsburgh, PA	11.5	10.0	10.5	11.0	9.2	9.7	8.3	6.3	8.9	0.7	0.9	0.8
Portland, OR	5.4	5.4	5.7	5.1	5.1	5.5	4.0	6.8	5.7	1.2	0.8	1.0
Providence, RI	9.5	9.4	8.5	7.6	7.6	6.8	4.5	3.7	3.2	0.4	0.3	0.4
Provo, UT	n/a	n/a	n/a	n/a	n/a	n/a	n/a	n/a	n/a	n/a	n/a	n/a
Raleigh, NC	7.4	6.7	6.3	7.3	6.6	6.2	7.1	8.8	8.8	0.5	0.5	0.7
Reno, NV	n/a	n/a	n/a	n/a	n/a	n/a	n/a	n/a	n/a	n/a	n/a	n/a
Richmond, VA	6.1	5.9	7.7	6.1	5.9	7.7	3.0	5.2	7.9	0.7	0.2	0.7
Rochester, MN	n/a	n/a	n/a	n/a	n/a	n/a	n/a	n/a	n/a	n/a	n/a	n/a
Sacramento, CA	6.3	6.4	8.0	6.1	6.2	7.6	2.3	4.2	3.9	0.6	0.6	0.9
Saint Louis, MO	7.2	7.4	7.7	7.1	7.3	7.6	6.8	7.8	7.9	1.4	0.6	0.9
Saint Paul, MN	4.8	5.5	4.9	4.5	5.3	4.6	6.7	8.1	5.2	0.8	0.5	0.4
Salem, OR	n/a	n/a	n/a	n/a	n/a	n/a	n/a	n/a	n/a	n/a	n/a	n/a
Salt Lake City, UT	5.1	6.1	10.1	4.5	5.0	5.8	4.6	6.2	6.1	0.6	0.6	0.7
San Antonio, TX	7.5	7.4	9.9	7.1	6.9	7.9	8.1	8.8	10.0	0.9	1.3	1.9
San Diego, CA	6.9	6.8	6.4	6.6	6.2	6.0	3.6	4.1	5.2	0.6	0.2	0.5
San Francisco, CA	7.9	8.1	8.3	7.7	8.0	8.1	5.4	6.6	6.3	1.3	0.5	0.7
San Jose, CA	5.8	4.5	4.7	5.8	4.5	4.7	4.7	3.3	3.3	0.4	0.3	1.0
Santa Rosa, CA	n/a	n/a	n/a	n/a	n/a	n/a	n/a	n/a	n/a	n/a	n/a	n/a
Savannah, GA	n/a	n/a	n/a	n/a	n/a	n/a	n/a	n/a	n/a	n/a	n/a	n/a
Seattle, WA	5.7	5.1	6.2	5.2	4.7	5.9	4.9	4.0	6.5	0.7	0.6	1.1
Sioux Falls, SD	n/a	n/a	n/a	n/a	n/a	n/a	n/a	n/a	n/a	n/a	n/a	n/a
Tampa, FL	13.3	13.3	14.2	9.9	9.1	10.9	8.1	8.5	8.7	1.2	1.0	2.0
Tucson, AZ	13.5	14.2	10.1	10.3	11.2	8.7	8.0	10.2	9.3	1.4	1.3	1.1
Tulsa, OK	8.9	8.3	7.5	8.5	7.9	6.8	5.6	6.7	7.2	0.7	0.8	0.7
Virginia Beach, VA	8.1	5.9	9.2	7.3	5.4	8.5	6.3	5.1	9.1	1.0	0.5	1.4
Washington, DC	5.2	5.1	5.5	5.0	5.0	5.4	5.3	5.5	4.7	0.6	0.3	0.4
Wichita, KS	n/a	n/a	n/a	n/a	n/a	n/a	n/a	n/a	n/a	n/a	n/a	n/a
Wilmington, NC	n/a	n/a	n/a	n/a	n/a	n/a	n/a	n/a	n/a	n/a	n/a	n/a
Winston-Salem, NC	n/a	n/a	n/a	n/a	n/a	n/a	n/a	n/a	n/a	n/a	n/a	n/a
U.S.[5]	9.1	9.0	9.1	7.5	7.5	7.6	5.7	6.5	6.8	0.8	0.8	1.0

Note: Figures cover the Metropolitan Statistical Area (MSA); (1) The percentage of the total housing inventory that is vacant; (2) The percentage of the housing inventory (excluding seasonal units) that is year-round vacant; (3) The percentage of rental inventory that is vacant for rent; (4) The percentage of homeowner inventory that is vacant for sale; (5) Figures cover the 75 largest Metropolitan Statistical Areas; n/a not available
Source: U.S. Census Bureau, Housing Vacancies and Homeownership Annual Statistics: 2022, 2023, 2024

Bankruptcy Filings

City	Area Covered	Business Filings			Nonbusiness Filings		
		2023	2024	% Chg.	2023	2024	% Chg.
Albuquerque, NM	Bernalillo County	24	33	37.5	373	454	21.7
Anchorage, AK	Anchorage Borough	9	7	-22.2	113	90	-20.4
Ann Arbor, MI	Washtenaw County	7	8	14.3	396	404	2.0
Athens, GA	Clarke County	2	5	150.0	176	189	7.4
Atlanta, GA	Fulton County	318	251	-21.1	2,723	2,846	4.5
Austin, TX	Travis County	133	121	-9.0	408	619	51.7
Baltimore, MD	Baltimore City	35	43	22.9	1,502	1,656	10.3
Billings, MT	Yellowstone County	5	9	80.0	111	153	37.8
Boise City, ID	Ada County	18	26	44.4	350	466	33.1
Boston, MA	Suffolk County	53	63	18.9	233	316	35.6
Boulder, CO	Boulder County	25	35	40.0	228	247	8.3
Cape Coral, FL	Lee County	97	64	-34.0	860	1,216	41.4
Cedar Rapids, IA	Linn County	9	7	-22.2	224	278	24.1
Charleston, SC	Charleston County	7	13	85.7	195	215	10.3
Charlotte, NC	Mecklenburg County	69	60	-13.0	577	689	19.4
Chicago, IL	Cook County	361	479	32.7	12,419	13,840	11.4
Cincinnati, OH	Hamilton County	32	42	31.3	1,286	1,619	25.9
Clarksville, TN	Montgomery County	4	11	175.0	475	513	8.0
Cleveland, OH	Cuyahoga County	37	60	62.2	3,437	4,054	18.0
College Station, TX	Brazos County	5	7	40.0	65	80	23.1
Colorado Springs, CO	El Paso County	23	50	117.4	784	973	24.1
Columbia, MO	Boone County	3	5	66.7	191	201	5.2
Columbia, SC	Richland County	7	10	42.9	453	584	28.9
Columbus, OH	Franklin County	43	81	88.4	2,330	2,671	14.6
Dallas, TX	Dallas County	296	496	67.6	2,363	3,025	28.0
Davenport, IA	Scott County	9	4	-55.6	157	158	0.6
Denver, CO	Denver County	61	79	29.5	669	854	27.7
Des Moines, IA	Polk County	15	13	-13.3	566	594	4.9
Detroit, MI	Wayne County	43	58	34.9	6,087	6,501	6.8
Durham, NC	Durham County	14	42	200.0	162	195	20.4
El Paso, TX	El Paso County	65	72	10.8	1,351	1,512	11.9
Eugene, OR	Lane County	12	18	50.0	535	707	32.1
Fargo, ND	Cass County	5	14	180.0	129	132	2.3
Fort Collins, CO	Larimer County	21	28	33.3	347	417	20.2
Fort Wayne, IN	Allen County	17	17	0.0	924	959	3.8
Fort Worth, TX	Tarrant County	200	198	-1.0	2,934	3,513	19.7
Gainesville, FL	Alachua County	11	30	172.7	153	177	15.7
Green Bay, WI	Brown County	5	10	100.0	320	408	27.5
Greensboro, NC	Guilford County	11	16	45.5	375	473	26.1
Honolulu, HI	Honolulu County	36	38	5.6	757	840	11.0
Houston, TX	Harris County	356	426	19.7	3,285	3,853	17.3
Huntsville, AL	Madison County	20	35	75.0	902	946	4.9
Indianapolis, IN	Marion County	45	43	-4.4	2,601	3,166	21.7
Jacksonville, FL	Duval County	73	83	13.7	1,514	1,784	17.8
Kansas City, MO	Jackson County	22	27	22.7	1,186	1,166	-1.7
Lafayette, LA	Lafayette Parish	19	44	131.6	335	410	22.4
Las Vegas, NV	Clark County	194	178	-8.2	5,622	6,690	19.0
Lexington, KY	Fayette County	13	14	7.7	468	540	15.4
Lincoln, NE	Lancaster County	11	15	36.4	367	405	10.4
Little Rock, AR	Pulaski County	17	29	70.6	1,436	1,390	-3.2
Los Angeles, CA	Los Angeles County	815	977	19.9	10,059	12,169	21.0
Louisville, KY	Jefferson County	28	35	25.0	2,280	2,258	-1.0
Madison, WI	Dane County	25	21	-16.0	437	494	13.0
Manchester, NH	Hillsborough County	8	21	162.5	235	298	26.8
McAllen, TX	Hidalgo County	13	11	-15.4	263	274	4.2

Table continued on following page.

		Business Filings			Nonbusiness Filings		
City	Area Covered	2023	2024	% Chg.	2023	2024	% Chg.
Memphis, TN	Shelby County	48	45	-6.3	5,959	6,030	1.2
Miami, FL	Miami-Dade County	242	413	70.7	5,320	6,779	27.4
Midland, TX	Midland County	14	17	21.4	66	93	40.9
Milwaukee, WI	Milwaukee County	24	40	66.7	2,881	3,306	14.8
Minneapolis, MN	Hennepin County	64	77	20.3	1,473	1,952	32.5
Nashville, TN	Davidson County	303	123	-59.4	1,109	1,195	7.8
New Orleans, LA	Orleans Parish	28	35	25.0	388	446	14.9
New York, NY	Bronx County	25	44	76.0	1,071	1,319	23.2
New York, NY	Kings County	394	457	16.0	1,781	2,036	14.3
New York, NY	New York County	750	361	-51.9	684	793	15.9
New York, NY	Queens County	215	209	-2.8	1,921	2,120	10.4
New York, NY	Richmond County	23	29	26.1	490	494	0.8
Oklahoma City, OK	Oklahoma County	46	54	17.4	1,374	1,526	11.1
Omaha, NE	Douglas County	21	26	23.8	687	802	16.7
Orlando, FL	Orange County	152	231	52.0	1,832	2,279	24.4
Philadelphia, PA	Philadelphia County	227	131	-42.3	940	1,094	16.4
Phoenix, AZ	Maricopa County	252	355	40.9	6,085	7,026	15.5
Pittsburgh, PA	Allegheny County	59	111	88.1	1,217	1,424	17.0
Portland, OR	Multnomah County	35	61	74.3	938	1,078	14.9
Providence, RI	Providence County	13	22	69.2	520	581	11.7
Provo, UT	Utah County	33	36	9.1	925	1,070	15.7
Raleigh, NC	Wake County	51	76	49.0	653	830	27.1
Reno, NV	Washoe County	35	59	68.6	610	860	41.0
Richmond, VA	Richmond city	2	14	600.0	620	678	9.4
Rochester, MN	Olmsted County	8	6	-25.0	137	161	17.5
Sacramento, CA	Sacramento County	96	163	69.8	1,675	2,259	34.9
Saint Louis, MO	Saint Louis City	12	23	91.7	1,497	1,311	-12.4
Saint Paul, MN	Ramsey County	20	19	-5.0	694	840	21.0
Salem, OR	Marion County	10	11	10.0	599	674	12.5
Salt Lake City, UT	Salt Lake County	58	58	0.0	2,508	2,763	10.2
San Antonio, TX	Bexar County	126	169	34.1	1,270	1,813	42.8
San Diego, CA	San Diego County	214	267	24.8	3,866	4,558	17.9
San Francisco, CA	San Francisco County	68	140	105.9	348	417	19.8
San Jose, CA	Santa Clara County	86	105	22.1	782	1,008	28.9
Santa Rosa, CA	Sonoma County	17	56	229.4	338	378	11.8
Savannah, GA	Chatham County	8	3	-62.5	732	695	-5.1
Seattle, WA	King County	92	113	22.8	1,134	1,459	28.7
Sioux Falls, SD	Minnehaha County	10	8	-20.0	220	220	0.0
Tampa, FL	Hillsborough County	121	158	30.6	1,822	2,440	33.9
Tucson, AZ	Pima County	28	27	-3.6	1,402	1,638	16.8
Tulsa, OK	Tulsa County	46	44	-4.3	867	1,065	22.8
Virginia Beach, VA	Virginia Beach City	10	20	100.0	822	966	17.5
Washington, DC	District of Columbia	78	81	3.8	293	347	18.4
Wichita, KS	Sedgwick County	24	27	12.5	757	777	2.6
Wilmington, NC	New Hanover County	29	19	-34.5	145	183	26.2
Winston-Salem, NC	Forsyth County	7	18	157.1	263	330	25.5
U.S.	U.S.	18,926	23,107	22.1	434,064	494,201	13.9

Note: Business filings include Chapter 7, Chapter 9, Chapter 11, Chapter 12, Chapter 13, Chapter 15, and Section 304; Nonbusiness filings include Chapter 7, Chapter 11, and Chapter 13
Source: Administrative Office of the U.S. Courts, Business and Nonbusiness Bankruptcy, County Cases Commenced by Chapter of the Bankruptcy Code, During the 12-Month Period Ending December 31, 2023 and Business and Nonbusiness Bankruptcy, County Cases Commenced by Chapter of the Bankruptcy Code, During the 12-Month Period Ending December 31, 2024

Income: City

City	Per Capita ($)	Median Household ($)	Average Household ($)
Albuquerque, NM	39,117	65,604	88,262
Anchorage, AK	49,338	98,152	127,598
Ann Arbor, MI	54,604	81,089	121,561
Athens, GA	31,836	51,655	76,375
Atlanta, GA	64,063	81,938	135,218
Austin, TX	59,427	91,461	130,163
Baltimore, MD	39,195	59,623	87,339
Billings, MT	42,639	71,855	98,655
Boise City, ID	48,274	81,308	112,482
Boston, MA	60,001	94,755	140,807
Boulder, CO	59,450	85,364	140,662
Cape Coral, FL	39,603	76,062	97,070
Cedar Rapids, IA	39,824	67,859	91,040
Charleston, SC	58,583	90,038	129,666
Charlotte, NC	49,991	78,438	119,473
Chicago, IL	48,148	75,134	112,443
Cincinnati, OH	38,878	51,707	83,146
Clarksville, TN	31,266	66,786	79,769
Cleveland, OH	27,078	39,187	56,900
College Station, TX	32,123	51,776	84,849
Colorado Springs, CO	44,893	83,198	108,459
Columbia, MO	37,359	64,488	91,425
Columbia, SC	38,087	55,653	90,935
Columbus, OH	37,189	65,327	85,919
Dallas, TX	44,138	67,760	106,979
Davenport, IA	36,583	64,497	83,699
Denver, CO	61,202	91,681	131,349
Des Moines, IA	36,459	63,966	83,728
Detroit, MI	24,029	39,575	56,528
Durham, NC	47,246	79,234	108,538
El Paso, TX	28,942	58,734	78,842
Eugene, OR	41,035	63,836	94,063
Fargo, ND	42,212	66,029	91,129
Fort Collins, CO	46,341	83,598	110,629
Fort Wayne, IN	32,884	60,293	78,764
Fort Worth, TX	37,157	76,602	101,838
Gainesville, FL	30,282	45,611	71,640
Green Bay, WI	34,514	62,546	81,363
Greensboro, NC	35,858	58,884	85,861
Honolulu, HI	48,465	85,428	120,718
Houston, TX	41,142	62,894	101,848
Huntsville, AL	44,733	70,778	101,671
Indianapolis, IN	36,194	62,995	86,913
Jacksonville, FL	37,269	66,981	90,429
Kansas City, MO	40,112	67,449	91,703
Lafayette, LA	39,861	61,454	91,871
Las Vegas, NV	38,421	70,723	98,664
Lexington, KY	42,272	67,631	98,429
Lincoln, NE	39,187	69,991	94,181
Little Rock, AR	43,242	60,583	98,728
Los Angeles, CA	46,270	80,366	122,610
Louisville, KY	38,890	64,731	91,264
Madison, WI	48,557	76,983	104,969
Manchester, NH	44,220	77,415	100,102
McAllen, TX	29,406	60,165	86,175
Memphis, TN	32,314	51,211	77,102

Table continued on following page.

City	Per Capita ($)	Median Household ($)	Average Household ($)
Miami, FL	42,528	59,390	97,643
Midland, TX	49,327	91,169	126,317
Milwaukee, WI	29,679	51,888	70,559
Minneapolis, MN	50,605	80,269	112,607
Nashville, TN	46,820	75,197	106,483
New Orleans, LA	39,698	55,339	89,943
New York, NY	50,776	79,713	127,894
Oklahoma City, OK	37,109	66,702	91,131
Omaha, NE	42,515	72,708	103,010
Orlando, FL	41,985	69,268	100,135
Philadelphia, PA	37,669	60,698	88,307
Phoenix, AZ	40,309	77,041	106,845
Pittsburgh, PA	43,590	64,137	93,301
Portland, OR	55,312	88,792	122,267
Providence, RI	36,694	66,772	95,112
Provo, UT	26,755	62,800	86,072
Raleigh, NC	49,948	82,424	116,724
Reno, NV	45,180	78,448	107,386
Richmond, VA	44,249	62,671	94,647
Rochester, MN	49,727	87,767	119,510
Sacramento, CA	42,300	83,753	108,939
Saint Louis, MO	38,947	55,279	78,097
Saint Paul, MN	41,594	73,055	102,197
Salem, OR	36,477	71,900	94,087
Salt Lake City, UT	49,642	74,925	111,189
San Antonio, TX	32,983	62,917	85,107
San Diego, CA	54,678	104,321	139,707
San Francisco, CA	90,285	141,446	204,625
San Jose, CA	63,253	141,565	187,711
Santa Rosa, CA	50,520	97,410	129,680
Savannah, GA	32,004	56,782	77,786
Seattle, WA	82,508	121,984	170,038
Sioux Falls, SD	43,231	74,714	102,058
Tampa, FL	49,513	71,302	117,408
Tucson, AZ	31,152	54,546	73,528
Tulsa, OK	37,533	58,407	88,998
Virginia Beach, VA	47,372	90,685	118,081
Washington, DC	75,253	106,287	157,604
Wichita, KS	35,958	63,072	87,820
Wilmington, NC	46,062	63,900	98,401
Winston-Salem, NC	35,074	57,673	85,278
U.S.	43,289	78,538	110,491

Source: U.S. Census Bureau, 2019-2023 American Community Survey 5-Year Estimates

Income: Metro Area

Metro Area	Per Capita ($)	Median Household ($)	Average Household ($)
Albuquerque, NM	38,300	67,995	91,376
Anchorage, AK	47,015	95,918	123,232
Ann Arbor, MI	51,746	87,156	122,847
Athens, GA	36,105	62,897	91,841
Atlanta, GA	44,798	86,338	118,625
Austin, TX	53,550	97,638	132,189
Baltimore, MD	51,146	97,300	128,719
Billings, MT	43,176	74,599	102,275
Boise City, ID	41,793	82,694	110,044
Boston, MA	61,389	112,484	155,005
Boulder, CO	60,272	102,772	144,869
Cape Coral, FL	43,365	73,099	102,290
Cedar Rapids, IA	41,820	77,084	100,451
Charleston, SC	46,863	82,272	114,464
Charlotte, NC	44,995	80,201	113,387
Chicago, IL	48,107	88,850	122,980
Cincinnati, OH	43,371	79,490	107,457
Clarksville, TN	31,813	66,210	82,303
Cleveland, OH	41,791	68,507	96,273
College Station, TX	34,136	59,691	88,300
Colorado Springs, CO	44,315	87,180	112,662
Columbia, MO	37,799	69,463	93,435
Columbia, SC	37,159	66,146	90,520
Columbus, OH	43,665	79,847	108,257
Dallas, TX	44,447	87,155	120,397
Davenport, IA	39,357	71,925	93,006
Denver, CO	55,529	102,339	135,703
Des Moines, IA	44,796	84,209	109,864
Detroit, MI	42,145	75,123	102,705
Durham, NC	48,827	81,017	116,697
El Paso, TX	27,509	58,800	77,734
Eugene, OR	38,563	69,311	91,348
Fargo, ND	43,099	75,523	100,645
Fort Collins, CO	49,323	91,364	118,812
Fort Wayne, IN	36,444	69,378	90,705
Fort Worth, TX	44,447	87,155	120,397
Gainesville, FL	36,810	58,946	89,302
Green Bay, WI	40,606	77,459	98,052
Greensboro, NC	35,569	63,083	87,043
Honolulu, HI	46,361	104,264	133,753
Houston, TX	41,559	80,458	115,043
Huntsville, AL	45,250	83,529	110,607
Indianapolis, IN	42,522	77,065	106,219
Jacksonville, FL	41,987	77,013	104,828
Kansas City, MO	44,205	81,927	108,186
Lafayette, LA	34,845	60,910	86,057
Las Vegas, NV	38,654	73,845	101,010
Lexington, KY	41,230	70,717	99,405
Lincoln, NE	40,527	73,095	99,081
Little Rock, AR	37,678	65,309	90,691
Los Angeles, CA	46,385	93,525	132,022
Louisville, KY	40,019	71,737	97,103
Madison, WI	49,799	86,827	113,809
Manchester, NH	52,243	100,436	128,567
McAllen, TX	22,005	52,281	71,722
Memphis, TN	36,519	64,743	92,389

Table continued on following page.

Metro Area	Per Capita ($)	Median Household ($)	Average Household ($)
Miami, FL	42,369	73,481	109,356
Midland, TX	48,843	93,442	126,152
Milwaukee, WI	44,476	76,404	104,403
Minneapolis, MN	51,500	98,180	128,647
Nashville, TN	45,266	82,499	113,441
New Orleans, LA	37,547	62,271	90,627
New York, NY	54,510	97,334	144,032
Oklahoma City, OK	38,240	70,499	95,891
Omaha, NE	44,338	83,023	111,142
Orlando, FL	38,776	75,611	103,312
Philadelphia, PA	49,178	89,273	123,454
Phoenix, AZ	43,395	84,703	113,623
Pittsburgh, PA	44,726	73,942	101,289
Portland, OR	50,158	94,573	124,372
Providence, RI	45,170	85,646	111,377
Provo, UT	35,045	96,745	121,112
Raleigh, NC	49,462	96,066	126,566
Reno, NV	45,849	84,684	114,037
Richmond, VA	46,237	84,405	114,424
Rochester, MN	48,977	89,675	120,598
Sacramento, CA	45,964	93,986	123,767
Saint Louis, MO	44,689	78,225	107,013
Saint Paul, MN	51,500	98,180	128,647
Salem, OR	36,260	76,010	97,771
Salt Lake City, UT	43,026	95,045	121,478
San Antonio, TX	37,425	74,297	100,400
San Diego, CA	49,891	102,285	136,236
San Francisco, CA	72,306	133,780	190,258
San Jose, CA	75,895	157,444	217,226
Santa Rosa, CA	54,941	102,840	138,572
Savannah, GA	39,158	74,632	99,643
Seattle, WA	61,286	112,594	152,753
Sioux Falls, SD	43,434	81,418	106,253
Tampa, FL	42,023	71,254	100,901
Tucson, AZ	38,564	67,929	92,561
Tulsa, OK	37,865	67,823	94,114
Virginia Beach, VA	42,791	80,533	105,690
Washington, DC	62,026	123,896	162,905
Wichita, KS	36,529	68,930	91,559
Wilmington, NC	44,459	73,687	100,847
Winston-Salem, NC	35,829	64,282	87,020
U.S.	43,289	78,538	110,491

Note: Figures cover the Metropolitan Statistical Area (MSA)
Source: U.S. Census Bureau, 2019-2023 American Community Survey 5-Year Estimates

Household Income Distribution: City

City	Percent of Households Earning							
	Under $15,000	$15,000 -$24,999	$25,000 -$34,999	$35,000 -$49,999	$50,000 -$74,999	$75,000 -$99,999	$100,000 -$149,999	$150,000 and up
Albuquerque, NM	10.9	8.5	7.9	11.5	17.5	12.6	16.0	15.2
Anchorage, AK	5.2	4.6	4.4	8.3	14.6	13.7	19.5	29.7
Ann Arbor, MI	12.8	5.7	5.8	8.8	14.4	10.6	15.2	26.8
Athens, GA	15.5	10.4	10.3	12.4	16.1	10.9	12.9	11.6
Atlanta, GA	13.2	6.7	6.1	8.2	12.8	11.5	15.0	26.5
Austin, TX	7.8	4.6	4.9	9.3	15.1	12.4	17.2	28.7
Baltimore, MD	15.7	8.4	7.4	11.4	16.6	11.3	13.5	15.7
Billings, MT	7.2	7.0	7.4	12.6	18.1	13.0	17.9	16.9
Boise City, ID	5.7	6.0	6.3	11.2	16.6	15.1	17.4	21.6
Boston, MA	12.9	6.5	5.1	7.1	10.6	9.9	15.5	32.5
Boulder, CO	12.4	6.7	7.3	7.7	11.5	9.5	14.0	30.9
Cape Coral, FL	6.2	5.0	7.7	10.6	19.9	15.6	19.3	15.7
Cedar Rapids, IA	7.3	6.6	8.9	14.1	18.3	14.2	16.0	14.8
Charleston, SC	7.7	6.1	4.3	9.6	14.7	12.7	18.6	26.4
Charlotte, NC	7.0	5.6	6.2	11.6	17.6	12.7	16.9	22.5
Chicago, IL	12.1	7.2	6.9	9.8	14.0	11.7	16.0	22.4
Cincinnati, OH	16.9	10.2	8.7	12.9	15.0	10.3	11.8	14.2
Clarksville, TN	7.7	5.7	7.7	13.4	21.0	16.7	17.8	10.0
Cleveland, OH	22.1	12.6	10.7	14.2	16.0	9.2	8.9	6.4
College Station, TX	18.3	8.3	9.5	12.9	12.2	11.0	12.2	15.6
Colorado Springs, CO	6.2	5.3	5.8	10.4	17.7	13.6	19.8	21.3
Columbia, MO	12.4	8.3	8.5	10.8	17.1	11.8	14.3	17.0
Columbia, SC	16.5	8.6	8.2	11.7	16.7	10.7	11.7	15.8
Columbus, OH	10.0	7.1	7.4	13.3	18.5	13.5	16.6	13.5
Dallas, TX	10.2	6.8	7.7	12.3	17.9	12.5	13.7	18.8
Davenport, IA	10.8	7.0	8.8	11.5	19.0	13.5	17.4	12.0
Denver, CO	7.8	5.2	5.1	8.6	14.4	12.6	17.9	28.4
Des Moines, IA	8.8	7.7	7.2	14.3	19.3	15.4	15.2	12.1
Detroit, MI	22.8	12.2	10.2	15.2	15.1	9.5	9.2	5.8
Durham, NC	7.7	5.8	6.4	10.6	16.9	12.9	17.9	21.7
El Paso, TX	12.9	9.1	8.9	12.8	18.2	12.6	14.2	11.5
Eugene, OR	11.3	7.8	7.6	13.2	15.5	12.5	15.8	16.3
Fargo, ND	8.5	7.3	9.2	12.9	18.1	13.8	15.2	15.0
Fort Collins, CO	9.5	5.7	5.5	10.0	14.9	12.5	18.4	23.5
Fort Wayne, IN	9.3	7.9	9.6	14.5	19.5	14.1	15.2	9.9
Fort Worth, TX	7.4	5.9	6.9	11.1	17.3	13.7	18.1	19.4
Gainesville, FL	18.0	10.4	11.2	14.8	14.8	10.2	10.4	10.2
Green Bay, WI	9.5	8.6	7.4	13.6	19.7	14.6	16.2	10.4
Greensboro, NC	11.7	8.0	9.0	13.8	17.8	12.2	15.0	12.6
Honolulu, HI	8.8	5.7	5.1	9.4	15.2	12.7	17.4	25.7
Houston, TX	10.9	8.2	8.5	12.6	17.4	11.6	13.1	17.7
Huntsville, AL	9.2	8.0	8.7	11.3	15.0	12.6	15.6	19.6
Indianapolis, IN	10.7	7.5	8.2	13.5	18.7	12.5	15.0	13.8
Jacksonville, FL	10.0	7.3	7.5	12.7	17.9	13.3	16.9	14.5
Kansas City, MO	10.3	7.2	7.5	12.5	17.2	12.6	16.9	15.7
Lafayette, LA	13.8	8.8	8.0	11.5	14.6	12.8	14.9	15.6
Las Vegas, NV	10.0	6.7	7.5	11.4	17.3	12.9	16.8	17.4
Lexington, KY	9.8	7.2	8.6	11.9	16.8	11.9	15.7	18.1
Lincoln, NE	8.1	6.4	8.2	12.5	18.3	14.0	17.1	15.6
Little Rock, AR	10.7	8.2	9.9	13.9	15.6	11.3	13.1	17.2
Los Angeles, CA	10.8	6.7	6.5	9.4	14.0	11.5	16.0	25.1
Louisville, KY	10.6	7.6	8.2	12.7	17.2	12.8	15.9	15.0
Madison, WI	9.4	6.2	7.2	10.3	15.5	12.8	17.6	20.9
Manchester, NH	6.0	6.9	5.7	11.7	18.0	14.3	19.3	18.1

Table continued on following page.

	Percent of Households Earning							
City	Under $15,000	$15,000 -$24,999	$25,000 -$34,999	$35,000 -$49,999	$50,000 -$74,999	$75,000 -$99,999	$100,000 -$149,999	$150,000 and up
McAllen, TX	11.9	10.2	9.3	11.4	16.1	11.7	15.7	13.7
Memphis, TN	14.7	9.9	10.1	14.4	17.9	10.9	11.6	10.5
Miami, FL	14.4	9.3	8.1	11.9	15.7	10.2	13.1	17.4
Midland, TX	9.1	4.8	5.8	9.2	14.3	10.1	18.0	28.6
Milwaukee, WI	14.5	9.7	10.4	13.8	18.0	12.0	12.7	8.9
Minneapolis, MN	9.5	6.6	6.2	9.7	15.2	12.3	17.3	23.1
Nashville, TN	8.5	5.6	6.6	11.8	17.4	13.6	17.2	19.3
New Orleans, LA	18.7	9.7	7.7	10.8	14.8	9.6	12.8	15.8
New York, NY	12.3	7.0	6.3	8.9	13.3	10.8	15.3	26.1
Oklahoma City, OK	10.0	7.0	7.9	12.4	18.1	13.3	15.9	15.4
Omaha, NE	8.8	6.5	7.2	11.4	17.6	13.1	17.1	18.2
Orlando, FL	9.5	7.0	8.7	11.7	17.1	12.5	16.3	17.2
Philadelphia, PA	15.1	8.7	8.2	11.0	15.8	11.8	14.0	15.3
Phoenix, AZ	7.7	5.6	6.7	11.5	17.3	13.7	17.4	20.1
Pittsburgh, PA	14.2	8.1	7.4	11.0	16.6	11.4	14.6	16.8
Portland, OR	8.8	5.3	5.6	9.2	14.2	11.9	17.6	27.3
Providence, RI	13.7	8.4	6.6	10.7	16.0	11.7	15.8	17.1
Provo, UT	9.4	8.2	9.2	13.5	17.7	13.6	14.5	13.8
Raleigh, NC	7.0	5.6	6.0	11.2	15.9	13.0	17.2	24.1
Reno, NV	7.9	6.4	6.9	10.2	16.6	13.2	18.7	19.9
Richmond, VA	13.0	8.4	7.7	12.7	16.6	12.0	12.4	17.1
Rochester, MN	5.2	5.8	5.7	9.1	16.3	13.5	19.9	24.5
Sacramento, CA	9.1	6.1	5.2	9.5	15.1	13.6	18.7	22.7
Saint Louis, MO	15.5	8.8	9.1	12.5	17.5	11.3	13.1	12.4
Saint Paul, MN	9.0	6.6	6.9	10.4	18.4	13.2	16.1	19.4
Salem, OR	9.0	6.5	7.5	11.2	17.5	12.6	19.0	16.5
Salt Lake City, UT	9.0	6.7	6.5	11.1	16.8	13.5	15.9	20.5
San Antonio, TX	10.3	7.9	9.2	12.4	18.6	13.4	15.0	13.4
San Diego, CA	6.7	4.4	4.8	7.3	12.5	12.4	19.4	32.5
San Francisco, CA	8.5	4.8	3.9	5.2	8.1	8.4	13.4	47.7
San Jose, CA	4.9	3.6	3.5	5.5	9.2	9.3	16.6	47.3
Santa Rosa, CA	6.3	4.1	4.4	7.7	15.6	13.4	19.5	29.1
Savannah, GA	13.4	8.3	9.8	13.0	18.8	11.7	13.9	11.2
Seattle, WA	7.3	3.9	4.0	6.5	11.4	9.5	16.3	41.1
Sioux Falls, SD	6.0	5.5	7.5	12.3	18.8	14.3	18.6	16.9
Tampa, FL	11.1	7.2	7.2	11.2	15.6	11.2	14.4	22.1
Tucson, AZ	12.0	9.6	10.2	14.6	17.5	12.7	14.1	9.5
Tulsa, OK	11.9	7.6	10.1	13.5	17.8	11.5	13.4	14.2
Virginia Beach, VA	5.7	3.9	5.1	8.5	18.1	13.7	20.8	24.2
Washington, DC	10.5	4.6	3.8	6.8	11.4	10.4	15.7	36.9
Wichita, KS	9.5	7.6	9.6	13.0	18.1	13.3	15.6	13.3
Wilmington, NC	11.3	6.8	8.3	13.0	17.6	11.9	14.2	16.8
Winston-Salem, NC	11.3	8.9	10.0	13.2	17.2	12.5	13.8	13.0
U.S.	8.5	6.6	6.8	10.4	15.7	12.7	17.4	21.9

Source: U.S. Census Bureau, 2019-2023 American Community Survey 5-Year Estimates

Household Income Distribution: Metro Area

Metro Area	Percent of Households Earning							
	Under $15,000	$15,000 -$24,999	$25,000 -$34,999	$35,000 -$49,999	$50,000 -$74,999	$75,000 -$99,999	$100,000 -$149,999	$150,000 and up
Albuquerque, NM	10.3	7.9	7.6	11.2	17.5	12.8	16.6	16.0
Anchorage, AK	5.4	4.9	4.7	8.5	14.6	13.8	19.8	28.2
Ann Arbor, MI	8.8	5.3	5.8	9.3	14.9	11.8	17.5	26.6
Athens, GA	12.6	8.5	9.0	11.3	15.5	12.1	14.8	16.2
Atlanta, GA	6.9	5.4	6.0	9.8	15.4	13.4	18.3	24.8
Austin, TX	6.3	4.1	4.8	8.6	14.8	12.4	19.2	29.9
Baltimore, MD	7.6	4.9	5.0	8.3	13.3	12.0	18.8	30.1
Billings, MT	6.6	6.8	7.6	11.5	17.6	13.4	18.1	18.2
Boise City, ID	5.3	5.3	5.6	10.5	18.4	15.3	19.7	19.8
Boston, MA	7.2	4.9	4.5	6.7	11.2	10.5	17.7	37.2
Boulder, CO	7.5	5.3	5.2	7.4	12.4	11.1	17.3	33.9
Cape Coral, FL	7.9	6.2	7.5	11.7	18.0	14.2	17.3	17.2
Cedar Rapids, IA	6.1	6.2	7.2	12.0	17.3	14.5	18.2	18.5
Charleston, SC	7.2	6.1	6.1	10.0	16.8	13.0	19.2	21.6
Charlotte, NC	6.8	6.1	6.5	10.9	16.7	13.0	17.7	22.2
Chicago, IL	8.1	5.6	5.9	9.0	14.2	12.5	18.4	26.4
Cincinnati, OH	8.4	6.5	6.7	10.4	15.5	13.0	18.7	20.9
Clarksville, TN	9.1	6.6	8.1	12.3	20.0	15.2	17.1	11.5
Cleveland, OH	10.1	7.6	7.8	11.6	16.9	12.5	16.0	17.3
College Station, TX	14.7	7.7	8.7	12.5	14.6	12.2	14.2	15.4
Colorado Springs, CO	5.7	4.8	5.6	9.8	16.9	13.7	20.3	23.3
Columbia, MO	10.3	7.4	7.6	11.1	17.3	13.3	16.6	16.2
Columbia, SC	10.1	7.3	8.1	12.5	17.5	13.0	15.8	15.7
Columbus, OH	7.6	5.8	6.4	11.0	16.6	12.9	18.2	21.5
Dallas, TX	6.3	4.9	5.8	10.0	16.1	13.1	18.5	25.2
Davenport, IA	9.0	6.9	7.5	11.5	17.0	13.6	18.6	16.0
Denver, CO	5.7	4.1	4.5	7.9	14.0	12.8	19.7	31.4
Des Moines, IA	5.6	5.4	6.1	11.0	16.5	14.0	19.1	22.4
Detroit, MI	9.3	6.7	7.0	11.1	15.7	12.8	17.0	20.2
Durham, NC	7.8	6.2	6.4	10.3	16.0	12.0	17.3	23.9
El Paso, TX	12.8	8.9	8.9	12.8	18.6	12.6	14.4	11.1
Eugene, OR	10.0	7.3	7.5	12.5	16.2	14.2	17.8	14.6
Fargo, ND	7.8	6.5	7.5	11.4	16.5	13.8	18.0	18.5
Fort Collins, CO	7.2	5.1	5.3	8.9	14.9	13.5	19.9	25.2
Fort Wayne, IN	7.2	6.9	7.9	12.8	18.9	15.0	17.0	14.1
Fort Worth, TX	6.3	4.9	5.8	10.0	16.1	13.1	18.5	25.2
Gainesville, FL	13.2	8.5	9.1	12.6	16.2	11.1	14.0	15.2
Green Bay, WI	6.7	5.6	7.0	11.1	17.9	14.8	20.8	16.1
Greensboro, NC	10.1	8.0	8.3	13.7	17.6	12.6	16.3	13.5
Honolulu, HI	6.3	4.2	4.2	7.9	12.9	12.6	20.4	31.6
Houston, TX	7.7	6.2	6.7	10.5	15.9	12.5	16.9	23.6
Huntsville, AL	7.3	6.6	6.8	10.1	15.1	12.5	18.2	23.4
Indianapolis, IN	7.7	6.0	6.6	11.2	17.3	13.2	17.5	20.5
Jacksonville, FL	8.0	6.1	6.7	11.1	16.9	13.3	18.3	19.7
Kansas City, MO	6.9	5.7	6.4	10.4	16.6	13.3	19.1	21.3
Lafayette, LA	13.1	9.6	8.3	12.0	14.7	12.2	15.8	14.3
Las Vegas, NV	8.6	6.4	7.2	11.3	17.2	13.6	17.4	18.2
Lexington, KY	9.1	6.8	8.1	11.7	17.0	12.5	17.0	17.6
Lincoln, NE	7.4	6.1	7.7	12.0	17.9	13.8	18.0	17.1
Little Rock, AR	9.9	7.9	8.8	12.9	17.0	12.7	16.1	14.8
Los Angeles, CA	8.3	5.4	5.6	8.5	13.4	11.7	17.9	29.3
Louisville, KY	8.5	6.8	7.4	12.0	17.2	13.5	17.6	17.0
Madison, WI	6.5	5.2	6.1	9.4	16.1	13.5	19.4	23.8
Manchester, NH	4.5	4.5	4.6	8.8	14.6	12.8	19.9	30.3

Table continued on following page.

	Percent of Households Earning							
Metro Area	Under $15,000	$15,000 -$24,999	$25,000 -$34,999	$35,000 -$49,999	$50,000 -$74,999	$75,000 -$99,999	$100,000 -$149,999	$150,000 and up
McAllen, TX	14.0	11.7	10.0	12.6	16.7	11.7	13.8	9.5
Memphis, TN	10.9	8.0	8.2	12.2	16.7	12.1	16.0	15.9
Miami, FL	9.3	7.1	7.4	10.9	16.1	12.6	16.3	20.1
Midland, TX	8.0	4.3	5.9	9.4	13.7	11.6	18.6	28.4
Milwaukee, WI	8.5	6.5	7.4	10.4	16.3	13.1	17.8	20.0
Minneapolis, MN	5.5	4.5	4.9	8.5	14.5	13.0	20.3	28.9
Nashville, TN	6.6	5.5	5.8	10.7	16.8	13.9	19.0	21.7
New Orleans, LA	13.6	8.8	8.5	11.2	15.6	11.7	14.6	15.9
New York, NY	9.0	5.6	5.4	7.9	12.4	10.7	16.7	32.4
Oklahoma City, OK	8.9	6.7	7.8	11.9	17.6	13.5	17.0	16.6
Omaha, NE	6.9	5.6	6.3	10.1	16.6	13.2	19.6	21.7
Orlando, FL	7.3	6.3	7.3	11.1	17.7	13.5	18.0	18.9
Philadelphia, PA	8.4	5.8	6.0	8.9	14.0	11.9	17.9	27.1
Phoenix, AZ	6.6	5.0	5.9	10.1	16.6	13.9	19.3	22.5
Pittsburgh, PA	8.8	7.3	7.3	10.9	16.2	12.9	17.2	19.3
Portland, OR	6.4	4.7	5.1	8.8	14.6	13.1	19.7	27.6
Providence, RI	8.7	6.7	6.0	9.1	14.0	12.6	19.0	23.8
Provo, UT	4.4	4.1	4.6	8.5	15.1	15.0	22.7	25.6
Raleigh, NC	5.6	4.9	5.4	9.0	14.6	12.1	19.5	28.8
Reno, NV	6.9	5.4	6.0	9.9	16.4	13.4	20.5	21.6
Richmond, VA	7.2	5.6	5.9	10.0	16.3	12.7	18.9	23.4
Rochester, MN	5.2	5.4	5.6	9.0	16.3	13.4	20.4	24.7
Sacramento, CA	7.3	5.2	5.3	8.5	13.9	12.7	19.3	27.9
Saint Louis, MO	7.6	6.2	6.8	11.1	16.4	13.1	18.1	20.7
Saint Paul, MN	5.5	4.5	4.9	8.5	14.5	13.0	20.3	28.9
Salem, OR	7.7	6.4	6.9	11.0	17.3	13.4	19.7	17.5
Salt Lake City, UT	5.3	4.0	4.7	8.8	15.3	14.6	21.5	25.8
San Antonio, TX	8.2	6.5	7.5	10.9	17.2	13.3	17.4	18.9
San Diego, CA	6.3	4.7	5.0	7.8	13.1	12.1	19.1	31.9
San Francisco, CA	6.3	3.8	3.8	5.9	9.6	9.3	15.9	45.4
San Jose, CA	4.6	3.0	3.1	4.8	8.4	8.5	15.5	52.0
Santa Rosa, CA	5.9	4.1	4.7	7.8	13.4	12.7	19.3	32.2
Savannah, GA	8.5	6.0	7.5	11.0	17.3	13.8	18.5	17.4
Seattle, WA	5.6	3.8	4.2	7.0	12.6	11.5	19.2	36.1
Sioux Falls, SD	5.4	5.2	6.6	11.6	17.7	14.7	20.0	18.9
Tampa, FL	8.6	6.9	7.6	11.6	17.6	12.8	16.6	18.3
Tucson, AZ	9.3	7.6	8.5	12.3	16.7	12.8	16.7	16.0
Tulsa, OK	8.9	7.1	8.4	12.3	17.8	12.9	16.9	15.8
Virginia Beach, VA	7.5	5.5	6.6	10.0	17.3	13.3	19.2	20.7
Washington, DC	5.4	3.2	3.5	5.9	11.0	11.0	18.9	41.0
Wichita, KS	8.3	6.6	8.7	12.2	18.3	13.9	17.0	14.8
Wilmington, NC	8.2	6.4	6.8	11.5	18.0	13.4	17.6	18.0
Winston-Salem, NC	9.2	8.1	9.0	12.8	18.0	13.7	15.4	13.9
U.S.	8.5	6.6	6.8	10.4	15.7	12.7	17.4	21.9

Note: Figures cover the Metropolitan Statistical Area (MSA)
Source: U.S. Census Bureau, 2019-2023 American Community Survey 5-Year Estimates

Poverty Rate: City

City	All Ages	Under 18 Years Old	18 to 64 Years Old	65 Years and Over
Albuquerque, NM	16.0	20.8	15.3	12.6
Anchorage, AK	9.3	11.3	8.8	7.8
Ann Arbor, MI	23.0	13.5	27.9	6.0
Athens, GA	26.3	24.3	29.5	11.7
Atlanta, GA	17.9	25.9	15.6	18.7
Austin, TX	12.3	15.7	11.6	10.9
Baltimore, MD	20.1	26.4	17.8	20.9
Billings, MT	10.6	13.0	10.2	8.9
Boise City, ID	10.6	12.7	10.8	7.3
Boston, MA	16.9	21.8	15.0	21.0
Boulder, CO	21.8	9.7	26.8	6.2
Cape Coral, FL	9.8	13.1	9.1	9.2
Cedar Rapids, IA	11.8	14.3	11.9	7.8
Charleston, SC	12.0	15.4	12.2	7.3
Charlotte, NC	11.7	16.9	10.1	10.4
Chicago, IL	16.8	24.0	14.6	17.1
Cincinnati, OH	24.5	34.2	22.8	17.1
Clarksville, TN	12.8	16.8	11.8	7.7
Cleveland, OH	30.8	45.3	27.4	24.5
College Station, TX	28.6	14.8	34.5	5.8
Colorado Springs, CO	9.3	10.8	9.2	7.7
Columbia, MO	20.0	13.4	23.5	10.7
Columbia, SC	23.3	29.4	22.6	17.2
Columbus, OH	17.8	25.9	16.1	12.1
Dallas, TX	17.2	25.7	14.3	15.0
Davenport, IA	15.6	20.7	15.0	11.3
Denver, CO	11.2	14.9	10.2	11.5
Des Moines, IA	14.9	22.1	13.1	10.8
Detroit, MI	31.5	44.2	28.8	20.9
Durham, NC	12.2	16.9	11.5	8.2
El Paso, TX	18.4	24.8	15.4	20.0
Eugene, OR	18.2	15.1	21.4	9.4
Fargo, ND	12.8	14.6	13.7	6.0
Fort Collins, CO	16.0	9.2	19.1	8.0
Fort Wayne, IN	15.6	22.5	14.3	9.1
Fort Worth, TX	12.9	18.0	11.1	10.2
Gainesville, FL	28.0	18.0	32.8	11.4
Green Bay, WI	16.5	23.4	15.0	11.0
Greensboro, NC	18.4	26.0	16.5	14.2
Honolulu, HI	11.9	15.0	11.1	11.7
Houston, TX	19.7	29.9	16.6	16.0
Huntsville, AL	13.8	19.5	13.3	8.9
Indianapolis, IN	15.7	21.2	14.3	11.5
Jacksonville, FL	15.0	20.9	13.1	14.2
Kansas City, MO	14.6	20.5	12.9	12.4
Lafayette, LA	19.1	28.3	17.1	14.8
Las Vegas, NV	14.2	18.8	13.2	11.7
Lexington, KY	15.7	19.3	16.3	7.7
Lincoln, NE	12.6	13.0	13.6	8.0
Little Rock, AR	16.4	25.1	15.1	7.8
Los Angeles, CA	16.5	22.1	14.8	16.9
Louisville, KY	16.1	23.2	14.9	10.8
Madison, WI	16.2	13.1	18.7	7.0
Manchester, NH	10.7	17.2	9.3	9.5
McAllen, TX	20.2	27.2	17.6	17.0

Table continued on following page.

City	All Ages	Under 18 Years Old	18 to 64 Years Old	65 Years and Over
Memphis, TN	22.5	34.7	18.9	16.4
Miami, FL	19.2	23.4	15.3	31.4
Midland, TX	11.7	14.0	10.6	11.5
Milwaukee, WI	23.3	32.5	20.7	16.7
Minneapolis, MN	16.4	19.8	15.7	14.2
Nashville, TN	14.1	21.2	12.5	11.2
New Orleans, LA	22.6	32.2	20.1	20.7
New York, NY	17.4	23.2	15.1	18.9
Oklahoma City, OK	15.2	20.6	14.2	9.4
Omaha, NE	12.8	15.9	12.3	9.3
Orlando, FL	15.5	23.0	12.9	16.8
Philadelphia, PA	22.0	30.1	19.5	21.1
Phoenix, AZ	14.3	20.3	12.5	11.7
Pittsburgh, PA	19.5	29.5	18.4	14.1
Portland, OR	12.8	14.5	12.5	11.8
Providence, RI	20.1	26.0	18.2	19.9
Provo, UT	22.3	12.8	26.3	9.4
Raleigh, NC	11.4	14.6	10.9	9.1
Reno, NV	12.5	13.9	12.2	11.8
Richmond, VA	18.8	28.3	17.2	14.6
Rochester, MN	9.1	9.0	9.4	7.6
Sacramento, CA	14.4	17.9	13.5	12.8
Saint Louis, MO	19.8	26.9	18.2	17.8
Saint Paul, MN	15.7	22.9	13.8	11.7
Salem, OR	14.7	17.2	14.4	11.8
Salt Lake City, UT	13.4	12.3	14.1	11.0
San Antonio, TX	17.1	24.8	14.8	14.2
San Diego, CA	11.1	12.3	11.0	10.2
San Francisco, CA	10.6	8.2	9.6	16.4
San Jose, CA	7.8	7.6	7.4	10.5
Santa Rosa, CA	9.5	10.8	9.1	9.5
Savannah, GA	19.5	28.9	17.6	14.0
Seattle, WA	9.9	8.6	9.7	12.3
Sioux Falls, SD	9.6	12.3	9.1	7.1
Tampa, FL	15.9	20.3	13.5	21.2
Tucson, AZ	18.8	24.3	18.7	12.5
Tulsa, OK	18.6	27.0	17.3	10.4
Virginia Beach, VA	8.4	11.2	8.0	5.9
Washington, DC	14.5	20.4	12.9	14.6
Wichita, KS	15.9	21.6	15.0	10.3
Wilmington, NC	16.3	18.1	17.3	11.0
Winston-Salem, NC	17.9	27.1	16.0	10.7
U.S.	12.4	16.3	11.6	10.4

Note: Figures are percentage of people whose income during the past 12 months was below the poverty level
Source: U.S. Census Bureau, 2019-2023 American Community Survey 5-Year Estimates

Poverty Rate: Metro Area

Metro Area	All Ages	Under 18 Years Old	18 to 64 Years Old	65 Years and Over
Albuquerque, NM	15.1	19.6	14.5	12.0
Anchorage, AK	9.6	11.6	9.1	7.9
Ann Arbor, MI	13.8	12.5	16.2	5.9
Athens, GA	19.7	19.0	22.1	10.1
Atlanta, GA	11.0	15.0	9.7	9.3
Austin, TX	9.9	11.5	9.6	8.7
Baltimore, MD	9.9	12.0	9.0	10.2
Billings, MT	10.0	12.0	9.9	8.2
Boise City, ID	9.1	10.7	8.9	7.7
Boston, MA	8.9	9.7	8.3	10.3
Boulder, CO	11.4	7.5	13.7	7.1
Cape Coral, FL	11.7	17.1	11.2	9.5
Cedar Rapids, IA	9.7	11.5	9.7	7.5
Charleston, SC	11.2	15.6	10.3	9.0
Charlotte, NC	10.5	14.2	9.4	9.3
Chicago, IL	11.1	14.8	10.0	10.2
Cincinnati, OH	11.6	14.7	11.1	9.2
Clarksville, TN	13.2	16.4	12.3	10.5
Cleveland, OH	13.6	19.3	12.6	10.6
College Station, TX	22.6	19.9	26.0	8.5
Colorado Springs, CO	8.5	10.2	8.2	6.9
Columbia, MO	16.5	14.6	18.8	9.0
Columbia, SC	14.7	19.8	13.9	10.6
Columbus, OH	12.2	16.5	11.4	8.7
Dallas, TX	10.5	14.5	9.2	9.3
Davenport, IA	12.4	16.9	12.0	8.3
Denver, CO	8.2	10.3	7.6	7.6
Des Moines, IA	8.9	11.0	8.5	7.1
Detroit, MI	13.2	19.1	12.0	10.2
Durham, NC	12.3	16.2	12.2	7.9
El Paso, TX	18.9	25.1	15.8	20.6
Eugene, OR	15.3	14.3	17.4	9.7
Fargo, ND	11.4	11.8	12.2	6.7
Fort Collins, CO	11.1	8.5	12.9	7.1
Fort Wayne, IN	11.8	16.1	11.1	7.3
Fort Worth, TX	10.5	14.5	9.2	9.3
Gainesville, FL	18.9	16.3	21.8	10.7
Green Bay, WI	9.5	11.6	9.3	7.5
Greensboro, NC	15.3	21.4	14.1	11.6
Honolulu, HI	9.1	11.4	8.5	8.7
Houston, TX	13.6	19.1	11.7	11.3
Huntsville, AL	10.4	13.1	9.8	9.1
Indianapolis, IN	10.5	13.6	9.8	8.3
Jacksonville, FL	12.1	16.9	10.9	10.2
Kansas City, MO	10.0	13.2	9.2	8.5
Lafayette, LA	18.5	25.0	16.8	14.8
Las Vegas, NV	13.2	18.1	12.1	10.6
Lexington, KY	14.0	17.4	14.1	8.6
Lincoln, NE	11.4	11.3	12.5	7.6
Little Rock, AR	14.2	19.7	13.5	8.7
Los Angeles, CA	12.6	16.0	11.4	13.1
Louisville, KY	12.3	17.0	11.4	9.2
Madison, WI	10.0	8.5	11.4	6.1
Manchester, NH	6.5	8.1	6.0	6.7
McAllen, TX	27.2	37.1	22.6	22.9

Table continued on following page.

Metro Area	All Ages	Under 18 Years Old	18 to 64 Years Old	65 Years and Over
Memphis, TN	16.3	24.2	14.0	12.2
Miami, FL	13.1	16.9	11.0	15.9
Midland, TX	10.6	12.7	9.3	11.6
Milwaukee, WI	12.4	17.0	11.2	10.3
Minneapolis, MN	8.2	9.6	7.7	7.7
Nashville, TN	10.4	13.6	9.5	8.9
New Orleans, LA	18.3	25.6	16.5	14.9
New York, NY	12.4	16.4	10.9	13.0
Oklahoma City, OK	13.9	18.3	13.3	8.8
Omaha, NE	9.5	11.2	9.1	8.1
Orlando, FL	11.8	15.0	11.0	10.5
Philadelphia, PA	11.7	15.7	10.6	10.3
Phoenix, AZ	11.2	15.1	10.3	9.2
Pittsburgh, PA	10.9	14.4	10.5	8.9
Portland, OR	9.5	10.5	9.4	9.0
Providence, RI	11.2	14.2	10.3	10.6
Provo, UT	8.7	7.2	10.0	5.5
Raleigh, NC	8.6	10.3	8.0	7.9
Reno, NV	10.7	12.1	10.3	10.3
Richmond, VA	10.0	13.4	9.3	8.0
Rochester, MN	7.8	8.3	7.8	7.1
Sacramento, CA	11.6	13.6	11.4	9.3
Saint Louis, MO	10.3	13.3	9.7	8.7
Saint Paul, MN	8.2	9.6	7.7	7.7
Salem, OR	12.9	16.0	12.5	10.2
Salt Lake City, UT	8.1	8.8	8.0	7.5
San Antonio, TX	13.4	18.5	11.9	11.4
San Diego, CA	10.4	12.0	10.0	9.4
San Francisco, CA	8.7	8.8	8.2	10.4
San Jose, CA	6.9	6.6	6.5	9.0
Santa Rosa, CA	8.6	9.3	8.4	8.4
Savannah, GA	12.4	16.6	11.4	9.9
Seattle, WA	8.4	9.5	7.9	8.8
Sioux Falls, SD	8.1	9.7	7.7	6.8
Tampa, FL	12.2	15.5	11.3	11.9
Tucson, AZ	14.4	18.7	14.9	8.9
Tulsa, OK	13.7	18.9	12.9	8.9
Virginia Beach, VA	10.9	15.4	9.9	8.4
Washington, DC	7.9	9.8	7.2	7.6
Wichita, KS	13.1	17.4	12.4	8.8
Wilmington, NC	11.1	13.9	11.9	7.0
Winston-Salem, NC	13.9	21.2	12.5	9.7
U.S.	12.4	16.3	11.6	10.4

Note: Figures are percentage of people whose income during the past 12 months was below the poverty level; Figures cover the Metropolitan Statistical Area (MSA)
Source: U.S. Census Bureau, 2019-2023 American Community Survey 5-Year Estimates

Employment by Industry

Metro Area	(A)	(B)	(C)	(D)	(E)	(F)	(G)	(H)	(I)	(J)	(K)	(L)	(M)	(N)
Albuquerque, NM	6.6	n/a	4.6	19.8	1.3	10.4	4.0	n/a	3.1	17.3	16.0	10.3	3.9	2.7
Anchorage, AK	7.3	6.2	4.0	19.3	1.7	10.9	1.3	1.1	3.7	19.1	11.0	10.9	8.0	2.8
Ann Arbor, MI	2.2	n/a	2.9	37.3	2.5	7.1	5.1	n/a	2.8	15.0	12.4	7.3	2.2	3.1
Athens, GA	3.9	n/a	3.3	28.7	0.7	11.4	6.7	n/a	3.6	16.0	8.8	11.1	1.8	4.0
Atlanta, GA[1]	4.2	4.1	7.0	11.9	3.8	9.7	5.3	0.1	3.6	14.6	18.3	9.4	7.1	5.1
Austin, TX	6.5	n/a	6.5	15.3	3.6	10.7	5.3	n/a	3.9	12.0	20.5	9.0	2.7	4.1
Baltimore, MD	5.4	n/a	5.3	16.6	1.1	8.4	3.9	n/a	3.7	20.0	17.5	9.0	5.3	3.7
Billings, MT	8.0	n/a	5.4	11.1	0.9	14.6	4.3	n/a	4.2	18.0	9.8	12.6	5.0	6.0
Boise City, ID	9.1	n/a	5.8	13.3	1.1	10.0	7.6	n/a	3.5	15.4	14.6	10.0	4.6	4.7
Boston, MA[1]	4.1	n/a	9.6	12.2	2.6	10.5	2.8	n/a	3.6	24.6	16.3	7.8	3.4	2.5
Boulder, CO	2.7	n/a	3.3	19.7	4.0	9.6	10.0	n/a	4.3	13.2	20.1	8.2	1.1	3.7
Cape Coral, FL	13.6	n/a	4.9	15.3	1.1	13.0	2.6	n/a	4.0	11.5	14.2	14.3	2.5	3.0
Cedar Rapids, IA	6.3	n/a	6.6	11.9	2.0	8.4	14.2	n/a	3.6	16.3	11.1	10.4	5.1	4.1
Charleston, SC	5.7	n/a	5.1	16.7	1.8	12.4	8.1	n/a	3.9	11.9	15.8	10.9	4.7	3.0
Charlotte, NC	5.9	n/a	8.8	12.9	1.9	10.9	7.7	n/a	4.0	11.1	16.2	10.0	6.1	4.7
Chicago, IL[1]	3.4	3.4	7.2	11.2	1.8	9.8	7.3	<0.1	4.1	17.0	18.0	8.7	6.5	4.9
Cincinnati, OH	4.6	n/a	6.8	11.6	1.1	10.6	10.4	n/a	3.6	15.9	15.3	9.0	5.8	5.3
Clarksville, TN	4.5	n/a	3.8	20.6	1.3	12.1	12.9	n/a	3.3	13.1	8.4	13.2	4.5	2.3
Cleveland, OH	3.7	n/a	6.5	12.5	1.3	9.5	11.6	n/a	3.5	19.7	13.9	9.1	3.8	4.9
College Station, TX	5.3	n/a	3.3	35.1	1.1	14.4	4.2	n/a	2.8	10.9	9.8	9.1	1.9	2.2
Colorado Springs, CO	5.4	n/a	5.8	17.9	1.5	12.4	3.6	n/a	7.0	14.6	16.0	10.2	3.8	2.0
Columbia, MO	3.6	3.5	7.6	31.5	1.1	10.6	4.7	0.1	2.8	13.9	9.1	10.1	2.6	2.5
Columbia, SC	4.3	n/a	8.3	19.4	1.1	9.4	7.4	n/a	4.2	13.9	13.6	10.5	4.2	3.7
Columbus, OH	4.5	n/a	6.9	16.6	1.5	9.1	6.5	n/a	3.8	15.5	16.3	9.2	6.7	3.6
Dallas, TX[1]	5.4	n/a	10.0	11.3	2.5	9.4	6.6	n/a	3.1	11.5	20.2	9.0	5.4	5.6
Davenport, IA	5.7	n/a	4.1	14.4	0.8	9.7	12.8	n/a	3.7	15.0	11.3	11.7	4.2	6.5
Denver, CO	6.9	n/a	7.1	13.7	3.0	10.4	4.0	n/a	4.2	12.9	19.4	8.5	5.3	4.7
Des Moines, IA	5.9	n/a	13.6	12.8	1.5	8.8	5.4	n/a	3.3	15.2	13.4	10.6	4.8	4.8
Detroit, MI[1]	4.0	n/a	6.2	9.6	1.4	9.1	12.1	n/a	3.8	16.2	18.4	9.9	5.2	4.1
Durham, NC	3.1	n/a	4.8	19.3	1.6	7.8	7.9	n/a	3.7	21.8	17.8	6.9	2.4	2.8
El Paso, TX	4.5	n/a	4.1	20.8	1.8	11.6	4.8	n/a	2.8	15.5	12.6	11.4	6.0	4.0
Eugene, OR	5.0	4.4	5.2	19.8	1.2	10.1	8.5	0.6	3.1	18.6	10.9	11.7	2.3	3.5
Fargo, ND	6.0	n/a	7.1	14.0	1.5	9.6	8.0	n/a	3.3	19.6	9.5	10.3	5.2	5.9
Fort Collins, CO	6.0	n/a	3.8	26.3	1.3	12.1	8.0	n/a	3.6	11.3	11.6	10.5	2.5	3.2
Fort Wayne, IN	5.5	n/a	5.1	9.6	0.8	8.8	15.8	n/a	5.6	19.2	9.6	10.4	5.0	4.6
Fort Worth, TX[1]	7.1	n/a	6.4	11.7	1.0	11.1	8.9	n/a	3.5	12.9	12.8	10.9	8.7	5.0
Gainesville, FL	4.3	n/a	4.0	28.7	1.2	10.5	3.1	n/a	3.0	19.7	10.7	10.0	2.8	2.1
Green Bay, WI	4.8	n/a	4.7	11.8	0.9	9.8	18.1	n/a	4.4	15.8	10.5	9.5	4.8	4.9
Greensboro, NC	5.3	n/a	4.3	12.6	1.0	9.9	12.8	n/a	3.7	14.9	12.6	11.3	5.7	5.8
Honolulu, HI	6.0	n/a	4.5	21.0	1.5	15.8	2.1	n/a	4.4	14.9	12.1	9.3	5.5	2.9
Houston, TX	9.0	6.7	5.2	13.4	0.9	10.4	6.9	2.3	3.9	13.3	16.4	9.6	5.8	5.2
Huntsville, AL	4.0	n/a	3.1	20.8	1.0	8.4	12.4	n/a	3.3	9.0	23.6	9.9	2.2	2.5
Indianapolis, IN	5.5	5.5	6.3	12.6	1.0	9.1	8.1	0.1	4.1	15.8	15.7	8.8	8.3	4.7
Jacksonville, FL	6.6	6.6	9.0	10.1	1.8	11.3	4.5	<0.1	3.6	16.3	14.9	11.0	7.3	3.7
Kansas City, MO	5.3	5.2	6.9	13.4	1.5	9.6	7.9	0.1	3.7	15.3	16.0	9.9	6.0	4.6
Lafayette, LA	9.6	5.5	4.7	12.6	0.8	11.1	7.7	4.1	3.6	18.3	11.3	12.6	3.3	4.4
Las Vegas, NV	6.8	6.8	5.3	10.7	1.3	25.8	2.6	<0.1	3.0	11.4	14.3	9.8	6.7	2.3
Lexington, KY	4.9	n/a	4.0	19.6	1.0	10.7	10.5	n/a	4.8	13.2	13.5	9.6	4.2	3.9
Lincoln, NE	5.4	n/a	5.4	21.8	2.0	9.7	7.4	n/a	4.3	17.0	10.3	9.3	5.3	2.2
Little Rock, AR	5.4	n/a	7.1	17.8	1.3	8.5	5.4	n/a	4.8	16.9	12.4	10.0	6.0	4.6
Los Angeles, CA[1]	3.2	3.2	4.5	12.9	4.1	11.6	6.5	<0.1	3.4	21.4	14.4	8.9	4.9	4.2
Louisville, KY	5.1	n/a	6.4	10.6	1.1	9.6	11.8	n/a	3.8	15.4	12.2	9.5	9.8	4.7
Madison, WI	4.6	n/a	5.5	22.4	5.0	8.4	8.7	n/a	5.0	13.1	12.2	9.1	2.5	3.6
Manchester, NH	4.3	n/a	5.6	10.8	2.4	9.0	12.0	n/a	3.8	20.1	14.1	12.5	2.4	3.1
McAllen, TX	3.0	n/a	3.3	20.3	1.0	9.8	2.3	n/a	2.2	30.1	8.9	12.7	3.3	3.1
Memphis, TN	3.8	n/a	4.5	13.2	0.8	9.3	6.1	n/a	4.2	15.2	13.5	9.4	14.1	5.8

Table continued on following page.

Metro Area	(A)	(B)	(C)	(D)	(E)	(F)	(G)	(H)	(I)	(J)	(K)	(L)	(M)	(N)
Miami, FL[1]	4.5	4.5	7.1	10.6	1.7	11.4	3.5	<0.1	3.7	16.6	15.7	11.2	7.8	6.2
Midland, TX	33.1	n/a	5.0	8.7	0.8	9.2	3.7	n/a	3.4	7.7	9.5	7.9	5.2	5.8
Milwaukee, WI	4.3	4.2	5.5	9.6	1.3	9.2	12.8	0.1	5.1	20.8	14.0	9.0	4.0	4.5
Minneapolis, MN	4.3	n/a	7.2	13.2	1.4	8.9	10.0	n/a	3.9	19.0	14.4	9.2	4.4	4.2
Nashville, TN	5.5	n/a	6.8	11.2	2.7	11.2	7.4	n/a	4.2	15.1	16.1	9.2	6.4	4.2
New Orleans, LA	6.0	5.6	5.0	11.6	1.4	14.5	5.5	0.4	4.3	20.3	12.9	9.3	5.6	3.6
New York, NY[1]	3.3	n/a	9.8	12.5	4.0	9.0	2.1	n/a	3.8	25.2	16.1	7.3	3.7	3.3
Oklahoma City, OK	6.5	5.0	5.2	19.0	0.9	11.4	4.9	1.4	4.3	16.7	12.7	10.2	4.7	3.5
Omaha, NE	6.2	n/a	7.7	13.5	1.7	10.7	6.9	n/a	3.5	17.6	13.6	10.2	5.2	3.2
Orlando, FL	6.3	6.3	6.1	8.9	1.8	19.2	3.5	<0.1	3.7	12.9	19.1	10.5	4.5	3.5
Philadelphia, PA[1]	2.4	n/a	6.1	13.0	1.8	9.3	3.1	n/a	4.2	32.9	14.4	6.7	3.9	2.2
Phoenix, AZ	7.3	7.2	8.5	10.5	1.6	10.7	6.0	0.1	3.2	16.9	15.6	10.3	5.3	4.1
Pittsburgh, PA	5.3	4.7	6.5	9.9	1.7	9.8	7.1	0.7	4.1	22.2	15.4	10.0	4.5	3.5
Portland, OR	6.4	6.3	5.8	12.9	2.1	9.4	9.6	0.1	3.5	16.6	15.5	9.3	4.3	4.6
Providence, RI	4.5	4.5	5.5	13.3	1.0	10.7	8.5	<0.1	4.2	21.6	12.1	11.0	3.6	3.8
Provo, UT	9.5	n/a	4.0	11.9	3.9	9.1	7.8	n/a	2.3	22.1	14.4	10.8	2.0	2.2
Raleigh, NC	7.0	n/a	5.5	14.4	3.3	10.5	4.5	n/a	4.4	13.8	19.4	10.1	3.5	3.8
Reno, NV	8.8	8.5	4.2	12.8	1.4	14.2	10.6	0.3	2.7	11.6	12.1	9.4	8.8	3.5
Richmond, VA	5.9	n/a	7.9	15.7	0.9	9.3	4.4	n/a	4.6	15.3	17.0	9.2	6.0	3.8
Rochester, MN	4.1	n/a	2.2	10.5	0.8	8.2	6.9	n/a	3.0	45.2	5.3	9.6	2.1	2.1
Sacramento, CA	6.9	6.8	4.2	24.0	0.9	10.1	3.6	<0.1	3.5	18.7	12.2	9.2	4.0	2.6
Saint Louis, MO	5.4	n/a	6.7	11.2	2.0	9.7	8.2	n/a	3.6	19.5	14.9	9.6	4.8	4.6
Saint Paul, MN	4.3	n/a	7.2	13.2	1.4	8.9	10.0	n/a	3.9	19.0	14.4	9.2	4.4	4.2
Salem, OR	7.4	7.1	3.2	24.5	1.0	8.5	6.2	0.3	3.0	19.9	10.0	10.1	3.9	2.2
Salt Lake City, UT	7.2	n/a	7.7	14.3	2.8	8.3	7.7	n/a	2.7	12.2	17.1	9.2	6.0	4.9
San Antonio, TX	6.3	5.7	8.5	16.1	1.6	12.2	5.2	0.6	3.5	15.2	13.3	10.7	4.0	3.2
San Diego, CA	5.8	5.7	4.5	16.6	1.3	12.9	7.0	<0.1	3.6	16.6	17.0	9.1	2.9	2.7
San Francisco, CA[1]	3.4	3.3	6.7	12.4	9.7	10.6	2.6	<0.1	3.3	14.3	25.1	5.5	4.4	2.0
San Jose, CA	4.6	4.5	3.1	8.8	8.1	9.0	10.6	<0.1	2.4	18.4	24.6	6.5	1.5	2.5
Santa Rosa, CA	8.0	7.9	3.3	13.9	1.3	12.4	10.5	0.1	3.8	18.6	11.5	11.2	2.3	3.2
Savannah, GA	4.8	n/a	3.7	12.3	0.7	13.1	11.0	n/a	4.1	14.2	11.2	11.5	9.8	3.7
Seattle, WA[1]	4.8	4.8	4.9	12.8	8.7	9.3	6.2	<0.1	3.2	13.7	20.9	7.2	4.5	4.0
Sioux Falls, SD	6.8	n/a	8.2	9.5	1.5	9.1	8.7	n/a	3.7	21.6	9.7	11.4	4.6	5.2
Tampa, FL[1]	n/a	6.6	10.2	10.4	1.8	10.3	3.7	n/a	3.3	16.0	18.1	10.9	4.3	4.3
Tucson, AZ	5.7	5.0	4.3	19.9	1.3	11.2	7.0	0.6	3.7	17.9	11.1	10.9	5.1	2.0
Tulsa, OK	6.4	5.7	5.1	13.2	1.0	9.9	11.1	0.7	4.5	17.0	13.2	10.3	4.6	3.7
Virginia Beach, VA	5.0	n/a	4.9	20.1	1.0	11.1	7.0	n/a	4.3	15.4	14.8	10.0	3.9	2.4
Washington, DC[1]	4.2	n/a	3.3	30.2	1.8	9.9	0.8	n/a	6.7	14.8	19.4	5.6	1.9	1.4
Wichita, KS	5.5	n/a	4.1	14.0	1.1	10.2	16.7	n/a	4.0	15.9	10.8	10.1	4.4	3.2
Wilmington, NC	7.3	n/a	4.9	12.9	1.6	15.5	4.5	n/a	4.6	16.9	12.2	13.3	3.6	2.8
Winston-Salem, NC	4.7	n/a	4.5	12.3	0.7	10.7	11.7	n/a	3.9	21.5	11.9	11.4	3.6	3.2
U.S.	5.5	5.1	5.8	14.9	1.9	10.4	8.0	0.4	3.7	16.9	14.2	10.0	4.8	3.9

Note: All figures are percentages covering non-farm employment as of December 2024 and are not seasonally adjusted; Figures cover the Metropolitan Statistical Area (MSA) except where noted; (1) Metropolitan Division; (A) Construction, Mining, and Logging (some areas report Construction separate from Mining and Logging); (B) Construction; (C) Financial Activities; (D) Government; (E) Information; (F) Leisure and Hospitality; (G) Manufacturing; (H) Mining and Logging; (I) Other Services; (J) Private Education and Health Services; (K) Professional and Business Services; (L) Retail Trade; (M) Transportation and Utilities; (N) Wholesale Trade; n/a not available
Source: Bureau of Labor Statistics, Current Employment Statistics, Employment, Hours, and Earnings, December 2024

Appendix A: Comparative Statistics

Labor Force, Employment and Job Growth: City

City	Civilian Labor Force			Workers Employed		
	Dec. 2023	Dec. 2024	% Chg.	Dec. 2023	Dec. 2024	% Chg.
Albuquerque, NM	295,286	297,348	0.7	286,112	286,738	0.2
Anchorage, AK	153,020	155,068	1.3	147,538	149,604	1.4
Ann Arbor, MI	66,518	68,304	2.6	64,986	66,059	1.6
Athens, GA	61,309	61,837	0.8	59,338	59,852	0.8
Atlanta, GA	278,364	279,245	0.3	268,161	267,879	-0.1
Austin, TX	692,732	711,010	2.6	671,863	690,459	2.7
Baltimore, MD	276,136	279,771	1.3	267,011	268,805	0.6
Billings, MT	59,483	58,785	-1.1	57,662	57,121	-0.9
Boise City, ID	146,113	151,831	3.9	142,029	147,110	3.5
Boston, MA	403,771	411,958	2.0	390,365	395,765	1.3
Boulder, CO	68,299	68,728	0.6	66,297	66,171	-0.1
Cape Coral, FL	100,486	101,752	1.2	97,397	98,477	1.1
Cedar Rapids, IA	70,086	70,636	0.7	67,783	68,276	0.7
Charleston, SC	81,443	83,687	2.7	79,209	80,914	2.1
Charlotte, NC	531,420	537,158	1.0	513,465	519,577	1.1
Chicago, IL	1,391,216	1,432,019	2.9	1,330,946	1,363,159	2.4
Cincinnati, OH	150,446	153,060	1.7	145,104	146,196	0.7
Clarksville, TN	65,211	66,900	2.5	62,910	64,067	1.8
Cleveland, OH	154,882	158,055	2.0	148,680	151,454	1.8
College Station, TX	70,826	73,610	3.9	68,915	71,605	3.9
Colorado Springs, CO	254,636	258,951	1.6	245,377	247,188	0.7
Columbia, MO	69,206	70,699	2.1	67,566	68,998	2.1
Columbia, SC	59,838	60,914	1.8	57,599	58,055	0.7
Columbus, OH	490,638	493,589	0.6	474,627	473,223	-0.3
Dallas, TX	753,950	773,828	2.6	727,021	746,370	2.6
Davenport, IA	49,490	49,873	0.7	47,766	47,656	-0.2
Denver, CO	439,297	444,521	1.1	421,359	422,120	0.1
Des Moines, IA	113,506	113,721	0.1	109,944	109,495	-0.4
Detroit, MI	252,407	254,935	1.0	235,064	230,371	-2.0
Durham, NC	161,695	163,549	1.1	156,943	158,778	1.1
El Paso, TX	321,869	330,289	2.6	309,686	317,905	2.6
Eugene, OR	86,438	87,547	1.2	82,952	83,877	1.1
Fargo, ND	75,385	76,672	1.7	73,971	74,762	1.0
Fort Collins, CO	104,877	106,076	1.1	101,643	102,156	0.5
Fort Wayne, IN	130,643	133,106	1.8	126,751	127,554	0.6
Fort Worth, TX	492,810	506,338	2.7	474,900	487,778	2.7
Gainesville, FL	71,265	72,407	1.6	68,797	69,722	1.3
Green Bay, WI	53,842	54,171	0.6	52,558	52,661	0.2
Greensboro, NC	145,300	143,645	-1.1	139,667	137,971	-1.2
Honolulu, HI	458,516	467,102	1.8	447,781	454,669	1.5
Houston, TX	1,221,575	1,251,524	2.4	1,168,408	1,201,001	2.7
Huntsville, AL	110,121	113,202	2.8	107,585	109,886	2.1
Indianapolis, IN	468,727	483,276	3.1	453,754	464,036	2.2
Jacksonville, FL	491,737	495,209	0.7	476,373	479,227	0.6
Kansas City, MO	261,274	264,629	1.2	252,452	255,316	1.1
Lafayette, LA	59,760	59,993	0.3	57,644	57,720	0.1
Las Vegas, NV	330,736	337,672	2.1	312,658	317,296	1.4
Lexington, KY	178,351	182,353	2.2	172,195	175,041	1.6
Lincoln, NE	164,857	168,647	2.3	161,204	164,571	2.0
Little Rock, AR	100,778	102,786	1.9	97,463	99,326	1.9
Los Angeles, CA	2,074,549	2,094,633	0.9	1,964,638	1,972,226	0.3
Louisville, KY	394,849	401,525	1.6	379,511	382,789	0.8
Madison, WI	167,700	168,775	0.6	164,752	165,214	0.2
Manchester, NH	64,039	66,140	3.2	62,588	64,103	2.4
McAllen, TX	72,499	74,052	2.1	69,572	71,063	2.1

Table continued on following page.

City	Civilian Labor Force			Workers Employed		
	Dec. 2023	Dec. 2024	% Chg.	Dec. 2023	Dec. 2024	% Chg.
Memphis, TN	283,933	286,196	0.8	271,779	271,426	-0.1
Miami, FL	247,114	249,197	0.8	242,276	243,343	0.4
Midland, TX	93,937	96,111	2.3	91,915	93,872	2.1
Milwaukee, WI	273,443	274,723	0.4	264,071	263,797	-0.1
Minneapolis, MN	244,672	245,657	0.4	238,965	239,886	0.3
Nashville, TN	421,198	426,189	1.1	411,304	413,569	0.5
New Orleans, LA	173,294	173,800	0.2	165,506	165,809	0.1
New York, NY	4,197,201	4,289,830	2.2	4,004,371	4,065,287	1.5
Oklahoma City, OK	352,331	357,109	1.3	341,478	346,634	1.5
Omaha, NE	251,851	256,156	1.7	245,154	248,481	1.3
Orlando, FL	181,418	181,948	0.2	176,377	176,719	0.1
Philadelphia, PA	750,976	745,485	-0.7	719,837	713,546	-0.8
Phoenix, AZ	913,817	927,572	1.5	887,451	898,365	1.2
Pittsburgh, PA	152,654	151,757	-0.5	148,435	147,774	-0.4
Portland, OR	386,871	388,825	0.5	372,067	372,849	0.2
Providence, RI	90,820	92,307	1.6	86,757	87,271	0.5
Provo, UT	73,763	74,411	0.8	72,156	72,484	0.4
Raleigh, NC	276,576	277,882	0.4	267,801	269,378	0.5
Reno, NV	144,664	147,939	2.2	138,887	141,134	1.6
Richmond, VA	123,724	126,447	2.2	120,027	122,541	2.0
Rochester, MN	68,874	73,886	7.2	67,640	72,557	7.2
Sacramento, CA	246,247	248,837	1.0	234,662	236,718	0.8
Saint Louis, MO	150,472	152,715	1.4	144,679	146,505	1.2
Saint Paul, MN	156,382	157,144	0.4	152,569	153,219	0.4
Salem, OR	86,857	88,580	1.9	83,316	84,776	1.7
Salt Lake City, UT	128,957	131,406	1.9	125,261	127,540	1.8
San Antonio, TX	780,314	813,666	4.2	753,069	786,995	4.5
San Diego, CA	730,171	734,863	0.6	701,246	703,991	0.3
San Francisco, CA	564,822	561,032	-0.6	545,573	541,446	-0.7
San Jose, CA	550,266	551,509	0.2	528,718	529,659	0.1
Santa Rosa, CA	87,410	88,152	0.8	84,056	84,516	0.5
Savannah, GA	69,925	69,887	0.0	67,803	67,610	-0.2
Seattle, WA	511,941	526,448	2.8	495,245	511,570	3.3
Sioux Falls, SD	113,602	115,243	1.4	111,615	112,947	1.1
Tampa, FL	222,684	223,321	0.2	215,665	215,892	0.1
Tucson, AZ	263,211	266,440	1.2	254,477	256,864	0.9
Tulsa, OK	206,897	209,496	1.2	199,811	203,133	1.6
Virginia Beach, VA	237,550	239,534	0.8	231,972	233,678	0.7
Washington, DC	411,135	417,094	1.4	391,912	396,492	1.1
Wichita, KS	194,170	197,795	1.8	188,497	190,038	0.8
Wilmington, NC	69,827	69,943	0.1	67,604	67,846	0.3
Winston-Salem, NC	118,508	118,217	-0.2	114,267	114,055	-0.1
U.S.	166,661,000	167,746,000	0.7	160,754,000	161,294,000	0.3

Note: Data is not seasonally adjusted and covers workers 16 years of age and older
Source: Bureau of Labor Statistics, Local Area Unemployment Statistics

Labor Force, Employment and Job Growth: Metro Area

Metro Area	Civilian Labor Force			Workers Employed		
	Dec. 2023	Dec. 2024	% Chg.	Dec. 2023	Dec. 2024	% Chg.
Albuquerque, NM	459,168	462,519	0.7	444,472	445,570	0.2
Anchorage, AK	203,512	206,186	1.3	195,498	198,110	1.3
Ann Arbor, MI	201,644	207,512	2.9	195,986	199,223	1.6
Athens, GA	103,836	104,775	0.9	100,776	101,698	0.9
Atlanta, GA[1]	2,520,105	2,525,607	0.2	2,441,223	2,439,016	0.0
Austin, TX	1,480,563	1,521,172	2.7	1,434,717	1,474,387	2.7
Baltimore, MD	1,496,175	1,509,109	0.8	1,460,563	1,468,370	0.5
Billings, MT	99,307	98,165	-1.1	96,370	95,349	-1.0
Boise City, ID	432,273	448,781	3.8	418,731	433,330	3.4
Boston, MA[1]	1,158,650	1,182,153	2.0	1,119,472	1,135,105	1.4
Boulder, CO	204,348	205,677	0.6	197,756	197,382	-0.1
Cape Coral, FL	376,769	381,593	1.2	365,271	369,323	1.1
Cedar Rapids, IA	141,248	142,473	0.8	136,873	137,885	0.7
Charleston, SC	433,190	445,523	2.8	421,406	430,483	2.1
Charlotte, NC	1,472,294	1,492,625	1.3	1,424,686	1,443,425	1.3
Chicago, IL[1]	3,780,647	3,890,015	2.8	3,630,697	3,719,159	2.4
Cincinnati, OH	1,154,630	1,170,746	1.4	1,116,229	1,123,236	0.6
Clarksville, TN	126,537	129,924	2.6	121,844	124,244	1.9
Cleveland, OH	1,067,052	1,088,179	1.9	1,033,451	1,051,761	1.7
College Station, TX	154,708	160,796	3.9	150,546	156,418	3.9
Colorado Springs, CO	380,947	387,217	1.6	366,679	369,336	0.7
Columbia, MO	113,118	115,648	2.2	110,484	112,817	2.1
Columbia, SC	419,770	426,736	1.6	406,945	410,354	0.8
Columbus, OH	1,134,646	1,141,335	0.5	1,099,340	1,096,249	-0.2
Dallas, TX[1]	3,019,102	3,099,037	2.6	2,914,521	2,992,023	2.6
Davenport, IA	184,725	184,714	0.0	177,254	176,542	-0.4
Denver, CO	1,731,722	1,751,255	1.1	1,667,215	1,670,077	0.1
Des Moines, IA	394,185	394,876	0.1	384,347	382,847	-0.3
Detroit, MI[1]	816,930	814,679	-0.2	784,713	769,048	-2.0
Durham, NC	323,131	326,577	1.0	313,852	317,268	1.0
El Paso, TX	388,422	398,643	2.6	372,959	382,859	2.6
Eugene, OR	184,890	187,239	1.2	177,117	179,091	1.1
Fargo, ND	149,293	152,175	1.9	146,516	148,732	1.5
Fort Collins, CO	216,529	219,305	1.2	209,634	210,691	0.5
Fort Wayne, IN	220,472	224,223	1.7	214,223	215,591	0.6
Fort Worth, TX[1]	1,397,596	1,435,889	2.7	1,349,809	1,386,446	2.7
Gainesville, FL	168,667	171,235	1.5	163,355	165,582	1.3
Green Bay, WI	174,722	175,808	0.6	170,734	171,226	0.2
Greensboro, NC	366,503	362,230	-1.1	353,122	348,882	-1.2
Honolulu, HI	458,516	467,102	1.8	447,781	454,669	1.5
Houston, TX	3,704,314	3,811,882	2.9	3,557,779	3,657,192	2.7
Huntsville, AL	257,532	264,722	2.7	252,062	257,486	2.1
Indianapolis, IN	1,114,296	1,147,341	2.9	1,082,623	1,106,085	2.1
Jacksonville, FL	845,904	852,367	0.7	820,842	825,781	0.6
Kansas City, MO	1,160,004	1,182,211	1.9	1,127,092	1,144,249	1.5
Lafayette, LA	185,004	185,747	0.4	178,352	178,532	0.1
Las Vegas, NV	1,199,294	1,224,775	2.1	1,135,389	1,152,230	1.4
Lexington, KY	278,181	284,384	2.2	268,513	272,804	1.6
Lincoln, NE	191,591	195,942	2.2	187,422	191,304	2.0
Little Rock, AR	371,026	378,813	2.1	359,838	366,941	1.9
Los Angeles, CA[1]	5,037,643	5,091,130	1.0	4,782,176	4,800,645	0.3
Louisville, KY	691,184	703,358	1.7	666,258	672,517	0.9
Madison, WI	410,987	413,894	0.7	403,502	404,881	0.3
Manchester, NH	238,986	245,151	2.5	233,791	237,759	1.7
McAllen, TX	385,693	394,540	2.2	362,243	370,007	2.1

Table continued on following page.

Metro Area	Civilian Labor Force			Workers Employed		
	Dec. 2023	Dec. 2024	% Chg.	Dec. 2023	Dec. 2024	% Chg.
Memphis, TN	620,716	627,549	1.1	598,585	600,246	0.2
Miami, FL[1]	1,433,283	1,445,779	0.8	1,404,765	1,410,954	0.4
Midland, TX	116,721	119,415	2.3	114,162	116,595	2.1
Milwaukee, WI	822,104	825,110	0.3	800,656	800,116	0.0
Minneapolis, MN	2,005,284	2,015,070	0.4	1,956,084	1,964,999	0.4
Nashville, TN	1,150,386	1,163,681	1.1	1,123,659	1,129,538	0.5
New Orleans, LA	461,088	463,007	0.4	442,552	443,450	0.2
New York, NY[1]	6,077,969	6,169,474	1.5	5,813,964	5,874,694	1.0
Oklahoma City, OK	752,168	762,662	1.4	729,908	740,966	1.5
Omaha, NE	505,378	514,350	1.7	492,693	499,953	1.4
Orlando, FL	1,476,354	1,481,986	0.3	1,432,973	1,435,926	0.2
Philadelphia, PA[1]	1,055,097	1,047,116	-0.7	1,014,794	1,006,018	-0.8
Phoenix, AZ	2,660,126	2,699,326	1.4	2,583,768	2,614,930	1.2
Pittsburgh, PA	1,218,768	1,213,214	-0.4	1,179,001	1,172,526	-0.5
Portland, OR	1,358,801	1,358,994	0.0	1,305,393	1,301,850	-0.2
Providence, RI	887,464	901,729	1.6	854,672	862,458	0.9
Provo, UT	363,569	366,874	0.9	354,453	356,068	0.4
Raleigh, NC	799,354	803,302	0.4	775,484	780,100	0.6
Reno, NV	291,520	298,309	2.3	279,599	284,384	1.7
Richmond, VA	703,806	718,292	2.0	685,441	699,371	2.0
Rochester, MN	128,702	138,168	7.3	126,091	135,339	7.3
Sacramento, CA	1,144,784	1,156,797	1.0	1,094,502	1,103,633	0.8
Saint Louis, MO	1,476,468	1,495,860	1.3	1,428,392	1,447,762	1.3
Saint Paul, MN	2,005,284	2,015,070	0.4	1,956,084	1,964,999	0.4
Salem, OR	215,316	219,611	1.9	206,688	210,311	1.7
Salt Lake City, UT	738,638	754,401	2.1	719,094	732,202	1.8
San Antonio, TX	1,308,187	1,349,973	3.1	1,265,057	1,304,101	3.0
San Diego, CA	1,608,713	1,619,332	0.6	1,543,490	1,549,532	0.3
San Francisco, CA[1]	1,011,370	1,004,815	-0.6	978,032	970,469	-0.7
San Jose, CA	1,075,900	1,078,520	0.2	1,034,963	1,036,708	0.1
Santa Rosa, CA	249,694	251,825	0.8	240,531	241,848	0.5
Savannah, GA	202,550	202,333	-0.1	197,273	196,748	-0.2
Seattle, WA[1]	1,366,721	1,405,582	2.8	1,318,947	1,362,424	3.3
Sioux Falls, SD	171,226	173,604	1.3	168,466	170,431	1.1
Tampa, FL[1]	1,167,354	1,171,736	0.3	1,130,613	1,132,522	0.1
Tucson, AZ	493,139	499,226	1.2	477,781	482,263	0.9
Tulsa, OK	510,676	517,614	1.3	494,038	502,372	1.6
Virginia Beach, VA	883,468	890,934	0.8	860,628	866,842	0.7
Washington, DC[1]	1,000,003	1,013,650	1.3	966,020	974,957	0.9
Wichita, KS	320,952	326,697	1.7	311,687	314,280	0.8
Wilmington, NC	222,997	222,642	-0.1	215,630	215,604	0.0
Winston-Salem, NC	329,205	328,631	-0.1	318,577	317,977	-0.1
U.S.	166,661,000	167,746,000	0.7	160,754,000	161,294,000	0.3

Note: Data is not seasonally adjusted and covers workers 16 years of age and older; Figures cover the Metropolitan Statistical Area (MSA) except where noted; (1) Metropolitan Division
Source: Bureau of Labor Statistics, Local Area Unemployment Statistics

Unemployment Rate: City

City	2024											
	Jan.	Feb.	Mar.	Apr.	May	Jun.	Jul.	Aug.	Sep.	Oct.	Nov.	Dec.
Albuquerque, NM	3.5	3.4	3.1	3.1	3.5	4.4	4.9	4.3	3.8	3.9	3.9	3.6
Anchorage, AK	4.0	4.2	3.8	3.7	3.6	4.2	3.8	3.5	3.5	3.6	3.8	3.5
Ann Arbor, MI	2.5	2.7	2.8	2.6	3.2	3.8	4.2	3.7	3.2	3.1	3.2	3.3
Athens, GA	3.7	3.5	3.6	2.8	3.7	4.6	4.5	4.5	3.8	4.0	3.3	3.2
Atlanta, GA	3.9	3.9	3.8	3.6	4.0	4.5	4.5	4.6	4.1	4.2	4.2	4.1
Austin, TX	3.3	3.5	3.2	2.9	3.1	3.5	3.5	3.5	3.3	3.2	3.2	2.9
Baltimore, MD	4.2	4.2	4.0	3.6	3.8	4.5	4.8	4.8	4.0	4.3	4.2	3.9
Billings, MT	3.5	3.3	3.0	2.6	2.6	3.2	3.1	3.0	2.5	2.5	2.6	2.8
Boise City, ID	3.3	3.4	3.3	2.9	3.0	3.3	3.5	3.3	3.1	3.1	3.3	3.1
Boston, MA	3.7	3.7	3.5	3.2	3.8	4.3	4.6	4.4	3.8	3.9	3.9	3.9
Boulder, CO	3.3	3.5	3.4	3.2	4.0	4.5	4.5	4.5	4.1	4.1	4.4	3.7
Cape Coral, FL	3.4	3.2	3.2	3.0	3.2	3.8	3.9	3.9	3.6	3.5	3.6	3.2
Cedar Rapids, IA	3.9	4.3	3.2	2.7	3.6	4.5	4.2	4.0	3.3	3.5	3.6	3.3
Charleston, SC	3.0	3.3	3.0	2.7	3.2	3.9	4.0	4.1	3.5	3.7	3.6	3.3
Charlotte, NC	3.8	3.9	3.6	3.2	3.4	3.8	4.1	3.9	3.2	3.3	3.5	3.3
Chicago, IL	5.0	5.5	5.1	5.1	5.6	6.9	6.7	6.4	5.8	5.8	5.4	4.8
Cincinnati, OH	4.3	4.4	4.3	4.1	4.5	5.2	5.3	5.0	4.6	4.3	4.6	4.5
Clarksville, TN	4.0	3.7	3.8	3.3	3.5	4.6	4.6	4.4	4.2	4.2	4.3	4.2
Cleveland, OH	5.0	5.8	5.2	4.7	5.0	5.5	5.5	4.7	4.1	3.8	4.0	4.2
College Station, TX	3.4	3.6	3.0	2.5	3.0	3.7	3.8	3.7	3.3	3.2	3.1	2.7
Colorado Springs, CO	4.1	4.2	3.8	3.7	3.9	4.4	4.7	4.6	4.3	4.4	4.7	4.5
Columbia, MO	3.1	2.9	3.2	2.7	3.3	3.6	3.8	3.4	2.4	2.7	2.8	2.4
Columbia, SC	4.1	4.4	4.1	3.8	5.0	5.8	6.1	5.8	4.9	5.7	5.3	4.7
Columbus, OH	4.0	4.0	4.0	3.8	4.0	4.5	4.5	4.3	4.2	3.9	4.2	4.1
Dallas, TX	4.0	4.1	3.9	3.5	3.7	4.3	4.3	4.3	4.0	4.0	4.0	3.5
Davenport, IA	4.2	3.6	3.5	3.0	3.8	4.5	4.8	4.9	5.1	4.9	4.9	4.4
Denver, CO	4.5	4.5	4.0	4.1	4.1	4.5	4.9	4.9	4.6	4.8	5.0	5.0
Des Moines, IA	4.3	3.8	3.5	2.6	3.1	3.6	4.1	4.4	3.5	3.7	3.9	3.7
Detroit, MI	8.3	8.3	8.1	7.4	8.6	10.0	12.7	9.7	9.6	10.8	10.6	9.6
Durham, NC	3.3	3.3	3.2	2.8	3.1	3.4	3.6	3.5	2.9	2.9	3.1	2.9
El Paso, TX	4.3	4.5	4.1	3.7	3.9	4.5	4.5	4.5	4.2	4.2	4.2	3.7
Eugene, OR	4.6	4.5	4.2	3.6	3.6	4.1	4.5	4.4	4.0	3.9	3.8	4.2
Fargo, ND	2.5	2.6	2.7	2.3	2.0	2.5	2.2	2.3	1.9	1.9	2.2	2.5
Fort Collins, CO	3.5	3.6	3.3	3.1	3.5	3.9	4.1	4.1	3.8	3.7	4.1	3.7
Fort Wayne, IN	3.9	4.3	4.1	3.4	3.9	4.4	6.0	4.4	4.0	4.1	4.4	4.2
Fort Worth, TX	4.1	4.3	4.1	3.6	3.9	4.6	4.6	4.4	4.1	4.1	4.1	3.7
Gainesville, FL	3.8	3.6	4.0	3.4	3.8	4.6	4.4	4.6	3.9	4.2	4.4	3.7
Green Bay, WI	2.7	3.2	3.3	2.8	2.8	3.3	3.1	2.8	2.5	2.5	2.6	2.8
Greensboro, NC	4.4	4.4	4.3	3.7	4.0	4.8	5.2	4.9	4.0	3.9	4.2	4.0
Honolulu, HI	2.5	2.5	2.4	2.4	2.3	3.2	3.0	3.1	3.1	2.9	3.0	2.7
Houston, TX	4.4	4.4	4.2	3.8	4.0	4.7	5.1	4.9	4.5	4.4	4.5	4.0
Huntsville, AL	2.8	2.8	2.6	2.1	2.1	2.9	3.1	3.1	2.7	2.8	2.9	2.9
Indianapolis, IN	3.9	4.3	4.2	3.6	4.0	4.4	4.7	4.5	4.1	4.0	4.2	4.0
Jacksonville, FL	3.5	3.4	3.3	3.1	3.3	3.9	4.1	4.0	3.6	3.6	3.5	3.2
Kansas City, MO	3.9	4.1	4.1	3.5	4.0	4.1	4.6	4.2	3.3	3.6	3.6	3.5
Lafayette, LA	4.0	3.9	3.8	3.4	3.6	4.5	4.4	4.4	4.3	4.3	4.1	3.8
Las Vegas, NV	5.7	5.8	5.7	5.5	5.6	6.2	6.5	6.3	5.9	6.0	6.1	6.0
Lexington, KY	3.9	4.3	4.2	3.5	3.9	4.5	4.7	4.4	4.1	4.0	4.1	4.0
Lincoln, NE	2.5	2.7	2.5	2.2	2.5	3.0	2.7	2.8	2.4	2.6	2.6	2.4
Little Rock, AR	3.8	3.8	3.6	3.3	3.4	3.8	4.0	3.6	3.3	3.3	3.4	3.4
Los Angeles, CA	5.8	5.5	5.4	5.1	5.5	6.2	6.8	6.8	6.1	6.1	6.1	5.8
Louisville, KY	4.5	4.9	4.7	4.2	4.3	4.9	5.9	4.9	4.6	4.7	4.7	4.7
Madison, WI	1.9	2.2	2.4	2.2	2.3	2.8	2.6	2.3	2.2	2.1	2.1	2.1
Manchester, NH	2.8	3.1	2.9	2.5	2.4	2.7	3.0	2.9	2.5	2.6	3.2	3.1
McAllen, TX	4.5	4.6	4.3	4.0	4.2	4.9	4.9	4.8	4.3	4.2	4.3	4.0

Table continued on following page.

City	2024											
	Jan.	Feb.	Mar.	Apr.	May	Jun.	Jul.	Aug.	Sep.	Oct.	Nov.	Dec.
Memphis, TN	4.9	4.5	4.7	4.2	4.4	5.8	6.2	5.8	5.3	5.4	5.3	5.2
Miami, FL	1.8	2.0	2.2	2.2	2.2	2.4	2.8	2.8	2.4	2.4	2.3	2.3
Midland, TX	2.6	2.8	2.4	2.2	2.4	2.8	2.8	2.9	2.6	2.7	2.7	2.3
Milwaukee, WI	3.9	4.5	4.6	4.2	4.0	4.9	4.9	4.8	3.8	3.9	4.1	4.0
Minneapolis, MN	2.8	3.0	2.8	2.6	2.5	3.3	3.4	3.4	2.9	2.7	2.5	2.3
Nashville, TN	2.6	2.5	2.6	2.4	2.5	3.1	3.2	3.1	2.9	3.0	3.1	3.0
New Orleans, LA	5.3	4.8	4.7	4.3	4.4	5.7	5.8	5.5	5.2	5.3	4.9	4.6
New York, NY	4.8	5.1	4.8	4.6	4.9	5.4	6.1	6.1	5.3	5.5	5.5	5.2
Oklahoma City, OK	3.4	3.4	3.1	2.7	3.2	3.4	3.4	3.3	3.1	3.1	3.1	2.9
Omaha, NE	3.2	3.5	3.2	3.1	3.1	3.5	3.6	3.3	3.0	3.2	3.0	3.0
Orlando, FL	3.0	2.8	2.7	2.7	2.9	3.3	3.5	3.5	3.2	3.1	3.1	2.9
Philadelphia, PA	4.7	4.9	4.4	4.0	4.4	4.9	5.5	5.7	4.4	4.6	4.5	4.3
Phoenix, AZ	3.0	3.0	2.7	2.5	2.9	3.5	3.8	3.7	3.4	3.4	3.4	3.1
Pittsburgh, PA	3.2	3.2	3.1	2.5	3.0	3.5	3.7	4.0	2.8	3.0	2.9	2.6
Portland, OR	4.5	4.4	4.3	3.6	3.6	4.0	4.4	4.3	3.9	3.9	4.0	4.1
Providence, RI	5.7	6.4	5.6	4.7	5.4	5.4	6.3	6.7	5.2	5.3	5.8	5.5
Provo, UT	2.6	2.6	2.4	2.4	3.2	3.8	3.2	3.4	2.9	2.6	2.8	2.6
Raleigh, NC	3.5	3.6	3.5	3.0	3.2	3.6	3.8	3.6	3.0	3.0	3.3	3.1
Reno, NV	4.5	4.6	4.6	4.4	4.6	4.9	5.1	4.9	4.4	4.6	4.5	4.6
Richmond, VA	3.4	3.4	3.4	3.0	3.4	3.6	3.8	3.9	3.5	3.4	3.4	3.1
Rochester, MN	2.2	2.5	2.1	2.0	1.9	2.6	2.6	2.5	2.0	1.9	1.9	1.8
Sacramento, CA	5.2	5.2	4.9	4.5	4.3	5.1	5.5	5.6	5.0	5.1	5.2	4.9
Saint Louis, MO	4.4	4.8	4.6	3.9	4.3	4.6	4.9	4.8	3.8	4.0	4.0	4.1
Saint Paul, MN	3.0	3.3	3.1	2.8	2.7	3.6	3.7	3.7	3.1	2.8	2.6	2.5
Salem, OR	4.7	4.6	4.5	3.8	3.7	4.2	4.6	4.5	4.0	4.0	4.1	4.3
Salt Lake City, UT	3.0	3.4	3.2	3.0	3.0	3.3	3.5	3.5	3.0	3.1	3.1	2.9
San Antonio, TX	3.9	4.1	3.6	3.4	3.4	4.5	4.3	4.2	3.8	3.8	4.0	3.3
San Diego, CA	4.4	4.4	4.2	3.8	3.7	4.4	4.8	4.9	4.3	4.4	4.5	4.2
San Francisco, CA	3.8	3.6	3.5	3.3	3.1	3.7	4.0	4.1	3.6	3.7	3.7	3.5
San Jose, CA	4.3	4.2	4.1	3.8	3.6	4.4	4.7	4.7	4.2	4.3	4.3	4.0
Santa Rosa, CA	4.5	4.3	4.2	3.8	3.6	4.3	4.7	4.7	4.1	4.3	4.4	4.1
Savannah, GA	3.5	3.5	3.5	3.0	3.6	4.1	4.0	4.2	3.5	3.6	3.4	3.3
Seattle, WA	4.0	3.6	3.5	3.5	3.7	4.5	4.2	4.1	3.9	3.7	3.4	2.8
Sioux Falls, SD	1.9	2.2	1.7	1.7	1.6	1.8	1.6	1.8	1.4	1.6	1.6	2.0
Tampa, FL	3.5	3.3	3.4	3.1	3.3	3.8	3.9	4.0	3.6	3.7	3.8	3.3
Tucson, AZ	3.5	3.4	3.1	2.9	3.4	4.2	4.4	4.3	3.9	3.8	3.9	3.6
Tulsa, OK	4.0	4.0	3.3	3.0	3.5	3.7	3.7	3.6	3.2	3.3	3.3	3.0
Virginia Beach, VA	2.6	2.7	2.5	2.3	2.7	2.9	3.0	3.1	2.8	2.7	2.8	2.4
Washington, DC	5.1	5.3	5.0	4.5	5.0	5.7	6.0	6.0	5.2	5.2	5.0	4.9
Wichita, KS	3.7	4.1	3.9	3.5	3.9	4.4	5.1	4.7	3.9	4.4	4.5	3.9
Wilmington, NC	3.6	3.5	3.3	2.8	3.1	3.5	3.7	3.5	2.9	2.9	3.2	3.0
Winston-Salem, NC	4.0	4.0	4.0	3.4	3.8	4.3	4.6	4.4	3.5	3.6	3.8	3.5
U.S.	4.1	4.2	3.9	3.5	3.7	4.3	4.5	4.4	3.9	3.9	4.0	3.8

Note: Data is not seasonally adjusted and covers workers 16 years of age and older; All figures are percentages
Source: Bureau of Labor Statistics, Local Area Unemployment Statistics

Unemployment Rate: Metro Area

Metro Area	2024											
	Jan.	Feb.	Mar.	Apr.	May	Jun.	Jul.	Aug.	Sep.	Oct.	Nov.	Dec.
Albuquerque, NM	3.6	3.5	3.2	3.3	3.6	4.6	5.1	4.4	3.9	4.0	4.1	3.7
Anchorage, AK	4.4	4.6	4.2	4.0	3.9	4.5	4.1	3.7	3.7	3.9	4.2	3.9
Ann Arbor, MI	3.1	3.3	3.4	3.2	3.9	4.6	5.1	4.5	3.9	3.8	3.8	4.0
Athens, GA	3.4	3.2	3.3	2.6	3.4	4.1	4.0	4.1	3.4	3.6	3.1	2.9
Atlanta, GA[1]	3.4	3.4	3.4	3.1	3.5	4.0	3.9	4.0	3.5	3.6	3.6	3.4
Austin, TX	3.5	3.6	3.4	3.0	3.2	3.7	3.7	3.7	3.5	3.4	3.4	3.1
Baltimore, MD	3.0	3.1	2.9	2.5	2.7	3.4	3.5	3.5	2.9	3.1	3.0	2.7
Billings, MT	3.3	3.3	2.9	2.6	2.5	3.1	3.0	2.9	2.4	2.3	2.4	2.9
Boise City, ID	3.8	3.9	3.7	3.2	3.3	3.6	3.8	3.7	3.3	3.4	3.6	3.4
Boston, MA[1]	3.9	4.0	3.7	3.2	3.8	4.2	4.5	4.3	3.7	3.9	3.9	4.0
Boulder, CO	3.6	3.7	3.4	3.3	3.7	4.2	4.4	4.3	4.0	4.1	4.3	4.0
Cape Coral, FL	3.4	3.3	3.2	3.0	3.2	3.7	4.0	3.9	3.7	3.6	3.6	3.2
Cedar Rapids, IA	3.9	4.0	3.2	2.5	3.2	3.8	3.8	3.7	3.0	3.3	3.4	3.2
Charleston, SC	3.1	3.4	3.1	2.7	3.3	4.0	4.2	4.3	3.6	3.8	3.6	3.4
Charlotte, NC	3.6	3.8	3.5	3.1	3.4	3.8	4.0	3.9	3.3	3.4	3.5	3.3
Chicago, IL[1]	4.7	5.2	4.8	4.6	5.1	6.2	6.0	5.7	5.1	5.1	4.8	4.4
Cincinnati, OH	4.1	4.2	4.2	3.8	4.0	4.6	4.6	4.3	4.1	3.9	4.1	4.1
Clarksville, TN	4.2	4.1	4.1	3.6	3.8	4.8	4.9	4.6	4.4	4.4	4.5	4.4
Cleveland, OH	4.0	4.7	4.2	3.6	3.9	4.4	4.4	3.7	3.3	3.0	3.2	3.3
College Station, TX	3.3	3.4	3.0	2.6	3.0	3.6	3.7	3.6	3.2	3.1	3.1	2.7
Colorado Springs, CO	4.2	4.3	3.9	3.8	4.0	4.5	4.8	4.8	4.4	4.5	4.8	4.6
Columbia, MO	3.2	3.0	3.2	2.7	3.2	3.5	3.7	3.3	2.4	2.7	2.7	2.4
Columbia, SC	3.5	3.7	3.5	3.1	3.8	4.5	4.7	4.8	4.1	4.3	4.1	3.8
Columbus, OH	3.9	3.9	3.9	3.6	3.8	4.3	4.3	4.1	4.0	3.7	4.0	4.0
Dallas, TX[1]	3.9	4.0	3.8	3.4	3.6	4.2	4.2	4.2	3.9	3.8	3.8	3.5
Davenport, IA	5.2	4.8	4.5	4.0	4.2	4.7	4.8	4.9	5.2	5.0	4.8	4.4
Denver, CO	4.1	4.2	3.8	3.8	3.9	4.4	4.6	4.7	4.3	4.5	4.7	4.6
Des Moines, IA	3.3	2.9	2.7	2.1	2.6	3.1	3.5	3.6	3.0	3.1	3.2	3.0
Detroit, MI[1]	4.8	4.8	4.7	4.3	5.0	5.8	7.5	5.6	5.6	6.3	6.2	5.6
Durham, NC	3.2	3.2	3.2	2.8	3.0	3.4	3.6	3.4	2.8	2.9	3.1	2.9
El Paso, TX	4.5	4.7	4.3	3.9	4.1	4.8	4.8	4.7	4.4	4.4	4.4	4.0
Eugene, OR	4.9	4.7	4.4	3.8	3.8	4.2	4.7	4.6	4.1	4.1	4.1	4.4
Fargo, ND	2.5	2.7	2.7	2.2	2.0	2.6	2.3	2.3	1.8	1.8	2.0	2.3
Fort Collins, CO	3.6	3.8	3.4	3.3	3.5	3.9	4.1	4.2	3.8	3.9	4.2	3.9
Fort Wayne, IN	3.8	4.1	3.9	3.2	3.7	4.2	5.8	4.1	3.7	3.8	4.1	3.8
Fort Worth, TX[1]	3.9	4.1	3.8	3.4	3.6	4.2	4.3	4.2	3.9	3.9	3.9	3.4
Gainesville, FL	3.5	3.3	3.5	3.1	3.4	4.0	4.0	4.0	3.5	3.7	3.8	3.3
Green Bay, WI	2.6	3.1	3.1	2.6	2.6	3.0	2.9	2.6	2.3	2.3	2.4	2.6
Greensboro, NC	4.2	4.2	4.0	3.5	3.9	4.5	4.8	4.5	3.7	3.7	4.0	3.7
Honolulu, HI	2.5	2.5	2.4	2.4	2.3	3.2	3.0	3.1	3.1	2.9	3.0	2.7
Houston, TX	4.4	4.5	4.1	3.8	4.0	4.7	5.0	4.8	4.5	4.4	4.4	4.1
Huntsville, AL	2.6	2.7	2.4	2.0	2.0	2.7	2.9	3.0	2.6	2.7	2.8	2.7
Indianapolis, IN	3.6	3.9	3.9	3.2	3.6	4.0	4.3	4.0	3.6	3.6	3.9	3.6
Jacksonville, FL	3.3	3.2	3.2	2.9	3.1	3.7	3.9	3.8	3.4	3.4	3.5	3.1
Kansas City, MO	3.5	3.8	3.8	3.2	3.6	3.8	4.2	3.9	3.2	3.5	3.3	3.2
Lafayette, LA	4.1	4.0	3.8	3.4	3.6	4.5	4.4	4.4	4.3	4.3	4.2	3.9
Las Vegas, NV	5.6	5.6	5.5	5.4	5.5	6.1	6.4	6.2	5.8	5.9	6.0	5.9
Lexington, KY	4.0	4.4	4.2	3.5	3.9	4.6	4.7	4.5	4.1	4.1	4.2	4.1
Lincoln, NE	2.4	2.6	2.4	2.2	2.5	3.0	2.6	2.7	2.4	2.6	2.5	2.4
Little Rock, AR	3.5	3.5	3.2	2.9	3.1	3.5	3.7	3.3	3.0	2.9	3.0	3.1
Los Angeles, CA[1]	5.6	5.3	5.3	5.0	5.4	6.1	6.7	6.7	6.0	6.0	6.0	5.7
Louisville, KY	4.3	4.7	4.4	3.9	4.1	4.7	5.6	4.6	4.3	4.4	4.5	4.4
Madison, WI	2.1	2.5	2.5	2.2	2.3	2.7	2.6	2.3	2.1	2.1	2.2	2.2
Manchester, NH	2.7	3.0	2.9	2.4	2.3	2.6	3.0	2.9	2.5	2.6	3.1	3.0
McAllen, TX	6.5	6.0	5.8	5.4	5.7	6.9	6.9	6.5	5.9	5.4	6.0	6.2

Table continued on following page.

Metro Area	2024											
	Jan.	Feb.	Mar.	Apr.	May	Jun.	Jul.	Aug.	Sep.	Oct.	Nov.	Dec.
Memphis, TN	4.0	3.7	3.8	3.4	3.7	4.9	5.0	4.8	4.4	4.5	4.5	4.4
Miami, FL[1]	1.9	2.0	2.3	2.3	2.3	2.6	2.8	2.9	2.4	2.4	2.4	2.4
Midland, TX	2.6	2.8	2.5	2.2	2.5	2.8	2.9	2.9	2.7	2.7	2.7	2.4
Milwaukee, WI	3.0	3.5	3.6	3.2	3.1	3.8	3.7	3.4	2.9	2.9	3.1	3.0
Minneapolis, MN	3.1	3.3	3.1	2.7	2.6	3.5	3.4	3.4	2.7	2.4	2.4	2.5
Nashville, TN	2.6	2.5	2.5	2.3	2.4	3.1	3.2	3.1	2.9	3.0	3.0	2.9
New Orleans, LA	4.6	4.3	4.2	3.8	3.9	5.0	5.0	4.9	4.7	4.7	4.5	4.2
New York, NY[1]	4.6	4.9	4.6	4.3	4.6	5.1	5.7	5.6	4.8	5.0	5.0	4.8
Oklahoma City, OK	3.3	3.4	3.0	2.6	3.0	3.3	3.3	3.2	3.0	3.0	3.0	2.8
Omaha, NE	3.1	3.2	2.9	2.7	2.9	3.3	3.4	3.1	2.8	3.0	2.9	2.8
Orlando, FL	3.2	3.1	3.1	2.9	3.1	3.6	3.8	3.8	3.4	3.4	3.5	3.1
Philadelphia, PA[1]	4.3	4.6	4.1	3.7	4.1	4.5	5.1	5.3	4.1	4.2	4.2	3.9
Phoenix, AZ	3.0	3.0	2.7	2.6	3.0	3.5	3.8	3.6	3.4	3.4	3.3	3.1
Pittsburgh, PA	3.9	4.1	3.6	3.1	3.3	3.9	4.2	4.4	3.1	3.4	3.3	3.4
Portland, OR	4.4	4.5	4.2	3.6	3.7	3.9	4.4	4.3	3.9	3.9	4.0	4.2
Providence, RI	4.8	5.2	4.5	3.8	4.1	4.3	4.9	5.0	4.0	4.2	4.4	4.4
Provo, UT	3.0	3.2	3.0	2.9	3.2	3.7	3.6	3.7	3.1	3.0	3.1	2.9
Raleigh, NC	3.3	3.4	3.2	2.9	3.1	3.4	3.6	3.5	2.9	2.9	3.1	2.9
Reno, NV	4.7	4.8	4.7	4.5	4.6	5.0	5.1	4.9	4.5	4.6	4.6	4.7
Richmond, VA	3.0	3.0	2.9	2.6	2.9	3.2	3.3	3.4	3.0	2.9	3.0	2.6
Rochester, MN	2.8	3.0	2.6	2.2	2.2	2.8	2.7	2.6	2.0	1.8	1.9	2.0
Sacramento, CA	4.9	4.9	4.7	4.2	4.0	4.8	5.1	5.2	4.6	4.7	4.8	4.6
Saint Louis, MO	3.9	4.1	3.9	3.4	3.7	4.0	4.2	3.9	3.2	3.3	3.3	3.2
Saint Paul, MN	3.1	3.3	3.1	2.7	2.6	3.5	3.4	3.4	2.7	2.4	2.4	2.5
Salem, OR	4.7	4.6	4.3	3.6	3.6	4.0	4.6	4.4	3.9	3.9	4.0	4.2
Salt Lake City, UT	3.0	3.4	3.2	3.0	3.1	3.5	3.5	3.6	3.0	3.1	3.0	2.9
San Antonio, TX	3.8	4.0	3.6	3.3	3.5	4.1	4.2	4.1	3.8	3.8	3.8	3.4
San Diego, CA	4.5	4.5	4.2	3.9	3.7	4.6	4.9	5.0	4.5	4.6	4.6	4.3
San Francisco, CA[1]	3.7	3.6	3.4	3.2	3.1	3.6	3.9	4.0	3.5	3.6	3.7	3.4
San Jose, CA	4.2	4.2	4.0	3.7	3.6	4.2	4.5	4.5	4.1	4.1	4.1	3.9
Santa Rosa, CA	4.3	4.2	4.0	3.6	3.4	4.1	4.4	4.5	3.9	4.1	4.2	4.0
Savannah, GA	2.9	3.0	3.0	2.5	3.1	3.5	3.4	3.7	2.9	3.0	2.9	2.8
Seattle, WA[1]	4.2	3.8	3.7	3.7	3.8	4.7	4.4	4.2	4.1	4.0	3.7	3.1
Sioux Falls, SD	1.8	2.1	1.6	1.6	1.6	1.8	1.5	1.8	1.3	1.5	1.5	1.8
Tampa, FL[1]	3.5	3.4	3.3	3.1	3.3	3.8	4.0	4.0	3.7	3.7	3.8	3.3
Tucson, AZ	3.3	3.3	3.0	2.8	3.3	4.0	4.3	4.0	3.7	3.7	3.6	3.4
Tulsa, OK	3.8	3.8	3.2	2.8	3.3	3.6	3.5	3.4	3.1	3.2	3.2	2.9
Virginia Beach, VA	3.0	3.0	2.9	2.6	3.0	3.2	3.4	3.4	3.1	3.0	3.1	2.7
Washington, DC[1]	3.9	4.1	3.9	3.4	3.7	4.4	4.6	4.7	4.0	4.1	4.1	3.8
Wichita, KS	3.6	3.8	3.7	3.4	3.7	4.2	5.0	4.6	3.8	4.2	4.3	3.8
Wilmington, NC	3.8	3.8	3.4	3.0	3.3	3.6	3.7	3.7	3.1	3.2	3.4	3.2
Winston-Salem, NC	3.6	3.7	3.6	3.1	3.4	3.9	4.1	4.0	3.3	3.3	3.6	3.2
U.S.	4.1	4.2	3.9	3.5	3.7	4.3	4.5	4.4	3.9	3.9	4.0	3.8

Note: Data is not seasonally adjusted and covers workers 16 years of age and older; All figures are percentages; (1) Figures cover the Metropolitan Statistical Area (MSA) except where noted; (1) Metropolitan Division
Source: Bureau of Labor Statistics, Local Area Unemployment Statistics

Average Hourly Wages: Occupations A – C

Metro Area	Accountants/ Auditors	Automotive Mechanics	Book-keepers	Carpenters	Cashiers	Computer Programmers	Computer Systems Analysts
Albuquerque, NM	40.90	25.69	23.51	26.42	14.93	43.80	46.83
Anchorage, AK	42.24	31.29	26.96	36.09	17.64	44.68	45.88
Ann Arbor, MI	41.19	27.70	24.68	30.96	15.32	39.67	53.91
Athens, GA	39.24	25.81	21.79	22.39	12.95	36.03	36.11
Atlanta, GA	46.20	28.17	24.88	24.84	13.99	49.60	53.95
Austin, TX	44.19	27.17	26.04	24.84	15.10	45.82	53.57
Baltimore, MD	44.96	27.65	26.87	28.13	16.18	52.85	56.04
Billings, MT	39.29	28.20	22.49	27.02	14.91	48.63	46.01
Boise City, ID	35.88	24.94	23.92	24.55	15.24	43.27	44.48
Boston, MA	49.79	29.49	28.51	38.40	17.37	57.83	60.98
Boulder, CO[2]	46.39	28.81	26.63	29.94	17.71	71.62	67.66
Cape Coral, FL	39.76	25.28	24.21	23.36	14.53	43.02	46.99
Cedar Rapids, IA	39.80	26.02	24.03	27.03	14.47	39.50	44.19
Charleston, SC	44.26	24.26	23.80	25.54	13.77	53.17	52.43
Charlotte, NC	47.13	27.27	24.68	25.51	14.02	44.72	57.50
Chicago, IL	44.28	28.71	25.75	38.11	16.33	46.08	48.09
Cincinnati, OH	41.81	24.64	24.76	27.72	14.23	56.17	52.48
Clarksville, TN	35.41	23.62	22.04	24.61	13.04	n/a	39.08
Cleveland, OH	41.49	26.14	24.08	29.35	14.16	44.94	47.53
College Station, TX	36.32	24.82	21.78	22.38	13.30	39.46	42.81
Colorado Springs, CO[2]	41.44	26.83	23.32	26.46	16.36	53.50	54.60
Columbia, MO	35.97	23.99	23.55	26.93	14.42	n/a	44.38
Columbia, SC	34.91	23.93	22.33	24.28	12.66	54.49	41.80
Columbus, OH	44.22	27.22	24.48	29.44	14.46	48.11	49.66
Dallas, TX	45.03	27.86	25.94	24.01	14.32	47.68	57.86
Davenport, IA	39.77	25.81	23.07	28.79	14.78	38.43	42.15
Denver, CO[2]	46.80	28.10	26.85	27.44	17.46	54.01	56.16
Des Moines, IA	40.26	26.59	24.64	28.46	14.74	45.02	47.37
Detroit, MI	43.77	27.01	25.39	31.70	14.88	39.07	50.95
Durham, NC	46.33	26.94	26.20	24.03	14.15	51.55	54.64
El Paso, TX	35.86	22.04	20.35	20.00	12.41	34.05	44.84
Eugene, OR	40.17	26.31	23.97	29.35	16.41	44.82	51.80
Fargo, ND	36.22	26.79	24.09	29.49	15.21	43.27	50.62
Fort Collins, CO[2]	43.11	27.93	24.64	26.93	16.61	54.48	53.23
Fort Wayne, IN	38.36	24.39	22.76	27.40	13.68	39.45	44.73
Fort Worth, TX	45.03	27.86	25.94	24.01	14.32	47.68	57.86
Gainesville, FL	38.54	24.87	23.70	23.37	14.25	44.12	41.84
Green Bay, WI	40.76	27.11	23.58	30.80	14.24	45.19	48.58
Greensboro, NC	41.27	25.40	22.80	21.70	13.29	43.91	50.14
Honolulu, HI	36.77	27.01	23.29	42.67	17.05	50.07	44.25
Houston, TX	45.33	27.12	24.69	24.93	14.10	n/a	56.46
Huntsville, AL	41.06	25.69	22.10	23.65	13.43	52.24	59.51
Indianapolis, IN	41.42	25.35	23.97	30.07	13.91	47.00	50.67
Jacksonville, FL	41.72	25.10	23.66	24.55	14.62	50.71	50.41
Kansas City, MO	41.41	26.51	24.38	31.38	15.02	46.73	48.94
Lafayette, LA	35.63	23.75	20.97	22.46	11.84	40.56	49.57
Las Vegas, NV	39.57	25.88	24.90	32.87	14.94	44.52	47.58
Lexington, KY	36.98	22.15	23.60	25.79	13.44	52.20	41.98
Lincoln, NE	34.67	25.66	22.74	25.07	14.50	43.25	40.47
Little Rock, AR	36.16	23.85	22.54	23.06	13.71	45.30	29.95
Los Angeles, CA	48.45	30.20	28.58	36.97	18.47	50.36	59.72
Louisville, KY	39.40	23.99	24.07	26.54	14.14	52.89	45.74
Madison, WI	41.87	28.99	25.40	32.44	15.63	42.40	46.04
Manchester, NH	42.84	28.99	25.41	28.98	14.89	41.19	52.98
McAllen, TX	33.75	22.30	19.81	18.97	12.40	38.07	37.09

Table continued on following page.

Metro Area	Accountants/ Auditors	Automotive Mechanics	Book-keepers	Carpenters	Cashiers	Computer Programmers	Computer Systems Analysts
Memphis, TN	39.28	25.26	23.48	25.20	13.30	43.86	48.38
Miami, FL	43.02	26.45	24.75	24.57	14.99	57.85	54.87
Midland, TX	47.51	26.20	25.44	24.81	14.69	42.10	57.62
Milwaukee, WI	43.31	28.74	24.38	32.43	14.53	43.19	50.52
Minneapolis, MN	45.40	29.52	26.89	35.62	16.35	50.83	53.62
Nashville, TN	41.77	26.05	24.43	25.67	14.57	n/a	42.96
New Orleans, LA	40.08	24.79	22.70	25.98	13.04	39.98	48.21
New York, NY	58.64	29.75	29.11	37.32	17.91	58.71	61.28
Oklahoma City, OK	41.96	23.62	22.88	25.29	13.24	57.04	47.08
Omaha, NE	37.98	26.58	24.02	26.11	14.93	46.38	46.14
Orlando, FL	42.38	25.24	23.73	24.25	15.21	46.42	49.67
Philadelphia, PA	46.34	27.57	26.12	32.62	15.31	46.77	51.52
Phoenix, AZ	42.29	28.52	25.59	28.74	16.53	40.51	51.41
Pittsburgh, PA	39.21	24.59	23.05	31.17	14.11	42.07	47.00
Portland, OR	44.95	29.63	26.60	35.28	17.91	57.44	60.32
Providence, RI	46.37	26.05	26.20	32.98	16.12	49.33	57.45
Provo, UT	38.12	23.63	23.58	25.60	15.11	43.63	48.54
Raleigh, NC	44.26	26.71	24.19	23.43	13.98	41.74	52.76
Reno, NV	41.47	27.04	25.86	32.80	15.27	49.79	47.77
Richmond, VA	42.37	27.70	24.33	24.90	15.01	46.29	51.27
Rochester, MN	46.22	27.15	27.32	32.24	15.88	n/a	n/a
Sacramento, CA	45.29	31.97	28.08	37.87	18.42	56.85	57.48
Saint Louis, MO	40.41	25.56	25.12	33.56	15.63	48.91	46.89
Saint Paul, MN	45.40	29.52	26.89	35.62	16.35	50.83	53.62
Salem, OR	42.14	27.01	26.35	27.76	16.54	52.83	53.95
Salt Lake City, UT	41.61	25.97	24.91	27.86	15.51	46.78	45.51
San Antonio, TX	41.41	25.74	23.19	23.06	14.39	62.03	51.53
San Diego, CA	50.36	29.84	28.01	36.37	18.50	60.74	57.81
San Francisco, CA	57.63	35.20	32.85	41.44	20.07	62.74	71.92
San Jose, CA	61.89	39.24	32.88	41.63	20.75	76.50	77.64
Santa Rosa, CA	47.74	31.99	29.51	40.36	19.48	48.16	55.29
Savannah, GA	40.41	27.16	23.06	24.58	13.64	46.30	52.25
Seattle, WA	51.01	30.63	28.45	39.76	20.63	80.47	66.53
Sioux Falls, SD	40.80	28.20	21.98	23.96	14.91	n/a	48.25
Tampa, FL	42.37	25.41	25.17	24.57	14.51	46.54	53.50
Tucson, AZ	39.27	26.22	24.08	25.46	15.74	46.55	51.81
Tulsa, OK	40.70	24.36	23.49	24.64	13.45	47.67	55.21
Virginia Beach, VA	41.24	26.43	23.13	24.88	14.28	50.07	50.99
Washington, DC	52.24	31.94	28.25	30.71	17.17	54.17	62.36
Wichita, KS	37.74	24.13	21.79	25.64	13.10	50.82	48.92
Wilmington, NC	37.67	23.96	22.76	24.06	13.23	37.74	46.73
Winston-Salem, NC	40.27	25.20	22.66	23.60	13.15	44.83	50.74

Notes: Figures cover the Metropolitan Statistical Area (MSA); (1) Data is from 2023 due to data quality issues in the state of Colorado and its substate areas in 2024; n/a not available
Source: Bureau of Labor Statistics, Metro Area Occupational Employment and Wage Estimates, May 2024

Average Hourly Wages: Occupations C – E

Metro Area	Comp. User Support Specialists	Construction Laborers	Cooks, Restaurant	Customer Service Reps.	Dentists	Electricians	Engineers, Electrical
Albuquerque, NM	24.18	20.58	16.62	20.23	92.52	28.48	71.65
Anchorage, AK	30.11	30.31	19.67	22.30	96.63	38.60	57.20
Ann Arbor, MI	27.63	24.45	18.17	20.90	n/a	37.90	52.52
Athens, GA	24.25	19.20	15.36	17.62	86.37	28.38	52.45
Atlanta, GA	31.11	20.30	16.66	21.35	102.19	30.62	56.08
Austin, TX	29.47	20.17	17.40	20.72	105.18	28.24	67.90
Baltimore, MD	33.50	22.42	18.38	21.60	108.70	33.58	59.60
Billings, MT	26.60	24.46	18.09	21.17	118.06	34.75	51.14
Boise City, ID	26.79	22.50	16.50	21.14	85.60	29.13	65.01
Boston, MA	37.62	33.95	21.98	25.48	n/a	40.10	64.82
Boulder, CO[1]	36.17	22.30	20.42	22.82	85.12	31.85	63.49
Cape Coral, FL	28.07	21.08	17.88	19.48	132.27	25.82	49.73
Cedar Rapids, IA	28.20	23.76	16.74	21.95	76.51	26.89	53.76
Charleston, SC	28.38	21.91	17.47	20.80	78.30	28.18	56.11
Charlotte, NC	30.08	21.52	17.64	21.55	106.87	27.55	58.48
Chicago, IL	30.31	34.99	18.66	23.30	89.54	44.39	57.06
Cincinnati, OH	28.23	26.28	15.92	21.20	103.59	30.46	51.81
Clarksville, TN	25.48	20.62	15.08	18.84	87.66	28.77	45.74
Cleveland, OH	28.26	27.82	17.24	22.13	81.41	32.62	49.77
College Station, TX	24.10	17.72	14.89	17.74	103.68	25.02	50.62
Colorado Springs, CO[1]	30.73	21.28	19.05	20.87	88.76	28.83	56.23
Columbia, MO	27.69	28.79	16.00	20.94	105.42	30.08	n/a
Columbia, SC	27.54	21.14	16.57	19.31	120.35	29.62	51.67
Columbus, OH	30.19	27.99	16.81	22.27	78.07	31.75	49.68
Dallas, TX	29.72	19.90	17.09	21.47	96.90	28.56	56.38
Davenport, IA	27.46	27.61	16.58	20.62	95.43	34.34	54.36
Denver, CO[1]	36.27	22.62	20.14	22.82	64.29	30.65	55.39
Des Moines, IA	29.14	24.89	17.75	24.02	93.83	32.28	69.53
Detroit, MI	29.25	26.26	18.06	22.70	93.92	36.41	53.76
Durham, NC	32.70	22.51	17.45	22.07	96.79	29.52	58.62
El Paso, TX	22.07	17.25	14.12	17.31	101.96	23.92	44.54
Eugene, OR	30.29	24.26	18.28	21.66	107.76	40.45	54.89
Fargo, ND	30.52	25.14	17.42	21.49	100.00	33.30	50.36
Fort Collins, CO[1]	32.68	21.53	18.75	20.21	100.41	29.77	55.88
Fort Wayne, IN	26.58	23.81	15.90	21.57	98.97	31.08	49.63
Fort Worth, TX	29.72	19.90	17.09	21.47	96.90	28.56	56.38
Gainesville, FL	25.88	19.68	16.92	19.63	98.53	25.55	51.00
Green Bay, WI	28.66	26.49	17.71	22.50	81.11	33.62	47.47
Greensboro, NC	26.94	20.44	16.19	20.71	85.23	26.42	53.13
Honolulu, HI	28.29	33.27	21.30	21.38	65.12	42.47	50.66
Houston, TX	29.02	20.13	15.99	20.40	115.55	28.39	57.48
Huntsville, AL	25.12	18.37	16.05	19.29	n/a	27.47	63.59
Indianapolis, IN	29.12	25.60	16.96	22.07	89.99	32.56	53.74
Jacksonville, FL	28.60	20.35	16.89	20.86	86.80	27.03	52.71
Kansas City, MO	28.37	26.74	18.07	21.64	89.46	35.72	51.97
Lafayette, LA	30.51	20.27	13.44	18.01	82.38	26.35	47.69
Las Vegas, NV	27.07	24.69	19.59	19.65	69.07	34.73	51.25
Lexington, KY	27.96	21.98	15.85	20.23	86.12	27.82	50.32
Lincoln, NE	28.07	21.86	17.81	19.65	85.28	29.82	47.88
Little Rock, AR	26.42	18.42	15.24	19.85	92.76	24.62	51.32
Los Angeles, CA	35.73	31.23	21.28	25.04	83.74	39.39	65.77
Louisville, KY	27.34	23.10	16.46	20.93	90.25	30.65	47.48
Madison, WI	29.81	27.12	18.70	23.53	98.38	36.51	51.89
Manchester, NH	34.06	22.66	18.60	23.92	77.22	30.59	70.89
McAllen, TX	21.73	15.75	13.57	17.73	106.72	21.99	46.39

Table continued on following page.

Metro Area	Comp. User Support Specialists	Construction Laborers	Cooks, Restaurant	Customer Service Reps.	Dentists	Electricians	Engineers, Electrical
Memphis, TN	28.25	22.21	16.20	21.10	91.70	27.81	53.37
Miami, FL	32.66	21.69	17.30	20.41	89.88	27.58	53.23
Midland, TX	27.70	20.63	16.62	20.78	n/a	28.92	61.86
Milwaukee, WI	30.47	28.30	18.61	23.48	97.31	35.83	50.13
Minneapolis, MN	33.76	30.67	20.11	24.54	108.57	41.70	54.81
Nashville, TN	29.95	22.45	18.35	21.72	97.05	29.83	55.61
New Orleans, LA	28.92	21.90	15.42	19.43	97.54	29.41	56.07
New York, NY	35.37	34.43	20.82	25.80	89.32	41.08	60.31
Oklahoma City, OK	26.99	20.63	17.14	20.02	112.93	30.47	53.72
Omaha, NE	29.50	23.84	18.03	21.38	103.65	31.36	48.89
Orlando, FL	28.57	21.13	18.25	19.99	85.11	26.17	56.13
Philadelphia, PA	31.66	28.19	17.84	23.03	87.74	38.14	61.83
Phoenix, AZ	32.43	23.17	19.56	22.50	98.52	29.58	59.00
Pittsburgh, PA	29.05	25.52	15.76	21.46	78.26	34.21	53.62
Portland, OR	31.89	27.95	20.13	23.78	94.71	46.08	57.53
Providence, RI	30.62	30.51	19.97	22.77	n/a	34.24	54.44
Provo, UT	28.65	22.38	17.58	19.85	66.32	29.16	60.54
Raleigh, NC	29.83	22.02	17.14	21.36	104.78	26.83	65.68
Reno, NV	28.19	27.64	18.27	20.68	74.31	32.97	57.15
Richmond, VA	29.64	19.84	17.56	20.92	103.90	29.24	56.26
Rochester, MN	33.24	28.42	18.68	23.08	122.85	39.75	50.77
Sacramento, CA	47.62	31.16	20.88	24.98	89.82	39.30	65.09
Saint Louis, MO	29.80	31.00	18.07	22.36	n/a	36.65	56.55
Saint Paul, MN	33.76	30.67	20.11	24.54	108.57	41.70	54.81
Salem, OR	31.51	25.90	18.91	22.72	104.28	40.07	55.99
Salt Lake City, UT	32.60	23.53	18.51	21.44	80.35	31.02	55.43
San Antonio, TX	27.32	19.44	15.83	20.34	78.33	26.69	55.23
San Diego, CA	35.01	30.44	21.15	24.53	87.88	39.61	65.99
San Francisco, CA	43.40	36.32	22.87	29.30	109.18	50.12	77.50
San Jose, CA	43.29	35.06	24.13	30.67	90.06	49.71	90.89
Santa Rosa, CA	37.08	32.20	21.98	25.04	82.86	42.00	63.20
Savannah, GA	31.48	19.01	16.30	18.64	98.92	28.43	57.20
Seattle, WA	37.28	31.08	22.67	27.52	97.55	48.19	67.55
Sioux Falls, SD	23.81	20.75	17.44	21.01	89.53	28.14	48.75
Tampa, FL	29.29	21.37	17.47	20.59	112.24	26.80	55.02
Tucson, AZ	28.35	21.11	17.71	19.74	92.54	28.60	62.08
Tulsa, OK	27.43	21.54	16.20	19.80	97.17	30.23	53.92
Virginia Beach, VA	29.01	19.76	17.15	19.47	87.77	29.26	53.55
Washington, DC	38.26	23.15	20.33	23.55	109.72	37.78	67.24
Wichita, KS	24.62	20.29	15.63	19.26	82.76	31.51	46.39
Wilmington, NC	28.36	21.81	16.50	19.57	104.98	26.12	54.21
Winston-Salem, NC	27.29	21.31	15.89	19.29	77.83	26.05	42.46

Notes: Figures cover the Metropolitan Statistical Area (MSA); (1) Data is from 2023 due to data quality issues in the state of Colorado and its substate areas in 2024; n/a not available
Source: Bureau of Labor Statistics, Metro Area Occupational Employment and Wage Estimates, May 2024

Average Hourly Wages: Occupations F – J

Metro Area	Fast Food and Counter Workers	Financial Managers	First-Line Supervisors/ of Office Workers	General and Operations Managers	Hair- dressers/ Cosme- tologists	Home Health and Personal Care Aides	Janitors/ Cleaners
Albuquerque, NM	14.78	67.06	31.40	59.24	18.37	14.44	16.27
Anchorage, AK	16.07	66.10	34.12	67.82	n/a	18.20	19.57
Ann Arbor, MI	15.01	78.28	33.10	66.91	21.16	17.05	18.60
Athens, GA	12.25	70.43	29.73	48.33	20.63	13.58	14.96
Atlanta, GA	13.55	92.61	34.57	65.51	22.26	14.69	16.89
Austin, TX	14.09	89.92	36.88	68.18	20.93	13.82	16.90
Baltimore, MD	15.89	80.29	35.89	61.48	20.61	18.43	18.03
Billings, MT	14.42	73.01	31.75	52.57	21.23	16.16	18.70
Boise City, ID	13.54	68.45	30.86	47.05	15.23	16.17	16.90
Boston, MA	17.43	100.73	38.59	78.73	24.97	19.58	21.75
Boulder, CO[1]	17.78	93.87	36.12	81.98	25.46	19.56	19.68
Cape Coral, FL	14.23	82.00	32.80	57.19	17.77	16.30	16.54
Cedar Rapids, IA	13.79	67.28	31.58	49.70	22.37	17.35	17.85
Charleston, SC	13.83	72.75	33.77	59.32	18.76	15.46	15.59
Charlotte, NC	14.27	91.39	33.22	66.57	20.12	15.34	16.27
Chicago, IL	16.05	88.31	35.22	68.58	20.23	17.79	19.25
Cincinnati, OH	14.06	77.39	32.81	58.30	20.06	15.99	17.45
Clarksville, TN	12.79	65.73	29.27	48.25	16.23	15.17	15.39
Cleveland, OH	14.06	76.95	33.00	57.91	17.62	15.55	17.41
College Station, TX	12.43	70.24	29.93	51.36	16.38	12.18	15.33
Colorado Springs, CO[1]	15.91	84.63	32.60	70.11	22.98	17.68	17.57
Columbia, MO	14.25	67.68	31.10	46.12	20.40	17.18	16.98
Columbia, SC	12.71	64.62	33.15	54.00	16.41	14.20	15.80
Columbus, OH	14.24	75.71	33.43	60.59	18.45	15.89	17.74
Dallas, TX	13.48	83.96	36.12	67.98	17.46	13.45	16.43
Davenport, IA	14.11	69.21	30.67	52.32	21.43	16.37	17.91
Denver, CO[1]	16.95	93.78	36.61	79.34	23.38	18.27	18.56
Des Moines, IA	14.21	77.18	33.94	54.24	22.00	17.30	17.35
Detroit, MI	14.34	77.60	33.92	65.30	21.26	15.95	17.41
Durham, NC	14.66	87.22	34.76	68.52	24.56	15.58	17.12
El Paso, TX	11.61	67.83	27.70	46.07	15.79	11.14	13.49
Eugene, OR	16.00	72.01	33.88	52.88	21.53	19.39	18.09
Fargo, ND	14.66	75.72	33.25	56.75	20.05	18.76	18.02
Fort Collins, CO[1]	16.21	90.82	32.90	67.45	28.72	18.19	18.27
Fort Wayne, IN	13.24	65.40	33.46	64.53	16.40	15.55	16.97
Fort Worth, TX	13.48	83.96	36.12	67.98	17.46	13.45	16.43
Gainesville, FL	14.25	67.20	30.71	55.75	15.92	15.70	16.07
Green Bay, WI	13.45	72.06	32.86	64.79	18.07	15.70	16.94
Greensboro, NC	13.39	82.48	31.23	58.89	18.93	14.32	15.59
Honolulu, HI	16.01	67.37	32.34	60.89	24.25	17.39	18.20
Houston, TX	12.78	88.07	35.05	66.82	19.05	12.11	15.20
Huntsville, AL	13.10	78.84	31.88	74.54	15.09	13.34	15.09
Indianapolis, IN	14.01	75.66	36.11	72.23	17.77	15.78	16.98
Jacksonville, FL	13.94	80.15	33.12	59.57	17.54	15.94	16.39
Kansas City, MO	14.34	76.99	34.02	53.13	20.28	15.65	17.70
Lafayette, LA	12.06	57.76	27.80	57.89	12.82	10.36	13.40
Las Vegas, NV	14.78	68.81	30.93	60.08	16.64	14.71	18.25
Lexington, KY	13.35	70.52	31.52	48.11	21.66	16.98	16.37
Lincoln, NE	14.42	68.94	30.73	50.12	17.48	16.47	16.83
Little Rock, AR	13.24	60.66	28.31	42.89	14.46	13.31	15.15
Los Angeles, CA	18.75	96.29	37.23	81.25	27.74	17.43	19.78
Louisville, KY	13.57	71.03	33.66	51.34	24.77	17.39	16.81
Madison, WI	14.40	77.53	36.80	69.40	17.58	17.03	18.27
Manchester, NH	14.45	76.66	37.63	74.48	18.36	18.05	18.24

Table continued on following page.

Metro Area	Fast Food and Counter Workers	Financial Managers	First-Line Supervisors/ of Office Workers	General and Operations Managers	Hair-dressers/ Cosme-tologists	Home Health and Personal Care Aides	Janitors/ Cleaners
McAllen, TX	11.81	63.80	28.02	44.25	14.51	11.34	14.44
Memphis, TN	13.12	76.07	34.04	61.94	17.10	15.01	15.76
Miami, FL	14.62	85.42	34.06	64.93	18.78	16.09	15.94
Midland, TX	13.82	87.54	36.53	69.94	n/a	12.83	16.27
Milwaukee, WI	13.86	78.61	35.29	68.07	19.57	15.84	17.69
Minneapolis, MN	16.17	85.12	37.88	59.75	22.01	17.88	19.66
Nashville, TN	14.12	79.15	35.70	66.64	20.68	16.69	17.04
New Orleans, LA	13.66	67.51	30.04	62.93	14.33	11.68	14.73
New York, NY	17.50	119.16	39.92	89.97	24.83	19.02	21.61
Oklahoma City, OK	12.18	71.53	32.48	52.56	18.80	13.47	15.40
Omaha, NE	14.83	75.03	31.66	51.15	21.52	17.13	17.41
Orlando, FL	14.19	78.11	32.58	58.33	17.70	16.03	16.19
Philadelphia, PA	15.05	85.35	35.52	66.76	19.65	15.40	18.54
Phoenix, AZ	16.50	75.51	33.09	59.06	19.33	17.28	18.02
Pittsburgh, PA	13.48	73.83	32.42	57.41	17.44	14.92	17.29
Portland, OR	17.61	86.12	36.29	70.26	25.82	21.37	20.22
Providence, RI	15.96	82.12	36.46	63.72	19.74	19.36	19.58
Provo, UT	13.85	75.16	33.39	54.43	18.78	17.59	15.34
Raleigh, NC	14.64	85.21	31.78	66.79	22.26	15.48	16.07
Reno, NV	15.29	67.77	32.24	59.24	23.92	16.38	17.04
Richmond, VA	14.48	88.63	33.36	63.23	25.31	14.98	16.42
Rochester, MN	15.53	77.53	34.14	50.21	22.80	17.71	20.40
Sacramento, CA	19.02	82.16	37.86	67.60	20.39	16.89	20.72
Saint Louis, MO	15.19	76.57	34.31	53.75	20.57	15.72	17.54
Saint Paul, MN	16.17	85.12	37.88	59.75	22.01	17.88	19.66
Salem, OR	16.51	80.64	34.43	56.23	22.06	20.60	19.35
Salt Lake City, UT	13.99	78.19	35.75	60.12	21.89	18.64	16.02
San Antonio, TX	13.32	77.30	32.68	57.15	16.98	12.52	15.75
San Diego, CA	18.39	92.64	36.65	n/a	22.37	17.55	19.51
San Francisco, CA	20.67	117.20	43.48	85.95	23.49	18.28	23.06
San Jose, CA	20.83	142.60	46.77	94.44	21.94	18.62	21.80
Santa Rosa, CA	19.46	82.80	36.40	66.12	22.13	18.18	21.32
Savannah, GA	13.18	76.60	32.20	55.21	19.33	14.47	15.78
Seattle, WA	19.74	96.69	42.38	82.62	33.56	23.17	22.62
Sioux Falls, SD	15.01	86.95	31.03	76.69	23.12	18.16	16.68
Tampa, FL	14.40	81.07	32.48	65.80	18.35	16.19	16.47
Tucson, AZ	15.89	66.97	29.60	57.34	19.10	16.54	17.29
Tulsa, OK	12.63	71.47	31.71	53.60	17.42	13.24	15.65
Virginia Beach, VA	14.30	78.26	32.80	57.87	23.44	14.33	16.05
Washington, DC	16.65	93.22	38.57	77.26	25.20	18.26	18.52
Wichita, KS	12.56	75.40	30.36	48.65	17.46	14.72	15.77
Wilmington, NC	13.68	73.03	29.78	55.43	19.37	14.82	16.04
Winston-Salem, NC	13.91	77.03	30.59	59.42	18.68	14.44	15.37

Notes: Figures cover the Metropolitan Statistical Area (MSA); (1) Data is from 2023 due to data quality issues in the state of Colorado and its substate areas in 2024; n/a not available
Source: Bureau of Labor Statistics, Metro Area Occupational Employment and Wage Estimates, May 2024

Average Hourly Wages: Occupations L – N

Metro Area	Landscapers	Lawyers	Maids/House-keepers	Maintenance/Repairers	Marketing Managers	Network Admin.	Nurses, Licensed Practical
Albuquerque, NM	18.15	67.75	15.65	23.82	62.50	44.51	26.25
Anchorage, AK	21.86	65.58	18.49	27.18	60.07	45.18	37.16
Ann Arbor, MI	19.91	80.54	17.03	24.12	70.18	46.70	33.06
Athens, GA	17.53	49.61	13.10	20.51	72.47	40.57	27.62
Atlanta, GA	18.84	98.50	15.44	25.02	82.69	48.68	29.80
Austin, TX	18.93	83.20	15.47	24.12	79.43	50.49	30.98
Baltimore, MD	19.36	76.50	16.48	25.58	76.43	60.34	34.04
Billings, MT	19.81	52.20	17.08	22.86	66.97	39.58	26.99
Boise City, ID	20.23	67.91	16.90	24.14	62.17	49.66	30.70
Boston, MA	24.09	109.06	21.01	28.49	98.23	53.85	37.85
Boulder, CO[1]	23.16	120.91	18.76	28.09	89.78	53.52	32.93
Cape Coral, FL	17.78	72.21	16.09	23.30	65.95	46.21	29.34
Cedar Rapids, IA	18.72	61.80	15.71	26.12	66.98	41.23	29.02
Charleston, SC	18.21	62.85	15.15	23.84	66.50	46.44	29.19
Charlotte, NC	18.72	89.69	16.06	25.50	77.80	48.36	30.80
Chicago, IL	21.26	89.56	19.33	27.90	78.03	49.76	34.69
Cincinnati, OH	18.59	69.29	15.43	26.32	72.86	48.96	29.78
Clarksville, TN	17.20	67.51	13.62	22.72	56.80	57.61	26.97
Cleveland, OH	18.91	71.42	15.21	25.41	67.80	46.55	30.00
College Station, TX	16.48	67.99	13.30	20.21	61.86	38.10	26.76
Colorado Springs, CO[1]	20.66	69.39	16.92	23.63	81.56	49.17	30.52
Columbia, MO	17.79	71.41	15.77	22.42	59.28	43.70	28.34
Columbia, SC	17.37	65.86	13.97	23.42	63.36	43.01	28.97
Columbus, OH	19.22	72.24	15.53	25.88	70.72	48.31	30.09
Dallas, TX	18.42	85.71	15.45	24.02	74.76	50.61	30.36
Davenport, IA	18.79	67.21	15.51	25.55	69.88	40.45	28.99
Denver, CO[1]	21.35	95.55	18.17	26.82	89.00	51.25	31.94
Des Moines, IA	19.53	64.42	15.83	25.62	70.53	44.92	30.46
Detroit, MI	19.93	69.97	16.33	24.30	72.83	48.72	32.31
Durham, NC	19.05	73.55	17.00	25.50	82.71	53.21	30.26
El Paso, TX	15.24	61.03	12.61	19.68	55.59	39.84	27.06
Eugene, OR	19.74	68.79	17.08	24.77	64.41	45.54	35.15
Fargo, ND	20.93	60.13	16.65	25.20	66.41	40.53	28.38
Fort Collins, CO[1]	20.58	104.22	17.22	24.61	88.03	47.68	30.10
Fort Wayne, IN	17.85	65.81	14.93	25.25	n/a	39.62	29.69
Fort Worth, TX	18.42	85.71	15.45	24.02	74.76	50.61	30.36
Gainesville, FL	17.73	53.79	15.37	23.13	64.71	41.00	27.62
Green Bay, WI	19.50	69.46	16.12	25.64	75.74	41.79	28.26
Greensboro, NC	17.87	68.03	14.93	23.70	80.15	41.61	30.11
Honolulu, HI	20.46	58.87	25.07	27.07	63.78	48.37	32.75
Houston, TX	17.42	78.80	14.99	23.29	75.23	48.11	30.16
Huntsville, AL	17.69	69.83	13.23	22.69	67.44	48.12	25.96
Indianapolis, IN	18.81	82.32	15.57	25.58	64.61	43.51	30.93
Jacksonville, FL	17.93	62.65	15.49	23.93	69.06	44.92	28.41
Kansas City, MO	20.15	84.26	16.32	25.52	69.71	44.91	30.67
Lafayette, LA	15.75	66.98	12.04	19.43	52.19	45.64	24.52
Las Vegas, NV	19.84	n/a	20.07	26.40	59.85	49.09	34.18
Lexington, KY	18.10	57.22	14.59	22.68	59.96	41.66	28.18
Lincoln, NE	18.75	54.48	15.57	24.63	54.33	42.93	28.51
Little Rock, AR	16.67	65.50	13.80	22.43	55.96	40.49	26.10
Los Angeles, CA	21.42	130.10	21.39	27.74	87.09	53.71	37.14
Louisville, KY	18.54	58.69	15.46	25.41	68.75	43.31	29.46
Madison, WI	21.04	69.54	16.72	26.12	67.95	41.94	30.71
Manchester, NH	21.01	90.60	16.93	26.41	79.04	50.29	34.71
McAllen, TX	14.92	57.98	12.70	17.79	54.38	37.41	24.78

Table continued on following page.

Metro Area	Landscapers	Lawyers	Maids/House-keepers	Maintenance/Repairers	Marketing Managers	Network Admin.	Nurses, Licensed Practical
Memphis, TN	18.30	71.60	15.17	23.77	70.27	43.88	25.70
Miami, FL	18.25	78.54	16.01	23.66	69.64	47.57	30.32
Midland, TX	18.44	95.87	14.15	23.89	73.71	47.24	30.11
Milwaukee, WI	19.82	86.63	17.09	26.01	71.02	46.35	30.73
Minneapolis, MN	22.32	79.57	19.15	28.72	85.36	48.14	30.75
Nashville, TN	19.47	80.00	15.97	24.27	70.23	54.49	28.30
New Orleans, LA	16.51	66.68	14.95	22.29	60.16	47.36	28.31
New York, NY	21.91	103.90	24.09	28.95	96.08	57.33	34.69
Oklahoma City, OK	17.06	59.75	13.86	21.81	69.08	41.11	26.98
Omaha, NE	20.04	68.96	16.54	25.08	63.75	45.55	29.24
Orlando, FL	17.82	68.56	16.98	23.02	75.25	45.79	28.81
Philadelphia, PA	19.86	82.76	16.94	26.00	81.62	49.02	32.87
Phoenix, AZ	19.42	81.05	17.66	25.41	74.34	46.72	35.33
Pittsburgh, PA	18.69	72.59	15.75	24.30	63.96	44.03	28.96
Portland, OR	21.90	76.99	19.20	28.31	81.04	50.92	38.94
Providence, RI	21.36	73.53	17.71	25.96	82.62	50.61	35.27
Provo, UT	20.19	70.82	16.07	24.23	70.63	46.73	28.85
Raleigh, NC	19.00	71.98	15.98	24.47	81.03	50.43	30.60
Reno, NV	21.79	96.52	18.19	25.86	73.52	48.59	35.06
Richmond, VA	18.50	80.01	15.53	25.46	84.07	49.36	30.78
Rochester, MN	21.83	65.23	18.18	26.25	80.62	52.13	29.80
Sacramento, CA	22.37	97.12	21.69	27.33	84.16	52.73	39.66
Saint Louis, MO	19.80	73.53	16.55	26.56	66.03	43.67	30.72
Saint Paul, MN	22.32	79.57	19.15	28.72	85.36	48.14	30.75
Salem, OR	20.37	76.23	19.11	25.44	64.66	52.82	35.99
Salt Lake City, UT	20.01	76.47	17.31	25.87	72.64	49.94	31.60
San Antonio, TX	17.39	73.65	14.28	22.06	67.10	43.87	29.23
San Diego, CA	21.52	93.11	20.83	27.48	93.41	50.55	37.47
San Francisco, CA	25.75	132.29	25.07	33.69	109.71	64.21	43.56
San Jose, CA	25.28	151.17	27.28	33.50	137.00	63.55	44.06
Santa Rosa, CA	23.68	124.30	22.21	28.52	80.50	50.04	41.93
Savannah, GA	17.56	67.70	13.59	23.15	75.38	45.56	27.56
Seattle, WA	24.35	88.39	20.95	30.02	94.44	55.61	39.88
Sioux Falls, SD	17.48	64.81	15.77	23.21	78.00	37.26	24.52
Tampa, FL	17.89	67.66	16.79	22.66	73.93	48.19	29.09
Tucson, AZ	18.04	67.35	16.29	22.70	65.42	44.42	34.81
Tulsa, OK	17.01	57.59	13.86	22.39	70.25	51.21	27.71
Virginia Beach, VA	17.88	71.39	15.26	24.23	77.38	47.60	29.68
Washington, DC	20.84	105.48	18.53	27.76	91.27	60.06	34.17
Wichita, KS	18.31	60.10	14.70	22.57	67.18	39.93	27.76
Wilmington, NC	17.61	60.44	14.71	22.36	72.18	42.11	29.97
Winston-Salem, NC	17.78	83.92	15.70	24.06	74.45	43.84	28.98

Notes: Figures cover the Metropolitan Statistical Area (MSA); (1) Data is from 2023 due to data quality issues in the state of Colorado and its substate areas in 2024; n/a not available
Source: Bureau of Labor Statistics, Metro Area Occupational Employment and Wage Estimates, May 2024

Average Hourly Wages: Occupations N – P

Metro Area	Nurses, Registered	Nursing Assistants	Office Clerks	Physical Therapists	Physicians	Plumbers	Police Officers
Albuquerque, NM	45.99	18.59	18.52	48.32	146.53	30.61	33.46
Anchorage, AK	54.49	22.44	25.42	54.28	n/a	40.27	52.82
Ann Arbor, MI	46.65	19.82	21.46	47.54	117.60	35.47	37.47
Athens, GA	40.42	17.28	20.80	45.86	148.79	26.20	28.56
Atlanta, GA	46.46	18.72	20.88	50.04	128.59	29.64	30.37
Austin, TX	44.74	18.68	21.24	50.22	140.23	30.87	40.67
Baltimore, MD	46.70	20.15	22.45	50.65	111.79	32.84	38.57
Billings, MT	43.06	20.43	21.25	46.45	n/a	37.35	35.12
Boise City, ID	44.68	18.92	21.13	46.02	150.09	28.71	36.96
Boston, MA	55.63	22.73	25.39	49.54	104.76	42.81	39.16
Boulder, CO[1]	47.77	22.19	27.23	47.73	157.65	33.25	43.85
Cape Coral, FL	41.84	18.75	22.60	46.75	178.53	25.11	36.26
Cedar Rapids, IA	37.78	19.56	21.03	42.76	148.31	33.30	35.70
Charleston, SC	42.57	18.63	20.56	47.07	142.06	26.91	30.52
Charlotte, NC	42.86	19.15	20.94	48.26	150.06	27.07	32.47
Chicago, IL	45.47	21.85	23.22	52.46	109.22	44.43	47.28
Cincinnati, OH	41.93	19.66	21.56	48.99	137.38	32.13	38.17
Clarksville, TN	37.88	17.59	18.67	45.46	154.95	31.80	26.37
Cleveland, OH	43.24	19.22	22.21	48.56	117.07	33.28	37.16
College Station, TX	40.15	16.34	n/a	49.86	118.72	26.89	36.08
Colorado Springs, CO[1]	41.57	20.55	25.08	47.11	145.41	29.44	40.85
Columbia, MO	39.72	18.73	20.78	43.86	149.57	30.64	28.96
Columbia, SC	40.80	17.13	19.07	45.02	172.10	25.12	32.54
Columbus, OH	42.87	19.72	22.35	47.24	129.01	32.38	42.38
Dallas, TX	46.50	18.80	21.12	52.68	105.52	30.24	41.90
Davenport, IA	36.47	18.90	20.19	45.91	133.88	34.59	34.22
Denver, CO[1]	44.80	21.50	27.01	47.63	148.66	32.33	44.76
Des Moines, IA	38.30	20.34	21.64	46.36	117.95	32.51	39.83
Detroit, MI	44.56	19.58	22.38	47.96	79.84	36.88	36.19
Durham, NC	n/a	19.70	21.79	44.30	69.93	28.13	30.46
El Paso, TX	42.08	16.41	16.95	46.74	120.70	25.72	36.19
Eugene, OR	54.25	23.01	22.54	47.48	165.85	40.25	42.81
Fargo, ND	39.76	19.70	24.78	43.52	165.27	31.67	36.83
Fort Collins, CO[1]	43.16	20.38	25.12	44.64	119.01	30.07	44.59
Fort Wayne, IN	39.85	18.10	21.10	46.11	144.14	35.26	36.57
Fort Worth, TX	46.50	18.80	21.12	52.68	105.52	30.24	41.90
Gainesville, FL	42.66	18.80	21.26	46.21	130.80	24.73	29.02
Green Bay, WI	41.77	19.98	21.47	47.00	196.56	39.90	39.06
Greensboro, NC	41.93	18.27	19.68	44.25	144.60	25.64	30.89
Honolulu, HI	60.17	21.81	21.33	48.19	152.85	40.69	45.53
Houston, TX	46.51	18.77	19.64	53.94	123.51	29.30	35.97
Huntsville, AL	35.22	16.31	16.03	47.20	140.44	26.63	30.79
Indianapolis, IN	42.93	18.85	22.26	47.40	154.93	33.46	38.34
Jacksonville, FL	41.31	18.27	21.57	46.05	130.38	26.34	33.29
Kansas City, MO	41.12	20.02	22.34	46.79	76.04	36.37	33.12
Lafayette, LA	38.87	14.75	15.09	45.77	127.73	26.64	26.21
Las Vegas, NV	49.23	21.32	21.50	55.52	108.49	31.52	41.22
Lexington, KY	40.98	19.39	19.89	44.65	134.53	31.89	32.13
Lincoln, NE	39.04	19.33	18.58	44.86	136.23	30.39	40.64
Little Rock, AR	39.00	16.82	19.51	45.58	113.68	25.08	28.58
Los Angeles, CA	66.35	23.03	23.99	56.57	82.19	37.49	52.17
Louisville, KY	42.06	19.38	18.96	44.32	137.23	33.07	31.32
Madison, WI	46.09	21.62	21.81	47.86	156.17	42.99	38.38
Manchester, NH	44.26	22.36	24.15	44.89	148.76	31.71	36.87
McAllen, TX	36.77	15.66	16.04	50.03	144.98	22.61	29.67

Table continued on following page.

Metro Area	Nurses, Registered	Nursing Assistants	Office Clerks	Physical Therapists	Physicians	Plumbers	Police Officers
Memphis, TN	40.79	17.76	19.17	48.19	143.52	28.45	32.26
Miami, FL	44.26	19.01	22.54	42.79	117.21	27.27	50.84
Midland, TX	42.82	18.39	23.20	54.19	n/a	27.83	40.49
Milwaukee, WI	43.77	21.00	21.09	48.16	115.37	41.81	41.03
Minneapolis, MN	49.42	22.60	24.20	47.65	159.99	42.95	42.99
Nashville, TN	42.71	19.32	20.60	47.86	134.22	29.46	30.96
New Orleans, LA	43.12	16.45	16.23	51.00	147.27	29.90	27.76
New York, NY	55.60	23.60	24.07	52.54	125.08	43.78	44.53
Oklahoma City, OK	41.29	17.28	19.03	48.05	113.07	27.59	35.39
Omaha, NE	40.84	20.08	19.65	45.26	132.45	34.64	39.22
Orlando, FL	41.57	17.96	21.36	47.77	152.34	26.02	32.01
Philadelphia, PA	46.88	20.72	22.87	50.29	103.98	38.73	41.45
Phoenix, AZ	46.26	21.03	24.26	50.72	101.37	33.45	42.24
Pittsburgh, PA	41.36	19.62	21.43	45.46	106.62	34.88	39.89
Portland, OR	59.41	24.32	24.99	51.26	145.16	46.10	45.23
Providence, RI	47.85	20.93	23.21	47.81	115.77	36.48	37.31
Provo, UT	40.74	18.10	20.61	47.91	138.71	27.75	34.98
Raleigh, NC	43.18	18.76	20.44	45.60	140.88	27.06	31.94
Reno, NV	49.60	21.66	22.82	51.17	119.36	34.61	40.69
Richmond, VA	43.52	19.49	22.18	49.10	124.83	28.27	33.25
Rochester, MN	50.31	21.62	23.84	46.20	142.26	41.69	38.02
Sacramento, CA	78.37	23.25	25.08	60.12	165.05	35.78	53.46
Saint Louis, MO	40.74	19.04	21.94	46.78	n/a	37.26	34.71
Saint Paul, MN	49.42	22.60	24.20	47.65	159.99	42.95	42.99
Salem, OR	58.70	24.31	23.22	46.55	156.96	38.33	41.55
Salt Lake City, UT	44.02	19.66	22.49	47.44	112.68	32.12	40.23
San Antonio, TX	42.93	17.50	19.72	48.60	148.25	28.13	33.62
San Diego, CA	67.00	23.07	23.88	52.74	133.58	36.03	53.06
San Francisco, CA	85.79	27.59	27.96	65.53	127.97	41.48	61.75
San Jose, CA	91.29	27.97	28.51	68.75	89.33	49.42	69.86
Santa Rosa, CA	82.45	23.29	26.18	62.99	96.04	38.02	53.85
Savannah, GA	41.90	17.49	19.60	47.93	140.56	29.86	30.08
Seattle, WA	57.82	25.24	26.95	50.63	142.83	45.49	53.76
Sioux Falls, SD	34.16	18.18	18.51	42.66	n/a	27.31	37.35
Tampa, FL	43.40	18.54	21.94	47.43	143.21	26.24	37.66
Tucson, AZ	44.18	20.24	22.28	47.48	134.43	27.72	37.95
Tulsa, OK	43.20	17.41	19.08	46.55	83.29	28.27	31.70
Virginia Beach, VA	42.13	18.43	21.17	48.12	125.27	27.83	32.02
Washington, DC	49.29	20.85	26.37	53.25	100.51	34.13	41.76
Wichita, KS	36.06	17.82	16.54	46.81	100.27	29.54	28.31
Wilmington, NC	39.17	18.20	18.96	41.99	129.60	25.08	26.40
Winston-Salem, NC	42.11	18.13	19.25	47.50	n/a	25.08	27.78

Notes: Figures cover the Metropolitan Statistical Area (MSA); (1) Data is from 2023 due to data quality issues in the state of Colorado and its substate areas in 2024; n/a not available
Source: Bureau of Labor Statistics, Metro Area Occupational Employment and Wage Estimates, May 2024

Average Hourly Wages: Occupations P – S

Metro Area	Postal Mail Carriers	R.E. Sales Agents	Retail Sales-persons	Sales Reps., Technical/ Scientific	Secretaries, Exc. Leg./ Med./Exec.	Security Guards	Surgeons
Albuquerque, NM	28.74	40.95	16.73	41.73	21.86	21.72	219.96
Anchorage, AK	27.61	43.45	19.57	40.10	21.78	26.71	n/a
Ann Arbor, MI	28.15	31.11	18.46	105.25	24.23	21.89	n/a
Athens, GA	28.08	27.38	14.88	n/a	17.77	21.83	n/a
Atlanta, GA	28.20	34.66	16.55	55.13	20.91	19.64	216.10
Austin, TX	29.21	41.46	17.04	45.57	22.22	19.26	n/a
Baltimore, MD	28.82	27.82	17.59	44.15	23.24	20.69	171.05
Billings, MT	28.52	37.77	17.80	49.31	21.21	19.51	n/a
Boise City, ID	28.72	n/a	18.06	59.59	20.77	20.32	n/a
Boston, MA	29.71	46.11	19.71	54.45	27.63	22.25	161.25
Boulder, CO[1]	29.62	37.36	20.20	68.73	23.54	25.69	n/a
Cape Coral, FL	29.05	37.59	16.92	57.39	20.71	17.45	n/a
Cedar Rapids, IA	28.91	21.00	16.36	49.65	21.59	19.04	n/a
Charleston, SC	29.37	n/a	16.45	50.27	21.83	18.35	n/a
Charlotte, NC	29.03	30.17	16.65	63.70	20.49	19.12	248.26
Chicago, IL	29.11	29.28	18.67	58.57	25.84	21.16	161.04
Cincinnati, OH	29.19	24.40	17.19	57.27	23.98	19.14	n/a
Clarksville, TN	27.83	25.11	16.33	34.76	19.85	19.00	n/a
Cleveland, OH	28.67	23.45	17.25	47.42	22.52	19.46	n/a
College Station, TX	27.95	29.01	15.01	41.37	19.66	16.89	n/a
Colorado Springs, CO[1]	27.18	33.25	18.80	53.78	21.04	19.20	n/a
Columbia, MO	28.47	24.50	16.22	46.86	20.78	18.70	n/a
Columbia, SC	27.58	25.47	15.69	55.80	20.60	16.75	n/a
Columbus, OH	29.11	25.57	17.40	54.37	23.47	19.81	n/a
Dallas, TX	29.14	35.39	16.85	49.39	22.33	19.16	172.43
Davenport, IA	28.67	31.72	16.82	46.92	21.95	19.78	n/a
Denver, CO[1]	29.38	n/a	20.04	57.52	23.31	22.24	n/a
Des Moines, IA	30.06	20.22	17.08	60.11	22.86	19.84	207.59
Detroit, MI	28.48	32.41	19.31	68.16	23.38	19.17	n/a
Durham, NC	29.34	28.62	16.63	57.68	23.09	21.40	n/a
El Paso, TX	28.75	31.06	14.45	41.79	18.76	14.38	n/a
Eugene, OR	27.06	26.12	18.58	52.14	23.51	19.91	186.25
Fargo, ND	30.03	34.07	18.57	54.80	21.50	20.01	n/a
Fort Collins, CO[1]	28.36	32.17	18.87	52.65	21.68	19.32	n/a
Fort Wayne, IN	28.41	37.39	16.08	52.60	20.58	20.23	n/a
Fort Worth, TX	29.14	35.39	16.85	49.39	22.33	19.16	172.43
Gainesville, FL	28.67	29.50	16.05	48.82	21.09	17.73	n/a
Green Bay, WI	29.14	28.56	17.47	31.64	22.49	20.67	n/a
Greensboro, NC	29.19	31.36	15.70	47.29	21.42	17.81	n/a
Honolulu, HI	27.98	33.03	19.06	58.17	25.07	20.40	n/a
Houston, TX	28.58	36.58	16.26	50.66	22.14	18.23	n/a
Huntsville, AL	27.93	22.98	16.48	52.53	21.47	19.04	n/a
Indianapolis, IN	29.29	36.12	16.89	55.71	21.53	21.17	222.23
Jacksonville, FL	29.28	35.39	16.85	47.51	21.36	17.65	n/a
Kansas City, MO	29.08	40.62	17.76	57.49	21.49	22.78	n/a
Lafayette, LA	28.33	20.17	14.62	53.76	19.61	15.29	n/a
Las Vegas, NV	28.67	32.12	17.32	51.43	22.21	19.00	n/a
Lexington, KY	28.80	31.80	16.41	45.46	21.53	17.37	n/a
Lincoln, NE	30.57	27.17	16.38	40.00	22.03	20.05	n/a
Little Rock, AR	29.24	n/a	15.97	38.95	19.79	18.85	n/a
Los Angeles, CA	29.11	36.15	20.52	56.19	26.51	21.76	181.61
Louisville, KY	28.87	25.01	16.47	51.44	22.05	18.78	n/a
Madison, WI	29.38	32.13	17.90	43.29	24.50	21.74	n/a
Manchester, NH	29.69	25.56	18.32	57.21	22.59	22.02	n/a
McAllen, TX	30.28	28.28	14.03	39.87	18.47	13.98	n/a

Table continued on following page.

Appendix A: Comparative Statistics

Metro Area	Postal Mail Carriers	R.E. Sales Agents	Retail Salespersons	Sales Reps., Technical/ Scientific	Secretaries, Exc. Leg./ Med./Exec.	Security Guards	Surgeons
Memphis, TN	28.14	27.09	16.86	48.33	21.52	18.00	n/a
Miami, FL	28.58	35.78	17.72	72.39	22.74	19.47	n/a
Midland, TX	27.68	57.72	17.23	n/a	22.14	23.02	n/a
Milwaukee, WI	28.92	36.71	17.62	43.52	23.21	21.24	n/a
Minneapolis, MN	29.62	34.01	18.56	50.40	25.28	24.99	180.26
Nashville, TN	29.67	24.17	17.69	49.18	22.79	20.23	n/a
New Orleans, LA	28.47	24.83	15.83	70.24	20.08	17.58	n/a
New York, NY	28.97	50.92	21.03	71.17	25.44	21.96	153.50
Oklahoma City, OK	28.83	n/a	16.29	44.00	19.75	20.95	n/a
Omaha, NE	29.45	23.46	16.96	41.73	22.46	21.05	165.50
Orlando, FL	28.68	33.44	16.93	50.60	21.59	18.05	n/a
Philadelphia, PA	28.61	31.43	17.58	57.13	23.47	20.88	n/a
Phoenix, AZ	29.45	33.31	18.61	47.67	23.90	20.06	201.58
Pittsburgh, PA	28.52	31.38	16.07	51.43	20.70	18.83	n/a
Portland, OR	28.58	33.65	20.03	60.80	26.92	23.38	n/a
Providence, RI	29.03	31.86	18.21	51.21	24.94	19.43	n/a
Provo, UT	29.07	24.11	17.69	38.31	20.88	20.05	n/a
Raleigh, NC	29.38	33.92	16.98	55.52	22.71	20.01	n/a
Reno, NV	28.83	27.04	18.04	54.60	23.35	20.48	n/a
Richmond, VA	29.19	34.95	17.09	54.94	22.38	21.69	n/a
Rochester, MN	30.26	32.82	18.61	63.87	25.11	23.45	n/a
Sacramento, CA	29.98	35.09	20.50	56.67	26.05	21.11	n/a
Saint Louis, MO	28.63	22.92	17.47	49.86	21.95	21.78	n/a
Saint Paul, MN	29.62	34.01	18.56	50.40	25.28	24.99	180.26
Salem, OR	28.32	31.93	18.59	51.43	25.45	21.67	n/a
Salt Lake City, UT	29.32	31.26	19.37	49.93	22.46	21.09	n/a
San Antonio, TX	28.61	27.84	16.14	48.30	21.21	17.26	n/a
San Diego, CA	28.81	33.54	20.16	56.30	26.29	21.29	215.16
San Francisco, CA	29.93	39.65	22.87	70.21	31.24	24.81	n/a
San Jose, CA	29.61	49.32	23.09	78.15	31.07	24.80	n/a
Santa Rosa, CA	28.63	39.71	21.77	56.13	27.28	22.66	n/a
Savannah, GA	28.40	31.87	15.49	43.92	19.62	17.54	n/a
Seattle, WA	29.52	40.04	21.76	71.82	28.37	25.48	164.19
Sioux Falls, SD	29.60	44.83	20.29	72.14	19.77	19.11	n/a
Tampa, FL	28.84	34.03	16.81	55.31	22.08	18.32	210.11
Tucson, AZ	29.27	30.47	18.32	47.81	21.86	18.88	n/a
Tulsa, OK	29.17	29.25	16.41	43.73	19.75	19.04	n/a
Virginia Beach, VA	28.31	31.93	16.44	52.97	21.87	20.46	n/a
Washington, DC	29.66	34.90	18.96	54.33	26.32	26.46	178.95
Wichita, KS	28.32	n/a	16.72	58.23	19.03	18.73	n/a
Wilmington, NC	29.33	24.73	16.08	51.06	21.11	21.00	n/a
Winston-Salem, NC	28.87	23.59	15.88	51.83	21.50	20.24	n/a

Notes: Figures cover the Metropolitan Statistical Area (MSA); (1) Data is from 2023 due to data quality issues in the state of Colorado and its substate areas in 2024; n/a not available
Source: Bureau of Labor Statistics, Metro Area Occupational Employment and Wage Estimates, May 2024

Average Hourly Wages: Occupations T – W

Metro Area	Teacher Assistants[2]	Teachers, Secondary School[2]	Telemarketers	Truck Drivers, Heavy	Truck Drivers, Light	Waiters/ Waitresses
Albuquerque, NM	15.58	32.70	33.59	25.68	20.59	18.83
Anchorage, AK	16.43	39.21	n/a	31.27	29.20	20.08
Ann Arbor, MI	16.34	35.96	n/a	28.12	23.79	20.05
Athens, GA	12.66	31.86	n/a	26.99	22.11	12.40
Atlanta, GA	14.65	35.49	16.14	28.06	23.97	13.74
Austin, TX	15.99	29.94	16.65	28.00	23.95	17.05
Baltimore, MD	18.88	36.16	16.80	28.16	23.74	19.68
Billings, MT	15.66	31.64	n/a	29.65	24.41	14.05
Boise City, ID	15.78	32.07	18.37	27.48	27.08	16.87
Boston, MA	20.03	42.74	18.61	29.10	25.46	22.07
Boulder, CO[1]	19.34	37.59	n/a	28.09	24.74	22.52
Cape Coral, FL	17.30	27.48	17.59	24.75	21.61	18.95
Cedar Rapids, IA	14.24	28.68	15.78	29.58	24.80	14.45
Charleston, SC	13.41	31.47	n/a	27.48	22.40	12.20
Charlotte, NC	14.49	27.70	19.21	27.14	21.73	16.65
Chicago, IL	18.41	42.55	17.05	31.25	25.40	16.76
Cincinnati, OH	17.09	33.20	16.50	30.56	24.16	18.39
Clarksville, TN	15.35	26.88	n/a	26.20	18.98	13.57
Cleveland, OH	17.13	37.67	15.51	28.14	21.75	18.81
College Station, TX	14.65	28.00	n/a	24.31	25.81	15.16
Colorado Springs, CO[1]	16.56	28.08	25.27	26.24	21.53	21.16
Columbia, MO	15.25	26.79	n/a	26.84	22.33	15.03
Columbia, SC	14.58	28.10	13.70	26.77	22.11	11.85
Columbus, OH	16.73	38.26	15.60	30.84	23.64	19.12
Dallas, TX	14.37	31.75	17.73	28.88	23.68	15.52
Davenport, IA	15.98	32.25	15.38	26.97	22.49	14.76
Denver, CO[1]	18.20	34.07	24.12	29.22	24.04	18.83
Des Moines, IA	15.17	29.25	15.86	29.34	22.55	15.00
Detroit, MI	15.96	34.65	16.11	27.01	21.91	19.88
Durham, NC	14.99	27.78	17.39	26.62	21.88	16.09
El Paso, TX	13.36	29.30	n/a	25.51	19.26	13.84
Eugene, OR	18.52	38.08	n/a	28.02	23.03	18.82
Fargo, ND	18.13	29.54	n/a	27.21	24.35	16.96
Fort Collins, CO[1]	17.53	31.75	n/a	26.38	22.67	21.70
Fort Wayne, IN	15.68	30.99	n/a	28.99	21.73	14.84
Fort Worth, TX	14.37	31.75	17.73	28.88	23.68	15.52
Gainesville, FL	15.81	33.04	n/a	24.90	21.27	18.15
Green Bay, WI	17.43	29.58	n/a	27.16	22.51	14.93
Greensboro, NC	13.56	25.65	16.15	26.84	21.55	15.80
Honolulu, HI	17.06	30.19	n/a	27.42	23.32	25.96
Houston, TX	14.01	31.15	18.64	27.49	23.30	15.23
Huntsville, AL	11.76	30.28	n/a	27.09	22.62	12.42
Indianapolis, IN	16.14	32.97	18.55	30.71	24.66	15.51
Jacksonville, FL	16.11	33.35	17.68	27.47	22.53	18.38
Kansas City, MO	15.24	29.47	18.48	28.62	23.71	17.04
Lafayette, LA	12.65	24.74	n/a	26.47	19.63	11.17
Las Vegas, NV	15.55	31.27	16.68	28.15	22.31	15.55
Lexington, KY	17.74	30.50	n/a	29.78	22.45	14.52
Lincoln, NE	13.52	29.94	14.12	38.54	22.72	19.50
Little Rock, AR	15.65	27.84	n/a	28.31	21.58	14.13
Los Angeles, CA	21.70	49.74	19.37	28.59	24.21	20.65
Louisville, KY	16.51	31.82	n/a	30.63	24.78	14.86
Madison, WI	18.13	30.40	17.61	27.62	23.52	17.52
Manchester, NH	18.04	34.04	15.89	27.49	22.94	21.07
McAllen, TX	13.28	30.53	n/a	24.00	19.17	13.40

Table continued on following page.

Metro Area	Teacher Assistants[2]	Teachers, Secondary School[2]	Telemarketers	Truck Drivers, Heavy	Truck Drivers, Light	Waiters/ Waitresses
Memphis, TN	14.32	28.90	13.76	29.58	29.29	13.80
Miami, FL	15.86	28.86	18.31	26.65	23.18	18.71
Midland, TX	15.30	31.99	n/a	28.32	23.98	15.93
Milwaukee, WI	17.98	34.09	17.30	28.14	22.92	16.18
Minneapolis, MN	20.05	35.70	22.16	31.39	25.01	13.95
Nashville, TN	14.83	29.56	15.16	28.95	23.69	15.99
New Orleans, LA	14.58	28.89	n/a	25.97	22.33	12.40
New York, NY	19.26	48.38	19.76	33.26	25.01	25.65
Oklahoma City, OK	14.11	27.06	16.04	27.43	20.70	14.43
Omaha, NE	14.60	29.23	14.96	27.64	23.61	19.47
Orlando, FL	15.02	27.08	17.71	26.28	22.34	18.62
Philadelphia, PA	16.42	37.57	18.66	29.70	23.32	19.57
Phoenix, AZ	17.41	33.10	25.15	27.04	25.25	23.73
Pittsburgh, PA	15.48	37.69	18.78	27.85	20.24	16.99
Portland, OR	19.63	42.02	19.64	31.98	24.55	22.74
Providence, RI	17.96	39.10	18.03	28.07	23.04	20.77
Provo, UT	15.72	32.55	19.36	27.39	21.30	16.73
Raleigh, NC	15.69	26.95	n/a	26.45	20.95	16.07
Reno, NV	17.00	36.97	16.27	31.35	24.02	13.93
Richmond, VA	16.87	30.92	n/a	29.88	21.77	19.74
Rochester, MN	18.97	34.45	n/a	30.88	23.86	12.89
Sacramento, CA	21.20	45.34	19.22	29.27	24.31	21.77
Saint Louis, MO	16.42	31.39	15.91	27.24	23.38	15.95
Saint Paul, MN	20.05	35.70	22.16	31.39	25.01	13.95
Salem, OR	18.55	36.88	n/a	29.67	22.75	20.45
Salt Lake City, UT	15.41	35.90	17.54	29.38	23.05	16.60
San Antonio, TX	12.78	29.49	16.58	25.47	21.43	15.16
San Diego, CA	20.95	54.30	19.47	28.38	23.68	22.56
San Francisco, CA	24.02	55.15	23.72	32.89	27.39	22.18
San Jose, CA	24.13	52.38	23.11	33.44	26.28	24.41
Santa Rosa, CA	22.92	47.05	n/a	29.46	25.70	21.12
Savannah, GA	13.88	32.08	13.85	27.26	24.37	13.65
Seattle, WA	24.88	47.37	21.66	33.99	26.42	27.97
Sioux Falls, SD	13.44	24.78	n/a	28.36	21.88	15.30
Tampa, FL	14.20	30.50	17.64	25.87	21.83	19.64
Tucson, AZ	16.88	25.54	n/a	25.42	23.43	20.95
Tulsa, OK	13.50	28.84	16.76	27.89	20.63	14.21
Virginia Beach, VA	18.39	34.95	20.17	24.69	20.85	19.88
Washington, DC	20.42	38.87	19.03	29.14	24.85	22.84
Wichita, KS	14.38	28.72	n/a	26.88	19.57	17.67
Wilmington, NC	14.70	25.61	16.58	24.77	19.92	14.23
Winston-Salem, NC	13.12	26.41	n/a	25.99	20.43	14.25

Notes: Figures cover the Metropolitan Statistical Area (MSA); (1) Data is from 2023 due to data quality issues in the state of Colorado and its substate areas in 2024; (2) Hourly wages were calculated from annual wage data based on a 40 hour work week; n/a not available
Source: Bureau of Labor Statistics, Metro Area Occupational Employment and Wage Estimates, May 2024

Means of Transportation to Work: City

City	Car/Truck/Van		Public Transportation			Bicycle	Walked	Other Means	Worked at Home
	Drove Alone	Car-pooled	Bus	Subway	Railroad				
Albuquerque, NM	73.2	8.8	1.2	0.0	0.1	0.9	1.9	1.2	12.8
Anchorage, AK	71.0	12.4	1.3	0.0	0.0	0.6	2.6	2.5	9.6
Ann Arbor, MI	45.6	5.0	7.3	0.1	0.0	2.4	13.1	0.5	26.2
Athens, GA	72.0	7.8	2.1	0.0	0.0	0.9	4.5	0.8	11.9
Atlanta, GA	55.2	4.6	3.6	2.5	0.1	0.7	4.2	2.4	26.6
Austin, TX	58.8	6.9	1.9	0.0	0.0	0.8	2.4	1.6	27.5
Baltimore, MD	56.8	6.9	9.3	1.0	0.8	0.6	5.6	3.1	15.9
Billings, MT	78.5	9.1	1.0	0.0	0.0	0.7	2.0	1.0	7.6
Boise City, ID	68.6	7.6	0.5	0.0	0.0	2.3	3.4	1.6	15.8
Boston, MA	34.1	5.4	8.6	13.6	1.2	2.1	13.8	2.4	18.8
Boulder, CO	41.9	3.6	5.8	0.0	0.0	7.6	8.6	0.9	31.6
Cape Coral, FL	76.0	8.1	0.2	0.0	0.0	0.1	1.0	1.4	13.1
Cedar Rapids, IA	77.0	6.5	0.6	0.0	0.0	0.3	2.2	0.8	12.6
Charleston, SC	68.1	6.5	0.9	0.0	0.0	1.5	4.1	1.2	17.6
Charlotte, NC	61.0	8.1	1.4	0.1	0.0	0.2	1.7	2.0	25.5
Chicago, IL	46.0	7.4	9.5	8.5	1.2	1.4	5.7	2.1	18.3
Cincinnati, OH	66.2	7.5	5.7	0.0	0.0	0.3	5.3	1.8	13.2
Clarksville, TN	81.0	8.7	0.5	0.0	0.0	0.0	1.2	1.5	7.1
Cleveland, OH	65.4	10.0	6.3	0.4	0.0	0.5	5.3	1.9	10.1
College Station, TX	70.8	8.0	2.3	0.0	0.0	1.9	3.9	1.1	12.1
Colorado Springs, CO	71.1	9.0	0.4	0.0	0.0	0.5	1.8	1.1	16.1
Columbia, MO	74.1	7.6	1.1	0.0	0.0	1.0	5.6	0.9	9.6
Columbia, SC	62.9	6.9	1.4	0.0	0.0	0.3	16.4	2.2	9.8
Columbus, OH	70.1	7.5	2.1	0.0	0.0	0.4	2.6	1.2	16.1
Dallas, TX	68.5	11.4	1.7	0.2	0.1	0.2	2.2	1.7	14.0
Davenport, IA	78.8	7.3	0.8	0.0	0.1	0.2	2.7	1.1	8.9
Denver, CO	57.7	6.5	2.8	0.3	0.1	1.6	3.9	2.7	24.4
Des Moines, IA	72.3	11.2	1.1	0.0	0.0	0.4	2.2	1.3	11.4
Detroit, MI	66.3	11.0	5.9	0.0	0.0	0.5	3.1	3.1	10.1
Durham, NC	65.2	8.0	2.2	0.0	0.0	0.5	2.3	1.4	20.6
El Paso, TX	76.5	11.1	1.0	0.0	0.0	0.1	1.1	2.3	7.8
Eugene, OR	63.0	7.9	2.6	0.0	0.0	4.7	5.3	1.1	15.3
Fargo, ND	78.7	6.6	0.7	0.0	0.1	0.3	3.5	2.0	8.1
Fort Collins, CO	63.3	5.6	1.4	0.0	0.0	4.2	4.2	1.0	20.2
Fort Wayne, IN	78.1	9.9	1.1	0.0	0.0	0.3	1.5	0.8	8.2
Fort Worth, TX	72.9	10.9	0.4	0.0	0.1	0.2	1.2	1.5	12.9
Gainesville, FL	62.9	9.0	4.9	0.0	0.0	3.5	5.0	2.3	12.4
Green Bay, WI	75.9	10.7	1.0	0.0	0.0	0.4	2.3	1.1	8.5
Greensboro, NC	73.7	8.2	2.4	0.0	0.0	0.2	2.3	1.4	11.8
Honolulu, HI	55.7	14.2	7.9	0.0	0.0	1.8	7.7	3.7	8.9
Houston, TX	69.7	10.1	2.9	0.1	0.0	0.4	1.9	3.1	11.7
Huntsville, AL	77.5	6.8	0.3	0.0	0.0	0.0	1.3	1.0	13.1
Indianapolis, IN	73.7	9.6	1.4	0.0	0.0	0.4	1.8	0.9	12.3
Jacksonville, FL	72.8	9.0	1.2	0.0	0.0	0.4	1.2	2.0	13.5
Kansas City, MO	72.7	7.4	1.9	0.0	0.0	0.2	1.5	1.5	14.8
Lafayette, LA	80.4	5.6	0.6	0.0	0.0	0.5	2.2	1.2	9.5
Las Vegas, NV	72.6	10.0	2.4	0.0	0.0	0.3	1.3	2.9	10.5
Lexington, KY	74.8	8.4	1.3	0.0	0.0	0.5	3.0	1.0	10.9
Lincoln, NE	75.7	8.6	0.9	0.0	0.0	0.9	3.2	0.8	10.0
Little Rock, AR	76.5	8.9	1.0	0.0	0.0	0.2	1.8	0.9	10.8
Los Angeles, CA	61.4	8.8	5.7	0.6	0.1	0.7	3.1	2.3	17.3
Louisville, KY	73.5	8.7	2.2	0.0	0.0	0.3	2.0	1.7	11.6
Madison, WI	57.6	5.9	5.6	0.0	0.1	3.1	8.2	1.3	18.2
Manchester, NH	74.2	9.1	0.4	0.1	0.0	0.3	2.4	1.5	12.1

Table continued on following page.

City	Car/Truck/Van		Public Transportation			Bicycle	Walked	Other Means	Worked at Home
	Drove Alone	Car-pooled	Bus	Subway	Railroad				
McAllen, TX	72.2	10.4	0.4	0.0	0.0	0.3	0.9	4.3	11.5
Memphis, TN	77.8	10.0	0.8	0.0	0.0	0.2	1.7	1.5	8.0
Miami, FL	61.7	7.9	5.4	1.1	0.1	0.8	5.4	3.5	14.2
Midland, TX	79.9	12.2	0.4	0.0	0.0	0.2	0.7	1.0	5.6
Milwaukee, WI	67.8	10.0	5.3	0.0	0.0	0.5	4.0	1.2	11.2
Minneapolis, MN	53.4	5.9	6.3	0.2	0.0	2.3	6.0	2.5	23.3
Nashville, TN	68.1	8.3	1.6	0.0	0.0	0.3	1.9	1.5	18.3
New Orleans, LA	63.2	8.7	3.8	0.1	0.0	1.9	5.6	3.0	13.7
New York, NY	21.9	4.3	9.8	34.4	1.0	1.5	9.4	2.7	15.0
Oklahoma City, OK	77.0	9.6	0.4	0.0	0.0	0.2	1.4	1.6	9.8
Omaha, NE	73.3	8.7	1.1	0.0	0.0	0.2	1.8	1.3	13.6
Orlando, FL	69.5	8.9	1.8	0.0	0.0	0.5	1.6	2.5	15.1
Philadelphia, PA	46.7	7.6	10.9	4.7	1.6	1.9	7.5	2.8	16.4
Phoenix, AZ	66.1	10.9	1.8	0.0	0.0	0.4	1.6	2.2	16.9
Pittsburgh, PA	48.2	6.2	11.6	0.3	0.0	1.1	9.8	2.3	20.4
Portland, OR	50.5	7.0	5.4	0.2	0.1	3.7	4.8	3.0	25.3
Providence, RI	62.6	9.8	3.1	0.0	1.1	0.8	7.3	2.6	12.7
Provo, UT	57.4	10.4	4.3	0.1	0.9	1.4	10.3	1.1	14.2
Raleigh, NC	65.1	6.6	1.3	0.0	0.0	0.4	1.6	1.6	23.4
Reno, NV	67.6	12.6	2.4	0.0	0.0	0.6	3.2	2.8	10.8
Richmond, VA	64.9	7.8	3.6	0.0	0.0	1.1	4.2	1.5	16.9
Rochester, MN	65.5	11.1	4.1	0.0	0.0	0.8	4.3	1.3	12.9
Sacramento, CA	65.5	9.0	1.0	0.2	0.1	1.4	2.7	2.4	17.7
Saint Louis, MO	66.6	6.7	4.4	0.4	0.1	0.9	4.0	1.9	15.0
Saint Paul, MN	59.3	10.0	5.0	0.1	0.0	0.8	3.7	2.7	18.3
Salem, OR	68.4	10.4	1.8	0.0	0.0	1.1	3.0	1.4	14.0
Salt Lake City, UT	60.2	8.1	3.1	0.3	0.3	1.6	4.8	2.9	18.5
San Antonio, TX	70.5	12.1	2.1	0.0	0.0	0.2	1.7	1.6	11.8
San Diego, CA	64.2	7.8	2.3	0.1	0.1	0.7	3.4	2.2	19.2
San Francisco, CA	28.6	6.0	14.1	4.8	1.1	3.3	10.0	4.5	27.5
San Jose, CA	64.6	10.5	1.6	0.2	0.5	0.5	1.8	1.7	18.5
Santa Rosa, CA	73.1	11.1	0.9	0.0	0.2	0.6	2.3	1.3	10.5
Savannah, GA	70.4	10.3	2.5	0.1	0.0	1.5	3.8	1.4	10.1
Seattle, WA	37.6	5.1	11.2	0.5	0.0	2.5	8.3	3.5	31.3
Sioux Falls, SD	79.4	7.7	0.7	0.0	0.0	0.2	1.9	0.9	9.4
Tampa, FL	66.1	8.2	1.3	0.0	0.0	0.8	2.3	2.1	19.3
Tucson, AZ	69.5	9.9	2.3	0.0	0.0	1.6	2.7	1.6	12.4
Tulsa, OK	75.4	10.2	0.5	0.0	0.0	0.3	1.7	1.8	10.1
Virginia Beach, VA	75.3	7.5	0.8	0.0	0.0	0.4	1.8	1.6	12.7
Washington, DC	28.2	4.3	8.1	13.8	0.3	3.3	10.0	2.7	29.4
Wichita, KS	80.0	9.6	0.6	0.0	0.0	0.4	0.9	1.5	6.9
Wilmington, NC	70.9	7.0	0.4	0.0	0.0	0.8	2.2	1.0	17.7
Winston-Salem, NC	73.2	9.5	1.1	0.0	0.0	0.3	2.0	1.6	12.3
U.S.	70.2	8.5	1.7	1.3	0.4	0.4	2.4	1.6	13.5

Note: Figures are percentages and cover workers 16 years of age and older
Source: U.S. Census Bureau, 2019-2023 American Community Survey 5-Year Estimates

Means of Transportation to Work: Metro Area

Metro Area	Car/Truck/Van		Public Transportation			Bicycle	Walked	Other Means	Worked at Home
	Drove Alone	Car-pooled	Bus	Subway	Railroad				
Albuquerque, NM	73.5	9.1	0.8	0.0	0.1	0.6	1.6	1.3	12.9
Anchorage, AK	71.3	11.7	1.1	0.0	0.0	0.5	2.4	3.1	9.8
Ann Arbor, MI	61.9	6.3	3.7	0.0	0.0	1.0	5.8	0.8	20.3
Athens, GA	74.7	7.3	1.3	0.0	0.0	0.6	3.3	0.9	12.1
Atlanta, GA	68.0	8.7	1.2	0.5	0.1	0.1	1.2	1.8	18.5
Austin, TX	63.4	7.7	1.0	0.0	0.0	0.4	1.8	1.4	24.2
Baltimore, MD	69.2	6.9	2.7	0.5	0.5	0.2	2.2	1.6	16.1
Billings, MT	76.5	10.5	1.0	0.0	0.0	0.5	2.3	1.0	8.2
Boise City, ID	71.7	8.3	0.3	0.0	0.0	1.1	2.2	1.4	15.1
Boston, MA	58.6	6.3	2.6	4.6	1.4	1.0	4.7	2.0	18.7
Boulder, CO	55.6	5.7	3.1	0.0	0.0	3.0	3.8	0.9	27.9
Cape Coral, FL	72.7	9.4	0.4	0.0	0.0	0.6	1.1	1.8	13.8
Cedar Rapids, IA	76.8	6.5	0.5	0.0	0.0	0.2	1.9	0.8	13.3
Charleston, SC	75.3	7.8	0.6	0.0	0.0	0.5	1.7	1.2	12.9
Charlotte, NC	69.3	8.1	0.7	0.1	0.0	0.1	1.2	1.5	19.0
Chicago, IL	63.6	7.8	3.3	2.9	2.0	0.6	2.8	1.6	15.6
Cincinnati, OH	75.0	7.7	1.3	0.0	0.0	0.2	1.8	1.1	12.9
Clarksville, TN	79.6	9.5	0.4	0.0	0.0	0.2	2.4	1.5	6.5
Cleveland, OH	74.3	7.4	1.9	0.1	0.0	0.2	2.1	1.3	12.6
College Station, TX	75.1	9.5	1.3	0.0	0.0	1.0	2.1	1.3	9.7
Colorado Springs, CO	70.5	9.0	0.3	0.0	0.0	0.4	3.3	1.1	15.4
Columbia, MO	76.0	8.8	0.7	0.0	0.0	0.7	3.8	1.0	8.9
Columbia, SC	76.2	8.1	0.5	0.0	0.0	0.1	3.5	1.7	9.9
Columbus, OH	72.2	6.8	1.1	0.0	0.0	0.2	1.9	1.1	16.6
Dallas, TX	71.2	9.4	0.5	0.1	0.1	0.1	1.2	1.5	15.9
Davenport, IA	80.1	7.2	0.8	0.0	0.0	0.1	2.4	0.9	8.4
Denver, CO	65.0	7.3	1.6	0.1	0.1	0.7	2.0	2.0	21.2
Des Moines, IA	74.3	7.9	0.4	0.0	0.0	0.2	1.6	1.2	14.3
Detroit, MI	74.8	7.6	1.0	0.0	0.0	0.2	1.3	1.2	13.8
Durham, NC	65.1	7.4	2.2	0.0	0.0	0.7	2.5	1.5	20.6
El Paso, TX	76.3	11.4	0.9	0.0	0.0	0.1	1.5	2.0	7.8
Eugene, OR	67.4	8.9	1.9	0.0	0.0	2.8	4.1	1.1	13.9
Fargo, ND	78.5	6.8	0.7	0.0	0.0	0.3	2.8	1.6	9.3
Fort Collins, CO	68.4	5.6	0.9	0.0	0.0	2.4	2.8	1.1	18.9
Fort Wayne, IN	79.9	9.1	0.7	0.0	0.0	0.3	1.2	0.7	8.1
Fort Worth, TX	71.2	9.4	0.5	0.1	0.1	0.1	1.2	1.5	15.9
Gainesville, FL	71.5	8.8	2.4	0.0	0.0	1.6	2.9	1.5	11.2
Green Bay, WI	78.7	7.8	0.4	0.0	0.0	0.2	1.7	0.9	10.4
Greensboro, NC	76.6	8.9	1.0	0.0	0.0	0.1	1.6	1.6	10.3
Honolulu, HI	64.0	13.7	5.2	0.0	0.0	1.0	5.0	2.6	8.4
Houston, TX	73.5	9.7	1.4	0.0	0.0	0.2	1.2	2.0	11.9
Huntsville, AL	78.3	6.8	0.2	0.0	0.0	0.0	0.8	1.1	12.7
Indianapolis, IN	74.5	8.4	0.6	0.0	0.0	0.3	1.3	0.9	14.0
Jacksonville, FL	72.1	8.2	0.7	0.0	0.0	0.4	1.1	1.8	15.6
Kansas City, MO	75.0	6.9	0.6	0.0	0.0	0.1	1.1	1.1	15.2
Lafayette, LA	82.4	6.3	0.3	0.0	0.0	0.3	1.8	1.3	7.7
Las Vegas, NV	72.6	10.3	2.3	0.0	0.0	0.2	1.2	2.6	10.7
Lexington, KY	76.1	8.6	0.9	0.0	0.0	0.4	2.5	0.8	10.7
Lincoln, NE	76.3	8.5	0.8	0.0	0.0	0.8	3.0	0.7	9.9
Little Rock, AR	79.2	8.8	0.5	0.0	0.0	0.1	1.2	1.0	9.1
Los Angeles, CA	67.1	9.2	2.9	0.3	0.1	0.6	2.3	1.9	15.5
Louisville, KY	76.0	8.4	1.1	0.0	0.0	0.2	1.5	1.2	11.6
Madison, WI	67.3	5.9	2.6	0.0	0.0	1.6	4.8	1.1	16.7
Manchester, NH	72.9	7.4	0.4	0.1	0.1	0.2	1.7	1.1	16.1

Table continued on following page.

Metro Area	Car/Truck/Van		Public Transportation			Bicycle	Walked	Other Means	Worked at Home
	Drove Alone	Car-pooled	Bus	Subway	Railroad				
McAllen, TX	75.8	10.3	0.2	0.0	0.0	0.1	1.2	3.7	8.6
Memphis, TN	79.5	9.2	0.4	0.0	0.0	0.1	1.0	1.1	8.6
Miami, FL	71.3	9.2	2.0	0.2	0.1	0.4	1.6	2.3	12.9
Midland, TX	79.8	12.0	0.3	0.0	0.0	0.2	1.1	1.3	5.2
Milwaukee, WI	73.8	7.1	2.1	0.0	0.0	0.3	2.2	0.9	13.5
Minneapolis, MN	67.7	7.1	2.2	0.0	0.0	0.5	2.0	1.4	19.0
Nashville, TN	72.4	8.2	0.7	0.0	0.0	0.1	1.1	1.2	16.3
New Orleans, LA	73.0	9.7	1.8	0.0	0.0	0.9	3.1	1.9	9.6
New York, NY	45.5	6.1	6.4	15.6	2.6	0.8	5.4	2.7	14.9
Oklahoma City, OK	78.1	9.0	0.3	0.0	0.0	0.2	1.6	1.3	9.5
Omaha, NE	75.8	7.8	0.6	0.0	0.0	0.1	1.5	1.1	13.0
Orlando, FL	70.8	9.2	1.0	0.0	0.1	0.3	1.2	1.8	15.6
Philadelphia, PA	64.4	7.0	3.4	1.5	1.3	0.6	3.2	1.7	16.8
Phoenix, AZ	66.9	9.7	1.0	0.0	0.0	0.5	1.4	2.0	18.5
Pittsburgh, PA	69.9	6.9	3.2	0.2	0.0	0.2	2.9	1.4	15.4
Portland, OR	62.7	7.7	2.6	0.2	0.1	1.4	3.1	2.0	20.4
Providence, RI	74.9	8.1	1.1	0.1	0.7	0.3	2.6	1.5	10.9
Provo, UT	66.7	10.1	1.2	0.0	0.6	0.5	2.9	1.0	17.1
Raleigh, NC	67.0	6.5	0.5	0.0	0.0	0.2	1.1	1.3	23.4
Reno, NV	70.2	12.5	1.8	0.0	0.0	0.4	2.2	2.1	10.8
Richmond, VA	71.6	7.3	1.0	0.0	0.1	0.3	1.7	1.2	16.7
Rochester, MN	69.6	9.9	2.4	0.0	0.0	0.6	3.5	1.1	12.8
Sacramento, CA	67.7	8.6	0.8	0.1	0.1	1.1	1.8	1.9	17.9
Saint Louis, MO	75.6	6.6	1.1	0.1	0.0	0.2	1.5	1.1	13.8
Saint Paul, MN	67.7	7.1	2.2	0.0	0.0	0.5	2.0	1.4	19.0
Salem, OR	70.9	11.0	1.1	0.0	0.0	0.7	2.4	1.3	12.6
Salt Lake City, UT	67.0	10.0	1.2	0.2	0.2	0.5	1.7	1.7	17.5
San Antonio, TX	71.5	10.9	1.3	0.0	0.0	0.2	1.5	1.5	13.0
San Diego, CA	67.6	8.2	1.6	0.1	0.1	0.5	3.1	2.0	16.9
San Francisco, CA	50.9	8.2	4.7	3.9	1.1	1.5	3.9	2.6	23.2
San Jose, CA	62.1	9.0	1.5	0.2	0.6	1.3	2.0	1.7	21.5
Santa Rosa, CA	71.0	9.2	0.7	0.1	0.2	0.7	2.4	1.4	14.4
Savannah, GA	76.6	9.4	1.0	0.0	0.0	0.7	1.7	1.5	9.0
Seattle, WA	59.1	8.2	4.7	0.1	0.3	0.8	3.3	1.8	21.6
Sioux Falls, SD	79.3	7.2	0.5	0.0	0.0	0.1	2.0	0.8	10.1
Tampa, FL	69.7	8.1	0.8	0.0	0.0	0.5	1.2	1.8	17.8
Tucson, AZ	70.7	9.6	1.5	0.0	0.0	1.0	1.9	1.5	13.8
Tulsa, OK	78.2	9.0	0.3	0.0	0.0	0.2	1.2	1.2	9.8
Virginia Beach, VA	75.8	8.2	1.0	0.0	0.0	0.3	2.4	1.6	10.7
Washington, DC	56.4	8.0	2.9	4.4	0.4	0.7	2.7	1.9	22.6
Wichita, KS	80.6	8.6	0.4	0.0	0.0	0.3	1.4	1.3	7.3
Wilmington, NC	73.9	7.8	0.2	0.0	0.0	0.3	1.2	1.1	15.5
Winston-Salem, NC	77.9	8.7	0.5	0.0	0.0	0.1	1.2	1.1	10.6
U.S.	70.2	8.5	1.7	1.3	0.4	0.4	2.4	1.6	13.5

Note: Figures are percentages and cover workers 16 years of age and older; Figures cover the Metropolitan Statistical Area (MSA)
Source: U.S. Census Bureau, 2019-2023 American Community Survey 5-Year Estimates

Travel Time to Work: City

City	Less Than 10 Minutes	10 to 19 Minutes	20 to 29 Minutes	30 to 44 Minutes	45 to 59 Minutes	60 to 89 Minutes	90 Minutes or More
Albuquerque, NM	11.7	36.0	27.6	17.3	3.0	2.5	1.9
Anchorage, AK	15.6	44.8	23.3	11.1	2.3	1.4	1.5
Ann Arbor, MI	12.9	45.8	18.9	13.6	5.8	2.3	0.7
Athens, GA	17.2	45.0	17.6	10.5	3.8	3.6	2.3
Atlanta, GA	7.8	29.8	25.5	22.5	6.3	5.1	3.0
Austin, TX	9.6	33.4	24.5	21.5	6.1	3.5	1.4
Baltimore, MD	7.2	24.8	24.3	24.3	8.5	6.9	4.0
Billings, MT	19.3	51.9	18.3	6.8	1.2	1.2	1.2
Boise City, ID	14.3	44.2	25.5	11.5	1.7	1.6	1.2
Boston, MA	6.9	21.3	20.7	28.8	11.4	8.6	2.3
Boulder, CO	20.2	44.2	16.9	9.4	5.0	2.9	1.3
Cape Coral, FL	7.8	24.9	22.7	24.9	10.5	6.5	2.7
Cedar Rapids, IA	19.8	47.9	17.9	8.7	1.8	2.5	1.4
Charleston, SC	11.8	32.8	24.8	19.0	7.2	2.5	1.8
Charlotte, NC	9.1	29.7	27.1	23.2	6.1	3.0	1.9
Chicago, IL	5.2	17.2	19.2	29.8	14.6	10.9	3.0
Cincinnati, OH	11.2	34.5	26.3	19.1	3.8	2.8	2.2
Clarksville, TN	10.5	32.6	25.9	13.1	7.3	8.3	2.3
Cleveland, OH	10.5	35.0	27.3	19.4	3.3	2.6	1.9
College Station, TX	17.5	54.7	15.3	7.9	1.4	1.8	1.5
Colorado Springs, CO	11.6	35.7	27.6	16.9	3.0	3.0	2.1
Columbia, MO	19.5	54.4	14.3	7.2	2.1	1.2	1.3
Columbia, SC	27.7	37.4	19.1	10.0	2.7	1.2	1.8
Columbus, OH	10.3	35.1	31.0	17.2	3.1	2.1	1.3
Dallas, TX	8.8	28.5	23.6	24.7	7.4	5.6	1.5
Davenport, IA	15.3	45.9	24.3	8.4	2.9	2.0	1.1
Denver, CO	8.6	28.3	25.3	25.9	6.5	3.9	1.5
Des Moines, IA	14.1	43.0	25.7	11.9	2.0	1.9	1.5
Detroit, MI	8.1	30.2	27.0	22.3	6.0	4.0	2.3
Durham, NC	10.2	37.8	25.1	17.8	4.8	2.6	1.6
El Paso, TX	9.3	33.5	28.5	20.1	4.3	2.4	1.9
Eugene, OR	16.3	50.9	19.5	7.2	2.2	2.1	1.9
Fargo, ND	20.1	56.1	15.1	4.6	1.5	1.7	0.9
Fort Collins, CO	15.6	45.7	19.3	10.1	4.6	3.3	1.4
Fort Wayne, IN	13.1	38.1	27.8	13.7	2.9	2.2	2.2
Fort Worth, TX	7.4	29.2	23.5	23.5	8.9	5.7	1.8
Gainesville, FL	16.1	43.8	23.4	11.6	2.6	1.6	0.9
Green Bay, WI	18.1	47.5	18.0	9.1	3.9	1.9	1.5
Greensboro, NC	13.4	40.9	22.3	14.6	3.5	3.0	2.4
Honolulu, HI	9.0	39.2	22.3	20.5	4.5	3.4	1.2
Houston, TX	7.5	25.3	23.6	27.7	8.6	5.5	1.8
Huntsville, AL	13.9	39.8	27.2	14.9	2.2	1.2	0.7
Indianapolis, IN	9.8	29.6	28.6	23.1	4.5	2.5	2.0
Jacksonville, FL	8.7	29.0	28.0	24.9	5.6	2.5	1.3
Kansas City, MO	11.7	35.0	28.3	18.3	3.5	1.8	1.4
Lafayette, LA	16.4	44.8	19.9	11.5	2.3	3.6	1.6
Las Vegas, NV	7.3	24.0	30.9	27.3	6.0	2.6	1.9
Lexington, KY	13.0	40.1	26.4	13.7	2.7	2.3	1.9
Lincoln, NE	16.8	46.0	22.5	8.9	2.9	2.1	1.0
Little Rock, AR	15.3	46.6	22.6	10.7	2.2	1.7	0.9
Los Angeles, CA	6.3	22.2	19.9	28.5	10.4	9.4	3.3
Louisville, KY	10.1	31.8	31.9	19.1	3.6	2.0	1.4
Madison, WI	14.4	40.3	25.5	14.3	3.2	1.7	0.6
Manchester, NH	12.9	35.1	23.0	16.0	6.2	5.1	1.9
McAllen, TX	14.6	39.5	23.9	15.2	2.9	2.1	1.7

Table continued on following page.

City	Less Than 10 Minutes	10 to 19 Minutes	20 to 29 Minutes	30 to 44 Minutes	45 to 59 Minutes	60 to 89 Minutes	90 Minutes or More
Memphis, TN	11.2	31.8	33.7	18.2	2.7	1.5	1.0
Miami, FL	6.4	24.1	25.7	27.6	8.7	6.0	1.5
Midland, TX	16.2	45.2	18.6	11.9	4.0	2.3	1.9
Milwaukee, WI	10.6	36.2	26.5	18.9	3.4	2.9	1.6
Minneapolis, MN	8.3	36.1	28.8	19.2	4.2	2.4	1.0
Nashville, TN	9.2	28.7	26.8	23.2	7.0	3.8	1.3
New Orleans, LA	11.9	35.1	24.3	18.7	5.2	3.1	1.7
New York, NY	4.4	12.7	14.0	27.0	16.1	18.7	7.1
Oklahoma City, OK	10.4	35.0	28.8	19.2	3.6	1.5	1.6
Omaha, NE	14.6	41.3	26.4	12.4	2.3	1.8	1.2
Orlando, FL	7.5	26.1	27.4	26.5	6.4	3.9	2.2
Philadelphia, PA	6.7	19.7	20.8	28.1	12.0	9.2	3.5
Phoenix, AZ	9.0	26.7	26.8	24.6	7.1	4.2	1.6
Pittsburgh, PA	10.3	34.0	26.0	20.5	4.6	3.2	1.5
Portland, OR	9.3	29.9	27.1	22.5	6.1	3.7	1.5
Providence, RI	11.0	36.1	20.6	16.8	6.7	6.1	2.7
Provo, UT	20.5	44.9	16.6	10.2	4.4	2.3	1.1
Raleigh, NC	10.3	33.4	26.8	19.9	5.4	2.5	1.7
Reno, NV	15.1	39.7	23.5	13.2	4.9	2.4	1.2
Richmond, VA	11.4	37.4	27.0	16.8	2.9	2.8	1.7
Rochester, MN	18.3	54.5	14.7	6.1	2.8	2.7	0.9
Sacramento, CA	8.9	32.2	25.8	21.3	5.1	3.5	3.2
Saint Louis, MO	9.9	36.2	27.2	19.5	3.2	2.5	1.6
Saint Paul, MN	10.5	35.0	27.6	19.0	4.4	2.1	1.4
Salem, OR	14.6	41.5	18.2	12.3	5.5	6.3	1.6
Salt Lake City, UT	14.6	45.2	20.6	12.7	3.5	2.1	1.3
San Antonio, TX	9.5	30.7	26.1	22.2	5.9	3.7	1.8
San Diego, CA	8.2	33.2	27.9	20.4	5.4	3.3	1.7
San Francisco, CA	5.3	21.2	22.1	28.8	10.6	8.9	3.1
San Jose, CA	5.9	26.5	25.5	25.0	8.6	5.7	2.7
Santa Rosa, CA	13.1	42.1	19.4	14.4	4.5	3.6	2.9
Savannah, GA	14.0	40.1	23.5	14.7	4.4	2.3	1.0
Seattle, WA	8.0	26.0	24.5	26.4	9.2	4.4	1.4
Sioux Falls, SD	15.9	52.2	22.0	6.2	1.5	1.0	1.2
Tampa, FL	10.8	31.4	22.8	22.5	6.5	4.2	1.8
Tucson, AZ	12.3	34.4	25.8	19.3	4.6	2.1	1.4
Tulsa, OK	14.0	46.0	25.7	9.8	1.8	1.4	1.3
Virginia Beach, VA	10.2	31.3	27.8	21.8	5.4	2.1	1.4
Washington, DC	5.2	19.2	22.5	33.1	11.8	6.3	1.9
Wichita, KS	14.0	46.0	25.9	9.5	1.8	1.4	1.4
Wilmington, NC	16.7	46.7	20.7	10.2	2.9	1.2	1.6
Winston-Salem, NC	14.4	39.6	23.0	14.0	4.1	2.9	2.0
U.S.	12.6	28.6	21.2	20.8	8.1	6.0	2.8

Note: Figures are percentages and include workers 16 years old and over
Source: U.S. Census Bureau, 2019-2023 American Community Survey 5-Year Estimates

Travel Time to Work: Metro Area

Metro Area	Less Than 10 Minutes	10 to 19 Minutes	20 to 29 Minutes	30 to 44 Minutes	45 to 59 Minutes	60 to 89 Minutes	90 Minutes or More
Albuquerque, NM	11.5	31.1	25.0	20.6	5.8	3.8	2.3
Anchorage, AK	14.7	40.5	21.8	11.4	5.1	4.0	2.6
Ann Arbor, MI	11.2	33.3	25.2	18.5	7.2	3.5	1.2
Athens, GA	13.4	38.2	22.3	13.7	5.2	4.1	3.0
Atlanta, GA	7.3	22.7	20.1	25.5	12.0	9.0	3.3
Austin, TX	9.5	27.1	21.8	24.0	9.7	6.0	1.9
Baltimore, MD	8.2	24.1	21.7	24.6	10.7	7.5	3.1
Billings, MT	18.7	42.7	20.8	11.0	2.7	2.1	2.0
Boise City, ID	13.4	31.8	25.2	19.9	5.8	2.3	1.5
Boston, MA	9.4	22.9	19.3	24.4	11.2	9.6	3.1
Boulder, CO	15.0	34.3	20.7	17.0	6.9	4.4	1.6
Cape Coral, FL	8.8	24.5	22.6	25.2	10.2	6.3	2.4
Cedar Rapids, IA	19.1	39.1	20.6	13.0	4.3	2.6	1.3
Charleston, SC	9.1	26.3	23.3	24.0	9.9	5.4	2.1
Charlotte, NC	9.8	27.9	22.9	23.4	9.2	4.9	2.0
Chicago, IL	8.9	22.3	19.5	25.3	11.9	9.3	2.9
Cincinnati, OH	10.7	28.7	25.2	23.3	6.9	3.4	1.7
Clarksville, TN	14.1	30.9	22.8	15.1	7.2	6.9	3.0
Cleveland, OH	12.0	28.7	25.7	22.7	6.4	2.8	1.7
College Station, TX	16.2	48.4	17.1	11.0	3.2	2.3	1.9
Colorado Springs, CO	12.1	32.3	26.6	19.0	4.3	3.5	2.2
Columbia, MO	17.1	44.0	20.2	11.8	3.4	1.7	1.8
Columbia, SC	12.7	28.9	23.6	22.0	7.3	3.2	2.3
Columbus, OH	11.7	29.8	27.5	20.7	5.8	3.1	1.5
Dallas, TX	8.8	25.5	21.7	25.3	10.2	6.5	2.0
Davenport, IA	18.0	35.9	26.0	12.4	3.7	2.6	1.4
Denver, CO	8.8	25.1	23.7	26.4	9.0	5.1	1.9
Des Moines, IA	15.2	35.6	26.7	15.6	3.8	1.7	1.3
Detroit, MI	10.0	27.0	23.7	24.2	8.5	4.8	1.7
Durham, NC	10.6	32.7	25.3	20.0	6.2	3.8	1.5
El Paso, TX	9.7	32.0	27.4	21.6	4.9	2.4	2.0
Eugene, OR	16.0	43.1	21.9	11.6	3.0	2.6	1.8
Fargo, ND	17.7	51.4	18.0	7.1	2.4	1.9	1.5
Fort Collins, CO	13.9	36.1	21.5	15.8	6.0	4.6	2.1
Fort Wayne, IN	13.8	34.9	28.2	15.9	3.4	1.9	2.0
Fort Worth, TX	8.8	25.5	21.7	25.3	10.2	6.5	2.0
Gainesville, FL	12.2	32.8	25.2	19.2	5.7	3.2	1.7
Green Bay, WI	16.8	39.6	22.4	13.1	4.3	2.1	1.7
Greensboro, NC	13.3	34.4	23.7	18.1	5.0	3.2	2.2
Honolulu, HI	9.9	27.1	20.0	25.2	9.1	6.5	2.1
Houston, TX	7.7	22.9	20.7	26.9	11.5	7.9	2.5
Huntsville, AL	10.8	30.8	28.1	22.2	4.9	1.9	1.2
Indianapolis, IN	11.3	27.6	24.2	24.6	7.2	3.3	1.9
Jacksonville, FL	9.2	26.2	24.8	26.0	8.2	3.9	1.7
Kansas City, MO	12.4	30.9	26.3	20.9	5.7	2.4	1.4
Lafayette, LA	13.7	32.9	21.8	19.4	5.2	3.8	3.2
Las Vegas, NV	7.9	27.2	29.2	25.9	5.3	2.6	2.0
Lexington, KY	14.4	35.7	24.4	16.8	4.4	2.5	1.8
Lincoln, NE	17.0	42.8	23.2	10.6	3.2	2.3	1.0
Little Rock, AR	13.2	32.4	22.2	21.1	6.6	3.1	1.5
Los Angeles, CA	7.3	25.0	20.8	25.4	9.7	8.5	3.3
Louisville, KY	10.6	29.6	28.4	20.9	6.1	2.9	1.5
Madison, WI	15.8	32.4	25.5	17.6	5.0	2.5	1.1
Manchester, NH	11.5	29.3	21.6	19.8	8.2	6.9	2.8
McAllen, TX	15.4	33.5	24.2	18.6	3.8	2.4	2.2

Table continued on following page.

Metro Area	Less Than 10 Minutes	10 to 19 Minutes	20 to 29 Minutes	30 to 44 Minutes	45 to 59 Minutes	60 to 89 Minutes	90 Minutes or More
Memphis, TN	11.0	26.8	27.9	23.6	6.6	2.6	1.4
Miami, FL	6.8	23.2	23.1	27.1	9.9	7.2	2.6
Midland, TX	15.7	40.3	20.4	14.4	4.2	2.3	2.7
Milwaukee, WI	12.3	32.4	26.0	20.7	4.7	2.5	1.4
Minneapolis, MN	11.1	29.6	25.3	22.3	6.9	3.5	1.4
Nashville, TN	9.6	26.0	21.1	24.2	10.7	6.6	1.8
New Orleans, LA	11.4	31.5	22.9	21.7	6.6	3.9	2.0
New York, NY	7.3	19.0	16.6	23.9	12.6	14.2	6.4
Oklahoma City, OK	12.2	31.4	25.4	21.2	5.6	2.6	1.7
Omaha, NE	14.0	36.2	27.4	15.9	3.5	1.8	1.2
Orlando, FL	7.1	23.4	22.2	27.8	10.6	6.3	2.5
Philadelphia, PA	10.0	24.4	20.8	24.1	10.6	7.3	2.8
Phoenix, AZ	10.2	26.0	24.3	23.7	8.7	5.3	1.8
Pittsburgh, PA	12.3	27.5	21.7	22.5	8.7	5.3	2.0
Portland, OR	11.5	29.0	23.7	21.7	7.7	4.5	1.8
Providence, RI	11.7	30.0	21.3	20.3	7.9	6.1	2.9
Provo, UT	17.2	34.7	19.9	17.0	6.2	3.7	1.3
Raleigh, NC	9.0	26.8	23.5	24.3	9.6	5.0	1.8
Reno, NV	12.8	34.1	24.2	17.6	6.0	3.6	1.6
Richmond, VA	9.7	28.3	26.8	23.2	6.5	3.2	2.2
Rochester, MN	18.1	41.6	18.7	12.5	4.6	2.9	1.6
Sacramento, CA	10.3	28.8	22.7	22.9	7.1	4.4	3.8
Saint Louis, MO	11.3	28.2	24.6	23.4	7.3	3.5	1.6
Saint Paul, MN	11.1	29.6	25.3	22.3	6.9	3.5	1.4
Salem, OR	15.0	32.4	19.8	17.1	7.4	6.5	1.8
Salt Lake City, UT	11.1	33.7	26.6	19.0	5.5	2.9	1.3
San Antonio, TX	9.5	27.1	24.0	23.8	8.3	5.1	2.3
San Diego, CA	8.5	29.3	25.1	23.4	7.1	4.5	2.1
San Francisco, CA	7.5	24.2	18.7	23.7	11.0	10.8	4.1
San Jose, CA	7.5	28.4	24.3	23.1	8.2	5.8	2.7
Santa Rosa, CA	14.0	34.1	19.3	17.3	6.3	5.6	3.4
Savannah, GA	10.5	29.3	23.7	22.8	8.5	3.7	1.5
Seattle, WA	8.7	23.7	21.6	24.7	10.5	7.8	3.0
Sioux Falls, SD	17.3	43.1	23.9	10.5	2.5	1.3	1.3
Tampa, FL	9.6	26.6	20.9	23.8	10.2	6.5	2.5
Tucson, AZ	11.0	29.4	25.2	23.2	6.8	2.6	1.7
Tulsa, OK	13.4	34.0	26.6	17.7	4.7	2.2	1.5
Virginia Beach, VA	10.5	31.2	24.1	21.7	6.9	3.9	1.8
Washington, DC	6.5	20.1	19.2	26.3	13.2	11.0	3.6
Wichita, KS	15.7	38.0	25.6	14.9	2.8	1.6	1.4
Wilmington, NC	12.4	35.0	23.4	18.2	5.8	3.0	2.3
Winston-Salem, NC	12.5	32.1	24.5	19.3	5.8	3.5	2.2
U.S.	12.6	28.6	21.2	20.8	8.1	6.0	2.8

Note: Figures are percentages and include workers 16 years old and over; Figures cover the Metropolitan Statistical Area (MSA)
Source: U.S. Census Bureau, 2019-2023 American Community Survey 5-Year Estimates

2024 Presidential Election Results

City	Area Covered	Trump (Rep.)	Harris (Dem.)	Stein (Green)	Kennedy (Ind.)	Oliver (Lib.)	Other
Albuquerque, NM	Bernalillo County	38.2	59.2	0.7	1.0	0.5	0.5
Anchorage, AK	State of Alaska	54.5	41.4	0.7	1.7	0.9	0.8
Ann Arbor, MI	Washtenaw County	26.5	70.7	1.3	0.4	0.4	0.7
Athens, GA	Clarke County	30.2	68.3	0.5	0.0	0.6	0.4
Atlanta, GA	Fulton County	26.8	71.3	0.6	0.0	0.5	0.8
Austin, TX	Travis County	29.2	68.3	1.0	0.0	0.8	0.6
Baltimore, MD	Baltimore City	12.1	84.6	1.4	0.8	0.4	0.7
Billings, MT	Yellowstone County	62.0	34.9	0.4	1.9	0.8	0.0
Boise City, ID	Ada County	53.8	43.4	0.4	1.3	0.6	0.5
Boston, MA	Suffolk County	22.2	74.3	1.1	0.0	0.4	2.0
Boulder, CO	Boulder County	20.8	76.5	0.8	0.9	0.6	0.4
Cape Coral, FL	Lee County	63.6	35.3	0.2	0.0	0.2	0.6
Cedar Rapids, IA	Linn County	44.1	54.0	0.0	0.8	0.5	0.6
Charleston, SC	Charleston County	46.3	51.9	0.5	0.0	0.8	0.6
Charlotte, NC	Mecklenburg County	32.5	65.2	0.7	0.0	0.5	1.1
Chicago, IL	Cook County	28.1	69.6	0.9	1.2	0.1	0.2
Cincinnati, OH	Hamilton County	41.7	56.5	0.4	0.0	0.6	0.8
Clarksville, TN	Montgomery County	58.3	39.9	0.3	0.8	0.0	0.7
Cleveland, OH	Cuyahoga County	33.6	64.7	0.5	0.0	0.4	0.8
College Station, TX	Brazos County	61.6	36.8	0.6	0.0	0.9	0.1
Colorado Springs, CO	El Paso County	53.5	43.7	0.5	1.1	0.8	0.4
Columbia, MO	Boone County	43.9	53.6	0.9	0.0	1.1	0.4
Columbia, SC	Richland County	31.8	66.4	0.4	0.0	0.5	0.9
Columbus, OH	Franklin County	34.9	63.0	0.6	0.0	0.6	0.9
Dallas, TX	Dallas County	37.8	59.9	1.1	0.0	0.7	0.5
Davenport, IA	Scott County	51.0	47.1	0.0	0.8	0.5	0.6
Denver, CO	Denver County	20.6	76.6	0.9	0.8	0.6	0.5
Des Moines, IA	Polk County	43.7	54.5	0.0	0.6	0.5	0.7
Detroit, MI	Wayne County	33.6	62.5	2.4	0.4	0.3	0.8
Durham, NC	Durham County	18.2	79.8	0.7	0.0	0.4	0.8
El Paso, TX	El Paso County	41.7	56.8	0.6	0.0	0.6	0.3
Eugene, OR	Lane County	36.6	59.5	0.9	1.5	0.4	1.1
Fargo, ND	Cass County	52.7	44.4	0.0	0.0	1.8	1.1
Fort Collins, CO	Larimer County	39.7	57.3	0.5	1.2	0.8	0.5
Fort Wayne, IN	Allen County	55.2	42.7	0.0	0.9	0.8	0.4
Fort Worth, TX	Tarrant County	51.8	46.7	0.7	0.0	0.7	0.1
Gainesville, FL	Alachua County	38.6	59.4	0.6	0.0	0.5	0.9
Green Bay, WI	Brown County	53.0	45.5	0.2	0.5	0.3	0.5
Greensboro, NC	Guilford County	38.3	60.0	0.5	0.0	0.4	0.8
Honolulu, HI	Honolulu County	38.3	59.9	0.7	0.0	0.5	0.5
Houston, TX	Harris County	46.4	51.9	1.0	0.0	0.6	0.1
Huntsville, AL	Madison County	53.4	44.4	0.3	0.8	0.5	0.6
Indianapolis, IN	Marion County	35.1	62.6	0.0	0.9	0.8	0.7
Jacksonville, FL	Duval County	49.9	48.5	0.5	0.0	0.4	0.7
Kansas City, MO	Jackson County	39.3	58.5	0.8	0.0	0.8	0.6
Lafayette, LA	Lafayette Parish	64.8	33.5	0.4	0.4	0.4	0.5
Las Vegas, NV	Clark County	47.8	50.4	0.0	0.0	0.4	1.4
Lexington, KY	Fayette County	39.8	57.9	0.7	0.9	0.5	0.2
Lincoln, NE	Lancaster County	46.8	51.0	0.4	0.0	0.8	1.1
Little Rock, AR	Pulaski County	37.7	59.8	0.6	1.1	0.5	0.3
Los Angeles, CA	Los Angeles County	31.9	64.8	1.1	1.2	0.3	0.6
Louisville, KY	Jefferson County	40.6	57.1	0.6	0.7	0.3	0.6
Madison, WI	Dane County	23.4	74.9	0.5	0.4	0.3	0.6
Manchester, NH	Hillsborough County	47.8	50.7	0.5	0.0	0.5	0.5
McAllen, TX	Hidalgo County	51.0	48.1	0.5	0.0	0.4	0.0

Table continued on following page.

City	Area Covered	Trump (Rep.)	Harris (Dem.)	Stein (Green)	Kennedy (Ind.)	Oliver (Lib.)	Other
Memphis, TN	Shelby County	36.2	61.5	0.6	0.8	0.0	1.0
Miami, FL	Miami-Dade County	55.2	43.8	0.3	0.0	0.2	0.5
Midland, TX	Midland County	79.6	19.2	0.2	0.0	0.6	0.3
Milwaukee, WI	Milwaukee County	29.7	68.2	0.7	0.4	0.2	0.7
Minneapolis, MN	Hennepin County	27.4	69.8	0.8	0.6	0.5	1.0
Nashville, TN	Davidson County	35.0	62.2	0.6	0.9	0.0	1.2
New Orleans, LA	Orleans Parish	15.2	82.2	0.9	0.3	0.5	1.0
New York, NY	New York City	30.0	68.1	0.9	0.0	0.0	1.0
New York, NY	Bronx County	27.0	71.9	0.6	0.0	0.0	0.5
New York, NY	Kings County	27.4	70.4	1.1	0.0	0.0	1.1
New York, NY	New York County	17.2	80.8	0.7	0.0	0.0	1.3
New York, NY	Queens County	37.0	61.1	1.2	0.0	0.0	0.7
New York, NY	Richmond County	63.9	34.6	0.9	0.0	0.0	0.6
Oklahoma City, OK	Oklahoma County	49.7	48.0	0.0	1.1	0.8	0.4
Omaha, NE	Douglas County	43.9	54.1	0.4	0.0	0.6	1.0
Orlando, FL	Orange County	42.4	55.9	0.7	0.0	0.3	0.7
Philadelphia, PA	Philadelphia County	19.9	78.6	0.9	0.0	0.3	0.3
Phoenix, AZ	Maricopa County	51.0	47.5	0.6	0.0	0.5	0.4
Pittsburgh, PA	Allegheny County	39.2	59.4	0.5	0.0	0.5	0.5
Portland, OR	Multnomah County	17.1	78.7	1.5	1.0	0.3	1.4
Providence, RI	Providence County	41.7	55.7	0.6	0.9	0.3	0.8
Provo, UT	Utah County	66.7	27.8	0.5	0.0	1.4	3.6
Raleigh, NC	Wake County	36.2	61.7	0.8	0.0	0.5	0.8
Reno, NV	Washoe County	48.3	49.3	0.0	0.0	0.5	1.8
Richmond, VA	Richmond City	64.7	34.5	0.2	0.0	0.2	0.3
Rochester, MN	Olmsted County	43.4	54.0	0.6	0.8	0.5	0.7
Sacramento, CA	Sacramento County	38.4	58.1	1.2	1.4	0.5	0.5
Saint Louis, MO	St. Louis City	16.5	80.7	1.2	0.0	0.7	0.8
Saint Paul, MN	Ramsey County	27.1	70.2	0.8	0.5	0.5	0.9
Salem, OR	Marion County	49.2	47.2	0.6	1.7	0.4	0.9
Salt Lake City, UT	Salt Lake County	42.9	52.9	0.7	0.0	1.0	2.5
San Antonio, TX	Bexar County	44.4	54.1	0.6	0.0	0.6	0.4
San Diego, CA	San Diego County	40.1	56.9	1.0	1.1	0.5	0.4
San Francisco, CA	San Francisco County	15.5	80.3	1.7	1.1	0.5	0.9
San Jose, CA	Santa Clara County	28.1	68.0	1.6	1.2	0.5	0.5
Santa Rosa, CA	Sonoma County	25.2	71.4	0.9	1.5	0.4	0.4
Savannah, GA	Chatham County	40.4	58.3	0.3	0.0	0.4	0.7
Seattle, WA	King County	22.3	73.6	1.2	1.0	0.4	1.4
Sioux Falls, SD	Minnehaha County	55.2	42.5	0.0	1.6	0.7	0.0
Tampa, FL	Hillsborough County	50.7	47.6	0.6	0.0	0.4	0.7
Tucson, AZ	Pima County	41.7	56.8	0.6	0.0	0.6	0.4
Tulsa, OK	Tulsa County	56.5	41.3	0.0	1.1	0.7	0.4
Virginia Beach, VA	Virginia Beach City	47.8	50.4	0.4	0.0	0.5	0.9
Washington, DC	District of Columbia	6.5	90.3	0.0	0.9	0.0	2.4
Wichita, KS	Sedgwick County	55.7	42.0	0.1	1.1	0.6	0.5
Wilmington, NC	New Hanover County	49.0	49.6	0.4	0.0	0.4	0.6
Winston-Salem, NC	Forsyth County	42.6	55.8	0.4	0.0	0.4	0.8
U.S.	U.S.	49.7	48.2	0.6	0.5	0.4	0.6

Note: Results are percentages and may not add to 100% due to rounding
Source: Dave Leip's Atlas of U.S. Presidential Elections

House Price Index (HPI)

Metro Area	National Ranking[2]	Quarterly Change (%)	One-Year Change (%)	Five-Year Change (%)	Since 1991Q1 (%)
Albuquerque, NM	152	0.28	4.68	60.38	291.99
Anchorage, AK	120	-2.19	5.44	38.20	272.70
Ann Arbor, MI	111	0.79	5.63	45.12	265.98
Athens, GA	145	0.95	4.82	77.54	363.29
Atlanta, GA	169	-0.09	4.19	66.19	310.49
Austin, TX	237	-1.06	-0.80	47.35	579.98
Baltimore, MD	113	0.13	5.59	41.90	246.61
Billings, MT	211	-0.95	2.58	54.45	434.47
Boise City, ID	156	0.77	4.58	63.16	546.52
Boston, MA[1]	123	0.36	5.29	50.28	365.78
Boulder, CO	218	0.54	2.49	40.60	618.40
Cape Coral, FL	240	-0.39	-2.44	67.84	353.01
Cedar Rapids, IA	204	-0.20	3.04	39.04	206.71
Charleston, SC	84	2.18	6.43	77.86	536.36
Charlotte, NC	175	0.39	4.07	71.74	349.74
Chicago, IL[1]	70	0.05	6.77	43.67	208.59
Cincinnati, OH	93	0.82	6.08	61.42	247.18
Clarksville, TN	(a)	n/a	3.55	67.67	n/a
Cleveland, OH	71	0.34	6.77	57.08	194.72
College Station, TX	(a)	n/a	1.96	50.70	n/a
Colorado Springs, CO	196	-0.38	3.24	49.58	453.42
Columbia, MO	24	0.09	8.46	58.84	279.40
Columbia, SC	61	0.87	6.97	64.02	248.40
Columbus, OH	63	1.20	6.96	61.81	293.84
Dallas, TX[1]	181	0.68	3.91	56.27	350.14
Davenport, IA	143	-0.86	4.87	39.11	236.99
Denver, CO	193	0.30	3.30	43.23	580.34
Des Moines, IA	174	-0.70	4.10	43.67	253.81
Detroit, MI[1]	40	0.25	7.71	52.17	227.11
Durham, NC	150	0.26	4.76	67.43	344.03
El Paso, TX	67	1.00	6.86	63.01	237.09
Eugene, OR	220	-1.37	2.45	48.27	459.38
Fargo, ND	214	-1.86	2.52	33.66	292.25
Fort Collins, CO	215	-0.72	2.52	44.72	544.83
Fort Wayne, IN	32	1.26	7.98	72.59	239.64
Fort Worth, TX[1]	194	0.54	3.30	53.69	324.24
Gainesville, FL	(a)	n/a	5.55	65.26	n/a
Green Bay, WI	103	-1.16	5.89	63.68	299.15
Greensboro, NC	65	0.24	6.92	68.92	226.57
Honolulu, HI	183	-0.33	3.85	35.89	242.48
Houston, TX	195	0.35	3.29	44.19	326.50
Huntsville, AL	76	-1.12	6.65	66.60	239.11
Indianapolis, IN	136	1.08	4.99	59.79	247.41
Jacksonville, FL	168	-0.18	4.19	65.48	401.54
Kansas City, MO	149	-0.76	4.78	56.68	300.63
Lafayette, LA	132	3.26	5.15	25.86	238.79
Las Vegas, NV	44	1.27	7.43	58.90	295.91
Lexington, KY	147	-0.02	4.79	58.94	282.27
Lincoln, NE	60	0.91	6.97	52.28	300.89
Little Rock, AR	197	-1.14	3.23	47.11	222.55
Los Angeles, CA[1]	114	0.65	5.59	48.41	341.40
Louisville, KY	81	0.59	6.45	50.59	291.73
Madison, WI	118	0.61	5.50	54.87	369.35
Manchester, NH	25	-0.15	8.25	67.31	310.83
McAllen, TX	(a)	n/a	8.58	59.26	n/a

Table continued on following page.

Metro Area	National Ranking[2]	Quarterly Change (%)	One-Year Change (%)	Five-Year Change (%)	Since 1991Q1 (%)
Memphis, TN	206	-0.64	2.99	49.80	207.31
Miami, FL[1]	19	2.12	8.69	89.36	668.91
Midland, TX	(a)	n/a	1.09	21.00	n/a
Milwaukee, WI	49	0.11	7.27	55.07	296.31
Minneapolis, MN	153	0.20	4.68	37.75	302.55
Nashville, TN	164	-0.12	4.28	65.94	467.10
New Orleans, LA	233	0.13	0.85	25.47	285.27
New York, NY[1]	34	0.62	7.86	43.82	309.75
Oklahoma City, OK	129	-0.57	5.22	50.62	294.07
Omaha, NE	154	0.12	4.63	51.76	295.39
Orlando, FL	56	2.87	7.06	70.73	377.10
Philadelphia, PA[1]	110	0.84	5.64	41.74	286.32
Phoenix, AZ	200	0.13	3.14	69.09	488.41
Pittsburgh, PA	104	0.17	5.87	45.46	262.85
Portland, OR	182	0.32	3.88	37.41	518.30
Providence, RI	41	0.25	7.70	64.34	289.70
Provo, UT	139	-1.41	4.94	59.50	545.94
Raleigh, NC	185	0.14	3.78	65.05	335.12
Reno, NV	121	0.31	5.40	49.95	361.77
Richmond, VA	98	0.07	5.98	59.60	306.38
Rochester, MN	160	-1.25	4.39	42.16	268.82
Sacramento, CA	198	0.32	3.19	42.05	255.25
Saint Louis, MO	92	1.02	6.12	48.75	237.26
Saint Paul, MN	153	0.20	4.68	37.75	302.55
Salem, OR	209	0.85	2.90	48.54	494.72
Salt Lake City, UT	115	0.53	5.58	59.66	644.94
San Antonio, TX	228	4.07	1.99	49.58	357.13
San Diego, CA	102	1.05	5.91	61.16	410.00
San Francisco, CA[1]	191	0.32	3.50	15.70	376.10
San Jose, CA	221	-0.52	2.35	36.42	433.00
Santa Rosa, CA	192	-0.37	3.47	28.24	304.85
Savannah, GA	225	-1.45	2.18	77.13	438.29
Seattle, WA[1]	91	-0.16	6.14	47.96	484.10
Sioux Falls, SD	224	0.06	2.21	52.27	347.79
Tampa, FL	229	-0.90	1.88	77.61	480.18
Tucson, AZ	223	-1.32	2.30	65.72	364.15
Tulsa, OK	116	1.84	5.52	56.84	272.73
Virginia Beach, VA	64	1.54	6.94	53.57	289.47
Washington, DC[1]	106	-0.50	5.79	38.73	288.38
Wichita, KS	170	-0.42	4.15	57.02	241.93
Wilmington, NC	137	0.32	4.98	74.07	421.24
Winston-Salem, NC	33	1.41	7.91	70.24	245.21
U.S.[3]	–	1.43	4.51	57.13	327.82

Note: The HPI is a weighted repeat sales index. It measures average price changes in repeat sales or refinancings on the same properties. This information is obtained by reviewing repeat mortgage transactions on single-family properties whose mortgages have been purchased or securitized by Fannie Mae or Freddie Mac since January 1975; all figures are for the period ended December 31, 2024; Figures cover the Metropolitan Statistical Area (MSA) unless noted otherwise; (1) Metropolitan Division; (2) Rankings are based on annual percentage change, for all MSAs containing at least 15,000 transactions over the last 10 years and ranges from 1 to 241; (3) Figures based on a weighted division average; (a) Not ranked because of increased index variability due to smaller sample size; n/a not available
Source: Federal Housing Finance Agency, Change in FHFA Metropolitan Area House Price Indexes, All Transactions Index, 2024Q4

Home Value: City

City	Under $100,000	$100,000 -$199,999	$200,000 -$299,999	$300,000 -$399,999	$400,000 -$499,999	$500,000 -$999,999	$1,000,000 or more	Median ($)
Albuquerque, NM	6.9	18.8	34.6	19.9	10.2	8.7	0.9	266,700
Anchorage, AK	5.3	7.4	17.7	25.8	19.8	21.8	2.2	375,900
Ann Arbor, MI	1.8	5.6	14.3	20.1	23.3	29.4	5.4	435,100
Athens, GA	8.3	18.2	31.4	20.3	9.1	11.0	1.8	271,800
Atlanta, GA	4.8	10.7	17.8	14.5	11.2	27.8	13.3	420,600
Austin, TX	2.9	2.8	11.0	14.7	17.1	39.2	12.2	512,700
Baltimore, MD	15.5	28.6	26.5	13.5	6.5	7.8	1.5	219,300
Billings, MT	6.6	10.2	30.1	25.7	15.5	10.6	1.3	311,800
Boise City, ID	4.2	3.9	12.0	18.2	21.0	33.8	6.9	456,000
Boston, MA	3.4	0.7	3.2	5.8	9.4	53.3	24.2	710,400
Boulder, CO	4.3	2.6	2.6	3.9	4.0	33.9	48.6	982,600
Cape Coral, FL	3.1	8.9	28.1	25.5	15.2	16.3	3.0	339,200
Cedar Rapids, IA	12.5	47.4	24.5	8.5	3.9	2.7	0.5	177,100
Charleston, SC	2.0	3.6	12.8	18.9	18.2	31.3	13.1	469,100
Charlotte, NC	4.4	13.0	22.8	19.2	12.6	20.8	7.2	351,500
Chicago, IL	6.6	16.0	24.7	17.7	11.1	18.1	5.8	315,200
Cincinnati, OH	14.9	31.5	20.8	12.4	7.1	10.7	2.6	215,300
Clarksville, TN	7.4	25.5	40.9	15.0	6.3	4.1	0.7	236,100
Cleveland, OH	53.4	31.8	8.1	3.0	1.6	1.7	0.5	94,100
College Station, TX	2.4	7.5	32.9	27.0	15.6	12.5	2.1	326,500
Colorado Springs, CO	4.1	3.5	14.0	23.8	22.3	29.5	2.8	420,700
Columbia, MO	6.6	23.2	30.2	18.4	10.8	10.1	0.8	268,300
Columbia, SC	12.4	26.0	23.5	11.7	8.3	14.7	3.5	243,500
Columbus, OH	11.3	27.4	31.0	18.0	6.6	4.9	0.8	234,500
Dallas, TX	9.9	20.3	20.7	12.2	8.8	19.9	8.2	295,300
Davenport, IA	18.4	45.7	19.6	9.4	3.8	2.8	0.3	162,900
Denver, CO	2.3	2.1	6.6	11.4	17.3	44.6	15.7	586,700
Des Moines, IA	13.7	44.2	27.4	8.7	2.6	2.7	0.7	183,700
Detroit, MI	63.8	21.8	7.7	3.4	1.3	1.6	0.4	76,800
Durham, NC	3.1	10.7	22.2	25.3	16.4	20.2	2.1	355,300
El Paso, TX	14.2	47.6	24.4	7.7	2.7	2.8	0.7	171,700
Eugene, OR	6.5	3.0	11.6	20.1	24.6	31.0	3.0	435,400
Fargo, ND	6.0	16.7	36.1	22.1	9.0	8.7	1.4	269,800
Fort Collins, CO	3.7	1.7	4.2	9.6	22.7	52.5	5.6	548,400
Fort Wayne, IN	19.8	42.0	25.3	7.7	2.8	2.0	0.3	169,700
Fort Worth, TX	8.5	18.0	31.0	21.0	10.5	8.9	2.0	277,300
Gainesville, FL	7.9	27.4	35.1	16.9	5.7	6.3	0.7	235,000
Green Bay, WI	8.5	46.2	29.0	8.4	4.0	3.6	0.3	191,500
Greensboro, NC	10.1	33.8	25.7	14.3	6.6	8.2	1.4	221,300
Honolulu, HI	2.1	1.6	3.1	8.6	10.6	35.0	39.0	834,100
Houston, TX	11.1	24.9	22.9	12.3	8.6	14.1	6.1	253,400
Huntsville, AL	11.8	23.6	22.4	17.3	9.3	12.8	2.7	263,100
Indianapolis, IN	14.2	33.3	28.5	11.6	5.2	6.1	1.1	207,000
Jacksonville, FL	11.0	20.4	27.6	19.5	10.1	9.1	2.2	266,100
Kansas City, MO	16.8	25.8	25.2	14.7	8.5	7.8	1.2	227,000
Lafayette, LA	11.2	23.8	28.6	14.9	9.3	10.0	2.2	251,300
Las Vegas, NV	3.9	4.5	17.2	25.6	19.7	24.9	4.2	395,300
Lexington, KY	5.4	22.4	29.2	18.8	10.0	11.8	2.4	272,100
Lincoln, NE	5.9	26.1	34.7	18.1	7.5	6.6	1.1	248,200
Little Rock, AR	15.5	28.7	22.6	12.2	8.1	10.2	2.6	221,200
Los Angeles, CA	2.5	1.2	1.2	2.5	5.7	47.7	39.2	879,500
Louisville, KY	11.8	32.0	25.5	13.2	7.6	8.4	1.5	221,500
Madison, WI	2.9	9.1	25.1	27.7	16.5	17.0	1.8	346,900
Manchester, NH	3.9	10.2	24.0	32.7	19.8	8.6	0.7	336,300
McAllen, TX	20.0	40.0	22.5	10.6	3.3	3.0	0.8	173,800

Table continued on following page.

City	Under $100,000	$100,000 -$199,999	$200,000 -$299,999	$300,000 -$399,999	$400,000 -$499,999	$500,000 -$999,999	$1,000,000 or more	Median ($)
Memphis, TN	31.7	28.3	18.4	8.8	4.5	6.3	1.9	157,100
Miami, FL	2.9	5.9	12.9	14.6	18.1	31.4	14.1	475,200
Midland, TX	7.8	12.9	29.7	24.9	10.4	11.8	2.5	298,600
Milwaukee, WI	19.7	43.3	25.1	5.9	2.6	2.6	0.8	172,000
Minneapolis, MN	2.9	10.4	25.0	25.6	14.0	18.1	4.0	345,600
Nashville, TN	3.4	6.6	21.4	22.5	16.9	22.1	7.1	383,100
New Orleans, LA	6.4	21.2	23.1	13.8	9.7	19.4	6.4	296,400
New York, NY	4.7	2.9	4.7	5.6	7.1	44.9	30.1	751,700
Oklahoma City, OK	14.8	30.5	27.8	13.1	5.7	6.6	1.6	215,100
Omaha, NE	9.8	29.2	31.6	14.2	7.4	6.7	1.2	230,100
Orlando, FL	3.5	15.0	19.9	19.6	14.5	22.0	5.4	359,000
Philadelphia, PA	14.0	26.4	26.8	14.6	6.6	9.5	2.0	232,400
Phoenix, AZ	5.7	6.6	20.5	21.1	16.0	24.9	5.2	381,900
Pittsburgh, PA	22.7	29.2	19.5	10.3	5.6	10.3	2.2	193,200
Portland, OR	2.5	1.5	4.8	11.9	21.2	50.0	8.1	557,600
Providence, RI	4.1	9.3	30.8	25.2	11.6	14.5	4.4	322,800
Provo, UT	5.1	1.8	10.4	24.4	22.4	31.3	4.6	437,100
Raleigh, NC	3.1	7.7	22.7	21.2	15.2	24.4	5.7	377,800
Reno, NV	6.1	3.0	6.9	14.9	19.3	42.7	7.1	498,600
Richmond, VA	4.9	17.9	22.4	17.1	13.0	19.0	5.7	328,100
Rochester, MN	4.4	16.0	33.6	19.2	12.2	13.4	1.1	287,500
Sacramento, CA	4.3	2.4	7.6	17.7	21.3	41.5	5.2	484,600
Saint Louis, MO	22.9	31.6	22.8	11.1	5.1	5.2	1.2	185,100
Saint Paul, MN	3.5	15.9	37.6	19.5	9.9	11.4	2.0	280,300
Salem, OR	6.8	5.2	14.1	29.1	22.7	21.4	0.8	382,400
Salt Lake City, UT	4.1	3.4	11.3	15.5	16.4	37.9	11.4	495,700
San Antonio, TX	13.7	29.8	29.2	14.1	6.3	5.9	1.0	219,700
San Diego, CA	2.6	1.2	1.5	3.4	7.1	48.7	35.6	848,500
San Francisco, CA	1.5	1.2	0.7	1.3	1.6	16.0	77.8	1,380,500
San Jose, CA	2.2	2.2	2.3	1.5	1.3	22.4	68.0	1,187,800
Santa Rosa, CA	3.7	2.8	2.7	3.8	7.2	65.4	14.3	685,000
Savannah, GA	12.1	29.9	27.2	12.5	6.6	9.4	2.4	225,200
Seattle, WA	1.1	0.6	1.2	3.6	5.2	47.4	40.8	912,100
Sioux Falls, SD	7.9	18.0	32.8	18.7	10.0	10.5	2.2	271,400
Tampa, FL	4.8	12.4	20.8	16.0	12.1	24.0	10.0	375,300
Tucson, AZ	12.9	21.2	34.4	17.5	7.6	5.4	1.1	242,200
Tulsa, OK	20.0	33.1	20.0	10.7	5.6	8.3	2.3	189,600
Virginia Beach, VA	3.1	7.5	23.9	23.4	16.1	21.5	4.5	366,300
Washington, DC	1.4	1.8	4.6	9.1	11.2	41.8	30.1	724,600
Wichita, KS	21.6	34.9	24.3	9.6	4.5	4.2	0.9	179,500
Wilmington, NC	3.3	13.2	23.0	21.1	14.2	19.1	6.2	350,300
Winston-Salem, NC	12.9	34.6	25.9	12.1	4.6	8.3	1.7	208,200
U.S.	12.1	17.8	19.5	14.4	10.5	19.1	6.5	303,400

Note: Figures are percentages except for median and cover owner-occupied housing units.
Source: U.S. Census Bureau, 2019-2023 American Community Survey 5-Year Estimates

Home Value: Metro Area

Metro Area	Under $100,000	$100,000 -$199,999	$200,000 -$299,999	$300,000 -$399,999	$400,000 -$499,999	$500,000 -$999,999	$1,000,000 or more	Median ($)
Albuquerque, NM	9.6	19.3	31.5	17.9	9.9	10.1	1.6	263,500
Anchorage, AK	5.4	8.2	21.3	25.5	18.1	19.7	1.8	358,900
Ann Arbor, MI	7.1	11.0	21.8	19.2	16.2	21.4	3.4	353,000
Athens, GA	10.5	18.0	26.3	18.0	10.1	14.3	2.8	280,900
Atlanta, GA	5.5	13.6	23.9	19.8	13.6	19.9	3.6	335,100
Austin, TX	5.1	5.2	15.7	18.2	16.6	30.5	8.6	434,800
Baltimore, MD	5.5	10.2	19.7	19.9	15.1	25.5	4.1	373,300
Billings, MT	8.9	10.1	25.9	22.6	14.8	15.5	2.2	322,700
Boise City, ID	5.0	4.9	13.8	19.8	19.1	31.9	5.6	434,400
Boston, MA	2.6	1.9	5.8	10.4	15.0	48.7	15.6	610,900
Boulder, CO	3.9	1.2	2.5	6.2	10.6	49.6	25.9	713,900
Cape Coral, FL	8.7	12.9	23.1	19.9	12.6	17.6	5.1	326,300
Cedar Rapids, IA	11.7	37.7	25.8	12.6	6.1	5.0	1.0	202,100
Charleston, SC	8.4	11.0	22.2	18.2	12.1	19.8	8.1	345,400
Charlotte, NC	8.7	15.9	21.8	18.3	12.5	18.3	4.4	319,400
Chicago, IL	6.2	16.9	26.5	19.9	12.0	15.0	3.5	301,900
Cincinnati, OH	10.2	28.0	26.6	15.7	8.7	9.3	1.5	240,200
Clarksville, TN	13.8	25.6	31.2	14.6	7.2	6.3	1.2	229,400
Cleveland, OH	16.6	33.1	23.9	12.6	6.4	6.4	1.0	201,000
College Station, TX	15.0	18.5	26.1	17.3	9.5	11.2	2.3	261,900
Colorado Springs, CO	4.0	3.9	13.2	22.2	21.5	31.2	4.1	431,600
Columbia, MO	11.1	26.8	26.5	15.4	9.6	9.0	1.6	242,500
Columbia, SC	15.7	30.4	25.4	12.9	6.5	7.4	1.7	213,400
Columbus, OH	9.2	20.9	26.3	18.4	10.8	12.8	1.6	274,300
Dallas, TX	6.8	13.3	23.8	20.1	13.1	18.8	4.1	330,300
Davenport, IA	20.4	38.7	21.3	9.7	5.0	4.2	0.7	170,000
Denver, CO	3.2	1.7	5.1	11.3	18.6	49.8	10.3	570,300
Des Moines, IA	8.7	25.7	28.2	18.3	9.0	9.0	1.1	252,400
Detroit, MI	16.3	23.8	24.2	15.1	9.2	9.8	1.5	237,100
Durham, NC	6.8	12.7	19.0	19.3	14.3	23.7	4.1	359,400
El Paso, TX	17.9	45.6	23.7	7.1	2.7	2.4	0.6	167,000
Eugene, OR	7.7	4.1	16.6	22.5	19.7	25.8	3.5	395,800
Fargo, ND	6.0	16.9	33.8	21.7	10.4	9.8	1.5	276,600
Fort Collins, CO	4.8	1.6	4.6	11.8	22.6	47.6	6.9	532,200
Fort Wayne, IN	16.3	35.8	25.6	11.4	5.1	5.0	0.7	194,000
Fort Worth, TX	6.8	13.3	23.8	20.1	13.1	18.8	4.1	330,300
Gainesville, FL	13.9	23.8	25.3	16.2	9.0	10.1	1.6	245,800
Green Bay, WI	7.8	29.2	31.1	15.7	8.0	7.3	0.9	238,700
Greensboro, NC	15.0	33.0	23.9	13.1	6.3	7.9	1.0	207,600
Honolulu, HI	2.2	1.5	2.2	5.1	7.6	43.9	37.6	873,000
Houston, TX	9.2	18.8	28.6	17.5	10.0	12.4	3.6	275,200
Huntsville, AL	10.6	22.2	26.0	17.6	10.3	11.7	1.6	265,000
Indianapolis, IN	10.9	25.6	27.2	15.9	8.9	9.9	1.7	244,000
Jacksonville, FL	8.7	15.7	24.0	19.1	12.4	16.2	4.0	308,900
Kansas City, MO	10.8	22.1	25.5	17.5	10.4	11.8	1.8	265,400
Lafayette, LA	22.9	24.9	27.1	12.6	6.3	5.2	1.0	206,900
Las Vegas, NV	4.7	4.8	15.2	25.2	21.6	24.5	4.1	400,800
Lexington, KY	6.9	24.4	28.6	17.8	9.1	10.7	2.5	258,900
Lincoln, NE	5.8	24.3	32.7	18.0	8.9	8.9	1.3	257,500
Little Rock, AR	17.5	32.8	24.9	11.9	5.4	6.1	1.5	199,300
Los Angeles, CA	3.2	1.7	1.8	3.2	6.3	50.5	33.3	825,300
Louisville, KY	10.5	28.4	27.1	15.9	8.1	8.6	1.3	236,400
Madison, WI	3.7	11.6	24.1	23.9	16.0	18.4	2.3	344,600
Manchester, NH	3.8	6.2	18.2	25.4	21.4	23.3	1.5	385,500
McAllen, TX	39.7	34.5	16.0	5.7	2.2	1.6	0.4	124,000

Table continued on following page.

Metro Area	Under $100,000	$100,000 -$199,999	$200,000 -$299,999	$300,000 -$399,999	$400,000 -$499,999	$500,000 -$999,999	$1,000,000 or more	Median ($)
Memphis, TN	18.7	24.3	22.8	15.3	8.1	9.3	1.6	228,100
Miami, FL	6.3	9.6	15.7	17.5	16.5	26.1	8.3	405,600
Midland, TX	12.7	13.2	26.8	21.6	10.8	12.6	2.4	290,300
Milwaukee, WI	7.4	19.6	27.2	19.0	11.7	13.0	2.1	283,800
Minneapolis, MN	4.0	7.4	24.9	25.1	16.1	19.6	2.9	354,400
Nashville, TN	4.8	8.7	20.9	20.4	15.0	23.6	6.7	376,800
New Orleans, LA	8.9	25.9	28.3	15.3	7.8	10.8	3.0	248,000
New York, NY	3.6	3.3	7.3	11.1	14.3	44.4	16.0	587,400
Oklahoma City, OK	14.4	31.1	26.8	12.7	6.2	7.1	1.7	214,700
Omaha, NE	8.7	25.0	29.9	16.9	9.6	8.7	1.3	248,100
Orlando, FL	7.9	10.2	22.8	23.6	15.2	17.1	3.2	338,500
Philadelphia, PA	7.1	14.6	23.2	19.2	13.4	19.5	3.0	326,700
Phoenix, AZ	6.7	5.9	16.8	20.3	17.5	26.9	5.9	401,400
Pittsburgh, PA	19.2	29.5	23.7	12.0	6.6	7.6	1.3	204,500
Portland, OR	3.9	2.2	5.4	12.8	22.0	46.6	7.0	526,500
Providence, RI	3.3	4.7	20.9	24.5	18.9	24.2	3.4	385,900
Provo, UT	3.5	1.6	7.4	18.5	22.0	41.2	6.0	487,200
Raleigh, NC	5.3	9.2	19.3	20.0	16.2	26.2	3.9	381,000
Reno, NV	5.5	4.0	9.4	17.0	18.9	36.5	8.6	474,000
Richmond, VA	4.9	12.5	26.9	22.4	13.5	17.3	2.6	325,800
Rochester, MN	6.7	18.1	29.5	17.4	11.9	14.4	2.0	284,600
Sacramento, CA	4.1	2.1	5.1	12.0	18.3	49.6	8.8	559,000
Saint Louis, MO	14.9	26.3	25.0	14.9	8.2	8.9	1.8	232,100
Saint Paul, MN	4.0	7.4	24.9	25.1	16.1	19.6	2.9	354,400
Salem, OR	7.5	5.1	14.2	25.9	20.5	24.2	2.7	389,800
Salt Lake City, UT	4.0	2.6	9.9	17.6	20.3	38.7	6.9	478,200
San Antonio, TX	11.7	21.6	27.6	16.5	9.1	11.3	2.2	258,700
San Diego, CA	3.7	1.9	2.1	3.4	6.8	52.6	29.5	791,600
San Francisco, CA	2.1	1.4	1.3	1.7	3.4	31.8	58.4	1,113,800
San Jose, CA	2.1	1.7	1.8	1.3	1.2	19.3	72.6	1,342,700
Santa Rosa, CA	3.3	3.1	2.4	2.7	5.4	57.0	26.2	779,000
Savannah, GA	9.6	21.3	26.2	16.7	9.8	13.3	3.2	271,100
Seattle, WA	3.2	1.7	3.9	8.3	12.9	46.7	23.2	673,500
Sioux Falls, SD	8.4	18.3	30.7	18.5	10.4	11.8	1.9	274,800
Tampa, FL	11.5	14.4	22.9	19.3	12.1	16.0	3.8	306,100
Tucson, AZ	11.2	15.2	26.9	19.0	11.6	13.4	2.6	286,900
Tulsa, OK	17.5	31.2	25.4	12.1	5.9	6.5	1.4	204,400
Virginia Beach, VA	5.2	13.4	27.6	21.5	14.3	15.6	2.5	318,000
Washington, DC	2.5	2.4	8.4	14.5	16.2	42.5	13.4	553,000
Wichita, KS	20.1	33.8	25.4	10.2	4.8	4.9	0.8	188,200
Wilmington, NC	7.5	14.3	22.8	19.4	13.3	19.0	3.8	328,000
Winston-Salem, NC	14.0	32.0	26.0	13.0	6.5	7.3	1.2	213,300
U.S.	12.1	17.8	19.5	14.4	10.5	19.1	6.5	303,400

Note: Figures are percentages except for median and cover owner-occupied housing units; Figures cover the Metropolitan Statistical Area (MSA)
Source: U.S. Census Bureau, 2019-2023 American Community Survey 5-Year Estimates

Homeownership Rate

Metro Area	2017	2018	2019	2020	2021	2022	2023	2024
Albuquerque, NM	67.0	67.9	70.0	69.5	66.5	67.3	69.1	71.8
Anchorage, AK	n/a	n/a	n/a	n/a	n/a	n/a	n/a	n/a
Ann Arbor, MI	n/a	n/a	n/a	n/a	n/a	n/a	n/a	n/a
Athens, GA	n/a	n/a	n/a	n/a	n/a	n/a	n/a	n/a
Atlanta, GA	62.4	64.0	64.2	66.4	64.2	64.4	67.5	67.5
Austin, TX	55.6	56.1	59.0	65.4	62.2	62.4	60.3	56.2
Baltimore, MD	67.5	63.5	66.5	70.7	67.5	70.4	72.9	70.0
Billings, MT	n/a	n/a	n/a	n/a	n/a	n/a	n/a	n/a
Boise City, ID	n/a	n/a	n/a	n/a	n/a	n/a	n/a	n/a
Boston, MA	58.8	61.0	60.9	61.2	60.7	59.4	59.9	60.7
Boulder, CO	n/a	n/a	n/a	n/a	n/a	n/a	n/a	n/a
Cape Coral, FL	65.5	75.1	72.0	77.4	76.1	70.8	78.5	77.1
Cedar Rapids, IA	n/a	n/a	n/a	n/a	n/a	n/a	n/a	n/a
Charleston, SC	67.7	68.8	70.7	75.5	73.2	71.9	69.6	68.1
Charlotte, NC	64.6	67.9	72.3	73.3	70.0	68.7	64.8	62.7
Chicago, IL	64.1	64.6	63.4	66.0	67.5	66.8	67.3	68.0
Cincinnati, OH	65.7	67.3	67.4	71.1	72.1	67.1	69.6	72.3
Clarksville, TN	n/a	n/a	n/a	n/a	n/a	n/a	n/a	n/a
Cleveland, OH	66.6	66.7	64.4	66.3	64.7	63.0	63.1	65.6
College Station, TX	n/a	n/a	n/a	n/a	n/a	n/a	n/a	n/a
Colorado Springs, CO	n/a	n/a	n/a	n/a	n/a	n/a	n/a	n/a
Columbia, MO	n/a	n/a	n/a	n/a	n/a	n/a	n/a	n/a
Columbia, SC	70.7	69.3	65.9	69.7	69.4	70.9	69.2	73.4
Columbus, OH	57.9	64.8	65.7	65.6	64.6	61.5	58.6	61.5
Dallas, TX	61.8	62.0	60.6	64.7	61.8	60.4	61.7	61.1
Davenport, IA	n/a	n/a	n/a	n/a	n/a	n/a	n/a	n/a
Denver, CO	59.3	60.1	63.5	62.9	62.8	64.6	65.9	61.6
Des Moines, IA	n/a	n/a	n/a	n/a	n/a	n/a	n/a	n/a
Detroit, MI	70.2	70.9	70.2	71.8	71.6	71.9	73.5	72.0
Durham, NC	n/a	n/a	n/a	n/a	n/a	n/a	n/a	n/a
El Paso, TX	n/a	n/a	n/a	n/a	n/a	n/a	n/a	n/a
Eugene, OR	n/a	n/a	n/a	n/a	n/a	n/a	n/a	n/a
Fargo, ND	n/a	n/a	n/a	n/a	n/a	n/a	n/a	n/a
Fort Collins, CO	n/a	n/a	n/a	n/a	n/a	n/a	n/a	n/a
Fort Wayne, IN	n/a	n/a	n/a	n/a	n/a	n/a	n/a	n/a
Fort Worth, TX	61.8	62.0	60.6	64.7	61.8	60.4	61.7	61.1
Gainesville, FL	n/a	n/a	n/a	n/a	n/a	n/a	n/a	n/a
Green Bay, WI	n/a	n/a	n/a	n/a	n/a	n/a	n/a	n/a
Greensboro, NC	61.9	63.2	61.7	65.8	61.9	70.0	69.4	67.0
Honolulu, HI	53.8	57.7	59.0	56.9	55.9	57.7	60.4	58.5
Houston, TX	58.9	60.1	61.3	65.3	64.1	63.7	61.8	61.6
Huntsville, AL	n/a	n/a	n/a	n/a	n/a	n/a	n/a	n/a
Indianapolis, IN	63.9	64.3	66.2	70.0	70.1	68.8	70.2	69.6
Jacksonville, FL	65.2	61.4	63.1	64.8	68.1	70.6	72.9	67.0
Kansas City, MO	62.4	64.3	65.0	66.7	63.8	63.8	64.1	65.3
Lafayette, LA	n/a	n/a	n/a	n/a	n/a	n/a	n/a	n/a
Las Vegas, NV	54.4	58.1	56.0	57.3	57.7	58.7	58.9	58.5
Lexington, KY	n/a	n/a	n/a	n/a	n/a	n/a	n/a	n/a
Lincoln, NE	n/a	n/a	n/a	n/a	n/a	n/a	n/a	n/a
Little Rock, AR	61.0	62.2	65.0	67.7	64.6	64.4	62.6	61.7
Los Angeles, CA	49.1	49.5	48.2	48.5	47.9	48.3	48.0	48.3
Louisville, KY	71.7	67.9	64.9	69.3	71.4	71.7	68.3	67.0
Madison, WI	n/a	n/a	n/a	n/a	n/a	n/a	n/a	n/a
Manchester, NH	n/a	n/a	n/a	n/a	n/a	n/a	n/a	n/a
McAllen, TX	n/a	n/a	n/a	n/a	n/a	n/a	n/a	n/a
Memphis, TN	62.4	63.5	63.7	62.5	60.7	59.7	63.2	60.1

Table continued on following page.

Metro Area	2017	2018	2019	2020	2021	2022	2023	2024
Miami, FL	57.9	59.9	60.4	60.6	59.4	58.3	58.6	60.8
Midland, TX	n/a	n/a	n/a	n/a	n/a	n/a	n/a	n/a
Milwaukee, WI	63.9	62.3	56.9	58.5	56.8	57.3	60.0	62.7
Minneapolis, MN	70.1	67.8	70.2	73.0	75.0	73.0	72.0	67.8
Nashville, TN	69.4	68.3	69.8	69.8	65.7	70.4	70.7	71.6
New Orleans, LA	61.7	62.6	61.1	66.3	66.2	66.3	63.2	63.2
New York, NY	49.9	49.7	50.4	50.9	50.7	50.5	50.2	49.4
Oklahoma City, OK	64.7	64.6	64.3	68.3	61.9	64.8	68.1	65.0
Omaha, NE	65.5	67.8	66.9	68.6	68.6	67.9	67.0	67.4
Orlando, FL	59.5	58.5	56.1	64.2	63.0	62.1	61.9	62.6
Philadelphia, PA	65.6	67.4	67.4	69.2	69.8	68.2	67.4	69.6
Phoenix, AZ	64.0	65.3	65.9	67.9	65.2	68.0	69.7	69.4
Pittsburgh, PA	72.7	71.7	71.5	69.8	69.1	72.7	72.4	71.7
Portland, OR	61.1	59.2	60.0	62.5	64.1	65.2	65.6	61.1
Providence, RI	58.6	61.3	63.5	64.8	64.1	66.3	65.4	63.2
Provo, UT	n/a	n/a	n/a	n/a	n/a	n/a	n/a	n/a
Raleigh, NC	68.2	64.9	63.0	68.2	62.7	65.1	68.8	65.0
Reno, NV	n/a	n/a	n/a	n/a	n/a	n/a	n/a	n/a
Richmond, VA	63.1	62.9	66.4	66.5	64.9	66.3	64.9	65.4
Rochester, MN	n/a	n/a	n/a	n/a	n/a	n/a	n/a	n/a
Sacramento, CA	60.1	64.1	61.6	63.4	63.2	63.5	64.4	63.0
Saint Louis, MO	65.6	65.8	68.1	71.1	73.8	69.9	69.4	68.2
Saint Paul, MN	70.1	67.8	70.2	73.0	75.0	73.0	72.0	67.8
Salem, OR	n/a	n/a	n/a	n/a	n/a	n/a	n/a	n/a
Salt Lake City, UT	68.1	69.5	69.2	68.0	64.1	66.6	62.9	61.0
San Antonio, TX	62.5	64.4	62.6	64.2	62.7	62.9	66.9	63.3
San Diego, CA	56.0	56.1	56.7	57.8	52.6	51.6	54.5	51.4
San Francisco, CA	55.7	55.6	52.8	53.0	54.7	56.4	55.0	56.4
San Jose, CA	50.4	50.4	52.4	52.6	48.4	53.1	53.5	52.3
Santa Rosa, CA	n/a	n/a	n/a	n/a	n/a	n/a	n/a	n/a
Savannah, GA	n/a	n/a	n/a	n/a	n/a	n/a	n/a	n/a
Seattle, WA	59.5	62.5	61.5	59.4	58.0	62.7	62.7	61.1
Sioux Falls, SD	n/a	n/a	n/a	n/a	n/a	n/a	n/a	n/a
Tampa, FL	60.4	64.9	68.0	72.2	68.3	68.4	66.9	68.9
Tucson, AZ	60.1	63.8	60.1	67.1	63.5	71.6	73.3	66.4
Tulsa, OK	66.8	68.3	70.5	70.1	63.8	63.7	62.8	65.3
Virginia Beach, VA	65.3	62.8	63.0	65.8	64.4	61.4	67.8	69.8
Washington, DC	63.3	62.9	64.7	67.9	65.8	66.2	65.1	64.0
Wichita, KS	n/a	n/a	n/a	n/a	n/a	n/a	n/a	n/a
Wilmington, NC	n/a	n/a	n/a	n/a	n/a	n/a	n/a	n/a
Winston-Salem, NC	n/a	n/a	n/a	n/a	n/a	n/a	n/a	n/a
U.S.	63.9	64.4	64.6	66.6	65.5	65.8	65.9	65.6

Note: Figures are percentages and cover the Metropolitan Statistical Area (MSA); n/a not available
Source: U.S. Census Bureau, Housing Vacancies and Homeownership Annual Statistics: 2017-2024

Year Housing Structure Built: City

City	2020 or Later	2010 -2019	2000 -2009	1990 -1999	1980 -1989	1970 -1979	1960 -1969	1950 -1959	1940 -1949	Before 1940	Median Year
Albuquerque, NM	0.7	6.9	16.2	14.2	14.1	19.2	9.5	12.3	3.9	3.0	1982
Anchorage, AK	0.2	6.6	12.1	11.6	24.8	27.5	9.7	5.8	0.9	0.8	1982
Ann Arbor, MI	1.3	6.5	6.8	11.2	9.9	16.0	17.9	10.6	4.8	15.2	1971
Athens, GA	1.6	8.9	19.0	16.3	14.5	14.3	12.0	5.8	2.7	4.9	1987
Atlanta, GA	2.3	15.8	21.0	8.9	7.8	7.8	10.2	8.8	5.3	12.1	1987
Austin, TX	2.5	20.7	17.2	13.0	17.3	13.7	7.2	4.1	2.0	2.3	1993
Baltimore, MD	0.3	4.3	4.1	4.1	4.6	5.8	8.6	15.3	11.6	41.1	1948
Billings, MT	2.3	12.7	10.6	11.9	11.3	16.3	9.0	13.1	5.5	7.4	1979
Boise City, ID	1.3	10.8	11.4	19.6	14.4	17.8	7.8	7.2	3.7	6.3	1985
Boston, MA	0.9	9.2	6.5	4.3	5.6	7.6	7.2	7.1	4.9	46.8	1947
Boulder, CO	0.5	8.5	8.8	12.4	15.5	19.8	16.2	9.0	1.5	7.7	1978
Cape Coral, FL	2.0	11.6	34.3	15.2	21.1	10.3	4.5	0.8	0.3	0.0	1999
Cedar Rapids, IA	0.8	9.6	11.3	10.9	7.5	14.7	13.9	12.4	4.3	14.7	1973
Charleston, SC	2.6	22.7	19.1	10.1	10.5	7.5	8.2	5.6	3.0	10.8	1994
Charlotte, NC	1.8	16.9	20.9	17.3	13.9	10.2	8.2	5.8	2.4	2.6	1994
Chicago, IL	0.4	5.1	8.2	4.9	5.0	7.9	9.7	11.6	8.2	39.1	1952
Cincinnati, OH	0.5	4.4	4.1	4.0	6.3	9.3	12.0	10.9	8.3	40.3	1951
Clarksville, TN	3.3	18.0	21.2	18.8	12.9	11.3	6.2	4.2	2.3	1.7	1996
Cleveland, OH	0.6	3.8	3.8	2.9	3.0	5.6	7.8	12.1	10.8	49.6	1940
College Station, TX	2.4	23.2	20.3	16.5	18.5	12.2	3.9	1.7	0.5	0.7	1998
Colorado Springs, CO	1.9	11.6	14.9	14.2	17.5	16.8	9.3	7.0	1.7	5.3	1986
Columbia, MO	0.8	17.5	20.3	17.0	12.3	9.9	10.3	4.5	2.4	5.0	1993
Columbia, SC	1.0	12.9	14.8	9.8	9.6	9.6	10.1	13.3	8.9	10.1	1978
Columbus, OH	1.0	9.6	11.8	13.7	13.3	14.4	10.7	9.6	4.0	12.0	1980
Dallas, TX	1.0	12.0	11.0	10.0	16.3	15.0	12.0	12.7	4.6	5.2	1980
Davenport, IA	0.6	4.8	9.1	8.4	6.9	15.3	12.8	11.8	6.0	24.2	1966
Denver, CO	2.3	15.5	10.9	6.6	7.4	12.0	9.9	13.0	5.2	17.2	1974
Des Moines, IA	0.6	6.9	7.3	6.8	6.4	12.8	9.5	14.6	7.3	27.8	1960
Detroit, MI	0.1	1.5	2.7	2.3	3.2	4.9	7.8	21.8	20.4	35.2	1947
Durham, NC	2.6	21.5	17.1	14.2	14.0	9.6	7.1	5.3	3.4	5.2	1994
El Paso, TX	0.9	14.1	13.5	11.7	14.9	15.9	10.2	10.9	3.2	4.7	1983
Eugene, OR	0.7	10.2	13.3	15.0	9.2	19.9	11.7	8.5	5.5	6.0	1979
Fargo, ND	1.3	20.3	14.9	14.5	11.5	13.7	5.8	7.7	2.5	7.9	1991
Fort Collins, CO	1.5	15.0	18.9	19.0	14.5	15.7	6.5	3.0	1.3	4.5	1992
Fort Wayne, IN	0.5	3.4	7.4	12.9	11.3	16.9	15.5	12.0	5.7	14.4	1971
Fort Worth, TX	2.4	17.7	20.8	11.1	13.2	8.7	6.9	9.3	4.5	5.6	1992
Gainesville, FL	1.3	6.5	14.0	14.2	19.5	20.2	11.8	7.0	2.7	2.9	1983
Green Bay, WI	0.4	3.2	7.3	9.8	12.5	17.9	12.6	16.1	5.9	14.4	1971
Greensboro, NC	0.8	9.8	14.7	14.5	15.6	13.9	11.0	10.1	3.8	5.7	1983
Honolulu, HI	0.5	7.5	6.7	7.8	10.5	25.9	19.6	11.6	5.1	4.8	1973
Houston, TX	1.4	14.0	13.0	9.3	14.1	19.0	12.1	9.4	3.7	4.1	1981
Huntsville, AL	2.3	15.6	12.4	10.8	14.8	11.9	20.1	7.8	1.8	2.6	1984
Indianapolis, IN	0.6	6.5	9.9	12.0	11.2	12.1	13.4	12.1	6.0	16.1	1972
Jacksonville, FL	2.4	10.6	17.4	13.1	15.9	11.9	9.3	10.3	4.1	5.0	1986
Kansas City, MO	1.0	8.2	10.1	8.5	8.6	11.4	12.0	13.2	5.5	21.6	1968
Lafayette, LA	0.8	12.4	11.5	9.3	18.6	21.5	12.8	8.7	2.7	1.6	1981
Las Vegas, NV	1.4	8.8	21.4	29.3	16.3	10.2	7.0	4.1	1.0	0.5	1994
Lexington, KY	1.1	10.0	14.5	15.6	13.0	14.5	13.4	8.5	2.7	6.7	1983
Lincoln, NE	1.0	11.9	14.2	13.6	10.1	14.5	8.7	10.3	3.2	12.4	1981
Little Rock, AR	0.4	9.7	11.7	11.8	13.1	17.9	14.7	8.5	4.9	7.2	1978
Los Angeles, CA	0.8	6.1	5.6	5.7	10.8	13.4	13.2	16.2	9.1	19.2	1964
Louisville, KY	0.8	7.7	11.8	10.4	6.9	13.0	12.7	14.2	6.6	15.9	1970
Madison, WI	0.9	11.8	14.3	11.8	9.5	12.8	11.9	9.2	4.3	13.4	1979
Manchester, NH	0.5	3.5	6.5	7.7	15.5	11.5	8.1	10.7	6.6	29.4	1964
McAllen, TX	1.2	13.0	24.8	16.8	18.5	15.3	5.0	2.3	1.2	1.9	1993

Table continued on following page.

City	2020 or Later	2010-2019	2000-2009	1990-1999	1980-1989	1970-1979	1960-1969	1950-1959	1940-1949	Before 1940	Median Year
Memphis, TN	0.5	3.6	6.5	9.7	12.4	17.3	14.6	20.0	7.7	7.7	1970
Miami, FL	1.8	15.4	17.0	6.0	7.4	11.9	10.0	13.5	9.1	7.9	1978
Midland, TX	2.2	21.9	10.1	9.7	17.3	10.9	7.7	16.6	2.5	1.1	1986
Milwaukee, WI	0.3	3.5	3.7	3.5	3.8	9.2	11.6	18.8	10.9	34.7	1952
Minneapolis, MN	1.0	8.8	6.2	4.2	6.8	8.2	6.8	8.2	6.2	43.6	1950
Nashville, TN	3.2	15.4	13.9	11.0	14.2	12.8	10.9	9.0	3.4	6.2	1985
New Orleans, LA	0.4	5.7	7.6	3.0	7.8	13.9	10.2	12.0	7.1	32.1	1959
New York, NY	0.4	5.5	5.5	3.7	5.0	7.0	12.2	12.8	9.4	38.4	1952
Oklahoma City, OK	1.6	13.7	13.3	9.3	13.4	15.6	11.3	9.2	5.0	7.4	1981
Omaha, NE	0.4	6.4	8.7	11.9	10.8	15.1	13.9	10.5	4.2	18.1	1972
Orlando, FL	1.3	16.1	21.0	13.1	15.1	12.7	7.2	8.4	2.6	2.6	1991
Philadelphia, PA	0.6	4.8	3.2	2.7	4.5	7.8	10.9	15.0	10.7	39.9	1949
Phoenix, AZ	1.1	8.6	16.4	14.3	17.3	18.9	9.5	9.6	2.4	1.9	1984
Pittsburgh, PA	0.5	4.8	3.7	3.4	4.2	6.5	7.9	13.0	7.6	48.4	1942
Portland, OR	0.9	11.0	10.1	7.3	6.4	10.5	8.4	11.0	7.2	27.1	1966
Providence, RI	0.4	2.2	4.9	4.5	5.6	7.8	5.4	7.5	6.3	55.6	1938
Provo, UT	1.1	7.6	11.6	18.7	14.7	17.7	9.7	7.3	5.0	6.6	1982
Raleigh, NC	1.6	17.5	23.5	17.1	16.0	9.6	6.8	3.7	1.3	2.9	1996
Reno, NV	3.0	11.6	19.1	15.0	13.3	17.7	8.5	5.7	3.1	2.9	1989
Richmond, VA	1.1	8.6	5.9	5.7	7.3	8.7	11.1	14.1	9.0	28.6	1959
Rochester, MN	1.2	12.9	18.5	14.1	11.1	12.4	9.9	9.0	3.7	7.2	1987
Sacramento, CA	0.9	6.3	15.0	7.8	15.2	13.3	11.3	11.9	7.2	11.0	1976
Saint Louis, MO	0.2	3.2	4.0	3.0	3.7	4.3	6.1	9.7	7.6	58.3	1938
Saint Paul, MN	0.7	4.5	5.1	3.5	7.3	9.8	9.4	11.7	6.7	41.2	1952
Salem, OR	1.8	9.1	13.5	15.9	9.5	18.5	9.3	9.3	4.5	8.6	1980
Salt Lake City, UT	1.8	10.6	6.8	5.5	7.4	11.4	9.8	12.2	8.2	26.3	1963
San Antonio, TX	1.6	11.9	15.2	11.3	16.2	13.8	10.1	9.5	5.2	5.2	1984
San Diego, CA	0.8	7.1	10.2	10.6	17.7	20.2	12.2	11.0	3.7	6.6	1978
San Francisco, CA	0.7	6.4	6.5	4.0	5.3	7.1	8.1	7.9	8.7	45.4	1945
San Jose, CA	0.6	7.3	9.6	9.6	12.1	23.6	18.5	10.9	2.7	5.2	1975
Santa Rosa, CA	1.0	6.2	12.3	12.5	17.9	20.9	11.9	8.1	4.4	4.9	1980
Savannah, GA	1.3	11.9	9.0	6.3	11.5	11.7	10.7	13.9	6.9	16.7	1971
Seattle, WA	1.2	17.6	12.0	7.4	7.5	7.2	7.7	8.4	7.4	23.4	1974
Sioux Falls, SD	2.0	19.1	18.4	13.3	10.6	10.4	6.5	8.0	3.0	8.6	1992
Tampa, FL	1.8	13.8	16.5	10.7	11.7	10.3	9.1	12.9	4.9	8.3	1984
Tucson, AZ	0.7	4.6	13.0	12.7	16.5	20.2	11.0	13.4	4.8	3.2	1979
Tulsa, OK	0.4	6.0	6.5	8.2	13.8	20.0	14.5	15.5	6.2	8.9	1972
Virginia Beach, VA	0.4	8.2	10.9	13.1	27.2	19.7	12.3	5.7	1.3	1.1	1984
Washington, DC	1.7	12.5	7.7	3.0	4.7	6.7	9.9	11.6	10.3	31.7	1957
Wichita, KS	0.7	6.9	10.1	11.2	12.8	13.3	9.1	18.0	7.7	10.3	1974
Wilmington, NC	2.3	13.1	14.9	16.2	15.2	11.1	6.2	6.3	5.7	9.1	1988
Winston-Salem, NC	1.1	8.6	13.2	12.5	15.0	14.4	11.0	12.2	4.1	7.7	1980
U.S.	1.2	8.9	13.6	12.8	13.0	14.4	10.0	9.7	4.5	11.9	1980

Note: Figures are percentages except for median year
Source: U.S. Census Bureau, 2019-2023 American Community Survey 5-Year Estimates

Year Housing Structure Built: Metro Area

Metro Area	2020 or Later	2010-2019	2000-2009	1990-1999	1980-1989	1970-1979	1960-1969	1950-1959	1940-1949	Before 1940	Median Year
Albuquerque, NM	0.9	7.5	17.4	16.2	15.7	17.7	8.6	9.5	3.3	3.2	1985
Anchorage, AK	0.5	9.5	16.8	12.5	23.9	22.9	7.8	4.6	0.8	0.7	1986
Ann Arbor, MI	1.2	6.4	13.0	16.0	10.5	15.4	12.3	9.1	4.3	11.8	1978
Athens, GA	1.8	10.2	19.4	18.1	15.0	14.1	9.5	4.6	2.2	5.1	1990
Atlanta, GA	1.7	11.8	23.5	19.3	16.7	11.5	6.8	4.2	1.7	2.8	1993
Austin, TX	4.0	25.5	21.4	14.6	14.3	9.7	4.5	2.8	1.3	2.0	2000
Baltimore, MD	0.6	7.2	9.6	13.0	13.4	12.8	10.3	12.4	6.0	14.6	1975
Billings, MT	2.1	12.3	12.8	12.9	11.6	16.7	7.7	10.1	4.8	9.1	1981
Boise City, ID	3.5	17.3	22.2	17.7	8.9	13.4	4.7	4.2	2.8	5.2	1996
Boston, MA	0.8	7.1	7.5	7.1	10.5	10.6	9.8	10.4	4.8	31.5	1963
Boulder, CO	1.5	11.2	12.5	18.7	14.7	19.1	9.9	5.0	1.4	6.2	1986
Cape Coral, FL	1.9	11.4	29.2	16.2	20.5	12.9	5.0	1.8	0.4	0.6	1995
Cedar Rapids, IA	0.9	10.2	13.2	12.8	7.4	13.6	11.6	10.2	3.6	16.6	1976
Charleston, SC	2.9	19.5	20.3	14.1	14.6	11.3	7.2	4.5	2.2	3.4	1995
Charlotte, NC	2.2	16.8	21.6	17.2	12.3	10.0	7.2	5.8	2.9	4.1	1994
Chicago, IL	0.5	4.6	11.5	10.7	9.2	13.9	11.6	12.4	5.5	20.1	1970
Cincinnati, OH	0.9	6.6	12.1	13.5	10.7	13.4	10.4	11.3	4.7	16.5	1975
Clarksville, TN	2.6	16.3	19.0	18.9	12.1	12.6	7.3	5.5	2.6	3.0	1994
Cleveland, OH	0.5	4.0	7.0	8.8	7.1	12.5	13.3	17.0	7.3	22.6	1962
College Station, TX	2.6	20.0	19.0	15.1	17.1	12.3	5.7	3.9	2.1	2.2	1994
Colorado Springs, CO	1.9	12.9	17.5	15.2	16.4	15.8	8.0	5.9	1.4	4.9	1988
Columbia, MO	1.0	14.0	17.9	16.8	13.2	13.1	9.7	4.6	2.4	7.3	1990
Columbia, SC	1.6	13.8	18.3	16.7	13.5	14.1	8.8	6.7	2.8	3.7	1990
Columbus, OH	1.4	9.5	14.1	14.9	11.5	13.7	10.1	9.2	3.5	12.1	1981
Dallas, TX	2.6	16.9	18.6	14.3	16.5	12.2	7.6	6.6	2.2	2.5	1992
Davenport, IA	0.6	5.3	8.4	7.9	7.0	16.0	13.7	12.1	6.9	22.1	1966
Denver, CO	1.9	13.0	15.6	13.8	13.5	16.4	8.7	8.4	2.4	6.3	1986
Des Moines, IA	2.2	15.6	15.3	12.1	7.8	12.5	7.5	8.3	3.5	15.3	1984
Detroit, MI	0.5	4.0	8.7	11.1	9.0	14.5	12.4	18.3	8.8	12.8	1968
Durham, NC	2.3	17.4	17.1	16.3	14.5	11.4	7.5	5.9	2.9	4.7	1992
El Paso, TX	1.4	16.4	15.2	12.8	14.7	14.6	8.7	9.3	2.8	4.1	1987
Eugene, OR	0.8	7.5	12.2	14.5	9.1	21.0	13.2	8.5	6.7	6.4	1977
Fargo, ND	1.9	19.2	17.1	13.2	9.8	14.3	6.5	7.4	2.2	8.2	1991
Fort Collins, CO	2.2	16.8	18.4	17.5	12.3	16.7	5.8	3.2	1.8	5.3	1993
Fort Wayne, IN	1.0	7.6	11.5	13.5	10.2	14.7	12.3	9.9	4.7	14.5	1976
Fort Worth, TX	2.6	16.9	18.6	14.3	16.5	12.2	7.6	6.6	2.2	2.5	1992
Gainesville, FL	1.8	9.8	17.7	17.7	18.9	16.6	8.4	4.7	1.9	2.5	1988
Green Bay, WI	1.0	8.5	13.4	15.1	11.6	15.5	9.9	9.3	4.0	11.7	1980
Greensboro, NC	0.9	9.0	15.8	16.5	14.4	14.3	10.1	8.9	4.1	6.0	1985
Honolulu, HI	0.6	7.7	9.6	11.4	12.8	23.9	17.3	10.0	3.8	3.0	1977
Houston, TX	2.3	18.1	19.6	12.8	14.7	15.1	7.6	5.4	2.1	2.3	1992
Huntsville, AL	2.9	16.7	18.5	15.2	14.9	9.8	12.7	5.5	1.4	2.3	1992
Indianapolis, IN	1.4	10.4	14.9	15.5	9.9	11.7	10.3	9.4	4.3	12.2	1982
Jacksonville, FL	3.2	13.5	20.2	14.3	16.1	11.4	7.3	7.2	2.9	3.8	1991
Kansas City, MO	1.2	8.8	13.5	13.3	12.0	14.1	11.2	10.6	4.0	11.4	1979
Lafayette, LA	1.4	15.7	15.9	12.0	15.0	15.9	9.4	8.3	3.2	3.4	1987
Las Vegas, NV	1.9	12.3	28.8	25.5	13.7	10.1	4.7	2.0	0.6	0.4	1997
Lexington, KY	1.2	10.3	15.9	16.7	13.1	14.2	10.8	7.5	2.8	7.5	1985
Lincoln, NE	1.1	11.9	14.3	13.5	9.6	14.7	8.9	9.5	3.2	13.1	1981
Little Rock, AR	1.3	13.5	17.7	15.3	13.9	15.3	9.9	6.3	3.2	3.7	1988
Los Angeles, CA	0.6	5.3	6.3	7.4	12.6	15.9	15.0	17.6	7.8	11.5	1969
Louisville, KY	1.1	8.4	13.5	13.4	9.3	14.8	11.1	11.7	5.1	11.6	1977
Madison, WI	1.2	11.5	15.9	14.2	10.4	13.6	9.2	7.5	3.3	13.1	1983
Manchester, NH	0.5	5.4	9.6	10.5	20.2	15.3	9.2	7.3	3.6	18.6	1977
McAllen, TX	1.6	18.0	27.8	19.0	15.8	9.7	3.9	2.1	1.1	1.1	1999

Table continued on following page.

Metro Area	2020 or Later	2010-2019	2000-2009	1990-1999	1980-1989	1970-1979	1960-1969	1950-1959	1940-1949	Before 1940	Median Year
Memphis, TN	0.9	7.4	15.0	16.1	13.3	15.3	10.5	11.7	4.8	4.9	1982
Miami, FL	1.0	7.4	12.8	13.8	19.0	20.4	11.5	9.6	2.6	2.0	1982
Midland, TX	2.4	24.0	11.8	9.7	17.4	10.3	6.8	13.7	2.4	1.3	1989
Milwaukee, WI	0.7	5.5	8.2	10.4	7.6	13.1	11.6	15.3	7.0	20.7	1966
Minneapolis, MN	1.3	8.6	13.3	13.4	13.8	13.9	9.3	9.1	3.6	13.6	1980
Nashville, TN	3.1	17.7	18.1	15.3	13.0	11.9	8.2	6.0	2.5	4.3	1993
New Orleans, LA	0.4	5.1	9.9	6.8	13.1	19.6	13.9	10.8	5.1	15.2	1973
New York, NY	0.5	5.3	6.6	5.9	7.8	9.6	13.3	15.3	8.3	27.3	1959
Oklahoma City, OK	1.7	13.5	14.4	10.3	13.8	16.5	11.2	8.6	4.3	5.6	1983
Omaha, NE	1.3	10.7	14.3	11.8	9.6	13.9	11.2	8.2	3.4	15.6	1978
Orlando, FL	2.1	15.3	21.5	17.9	18.5	11.6	5.5	4.9	1.1	1.5	1994
Philadelphia, PA	0.7	5.3	7.9	8.9	9.9	12.2	11.7	14.9	7.0	21.5	1966
Phoenix, AZ	1.9	12.2	23.7	17.9	16.2	14.9	6.3	4.8	1.1	0.9	1993
Pittsburgh, PA	0.6	4.6	6.4	7.3	7.7	11.8	11.3	16.3	8.2	25.8	1960
Portland, OR	1.4	11.1	14.0	16.3	10.9	16.0	8.0	6.7	4.2	11.3	1983
Providence, RI	0.4	3.6	6.3	7.6	11.6	11.9	10.3	11.6	5.9	30.8	1962
Provo, UT	3.7	22.3	22.9	16.1	8.5	11.7	4.3	4.2	2.6	3.9	1999
Raleigh, NC	2.9	20.7	23.7	19.4	13.7	8.2	4.8	3.0	1.2	2.5	1999
Reno, NV	2.3	10.8	21.1	16.9	14.2	17.6	7.9	4.6	2.3	2.3	1991
Richmond, VA	1.3	10.3	14.2	14.3	15.3	13.7	9.3	8.5	4.2	8.8	1984
Rochester, MN	1.2	10.4	18.3	13.5	10.5	13.0	8.9	7.5	3.4	13.3	1984
Sacramento, CA	1.2	6.8	17.1	14.0	16.3	17.3	10.4	9.3	3.3	4.2	1983
Saint Louis, MO	0.8	6.3	11.4	11.6	11.1	12.8	12.2	12.3	5.4	16.1	1973
Saint Paul, MN	1.3	8.6	13.3	13.4	13.8	13.9	9.3	9.1	3.6	13.6	1980
Salem, OR	1.6	8.1	14.1	16.7	9.7	21.1	9.8	7.1	3.9	7.9	1980
Salt Lake City, UT	1.9	14.7	14.4	14.0	11.3	16.8	8.3	8.1	3.2	7.2	1986
San Antonio, TX	3.0	18.3	18.5	12.4	13.9	11.8	7.6	6.7	3.7	4.0	1992
San Diego, CA	0.8	6.5	12.0	11.5	18.6	21.7	11.6	10.1	3.1	4.1	1980
San Francisco, CA	0.7	5.6	7.7	7.8	10.6	14.2	12.8	13.4	7.7	19.5	1967
San Jose, CA	0.9	8.8	9.2	9.6	11.7	20.4	17.4	13.7	3.4	4.8	1975
Santa Rosa, CA	1.0	5.3	10.1	13.2	18.0	19.8	11.8	8.5	4.2	8.0	1979
Savannah, GA	2.2	15.8	19.4	13.1	12.7	11.0	6.7	7.5	3.8	7.7	1990
Seattle, WA	1.3	12.4	14.7	14.0	13.7	12.9	10.5	6.8	3.9	9.7	1985
Sioux Falls, SD	1.9	17.3	17.9	13.6	9.2	11.2	6.3	7.4	3.1	12.2	1990
Tampa, FL	1.6	10.2	15.4	13.0	19.8	18.9	8.7	7.9	1.9	2.5	1985
Tucson, AZ	1.2	7.5	18.2	16.5	17.1	18.6	8.3	7.9	2.8	1.9	1986
Tulsa, OK	1.2	11.0	13.9	11.1	13.9	18.2	10.3	9.8	4.1	6.7	1981
Virginia Beach, VA	1.0	9.6	12.6	14.0	18.1	14.3	11.5	9.1	4.2	5.6	1983
Washington, DC	1.2	10.7	14.1	12.9	15.2	13.0	11.5	8.7	4.7	8.1	1983
Wichita, KS	0.9	7.8	12.0	12.8	12.5	13.0	8.1	15.9	6.1	10.7	1977
Wilmington, NC	2.7	17.1	23.5	18.8	14.4	9.9	4.4	3.2	2.4	3.6	1996
Winston-Salem, NC	1.0	8.7	15.6	15.9	14.5	15.5	10.1	9.0	3.7	6.1	1984
U.S.	1.2	8.9	13.6	12.8	13.0	14.4	10.0	9.7	4.5	11.9	1980

Note: Figures are percentages except for median year; Figures cover the Metropolitan Statistical Area (MSA)
Source: U.S. Census Bureau, 2019-2023 American Community Survey 5-Year Estimates

Gross Monthly Rent: City

City	Under $500	$500 -$999	$1,000 -$1,499	$1,500 -$1,999	$2,000 -$2,499	$2,500 -$2,999	$3,000 and up	Median ($)
Albuquerque, NM	5.3	37.7	35.1	16.1	3.9	0.8	1.1	1,085
Anchorage, AK	3.5	14.0	35.7	25.6	12.6	5.5	3.0	1,453
Ann Arbor, MI	3.0	11.6	32.6	26.6	14.6	4.9	6.7	1,552
Athens, GA	3.8	33.4	37.8	17.1	5.0	1.5	1.3	1,162
Atlanta, GA	9.7	10.8	22.9	28.6	16.1	6.4	5.6	1,617
Austin, TX	2.5	4.7	32.4	33.5	15.4	6.4	5.0	1,655
Baltimore, MD	13.0	15.9	35.9	21.5	8.9	2.8	2.0	1,290
Billings, MT	7.9	34.2	37.7	14.4	3.3	0.7	1.7	1,097
Boise City, ID	4.1	15.0	41.7	26.5	9.3	1.9	1.6	1,359
Boston, MA	12.2	9.1	9.8	15.4	18.7	13.2	21.6	2,093
Boulder, CO	2.9	4.3	17.5	29.8	18.2	10.7	16.5	1,924
Cape Coral, FL	0.8	4.6	24.6	39.7	20.2	6.3	3.7	1,751
Cedar Rapids, IA	7.5	49.3	31.3	8.7	0.9	0.3	2.0	925
Charleston, SC	4.4	7.5	29.8	31.4	16.4	4.4	6.1	1,632
Charlotte, NC	2.7	10.1	36.9	33.9	10.9	3.2	2.3	1,504
Chicago, IL	7.2	17.6	32.2	20.1	11.6	5.4	5.9	1,380
Cincinnati, OH	11.8	43.6	26.9	11.1	3.9	1.5	1.3	953
Clarksville, TN	2.4	26.4	43.4	20.7	6.1	0.8	0.3	1,215
Cleveland, OH	17.2	43.0	26.0	9.4	2.6	0.9	0.8	894
College Station, TX	2.3	31.8	36.6	18.4	6.6	3.1	1.1	1,168
Colorado Springs, CO	2.7	10.7	32.8	30.0	15.9	4.3	3.6	1,562
Columbia, MO	4.0	39.3	38.9	9.8	5.8	1.4	0.8	1,067
Columbia, SC	8.4	26.7	42.3	16.5	5.4	0.5	0.2	1,158
Columbus, OH	4.5	22.1	46.5	19.4	5.3	1.2	0.9	1,224
Dallas, TX	3.1	12.2	42.5	25.9	9.5	3.4	3.4	1,403
Davenport, IA	7.1	52.5	29.5	6.8	1.6	0.1	2.4	930
Denver, CO	5.7	6.3	22.4	28.8	19.9	9.0	7.9	1,770
Des Moines, IA	5.4	39.0	40.2	12.9	2.0	0.2	0.3	1,054
Detroit, MI	11.7	35.1	39.5	10.0	2.5	0.8	0.4	1,034
Durham, NC	4.9	15.5	37.1	29.7	8.9	2.1	1.8	1,412
El Paso, TX	8.8	37.4	37.3	12.4	3.1	0.6	0.5	1,041
Eugene, OR	4.5	22.0	34.3	25.4	8.7	2.5	2.6	1,347
Fargo, ND	4.3	56.5	27.7	8.1	1.6	0.7	1.1	916
Fort Collins, CO	2.5	10.8	26.1	33.0	19.7	6.0	1.9	1,661
Fort Wayne, IN	6.7	48.7	37.3	5.3	1.4	0.4	0.3	959
Fort Worth, TX	2.6	13.5	40.6	25.3	12.3	3.4	2.2	1,412
Gainesville, FL	3.6	27.6	37.8	20.0	7.3	2.2	1.6	1,214
Green Bay, WI	6.7	55.0	31.7	5.1	0.7	0.1	0.6	904
Greensboro, NC	4.8	31.8	45.3	12.5	3.2	0.8	1.5	1,114
Honolulu, HI	5.7	7.6	21.8	26.2	16.6	7.5	14.5	1,783
Houston, TX	2.7	21.1	39.5	23.4	8.1	2.6	2.7	1,313
Huntsville, AL	4.8	38.7	37.7	14.0	2.9	0.5	1.3	1,078
Indianapolis, IN	4.8	32.8	43.9	13.7	3.2	1.0	0.6	1,112
Jacksonville, FL	4.9	16.1	38.9	26.9	9.7	2.3	1.2	1,375
Kansas City, MO	6.7	25.9	41.6	18.6	4.6	1.5	1.2	1,186
Lafayette, LA	6.5	37.0	39.7	13.7	2.6	0.2	0.4	1,065
Las Vegas, NV	3.1	14.4	35.9	29.4	11.7	3.5	1.9	1,456
Lexington, KY	4.4	36.0	40.3	13.9	3.8	1.2	0.5	1,101
Lincoln, NE	4.7	41.3	37.3	12.0	3.0	0.5	1.4	1,045
Little Rock, AR	5.2	38.1	39.8	12.0	2.8	0.8	1.2	1,067
Los Angeles, CA	4.6	7.2	20.1	23.9	18.3	10.6	15.3	1,879
Louisville, KY	9.7	34.0	39.6	12.5	2.8	0.7	0.7	1,069
Madison, WI	3.6	15.5	41.6	26.0	8.2	2.4	2.7	1,364
Manchester, NH	5.5	12.8	34.2	31.7	12.5	1.9	1.3	1,465
McAllen, TX	8.3	40.3	37.2	11.2	2.0	0.9	0.0	1,017

Table continued on following page.

City	Under $500	$500 -$999	$1,000 -$1,499	$1,500 -$1,999	$2,000 -$2,499	$2,500 -$2,999	$3,000 and up	Median ($)
Memphis, TN	4.9	32.5	43.3	15.2	2.8	0.7	0.6	1,123
Miami, FL	8.4	9.2	25.4	22.3	16.1	8.1	10.5	1,657
Midland, TX	3.2	15.5	38.6	24.4	11.7	4.2	2.3	1,407
Milwaukee, WI	7.0	39.6	38.2	10.7	2.4	1.0	1.1	1,033
Minneapolis, MN	8.7	16.4	35.0	22.5	10.8	3.3	3.3	1,329
Nashville, TN	6.2	10.7	34.1	28.4	12.8	4.5	3.3	1,486
New Orleans, LA	10.0	21.7	38.2	19.5	6.2	2.7	1.7	1,211
New York, NY	8.3	10.0	19.2	22.4	16.2	8.5	15.4	1,779
Oklahoma City, OK	5.3	36.3	40.4	13.3	2.8	1.1	0.7	1,083
Omaha, NE	4.4	29.7	43.5	16.1	4.3	0.8	1.3	1,150
Orlando, FL	3.1	6.0	30.0	36.5	17.1	4.7	2.6	1,650
Philadelphia, PA	8.5	18.1	35.8	22.6	8.7	3.1	3.2	1,323
Phoenix, AZ	3.5	13.5	36.2	29.1	12.0	3.7	2.0	1,458
Pittsburgh, PA	10.6	21.9	35.1	18.4	8.3	3.3	2.4	1,221
Portland, OR	4.6	9.6	30.1	29.6	15.0	6.3	4.8	1,596
Providence, RI	16.9	11.3	33.2	22.3	10.5	3.4	2.4	1,333
Provo, UT	5.6	28.6	40.3	16.6	6.4	1.9	0.5	1,152
Raleigh, NC	2.5	9.3	41.1	33.8	8.8	2.7	1.8	1,468
Reno, NV	4.9	15.0	33.3	26.7	13.4	4.0	2.7	1,453
Richmond, VA	9.4	14.9	41.0	24.1	7.9	1.9	0.8	1,314
Rochester, MN	6.3	23.1	32.8	23.3	8.8	1.7	4.0	1,316
Sacramento, CA	4.4	10.1	23.1	31.7	19.4	7.9	3.3	1,694
Saint Louis, MO	9.1	43.5	33.0	9.9	3.0	0.9	0.7	978
Saint Paul, MN	9.5	16.7	41.4	20.1	9.0	1.6	1.7	1,248
Salem, OR	5.6	16.1	43.1	24.0	8.2	1.8	1.2	1,323
Salt Lake City, UT	6.7	16.6	37.5	23.0	10.1	3.7	2.5	1,343
San Antonio, TX	4.8	21.4	43.5	21.8	5.7	1.6	1.2	1,258
San Diego, CA	2.3	3.9	11.3	22.8	21.9	16.0	21.8	2,223
San Francisco, CA	7.8	8.1	11.1	11.9	13.2	10.9	36.9	2,419
San Jose, CA	3.7	4.7	6.6	12.7	18.3	17.6	36.5	2,617
Santa Rosa, CA	4.1	5.1	12.9	24.0	23.2	15.4	15.3	2,084
Savannah, GA	6.6	17.0	41.8	23.1	7.7	1.9	2.0	1,302
Seattle, WA	5.0	4.2	15.6	25.4	21.5	13.0	15.5	1,998
Sioux Falls, SD	4.5	46.5	36.9	8.1	2.4	0.3	1.2	993
Tampa, FL	6.5	11.9	27.9	27.1	14.9	6.8	4.9	1,567
Tucson, AZ	4.5	38.5	36.3	15.0	3.5	0.8	1.3	1,079
Tulsa, OK	7.3	42.9	36.4	9.1	2.1	1.0	1.2	998
Virginia Beach, VA	1.9	5.3	31.3	38.7	14.9	3.9	4.0	1,649
Washington, DC	7.4	7.8	17.8	21.2	16.8	11.4	17.6	1,900
Wichita, KS	4.8	50.2	34.2	7.8	2.1	0.3	0.7	960
Wilmington, NC	6.3	17.3	40.7	25.1	7.1	1.9	1.5	1,311
Winston-Salem, NC	6.7	40.1	36.5	11.4	3.5	0.8	1.0	1,033
U.S.	6.5	22.3	29.5	20.2	10.8	4.8	5.9	1,348

Note: Figures are percentages except for Median; Gross rent is the contract rent plus the estimated average monthly cost of utilities (electricity, gas, and water and sewer) and fuels (oil, coal, kerosene, wood, etc.) if these are paid by the renter (or paid for the renter by someone else).
Source: U.S. Census Bureau, 2019-2023 American Community Survey 5-Year Estimates

Gross Monthly Rent: Metro Area

Metro Area	Under $500	$500 -$999	$1,000 -$1,499	$1,500 -$1,999	$2,000 -$2,499	$2,500 -2,999	$3,000 and up	Median ($)
Albuquerque, NM	5.5	36.2	35.3	16.7	4.3	0.9	1.1	1,102
Anchorage, AK	3.9	15.2	36.0	25.1	12.2	4.8	2.7	1,422
Ann Arbor, MI	4.3	14.9	39.0	23.1	10.3	3.5	4.7	1,400
Athens, GA	4.0	34.6	36.7	16.4	4.9	2.0	1.4	1,144
Atlanta, GA	3.5	10.4	31.9	33.0	14.4	4.1	2.7	1,563
Austin, TX	2.2	6.5	32.0	32.0	16.4	6.3	4.6	1,646
Baltimore, MD	6.9	10.5	29.1	28.1	15.8	5.6	3.9	1,562
Billings, MT	8.5	35.8	36.1	14.7	2.8	0.7	1.4	1,072
Boise City, ID	4.7	16.9	37.0	26.4	10.2	2.7	2.2	1,383
Boston, MA	9.4	8.3	13.6	21.1	19.8	12.2	15.5	1,940
Boulder, CO	3.0	4.7	17.7	31.3	20.8	10.0	12.5	1,893
Cape Coral, FL	2.9	8.6	31.7	34.5	14.0	4.2	4.1	1,597
Cedar Rapids, IA	7.8	50.9	29.5	8.0	1.3	0.3	2.2	899
Charleston, SC	3.1	11.1	36.7	27.9	13.4	4.0	3.8	1,488
Charlotte, NC	3.8	18.7	36.7	27.1	9.1	2.5	2.0	1,377
Chicago, IL	5.8	16.7	35.4	21.8	11.0	4.6	4.6	1,378
Cincinnati, OH	8.2	37.8	34.1	12.7	4.4	1.5	1.4	1,047
Clarksville, TN	4.4	33.0	39.4	17.7	4.4	0.6	0.5	1,141
Cleveland, OH	9.8	40.6	34.0	10.8	2.6	0.9	1.3	996
College Station, TX	4.0	32.0	38.0	16.6	5.7	2.2	1.4	1,146
Colorado Springs, CO	2.7	10.6	30.1	29.6	18.6	5.0	3.4	1,611
Columbia, MO	4.7	41.2	38.4	9.2	4.6	1.1	0.8	1,041
Columbia, SC	5.2	31.0	41.5	15.6	5.0	0.9	0.9	1,145
Columbus, OH	5.1	24.3	43.9	18.5	5.5	1.4	1.2	1,208
Dallas, TX	2.1	9.7	37.7	28.7	13.8	4.7	3.3	1,509
Davenport, IA	11.1	50.2	27.2	7.3	1.5	0.8	1.9	899
Denver, CO	3.6	5.3	21.2	32.6	21.1	9.5	6.7	1,805
Des Moines, IA	4.6	33.5	42.0	15.1	3.4	0.5	0.9	1,113
Detroit, MI	7.5	26.8	41.4	16.4	4.7	1.3	1.8	1,162
Durham, NC	5.0	18.6	36.6	26.5	8.7	2.4	2.3	1,374
El Paso, TX	8.7	37.2	37.0	13.0	3.1	0.5	0.4	1,045
Eugene, OR	5.4	23.6	36.5	23.0	7.6	1.9	1.9	1,287
Fargo, ND	4.7	52.7	29.3	9.2	2.5	0.8	0.9	940
Fort Collins, CO	2.6	10.0	25.7	33.1	18.9	6.6	3.1	1,677
Fort Wayne, IN	6.6	48.2	36.5	6.1	1.7	0.5	0.4	963
Fort Worth, TX	2.1	9.7	37.7	28.7	13.8	4.7	3.3	1,509
Gainesville, FL	3.9	27.5	36.4	20.0	7.2	2.6	2.3	1,219
Green Bay, WI	4.8	50.7	35.3	6.6	1.4	0.4	0.8	959
Greensboro, NC	7.6	37.7	39.7	10.5	2.6	0.7	1.2	1,045
Honolulu, HI	4.7	6.3	16.7	20.6	15.8	11.3	24.6	2,054
Houston, TX	2.6	17.5	39.1	24.9	10.1	3.2	2.6	1,378
Huntsville, AL	4.8	37.6	36.8	14.6	4.3	0.6	1.2	1,091
Indianapolis, IN	4.8	30.7	41.9	15.6	4.7	1.4	0.9	1,142
Jacksonville, FL	4.3	15.8	36.2	27.0	11.0	2.9	2.7	1,416
Kansas City, MO	5.4	25.3	41.7	18.9	5.6	1.4	1.6	1,201
Lafayette, LA	11.3	44.1	33.2	9.1	1.7	0.3	0.2	954
Las Vegas, NV	1.8	12.2	34.8	31.6	13.6	3.7	2.2	1,518
Lexington, KY	5.5	38.0	38.7	13.0	3.1	1.1	0.5	1,070
Lincoln, NE	4.8	41.4	37.2	11.8	2.9	0.5	1.4	1,043
Little Rock, AR	6.2	43.2	37.0	10.4	1.7	0.6	0.9	1,007
Los Angeles, CA	3.5	5.8	16.8	24.5	21.1	12.0	16.3	1,987
Louisville, KY	9.1	34.6	40.1	12.2	2.6	0.7	0.8	1,064
Madison, WI	3.9	19.6	41.6	23.8	6.9	1.9	2.2	1,300
Manchester, NH	5.5	11.2	31.2	31.7	14.5	3.8	2.0	1,532
McAllen, TX	11.1	48.5	30.9	7.4	1.4	0.5	0.2	925

Table continued on following page.

Metro Area	Under $500	$500 -$999	$1,000 -$1,499	$1,500 -$1,999	$2,000 -$2,499	$2,500 -2,999	$3,000 and up	Median ($)
Memphis, TN	4.9	30.4	42.2	16.0	4.3	1.2	1.0	1,153
Miami, FL	3.9	6.5	23.2	30.3	19.3	8.6	8.2	1,770
Midland, TX	3.7	17.8	38.4	23.7	10.7	3.8	2.0	1,377
Milwaukee, WI	6.0	33.5	39.6	14.3	3.8	1.5	1.3	1,105
Minneapolis, MN	6.6	14.0	36.6	25.6	10.8	3.3	3.2	1,396
Nashville, TN	5.4	15.0	34.3	27.1	11.6	3.7	2.8	1,434
New Orleans, LA	7.3	24.9	41.7	18.2	5.0	1.7	1.1	1,182
New York, NY	7.3	9.0	20.0	24.4	16.9	8.6	13.8	1,780
Oklahoma City, OK	5.3	36.8	39.1	13.4	3.1	1.1	1.1	1,081
Omaha, NE	5.0	29.1	42.6	16.6	4.3	0.9	1.5	1,152
Orlando, FL	2.1	8.2	28.7	34.6	18.0	5.3	3.0	1,659
Philadelphia, PA	6.4	14.6	35.3	25.2	11.2	3.7	3.7	1,413
Phoenix, AZ	2.7	10.8	31.5	30.9	15.3	5.2	3.5	1,581
Pittsburgh, PA	11.8	37.3	32.0	11.5	4.4	1.5	1.6	1,011
Portland, OR	3.4	7.7	28.4	33.9	16.2	6.3	4.1	1,654
Providence, RI	12.9	18.9	35.1	20.9	7.8	2.5	1.9	1,236
Provo, UT	3.1	16.5	34.5	27.9	12.6	3.7	1.8	1,434
Raleigh, NC	3.4	13.4	36.5	31.2	10.0	3.4	2.1	1,459
Reno, NV	4.2	14.7	31.6	27.3	14.8	4.0	3.4	1,491
Richmond, VA	5.5	14.0	39.6	27.9	9.1	1.8	2.0	1,388
Rochester, MN	7.9	29.2	31.6	19.9	7.1	1.3	3.0	1,195
Sacramento, CA	3.6	8.3	24.6	29.4	19.8	8.6	5.7	1,729
Saint Louis, MO	6.4	36.8	37.9	12.7	3.4	1.2	1.8	1,073
Saint Paul, MN	6.6	14.0	36.6	25.6	10.8	3.3	3.2	1,396
Salem, OR	4.9	16.5	43.8	24.6	7.3	1.8	1.1	1,324
Salt Lake City, UT	3.9	11.4	35.8	29.9	13.2	3.6	2.2	1,486
San Antonio, TX	4.4	19.8	41.8	22.8	7.7	2.0	1.4	1,299
San Diego, CA	2.2	4.0	12.0	24.8	22.5	14.8	19.6	2,154
San Francisco, CA	5.1	5.6	9.5	14.1	18.4	15.0	32.3	2,426
San Jose, CA	2.7	3.7	5.4	10.8	16.8	17.8	42.7	2,794
Santa Rosa, CA	4.1	6.8	13.4	21.5	22.3	14.4	17.4	2,093
Savannah, GA	4.2	17.2	38.3	28.2	8.4	1.9	1.8	1,370
Seattle, WA	4.0	4.8	16.7	28.3	22.6	11.5	12.2	1,932
Sioux Falls, SD	5.6	46.3	36.0	8.1	2.6	0.3	1.1	987
Tampa, FL	3.2	13.0	34.1	27.7	13.7	4.8	3.5	1,497
Tucson, AZ	4.3	32.8	35.8	18.7	4.9	1.4	2.1	1,154
Tulsa, OK	7.1	39.7	37.8	10.4	2.9	1.0	1.1	1,034
Virginia Beach, VA	5.0	13.8	37.7	28.0	10.3	2.6	2.7	1,416
Washington, DC	3.7	4.7	14.3	28.7	23.5	12.3	12.9	1,975
Wichita, KS	5.7	48.1	34.1	8.5	2.5	0.5	0.6	969
Wilmington, NC	5.1	19.5	40.4	23.1	7.7	2.0	2.3	1,313
Winston-Salem, NC	7.6	45.5	32.7	10.3	2.5	0.7	0.6	973
U.S.	6.5	22.3	29.5	20.2	10.8	4.8	5.9	1,348

Note: Figures are percentages except for Median; Gross rent is the contract rent plus the estimated average monthly cost of utilities (electricity, gas, and water and sewer) and fuels (oil, coal, kerosene, wood, etc.) if these are paid by the renter (or paid for the renter by someone else); Figures cover the Metropolitan Statistical Area (MSA)
Source: U.S. Census Bureau, 2019-2023 American Community Survey 5-Year Estimates

Highest Level of Education: City

City	Less than H.S.	H.S. Diploma	Some College, No Deg.	Associate Degree	Bachelors Degree	Masters Degree	Profess. School Degree	Doctorate Degree
Albuquerque, NM	9.1	21.6	21.2	9.5	20.9	12.0	2.8	2.9
Anchorage, AK	6.0	24.5	23.2	8.6	23.4	9.9	2.7	1.7
Ann Arbor, MI	2.4	7.0	8.9	4.0	30.5	26.4	8.7	12.1
Athens, GA	10.1	17.7	16.5	7.0	24.3	15.3	2.9	6.2
Atlanta, GA	7.0	16.0	13.6	5.0	32.8	16.8	5.7	3.0
Austin, TX	8.4	13.2	14.8	5.4	36.2	15.9	3.6	2.5
Baltimore, MD	12.8	27.9	18.4	5.5	18.1	11.7	3.1	2.5
Billings, MT	4.5	27.6	22.5	8.3	25.0	7.7	2.6	1.7
Boise City, ID	5.2	19.3	21.5	7.3	29.2	12.0	3.1	2.2
Boston, MA	11.1	18.3	11.6	4.9	28.5	16.4	5.2	3.9
Boulder, CO	3.1	6.4	10.2	3.5	36.9	25.7	5.1	9.1
Cape Coral, FL	6.8	35.3	22.6	9.5	16.7	6.0	1.7	1.3
Cedar Rapids, IA	5.9	25.9	22.4	12.9	22.2	7.8	2.1	0.8
Charleston, SC	4.1	15.4	16.0	6.8	35.5	13.8	5.2	3.2
Charlotte, NC	10.4	16.6	17.5	8.0	30.4	12.8	2.9	1.3
Chicago, IL	13.2	21.3	16.4	5.8	24.9	12.8	3.6	2.0
Cincinnati, OH	10.3	24.1	17.0	7.3	23.2	11.7	3.8	2.5
Clarksville, TN	5.8	27.4	24.2	12.0	18.9	9.4	1.2	1.1
Cleveland, OH	16.5	33.5	21.6	7.1	12.5	5.8	2.2	0.9
College Station, TX	5.4	14.4	16.9	6.2	29.5	16.1	2.0	9.5
Colorado Springs, CO	5.4	19.2	23.0	10.6	25.2	12.8	2.1	1.9
Columbia, MO	4.7	16.9	15.7	6.2	30.1	15.7	4.8	5.9
Columbia, SC	9.1	19.2	18.2	7.4	25.2	12.7	5.0	3.1
Columbus, OH	10.2	25.2	19.2	7.2	24.1	10.2	2.1	1.8
Dallas, TX	19.2	21.5	16.7	5.1	22.9	9.7	3.4	1.4
Davenport, IA	7.4	28.8	22.1	11.7	18.9	8.2	1.8	1.1
Denver, CO	8.6	14.8	15.7	5.3	33.8	15.0	4.7	2.2
Des Moines, IA	12.7	29.1	20.0	9.1	19.9	6.3	1.8	0.9
Detroit, MI	16.6	33.2	25.4	7.2	10.5	5.4	1.0	0.7
Durham, NC	8.6	15.4	13.7	6.6	28.8	16.9	4.5	5.5
El Paso, TX	18.1	24.4	21.3	8.8	18.3	6.7	1.4	1.0
Eugene, OR	5.2	17.4	24.3	8.8	23.7	13.5	3.6	3.5
Fargo, ND	4.7	18.7	20.7	12.7	29.0	9.9	2.0	2.3
Fort Collins, CO	2.4	13.5	16.1	8.2	34.3	18.9	2.8	3.9
Fort Wayne, IN	11.1	28.7	21.8	9.9	19.4	7.2	1.1	0.9
Fort Worth, TX	15.7	24.7	20.5	7.4	20.6	8.4	1.6	1.1
Gainesville, FL	5.7	17.7	14.9	10.0	25.7	15.1	4.2	6.8
Green Bay, WI	11.0	31.4	20.4	11.7	18.4	5.3	1.2	0.7
Greensboro, NC	9.9	21.5	20.1	8.7	24.2	11.3	2.3	2.1
Honolulu, HI	9.1	22.8	17.2	10.1	25.2	9.9	3.4	2.2
Houston, TX	19.7	21.5	16.6	6.2	21.3	9.6	3.2	1.9
Huntsville, AL	8.4	17.3	20.8	7.3	26.7	14.8	2.3	2.3
Indianapolis, IN	12.5	26.8	18.9	7.7	21.7	8.8	2.3	1.4
Jacksonville, FL	9.2	28.2	20.7	10.0	21.6	7.4	1.7	1.1
Kansas City, MO	8.2	25.0	21.6	7.4	23.8	10.1	2.7	1.2
Lafayette, LA	9.1	25.3	18.9	6.0	27.1	7.7	4.0	1.9
Las Vegas, NV	14.2	26.7	23.7	8.1	17.3	6.9	2.1	1.0
Lexington, KY	7.6	19.0	18.5	7.6	26.5	12.9	4.3	3.6
Lincoln, NE	7.0	20.4	20.3	11.4	26.4	9.8	2.3	2.5
Little Rock, AR	7.7	21.2	20.7	6.5	25.0	11.7	4.7	2.6
Los Angeles, CA	20.7	18.5	16.6	6.3	24.5	8.7	3.1	1.6
Louisville, KY	9.5	27.7	21.0	8.4	19.9	9.6	2.4	1.5
Madison, WI	4.3	14.6	14.4	7.5	33.5	16.0	3.7	6.0
Manchester, NH	11.3	29.1	18.1	8.0	22.5	8.8	1.3	0.9
McAllen, TX	20.1	20.7	20.6	6.5	20.3	7.6	2.9	1.2

Table continued on following page.

City	Less than H.S.	H.S. Diploma	Some College, No Deg.	Associate Degree	Bachelors Degree	Masters Degree	Profess. School Degree	Doctorate Degree
Memphis, TN	12.6	30.6	22.5	6.1	16.9	7.9	2.0	1.4
Miami, FL	20.0	25.2	11.6	7.5	21.5	8.8	4.1	1.3
Midland, TX	13.5	22.5	22.4	8.0	23.9	7.4	1.4	1.0
Milwaukee, WI	14.5	30.8	20.9	7.3	17.2	7.0	1.4	1.0
Minneapolis, MN	8.9	13.8	15.7	7.2	32.7	14.8	4.1	2.9
Nashville, TN	9.8	20.2	17.0	6.0	29.1	11.7	3.4	2.7
New Orleans, LA	10.9	21.3	20.7	5.2	22.5	12.0	4.8	2.6
New York, NY	16.3	23.0	13.2	6.5	23.6	12.4	3.3	1.7
Oklahoma City, OK	12.2	24.5	21.3	8.0	21.5	8.5	2.6	1.3
Omaha, NE	9.5	21.3	21.3	7.7	25.6	9.7	3.2	1.8
Orlando, FL	8.1	23.1	15.7	10.9	26.1	11.2	3.2	1.8
Philadelphia, PA	12.6	29.8	16.4	6.5	19.4	10.2	3.0	2.1
Phoenix, AZ	15.6	23.1	21.1	7.9	19.9	8.9	2.3	1.3
Pittsburgh, PA	5.7	23.7	14.7	8.0	24.6	14.1	4.5	4.6
Portland, OR	6.7	14.7	18.5	6.7	32.1	14.2	4.5	2.7
Providence, RI	18.1	27.5	14.8	4.9	18.3	9.7	3.5	3.3
Provo, UT	7.5	14.4	24.4	8.7	31.1	9.5	1.7	2.6
Raleigh, NC	7.5	15.9	16.2	7.4	32.5	14.3	3.5	2.6
Reno, NV	10.7	22.8	22.6	8.3	21.4	9.4	2.8	2.2
Richmond, VA	10.7	21.2	18.8	5.3	26.0	12.3	3.5	2.2
Rochester, MN	5.5	18.9	14.9	10.6	27.7	13.2	5.2	3.9
Sacramento, CA	13.1	20.5	21.6	8.4	22.9	8.7	3.3	1.6
Saint Louis, MO	9.5	24.5	19.7	6.1	22.0	12.1	3.4	2.7
Saint Paul, MN	11.1	20.8	16.9	7.7	25.2	12.3	3.3	2.8
Salem, OR	11.3	22.4	25.4	9.3	19.3	8.6	2.1	1.5
Salt Lake City, UT	8.4	17.1	16.9	6.7	28.9	13.6	4.7	3.7
San Antonio, TX	15.7	25.6	21.8	8.2	17.7	7.7	2.1	1.3
San Diego, CA	9.8	15.0	17.8	7.5	28.8	13.6	3.6	3.8
San Francisco, CA	11.2	11.3	12.0	5.3	35.1	16.7	4.9	3.4
San Jose, CA	14.5	16.4	15.5	7.1	26.2	15.1	2.1	3.1
Santa Rosa, CA	14.5	19.2	21.9	9.7	21.3	9.0	3.2	1.2
Savannah, GA	10.1	27.0	23.7	7.2	20.6	8.1	2.0	1.3
Seattle, WA	4.3	9.5	12.9	5.8	37.6	20.5	5.3	4.2
Sioux Falls, SD	6.9	24.3	20.1	11.2	25.4	8.2	2.5	1.3
Tampa, FL	10.2	22.5	14.7	8.0	26.3	11.7	4.4	2.2
Tucson, AZ	12.7	23.0	25.2	9.0	17.7	9.0	1.6	1.9
Tulsa, OK	12.4	25.0	21.2	8.2	20.8	8.0	3.0	1.5
Virginia Beach, VA	5.3	21.3	22.4	10.5	25.0	11.4	2.3	1.8
Washington, DC	7.2	14.5	11.8	2.9	26.1	22.7	10.3	4.6
Wichita, KS	12.0	26.0	23.0	8.1	19.7	8.5	1.6	1.1
Wilmington, NC	6.5	18.0	18.9	10.8	29.2	11.1	3.3	2.3
Winston-Salem, NC	11.6	23.7	19.5	7.9	21.6	10.2	2.8	2.6
U.S.	10.6	26.2	19.4	8.8	21.3	9.8	2.3	1.6

Note: Figures cover persons age 25 and over
Source: U.S. Census Bureau, 2019-2023 American Community Survey 5-Year Estimates

Highest Level of Education: Metro Area

Metro Area	Less than H.S.	H.S. Diploma	Some College, No Deg.	Associate Degree	Bachelors Degree	Masters Degree	Profess. School Degree	Doctorate Degree
Albuquerque, NM	9.7	23.6	22.0	9.7	19.2	11.0	2.4	2.5
Anchorage, AK	5.9	27.1	23.6	9.4	21.3	9.0	2.3	1.4
Ann Arbor, MI	4.2	14.2	16.8	6.7	27.1	19.4	5.1	6.5
Athens, GA	10.2	21.4	17.5	7.5	21.9	13.4	3.3	4.9
Atlanta, GA	9.2	23.0	18.4	7.9	25.4	11.7	2.6	1.8
Austin, TX	8.4	17.1	18.0	6.6	31.6	13.6	2.7	2.1
Baltimore, MD	7.9	23.6	18.2	7.0	23.4	14.4	3.1	2.5
Billings, MT	4.8	30.1	22.7	9.0	22.8	7.0	2.2	1.5
Boise City, ID	7.5	23.3	24.0	8.6	24.3	8.8	2.1	1.4
Boston, MA	7.7	20.8	13.3	7.0	27.5	16.4	3.6	3.7
Boulder, CO	4.5	11.0	14.5	6.1	34.5	20.0	3.8	5.6
Cape Coral, FL	9.6	30.0	19.8	9.8	18.8	8.2	2.3	1.4
Cedar Rapids, IA	4.8	27.8	20.7	13.9	22.2	8.0	1.7	0.9
Charleston, SC	8.1	22.9	19.8	9.3	24.9	10.7	2.8	1.6
Charlotte, NC	9.6	22.6	19.4	9.5	25.4	10.4	2.1	1.1
Chicago, IL	10.3	23.2	18.4	7.3	24.4	12.1	2.8	1.6
Cincinnati, OH	7.7	28.8	18.0	8.6	22.7	10.4	2.2	1.6
Clarksville, TN	7.7	29.5	23.6	11.2	17.4	8.2	1.3	1.1
Cleveland, OH	8.3	29.0	20.4	8.8	20.0	9.6	2.5	1.4
College Station, TX	11.7	23.8	18.7	6.8	22.2	10.2	1.7	5.0
Colorado Springs, CO	4.9	19.7	23.4	11.0	24.9	12.6	1.8	1.7
Columbia, MO	6.0	22.6	16.6	7.3	26.7	13.0	3.5	4.2
Columbia, SC	8.9	25.3	21.2	9.6	20.8	10.2	2.2	1.8
Columbus, OH	7.9	26.7	18.4	7.5	24.4	10.8	2.5	1.7
Dallas, TX	12.7	21.7	19.7	7.4	24.5	10.7	2.0	1.3
Davenport, IA	7.6	29.3	22.7	11.1	18.6	8.2	1.5	1.1
Denver, CO	7.7	18.4	18.2	7.3	30.3	13.3	2.9	1.9
Des Moines, IA	6.5	25.0	19.0	10.4	26.4	9.0	2.1	1.5
Detroit, MI	8.8	26.0	22.0	9.2	20.4	10.3	2.2	1.1
Durham, NC	8.9	17.0	14.3	7.5	26.3	15.5	4.8	5.6
El Paso, TX	19.4	24.9	21.1	9.2	17.1	6.1	1.2	0.9
Eugene, OR	6.9	22.8	27.0	9.9	19.7	9.4	2.3	2.1
Fargo, ND	4.4	19.1	20.8	13.5	28.4	9.7	1.9	2.3
Fort Collins, CO	3.4	16.8	19.3	8.8	31.0	14.9	2.7	3.1
Fort Wayne, IN	9.3	29.7	20.7	10.6	20.0	7.3	1.5	0.9
Fort Worth, TX	12.7	21.7	19.7	7.4	24.5	10.7	2.0	1.3
Gainesville, FL	7.3	24.2	16.4	11.1	20.3	11.8	4.0	4.8
Green Bay, WI	6.7	31.3	19.1	13.0	21.0	6.8	1.3	0.8
Greensboro, NC	11.7	26.5	20.8	9.6	20.0	8.5	1.5	1.4
Honolulu, HI	7.1	25.2	19.0	11.0	23.7	9.4	2.8	1.8
Houston, TX	14.9	22.7	19.5	7.5	22.1	9.3	2.3	1.7
Huntsville, AL	8.5	20.7	20.4	8.0	25.3	13.5	1.7	1.9
Indianapolis, IN	8.9	26.7	18.4	8.1	24.1	9.9	2.4	1.5
Jacksonville, FL	7.9	26.4	20.5	10.0	23.0	8.9	2.0	1.3
Kansas City, MO	6.9	24.9	21.1	7.9	24.4	11.0	2.5	1.3
Lafayette, LA	13.0	34.8	17.9	7.3	19.0	5.3	1.8	0.9
Las Vegas, NV	13.2	27.6	23.4	8.5	18.0	6.6	1.7	1.0
Lexington, KY	8.1	23.5	19.2	8.1	23.4	11.4	3.5	2.8
Lincoln, NE	6.4	20.9	20.1	11.9	26.2	9.8	2.1	2.4
Little Rock, AR	7.9	29.1	21.7	8.4	20.3	8.8	2.4	1.4
Los Angeles, CA	17.8	19.5	18.1	7.1	23.9	9.2	2.8	1.6
Louisville, KY	8.7	29.4	20.8	8.9	19.5	9.2	2.2	1.3
Madison, WI	4.1	20.2	16.6	9.7	29.9	12.7	2.9	3.8
Manchester, NH	7.0	25.6	17.2	9.6	25.4	12.1	1.6	1.5
McAllen, TX	30.7	25.2	18.3	5.6	13.9	4.8	1.0	0.6

Table continued on following page.

Metro Area	Less than H.S.	H.S. Diploma	Some College, No Deg.	Associate Degree	Bachelors Degree	Masters Degree	Profess. School Degree	Doctorate Degree
Memphis, TN	10.5	29.1	22.1	7.6	18.5	8.9	2.0	1.4
Miami, FL	13.1	25.7	16.0	9.5	21.8	9.0	3.4	1.4
Midland, TX	13.8	24.0	23.3	8.2	20.9	7.4	1.4	0.8
Milwaukee, WI	7.3	25.6	19.3	9.0	25.2	9.8	2.2	1.5
Minneapolis, MN	5.8	20.2	18.7	10.5	29.1	11.3	2.7	1.9
Nashville, TN	8.5	25.7	18.7	7.3	25.6	10.0	2.4	1.9
New Orleans, LA	12.5	26.2	21.5	6.7	19.6	8.7	3.1	1.6
New York, NY	12.4	23.2	14.0	6.8	24.9	13.3	3.5	1.8
Oklahoma City, OK	10.1	26.2	22.3	8.0	21.3	8.4	2.2	1.5
Omaha, NE	7.3	22.5	21.7	9.4	24.9	10.2	2.5	1.5
Orlando, FL	9.3	25.1	18.5	11.2	23.2	9.2	2.1	1.3
Philadelphia, PA	7.9	27.0	16.1	7.5	24.1	12.2	3.0	2.2
Phoenix, AZ	10.5	22.7	23.0	9.2	21.6	9.4	2.1	1.4
Pittsburgh, PA	5.1	31.4	15.5	10.6	22.6	10.6	2.3	1.9
Portland, OR	7.2	19.8	22.1	8.8	26.0	11.1	2.8	2.1
Providence, RI	11.6	27.8	17.2	8.4	21.3	9.9	2.1	1.7
Provo, UT	4.7	17.1	24.8	10.1	30.1	9.9	1.7	1.6
Raleigh, NC	7.1	17.3	16.6	8.8	30.8	14.4	2.6	2.4
Reno, NV	11.4	24.4	24.0	8.8	19.2	8.4	2.2	1.6
Richmond, VA	8.1	24.4	19.5	7.8	24.4	11.7	2.5	1.7
Rochester, MN	5.2	23.0	17.1	12.5	24.7	10.8	4.1	2.7
Sacramento, CA	9.9	20.6	23.3	9.9	23.0	8.7	3.0	1.6
Saint Louis, MO	6.7	25.5	21.0	9.3	22.3	11.2	2.3	1.7
Saint Paul, MN	5.8	20.2	18.7	10.5	29.1	11.3	2.7	1.9
Salem, OR	12.8	24.9	25.6	9.8	17.4	6.9	1.6	1.0
Salt Lake City, UT	8.2	22.7	22.1	9.2	24.1	9.7	2.3	1.7
San Antonio, TX	12.7	25.0	21.8	8.6	20.0	8.7	1.9	1.3
San Diego, CA	11.0	17.9	20.6	8.3	25.6	11.0	2.9	2.6
San Francisco, CA	10.5	15.0	15.5	6.6	30.0	15.1	3.9	3.4
San Jose, CA	10.9	13.9	13.9	6.5	27.8	19.3	2.9	4.8
Santa Rosa, CA	11.1	18.6	23.0	9.4	23.5	9.4	3.4	1.5
Savannah, GA	8.7	25.9	22.4	8.0	21.6	9.6	2.3	1.5
Seattle, WA	6.7	18.8	19.2	9.1	27.8	13.5	2.8	2.2
Sioux Falls, SD	6.3	25.7	19.7	12.6	24.8	7.7	2.0	1.2
Tampa, FL	9.1	27.4	19.4	10.0	21.5	8.9	2.2	1.3
Tucson, AZ	10.1	21.2	23.9	9.0	20.4	10.7	2.4	2.4
Tulsa, OK	9.9	28.6	22.4	9.4	19.7	7.0	1.9	1.1
Virginia Beach, VA	7.2	25.1	22.8	9.8	21.2	10.4	1.9	1.6
Washington, DC	8.5	17.3	14.6	5.8	27.0	18.7	4.7	3.4
Wichita, KS	9.7	26.4	23.4	9.0	20.2	8.8	1.5	1.0
Wilmington, NC	6.9	22.3	20.8	11.4	24.9	9.7	2.5	1.4
Winston-Salem, NC	10.8	28.4	21.4	9.8	18.9	7.3	1.9	1.5
U.S.	10.6	26.2	19.4	8.8	21.3	9.8	2.3	1.6

Note: Figures cover persons age 25 and over; Figures cover the Metropolitan Statistical Area (MSA)
Source: U.S. Census Bureau, 2019-2023 American Community Survey 5-Year Estimates

School Enrollment by Grade and Control: City

City	Preschool (%)		Kindergarten (%)		Grades 1 - 4 (%)		Grades 5 - 8 (%)		Grades 9 - 12 (%)	
	Public	Private	Public	Private	Public	Private	Public	Private	Public	Private
Albuquerque, NM	51.7	48.3	85.1	14.9	87.2	12.8	89.7	10.3	91.4	8.6
Anchorage, AK	53.5	46.5	89.2	10.8	84.1	15.9	87.8	12.2	91.8	8.2
Ann Arbor, MI	44.3	55.7	86.7	13.3	89.6	10.4	87.0	13.0	91.2	8.8
Athens, GA	65.1	34.9	95.8	4.2	88.4	11.6	86.4	13.6	89.2	10.8
Atlanta, GA	44.5	55.5	67.2	32.8	82.9	17.1	77.0	23.0	78.1	21.9
Austin, TX	51.1	48.9	85.1	14.9	87.7	12.3	86.7	13.3	90.3	9.7
Baltimore, MD	65.6	34.4	85.0	15.0	83.9	16.1	85.1	14.9	85.3	14.7
Billings, MT	39.2	60.8	80.1	19.9	84.7	15.3	84.3	15.7	86.1	13.9
Boise City, ID	34.8	65.2	80.0	20.0	85.7	14.3	89.3	10.7	86.4	13.6
Boston, MA	46.4	53.6	83.7	16.3	86.5	13.5	85.2	14.8	85.4	14.6
Boulder, CO	43.0	57.0	93.0	7.0	86.9	13.1	92.7	7.3	90.7	9.3
Cape Coral, FL	65.1	34.9	94.7	5.3	84.1	15.9	91.1	8.9	88.5	11.5
Cedar Rapids, IA	73.1	26.9	85.9	14.1	88.2	11.8	87.2	12.8	86.4	13.6
Charleston, SC	55.1	44.9	79.8	20.2	86.0	14.0	85.5	14.5	80.9	19.1
Charlotte, NC	50.8	49.2	86.8	13.2	88.6	11.4	87.4	12.6	88.8	11.2
Chicago, IL	56.4	43.6	81.6	18.4	82.8	17.2	83.6	16.4	85.2	14.8
Cincinnati, OH	60.9	39.1	77.2	22.8	78.5	21.5	78.9	21.1	81.8	18.2
Clarksville, TN	65.2	34.8	88.2	11.8	93.2	6.8	91.6	8.4	88.3	11.7
Cleveland, OH	68.9	31.1	68.7	31.3	78.2	21.8	77.9	22.1	77.6	22.4
College Station, TX	57.7	42.3	82.6	17.4	90.0	10.0	87.4	12.6	86.2	13.8
Colorado Springs, CO	64.6	35.4	88.0	12.0	87.3	12.7	88.4	11.6	90.7	9.3
Columbia, MO	49.7	50.3	85.6	14.4	87.0	13.0	89.5	10.5	91.0	9.0
Columbia, SC	33.0	67.0	81.8	18.2	76.7	23.3	85.6	14.4	84.0	16.0
Columbus, OH	64.5	35.5	79.2	20.8	84.3	15.7	85.7	14.3	87.2	12.8
Dallas, TX	69.0	31.0	88.5	11.5	89.5	10.5	91.1	8.9	89.8	10.2
Davenport, IA	52.6	47.4	86.2	13.8	79.3	20.7	86.4	13.6	92.5	7.5
Denver, CO	56.0	44.0	85.1	14.9	89.4	10.6	88.2	11.8	92.7	7.3
Des Moines, IA	76.4	23.6	88.0	12.0	90.8	9.2	91.8	8.2	93.8	6.2
Detroit, MI	81.6	18.4	91.8	8.2	93.4	6.6	92.1	7.9	92.4	7.6
Durham, NC	51.3	48.7	86.2	13.8	86.0	14.0	85.2	14.8	87.8	12.2
El Paso, TX	87.0	13.0	91.9	8.1	92.8	7.2	94.1	5.9	95.7	4.3
Eugene, OR	52.8	47.2	85.1	14.9	88.6	11.4	89.0	11.0	93.6	6.4
Fargo, ND	46.4	53.6	89.8	10.2	91.9	8.1	92.1	7.9	94.3	5.7
Fort Collins, CO	48.1	51.9	87.7	12.3	89.2	10.8	92.4	7.6	94.5	5.5
Fort Wayne, IN	45.6	54.4	70.8	29.2	78.5	21.5	82.0	18.0	79.2	20.8
Fort Worth, TX	61.4	38.6	86.8	13.2	90.9	9.1	91.0	9.0	91.3	8.7
Gainesville, FL	61.4	38.6	70.4	29.6	82.4	17.6	88.7	11.3	92.3	7.7
Green Bay, WI	71.0	29.0	86.2	13.8	87.3	12.7	89.8	10.2	90.4	9.6
Greensboro, NC	56.8	43.2	89.0	11.0	88.9	11.1	89.3	10.7	88.6	11.4
Honolulu, HI	36.4	63.6	74.0	26.0	79.9	20.1	76.4	23.6	69.1	30.9
Houston, TX	65.2	34.8	87.6	12.4	91.1	8.9	91.5	8.5	91.7	8.3
Huntsville, AL	63.7	36.3	80.9	19.1	81.8	18.2	78.2	21.8	84.2	15.8
Indianapolis, IN	61.1	38.9	85.4	14.6	82.9	17.1	83.7	16.3	85.2	14.8
Jacksonville, FL	56.5	43.5	83.5	16.5	83.4	16.6	80.0	20.0	83.7	16.3
Kansas City, MO	61.2	38.8	86.8	13.2	85.4	14.6	87.0	13.0	83.4	16.6
Lafayette, LA	55.1	44.9	71.4	28.6	76.8	23.2	72.2	27.8	78.4	21.6
Las Vegas, NV	68.6	31.4	91.1	8.9	87.6	12.4	89.3	10.7	91.2	8.8
Lexington, KY	29.5	70.5	81.0	19.0	82.3	17.7	85.7	14.3	85.4	14.6
Lincoln, NE	53.4	46.6	79.0	21.0	82.6	17.4	84.2	15.8	90.3	9.7
Little Rock, AR	66.2	33.8	86.5	13.5	78.2	21.8	76.0	24.0	77.5	22.5
Los Angeles, CA	55.2	44.8	85.7	14.3	87.7	12.3	87.5	12.5	88.0	12.0
Louisville, KY	50.3	49.7	77.2	22.8	81.9	18.1	81.0	19.0	78.2	21.8
Madison, WI	47.1	52.9	87.9	12.1	88.1	11.9	89.4	10.6	89.8	10.2
Manchester, NH	51.8	48.2	85.9	14.1	88.1	11.9	92.7	7.3	92.2	7.8
McAllen, TX	81.6	18.4	90.0	10.0	94.4	5.6	96.7	3.3	98.3	1.7

Table continued on following page.

City	Preschool (%)		Kindergarten (%)		Grades 1 - 4 (%)		Grades 5 - 8 (%)		Grades 9 - 12 (%)	
	Public	Private	Public	Private	Public	Private	Public	Private	Public	Private
Memphis, TN	60.2	39.8	87.7	12.3	88.1	11.9	88.5	11.5	85.6	14.4
Miami, FL	61.1	38.9	80.7	19.3	85.9	14.1	86.9	13.1	91.6	8.4
Midland, TX	57.2	42.8	67.9	32.1	78.9	21.1	76.4	23.6	84.3	15.7
Milwaukee, WI	77.0	23.0	73.9	26.1	75.5	24.5	73.9	26.1	79.9	20.1
Minneapolis, MN	53.1	46.9	86.3	13.7	86.2	13.8	87.0	13.0	88.8	11.2
Nashville, TN	51.0	49.0	82.7	17.3	82.9	17.1	78.2	21.8	81.2	18.8
New Orleans, LA	42.8	57.2	76.0	24.0	75.5	24.5	80.0	20.0	78.6	21.4
New York, NY	67.6	32.4	78.2	21.8	80.9	19.1	80.6	19.4	80.3	19.7
Oklahoma City, OK	69.7	30.3	86.9	13.1	87.9	12.1	86.4	13.6	86.9	13.1
Omaha, NE	54.5	45.5	79.9	20.1	82.7	17.3	82.7	17.3	83.3	16.7
Orlando, FL	60.7	39.3	81.8	18.2	85.9	14.1	90.0	10.0	88.0	12.0
Philadelphia, PA	54.5	45.5	78.0	22.0	79.4	20.6	79.1	20.9	77.6	22.4
Phoenix, AZ	62.6	37.4	86.7	13.3	88.9	11.1	91.5	8.5	92.2	7.8
Pittsburgh, PA	53.9	46.1	71.0	29.0	75.1	24.9	79.8	20.2	79.1	20.9
Portland, OR	36.8	63.2	84.3	15.7	87.0	13.0	86.9	13.1	85.7	14.3
Providence, RI	58.9	41.1	80.8	19.2	89.3	10.7	86.2	13.8	90.1	9.9
Provo, UT	64.9	35.1	88.2	11.8	91.6	8.4	95.6	4.4	91.6	8.4
Raleigh, NC	33.6	66.4	86.9	13.1	85.2	14.8	87.2	12.8	86.8	13.2
Reno, NV	54.6	45.4	96.7	3.3	89.2	10.8	88.3	11.7	93.6	6.4
Richmond, VA	53.2	46.8	90.2	9.8	87.7	12.3	84.7	15.3	82.7	17.3
Rochester, MN	43.6	56.4	90.6	9.4	86.3	13.7	84.5	15.5	90.2	9.8
Sacramento, CA	56.9	43.1	92.4	7.6	91.3	8.7	92.3	7.7	89.5	10.5
Saint Louis, MO	56.5	43.5	85.1	14.9	83.3	16.7	82.7	17.3	84.0	16.0
Saint Paul, MN	64.7	35.3	82.1	17.9	89.2	10.8	87.3	12.7	90.7	9.3
Salem, OR	70.2	29.8	88.8	11.2	88.5	11.5	91.6	8.4	97.2	2.8
Salt Lake City, UT	52.1	47.9	81.8	18.2	85.6	14.4	90.6	9.4	93.7	6.3
San Antonio, TX	73.0	27.0	89.7	10.3	90.7	9.3	92.1	7.9	91.8	8.2
San Diego, CA	47.0	53.0	84.6	15.4	88.6	11.4	91.3	8.7	90.8	9.2
San Francisco, CA	25.0	75.0	67.5	32.5	69.1	30.9	68.5	31.5	72.8	27.2
San Jose, CA	43.5	56.5	83.1	16.9	86.1	13.9	87.4	12.6	87.1	12.9
Santa Rosa, CA	55.2	44.8	90.3	9.7	92.4	7.6	88.6	11.4	92.8	7.2
Savannah, GA	76.3	23.7	85.4	14.6	88.1	11.9	88.2	11.8	88.6	11.4
Seattle, WA	35.0	65.0	76.0	24.0	77.9	22.1	74.8	25.2	78.3	21.7
Sioux Falls, SD	59.5	40.5	86.0	14.0	85.9	14.1	86.2	13.8	86.7	13.3
Tampa, FL	46.6	53.4	86.5	13.5	86.6	13.4	81.5	18.5	83.5	16.5
Tucson, AZ	71.7	28.3	90.3	9.7	88.2	11.8	88.1	11.9	91.9	8.1
Tulsa, OK	65.1	34.9	83.2	16.8	82.9	17.1	82.2	17.8	82.6	17.4
Virginia Beach, VA	39.5	60.5	77.6	22.4	88.8	11.2	88.5	11.5	91.2	8.8
Washington, DC	74.8	25.2	90.5	9.5	85.6	14.4	83.0	17.0	79.9	20.1
Wichita, KS	61.8	38.2	82.0	18.0	84.6	15.4	84.4	15.6	86.3	13.7
Wilmington, NC	55.8	44.2	84.8	15.2	79.3	20.7	75.6	24.4	87.1	12.9
Winston-Salem, NC	60.4	39.6	88.7	11.3	88.2	11.8	90.5	9.5	90.4	9.6
U.S.	58.7	41.3	85.2	14.8	87.2	12.8	87.9	12.1	89.0	11.0

Note: Figures shown cover persons 3 years old and over
Source: U.S. Census Bureau, 2019-2023 American Community Survey 5-Year Estimates

School Enrollment by Grade and Control: Metro Area

Metro Area	Preschool (%)		Kindergarten (%)		Grades 1 - 4 (%)		Grades 5 - 8 (%)		Grades 9 - 12 (%)	
	Public	Private	Public	Private	Public	Private	Public	Private	Public	Private
Albuquerque, NM	60.4	39.6	84.3	15.7	86.3	13.7	88.4	11.6	90.3	9.7
Anchorage, AK	51.9	48.1	87.7	12.3	83.6	16.4	86.9	13.1	89.7	10.3
Ann Arbor, MI	53.0	47.0	89.6	10.4	85.0	15.0	84.6	15.4	91.8	8.2
Athens, GA	63.8	36.2	93.2	6.8	88.2	11.8	87.2	12.8	88.5	11.5
Atlanta, GA	56.1	43.9	84.1	15.9	88.3	11.7	87.2	12.8	88.5	11.5
Austin, TX	49.6	50.4	87.0	13.0	90.0	10.0	89.2	10.8	91.1	8.9
Baltimore, MD	47.0	53.0	82.9	17.1	84.6	15.4	84.0	16.0	84.2	15.8
Billings, MT	41.5	58.5	84.1	15.9	87.0	13.0	87.1	12.9	88.2	11.8
Boise City, ID	40.0	60.0	86.5	13.5	85.6	14.4	88.0	12.0	88.4	11.6
Boston, MA	45.6	54.4	87.8	12.2	90.3	9.7	89.1	10.9	85.9	14.1
Boulder, CO	48.1	51.9	87.6	12.4	88.7	11.3	91.5	8.5	93.0	7.0
Cape Coral, FL	61.4	38.6	86.9	13.1	88.2	11.8	88.7	11.3	90.3	9.7
Cedar Rapids, IA	74.7	25.3	87.6	12.4	88.4	11.6	88.3	11.7	89.7	10.3
Charleston, SC	47.5	52.5	82.7	17.3	86.5	13.5	87.9	12.1	87.7	12.3
Charlotte, NC	50.5	49.5	86.2	13.8	87.8	12.2	87.3	12.7	88.6	11.4
Chicago, IL	56.8	43.2	84.8	15.2	87.6	12.4	88.1	11.9	90.0	10.0
Cincinnati, OH	50.7	49.3	79.1	20.9	81.9	18.1	82.2	17.8	83.0	17.0
Clarksville, TN	62.8	37.2	85.3	14.7	86.8	13.2	86.0	14.0	87.6	12.4
Cleveland, OH	53.0	47.0	75.5	24.5	80.6	19.4	80.7	19.3	82.4	17.6
College Station, TX	61.4	38.6	87.5	12.5	90.5	9.5	87.7	12.3	90.5	9.5
Colorado Springs, CO	66.9	33.1	86.3	13.7	87.4	12.6	88.5	11.5	89.8	10.2
Columbia, MO	55.0	45.0	87.6	12.4	84.6	15.4	90.4	9.6	90.7	9.3
Columbia, SC	51.6	48.4	88.3	11.7	87.8	12.2	90.4	9.6	91.7	8.3
Columbus, OH	56.4	43.6	81.4	18.6	87.0	13.0	88.1	11.9	88.9	11.1
Dallas, TX	57.4	42.6	88.0	12.0	90.4	9.6	91.4	8.6	91.5	8.5
Davenport, IA	65.1	34.9	87.2	12.8	87.0	13.0	91.2	8.8	92.2	7.8
Denver, CO	58.5	41.5	86.4	13.6	89.3	10.7	89.9	10.1	91.6	8.4
Des Moines, IA	68.1	31.9	87.6	12.4	91.2	8.8	89.9	10.1	91.5	8.5
Detroit, MI	62.5	37.5	86.9	13.1	88.7	11.3	89.8	10.2	89.9	10.1
Durham, NC	43.5	56.5	80.2	19.8	85.4	14.6	85.0	15.0	89.7	10.3
El Paso, TX	87.0	13.0	94.1	5.9	93.1	6.9	94.4	5.6	96.2	3.8
Eugene, OR	54.2	45.8	84.1	15.9	87.0	13.0	89.6	10.4	91.4	8.6
Fargo, ND	65.0	35.0	90.0	10.0	89.1	10.9	90.7	9.3	91.7	8.3
Fort Collins, CO	52.8	47.2	85.7	14.3	85.4	14.6	86.7	13.3	88.2	11.8
Fort Wayne, IN	44.1	55.9	73.2	26.8	75.7	24.3	76.8	23.2	81.3	18.7
Fort Worth, TX	57.4	42.6	88.0	12.0	90.4	9.6	91.4	8.6	91.5	8.5
Gainesville, FL	53.9	46.1	72.0	28.0	76.7	23.3	78.1	21.9	86.5	13.5
Green Bay, WI	68.0	32.0	84.2	15.8	86.1	13.9	87.0	13.0	90.5	9.5
Greensboro, NC	56.8	43.2	86.7	13.3	85.9	14.1	85.7	14.3	87.9	12.1
Honolulu, HI	34.7	65.3	79.0	21.0	79.9	20.1	78.2	21.8	74.9	25.1
Houston, TX	57.2	42.8	88.1	11.9	90.9	9.1	92.0	8.0	91.7	8.3
Huntsville, AL	56.0	44.0	79.7	20.3	82.9	17.1	82.3	17.7	83.1	16.9
Indianapolis, IN	53.8	46.2	84.3	15.7	85.1	14.9	85.7	14.3	87.4	12.6
Jacksonville, FL	56.0	44.0	85.4	14.6	84.0	16.0	82.8	17.2	85.6	14.4
Kansas City, MO	60.8	39.2	86.2	13.8	87.9	12.1	88.5	11.5	88.5	11.5
Lafayette, LA	56.7	43.3	78.8	21.2	77.7	22.3	77.9	22.1	79.1	20.9
Las Vegas, NV	64.0	36.0	87.1	12.9	88.8	11.2	90.1	9.9	91.8	8.2
Lexington, KY	40.9	59.1	82.4	17.6	83.7	16.3	84.8	15.2	85.9	14.1
Lincoln, NE	54.3	45.7	79.6	20.4	81.9	18.1	84.4	15.6	90.5	9.5
Little Rock, AR	69.9	30.1	86.8	13.2	86.2	13.8	85.4	14.6	87.1	12.9
Los Angeles, CA	54.7	45.3	86.6	13.4	89.1	10.9	89.9	10.1	90.6	9.4
Louisville, KY	53.0	47.0	79.7	20.3	81.8	18.2	82.4	17.6	81.0	19.0
Madison, WI	64.6	35.4	89.5	10.5	88.4	11.6	90.8	9.2	93.5	6.5
Manchester, NH	45.6	54.4	81.4	18.6	85.2	14.8	87.5	12.5	89.8	10.2
McAllen, TX	93.3	6.7	96.4	3.6	97.7	2.3	98.1	1.9	98.7	1.3

Table continued on following page.

Metro Area	Preschool (%) Public	Preschool (%) Private	Kindergarten (%) Public	Kindergarten (%) Private	Grades 1 - 4 (%) Public	Grades 1 - 4 (%) Private	Grades 5 - 8 (%) Public	Grades 5 - 8 (%) Private	Grades 9 - 12 (%) Public	Grades 9 - 12 (%) Private
Memphis, TN	59.8	40.2	87.5	12.5	86.3	13.7	87.0	13.0	84.8	15.2
Miami, FL	50.2	49.8	80.4	19.6	84.2	15.8	85.0	15.0	85.7	14.3
Midland, TX	65.0	35.0	65.8	34.2	80.9	19.1	78.8	21.2	83.9	16.1
Milwaukee, WI	59.4	40.6	75.9	24.1	78.5	21.5	78.7	21.3	84.9	15.1
Minneapolis, MN	60.7	39.3	85.8	14.2	88.3	11.7	88.7	11.3	91.5	8.5
Nashville, TN	50.1	49.9	82.5	17.5	84.8	15.2	83.3	16.7	83.0	17.0
New Orleans, LA	50.8	49.2	76.7	23.3	76.5	23.5	78.6	21.4	75.1	24.9
New York, NY	58.7	41.3	80.9	19.1	83.9	16.1	84.6	15.4	83.7	16.3
Oklahoma City, OK	70.9	29.1	86.9	13.1	87.7	12.3	87.4	12.6	87.8	12.2
Omaha, NE	58.9	41.1	81.9	18.1	84.5	15.5	85.7	14.3	85.5	14.5
Orlando, FL	48.9	51.1	79.8	20.2	82.1	17.9	85.3	14.7	87.0	13.0
Philadelphia, PA	47.4	52.6	81.4	18.6	85.0	15.0	84.4	15.6	83.6	16.4
Phoenix, AZ	60.3	39.7	85.5	14.5	88.1	11.9	90.4	9.6	91.9	8.1
Pittsburgh, PA	52.6	47.4	81.9	18.1	87.4	12.6	89.1	10.9	89.6	10.4
Portland, OR	40.0	60.0	83.8	16.2	85.8	14.2	88.1	11.9	89.6	10.4
Providence, RI	57.9	42.1	85.5	14.5	89.4	10.6	88.9	11.1	88.7	11.3
Provo, UT	55.5	44.5	87.9	12.1	90.3	9.7	92.6	7.4	94.0	6.0
Raleigh, NC	33.6	66.4	82.6	17.4	85.2	14.8	85.7	14.3	87.6	12.4
Reno, NV	51.8	48.2	90.8	9.2	90.9	9.1	89.7	10.3	92.1	7.9
Richmond, VA	44.4	55.6	86.4	13.6	87.5	12.5	89.1	10.9	90.0	10.0
Rochester, MN	61.3	38.7	91.0	9.0	88.1	11.9	87.9	12.1	91.8	8.2
Sacramento, CA	55.0	45.0	87.3	12.7	89.8	10.2	90.5	9.5	90.7	9.3
Saint Louis, MO	53.9	46.1	82.1	17.9	82.1	17.9	83.2	16.8	84.7	15.3
Saint Paul, MN	60.7	39.3	85.8	14.2	88.3	11.7	88.7	11.3	91.5	8.5
Salem, OR	59.8	40.2	86.8	13.2	86.0	14.0	90.3	9.7	92.4	7.6
Salt Lake City, UT	57.4	42.6	84.7	15.3	89.9	10.1	93.4	6.6	93.9	6.1
San Antonio, TX	65.5	34.5	87.7	12.3	89.4	10.6	90.3	9.7	90.5	9.5
San Diego, CA	50.7	49.3	86.1	13.9	89.3	10.7	90.8	9.2	91.9	8.1
San Francisco, CA	38.9	61.1	81.4	18.6	84.7	15.3	83.8	16.2	85.8	14.2
San Jose, CA	36.2	63.8	80.1	19.9	84.7	15.3	85.9	14.1	86.5	13.5
Santa Rosa, CA	53.1	46.9	91.2	8.8	92.9	7.1	89.9	10.1	91.1	8.9
Savannah, GA	57.5	42.5	79.1	20.9	84.4	15.6	84.9	15.1	85.2	14.8
Seattle, WA	40.8	59.2	79.5	20.5	85.6	14.4	86.7	13.3	90.0	10.0
Sioux Falls, SD	64.5	35.5	86.8	13.2	86.8	13.2	87.8	12.2	87.7	12.3
Tampa, FL	54.3	45.7	82.4	17.6	84.7	15.3	84.3	15.7	86.4	13.6
Tucson, AZ	71.3	28.7	88.0	12.0	87.2	12.8	87.8	12.2	89.8	10.2
Tulsa, OK	67.2	32.8	84.6	15.4	84.2	15.8	85.3	14.7	85.5	14.5
Virginia Beach, VA	50.5	49.5	80.8	19.2	87.9	12.1	88.8	11.2	89.9	10.1
Washington, DC	45.5	54.5	82.8	17.2	86.8	13.2	87.5	12.5	88.2	11.8
Wichita, KS	63.2	36.8	80.5	19.5	85.1	14.9	86.3	13.7	87.5	12.5
Wilmington, NC	52.1	47.9	83.4	16.6	83.8	16.2	84.3	15.7	88.3	11.7
Winston-Salem, NC	48.5	51.5	85.5	14.5	87.3	12.7	89.0	11.0	86.7	13.3
U.S.	58.7	41.3	85.2	14.8	87.2	12.8	87.9	12.1	89.0	11.0

Note: Figures shown cover persons 3 years old and over; Figures cover the Metropolitan Statistical Area (MSA)
Source: U.S. Census Bureau, 2019-2023 American Community Survey 5-Year Estimates

Educational Attainment by Race: City

City	High School Graduate or Higher (%)					Bachelor's Degree or Higher (%)				
	Total	White	Black	Asian	Hisp.[1]	Total	White	Black	Asian	Hisp.[1]
Albuquerque, NM	90.9	94.6	94.0	88.3	84.4	38.7	45.2	38.8	51.0	25.4
Anchorage, AK	94.0	96.7	91.7	86.6	86.6	37.7	45.2	23.6	30.5	23.8
Ann Arbor, MI	97.6	98.6	92.7	97.2	92.8	77.7	79.7	44.8	85.2	75.5
Athens, GA	89.9	96.9	82.5	88.5	66.8	48.7	62.8	22.6	67.8	31.7
Atlanta, GA	93.0	98.5	87.9	97.7	86.1	58.4	81.2	34.6	86.7	50.5
Austin, TX	91.6	95.1	90.6	93.6	78.3	58.2	63.9	36.7	78.4	35.6
Baltimore, MD	87.2	92.9	85.7	92.2	70.0	35.4	62.2	20.0	73.3	31.3
Billings, MT	95.5	96.2	98.6	89.9	85.1	37.0	38.3	35.8	56.4	14.6
Boise City, ID	94.8	96.2	73.7	89.9	80.6	46.6	47.4	24.4	60.1	30.3
Boston, MA	88.9	96.4	86.4	80.9	72.8	54.1	72.5	26.7	57.4	26.6
Boulder, CO	96.9	98.3	95.0	95.1	78.4	76.8	79.1	43.7	79.9	48.6
Cape Coral, FL	93.2	94.9	87.7	90.2	87.3	25.7	26.8	21.3	50.2	18.9
Cedar Rapids, IA	94.1	95.5	81.1	88.4	90.0	32.9	33.6	15.5	55.7	25.0
Charleston, SC	95.9	98.3	86.7	92.1	87.9	57.7	65.3	22.9	67.6	39.8
Charlotte, NC	89.6	95.9	91.6	85.3	60.5	47.4	63.1	33.3	61.3	20.5
Chicago, IL	86.8	93.4	87.4	88.3	71.9	43.3	61.9	25.2	65.0	20.4
Cincinnati, OH	89.7	94.6	83.8	93.1	81.1	41.3	57.9	16.2	80.1	36.2
Clarksville, TN	94.2	95.8	95.2	84.5	84.8	30.6	33.8	27.3	27.8	19.9
Cleveland, OH	83.5	87.5	82.3	78.8	70.9	21.3	31.8	12.7	55.6	10.6
College Station, TX	94.6	97.4	88.7	95.6	83.0	57.1	60.8	24.5	79.1	40.4
Colorado Springs, CO	94.6	96.4	94.1	89.0	84.6	41.9	45.3	32.1	43.8	21.6
Columbia, MO	95.3	96.4	92.0	94.2	86.7	56.5	59.4	33.9	72.5	48.5
Columbia, SC	90.9	96.0	85.2	89.9	85.6	46.1	62.6	25.4	73.0	39.5
Columbus, OH	89.8	93.6	86.6	82.8	71.2	38.2	45.8	21.1	57.8	25.2
Dallas, TX	80.8	87.6	89.0	89.3	58.2	37.4	53.6	23.6	68.5	15.3
Davenport, IA	92.6	94.7	87.4	84.3	78.3	30.0	31.7	16.8	59.3	15.0
Denver, CO	91.4	96.4	91.5	87.1	72.5	55.6	66.7	31.4	58.1	23.3
Des Moines, IA	87.3	93.7	79.3	61.3	60.1	29.0	33.5	15.8	23.0	10.8
Detroit, MI	83.4	84.3	85.3	75.5	56.8	17.6	37.4	14.1	43.5	11.6
Durham, NC	91.4	96.1	91.7	92.8	59.7	55.7	70.7	39.4	76.8	22.1
El Paso, TX	81.9	87.0	94.8	88.4	78.7	27.5	31.5	30.8	52.7	23.9
Eugene, OR	94.8	95.7	98.0	92.9	86.2	44.2	44.8	37.2	59.1	33.3
Fargo, ND	95.3	96.6	82.3	87.0	95.2	43.2	44.3	20.1	69.9	31.7
Fort Collins, CO	97.6	98.4	87.7	95.1	91.1	59.9	62.0	34.6	76.2	37.0
Fort Wayne, IN	88.9	94.1	87.7	49.2	65.7	28.5	33.1	13.9	19.7	15.4
Fort Worth, TX	84.3	91.2	90.0	82.7	64.6	31.7	41.0	23.0	46.0	14.7
Gainesville, FL	94.3	96.5	87.4	96.9	94.7	51.7	57.0	28.8	77.5	61.4
Green Bay, WI	89.0	92.6	69.5	84.3	65.8	25.5	27.8	16.2	32.8	11.5
Greensboro, NC	90.1	95.2	89.5	75.7	70.2	39.9	52.3	28.0	46.5	19.4
Honolulu, HI	90.9	97.6	91.5	88.1	93.6	40.8	54.6	32.5	40.7	30.5
Houston, TX	80.3	88.5	89.9	86.6	60.7	36.0	50.8	27.4	61.7	16.7
Huntsville, AL	91.6	94.8	86.8	91.0	77.4	46.2	54.1	30.1	57.6	29.7
Indianapolis, IN	87.5	91.3	87.9	70.4	64.5	34.2	41.0	22.1	41.0	18.6
Jacksonville, FL	90.8	93.0	88.6	88.9	84.8	31.8	35.1	22.6	52.6	28.1
Kansas City, MO	91.8	94.9	89.8	89.9	73.9	37.8	47.4	17.5	49.5	20.7
Lafayette, LA	90.9	95.4	81.2	91.6	83.8	40.6	50.4	17.4	55.0	36.6
Las Vegas, NV	85.8	91.7	88.5	91.7	66.8	27.3	32.2	19.5	44.8	12.5
Lexington, KY	92.4	95.3	90.4	89.9	65.1	47.3	51.9	27.1	72.2	25.3
Lincoln, NE	93.0	95.2	86.6	81.2	70.7	41.0	42.7	25.0	43.3	21.1
Little Rock, AR	92.3	96.3	91.5	92.7	63.7	44.0	58.0	26.6	73.5	13.5
Los Angeles, CA	79.3	89.6	90.1	91.1	59.4	37.8	51.6	31.9	57.6	15.1
Louisville, KY	90.5	92.9	87.6	83.3	78.7	33.4	37.4	20.2	56.1	27.5
Madison, WI	95.7	97.7	91.9	92.5	78.5	59.2	62.9	25.6	70.4	37.4
Manchester, NH	88.7	91.3	75.7	81.2	68.7	33.5	35.4	22.8	35.6	13.5
McAllen, TX	79.9	85.7	99.5	89.7	77.2	32.0	35.4	31.6	64.7	28.6

Table continued on following page.

City	High School Graduate or Higher (%)					Bachelor's Degree or Higher (%)				
	Total	White	Black	Asian	Hisp.[1]	Total	White	Black	Asian	Hisp.[1]
Memphis, TN	87.4	93.9	87.8	86.8	52.0	28.2	49.9	17.9	60.0	17.8
Miami, FL	80.0	82.6	78.1	95.4	76.7	35.6	44.7	17.5	69.4	31.3
Midland, TX	86.5	91.9	90.5	70.2	74.6	33.7	40.3	20.1	39.1	22.1
Milwaukee, WI	85.5	92.8	86.0	74.3	64.6	26.6	41.0	13.7	32.7	12.0
Minneapolis, MN	91.1	97.2	74.9	86.3	71.6	54.5	65.6	19.1	62.7	31.0
Nashville, TN	90.2	93.9	89.5	83.4	61.8	46.9	56.0	29.8	55.1	20.5
New Orleans, LA	89.1	96.8	85.9	77.4	79.1	42.0	68.0	24.1	50.4	42.2
New York, NY	83.7	92.5	85.1	77.3	71.7	41.0	59.2	26.7	45.2	21.5
Oklahoma City, OK	87.8	91.4	90.7	81.6	61.7	34.0	38.4	26.1	48.0	12.8
Omaha, NE	90.5	95.1	86.9	71.7	61.9	40.3	45.7	18.6	50.2	15.0
Orlando, FL	91.9	95.6	84.1	93.4	90.9	42.2	53.5	21.7	59.3	33.9
Philadelphia, PA	87.4	93.5	88.1	74.3	72.6	34.6	51.0	20.4	42.0	19.5
Phoenix, AZ	84.4	91.2	89.2	89.2	66.9	32.3	38.9	27.3	62.6	13.6
Pittsburgh, PA	94.3	95.7	90.6	92.3	87.4	47.8	53.2	20.3	82.0	55.8
Portland, OR	93.3	96.2	88.6	81.7	80.0	53.5	58.1	29.8	47.3	35.7
Providence, RI	81.9	89.9	87.0	87.7	69.5	34.7	51.7	23.6	58.3	12.9
Provo, UT	92.5	95.3	99.6	84.9	75.2	45.0	49.0	29.9	52.7	20.8
Raleigh, NC	92.5	96.8	92.0	90.0	67.3	52.9	66.4	32.5	62.5	23.7
Reno, NV	89.3	94.9	91.5	90.5	65.3	35.7	39.9	26.6	49.2	15.2
Richmond, VA	89.3	96.6	85.0	90.3	61.4	44.1	70.1	16.1	64.9	25.2
Rochester, MN	94.5	97.2	73.9	86.1	78.6	50.1	51.6	25.7	61.6	34.9
Sacramento, CA	86.9	93.0	91.4	82.5	76.4	36.4	45.2	24.4	38.9	23.7
Saint Louis, MO	90.5	95.0	85.7	86.9	81.7	40.2	56.0	18.1	63.5	35.3
Saint Paul, MN	88.9	96.6	81.4	67.4	73.7	43.5	55.6	21.2	23.6	24.2
Salem, OR	88.7	93.5	94.1	86.4	63.7	31.4	35.1	27.7	46.3	12.8
Salt Lake City, UT	91.6	95.7	86.1	85.3	72.5	50.9	56.2	30.7	62.6	24.5
San Antonio, TX	84.3	88.4	91.0	85.7	78.0	28.7	33.7	25.0	56.5	19.4
San Diego, CA	90.2	95.2	90.0	90.2	76.2	49.9	57.6	31.3	57.3	25.4
San Francisco, CA	88.8	97.5	88.8	80.8	80.1	60.1	76.3	30.9	51.0	40.1
San Jose, CA	85.5	93.1	90.1	88.3	69.6	46.5	51.5	37.5	59.7	17.5
Santa Rosa, CA	85.5	94.7	85.7	83.6	63.0	34.8	42.5	21.8	45.8	14.6
Savannah, GA	89.9	95.3	86.3	81.6	86.9	32.0	47.8	17.9	46.9	32.4
Seattle, WA	95.7	98.4	89.9	91.2	87.8	67.5	72.6	33.8	69.8	49.3
Sioux Falls, SD	93.1	95.7	83.0	76.0	64.7	37.4	40.0	21.0	42.2	14.8
Tampa, FL	89.8	94.4	85.6	90.4	80.9	44.6	56.0	20.5	68.9	29.4
Tucson, AZ	87.3	91.8	87.3	88.4	76.7	30.2	35.6	17.5	51.9	17.3
Tulsa, OK	87.6	92.1	90.0	77.0	59.5	33.3	39.7	19.7	38.0	12.4
Virginia Beach, VA	94.7	96.4	92.7	89.4	89.9	40.4	44.2	27.9	46.6	32.5
Washington, DC	92.8	99.1	88.5	95.8	81.3	63.6	92.0	33.3	84.7	56.7
Wichita, KS	88.0	92.3	87.4	74.0	63.9	30.9	34.8	19.0	31.6	14.7
Wilmington, NC	93.5	96.4	84.9	87.8	77.5	45.8	51.7	23.0	61.8	30.2
Winston-Salem, NC	88.4	91.9	89.4	96.1	61.1	37.2	47.5	24.1	70.3	16.3
U.S.	89.4	92.9	88.1	88.0	72.5	35.0	37.7	24.7	57.0	19.9

Note: Figures shown cover persons 25 years old and over; (1) People of Hispanic origin can be of any race
Source: U.S. Census Bureau, 2019-2023 American Community Survey 5-Year Estimates

Educational Attainment by Race: Metro Area

Metro Area	High School Graduate or Higher (%)					Bachelor's Degree or Higher (%)				
	Total	White	Black	Asian	Hisp.[1]	Total	White	Black	Asian	Hisp.[1]
Albuquerque, NM	90.3	94.2	93.1	88.8	84.0	35.0	41.5	38.7	52.7	22.6
Anchorage, AK	94.1	96.2	91.7	86.6	87.7	34.0	38.9	23.5	29.7	23.9
Ann Arbor, MI	95.8	97.1	90.9	95.6	85.8	58.1	60.0	31.5	82.0	47.3
Athens, GA	89.8	94.2	82.4	85.0	66.0	43.5	49.5	21.4	64.9	30.8
Atlanta, GA	90.8	93.8	91.9	87.8	69.6	41.5	46.4	34.0	61.2	24.7
Austin, TX	91.6	94.9	93.3	93.8	78.2	49.9	54.2	36.5	76.1	29.0
Baltimore, MD	92.1	94.7	90.2	89.3	77.0	43.3	48.4	30.1	64.0	32.9
Billings, MT	95.2	95.8	99.0	87.5	84.4	33.5	34.3	31.1	47.3	15.7
Boise City, ID	92.5	94.9	80.7	90.9	72.9	36.6	38.2	24.7	55.8	19.1
Boston, MA	92.3	95.8	87.4	87.0	74.8	51.2	54.8	31.8	65.0	26.6
Boulder, CO	95.5	97.6	93.4	92.4	76.4	63.9	67.0	40.6	70.1	30.8
Cape Coral, FL	90.4	94.0	82.6	89.5	75.7	30.8	34.0	16.7	50.3	17.1
Cedar Rapids, IA	95.2	96.1	83.2	90.9	85.2	32.8	33.3	16.5	53.6	24.3
Charleston, SC	91.9	95.4	86.5	90.2	72.3	40.0	47.6	20.1	51.7	25.5
Charlotte, NC	90.4	93.4	90.6	88.0	67.0	39.0	42.6	30.0	61.9	21.4
Chicago, IL	89.7	94.4	89.4	91.3	71.8	40.9	47.4	25.8	67.0	18.6
Cincinnati, OH	92.3	93.5	87.9	88.6	76.7	36.9	38.1	22.8	63.4	31.1
Clarksville, TN	92.3	92.8	93.3	87.6	84.0	28.0	29.3	25.3	35.5	20.5
Cleveland, OH	91.7	93.6	87.0	87.8	78.0	33.4	36.9	18.3	63.6	19.0
College Station, TX	88.3	91.8	87.1	96.0	69.9	39.1	43.4	15.1	77.8	18.7
Colorado Springs, CO	95.1	96.6	95.2	90.1	86.4	41.0	43.8	32.5	44.9	23.2
Columbia, MO	94.0	94.6	91.5	92.8	87.6	47.5	48.9	28.5	71.0	38.4
Columbia, SC	91.1	93.5	88.9	91.0	75.3	35.0	39.2	27.3	64.1	22.7
Columbus, OH	92.1	94.2	87.4	86.3	75.0	39.4	41.8	23.9	62.6	27.7
Dallas, TX	87.3	92.0	92.2	90.0	66.3	38.5	42.8	31.6	65.4	17.8
Davenport, IA	92.4	94.5	83.5	82.5	77.4	29.4	30.4	14.2	61.6	16.8
Denver, CO	92.3	96.0	90.8	86.3	75.5	48.4	54.4	30.3	55.4	21.7
Des Moines, IA	93.5	96.3	82.0	73.9	69.3	39.1	40.8	20.1	44.7	17.4
Detroit, MI	91.2	92.9	88.4	89.5	76.9	34.1	36.5	19.4	66.4	26.5
Durham, NC	91.1	95.0	90.1	92.2	59.9	52.3	60.5	35.3	77.4	23.4
El Paso, TX	80.6	85.8	95.3	88.8	77.4	25.3	29.4	32.0	50.5	21.9
Eugene, OR	93.1	94.1	96.1	90.4	81.3	33.4	33.6	33.2	53.7	25.3
Fargo, ND	95.6	96.6	84.7	88.7	89.2	42.2	43.0	24.6	67.9	30.1
Fort Collins, CO	96.6	97.7	91.5	95.6	85.2	51.7	53.4	37.7	69.3	29.5
Fort Wayne, IN	90.7	93.8	88.5	59.3	68.5	29.7	32.0	15.8	29.2	16.9
Fort Worth, TX	87.3	92.0	92.2	90.0	66.3	38.5	42.8	31.6	65.4	17.8
Gainesville, FL	92.7	93.9	87.4	94.6	89.8	40.9	41.6	24.2	73.6	49.6
Green Bay, WI	93.3	95.2	74.2	85.9	69.6	29.9	30.8	18.3	44.5	15.5
Greensboro, NC	88.3	91.1	88.5	78.6	63.3	31.4	34.4	24.7	49.1	16.3
Honolulu, HI	92.9	97.2	95.8	90.6	94.5	37.7	51.2	32.8	39.2	29.2
Houston, TX	85.1	90.6	92.3	87.6	67.9	35.4	40.8	32.1	58.0	17.8
Huntsville, AL	91.5	93.3	88.5	91.9	77.4	42.4	45.2	33.2	63.5	30.7
Indianapolis, IN	91.1	93.5	88.2	81.4	70.5	37.8	40.4	24.9	54.4	24.0
Jacksonville, FL	92.1	93.8	88.5	89.6	87.1	35.1	37.9	23.6	52.4	30.2
Kansas City, MO	93.1	95.0	90.9	89.1	75.0	39.2	42.6	21.9	56.7	20.9
Lafayette, LA	87.0	90.1	79.6	72.7	76.8	27.0	30.1	15.1	36.6	27.1
Las Vegas, NV	86.8	91.8	90.6	90.6	69.6	27.3	31.1	21.2	42.9	12.7
Lexington, KY	91.9	93.9	90.6	89.7	65.7	41.1	43.4	25.4	67.8	23.0
Lincoln, NE	93.6	95.4	86.4	81.1	71.1	40.6	42.0	24.8	43.2	20.9
Little Rock, AR	92.1	93.9	91.4	89.9	68.2	32.9	35.4	25.8	55.9	17.4
Los Angeles, CA	82.2	90.4	91.1	89.2	65.7	37.4	46.4	31.8	55.5	16.2
Louisville, KY	91.3	92.7	87.7	86.4	77.4	32.1	33.7	20.6	60.2	25.4
Madison, WI	95.9	97.1	91.4	92.5	78.5	49.3	50.1	25.9	69.7	33.2
Manchester, NH	93.0	94.3	83.0	90.5	74.3	40.6	41.1	26.8	60.6	20.1
McAllen, TX	69.3	76.0	84.4	92.3	66.7	20.3	22.9	23.5	67.0	18.2

Table continued on following page.

Metro Area	High School Graduate or Higher (%)					Bachelor's Degree or Higher (%)				
	Total	White	Black	Asian	Hisp.[1]	Total	White	Black	Asian	Hisp.[1]
Memphis, TN	89.5	93.3	88.5	88.2	57.9	30.7	39.1	21.4	64.8	19.0
Miami, FL	86.9	90.6	84.2	88.6	81.7	35.6	42.4	22.4	56.3	31.2
Midland, TX	86.2	91.5	91.3	74.8	74.3	30.6	35.7	20.6	48.7	19.3
Milwaukee, WI	92.7	96.2	86.7	86.3	72.7	38.8	44.4	15.3	53.9	18.1
Minneapolis, MN	94.2	97.0	84.0	83.5	76.4	44.9	47.7	25.1	47.6	27.2
Nashville, TN	91.5	93.4	90.4	85.7	68.4	39.9	42.0	30.5	56.8	22.2
New Orleans, LA	87.5	92.2	85.3	80.0	74.8	33.0	41.2	22.5	47.7	25.0
New York, NY	87.6	93.7	86.9	84.4	74.1	43.5	52.7	28.4	57.0	22.8
Oklahoma City, OK	89.9	92.3	91.0	83.8	65.5	33.4	36.0	25.3	50.9	14.8
Omaha, NE	92.7	95.6	88.8	74.3	68.3	39.1	41.8	21.4	48.0	18.5
Orlando, FL	90.7	93.5	85.8	90.2	86.5	35.8	39.4	25.0	54.9	28.8
Philadelphia, PA	92.1	95.3	89.7	85.5	74.5	41.5	46.8	24.3	59.2	22.5
Phoenix, AZ	89.5	93.7	91.6	90.3	73.5	34.6	38.2	29.8	60.9	16.4
Pittsburgh, PA	94.9	95.4	91.7	87.5	86.9	37.4	37.8	21.5	69.8	39.9
Portland, OR	92.8	95.2	90.7	88.4	74.5	42.1	43.3	31.8	55.8	23.6
Providence, RI	88.4	90.8	85.6	88.6	72.1	35.0	37.5	25.4	56.3	16.8
Provo, UT	95.3	96.5	97.2	94.6	83.1	43.4	44.7	38.3	62.7	26.4
Raleigh, NC	92.9	96.0	92.2	93.3	69.1	50.2	55.5	33.9	76.2	22.7
Reno, NV	88.6	93.5	90.2	90.5	65.8	31.4	34.6	21.8	45.8	14.4
Richmond, VA	91.9	95.0	89.7	90.1	71.2	40.2	47.4	24.6	63.9	22.8
Rochester, MN	94.8	96.5	74.4	85.8	79.8	42.3	42.2	25.1	60.4	33.9
Sacramento, CA	90.1	94.4	91.4	85.1	78.1	36.3	39.2	26.0	45.0	22.0
Saint Louis, MO	93.3	94.7	88.8	90.9	82.6	37.6	40.1	22.0	68.6	31.0
Saint Paul, MN	94.2	97.0	84.0	83.5	76.4	44.9	47.7	25.1	47.6	27.2
Salem, OR	87.2	92.5	91.1	85.4	62.2	26.9	30.0	28.2	43.5	11.0
Salt Lake City, UT	91.8	95.2	84.3	86.9	74.6	37.8	40.9	25.4	52.0	18.6
San Antonio, TX	87.3	91.2	92.4	88.2	79.8	31.9	36.6	30.1	53.8	21.2
San Diego, CA	89.0	93.8	91.0	91.1	75.0	42.1	48.0	29.6	55.2	21.5
San Francisco, CA	89.5	96.2	91.4	88.4	73.3	52.4	61.6	32.3	59.9	25.1
San Jose, CA	89.1	94.7	92.0	91.9	72.1	54.8	57.5	42.1	69.5	20.2
Santa Rosa, CA	88.9	95.8	88.8	86.2	66.2	37.8	44.2	29.4	46.1	16.0
Savannah, GA	91.3	94.0	88.9	82.3	84.1	34.9	41.2	23.4	50.9	27.4
Seattle, WA	93.3	96.0	90.4	91.0	77.4	46.3	47.0	28.6	61.7	27.5
Sioux Falls, SD	93.7	95.6	83.4	76.1	66.5	35.7	37.4	20.1	40.3	16.0
Tampa, FL	90.9	93.1	89.2	86.4	82.3	34.0	35.4	26.6	54.2	25.9
Tucson, AZ	89.9	93.9	89.2	89.8	78.6	35.9	41.0	25.7	56.3	19.7
Tulsa, OK	90.1	92.7	90.7	77.9	66.0	29.8	32.6	21.1	33.6	15.1
Virginia Beach, VA	92.8	95.3	89.6	88.9	86.0	35.1	39.9	24.9	47.4	29.2
Washington, DC	91.5	96.2	92.8	91.8	70.7	53.8	64.4	39.1	67.2	29.3
Wichita, KS	90.3	93.5	87.6	75.1	67.1	31.5	34.2	19.0	32.5	16.4
Wilmington, NC	93.1	95.0	86.8	85.4	75.6	38.5	41.1	23.8	56.4	25.1
Winston-Salem, NC	89.2	91.0	90.0	88.5	63.8	29.6	31.4	24.6	54.1	14.7
U.S.	89.4	92.9	88.1	88.0	72.5	35.0	37.7	24.7	57.0	19.9

Note: Figures shown cover persons 25 years old and over; Figures cover the Metropolitan Statistical Area (MSA); (1) People of Hispanic origin can be of any race
Source: U.S. Census Bureau, 2019-2023 American Community Survey 5-Year Estimates

Cost of Living Index

Urban Area	Composite	Groceries	Housing	Utilities	Transp.	Health	Misc.
Albuquerque, NM	94.9	97.4	89.1	87.3	85.9	102.0	101.8
Anchorage, AK	122.8	126.5	133.1	112.4	113.6	147.1	114.1
Ann Arbor, MI	n/a	n/a	n/a	n/a	n/a	n/a	n/a
Athens, GA	98.9	100.4	97.3	99.4	95.0	96.7	100.8
Atlanta, GA	96.0	100.9	86.9	99.7	100.2	107.9	97.6
Austin, TX	97.3	96.6	104.1	98.6	94.9	98.6	92.2
Baltimore, MD	100.5	102.8	86.5	110.6	104.2	94.2	108.4
Billings, MT	99.8	103.5	95.3	82.7	120.0	114.8	98.9
Boise City, ID	102.1	103.7	101.0	77.8	109.9	98.2	106.6
Boston, MA	145.9	104.4	218.9	149.7	109.8	125.3	115.2
Boulder, CO	n/a	n/a	n/a	n/a	n/a	n/a	n/a
Cape Coral, FL	104.9	104.0	105.1	106.5	105.9	111.8	103.5
Cedar Rapids, IA	n/a	n/a	n/a	n/a	n/a	n/a	n/a
Charleston, SC	101.9	102.1	103.8	113.9	94.9	85.7	101.2
Charlotte, NC	98.9	101.1	84.8	101.3	94.4	99.6	110.0
Chicago, IL	115.1	103.9	140.1	96.7	107.3	107.9	107.0
Cincinnati, OH	96.0	100.7	87.3	99.6	96.2	94.8	100.4
Clarksville, TN	n/a	n/a	n/a	n/a	n/a	n/a	n/a
Cleveland, OH	91.4	99.8	81.2	85.5	96.7	92.2	96.1
College Station, TX	n/a	n/a	n/a	n/a	n/a	n/a	n/a
Colorado Springs, CO	101.9	101.9	110.2	75.7	95.1	95.5	104.0
Columbia, MO	90.0	96.2	79.7	96.8	84.8	98.8	94.3
Columbia, SC	89.2	99.1	69.2	117.6	80.6	75.6	98.3
Columbus, OH	95.3	100.6	96.5	104.2	87.5	82.3	93.6
Dallas, TX	101.7	98.9	95.1	115.6	91.2	104.5	107.4
Davenport, IA	90.1	97.4	76.8	83.2	105.1	97.3	94.6
Denver, CO	108.6	101.3	123.4	89.3	94.7	109.6	107.7
Des Moines, IA	85.8	99.6	66.1	80.8	93.2	87.2	94.9
Detroit, MI	103.3	101.0	106.0	100.6	103.7	107.0	102.0
Durham, NC	98.5	102.0	101.6	93.4	93.8	103.8	96.2
El Paso, TX	88.1	96.7	70.7	91.5	101.2	88.7	94.3
Eugene, OR	107.3	105.2	120.6	92.5	110.3	108.2	100.0
Fargo, ND	97.3	97.9	85.1	80.1	98.8	118.1	108.0
Fort Collins, CO	n/a	n/a	n/a	n/a	n/a	n/a	n/a
Fort Wayne, IN	90.3	99.0	77.5	91.0	100.4	97.4	93.1
Fort Worth, TX	96.0	99.3	85.8	116.7	94.7	105.7	97.0
Gainesville, FL	n/a	n/a	n/a	n/a	n/a	n/a	n/a
Green Bay, WI	90.5	97.9	80.9	82.0	102.8	95.1	93.4
Greensboro, NC	n/a	n/a	n/a	n/a	n/a	n/a	n/a
Honolulu, HI	186.8	130.4	310.0	197.6	133.6	120.8	130.4
Houston, TX	94.1	99.3	79.2	92.4	94.0	97.5	104.1
Huntsville, AL	90.8	100.2	72.3	88.7	96.5	92.5	100.7
Indianapolis, IN	88.8	98.0	76.9	88.4	98.0	86.9	92.5
Jacksonville, FL	92.9	104.0	87.1	89.7	87.2	85.2	96.0
Kansas City, MO	91.1	97.3	87.5	105.6	89.3	83.8	89.1
Lafayette, LA	87.2	97.1	64.5	84.1	97.9	80.7	100.5
Las Vegas, NV	98.5	103.7	104.6	113.8	115.0	85.2	85.1
Lexington, KY	91.9	100.5	77.2	84.4	97.3	97.6	99.7
Lincoln, NE	94.3	99.3	77.6	92.2	99.5	105.4	103.5
Little Rock, AR	93.4	97.3	77.6	84.2	94.5	84.6	107.8
Los Angeles, CA	149.4	109.3	232.5	107.2	136.1	101.1	118.9
Louisville, KY	94.1	99.1	80.1	83.2	96.7	114.9	102.4
Madison, WI	104.7	98.8	106.4	98.8	98.3	113.2	107.8
Manchester, NH	112.6	99.9	117.6	112.2	105.9	103.9	117.0
McAllen, TX	85.1	93.4	60.2	119.6	94.1	79.2	92.1
Memphis, TN	89.8	98.8	86.2	80.9	88.8	86.0	91.7

Table continued on following page.

Urban Area	Composite	Groceries	Housing	Utilities	Transp.	Health	Misc.
Miami, FL	120.9	110.8	157.4	104.9	100.6	98.1	107.4
Midland, TX	96.4	96.2	83.8	100.9	94.3	87.6	107.5
Milwaukee, WI	100.5	100.8	104.2	94.0	102.7	105.0	97.7
Minneapolis, MN	93.6	102.6	82.9	96.6	96.4	96.0	96.5
Nashville, TN	98.7	99.5	101.4	98.2	90.8	95.5	98.7
New Orleans, LA	112.4	99.2	148.7	71.6	95.6	102.6	104.0
New York, NY[2]	161.1	113.0	276.5	115.1	114.9	128.1	114.9
Oklahoma City, OK	82.2	94.9	60.1	96.8	91.3	103.9	86.0
Omaha, NE	91.9	99.1	82.5	84.2	94.4	94.0	97.5
Orlando, FL	96.4	104.7	91.7	103.7	97.4	91.9	95.2
Philadelphia, PA	103.2	104.1	99.2	105.5	105.3	96.2	106.0
Phoenix, AZ	106.3	102.8	115.6	106.6	105.4	91.6	102.2
Pittsburgh, PA	98.1	97.8	94.9	119.9	107.2	99.2	93.2
Portland, OR	116.6	107.2	146.0	86.6	127.4	110.5	101.9
Providence, RI	112.2	102.0	113.4	139.7	96.5	104.4	114.1
Provo, UT	102.5	96.7	111.3	93.2	107.4	89.9	100.5
Raleigh, NC	97.2	100.6	91.9	89.8	92.1	112.2	101.0
Reno, NV	104.0	102.9	110.9	93.4	123.5	88.5	98.6
Richmond, VA	94.2	99.9	84.6	96.2	95.3	91.1	99.2
Rochester, MN	n/a	n/a	n/a	n/a	n/a	n/a	n/a
Sacramento, CA	128.8	106.9	139.2	174.4	152.0	99.7	116.9
Saint Louis, MO	89.1	98.8	78.0	97.9	93.3	87.6	90.9
Saint Paul, MN	94.0	105.2	81.3	95.6	96.0	96.7	98.1
Salem, OR	n/a	n/a	n/a	n/a	n/a	n/a	n/a
Salt Lake City, UT	109.0	98.1	128.7	95.4	111.4	88.5	103.0
San Antonio, TX	91.2	94.5	79.0	81.8	94.3	111.3	98.5
San Diego, CA	145.3	111.1	212.1	139.4	140.9	102.2	113.9
San Francisco, CA	166.8	123.6	263.3	160.1	143.6	127.6	119.3
San Jose, CA	180.6	115.0	321.1	158.6	140.7	120.1	117.9
Santa Rosa, CA	n/a	n/a	n/a	n/a	n/a	n/a	n/a
Savannah, GA	93.8	102.5	78.1	99.5	102.7	113.7	96.4
Seattle, WA	145.1	110.3	212.2	101.4	128.4	128.5	122.4
Sioux Falls, SD	91.0	96.4	88.5	91.3	89.9	92.6	90.7
Tampa, FL	97.6	105.7	95.8	99.9	102.1	93.1	94.4
Tucson, AZ	n/a	n/a	n/a	n/a	n/a	n/a	n/a
Tulsa, OK	84.7	95.9	65.1	98.3	88.4	93.5	90.3
Virginia Beach, VA[3]	94.0	98.5	82.4	104.2	96.0	110.6	96.4
Washington, DC	141.9	105.9	222.4	102.4	107.9	117.0	113.2
Wichita, KS	88.8	94.9	65.9	98.2	97.5	94.3	99.6
Wilmington, NC	n/a	n/a	n/a	n/a	n/a	n/a	n/a
Winston-Salem, NC	93.4	97.0	77.5	101.7	92.1	105.8	101.5
U.S.	100.0	100.0	100.0	100.0	100.0	100.0	100.0

Note: The Cost of Living Index measures regional differences in the cost of consumer goods and services, excluding taxes and non-consumer expenditures, for professional and managerial households in the top income quintile. It is based on more than 50,000 prices covering almost 60 different items for which prices are collected three times a year by chambers of commerce, economic development organizations or university applied economic centers in each participating urban area. The numbers shown should be read as a percentage above or below the national average of 100. For example, a value of 115.4 in the groceries column indicates that grocery prices are 15.4% higher than the national average. Small differences in the index numbers should not be interpreted as significant. In cases where data is not available for the city, data for the metro area or for a neighboring city has been provided and noted as follows: (2) Brooklyn, NY; (3) Hampton Roads-SE Virginia
Source: The Council for Community and Economic Research, Cost of Living Index, 2024

Grocery Prices

Urban Area	T-Bone Steak ($/pound)	Frying Chicken ($/pound)	Whole Milk ($/half gal.)	Eggs ($/dozen)	Orange Juice ($/64 oz.)	Coffee ($/11.5 oz.)
Albuquerque, NM	14.86	1.51	4.61	3.01	4.27	5.45
Anchorage, AK	17.56	2.89	5.34	4.09	5.40	7.86
Ann Arbor, MI	n/a	n/a	n/a	n/a	n/a	n/a
Athens, GA	15.55	1.45	4.70	3.57	4.49	5.28
Atlanta, GA	15.52	1.44	4.67	3.38	4.47	5.59
Austin, TX	14.52	1.37	4.62	3.05	4.27	5.19
Baltimore, MD	15.52	1.44	4.64	3.35	4.34	5.56
Billings, MT	15.52	1.47	4.72	3.46	4.19	6.92
Boise City, ID	15.52	1.52	4.75	3.63	4.45	6.38
Boston, MA	15.52	1.51	4.76	3.03	4.54	5.39
Boulder, CO	n/a	n/a	n/a	n/a	n/a	n/a
Cape Coral, FL	15.51	1.46	4.69	3.46	4.51	5.45
Cedar Rapids, IA	n/a	n/a	n/a	n/a	n/a	n/a
Charleston, SC	15.51	1.64	4.54	3.41	4.43	5.46
Charlotte, NC	15.53	1.61	4.69	3.30	4.33	5.36
Chicago, IL	15.52	1.45	4.88	3.50	4.50	5.80
Cincinnati, OH	15.52	1.74	4.74	3.73	4.36	5.67
Clarksville, TN	n/a	n/a	n/a	n/a	n/a	n/a
Cleveland, OH	15.51	1.42	4.58	3.24	4.44	5.24
College Station, TX	n/a	n/a	n/a	n/a	n/a	n/a
Colorado Springs, CO	15.53	1.46	4.60	2.91	4.42	6.03
Columbia, MO	15.51	1.47	4.69	3.41	4.45	5.17
Columbia, SC	15.51	1.66	4.62	3.28	4.38	5.27
Columbus, OH	15.51	1.72	4.72	3.39	4.39	5.52
Dallas, TX	14.56	1.54	4.61	3.13	4.31	5.41
Davenport, IA	15.52	1.43	4.92	3.35	4.44	5.02
Denver, CO	15.52	1.45	4.62	2.98	4.42	6.16
Des Moines, IA	15.52	1.44	4.76	3.47	4.47	4.94
Detroit, MI	15.53	1.73	4.80	3.37	4.41	5.64
Durham, NC	15.53	1.48	4.61	3.25	4.39	5.40
El Paso, TX	14.86	1.41	4.63	2.97	4.27	5.42
Eugene, OR	15.53	1.92	4.92	3.47	4.49	6.40
Fargo, ND	15.51	1.46	4.85	3.12	4.28	5.46
Fort Collins, CO	n/a	n/a	n/a	n/a	n/a	n/a
Fort Wayne, IN	15.51	1.66	4.69	3.49	4.36	5.41
Fort Worth, TX	14.52	1.56	4.61	3.13	4.28	5.46
Gainesville, FL	n/a	n/a	n/a	n/a	n/a	n/a
Green Bay, WI	15.51	1.42	4.70	3.25	4.43	5.29
Greensboro, NC	n/a	n/a	n/a	n/a	n/a	n/a
Honolulu, HI	16.57	2.86	5.49	3.98	5.19	7.89
Houston, TX	14.53	1.62	4.64	3.18	4.33	5.40
Huntsville, AL	15.52	1.41	4.54	3.35	4.41	5.49
Indianapolis, IN	15.51	1.63	4.67	3.40	4.33	5.39
Jacksonville, FL	15.52	1.42	4.72	3.41	4.53	5.38
Kansas City, MO	15.52	1.45	4.70	3.17	4.38	5.06
Lafayette, LA	15.29	1.41	4.60	3.05	4.38	5.07
Las Vegas, NV	15.54	1.74	4.78	3.08	4.43	6.31
Lexington, KY	15.52	1.44	4.69	3.40	4.30	5.70
Lincoln, NE	15.51	1.44	4.68	3.13	4.43	5.17
Little Rock, AR	14.86	1.43	4.62	3.40	4.31	5.24
Los Angeles, CA	15.55	2.45	5.00	3.14	4.55	6.68
Louisville, KY	15.51	1.48	4.71	3.39	4.37	5.37
Madison, WI	15.51	1.43	4.77	3.34	4.44	5.60
Manchester, NH	15.51	1.42	4.71	2.98	4.42	5.31
McAllen, TX	14.52	1.28	4.54	2.96	4.22	5.08

Table continued on following page.

Urban Area	T-Bone Steak ($/pound)	Frying Chicken ($/pound)	Whole Milk ($/half gal.)	Eggs ($/dozen)	Orange Juice ($/64 oz.)	Coffee ($/11.5 oz.)
Memphis, TN	15.53	1.31	4.67	3.47	4.35	5.24
Miami, FL	15.52	1.45	4.80	3.77	4.78	5.91
Midland, TX	14.53	1.41	4.61	3.04	4.30	4.99
Milwaukee, WI	15.50	1.43	4.80	3.34	4.45	5.96
Minneapolis, MN	15.53	1.44	4.66	3.56	4.49	5.23
Nashville, TN	15.51	1.43	4.63	3.32	4.40	5.35
New Orleans, LA	15.51	1.36	4.66	3.19	4.38	4.94
New York, NY[2]	15.52	1.56	5.14	3.63	4.79	5.93
Oklahoma City, OK	15.34	1.46	4.55	2.97	4.28	5.16
Omaha, NE	15.51	1.44	4.87	3.22	4.43	5.50
Orlando, FL	15.52	1.45	4.63	3.47	4.53	5.53
Philadelphia, PA	15.46	1.52	4.70	3.48	4.41	5.43
Phoenix, AZ	15.53	1.77	4.76	2.95	4.40	6.24
Pittsburgh, PA	15.52	1.43	4.52	3.27	4.44	5.15
Portland, OR	15.52	1.89	4.93	3.57	4.49	6.85
Providence, RI	15.51	1.68	4.70	3.55	4.43	4.91
Provo, UT	15.52	1.54	4.57	2.91	4.17	5.79
Raleigh, NC	15.51	1.45	4.58	3.33	4.31	5.44
Reno, NV	15.53	2.26	4.66	2.91	4.36	5.88
Richmond, VA	15.51	1.43	4.65	3.38	4.37	5.55
Rochester, MN	n/a	n/a	n/a	n/a	n/a	n/a
Sacramento, CA	15.53	2.13	5.01	2.90	4.40	6.44
Saint Louis, MO	15.51	1.44	4.67	3.37	4.43	5.05
Saint Paul, MN	15.52	1.44	4.64	3.81	4.58	5.13
Salem, OR	n/a	n/a	n/a	n/a	n/a	n/a
Salt Lake City, UT	15.51	1.53	4.62	3.03	4.19	6.11
San Antonio, TX	14.53	1.33	4.57	2.98	4.25	5.05
San Diego, CA	15.56	2.40	5.07	3.17	4.63	6.78
San Francisco, CA	15.55	2.66	5.03	3.35	4.86	7.53
San Jose, CA	15.54	2.57	5.09	3.10	4.64	6.92
Santa Rosa, CA	n/a	n/a	n/a	n/a	n/a	n/a
Savannah, GA	15.52	1.43	4.72	3.53	4.53	5.62
Seattle, WA	15.51	1.98	4.94	3.87	4.58	7.06
Sioux Falls, SD	15.53	1.49	4.52	3.10	4.37	5.10
Tampa, FL	15.52	1.46	4.73	3.60	4.59	5.56
Tucson, AZ	n/a	n/a	n/a	n/a	n/a	n/a
Tulsa, OK	15.52	1.45	4.59	2.97	4.32	5.06
Virginia Beach, VA[3]	15.52	1.46	4.58	3.35	4.34	5.34
Washington, DC	15.51	1.42	4.62	3.47	4.44	5.77
Wichita, KS	15.50	1.43	4.66	3.16	4.30	5.36
Wilmington, NC	n/a	n/a	n/a	n/a	n/a	n/a
Winston-Salem, NC	15.51	1.46	4.60	3.19	4.30	5.15
Average[1]	15.42	1.55	4.69	3.25	4.41	5.46
Minimum[1]	14.50	1.16	4.43	2.75	4.00	4.85
Maximum[1]	17.56	2.89	5.49	4.78	5.54	7.89

Note: **T-Bone Steak** *(price per pound);* **Frying Chicken** *(price per pound, whole fryer);* **Whole Milk** *(half gallon carton);* **Eggs** *(price per dozen, Grade A, large);* **Orange Juice** *(64 oz. Tropicana or Florida Natural);* **Coffee** *(11.5 oz. can, vacuum-packed, Maxwell House, Hills Bros, or Folgers); (1) Average, minimum, and maximum values for all 276 areas in the Cost of Living Index report; n/a not available; In cases where data is not available for the city, data for the metro area or for a neighboring city has been provided and noted as follows: (2) Brooklyn, NY; (3) Hampton Roads-SE Virginia*
Source: The Council for Community and Economic Research, Cost of Living Index, 2024

Housing and Utility Costs

Urban Area	New Home Price ($)	Apartment Rent ($/month)	All Electric ($/month)	Part Electric ($/month)	Other Energy ($/month)	Telephone ($/month)
Albuquerque, NM	424,687	1,574	-	115.74	50.09	192.92
Anchorage, AK	758,772	1,670	-	108.68	138.69	193.41
Ann Arbor, MI	n/a	n/a	n/a	n/a	n/a	n/a
Athens, GA	483,427	1,622	-	113.87	91.54	192.87
Atlanta, GA	428,946	1,464	-	113.87	91.54	194.22
Austin, TX	500,842	1,849	-	137.02	59.06	203.47
Baltimore, MD	390,678	1,695	-	134.88	101.43	201.97
Billings, MT	517,409	1,317	-	94.77	60.66	185.25
Boise City, ID	514,076	1,611	-	83.70	59.41	179.42
Boston, MA	1,039,939	3,993	-	190.85	180.18	190.24
Boulder, CO	n/a	n/a	n/a	n/a	n/a	n/a
Cape Coral, FL	509,774	1,897	225.95	-	-	197.01
Cedar Rapids, IA	n/a	n/a	n/a	n/a	n/a	n/a
Charleston, SC	526,080	1,748	249.82	-	-	197.48
Charlotte, NC	398,825	1,562	213.43	-	-	189.47
Chicago, IL	566,384	3,240	-	113.94	70.31	212.43
Cincinnati, OH	443,467	1,416	-	116.95	90.88	189.55
Clarksville, TN	n/a	n/a	n/a	n/a	n/a	n/a
Cleveland, OH	391,639	1,431	-	83.27	78.55	189.85
College Station, TX	n/a	n/a	n/a	n/a	n/a	n/a
Colorado Springs, CO	557,240	1,828	-	86.01	42.49	192.15
Columbia, MO	451,668	1,041	-	114.12	78.36	199.61
Columbia, SC	328,383	1,205	-	119.24	143.41	195.98
Columbus, OH	482,718	1,613	-	146.60	76.69	189.10
Dallas, TX	477,656	1,572	-	171.06	80.72	203.47
Davenport, IA	387,652	1,218	-	85.51	62.12	200.43
Denver, CO	650,555	1,899	-	93.55	76.25	197.22
Des Moines, IA	359,756	846	-	84.52	63.10	188.12
Detroit, MI	568,077	1,560	-	134.21	78.36	187.38
Durham, NC	521,333	1,650	187.89	-	-	189.44
El Paso, TX	354,072	1,146	-	111.01	62.07	203.47
Eugene, OR	666,539	1,654	-	89.38	96.37	187.81
Fargo, ND	390,066	1,596	-	81.39	58.17	197.46
Fort Collins, CO	n/a	n/a	n/a	n/a	n/a	n/a
Fort Wayne, IN	364,871	1,370	-	109.31	68.72	192.42
Fort Worth, TX	422,585	1,470	-	170.29	80.72	210.13
Gainesville, FL	n/a	n/a	n/a	n/a	n/a	n/a
Green Bay, WI	447,400	1,055	-	90.06	61.14	188.34
Greensboro, NC	n/a	n/a	n/a	n/a	n/a	n/a
Honolulu, HI	1,681,170	4,424	529.02	-	-	187.39
Houston, TX	388,197	1,322	-	124.12	48.31	209.27
Huntsville, AL	361,221	1,123	172.74	-	-	189.28
Indianapolis, IN	360,369	1,336	-	99.46	70.12	192.42
Jacksonville, FL	391,862	1,714	170.55	-	-	197.76
Kansas City, MO	429,449	1,506	-	103.82	115.85	202.40
Lafayette, LA	306,872	1,150	-	96.15	60.82	190.09
Las Vegas, NV	554,723	1,576	-	160.52	94.44	188.64
Lexington, KY	380,651	1,239	-	82.51	72.69	194.48
Lincoln, NE	390,814	1,216	-	90.57	84.28	204.27
Little Rock, AR	407,536	1,155	-	76.85	69.20	208.40
Los Angeles, CA	1,311,286	2,988	-	163.45	65.93	194.86
Louisville, KY	388,161	1,369	-	82.51	72.69	188.14
Madison, WI	622,141	1,233	-	126.81	79.79	187.45
Manchester, NH	552,244	2,205	-	135.10	114.30	189.12
McAllen, TX	291,921	981	-	176.13	88.49	203.47

Table continued on following page.

Urban Area	New Home Price ($)	Apartment Rent ($/month)	All Electric ($/month)	Part Electric ($/month)	Other Energy ($/month)	Telephone ($/month)
Memphis, TN	404,407	1,598	-	105.22	38.46	195.12
Miami, FL	711,025	3,211	220.47	-	-	197.31
Midland, TX	400,707	1,483	-	150.59	53.85	202.34
Milwaukee, WI	541,477	1,627	-	123.28	67.66	187.62
Minneapolis, MN	405,152	1,419	-	98.70	98.25	191.53
Nashville, TN	519,432	1,670	-	105.42	77.00	223.33
New Orleans, LA	812,851	2,128	-	68.38	47.92	190.09
New York, NY[2]	1,411,780	3,995	-	157.71	92.60	203.07
Oklahoma City, OK	320,395	811	-	115.46	78.66	197.38
Omaha, NE	385,889	1,500	-	93.49	55.47	203.73
Orlando, FL	441,765	1,690	216.79	-	-	197.01
Philadelphia, PA	470,985	1,851	-	138.01	81.94	201.51
Phoenix, AZ	609,926	1,792	232.03	-	-	187.62
Pittsburgh, PA	478,461	1,602	-	137.23	130.44	200.01
Portland, OR	723,737	2,574	-	70.81	96.37	186.81
Providence, RI	474,141	2,453	-	171.99	161.54	198.12
Provo, UT	612,973	1,544	-	77.11	106.23	195.59
Raleigh, NC	466,683	1,514	-	107.05	69.13	189.30
Reno, NV	596,654	1,646	-	129.17	59.21	188.64
Richmond, VA	418,775	1,466	-	117.64	80.21	187.77
Rochester, MN	n/a	n/a	n/a	n/a	n/a	n/a
Sacramento, CA	718,604	2,241	-	397.28	53.75	191.51
Saint Louis, MO	427,558	1,128	-	100.98	92.58	203.68
Saint Paul, MN	404,109	1,358	-	92.16	101.15	192.06
Salem, OR	n/a	n/a	n/a	n/a	n/a	n/a
Salt Lake City, UT	717,422	1,758	-	96.56	93.13	196.83
San Antonio, TX	357,072	1,521	-	105.82	36.26	202.34
San Diego, CA	1,113,702	3,153	-	255.41	87.52	181.36
San Francisco, CA	1,383,739	3,749	-	264.12	131.73	205.06
San Jose, CA	1,860,932	3,311	-	267.58	131.25	192.30
Santa Rosa, CA	n/a	n/a	n/a	n/a	n/a	n/a
Savannah, GA	379,397	1,313	206.53	-	-	191.37
Seattle, WA	1,093,157	3,259	204.50	-	-	204.74
Sioux Falls, SD	509,371	977	-	103.68	71.55	198.68
Tampa, FL	455,535	1,796	203.80	-	-	197.76
Tucson, AZ	n/a	n/a	n/a	n/a	n/a	n/a
Tulsa, OK	339,822	935	-	118.37	80.52	197.22
Virginia Beach, VA[3]	389,841	1,484	-	120.02	103.90	187.93
Washington, DC	1,149,206	3,212	-	122.00	92.52	193.65
Wichita, KS	334,425	1,007	-	113.92	81.43	202.42
Wilmington, NC	n/a	n/a	n/a	n/a	n/a	n/a
Winston-Salem, NC	383,928	1,301	214.90	-	-	189.30
Average[1]	515,975	1,550	210.99	123.07	82.07	194.99
Minimum[1]	265,375	692	104.33	53.68	36.26	179.42
Maximum[1]	2,775,821	5,719	529.02	397.28	361.63	223.33

Note: **New Home Price** (2,400 sf living area, 8,000 sf lot, in urban area with full utilities); **Apartment Rent** (950 sf 2 bedroom/1.5 or 2 bath, unfurnished, excluding all utilities except water); **All Electric** (average monthly cost for an all-electric home); **Part Electric** (average monthly cost for a part-electric home); **Other Energy** (average monthly cost for natural gas, fuel oil, coal, wood, and any other forms of energy except electricity); **Telephone** (price includes the base monthly rate plus taxes and fees for three lines of mobile phone service); (1) Average, minimum, and maximum values for all 276 areas in the Cost of Living Index report; n/a not available; In cases where data is not available for the city, data for the metro area or for a neighboring city has been provided and noted as follows: (2) Brooklyn, NY; (3) Hampton Roads-SE Virginia
Source: The Council for Community and Economic Research, Cost of Living Index, 2024

Health Care, Transportation, and Other Costs

Urban Area	Doctor ($/visit)	Dentist ($/visit)	Optometrist ($/visit)	Gasoline ($/gallon)	Beauty Salon ($/visit)	Men's Shirt ($)
Albuquerque, NM	133.41	115.32	145.00	3.10	47.25	37.35
Anchorage, AK	243.83	173.17	265.00	3.68	50.00	45.44
Ann Arbor, MI	n/a	n/a	n/a	n/a	n/a	n/a
Athens, GA	123.75	128.33	97.63	3.12	56.40	40.51
Atlanta, GA	132.58	142.21	130.44	3.22	56.70	30.32
Austin, TX	109.05	135.58	126.98	2.98	67.39	27.11
Baltimore, MD	135.14	116.91	119.20	3.41	61.43	41.00
Billings, MT	215.23	110.57	164.07	3.33	38.78	36.85
Boise City, ID	169.88	102.77	145.10	3.61	52.55	48.06
Boston, MA	222.77	144.00	161.33	3.33	66.76	39.88
Boulder, CO	n/a	n/a	n/a	n/a	n/a	n/a
Cape Coral, FL	178.39	133.21	101.13	3.36	54.67	30.93
Cedar Rapids, IA	n/a	n/a	n/a	n/a	n/a	n/a
Charleston, SC	123.53	99.17	82.86	3.03	56.00	24.77
Charlotte, NC	157.61	120.57	92.08	3.12	79.44	57.64
Chicago, IL	179.67	126.00	113.83	3.55	62.23	34.52
Cincinnati, OH	158.21	98.92	97.57	3.18	39.43	41.70
Clarksville, TN	n/a	n/a	n/a	n/a	n/a	n/a
Cleveland, OH	117.00	111.33	110.47	3.21	40.20	39.79
College Station, TX	n/a	n/a	n/a	n/a	n/a	n/a
Colorado Springs, CO	134.99	106.17	132.00	3.04	50.14	30.58
Columbia, MO	182.67	95.67	138.50	3.10	45.42	37.14
Columbia, SC	150.00	58.67	67.33	3.12	38.83	34.56
Columbus, OH	115.70	94.35	93.20	3.19	49.51	36.47
Dallas, TX	138.26	133.49	135.65	3.07	72.78	43.45
Davenport, IA	167.17	105.92	108.62	3.41	39.87	34.38
Denver, CO	134.18	140.57	122.31	3.05	50.44	22.71
Des Moines, IA	119.38	101.96	128.70	3.15	42.46	37.61
Detroit, MI	183.09	126.33	95.64	3.42	60.83	52.14
Durham, NC	179.33	112.78	133.40	3.38	54.35	30.66
El Paso, TX	129.11	95.03	101.95	3.23	33.64	34.89
Eugene, OR	196.75	117.67	126.00	3.83	40.19	36.32
Fargo, ND	230.71	124.67	113.44	3.12	40.47	44.83
Fort Collins, CO	n/a	n/a	n/a	n/a	n/a	n/a
Fort Wayne, IN	137.75	106.33	122.67	3.32	33.28	39.34
Fort Worth, TX	138.71	136.11	137.89	3.03	52.39	37.44
Gainesville, FL	n/a	n/a	n/a	n/a	n/a	n/a
Green Bay, WI	167.58	112.11	84.28	3.14	30.42	26.22
Greensboro, NC	n/a	n/a	n/a	n/a	n/a	n/a
Honolulu, HI	201.94	127.00	258.67	4.58	75.33	58.48
Houston, TX	97.07	129.17	137.54	2.98	73.30	50.68
Huntsville, AL	121.00	115.28	99.56	3.04	58.56	30.30
Indianapolis, IN	112.66	105.53	77.80	3.35	39.07	43.61
Jacksonville, FL	106.53	98.40	97.76	3.34	79.67	30.27
Kansas City, MO	95.79	108.20	95.10	3.06	34.80	29.79
Lafayette, LA	95.33	95.87	120.20	3.01	40.73	44.86
Las Vegas, NV	110.44	99.25	100.78	4.13	48.86	25.05
Lexington, KY	144.23	113.73	92.42	3.19	60.23	44.97
Lincoln, NE	183.29	113.07	119.17	3.25	42.20	52.31
Little Rock, AR	133.00	83.67	105.53	2.95	52.55	47.99
Los Angeles, CA	130.00	133.17	127.53	4.85	94.00	38.64
Louisville, KY	152.10	159.00	107.05	3.21	43.89	48.00
Madison, WI	236.64	124.37	72.86	3.27	76.22	41.80
Manchester, NH	183.83	108.17	116.33	3.24	56.33	42.69
McAllen, TX	91.69	88.11	100.21	2.96	47.50	32.95

Table continued on following page.

Urban Area	Doctor ($/visit)	Dentist ($/visit)	Optometrist ($/visit)	Gasoline ($/gallon)	Beauty Salon ($/visit)	Men's Shirt ($)
Memphis, TN	112.80	97.80	83.95	3.00	46.92	27.44
Miami, FL	134.75	118.47	110.39	3.43	87.63	28.46
Midland, TX	97.50	108.17	132.67	3.13	69.08	43.45
Milwaukee, WI	174.22	122.03	86.17	3.30	44.20	32.41
Minneapolis, MN	170.09	100.86	120.48	3.16	40.96	41.19
Nashville, TN	122.71	110.37	114.45	3.08	48.65	32.66
New Orleans, LA	161.78	121.36	115.44	3.11	48.33	49.00
New York, NY[2]	192.84	171.93	152.60	3.43	68.80	44.04
Oklahoma City, OK	149.53	124.67	99.96	3.02	51.40	22.45
Omaha, NE	151.64	90.62	117.00	3.08	33.92	35.09
Orlando, FL	123.06	110.00	97.28	3.34	53.19	32.49
Philadelphia, PA	148.84	111.61	125.00	3.33	67.25	36.90
Phoenix, AZ	99.00	127.08	103.50	3.64	55.36	22.95
Pittsburgh, PA	96.56	128.63	105.71	3.67	44.32	28.77
Portland, OR	218.48	116.33	147.50	4.17	60.17	35.98
Providence, RI	168.33	117.58	111.08	3.28	50.22	31.37
Provo, UT	113.66	105.45	127.59	3.41	51.34	49.04
Raleigh, NC	146.67	153.61	109.33	3.23	55.17	32.17
Reno, NV	115.00	105.00	118.17	4.35	49.17	27.27
Richmond, VA	120.19	104.13	133.02	3.24	48.38	20.26
Rochester, MN	n/a	n/a	n/a	n/a	n/a	n/a
Sacramento, CA	151.58	121.82	173.55	5.28	71.49	36.48
Saint Louis, MO	92.32	115.88	95.55	3.38	41.97	28.19
Saint Paul, MN	169.08	101.40	118.46	3.16	41.44	42.25
Salem, OR	n/a	n/a	n/a	n/a	n/a	n/a
Salt Lake City, UT	129.02	100.40	125.47	3.38	56.68	44.66
San Antonio, TX	149.40	139.78	139.25	2.97	69.33	39.95
San Diego, CA	139.44	126.00	143.70	4.93	67.95	39.49
San Francisco, CA	183.65	160.37	168.34	5.07	86.22	48.81
San Jose, CA	212.00	131.83	166.92	5.00	65.28	32.93
Santa Rosa, CA	n/a	n/a	n/a	n/a	n/a	n/a
Savannah, GA	150.00	152.87	91.31	3.29	39.61	38.61
Seattle, WA	208.77	157.05	179.39	4.49	85.33	49.17
Sioux Falls, SD	116.42	116.32	140.94	3.04	40.11	30.74
Tampa, FL	126.57	112.70	118.00	3.36	48.00	27.91
Tucson, AZ	n/a	n/a	n/a	n/a	n/a	n/a
Tulsa, OK	109.57	109.83	111.11	2.95	35.40	29.28
Virginia Beach, VA[3]	144.92	148.93	69.03	3.20	42.70	32.71
Washington, DC	177.67	151.33	125.50	3.36	78.76	37.95
Wichita, KS	111.32	102.90	144.60	3.09	48.13	54.27
Wilmington, NC	n/a	n/a	n/a	n/a	n/a	n/a
Winston-Salem, NC	152.89	120.67	145.61	3.15	50.94	38.49
Average[1]	143.77	117.51	129.23	3.32	48.57	38.14
Minimum[1]	36.74	58.67	67.33	2.80	24.00	13.41
Maximum[1]	270.44	216.82	307.33	5.28	94.00	63.89

Note: **Doctor** (general practitioners routine exam of an established patient); **Dentist** (adult teeth cleaning and periodic oral examination); **Optometrist** (full vision eye exam for established adult patient); **Gasoline** (one gallon regular unleaded, national brand, including all taxes, cash price at self-service pump if available); **Beauty Salon** (woman's shampoo, trim, and blow-dry); **Men's Shirt** (cotton/polyester dress shirt, pinpoint weave, long sleeves); (1) Average, minimum, and maximum values for all 276 areas in the Cost of Living Index report; n/a not available; In cases where data is not available for the city, data for the metro area or for a neighboring city has been provided and noted as follows: (2) Brooklyn, NY; (3) Hampton Roads-SE Virginia
Source: The Council for Community and Economic Research, Cost of Living Index, 2024

Number of Medical Professionals

City	Area Covered	MDs[1]	DOs[1,2]	Dentists	Podiatrists	Chiropractors	Optometrists
Albuquerque, NM	Bernalillo County	503.5	30.6	87.4	9.4	24.9	17.7
Anchorage, AK	Anchorage Borough	384.5	55.4	134.9	5.9	65.7	31.5
Ann Arbor, MI	Washtenaw County	1,420.9	52.7	208.7	9.0	26.5	19.4
Athens, GA	Clarke County	392.7	17.7	50.0	3.8	21.5	16.2
Atlanta, GA	Fulton County	548.6	18.3	76.9	5.1	60.5	21.3
Austin, TX	Travis County	332.0	21.9	76.9	4.4	36.6	18.8
Baltimore, MD	Baltimore City	1,247.2	36.1	88.5	8.0	16.8	16.6
Billings, MT	Yellowstone County	379.2	40.0	101.3	9.4	38.6	26.9
Boise City, ID	Ada County	286.2	40.1	83.7	4.6	54.9	23.1
Boston, MA	Suffolk County	1,797.9	24.3	251.7	9.0	16.9	39.0
Boulder, CO	Boulder County	365.5	34.2	116.9	6.4	84.4	30.0
Cape Coral, FL	Lee County	198.8	29.9	56.1	7.9	28.8	13.3
Cedar Rapids, IA	Linn County	181.2	25.3	77.7	8.7	62.5	17.9
Charleston, SC	Charleston County	881.5	45.6	117.8	5.7	54.7	25.9
Charlotte, NC	Mecklenburg County	352.8	20.9	72.1	3.7	37.2	14.5
Chicago, IL	Cook County	472.9	34.3	100.5	12.9	30.1	22.5
Cincinnati, OH	Hamilton County	662.9	36.0	77.1	10.4	21.6	23.3
Clarksville, TN	Montgomery County	91.4	16.6	45.0	2.9	12.9	10.4
Cleveland, OH	Cuyahoga County	799.3	74.0	110.6	18.8	20.5	18.2
College Station, TX	Brazos County	254.5	20.2	58.0	3.3	19.6	18.0
Colorado Springs, CO	El Paso County	214.0	37.9	107.1	5.4	47.7	25.7
Columbia, MO	Boone County	864.2	95.9	78.6	5.8	41.2	28.0
Columbia, SC	Richland County	358.7	21.6	93.1	6.8	22.8	18.8
Columbus, OH	Franklin County	473.2	78.8	99.2	8.0	26.5	29.9
Dallas, TX	Dallas County	380.9	24.6	96.6	4.5	40.3	15.6
Davenport, IA	Scott County	256.4	56.3	85.5	5.2	190.5	16.6
Denver, CO	Denver County	610.0	36.3	84.8	6.8	40.6	17.3
Des Moines, IA	Polk County	221.1	118.9	80.8	12.3	63.7	21.2
Detroit, MI	Wayne County	348.3	61.0	80.1	9.8	19.1	12.4
Durham, NC	Durham County	1,206.3	21.9	77.2	4.2	21.1	13.7
El Paso, TX	El Paso County	231.2	22.1	49.5	4.7	9.2	10.8
Eugene, OR	Lane County	250.6	16.5	75.6	5.2	29.4	17.3
Fargo, ND	Cass County	401.6	26.5	78.4	5.1	75.9	33.6
Fort Collins, CO	Larimer County	251.9	39.3	85.2	6.5	57.4	21.3
Fort Wayne, IN	Allen County	272.1	33.5	72.7	5.6	23.8	26.6
Fort Worth, TX	Tarrant County	197.7	39.4	64.9	4.5	30.4	17.3
Gainesville, FL	Alachua County	1,059.4	68.3	193.4	5.6	26.9	19.2
Green Bay, WI	Brown County	265.5	25.6	80.7	3.3	50.5	19.9
Greensboro, NC	Guilford County	262.2	18.9	62.9	4.7	15.1	10.2
Honolulu, HI	Honolulu County	357.2	23.8	103.9	3.9	22.6	25.8
Houston, TX	Harris County	363.6	16.0	75.3	5.0	24.0	21.6
Huntsville, AL	Madison County	275.3	16.1	53.3	2.9	23.0	20.1
Indianapolis, IN	Marion County	475.0	31.6	95.4	6.9	17.5	22.1
Jacksonville, FL	Duval County	369.2	38.0	77.4	6.9	27.6	16.4
Kansas City, MO	Jackson County	343.6	110.1	94.5	7.1	49.3	20.2
Lafayette, LA	Lafayette Parish	383.7	17.3	71.3	4.0	33.6	14.4
Las Vegas, NV	Clark County	188.3	42.2	69.1	4.7	21.1	14.8
Lexington, KY	Fayette County	844.1	66.5	149.6	8.1	25.9	29.4
Lincoln, NE	Lancaster County	215.9	16.9	109.0	5.5	49.9	20.5
Little Rock, AR	Pulaski County	822.8	30.3	80.2	5.2	24.0	22.7
Los Angeles, CA	Los Angeles County	336.3	17.6	99.4	6.9	32.1	20.8
Louisville, KY	Jefferson County	506.3	25.2	107.8	8.5	28.2	17.9
Madison, WI	Dane County	669.0	28.0	77.3	5.2	45.9	21.9
Manchester, NH	Hillsborough County	235.1	26.7	85.2	6.6	26.9	22.5
McAllen, TX	Hidalgo County	145.8	4.7	31.4	1.6	8.0	7.2
Memphis, TN	Shelby County	429.3	17.8	78.8	4.0	15.5	33.0

Table continued on following page.

City	Area Covered	MDs[1]	DOs[1,2]	Dentists	Podiatrists	Chiropractors	Optometrists
Miami, FL	Miami-Dade County	415.2	27.2	81.5	10.0	20.1	16.3
Midland, TX	Midland County	154.1	6.4	60.4	2.3	14.1	11.9
Milwaukee, WI	Milwaukee County	431.6	36.6	92.8	7.1	22.0	12.1
Minneapolis, MN	Hennepin County	570.7	32.9	106.5	5.7	80.2	23.3
Nashville, TN	Davidson County	698.9	19.2	84.9	5.3	29.8	17.8
New Orleans, LA	Orleans Parish	1,005.0	33.8	86.5	4.9	10.2	8.8
New York, NY	New York City	545.5	24.3	90.9	13.8	16.8	19.8
Oklahoma City, OK	Oklahoma County	432.6	52.2	111.5	4.8	29.7	21.3
Omaha, NE	Douglas County	600.0	44.3	105.5	5.4	44.4	23.6
Orlando, FL	Orange County	349.3	28.9	54.1	4.1	29.8	14.1
Philadelphia, PA	Philadelphia County	663.2	66.9	86.4	16.3	15.6	20.8
Phoenix, AZ	Maricopa County	258.2	37.8	73.7	7.4	34.3	17.5
Pittsburgh, PA	Allegheny County	677.7	59.4	99.5	9.3	44.9	21.1
Portland, OR	Multnomah County	687.2	44.4	105.1	5.1	80.2	26.2
Providence, RI	Providence County	526.4	19.5	59.8	10.1	21.2	22.4
Provo, UT	Utah County	115.9	24.3	60.3	4.7	26.7	11.4
Raleigh, NC	Wake County	293.0	15.8	75.8	3.8	29.7	16.6
Reno, NV	Washoe County	310.2	25.2	72.1	4.4	30.7	23.7
Richmond, VA	Richmond City	822.6	63.6	155.7	13.5	7.4	15.7
Rochester, MN	Olmsted County	2,670.4	71.3	137.1	7.3	45.5	24.9
Sacramento, CA	Sacramento County	344.7	20.3	84.3	4.5	22.0	19.4
Saint Louis, MO	St. Louis City	1,491.0	56.9	71.0	4.3	23.4	21.7
Saint Paul, MN	Ramsey County	379.6	17.2	95.7	5.8	71.4	14.7
Salem, OR	Marion County	180.0	18.7	88.3	6.6	35.5	16.7
Salt Lake City, UT	Salt Lake County	422.6	23.4	83.1	6.6	29.7	15.1
San Antonio, TX	Bexar County	330.0	28.5	95.3	6.0	17.4	19.0
San Diego, CA	San Diego County	364.2	22.2	100.8	5.0	36.4	21.2
San Francisco, CA	San Francisco County	942.4	16.7	175.9	11.4	44.0	34.6
San Jose, CA	Santa Clara County	483.8	14.5	129.4	7.4	47.0	30.7
Santa Rosa, CA	Sonoma County	289.0	21.3	99.6	6.8	44.8	18.9
Savannah, GA	Chatham County	384.6	28.2	73.4	6.9	21.4	14.8
Seattle, WA	King County	521.6	19.0	118.3	6.4	48.4	24.3
Sioux Falls, SD	Minnehaha County	395.6	31.4	56.1	5.8	57.5	18.4
Tampa, FL	Hillsborough County	375.2	41.2	66.1	6.7	29.3	16.2
Tucson, AZ	Pima County	387.9	35.6	67.8	5.6	19.4	17.6
Tulsa, OK	Tulsa County	265.4	153.1	71.8	4.2	40.1	25.0
Virginia Beach, VA	Virginia Beach City	263.4	14.9	82.0	7.5	26.7	16.3
Washington, DC	District of Columbia	928.4	29.2	130.5	9.3	11.2	15.2
Wichita, KS	Sedgwick County	266.0	42.1	71.3	1.9	43.9	29.0
Wilmington, NC	New Hanover County	367.8	37.9	82.9	8.4	36.0	24.3
Winston-Salem, NC	Forsyth County	716.2	41.1	64.9	6.9	19.1	18.6
U.S.	U.S.	302.5	29.2	74.6	6.4	29.5	18.0

Note: All figures are the number of medical professionals per 100,000 population; Data as of 2023 unless noted; (1) Data as of 2022 and includes all active, non-federal physicians; (2) Doctor of Osteopathic Medicine
Source: U.S. Department of Health and Human Services, Health Resources and Services Administration, Bureau of Health Professions, Area Resource File (ARF) 2023-2024

Health Insurance Coverage: City

City	With Health Insurance	With Private Health Insurance	With Public Health Insurance	Without Health Insurance	Population Under Age 19 Without Health Insurance
Albuquerque, NM	91.7	60.1	45.1	8.3	5.0
Anchorage, AK	90.0	70.0	34.0	10.0	7.4
Ann Arbor, MI	97.2	86.7	20.9	2.8	2.1
Athens, GA	88.8	72.8	25.0	11.2	8.1
Atlanta, GA	89.5	70.4	27.2	10.5	6.2
Austin, TX	87.6	74.8	20.6	12.4	9.2
Baltimore, MD	94.2	58.5	46.8	5.8	3.8
Billings, MT	93.1	67.1	39.9	6.9	4.8
Boise City, ID	92.3	74.4	29.4	7.7	4.9
Boston, MA	97.0	69.9	35.8	3.0	1.9
Boulder, CO	96.5	83.8	21.0	3.5	1.0
Cape Coral, FL	88.4	65.5	38.4	11.6	10.1
Cedar Rapids, IA	95.5	71.1	36.8	4.5	1.6
Charleston, SC	93.6	79.0	27.0	6.4	2.0
Charlotte, NC	87.1	67.8	26.5	12.9	8.3
Chicago, IL	90.2	61.6	35.8	9.8	4.0
Cincinnati, OH	92.4	61.1	40.3	7.6	5.7
Clarksville, TN	90.7	72.1	34.3	9.3	4.3
Cleveland, OH	92.3	43.8	57.2	7.7	3.7
College Station, TX	91.9	83.0	16.5	8.1	4.7
Colorado Springs, CO	92.3	69.8	36.4	7.7	4.7
Columbia, MO	93.6	79.1	23.3	6.4	4.7
Columbia, SC	91.9	71.0	31.4	8.1	3.2
Columbus, OH	90.2	62.3	35.5	9.8	5.8
Dallas, TX	77.0	54.1	29.3	23.0	15.7
Davenport, IA	92.8	65.0	41.1	7.2	4.7
Denver, CO	91.2	68.3	30.8	8.8	5.3
Des Moines, IA	93.3	62.0	42.7	6.7	2.2
Detroit, MI	92.5	41.8	62.6	7.5	2.7
Durham, NC	88.4	70.6	27.4	11.6	8.6
El Paso, TX	79.0	53.1	34.9	21.0	11.9
Eugene, OR	94.5	68.2	39.0	5.5	2.3
Fargo, ND	93.9	79.5	26.0	6.1	4.5
Fort Collins, CO	94.4	78.3	25.0	5.6	4.8
Fort Wayne, IN	90.6	62.9	38.1	9.4	6.7
Fort Worth, TX	81.4	61.7	26.4	18.6	12.7
Gainesville, FL	91.8	76.6	23.8	8.2	5.0
Green Bay, WI	91.6	59.8	40.9	8.4	4.9
Greensboro, NC	90.9	65.5	35.7	9.1	4.1
Honolulu, HI	96.2	75.5	38.3	3.8	2.4
Houston, TX	76.0	52.1	30.3	24.0	16.0
Huntsville, AL	90.6	73.2	32.5	9.4	3.2
Indianapolis, IN	91.0	62.3	38.6	9.0	5.7
Jacksonville, FL	88.3	64.4	34.4	11.7	7.1
Kansas City, MO	88.7	68.3	29.8	11.3	7.4
Lafayette, LA	90.5	60.7	41.3	9.5	4.4
Las Vegas, NV	86.8	60.3	36.5	13.2	8.8
Lexington, KY	93.2	69.8	34.5	6.8	2.9
Lincoln, NE	93.3	76.3	28.6	6.7	3.9
Little Rock, AR	90.0	62.0	39.1	10.0	7.0
Los Angeles, CA	90.0	55.2	41.9	10.0	3.6
Louisville, KY	94.2	64.2	43.1	5.8	3.8
Madison, WI	95.7	81.9	24.1	4.3	2.9
Manchester, NH	91.2	66.6	35.0	8.8	4.9
McAllen, TX	74.2	48.4	32.3	25.8	14.9

Table continued on following page.

City	With Health Insurance	With Private Health Insurance	With Public Health Insurance	Without Health Insurance	Population Under Age 19 Without Health Insurance
Memphis, TN	85.2	55.1	41.3	14.8	8.6
Miami, FL	82.4	52.6	33.5	17.6	8.8
Midland, TX	85.2	72.0	21.3	14.8	11.7
Milwaukee, WI	90.9	52.2	46.7	9.1	3.6
Minneapolis, MN	94.1	69.5	32.8	5.9	2.8
Nashville, TN	87.4	69.0	29.0	12.6	9.0
New Orleans, LA	91.6	55.4	45.3	8.4	5.4
New York, NY	93.6	58.2	45.3	6.4	2.3
Oklahoma City, OK	86.0	63.0	34.4	14.0	7.6
Omaha, NE	90.3	69.2	31.0	9.7	6.9
Orlando, FL	86.1	64.6	27.6	13.9	8.0
Philadelphia, PA	92.8	58.8	45.9	7.2	4.5
Phoenix, AZ	85.5	58.6	34.6	14.5	9.8
Pittsburgh, PA	94.8	72.9	33.5	5.2	3.8
Portland, OR	94.5	71.5	33.1	5.5	2.1
Providence, RI	92.6	57.0	44.1	7.4	5.1
Provo, UT	90.6	78.6	17.5	9.4	9.8
Raleigh, NC	89.9	73.5	26.0	10.1	6.0
Reno, NV	89.5	67.9	31.5	10.5	7.0
Richmond, VA	90.2	63.3	36.9	9.8	7.2
Rochester, MN	95.7	79.7	30.5	4.3	3.7
Sacramento, CA	94.5	65.3	40.5	5.5	3.2
Saint Louis, MO	90.7	63.5	35.7	9.3	3.7
Saint Paul, MN	93.6	62.5	41.0	6.4	4.5
Salem, OR	92.6	63.9	41.9	7.4	1.9
Salt Lake City, UT	89.0	73.9	22.8	11.0	10.2
San Antonio, TX	82.5	58.4	33.8	17.5	9.8
San Diego, CA	93.7	71.9	31.7	6.3	3.6
San Francisco, CA	96.5	75.8	30.7	3.5	2.0
San Jose, CA	95.1	72.5	30.6	4.9	1.8
Santa Rosa, CA	93.6	67.8	39.1	6.4	3.9
Savannah, GA	86.2	59.3	36.7	13.8	5.7
Seattle, WA	95.6	80.5	23.5	4.4	1.8
Sioux Falls, SD	92.2	77.7	25.8	7.8	5.6
Tampa, FL	89.0	64.5	32.0	11.0	5.7
Tucson, AZ	89.0	57.0	42.7	11.0	7.4
Tulsa, OK	83.5	56.6	37.7	16.5	8.4
Virginia Beach, VA	93.5	78.0	30.8	6.5	3.8
Washington, DC	96.6	72.4	34.2	3.4	2.7
Wichita, KS	87.6	65.3	34.1	12.4	6.1
Wilmington, NC	88.4	69.5	32.5	11.6	8.0
Winston-Salem, NC	88.1	61.8	37.5	11.9	4.7
U.S.	91.4	67.3	36.3	8.6	5.4

Note: Figures are percentages that cover the civilian noninstitutionalized population
Source: U.S. Census Bureau, 2019-2023 American Community Survey 5-Year Estimates

Health Insurance Coverage: Metro Area

Metro Area	With Health Insurance	With Private Health Insurance	With Public Health Insurance	Without Health Insurance	Population Under Age 19 Without Health Insurance
Albuquerque, NM	91.9	59.2	47.2	8.1	5.0
Anchorage, AK	89.4	68.4	35.1	10.6	8.2
Ann Arbor, MI	96.7	81.5	28.7	3.3	2.0
Athens, GA	89.0	71.4	27.8	11.0	7.2
Atlanta, GA	87.8	69.1	28.2	12.2	7.2
Austin, TX	87.9	75.2	21.9	12.1	9.0
Baltimore, MD	95.1	74.5	34.4	4.9	3.6
Billings, MT	93.2	68.2	39.6	6.8	5.2
Boise City, ID	91.4	72.1	31.8	8.6	6.2
Boston, MA	97.2	76.4	33.5	2.8	1.6
Boulder, CO	95.6	79.6	26.6	4.4	2.0
Cape Coral, FL	87.5	62.0	43.6	12.5	9.7
Cedar Rapids, IA	96.3	74.8	35.1	3.7	1.4
Charleston, SC	90.3	71.9	32.2	9.7	6.8
Charlotte, NC	89.9	70.0	29.9	10.1	5.9
Chicago, IL	92.4	69.8	32.5	7.6	3.5
Cincinnati, OH	94.5	72.3	33.5	5.5	3.8
Clarksville, TN	90.7	69.7	36.3	9.3	6.7
Cleveland, OH	94.4	67.4	40.0	5.6	3.9
College Station, TX	88.1	73.2	24.7	11.9	7.6
Colorado Springs, CO	92.9	71.5	35.9	7.1	4.6
Columbia, MO	93.4	77.7	26.6	6.6	4.4
Columbia, SC	91.0	69.6	36.0	9.0	5.2
Columbus, OH	92.6	70.0	32.5	7.4	4.5
Dallas, TX	83.7	66.7	24.5	16.3	11.8
Davenport, IA	94.5	71.3	38.0	5.5	3.7
Denver, CO	92.2	72.2	29.4	7.8	5.0
Des Moines, IA	95.5	75.1	32.5	4.5	2.3
Detroit, MI	95.1	70.0	40.0	4.9	2.6
Durham, NC	90.2	72.6	29.5	9.8	6.1
El Paso, TX	78.1	52.1	34.3	21.9	12.9
Eugene, OR	94.1	63.9	44.5	5.9	2.9
Fargo, ND	94.8	80.6	25.8	5.2	4.2
Fort Collins, CO	94.3	74.9	31.0	5.7	3.8
Fort Wayne, IN	92.0	68.5	34.5	8.0	6.3
Fort Worth, TX	83.7	66.7	24.5	16.3	11.8
Gainesville, FL	90.9	71.2	30.8	9.1	5.2
Green Bay, WI	94.8	72.2	34.1	5.2	3.4
Greensboro, NC	90.2	64.1	37.2	9.8	4.2
Honolulu, HI	96.6	78.2	36.3	3.4	2.6
Houston, TX	81.3	61.4	27.1	18.7	12.6
Huntsville, AL	92.2	77.5	29.4	7.8	2.8
Indianapolis, IN	93.0	70.9	32.9	7.0	4.6
Jacksonville, FL	90.1	69.3	33.4	9.9	6.3
Kansas City, MO	91.1	74.1	27.9	8.9	5.6
Lafayette, LA	92.3	60.4	42.4	7.7	3.2
Las Vegas, NV	87.9	62.5	35.9	12.1	8.3
Lexington, KY	93.9	69.8	36.2	6.1	3.2
Lincoln, NE	93.7	77.6	28.1	6.3	3.8
Little Rock, AR	91.7	65.3	39.2	8.3	5.1
Los Angeles, CA	91.8	60.8	38.8	8.2	3.5
Louisville, KY	94.7	69.5	38.9	5.3	3.6
Madison, WI	96.3	82.6	26.5	3.7	2.8
Manchester, NH	94.0	77.1	29.3	6.0	4.0
McAllen, TX	70.3	37.7	37.5	29.7	15.7

Table continued on following page.

Metro Area	With Health Insurance	With Private Health Insurance	With Public Health Insurance	Without Health Insurance	Population Under Age 19 Without Health Insurance
Memphis, TN	88.9	64.1	36.1	11.1	6.4
Miami, FL	86.3	60.5	33.6	13.7	8.2
Midland, TX	84.7	70.7	21.7	15.3	12.1
Milwaukee, WI	94.6	70.6	35.5	5.4	2.8
Minneapolis, MN	95.7	77.3	30.9	4.3	2.7
Nashville, TN	90.6	72.8	28.6	9.4	5.8
New Orleans, LA	90.8	55.9	45.1	9.2	5.6
New York, NY	93.5	66.6	37.8	6.5	3.1
Oklahoma City, OK	87.7	66.8	33.5	12.3	7.3
Omaha, NE	92.9	74.5	29.2	7.1	4.7
Orlando, FL	88.7	66.6	31.4	11.3	6.3
Philadelphia, PA	94.7	72.5	35.5	5.3	3.4
Phoenix, AZ	89.3	66.2	34.1	10.7	8.6
Pittsburgh, PA	96.2	74.5	37.9	3.8	2.4
Portland, OR	94.2	72.3	34.0	5.8	3.2
Providence, RI	96.1	70.1	39.7	3.9	2.4
Provo, UT	92.3	82.1	17.4	7.7	6.0
Raleigh, NC	91.3	76.0	25.6	8.7	5.0
Reno, NV	90.4	69.0	32.8	9.6	6.8
Richmond, VA	93.2	73.3	33.5	6.8	5.0
Rochester, MN	95.6	79.5	31.1	4.4	4.0
Sacramento, CA	95.3	70.1	38.7	4.7	2.7
Saint Louis, MO	94.0	73.7	31.5	6.0	3.5
Saint Paul, MN	95.7	77.3	30.9	4.3	2.7
Salem, OR	92.0	63.0	42.6	8.0	3.3
Salt Lake City, UT	90.6	77.4	20.8	9.4	7.7
San Antonio, TX	85.0	64.6	31.8	15.0	9.1
San Diego, CA	93.2	69.6	34.3	6.8	3.8
San Francisco, CA	95.9	75.5	31.5	4.1	2.4
San Jose, CA	95.9	77.1	27.4	4.1	1.8
Santa Rosa, CA	94.6	71.3	38.3	5.4	3.2
Savannah, GA	88.0	67.8	32.8	12.0	6.6
Seattle, WA	94.4	75.5	29.6	5.6	2.7
Sioux Falls, SD	93.1	79.1	25.6	6.9	4.8
Tampa, FL	88.9	64.2	36.5	11.1	6.0
Tucson, AZ	91.1	62.8	42.8	8.9	7.0
Tulsa, OK	86.8	63.7	35.3	13.2	7.6
Virginia Beach, VA	93.3	73.2	35.8	6.7	4.0
Washington, DC	92.6	76.7	27.8	7.4	4.9
Wichita, KS	89.7	69.9	32.5	10.3	5.3
Wilmington, NC	90.4	71.3	38.0	9.6	6.8
Winston-Salem, NC	89.6	64.5	37.6	10.4	4.6
U.S.	91.4	67.3	36.3	8.6	5.4

Note: Figures are percentages that cover the civilian noninstitutionalized population; Figures cover the Metropolitan Statistical Area (MSA)
Source: U.S. Census Bureau, 2019-2023 American Community Survey 5-Year Estimates

Crime Rate: City

City	Total Crime	Violent Crime Rate				Property Crime Rate		
		Murder	Rape	Robbery	Aggrav. Assault	Burglary	Larceny -Theft	Motor Vehicle Theft
Albuquerque, NM	6,021.7	19.3	54.2	175.5	1,068.0	671.8	3,003.1	1,029.9
Anchorage, AK	3,953.3	7.7	150.2	161.7	742.0	334.0	2,132.4	425.2
Ann Arbor, MI	2,058.1	3.4	37.3	39.0	232.1	171.1	1,438.1	137.2
Athens, GA	2,950.7	3.9	60.2	61.7	305.6	238.4	2,063.4	217.6
Atlanta, GA	4,599.8	26.4	23.2	120.3	537.4	346.9	2,500.1	1,045.6
Austin, TX	3,804.7	6.7	50.3	93.3	348.8	468.0	2,125.2	712.4
Baltimore, MD	5,850.2	41.2	45.1	577.9	908.2	445.5	1,987.6	1,844.7
Billings, MT	4,487.3	7.4	83.2	123.6	674.0	346.1	2,723.2	529.8
Boise City, ID	1,512.1	2.1	67.9	21.9	177.7	131.7	971.9	138.8
Boston, MA	2,571.3	5.3	32.5	136.6	452.5	180.9	1,589.2	174.2
Boulder, CO	3,414.5	2.9	38.4	36.5	279.2	457.6	2,276.7	323.3
Cape Coral, FL	n/a	n/a	n/a	n/a	n/a	n/a	n/a	n/a
Cedar Rapids, IA	3,184.6	5.9	8.1	30.2	255.6	345.4	2,281.7	257.8
Charleston, SC	2,379.5	6.4	28.4	52.8	314.5	164.3	1,501.0	311.9
Charlotte, NC	4,562.0	9.4	25.4	128.4	563.0	430.0	2,578.2	827.7
Chicago, IL	4,038.7	19.0	47.3	412.3	128.1	280.1	2,145.0	1,006.8
Cincinnati, OH	4,956.6	22.0	71.4	208.4	426.2	617.2	2,416.3	1,195.2
Clarksville, TN	2,193.3	6.0	57.7	29.7	373.8	214.9	1,285.8	225.4
Cleveland, OH	6,515.8	38.8	119.5	448.1	1,096.8	894.3	2,475.2	1,443.0
College Station, TX	1,493.6	3.2	49.2	17.4	88.8	141.9	1,086.9	106.2
Colorado Springs, CO	4,386.7	4.9	104.2	76.4	506.5	521.6	2,354.6	818.4
Columbia, MO	2,897.3	7.7	59.4	33.2	285.5	307.1	1,859.5	344.9
Columbia, SC	4,223.4	7.8	45.2	107.4	596.5	455.8	2,537.2	473.5
Columbus, OH	3,089.1	10.5	115.3	117.5	141.8	412.2	1,553.0	738.9
Dallas, TX	4,701.5	18.5	36.8	157.8	458.4	470.3	2,126.6	1,433.1
Davenport, IA	4,501.0	9.0	102.1	91.1	488.4	688.6	2,601.3	520.5
Denver, CO	6,772.3	11.9	93.2	175.8	740.8	716.9	3,284.7	1,749.0
Des Moines, IA	4,056.1	4.3	69.2	90.6	542.8	451.2	2,271.3	626.7
Detroit, MI	6,785.7	40.6	109.3	225.5	1,676.7	756.9	2,485.8	1,490.8
Durham, NC	4,397.4	15.2	53.4	168.4	399.3	497.0	2,574.8	689.3
El Paso, TX	1,955.2	5.0	40.9	48.0	242.2	157.2	1,116.4	345.4
Eugene, OR	3,545.1	3.4	56.7	77.4	210.4	497.8	2,306.5	392.8
Fargo, ND	4,394.2	1.5	71.5	75.2	367.2	768.6	2,690.1	420.1
Fort Collins, CO	2,736.2	0.6	29.0	36.7	229.7	273.6	1,958.1	208.4
Fort Wayne, IN	2,623.8	9.6	43.7	64.9	153.1	251.0	1,800.3	301.0
Fort Worth, TX	3,135.9	8.7	69.1	71.2	340.8	391.4	1,763.5	491.2
Gainesville, FL	3,608.3	10.9	100.9	119.3	507.7	286.2	2,572.5	10.9
Green Bay, WI	1,915.3	5.7	66.3	31.3	283.4	215.1	1,029.2	284.3
Greensboro, NC	4,560.5	24.7	24.4	164.9	612.1	555.0	2,682.7	496.6
Honolulu, HI	2,128.6	0.6	28.0	51.7	105.8	193.1	1,377.3	372.0
Houston, TX	5,599.2	14.9	61.1	295.7	720.0	606.3	3,034.5	866.7
Huntsville, AL	834.6	2.7	15.1	17.4	94.8	101.9	521.4	81.4
Indianapolis, IN	4,653.4	18.9	55.9	174.2	782.0	615.8	2,229.9	776.8
Jacksonville, FL	n/a	n/a	n/a	n/a	n/a	n/a	n/a	n/a
Kansas City, MO	6,436.1	35.5	78.5	241.2	1,122.5	549.6	2,633.3	1,775.6
Lafayette, LA	5,421.0	23.1	24.7	98.1	672.4	1,017.6	3,291.8	293.3
Las Vegas, NV	3,551.8	8.0	49.8	77.6	334.6	524.7	1,681.3	875.9
Lexington, KY	3,004.7	4.4	56.6	76.9	115.9	337.8	2,022.9	390.3
Lincoln, NE	3,052.3	2.4	90.4	52.9	220.4	252.4	2,106.4	327.5
Little Rock, AR	7,228.6	30.5	122.2	223.2	1,425.2	925.7	4,003.7	498.1
Los Angeles, CA	3,666.8	8.6	51.4	230.1	530.0	406.4	1,764.3	676.0
Louisville, KY	4,385.4	22.9	32.7	148.2	561.8	498.8	2,104.4	1,016.8
Madison, WI	2,636.1	3.6	27.7	44.5	225.4	280.4	1,859.0	195.5
Manchester, NH	2,061.5	7.0	59.1	87.9	229.6	147.9	1,342.2	187.9

Table continued on following page.

City	Total Crime	Violent Crime Rate				Property Crime Rate		
		Murder	Rape	Robbery	Aggrav. Assault	Burglary	Larceny-Theft	Motor Vehicle Theft
McAllen, TX	2,092.9	4.8	35.7	24.0	79.6	111.2	1,774.4	63.2
Memphis, TN	11,214.8	57.0	73.4	451.1	2,030.5	1,110.9	4,942.0	2,549.9
Miami, FL	3,436.7	7.1	28.3	109.7	346.9	254.1	2,223.1	467.6
Midland, TX	2,321.6	5.2	63.6	33.3	328.3	274.3	1,354.5	262.5
Milwaukee, WI	4,136.0	31.0	74.3	284.4	1,048.0	418.1	1,278.7	1,001.6
Minneapolis, MN	6,384.2	17.0	86.7	339.8	688.1	605.7	2,806.3	1,840.7
Nashville, TN	5,533.6	14.5	59.1	163.4	892.0	401.7	3,232.8	770.2
New Orleans, LA	6,450.6	53.0	187.0	180.1	941.0	478.3	2,770.8	1,840.5
New York, NY	3,066.4	4.2	25.3	200.0	438.8	167.2	2,006.8	224.2
Oklahoma City, OK	3,571.8	9.0	68.9	88.0	471.6	566.1	1,965.4	402.7
Omaha, NE[1]	4,029.5	6.0	61.6	69.5	424.0	259.6	2,514.4	694.4
Orlando, FL[1]	4,864.3	10.3	72.7	137.1	615.7	449.9	3,173.7	404.9
Philadelphia, PA	6,039.7	26.0	46.6	336.1	574.4	363.9	3,161.8	1,530.9
Phoenix, AZ	3,268.6	11.5	65.6	168.8	538.9	342.6	1,577.4	563.9
Pittsburgh, PA	n/a	n/a	n/a	n/a	n/a	n/a	n/a	n/a
Portland, OR	6,575.8	11.8	51.1	193.1	459.2	792.8	3,756.6	1,311.2
Providence, RI	2,215.3	5.8	34.3	59.6	209.9	157.2	1,482.7	265.8
Provo, UT	1,531.8	0.0	60.3	16.0	98.5	110.0	1,149.5	97.6
Raleigh, NC	3,117.6	5.4	32.1	87.2	403.4	306.3	1,891.3	391.8
Reno, NV	3,234.8	6.8	102.2	111.6	375.1	381.9	1,838.8	418.3
Richmond, VA	4,078.2	26.9	29.5	97.1	204.1	287.3	2,899.2	534.3
Rochester, MN	1,754.4	0.8	36.1	22.9	102.4	182.7	1,283.2	126.2
Sacramento, CA	3,692.9	7.7	32.1	225.3	535.6	520.1	1,672.4	699.8
Saint Louis, MO	7,844.8	56.4	70.3	260.3	1,058.2	751.1	3,434.0	2,214.5
Saint Paul, MN	3,714.1	9.0	67.3	126.8	420.8	434.5	1,962.9	692.8
Salem, OR	3,650.5	5.0	15.1	98.7	328.7	384.2	2,312.7	506.0
Salt Lake City, UT	6,514.5	7.7	159.7	175.6	524.9	555.4	4,504.8	586.4
San Antonio, TX	6,089.1	10.9	97.8	120.5	465.0	546.5	3,568.2	1,280.2
San Diego, CA	2,229.6	2.9	21.5	87.4	306.1	201.5	1,118.7	491.6
San Francisco, CA	6,422.7	6.6	37.3	349.7	316.5	720.8	4,135.3	856.4
San Jose, CA[1]	3,178.2	3.7	93.4	132.1	298.2	405.9	1,568.7	676.1
Santa Rosa, CA	1,799.8	5.7	65.0	63.9	196.2	257.8	1,004.2	206.9
Savannah, GA	n/a	n/a	n/a	n/a	n/a	n/a	n/a	n/a
Seattle, WA	5,789.3	9.0	36.2	221.7	510.2	1,126.3	2,662.2	1,223.7
Sioux Falls, SD	2,864.1	0.5	16.9	32.4	385.4	287.6	1,635.4	505.9
Tampa, FL	2,115.0	10.2	42.4	65.4	341.8	194.1	1,272.2	188.9
Tucson, AZ	n/a	n/a	n/a	n/a	n/a	n/a	n/a	n/a
Tulsa, OK	4,850.8	8.8	101.5	100.0	702.2	878.8	2,486.1	573.5
Virginia Beach, VA	1,751.8	3.7	22.0	29.5	40.1	86.6	1,431.3	138.5
Washington, DC	5,205.1	38.9	38.4	558.0	412.1	245.1	2,905.0	1,007.6
Wichita, KS	5,864.8	9.9	87.8	104.7	930.0	548.2	3,662.4	521.9
Wilmington, NC	3,995.9	8.2	31.0	99.4	348.9	455.7	2,763.4	289.4
Winston-Salem, NC	3,897.6	16.7	34.9	97.2	737.7	629.4	1,994.6	387.1
U.S.	2,290.9	5.7	38.0	66.5	264.1	250.7	1,347.2	318.7

Note: Figures are crimes per 100,000 population in 2023 except where noted; (1) 2022 data; n/a not available.
Source: FBI, Table 8, Offenses Known to Law Enforcement, by State by City, 2022, 2023

Temperature & Precipitation: Yearly Averages and Extremes

City	Extreme Low (°F)	Average Low (°F)	Average Temp. (°F)	Average High (°F)	Extreme High (°F)	Average Precip. (in.)	Average Snow (in.)
Albuquerque, NM	-17	43	57	70	105	8.5	11
Anchorage, AK	-34	29	36	43	85	15.7	71
Ann Arbor, MI	-21	39	49	58	104	32.4	41
Athens, GA	-8	52	62	72	105	49.8	2
Atlanta, GA	-8	52	62	72	105	49.8	2
Austin, TX	-2	58	69	79	109	31.1	1
Baltimore, MD	-7	45	56	65	105	41.2	21
Billings, MT	-32	36	47	59	105	14.6	59
Boise City, ID	-25	39	51	63	111	11.8	22
Boston, MA	-12	44	52	59	102	42.9	41
Boulder, CO	-25	37	51	64	103	15.5	63
Cape Coral, FL	26	65	75	84	103	53.9	0
Cedar Rapids, IA	-34	36	47	57	105	34.4	33
Charleston, SC	6	55	66	76	104	52.1	1
Charlotte, NC	-5	50	61	71	104	42.8	6
Chicago, IL	-27	40	49	59	104	35.4	39
Cincinnati, OH	-25	44	54	64	103	40.9	23
Clarksville, TN	-17	49	60	70	107	47.4	11
Cleveland, OH	-19	41	50	59	104	37.1	55
College Station, TX	-2	58	69	79	109	31.1	1
Colorado Springs, CO	-24	36	49	62	99	17.0	48
Columbia, MO	-20	44	54	64	111	40.6	25
Columbia, SC	-1	51	64	75	107	48.3	2
Columbus, OH	-19	42	52	62	104	37.9	28
Dallas, TX	-2	56	67	77	112	33.9	3
Davenport, IA	-24	40	50	60	108	31.8	33
Denver, CO	-25	37	51	64	103	15.5	63
Des Moines, IA	-24	40	50	60	108	31.8	33
Detroit, MI	-21	39	49	58	104	32.4	41
Durham, NC	-9	48	60	71	105	42.0	8
El Paso, TX	-8	50	64	78	114	8.6	6
Eugene, OR	-12	42	53	63	108	47.3	7
Fargo, ND	-36	31	41	52	106	19.6	40
Fort Collins, CO	-25	37	51	64	103	15.5	63
Fort Wayne, IN	-22	40	50	60	106	35.9	33
Fort Worth, TX	-1	55	66	76	113	32.3	3
Gainesville, FL	10	58	69	79	102	50.9	Trace
Green Bay, WI	-31	34	44	54	99	28.3	46
Greensboro, NC	-8	47	58	69	103	42.5	10
Honolulu, HI	52	70	77	84	94	22.4	0
Houston, TX	7	58	69	79	107	46.9	Trace
Huntsville, AL	-11	50	61	71	104	56.8	4
Indianapolis, IN	-23	42	53	62	104	40.2	25
Jacksonville, FL	7	58	69	79	103	52.0	0
Kansas City, MO	-23	44	54	64	109	38.1	21
Lafayette, LA	8	57	68	78	103	58.5	Trace
Las Vegas, NV	8	53	67	80	116	4.0	1
Lexington, KY	-21	45	55	65	103	45.1	17
Lincoln, NE	-33	39	51	62	108	29.1	27
Little Rock, AR	-5	51	62	73	112	50.7	5
Los Angeles, CA	27	55	63	70	110	11.3	Trace
Louisville, KY	-20	46	57	67	105	43.9	17
Madison, WI	-37	35	46	57	104	31.1	42
Manchester, NH	-33	34	46	57	102	36.9	63
McAllen, TX	16	65	74	83	106	25.8	Trace

Table continued on following page.

City	Extreme Low (°F)	Average Low (°F)	Average Temp. (°F)	Average High (°F)	Extreme High (°F)	Average Precip. (in.)	Average Snow (in.)
Memphis, TN	0	52	65	77	107	54.8	1
Miami, FL	30	69	76	83	98	57.1	0
Midland, TX	-11	50	64	77	116	14.6	4
Milwaukee, WI	-26	38	47	55	103	32.0	49
Minneapolis, MN	-34	35	45	54	105	27.1	52
Nashville, TN	-17	49	60	70	107	47.4	11
New Orleans, LA	11	59	69	78	102	60.6	Trace
New York, NY	-2	47	55	62	104	47.0	23
Oklahoma City, OK	-8	49	60	71	110	32.8	10
Omaha, NE	-23	40	51	62	110	30.1	29
Orlando, FL	19	62	72	82	100	47.7	Trace
Philadelphia, PA	-7	45	55	64	104	41.4	22
Phoenix, AZ	17	59	72	86	122	7.3	Trace
Pittsburgh, PA	-18	41	51	60	103	37.1	43
Portland, OR	-3	45	54	62	107	37.5	7
Providence, RI	-13	42	51	60	104	45.3	35
Provo, UT	-22	40	52	64	107	15.6	63
Raleigh, NC	-9	48	60	71	105	42.0	8
Reno, NV	-16	33	50	67	105	7.2	24
Richmond, VA	-8	48	58	69	105	43.0	13
Rochester, MN	-40	34	44	54	102	29.4	47
Sacramento, CA	18	48	61	73	115	17.3	Trace
Saint Louis, MO	-18	46	56	66	115	36.8	20
Saint Paul, MN	-34	35	45	54	105	27.1	52
Salem, OR	-12	41	52	63	108	40.2	7
Salt Lake City, UT	-22	40	52	64	107	15.6	63
San Antonio, TX	0	58	69	80	108	29.6	1
San Diego, CA	29	57	64	71	111	9.5	Trace
San Francisco, CA	24	49	57	65	106	19.3	Trace
San Jose, CA	21	50	59	68	105	13.5	Trace
Santa Rosa, CA	23	42	57	71	109	29.0	n/a
Savannah, GA	3	56	67	77	105	50.3	Trace
Seattle, WA	0	44	52	59	99	38.4	13
Sioux Falls, SD	-36	35	46	57	110	24.6	38
Tampa, FL	18	63	73	82	99	46.7	Trace
Tucson, AZ	16	55	69	82	117	11.6	2
Tulsa, OK	-8	50	61	71	112	38.9	10
Virginia Beach, VA	-3	51	60	69	104	44.8	8
Washington, DC	-5	49	58	67	104	39.5	18
Wichita, KS	-21	45	57	68	113	29.3	17
Wilmington, NC	0	53	64	74	104	55.0	2
Winston-Salem, NC	-8	47	58	69	103	42.5	10

Source: National Climatic Data Center, International Station Meteorological Climate Summary, 9/96; NOAA

Weather Conditions

City	Temperature			Daytime Sky			Precipitation		
	10°F & below	32°F & below	90°F & above	Clear	Partly cloudy	Cloudy	0.01 inch or more precip.	1.0 inch or more snow/ice	Thunder-storms
Albuquerque, NM	4	114	65	140	161	64	60	9	38
Anchorage, AK	n/a	194	n/a	50	115	200	113	49	2
Ann Arbor, MI	n/a	136	12	74	134	157	135	38	32
Athens, GA	1	49	38	98	147	120	116	3	48
Atlanta, GA	1	49	38	98	147	120	116	3	48
Austin, TX	<1	20	111	105	148	112	83	1	41
Baltimore, MD	6	97	31	91	143	131	113	13	27
Billings, MT	n/a	149	29	75	163	127	97	41	27
Boise City, ID	n/a	124	45	106	133	126	91	22	14
Boston, MA	n/a	97	12	88	127	150	253	48	18
Boulder, CO	24	155	33	99	177	89	90	38	39
Cape Coral, FL	n/a	n/a	115	93	220	52	110	0	92
Cedar Rapids, IA	n/a	156	16	89	132	144	109	28	42
Charleston, SC	<1	33	53	89	162	114	114	1	59
Charlotte, NC	1	65	44	98	142	125	113	3	41
Chicago, IL	n/a	132	17	83	136	146	125	31	38
Cincinnati, OH	14	107	23	80	126	159	127	25	39
Clarksville, TN	5	76	51	98	135	132	119	8	54
Cleveland, OH	n/a	123	12	63	127	175	157	48	34
College Station, TX	<1	20	111	105	148	112	83	1	41
Colorado Springs, CO	21	161	18	108	157	100	98	33	49
Columbia, MO	17	108	36	99	127	139	110	17	52
Columbia, SC	<1	58	77	97	149	119	110	1	53
Columbus, OH	n/a	118	19	72	137	156	136	29	40
Dallas, TX	1	34	102	108	160	97	78	2	49
Davenport, IA	n/a	137	26	99	129	137	106	25	46
Denver, CO	24	155	33	99	177	89	90	38	39
Des Moines, IA	n/a	137	26	99	129	137	106	25	46
Detroit, MI	n/a	136	12	74	134	157	135	38	32
Durham, NC	n/a	n/a	39	98	143	124	110	3	42
El Paso, TX	1	59	106	147	164	54	49	3	35
Eugene, OR	n/a	n/a	15	75	115	175	136	4	3
Fargo, ND	n/a	180	15	81	145	139	100	38	31
Fort Collins, CO	24	155	33	99	177	89	90	38	39
Fort Wayne, IN	n/a	131	16	75	140	150	131	31	39
Fort Worth, TX	1	40	100	123	136	106	79	3	47
Gainesville, FL	n/a	n/a	77	88	196	81	119	0	78
Green Bay, WI	n/a	163	7	86	125	154	120	40	33
Greensboro, NC	3	85	32	94	143	128	113	5	43
Honolulu, HI	n/a	n/a	23	25	286	54	98	0	7
Houston, TX	n/a	n/a	96	83	168	114	101	1	62
Huntsville, AL	2	66	49	70	118	177	116	2	54
Indianapolis, IN	19	119	19	83	128	154	127	24	43
Jacksonville, FL	<1	16	83	86	181	98	114	1	65
Kansas City, MO	22	110	39	112	134	119	103	17	51
Lafayette, LA	<1	21	86	99	150	116	113	<1	73
Las Vegas, NV	<1	37	134	185	132	48	27	2	13
Lexington, KY	11	96	22	86	136	143	129	17	44
Lincoln, NE	n/a	145	40	108	135	122	94	19	46
Little Rock, AR	1	57	73	110	142	113	104	4	57
Los Angeles, CA	0	<1	5	131	125	109	34	0	1
Louisville, KY	8	90	35	82	143	140	125	15	45
Madison, WI	n/a	161	14	88	119	158	118	38	40
Manchester, NH	n/a	171	12	87	131	147	125	32	19

Table continued on following page.

City	Temperature			Daytime Sky			Precipitation		
	10°F & below	32°F & below	90°F & above	Clear	Partly cloudy	Cloudy	0.01 inch or more precip.	1.0 inch or more snow/ice	Thunderstorms
McAllen, TX	n/a	n/a	116	86	180	99	72	0	27
Memphis, TN	1	53	86	101	152	112	104	2	59
Miami, FL	n/a	n/a	55	48	263	54	128	0	74
Midland, TX	1	62	102	144	138	83	52	3	38
Milwaukee, WI	n/a	141	10	90	118	157	126	38	35
Minneapolis, MN	n/a	156	16	93	125	147	113	41	37
Nashville, TN	5	76	51	98	135	132	119	8	54
New Orleans, LA	0	13	70	90	169	106	114	1	69
New York, NY	n/a	n/a	18	85	166	114	120	11	20
Oklahoma City, OK	5	79	70	124	131	110	80	8	50
Omaha, NE	n/a	139	35	100	142	123	97	20	46
Orlando, FL	n/a	n/a	90	76	208	81	115	0	80
Philadelphia, PA	5	94	23	81	146	138	117	14	27
Phoenix, AZ	0	10	167	186	125	54	37	< 1	23
Pittsburgh, PA	n/a	121	8	62	137	166	154	42	35
Portland, OR	n/a	37	11	67	116	182	152	4	7
Providence, RI	n/a	117	9	85	134	146	123	21	21
Provo, UT	n/a	128	56	94	152	119	92	38	38
Raleigh, NC	n/a	n/a	39	98	143	124	110	3	42
Reno, NV	14	178	50	143	139	83	50	17	14
Richmond, VA	3	79	41	90	147	128	115	7	43
Rochester, MN	n/a	165	9	87	126	152	114	40	41
Sacramento, CA	0	21	73	175	111	79	58	< 1	2
Saint Louis, MO	13	100	43	97	138	130	109	14	46
Saint Paul, MN	n/a	156	16	93	125	147	113	41	37
Salem, OR	n/a	66	16	78	118	169	146	6	5
Salt Lake City, UT	n/a	128	56	94	152	119	92	38	38
San Antonio, TX	n/a	n/a	112	97	153	115	81	1	36
San Diego, CA	0	< 1	4	115	126	124	40	0	5
San Francisco, CA	0	6	4	136	130	99	63	< 1	5
San Jose, CA	0	5	5	106	180	79	57	< 1	6
Santa Rosa, CA	n/a	43	30	n/a	365	n/a	n/a	n/a	2
Savannah, GA	< 1	29	70	97	155	113	111	< 1	63
Seattle, WA	n/a	38	3	57	121	187	157	8	8
Sioux Falls, SD	n/a	n/a	n/a	95	136	134	n/a	n/a	n/a
Tampa, FL	n/a	n/a	85	81	204	80	107	< 1	87
Tucson, AZ	0	18	140	177	119	69	54	2	42
Tulsa, OK	6	78	74	117	141	107	88	8	50
Virginia Beach, VA	< 1	53	33	89	149	127	115	5	38
Washington, DC	2	71	34	84	144	137	112	9	30
Wichita, KS	13	110	63	117	132	116	87	13	54
Wilmington, NC	< 1	42	46	96	150	119	115	1	47
Winston-Salem, NC	3	85	32	94	143	128	113	5	43

Note: Figures are average number of days per year
Source: National Climatic Data Center, International Station Meteorological Climate Summary, 9/96; NOAA

Air Quality Index

Metro Area (Days[1])	Percent of Days when Air Quality was...					AQI Statistics	
	Good	Moderate	Unhealthy for Sensitive Groups	Unhealthy	Very Unhealthy	Maximum	Median
Albuquerque, NM (365)	26.6	72.3	0.8	0.0	0.3	207	60
Anchorage, AK (365)	81.1	18.6	0.3	0.0	0.0	102	25
Ann Arbor, MI (365)	46.0	50.4	2.5	0.5	0.5	218	52
Athens, GA (365)	47.4	51.8	0.8	0.0	0.0	147	52
Atlanta, GA (365)	26.6	67.7	4.9	0.8	0.0	172	57
Austin, TX (365)	40.3	56.7	3.0	0.0	0.0	122	54
Baltimore, MD (365)	55.1	40.3	3.6	0.8	0.3	205	49
Billings, MT (357)	85.7	13.2	0.8	0.3	0.0	191	29
Boise City, ID (365)	49.3	49.9	0.8	0.0	0.0	120	51
Boston, MA (365)	52.1	46.0	1.9	0.0	0.0	136	50
Boulder, CO (365)	52.6	45.8	1.1	0.5	0.0	181	50
Cape Coral, FL (363)	94.5	5.2	0.3	0.0	0.0	101	35
Cedar Rapids, IA (365)	35.6	59.5	3.8	0.8	0.3	207	54
Charleston, SC (365)	57.8	41.6	0.5	0.0	0.0	105	47
Charlotte, NC (365)	39.7	58.1	2.2	0.0	0.0	150	53
Chicago, IL (365)	20.8	67.4	9.0	2.2	0.5	246	60
Cincinnati, OH (365)	25.2	68.2	5.2	1.4	0.0	197	57
Clarksville, TN (365)	56.2	42.5	1.4	0.0	0.0	117	47
Cleveland, OH (365)	31.5	64.1	3.0	1.1	0.3	285	57
College Station, TX (348)	67.0	33.0	0.0	0.0	0.0	79	39
Colorado Springs, CO (365)	65.8	33.7	0.3	0.3	0.0	154	47
Columbia, MO (244)	79.9	18.0	2.0	0.0	0.0	143	42
Columbia, SC (365)	54.5	44.4	1.1	0.0	0.0	123	48
Columbus, OH (365)	37.0	59.5	2.5	0.8	0.3	210	54
Dallas, TX (365)	20.5	64.9	12.1	2.5	0.0	177	60
Davenport, IA (365)	37.3	56.4	5.2	0.8	0.3	232	54
Denver, CO (365)	19.7	72.3	7.4	0.5	0.0	179	64
Des Moines, IA (365)	46.0	49.9	3.3	0.8	0.0	166	52
Detroit, MI (365)	18.6	74.0	6.3	0.8	0.3	226	61
Durham, NC (361)	69.5	29.4	1.1	0.0	0.0	121	44
El Paso, TX (365)	18.9	75.9	4.9	0.3	0.0	155	64
Eugene, OR (365)	52.1	43.6	2.5	1.6	0.3	211	49
Fargo, ND (358)	50.3	46.4	2.8	0.6	0.0	175	50
Fort Collins, CO (365)	47.9	50.7	1.1	0.3	0.0	156	51
Fort Wayne, IN (365)	45.2	52.1	1.9	0.5	0.3	223	52
Fort Worth, TX (365)	20.5	64.9	12.1	2.5	0.0	177	60
Gainesville, FL (365)	74.0	25.8	0.3	0.0	0.0	104	40
Green Bay, WI (365)	57.0	38.1	3.3	1.6	0.0	182	46
Greensboro, NC (365)	50.1	48.8	1.1	0.0	0.0	131	50
Honolulu, HI (365)	92.3	7.4	0.3	0.0	0.0	117	31
Houston, TX (365)	9.9	74.5	12.3	3.0	0.3	205	65
Huntsville, AL (364)	56.0	43.1	0.8	0.0	0.0	135	49
Indianapolis, IN (365)	21.9	71.5	5.5	0.5	0.5	259	60
Jacksonville, FL (365)	41.6	57.8	0.5	0.0	0.0	124	52
Kansas City, MO (365)	34.0	58.1	6.8	1.1	0.0	166	55
Lafayette, LA (365)	56.7	43.0	0.3	0.0	0.0	112	47
Las Vegas, NV (365)	29.0	63.8	6.8	0.3	0.0	197	61
Lexington, KY (365)	63.3	35.9	0.5	0.3	0.0	167	45
Lincoln, NE (283)	69.6	29.3	0.7	0.4	0.0	160	42
Little Rock, AR (365)	33.4	65.2	1.1	0.3	0.0	174	55
Los Angeles, CA (365)	11.2	64.9	14.2	8.8	0.8	210	67
Louisville, KY (365)	32.1	62.2	5.5	0.3	0.0	182	55
Madison, WI (365)	49.6	43.6	5.5	0.5	0.8	268	51
Manchester, NH (365)	83.6	15.1	1.4	0.0	0.0	119	39

Table continued on following page.

Metro Area (Days[1])	Percent of Days when Air Quality was...					AQI Statistics	
	Good	Moderate	Unhealthy for Sensitive Groups	Unhealthy	Very Unhealthy	Maximum	Median
McAllen, TX (357)	57.7	42.3	0.0	0.0	0.0	95	44
Memphis, TN (365)	28.5	67.4	4.1	0.0	0.0	140	55
Miami, FL (365)	37.3	61.6	0.3	0.8	0.0	170	53
Midland, TX (n/a)	n/a	n/a	n/a	n/a	n/a	n/a	n/a
Milwaukee, WI (365)	43.6	48.8	6.6	0.3	0.8	270	53
Minneapolis, MN (365)	36.7	55.1	6.6	1.6	0.0	190	55
Nashville, TN (365)	34.8	62.5	2.7	0.0	0.0	133	54
New Orleans, LA (365)	38.1	59.2	2.7	0.0	0.0	126	53
New York, NY (365)	29.3	64.1	4.7	1.6	0.3	278	56
Oklahoma City, OK (365)	35.1	60.8	4.1	0.0	0.0	143	54
Omaha, NE (365)	50.4	42.7	6.3	0.5	0.0	169	50
Orlando, FL (365)	71.0	28.2	0.8	0.0	0.0	115	44
Philadelphia, PA (365)	17.8	75.3	5.2	1.1	0.3	331	59
Phoenix, AZ (365)	8.5	67.9	20.3	2.7	0.3	709	78
Pittsburgh, PA (365)	26.8	66.6	5.5	0.5	0.5	237	58
Portland, OR (365)	60.0	38.4	1.1	0.5	0.0	153	43
Providence, RI (365)	54.8	42.2	3.0	0.0	0.0	140	48
Provo, UT (365)	55.1	44.7	0.3	0.0	0.0	104	48
Raleigh, NC (365)	50.4	48.2	1.4	0.0	0.0	130	50
Reno, NV (365)	52.3	47.7	0.0	0.0	0.0	97	50
Richmond, VA (365)	55.9	42.7	0.5	0.8	0.0	159	48
Rochester, MN (365)	51.8	44.1	3.8	0.3	0.0	167	49
Sacramento, CA (365)	35.3	60.8	3.8	0.0	0.0	143	58
Saint Louis, MO (365)	14.0	79.5	5.8	0.8	0.0	185	60
Saint Paul, MN (365)	36.7	55.1	6.6	1.6	0.0	190	55
Salem, OR (365)	73.4	25.5	1.1	0.0	0.0	128	38
Salt Lake City, UT (365)	40.5	55.1	4.1	0.3	0.0	154	54
San Antonio, TX (365)	41.6	55.1	2.7	0.3	0.0	309	53
San Diego, CA (365)	16.7	71.2	12.1	0.0	0.0	150	67
San Francisco, CA (365)	34.0	62.5	3.6	0.0	0.0	130	54
San Jose, CA (365)	61.6	37.3	1.1	0.0	0.0	134	45
Santa Rosa, CA (365)	88.5	11.0	0.5	0.0	0.0	117	33
Savannah, GA (352)	56.0	43.5	0.6	0.0	0.0	108	48
Seattle, WA (365)	51.0	47.1	1.1	0.8	0.0	195	50
Sioux Falls, SD (365)	64.4	28.2	6.3	1.1	0.0	181	44
Tampa, FL (365)	39.5	59.2	1.4	0.0	0.0	114	52
Tucson, AZ (365)	33.7	64.4	1.9	0.0	0.0	147	54
Tulsa, OK (365)	37.8	56.7	4.9	0.5	0.0	197	53
Virginia Beach, VA (365)	62.7	36.4	0.5	0.3	0.0	174	44
Washington, DC (365)	43.3	51.2	4.4	0.8	0.3	222	52
Wichita, KS (365)	44.7	54.0	1.1	0.3	0.0	157	52
Wilmington, NC (362)	65.5	34.3	0.3	0.0	0.0	142	44
Winston-Salem, NC (365)	40.3	57.8	1.6	0.3	0.0	154	53

Note: The Air Quality Index (AQI) is an index for reporting daily air quality. EPA calculates the AQI for five major air pollutants regulated by the Clean Air Act: ground-level ozone, particle pollution (also known as particulate matter), carbon monoxide, sulfur dioxide, and nitrogen dioxide. The AQI runs from 0 to 500. The higher the AQI value, the greater the level of air pollution and the greater the health concern. There are six AQI categories: "Good" The AQI is between 0 and 50. Air quality is considered satisfactory; "Moderate" The AQI is between 51 and 100. Air quality is acceptable; "Unhealthy for Sensitive Groups" When AQI values are between 101 and 150, members of sensitive groups may experience health effects; "Unhealthy" When AQI values are between 151 and 200 everyone may begin to experience health effects; "Very Unhealthy" AQI values between 201 and 300 trigger a health alert; "Hazardous" AQI values over 300 trigger health warnings of emergency conditions; Figures cover the Metropolitan Statistical Area (MSA); (1) Number of days with AQI data in 2023
Source: U.S. Environmental Protection Agency, Air Quality Index Report, 2023

Air Quality Index Pollutants

Metro Area (Days)[1]	Percent of Days when AQI Pollutant was...					
	Carbon Monoxide	Nitrogen Dioxide	Ozone	Sulfur Dioxide[2]	Particulate Matter 2.5	Particulate Matter 10
Albuquerque, NM (365)	0.0	0.3	53.2	–	23.8	22.7
Anchorage, AK (365)	0.8	0.0	0.0	–	70.1	29.0
Ann Arbor, MI (365)	0.0	0.0	33.2	–	66.8	0.0
Athens, GA (365)	0.0	0.0	26.8	–	73.2	0.0
Atlanta, GA (365)	0.0	0.8	31.5	–	67.7	0.0
Austin, TX (365)	0.0	1.1	29.3	–	69.6	0.0
Baltimore, MD (365)	0.0	1.1	54.5	–	44.4	0.0
Billings, MT (357)	0.0	0.0	0.0	–	100.0	0.0
Boise City, ID (365)	0.0	0.3	44.9	–	54.0	0.8
Boston, MA (365)	0.0	0.5	36.7	–	62.7	0.0
Boulder, CO (365)	0.0	0.0	74.5	–	25.5	0.0
Cape Coral, FL (363)	0.0	0.0	100.0	–	0.0	0.0
Cedar Rapids, IA (365)	0.0	0.0	23.6	–	76.4	0.0
Charleston, SC (365)	0.0	0.0	24.4	–	75.1	0.5
Charlotte, NC (365)	0.0	0.0	45.8	–	54.2	0.0
Chicago, IL (365)	0.0	1.6	27.1	–	67.7	3.6
Cincinnati, OH (365)	0.0	0.5	25.5	–	72.1	1.9
Clarksville, TN (365)	0.0	0.0	23.3	–	76.7	0.0
Cleveland, OH (365)	0.5	0.0	27.1	–	71.2	1.1
College Station, TX (348)	0.0	0.0	0.0	–	100.0	0.0
Colorado Springs, CO (365)	0.0	0.0	91.5	–	8.5	0.0
Columbia, MO (244)	0.0	0.0	100.0	–	0.0	0.0
Columbia, SC (365)	0.0	0.3	32.9	–	66.8	0.0
Columbus, OH (365)	0.0	0.0	26.6	–	71.2	2.2
Dallas, TX (365)	0.0	0.5	40.5	–	58.4	0.5
Davenport, IA (365)	0.0	0.0	30.4	–	62.2	7.4
Denver, CO (365)	0.0	5.5	66.6	–	23.3	4.7
Des Moines, IA (365)	0.0	0.8	22.2	–	77.0	0.0
Detroit, MI (365)	0.0	0.5	11.5	–	87.9	0.0
Durham, NC (361)	0.0	0.0	45.2	–	52.4	2.5
El Paso, TX (365)	0.0	1.4	29.9	–	56.4	12.3
Eugene, OR (365)	0.0	0.0	21.4	–	78.6	0.0
Fargo, ND (358)	0.0	0.3	31.3	–	68.4	0.0
Fort Collins, CO (365)	0.0	0.0	83.3	–	16.7	0.0
Fort Wayne, IN (365)	0.0	0.0	38.9	–	61.1	0.0
Fort Worth, TX (365)	0.0	0.5	40.5	–	58.4	0.5
Gainesville, FL (365)	0.0	0.0	38.1	–	61.9	0.0
Green Bay, WI (365)	0.0	0.0	35.9	–	64.1	0.0
Greensboro, NC (365)	0.0	0.0	31.8	–	66.8	1.4
Honolulu, HI (365)	0.0	0.0	47.7	–	51.2	1.1
Houston, TX (365)	0.0	0.3	31.5	–	62.7	5.5
Huntsville, AL (364)	0.0	0.0	25.3	–	74.7	0.0
Indianapolis, IN (365)	0.0	0.0	19.2	–	80.8	0.0
Jacksonville, FL (365)	0.0	0.0	17.0	–	83.0	0.0
Kansas City, MO (365)	0.0	1.4	39.5	–	55.6	3.6
Lafayette, LA (365)	0.0	0.0	54.8	–	44.7	0.5
Las Vegas, NV (365)	0.0	0.3	67.7	–	27.7	4.4
Lexington, KY (365)	0.0	1.1	40.0	–	58.9	0.0
Lincoln, NE (283)	0.0	0.0	74.9	–	25.1	0.0
Little Rock, AR (365)	0.0	0.0	16.4	–	83.6	0.0
Los Angeles, CA (365)	0.0	1.4	41.1	–	55.6	1.9
Louisville, KY (365)	0.0	0.5	28.2	–	71.2	0.0
Madison, WI (365)	0.0	0.0	31.5	–	68.5	0.0
Manchester, NH (365)	0.8	0.0	80.3	–	18.9	0.0

Table continued on following page.

Metro Area (Days[1])	Percent of Days when AQI Pollutant was...					
	Carbon Monoxide	Nitrogen Dioxide	Ozone	Sulfur Dioxide[2]	Particulate Matter 2.5	Particulate Matter 10
McAllen, TX (357)	0.0	0.0	5.3	–	94.7	0.0
Memphis, TN (365)	0.0	0.0	34.2	–	65.8	0.0
Miami, FL (365)	0.0	3.6	13.7	–	82.7	0.0
Midland, TX (n/a)	n/a	n/a	n/a	–	n/a	n/a
Milwaukee, WI (365)	0.0	1.4	31.5	–	67.1	0.0
Minneapolis, MN (365)	0.3	0.8	33.4	–	61.1	4.4
Nashville, TN (365)	0.0	0.5	26.0	–	73.4	0.0
New Orleans, LA (365)	0.0	0.3	37.5	–	62.2	0.0
New York, NY (365)	0.0	4.1	27.7	–	68.2	0.0
Oklahoma City, OK (365)	0.0	2.2	42.7	–	54.2	0.8
Omaha, NE (365)	0.0	0.0	48.2	–	47.4	4.4
Orlando, FL (365)	0.0	0.5	55.1	–	44.4	0.0
Philadelphia, PA (365)	0.0	0.3	22.5	–	77.3	0.0
Phoenix, AZ (365)	0.0	0.0	41.9	–	24.1	34.0
Pittsburgh, PA (365)	0.0	0.0	19.7	–	80.3	0.0
Portland, OR (365)	0.0	1.1	42.7	–	56.2	0.0
Providence, RI (365)	0.0	0.3	41.9	–	57.8	0.0
Provo, UT (365)	0.0	0.3	63.3	–	36.2	0.3
Raleigh, NC (365)	0.0	0.3	32.1	–	67.7	0.0
Reno, NV (365)	0.0	1.1	67.9	–	30.7	0.3
Richmond, VA (365)	0.0	4.4	34.8	–	60.8	0.0
Rochester, MN (365)	0.0	0.0	32.6	–	67.4	0.0
Sacramento, CA (365)	0.0	0.0	60.5	–	39.5	0.0
Saint Louis, MO (365)	0.0	0.0	27.7	–	67.4	4.9
Saint Paul, MN (365)	0.3	0.8	33.4	–	61.1	4.4
Salem, OR (365)	0.0	0.0	35.6	–	64.4	0.0
Salt Lake City, UT (365)	0.0	5.5	60.0	–	32.3	2.2
San Antonio, TX (365)	0.0	0.3	37.5	–	62.2	0.0
San Diego, CA (365)	0.0	0.3	50.7	–	41.4	7.7
San Francisco, CA (365)	0.3	4.4	17.8	–	77.5	0.0
San Jose, CA (365)	0.0	0.0	57.5	–	41.9	0.5
Santa Rosa, CA (365)	0.3	0.0	64.9	–	34.5	0.3
Savannah, GA (352)	0.0	0.0	14.8	–	85.2	0.0
Seattle, WA (365)	0.0	0.8	32.9	–	66.3	0.0
Sioux Falls, SD (365)	0.0	1.6	69.6	–	26.3	2.5
Tampa, FL (365)	0.0	0.0	27.7	–	71.5	0.8
Tucson, AZ (365)	0.0	0.0	49.0	–	33.7	17.3
Tulsa, OK (365)	0.0	0.0	45.2	–	52.9	1.9
Virginia Beach, VA (365)	0.0	1.6	33.7	–	64.7	0.0
Washington, DC (365)	0.0	1.4	44.1	–	54.2	0.3
Wichita, KS (365)	0.0	0.5	45.2	–	51.2	3.0
Wilmington, NC (362)	0.0	0.0	25.1	–	74.9	0.0
Winston-Salem, NC (365)	0.0	0.0	27.7	–	72.3	0.0

Note: The Air Quality Index (AQI) is an index for reporting daily air quality. EPA calculates the AQI for five major air pollutants regulated by the Clean Air Act: ground-level ozone, particle pollution (also known as particulate matter), carbon monoxide, sulfur dioxide, and nitrogen dioxide. The AQI runs from 0 to 500. The higher the AQI value, the greater the level of air pollution and the greater the health concern; Figures cover the Metropolitan Statistical Area (MSA); (1) Number of days with AQI data in 2023; (2) Sulfur dioxide is no longer included in this table because SO_2 concentrations tend to be very localized and not necessarily representative of broad geographical areas like counties and CBSAs

Source: U.S. Environmental Protection Agency, Air Quality Index Report, 2023

Air Quality Trends: Ozone

Metro Area	1990	1995	2000	2005	2010	2015	2020	2021	2022	2023
Albuquerque, NM	0.072	0.070	0.072	0.073	0.066	0.066	0.071	0.071	0.071	0.067
Anchorage, AK	n/a	n/a	n/a	n/a	n/a	n/a	n/a	n/a	n/a	n/a
Ann Arbor, MI	0.025	0.034	0.035	0.023	0.034	0.064	0.067	0.063	0.066	0.072
Athens, GA	n/a	n/a	n/a	n/a	n/a	n/a	n/a	n/a	n/a	n/a
Atlanta, GA	0.088	0.089	0.089	0.077	0.067	0.069	0.059	0.064	0.063	0.072
Austin, TX	0.088	0.089	0.088	0.082	0.074	0.073	0.066	0.066	0.073	0.074
Baltimore, MD	0.100	0.103	0.088	0.089	0.084	0.073	0.064	0.071	0.066	0.073
Billings, MT	n/a	n/a	n/a	n/a	n/a	n/a	n/a	n/a	n/a	n/a
Boise City, ID	n/a	n/a	n/a	n/a	n/a	n/a	n/a	n/a	n/a	n/a
Boston, MA	0.078	0.085	0.067	0.075	0.066	0.065	0.053	0.059	0.066	0.060
Boulder, CO	n/a	n/a	n/a	n/a	n/a	n/a	n/a	n/a	n/a	n/a
Cape Coral, FL	0.069	0.066	0.073	0.071	0.065	0.058	0.061	0.055	0.058	0.064
Cedar Rapids, IA	n/a	n/a	n/a	n/a	n/a	n/a	n/a	n/a	n/a	n/a
Charleston, SC	0.059	0.075	0.076	0.077	0.068	0.054	0.053	0.059	0.059	0.056
Charlotte, NC	0.094	0.091	0.099	0.089	0.082	0.071	0.060	0.067	0.068	0.072
Chicago, IL	0.074	0.094	0.073	0.084	0.070	0.066	0.076	0.071	0.070	0.081
Cincinnati, OH	0.083	0.082	0.074	0.075	0.069	0.069	0.067	0.065	0.068	0.072
Clarksville, TN	n/a	n/a	n/a	n/a	n/a	n/a	n/a	n/a	n/a	n/a
Cleveland, OH	0.084	0.090	0.079	0.084	0.074	0.069	0.069	0.066	0.068	0.071
College Station, TX	n/a	n/a	n/a	n/a	n/a	n/a	n/a	n/a	n/a	n/a
Colorado Springs, CO	n/a	n/a	n/a	n/a	n/a	n/a	n/a	n/a	n/a	n/a
Columbia, MO	n/a	n/a	n/a	n/a	n/a	n/a	n/a	n/a	n/a	n/a
Columbia, SC	0.091	0.079	0.089	0.082	0.069	0.058	0.053	0.061	0.061	0.064
Columbus, OH	0.090	0.091	0.085	0.084	0.073	0.066	0.062	0.061	0.061	0.066
Dallas, TX	0.094	0.103	0.096	0.096	0.079	0.078	0.070	0.076	0.072	0.081
Davenport, IA	0.065	0.072	0.064	0.065	0.057	0.060	0.063	0.066	0.061	0.079
Denver, CO	0.076	0.070	0.069	0.077	0.069	0.072	0.081	0.082	0.074	0.073
Des Moines, IA	n/a	n/a	n/a	n/a	n/a	n/a	n/a	n/a	n/a	n/a
Detroit, MI	0.083	0.088	0.076	0.083	0.074	0.068	0.072	0.069	0.068	0.074
Durham, NC	0.078	0.080	0.082	0.079	0.074	0.061	0.051	0.063	0.058	0.066
El Paso, TX	0.080	0.078	0.082	0.074	0.072	0.071	0.076	0.071	0.071	0.071
Eugene, OR	0.068	0.062	0.056	0.068	0.058	0.070	0.054	0.061	0.058	0.060
Fargo, ND	n/a	n/a	n/a	n/a	n/a	n/a	n/a	n/a	n/a	n/a
Fort Collins, CO	0.066	0.072	0.074	0.075	0.072	0.070	0.070	0.077	0.070	0.067
Fort Wayne, IN	0.086	0.094	0.086	0.081	0.067	0.061	0.064	0.062	0.064	0.067
Fort Worth, TX	0.094	0.103	0.096	0.096	0.079	0.078	0.070	0.076	0.072	0.081
Gainesville, FL	n/a	n/a	n/a	n/a	n/a	n/a	n/a	n/a	n/a	n/a
Green Bay, WI	n/a	n/a	n/a	n/a	n/a	n/a	n/a	n/a	n/a	n/a
Greensboro, NC	0.097	0.089	0.089	0.082	0.076	0.064	0.057	0.066	0.063	0.067
Honolulu, HI	0.034	0.049	0.044	0.042	0.046	0.048	0.044	0.045	0.044	0.046
Houston, TX	0.119	0.114	0.102	0.087	0.079	0.083	0.067	0.072	0.068	0.079
Huntsville, AL	0.079	0.080	0.088	0.075	0.071	0.063	0.057	0.061	0.065	0.064
Indianapolis, IN	0.085	0.095	0.081	0.081	0.070	0.065	0.065	0.067	0.070	0.073
Jacksonville, FL	0.080	0.068	0.072	0.076	0.068	0.060	0.057	0.061	0.062	0.060
Kansas City, MO	0.075	0.095	0.087	0.082	0.067	0.063	0.064	0.067	0.066	0.074
Lafayette, LA	n/a	n/a	n/a	n/a	n/a	n/a	n/a	n/a	n/a	n/a
Las Vegas, NV	n/a	n/a	n/a	n/a	n/a	n/a	n/a	n/a	n/a	n/a
Lexington, KY	0.078	0.088	0.077	0.078	0.070	0.069	0.060	0.064	0.065	0.070
Lincoln, NE	0.057	0.060	0.057	0.056	0.050	0.061	0.054	0.059	0.055	0.068
Little Rock, AR	0.080	0.086	0.090	0.083	0.072	0.063	0.062	0.066	0.063	0.067
Los Angeles, CA	0.128	0.109	0.090	0.086	0.074	0.082	0.096	0.076	0.077	0.081
Louisville, KY	0.082	0.091	0.087	0.083	0.076	0.071	0.063	0.064	0.063	0.072
Madison, WI	0.077	0.084	0.072	0.079	0.062	0.064	0.070	0.066	0.062	0.082
Manchester, NH	0.085	0.088	0.070	0.082	0.067	0.061	0.055	0.061	0.058	0.065
McAllen, TX	n/a	n/a	n/a	n/a	n/a	n/a	n/a	n/a	n/a	n/a
Memphis, TN	0.088	0.095	0.092	0.086	0.076	0.065	0.063	0.067	0.071	0.071

Table continued on following page.

Metro Area	1990	1995	2000	2005	2010	2015	2020	2021	2022	2023
Miami, FL	0.068	0.072	0.075	0.065	0.064	0.061	0.058	0.057	0.063	0.061
Midland, TX	n/a	n/a	n/a	n/a	n/a	n/a	n/a	n/a	n/a	n/a
Milwaukee, WI	0.095	0.106	0.082	0.092	0.079	0.069	0.074	0.072	0.073	0.077
Minneapolis, MN	0.068	0.084	0.065	0.074	0.066	0.061	0.060	0.067	0.057	0.077
Nashville, TN	0.089	0.092	0.084	0.078	0.073	0.065	0.061	0.064	0.065	0.071
New Orleans, LA	0.082	0.088	0.091	0.079	0.074	0.067	0.061	0.060	0.061	0.068
New York, NY	0.101	0.105	0.089	0.090	0.080	0.074	0.064	0.069	0.067	0.071
Oklahoma City, OK	0.080	0.087	0.083	0.077	0.071	0.067	0.066	0.068	0.071	0.072
Omaha, NE	n/a	n/a	n/a	n/a	n/a	n/a	n/a	n/a	n/a	n/a
Orlando, FL	0.081	0.075	0.080	0.083	0.069	0.060	0.059	0.061	0.062	0.066
Philadelphia, PA	0.102	0.109	0.099	0.091	0.083	0.074	0.065	0.069	0.067	0.071
Phoenix, AZ	0.080	0.086	0.082	0.077	0.075	0.072	0.079	0.079	0.074	0.077
Pittsburgh, PA	0.080	0.100	0.084	0.083	0.077	0.070	0.066	0.066	0.064	0.067
Portland, OR	0.081	0.065	0.059	0.059	0.056	0.064	0.058	0.058	0.059	0.062
Providence, RI	0.106	0.107	0.087	0.090	0.072	0.070	0.065	0.067	0.060	0.066
Provo, UT	n/a	n/a	n/a	n/a	n/a	n/a	n/a	n/a	n/a	n/a
Raleigh, NC	0.093	0.081	0.087	0.082	0.071	0.065	0.054	0.062	0.064	0.064
Reno, NV	0.074	0.069	0.067	0.069	0.068	0.071	0.073	0.078	0.064	0.065
Richmond, VA	0.083	0.089	0.080	0.082	0.079	0.062	0.054	0.061	0.060	0.063
Rochester, MN	n/a	n/a	n/a	n/a	n/a	n/a	n/a	n/a	n/a	n/a
Sacramento, CA	0.087	0.092	0.085	0.084	0.072	0.073	0.072	0.072	0.067	0.069
Saint Louis, MO	0.077	0.084	0.074	0.078	0.069	0.067	0.066	0.067	0.070	0.077
Saint Paul, MN	0.068	0.084	0.065	0.074	0.066	0.061	0.060	0.067	0.057	0.077
Salem, OR	n/a	n/a	n/a	n/a	n/a	n/a	n/a	n/a	n/a	n/a
Salt Lake City, UT	n/a	n/a	n/a	n/a	n/a	n/a	n/a	n/a	n/a	n/a
San Antonio, TX	0.090	0.095	0.078	0.084	0.072	0.079	0.069	0.070	0.076	0.074
San Diego, CA	0.110	0.085	0.079	0.074	0.073	0.068	0.078	0.068	0.067	0.072
San Francisco, CA	0.062	0.077	0.060	0.060	0.063	0.064	0.062	0.064	0.057	0.053
San Jose, CA	0.078	0.084	0.065	0.063	0.072	0.067	0.066	0.067	0.062	0.057
Santa Rosa, CA	n/a	n/a	n/a	n/a	n/a	n/a	n/a	n/a	n/a	n/a
Savannah, GA	n/a	n/a	n/a	n/a	n/a	n/a	n/a	n/a	n/a	n/a
Seattle, WA	0.082	0.062	0.056	0.053	0.053	0.059	0.056	0.061	0.065	0.056
Sioux Falls, SD	n/a	n/a	n/a	n/a	n/a	n/a	n/a	n/a	n/a	n/a
Tampa, FL	0.080	0.075	0.081	0.075	0.067	0.062	0.063	0.060	0.061	0.066
Tucson, AZ	0.073	0.078	0.074	0.075	0.068	0.065	0.070	0.068	0.069	0.069
Tulsa, OK	0.086	0.091	0.081	0.072	0.069	0.061	0.061	0.063	0.070	0.072
Virginia Beach, VA	0.085	0.084	0.083	0.078	0.074	0.061	0.053	0.057	0.057	0.059
Washington, DC	0.075	0.083	0.073	0.069	0.069	0.067	0.057	0.066	0.061	0.069
Wichita, KS	0.077	0.069	0.080	0.074	0.075	0.064	0.059	0.061	0.072	0.066
Wilmington, NC	0.082	0.079	0.080	0.075	0.062	0.057	0.054	0.062	0.058	0.067
Winston-Salem, NC	0.084	0.086	0.089	0.080	0.078	0.065	0.058	0.062	0.057	0.066
U.S.	0.087	0.089	0.081	0.080	0.072	0.068	0.066	0.067	0.067	0.070

Note: Figures cover the Metropolitan Statistical Area (MSA); n/a not available. The values shown are the composite ozone concentration averages among trend sites based on the highest fourth daily maximum 8-hour concentration in parts per million. These trends are based on sites having an adequate record of monitoring data during the trend period. Data from exceptional events are included.
Source: U.S. Environmental Protection Agency, Air Quality Monitoring Information, "Air Quality Trends by City, 1990-2023"

Maximum Air Pollutant Concentrations: Particulate Matter, Ozone, CO and Lead

Metro Area	PM 10 (ug/m³)	PM 2.5 Wtd AM (ug/m³)	PM 2.5 24-Hr (ug/m³)	Ozone (ppm)	Carbon Monoxide (ppm)	Lead (ug/m³)
Albuquerque, NM	182	7.5	23	0.069	2	n/a
Anchorage, AK	130	4.2	18	n/a	2	n/a
Ann Arbor, MI	n/a	10.6	33	0.073	n/a	n/a
Athens, GA	n/a	9.3	26	0.068	n/a	n/a
Atlanta, GA	60	10.6	28	0.077	2	n/a
Austin, TX	53	10.4	25	0.074	2	n/a
Baltimore, MD	42	10.1	32	0.075	1	n/a
Billings, MT	n/a	6.7	29	n/a	n/a	n/a
Boise City, ID	84	n/a	n/a	0.066	1	n/a
Boston, MA	47	7.8	22	0.071	1	n/a
Boulder, CO	39	6.8	19	0.071	n/a	n/a
Cape Coral, FL	n/a	n/a	n/a	0.064	n/a	n/a
Cedar Rapids, IA	68	9.9	25	0.08	n/a	n/a
Charleston, SC	70	8.1	20	0.062	n/a	n/a
Charlotte, NC	51	10	26	0.073	2	n/a
Chicago, IL	137	11.2	31	0.086	1	0.1
Cincinnati, OH	111	12.2	44	0.077	1	n/a
Clarksville, TN	n/a	8.6	22	0.07	n/a	n/a
Cleveland, OH	147	12.8	40	0.075	5	0.04
College Station, TX	n/a	8	20	n/a	n/a	n/a
Colorado Springs, CO	32	5.4	13	0.069	1	n/a
Columbia, MO	n/a	n/a	n/a	0.072	n/a	n/a
Columbia, SC	44	8.2	22	0.069	1	n/a
Columbus, OH	97	10.9	36	0.069	1	0
Dallas, TX	70	10.7	23	0.084	2	0.07
Davenport, IA	109	10.4	28	0.08	1	n/a
Denver, CO	89	8.7	24	0.077	2	n/a
Des Moines, IA	56	10.2	31	0.077	n/a	n/a
Detroit, MI	161	14.7	46	0.079	2	0.03
Durham, NC	42	8	24	0.066	n/a	n/a
El Paso, TX	180	8.6	23	0.074	2	n/a
Eugene, OR	118	10.1	46	0.06	n/a	n/a
Fargo, ND	n/a	11.5	39	0.07	n/a	n/a
Fort Collins, CO	n/a	n/a	n/a	0.071	1	n/a
Fort Wayne, IN	n/a	10	33	0.075	n/a	n/a
Fort Worth, TX	70	10.7	23	0.084	2	0.07
Gainesville, FL	n/a	6.3	17	0.058	n/a	n/a
Green Bay, WI	n/a	9.5	38	0.075	n/a	n/a
Greensboro, NC	39	9.8	25	0.067	n/a	n/a
Honolulu, HI	46	4.1	10	0.046	0	n/a
Houston, TX	161	13.1	28	0.09	2	n/a
Huntsville, AL	61	8.6	21	0.067	n/a	n/a
Indianapolis, IN	147	13.7	44	0.077	2	n/a
Jacksonville, FL	55	7.9	20	0.062	1	n/a
Kansas City, MO	256	9.6	27	0.077	1	n/a
Lafayette, LA	48	8.2	15	0.068	n/a	n/a
Las Vegas, NV	209	8.2	27	0.074	2	n/a
Lexington, KY	28	8.3	27	0.07	n/a	n/a
Lincoln, NE	n/a	n/a	n/a	0.068	n/a	n/a
Little Rock, AR	39	10.8	23	0.07	1	n/a
Los Angeles, CA	124	11.1	28	0.103	3	0.02
Louisville, KY	96	10.7	32	0.075	2	n/a
Madison, WI	208	10.7	39	0.082	n/a	n/a
Manchester, NH	n/a	4.5	20	0.067	1	n/a
McAllen, TX	47	n/a	n/a	0.051	n/a	n/a

Table continued on following page.

Metro Area	PM 10 (ug/m³)	PM 2.5 Wtd AM (ug/m³)	PM 2.5 24-Hr (ug/m³)	Ozone (ppm)	Carbon Monoxide (ppm)	Lead (ug/m³)
Memphis, TN	67	10.6	27	0.074	1	n/a
Miami, FL	65	9.4	24	0.066	2	n/a
Midland, TX	n/a	n/a	n/a	n/a	n/a	n/a
Milwaukee, WI	209	11	39	0.08	1	n/a
Minneapolis, MN	118	10.6	41	0.079	4	0.46
Nashville, TN	57	10.2	25	0.076	2	n/a
New Orleans, LA	49	9.4	19	0.071	2	0.02
New York, NY	41	10.5	40	0.076	2	n/a
Oklahoma City, OK	89	9.2	21	0.074	1	n/a
Omaha, NE	79	9.7	33	0.082	1	0.06
Orlando, FL	54	6.8	16	0.069	1	n/a
Philadelphia, PA	174	13.3	37	0.074	1	0
Phoenix, AZ	387	9.8	32	0.083	2	n/a
Pittsburgh, PA	168	12	36	0.071	3	0
Portland, OR	27	6.5	25	0.068	1	n/a
Providence, RI	29	8.2	29	0.075	2	n/a
Provo, UT	76	6.8	21	0.066	1	n/a
Raleigh, NC	60	9.2	31	0.064	1	n/a
Reno, NV	63	7.2	18	0.067	2	n/a
Richmond, VA	65	8.7	28	0.067	1	n/a
Rochester, MN	n/a	9.6	33	0.074	n/a	n/a
Sacramento, CA	57	9.4	28	0.077	n/a	n/a
Saint Louis, MO	160	11.3	26	0.082	2	0.1
Saint Paul, MN	118	10.6	41	0.079	4	0.46
Salem, OR	n/a	n/a	n/a	0.064	n/a	n/a
Salt Lake City, UT	79	8.6	31	0.076	1	n/a
San Antonio, TX	50	9	26	0.076	1	n/a
San Diego, CA	142	12.5	24	0.08	1	0.02
San Francisco, CA	48	9.9	23	0.069	4	n/a
San Jose, CA	59	8.2	25	0.067	1	0.02
Santa Rosa, CA	48	5	17	0.046	1	n/a
Savannah, GA	n/a	8.8	24	0.061	n/a	n/a
Seattle, WA	17	8.5	29	0.068	1	n/a
Sioux Falls, SD	80	n/a	n/a	0.082	n/a	n/a
Tampa, FL	76	7.8	16	0.069	1	0.05
Tucson, AZ	201	7.8	16	0.07	1	n/a
Tulsa, OK	101	9.3	20	0.078	1	n/a
Virginia Beach, VA	62	8.1	28	0.066	1	n/a
Washington, DC	142	9.7	33	0.076	2	n/a
Wichita, KS	99	n/a	n/a	0.068	n/a	n/a
Wilmington, NC	45	6.8	19	0.067	n/a	n/a
Winston-Salem, NC	72	9.5	31	0.069	n/a	n/a
NAAQS[1]	150	15.0	35	0.075	9	0.15

Note: Data from exceptional events are included; Figures cover the Metropolitan Statistical Area (MSA); (1) National Ambient Air Quality Standards; ppm = parts per million; ug/m³ = micrograms per cubic meter; n/a not available
Concentrations: Particulate Matter 10 (coarse particulate)—highest second maximum 24-hour concentration; Particulate Matter 2.5 Wtd AM (fine particulate)—highest weighted annual mean concentration; Particulate Matter 2.5 24-Hour (fine particulate)—highest 98th percentile 24-hour concentration; Ozone—highest fourth daily maximum 8-hour concentration; Carbon Monoxide—highest second maximum non-overlapping 8-hour concentration; Lead—maximum running 3-month average
Source: U.S. Environmental Protection Agency, Air Quality Monitoring Information, "Air Quality Statistics by City, 2023"

Maximum Air Pollutant Concentrations: Nitrogen Dioxide and Sulfur Dioxide

Metro Area	Nitrogen Dioxide AM (ppb)	Nitrogen Dioxide 1-Hr (ppb)	Sulfur Dioxide AM (ppb)	Sulfur Dioxide 1-Hr (ppb)	Sulfur Dioxide 24-Hr (ppb)
Albuquerque, NM	8	43	n/a	n/a	n/a
Anchorage, AK	n/a	n/a	n/a	n/a	n/a
Ann Arbor, MI	n/a	n/a	n/a	n/a	n/a
Athens, GA	n/a	n/a	n/a	n/a	n/a
Atlanta, GA	15	48	n/a	5	n/a
Austin, TX	13	n/a	n/a	n/a	n/a
Baltimore, MD	15	45	n/a	4	n/a
Billings, MT	n/a	n/a	n/a	19	n/a
Boise City, ID	8	38	n/a	3	n/a
Boston, MA	11	45	n/a	5	n/a
Boulder, CO	n/a	n/a	n/a	n/a	n/a
Cape Coral, FL	n/a	n/a	n/a	n/a	n/a
Cedar Rapids, IA	n/a	n/a	n/a	10	n/a
Charleston, SC	7	n/a	n/a	6	n/a
Charlotte, NC	11	37	n/a	2	n/a
Chicago, IL	17	54	n/a	79	n/a
Cincinnati, OH	18	49	n/a	21	n/a
Clarksville, TN	n/a	n/a	n/a	n/a	n/a
Cleveland, OH	9	44	n/a	27	n/a
College Station, TX	n/a	n/a	n/a	29	n/a
Colorado Springs, CO	n/a	n/a	n/a	5	n/a
Columbia, MO	n/a	n/a	n/a	n/a	n/a
Columbia, SC	3	28	n/a	2	n/a
Columbus, OH	9	43	n/a	4	n/a
Dallas, TX	14	46	n/a	17	n/a
Davenport, IA	n/a	n/a	n/a	4	n/a
Denver, CO	24	65	n/a	6	n/a
Des Moines, IA	n/a	n/a	n/a	n/a	n/a
Detroit, MI	14	50	n/a	55	n/a
Durham, NC	n/a	n/a	n/a	3	n/a
El Paso, TX	15	57	n/a	6	n/a
Eugene, OR	n/a	n/a	n/a	n/a	n/a
Fargo, ND	4	n/a	n/a	3	n/a
Fort Collins, CO	n/a	n/a	n/a	n/a	n/a
Fort Wayne, IN	n/a	n/a	n/a	n/a	n/a
Fort Worth, TX	14	46	n/a	17	n/a
Gainesville, FL	n/a	n/a	n/a	n/a	n/a
Green Bay, WI	n/a	n/a	n/a	n/a	n/a
Greensboro, NC	n/a	n/a	n/a	4	n/a
Honolulu, HI	3	23	n/a	60	n/a
Houston, TX	18	60	n/a	13	n/a
Huntsville, AL	n/a	n/a	n/a	n/a	n/a
Indianapolis, IN	13	44	n/a	3	n/a
Jacksonville, FL	10	40	n/a	40	n/a
Kansas City, MO	11	45	n/a	6	n/a
Lafayette, LA	n/a	n/a	n/a	n/a	n/a
Las Vegas, NV	20	52	n/a	5	n/a
Lexington, KY	6	39	n/a	7	n/a
Lincoln, NE	n/a	n/a	n/a	n/a	n/a
Little Rock, AR	3	13	n/a	4	n/a
Los Angeles, CA	21	61	n/a	8	n/a
Louisville, KY	13	47	n/a	13	n/a
Madison, WI	n/a	n/a	n/a	n/a	n/a
Manchester, NH	n/a	n/a	n/a	1	n/a
McAllen, TX	n/a	n/a	n/a	n/a	n/a

Table continued on following page.

Metro Area	Nitrogen Dioxide AM (ppb)	Nitrogen Dioxide 1-Hr (ppb)	Sulfur Dioxide AM (ppb)	Sulfur Dioxide 1-Hr (ppb)	Sulfur Dioxide 24-Hr (ppb)
Memphis, TN	9	38	n/a	2	n/a
Miami, FL	15	53	n/a	2	n/a
Midland, TX	n/a	n/a	n/a	n/a	n/a
Milwaukee, WI	11	46	n/a	3	n/a
Minneapolis, MN	12	45	n/a	14	n/a
Nashville, TN	13	52	n/a	6	n/a
New Orleans, LA	8	39	n/a	52	n/a
New York, NY	19	60	n/a	5	n/a
Oklahoma City, OK	12	29	n/a	1	n/a
Omaha, NE	n/a	n/a	n/a	39	n/a
Orlando, FL	n/a	n/a	n/a	4	n/a
Philadelphia, PA	15	48	n/a	5	n/a
Phoenix, AZ	24	58	n/a	4	n/a
Pittsburgh, PA	9	38	n/a	65	n/a
Portland, OR	9	29	n/a	n/a	n/a
Providence, RI	13	35	n/a	3	n/a
Provo, UT	8	39	n/a	n/a	n/a
Raleigh, NC	9	36	n/a	2	n/a
Reno, NV	11	49	n/a	3	n/a
Richmond, VA	13	47	n/a	3	n/a
Rochester, MN	n/a	n/a	n/a	n/a	n/a
Sacramento, CA	9	33	n/a	2	n/a
Saint Louis, MO	10	43	n/a	38	n/a
Saint Paul, MN	12	45	n/a	14	n/a
Salem, OR	n/a	n/a	n/a	n/a	n/a
Salt Lake City, UT	16	57	n/a	5	n/a
San Antonio, TX	8	37	n/a	2	n/a
San Diego, CA	14	49	n/a	n/a	n/a
San Francisco, CA	11	102	n/a	18	n/a
San Jose, CA	13	44	n/a	2	n/a
Santa Rosa, CA	3	25	n/a	n/a	n/a
Savannah, GA	n/a	n/a	n/a	44	n/a
Seattle, WA	15	50	n/a	3	n/a
Sioux Falls, SD	5	40	n/a	1	n/a
Tampa, FL	9	36	n/a	48	n/a
Tucson, AZ	13	39	n/a	1	n/a
Tulsa, OK	6	33	n/a	3	n/a
Virginia Beach, VA	8	37	n/a	3	n/a
Washington, DC	16	47	n/a	3	n/a
Wichita, KS	6	23	n/a	2	n/a
Wilmington, NC	n/a	n/a	n/a	n/a	n/a
Winston-Salem, NC	7	40	n/a	2	n/a
NAAQS[1]	53	100	30	75	140

Note: Data from exceptional events are included; Figures cover the Metropolitan Statistical Area (MSA); (1) National Ambient Air Quality Standards; ppb = parts per billion; n/a not available
Concentrations: Nitrogen Dioxide AM—highest arithmetic mean concentration; Nitrogen Dioxide 1-Hr—highest 98th percentile 1-hour daily maximum concentration; Sulfur Dioxide AM—highest annual mean concentration; Sulfur Dioxide 1-Hr—highest 99th percentile 1-hour daily maximum concentration; Sulfur Dioxide 24-Hr—highest second maximum 24-hour concentration
Source: U.S. Environmental Protection Agency, Air Quality Monitoring Information, "Air Quality Statistics by City, 2023"

Appendix B: Metropolitan Area Definitions

Includes Metropolitan Statistical Areas (MSA) and Metropolitan Divisions (MD) referenced in this book.

Note: On July 21, 2023, the Office of Management and Budget (OMB) announced changes to metropolitan and micropolitan statistical area definitions. The current definitions are shown below.

Albuquerque, NM MSA
Bernalillo, Sandoval, Torrance, and Valencia Counties

Anchorage, AK MSA
Anchorage Municipality and Matanuska-Susitna Borough

Ann Arbor, MI MSA
Washtenaw County

Athens-Clarke County, GA MSA
Clarke, Madison, Oconee, and Oglethorpe Counties

Atlanta, GA
Atlanta-Sandy Springs-Roswell, GA MSA
Barrow, Bartow, Butts, Carroll, Cherokee, Clayton, Cobb, Coweta, Dawson, DeKalb, Douglas, Fayette, Forsyth, Fulton, Gwinnett, Haralson, Heard, Henry, Jasper, Lumpkin, Meriwether, Morgan, Newton, Paulding, Pickens, Pike, Rockdale, Spalding, and Walton Counties
Atlanta-Sandy Springs-Roswell, GA MD
Barrow, Butts, Carroll, Clayton, Coweta, Dawson, DeKalb, Douglas, Fayette, Forsyth, Fulton, Gwinnett, Heard, Henry, Jasper, Lumpkin, Meriwether, Morgan, Newton, Pickens, Pike, Rockdale, Spalding, and Walton Counties

Austin-Round Rock-San Marcos, TX MSA
Bastrop, Caldwell, Hays, Travis, and Williamson Counties

Baltimore-Columbia-Towson, MD MSA
Baltimore city; Anne Arundel, Baltimore, Carroll, Harford, Howard, and Queen Anne's Counties

Billings, MT MSA
Carbon, Stillwater, and Yellowstone Counties

Boise City, ID MSA
Previously Boise City-Nampa, ID MSA
Ada, Boise, Canyon, Gem, and Owyhee Counties

Boston, MA
Boston-Cambridge-Newton, MA-NH MSA
Essex, Middlesex, Norfolk, Plymouth, and Suffolk Counties, MA; Rockingham and Strafford Counties, NH
Boston, MA MD
Norfolk, Plymouth, and Suffolk Counties

Boulder, CO MSA
Boulder County

Cape Coral-Fort Myers, FL MSA
Lee County

Cedar Rapids, IA, MSA
Benton, Jones, and Linn Counties

Charleston-North Charleston, SC MSA
Berkeley, Charleston, and Dorchester Counties

Charlotte-Concord-Gastonia, NC-SC MSA
Anson, Cabarrus, Gaston, Iredell, Lincoln, Mecklenburg, Rowan, and Union Counties, NC; Chester, Lancaster, and York Counties, SC

Chicago, IL
Chicago-Naperville-Elgin, IL-IN MSA
Cook, DeKalb, DuPage, Grundy, Kane, Kendall, Lake, McHenry, and Will Counties, IL; Jasper, Lake, Newton, and Porter Counties, IN
Chicago-Naperville-Schaumburg, IL MD
Cook, DuPage, Grundy, McHenry, and Will Counties

Cincinnati, OH-KY-IN MSA
Brown, Butler, Clermont, Hamilton, and Warren Counties, OH; Boone, Bracken, Campbell, Gallatin, Grant, Kenton, and Pendleton County, KY; Dearborn, Franklin, and Ohio Counties, IN

Clarksville, TN-KY MSA
Montgomery and Stewart Counties, TN; Christian and Trigg Counties, KY

Cleveland, OH MSA
Ashtabula, Cuyahoga, Geauga, Lake, Lorain, and Medina Counties

College Station-Bryan, TX MSA
Brazos, Burleson, and Robertson Counties

Colorado Springs, CO MSA
El Paso and Teller Counties

Columbia, MO MSA
Boone, Cooper, and Howard Counties

Columbia, SC MSA
Calhoun, Fairfield, Kershaw, Lexington, Richland, and Saluda Counties

Columbus, OH MSA
Delaware, Fairfield, Franklin, Hocking, Licking, Madison, Morrow, Perry, Pickaway, and Union Counties

Dallas, TX
Dallas-Fort Worth-Arlington, TX MSA
Collin, Dallas, Denton, Ellis, Hunt, Johnson, Kaufman, Parker, Rockwall, Tarrant, and Wise Counties
Dallas-Plano-Irving, TX MD
Collin, Dallas, Denton, Ellis, Hunt, Kaufman, and Rockwall Counties

Davenport-Moline-Rock Island, IA-IL MSA
Scott County, IA; Henry, Mercer, and Rock Island Counties, IL

Denver-Aurora-Centennial, CO MSA
Adams, Arapahoe, Broomfield, Clear Creek, Denver, Douglas, Elbert, Gilpin, Jefferson, and Park Counties

Des Moines-West Des Moines, IA MSA
Dallas, Guthrie, Jasper, Madison, Polk, and Warren Counties

Detroit, MI
Detroit-Warren-Dearborn, MI MSA
Lapeer, Livingston, Macomb, Oakland, St. Clair, and Wayne Counties
Detroit-Dearborn-Livonia, MI MD
Wayne County

Durham-Chapel Hill, NC MSA
Chatham, Durham, Orange, and Person Counties

El Paso, TX MSA
El Paso and Hudspeth Counties

Eugene-Springfield, OR MSA
Lane County

Fargo, ND-MN MSA
Cass County, ND; Clay County, MN

Fort Collins-Loveland, CO MSA
Larimer County

Fort Wayne, IN MSA
Allen, Wells, and Whitley Counties

Fort Worth, TX

Dallas-Fort Worth-Arlington, TX MSA
Collin, Dallas, Denton, Ellis, Hunt, Johnson, Kaufman, Parker, Rockwall, Tarrant, and Wise Counties

Fort Worth-Arlington-Grapevine, TX MD
Johnson, Parker, Tarrant, and Wise Counties

Gainesville, FL MSA
Alachua, Gilchrist, and Levy Counties

Green Bay, WI MSA
Brown, Kewaunee, and Oconto Counties

Greensboro-High Point, NC MSA
Guilford, Randolph, and Rockingham Counties

Honolulu, HI
See Urban Honolulu, HI

Houston-Pasadena-The Woodlands, TX MSA
Austin, Brazoria, Chambers, Fort Bend, Galveston, Harris, Liberty, Montgomery, San Jacinto, and Waller Counties

Huntsville, AL MSA
Limestone and Madison Counties

Indianapolis-Carmel-Greenwood, IN MSA
Boone, Brown, Hamilton, Hancock, Hendricks, Johnson, Madison, Marion, Morgan, Shelby, and Tipton Counties

Jacksonville, FL MSA
Baker, Clay, Duval, Nassau, and St. Johns Counties

Kansas City, MO-KS MSA
Johnson, Leavenworth, Linn, Miami, and Wyandotte Counties, KS; Bates, Caldwell, Cass, Clay, Clinton, Jackson, Lafayette, Platte, and Ray Counties, MO

Lafayette, LA MSA
Acadia, Lafayette, St. Martin, and Vermilion Parishes

Las Vegas-Henderson-North Las Vegas, NV MSA
Clark County

Lexington-Fayette, KY MSA
Bourbon, Clark, Fayette, Jessamine, Scott, and Woodford Counties

Lincoln, NE MSA
Lancaster and Seward Counties

Little Rock-North Little Rock-Conway, AR MSA
Faulkner, Grant, Lonoke, Perry, Pulaski, and Saline Counties

Los Angeles, CA

Los Angeles-Long Beach-Anaheim, CA MSA
Los Angeles and Orange Counties

Los Angeles-Long Beach-Glendale, CA MD
Los Angeles County

Louisville/Jefferson County, KY-IN MSA
Clark, Floyd, Harrison, and Washington Counties, IN; Bullitt, Henry, Jefferson, Meade, Nelson, Oldham, Shelby, and Spencer Counties, KY

Madison, WI MSA
Columbia, Dane, Green, and Iowa Counties

Manchester-Nashua, NH MSA
Hillsborough County

McAllen-Edinburg-Mission, TX
Hidalgo County

Memphis, TN-AR-MS MSA
Fayette, Shelby and Tipton Counties, TN; Crittenden County, AR; Benton, DeSoto, Marshall, Tate and Tunica Counties, MS

Miami, FL

Miami-Fort Lauderdale-West Palm Beach, FL MSA
Broward, Miami-Dade, and Palm Beach Counties

Miami-Miami Beach-Kendall, FL MD
Miami-Dade County

Midland, TX MSA
Martin and Midland Counties

Milwaukee-Waukesha, WI MSA
Milwaukee, Ozaukee, Washington, and Waukesha Counties

Minneapolis-St. Paul-Bloomington, MN-WI MSA
Anoka, Carver, Chisago, Dakota, Hennepin, Isanti, Le Sueur, Mille Lacs, Ramsey, Scott, Sherburne, Washington, and Wright Counties, MN; Pierce and St. Croix Counties, WI

Nashville-Davidson–Murfreesboro–Franklin, TN MSA
Cannon, Cheatham, Davidson, Dickson, Hickman, Macon, Maury, Robertson, Rutherford, Smith, Sumner, Trousdale, Williamson, and Wilson Counties

New Orleans-Metarie, LA MSA
Jefferson, Orleans, Plaquemines, St. Bernard, St. Charles, St. James, and St. John the Baptist Parishes

New York, NY

New York-Newark-Jersey City, NY-NJ MSA
Bergen, Essex, Hudson, Hunterdon, Middlesex, Monmouth, Morris, Ocean, Passaic, Somerset, Sussex, and Union Counties, NJ; Bronx, Kings, Nassau, New York, Putnam, Queens, Richmond, Rockland, Suffolk, and Westchester Counties, NY

New York-Jersey City-White Plains, NY-NJ MD
Bergen, Hudson, and Passaic Counties, NJ; Bronx, Kings, New York, Putnam, Queens, Richmond, Rockland, and Westchester Counties, NY

Oklahoma City, OK MSA
Canadian, Cleveland, Grady, Lincoln, Logan, McClain, and Oklahoma Counties

Omaha, NE-IA MSA
Harrison, Mills, and Pottawattamie Counties, IA; Cass, Douglas, Sarpy, Saunders, and Washington Counties, NE

Orlando-Kissimmee-Sanford, FL MSA
Lake, Orange, Osceola, and Seminole Counties

Appendix B: Metropolitan Area Definitions   A-173

Philadelphia, PA

Philadelphia-Camden-Wilmington, PA-NJ-DE-MD MSA
New Castle County, DE; Cecil County, MD; Burlington, Camden, Gloucester, and Salem Counties, NJ; Bucks, Chester, Delaware, Montgomery, and Philadelphia Counties, PA

Philadelphia, PA MD
Delaware and Philadelphia Counties

Phoenix-Mesa-Chandler, AZ MSA
Maricopa and Pinal Counties

Pittsburgh, PA MSA
Allegheny, Armstrong, Beaver, Butler, Fayette, Lawrence, Washington, and Westmoreland Counties

Portland-Vancouver-Hillsboro, OR-WA MSA
Clackamas, Columbia, Multnomah, Washington, and Yamhill Counties, OR; Clark and Skamania Counties, WA

Providence-Warwick, RI MSA
Bristol County, MA; Bristol, Kent, Newport, Providence, and Washington Counties, RI

Provo-Orem-Lehi, UT MSA
Juab and Utah Counties

Raleigh-Cary, NC MSA
Franklin, Johnston, and Wake Counties

Reno, NV MSA
Lyon, Storey, and Washoe Counties

Richmond, VA MSA
Amelia, Charles City, Chesterfield, Dinwiddie, Goochland, Hanover, Henrico, King and Queen, King William, New Kent, Powhatan, Prince George, and Sussex Counties; Colonial Heights, Hopewell, Petersburg, and Richmond Cities

Rochester, MN MSA
Dodge, Fillmore, Olmsted, and Wabasha Counties

Sacramento-Roseville-Folsom, CA MSA
El Dorado, Placer, Sacramento, and Yolo Counties

Saint Louis, MO-IL MSA
Bond, Calhoun, Clinton, Jersey, Macoupin, Madison, Monroe, and St. Clair Counties, IL; St. Louis city; Crawford (part–Sullivan city), Franklin, Jefferson, Lincoln, St. Charles, St. Louis, and Warren Counties, MO

Saint Paul, MN
See Minneapolis-St. Paul-Bloomington, MN-WI MSA

Salem, OR MSA
Marion and Polk Counties

Salt Lake City-Murray, UT MSA
Salt Lake and Tooele Counties

San Antonio-New Braunfels, TX MSA
Atascosa, Bandera, Bexar, Comal, Guadalupe, Kendall, Medina, and Wilson Counties

San Diego-Chula Vista-Carlsbad, CA MSA
San Diego County

San Francisco, CA

San Francisco-Oakland-Fremont, CA MSA
Alameda, Contra Costa, Marin, San Francisco, and San Mateo Counties

San Francisco-San Mateo-Redwood City, CA MD
San Francisco and San Mateo Counties

San Jose-Sunnyvale-Santa Clara, CA MSA
San Benito and Santa Clara Counties

Santa Rosa-Petaluma, CA MSA
Sonoma County

Savannah, GA MSA
Bryan, Chatham, and Effingham Counties

Seattle, WA

Seattle-Tacoma-Bellevue, WA MSA
King, Pierce, and Snohomish Counties

Seattle-Bellevue-Kent, WA MD
King County

Sioux Falls, SD-MN MSA
Lincoln, McCook, Minnehaha, and Turner Counties, SD; Rock County, MN

Tampa, FL

Tampa-St. Petersburg-Clearwater, FL MSA
Hernando, Hillsborough, Pasco, and Pinellas Counties

Tampa, FL MD
Hernando, Hillsborough, and Pasco Counties

Tucson, AZ MSA
Pima County

Tulsa, OK MSA
Creek, Okmulgee, Osage, Pawnee, Rogers, Tulsa, and Wagoner Counties

Urban Honolulu, HI MSA
Honolulu County

Virginia Beach-Chesapeake-Norfolk, VA-NC MSA
Camden, Currituck, and Gates Counties, NC; Chesapeake, Hampton, Newport News, Norfolk, Poquoson, Portsmouth, Suffolk, Virginia Beach and Williamsburg cities, VA; Gloucester, Isle of Wight, James City, Mathews, Surry, and York Counties, VA

Washington, DC

Washington-Arlington-Alexandria, DC-VA-MD-WV MSA
District of Columbia; Calvert, Charles, Frederick, Montgomery, and Prince George's Counties, MD; Alexandria, Fairfax, Falls Church, Fredericksburg, Manassas, and Manassas Park cities, VA; Arlington, Clarke, Culpeper, Fairfax, Fauquier, Loudoun, Prince William, Rappahannock, Spotsylvania, Stafford, and Warren Counties, VA; Jefferson County, WV

Washington, DC-MD MD
District of Columbia; Charles and Prince George's Counties, MD

Wichita, KS MSA
Butler, Harvey, Sedgwick, and Sumner Counties

Wilmington, NC MSA
Brunswick, New Hanover and Pender Counties

Winston-Salem, NC MSA
Davidson, Davie, Forsyth, Stokes, and Yadkin Counties

Appendix C: Government Type and Primary County

This appendix includes the government structure of each place included in this book. It also includes the county or county equivalent in which each place is located. If a place spans more than one county, the county in which the majority of the population resides is shown.

Albuquerque, NM
Government Type: City
County: Bernalillo

Anchorage, AK
Government Type: Municipality
Borough: Anchorage

Ann Arbor, MI
Government Type: City
County: Washtenaw

Athens, GA
Government Type: Consolidated city-county
County: Clarke

Atlanta, GA
Government Type: City
County: Fulton

Austin, TX
Government Type: City
County: Travis

Baltimore, MD
Government Type: Independent city

Baton Rouge, LA
Government Type: Consolidated city-parish
Parish: East Baton Rouge

Billings, MT
Government Type: City
County: Yellowstone

Boise City, ID
Government Type: City
County: Ada

Boston, MA
Government Type: City
County: Suffolk

Boulder, CO
Government Type: City
County: Boulder

Cape Coral, FL
Government Type: City
County: Lee

Cedar Rapids, IA
Government Type: City
County: Linn

Charleston, SC
Government Type: City
County: Charleston

Charlotte, NC
Government Type: City
County: Mecklenburg

Chicago, IL
Government Type: City
County: Cook

Cincinnati, OH
Government Type: City
County: Hamilton

Clarksville, TN
Government Type: City
County: Montgomery

Cleveland, OH
Government Type: City
County: Cuyahoga

College Station, TX
Government Type: City
County: Brazos

Colorado Springs, CO
Government Type: City
County: El Paso

Columbia, MO
Government Type: City
County: Boone

Columbia, SC
Government Type: City
County: Richland

Columbus, OH
Government Type: City
County: Franklin

Dallas, TX
Government Type: City
County: Dallas

Davenport, IA
Government Type: City
County: Scott

Denver, CO
Government Type: City
County: Denver

Des Moines, IA
Government Type: City
County: Polk

Detroit, MI
Government Type: City
County: Wayne

Durham, NC
Government Type: City
County: Durham

El Paso, TX
Government Type: City
County: El Paso

Eugene, OR
Government Type: City
County: Lane

Fargo, ND
Government Type: City
County: Cass

Fort Collins, CO
Government Type: City
County: Larimer

Fort Wayne, IN
Government Type: City
County: Allen

Fort Worth, TX
Government Type: City
County: Tarrant

Gainesville, FL
Government Type: City
County: Alachua

Green Bay, WI
Government Type: City
County: Brown

Greensboro, NC
Government Type: City
County: Guilford

Honolulu, HI
Government Type: Census Designated Place (CDP)
County: Honolulu

Houston, TX
Government Type: City
County: Harris

Huntsville, AL
Government Type: City
County: Madison

Indianapolis, IN
Government Type: City
County: Marion

Jacksonville, FL
Government Type: City
County: Duval

Kansas City, MO
Government Type: City
County: Jackson

Lafayette, LA
Government Type: City
Parish: Lafayette

Las Vegas, NV
Government Type: City
County: Clark

Lexington, KY
Government Type: Consolidated city-county
County: Fayette

Lincoln, NE
Government Type: City
County: Lancaster

Little Rock, AR
Government Type: City
County: Pulaski

Los Angeles, CA
Government Type: City
County: Los Angeles

Louisville, KY
Government Type: Consolidated city-county
County: Jefferson

Madison, WI
Government Type: City
County: Dane

Manchester, NH
Government Type: City
County: Hillsborough

McAllen, TX
Government Type: City
County: Hidalgo

Memphis, TN
Government Type: City
County: Shelby

Miami, FL
Government Type: City
County: Miami-Dade

Midland, TX
Government Type: City
County: Midland

Milwaukee, WI
Government Type: City
County: Milwaukee

Minneapolis, MN
Government Type: City
County: Hennepin

Nashville, TN
Government Type: Consolidated city-county
County: Davidson

New Orleans, LA
Government Type: City
Parish: Orleans

New York, NY
Government Type: City
Counties: Bronx; Kings; New York; Queens; Staten Island

Oklahoma City, OK
Government Type: City
County: Oklahoma

Omaha, NE
Government Type: City
County: Douglas

Orlando, FL
Government Type: City
County: Orange

Philadelphia, PA
Government Type: City
County: Philadelphia

Phoenix, AZ
Government Type: City
County: Maricopa

Pittsburgh, PA
Government Type: City
County: Allegheny

Portland, OR
Government Type: City
County: Multnomah

Providence, RI
Government Type: City
County: Providence

Provo, UT
Government Type: City
County: Utah

Raleigh, NC
Government Type: City
County: Wake

Reno, NV
Government Type: City
County: Washoe

Richmond, VA
Government Type: Independent city

Riverside, CA
Government Type: City
County: Riverside

Rochester, MN
Government Type: City
County: Olmsted

Rochester, NY
Government Type: City
County: Monroe

Sacramento, CA
Government Type: City
County: Sacramento

Saint Louis, MO
Government Type: Independent city

Saint Paul, MN
Government Type: City
County: Ramsey

Salem, OR
Government Type: City
County: Marion

Salt Lake City, UT
Government Type: City
County: Salt Lake

San Antonio, TX
Government Type: City
County: Bexar

San Diego, CA
Government Type: City
County: San Diego

San Francisco, CA
Government Type: City
County: San Francisco

San Jose, CA
Government Type: City
County: Santa Clara

Santa Rosa, CA
Government Type: City
County: Sonoma

Savannah, GA
Government Type: City
County: Chatham

Seattle, WA
Government Type: City
County: King

Sioux Falls, SD
Government Type: City
County: Minnehaha

Tampa, FL
Government Type: City
County: Hillsborough

Tucson, AZ
Government Type: City
County: Pima

Tulsa, OK
Government Type: City
County: Tulsa

Virginia Beach, VA
Government Type: Independent city

Washington, DC
Government Type: City
County: District of Columbia

Wichita, KS
Government Type: City
County: Sedgwick

Wilmington, NC
Government Type: City
County: New Hanover

Winston-Salem, NC
Government Type: City
County: Forsyth

Appendix D: Chambers of Commerce

Albuquerque, NM
Albuquerque Chamber of Commerce
P.O. Box 25100
Albuquerque, NM 87125
Phone: (505) 764-3700
Fax: (505) 764-3714
www.abqchamber.com

Albuquerque Economic Development Dept
851 University Blvd SE, Suite 203
Albuquerque, NM 87106
Phone: (505) 246-6200
Fax: (505) 246-6219
www.cabq.gov/econdev

Anchorage, AK
Anchorage Chamber of Commerce
1016 W Sixth Avenue, Suite 303
Anchorage, AK 99501
Phone: (907) 272-2401
Fax: (907) 272-4117
www.anchoragechamber.org

Anchorage Economic Development Department
900 W 5th Avenue, Suite 300
Anchorage, AK 99501
Phone: (907) 258-3700
Fax: (907) 258-6646
aedcweb.com

Ann Arbor, MI
Ann Arbor Area Chamber of Commerce
115 West Huron, 3rd Floor
Ann Arbor, MI 48104
Phone: (734) 665-4433
Fax: (734) 665-4191
www.annarborchamber.org

Ann Arbor Economic Development Department
201 S Division, Suite 430
Ann Arbor, MI 48104
Phone: (734) 761-9317
www.annarborspark.org

Athens, GA
Athens Area Chamber of Commerce
246 W Hancock Avenue
Athens, GA 30601
Phone: (706) 549-6800
Fax: (706) 549-5636
www.aacoc.org

Athens-Clarke County Economic Development Department
246 W. Hancock Avenue
Athens, GA 30601
Phone: (706) 613-3233
Fax: (706) 613-3812
www.athensbusiness.org

Atlanta, GA
Metro Atlanta Chamber of Commerce
235 Andrew Young International Blvd NW
Atlanta, GA 30303
Phone: (404) 880-9000
Fax: (404) 586-8464
www.metroatlantachamber.com

Austin, TX
Greater Austin Chamber of Commerce
210 Barton Springs Road, Suite 400
Austin, TX 78704
Phone: (512) 478-9383
Fax: (512) 478-6389
www.austin-chamber.org

Baltimore, MD
Baltimore City Chamber of Commerce
P.O. Box 43121
Baltimore, MD 21236
443-860-2020
baltimorecitychamber.org

Baltimore County Chamber of Commerce
102 W. Pennsylvania Avenue, Suite 305
Towson, MD, 21204
Phone: (410) 825-6200
Fax: (410) 821-9901
www.baltcountychamber.com

Billings, MT
Billings Chamber of Commerce
815 S. 27th St
Billings, MT 59101
Phone: (406) 245-4111
Fax: (406) 245-7333
www.billingschamber.com

Boise City, ID
Boise Metro Chamber of Commerce
250 S. 5th Street, Suite 800
Boise City, ID 83701
Phone: (208) 472-5200
Fax: (208) 472-5201
www.boisechamber.org

Boston, MA
Greater Boston Chamber of Commerce
265 Franklin Street, 12th Floor
Boston, MA 02110
Phone: (617) 227-4500
Fax: (617) 227-7505
www.bostonchamber.com

Boulder, CO
Boulder Chamber of Commerce
2440 Pearl Street
Boulder, CO 80302
Phone: (303) 442-1044
Fax: (303) 938-8837
www.boulderchamber.com

Cape Coral, FL
Chamber of Commerce of Cape Coral
2051 Cape Coral Parkway East
Cape Coral, FL 33904
Phone: (239) 549-6900
www.capecoralchamber.com

Cedar Rapids, IA
Cedar Rapids Chamber of Commerce
424 First Avenue NE
Cedar Rapids, IA 52401
Phone: (319) 398-5317
Fax: (319) 398-5228
www.cedarrapids.org

Cedar Rapids Economic Development
50 Second Avenue Bridge, Sixth Floor
Cedar Rapids, IA 52401-1256
Phone: (319) 286-5041
Fax: (319) 286-5141
www.cedar-rapids.org

Charleston, SC
Charleston Metro Chamber of Commerce
P.O. Box 975
Charleston, SC 29402
Phone: (843) 577-2510
www.charlestonchamber.net

Charlotte, NC
Charlotte Chamber of Commerce
330 S Tryon Street
P.O. Box 32785
Charlotte, NC 28232
Phone: (704) 378-1300
Fax: (704) 374-1903
www.charlottechamber.com

Charlotte Regional Partnership
1001 Morehead Square Drive, Suite 200
Charlotte, NC 28203
Phone: (704) 347-8942
Fax: (704) 347-8981
www.charlotteusa.com

Chicago, IL
Chicagoland Chamber of Commerce
200 E Randolph Street, Suite 2200
Chicago, IL 60601-6436
Phone: (312) 494-6700
Fax: (312) 861-0660
www.chicagolandchamber.org

City of Chicago Department of Planning and Development
City Hall, Room 1000
121 North La Salle Street
Chicago, IL 60602
Phone: (312) 744-4190
Fax: (312) 744-2271
www.cityofchicago.org/city/en/depts/dcd.html

Cincinnati, OH
Cincinnati USA Regional Chamber
3 East 4th Street, Suite 200
Cincinnati, Ohio 45202
Phone: (513) 579-3111
www.cincinnatichamber.com

Clarksville, TN
Clarksville Area Chamber of Commerce
25 Jefferson Street, Suite 300
Clarksville, TN 37040
Phone: (931) 647-2331
www.clarksvillechamber.com

Cleveland, OH
Greater Cleveland Partnership
1240 Huron Rd. E, Suite 300
Cleveland, OH 44115
Phone: (216) 621-3300
www.gcpartnership.com

Appendix D: Chambers of Commerce

College Station, TX
Bryan-College Station Chamber of Commerce
4001 East 29th St, Suite 175
Bryan, TX 77802
Phone: (979) 260-5200
www.bcschamber.org

Colorado Springs, CO
Colorado Springs Chamber and EDC
102 South Tejon Street, Suite 430
Colorado Springs, CO 80903
Phone: (719) 471-8183
coloradospringschamberedc.com

Columbia, MO
Columbia Chamber of Commerce
300 South Providence Rd.
P.O. Box 1016
Columbia, MO 65205-1016
Phone: (573) 874-1132
Fax: (573) 443-3986
www.columbiamochamber.com

Columbia, SC
The Columbia Chamber
930 Richland Street
Columbia, SC 29201
Phone: (803) 733-1110
Fax: (803) 733-1113
www.columbiachamber.com

Columbus, OH
Greater Columbus Chamber
37 North High Street
Columbus, OH 43215
Phone: (614) 221-1321
Fax: (614) 221-1408
www.columbus.org

Dallas, TX
City of Dallas Economic Development Department
1500 Marilla Street, 5C South
Dallas, TX 75201
Phone: (214) 670-1685
Fax: (214) 670-0158
www.dallas-edd.org

Greater Dallas Chamber of Commerce
700 North Pearl Street, Suite 1200
Dallas, TX 75201
Phone: (214) 746-6600
Fax: (214) 746-6799
www.dallaschamber.org

Davenport, IA
Quad Cities Chamber
331 W. 3rd Street, Suite 100
Davenport, IA 52801
Phone: (563) 322-1706
quadcitieschamber.com

Denver, CO
Denver Metro Chamber of Commerce
1445 Market Street
Denver, CO 80202
Phone: (303) 534-8500
Fax: (303) 534-3200
www.denverchamber.org

Downtown Denver Partnership
511 16th Street, Suite 200
Denver, CO 80202
Phone: (303) 534-6161
Fax: (303) 534-2803
www.downtowndenver.com

Des Moines, IA
Des Moines Downtown Chamber
301 Grand Ave
Des Moines, IA 50309
Phone: (515) 309-3229
desmoinesdowntownchamber.com

Greater Des Moines Partnership
700 Locust Street, Suite 100
Des Moines, IA 50309
Phone: (515) 286-4950
Fax: (515) 286-4974
www.desmoinesmetro.com

Durham, NC
Durham Chamber of Commerce
P.O. Box 3829
Durham, NC 27702
Phone: (919) 682-2133
Fax: (919) 688-8351
www.durhamchamber.org

North Carolina Institute of Minority Economic Development
114 W Parish Street
Durham, NC 27701
Phone: (919) 956-8889
Fax: (919) 688-7668
www.ncimed.com

El Paso, TX
City of El Paso Department of Economic Development
2 Civic Center Plaza
El Paso, TX 79901
Phone: (915) 541-4000
Fax: (915) 541-1316
www.elpasotexas.gov

Greater El Paso Chamber of Commerce
10 Civic Center Plaza
El Paso, TX 79901
Phone: (915) 534-0500
Fax: (915) 534-0510
www.elpaso.org

Eugene, OR
Eugene Area Chamber of Commerce
1401 Williamette Street
Eugene, OR 97401
Phone: (541) 484-1314
Fax: (541) 484-4942
www.eugenechamber.com

Fargo, ND
Chamber of Commerce of Fargo Moorhead
202 First Avenue North
Fargo, ND 56560
Phone: (218) 233-1100
Fax: (218) 233-1200
www.fmchamber.com

Greater Fargo-Moorhead Economic Development Corporation
51 Broadway, Suite 500
Fargo, ND 58102
Phone: (701) 364-1900
Fax: (701) 293-7819
www.gfmedc.com

Fort Collins, CO
Fort Collins Chamber of Commerce
225 South Meldrum
Fort Collins, CO 80521
Phone: (970) 482-3746
Fax: (970) 482-3774
fortcollinschamber.com

Fort Wayne, IN
City of Fort Wayne Economic Development
1 Main Street
Fort Wayne, IN 46802
Phone: (260) 427-1111
Fax: (260) 427-1375
www.cityoffortwayne.org

Greater Fort Wayne Chamber of Commerce
826 Ewing Street
Fort Wayne, IN 46802
Phone: (260) 424-1435
Fax: (260) 426-7232
www.fwchamber.org

Fort Worth, TX
Fort Worth Chamber of Commerce
777 Taylor Street, Suite 900
Fort Worth, TX 76102-4997
Phone: (817) 336-2491
Fax: (817) 877-4034
www.fortworthchamber.com

City of Fort Worth Economic Development
City Hall
900 Monroe Street, Suite 301
Fort Worth, TX 76102
Phone: (817) 392-6103
Fax: (817) 392-2431
www.fortworthgov.org

Gainesville, FL
Greater Gainesville Chamber
300 East University Avenue, Suite 100
Gainesville, FL 32601
Phone: (352) 334-7100
Fax: (352) 334-7141
www.gainesvillechamber.com

Green Bay, WI
Greater Green Bay Chamber
300 N. Broadway, Suite 3A
Green Bay, WI 54303
Phone: (920) 593-3400
www.greatergbc.org

Greensboro, NC
Greensboro Chamber of Commerce
111 W. February One Place
Greensboro, NC 27401
Phone: (336) 387-8301
greensboro.org

Honolulu, HI
The Chamber of Commerce of Hawaii
1132 Bishop Street, Suite 402
Honolulu, HI 96813
Phone: (808) 545-4300
Fax: (808) 545-4369
www.cochawaii.com

Houston, TX
Greater Houston Partnership
1200 Smith Street, Suite 700
Houston, TX 77002-4400
Phone: (713) 844-3600
Fax: (713) 844-0200
www.houston.org

Huntsville, AL
Chamber of Commerce of
Huntsville/Madison County
225 Church Street
Huntsville, AL 35801
Phone: (256) 535-2000
www.huntsvillealabamausa.com

Indianapolis, IN
Greater Indianapolis Chamber of Commerce
111 Monument Circle, Suite 1950
Indianapolis, IN 46204
Phone: (317) 464-2222
Fax: (317) 464-2217
www.indychamber.com

Jacksonville, FL
Jacksonville Chamber of Commerce
3 Independent Drive
Jacksonville, FL 32202
Phone: (904) 366-6600
Fax: (904) 632-0617
www.myjaxchamber.com

Kansas City, MO
Greater Kansas City Chamber of Commerce
2600 Commerce Tower
911 Main Street
Kansas City, MO 64105
Phone: (816) 221-2424
Fax: (816) 221-7440
www.kcchamber.com

Kansas City Area Development Council
2600 Commerce Tower
911 Main Street
Kansas City, MO 64105
Phone: (816) 221-2121
www.thinkkc.com

Lafayette, LA
Greater Lafayette Chamber of Commerce
804 East Saint Mary Blvd.
Lafayette, LA 70503
Phone: (337) 233-2705
Fax: (337) 234-8671
www.lafchamber.org

Las Vegas, NV
Las Vegas Chamber of Commerce
6671 Las Vegas Blvd South, Suite 300
Las Vegas, NV 89119
Phone: (702) 735-1616
Fax: (702) 735-0406
www.lvchamber.org

Las Vegas Office of Business Development
400 Stewart Avenue
City Hall
Las Vegas, NV 89101
Phone: (702) 229-6011
Fax: (702) 385-3128
www.lasvegasnevada.gov

Lexington, KY
Greater Lexington Chamber of Commerce
330 East Main Street, Suite 100
Lexington, KY 40507
Phone: (859) 254-4447
Fax: (859) 233-3304
www.commercelexington.com

Lexington Downtown Development
Authority
101 East Vine Street, Suite 500
Lexington, KY 40507
Phone: (859) 425-2296
Fax: (859) 425-2292
www.lexingtondda.com

Lincoln, NE
Lincoln Chamber of Commerce
1135 M Street, Suite 200
Lincoln, NE 68508
Phone: (402) 436-2350
www.lcoc.com

Little Rock, AR
Little Rock Regional Chamber
One Chamber Plaza
Little Rock, AR 72201
Phone: (501) 374-2001
Fax: (501) 374-6018
www.littlerockchamber.com

Los Angeles, CA
Los Angeles Area Chamber of Commerce
350 South Bixel Street
Los Angeles, CA 90017
Phone: (213) 580-7500
Fax: (213) 580-7511
www.lachamber.org

Los Angeles County Economic
Development Corporation
444 South Flower Street, 34th Floor
Los Angeles, CA 90071
Phone: (213) 622-4300
Fax: (213) 622-7100
www.laedc.org

Louisville, KY
The Greater Louisville Chamber of
Commerce
614 West Main Street, Suite 6000
Louisville, KY 40202
Phone: (502) 625-0000
Fax: (502) 625-0010
www.greaterlouisville.com

Madison, WI
Greater Madison Chamber of Commerce
615 East Washington Avenue
P.O. Box 71
Madison, WI 53701-0071
Phone: (608) 256-8348
Fax: (608) 256-0333
www.greatermadisonchamber.com

Manchester, NH
Greater Manchester Chamber of Commerce
889 Elm Street
Manchester, NH 03101
Phone: (603) 666-6600
Fax: (603) 626-0910
www.manchester-chamber.org

Manchester Economic Development Office
One City Hall Plaza
Manchester, NH 03101
Phone: (603) 624-6505
Fax: (603) 624-6308
www.yourmanchesternh.com

McAllen, TX
McAllen Chamber of Commerce
1200 Ash Avenue
McAllen, TX 78501
Phone: (956) 682-2871
Fax: (956) 687-2917
mcallenchamber.com

Memphis, TN
Greater Memphis Chamber
22 North Front Street, Suite 200
Memphis, TN 38103-2100
Phone: (901) 543-3500
memphischamber.com

Miami, FL
Greater Miami Chamber of Commerce
1601 Biscayne Boulevard
Miami, FL 33132-1260
Phone: (305) 350-7700
Fax: (305) 374-6902
www.miamichamber.com

The Beacon Council
80 Southwest 8th Street, Suite 2400
Miami, FL 33130
Phone: (305) 579-1300
Fax: (305) 375-0271
www.beaconcouncil.com

Midland, TX
Midland Chamber of Commerce
303 W. Wall Street, Suite 200
Midland, TX 79701
Phone: (432) 683-3381
www.midlandtxchamber.com

Milwaukee, WI
Greater Milwaukee Chamber of Commerce
6815 W. Capitol Drive, Suite 300
Milwaukee, WI 53216
Phone: (414) 465-2422
www.gmcofc.org

Minneapolis, MN
Minneapolis Regional Chamber
81 South Ninth Street, Suite 200
Minneapolis, MN 55402
Phone: (612) 370-9100
Fax: (612) 370-9195
www.minneapolischamber.org

Minneapolis Community Development
Agency
Crown Roller Mill
105 5th Avenue South, Suite 200
Minneapolis, MN 55401
Phone: (612) 673-5095
Fax: (612) 673-5100
www.ci.minneapolis.mn.us

Nashville, TN
Nashville Area Chamber of Commerce
211 Commerce Street, Suite 100
Nashville, TN 37201
Phone: (615) 743-3000
Fax: (615) 256-3074
www.nashvillechamber.com

TVA Economic Development
400 West Summit Hill Drive
Knoxville TN 37902
Phone: (865) 632-2101
www.tvaed.com

New Orleans, LA
New Orleans Chamber of Commerce
1515 Poydras Street, Suite 1010
New Orleans, LA 70112
Phone: (504) 799-4260
Fax: (504) 799-4259
www.neworleanschamber.org

New York, NY
New York City Economic Development
Corporation
110 William Street
New York, NY 10038
Phone: (212) 619-5000
www.nycedc.com

The Partnership for New York City
One Battery Park Plaza
5th Floor
New York, NY 10004
Phone: (212) 493-7400
Fax: (212) 344-3344
www.pfnyc.org

Oklahoma City, OK
Greater Oklahoma City Chamber of
Commerce
123 Park Avenue
Oklahoma City, OK 73102
Phone: (405) 297-8900
Fax: (405) 297-8916
www.okcchamber.com

Omaha, NE
Omaha Chamber of Commerce
1301 Harney Street
Omaha, NE 68102
Phone: (402) 346-5000
Fax: (402) 346-7050
www.omahachamber.org

Orlando, FL
Metro Orlando Economic Development
Commission of Mid-Florida
301 East Pine Street, Suite 900
Orlando, FL 32801
Phone: (407) 422-7159
Fax: (407) 425.6428
www.orlandoedc.com

Orlando Regional Chamber of Commerce
75 South Ivanhoe Boulevard
P.O. Box 1234
Orlando, FL 32802
Phone: (407) 425-1234
Fax: (407) 839-5020
www.orlando.org

Philadelphia, PA
Greater Philadelphia Chamber of
Commerce
200 South Broad Street, Suite 700
Philadelphia, PA 19102
Phone: (215) 545-1234
Fax: (215) 790-3600
www.greaterphilachamber.com

Phoenix, AZ
Greater Phoenix Chamber of Commerce
201 North Central Avenue, 27th Floor
Phoenix, AZ 85073
Phone: (602) 495-2195
Fax: (602) 495-8913
www.phoenixchamber.com

Greater Phoenix Economic Council
2 North Central Avenue, Suite 2500
Phoenix, AZ 85004
Phone: (602) 256-7700
Fax: (602) 256-7744
www.gpec.org

Pittsburgh, PA
Allegheny County Industrial Development
Authority
425 6th Avenue, Suite 800
Pittsburgh, PA 15219
Phone: (412) 350-1067
Fax: (412) 642-2217
www.alleghenycounty.us

Greater Pittsburgh Chamber of Commerce
425 6th Avenue, 12th Floor
Pittsburgh, PA 15219
Phone: (412) 392-4500
Fax: (412) 392-4520
www.alleghenyconference.org

Portland, OR
Portland Business Alliance
200 SW Market Street, Suite 1770
Portland, OR 97201
Phone: (503) 224-8684
Fax: (503) 323-9186
www.portlandalliance.com

Providence, RI
Greater Providence Chamber of Commerce
30 Exchange Terrace, Fourth Floor
Providence, RI 02903
Phone: (401) 521-5000
Fax: (401) 351-2090
www.provchamber.com

Rhode Island Economic Development
Corporation
Providence City Hall
25 Dorrance Street
Providence, RI 02903
Phone: (401) 421-7740
Fax: (401) 751-0203
www.providenceri.com

Provo, UT
Provo-Orem Chamber of Commerce
51 South University Avenue, Suite 215
Provo, UT 84601
Phone: (801) 851-2555
Fax: (801) 851-2557
www.thechamber.org

Raleigh, NC
Greater Raleigh Chamber of Commerce
800 South Salisbury Street
Raleigh, NC 27601-2978
Phone: (919) 664-7000
Fax: (919) 664-7099
www.raleighchamber.org

Reno, NV
Reno + Sparks Chamber of Commerce
449 S. Virginia Street, 2nd Floor
Reno, NV 89501
Phone: (775) 636-9550
www.thechambernv.org

Richmond, VA
Greater Richmond Chamber
600 East Main Street, Suite 700
Richmond, VA 23219
Phone: (804) 648-1234
www.grcc.com

Greater Richmond Partnership
901 East Byrd Street, Suite 801
Richmond, VA 23219-4070
Phone: (804) 643-3227
Fax: (804) 343-7167
www.grpva.com

Rochester, MN
Rochester Area Chamber of Commerce
220 South Broadway, Suite 100
Rochester, MN 55904
Phone: (507) 288-1122
www.rochestermnchamber.com

Sacramento, CA
Sacramento Metro Chamber
One Capitol Mall, Suite 700
Sacramento, CA 95814
Phone: (916) 552-6800
metrochamber.org

Saint Louis, MO
St. Louis Regional Chamber
One Metropolitan Square, Suite 1300
St. Louis, MO 63102
Phone: (314) 231-5555
www.stlregionalchamber.com

Saint Paul, OR
St. Paul Area Chamber
401 Robert Street N, Suite 150
St. Paul, MN 55101
Phone: (651) 223-5000
www.stpaulchamber.com

Salem, OR
Salem Area Chamber of Commerce
1110 Commercial Street NE
Salem, OR 97301
Phone: (503) 581-1466
www.salemchamber.org

Salt Lake City, UT
Salt Lake Chamber
175 E. University Blvd. (400 S), Suite 600
Salt Lake City, UT 84111
Phone: (801) 364-3631
www.slchamber.com

San Antonio, TX
The Greater San Antonio Chamber of Commerce
602 E. Commerce Street
San Antonio, TX 78205
Phone: (210) 229-2100
Fax: (210) 229-1600
www.sachamber.org

San Antonio Economic Development Department
P.O. Box 839966
San Antonio, TX 78283-3966
Phone: (210) 207-8080
Fax: (210) 207-8151
www.sanantonio.gov/edd

San Diego, CA
San Diego Economic Development Corp.
401 B Street, Suite 1100
San Diego, CA 92101
Phone: (619) 234-8484
Fax: (619) 234-1935
www.sandiegobusiness.org

San Diego Regional Chamber of Commerce
402 West Broadway, Suite 1000
San Diego, CA 92101-3585
Phone: (619) 544-1300
Fax: (619) 744-7481
www.sdchamber.org

San Francisco, CA
San Francisco Chamber of Commerce
235 Montgomery Street, 12th Floor
San Francisco, CA 94104
Phone: (415) 392-4520
Fax: (415) 392-0485
www.sfchamber.com

San Jose, CA
Office of Economic Development
60 South Market Street, Suite 470
San Jose, CA 95113
Phone: (408) 277-5880
Fax: (408) 277-3615
www.sba.gov

The Silicon Valley Organization
101 W Santa Clara Street
San Jose, CA 95113
Phone: (408) 291-5250
www.thesvo.com

Santa Rosa, CA
Santa Rosa Chamber of Commerce
1260 North Dutton Avenue, Suite 272
Santa Rosa, CA 95401
Phone: (707) 545-1414
www.santarosachamber.com

Savannah, GA
Savannah Chamber of Commerce
101 E. Bay Street
Savannah, GA 31402
Phone: (912) 644-6400
Fax: (912) 644-6499
www.savannahchamber.com

Seattle, WA
Greater Seattle Chamber of Commerce
1301 Fifth Avenue, Suite 2500
Seattle, WA 98101
Phone: (206) 389-7200
Fax: (206) 389-7288
www.seattlechamber.com

Sioux Falls, SD
Sioux Falls Area Chamber of Commerce
200 N. Phillips Avenue, Suite 102
Sioux Falls, SD 57104
Phone: (605) 336-1620
Fax: (605) 336-6499
www.siouxfallschamber.com

Tampa, FL
Greater Tampa Chamber of Commerce
P.O. Box 420
Tampa, FL 33601-0420
Phone: (813) 276-9401
Fax: (813) 229-7855
www.tampachamber.com

Tucson, AZ
Tucson Metro Chamber
212 E. Broadway Blvd
Tucson, AZ 85701
Phone: (520) 792-1212
tucsonchamber.org

Tulsa, OK
Tulsa Regional Chamber
One West Third Street, Suite 100
Tulsa, OK 74103
Phone: (918) 585-1201
www.tulsachamber.com

Virginia Beach, VA
Hampton Roads Chamber of Commerce
500 East Main Street, Suite 700
Virginia Beach, VA 23510
Phone: (757) 664-2531
www.hamptonroadschamber.com

Washington, DC
District of Columbia Chamber of Commerce
1213 K Street NW
Washington, DC 20005
Phone: (202) 347-7201
Fax: (202) 638-6762
www.dcchamber.org

District of Columbia Office of Planning and Economic Development
J.A. Wilson Building
1350 Pennsylvania Ave NW, Suite 317
Washington, DC 20004
Phone: (202) 727-6365
Fax: (202) 727-6703
www.dcbiz.dc.gov

Wichita, KS
Wichita Regional Chamber of Commerce
350 W Douglas Avennue
Wichita, KS 67202
Phone: (316) 265-7771
www.wichitachamber.org

Wilmington, NC
Wilmington Chamber of Commerce
One Estell Lee Place
Wilmington, NC 28401
Phone: (910) 762-2611
www.wilmingtonchamber.org

Winston-Salem, NC
Winston-Salem Chamber of Commerce
411 West Fourth Street, Suite 211
Winston-Salem, NC 27101
Phone: (336) 728-9200
www.winstonsalem.com

Appendix E: State Departments of Labor

Alabama
Alabama Department of Labor
P.O. Box 303500
Montgomery, AL 36130-3500
Phone: (334) 242-3072
adol.alabama.gov

Alaska
Dept of Labor and Workforce Development
P.O. Box 11149
Juneau, AK 99822-2249
Phone: (907) 465-2700
www.labor.state.ak.us

Arizona
Industrial Commission or Arizona
800 West Washington Street
Phoenix, AZ 85007
Phone: (602) 542-4661
www.azica.gov

Arkansas
Department of Labor
10421 West Markham
Little Rock, AR 72205
Phone: (501) 682-4500
www.labor.ar.gov

California
Labor and Workforce Development
445 Golden Gate Ave., 10th Floor
San Francisco, CA 94102
Phone: (916) 263-1811
www.labor.ca.gov

Colorado
Dept of Labor and Employment
633 17th St., 2nd Floor
Denver, CO 80202-3660
Phone: (888) 390-7936
cdle.colorado.gov

Connecticut
Department of Labor
200 Folly Brook Blvd.
Wethersfield, CT 06109-1114
Phone: (860) 263-6000
www.ctdol.state.ct.us

Delaware
Department of Labor
4425 N. Market St., 4th Floor
Wilmington, DE 19802
Phone: (302) 451-3423
dol.delaware.gov

District of Columbia
Department of Employment Services
614 New York Ave., NE, Suite 300
Washington, DC 20002
Phone: (202) 671-1900
does.dc.gov

Florida
Florida Department of Economic Opportunity
The Caldwell Building
107 East Madison St. Suite 100
Tallahassee, FL 32399-4120
Phone: (800) 342-3450
www.floridajobs.org

Georgia
Department of Labor
Sussex Place, Room 600
148 Andrew Young Intl Blvd., NE
Atlanta, GA 30303
Phone: (404) 656-3011
dol.georgia.gov

Hawaii
Dept of Labor & Industrial Relations
830 Punchbowl Street
Honolulu, HI 96813
Phone: (808) 586-8842
labor.hawaii.gov

Idaho
Department of Labor
317 W. Main St.
Boise, ID 83735-0001
Phone: (208) 332-3579
www.labor.idaho.gov

Illinois
Department of Labor
160 N. LaSalle Street, 13th Floor
Suite C-1300
Chicago, IL 60601
Phone: (312) 793-2800
www.illinois.gov/idol

Indiana
Indiana Department of Labor
402 West Washington Street, Room W195
Indianapolis, IN 46204
Phone: (317) 232-2655
www.in.gov/dol

Iowa
Iowa Workforce Development
1000 East Grand Avenue
Des Moines, IA 50319-0209
Phone: (515) 242-5870
www.iowadivisionoflabor.gov

Kansas
Department of Labor
401 S.W. Topeka Blvd.
Topeka, KS 66603-3182
Phone: (785) 296-5000
www.dol.ks.gov

Kentucky
Department of Labor
1047 U.S. Hwy 127 South, Suite 4
Frankfort, KY 40601-4381
Phone: (502) 564-3070
www.labor.ky.gov

Louisiana
Louisiana Workforce Commission
1001 N. 23rd Street
Baton Rouge, LA 70804-9094
Phone: (225) 342-3111
www.laworks.net

Maine
Department of Labor
45 Commerce Street
Augusta, ME 04330
Phone: (207) 623-7900
www.state.me.us/labor

Maryland
Department of Labor, Licensing & Regulation
500 N. Calvert Street
Suite 401
Baltimore, MD 21202
Phone: (410) 767-2357
www.dllr.state.md.us

Massachusetts
Dept of Labor & Workforce Development
One Ashburton Place
Room 2112
Boston, MA 02108
Phone: (617) 626-7100
www.mass.gov/lwd

Michigan
Department of Licensing and Regulatory Affairs
611 W. Ottawa
P.O. Box 30004
Lansing, MI 48909
Phone: (517) 373-1820
www.michigan.gov/lara

Minnesota
Dept of Labor and Industry
443 Lafayette Road North
Saint Paul, MN 55155
Phone: (651) 284-5070
www.doli.state.mn.us

Mississippi
Dept of Employment Security
P.O. Box 1699
Jackson, MS 39215-1699
Phone: (601) 321-6000
www.mdes.ms.gov

Missouri
Labor and Industrial Relations
P.O. Box 599
3315 W. Truman Boulevard
Jefferson City, MO 65102-0599
Phone: (573) 751-7500
labor.mo.gov

Montana
Dept of Labor and Industry
P.O. Box 1728
Helena, MT 59624-1728
Phone: (406) 444-9091
www.dli.mt.gov

Nebraska
Department of Labor
550 S 16th Street
Lincoln, NE 68508
Phone: (402) 471-9000
dol.nebraska.gov

Nevada
Dept of Business and Industry
3300 W. Sahara Ave, Suite 425
Las Vegas, NV 89102
Phone: (702) 486-2750
business.nv.gov

New Hampshire
Department of Labor
State Office Park South
95 Pleasant Street
Concord, NH 03301
Phone: (603) 271-3176
www.nh.gov/labor

New Jersey
Department of Labor & Workforce Devel.
John Fitch Plaza, 13th Floor, Suite D
Trenton, NJ 08625-0110
Phone: (609) 777-3200
lwd.dol.state.nj.us/labor

New Mexico
Department of Workforce Solutions
401 Broadway, NE
Albuquerque, NM 87103-1928
Phone: (505) 841-8450
www.dws.state.nm.us

New York
Department of Labor
State Office Bldg. # 12
W.A. Harriman Campus
Albany, NY 12240
Phone: (518) 457-9000
www.labor.ny.gov

North Carolina
Department of Labor
4 West Edenton Street
Raleigh, NC 27601-1092
Phone: (919) 733-7166
www.labor.nc.gov

North Dakota
North Dakota Department of Labor and Human Rights
State Capitol Building
600 East Boulevard, Dept 406
Bismark, ND 58505-0340
Phone: (701) 328-2660
www.nd.gov/labor

Ohio
Department of Commerce
77 South High Street, 22nd Floor
Columbus, OH 43215
Phone: (614) 644-2239
www.com.state.oh.us

Oklahoma
Department of Labor
4001 N. Lincoln Blvd.
Oklahoma City, OK 73105-5212
Phone: (405) 528-1500
www.ok.gov/odol

Oregon
Bureau of Labor and Industries
800 NE Oregon St., #32
Portland, OR 97232
Phone: (971) 673-0761
www.oregon.gov/boli

Pennsylvania
Dept of Labor and Industry
1700 Labor and Industry Bldg
7th and Forster Streets
Harrisburg, PA 17120
Phone: (717) 787-5279
www.dli.pa.gov

Rhode Island
Department of Labor and Training
1511 Pontiac Avenue
Cranston, RI 02920
Phone: (401) 462-8000
www.dlt.state.ri.us

South Carolina
Dept of Labor, Licensing & Regulations
P.O. Box 11329
Columbia, SC 29211-1329
Phone: (803) 896-4300
www.llr.state.sc.us

South Dakota
Department of Labor & Regulation
700 Governors Drive
Pierre, SD 57501-2291
Phone: (605) 773-3682
dlr.sd.gov

Tennessee
Dept of Labor & Workforce Development
Andrew Johnson Tower
710 James Robertson Pkwy
Nashville, TN 37243-0655
Phone: (615) 741-6642
www.tn.gov/workforce

Texas
Texas Workforce Commission
101 East 15th St.
Austin, TX 78778
Phone: (512) 475-2670
www.twc.state.tx.us

Utah
Utah Labor Commission
160 East 300 South, 3rd Floor
Salt Lake City, UT 84114-6600
Phone: (801) 530-6800
laborcommission.utah.gov

Vermont
Department of Labor
5 Green Mountain Drive
P.O. Box 488
Montpelier, VT 05601-0488
Phone: (802) 828-4000
labor.vermont.gov

Virginia
Dept of Labor and Industry
Powers-Taylor Building
13 S. 13th Street
Richmond, VA 23219
Phone: (804) 371-2327
www.doli.virginia.gov

Washington
Dept of Labor and Industries
P.O. Box 44001
Olympia, WA 98504-4001
Phone: (360) 902-4200
www.lni.wa.gov

West Virginia
Division of Labor
749 B Building 6
Capitol Complex
Charleston, WV 25305
Phone: (304) 558-7890
labor.wv.gov

Wisconsin
Dept of Workforce Development
201 E. Washington Ave., #A400
P.O. Box 7946
Madison, WI 53707-7946
Phone: (608) 266-6861
dwd.wisconsin.gov

Wyoming
Department of Workforce Services
1510 East Pershing Blvd.
Cheyenne, WY 82002
Phone: (307) 777-7261
www.wyomingworkforce.org

Titles from Grey House

Visit www.GreyHouse.com for Product Information, Table of Contents, and Sample Pages.

Opinions Throughout History

Opinions Throughout History: Church & State
Opinions Throughout History: Conspiracy Theories
Opinions Throughout History: The Death Penalty
Opinions Throughout History: Diseases & Epidemics
Opinions Throughout History: Domestic Terrorism
Opinions Throughout History: Drug Use & Abuse
Opinions Throughout History: The Environment
Opinions Throughout History: Fame & Celebrity in America
Opinions Throughout History: Free Speech & Censorship
Opinions Throughout History: Gender: Roles & Rights
Opinions Throughout History: Globalization
Opinions Throughout History: Guns in America
Opinions Throughout History: Immigration
Opinions Throughout History: Law Enforcement in America
Opinions Throughout History: LGBTQ+ Rights
Opinions Throughout History: Mental Health
Opinions Throughout History: Nat'l Security vs. Civil & Privacy Rights
Opinions Throughout History: Presidential Authority
Opinions Throughout History: Refugees & Asylum Seekers
Opinions Throughout History: Robotics & Artificial Intelligence
Opinions Throughout History: Social Media Issues
Opinions Throughout History: Spies & Espionage
Opinions Throughout History: The Supreme Court
Opinions Throughout History: Truth & Lies in the Media
Opinions Throughout History: Voters' Rights
Opinions Throughout History: War & the Military
Opinions Throughout History: Workers Rights & Wages

General Reference

American Environmental Leaders
Constitutional Amendments
Encyclopedia of African-American Writing
Encyclopedia of Invasions & Conquests
Encyclopedia of Prisoners of War & Internment
Encyclopedia of the Continental Congresses
Encyclopedia of the United States Cabinet
Encyclopedia of War Journalism
The Environmental Debate
Environmental Sustainability: Skills & Strategies
Financial Literacy Starter Kit
From Suffrage to the Senate
The Gun Debate: Gun Rights & Gun Control in the U.S.
Historical Warrior Peoples & Modern Fighting Groups
Human Rights and the United States
Political Corruption in America
Privacy Rights in the Digital Age
The Religious Right and American Politics
Speakers of the House of Representatives, 1789-2021
US Land & Natural Resources Policy
The Value of a Dollar 1600-1865 Colonial to Civil War
The Value of a Dollar 1860-2024

This is Who We Were

This is Who We Were: Colonial America (1492-1775)
This is Who We Were: Civil War & Reconstruction
This is Who We Were: 1880-1899
This is Who We Were: In the 1900s
This is Who We Were: In the 1910s
This is Who We Were: In the 1920s
This is Who We Were: A Companion to the 1940 Census
This is Who We Were: In the 1940s (1940-1949)
This is Who We Were: In the 1950s
This is Who We Were: In the 1960s
This is Who We Were: In the 1970s
This is Who We Were: In the 1980s
This is Who We Were: In the 1990s
This is Who We Were: In the 2000s
This is Who We Were: In the 2010s

Working Americans

Working Americans—Vol. 1: The Working Class
Working Americans—Vol. 2: The Middle Class
Working Americans—Vol. 3: The Upper Class
Working Americans—Vol. 4: Children
Working Americans—Vol. 5: At War
Working Americans—Vol. 6: Working Women
Working Americans—Vol. 7: Social Movements
Working Americans—Vol. 8: Immigrants
Working Americans—Vol. 9: Revolutionary War to the Civil War
Working Americans—Vol. 10: Sports & Recreation
Working Americans—Vol. 11: Inventors & Entrepreneurs
Working Americans—Vol. 12: Our History through Music
Working Americans—Vol. 13: Education & Educators
Working Americans—Vol. 14: African Americans
Working Americans—Vol. 15: Politics & Politicians
Working Americans—Vol. 16: Farming & Ranching
Working Americans—Vol. 17: Teens in America
Working Americans—Vol. 18: Health Care Workers
Working Americans—Vol. 19: The Performing Arts

Grey House Health & Wellness Guides

Addiction Handbook & Resource Guide
Adolescent Mental Health Handbook & Resource Guide
Anxiety & Stress Handbook & Resource Guide
Attention Disorders Handbook & Resource Guide
The Autism Spectrum Handbook & Resource Guide
Autoimmune Disorders Handbook & Resource Guide
Breast Cancer Handbook & Resource Guide
Cardiovascular Disease Handbook & Resource Guide
Chronic Pain Handbook & Resource Guide
Dementia Handbook & Resource Guide
Depression Handbook & Resource Guide
Diabetes Handbook & Resource Guide
Nutrition, Obesity & Eating Disorders Handbook & Resource Guide

Consumer Health

Complete Mental Health Resource Guide
Complete Resource Guide for Pediatric Disorders
Complete Resource Guide for People with Chronic Illness
Complete Resource Guide for People with Disabilities
Older Americans Information Resource
Parenting: Styles & Strategies
Social Media & Your Mental Health
Teens: Growing Up, Skills & Strategies

Guide to Venture Capital & Private Equity Firms
Hudson's Washington News Media Contacts Guide
New York State Directory
Sports Market Place

Grey House Publishing | Salem Press | H.W. Wilson | 4919 Route 22, PO Box 56, Amenia NY 12501-0056

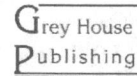

Grey House Imprints

Visit www.GreyHouse.com for Product Information, Table of Contents, and Sample Pages.

Grey House Titles, continued

Business Information
Business Information Resources
Complete Broadcasting Industry Guide: TV, Radio, Cable & Streaming
Directory of Mail Order Catalogs
Environmental Resource Handbook
Food & Beverage Market Place
Guide to Healthcare Group Purchasing Organizations
Guide to U.S. HMOs and PPOs

Education
Complete Learning Disabilities Resource Guide
Digital Literacy: Skills & Strategies

Statistics & Demographics
America's Top-Rated Cities
America's Top-Rated Smaller Cities
Profiles of California
Profiles of Florida
Profiles of Illinois
Profiles of Indiana
Profiles of Massachusetts
Profiles of Michigan
Profiles of New Jersey
Profiles of New York
Profiles of North Carolina & South Carolina
Profiles of Ohio
Profiles of Pennsylvania
Profiles of Texas
Profiles of Virginia
Profiles of Wisconsin

Canadian Resources
Associations Canada
Canadian Almanac & Directory
Canadian Environmental Resource Guide
Canadian Parliamentary Guide
Canadian Venture Capital & Private Equity Firms
Canadian Who's Who
Cannabis Canada
Careers & Employment Canada
Financial Post: Directory of Directors
Financial Services Canada
FP Bonds: Corporate
FP Bonds: Government
FP Equities: Preferreds & Derivatives
FP Survey: Industrials
FP Survey: Mines & Energy
FP Survey: Predecessor & Defunct
Health Guide Canada
Indigenous History & Culture in Canada
Libraries Canada
Major Canadian Cities: 50 Cities Compared, Ranked & Profiled

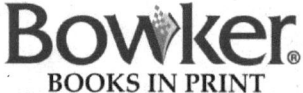

Books in Print Series
American Book Publishing Record® Annual
American Book Publishing Record® Monthly
Books In Print®
Books In Print® Supplement
Books Out Loud™
Bowker's Complete Video Directory™
Children's Books In Print®
El-Hi Textbooks & Serials In Print®
Forthcoming Books®
Law Books & Serials In Print™
Medical & Health Care Books In Print™
Publishers, Distributors & Wholesalers of the US™
Subject Guide to Books In Print®
Subject Guide to Children's Books In Print®

Weiss Financial Ratings
Financial Literacy Basics
Financial Literacy: How to Become an Investor
Financial Literacy: Planning for the Future
Weiss Ratings Consumer Guides
Weiss Ratings Guide to Banks
Weiss Ratings Guide to Credit Unions
Weiss Ratings Guide to Health Insurers
Weiss Ratings Guide to Life & Annuity Insurers
Weiss Ratings Guide to Property & Casualty Insurers
Weiss Ratings Investment Research Guide to Bond & Money Market Mutual Funds
Weiss Ratings Investment Research Guide to Exchange-Traded Funds
Weiss Ratings Investment Research Guide to Stock Mutual Funds
Weiss Ratings Investment Research Guide to Stocks

Grey House Publishing | Salem Press | H.W. Wilson | 4919 Route 22, PO Box 56, Amenia NY 12501-0056

Titles from Salem Press

Visit www.SalemPress.com for Product Information, Table of Contents, and Sample Pages.

LITERATURE

Critical Insights: Authors

Louisa May Alcott
Sherman Alexie
Dante Alighieri
Isabel Allende
Maya Angelou
Isaac Asimov
Margaret Atwood
Jane Austen
James Baldwin
Saul Bellow
Roberto Bolano
Ray Bradbury
The Brontë Sisters
Gwendolyn Brooks
Albert Camus
Raymond Carver
Willa Cather
Geoffrey Chaucer
John Cheever
Kate Chopin
Joseph Conrad
Charles Dickens
Emily Dickinson
Frederick Douglass
T. S. Eliot
George Eliot
Harlan Ellison
Ralph Waldo Emerson
Louise Erdrich
William Faulkner
F. Scott Fitzgerald
Gustave Flaubert
Horton Foote
Benjamin Franklin
Robert Frost
Neil Gaiman
Gabriel Garcia Marquez
Thomas Hardy
Nathaniel Hawthorne
Robert A. Heinlein
Lillian Hellman
Ernest Hemingway
Langston Hughes
Zora Neale Hurston
Henry James
Thomas Jefferson
James Joyce
Jamaica Kincaid
Stephen King
Martin Luther King, Jr.
Barbara Kingsolver
Abraham Lincoln
C.S. Lewis
Mario Vargas Llosa
Jack London
James McBride
Cormac McCarthy
Herman Melville
Arthur Miller
Toni Morrison
Alice Munro
Tim O'Brien
Flannery O'Connor
Eugene O'Neill
George Orwell
Sylvia Plath
Edgar Allan Poe
Philip Roth
Salman Rushdie
J.D. Salinger
Mary Shelley
John Steinbeck
Amy Tan
Leo Tolstoy
Mark Twain
John Updike
Kurt Vonnegut
Alice Walker
David Foster Wallace
H. G. Wells
Edith Wharton
Walt Whitman
Oscar Wilde
Tennessee Williams
Virginia Woolf
Richard Wright
Malcolm X

Critical Insights: Works

Absalom, Absalom!
Adventures of Huckleberry Finn
The Adventures of Tom Sawyer
Aeneid
All Quiet on the Western Front
All the Pretty Horses
Animal Farm
Anna Karenina
As You Like It
The Awakening
The Bell Jar
Beloved
Billy Budd, Sailor
The Bluest Eye
The Book Thief
Brave New World
The Canterbury Tales
Catch-22
The Catcher in the Rye
The Color Purple
Crime and Punishment
The Crucible
Death of a Salesman
The Diary of a Young Girl
Dracula
Fahrenheit 451
A Farewell to Arms
Frankenstein; or, The Modern Prometheus
The Grapes of Wrath
Great Expectations
The Great Gatsby
Hamlet
The Handmaid's Tale
Harry Potter Series
Heart of Darkness
The Hobbit
The House on Mango Street
How the Garcia Girls Lost Their Accents
The Hunger Games Trilogy
I Know Why the Caged Bird Sings
In Cold Blood
The Inferno
Invisible Man
Jane Eyre
The Joy Luck Club
Julius Caesar
King Lear
The Kite Runner
Life of Pi
Little Women
Lolita
Lord of the Flies
The Lord of the Rings
Macbeth
The Merchant of Venice
The Metamorphosis
Midnight's Children
A Midsummer Night's Dream
Moby-Dick
Mrs. Dalloway
Native Son
Nineteen Eighty-Four
The Odyssey
Of Mice and Men
The Old Man and the Sea
On the Road
One Flew Over the Cuckoo's Nest
One Hundred Years of Solitude
Othello
The Outsiders
Paradise Lost
The Pearl
The Plague
The Poetry of Baudelaire
The Poetry of Edgar Allan Poe
A Portrait of the Artist as a Young Man
Pride and Prejudice
A Raisin in the Sun
The Red Badge of Courage
Romeo and Juliet
The Scarlet Letter
Sense and Sensibility
Short Fiction of Flannery O'Connor
Slaughterhouse-Five
The Sound and the Fury
A Streetcar Named Desire
The Sun Also Rises
A Tale of Two Cities
The Tales of Edgar Allan Poe
Their Eyes Were Watching God
Things Fall Apart
To Kill a Mockingbird
Twelfth Night, or What You Will
Twelve Years a Slave
War and Peace
The Woman Warrior
Wuthering Heights

Grey House Publishing | Salem Press | H.W. Wilson | 4919 Route 22, PO Box 56, Amenia NY 12501-0056

Titles from Salem Press

Visit www.SalemPress.com for Product Information, Table of Contents, and Sample Pages.

Critical Insights: Themes
The American Comic Book
American Creative Non-Fiction
The American Dream
American Multicultural Identity
American Road Literature
American Short Story
American Sports Fiction
The American Thriller
American Writers in Exile
Censored & Banned Literature
Civil Rights Literature, Past & Present
Coming of Age
Conspiracies
Contemporary Canadian Fiction
Contemporary Immigrant Short Fiction
Contemporary Latin American Fiction
Contemporary Speculative Fiction
Crime and Detective Fiction
Crisis of Faith
Cultural Encounters
Dystopia
Family
The Fantastic
Feminism Flash Fiction
Friendship
Gender, Sex and Sexuality
Going Into the Woods
Good & Evil
The Graphic Novel
Greed
Harlem Renaissance
The Hero's Quest
Historical Fiction
Holocaust Literature
The Immigrant Experience
Inequality
LGBTQ Literature
Literature in Times of Crisis
Literature of Protest
Love
Magical Realism
Midwestern Literature
Modern Japanese Literature
Nature & the Environment
Paranoia, Fear & Alienation
Patriotism
Political Fiction
Postcolonial Literature
Power & Corruption
Pulp Fiction of the '20s and '30s
Rebellion
Russia's Golden Age
Satire
The Slave Narrative
Social Justice and American Literature
Southern Gothic Literature
Southwestern Literature
The Supernatural
Survival
Technology & Humanity
Truth & Lies
Violence in Literature
Virginia Woolf & 20th Century Women Writers
War

Critical Insights: Film
Bonnie & Clyde
Casablanca
Alfred Hitchcock
Stanley Kubrick

Critical Approaches to Literature
Critical Approaches to Literature: Feminist
Critical Approaches to Literature: Moral
Critical Approaches to Literature: Multicultural
Critical Approaches to Literature: Psychological

Literary Classics
Recommended Reading: 600 Classics Reviewed

Novels into Film
Novels into Film: Adaptations & Interpretation
Novels into Film: Adaptations & Interpretation, Volume 2

Critical Surveys of Literature
Critical Survey of American Literature
Critical Survey of Drama
Critical Survey of Long Fiction
Critical Survey of Mystery and Detective Fiction
Critical Survey of Poetry
Critical Survey of Poetry: Contemporary Poets
Critical Survey of Science Fiction & Fantasy Literature
Critical Survey of Shakespeare's Film Adaptations
Critical Survey of Shakespeare's Plays
Critical Survey of Shakespeare's Sonnets
Critical Survey of Short Fiction
Critical Survey of World Literature
Critical Survey of Young Adult Literature

Critical Surveys of Graphic Novels
Heroes & Superheroes
History, Theme, and Technique
Independents & Underground Classics
Manga

Critical Surveys of Mythology & Folklore
Creation Myths
Deadly Battles & Warring Enemies
Gods & Goddesses
Heroes and Heroines
Legendary Creatures
Love, Sexuality, and Desire
World Mythology

Cyclopedia of Literary Characters & Places
Cyclopedia of Literary Characters
Cyclopedia of Literary Places

Grey House Publishing | Salem Press | H.W. Wilson | 4919 Route 22, PO Box 56, Amenia NY 12501-0056

Titles from Salem Press

Visit www.SalemPress.com for Product Information, Table of Contents, and Sample Pages.

Introduction to Literary Context
American Poetry of the 20th Century
American Post-Modernist Novels
American Short Fiction
English Literature
Plays
World Literature

Magill's Literary Annual
Magill's Literary Annual, Annual Editions 1977-2024

Masterplots
Masterplots, Fourth Edition
Masterplots, 2010-2018 Supplement

Notable Writers
Notable African American Writers
Notable American Women Writers
Notable Horror Fiction Writers
Notable Mystery & Detective Fiction Writers
Notable Writers of the American West & the Native American Experience
Notable Writers of LGBTQ+ Literature

HISTORY
The Decades
The 1900s in America
The 1910s in America
The Twenties in America
The Thirties in America
The Forties in America
The Fifties in America
The Sixties in America
The Seventies in America
The Eighties in America
The Nineties in America
The 2000s in America
The 2010s in America

Defining Documents in American History
Defining Documents: The 1900s
Defining Documents: The 1910s
Defining Documents: The 1920s
Defining Documents: The 1930s
Defining Documents: The 1950s
Defining Documents: The 1960s
Defining Documents: The 1970s
Defining Documents: The 1980s
Defining Documents: American Citizenship
Defining Documents: The American Economy
Defining Documents: The American Revolution
Defining Documents: The American West
Defining Documents: Business Ethics
Defining Documents: Capital Punishment
Defining Documents: Censorship
Defining Documents: Civil Rights
Defining Documents: Civil War
Defining Documents: Conservatism
Defining Documents: The Constitution
Defining Documents: The Cold War
Defining Documents: Dissent & Protest
Defining Documents: Domestic Terrorism & Extremism
Defining Documents: Drug Policy
Defining Documents: The Emergence of Modern America
Defining Documents: Environment & Conservation
Defining Documents: Espionage & Intrigue
Defining Documents: Exploration and Colonial America
Defining Documents: The First Amendment
Defining Documents: The Free Press
Defining Documents: The Great Depression
Defining Documents: The Great Migration
Defining Documents: The Gun Debate
Defining Documents: Immigration & Immigrant Communities
Defining Documents: The Legacy of 9/11
Defining Documents: LGBTQ+
Defining Documents: Liberalism
Defining Documents: Manifest Destiny and the New Nation
Defining Documents: Native Americans
Defining Documents: Political Campaigns, Candidates & Discourse
Defining Documents: Postwar 1940s
Defining Documents: Prison Reform
Defining Documents: The Salem Witch Trials
Defining Documents: Secrets, Leaks & Scandals
Defining Documents: Slavery
Defining Documents: Supreme Court Decisions
Defining Documents: Reconstruction Era
Defining Documents: The Vietnam War
Defining Documents: The Underground Railroad
Defining Documents: U.S. Involvement in the Middle East
Defining Documents: Voters' Rights
Defining Documents: Watergate
Defining Documents: Workers' Rights
Defining Documents: World War I
Defining Documents: World War II

Defining Documents in World History
Defining Documents: The 17th Century
Defining Documents: The 18th Century
Defining Documents: The 19th Century
Defining Documents: The 20th Century (1900-1950)
Defining Documents: The Ancient World
Defining Documents: Asia
Defining Documents: Genocide & the Holocaust
Defining Documents: Human Rights
Defining Documents: The Middle Ages
Defining Documents: The Middle East
Defining Documents: Nationalism & Populism
Defining Documents: The Nuclear Age
Defining Documents: Pandemics, Plagues & Public Health
Defining Documents: Religious Freedom & Religious Persecution
Defining Documents: Renaissance & Early Modern Era
Defining Documents: Revolutions
Defining Documents: The Rise & Fall of the Soviet Union
Defining Documents: Treason
Defining Documents: Women's Rights

Grey House Publishing | Salem Press | H.W. Wilson | 4919 Route 22, PO Box 56, Amenia NY 12501-0056

Titles from Salem Press

Visit www.SalemPress.com for Product Information, Table of Contents, and Sample Pages.

Great Events from History
Great Events from History: American History, Exploration to the Colonial Era, 1492-1775
Great Events from History: American History, Forging a New Nation, 1775-1850
Great Events from History: American History, War, Peace & Growth, 1850-1918
Great Events from History: The Ancient World
Great Events from History: The Middle Ages
Great Events from History: The Renaissance & Early Modern Era
Great Events from History: The 17th Century
Great Events from History: The 18th Century
Great Events from History: The 19th Century
Great Events from History: The 20th Century, 1901-1940
Great Events from History: The 20th Century, 1941-1970
Great Events from History: The 20th Century, 1971-2000
Great Events from History: Modern Scandals
Great Events from History: African American History
Great Events from History: The 21st Century, 2000-2016
Great Events from History: LGBTQ Events
Great Events from History: Human Rights
Great Events from History: Women's History

Great Lives from History
Great Athletes
Great Athletes of the Twenty-First Century
Great Lives from History: The 17th Century
Great Lives from History: The 18th Century
Great Lives from History: The 19th Century
Great Lives from History: The 20th Century
Great Lives from History: The 21st Century, 2000-2017
Great Lives from History: African Americans
Great Lives from History: The Ancient World
Great Lives from History: American Heroes
Great Lives from History: American Women
Great Lives from History: Asian and Pacific Islander Americans
Great Lives from History: Autocrats & Dictators
Great Lives from History: The Incredibly Wealthy
Great Lives from History: Inventors & Inventions
Great Lives from History: Jewish Americans
Great Lives from History: Latinos
Great Lives from History: LGBTQ+
Great Lives from History: The Middle Ages
Great Lives from History: The Renaissance & Early Modern Era
Great Lives from History: Scientists and Science

History & Government
American First Ladies
American Presidents
The 50 States
The Ancient World: Extraordinary People in Extraordinary Societies
The Bill of Rights
The Criminal Justice System
U.S. Court Cases
The U.S. Supreme Court

SOCIAL SCIENCES
Civil Rights Movements: Past & Present
Countries, Peoples and Cultures
Countries: Their Wars & Conflicts: A World Survey
Education Today: Issues, Policies & Practices
Encyclopedia of American Immigration
Ethics: Questions & Morality of Human Actions
Issues in U.S. Immigration
Principles of Sociology: Group Relationships & Behavior
Principles of Sociology: Personal Relationships & Behavior
Principles of Sociology: Societal Issues & Behavior
Racial & Ethnic Relations in America
Weapons, Warfare & Military Technology
World Geography

HEALTH
Addictions, Substance Abuse & Alcoholism
Adolescent Health & Wellness
Aging
Cancer
Community & Family Health Issues
Integrative, Alternative & Complementary Medicine
Genetics and Inherited Conditions
Infectious Diseases and Conditions
Magill's Medical Guide
Men's Health
Nutrition
Parenting: Styles & Strategies
Psychology & Behavioral Health
Social Media & Your Mental Health
Teens: Growing Up, Skills & Strategies
Women's Health

Principles of Health
Principles of Health: Allergies & Immune Disorders
Principles of Health: Anxiety & Stress
Principles of Health: Depression
Principles of Health: Diabetes
Principles of Health: Hypertension
Principles of Health: Nursing
Principles of Health: Obesity
Principles of Health: Occupational Therapy & Physical Therapy
Principles of Health: Pain Management
Principles of Health: Prescription Drug Abuse
Principles of Health: Whole Body Wellness

BUSINESS
Principles of Business: Accounting
Principles of Business: Economics
Principles of Business: Entrepreneurship
Principles of Business: Finance
Principles of Business: Globalization
Principles of Business: Leadership
Principles of Business: Management
Principles of Business: Marketing

Titles from Salem Press

Visit www.SalemPress.com for Product Information, Table of Contents, and Sample Pages.

SCIENCE
Ancient Creatures
Applied Science
Applied Science: Engineering & Mathematics
Applied Science: Science & Medicine
Applied Science: Technology
Biomes and Ecosystems
Digital Literacy: Skills & Strategies
Earth Science: Earth Materials and Resources
Earth Science: Earth's Surface and History
Earth Science: Earth's Weather, Water and Atmosphere
Earth Science: Physics and Chemistry of the Earth
Encyclopedia of Climate Change
Encyclopedia of Energy
Encyclopedia of Environmental Issues
Encyclopedia of Global Resources
Encyclopedia of Mathematics and Society
Environmental Sustainability: Skills & Strategies
Forensic Science
Notable Natural Disasters
The Solar System
USA in Space

Principles of Science
Principles of Aeronautics
Principles of Anatomy
Principles of Archaeology
Principles of Architecture
Principles of Astronomy
Principles of Behavioral Science
Principles of Biology
Principles of Biotechnology
Principles of Botany
Principles of Chemistry
Principles of Climatology
Principles of Computer-aided Design
Principles of Computer Science
Principles of Cybersecurity
Principles of Digital Arts & Multimedia
Principles of Ecology
Principles of Energy
Principles of Environmental Engineering
Principles of Fire Science
Principles of Food Science
Principles of Forestry & Conservation
Principles of Geology
Principles of Graphic Design & Typography
Principles of Information Technology
Principles of Marine Science
Principles of Mass Communication
Principles of Mathematics
Principles of Mechanics
Principles of Microbiology
Principles of Modern Agriculture
Principles of Pharmacology
Principles of Physical Science
Principles of Physics
Principles of Probability & Statistics
Principles of Programming & Coding
Principles of Robotics & Artificial Intelligence
Principles of Scientific Research
Principles of Sports Medicine & Exercise Science
Principles of Sustainability

Principles of Zoology

CAREERS
Careers: Paths to Entrepreneurship
Careers in Archaeology & Museum Services
Careers in Artificial Intelligence
Careers in the Arts: Fine, Performing & Visual
Careers in the Automotive Industry
Careers in Biology
Careers in Biotechnology
Careers in Building Construction
Careers in Business
Careers in Chemistry
Careers in Communications & Media
Careers in Criminal Justice
Careers in Culinary Arts
Careers in Cybersecurity
Careers in Earth Science
Careers in Education & Training
Careers in Engineering
Careers in Environment & Conservation
Careers in Financial Services
Careers in Fish & Wildlife
Careers in Forensic Science
Careers in Gaming
Careers in Green Energy
Careers in Healthcare
Careers in Heavy Equipment Operation, Maintenance & Repair
Careers in Hospitality & Tourism
Careers in Human Services
Careers in Illustration & Animation
Careers in Information Technology
Careers in Intelligence & National Security
Careers in Law, Criminal Justice & Emergency Services
Careers in Mass Communication
Careers in the Music Industry
Careers in Manufacturing & Production
Careers in Medical Technology
Careers in Nursing
Careers in Physics
Careers in Protective Services
Careers in Psychology & Behavioral Health
Careers in Public Administration
Careers in Sales, Insurance & Real Estate
Careers in Science & Engineering
Careers in Social Media
Careers in Sports & Fitness
Careers in Sports Medicine & Training
Careers in Technical Services & Equipment Repair
Careers in Transportation
Careers in Travel & Adventure
Careers in Writing & Editing
Careers Outdoors
Careers Overseas
Careers Working with Infants & Children
Careers Working with Animals

Grey House Publishing | Salem Press | H.W. Wilson | 4919 Route 22, PO Box 56, Amenia NY 12501-0056

Titles from H.W. Wilson

Visit www.HWWilsonInPrint.com for Product Information, Table of Contents, and Sample Pages.

The Reference Shelf
Affordable Housing
Aging in America
Alternative Facts, Post-Truth and the Information War
The American Dream
Artificial Intelligence
Book Bans & Censorship
The Business of Food
Campaign Trends & Election Law
College Sports
Democracy Evolving
The Digital Age
Embracing New Paradigms in Education
Food Insecurity & Hunger in the United States
Future of U.S. Economic Relations: Mexico, Cuba, & Venezuela
Gene Editing & Genetic Engineering
Global Climate Change
Guns in America
Hacktivism
Hate Crimes
Health Conspiracies
Immigration & Border Control in the 21st Century
Income Inequality
Internet Abuses & Privacy Rights
Internet Law
Labor Unions
LGBTQ in the 21st Century
Marijuana Reform
Mental Health Awareness
Money in Politics
National Debate Topic 2020/2021: Criminal Justice Reform
National Debate Topic 2021/2022: Water Resources
National Debate Topic 2022/2023: Emerging Technologies & International Security
National Debate Topic 2023/2024: Economic Inequality
National Debate Topic 2024/2025: Intellectual Property Rights
National Debate Topic 2025/2026: The Arctic
New Developments in Artificial Intelligence
New Frontiers in Space
Policing in 2020
Pollution
Prescription Drug Abuse
Propaganda and Misinformation
Racial Tension in a Postracial Age
Reality Television
Renewable Energy
Representative American Speeches, Annual Editions
Reproductive Rights
Rethinking Work
Revisiting Gender
Russia & Ukraine
The South China Sea Conflict
Space Exploration
Sports in America
The Supreme Court
The Transformation of American Cities
The Two Koreas
UFOs
Vaccinations
Voting Rights
Whistleblowers

Core Collections
Children's Core Collection
Fiction Core Collection
Graphic Novels Core Collection
Middle & Junior High School Core
Public Library Core Collection: Nonfiction
Senior High Core Collection
Young Adult Fiction Core Collection

Current Biography
Current Biography Cumulative Index 1946-2025
Current Biography Magazine
Current Biography Yearbook

Readers' Guide to Periodical Literature
Abridged Readers' Guide to Periodical Literature
Readers' Guide to Periodical Literature

Indexes
Index to Legal Periodicals & Books
Short Story Index

Sears List
Sears List of Subject Headings
Sears List of Subject Headings, Online Database

History
American Game Changers: Invention, Innovation & Transformation
American Reformers
Speeches of the American Presidents

Facts About Series
Facts About the 20th Century
Facts About American Immigration
Facts About China
Facts About the Presidents
Facts About the World's Languages

Nobel Prize Winners
Nobel Prize Winners: 1901-1986
Nobel Prize Winners: 1987-1991
Nobel Prize Winners: 1992-1996
Nobel Prize Winners: 1997-2001
Nobel Prize Winners: 2002-2018

Famous First Facts
Famous First Facts
Famous First Facts About American Politics
Famous First Facts About Sports
Famous First Facts About the Environment
Famous First Facts: International Edition

American Book of Days
The American Book of Days
The International Book of Days

Grey House Publishing | Salem Press | H.W. Wilson | 4919 Route 22, PO Box 56, Amenia NY 12501-0056